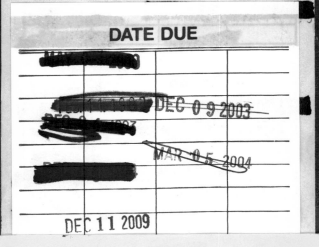

THE WORLD'S GREAT CLASSICS

William Shakespeare

THE COMPLETE
COMEDIES

Edited by GEORGE LYMAN KITTREDGE, Gurney Professor
of English Literature, Harvard University;
with an introduction by MICHAEL BENTHALL, Director of the
Old Vic Theatre, and a biography of the author by
EDWIN E. WILLOUGHBY of the Folger Shakespeare Library

THE KITTREDGE-PLAYERS EDITION
Illustrated with photographs of actual stage productions

Grolier
INCORPORATED
NEW YORK

Standard Book Number 7172-0000-0

PRINTED IN THE UNITED STATES OF AMERICA

Preface

THE present edition of SHAKESPEARE'S COMPLETE WORKS includes all the plays and poems that are ascribed to him, in whole or in part, on satisfactory evidence.

The text has been determined by a fresh collation of the original editions. To the First Folio (1623), even in those cases in which some Quarto is more authoritative, such respect is due as attaches to a volume sponsored by Shakespeare's literary executors. So-called 'bad Quartos' often preserve correct readings. The later Folios, especially the Second (1632), though they have no claim to be authoritative, serve, at least, to correct a considerable number of old misprints. Most of these corrections, to be sure, are not beyond the powers of a modern critic, but it is comforting, at times, to know how a corrupt passage looked to a proofreader of the early seventeenth century. For *Pericles* and *The Two Noble Kinsmen* we must depend on a Quarto text—bad in the first case, excellent in the second.

In accepting the conjectural emendations of modern scholars caution is manifestly necessary. Yet conservatism may be carried too far. One should not canonize the heedless type-setters of the Elizabethan printing house. That an old reading 'makes sense' of a sort is not in and for itself a sufficient guaranty. Thus Upton's 'Adam Cupid' (*Romeo and Juliet*, ii, 1, 13) must be right, though 'Abraham' is not absolutely unintelligible; Farmer's 'holy-ales' (*Pericles*, i, Gower, 6) is better than 'holy days'; Theobald's 'a babbled' (*Henry V*, ii, 3, 17) for 'a table' is a stroke of genius. An editor should never forget Bacon's inspired epigram: 'A froward retention of custom is as turbulent a thing as an innovation.'

Care has been taken to indicate elisions and contractions in accordance with what seems to have been Shakespeare's intent in each case. To substitute *the* for the old *th'*, *to* for *t'*, *on* or *of* for *o'*, *in* for *i'*, and so forth, frequently gives a wrong impression of the author's metrical scheme. This is especially noteworthy, for example, in *Coriolanus*, where the verses abound in such clipped forms. In the case of *-ed*, the apostrophe is used when elision is intended; full spelling indicates full pronunciation. In such words as *followed, borrowed, withered*, and the like, the full spelling is retained when the old texts justify it. Uniformity is not to be expected. The metrical problems involved cannot be settled beyond question; but there is no reason why *followed* (in full) should not satisfy the metre whenever such a form as *follower* would not violate it. In prose passages a common practice of editors has been to ignore many of the distinctions between full and clipped forms which the Quartos and Folios make. To maintain the euphony of the prose, this edition preserves such indications of the sort as the texts of Shakespeare's time supply.

Careful attention has been paid to the stage directions. No liberties are taken with the old texts in this regard. Additions are often imperative, but in such cases whatever is added is enclosed within square brackets. Thus the reader is in no danger of confusing the opinions of modern editors with the testimony of Shakespeare's own time. The same policy has been adopted in dividing the plays into Acts and Scenes and in designating the place of action. In most cases, the lists of *Dramatis Personæ* are bracketed for the same reason. When (as in *The Tempest*) the Folio prints *Names of the Actors*, these have been treated in the same way as the stage directions.

In a text that adopts modern spelling, logical procedure calls for modern punctuation. Hence the present edition has been repunctuated in strict accordance with the rules that Shakespeare would presumably observe if he were writing to-day. Theorists have dallied with the idea that what is called 'dramatic punctuation' may be discovered in the old texts; but this theory has had its day.

The Introductions which preface each play undertake to give, in brief, the pertinent facts. They discuss the basis of the text, the date of composition, the source of the plot, the dramatic method, and such other significant matters as space permits.

The Glossary is unusually full. In many cases where the usage is peculiar, or where there has been much discussion about the exact meaning, references are given to the place where the word or phrase occurs in the text.

The numbering of lines has been made to accord so far as possible with that commonly used in citing the plays. This method is preferred to a new counting in order to facilitate reference to such standard works as Bartlett's *Concordance* and Schmidt's *Shakespeare-Lexicon*.

G. L. K.

CAMBRIDGE, JULY 21, 1936

vi

Publisher's Preface

A popular pastime of some years ago, known as "Desert Island," was the compilation of lists of indispensable books which would constitute the sole reading of a castaway. Needless to say, the Bible and the works of Shakespeare were initial items on all such lists. They are regarded as the noblest of our cultural legacies, the *sine qua non* of the "well-stored mind."

Unfortunately, the standard editions of Shakespeare—the musty tomes of "the complete works" which gather dust on the family bookshelf—while they contain a fund of matchless poetry, cannot convey any impression of the color and atmosphere of the plays as Shakespeare intended them to be produced. And the hypothetical castaway, like the average reader, would receive from the plain text no more than a faint notion of what the plays are like when effectively staged.

The Kittredge-Players edition is designed to supply—as well as anything less than the actual productions can hope to—those elements which are consistently lacking in the usual editions of the plays. It supplements the best available modern text with over seven hundred photographs of the plays and players, illustrating the productions of the world's finest Shakespearean repertory theaters.

The text of this edition, the result of a lifetime of Shakespeare study by the late George Lyman Kittredge, Gurney Professor of English Literature at Harvard University, presents the plays in their most readable form, with modern spelling and punctuation.

Introductions to the individual plays provide the essential literary data and historical background and concisely discuss the sources of the play and its relation to other works of the dramatist. A compendious glossary explains some five thousand archaic and unusual terms used in the plays.

The illustrations are photographs of the most magnificently staged productions in the history of the Shakespearean theater, and include hundreds of scenes from gala performances of the Old Vic Company of London and the Memorial Theatre at Stratford-upon-Avon, world famous for their distinguished casts and the originality and richness of settings and costumes. Introducing the folio of photographs that accompanies each play are portrait studies of the principals, the most noted contemporary Shakespeareans pictured in the roles in which they have been most successful.

Mr. Michael Benthall, director of the Old Vic Theatre, has contributed an informative discussion on the problems of the actor and director in the staging of the plays of Shakespeare; and a biographical essay by Edwin E. Willoughby, chief bibliographer of the Folger Shakespeare Library, affords a view of Shakespeare and his works in relation to the political and cultural developments of the Elizabethan age.

The publisher gratefully acknowledges the co-operation of the directors of the Old Vic Theatre and the Memorial Theatre and the brilliant contribution of the photographers whose work illustrates this edition. Special thanks are also due to Miss Anne Bolton for her assistance in collecting and titling the photographs.

Chicago, 1958   LEONARD S. DAVIDOW

Contents

The Living Shakespeare

ONE of the really interesting phenomena in the theater of our time is that actors and managements everywhere are rediscovering Shakespeare as a living force. That scholars have never forgotten him is beside the point: poets and pedants can exhume and honor his dry bones, but it takes actors to breathe life into them. Tourists may regard Stratford as the shrine and gape at a few relics, but what really matters is the performances in the Memorial Theatre. It may well be that the performances in the giant marquee at Stratford, Ontario, or in the pinewood reconstruction of the Globe Theatre at Stratford, Connecticut, will in the long run matter just as much. Enterprise on that scale can scarcely be dismissed as one more fashionable trend in the theater; nor can the unfailing appearance of Shakespeare's name on the program of every Drama Festival which dares to style itself "international."

We don't have to dig deep to find out why the larger public today recognizes the performance of Shakespeare's plays as a prime theatrical attraction. The first reason is simply that higher standards of performance and of presentation have revealed the sheer entertainment value of the plays when they are properly done. The second reason is the reappearance of the less familiar plays, enabling audiences to reassess their worth by more reliable standards of comparison. We used to be told the difference between the good and the bad plays in the canon; later it became the difference between the best and the next best. Nowadays we are taught to distinguish between what is good and what is better. The public is becoming familiar with a larger part of Shakespeare; and though the public rarely knows what it likes, it usually likes what it knows.

To rebut any charge of oversimplification there is the curious parallel of Beethoven, whose music has gained enormously in popular favor during the last quarter of a century. Toscanini had demonstrated—simply by playing the music as it was written instead of "interpreting" it—that Beethoven was not meant to be revered so much as enjoyed. New standards of performance were set and Beethoven found an even larger audience than Tchaikovsky because so much more of Beethoven was found to be worth a permanent place in the concert repertory. It is vitally important to try to see a creative artist as a whole.

It was a grasp of this truth, more than the advent of the new Elizabethan Age, which inspired the London Old Vic to plan the production during five years of all the Shakespeare plays in the First Folio. The need was felt to provide the ordinary theater-goer with a more direct approach to Shakespeare, and such a plan, being the kind of long-term project which the "commercial" theater could hardly contemplate, seemed the right policy for a theater receiving part of its revenue from public funds. A keen schoolboy might thus see all the plays before graduation. This might not make it any easier for him to negotiate his paper in English Literature, but he would come to regard a visit to a performance of Shakespeare as an exciting theatrical experience instead of another excuse for getting out of algebra.

Clearly there is a new generation of audiences avid for Shakespeare. Can the demand be met by the new generation of actors?

Modern audiences will no longer tolerate Shakespeare played by actors with no classical training. Drawing room comedy is no preparation for an actor in the classics; nor is any kind of technique involving the use of a microphone or of any other meretricious aid. The young actor must be prepared to serve a long and rigorous apprenticeship before he can hope to mesmerize the informed public with his Hamlet. Yet there will always be plenty of intrepid young men ready to take up the challenge, perhaps because they so rarely see the size of the obstacles ahead. For although a would-be instrumentalist knows exactly what he must learn before he can qualify for membership in a great orchestra, paradoxically there is no accepted syllabus of teaching for acting in the classical drama, the art with the greatest of all English traditional associations. Whether the answer is bigger and better schools of drama or the opportunity to carry a spear in a classical company as a means of contact with experienced actors, the fact remains that there are no short cuts to playing or directing Shakespeare. An actor relying on an imposing profile and a talent for verse-speaking will soon be put in his place by an audience content with nothing less than a vibrant personality and a capacity for verse-*acting;* a director preoccupied with handsomely mounted production and adroit choreography will quickly be decried by a public insisting on being given the sense of the play and demanding a splendid vocal line to communicate it.

Probably a judicious mixture of academic training and practical experience is the right solution for the aspiring classical actor, but it takes a great deal to deter the young artist with the instinct and the will to succeed, and if he has talent plus a magnetic personality, nothing can prevent the public from making him a star. A young artist of this kind learns automatically that an enormously wide variety of Shakespearean roles can be rewarding in terms of themselves. With Shakespeare, as much as any playwright, it is the part which makes the actor; and for a good actor there is no such thing as a small part. Attention to the somewhat derogatory term, "star-quality," is important, because it cannot be denied that such a quality contributes just as much to the popularity of Shakespeare as the teamwork and sense of style which are prerequisites of any Shakespearean company. In fact, it is the business of managements to see that the professional careers of their actors are fully developed and that each artist is given the best possible presentation in terms of parts. Planning the order of the parts played has a lot to do with an artist's ultimate success, for when he reaches the major character parts, his admirers like to remember the romantic behind the whiskers. In any case, talent in the classical theater is not so plentiful that we can afford to let any of it wither away because of lack of proper attention and the right kind of encouragement.

This very edition of Shakespeare is in itself a form of encouragement. What distinguishes this edition from all others is that it is embellished with photographs of *living* artists. In that sense it also helps to keep Shakespeare alive. It shows, too, that the major Shakespearean roles can still be really well played by quite young artists.

One much cherished illusion is that some Shakespeare roles are unplayable. What we really mean is that we don't happen to have seen an entirely satisfactory performance of this or that part; the fact that different people cite different parts effectively disposes of that particular myth. In this context, too, it is worth remembering that the female parts most often called "unactable"—*Cleopatra, Lady Macbeth* and *Juliet*—were originally played by boys well enough to convince an Elizabethan audience. We may be reasonably sure that the accomplishments of

Dame Sybil Thorndike, Dame Edith Evans, Miss Peggy Ashcroft, and Miss Katherine Cornell can stand comparison with anything produced by those talented boy players. It is the same with the perennial claim that the major roles are never played today so well as they used to be. The only evidence we have of the truth of this is the sentimental memories of aging critics. (Not all critics mellow with the years, and it may well be self-disillusionment that induces some of them to sneer at failure and resent success.) But in the not too distant future it may be possible to demolish this defeatist attitude. The phonograph record companies are already experimenting with full-length recordings of classical plays, and they may yet provide at least some aural evidence that the new generation of actors can measure up to the old. Film producers, too, will find a way of presenting classical acting companies in a manner which records their best achievements and communicates their individual style. Meanwhile, such distinguished artists as Sir Laurence Olivier and Sir John Gielgud have provided us with film performances of Shakespeare which will long be treasured. On the other hand, there is nothing so far to suggest that film versions of Shakespeare will ever be anything more than a celluloid substitute for the living theater. Historians have it that Shakespeare owed much to the contact between actors and audience in the theater of his day, and even contemporary methods of staging allow an audience to enjoy a sense of participation entirely absent in motion pictures. The vitality of a live performance springs from the slight insecurity which exists in a theater until contact between players and audience has been established. Everyone knows that performances of the same play by the same company vary with different audiences; what is sometimes overlooked is that the disparities between one theatrical performance and another can be just as entertaining as the similarities.

Photographs of contemporary actors in well-known classical roles, such as are to be found in this book, evoke memories not only of the part played but of the whole play. It is extraordinary how the memory of an individual performance can color one's recollected impressions of the whole, and remarkable that the first performance seen is usually the one which remains longest in the memory. In the case of the classical drama it is, therefore, all the more important that the first impressions should be the right ones, lest the interest of younger audiences is dissipated forever. One makeshift performance of a Shakespeare play by an inadequate touring company is enough to form a prejudice in a child's mind against Shakespeare as lasting as any initiated in a schoolroom; the notion that the greatest of Shakespeare's plays are indestructible and proof against demonstrably bad performance is pitifully inept and must be ruthlessly exposed wherever it is met. Where Shakespeare is concerned, say the theorists, we can't have too much of a good thing. Audiences reply (through the box office) that it depends on what you mean by "a good thing." For them the best is just good enough.

It follows that if the new popularity of Shakespeare is to be consolidated into something more permanent, enough directors will have to be found who are capable of presenting the plays properly. The shortage of directors well-versed in the classics is acute, and the services of those available have to be spread out among more and more theater organizations. Shortages usually act as a spur to newcomers, and when talented young directors are found they will continue to disagree between themselves—just as their predecessors have always done—about the right way to set about presenting the plays. The disagreements will be stimulating. There will always be convinced geniuses determined to experiment with every play from *King Lear* to *The Comedy of Errors* and to treat all known methods of production as a point of departure; there will always be plenty of charlatans resorting to every trick of the theater to "improve" Shakespeare—or at least to divert attention from the poverty of their own invention. Then there will also be the very few with an instinctive feeling for the truth of a play—and it is they who will always win the arguments in the end. The decision will be made, not by the critics nor by the acting profession, but by the audience.

The director's function during the production of a play should be to take the place of the audience. Whether he is considered a good director or not depends on whether the performance for which he is responsible gives the maximum amount of satisfaction to the largest number of people. He has to work on his own instinct and to have the confidence to believe that the audience will like what he likes. The director's "instinct" however can often so dominate a production that he directs the audience's attention from the real truth of the play; to take a broad example, he can turn a tragedy scene to comedy or vice versa, either because his instinct is awry or because he wishes to show off his own invention powers instead of relying on those of his author. Sometimes there is good reason for tampering with the text itself and a director of discretion should have the confidence to cut or rearrange a script as if the author were there himself for discussion; but, on the whole, if the play is acted and spoken with true understanding and a sense of the rhythm of the lines and scenes, no audience will fail to rise to it. A lot of nonsense is written and talked about the speaking of the verse, but it must be remembered that Shakespeare was an actor and wrote his plays to be acted, and there is one basic rule, with which Sir John Gielgud, our greatest verse speaker, concurs, which is that if you make sense of the lines and pay attention to Shakespeare's punctuation, the verse will take care of itself.

Technical problems—of staging or decor, accent or incidental music—are quite a different matter and of relatively less importance. These are the aspects most susceptible to the fashionable trends in the theater, which are mercifully short-lived and which occur among amateur societies as well as professional organizations— but most of all among the paid amateurs working in the professional theater. Directors will continue to struggle with variations of the platform theater while most theaters have a proscenium arch and most audiences are demanding the maximum illusion that the theater has to give. From time to time we shall be favored with "authentic" Elizabethan pronunciation for the delight of audiences reared on radio announcers' English. That kind of thing is always enlivening and every *enfant terrible* may at least be a catalyst for ideas.

The fundamental problems remain: the problems relating to the structure of the plays and to the poetical language that transfigures every plot and situation. These are the problems that eternally fascinate actor and director alike. Their success in solving them will make something permanent of the renewed interest in the living Shakespeare. It will help us toward a fuller appreciation of Shakespeare's greatness as a poet, his towering genius as a playwright. Above all it will teach us once again to marvel at his infinite knowledge of human nature.

September 1, 1955.

MICHAEL BENTHALL
Director,
The Old Vic Theatre

Note: Mr. Benthall wishes to acknowledge the assistance of his colleague, Alfred Francis, administrative director of the Old Vic Theatre, in compiling and co-ordinating his views.

The Man and the Playwright

WILLIAM Shakespeare was born in Stratford-upon-Avon. He was baptized in the Stratford church on April 25, 1564. As children then were usually baptized about three days after birth, it is probable that April 23, 1564, the traditional date of Shakespeare's birth is the correct one. This day, dedicated to St. George, the patron saint of England, has long been celebrated as the birthday of Shakespeare.

Shakespeare was a middle-class, small-town man. In Stratford he spent his childhood and youth. While he was away from it, he still maintained his family there. After he had become a successful dramatist and a wealthy business man, he retired to it.

Stratford, even in the 16th century, was an old historic town. It is in Warwickshire, 110 miles northwest of London. One road from Stratford to London goes through Oxford, 50 miles away—past the gray towers of the university, which was as famous then as it is now as a seat of learning.

Youth

John Shakespeare, the poet's father, came to Stratford about 1552, 12 years before the birth of his famous son. With the same enterprise which later was to characterize his son, John Shakespeare married Mary Arden, the daughter of his father's landlord, soon after he left his father's farm. He went into business as a glover and whittawer; that is, he tanned and whitened skins, then made from them gloves and other articles. Prospering in his business, John Shakespeare was elected in 1561 and in 1562 one of the two chamberlains who managed the financial affairs of Stratford. In 1568, he was chosen high bailiff or mayor of Stratford and in 1571, chief alderman. As the bailiff and the chief alderman of Stratford, John Shakespeare held the office of justice of the peace. It is not unlikely that Shakespeare's love of depicting comic country constables and solemn courtroom scenes had its origin in watching his father preside over a justice's court.

Education

As Shakespeare grew into childhood, he probably was sent to an elementary school for a short time and then at about the age of seven, as almost every boy of Stratford did, he entered the King's New School at Stratford-upon-Avon, a school which unfortunately has none of its early attendance records. The curriculum of the school was by modern standards narrow. Latin was the most emphasized subject. Taught for long hours each day, a graduate was able not only to read Latin authors but to write the language—an accomplishment necessary for success in law, medicine, the church, and the government service, and which was often of value in business. Stratford Grammar School was an excellent school. The three masters who taught there during Shakespeare's youth were Oxford graduates. Two of these Stratford teachers had been fellows of colleges.

After Shakespeare left school, according to tradition, he began to learn his father's trade, the trade of a glover. This is probable; his plays and poems show an intimate knowledge of the terms of the glover's craft. Shakespeare, according to another tradition, became for a time a country school teacher—not an impossible attainment for a young man educated at the Stratford Grammar School. Other traditions about Shakespeare's early life have resulted from misunderstanding. A favorite variety act, for instance, was for an actor to pretend to kill a calf (cf. *Hamlet* III, 2, 100). From the tradition that Shakespeare would perform this entertainment in "a high style and make a speech," early biographers concluded that in his youth he was a butcher.

Marriage

Soon after he left school, Shakespeare married hastily, with a bishop's special license, Anne Hathaway, the daughter, in all probability, of one of his father's friends. He was 18; she was 25 or 26. The wedding took place about Dec. 1, 1582 (the records of it were possibly stolen by a souvenir hunter), and a daughter was baptized on May 26, 1583. These dates, plus a little arithmetic, have produced the appearance of a scandal. But marriages then were often entered into by precontract which preceded the formal wedding ceremony.

Before their father had reached the age of 21, twins, Hamnet (or Hamlet) and Judith Shakespeare, were born. Shortly after this Shakespeare left Stratford and for about 10 years—the so-called "10 lost years in London"—Shakespeare's name disappears from the records. When it reappears, Shakespeare had become a trained professional actor and dramatist.

London

A legend long circulated that Shakespeare fled because he was persecuted by the local magnate of Stratford, Sir Thomas Lucy, for killing his deer and for writing a satirical poem about him. But Lucy had no deer park and the poem, which was later produced, is clearly a forgery.

The natural explanation of Shakespeare's coming to London is that Stratford, like other small towns, offered few opportunities to ambitious young men. Like his fellow townsman Richard Field, later the printer of his first poems, Shakespeare probably went to London to seek his fortune, managed to get a minor job in the theater, then learned the art of acting. Which company of players he joined is not known—he may have connected with more than one—but the most probable company was that which had as its patron the Earl of Pembroke.

Shakespeare became a competent actor. A contemporary witness tells us that he played the parts of kings. Good tradition assigns to him the role of Adam in *As You Like It* and of the ghost in *Hamlet*.

Shakespeare also learned to write plays. By 1592, he was attracting so much attention that a contemporary poet, Robert Greene, as he was dying in poverty, wrote a bitter attack upon him, because he, a mere actor, was by his writings taking work away from Greene and his fellow university wits who had been supplying the players with their plays. He called Shakespeare "an upstart crow beautified with our feathers . . . the only Shake-scene in a country" and parodied a line from his *Henry VI, Part 2.*

The Early Plays

These plays of Shakespeare, the success of which aroused the wrath of Greene, were varied, for Shakespeare began by experimenting with different types of plays. And unfortunately it is difficult to fix their dates. Six plays—a comedy, a tragedy, and four histories—however, can reasonably be assigned to this early period.

The Comedy of Errors is based upon a comedy by the Latin poet, Plautus, which Shakespeare may well have read in the Stratford Grammar School. It concerns the misadventures of two pairs of twins.

In contrast with this comedy stands *Titus Andronicus.* Shakespeare saw the success that Thomas Kyd was scoring in *The Spanish Tragedy*, a play filled with blood and violence. With the true showman's desire to meet the public demand, he decided to write a tragedy like it. He may have adapted a play by Kyd which is now lost, or more probably, he may have imitated those elements of Kyd's style which he believed made his play successful. *Titus Andronicus* has its scene in Rome; it is a play of revenge, crammed full of murders, rape, and mutilation.

The histories were called forth by the wave of patriotic enthusiasm which swept England at the time when Shakespeare began writing. In 1588, England scored a glorious victory by defeating the Spanish Armada. The theatergoers demanded plays which would dramatize their country's history. But they feared rebellion within their country for unrest was pervading the land. The change of the national religion grieved and angered those who remained loyal to the old faith. And the changes in the national economy brought wealth to some but desperation to others. Shakespeare, no doubt with these conditions in mind, wrote three plays, *Henry VI*, *Parts 1*, *2*, and *3*, which depicted the sufferings caused by civil war by rebellion against a weak king, so unlike England's strong queen, Elizabeth. The theme of the value of a strong stable government is a theme also of *Richard III*. Here a tyrant is seen cunningly usurping the throne and killing many of his nobles until he finally is slain by Elizabeth's grandfather, Henry VII, who brought peace to England.

Poems

Beginning with the summer of 1592, the theaters were closed almost continuously for two years because of the bubonic plague. Shakespeare turned his attention to narrative poetry, which was considered by his fellow Elizabethans as serious literature in contrast with the drama which they esteemed mere popular entertainment. Again, he went back to a book which he had probably read in the Stratford Grammar School, the *Metamorphoses* of the Latin poet Ovid. Shakespeare took the manuscript of his *Venus and Adonis* to his Stratford friend, Richard Field, who in 1593 printed and published the volume. Shakespeare dedicated this poem to a young nobleman, Henry Wriothesley, the Earl of Southampton, then aged 20, who probably, as was customary, rewarded the author with a gift.

Venus and Adonis met with an immediate success, so great indeed that Shakespeare next year followed it with another long poem, *The Rape of Lucrece*. Again he went back to Ovid for a story, this time to his *Fasti*. This poem was also printed by Field in 1594, but it was published by John Harrison. Again Shakespeare dedicated the poem to the young Earl of Southampton but in terms which showed that a greater intimacy had grown up between the poet and the nobleman.

Sonnets

About this time also Shakespeare began writing a series of 154 poems, all but three of them 14-line sonnets. The composition of these sonnets was spread over a number of years. Possibly some even go back to 1588, the year of the attempted invasion of England by the Armada. Two were included in 1599 by William Jaggard in a collection, *The Passionate Pilgrim*, but the entire series of sonnets was not published until 1609, and then probably without the knowledge of Shakespeare. In that year Thomas Thorp by some means obtained possession of a manuscript of Shakespeare's *Sonnets* and had them published. He prefixed to them—it is not known by what authority—a dedication to a "Mr. W. H." Who "Mr. W. H." was is unknown. There have been many guesses, most of them ridiculous. "W. H." could be a reversal of the initials of Henry Wriothesley, Earl of Southampton, who is the favored candidate, and some of the sonnets fit Southampton well. But the initials and some of the other sonnets fit other candidates also.

In the *Sonnets* Shakespeare urges his patron to marry. He then speaks of a love affair between the author and a married woman, "the Dark Lady," whom his patron later takes away from him. Nevertheless he forgives his friend. Other episodes follow.

These *Sonnets* may be autobiographical or they may not be. If they describe incidents in the life of Shakespeare, it is easy to see why he did not desire to have them printed. But it is almost as unlikely, were they autobiographical, that he should be willing to have "his sugared *Sonnets*" circulated "among his private friends," as they were circulating in or before 1598. It is likely, therefore, that few, if any, of the episodes of Shakespeare's *Sonnets* were from real life. Certainly the episodes in the sonnets of Shakespeare's contemporaries were largely imaginary and those of his may well be also.

Member of Chamberlain's Company

When the plague ended late in 1594, Shakespeare is found in a new company, the Chamberlain's Men, which had as its patron, Henry Carey, Lord Hunsdon, the cousin and the closest living relative of the queen, and as the Lord Chamberlain, the master of her household. Shakespeare now had the great advantage not only of playing with the best actors of England but, even more important, of having his plays produced by a company which challenged his best efforts. This superior acting encouraged him to write better and better plays. He averaged now two plays a year.

Period of the Comedies

For his new company Shakespeare began by writing comedies, a type of play which has always appealed to English theatergoers. From about 1594 to 1603, roughly from his 30th until his 39th year, Shakespeare produced 11 comedies.

The earliest of these comedies was probably *The Taming of the Shrew*, a rollicking story of how a young husband changed his nagging, domineering bride into a sweet-tempered and dutiful wife.

Less successful was a comedy on the conflict of love and friendship, *Two Gentlemen of Verona*, and a satire on pedantry and affectation, *Love's Labour's Lost*. But in *A Midsummer-Night's Dream*, a more successful play, Shakespeare first made use of the supernatural element which he later employed so successfully in *Macbeth*, *Hamlet*, *The Tempest*, and other plays. In this comedy mortal love affairs are interrupted by a quarrel between the king and queen of fairies. In the course of this quarrel Oberon, the king, causes his wife Titania to fall madly in love with a weaver whose head he changes temporarily into that of an ass.

The next comedy, *The Merchant of Venice*, has the powerful character of the Jew, Shylock, the only major character of Shakespeare who is a business man. Its climax is the courtroom scene in which the heroine, Portia, disguised as a lawyer, successfully defends the life of her husband's friend.

Much Ado About Nothing, a play about a plot to blast the reputation of a woman, which is frustrated by a stupid constable and his watchmen, stands in contrast with *As You Like It*, probably written in the same year (1599 or 1600), a comedy with the idyllic background of the forest of Arden. Perhaps the most hilarious of Shakespeare's comedies is *Twelfth Night* in which the puritanical and officious manager of the household of a beautiful young woman is persuaded that his mistress is secretly in love with him. Consequently, he acts so strangely that he is confined as insane.

But Shakespeare did not restrict himself during this period entirely to comedies. Indeed, Shakespeare's comic art probably reached its greatest height in two of the histories. In *Henry IV, Part 1*, Shakespeare created Sir John Falstaff, one of his greatest characters. This fat, drunken old braggart, who is a clever, witty, and penetrating judge of men, proved so popular that Shakespeare immediately wrote *Part 2* so that he might continue his adventures. He described the death of the intriguing old rascal in *Henry V*, perhaps the greatest of his historical plays. This story of the conquest of France by England's hero-king appealed to the patriotic feelings of his audience with scenes of the battle of Agincourt. Shakespeare brought Falstaff back to life to become the hero of *The Merry Wives of Windsor*, Shakespeare's only picture of contemporary English middle-class life. In this comedy Falstaff assails the virtue of two middle-aged small-town women with disastrous consequence to himself.

During this period, Shakespeare also wrote *Richard II*, the story of a weakling who lost his throne. *King John* was a less successful play. The king who was forced to grant the Magna Carta did not appeal to a dramatist who admired the semi-absolutism of Elizabeth.

Shakespeare also wrote two tragedies during this period: one at the beginning of it, the other at its end. *Romeo and Juliet*, written about 1594, is the story of two "star-crossed lovers," the son and daughter of two quarreling families whose enmity brings death to their young children. *Julius Caesar*, written about 1599, is the story of a political assassination and the national disaster of civil war which followed it.

Landed Gentleman

While he was writing these comedies, histories, and tragedies, Shakespeare was achieving success as an actor and was growing in wealth. He desired, like many other middle-class men of his time, to be granted a coat of arms. This would entitle him to be styled "gentleman" and to occupy the rank in society next below a knight. On October 20, 1596, heralds granted to John Shakespeare and his children a coat of arms, the chief element of which is a falcon shaking a spear. The next year, 1597, Shakespeare purchased New Place, one of the largest houses in Stratford.

Globe Theatre

In 1599 he joined with four fellow-actors and with the brother of one of them to build a theater in Southwark, on the bank of the Thames. With a capacity of about 1,500 people, it was the largest theater in England. It was named "The Globe" from the sign painted above its door, a picture of Atlas holding the world on his shoulders. Shakespeare now was part owner of a theater in which he acted, and he sometimes appeared there in plays which he himself had written.

Near the end of the reign of Elizabeth occurred an event which could have ruined the dramatist. The Earl of Essex, a friend of Shakespeare's patron, Southampton, feeling aggrieved at the queen's counselors, determined to revolt against the government. He and his friends persuaded the Chamberlain's Men to present Shakespeare's *Richard II* at the Globe, hoping that the scene of the deposing of a king would inspire the people to revolt. They played it on the afternoon of February 7, 1601, the day before the attempted insurrection. But the revolt failed completely; Essex and Southampton were arrested. Fortunately the players were able to convince the authorities that they were ignorant of the intentions of the conspirators. Otherwise Shakespeare, who in *Henry V* had praised Essex, might even have been tried for treason.

Groom of the Court

Shakespeare's good fortune continued. The death of Elizabeth brought down from Scotland her successor, King James I, a lover of plays and a lavish, even extravagant, supporter of the stage. On May 19, 1603, a few weeks after his accession to the throne, he became the patron of Shakespeare's company, who became known as the King's Men. James appointed the major players to places in his household as Grooms of the Chamber. As such, Shakespeare and his fellows attended the king on various state functions. And they continued to perform at the Globe and at the court. Probably to please the king, Shakespeare wrote, about 1606, *Macbeth*, a play with a Scotch background which echoed James's political philosophy and paid the king a number of compliments.

From 1599 to the end of his residence in London (about 1610), Shakespeare lived comfortably, much of the time in the house of a Frenchman, Mountjoy, a maker of hair ornaments. He was on intimate terms with this family. Many of his evenings he spent with a group of prominent authors at the Mermaid Tavern.

Great Tragedies

It is strange to find Shakespeare, at the height of his success, changing from the comedies which he had been writing for about seven years to tragedies and to darkly serious comedies. About 1599, Shakespeare wrote his greatest drama, probably the greatest tragedy ever written, *Hamlet, Prince of Denmark*. In this play his father's ghost reveals to Hamlet that it is his duty to revenge his murder; that he had been poisoned by his brother, who desired his throne and his queen. But Hamlet hesitates to kill his own uncle, and by delaying brings death upon his beloved Ophelia, her family, his mother, and himself.

Other tragedies followed. *Othello, the Moor of Venice*, has as its hero a middle-aged general whom a subtle liar so excites with jealousy that he murders his young and innocent wife. *King Lear* is the story of an old king who is induced by flattery to disinherit a loving daughter in favor of two ungrateful older ones; they bring death to him, to their younger sister, and themselves. *Macbeth*, another tragedy of a political murder, has already been noticed. *Antony and Cleopatra* was the last of Shakespeare's great tragedies. This is the tragedy of a queen and a general who become enmeshed in an unchaste love affair which finally leads them both to disgrace and suicide. The last two tragedies which Shakespeare wrote alone are both, like *Lear*, on the theme of ingratitude. *Coriolanus* tells of the ingratitude of a commonwealth, Rome, to a general who had saved it; *Timon of Athens*, of the ingratitude of friends toward a lavish bestower of favors.

Shakespeare's turning from comedies to tragedies has called forth many explanations. Some scholars have professed to find explanations deep in the mind and philosophy of Shakespeare. Others have suggested some grief, such as the death of his son, Hamnet, in 1596, as the cause. Any of these are possible. A simpler explanation can also be advanced: *Hamlet* proved to be an outstanding box-office success. Shakespeare, a practical dramatist, might well have tried to gratify a public demand by writing more plays of this same type.

Somber Comedies

This explanation, however, only partially accounts for the comedies written at the time of these tragedies. *Troilus and Cressida*, the earliest of these, was probably written as a satirical answer to attacks by other dramatists on Shakespeare's company in the so-called "war of the theaters." The plot is a medievalized version of an episode in the Trojan war.

All's Well that Ends Well is the story of how a young woman after obtaining a husband by royal command pursues him when he flees from her and finally, disguised and in an ambiguous situation, wins his love. *Measure for Measure* is a problem play. A hypocritical official attempts to force a girl to save the life of her brother by yielding her virtue to him, but he is thwarted in this attempt by the duke, his sovereign, and is forgiven by the heroine.

Blackfriars Theatre

The King's Men were prospering under James I. But the Globe was an open air theater not suitable for winter performances. Some of the leading men of the company, Shakespeare among them, late in 1608 leased a theater situated in the old monastery of Blackfriars, which had become a fashionable residential section. With this completely roofed playhouse inside the city the King's Men could perform in both winter and summer. A wealthier group of theater-goers came to the Blackfriars Theatre, and as part lessee of this theater, Shakespeare enjoyed a considerable income.

The death, in 1607, of his youngest brother, Edmund, who had become an actor in London, at the age of 28 no doubt brought sorrow to the poet. William buried his brother in the chancel of what is now Southwark Cathedral, close to the Globe.

Late Tragi-comedies

After 1607, Shakespeare wrote on an average of but one play a year. Realizing the popularity of the tragi-comedies which Beaumont and Fletcher were producing, he turned his hand to this type of play. (Beaumont and Fletcher, in turn, may have patterned their own plays upon a romance, *Pericles, Prince of Tyre*, of which Shakespeare wrote but a part.) Alone Shakespeare wrote three romances. All of them are placed outside the bounds of definite time and space. All have improbable plots in keeping with their storyland settings. And all three voice a theme brought out before in *Measure for Measure*, the value of forgiveness on the part of the injured party, so strongly that it has even been conjectured that Shakespeare may have undergone an experience akin to a religious conversion about 1604. *Cymbeline*, the first of these tragi-comedies, has as its scene ancient Britain. Its plot concerns an attempt to slander a woman's honor. *The Winter's Tale*, the next of these, is a story of intense and causeless jealousy enacted in a land on "the sea coasts of Bohemia" and in Sicily in a time when the Greek gods were worshiped. Shakespeare's last play of his sole authorship, *The Tempest*, has as its scene an enchanted island where an exiled duke by magic power overcomes the usurper of his throne, effects a change in his moral nature, forgives him, and arranges a marriage between the usurper's son and his own daughter.

Retirement to Stratford

Shakespeare always seems to have planned to retire to Stratford. He continued investing in land in its vicinity and about 1610 he settled with his family in New Place. He was regarded by his fellow-townsmen as one of Stratford's leading citizens.

But he continued his interest in London. He leased the gate house, an old building in the Blackfriars' estate, on March 10, 1613. And he continued to write for the King's Men; in 1613, he completed two plays written in collaboration with the dramatist John Fletcher: *The Two Noble Kinsmen* and *King Henry VIII*. The first production of the latter play, on June 29, 1613, brought misfortune to its players. Guns fired during the play ignited the thatch on the roof of the Globe and set it on fire. The Globe was soon rebuilt, but the fire involved loss to the poet.

Death

Shakespeare was ill when a month before his death he made his will. He left token bequests to his fellow-players and Stratford friends, provided for his daughters, and in an interlined addition gave his wife his second-best bed. Anne Shakespeare was entitled to one-third of her husband's real estate and to other properties by her dower right; so there was no reason to mention them in the will. The second-best bed was probably that which she and her husband regularly occupied and she probably desired to possess it for sentimental reasons.

William Shakespeare died at New Place, Stratford, on April 23, 1616, and was buried in a place of honor by the high altar in the Stratford church. An expensive monument bearing his bust was placed above his grave.

Publication of Plays

Shakespeare wrote in all 39 plays, including those in which he collaborated. He probably revised a few more. Of these, 17 were published before his death, in small pamphlets (called from their size, quartos) each containing a single play. But Shakespeare's fellow-players to honor his memory collected his plays into a single large volume, now called from its size the First Folio. This, *The Comedies, Histories & Tragedies of Mr. William Shakespeare*, published in 1623, is considered the most important single volume in English literature. On its title page appears the best-known portrait of the poet.

Shakespeare lived quietly in Stratford during the last years of his life. Quite probably he was not well. His parents and probably all his brothers died before him. His eldest daughter, married in 1607 to a successful physician, John Hall, lived with him. His youngest daughter, Judith, also lived in New Place until she was 32. Then long past the usual age for marriage, she, like her mother before her, married a man six years younger than herself, Thomas Quiney, on February 10, 1616, without obtaining a required license. This caused her excommunication, which no doubt brought sorrow to her father in his last days.

Shakespeare's Unceasing Appeal

Shakespeare's plays have continued to be printed and performed for over three and a half centuries. Since the middle of the 17th century there probably has never been a decade in which Shakespeare's plays were not performed more than those of any other dramatist. For more than a century he has been a favorite dramatist in Germany. He has had an especial appeal to the Russians and the Italians. Even in the crowded cities of India adaptations of his plays are frequently performed.

Shakespeare more than any dramatist of the past has retained his hold on the ordinary man and woman of today. What is the secret of this appeal? Dr. Samuel Johnson has supplied the answer when he said, "This therefore is the praise of Shakespeare, that his drama is the mirror of life." The modern man when he sees or reads Shakespeare's plays recognizes himself in them. He sees problems growing out of faults and weaknesses like his own. He finds these problems resolved with great wisdom expressed in language of surpassing beauty. Because the problems presented in the plays of Shakespeare are fundamental ones and so essentially those of today, the appeal of Shakespeare still remains and may well remain for centuries to come.

EDWIN E. WILLOUGHBY
Folger Shakespeare Library
Washington, D. C.

The Complete Comedies

THE TEMPEST

THE TEMPEST was first printed in the Folio of 1623, which affords an excellent text with unusually elaborate stage directions (see, for example, iii, 3; iv, 1; v, 1). It was acted at court by the King's Players (Shakespeare's company) sometime in the winter of 1612–1613 (or in the late autumn of 1612) during the festivities incident to the visit of Frederick the Elector Palatine, who arrived at London on October 18, 1612, was betrothed to the King's daughter Elizabeth on December 27, and married her on February 14. There is evidence, however, that THE TEMPEST had already been presented before the King on Hallowmas (November 1), 1611. This fixes one limit for the date of composition. The other limit is fixed as the autumn of 1610 by the fact that for details of the storm, as well as for the description of Prospero's island, Shakespeare got suggestions from the Bermudan adventures and discoveries of Sir George Somers, no report of which reached England until September, 1610. The most probable date for THE TEMPEST, then, is 1611. It may well be the latest of all Shakespeare's plays, except for his share in *Henry VIII* and in *The Two Noble Kinsmen*. The passage, however, in which Prospero speaks of "breaking his staff" and "drowning his book" (v, 1, 54–57), though it sounds like a presentiment, can hardly be interpreted as a farewell to the stage. The Folio doubtless represents the play as it was acted at court in the winter. Some scholars believe that the masque in act iv was written or enlarged expressly for that occasion; others conjecture that the masque, in whole or in part, is not Shakespeare's own work. Probably there was some adaptation of the original text for court performance, but there is no good reason for supposing that THE TEMPEST is not all Shakespeare's or that it ever existed in an earlier form that differed, except for a touch here and there, from the text as we have it.

No source for the plot has been discovered. *Die Schöne Sidea*, a comedy by Jakob Ayrer, who died in 1605, bears some resemblance to THE TEMPEST in outline and agrees with it in several details; but the differences are more significant than the agreements. *Die Schöne Sidea* reproduces, in a rationalized form, the ancient and widespread folk-tale of 'The Forgotten Bride.' Like the ninth story of the fifth day in Basile's *Pentamerone*, it belongs to that group of versions which include the romantic incidents (foreign to Shakespeare) of the maiden in the tree and the face mirrored in the spring. There is no forgotten bride in THE TEMPEST. Shakespeare's plot may be remotely akin to the ancient *märchen*, but he owes nothing to the German drama, of which, indeed, he had probably never heard. Certain Italian *scenari* that resemble Shakespeare's plot may likewise be disregarded as sources. The incidents in question were the common property of novelists and playwrights.

That Shakespeare owes something to narratives of Somers's adventures is certain. In 1608 and the following years the Virginia Company and its designs were in the forefront of public interest. On June 2, 1609, a fleet of seven ships and two small vessels sailed from Plymouth for Virginia. The flagship, the Sea Adventure, carried the new Governor (Sir Thomas Gates), the Admiral (Sir George Somers), and Captain Christopher Newport. On July 24 a terrible storm scattered the fleet. It arrived at Jamestown in August, but the Sea Adventure was missing. She had run ashore on the Bermudas on July 28, but without loss of life. Gates, Somers, and the rest — some hundred and fifty in all — remained in the islands for about nine months. On May 10, 1610, they sailed away in two small pinnaces which they had built, arriving at Jamestown on the 23d. In the following July Gates and Newport sailed for England. They arrived in September, and thus the first news of the adventures of Gates and Somers in Bermuda reached the mother country.

In 1610, soon after their arrival, three narratives of these adventures were published: (1) *Newes from Virginia*, a ballad by Richard Rich; (2) *A Discovery of the Bermudas, otherwise called the Ile of Divels*, by Silvester Jourdan; and (3) *A True Declaration of the estate of the Colonie in Virginia*. Both Rich and Jourdan had been with Somers in the Sea Adventure when she was wrecked. The ballad has no Shakespearean significance. The other two narratives coincide with THE TEMPEST in some details which, though slight, warrant the inference that Shakespeare had read them, as, indeed, he was very likely to do if he felt any interest in the news of the day. More important, however, is a long letter from William Strachey, another of Somers's companions. This seems to be dated July 15, 1610, and doubtless came over with Gates in September. It was not printed until 1625, when Purchas included it in the fourth volume of his *Pilgrimes*; but it must have circulated in manuscript and we may be reasonably sure that Shakespeare read it.

These three narratives, however, are in no sense to be regarded as sources of THE TEMPEST. At most they furnished Shakespeare with a few items of information or with miscellaneous suggestions which he has followed after his own fashion. Strachey's account of the wreck, for instance, is in striking contrast to what we find in THE TEMPEST. The Sea Adventure has sprung a leak and is in imminent danger of foundering. Crew and passengers, exhausted by four days' desperate toil at the pumps, are in raptures when they sight Bermuda, which, by good fortune, is on their weather. They lay their course for the shore, run the ship aground, and make a safe landing — a hundred and fifty of them — in their boats. The situation in THE TEMPEST is utterly different. There is, in fact, no wreck at all. The sailors make every effort to weather Prospero's island, which is on their lee, for they can defy the storm if they have "room enough." They do not succeed, but by the help of Ariel the ship is not dashed to pieces upon the rocks, but makes her way into a "deep nook" or cove, where she rides in safety. Shakespeare's handling of the vessel shows an accurate knowledge of seamanship which he cannot have learned from the Bermuda narratives. Unquestionably he had talked with sailors in his time and he owes quite as much to such conversation as to anything that he read in the three narratives.

Setebos is several times mentioned as the "great devil" of the Patagonian giants by Pigafetta in his account of Magellan's circumnavigation, an English version of which Shakespeare could have seen in Richard Eden's well-known volume *The History of Trauayle in the West and East Indies* (1577). Caliban is more likely to have derived his name from 'cannibal' than from the Gypsy word *cauliban*, 'blackness.' For Gonzalo's ideal commonwealth (ii, 1, 147 ff.) Shakespeare is indebted to Florio's Montaigne (1603). Prospero and some of the other names he could have found in Thomas's *History of Italye* (1549).

4

THE TEMPEST

Names of the Actors.

Alonso, King of Naples.
Sebastian, his brother.
Prospero, the right Duke of Milan.
Antonio, his brother, the usurping Duke of Milan.
Ferdinand, son to the King of Naples.
Gonzalo, an honest old councillor.
Adrian and *Francisco*, lords.
Caliban, a salvage and deformed slave.
Trinculo, a jester.
Stephano, a drunken butler.

Master of a ship, Boatswain, Mariners.

Miranda, daughter to *Prospero*.
Ariel, an airy spirit.
Iris,
Ceres,
Juno, ⎫
Nymphs, ⎬ [presented by] spirits.
Reapers, ⎭

[Other Spirits attending on *Prospero*.]

THE SCENE. — [*On board a ship at sea; afterwards*] *an uninhabited island.*

ACT I. Scene I. [*On board a ship at sea.*]

A tempestuous noise of thunder and lightning heard. Enter a *Shipmaster* and a *Boatswain*.

Mast. Boatswain!
Boats. Here, master. What cheer?
Mast. Good, speak to th' mariners! Fall to't — yarely, or we run ourselves aground! Bestir, bestir! *Exit.*

Enter *Mariners*.

Boats. Heigh, my hearts! Cheerly, cheerly, my hearts! Yare, yare! Take in the topsail! Tend to th' master's whistle! Blow till thou burst thy wind, if room enough!

Enter *Alonso, Sebastian, Antonio, Ferdinand, Gonzalo*, and others.

Alon. Good boatswain, have care. Where's the master? Play the men. 11
Boats. I pray now, keep below.
Ant. Where is the master, bos'n?
Boats. Do you not hear him? You mar our labour. Keep your cabins! You do assist the storm.
Gon. Nay, good, be patient. 16
Boats. When the sea is. Hence! What cares these roarers for the name of king? To cabin! Silence! Trouble us not!
Gon. Good, yet remember whom thou hast aboard. 21
Boats. None that I more love than myself. You are a Councillor. If you can command these elements to silence and work the peace of the present, we will not hand a rope more; use your authority. If you cannot, give thanks you have liv'd so long, and make yourself ready in your cabin for the mischance of the hour, if it so hap. — Cheerly, good hearts! — Out of our way, I say. *Exit.*
Gon. I have great comfort from this fellow. Methinks he hath no drowning mark upon him; his complexion is perfect gallows. Stand fast, good Fate, to his hanging! Make the rope of his destiny our cable, for our own doth little advantage. If he be not born to be hang'd, our case is miserable. *Exeunt.*

Enter *Boatswain*.

Boats. Down with the topmast! Yare! Lower, lower! Bring her to try with maincourse! (*A cry within.*) A plague upon this howling! They are louder than the weather or our office. 40

Enter *Sebastian, Antonio*, and *Gonzalo*.

Yet again? What do you here? Shall we give o'er and drown? Have you a mind to sink?
Seb. A pox o' your throat, you bawling, blasphemous, incharitable dog!
Boats. Work you then. 45
Ant. Hang, cur, hang, you whoreson, insolent noisemaker! We are less afraid to be drown'd than thou art.
Gon. I'll warrant him for drowning, though the ship were no stronger than a nutshell and as leaky as an unstanched wench. 51

5

Boats. Lay her ahold, ahold! Set her two courses! Off to sea again! Lay her off!

Enter *Mariners* wet.

Mariners. All lost! To prayers, to prayers! All lost! [*Exeunt.*]

Boats. What, must our mouths be cold?

Gon. The King and Prince at prayers! Let's assist them,
For our case is as theirs.

Seb. I am out of patience.

Ant. We are merely cheated of our lives by drunkards.
This wide-chopp'd rascal — would thou mightst lie drowning 60
The washing of ten tides!

Gon. He'll be hang'd yet,
Though every drop of water swear against it
And gape at wid'st to glut him.

A confused noise within: 'Mercy on us! —
We split, we split! — Farewell, my wife and children! —
Farewell, brother! — We split, we split, we split!' 65
[*Exit Boatswain.*]

Ant. Let's all sink with th' King.

Seb. Let's take leave of him.
Exeunt [*Antonio and Sebastian*].

Gon. Now would I give a thousand furlongs of sea for an acre of barren ground — long heath, brown furze, anything. The wills above be done! but I would fain die a dry death. 70
Exit.

Scene II. [*The island. Before Prospero's cell.*]

Enter *Prospero* and *Miranda*.

Mir. If by your art, my dearest father, you have
Put the wild waters in this roar, allay them.
The sky, it seems, would pour down stinking pitch
But that the sea, mounting to th' welkin's cheek,
Dashes the fire out. O, I have suffered 5
With those that I saw suffer! a brave vessel
(Who had no doubt some noble creature in her)
Dash'd all to pieces! O, the cry did knock
Against my very heart! Poor souls, they perish'd!
Had I been any god of power, I would 10
Have sunk the sea within the earth or ere

It should the good ship so have swallow'd and
The fraughting souls within her.

Pros. Be collected.
No more amazement. Tell your piteous heart
There's no harm done.

Mir. O, woe the day!

Pros. No harm. 15
I have done nothing but in care of thee,
Of thee my dear one, thee my daughter, who
Art ignorant of what thou art, naught knowing
Of whence I am; nor that I am more better
Than Prospero, master of a full poor cell, 20
And thy no greater father.

Mir. More to know
Did never meddle with my thoughts.

Pros. 'Tis time
I should inform thee farther. Lend thy hand
And pluck my magic garment from me. So,
[*Lays down his robe.*]
Lie there, my art. Wipe thou thine eyes; have comfort. 25
The direful spectacle of the wrack, which touch'd
The very virtue of compassion in thee,
I have with such provision in mine art
So safely ordered that there is no soul —
No, not so much perdition as an hair 30
Betid to any creature in the vessel
Which thou heard'st cry, which thou saw'st sink. Sit down;
For thou must now know farther.

Mir. You have often
Begun to tell me what I am; but stopp'd
And left me to a bootless inquisition, 35
Concluding, 'Stay! Not yet.'

Pros. The hour's now come;
The very minute bids thee ope thine ear.
Obey, and be attentive. Canst thou remember
A time before we came unto this cell?
I do not think thou canst, for then thou wast not 40
Out three years old.

Mir. Certainly, sir, I can.

Pros. By what? By any other house or person?
Of any thing the image tell me that
Hath kept with thy remembrance.

Mir. 'Tis far off,
And rather like a dream than an assurance 45
That my remembrance warrants. Had I not
Four or five women once that tended me?

Pros. Thou hadst, and more, Miranda. But how is it
That this lives in thy mind? What seest thou else

6

In the dark backward and abysm of time?   50
If thou rememb'rest aught ere thou cam'st here,
How thou cam'st here thou mayst.
   Mir.   But that I do not.
   Pros. Twelve year since, Miranda, twelve
     year since,
Thy father was the Duke of Milan and
A prince of power.
   Mir.   Sir, are not you my father?   55
   Pros. Thy mother was a piece of virtue, and
She said thou wast my daughter; and thy
     father
Was Duke of Milan; and his only heir
A princess — no worse issued.
   Mir.   O the heavens!
What foul play had we that we came from
     thence?   60
Or blessed was't we did?
   Pros.   Both, both, my girl!
By foul play, as thou say'st, were we heav'd
     thence,
But blessedly holp hither.
   Mir.   O, my heart bleeds
To think o' th' teen that I have turn'd you to,
Which is from my remembrance! Please you,
     farther.   65
   Pros. My brother, and thy uncle, call'd
     Antonio —
I pray thee mark me — that a brother should
Be so perfidious! — he whom next thyself
Of all the world I lov'd, and to him put
The manage of my state, as at that time   70
Through all the signories it was the first,
And Prospero the prime duke, being so reputed
In dignity, and for the liberal arts
Without a parallel; those being all my study,
The government I cast upon my brother   75
And to my state grew stranger, being trans-
     ported
And rapt in secret studies — thy false uncle —
Dost thou attend me?
   Mir.   Sir, most heedfully.
   Pros. Being once perfected how to grant
     suits,
How to deny them, who t' advance, and who
To trash for over-topping, new-created   81
The creatures that were mine, I say, or chang'd
     'em,
Or else new-form'd 'em; having both the key
Of officer and office, set all hearts i' th' state
To what tune pleas'd his ear, that now he was
The ivy which had hid my princely trunk   86
And suck'd my verdure out on't. Thou at-
     tend'st not!
   Mir. O, good sir, I do.

   Pros.   I pray thee mark me.
I thus neglecting worldly ends, all dedicated
To closeness, and the bettering of my mind   90
With that which, but by being so retir'd,
O'er-priz'd all popular rate, in my false brother
Awak'd an evil nature, and my trust,
Like a good parent, did beget of him
A falsehood in its contrary as great   95
As my trust was, which had indeed no limit,
A confidence sans bound. He being thus lorded,
Not only with what my revenue yielded
But what my power might else exact, like one
Who having unto truth, by telling of it,   100
Made such a sinner of his memory
To credit his own lie, he did believe
He was indeed the Duke, out o' th' substi-
     tution
And executing th' outward face of royalty
With all prerogative. Hence his ambition
     growing —   105
Dost thou hear?
   Mir. Your tale, sir, would cure deafness.
   Pros. To have no screen between this part
     he play'd
And him he play'd it for, he needs will be
Absolute Milan. Me (poor man) my library
Was dukedom large enough! Of temporal
     royalties   110
He thinks me now incapable; confederates
(So dry he was for sway) with th' King of
     Naples
To give nim annual tribute, do him homage,
Subject his coronet to his crown, and bend
The dukedom yet unbow'd (alas, poor Milan!)
To most ignoble stooping.
   Mir.   O the heavens!   116
   Pros. Mark his condition, and th' event;
     then tell me
If this might be a brother.
   Mir.   I should sin
To think but nobly of my grandmother.
Good wombs have borne bad sons.
   Pros.   Now the condition.
This King of Naples, being an enemy   121
To me inveterate, hearkens my brother's suit;
Which was, that he, in lieu o' th' premises,
Of homage and I know not how much tribute,
Should presently extirpate me and mine   125
Out of the dukedom and confer fair Milan,
With all the honours, on my brother. Whereon,
A treacherous army levied, one midnight
Fated to th' purpose, did Antonio open   129
The gates of Milan; and, i' th' dead of darkness,
The ministers for th' purpose hurried thence
Me and thy crying self.

7

Mir.   Alack, for pity!
I, not rememb'ring how I cried out then,
Will cry it o'er again. It is a hint
That wrings mine eyes to't.
    Pros.   Hear a little further,
And then I'll bring thee to the present business
Which now 's upon 's ; without the which this
    story   137
Were most impertinent.
    Mir.   Wherefore did they not
That hour destroy us?
    Pros.   Well demanded, wench.
My tale provokes that question. Dear, they
    durst not,   140
So dear the love my people bore me; nor set
A mark so bloody on the business; but
With colours fairer painted their foul ends.
In few, they hurried us aboard a bark,
Bore us some leagues to sea; where they prepar'd
A rotten carcass of a butt, not rigg'd,   146
Nor tackle, sail, nor mast; the very rats
Instinctively have quit it. There they hoist us,
To cry to th' sea, that roar'd to us; to sigh
To th' winds, whose pity, sighing back again,
Did us but loving wrong.
    Mir.   Alack, what trouble
Was I then to you!
    Pros.   O, a cherubin   152
Thou wast that did preserve me! Thou didst
    smile,
Infused with a fortitude from heaven,
When I have deck'd the sea with drops full salt,
Under my burthen groan'd; which rais'd in me
An undergoing stomach, to bear up   157
Against what should ensue.
    Mir.   How came we ashore?
    Pros. By providence divine.
Some food we had, and some fresh water, that
A noble Neapolitan, Gonzalo,   161
Out of his charity, who being then appointed
Master of this design, did give us, with
Rich garments, linens, stuffs, and necessaries
Which since have steaded much. So, of his
    gentleness,   165
Knowing I lov'd my books, he furnish'd me
From mine own library with volumes that
I prize above my dukedom.
    Mir.   Would I might
But ever see that man!
    Pros.   Now I arise.
Sit still, and hear the last of our sea-sorrow.
Here in this island we arriv'd; and here   171
Have I, thy schoolmaster, made thee more profit
Than other princess can, that have more time
For vainer hours, and tutors not so careful.

Mir. Heavens thank you for't! And now I
    pray you, sir, —   175
For still 'tis beating in my mind, — your reason
For raising this sea-storm?
    Pros.   Know thus far forth.
By accident most strange, bountiful Fortune
(Now my dear lady) hath mine enemies
Brought to this shore; and by my prescience
I find my zenith doth depend upon   181
A most auspicious star, whose influence
If now I court not, but omit, my fortunes
Will ever after droop. Here cease more ques-
    tions.   184
Thou art inclin'd to sleep. 'Tis a good dulness,
And give it way. I know thou canst not choose.
                              [*Miranda sleeps.*]
Come away, servant, come! I am ready now.
Approach, my Ariel. Come!

Enter *Ariel.*

Ari. All hail, great master! Grave sir, hail!
    I come
To answer thy best pleasure; be't to fly,   190
To swim, to dive into the fire, to ride
On the curl'd clouds. To thy strong bidding
    task
Ariel and all his quality.
    Pros.   Hast thou, spirit,
Perform'd to point the tempest that I bade
    thee?
    Ari. To every article.   195
I boarded the King's ship. Now on the beak,
Now in the waist, the deck, in every cabin,
I flam'd amazement. Sometime I'ld divide
And burn in many places; on the topmast,
The yards, and boresprit would I flame dis-
    tinctly,   200
Then meet and join. Jove's lightnings, the
    precursors
O' th' dreadful thunderclaps, more momentary
And sight-outrunning were not. The fire and
    cracks
Of sulphurous roaring the most mighty Neptune
Seem to besiege and make his bold waves
    tremble;   205
Yea, his dread trident shake.
    Pros.   My brave spirit!
Who was so firm, so constant, that this coil
Would not infect his reason?
    Ari.   Not a soul
But felt a fever of the mad and play'd   209
Some tricks of desperation. All but mari-
    ners
Plung'd in the foaming brine and quit the
    vessel,

Then all afire with me. The King's son
   Ferdinand,
With hair up-staring (then like reeds, not hair),
Was the first man that leapt; cried 'Hell is
   empty,
And all the devils are here!'
   Pros.   Why, that's my spirit! 215
But was not this nigh shore?
   Ari.   Close by, my master.
   Pros. But are they, Ariel, safe?
   Ari.   Not a hair perish'd.
On their sustaining garments not a blemish,
But fresher than before; and as thou bad'st me,
In troops I have dispers'd them 'bout the isle.
The King's son have I landed by himself, 221
Whom I left cooling of the air with sighs
In an odd angle of the isle, and sitting,
His arms in this sad knot.
   Pros.   Of the King's ship
The mariners say how thou hast dispos'd, 225
And all the rest o' th' fleet.
   Ari.   Safely in harbour
Is the King's ship; in the deep nook where once
Thou call'dst me up at midnight to fetch dew
From the still-vex'd Bermoothes, there she's
   hid;
The mariners all under hatches stow'd, 230
Who, with a charm join'd to their suff'red
   labour,
I have left asleep; and for the rest o' th' fleet,
Which I dispers'd, they all have met again,
And are upon the Mediterranean flote
Bound sadly home for Naples, 235
Supposing that they saw the King's ship
   wrack'd
And his great person perish.
   Pros.   Ariel, thy charge
Exactly is perform'd; but there's more work.
What is the time o' th' day?
   Ari.   Past the mid season.
   Pros. At least two glasses. The time 'twixt
   six and now 240
Must by us both be spent most preciously.
   Ari. Is there more toil? Since thou dost give
   me pains,
Let me remember thee what thou hast prom-
   is'd,
Which is not yet perform'd me.
   Pros.   How now? moody?
What is't thou canst demand?
   Ari.   My liberty. 245
   Pros. Before the time be out? No more!
   Ari.   I prithee,
Remember I have done thee worthy service,
Told thee no lies, made no mistakings, serv'd

Without or grudge or grumblings. Thou didst
   promise
To bate me a full year.
   Pros.   Dost thou forget 250
From what a torment I did free thee?
   Ari.   No.
   Pros. Thou dost; and think'st it much t
   tread the ooze
Of the salt deep,
To run upon the sharp wind of the North,
To do me business in the veins o' th' earth 255
When it is bak'd with frost.
   Ari.   I do not, sir.
   Pros. Thou liest, malignant thing! Hast
   thou forgot
The foul witch Sycorax, who with age and envy
Was grown into a hoop? Hast thou forgot her?
   Ari. No, sir.
   Pros.   Thou hast. Where was she
   born? Speak! Tell me! 260
   Ari. Sir, in Argier.
   Pros.   O, was she so? I must
Once in a month recount what thou hast been,
Which thou forget'st. This damn'd witch
   Sycorax,
For mischiefs manifold, and sorceries terrible
To enter human hearing, from Argier 265
Thou know'st was banish'd. For one thing she
   did
They would not take her life. Is not this true?
   Ari. Ay, sir.
   Pros. This blue-ey'd hag was hither brought
   with child
And here was left by th' sailors. Thou, my
   slave, 270
As thou report'st thyself, wast then her servant;
And, for thou wast a spirit too delicate
To act her earthy and abhorr'd commands,
Refusing her grand hests, she did confine thee,
By help of her more potent ministers, 275
And in her most unmitigable rage,
Into a cloven pine; within which rift
Imprison'd thou didst painfully remain
A dozen years; within which space she died
And left thee there; where thou didst vent thy
   groans 280
As fast as millwheels strike. Then was this
   island
(Save for the son that she did litter here,
A freckled whelp, hag-born) not honour'd with
A human shape.
   Ari.   Yes, Caliban her son. 284
   Pros. Dull thing, I say so! he, that Caliban
Whom now I keep in service. Thou best know'st
What torment I did find thee in. Thy groans

9

Did make wolves howl and penetrate the breasts
Of ever-angry bears. It was a torment
To lay upon the damn'd, which Sycorax   290
Could not again undo. It was mine art,
When I arriv'd and heard thee, that made gape
The pine, and let thee out.
Ari.   I thank thee, master.
Pros. If thou more murmur'st, I will rend an oak
And peg thee in his knotty entrails till   295
Thou hast howl'd away twelve winters.
Ari.   Pardon, master.
I will be correspondent to command
And do my spriting gently.
Pros.   Do so; and after two days
I will discharge thee.
Ari.   That's my noble master!
What shall I do? Say what! What shall I do?
Pros. Go make thyself like a nymph o' th' sea. Be subject   301
To no sight but thine and mine; invisible
To every eyeball else. Go take this shape
And hither come in't. Go! Hence with diligence!   *Exit [Ariel].*
Awake, dear heart, awake! Thou hast slept well.   305
Awake!
Mir. The strangeness of your story put
Heaviness in me.
Pros.   Shake it off. Come on.
We'll visit Caliban, my slave, who never
Yields us kind answer.
Mir.   'Tis a villain, sir,
I do not love to look on.
Pros.   But as 'tis,   310
We cannot miss him. He does make our fire,
Fetch in our wood, and serves in offices
That profit us. What, ho! slave! Caliban!
Thou earth, thou! Speak!
Cal. (within) There's wood enough within.
Pros. Come forth, I say! There's other business for thee.   315
Come, thou tortoise! When?

Enter *Ariel* like a water nymph.

Fine apparition! My quaint Ariel,
Hark in thine ear.
Ari.   My lord, it shall be done.
                                          Exit.
Pros. Thou poisonous slave, got by the devil himself
Upon thy wicked dam, come forth!   320

Enter *Caliban.*

Cal. As wicked dew as e'er my mother brush'd
With raven's feather from unwholesome fen
Drop on you both! A south-west blow on ye
And blister you all o'er!
Pros. For this, be sure, to-night thou shalt have cramps,   325
Side-stitches that shall pen thy breath up; urchins
Shall, for that vast of night that they may work,
All exercise on thee; thou shalt be pinch'd
As thick as honeycomb, each pinch more stinging
Than bees that made 'em.
Cal.   I must eat my dinner.   330
This island 's mine by Sycorax my mother,
Which thou tak'st from me. When thou camest first,
Thou strok'dst me and mad'st much of me; wouldst give me
Water with berries in't; and teach me how
To name the bigger light, and how the less,   335
That burn by day, and night; and then I lov'd thee
And show'd thee all the qualities o' th' isle,
The fresh springs, brine-pits, barren place and fertile.
Cursed be I that did so! All the charms
Of Sycorax — toads, beetles, bats light on you!
For I am all the subjects that you have,   341
Which first was mine own king; and here you sty me
In this hard rock, whiles you do keep from me
The rest o' th' island.
Pros.   Thou most lying slave,
Whom stripes may move, not kindness! I have us'd thee,   345
(Filth as thou art) with humane care, and lodg'd thee
In mine own cell till thou didst seek to violate
The honour of my child.
Cal. O ho, O ho! Would 't had been done!
Thou didst prevent me; I had peopled else   350
This isle with Calibans.
Pros.   Abhorred slave,
Which any print of goodness wilt not take,
Being capable of all ill! I pitied thee,
Took pains to make thee speak, taught thee each hour
One thing or other. When thou didst not, savage,   355
Know thine own meaning, but wouldst gabble like

THE
TEMPEST

Above: "Your swords are now too massy for your strengths, and will not be uplifted." The fairy Ariel (Alan Badel), in the form of a harpy, disarms Alonso (Jack Gwillim) and his companions by casting a spell on them. At the right, Michael Redgrave as Prospero (Act III, Scene III)

Left: Prospero lays his commands upon the inhabitants of the haunted island

PHOTOGRAPHS BY ANGUS MCBEAN
PRODUCED BY THE MEMORIAL THEATRE COMPANY
STRATFORD-UPON-AVON

"Fall to 't yarely, or we run ourselves a-ground." The opening scene, in which the ship is wrecked on the mysterious isle

Right: "Dost thou forget from what a torment I did free thee?" Prospero rebukes the restless Ariel, whom he bound to a period of servitude after freeing him from the witch's spell (*Act I, Scene II*)

Below: "A cherubim thou wast, that did preserve me!" Prospero tells his daughter Miranda (Hazel Penwarden) how her company consoled him during the first lonely years of their isolation (*Act I, Scene II*)

Above: "You taught me language; and my profit on't is, I know how to curse: the red plague rid you, for learning me your language." The monster Caliban (Hugh Griffith) rebels against the domination of Prospero, his master (*Act I, Scene II*)

Right: Evil Caliban, monstrous offspring of the witch Sycorax, was once the ruler of the island and regards Prospero as a usurper of his power

"Beseech you, sir, be merry: you have cause." Gonzalo (Geoffrey Bayldon) reminds the king that he should be grateful that he has escaped death in the shipwreck (*Act II, Scene I*)

"Then let us both be sudden."
Finding King Alonso and his
followers asleep, under the
spell of Ariel, Sebastian
(William Squire) and Antonio
(William Fox) decide to kill
him (*Act II, Scene I*)

"If in Naples I should report
this now, would they believe
me?" Alonso and his retinue
are amazed at the banquet
set before them through the
magical powers of Prospero
(*Act III, Scene III*)

"Open your mouth; here is
that which will give lan-
guage to you." The drunken
butler, Trinculo (Michael
Gwynn), and the jester (Alexander Gauge) give Cali-
ban liquor (*Act II, Scene II*)

"I am your wife, if you will marry me." Miranda and Ferdinand (Richard Burton), Alonso's son, plight their troth (*Act III, Scene I*)

Right: "If I have too austerely punish'd you, your compensation makes amends." Having tried Ferdinand's mettle by assigning him menial tasks to perform, Prospero consents to his marriage with Miranda (*Act IV, Scene I*)

Below: "Juno sings her blessings on you." The goddess Juno (Barbara Jefford) is summoned to give her blessing at the formal betrothal of Miranda and Ferdinand (*Act IV, Scene I*)

Above: "There stand, for you are spell-stopp'd." Prospero addresses Alonso and his followers as they stand in the magic circle drawn before his cell (*Act V, Scene I*)

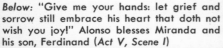

Right: "Sweet lord, you play me false." Miranda and Ferdinand are discovered playing chess in Prospero's cell (*Act V, Scene I*)

Below: "Give me your hands: let grief and sorrow still embrace his heart that doth not wish you joy!" Alonso blesses Miranda and his son, Ferdinand (*Act V, Scene I*)

"The best news is that we have safely found our king and company." The boatswain (Duncan Lamont) and master (David Orr) rejoice on discovering that King Alonso is alive (*Act V, Scene I*)

Left: "How beauteous mankind is! O brave new world, that has such people in 't!" Miranda is amazed at man's variety (*Act V, Scene I*)

Below: Prospero the magician. Always obsessed with the supernatural, he came to the island equipped with a whole library of necromancy

Above: "I'll break my staff, bury it certain fathoms in the earth." As he prepares a last spell, Prospero announces he is going to abjure practicing magic (*Act V, Scene I*)

Right: Light and swift, Ariel is Prospero's messenger and chief of the virtuous spirits which inhabit the magic isle

A thing most brutish, I endow'd thy purposes
With words that made them known. But thy
     vile race,
Though thou didst learn, had that in't which
     good natures
Could not abide to be with. Therefore wast
     thou   360
Deservedly confin'd into this rock, who hadst
Deserv'd more than a prison.
  Cal. You taught me language, and my
     profit on't
Is, I know how to curse. The red plague rid you
For learning me your language!
  Pros.   Hag-seed, hence!
Fetch us in fuel; and be quick, thou'rt best, 366
To answer other business. Shrug'st thou,
     malice?
If thou neglect'st or dost unwillingly
What I command, I'll rack thee with old cramps,
Fill all thy bones with achës, make thee roar
That beasts shall tremble at thy din.
  Cal.   No, pray thee.
[*Aside*] I must obey. His art is of such pow'r
It would control my dam's god, Setebos,
And make a vassal of him.
  Pros.   So, slave; hence! *Exit Caliban.*

     Enter *Ferdinand*; and *Ariel* (invisible),
          playing and singing.

          Ariel's song.

  Come unto these yellow sands,   375
     And then take hands.
  Curtsied when you have and kiss'd,
     The wild waves whist,
  Foot it featly here and there;
  And, sweet sprites, the burthen bear.   380
     Hark, hark!
        Burthen, dispersedly. Bowgh, wawgh!
     The watchdogs bark.
        Burthen, dispersedly. Bowgh, wawgh!
  Hark, hark! I hear
     The strain of strutting chanticleer   385
        Cry, cock-a-diddle-dowe.

  Fer. Where should this music be? I' th' air,
     or th' earth?
It sounds no more; and sure it waits upon
Some god o' th' island. Sitting on a bank,
Weeping again the King my father's wrack,
This music crept by me upon the waters,   391
Allaying both their fury and my passion
With its sweet air. Thence I have follow'd it,
Or it hath drawn me rather; but 'tis gone.
No, it begins again.   395

          Ariel's song.

  Full fadom five thy father lies;
     Of his bones are coral made;
  Those are pearls that were his eyes;
     Nothing of him that doth fade
  But doth suffer a sea-change   400
  Into something rich and strange.
  Sea nymphs hourly ring his knell:
        Burthen. Ding-dong.
  Hark! now I hear them — Ding-dong bell.

  Fer. The ditty does remember my drown'd
     father.   405
This is no mortal business, nor no sound
That the earth owes. I hear it now above me.
  Pros. The fringed curtains of thine eye ad-
     vance
And say what thou seest yond.
  Mir.   What is't? a spirit?
Lord, how it looks about! Believe me, sir, 410
It carries a brave form. But 'tis a spirit.
  Pros. No, wench. It eats, and sleeps, and
     hath such senses
As we have, such. This gallant which thou seest
Was in the wrack; and, but he's something
     stain'd
With grief (that's beauty's canker), thou
     mightst call him   415
A goodly person. He hath lost his fellows
And strays about to find 'em.
  Mir.   I might call him
A thing divine; for nothing natural
I ever saw so noble.
  Pros. [*aside*]   It goes on, I see,
As my soul prompts it. Spirit, fine spirit! I'll
     free thee   420
Within two days for this.
  Fer.   Most sure, the goddess
On whom these airs attend! Vouchsafe my
     pray'r
May know if you remain upon this island,
And that you will some good instruction give
How I may bear me here. My prime request,
Which I do last pronounce, is (O you wonder!)
If you be maid or no?
  Mir.   No wonder, sir,   427
But certainly a maid.
  Fer.   My language? Heavens!
I am the best of them that speak this speech,
Were I but where 'tis spoken.
  Pros.   How? the best?   430
What wert thou if the King of Naples heard
     thee?
  Fer. A single thing, as I am now, that won-
     ders

To hear thee speak of Naples. He does hear me;
And that he does I weep. Myself am Naples,
Who with mine eyes, never since at ebb, beheld
The King my father wrack'd.
 Mir.   Alack, for mercy!
 Fer. Yes, faith, and all his lords, the Duke
  of Milan   437
And his brave son being twain.
 Pros. [*aside*] The Duke of Milan
And his more braver daughter could control thee,
If now 'twere fit to do't. At the first sight 440
They have chang'd eyes. Delicate Ariel,
I'll set thee free for this! — A word, good sir.
I fear you have done yourself some wrong. A word!
 Mir. Why speaks my father so ungently? This
Is the third man that e'er I saw; the first 445
That e'er I sigh'd for. Pity move my father
To be inclin'd my way!
 Fer.   O, if a virgin,
And your affection not gone forth, I'll make you
The Queen of Naples.
 Pros. Soft, sir! one word more.
[*Aside*] They are both in either's pow'rs. But
  this swift business   450
I must uneasy make, lest too light winning
Make the prize light. — One word more! I charge thee
That thou attend me. Thou dost here usurp
The name thou ow'st not, and hast put thyself
Upon this island as a spy, to win it 455
From me, the lord on't.
 Fer.   No, as I am a man!
 Mir. There's nothing ill can dwell in such a temple.
If the ill spirit have so fair a house,
Good things will strive to dwell with't.
 Pros.   Follow me. —
Speak not you for him; he's a traitor. — Come!
I'll manacle thy neck and feet together; 461
Sea water shalt thou drink; thy food shall be
The fresh-brook mussels, wither'd roots, and husks
Wherein the acorn cradled. Follow.
 Fer.   No.
I will resist such entertainment till 465
Mine enemy has more power.
   He draws, and is charmed from moving.
 Mir.   O dear father,
Make not too rash a trial of him, for
He's gentle, and not fearful.

 Pros.   What, I say,
My foot my tutor? — Put thy sword up, traitor!
Who mak'st a show but dar'st not strike, thy conscience 470
Is so possess'd with guilt. Come, from thy ward!
For I can here disarm thee with this stick
And make thy weapon drop
 Mir.   Beseech you, father!
 Pros. Hence! Hang not on my garments.
 Mir.   Sir, have pity.
I'll be his surety.
 Pros. Silence! One word more 475
Shall make me chide thee, if not hate thee. What,
An advocate for an impostor? Hush!
Thou think'st there is no more such shapes as he,
Having seen but him and Caliban. Foolish wench!
To th' most of men this is a Caliban, 480
And they to him are angels.
 Mir.   My affections
Are then most humble. I have no ambition
To see a goodlier man.
 Pros.   Come on, obey!
Thy nerves are in their infancy again
And have no vigour in them.
 Fer.   So they are. 485
My spirits, as in a dream, are all bound up.
My father's loss, the weakness which I feel,
The wrack of all my friends, nor this man's threats
To whom I am subdu'd, are but light to me,
Might I but through my prison once a day 490
Behold this maid. All corners else o' th' earth
Let liberty make use of. Space enough
Have I in such a prison.
 Pros. [*aside*] It works. [*To Ferdinand*]
  Come on. —
Thou hast done well, fine Ariel! [*To Ferdinand*]
  Follow me. —
[*To Ariel*] Hark what thou else shalt do me.
 Mir.   Be of comfort.
My father's of a better nature, sir, 496
Than he appears by speech. This is unwonted
Which now came from him.
 Pros.   Thou shalt be as free
As mountain winds; but then exactly do
All points of my command.
 Ari.   To th' syllable. 500
 Pros. Come, follow. — Speak not for him.
          Exeunt.

ACT II. Scene I. [*Another part of the island.*]

Enter *Alonso, Sebastian, Antonio, Gonzalo, Adrian, Francisco*, and others.

Gon. Beseech you, sir, be merry. You have cause
(So have we all) of joy; for our escape
Is much beyond our loss. Our hint of woe
Is common. Every day some sailor's wife, 4
The master of some merchant, and the merchant,
Have just our theme of woe; but for the miracle,
I mean our preservation, few in millions
Can speak like us. Then wisely, good sir, weigh
Our sorrow with our comfort.

Alon.   Prithee peace.
Seb. He receives comfort like cold porridge.
Ant. The visitor will not give him o'er so. 11
Seb. Look, he's winding up the watch of his
wit; by-and-by it will strike.
Gon. Sir —
Seb. One. Tell. 15
Gon. When every grief is entertain'd that's offer'd,
Comes to th' entertainer —
Seb. A dollar.
Gon. Dolour comes to him, indeed. You have
spoken truer than you purpos'd. 20
Seb. You have taken it wiselier than I meant
you should.
Gon. Therefore, my lord —
Ant. Fie, what a spendthrift is he of his
tongue!
Alon. I prithee spare. 25
Gon. Well, I have done. But yet —
Seb. He will be talking.
Ant. Which, of he or Adrian, for a good
wager, first begins to crow?
Seb. The old cock. 30
Ant. The cock'rel.
Seb. Done! The wager?
Ant. A laughter.
Seb. A match!
Adr. Though this island seem to be desert —
Ant. Ha, ha, ha! 36
Seb. So, you're paid.
Adr. Uninhabitable and almost inaccessible—
Seb. Yet —
Adr. Yet —
Ant. He could not miss't. 40
Adr. It must needs be of subtle, tender, and
delicate temperance.
Ant. Temperance was a delicate wench.

Seb. Ay, and a subtle, as he most learnedly
deliver'd. 45
Adr. The air breathes upon us here most
sweetly.
Seb. As if it had lungs, and rotten ones.
Ant. Or as 'twere perfum'd by a fen.
Gon. Here is everything advantageous to
life.
Ant. True; save means to live. 50
Seb. Of that there's none, or little.
Gon. How lush and lusty the grass looks!
how green!
Ant. The ground indeed is tawny.
Seb. With an eye of green in't. 55
Ant. He misses not much.
Seb. No; he doth but mistake the truth
totally.
Gon. But the rarity of it is — which is indeed
almost beyond credit —
Seb. As many vouch'd rarities are. 60
Gon. That our garments, being, as they were,
drench'd in the sea, hold, notwithstanding,
their freshness and gloss, being rather new-dy'd
than stain'd with salt water.
Ant. If but one of his pockets could speak,
would it not say he lies? 66
Seb. Ay, or very falsely pocket up his report.
Gon. Methinks our garments are now as
fresh as when we put them on first in Afric, at
the marriage of the King's fair daughter Claribel to the King of Tunis. 71
Seb. 'Twas a sweet marriage, and we prosper
well in our return.
Adr. Tunis was never grac'd before with
such a paragon to their queen. 75
Gon. Not since widow Dido's time.
Ant. Widow? A pox o' that! How came
that 'widow' in? Widow Dido!
Seb. What if he had said 'widower Æneas'
too? Good Lord, how you take it! 80
Adr. 'Widow Dido,' said you? You make
me study of that. She was of Carthage, not of
Tunis.
Gon. This Tunis, sir, was Carthage.
Adr. Carthage?
Gon. I assure you, Carthage. 85
Ant. His word is more than the miraculous
harp.
Seb. He hath rais'd the wall, and houses too.
Ant. What impossible matter will he make
easy next?

Seb. I think he will carry this island home in
his pocket and give it his son for an apple. 91
Ant. And, sowing the kernels of it in the sea,
bring forth more islands.
Gon. Ay!
Ant. Why, in good time!   95
Gon. Sir, we were talking that our garments
seem now as fresh as when we were at Tunis at
the marriage of your daughter, who is now
Queen.
Ant. And the rarest that e'er came there.
Seb. Bate, I beseech you, widow Dido. 100
Ant. O, widow Dido? Ay, widow Dido!
Gon. Is not, sir, my doublet as fresh as the
first day I wore it? I mean, in a sort.
Ant. That 'sort' was well fish'd for.
Gon. When I wore it at your daughter's
marriage.   105
Alon. You cram these words into mine ears
against
The stomach of my sense. Would I had never
Married my daughter there! for, coming thence,
My son is lost; and, in my rate, she too,
Who is so far from Italy remov'd   110
I ne'er again shall see her. O thou mine heir
Of Naples and of Milan, what strange fish
Hath made his meal on thee?
Fran.   Sir, he may live.
I saw him beat the surges under him
And ride upon their backs. He trod the water,
Whose enmity he flung aside, and breasted 116
The surge most swol'n that met him. His bold
head
'Bove the contentious waves he kept, and oar'd
Himself with his good arms in lusty stroke
To th' shore, that o'er his wave-worn basis
bow'd,   120
As stooping to relieve him. I not doubt
He came alive to land.
Alon.   No, no, he's gone.
Seb. Sir, you may thank yourself for this
great loss,
That would not bless our Europe with your
daughter,
But rather lose her to an African,   125
Where she, at least, is banish'd from your eye
Who hath cause to wet the grief on't.
Alon.   Prithee peace.
Seb. You were kneel'd to and importun'd
otherwise
By all of us; and the fair soul herself   129
Weigh'd, between loathness and obedience, at
Which end o' th' beam should bow. We have
lost your son,
I fear, for ever. Milan and Naples have

Moe widows in them of this business' making
Than we bring men to comfort them.
The fault's your own.
Alon.   So is the dear'st o' th' loss.
Gon. My Lord Sebastian,   136
The truth you speak doth lack some gentleness,
And time to speak it in. You rub the sore
When you should bring the plaster.
Seb.   Very well.
Ant. And most chirurgeonly.   140
Gon. It is foul weather in us all, good sir,
When you are cloudy.
Seb.   Foul weather?
Ant.   Very foul.
Gon. Had I plantation of this isle, my lord —
Ant. He'd sow't with nettle seed.
Seb.   Or docks, or mallows.
Gon. And were the king on't, what would I
do?   145
Seb. Scape being drunk, for want of wine.
Gon. I' th' commonwealth I would by con-
traries
Execute all things; for no kind of traffic
Would I admit; no name of magistrate; 149
Letters should not be known; riches, poverty,
And use of service, none; contract, succession,
Bourn, bound of land, tilth, vineyard, none;
No use of metal, corn, or wine, or oil;
No occupation; all men idle, all;
And women too, but innocent and pure; 155
No sovereignty.
Seb.   Yet he would be king on't.
Ant. The latter end of his commonwealth
forgets the beginning.
Gon. All things in common nature should
produce   156
Without sweat or endeavour. Treason, felony,
Sword, pike, knife, gun, or need of any engine
Would I not have; but nature should bring
forth,
Of it own kind, all foison, all abundance,
To feed my innocent people.
Seb. No marrying 'mong his subjects? 165
Ant. None, man! All idle — whores and
knaves.
Gon. I would with such perfection govern,
sir,
T' excel the golden age.
Seb.   Save his Majesty!
Ant. Long live Gonzalo!
Gon.   And — do you mark me, sir?
Alon. Prithee no more. Thou dost talk
nothing to me.   171
Gon. I do well believe your Highness; and
did it to minister occasion to these gentlemen,

who are of such sensible and nimble lungs that
they always use to laugh at nothing.   175

Ant. 'Twas you we laugh'd at.

Gon. Who in this kind of merry fooling am
nothing to you. So you may continue, and
laugh at nothing still.

Ant. What a blow was there given!   180

Seb. An it had not fall'n flatlong.

Gon. You are gentlemen of brave metal.
You would lift the moon out of her sphere if
she would continue in it five weeks without
changing.

Enter *Ariel,* [invisible,] playing solemn music.

Seb. We would so, and then go a-batfowling.

Ant. Nay, good my lord, be not angry.   186

Gon. No, I warrant you. I will not adventure
my discretion so weakly. Will you laugh me
asleep, for I am very heavy?

Ant. Go sleep, and hear us.   190

[*All sleep except Alonso, Sebastian, and
Antonio.*]

Alon. What, all so soon asleep? I wish mine
eyes

Would, with themselves, shut up my thoughts.
I find

They are inclin'd to do so.

Seb.   Please you, sir,

Do not omit the heavy offer of it.

It seldom visits sorrow; when it doth,   195

It is a comforter.

Ant.   We two, my lord,

Will guard your person while you take your rest,
And watch your safety.

Alon.   Thank you. Wondrous heavy.

[*Alonso sleeps. Exit Ariel.*]

Seb. What a strange drowsiness possesses
them!

Ant. It is the quality o' th' climate.

Seb.   Why   200

Doth it not then our eyelids sink? I find not
Myself dispos'd to sleep.

Ant.   Nor I. My spirits are nimble.

They fell together all, as by consent.

They dropp'd as by a thunder-stroke. What
might,

Worthy Sebastian — O, what might? — No
more!   205

And yet methinks I see it in thy face,

What thou shouldst be. Th' occasion speaks
thee, and

My strong imagination sees a crown

Dropping upon thy head.

Seb.   What? Art thou waking?

Ant. Do you not hear me speak?

Seb.   I do; and surely   210
It is a sleepy language, and thou speak'st
Out of thy sleep. What is it thou didst say?
This is a strange repose, to be asleep
With eyes wide open; standing, speaking,
moving —
And yet so fast asleep.

Ant.   Noble Sebastian,   215
Thou let'st thy fortune sleep — die, rather;
wink'st
Whiles thou art waking.

Seb   Thou dost snore distinctly;
There's meaning in thy snores.

Ant. I am more serious than my custom.
You
Must be so too, if heed me; which to do   220
Trebles thee o'er.

Seb.   Well, I am standing water.

Ant. I'll teach you how to flow.

Seb.   Do so. To ebb
Hereditary sloth instructs me.

Ant.   O,
If you but knew how you the purpose cherish
Whiles thus you mock it! how, in stripping it,
You more invest it! Ebbing men indeed   226
(Most often) do so near the bottom run
By their own fear or sloth.

Seb.   Prithee say on.
The setting of thine eye and cheek proclaim
A matter from thee; and a birth, indeed,   230
Which throes thee much to yield.

Ant.   Thus, sir:
Although this lord of weak remembrance, this
Who shall be of as little memory
When he is earth'd, hath here almost persuaded
(For he's a spirit of persuasion, only   235
Professes to persuade) the King his son's alive,
'Tis as impossible that he's undrown'd
As he that sleeps here swims.

Seb.   I have no hope
That he's undrown'd.

Ant.   O, out of that no hope
What great hope have you! No hope that way
is   240
Another way so high a hope that even
Ambition cannot pierce a wink beyond,
But doubts discovery there. Will you grant
with me
That Ferdinand is drown'd?

Seb.   He's gone.

Ant.   Then tell me,
Who's the next heir of Naples?

Seb.   Claribel.   245

Ant. She that is Queen of Tunis; she that
dwells

15

Ten leagues beyond man's life; she that from
Naples
Can have no note, unless the sun were post —
The man i' th' moon 's too slow — till new-born
chins
Be rough and razorable; she that from whom
We all were sea-swallow'd, though some cast
again, 251
And, by that destiny, to perform an act
Whereof what's past is prologue, what to come,
In yours and my discharge.
   Seb.   What stuff is this? How say you?
'Tis true my brother's daughter 's Queen of
Tunis; 255
So is she heir of Naples; 'twixt which regions
There is some space.
   Ant.   A space whose ev'ry cubit
Seems to cry out 'How shall that Claribel
Measure us back to Naples? Keep in Tunis,
And let Sebastian wake!' Say this were death
That now hath seiz'd them, why, they were no
worse 261
Than now they are. There be that can rule
Naples
As well as he that sleeps; lords that can prate
As amply and unnecessarily
As this Gonzalo. I myself could make 265
A chough of as deep chat. O, that you bore
The mind that I do! What a sleep were this
For your advancement! Do you understand
me?
   Seb. Methinks I do.
   Ant.   And how does your content
Tender your own good fortune?
   Seb.   I remember 270
You did supplant your brother Prospero.
   Ant.   True.
And look how well my garments sit upon me,
Much feater than before! My brother's serv-
ants
Were then my fellows; now they are my men.
   Seb. But, for your conscience — 275
   Ant. Ay, sir! Where lies that? If 'twere a
kibe,
'Twould put me to my slipper; but I feel not
This deity in my bosom. Twenty consciences
That stand 'twixt me and Milan, candied be
they
And melt, ere they molest! Here lies your
brother, 280
No better than the earth he lies upon
If he were that which now he's like — that's
dead;
Whom I with this obedient steel (three inches
of it)

Can lay to bed for ever; whiles you, doing
thus,
To the perpetual wink for aye might put 285
This ancient morsel, this Sir Prudence, who
Should not upbraid our course. For all the rest,
They'll take suggestion as a cat laps milk;
They'll tell the clock to any business that 289
We say befits the hour.
   Seb.   Thy case, dear friend,
Shall be my precedent. As thou got'st Milan,
I'll come by Naples. Draw thy sword. One
stroke
Shall free thee from the tribute which thou
payest,
And I the King shall love thee.
   Ant.   Draw together;
And when I rear my hand, do you the like, 295
To fall it on Gonzalo.   *[They draw.]*
   Seb.   O, but one word!
          [They converse apart.]

Enter *Ariel*, [invisible,] with music and song.

   Ari. My master through his art foresees the
danger
That you, his friend, are in, and sends me forth
(For else his project dies) to keep them living.
          Sings in Gonzalo's ear.

    While you here do snoring lie,   300
    Open-ey'd conspiracy
      His time doth take.
    If of life you keep a care,
    Shake off slumber and beware.
      Awake, Awake!   305

   Ant. Then let us both be sudden.
   Gon. *[wakes]*   Now good angels
Preserve the King!
Why, how now? —*[Shakes Alonso.]* Ho, awake!
— Why are you drawn?
Wherefore this ghastly looking?
   Alon. *[wakes]*   What's the matter?
   Seb. Whiles we stood here securing your
repose, 310
Even now, we heard a hollow burst of bellowing
Like bulls, or rather lions. Did 't not wake you?
It struck mine ear most terribly.
   Alon.   I heard nothing.
   Ant. O, 'twas a din to fright a monster's ear,
To make an earthquake! Sure it was the roar
Of a whole herd of lions.
   Alon.   Heard you this, Gonzalo?
   Gon. Upon mine honour, sir, I heard a hum-
ming, 317
And that a strange one too, which did awake me.

I shak'd you, sir, and cried. As mine eyes
    open'd,
I saw their weapons drawn. There was a noise;
That's verily. 'Tis best we stand upon our
    guard,   321
Or that we quit this place. Let's draw our
    weapons.
Alon. Lead off this ground, and let's make
    further search
For my poor son.
Gon.   Heavens keep him from these beasts!
For he is sure i' th' island.
Alon.   Lead away.   325
Ari. Prospero my lord shall know what I
    have done.
So, King, go safely on to seek thy son. *Exeunt.*

Scene II. [*Another part of the island.*]

Enter *Caliban* with a burthen of wood.
A noise of thunder heard.

Cal. All the infections that the sun sucks up
From bogs, fens, flats, on Prosper fall and make
    him
By inchmeal a disease! His spirits hear me,
And yet I needs must curse. But they'll nor
    pinch,
Fright me with urchin-shows, pitch me i' th'
    mire,   5
Nor lead me, like a firebrand, in the dark
Out of my way, unless he bid 'em; but
For every trifle are they set upon me;
Sometime like apes that mow and chatter at me,
And after bite me; then like hedgehogs which
Lie tumbling in my barefoot way and mount 11
Their pricks at my footfall; sometime am I
All wound with adders, who with cloven tongues
Do hiss me into madness.

Enter *Trinculo.*
                   Lo, now, lo!
Here comes a spirit of his, and to torment me
For bringing wood in slowly. I'll fall flat.   16
Perchance he will not mind me. [*Lies down.*]
Trin. Here's neither bush nor shrub to bear
off any weather at all, and another storm
brewing. I hear it sing i' th' wind. Yond same
black cloud, yond huge one, looks like a foul
bombard that would shed his liquor. If it
should thunder as it did before, I know not
where to hide my head. Yond same cloud cannot choose but fall by pailfuls. What have we
here? a man or a fish? dead or alive? A fish:

he smells like a fish; a very ancient and fishlike
smell; a kind of, not of the newest, poor-John.
A strange fish! Were I in England now, as once
I was, and had but this fish painted, not a holiday fool there but would give a piece of silver.
There would this monster make a man. Any
strange beast there makes a man. When they
will not give a doit to relieve a lame beggar,
they will lay out ten to see a dead Indian.
Legg'd like a man! and his fins like arms!
Warm, o' my troth! I do now let loose my
opinion, hold it no longer: this is no fish, but
an islander, that hath lately suffered by a
thunderbolt. [*Thunder.*] Alas, the storm is
come again! My best way is to creep under his
gaberdine. There is no other shelter hereabout.
Misery acquaints a man with strange bedfellows.
I will here shroud till the dregs of the storm be
past.   [*Creeps under Caliban's garment.*]

Enter *Stephano*, singing; [a bottle in his hand].
  Ste. I shall no more to sea, to sea;
        Here shall I die ashore.   45

This is a very scurvy tune to sing at a man's
funeral. Well, here's my comfort.   *Drinks.*

The master, the swabber, the boatswain, and I,
    The gunner, and his mate,
Lov'd Mall, Meg, and Marian, and Margery, 50
    But none of us car'd for Kate.
For she had a tongue with a tang,
    Would cry to a sailor 'Go hang!'
She lov'd not the savour of tar nor of pitch;
    Yet a tailor might scratch her where'er she did itch.
    Then to sea, boys, and let her go hang!   56

This is a scurvy tune too; but here's my comfort.   *Drinks.*
Cal. Do not torment me! O!
Ste. What's the matter? Have we devils
here? Do you put tricks upon 's with salvages
and men of Inde, ha? I have not scap'd drowning to be afeard now of your four legs; for it
hath been said, 'As proper a man as ever went
on four legs cannot make him give ground';
and it shall be said so again, while Stephano
breathes at' nostrils.   65
Cal. The spirit torments me. O!
Ste. This is some monster of the isle, with
four legs, who hath got, as I take it, an ague.
Where the devil should he learn our language?
I will give him some relief, if it be but for that.
If I can recover him, and keep him tame, and
get to Naples with him, he's a present for any
emperor that ever trod on neat's leather.

17

Cal. Do not torment me prithee! I'll bring my wood home faster. 75

Ste. He's in his fit now and does not talk after the wisest. He shall taste of my bottle. If he have never drunk wine afore, it will go near to remove his fit. If I can recover him and keep him tame, I will not take too much for him; he shall pay for him that hath him, and that soundly. 81

Cal. Thou dost me yet but little hurt.
Thou wilt anon; I know it by thy trembling.
Now Prosper works upon thee.

Ste. Come on your ways. Open your mouth. Here is that which will give language to you, cat. Open your mouth. This will shake your shaking, I can tell you, and that soundly. [*Gives Caliban drink.*] You cannot tell who's your friend. Open your chaps again.

Trin. I should know that voice. It should be — but he is drown'd; and these are devils. O, defend me! 92

Ste. Four legs and two voices — a most delicate monster! His forward voice now is to speak well of his friend; his backward voice is to utter foul speeches and to detract. If all the wine in my bottle will recover him, I will help his ague. Come! [*Gives drink.*] Amen! I will pour some in thy other mouth.

Trin. Stephano! 100

Ste. Doth thy other mouth call me? Mercy, mercy! This is a devil, and no monster. I will leave him; I have no long spoon.

Trin. Stephano! If thou beest Stephano, touch me and speak to me; for I am Trinculo — be not afeard — thy good friend Trinculo.

Ste. If thou beest Trinculo, come forth. I'll pull thee by the lesser legs. If any be Trinculo's legs, these are they. [*Draws him out from under Caliban's garment.*] Thou art very Trinculo indeed! How cam'st thou to be the siege of this mooncalf? Can he vent Trinculos? 111

Trin. I took him to be kill'd with a thunderstroke. But art thou not drown'd, Stephano? I hope now thou art not drown'd. Is the storm overblown? I hid me under the dead mooncalf's gaberdine for fear of the storm. And art thou living, Stephano? O Stephano, two Neapolitans scap'd?

Ste. Prithee do not turn me about. My stomach is not constant.

Cal. [*aside*] These be fine things, an if they be not sprites. 120
That's a brave god and bears celestial liquor.
I will kneel to him.

Ste. How didst thou scape? How cam'st thou hither? Swear by this bottle how thou cam'st hither. I escap'd upon a butt of sack which the sailors heaved o'erboard, by this bottle! which I made of the bark of a tree with mine own hands since I was cast ashore.

Cal. I'll swear upon that bottle to be thy true subject, for the liquor is not earthly. 130

Ste. Here! Swear then how thou escap'dst.

Trin. Swum ashore, man, like a duck. I can swim like a duck, I'll be sworn.

Ste. Here, kiss the book. [*Gives him drink.*] Though thou canst swim like a duck, thou art made like a goose. 135

Trin. O Stephano, hast any more of this?

Ste. The whole butt, man. My cellar is in a rock by th' seaside, where my wine is hid. How now, mooncalf? How does thine ague?

Cal. Hast thou not dropp'd from heaven? 140

Ste. Out o' th' moon, I do assure thee. I was the Man i' th' Moon when time was.

Cal. I have seen thee in her, and I do adore thee.
My mistress show'd me thee, and thy dog, and thy bush. 144

Ste. Come, swear to that; kiss the book. I will furnish it anon with new contents. Swear.
[*Caliban drinks.*]

Trin. By this good light, this is a very shallow monster! I afeard of him? A very weak monster! The Man i' th' Moon? A most poor credulous monster! Well drawn, monster, in good sooth. 151

Cal. I'll show thee every fertile inch o' th' island;
And I will kiss thy foot. I prithee be my god.

Trin. By this light, a most perfidious and drunken monster! When's god's asleep he'll rob his bottle. 155

Cal. I'll kiss thy foot. I'll swear myself thy subject.

Ste. Come on then. Down, and swear!

Trin. I shall laugh myself to death at this puppy-headed monster. A most scurvy monster! I could find in my heart to beat him —

Ste. Come, kiss. 161

Trin. But that the poor monster's in drink. An abominable monster!

Cal. I'll show thee the best springs; I'll pluck thee berries;
I'll fish for thee, and get thee wood enough. 165
A plague upon the tyrant that I serve!
I'll bear him no more sticks, but follow thee,
Thou wondrous man.

Trin. A most ridiculous monster, to make a wonder of a poor drunkard! 170
Cal. I prithee let me bring thee where crabs grow;
And I with my long nails will dig thee pig-nuts,
Show thee a jay's nest, and instruct thee how
To snare the nimble marmoset; I'll bring thee
To clust'ring filberts, and sometimes I'll get thee 175
Young scamels from the rock. Wilt thou go with me?
Ste. I prithee now lead the way without any more talking. Trinculo, the King and all our company else being drown'd, we will inherit here. Here, bear my bottle. Fellow Trinculo, we'll fill him by-and-by again. 181
Caliban sings drunkenly.
Cal. Farewell, master; farewell, farewell!
Trin. A howling monster! a drunken monster!
Cal. No more dams I'll make for fish,
Nor fetch in firing 185
At requiring,
Nor scrape trenchering, nor wash dish.
'Ban, 'Ban, Ca — Caliban
Has a new master. Get a new man.
Freedom, high-day! high-day, freedom! freedom, high-day, freedom! 191
Ste. O brave monster! lead the way.
Exeunt.

ACT III. Scene I. [*Before* Prospero's *cell.*]

Enter *Ferdinand*, bearing a log.

Fer. There be some sports are painful, and their labour
Delight in them sets off; some kinds of base-ness
Are nobly undergone, and most poor matters
Point to rich ends. This my mean task
Would be as heavy to me as odious, but 5
The mistress which I serve quickens what's dead
And makes my labours pleasures. O, she is
Ten times more gentle than her father's crabbed;
And he's compos'd of harshness! I must remove
Some thousands of these logs and pile them up,
Upon a sore injunction. My sweet mistress 11
Weeps when she sees me work, and says such baseness
Had never like executor. I forget;
But these sweet thoughts do even refresh my labours
Most busiest when I do it.

Enter *Miranda*; and *Prospero* [behind, *unseen*].

Mir. Alas, now pray you 15
Work not so hard! I would the lightning had
Burnt up those logs that you are enjoin'd to pile!
Pray set it down and rest you. When this burns,
'Twill weep for having wearied you. My father
Is hard at study. Pray now rest yourself. 20
He's safe for these three hours.
Fer. O most dear mistress,
The sun will set before I shall discharge
What I must strive to do.
Mir. If you'll sit down,
I'll bear your logs the while. Pray give me that.
I'll carry it to the pile.
Fer. No, precious creature. 25
I had rather crack my sinews, break my back,
Than you should such dishonour undergo
While I sit lazy by.
Mir. It would become me
As well as it does you; and I should do it 29
With much more ease; for my good will is to it,
And yours it is against.
Pros. [*aside*] Poor worm, thou art infected!
This visitation shows it.
Mir. You look wearily.
Fer. No, noble mistress. 'Tis fresh morning with me
When you are by at night. I do beseech you,
Chiefly that I might set it in my prayers, 35
What is your name?
Mir. Miranda. O my father,
I have broke your hest to say so!
Fer. Admir'd Miranda!
Indeed the top of admiration, worth
What's dearest to the world! Full many a lady
I have ey'd with best regard, and many a time
Th' harmony of their tongues hath into bondage 41
Brought my too diligent ear; for several virtues
Have I lik'd several women; never any
With so full soul but some defect in her
Did quarrel with the noblest grace she ow'd, 45

And put it to the foil; but you, O you,
So perfect and so peerless, are created
Of every creature's best!

Mir.   I do not know
One of my sex; no woman's face remember,
Save, from my glass, mine own; nor have I
    seen   50
More that I may call men than you, good friend,
And my dear father. How features are abroad
I am skilless of; but, by my modesty
(The jewel in my dower), I would not wish
Any companion in the world but you;   55
Nor can imagination form a shape,
Besides yourself, to like of. But I prattle
Something too wildly, and my father's precepts
I therein do forget.

Fer.   I am, in my condition,
A prince, Miranda; I do think, a king   60
(I would not so!), and would no more endure
This wooden slavery than to suffer
The fleshfly blow my mouth. Hear my soul
    speak!
The very instant that I saw you, did
My heart fly to your service; there resides, 65
To make me slave to it; and for your sake
Am I this patient log-man.

Mir.   Do you love me?
Fer. O heaven, O earth, bear witness to this
    sound,
And crown what I profess with kind event
If I speak true! if hollowly, invert   70
What best is boded me to mischief! I,
Beyond all limit of what else i' th' world,
Do love, prize, honour you.

Mir.   I am a fool
To weep at what I am glad of.

Pros. [aside]   Fair encounter
Of two most rare affections! Heavens rain
    grace   75
On that which breeds between 'em!

Fer.   Wherefore weep you?
Mir. At mine unworthiness, that dare not
    offer
What I desire to give, and much less take
What I shall die to want. But this is trifling;
And all the more it seeks to hide itself,   80
The bigger bulk it shows. Hence, bashful
    cunning!
And prompt me plain and holy innocence!
I am your wife, if you will marry me;
If not, I'll die your maid. To be your fellow
You may deny me; but I'll be your servant,   85
Whether you will or no.

Fer.   My mistress, dearest!
And I thus humble ever.

Mir.   My husband then?
Fer. Ay, with a heart as willing
As bondage e'er of freedom. Here's my hand.
Mir. And mine, with my heart in't; and
    now farewell   90
Till half an hour hence.

Fer.   A thousand thousand!
Exeunt [*Ferdinand and Miranda severally*].
Pros. So glad of this as they I cannot
    be,
Who are surpris'd withal, but my rejoicing
At nothing can be more. I'll to my book;
For yet ere supper time must I perform   95
Much business appertaining.   *Exit.*

Scene II. [*Another part of the island.*]

Enter *Caliban, Stephano,* and *Trinculo.*

Ste. Tell not me! When the butt is out, we
will drink water; not a drop before. Therefore
bear up and board 'em! Servant monster,
drink to me.   4
Trin. Servant monster? The folly of this
island! They say there's but five upon this isle.
We are three of them. If th' other two be
brain'd like us, the state totters.
Ste. Drink, servant monster, when I bid
thee. Thy eyes are almost set in thy head.
Trin. Where should they be set else? He
were a brave monster indeed if they were set in
his tail.
Ste. My man-monster hath drown'd his
tongue in sack. For my part, the sea cannot
drown me. I swam, ere I could recover the
shore, five-and-thirty leagues off and on, by
this light. Thou shalt be my lieutenant, monster, or my standard.
Trin. Your lieutenant, if you list; he's no
standard.   20
Ste. We'll not run, Monsieur Monster.
Trin. Nor go neither; but you'll lie like
dogs, and yet say nothing neither.
Ste. Mooncalf, speak once in thy life, if
thou beest a good mooncalf.   25
Cal. How does thy honour? Let me lick
    thy shoe.
I'll not serve him; he is not valiant.
Trin. Thou liest, most ignorant monster! I
am in case to justle a constable. Why, thou
debosh'd fish thou, was there ever man a coward
that hath drunk so much sack as I to-day? Wilt
thou tell a monstrous lie, being but half a fish
and half a monster?

Cal. Lo, how he mocks me! Wilt thou let
him, my lord?   35
Trin. 'Lord' quoth he? That a monster
should be such a natural!
Cal. Lo, lo, again! Bite him to death I
prithee.
Ste. Trinculo, keep a good tongue in your
head. If you prove a mutineer — the next tree!
The poor monster's my subject, and he shall
not suffer indignity.   42
Cal. I thank my noble lord. Wilt thou be
pleas'd
To hearken once again to the suit I made to thee?
Ste. Marry, will I. Kneel and repeat it; I
will stand, and so shall Trinculo.

> Enter *Ariel*, invisible.

Cal. As I told thee before, I am subject to a
tyrant,
A sorcerer, that by his cunning hath
Cheated me of the island.   50
Ari. Thou liest.
Cal.   Thou liest, thou jesting mon-
key thou!
I would my valiant master would destroy thee.
I do not lie.
Ste. Trinculo, if you trouble him any more
in 's tale, by this hand, I will supplant some of
your teeth.
Trin. Why, I said nothing.
Ste. Mum then, and no more. — Proceed.
Cal. I say by sorcery he got this isle;   60
From me he got it. If thy greatness will
Revenge it on him — for I know thou dar'st,
But this thing dare not —
Ste. That's most certain.
Cal. Thou shalt be lord of it, and I'll serve
thee.   65
Ste. How now shall this be compass'd?
Canst thou bring me to the party?
Cal. Yea, yea, my lord! I'll yield him thee
asleep,
Where thou mayst knock a nail into his head.
Ari. Thou liest; thou canst not.   70
Cal. What a pied ninny's this! Thou scurvy
patch!
I do beseech thy greatness give him blows
And take his bottle from him. When that's gone,
He shall drink naught but brine, for I'll not
show him
Where the quick freshes are.   75
Ste. Trinculo, run into no further danger.
Interrupt the monster one word further and,
by this hand, I'll turn my mercy out o' doors
and make a stockfish of thee.

Trin. Why, what did I? I did nothing. I'll
go farther off.   81
Ste. Didst thou not say he lied?
Ari. Thou liest.
Ste. Do I so? Take thou that! [*Strikes
Trinculo.*] As you like this, give me the lie
another time.   85
Trin. I did not give thee the lie. Out o' your
wits, and hearing too? A pox o' your bottle!
This can sack and drinking do. A murrain on
your monster, and the devil take your fingers!
Cal. Ha, ha, ha!   90
Ste. Now forward with your tale. — Prithee
stand further off.
Cal. Beat him enough. After a little time
I'll beat him too.
Ste.   Stand farther. — Come, proceed.
Cal. Why, as I told thee, 'tis a custom with
him   95
I' th' afternoon to sleep. There thou mayst
brain him,
Having first seiz'd his books, or with a log
Batter his skull, or paunch him with a stake,
Or cut his wesand with thy knife. Remember
First to possess his books; for without them
He's but a sot, as I am, nor hath not   101
One spirit to command. They all do hate
him
As rootedly as I. Burn but his books.
He has brave utensils (for so he calls them)
Which, when he has a house, he'll deck withal.
And that most deeply to consider is   106
The beauty of his daughter. He himself
Calls her a nonpareil. I never saw a woman
But only Sycorax my dam and she;
But she as far surpasseth Sycorax   110
As great'st does least.
Ste.   Is it so brave â lass?
Cal. Ay, lord. She will become thy bed, I
warrant,
And bring thee forth brave brood.
Ste. Monster, I will kill this man. His daugh-
ter and I will be king and queen, save our
Graces! and Trinculo and thyself shall be
viceroys. Dost thou like the plot, Trinculo?
Trin. Excellent.   118
Ste. Give me thy hand. I am sorry I beat
thee; but while thou liv'st, keep a good tongue
in thy head.   121
Cal. Within this half hour will he be asleep.
Wilt thou destroy him then?
Ste.   Ay, on mine honour.
Ari. This will I tell my master.
Cal. Thou mak'st me merry; I am full of
pleasure.   125

21

Let us be jocund. Will you troll the catch
You taught me but whilere?
  Ste. At thy request, monster, I will do reason, any reason. Come on, Trinculo, let us
sing.   *Sings.*

    Flout 'em and scout 'em   130
    And scout 'em and flout 'em!
    Thought is free.

  Cal. That's not the tune.
   Ariel plays the tune on a tabor and pipe.
  Ste. What is this same?
  Trin. This is the tune of our catch, play'd
by the picture of No-body.   136
  Ste. If thou beest a man, show thyself in
thy likeness. If thou beest a devil, take't as
thou list.
  Trin. O, forgive me my sins!
  Ste. He that dies pays all debts. I defy thee.
Mercy upon us!   141
  Cal. Art thou afeard?
  Ste. No, monster, not I.
  Cal. Be not afeard. The isle is full of noises,
Sounds and sweet airs that give delight and
hurt not.   145
Sometimes a thousand twangling instruments
Will hum about mine ears; and sometime
  voices
That, if I then had wak'd after long sleep,
Will make me sleep again; and then, in dream-
  ing,
The clouds methought would open and show
  riches   150
Ready to drop upon me, that, when I wak'd,
I cried to dream again.
  Ste. This will prove a brave kingdom to me,
where I shall have my music for nothing.
  Cal. When Prospero is destroy'd.   155
  Ste. That shall be by-and-by. I remember
the story.
  Trin. The sound is going away. Let's fol-
low it, and after do our work.
  Ste. Lead, monster; we'll follow. I would
I could see this taborer! He lays it on. Wilt
come?   161
  Trin. I'll follow, Stephano.   *Exeunt.*

Scene III. [*Another part of the island.*]

Enter *Alonso, Sebastian, Antonio, Gonzalo,
Adrian, Francisco, &c.*

  Gon. By'r Lakin, I can go no further, sir!
My old bones ache. Here's a maze trod indeed
Through forthrights and meanders. By your
  patience,
I needs must rest me.
  Alon.   Old lord, I cannot blame thee,
Who am myself attach'd with weariness   5
To th' dulling of my spirits. Sit down and rest.
Even here I will put off my hope, and keep it
No longer for my flatterer. He is drown'd
Whom thus we stray to find; and the sea
  mocks
Our frustrate search on land. Well, let him
  go.   10
  Ant. [*aside to Sebastian*] I am right glad that
he's so out of hope.
Do not for one repulse forgo the purpose
That you resolv'd t' effect.
  Seb. [*aside to Antonio*] The next advantage
Will we take throughly.
  Ant. [*aside to Sebastian*] Let it be to-night;
For, now they are oppress'd with travel, they 15
Will not nor cannot use such vigilance
As when they are fresh.
  Seb. [*aside to Antonio*] I say to-night. No
  more.

  Solemn and strange music; and Prospero
  on the top (invisible).

  Alon. What harmony is this? My good
friends, hark!
  Gon. Marvellous sweet music!

Enter several *strange Shapes*, bringing in a
banquet; and dance about it with gentle actions of salutations; and, inviting the *King &c.*
  to eat, they depart.

  Alon. Give us kind keepers, heavens! What
  were these?   20
  Seb. A living drollery. Now I will believe
That there are unicorns; that in Arabia
There is one tree, the phœnix' throne; one
  phœnix
At this hour reigning there.
  Ant.   I'll believe both;
And what does else want credit, come to me, 25
And I'll be sworn 'tis true. Travellers ne'er
  did lie,
Though fools at home condemn 'em.
  Gon.   If in Naples
I should report this now, would they believe
  me?
If I should say, I saw such islanders
(For certes these are people of the island), 30
Who, though they are of monstrous shape, yet,
  note,

Their manners are more gentle, kind, than of
Our human generation you shall find
Many — nay, almost any.
　Pros. [*aside*]　　　Honest lord,
Thou hast said well; for some of you there
　　present　　　　　　　　　　　　　35
Are worse than devils.
　Alon.　　　　I cannot too much muse
Such shapes, such gesture, and such sound, ex-
　　pressing
(Although they want the use of tongue) a kind
Of excellent dumb discourse.
　Pros. [*aside*]　　　Praise in departing.
　Fran. They vanish'd strangely.
　Seb.　　　　No matter, since　40
They have left their viands behind; for we
　have stomachs.
Will't please you taste of what is here?
　Alon.　　　　　　　　Not I.
　Gon. Faith, sir, you need not fear. When
　we were boys,
Who would believe that there were mountain-
　eers
Dewlapp'd like bulls, whose throats had hang-
　ing at 'em　　　　　　　　　　45
Wallets of flesh? or that there were such men
Whose heads stood in their breasts? which
　now we find
Each putter-out of five for one will bring us
Good warrant of.
　Alon.　　　　I will stand to, and feed;
Although my last, no matter, since I feel　50
The best is past. Brother, my lord the Duke,
Stand to, and do as we.

Thunder and lightning. Enter *Ariel, like a
harpy*; claps his wings upon the table; and
with a quaint device *the banquet vanishes.*

　Ari. You are three men of sin, whom des-
　tiny —
That hath to instrument this lower world
And what is in't — the never-surfeited sea　55
Hath caus'd to belch up you, and on this
　island,
Where man doth not inhabit — you 'mongst
　men
Being most unfit to live. I have made you mad;
And even with such-like valour men hang and
　drown
Their proper selves.
　[*Alonso, Sebastian, &c. draw their swords.*]
　　　　　You fools! I and my fellows　60
Are ministers of Fate. The elements,
Of whom your swords are temper'd, may as
　well

Wound the loud winds, or with bemock'd-at
　stabs
Kill the still-closing waters, as diminish
One dowle that's in my plume. My fellow
　ministers　　　　　　　　　　　65
Are like invulnerable. If you could hurt,
Your swords are now too massy for your
　strengths
And will not be uplifted. But remember
(For that's my business to you) that you three
From Milan did supplant good Prospero;　70
Expos'd unto the sea, which hath requit it,
Him and his innocent child; for which foul
　deed
The powers, delaying (not forgetting), have
Incens'd the seas and shores, yea, all the crea-
　tures,
Against your peace. Thee of thy son, Alonso,　75
They have bereft; and do pronounce by me
Ling'ring perdition (worse than any death
Can be at once) shall step by step attend
You and your ways; whose wraths to guard
　you from,　　　　　　　　　　79
Which here, in this most desolate isle, else falls
Upon your heads, is nothing but heart's sorrow
And a clear life ensuing.

*He vanishes in thunder; then, to soft music,
enter the* Shapes *again, and dance, with mocks
and mows, and carrying out the table.*

　Pros. [*aside*] Bravely the figure of this harpy
　hast thou
Perform'd, my Ariel; a grace it had, devouring.
Of my instruction hast thou nothing bated　85
In what thou hadst to say. So, with good life
And observation strange, my meaner ministers
Their several kinds have done. My high charms
　work,
And these, mine enemies, are all knit up
In their distractions. They now are in my
　pow'r;　　　　　　　　　　　　90
And in these fits I leave them, while I visit
Young Ferdinand, whom they suppose is
　drown'd,
And his and mine lov'd darling.　[*Exit above.*]
　Gon. I' th' name of something holy, sir, why
　stand you
In this strange stare?
　Alon.　　　O, it is monstrous, monstrous!　95
Methought the billows spoke and told me of
　it;
The winds did sing it to me; and the thunder,
That deep and dreadful organ pipe, pronounc'd
The name of Prosper. It did bass my trespass.
Therefore my son i' th' ooze is bedded; and　100

23

I'll seek him deeper than e'er plummet sounded
And with him there lie mudded.   *Exit.*
  Seb.   But one fiend at a time,
I'll fight their legions o'er!
  Ant.   I'll be thy second.
              Exeunt [Sebastian and Antonio].
  Gon. All three of them are desperate. Their
  great guilt,   104

ACT IV. Scene I. [*Before* Prospero's *cell.*]

Enter *Prospero, Ferdinand,* and *Miranda.*

  Pros. If I have too austerely punish'd you,
Your compensation makes amends; for I
Have given you here a third of mine own life,
Or that for which I live; who once again
I tender to thy hand. All thy vexations   5
Were but my trials of thy love, and thou
Hast strangely stood the test. Here, afore
  heaven,
I ratify this my rich gift. O Ferdinand,
Do not smile at me that I boast her off,
For thou shalt find she will outstrip all praise
And make it halt behind her.
  Fer.   I do believe it 11
Against an oracle.
  Pros. Then, as my gift, and thine own ac-
  quisition
Worthily purchas'd, take my daughter. But
If thou dost break her virgin-knot before 15
All sanctimonious ceremonies may
With full and holy rite be minist'red,
No sweet aspersion shall the heavens let fall
To make this contract grow; but barren hate,
Sour-ey'd disdain, and discord shall bestrew 20
The union of your bed with weeds so loathly
That you shall hate it both. Therefore take
  heed,
As Hymen's lamp shall light you!
  Fer.   As I hope
For quiet days, fair issue, and long life,
With such love as 'tis now, the murkiest den, 25
The most opportune place, the strong'st sug-
  gestion
Our worser genius can, shall never melt
Mine honour into lust, to take away
The edge of that day's celebration
When I shall think or Phœbus' steeds are
  founder'd   30
Or Night kept chain'd below.
  Pros.   Fairly spoke.
Sit then and talk with her; she is thine own.
What, Ariel! my industrious servant, Ariel!

Enter *Ariel.*

  Ari. What would my potent master? Here
  I am.
  Pros. Thou and thy meaner fellows your
  last service   35
Did worthily perform; and I must use you
In such another trick. Go bring the rabble,
O'er whom I give thee pow'r, here to this place.
Incite them to quick motion; for I must
Bestow upon the eyes of this young couple 40
Some vanity of mine art. It is my promise,
And they expect it from me.
  Ari.   Presently?
  Pros. Ay, with a twink.
  Ari. Before you can say 'Come' and 'Go,'
And breathe twice and cry, 'So, so,'   45
Each one, tripping on his toe,
Will be here with mop and mow.
Do you love me, master? No?
  Pros. Dearly, my delicate Ariel. Do not
  approach
Till thou dost hear me call.
  Ari.   Well! I conceive. 50
                                            Exit.
  Pros. Look thou be true. Do not give dal-
  liance
Too much the rein. The strongest oaths are
  straw
To th' fire i' th' blood. Be more abstemious,
Or else good night your vow!
  Fer.   I warrant you, sir.
The white cold virgin snow upon my heart 55
Abates the ardour of my liver.
  Pros.   Well.
Now come, my Ariel! Bring a corollary
Rather than want a spirit. Appear, and pertly!
No tongue! All eyes! Be silent.   *Soft music.*

Enter *Iris.*

  Iris. Ceres, most bounteous lady, thy rich
  leas   60
Of wheat, rye, barley, fetches, oats, and pease;

Thy turfy mountains, where live nibbling sheep,
And flat meads thatch'd with stover, them to
    keep;
Thy banks with pioned and twilled brims,
Which spongy April at thy hest betrims   65
To make cold nymphs chaste crowns; and thy
    broom groves,
Whose shadow the dismissed bachelor loves,
Being lasslorn; thy pole-clipt vineyard;
And thy sea-marge, sterile and rocky-hard,
Where thou thyself dost air — the queen o' th'
    sky,   70
Whose wat'ry arch and messenger am I,
Bids thee leave these, and with her sovereign
    grace,
Here on this grass-plot, in this very place,
To come and sport. Her peacocks fly amain.
Approach, rich Ceres, her to entertain.   75

Enter *Ceres.*

Cer. Hail, many-coloured messenger, that
    ne'er
Dost disobey the wife of Jupiter,
Who, with thy saffron wings, upon my flow'rs
Diffusest honey drops, refreshing show'rs,
And with each end of thy blue bow dost crown
My bosky acres and my unshrubb'd down,   81
Rich scarf to my proud earth — why hath thy
    queen
Summon'd me hither to this short-grass'd
    green?
Iris. A contract of true love to celebrate
And some donation freely to estate   85
On the bless'd lovers.
Cer.   Tell me, heavenly bow,
If Venus or her son, as thou dost know,
Do now attend the Queen. Since they did plot
The means that dusky Dis my daughter got,
Her and her blind boy's scandal'd company 90
I have forsworn.
Iris.   Of her society
Be not afraid. I met her Deity
Cutting the clouds towards Paphos, and her
    son
Dove-drawn with her. Here thought they to
    have done   94
Some wanton charm upon this man and maid,
Whose vows are, that no bed-right shall be paid
Till Hymen's torch be lighted; but in vain.
Mars's hot minion is return'd again;
Her waspish-headed son has broke his arrows,
Swears he will shoot no more, but play with
    sparrows   100
And be a boy right out.

[Enter *Juno.*]
Cer.   Highest queen of state,
Great Juno, comes; I know her by her gait.
Juno. How does my bounteous sister? Go
    with me
To bless this twain, that they may prosperous
    be
And honour'd in their issue.   105

They sing.

Juno. Honour, riches, marriage blessing,
    Long continuance, and increasing,
    Hourly joys be still upon you!
    Juno sings her blessings on you.

Cer.   Earth's increase, foison plenty,   110
    Barns and garners never empty,
    Vines with clust'ring bunches growing,
    Plants with goodly burthen bowing;
    Spring come to you at the farthest
    In the very end of harvest!   115
    Scarcity and want shall shun you,
    Ceres' blessing so is on you.

Fer. This is a most majestic vision, and
Harmonious charmingly. May I be bold
To think these spirits?
Pros.   Spirits, which by mine art
I have from their confines call'd to enact   121
My present fancies.
Fer.   Let me live here ever!
So rare a wond'red father and a wise
Makes this place Paradise.
Juno and Ceres whisper, and send Iris on
    employment.
Pros.   Sweet now, silence!
Juno and Ceres whisper seriously.   125
There's something else to do. Hush and be
    mute,
Or else our spell is marr'd.
Iris. You nymphs, call'd Naiades, of the
    wand'ring brooks,
With your sedg'd crowns and ever-harmless
    looks,
Leave your crisp channels, and on this green
    land   130
Answer your summons. Juno does command.
Come, temperate nymphs, and help to celebrate
A contract of true love. Be not too late.

Enter certain *Nymphs.*

You sunburn'd sicklemen, of August weary,
Come hither from the furrow and be merry. 133
Make holiday. Your rye-straw hats put on,
And these fresh nymphs encounter every one
In country footing.

Enter certain *Reapers*, properly habited. They join with the *Nymphs* in a graceful dance; towards the end whereof *Prospero* starts suddenly and speaks; after which, to a strange, hollow, and confused noise, *they heavily vanish.*

Pros. [aside] I had forgot that foul conspiracy
Of the beast Caliban and his confederates 140
Against my life. The minute of their plot
Is almost come. — [To the Spirits] Well done!
   Avoid! No more!
Fer. This is strange. Your father's in some
   passion
That works him strongly.
Mir.   Never till this day
Saw I him touch'd with anger so distemper'd.
Pros. You do look, my son, in a mov'd sort,
As if you were dismay'd. Be cheerful, sir.
Our revels now are ended. These our actors,
As I foretold you, were all spirits and
Are melted into air, into thin air;   150
And, like the baseless fabric of this vision,
The cloud-capp'd towers, the gorgeous palaces,
The solemn temples, the great globe itself,
Yea, all which it inherit, shall dissolve,
And, like this insubstantial pageant faded, 155
Leave not a rack behind. We are such stuff
As dreams are made on, and our little life
Is rounded with a sleep. Sir, I am vex'd.
Bear with my weakness. My old brain is
   troubled.
Be not disturb'd with my infirmity.   160
If you be pleas'd, retire into my cell
And there repose. A turn or two I'll walk
To still my beating mind.
Fer., Mir.   We wish your peace.
                                   Exeunt.

      Enter *Ariel.*

Pros. Come with a thought! I thank thee,
   Ariel. Come.
Ari. Thy thoughts I cleave to. What's thy
   pleasure?
Pros.   Spirit,   165
We must prepare to meet with Caliban.
Ari. Ay, my commander. When I presented
   Ceres,
I thought to have told thee of it, but I fear'd
Lest I might anger thee.
Pros. Say again, where didst thou leave
   these varlets?   170
Ari. I told you, sir, they were redhot with
   drinking;
So full of valour that they smote the air
For breathing in their faces, beat the ground

For kissing of their feet; yet always bending
Towards their project. Then I beat my tabor;
At which like unback'd colts they prick'd their
   ears,   176
Advanc'd their eyelids, lifted up their noses
As they smelt music. So I charm'd their ears
That calf-like they my lowing follow'd through
Tooth'd briers, sharp furzes, pricking goss, and
   thorns,   180
Which ent'red their frail shins. At last I left
   them
I' th' filthy mantled pool beyond your cell,
There dancing up to th' chins, that the foul lake
O'erstunk their feet.
Pros.   This was well done, my bird.
Thy shape invisible retain thou still.   185
The trumpery in my house, go bring it hither
For stale to catch these thieves.
Ari.   I go, I go. *Exit.*
Pros. A devil, a born devil, on whose nature
Nurture can never stick! on whom my pains,
Humanely taken, all, all lost, quite lost! 190
And as with age his body uglier grows,
So his mind cankers. I will plague them all,
Even to roaring.

Enter *Ariel*, loaden with glistering apparel, etc.

   Come, hang them on this line.

[*Prospero* and *Ariel* remain, invisible.] Enter
   Caliban, Stephano, and *Trinculo*, all wet.

Cal. Pray you tread softly, that the blind
   mole may not
Hear a foot fall. We now are near his cell. 195
Ste. Monster, your fairy, which you say is a
harmless fairy, has done little better than play'd
the Jack with us.
Trin. Monster, I do smell all horse-piss, at
which my nose is in great indignation.   200
Ste. So is mine. Do you hear, monster? If
I should take a displeasure against you, look
you —
Trin. Thou wert but a lost monster.
Cal. Good my lord, give me thy favour still.
Be patient, for the prize I'll bring thee to 205
Shall hoodwink this mischance. Therefore
speak softly.
All's hush'd as midnight yet.
Trin. Ay, but to lose our bottles in the
pool —
Ste. There is not only disgrace and dishonour
in that, monster, but an infinite loss.   210
Trin. That's more to me than my wetting.
Yet this is your harmless fairy, monster.

Ste. I will fetch off my bottle, though I be o'er ears for my labour.

Cal. Prithee, my king, be quiet. Seest thou here?   215
This is the mouth o' th' cell. No noise, and enter.
Do that good mischief which may make this island
Thine own for ever, and I, thy Caliban,
For aye thy foot-licker.

Ste. Give me thy hand. I do begin to have bloody thoughts.   221

Trin. O King Stephano! O peer! O worthy Stephano, look what a wardrobe here is for thee!

Cal. Let it alone, thou fool! It is but trash.

Trin. O, ho, monster! we know what belongs to a frippery. O King Stephano!   226

Ste. Put off that gown, Trinculo. By this hand, I'll have that gown!

Trin. Thy Grace shall have it.

Cal. The dropsy drown this fool! What do you mean   230
To dote thus on such luggage? Let't alone,
And do the murther first. If he awake,
From toe to crown he'll fill our skins with pinches,
Make us strange stuff.

Ste. Be you quiet, monster. Mistress line, is not this my jerkin? [*Takes it down.*] Now is the jerkin under the line. Now, jerkin, you are like to lose your hair and prove a bald jerkin.

Trin. Do, do! We steal by line and level, an 't like your Grace.   240

Ste. I thank thee for that jest. Here's a garment for't. Wit shall not go unrewarded while I am king of this country. 'Steal by line and

level' is an excellent pass of pate. There's another garment for't.   245

Trin. Monster, come put some lime upon your fingers, and away with the rest!

Cal. I will have none on't. We shall lose our time
And all be turn'd to barnacles, or to apes
With foreheads villanous low.   250

Ste. Monster, lay-to your fingers. Help to bear this away where my hogshead of wine is, or I'll turn you out of my kingdom. Go to, carry this.

Trin. And this.

Ste. Ay, and this.   255

A noise of hunters heard. Enter divers *Spirits* in shape of dogs and hounds, hunting them about, *Prospero* and *Ariel setting them on.*

Pros. Hey, Mountain, hey!

Ari. Silver! there it goes, Silver!

Pros. Fury, Fury! There, Tyrant, there!
Hark, hark!
[*Caliban, Stephano, and Trinculo are driven out.*]
Go, charge my goblins that they grind their joints
With dry convulsions, shorten up their sinews
With aged cramps, and more pinch-spotted make them   261
Than pard or cat o' mountain.

Ari.   Hark, they roar.

Pros. Let them be hunted soundly. At this hour
Lie at my mercy all mine enemies.
Shortly shall all my labours end, and thou   265
Shalt have the air at freedom. For a little
Follow, and do me service.   *Exeunt.*

ACT V. Scene I. [*Before the cell of* Prospero.]

Enter *Prospero* in his magic robes, and *Ariel.*

Pros. Now does my project gather to a head.
My charms crack not, my spirits obey, and time
Goes upright with his carriage. How's the day?

Ari. On the sixth hour, at which time, my lord,
You said our work should cease.

Pros.   I did say so   5
When first I rais'd the tempest. Say, my spirit,
How fares the King and 's followers?

Ari.   Confin'd together
In the same fashion as you gave in charge,
Just as you left them — all prisoners, sir,   9

In the line grove which weather-fends your cell.
They cannot budge till your release. The King,
His brother, and yours abide all three distracted,
And the remainder mourning over them,
Brimful of sorrow and dismay; but chiefly
Him that you term'd, sir, the good old Lord Gonzalo.   15
His tears run down his beard like winter's drops
From eaves of reeds. Your charm so strongly works 'em,
That if you now beheld them, your affections
Would become tender.

Pros.   Dost thou think so, spirit?

Ari. Mine would, sir, were I human.

27

Pros. And mine shall. 20
Hast thou, which art but air, a touch, a feeling
Of their afflictions, and shall not myself,
One of their kind, that relish all as sharply
Passion as they, be kindlier mov'd than thou art?
Though with their high wrongs I am struck to
th' quick, 25
Yet with my nobler reason 'gainst my fury
Do I take part. The rarer action is
In virtue than in vengeance. They being
penitent,
The sole drift of my purpose doth extend 29
Not a frown further. Go, release them, Ariel.
My charms I'll break, their senses I'll restore,
And they shall be themselves.
Ari. I'll fetch them, sir. *Exit.*
Pros. [*makes a magic circle with his staff*] Ye
elves of hills, brooks, standing lakes, and
groves,
And ye that on the sands with printless foot
Do chase the ebbing Neptune, and do fly him 35
When he comes back; you demi-puppets that
By moonshine do the green sour ringlets make,
Whereof the ewe not bites; and you whose
pastime
Is to make midnight mushrumps, that rejoice
To hear the solemn curfew; by whose aid 40
(Weak masters though ye be) I have bedimm'd
The noontide sun, call'd forth the mutinous
winds,
And 'twixt the green sea and the azur'd vault
Set roaring war; to the dread rattling thunder
Have I given fire and rifted Jove's stout oak 45
With his own bolt; the strong-bas'd promontory
Have I made shake and by the spurs pluck'd up
The pine and cedar; graves at my command
Have wak'd their sleepers, op'd, and let 'em forth
By my so potent art. But this rough magic 50
I here abjure; and when I have requir'd
Some heavenly music (which even now I do)
To work mine end upon their senses that
This airy charm is for, I'll break my staff,
Bury it certain fadoms in the earth, 55
And deeper than did ever plummet sound
I'll drown my book. *Solemn music.*

Here enters *Ariel* before; then *Alonso*, with a
frantic gesture, attended by *Gonzalo*; *Sebastian*
and *Antonio* in like manner, attended by *Adrian*
and *Francisco*. They all enter the circle which
Prospero had made, and there stand charm'd;
which *Prospero* observing, speaks.

A solemn air, and the best comforter
To an unsettled fancy, cure thy brains

Now useless, boil'd within thy skull! There
stand, 60
For you are spell-stopp'd.
Holy Gonzalo, honourable man,
Mine eyes, ev'n sociable to the show of thine,
Fall fellowly drops. The charm dissolves apace;
And as the morning steals upon the night, 65
Melting the darkness, so their rising senses
Begin to chase the ignorant fumes that mantle
Their clearer reason. O good Gonzalo,
My true preserver, and a loyal sir
To him thou follow'st! I will pay thy graces 70
Home both in word and deed. Most cruelly
Didst thou, Alonso, use me and my daughter.
Thy brother was a furtherer in the act.
Thou art pinch'd for't now, Sebastian. Flesh
and blood,
You, brother mine, that entertain'd ambition,
Expell'd remorse and nature; who, with Se-
bastian 76
(Whose inward pinches therefore are most
strong),
Would here have kill'd your king, I do forgive thee,
Unnatural though thou art. Their understanding
Begins to swell, and the approaching tide 80
Will shortly fill the reasonable shore,
That now lies foul and muddy. Not one of
them
That yet looks on me or would know me. Ariel,
Fetch me the hat and rapier in my cell.
I will discase me, and myself present 85
As I was sometime Milan. Quickly, spirit!
Thou shalt ere long be free.

[Exit *Ariel* and returns immediately.]

Ariel sings and helps to attire him.

Where the bee sucks, there suck I;
In a cowslip's bell I lie;
There I couch when owls do cry. 90
On the bat's back I do fly
After summer merrily.
Merrily, merrily shall I live now
Under the blossom that hangs on the bough.

Pros. Why, that's my dainty Ariel! I shall
miss thee, 95
But yet thou shalt have freedom. So, so, so.
To the King's ship, invisible as thou art!
There shalt thou find the mariners asleep
Under the hatches. The master and the boat-
swain
Being awake, enforce them to this place, 100
And presently, I prithee.
Ari. I drink the air before me, and return
Or ere your pulse twice beat. *Exit.*

Gon. All torment, trouble, wonder, and amazement
Inhabits here. Some heavenly power guide us
Out of this fearful country!
Pros.   Behold, sir King, 106
The wronged Duke of Milan, Prospero.
For more assurance that a living prince
Does now speak to thee, I embrace thy body,
And to thee and thy company I bid   110
A hearty welcome.
Alon.   Whe'r thou be'st he or no,
Or some enchanted trifle to abuse me,
As late I have been, I not know. Thy pulse
Beats, as of flesh and blood; and, since I saw thee,
Th' affliction of my mind amends, with which,
I fear, a madness held me. This must crave 116
(An if this be at all) a most strange story.
Thy dukedom I resign and do entreat
Thou pardon me my wrongs. But how should Prospero
Be living and be here?
Pros.   First, noble friend, 120
Let me embrace thine age, whose honour cannot
Be measur'd or confin'd.
Gon.   Whether this be
Or be not, I'll not swear.
Pros.   You do yet taste
Some subtleties o' th' isle, that will not let you
Believe things certain. Welcome, my friends all.   125
[*Aside to Sebastian and Antonio*] But you, my brace of lords, were I so minded,
I here could pluck his Highness' frown upon you,
And justify you traitors. At this time
I will tell no tales.
Seb. [*aside*]   The devil speaks in him.
Pros.   No.
For you, most wicked sir, whom to call brother
Would even infect my mouth, I do forgive 131
Thy rankest fault — all of them; and require
My dukedom of thee, which perforce I know
Thou must restore.
Alon.   If thou beest Prospero,
Give us particulars of thy preservation;   135
How thou hast met us here, who three hours since
Were wrack'd upon this shore; where I have lost
(How sharp the point of this remembrance is!)
My dear son Ferdinand.
Pros.   I am woe for't, sir.
Alon. Irreparable is the loss, and patience
Says it is past her cure.

Pros.   I rather think   141
You have not sought her help, of whose soft grace
For the like loss I have her sovereign aid
And rest myself content.
Alon.   You the like loss?
Pros. As great to me as late; and, supportable
To make the dear loss, have I means much weaker   146
Than you may call to comfort you; for I
Have lost my daughter.
Alon.   A daughter?
O heavens, that they were living both in Naples,
The King and Queen there! That they were, I wish   150
Myself were mudded in that oozy bed
Where my son lies. When did you lose your daughter?
Pros. In this last tempest. I perceive these lords
At this encounter do so much admire
That they devour their reason, and scarce think
Their eyes do offices of truth, their words   156
Are natural breath. But, howsoev'r you have
Been justled from your senses, know for certain
That I am Prospero, and that very duke
Which was thrust forth of Milan, who most strangely   160
Upon this shore, where you were wrack'd, was landed
To be the lord on't. No more yet of this;
For 'tis a chronicle of day by day,
Not a relation for a breakfast, nor
Befitting this first meeting. Welcome, sir. 165
This cell's my court. Here have I few attendants,
And subjects none abroad. Pray you look in.
My dukedom since you have given me again,
I will requite you with as good a thing,
At least bring forth a wonder to content ye 170
As much as me my dukedom.
*Here Prospero discovers Ferdinand and Mi-
randa playing at chess.*
Mir. Sweet lord, you play me false.
Fer.   No, my dearest love,
I would not for the world.
Mir. Yes, for a score of kingdoms you should wrangle,
And I would call it fair play.
Alon.   If this prove 175
A vision of the island, one dear son
Shall I twice lose.
Seb.   A most high miracle!
Fer. Though the seas threaten, they are merciful.
I have curs'd them without cause. [*Kneels.*]

29

Alon.   Now all the blessings
Of a glad father compass thee about!   180
Arise, and say how thou cam'st here.
  Mir.   O, wonder!
How many goodly creatures are there here!
How beauteous mankind is! O brave new world
That has such people in't!
  Pros.   'Tis new to thee.
  Alon. What is this maid with whom thou
    wast at play?   185
Your eld'st acquaintance cannot be three hours.
Is she the goddess that hath sever'd us
And brought us thus together?
  Fer.   Sir, she is mortal;
But by immortal providence she's mine.
I chose her when I could not ask my father 190
For his advice, nor thought I had one. She
Is daughter to this famous Duke of Milan,
Of whom so often I have heard renown
But never saw before; of whom I have
Receiv'd a second life; and second father 195
This lady makes him to me.
  Alon.   I am hers.
But, O, how oddly will it sound that I
Must ask my child forgiveness!
  Pros.   There, sir, stop.
Let us not burthen our remembrance with
A heaviness that's gone.
  Gon.   I have inly wept, 200
Or should have spoke ere this. Look down,
    you gods,
And on this couple drop a blessed crown!
For it is you that have chalk'd forth the way
Which brought us hither.
  Alon.   I say amen, Gonzalo.
  Gon. Was Milan thrust from Milan that his
    issue   205
Should become kings of Naples? O, rejoice
Beyond a common joy, and set it down
With gold on lasting pillars: In one voyage
Did Claribel her husband find at Tunis,
And Ferdinand her brother found a wife 210
Where he himself was lost; Prospero his dukedom
In a poor isle; and all of us ourselves
When no man was his own.
  Alon. [*to Ferdinand and Miranda*] Give me
    your hands.
Let grief and sorrow still embrace his heart
That doth not wish you joy.
  Gon.   Be it so! Amen! 215

Enter *Ariel*, with the *Master* and *Boatswain*
    amazedly following.

O, look, sir; look, sir! Here is more of us!
I prophesied, if a gallows were on land,
This fellow could not drown. Now, blasphemy,
That swear'st grace o'erboard, not an oath on
    shore?
Hast thou no mouth by land? What is the
    news?   220
  Boats. The best news is that we have safely
    found
Our king and company; the next, our ship,
Which, but three glasses since, we gave out split,
Is tight and yare and bravely rigg'd as when
We first put out to sea.
  Ari. [*aside to Prospero*] Sir, all this service
Have I done since I went.
  Pros. [*aside to Ariel*] My tricksy spirit! 226
  Alon. These are not natural events; they
    strengthen
From strange to stranger. Say, how came you
    hither?
  Boats. If I did think, sir, I were well awake,
I'ld strive to tell you. We were dead of sleep
And (how we know not) all clapp'd under
    hatches;   231
Where, but even now, with strange and several
    noises
Of roaring, shrieking, howling, jingling chains,
And moe diversity of sounds, all horrible,
We were awak'd; straightway at liberty;   235
Where we, in all her trim, freshly beheld
Our royal, good, and gallant ship; our master
Cap'ring to eye her. On a trice, so please you,
Even in a dream, were we divided from them
And were brought moping hither.
  Ari. [*aside to Prospero*]   Was't well done?
  Pros. [*aside to Ariel*] Bravely, my diligence.
Thou shalt be free.   241
  Alon. This is as strange a maze as e'er men
    trod,
And there is in this business more than nature
Was ever conduct of. Some oracle
Must rectify our knowledge.
  Pros.   Sir, my liege, 245
Do not infest your mind with beating on
The strangeness of this business. At pick'd
    leisure,
Which shall be shortly, single I'll resolve you
(Which to you shall seem probable) of every
These happen'd accidents; till when, be cheer-
    ful   250
And think of each thing well. [*Aside to Ariel*]
Come hither, spirit.
Set Caliban and his companions free.
Untie the spell. [*Exit Ariel.*] How fares my
    gracious sir?
There are yet missing of your company
Some few odd lads that you remember not. 255

Enter *Ariel*, driving in *Caliban, Stephano*, and
     Trinculo, in their stol'n apparel.

Ste. Every man shift for all the rest, and let
no man take care for himself; for all is but
fortune. Coragio, bully-monster, coragio!

Trin. If these be true spies which I wear in
my head, here's a goodly sight.   260

Cal. O Setebos, these be brave spirits indeed!
How fine my master is! I am afraid
He will chastise me.

Seb.   Ha, ha!
What things are these, my Lord Antonio?
Will money buy 'em?

Ant.   Very like. One of them   265
Is a plain fish and no doubt marketable.

Pros. Mark but the badges of these men, my
     lords,
Then say if they be true. This misshapen knave,
His mother was a witch, and one so strong   269
That could control the moon, make flows and ebbs,
And deal in her command without her power.
These three have robb'd me, and this demi-
     devil
(For he's a bastard one) had plotted with them
To take my life. Two of these fellows you
Must know and own; this thing of darkness I
Acknowledge mine.

Cal.   I shall be pinch'd to death. 276
Alon. Is not this Stephano, my drunken
     butler?

Seb. He is drunk now. Where had he wine?
Alon. And Trinculo is reeling ripe. Where
     should they
Find this grand liquor that hath gilded 'em?
How cam'st thou in this pickle?   281

Trin. I have been in such a pickle, since I
saw you last, that I fear me will never out of
my bones. I shall not fear fly-blowing.

Seb. Why, how now, Stephano?   285
Ste. O, touch me not! I am not Stephano,
but a cramp.

Pros. You'ld be king o' the isle, sirrah?
Ste. I should have been a sore one then.
Alon. This is as strange a thing as e'er I
     look'd on.

Pros. He is as disproportion'd in his manners
As in his shape. Go, sirrah, to my cell;   291
Take with you your companions. As you look
To have my pardon, trim it handsomely.

Cal. Ay, that I will! and I'll be wise here-
     after,
And seek for grace. What a thrice-double ass
Was I to take this drunkard for a god   296
And worship this dull fool!

Pros.   Go to! Away!
Alon. Hence, and bestow your luggage where
     you found it.

Seb. Or stole it rather.
     [*Exeunt Caliban, Stephano, and Trinculo.*]
Pros. Sir, I invite your Highness and your
     train   300
To my poor cell, where you shall take your rest
For this one night; which, part of it, I'll waste
With such discourse as, I not doubt, shall make
     it
Go quick away — the story of my life,
And the particular accidents gone by   305
Since I came to this isle; and in the morn
I'll bring you to your ship, and so to Naples,
Where I have hope to see the nuptial
Of these our dear-belov'd solemnized;
And thence retire me to my Milan, where   310
Every third thought shall be my grave.

Alon.   I long
To hear the story of your life, which must
Take the ear strangely.

Pros.   I'll deliver all;
And promise you calm seas, auspicious gales,
And sail so expeditious that shall catch   315
Your royal fleet far off. — My Ariel, chick,
That is thy charge. Then to the elements
Be free, and fare thou well — Please you draw
     near.   *Exeunt omnes.*

EPILOGUE.

Spoken by *Prospero*.

Now my charms are all o'erthrown,
And what strength I have's mine own,
Which is most faint. Now 'tis true
I must be here confin'd by you,
Or sent to Naples. Let me not,   5
Since I have my dukedom got
And pardon'd the deceiver, dwell
In this bare island by your spell;
But release me from my bands
With the help of your good hands.   10
Gentle breath of yours my sails
Must fill, or else my project fails,
Which was to please. Now I want
Spirits to enforce, art to enchant;
And my ending is despair   15
Unless I be reliev'd by prayer,
Which pierces so that it assaults
Mercy itself and frees all faults.
As you from crimes would pardon'd be,
Let your indulgence set me free.   20
                              Exit.

31

THE TWO GENTLEMEN OF VERONA

The sole authority for the text of THE TWO GENTLEMEN is the First Folio (1623), in which the stage directions are limited to exits and entrances. In each scene the entrances are indicated at the outset by a single collective stage direction which enumerates the characters, once for all, in substantially the order of their appearance. No entrances and very few exits are marked within the scene, but the scene generally ends with *exeunt* or *exit*. The same plan is followed in *The Merry Wives of Windsor* and, to a limited extent, in *The Winter's Tale*. What this collective method signifies is by no means clear. Some critics regard it as evidence that THE TWO GENTLEMEN was printed from what is called an 'assembled' copy. The prompter's copy, they think, had been lost or destroyed, and a text was reconstructed by bringing together the manuscript 'parts' of the several actors and utilizing a so-called 'plot,' that is, an outline indicating the order of scenes and specifying the characters in each. This complicated and laborious process is no doubt possible, but there is no likelihood that the Folio owes its excellent text of THE TWO GENTLEMEN to any such hazardous patchwork. In modern editions the stage directions are regulated in accordance with Shakespeare's usual practice.

The date of the play is uncertain, but it is clearly one of Shakespeare's earliest comedies. This is indicated by the style and metre, and by lack of maturity in both characterization and management of the plot. The final scene, though it opens with a fine poetic soliloquy, sacrifices everything to crude sensationalism and leaves us at odds with both Valentine and Proteus. The comic element also suggests an early stage of Shakespeare's art. The quibbling dialogues, which remind one of *Love's Labour's Lost* and *The Comedy of Errors*, are good of their kind, but not extraordinary. They show the influence of Lyly and follow a classical convention to which Shakespeare was, of course, obedient at the outset of his career. More distinguished are Launce's comic monologues, which have never been surpassed. Launce in THE TWO GENTLEMEN looks forward to Launcelot Gobbo in *The Merchant of Venice*. There are other forecasts. Compare, for instance, the scene in which Julia asks Lucetta's opinion of 'the fair resort of gentlemen that every day with parle encounter me' (i, 2) with the conversation between Portia and Nerissa in *The Merchant of Venice* (i, 2). The disguised Julia's rôle in the service of Proteus is like Viola's in *Twelfth Night*. The only bit of direct evidence as to date is the passage in which Francis Meres pays tribute to Shakespeare in his *Palladis Tamia: Wits Treasury* (1598):

As *Plautus* and *Seneca* are accounted the best for Comedy and Tragedy among the Latines: so *Shakespeare* among the English is the most excellent in both kinds for the stage; for Comedy, witnes his *Gentlemen of Verona*, his *Errors*, his *Loue labors lost*, his *Loue labours wonne*, his *Midsummers night dreame*, & his *Merchant of Venice*: for Tragedy his *Richard the 2*. *Richard the 3*. *Henry the 4*. *King Iohn*, *Titus Andronicus* and his *Romeo and Iuliet*.

A probable date for the play is 1594.

There is no likelihood that THE TWO GENTLEMEN as we have it is a revision of an earlier form, though there may be some cuts in the Folio text; nor is there any foundation for the theory that Shakespeare had a collaborator. The merits and the defects are Shakespeare's own. That he wrote rapidly we know. This accounts well enough for some confusions of place, though these may be due to a copyist. Such slips of the pen or the mind need cause no surprise.

The main plot of THE TWO GENTLEMEN is based upon the episode of Felix and Felismena in the *Diana*, a Spanish pastoral romance by Jorge de Montemayor. The *Diana* was immensely popular. Several editions appeared before 1590. Bartholomew Yong's English translation, though finished by 1582, was not published until 1598. Shakespeare may have seen it in manuscript, though this seems unlikely, for Yong in his Preface indicates that he sent to the printer the only copy he had, which was 'verie darke and enterlined.' A French version by Nicolas Colin (1578, 1582, 1587) is also a possible intermediary. A play entitled *The History of Felix and Philiomena* was acted at court by the Queen's Players in 1585. Perhaps this was the link between Montemayor's romance and Shakespeare's comedy.

The story in the *Diana* runs as follows in Yong's translation:

Felix (Shakespeare's Proteus) is in love with Felismena (Shakespeare's Julia). When he has 'by sundrie signes, as by Tylt and Tourneyes, and by prauncing vp and down vpone his proude Iennet before [her] windowes' made his devotion manifest, he ventures to send her a letter by her maid, Rosina (Shakespeare's Lucetta). She declines to receive it and upbraids Rosina, who carries the letter away. Next morning, however, the sly Rosina drops it in her mistress's chamber, and Felismena, who is in fact eager to read the letter, pretends to believe that it is addressed to Rosina by some lover and bids her pick it up and let her see it. [Shakespeare (i, 2) follows the *Diana* rather closely in these incidents.] Felismena's reply to Felix's letter, though coy, is encouraging, and for 'almost a whole year' there is a constant exchange of 'amorous letters and verses.' But Felix's father, fearing a hasty marriage, sends him to the court of the Princess Augusta Cæsarina, telling him that 'it was not meet that a young gentleman, and of so noble a house as he was, should spend his youth idly at home' (cf. i, 3). Julia follows, disguised in male attire, and lodges at an inn. Shortly after midnight, the host suggests that she should open her window if she cares for music. Thus she hears the faithless Felix serenading his new love, Celia — Shakespeare's Sylvia (iv, 2). Felismena becomes Felix's page and wins his confidence. He tells her that Celia had shown him favour at first, but that she has turned against him because of a rumour that he loves a lady in his own country and is only amusing himself. He even shows Felismena Celia's reproachful letter and reads to her the reply which she is to carry to Celia.

The disguised Julia's conversation with Proteus (iv, 4), in which she describes her own feelings, and her soliloquy immediately after are strongly reminiscent of Felismena's story. The same is true of Julia's interview with Sylvia in the same scene. One notes particularly Sylvia's emphasis on the fickleness of Proteus and Julia's description of her own faded beauty. Verbal agreement, however, between the *Diana* and THE TWO GENTLEMEN is very slight. If Shakespeare had used the extant English version, such agreement would probably be conspicuous. Contrast, in this regard, the use he makes of Greene's *Pandosto* in *The Winter's Tale*. The remainder of Felismena's story is quite different from Shakespeare's plot. There is no Valentine in the *Diana*, and therefore no conflict between love and friendship. Celia falls in love with the supposed page and wooes her passionately (cf. *Twelfth Night*). Meeting with no response, she threatens to kill herself, falls in a swoon, and dies. Felix, in despair, wanders away and all trace of him is lost. Felismena assumes the habit of a shepherdess and seeks him in many countries. At last she comes to a little island where a knight is defending himself against three assailants. One of them he kills; the other two are shot to death by Felismena's arrows. When the knight takes off his helmet to thank his rescuer, she recognizes the faithless Felix. He is repentant; she forgives him, and they are happily married.

THE TWO GENTLEMEN OF VERONA

The Names of all the Actors.

Duke [of Milan], father to Silvia.
Valentine, } the Two Gentlemen.
Proteus,
Antonio, father to Proteus.
Thurio, a foolish rival to Valentine.
Eglamour, agent for Silvia in her escape.
Host, where Julia lodges.
Outlaws, with Valentine.

Speed, a clownish servant to Valentine.
Launce, the like to Proteus.
Panthino, servant to Antonio.

Julia, beloved of Proteus.
Silvia, beloved of Valentine.
Lucetta, waiting woman to Julia.

[Servants, Musicians.]

[SCENE. — Verona; Milan; and a forest on the Milan frontier.]

ACT I. [Scene I. Verona. An open place.]

Enter Valentine and Proteus.

Val. Cease to persuade, my loving Proteus:
Home-keeping youth have ever homely wits.
Were't not affection chains thy tender days
To the sweet glances of thy honour'd love,
I rather would entreat thy company 5
To see the wonders of the world abroad
Than (living dully sluggardiz'd at home)
Wear out thy youth with shapeless idleness.
But since thou lov'st, love still, and thrive
therein,
Even as I would when I to love begin. 10
  Pro. Wilt thou be gone? Sweet Valentine,
adieu!
Think on thy Proteus when thou (haply) seest
Some rare noteworthy object in thy travel.
Wish me partaker in thy happiness
When thou dost meet good hap; and in thy
danger, 15
If ever danger do environ thee,
Commend thy grievance to my holy prayers,
For I will be thy beadsman, Valentine.
  Val. And on a love-book pray for my success?
  Pro. Upon some book I love I'll pray for
thee.
  Val. That's on some shallow story of deep
love — 21
How young Leander cross'd the Hellespont.
  Pro. That's a deep story of a deeper love,
For he was more than over shoes in love.
  Val. 'Tis true; for you are over boots in love,
And yet you never swum the Hellespont. 26

  Pro. Over the boots? Nay, give me not the
boots!
  Val. No, I will not; for it boots thee not.
  Pro. What?
  Val. To be in love, where scorn is bought
with groans;
Coy looks with heart-sore sighs; one fading
moment's mirth 30
With twenty watchful, weary, tedious nights:
If haply won, perhaps a hapless gain;
If lost, why then a grievous labour won;
However — but a folly bought with wit,
Or else a wit by folly vanquished. 35
  Pro. So, by your circumstance, you call me
fool.
  Val. So, by your circumstance, I fear you'll
prove.
  Pro. 'Tis love you cavil at. I am not Love.
  Val. Love is your master, for he masters you;
And he that is so yoked by a fool, 40
Methinks should not be chronicled for wise.
  Pro. Yet writers say, as in the sweetest bud
The eating canker dwells, so eating love
Inhabits in the finest wits of all.
  Val. And writers say, as the most forward
bud 45
Is eaten by the canker ere it blow,
Even so by love the young and tender wit
Is turn'd to folly, blasting in the bud,
Losing his verdure, even in the prime,
And all the fair effects of future hopes. 50
But wherefore waste I time to counsel thee
That art a votary to fond desire?

35

Once more adieu! My father at the road
Expects my coming, there to see me shipp'd.
  Pro. And thither will I bring thee, Valentine.
  Val. Sweet Proteus, no. Now let us take our
    leave. 56
To Milan let me hear from thee by letters
Of thy success in love, and what news else
Betideth here in absence of thy friend;
And I likewise will visit thee with mine. 60
  Pro. All happiness bechance to thee in Milan!
  Val. As much to you at home! And so
    farewell. *Exit.*
  Pro. He after honour hunts, I after love.
He leaves his friends to dignify them more;
I leave myself, my friends, and all, for love. 65
Thou, Julia, thou, hast metamorphis'd me,
Made me neglect my studies, lose my time,
War with good counsel, set the world at naught;
Made wit with musing weak, heart sick with
    thought.

[Enter *Speed*.]

  Speed. Sir Proteus, save you! Saw you my
    master? 70
  Pro. But now he parted hence to embark for
    Milan.
  Speed. Twenty to one then he is shipp'd already,
And I have play'd the sheep in losing him.
  Pro. Indeed a sheep doth very often stray
An if the shepherd be awhile away. 75
  Speed. You conclude that my master is a
    shepherd then, and I a sheep?
  Pro. I do.
  Speed. Why then, my horns are his horns,
    whether I wake or sleep. 80
  Pro. A silly answer, and fitting well a sheep.
  Speed. This proves me still a sheep.
  Pro. True, and thy master a shepherd.
  Speed. Nay, that I can deny by a circumstance. 85
  Pro. It shall go hard but I'll prove it by
    another.
  Speed. The shepherd seeks the sheep, and
not the sheep the shepherd; but I seek my
master, and my master seeks not me. Therefore I am no sheep. 91
  Pro. The sheep for fodder follow the shepherd; the shepherd for food follows not the
sheep. Thou for wages followest thy master;
thy master for wages follows not thee. Therefore thou art a sheep. 96
  Speed. Such another proof will make me
cry 'baa.'

  Pro. But dost thou hear? Gav'st thou my
letter to Julia? 100
  Speed. Ay, sir. I (a lost mutton) gave your
letter to her (a lac'd mutton), and she (a lac'd
mutton) gave me (a lost mutton) nothing for
my labour.
  Pro. Here's too small a pasture for such store
of muttons. 106
  Speed. If the ground be overcharg'd, you
were best stick her.
  Pro. Nay; in that you are astray: 'twere
best pound you. 110
  Speed. Nay, sir. Less than a pound shall
serve me for carrying your letter.
  Pro. You mistake. I mean the pound — a
pinfold.
  Speed. From a pound to a pin? Fold it over
    and over, 115
'Tis threefold too little for carrying a letter to
your lover.
  Pro. But what said she?
  Speed. [*nods*] Ay.
  Pro. Nod-ay? Why, that's noddy.
  Speed. You mistook, sir. I say she did nod;
and you ask me if she did nod; and I say 'Ay.'
  Pro. And that set together is 'noddy.' 122
  Speed. Now you have taken the pains to set
it together, take it for your pains.
  Pro. No, no! You shall have it for bearing
the letter. 126
  Speed. Well, I perceive I must be fain to
bear with you.
  Pro. Why, sir, how do you bear with me?
  Speed. Marry, sir, the letter very orderly,
having nothing but the word 'noddy' for my
pains. 131
  Pro. Beshrew me, but you have a quick wit!
  Speed. And yet it cannot overtake your slow
purse.
  Pro. Come, come, open the matter in brief.
What said she? 136
  Speed. Open your purse, that the money and
the matter may be both at once delivered.
  Pro. Well, sir, here is for your pains. [*Gives
him money.*] What said she? 140
  Speed. Truly, sir, I think you'll hardly win
her.
  Pro. Why? Couldst thou perceive so much
from her?
  Speed. Sir, I could perceive nothing at all
from her; no, not so much as a ducat for delivering your letter; and being so hard to me
that brought your mind, I fear she'll prove as
hard to you in telling your mind. Give her no
token but stones, for she's as hard as steel.

Pro. What said she? nothing?   150
Speed. No, not so much as 'Take this for
thy pains.' To testify your bounty, I thank
you, you have testern'd me; in requital whereof,
henceforth carry your letters yourself. And
so, sir, I'll commend you to my master.   155
Pro. Go, go, be gone, to save your ship from
      wrack,
Which cannot perish, having thee aboard,
Being destin'd to a drier death on shore.
                                   [*Exit Speed.*]
I must go send some better messenger;
I fear my Julia would not deign my lines,   160
Receiving them from such a worthless post.
                                        Exit.

Scene II. [*Verona. The garden of
Julia's house.*]

Enter *Julia* and *Lucetta.*

Jul. But say, Lucetta, now we are alone,
Wouldst thou then counsel me to fall in love?
Luc. Ay, madam, so you stumble not un-
heedfully.
Jul. Of all the fair resort of gentlemen
That every day with parle encounter me,   5
In thy opinion which is worthiest love?
Luc. Please you repeat their names, I'll show
my mind
According to my shallow simple skill.
Jul. What think'st thou of the fair Sir
Eglamour?
Luc. As of a knight well-spoken, neat, and
fine;   10
But, were I you, he never should be mine.
Jul. What think'st thou of the rich Mer-
catio?
Luc. Well of his wealth; but of himself,
so so.
Jul. What think'st thou of the gentle
Proteus?
Luc. Lord, Lord! to see what folly reigns
in us!   15
Jul. How now? What means this passion
at his name?
Luc. Pardon, dear madam. 'Tis a passing
shame
That I, unworthy body as I am,
Should censure thus on lovely gentlemen.
Jul. Why not on Proteus, as of all the rest?
Luc. Then thus: of many good I think him
best.   21
Jul. Your reason?

Luc. I have no other but a woman's reason:
I think him so because I think him so.
Jul. And wouldst thou have me cast my love
on him?   25
Luc. Ay, if you thought your love not cast
away.
Jul. Why, he, of all the rest, hath never
mov'd me.
Luc. Yet he, of all the rest, I think best loves
ye.
Jul. His little speaking shows his love but
small.
Luc. Fire that's closest kept burns most of
all.   30
Jul. They do not love that do not show their
love.
Luc. O, they love least that let men know
their love.
Jul. I would I knew his mind.
Luc. Peruse this paper, madam.
                                 [*Gives a letter.*]
Jul. 'To Julia.' Say, from whom?   35
Luc. That the contents will show.
Jul. Say, say! Who gave it thee?
Luc. Sir Valentine's page; and sent, I think,
from Proteus.
He would have given it you; but I, being in
the way,
Did in your name receive it. Pardon the fault,
I pray.   40
Jul. Now, by my modesty, a goodly broker!
Dare you presume to harbour wanton lines?
To whisper, and conspire against my youth?
Now trust me, 'tis an office of great worth
And you an officer fit for the place.   45
There, take the paper. See it be return'd,
Or else return no more into my sight.
Luc. To plead for love deserves more fee
than hate.
Jul. Will ye be gone?
Luc.   That you may ruminate.
                                        Exit.
Jul. And yet I would I had o'erlook'd the
letter.   50
It were a shame to call her back again
And pray her to a fault for which I chid her.
What fool is she, that knows I am a maid
And would not force the letter to my view,
Since maids, in modesty, say 'no' to that   55
Which they would have the profferer construe
'ay'!
Fie, fie! how wayward is this foolish love,
That, like a testy babe, will scratch the nurse
And presently, all humbled, kiss the rod!
How churlishly I chid Lucetta hence   60

When willingly I would have had her here!
How angerly I taught my brow to frown
When inward joy enforc'd my heart to smile!
My penance is, to call Lucetta back
And ask remission for my folly past. 65
What ho! Lucetta!

[Enter *Lucetta*.]

Luc. What would your ladyship?
Jul. Is it near dinner time?
Luc. I would it were,
That you might kill your stomach on your
meat
And not upon your maid.
Jul. What is't that you took up so gingerly?
Luc. Nothing. 71
Jul. Why didst thou stoop then?
Luc. To take a paper up that I let fall.
Jul. And is that paper nothing?
Luc. Nothing concerning me. 75
Jul. Then let it lie, for those that it con-
cerns.
Luc. Madam, it will not lie where it concerns
Unless it have a false interpreter.
Jul. Some love of yours hath writ to you in
rhyme.
Luc. That I might sing it, madam, to a tune.
Give me a note; your ladyship can set. 81
Jul. As little by such toys as may be possible.
Best sing it to the tune of 'Light o' love.'
Luc. It is too heavy for so light a tune.
Jul. Heavy? Belike it hath some burden
then? 85
Luc. Ay! and melodious were it, would you
sing it.
Jul. And why not you?
Luc. I cannot reach so high.
Jul. Let's see your song. [*Takes the letter.*]
How now, minion?
Luc. Keep tune there still, so you will sing
it out.
And yet methinks I do not like this tune. 90
Jul. You do not?
Luc. No, madam. 'Tis too sharp.
Jul. You, minion, are too saucy.
Luc. Nay, now you are too flat
And mar the concord with too harsh a descant.
There wanteth but a mean to fill your song. 95
Jul. The mean is drown'd with your unruly
bass.
Luc. Indeed I bid the base for Proteus.
Jul. This babble shall not henceforth trouble
me.
Here is a coil with protestation!
[*Tears the letter.*]

Go, get you gone; and let the papers lie. 100
You would be fing'ring them to anger me.
Luc. She makes it strange, but she would
be best pleas'd
To be so ang'red with another letter. [*Exit.*]
Jul. Nay, would I were so ang'red with the
same!
O hateful hands, to tear such loving words! 105
Injurious wasps, to feed on such sweet honey
And kill the bees that yield it with your
stings!
I'll kiss each several paper for amends.
Look, here is writ 'kind Julia.' Unkind Julia,
As in revenge of thy ingratitude, 110
I throw thy name against the bruising stones,
Trampling contemptuously on thy disdain.
And here is writ 'love-wounded Proteus.'
Poor wounded name! My bosom, as a bed,
Shall lodge thee till thy wound be throughly
heal'd; 115
And thus I search it with a sovereign kiss.
But twice or thrice was 'Proteus' written
down.
Be calm, good wind, blow not a word away
Till I have found each letter in the letter,
Except mine own name. That some whirlwind
bear 120
Unto a ragged, fearful, hanging rock
And throw it thence into the raging sea!
Lo, here in one line is his name twice writ:
'Poor forlorn Proteus, passionate Proteus,
To the sweet Julia.' That I'll tear away; 125
And yet I will not, sith so prettily
He couples it to his complaining names.
Thus will I fold them one upon another.
Now kiss, embrace, contend, do what you
will.

[Enter *Lucetta*.]

Luc. Madam, 130
Dinner is ready, and your father stays.
Jul. Well, let us go.
Luc. What, shall these papers lie like tell-
tales here?
Jul. If you respect them, best to take them
up.
Luc. Nay, I was taken up for laying them
down. 135
Yet here they shall not lie, for catching cold.
Jul. I see you have a month's mind to them.
Luc. Ay, madam, you may say what sights
you see.
I see things too, although you judge I wink.
Jul. Come, come! Will't please you go? 140
Exeunt.

Scene III. [*Verona.* Antonio's *house.*]

Enter *Antonio* and *Panthino.*

Ant. Tell me, Panthino, what sad talk was that
Wherewith my brother held you in the cloister?
Pan. 'Twas of his nephew Proteus, your son.
Ant. Why, what of him?
Pan.   He wond'red that your lordship
Would suffer him to spend his youth at home
While other men, of slender reputation,   6
Put forth their sons to seek preferment out:
Some to the wars, to try their fortune there;
Some to discover islands far away;
Some to the studious universities.   10
For any or for all these exercises
He said that Proteus your son was meet;
And did request me to importune you
To let him spend his time no more at home,
Which would be great impeachment to his age,
In having known no travel in his youth.   16
Ant. Nor need'st thou much importune me to that
Whereon this month I have been hammering.
I have consider'd well his loss of time,
And how he cannot be a perfect man,   20
Not being tried and tutor'd in the world.
Experience is by industry achiev'd
And perfected by the swift course of time.
Then tell me, whither were I best to send him?
Pan. I think your lordship is not ignorant   25
How his companion, youthful Valentine,
Attends the Emperor in his royal court.
Ant. I know it well.
Pan. 'Twere good, I think, your lordship sent him thither.   29
There shall he practise tilts and tournaments,
Hear sweet discourse, converse with noblemen,
And be in eye of every exercise
Worthy his youth and nobleness of birth.
Ant. I like thy counsel; well hast thou advis'd.   34
And that thou mayst perceive how well I like it,
The execution of it shall make known.
Even with the speediest expedition
I will dispatch him to the Emperor's court.
Pan. To-morrow, may it please you, Don Alphonso,

With other gentlemen of good esteem,   40
Are journeying to salute the Emperor
And to commend their service to his will.
Ant. Good company. With them shall Proteus go.

[Enter *Proteus* with a letter.]

And in good time! Now will we break with him.
Pro. Sweet love, sweet lines, sweet life!   45
Here is her hand, the agent of her heart;
Here is her oath for love, her honour's pawn.
O that our fathers would applaud our loves,
To seal our happiness with their consents!
O heavenly Julia!   50
Ant. How now? What letter are you reading there?
Pro. May't please your lordship, 'tis a word or two
Of commendations sent from Valentine,
Deliver'd by a friend that came from him.
Ant. Lend me the letter. Let me see what news.   55
Pro. There is no news, my lord, but that he writes
How happily he lives, how well belov'd,
And daily graced by the Emperor;
Wishing me with him, partner of his fortune.
Ant. And how stand you affected to his wish?   60
Pro. As one relying on your lordship's will
And not depending on his friendly wish.
Ant. My will is something sorted with his wish.
Muse not that I thus suddenly proceed;
For what I will, I will, and there an end.   65
I am resolv'd that thou shalt spend some time
With Valentinus in the Emperor's court.
What maintenance he from his friends receives,
Like exhibition thou shalt have from me.
To-morrow be in readiness to go.   70
Excuse it not, for I am peremptory.
Pro. My lord, I cannot be so soon provided.
Please you deliberate a day or two.
Ant. Look, what thou want'st shall be sent after thee.
No more of stay! To-morrow thou must go.   75
Come on, Panthino. You shall be employ'd
To hasten on his expedition.
        [*Exeunt Antonio and Panthino.*]
Pro. Thus have I shunn'd the fire for fear of burning
And drench'd me in the sea, where I am drown'd.

I fear'd to show my father Julia's letter,   80
Lest he should take exceptions to my love;
And with the vantage of mine own excuse
Hath he excepted most against my love.
O, how this spring of love resembleth
  The uncertain glory of an April day,   85
Which now shows all the beauty of the sun,
  And by-and-by a cloud takes all away!

[Enter *Panthino*.]

Pan. Sir Proteus, your father calls for you.
He is in haste; therefore I pray you go.
Pro. Why, this it is! My heart accords
  thereto,   90
And yet a thousand times it answers 'no.'
                                        Exeunt.

ACT II. Scene I. [*Milan. The* Duke's *Palace.*]

Enter *Valentine, Speed.*

Speed. Sir, your glove.
Val.   Not mine. My gloves are on.
Speed. Why then, this may be yours, for
this is but one.
Val. Ha, let me see! Ay, give it me; it's
mine.
Sweet ornament that decks a thing divine!
Ah, Silvia, Silvia!   5
Speed. [*shouts*] Madam Silvia, Madam Silvia!
Val. How now, sirrah?
Speed. She is not within hearing, sir.
Val. Why, sir, who bade you call her?
Speed. Your worship, sir, or else I mistook.
Val. Well, you'll still be too forward.   11
Speed. And yet I was last chidden for being
too slow.
Val. Go to, sir. Tell me, do you know
Madam Silvia?   15
Speed. She that your worship loves?
Val. Why, how know you that I am in love?
Speed. Marry, by these special marks: first,
you have learn'd, like Sir Proteus, to wreathe
your arms like a malecontent; to relish a love
song like a robin redbreast; to walk alone like
one that had the pestilence; to sigh like a
schoolboy that had lost his A B C; to weep
like a young wench that had buried her
grandam; to fast like one that takes diet;
to watch like one that fears robbing; to speak
puling like a beggar at Hallowmas. You were
wont, when you laughed, to crow like a cock;
when you walk'd, to walk like one of the lions;
when you fasted, it was presently after dinner;
when you look'd sadly, it was for want of
money. And now you are metamorphis'd with
a mistress, that, when I look on you, I can
hardly think you my master.   34
Val. Are all these things perceiv'd in me?
Speed. They are all perceiv'd without ye.
Val. Without me? They canno*

Speed. Without you? Nay, that's certain,
for, without you were so simple, none else
would. But you are so without these follies
that these follies are within you and shine
through you like the water in an urinal, that
not an eye that sees you but is a physician to
comment on your malady.   44
Val. But tell me, dost thou know my lady
Silvia?
Speed. She that you gaze on so as she sits
at supper?
Val. Hast thou observ'd that? Even she I
mean.
Speed. Why, sir, I know her not.   50
Val. Dost thou know her by my gazing on
her, and yet know'st her not?
Speed. Is she not hard-favour'd, sir?
Val. Not so fair, boy, as well-favour'd.
Speed. Sir, I know that well enough.   55
Val. What dost thou know?
Speed. That she is not so fair as (of you) well
favour'd.
Val. I mean that her beauty is exquisite, but
her favour infinite.   60
Speed. That's because the one is painted,
and the other out of all count.
Val. How painted? and how out of count?
Speed. Marry, sir, so painted, to make her
fair, that no man counts of her beauty.   65
Val. How esteem'st thou me? I account of
her beauty.
Speed. You never saw her since she was de-
form'd.
Val. How long hath she been deform'd?   70
Speed. Ever since you lov'd her.
Val. I have lov'd her ever since I saw her,
and still I see her beautiful.
Speed. If you love her, you cannot see
her.
Val. Why?   75
Speed. Because Love is blind. O, that you
had mine eyes! or your own eyes had the lights

40

they were wont to have when you chid at Sir
Proteus for going ungarter'd!
Val. What should I see then?   80
Speed. Your own present folly and her pass-
ing deformity; for he, being in love, could not
see to garter his hose; and you, being in love,
cannot see to put on your hose.
Val. Belike, boy, then you are in love; for
last morning you could not see to wipe my shoes.
Speed. True, sir; I was in love with my bed.
I thank you, you swing'd me for my love, which
makes me the bolder to chide you for yours.
Val. In conclusion, I stand affected to her.
Speed. I would you were set; so your affec-
tion would cease.
Val. Last night she enjoin'd me to write
some lines to one she loves.
Speed. And have you?   95
Val. I have.
Speed. Are they not lamely writ?
Val. No, boy, but as well as I can do them.

[Enter *Silvia.*]

Peace! here she comes.
Speed. [*aside*] O excellent motion! O exceed-
ing puppet! Now will he interpret to her. 101
Val. Madam and mistress, a thousand good-
morrows!
Speed. [*aside*] O, give ye good ev'n! Here's
a million of manners.   105
Sil. Sir Valentine and servant, to you two
thousand.
Speed. [*aside*] He should give her interest,
and she gives it him.
Val. As you enjoin'd me, I have writ your
letter   110
Unto the secret nameless friend of yours;
Which I was much unwilling to proceed in,
But for my duty to your ladyship.
                        [*Gives a letter.*]
Sil. I thank you, gentle servant. 'Tis very
clerkly done.
Val. Now trust me, madam, it came hardly
off;   115
For, being ignorant to whom it goes,
I writ at random, very doubtfully.
Sil. Perchance you think too much of so
much pains?
Val. No, madam. So it stead you, I will
write
(Please you command) a thousand times as
much;   120
And yet —
Sil. A pretty period! Well, I guess the
sequel.

And yet I will not name it — and yet I care
not —
And yet take this again — and yet I thank
you —
Meaning henceforth to trouble you no more.
Speed. [*aside*] And yet you will; and yet,
another 'yet.'   126
Val. What means your ladyship? Do you
not like it?
Sil. Yes, yes. The lines are very quaintly
writ;
But, since unwillingly, take them again.
Nay, take them!   [*Gives back the letter.*]
Val. Madam, they are for you.   131
Sil. Ay, ay! you writ them, sir, at my re-
quest;
But I will none of them: they are for you.
I would have had them writ more movingly.
Val. Please you, I'll write your ladyship
another.   135
Sil. And when it's writ, for my sake read it
over;
And if it please you, so; if not, why, so!
Val. If it please me, madam, what then?
Sil. Why, if it please you, take it for your
labour;
And so good morrow, servant.   *Exit.*
Speed. [*aside*] O jest unseen, inscrutable,
invisible,   141
As a nose on a man's face or a weathercock on
a steeple!
My master sues to her; and she hath taught
her suitor,
He being her pupil, to become her tutor.
O, excellent device! Was there ever heard a
better,   145
That my master, being scribe, to himself should
write the letter?
Val. How now, sir? What are you reasoning
with yourself?
Speed. Nay, I was rhyming; 'tis you that
have the reason.
Val. To do what?   151
Speed. To be a spokesman from Madam
Silvia.
Val. To whom?
Speed. To yourself. Why, she wooes you by
a figure.
Val. What figure?   155
Speed. By a letter, I should say.
Val. Why, she hath not writ to me!
Speed. What need she, when she hath made
you write to yourself? Why, do you not per-
ceive the jest?
Val. No, believe me.   161

Speed. No believing you indeed, sir! But did you perceive her earnest?

Val. She gave me none, except an angry word.

Speed. Why, she hath given you a letter. 165

Val. That's the letter I writ to her friend.

Speed. And that letter hath she deliver'd, and there an end.

Val. I would it were no worse.

Speed. I'll warrant you 'tis as well; 170
For often have you writ to her; and she, in modesty,
Or else for want of idle time, could not again reply;
Or fearing else some messenger that might her mind discover,
Herself hath taught her love himself to write unto her lover.
All this I speak in print, for in print I found it.
Why muse you, sir? 'Tis dinner time. 176

Val. I have din'd.

Speed. Ay, but hearken, sir. Though the chameleon Love can feed on the air, I am one that am nourish'd by my victuals, and would fain have meat. O, be not like your mistress. Be moved, be moved. *Exeunt.*

Scene II. [*Verona.* Julia's *house.*]

Enter *Proteus, Julia.*

Pro. Have patience, gentle Julia.

Jul. I must, where is no remedy.

Pro. When possibly I can, I will return.

Jul. If you turn not, you will return the sooner.
Keep this remembrance for thy Julia's sake. 5
　　　　　　　　　[*Gives a ring.*]

Pro. Why then, we'll make exchange. Here take you this. [*Gives her another.*]

Jul. And seal the bargain with a holy kiss.

Pro. Here is my hand for my true constancy;
And when that hour o'erslips me in the day
Wherein I sigh not, Julia, for thy sake, 10
The next ensuing hour some foul mischance
Torment me for my love's forgetfulness!
My father stays my coming. Answer not.
The tide is now. Nay, not thy tide of tears!
That tide will stay me longer than I should. 15
Julia, farewell! [*Exit Julia.*]
　　　　What, gone without a word?
Ay, so true love should do. It cannot speak,
For truth hath better deeds than words to grace it.

[*Enter Panthino.*]

Pan. Sir Proteus, you are stay'd for.

Pro. Go. I come, I come! 20
Alas, this parting strikes poor lovers dumb!
　　　　　　　　　Exeunt.

Scene III. [*Verona. A street.*]

Enter *Launce,* [leading a dog].

Launce. Nay, 'twill be this hour ere I have done weeping; all the kind of the Launces have this very fault. I have receiv'd my proportion, like the Prodigious Son, and am going with Sir Proteus to the Imperial's court. I think Crab my dog be the sourest-natured dog that lives. My mother weeping; my father wailing; my sister crying; our maid howling; our cat wringing her hands, and all our house in a great perplexity — yet did not this cruelhearted cur shed one tear. He is a stone, a very pebble stone, and has no more pity in him than a dog. A Jew would have wept to have seen our parting. Why, my grandam, having no eyes, look you, wept herself blind at my parting! Nay, I'll show you tne manner of it. This shoe is my father. No, this left shoe is my father. No, no, this left shoe is my mother. Nay, that cannot be so neither. Yes, it is so, it is so! — it hath the worser sole. This shoe with the hole in it is my mother, and this my father. A vengeance on't! there 'tis! Now, sir, this staff is my sister; for, look you, she is as white as a lily and as small as a wand. This hat is Nan, our maid. I am the dog. No, the dog is himself, and I am the dog. O, the dog is me, and I am myself. Ay, so, so! Now come I to my father: 'Father, your blessing!' Now should not the shoe speak a word for weeping. Now should I kiss my father; well, he weeps on. Now come I to my mother. O that she could speak now like a wood woman! Well, I kiss her. Why, there 'tis! here's my mother's breath up and down. Now come I to my sister; mark the moan she makes. Now the dog all this while sheds not a tear, nor speaks a word; but see how I lay the dust with my tears. 35

[*Enter Panthino.*]

Pan. Launce, away, away! aboard! Thy master is shipp'd, and thou art to post after with oars. What's the matter? Why weep'st

John Neville in the role of the restless Valentine, who leaves home for adventure in Milan

Laurence Payne as the other gentleman, the fickle, perfidious Proteus, villain of the piece

THE TWO GENTLEMEN
OF VERONA

PHOTOGRAPHS BY DESMOND TRIPP
PRODUCED BY THE BRISTOL OLD VIC COMPANY

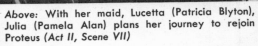

Above: With her maid, Lucetta (Patricia Blyton), Julia (Pamela Alan) plans her journey to rejoin Proteus (Act II, Scene VII)

Left: "What think'st thou of the gentle Proteus?" Julia seeks Lucetta's approval of Proteus (Act I, Scene II)

Below left: Newton Blick in the comic role of Speed, servant of Valentine.

Below right: Launce (Michael Aldridge), servant of Proteus, delivers a comic monologue which is patiently received by his dog (Act II, Scene III)

"I am resolv'd that thou shalt spend some time with Valentinus in the emperor's court."
Proteus is dismayed as his father, Antonio (Peter Howell), advised by his old steward,
Panthino (Norman Tyrrell), tells him he is to leave Verona for Milan (Act I, Scene III)

"Here is my hand for my true constancy."
Proteus' farewell to Julia (Act II, Scene II)

Speed haggles with Proteus over his fee for
giving information about Julia (Act I, Scene I)

Having learned through Proteus that Valentine is planning to elope with his daughter Silvia, the Duke of Milan (William Squire) banishes him from Milan (*Act III, Scene I*)

Valentine and Silvia (Gudrun Ure) are interrupted in a romantic scene by the jealous Thurio (John Warner), a favorite of the duke (*Act II, Scene IV*)

Valentine and his servant, Speed, are set upon by a band of outlaws (*Act IV, Scene I*)

Above: Disguised as a boy, Julia has taken service with Proteus. Here she punctuates the queries of the foppish Thurio with sarcastic asides (*Act V, Scene II*)

Left: Julia in her disguise as Sebastian

Below: At the bidding of Proteus, a band of musicians serenades Silvia in the courtyard of the duke's palace (*Act IV, Scene II*)

The duke assures his minion Thurio that Silvia's love will
return to him now that Valentine is banished (*Act III, Scene II*)

Valentine comes to the defense of Silvia when Proteus
seeks to force his attentions on her (*Act V, Scene IV*)

"Thou hast prevailed; I pardon them, and thee." The play's final scene: the lovers are united and the duke forgives both Valentine and the group of outlaws whom he joined in the forest after his banishment (*Act V, Scene IV*)

thou, man? Away, ass! You'll lose the tide
if you tarry any longer.   40
Launce. It is no matter if the tied were
lost, for it is the unkindest tied that ever any
man tied.
Pan. What's the unkindest tide?
Launce. Why, he that's tied here! Crab,
my dog.   45
Pan. Tut, man! I mean thou'lt lose the
flood, and in losing the flood, lose thy voyage,
and in losing thy voyage, lose thy master, and
in losing thy master, lose thy service, and in
losing thy service — Why dost thou stop my
mouth?
Launce. For fear thou shouldst lose thy
tongue.   52
Pan. Where should I lose my tongue?
Launce. In thy tale.
Pan. In my tail?   55
Launce. Lose the tide, and the voyage, and
the master, and the service, and the tied!
Why, man, if the river were dry, I am able to
fill it with my tears; if the wind were down,
I could drive the boat with my sighs.   60
Pan. Come! come away, man! I was sent
to call thee.
Launce. Sir, call me what thou dar'st.
Pan. Wilt thou go?
Launce. Well, I will go.   *Exeunt.*

Scene IV. [*Milan. The* Duke's *Palace.*]

Enter *Valentine, Silvia, Thurio, Speed.*
Sil. Servant!
Val. Mistress?
Speed. Master, Sir Thurio frowns on you.
Val. Ay, boy; it's for love.
Speed. Not of you.   5
Val. Of my mistress then.
Speed. 'Twere good you knock'd him. [*Exit.*]
Sil. Servant, you are sad.
Val. Indeed, madam, I seem so.
Thu. Seem you that you are not?   10
Val. Haply I do.
Thu. So do counterfeits.
Val. So do you.
Thu. What seem I that I am not?
Val. Wise.   15
Thu. What instance of the contrary?
Val. Your folly.
Thu. And how quote you my folly?
Val. I quote it in your jerkin.
Thu. My jerkin is a doublet.   20

Val. Well then, I'll double your folly.
Thu. How?
Sil. What, angry, Sir Thurio? Do you
change colour?
Val. Give him leave, madam; he is a kind
of chameleon.   26
Thu. That hath more mind to feed on your
blood than live in your air.
Val. You have said, sir.
Thu. Ay, sir, and done too, for this time. 30
Val. I know it well, sir. You always end
ere you begin.
Sil. A fine volley of words, gentlemen, and
quickly shot off.
Val. 'Tis indeed, madam. We thank the
giver.   35
Sil. Who is that, servant?
Val. Yourself, sweet lady; for you gave the
fire. Sir Thurio borrows his wit from your
ladyship's looks, and spends what he borrows
kindly in your company.   40
Thu. Sir, if you spend word for word with
me, I shall make your wit bankrupt.
Val. I know it well, sir. You have an ex-
chequer of words and, I think, no other treasure to give your followers; for it appears by
their bare liveries that they live by your bare
words.   46

[Enter *Duke.*]

Sil. No more, gentlemen, no more! Here
comes my father.
Duke. Now, daughter Silvia, you are hard
beset.
Sir Valentine, your father is in good health. 50
What say you to a letter from your friends
Of much good news?
Val.   My lord, I will be thankful
To any happy messenger from thence.
Duke. Know ye Don Antonio, your coun-
tryman?
Val. Ay, my good lord, I know the gentle-
man   55
To be of worth and worthy estimation,
And not without desert so well reputed.
Duke. Hath he not a son?
Val. Ay, my good lord; a son that well
deserves
The honour and regard of such a father.   60
Duke. You know him well?
Val. I know him as myself; for from our
infancy
We have convers'd, and spent our hours to-
gether;
And though myself have been an idle truant,

43

Omitting the sweet benefit of time 65
To clothe mine age with angel-like perfection,
Yet hath Sir Proteus (for that's his name)
Made use and fair advantage of his days —
His years but young, but his experience old;
His head unmellowed, but his judgment ripe;
And in a word (for far behind his worth 71
Comes all the praises that I now bestow)
He is complete in feature and in mind
With all good grace to grace a gentleman.
Duke. Beshrew me, sir, but if he make this
good, 75
He is as worthy for an empress' love
As meet to be an emperor's counsellor.
Well, sir, this gentleman is come to me
With commendation from great potentates,
And here he means to spend his time awhile. 80
I think 'tis no unwelcome news to you.
Val. Should I have wish'd a thing, it had
been he.
Duke. Welcome him then according to his
worth.
Silvia, I speak to you; and you, Sir Thurio;
For Valentine, I need not cite him to it. 85
I will send him hither to you presently. [*Exit.*]
Val. This is the gentleman I told your ladyship
Had come along with me, but that his mistress
Did hold his eyes lock'd in her crystal looks.
Sil. Belike that now she hath enfranchis'd
them 90
Upon some other pawn for fealty.
Val. Nay, sure, I think she holds them pris-
oners still.
Sil. Nay, then he should be blind, and being
blind,
How could he see his way to seek out you?
Val. Why, lady, love hath twenty pair of
eyes. 95
Thu. They say that Love hath not an eye at
all.
Val. To see such lovers, Thurio, as yourself.
Upon a homely object Love can wink.

[Enter *Proteus.*]

Sil. Have done, have done! Here comes the
gentleman.
Val. Welcome, dear Proteus! Mistress, I
beseech you 100
Confirm his welcome with some special favour.
Sil. His worth is warrant for his welcome
hither,
If this be he you oft have wish'd to hear from.
Val. Mistress, it is. Sweet lady, entertain
him
To be my fellow servant to your ladyship. 105

Sil. Too low a mistress for so high a servant.
Pro. Not so, sweet lady, but too mean a
servant
To have a look of such a worthy mistress.
Val. Leave off discourse of disability.
Sweet lady, entertain him for your servant. 110
Pro. My duty will I boast of, nothing else.
Sil. And duty never yet did want his meed.
Servant, you are welcome to a worthless mis-
tress.
Pro. I'll die on him that says so but yourself.
Sil. That you are welcome?
Pro. That you are worthless. 115

[Enter a *Servant.*]

Serv. Madam, my lord your father would
speak with you.
Sil. I wait upon his pleasure. [*Exit Servant.*]
Come, Sir Thurio,
Go with me. Once more, new servant, welcome.
I'll leave you to confer of home affairs; 119
When you have done, we look to hear from you.
Pro. We'll both attend upon your ladyship.
[*Exeunt Silvia and Thurio.*]
Val. Now tell me, how do all from whence
you came?
Pro. Your friends are well and have them
much commended.
Val. And how do yours?
Pro. I left them all in health.
Val. How does your lady, and how thrives
your love? 125
Pro. My tales of love were wont to weary
you;
I know you joy not in a love discourse.
Val. Ay, Proteus, but that life is alter'd now.
I have done penance for contemning Love,
Whose high imperious thoughts have punish'd
me 130
With bitter fasts, with penitential groans,
With nightly tears, and daily heartsore sighs,
For, in revenge of my contempt of love,
Love hath chas'd sleep from my enthralled eyes
And made them watchers of mine own heart's
sorrow. 135
O gentle Proteus, Love's a mighty lord,
And hath so humbled me as I confess
There is no woe to his correction,
Nor to his service no such joy on earth.
Now no discourse, except it be of love! 140
Now can I break my fast, dine, sup, and sleep
Upon the very naked name of love.
Pro. Enough! I read your fortune in your
eye.
Was this the idol that you worship so?

Val. Even she; and is she not a heavenly
saint?   145
Pro. No; but she is an earthly paragon.
Val. Call her divine.
Pro.   I will not flatter her.
Val. O, flatter me! for love delights in
praises.
Pro. When I was sick you gave me bitter
pills,
And I must minister the like to you.   150
Val. Then speak the truth by her. If not
divine,
Yet let her be a principality,
Sovereign to all the creatures on the earth.
Pro. Except my mistress.
Val.   Sweet, except not any,
Except thou wilt except against my love.   155
Pro. Have I not reason to prefer mine own?
Val. And I will help thee to prefer her too.
She shall be dignified with this high honour,
To bear my lady's train, lest the base earth
Should from her vesture chance to steal a kiss
And, of so great a favour growing proud,   161
Disdain to root the summer-swelling flow'r
And make rough winter everlastingly.
Pro. Why, Valentine! what braggardism is
this?
Val. Pardon me, Proteus. All I can is noth-
ing   165
To her, whose worth makes other worthies
nothing.
She is alone.
Pro.   Then let her alone.
Val. Not for the world! Why, man, she is
mine own,
And I as rich in having such a jewel
As twenty seas, if all their sand were pearl, 170
The water nectar, and the rocks pure gold.
Forgive me that I do not dream on thee,
Because thou seest me dote upon my love.
My foolish rival, that her father likes
(Only for his possessions are so huge),   175
Is gone with her along; and I must after,
For love, thou know'st, is full of jealousy.
Pro. But she loves you?
Val. Ay, and we are betroth'd; nay more,
our marriage hour,
With all the cunning manner of our flight, 180
Determin'd of: how I must climb her window,
The ladder made of cords, and all the means
Plotted and 'greed on for my happiness.
Good Proteus, go with me to my chamber,
In these affairs to aid me with thy counsel. 185
Pro. Go on before; I shall enquire you forth.
I must unto the road, to disembark

Some necessaries that I needs must use,
And then I'll presently attend you.
Val. Will you make haste?   190
Pro. I will.   *Exit* [*Valentine*].
Even as one heat another heat expels
Or as one nail by strength drives out another,
So the remembrance of my former love
Is by a newer object quite forgotten.   195
Is it mine eye, or Valentinus' praise,
Her true perfection, or my false transgression-
That makes me reasonless, to reason thus?
She is fair; and so is Julia that I love —
That I did love, for now my love is thaw'd, 200
Which, like a waxen image 'gainst a fire,
Bears no impression of the thing it was.
Methinks my zeal to Valentine is cold
And that I love him not as I was wont.
O, but I love his lady too too much,   205
And that's the reason I love him so little.
How shall I dote on her with more advice
That thus without advice begin to love her!
'Tis but her picture I have yet beheld,
And that hath dazzled my reason's light;   210
But when I look on her perfections,
There is no reason but I shall be blind.
If I can check my erring love, I will;
If not, to compass her I'll use my skill.   *Exit*

Scene V. [*Milan. A street.*]

Enter *Speed* and *Launce*, [meeting].

Speed. Launce! by mine honesty, welcome
to Milan!
Launce. Forswear not thyself, sweet youth,
for I am not welcome. I reckon this always:
that a man is never undone till he be hang'd,
nor never welcome to a place till some certain
shot be paid and the hostess say 'Welcome.'
Speed. Come on, you madcap. I'll to the
alehouse with you presently, where for one shot
of five pence thou shalt have five thousand welcomes. But, sirrah, how did thy master part
with Madam Julia?   12
Launce. Marry, after they clos'd in earnest,
they parted very fairly in jest.
Speed. But shall she marry him?   15
Launce. No.
Speed. How then? Shall he marry her?
Launce. No, neither.
Speed. What, are they broken?
Launce. No, they are both as whole as a fish.
Speed. Why then, how stands the matter
with them?   22

Launce. Marry, thus: when it stands well with him, it stands well with her.

Speed. What an ass art thou! I understand thee not.   26

Launce. What a block art thou that thou canst not! My staff understands me.

Speed. What thou say'st?

Launce. Ay, and what I do too. Look thee, I'll but lean, and my staff understands me. 31

Speed. It stands under thee indeed.

Launce. Why, stand-under and under-stand is all one.

Speed. But tell me true, will't be a match? 35

Launce. Ask my dog. If he say ay, it will; if he say no, it will; if he shake his tail and say nothing, it will.

Speed. The conclusion is, then, that it will.

Launce. Thou shalt never get such a secret from me but by a parable.   41

Speed. 'Tis well that I get it so. But, Launce, how say'st thou that my master is become a notable lover?

Launce. I never knew him otherwise.   45

Speed. Than how?

Launce. A notable lubber, as thou reportest him to be.

Speed. Why, thou whoreson ass, thou mistak'st me.   50

Launce. Why, fool, I meant not thee; I meant thy master.

Speed. I tell thee my master is become a hot lover.

Launce. Why, I tell thee I care not though he burn himself in love. If thou wilt, go with me to the alehouse; if not, thou art an Hebrew, a Jew, and not worth the name of a Christian.

Speed. Why?   59

Launce. Because thou hast not so much charity in thee as to go to the ale with a Christian. Wilt thou go?

Speed. At thy service.   *Exeunt.*

Scene VI. [*Milan. The* Duke's *Palace.*]

Enter *Proteus* solus.

Pro. To leave my Julia, shall I be forsworn;
To love fair Silvia, shall I be forsworn;
To wrong my friend, I shall be much forsworn;
And ev'n that pow'r which gave me first my oath

Provokes me to this threefold perjury.   5
Love bade me swear, and Love bids me forswear.
O sweet-suggesting Love, if thou hast sinn'd,
Teach me, thy tempted subject, to excuse it!
At first I did adore a twinkling star,
But now I worship a celestial sun.   10
Unheedful vows may heedfully be broken,
And he wants wit that wants resolved will
To learn his wit t' exchange the bad for better.
Fie, fie, unreverend tongue, to call her bad
Whose sovereignty so oft thou hast preferr'd 15
With twenty thousand soul-confirming oaths!
I cannot leave to love, and yet I do;
But there I leave to love where I should love.
Julia I lose, and Valentine I lose.
If I keep them, I needs must lose myself;   20
If I lose them, thus find I by their loss —
For Valentine, myself; for Julia, Silvia.
I to myself am dearer than a friend,
For love is still most precious in itself;
And Silvia (witness heaven, that made her fair!)
Shows Julia but a swarthy Ethiope.   26
I will forget that Julia is alive,
Rememb'ring that my love to her is dead;
And Valentine I'll hold an enemy,
Aiming at Silvia as a sweeter friend.   30
I cannot now prove constant to myself
Without some treachery us'd to Valentine.
This night he meaneth with a corded ladder
To climb celestial Silvia's chamber window,
Myself in counsel his competitor.   35
Now presently I'll give her father notice
Of their disguising and pretended flight;
Who, all enrag'd, will banish Valentine,
For Thurio he intends shall wed his daughter;
But, Valentine being gone, I'll quickly cross 40
By some sly trick blunt Thurio's dull proceeding.
Love, lend me wings to make my purpose swift,
As thou hast lent me wit to plot this drift!
                                       Exit.

Scene VII. [*Verona.* Julia's *house.*]

Enter *Julia* and *Lucetta.*

Jul. Counsel, Lucetta! gentle girl, assist me!
And ev'n in kind love I do conjure thee,

Who art the table wherein all my thoughts
Are visibly character'd and engrav'd,
To lesson me, and tell me some good mean   5
How with my honour I may undertake
A journey to my loving Proteus.
  Luc. Alas, the way is wearisome and long!
  Jul. A true-devoted pilgrim is not weary
To measure kingdoms with his feeble steps;   10
Much less shall she that hath Love's wings to
fly,
And when the flight is made to one so dear,
Of such divine perfection as Sir Proteus.
  Luc. Better forbear till Proteus make re-
turn.
  Jul. O, know'st thou not his looks are my
soul's food?   15
Pity the dearth that I have pined in
By longing for that food so long a time.
Didst thou but know the inly touch of love,
Thou wouldst as soon go kindle fire with snow
As seek to quench the fire of love with words.   20
  Luc. I do not seek to quench your love's hot
fire,
But qualify the fire's extreme rage,
Lest it should burn above the bounds of reason.
  Jul. The more thou dam'st it up, the more
it burns.
The current that with gentle murmur glides,   25
Thou know'st, being stopp'd, impatiently doth
rage;
But when his fair course is not hindered,
He makes sweet music with th' enamell'd
stones,
Giving a gentle kiss to every sedge
He overtaketh in his pilgrimage;   30
And so by many winding nooks he strays
With willing sport to the wide ocean.
Then let me go, and hinder not my course.
I'll be as patient as a gentle stream,
And make a pastime of each weary step   35
Till the last step have brought me to my
love,
And there I'll rest, as after much turmoil
A blessed soul doth in Elysium.
  Luc. But in what habit will you go along?
  Jul. Not like a woman, for I would prevent
The loose encounters of lascivious men.   41
Gentle Lucetta, fit me with such weeds
As may beseem some well-reputed page.
  Luc. Why then, your ladyship must cut
your hair.
  Jul. No, girl; I'll knit it up in silken strings
With twenty odd-conceited true-love knots.   46
To be fantastic may become a youth
Of greater time than I shall show to be.

  Luc. What fashion, madam, shall I make
your breeches?
  Jul. That fits as well as 'Tell me, good my
lord,   50
What compass will you wear your farthingale?'
Why, ev'n what fashion thou best lik'st, Lu-
cetta.
  Luc. You must needs have them with a cod-
piece, madam.
  Jul. Out, out, Lucetta! that will be ill-
favour'd.
  Luc. A round hose, madam, now's not worth
a pin   55
Unless you have a codpiece to stick pins on.
  Jul. Lucetta, as thou lov'st me, let me have
What thou think'st meet, and is most man-
nerly.
But tell me, wench, how will the world repute
me
For undertaking so unstaid a journey?   60
I fear me it will make me scandaliz'd.
  Luc. If you think so, then stay at home and
go not.
  Jul. Nay, that I will not.
  Luc. Then never dream on infamy, but go.
If Proteus like your journey when you come,   65
No matter who's displeas'd when you are gone.
I fear me he will scarce be pleas'd withal.
  Jul. That is the least, Lucetta, of my fear.
A thousand oaths, an ocean of his tears,
And instances of infinite of love   70
Warrant me welcome to my Proteus.
  Luc. All these are servants to deceitful men.
  Jul. Base men that use them to so base
effect!
But truer stars did govern Proteus' birth.
His words are bonds, his oaths are oracles,   75
His love sincere, his thoughts immaculate,
His tears pure messengers sent from his heart,
His heart as far from fraud as heaven from
earth.
  Luc. Pray heav'n he prove so when you come
to him!
  Jul. Now, as thou lov'st me, do him not
that wrong   80
To bear a hard opinion of his truth!
Only deserve my love by loving him.
And presently go with me to my chamber
To take a note of what I stand in need of
To furnish me upon my longing journey.   85
All that is mine I leave at thy dispose,
My goods, my lands, my reputation;
Only, in lieu thereof, dispatch me hence.
Come, answer not, but to it presently!   89
I am impatient of my tarriance.   *Exeunt.*

ACT III. Scene I. [*Milan. An anteroom in the* Duke's *Palace.*]

Enter *Duke, Thurio, Proteus.*

Duke. Sir Thurio, give us leave, I pray,
  awhile;
We have some secrets to confer about.
                      [*Exit Thurio.*]
Now, tell me, Proteus, what's your will with
  me?
Pro. My gracious lord, that which I would
  discover
The law of friendship bids me to conceal;   5
But when I call to mind your gracious favours
Done to me (undeserving as I am),
My duty pricks me on to utter that
Which else no worldly good should draw from
  me.   9
Know, worthy prince, Sir Valentine, my friend,
This night intends to steal away your daughter.
Myself am one made privy to the plot.
I know you have determin'd to bestow her
On Thurio, whom your gentle daughter hates;
And should she thus be stol'n away from you,
It would be much vexation to your age.   16
Thus, for my duty's sake, I rather chose
To cross my friend in his intended drift
Than, by concealing it, heap on your head
A pack of sorrows which would press you down,
Being unprevented, to your timeless grave.   21
Duke. Proteus, I thank thee for thine honest
  care,
Which to requite, command me while I live.
This love of theirs myself have often seen,
Haply when they have judg'd me fast asleep,   25
And oftentimes have purpos'd to forbid
Sir Valentine her company and my court;
But, fearing lest my jealous aim might err
And so (unworthily) disgrace the man
(A rashness that I ever yet have shunn'd),   30
I gave him gentle looks, thereby to find
That which thyself hast now disclos'd to me.
And, that thou mayst perceive my fear of this,
Knowing that tender youth is soon suggested,
I nightly lodge her in an upper tow'r,   35
The key whereof myself have ever kept,
And thence she cannot be convey'd away.
Pro. Know, noble lord, they have devis'd a
  mean
How he her chamber window will ascend
And with a corded ladder fetch her down;   40
For which the youthful lover now is gone,
And this way comes he with it presently,

Where, if it please you, you may intercept
  him.
But, good my lord, do it so cunningly
That my discovery be not aimed at;   45
For love of you, not hate unto my friend,
Hath made me publisher of this pretence.
Duke. Upon mine honour, he shall never
  know
That I had any light from thee of this.   49
Pro. Adieu, my lord. Sir Valentine is com-
  ing.   [*Exit.*]

[Enter *Valentine.*]

Duke. Sir Valentine, whither away so fast?
Val. Please it your Grace, there is a mes-
  senger
That stays to bear my letters to my friends,
And I am going to deliver them.
Duke. Be they of much import?   55
Val. The tenure of them doth but signify
My health, and happy being at your court.
Duke. Nay then, no matter. Stay with me
  awhile.
I am to break with thee of some affairs
That touch me near; wherein thou must be
  secret.   60
'Tis not unknown to thee that I have sought
To match my friend Sir Thurio to my daughter.
Val. I know it well, my lord; and sure the
  match
Were rich and honourable. Besides, the gen-
  tleman
Is full of virtue, bounty, worth, and qualities 65
Beseeming such a wife as your fair daughter.
Cannot your Grace win her to fancy him?
Duke. No, trust me. She is peevish, sullen,
  froward,
Proud, disobedient, stubborn, lacking duty;
Neither regarding that she is my child   70
Nor fearing me as if I were her father.
And may I say to thee this pride of hers,
Upon advice, hath drawn my love from her,
And where I thought the remnant of mine age
Should have been cherish'd by her childlike
  duty,   75
I now am full resolv'd to take a wife
And turn her out to who will take her in.
Then let her beauty be her wedding dow'r;
For me and my possessions she esteems not.
Val. What would your Grace have me to do
  in this?   80

Duke. There is a lady in Milano here
Whom I affect; but she is nice and coy
And naught esteems my aged eloquence.
Now therefore would I have thee to my tutor
(For long agone I have forgot to court;   85
Besides, the fashion of the time is chang'd)
How and which way I may bestow myself
To be regarded in her sun-bright eye.
Val. Win her with gifts, if she respect not
  words.
Dumb jewels often in their silent kind   90
More than quick words do move a woman's
  mind.
Duke. But she did scorn a present that I
  sent her.
Val. A woman sometime scorns what best
  contents her.
Send her another! Never give her o'er,
For scorn at first makes after-love the more. 95
If she do frown, 'tis not in hate of you,
But rather to beget more love in you.
If she do chide, 'tis not to have you gone,
For why, the fools are mad if left alone.
Take no repulse, whatever she doth say;   100
For 'Get you gone!' she doth not mean 'Away!'
Flatter and praise, commend, extol their graces;
Though ne'er so black, say they have angels'
  faces.
That man that hath a tongue, I say is no man
If with his tongue he cannot win a woman. 105
Duke. But she I mean is promis'd by her
  friends
Unto a youthful gentleman of worth,
And kept severely from resort of men,
That no man hath access by day to her.
Val. Why then, I would resort to her by
  night.   110
Duke. Ay, but the doors be lock'd and keys
  kept safe,
That no man hath recourse to her by night.
Val. What lets but one may enter at her
  window?
Duke. Her chamber is aloft, far from the
  ground,
And built so shelving that one cannot climb it
Without apparent hazard of his life.   116
Val. Why then, a ladder quaintly made of
  cords,
To cast up, with a pair of anchoring hooks,
Would serve to scale another Hero's tow'r,
So bold Leander would adventure it.   120
Duke. Now, as thou art a gentleman of blood,
Advise me where I may have such a ladder.
Val. When would you use it? Pray, sir, tell
me that.

Duke. This very night; for Love is like a
  child,
That longs for everything that he can come by.
Val. By seven o'clock I'll get you such a
  ladder.   126
Duke. But hark thee! I will go to her alone.
How shall I best convey the ladder thither?
Val. It will be light, my lord, that you may
  bear it
Under a cloak that is of any length.   130
Duke. A cloak as long as thine will serve the
  turn?
Val. Ay, my good lord.
Duke.   Then let me see thy cloak.
I'll get me one of such another length.
Val. Why, any cloak will serve the turn, my
  lord.
Duke. How shall I fashion me to wear a
  cloak?   135
I pray thee let me feel thy cloak upon me.
                    [Takes the cloak.]
What letter is this same? What's here? 'To
  Silvia'?
And here an engine fit for my proceeding!
I'll be so bold to break the seal for once. *[Reads.]*

'My thoughts do harbour with my Silvia nightly,
  And slaves they are to me, that send them
    flying.   141
O, could their master come and go as lightly,
  Himself would lodge where (senseless) they are
    lying!
My herald thoughts in thy pure bosom rest them,
  While I, their king, that thither them impor-
    tune,   145
Do curse the grace that with such grace hath
    blest them,
  Because myself do want my servants' fortune,
I curse myself, for they are sent by me,
That they should harbour where their lord would
    be.'

What's here?   150
'Silvia, this night I will enfranchise thee.'
'Tis so! and here's the ladder for the pur-
  pose.
Why, Phaëton (for thou art Merops' son),
Wilt thou aspire to guide the heavenly car
And with thy daring folly burn the world? 155
Wilt thou reach stars, because they shine on
  thee?
Go, base intruder, overweening slave!
Bestow thy fawning smiles on equal mates,
And think my patience, more than thy desert,
Is privilege for thy departure hence.   160
Thank me for this more than for all the favours
Which (all too much) I have bestow'd on thee.

But if thou linger in my territories
Longer than swiftest expedition
Will give thee time to leave our royal court, 165
By heaven, my wrath shall far exceed the love
I ever bore my daughter or thyself.
Be gone! I will not hear thy vain excuse,
But, as thou lov'st thy life, make speed from
hence.   [*Exit.*]
Val. And why not death rather than living
torment?   170
To die is to be banish'd from myself;
And Silvia is myself. Banish'd from her
Is self from self — a deadly banishment!
What light is light, if Silvia be not seen?
What joy is joy, if Silvia be not by?   175
Unless it be to think that she is by
And feed upon the shadow of perfection.
Except I be by Silvia in the night,
There is no music in the nightingale.
Unless I look on Silvia in the day,   180
There is no day for me to look upon.
She is my essence, and I leave to be
If I be not by her fair influence
Foster'd, illumin'd, cherish'd, kept alive.
I fly not death, to fly his deadly doom: 185
Tarry I here, I but attend on death;
But fly I hence, I fly away from life.

[*Enter Proteus and Launce.*]

Pro. Run, boy, run, run, and seek him out!
Launce. So-hough, so-hough!
Pro. What seest thou?   190
Launce. Him we go to find. There's not a
hair on 's head but 'tis a Valentine.
Pro. Valentine?
Val. No.
Pro. Who then? his spirit?   195
Val. Neither.
Pro. What then?
Val. Nothing.
Launce. Can nothing speak? Master, shall
I strike?
Pro. Who wouldst thou strike?   200
Launce. Nothing.
Pro. Villain, forbear!
Launce. Why, sir, I'll strike nothing. I
pray you —
Pro. Sirrah, I say forbear! — Friend Valen-
tine, a word.
Val. My ears are stopp'd and cannot hear
good news,   205
So much of bad already hath possess'd them.
Pro. Then in dumb silence will I bury mine,
For they are harsh, untuneable, and bad.
Val. Is Silvia dead?

Pro. No, Valentine.   210
Val. No Valentine indeed for sacred Silvia!
Hath she forsworn me?
Pro. No, Valentine.
Val. No Valentine, if Silvia have forsworn
me!
What is your news?   215
Launce. Sir, there is a proclamation that you
are vanished.
Pro. That thou art banished — O, that's the
news! —
From hence, from Silvia, and from me thy
friend.
Val. O, I have fed upon this woe already,
And now excess of it will make me surfeit. 220
Doth Silvia know that I am banished?
Pro. Ay, ay! and she hath offered to the
doom
(Which, unrevers'd, stands in effectual force)
A sea of melting pearl, which some call tears.
Those at her father's churlish feet she tender'd;
With them, upon her knees, her humble self,
Wringing her hands, whose whiteness so be-
came them   227
As if but now they waxed pale for woe.
But neither bended knees, pure hands held up,
Sad sighs, deep groans, nor silver-shedding tears
Could penetrate her uncompassionate sire; 231
But Valentine, if he be ta'en, must die.
Besides, her intercession chaf'd him so,
When she for thy repeal was suppliant,
That to close prison he commanded her,   235
With many bitter threats of biding there.
Val. No more! unless the next word that
thou speak'st
Have some malignant power upon my life;
If so, I pray thee breathe it in mine ear,
As ending anthem of my endless dolour.   240
Pro. Cease to lament for that thou canst not
help,
And study help for that which thou lament'st.
Time is the nurse and breeder of all good.
Here if thou stay, thou canst not see thy love;
Besides, thy staying will abridge thy life. 245
Hope is a lover's staff; walk hence with that
And manage it against despairing thoughts.
Thy letters may be here, though thou art hence,
Which, being writ to me, shall be deliver'd
Even in the milk-white bosom of thy love. 250
The time now serves not to expostulate.
Come, I'll convey thee through the city gate,
And, ere I part with thee, confer at large
Of all that may concern thy love affairs.
As thou lov'st Silvia (though not for thyself),
Regard thy danger, and along with me!   256

Val. I pray thee, Launce, an if thou seest my boy,
Bid him make haste and meet me at the North-
gate.
Pro. Go, sirrah, find him out. Come, Valentine.   259
Val. O my dear Silvia! Hapless Valentine!
            [*Exeunt Valentine and Proteus.*]
Launce. I am but a fool, look you, and yet I
have the wit to think my master is a kind of a
knave. But that's all one, if he be but one
knave. He lives not now that knows me to be
in love; yet I am in love. But a team of horse
shall not pluck that from me, nor who 'tis I
love. And yet 'tis a woman; but what woman,
I will not tell myself. And yet 'tis a milkmaid.
Yet 'tis not a maid, for she hath had gossips.
Yet 'tis a maid, for she is her master's maid and
serves for wages. She hath more qualities than
a water spaniel, which is much in a bare Christian. [*Pulls out a paper.*] Here is the cate-log
of her condition. 'Inprimis. She can fetch and
carry.' Why, a horse can do no more. Nay, a
horse cannot fetch, but only carry; therefore
is she better than a jade. 'Item. She can milk.'
Look you, a sweet virtue in a maid with clean
hands.

[Enter *Speed.*]

Speed. How now, Signior Launce? What
news with your mastership?   280
Launce. With my master's ship? Why, it is
at sea.
Speed. Well, your old vice still — mistake
the word. What news then in your paper?
Launce. The black'st news that ever thou
heard'st.   286
Speed. Why, man? how black?
Launce. Why, as black as ink.
Speed. Let me read them.
Launce. Fie on thee, jolthead! Thou canst
not read.   291
Speed. Thou liest! I can.
Launce. I will try thee. Tell me this: who
begot thee?
Speed. Marry, the son of my grandfather.
Launce. O illiterate loiterer! It was the son
of thy grandmother. This proves that thou
canst not read.
Speed. Come, fool, come! try me in thy
paper.
Launce. There! and Saint Nicholas be thy
speed!   301
Speed. [*reads*] 'Inprimis. She can milk.'
Launce. Ay, that she can.

Speed. 'Item. She brews good ale.'
Launce. And thereof comes the proverb,
'Blessing of your heart, you brew good ale.'
Speed. 'Item. She can sew.'
Launce. That's as much as to say 'Can she
so?'
Speed. 'Item. She can knit.'   310
Launce. What need a man care for a stock
with a wench, when she can knit him a stock?
Speed. 'Item. She can wash and scour.'
Launce. A special virtue; for then she need
not be wash'd and scour'd.   315
Speed. 'Item. She can spin.'
Launce. Then may I set the world on wheels,
when she can spin for her living.
Speed. 'Item. She hath many nameless vir-
tues.'   320
Launce. That's as much as to say 'bastard
virtues'; that indeed know not their fathers,
and therefore have no names.
Speed. Here follow her vices.   324
Launce. Close at the heels of her virtues.
Speed. 'Item. She is not to be kiss'd fasting,
in respect of her breath.'
Launce. Well, that fault may be mended
with a breakfast. Read on.
Speed. 'Item. She hath a sweet mouth.'   330
Launce. That makes amends for her sour
breath.
Speed. 'Item. She doth talk in her sleep.'
Launce. It's no matter for that, so she sleep
not in her talk.   335
Speed. 'Item. She is slow in words.'
Launce. O villain, that set this down among
her vices! To be slow in words is a woman's
only virtue. I pray thee, out with't, and place
it for her chief virtue.   340
Speed. 'Item. She is proud.'
Launce. Out with that too! It was Eve's
legacy and cannot be ta'en from her.
Speed. 'Item. She hath no teeth.'
Launce. I care not for that neither, because
I love crusts.   346
Speed. 'Item. She is curst.'
Launce. Well, the best is, she hath no teeth
to bite.
Speed. 'Item. She will often praise her
liquor.'   351
Launce. If her liquor be good, she shall. If
she will not, I will; for good things should be
praised.
Speed. 'Item. She is too liberal.'   355
Launce. Of her tongue she cannot, for that's
writ down she is slow of; of her purse she shall
not, for that I'll keep shut. Now of another

thing she may, and that cannot I help. Well,
proceed.   360
Speed. 'Item. She hath more hair than wit,
and more faults than hairs, and more wealth
than faults.'
Launce. Stop there! I'll have her! She was
mine, and not mine, twice or thrice in that last
article. Rehearse that once more.   366
Speed. 'Item. She hath more hair than wit'—
Launce. More hair than wit. It may be. I'll
prove it. The cover of the salt hides the salt,
and therefore it is more than the salt; the hair
that covers the wit is more than the wit, for the
greater hides the less. What's next?
Speed. 'And more faults than hairs' —
Launce. That's monstrous! O that that
were out!   375
Speed. 'And more wealth than faults.'
Launce. Why, that word makes the faults
gracious. Well, I'll have her. And if it be a
match, as nothing is impossible —
Speed. What then?   380
Launce. Why, then will I tell thee — that
thy master stays for thee at the North-gate.
Speed. For me?
Launce. For thee? Ay. Who art thou? He
hath stay'd for a better man than thee.
Speed. And must I go to him?
Launce. Thou must run to him, for thou
hast stay'd so long that going will scarce serve
the turn.   389
Speed. Why didst not tell me sooner? Pox
of your love letters!   [*Exit.*]
Launce. Now will he be swing'd for reading
my letter. An unmannerly slave, that will
thrust himself into secrets! I'll after, to rejoice
in the boy's correction.   *Exit.*

Scene II. [*Milan. The* Duke's *Palace.*]

Enter *Duke, Thurio.*

Duke. Sir Thurio, fear not but that she will
love you
Now Valentine is banish'd from her sight.
Thu. Since his exile she hath despis'd me
most,
Forsworn my company, and rail'd at me,
That I am desperate of obtaining her.   5
Duke. This weak impress of love is as a figure
Trenched in ice, which with an hour's heat
Dissolves to water and doth lose his form.
A little time will melt her frozen thoughts,
And worthless Valentine shall be forgot.   10

[Enter *Proteus.*]
How now, Sir Proteus? Is your countryman,
According to our proclamation, gone?
Pro. Gone, my good lord.
Duke. My daughter takes his going griev-
ously.
Pro. A little time, my lord, will kill that
grief.   15
Duke. So I believe, but Thurio thinks not so.
Proteus, the good conceit I hold of thee
(For thou hast shown some sign of good desert)
Makes me the better to confer with thee.
Pro. Longer than I prove loyal to your Grace
Let me not live to look upon your Grace.   21
Duke. Thou know'st how willingly I would
effect
The match between Sir Thurio and my daugh-
ter?
Pro. I do, my lord.
Duke. And also, I think, thou art not ig-
norant   25
How she opposes her against my will?
Pro. She did, my lord, when Valentine was
here.
Duke. Ay, and perversely she persevers so.
What might we do to make the girl forget
The love of Valentine and love Sir Thurio? 30
Pro. The best way is to slander Valentine
With falsehood, cowardice, and poor descent:
Three things that women highly hold in hate.
Duke. Ay, but she'll think that it is spoke
in hate.
Pro. Ay, if his enemy deliver it.   35
Therefore it must with circumstance be spoken
By one whom she esteemeth as his friend.
Duke Then you must undertake to slander
him.
Pro. And that, my lord, I shall be loath to
do.
'Tis an ill office for a gentleman,   40
Especially against his very friend.
Duke. Where your good word cannot advan-
tage him,
Your slander never can endamage him.
Therefore the office is indifferent,
Being entreated to it by your friend.   45
Pro. You have prevail'd, my lord. If I can
do it
By aught that I can speak in his dispraise,
She shall not long continue love to him.
But say this weed her love from Valentine,
It follows not that she will love Sir Thurio. 50
Thu. Therefore, as you unwind her love
from him,

Lest it should ravel and be good to none.
You must provide to bottom it on me;
Which must be done by praising me as much
As you in worth dispraise Sir Valentine.   55
  Duke. And, Proteus, we dare trust you in
    this kind,
Because we know, on Valentine's report,
You are already Love's firm votary
And cannot soon revolt and change your mind.
Upon this warrant shall you have access   60
Where you with Silvia may confer at large —
For she is lumpish, heavy, melancholy,
And, for your friend's sake, will be glad of you —
Where you may temper her by your persuasion
To hate young Valentine and love my friend. 65
  Pro. As much as I can do, I will effect.
But you, Sir Thurio, are not sharp enough.
You must lay lime to tangle her desires
By wailful sonnets, whose composed rhymes
Should be full fraught with serviceable vows. 70
  Duke. Ay!
Much is the force of heaven-bred poesy.
  Pro. Say that upon the altar of her beauty
You sacrifice your tears, your sighs, your heart.
Write till your ink be dry, and with your tears
Moist it again; and frame some feeling line
That may discover such integrity.   77
For Orpheus' lute was strung with poets'
    sinews,

Whose golden touch could soften steel and
    stones,
Make tigers tame, and huge leviathans   80
Forsake unsounded deeps to dance on sands.
After your dire-lamenting elegies,
Visit by night your lady's chamber window
With some sweet consort. To their instru-
    ments
Tune a deploring dump. The night's dead si-
    lence   85
Will well become such sweet-complaining
    grievance.
This, or else nothing, will inherit her.
  Duke. This discipline shows thou hast been
    in love.
  Thu. And thy advice this night I'll put in
    practice.
Therefore, sweet Proteus, my direction-giver, 90
Let us into the city presently
To sort some gentlemen well skill'd in music.
I have a sonnet that will serve the turn
To give the onset to thy good advice.
  Duke. About it, gentlemen!   95
  Pro. We'll wait upon your Grace till after
    supper
And afterward determine our proceedings.
  Duke. Even now about it! I will pardon you.
                                        Exeunt.

ACT IV. Scene I. [*A road in a forest on the Milan frontier.*]

Enter certain *Outlaws.*

1. Out. Fellows, stand fast! I see a passenger.
2. Out. If there be ten, shrink not, but down
    with 'em!

Enter *Valentine* and *Speed.*

3. Out. Stand, sir, and throw us that you
    have about ye!
If not, we'll make you sit, and rifle you.
  Speed. Sir, we are undone! These are the
    villains   5
That all the travellers do fear so much.
  Val. My friends —
1. Out. That's not so, sir! We are your
    enemies.
2. Out. Peace! we'll hear him.
3. Out. Ay, by my beard, will we! for he is
    a proper man.   10
  Val. Then know that I have little wealth to
    lose.
A man I am cross'd with adversity.

My riches are these poor habiliments,
Of which if you should here disfurnish me,
You take the sum and substance that I have. 15
  2. Out. Whither travel you?
  Val. To Verona.
  1. Out. Whence came you?
  Val. From Milan.
  3. Out. Have you long sojourn'd there?   20
  Val. Some sixteen months, and longer might
    have stay'd
If crooked fortune had not thwarted me.
  1. Out. What, were you banish'd thence?
  Val. I was.
  2. Out. For what offence?   25
  Val. For that which now torments me to re-
    hearse.
I kill'd a man, whose death I much repent;
But yet I slew him manfully, in fight,
Without false vantage or base treachery.
  1. Out. Why, ne'er repent it if it were done
    so.   30
But were you banish'd for so small a fault?

Val. I was, and held me glad of such a doom.
2. Out. Have you the tongues?
Val. My youthful travel therein made me
happy,
Or else I often had been miserable.   35
3. Out. By the bare scalp of Robin Hood's
fat friar,
This fellow were a king for our wild faction!
1. Out. We'll have him! Sirs, a word!
Speed. Master, be one of them. It's an honourable kind of thievery.   40
Val. Peace, villain!
2. Out. Tell us this: have you anything to
take to?
Val. Nothing but my fortune.
3. Out. Know then that some of us are
gentlemen,
Such as the fury of ungovern'd youth   45
Thrust from the company of awful men.
Myself was from Verona banished
For practising to steal away a lady,
An heir, and near allied unto the Duke.
2. Out. And I from Mantua, for a gentleman
Who, in my mood, I stabb'd unto the heart.   51
1. Out. And I for such-like petty crimes as
these.
But to the purpose! for we cite our faults
That they may hold excus'd our lawless lives;
And partly, seeing you are beautified   55
With goodly shape, and by your own report
A linguist, and a man of such perfection
As we do in our quality much want —
2. Out. Indeed, because you are a banish'd
man,
Therefore, above the rest, we parley to you. 60
Are you content to be our general?
To make a virtue of necessity
And live as we do in this wilderness?
3. Out. What say'st thou? Wilt thou be of
our consort?
Say ay, and be the captain of us all!   65
We'll do thee homage and be rul'd by thee,
Love thee as our commander and our king.
1. Out. But if thou scorn our courtesy, thou
diest.
2. Out. Thou shalt not live to brag what we
have offer'd.
Val. I take your offer and will live with you,
Provided that you do no outrages   71
On silly women or poor passengers.
3. Out. No, we detest such vile base practises.
Come, go with us; we'll bring thee to our crew
And show thee all the treasure we have got,   75
Which, with ourselves, all rest at thy dispose.
                                      Exeunt.

Scene II. [*Milan. Without the* Duke's
Palace, under Silvia's *window.*]

Enter *Proteus.*

Pro. Already have I been false to Valen-
tine,
And now I must be as unjust to Thurio.
Under the colour of commending him
I have access my own love to prefer.
But Silvia is too fair, too true, too holy,   5
To be corrupted with my worthless gifts.
When I protest true loyalty to her,
She twits me with my falsehood to my friend;
When to her beauty I commend my vows,
She bids me think how I have been forsworn   10
In breaking faith with Julia, whom I lov'd;
And notwithstanding all her sudden quips,
The least whereof would quell a lover's hope,
Yet, spaniel-like, the more she spurns my love,
The more it grows, and fawneth on her still. 15

[Enter *Thurio* and *Musicians.*]
But here comes Thurio. Now must we to her
window
And give some evening music to her ear.
Thu. How now, Sir Proteus? Are you crept
before us?
Pro. Ay, gentle Thurio; for you know that
love
Will creep in service where it cannot go.   20
Thu. Ay, but I hope, sir, that you love not
here.
Pro. Sir, but I do; or else I would be hence.
Thu. Who? Silvia?
Pro.   Ay, Silvia — for your sake.
Thu. I thank you for your own. Now, gentle-
men,
Let's tune; and to it lustily awhile.   25

[Enter, at a distance, *Host,* and *Julia* in
boy's clothes.]

Host. Now, my young guest — methinks
you're allycholly. I pray you, why is it?
Jul. Marry, mine host, because I cannot be
merry.   29
Host. Come, we'll have you merry! I'll
bring you where you shall hear music and see
the gentleman that you ask'd for.
Jul. But shall I hear him speak?
Host. Ay, that you shall.
Jul. That will be music.   [*Music plays.*]
Host. Hark, hark!   36
Jul. Is he among these?
Host. Ay; but, peace! let's hear 'em.

54

Song.

Who is Silvia? What is she,
    That all our swains commend her?   40
Holy, fair, and wise is she:
    The heaven such grace did lend her,
That she might admired be.

Is she kind as she is fair?
    For beauty lives with kindness.   45
Love doth to her eyes repair
    To help him of his blindness,
And being help'd, inhabits there.

Then to Silvia let us sing
    That Silvia is excelling;   50
She excels each mortal thing
    Upon the dull earth dwelling.
To her let us garlands bring.

Host. How now? Are you sadder than you were before? How do you, man? The music likes you not.   56
Jul. You mistake. The musician likes me not.
Host. Why, my pretty youth?
Jul. He plays false, father.
Host. How? Out of tune on the strings?   60
Jul. Not so; but yet so false that he grieves my very heartstrings.
Host. You have a quick ear.
Jul. Ay, I would I were deaf! It makes me have a slow heart.   65
Host. I perceive you delight not in music.
Jul. Not a whit, when it jars so.
Host. Hark, what fine change is in the music!
Jul. Ay, that change is the spite.
Host. You would have them always play but one thing?   71
Jul. I would always have one play but one thing.
But, host, doth this Sir Proteus that we talk on
Often resort unto this gentlewoman?   74
Host. I tell you what Launce, his man, told me: he lov'd her out of all nick.
Jul. Where is Launce?
Host. Gone to seek his dog, which to-morrow, by his master's command, he must carry for a present to his lady.   80
Jul. Peace, stand aside! The company parts.   [*They hide.*]
Pro. Sir Thurio, fear not you. I will so plead
That you shall say my cunning drift excels.
Thu. Where meet we?
Pro.   At Saint Gregory's Well.
Thu.   Farewell.
    [*Exeunt Thurio and Musicians.*]

[*Enter Silvia above, at her window.*]

Pro. Madam, good ev'n to your ladyship.   85
Sil. I thank you for your music, gentlemen.
Who is that that spake?
Pro. One, lady, if you knew his pure heart's truth,
You would quickly learn to know him by his voice.
Sil. Sir Proteus, as I take it.   90
Pro. Sir Proteus, gentle lady, and your servant.
Sil. What is your will?
Pro.   That I may compass yours.
Sil. You have your wish. My will is even this,
That presently you hie you home to bed.
Thou subtile, perjur'd, false, disloyal man!   95
Think'st thou I am so shallow, so conceitless,
To be seduced by thy flattery
That hast deceiv'd so many with thy vows?
Return, return, and make thy love amends!
For me (by this pale queen of night I swear),
I am so far from granting thy request   101
That I despise thee for thy wrongful suit,
And by-and-by intend to chide myself
Even for this time I spend in talking to thee.
Pro. I grant, sweet love, that I did love a lady;   105
But she is dead.
Jul. [*aside*] 'Twere false, if I should speak it;
For I am sure she is not buried.
Sil. Say that she be, yet Valentine, thy friend,
Survives; to whom (thyself art witness)   110
I am betroth'd; and art thou not asham'd
To wrong him with thy importunacy?
Pro. I likewise hear that Valentine is dead.
Sil. And so suppose am I; for in his grave
Assure thyself my love is buried.   115
Pro. Sweet lady, let me rake it from the earth.
Sil. Go to thy lady's grave, and call hers thence,
Or, at the least, in hers sepulcher thine.
Jul. [*aside*] He heard not that.
Pro. Madam, if your heart be so obdurate,
Vouchsafe me yet your picture for my love,   121
The picture that is hanging in your chamber.
To that I'll speak, to that I'll sigh and weep;
For since the substance of your perfect self
Is else devoted, I am but a shadow,   125
And to your shadow will I make true love.
Jul. [*aside*] If 'twere a substance, you would sure deceive it
And make it but a shadow, as I am.

55

Sil. I am very loath to be your idol, sir;
But since your falsehood shall become you well
To worship shadows and adore false shapes, 131
Send to me in the morning, and I'll send it.
And so, good rest!
　　Pro.　　　　As wretches have o'ernight
That wait for execution in the morn.
　　　　　　　[*Exeunt Silvia and Proteus.*]
Jul. Host, will you go? 135
Host. By my halidome, I was fast asleep.
Jul. Pray you, where lies Sir Proteus?
Host. Marry, at my house. Trust me, I
think 'tis almost day.
Jul. Not so; but it hath been the longest
night 140
That e'er I watch'd, and the most heaviest.
　　　　　　　　　　　　[*Exeunt.*]

Scene III. [*The same.*]

Enter Eglamour.

Egl. This is the hour that Madam Silvia
Entreated me to call and know her mind.
There's some great matter she'ld employ me in.
Madam, madam!

[*Enter Silvia above, at her window.*]

Sil.　　　　Who calls?
Egl.　　　　Your servant, and your friend;
One that attends your ladyship's command. 5
Sil. Sir Eglamour, a thousand times good
　　morrow!
Egl. As many, worthy lady, to yourself!
According to your ladyship's impose,
I am thus early come to know what service
It is your pleasure to command me in. 10
Sil. O Eglamour, thou art a gentleman —
Think not I flatter, for I swear I do not —
Valiant, wise, remorseful, well-accomplish'd.
Thou art not ignorant what dear good will
I bear unto the banish'd Valentine; 15
Nor how my father would enforce me marry
Vain Thurio, whom my very soul abhors.
Thyself hast lov'd; and I have heard thee say
No grief did ever come so near thy heart
As when thy lady and thy true-love died, 20
Upon whose grave thou vow'dst pure chastity.
Sir Eglamour, I would to Valentine,
To Mantua, where I hear he makes abode;
And, for the ways are dangerous to pass,
I do desire thy worthy company, 25
Upon whose faith and honour I repose.
Urge not my father's anger. Eglamour,

But think upon my grief (a lady's grief)
And on the justice of my flying hence
To keep me from a most unholy match, 30
Which heaven and fortune still rewards with
　　plagues.
I do desire thee, even from a heart
As full of sorrows as the sea of sands,
To bear me company and go with me;
If not, to hide what I have said to thee, 35
That I may venture to depart alone.
Egl. Madam, I pity much your grievances,
Which since I know they virtuously are plac'd,
I give consent to go along with you,
Recking as little what betideth me 40
As much I wish all good befortune you.
When will you go?
Sil.　　　　　　This evening coming.
Egl. Where shall I meet you?
Sil.　　　　　　　　At Friar Patrick's cell,
Where I intend holy confession.
Egl. I will not fail your ladyship. Good
　　morrow, gentle lady. 45
Sil. Good morrow, kind Sir Eglamour.
　　　　　　　　　　　　　　Exeunt.

Scene IV. [*The same.*]

Enter Launce [with his dog].

Launce. When a man's servant shall play
the cur with him, look you, it goes hard —
one that I brought up of a puppy; one that
I sav'd from drowning when three or four of
his blind brothers and sisters went to it. I have
taught him even as one would say precisely
'Thus I would teach a dog.' I was sent to deliver him in as a present to Mistress Silvia from
my master; and I came no sooner into the
dining chamber but he steps me to her trencher
and steals her capon's leg. O, 'tis a foul thing
when a cur cannot keep himself in all companies! I would have (as one should say) one
that takes upon him to be a dog indeed; to be,
as it were, a dog at all things. If I had not had
more wit than he, to take a fault upon me that
he did, I think verily he had been hang'd for't.
Sure as I live, he had suffer'd for't! You shall
judge. He thrusts me himself into the company
of three or four gentlemanlike dogs, under the
Duke's table. He had not been there (bless the
mark!) a pissing while but all the chamber
smelt him. 'Out with the dog!' says one. 'What
cur is that?' says another. 'Whip him out!'
says the third. 'Hang him up!' says the Duke.

I, having been acquainted with the smell before, knew it was Crab, and goes me to the fellow that whips the dogs. 'Friend,' quoth I, 'you mean to whip the dog?' 'Ay, marry, do I!' quoth he. 'You do him the more wrong,' quoth I. ''Twas I did the thing you wot of.' He makes me no more ado, but whips me out of the chamber. How many masters would do this for his servant? Nay, I'll be sworn I have sat in the stocks for puddings he hath stol'n, otherwise he had been executed; I have stood on the pillory for geese he hath kill'd, otherwise he had suffer'd for't. Thou think'st not of this now! Nay, I remember the trick you serv'd me when I took my leave of Madam Silvia! Did not I bid thee still mark me and do as I do? When didst thou see me heave up my leg and make water against a gentlewoman's farthingale? Didst thou ever see me do such a trick?

[*Enter Proteus, and Julia in boy's clothes.*]

Pro. Sebastian is thy name? I like thee well And will employ thee in some service presently.
Jul. In what you please. I'll do what I can.
Pro. I hope thou wilt. [*To Launce*] How now, you whoreson peasant?   47
Where have you been these two days loitering?
Launce. Marry, sir, I carried Mistress Silvia the dog you bade me.   50
Pro. And what says she to my little jewel?
Launce. Marry, she says your dog was a cur, and tells you currish thanks is good enough for such a present.
Pro. But she receiv'd my dog?   55
Launce. No indeed did she not! Here have I brought him back again.
Pro. What, didst thou offer her this from me?
Launce. Ay, sir. The other squirrel was stol'n from me by the hangman boys in the market place; and then I offer'd her mine own, who is a dog as big as ten of yours, and therefore the gift the greater.
Pro. Go, get thee hence, and find my dog again
Or ne'er return again into my sight.   65
Away, I say! Stayest thou to vex me here?
A slave that still an end turns me to shame!
                                   [*Exit Launce.*]
Sebastian, I have entertained thee,
Partly that I have need of such a youth
That can with some discretion do my business,
For 'tis no trusting to yond foolish lout;   71
But chiefly for thy face and thy behaviour,
Which (if my augury deceive me not)

Witness good bringing up, fortune, and truth.
Therefore know thou, for this I entertain thee.
Go presently, and take this ring with thee;   76
Deliver it to Madam Silvia.
She lov'd me well deliver'd it to me.
Jul. It seems you lov'd not her, to leave her token.
She is dead belike?
Pro.   Not so. I think she lives.
Jul. Alas!   81
Pro. Why dost thou cry 'Alas'?
Jul.   I cannot choose
But pity her.
Pro.   Wherefore shouldst thou pity her?
Jul. Because methinks that she lov'd you as well
As you do love your lady Silvia.   85
She dreams on him that has forgot her love;
You dote on her that cares not for your love.
'Tis pity love should be so contrary;
And thinking on it makes me cry 'Alas!'
Pro. Well, give her that ring, and therewithal   90
This letter. That's her chamber. Tell my lady
I claim the promise for her heavenly picture.
Your message done, hie home unto my chamber,
Where thou shalt find me sad and solitary.
                                   [*Exit.*]
Jul. How many women would do such a message?   95
Alas, poor Proteus! thou hast entertain'd
A fox to be the shepherd of thy lambs.
Alas, poor fool! Why do I pity him
That with his very heart despiseth me?
Because he loves her, he despiseth me;   100
Because I love him, I must pity him.
This ring I gave him when he parted from me,
To bind him to remember my good will;
And now am I (unhappy messenger!)
To plead for that which I would not obtain,
To carry that which I would have refus'd,   106
To praise his faith which I would have disprais'd.
I am my master's true confirmed love,
But cannot be true servant to my master
Unless I prove false traitor to myself.   110
Yet will I woo for him; but yet so coldly
As (heaven it knows) I would not have him speed.

[*Enter Silvia, attended.*]

Gentlewoman, good day! I pray you be my mean
To bring me where to speak with Madam Silvia.

Sil. What would you with her, if that I be she? 115

Jul. If you be she, I do entreat your patience To hear me speak the message I am sent on.

Sil. From whom?

Jul. From my master, Sir Proteus, madam.

Sil. O, he sends you for a picture? 120

Jul. Ay, madam.

Sil. Ursula, bring my picture there.

[*Picture brought.*]

Go give your master this. Tell him from me, One Julia, that his changing thoughts forget, Would better fit his chamber than this shadow.

Jul. Madam, please you peruse this letter.

[*Gives a letter.*]

Pardon me, madam! I have unadvis'd 127 Deliver'd you a paper that I should not. This is the letter to your ladyship.

[*Gives another.*]

Sil. I pray thee let me look on that again.

Jul. It may not be. Good madam, pardon me!

Sil. There, hold! [*Gives back the first letter.*] I will not look upon your master's lines. I know they are stuff'd with protestations And full of new-found oaths, which he will break As easily as I do tear his paper. 136

[*Tears the second letter.*]

Jul. Madam, he sends your ladyship this ring.

Sil. The more shame for him that he sends it me!

For I have heard him say a thousand times His Julia gave it him at his departure. 140 Though his false finger have profan'd the ring, Mine shall not do his Julia so much wrong.

Jul. She thanks you.

Sil. What say'st thou?

Jul. I thank you, madam, that you tender her.

Poor gentlewoman! my master wrongs her much. 146

Sil. Dost thou know her?

Jul. Almost as well as I do know myself.

To think upon her woes, I do protest That I have wept a hundred several times. 150

Sil. Belike she thinks that Proteus hath forsook her?

Jul. I think she doth; and that's her cause of sorrow.

Sil. Is she not passing fair?

Jul. She hath been fairer, madam, than she is.

When she did think my master lov'd her well, She, in my judgment, was as fair as you; 156 But since she did neglect her looking glass And threw her sun-expelling mask away, The air hath starv'd the roses in her cheeks And pinch'd the lily-tincture of her face, 160 That now she is become as black as I.

Sil. How tall was she?

Jul. About my stature; for at Pentecost, When all our pageants of delight were play'd, Our youth got me to play the woman's part, 165 And I was trimm'd in Madam Julia's gown, Which served me as fit, by all men's judgments, As if the garment had been made for me. Therefore I know she is about my height. And at that time I made her weep a good, 170 For I did play a lamentable part. Madam, 'twas Ariadne, passioning For Theseus' perjury and unjust flight; Which I so lively acted with my tears That my poor mistress, moved therewithal, 175 Wept bitterly; and would I might be dead If I in thought felt not her very sorrow!

Sil. She is beholding to thee, gentle youth. Alas, poor lady, desolate and left! I weep myself to think upon thy words. 180 Here, youth, there is my purse. I give thee this For thy sweet mistress' sake, because thou lov'st her.

Farewell. [*Exit Silvia with Attendants.*]

Jul. And she shall thank you for't, if e'er you know her.

A virtuous gentlewoman, mild and beautiful! I hope my master's suit will be but cold, 186 Since she respects my mistress' love so much. Alas, how love can trifle with itself! Here is her picture. Let me see. I think, If I had such a tire, this face of mine 190 Were full as lovely as is this of hers; And yet the painter flatter'd her a little, Unless I flatter with myself too much. Her hair is auburn, mine is perfect yellow. If that be all the difference in his love, 195 I'll get me such a colour'd periwig. Her eyes are grey as glass, and so are mine. Ay, but her forehead's low, and mine's as high. What should it be that he respects in her But I can make respective in myself 200 If this fond Love were not a blinded god? Come, shadow, come, and take this shadow up, For 'tis thy rival. O thou senseless form, Thou shalt be worshipp'd, kiss'd, lov'd, and ador'd! And, were there sense in his idolatry, 205 My substance should be statue in thy stead. I'll use thee kindly for thy mistress' sake That us'd me so; or else, by Jove I vow, I should have scratch'd out your unseeing eyes To make my master out of love with thee! 210

Exit.

ACT V. Scene I. [*Milan. An abbey.*]

Enter *Eglamour.*

Egl. The sun begins to gild the western sky,
And now it is about the very hour
That Silvia at Friar Patrick's cell should meet
me.
She will not fail; for lovers break not hours
Unless it be to come before their time,   5
So much they spur their expedition.

Enter *Silvia.*

See where she comes. Lady, a happy evening!
Sil. Amen, amen! Go on, good Eglamour,
Out at the postern by the abbey wall.
I fear I am attended by some spies.   10
Egl. Fear not. The forest is not three leagues
off.
If we recover that, we are sure enough.
Exeunt.

Scene II. [*Milan. The* Duke's *Palace.*]

Enter *Thurio, Proteus, Julia* [as *Sebastian*].

Thu. Sir Proteus, what says Silvia to my
suit?
Pro. O, sir, I find her milder than she was,
And yet she takes exceptions at your person.
Thu. What? that my leg is too long?
Pro. No; that it is too little.   5
Thu. I'll wear a boot to make it somewhat
rounder.
Jul. [*aside*] But love will not be spurr'd to
what it loathes.
Thu. What says she to my face?
Pro. She says it is a fair one.
Thu. Nay then, the wanton lies! My face
is black.   10
Pro. But pearls are fair; and the old saying
is,
'Black men are pearls in beauteous ladies' eyes.'
Jul. [*aside*] 'Tis true! such pearls as put out
ladies' eyes,
For I had rather wink than look on them.
Thu. How likes she my discourse?   15
Pro. Ill when you talk of war.
Thu. But well when I discourse of love and
peace?
Jul. [*aside*] But better indeed when you hold
your peace.

Thu. What says she to my valour?
Pro. O, sir, she makes
No doubt of that.   20
Jul. [*aside*] She needs not, when she knows
it cowardice.
Thu. What says she to my birth?
Pro. That you are well deriv'd.
Jul. [*aside*] True! from a gentleman to a fool.
Thu. Considers she my possessions?   25
Pro. O, ay! and pities them.
Thu. Wherefore?
Jul. [*aside*] That such an ass should owe
them.
Pro. That they are out by lease.
Jul. Here comes the Duke.   30

[Enter *Duke.*]

Duke. How now, Sir Proteus? How now,
Thurio?
Which of you saw Sir Eglamour of late?
Thu. Not I.
Pro. Nor I.
Duke. Saw you my daughter?
Pro. Neither.
Duke. Why then,
She's fled unto that peasant Valentine,   35
And Eglamour is in her company.
'Tis true; for Friar Laurence met them both
As he in penance wander'd through the forest.
Him he knew well, and guess'd that it was she,
But, being mask'd, he was not sure of it.   40
Besides, she did intend confession
At Patrick's cell this even, and there she was not.
These likelihoods confirm her flight from hence.
Therefore, I pray you, stand not to discourse,
But mount you presently, and meet with me   45
Upon the rising of the mountain foot
That leads toward Mantua, whither they are
fled.
Dispatch, sweet gentlemen, and follow me.
[*Exit.*]
Thu. Why, this it is to be a peevish girl
That flies her fortune when it follows her!   50
I'll after, more to be reveng'd on Eglamour
Than for the love of reckless Silvia.   [*Exit.*]
Pro. And I will follow, more for Silvia's love
Than hate of Eglamour, that goes with her.
[*Exit.*]
Jul. And I will follow, more to cross that
love   55
Than hate for Silvia, that is gone for love. *Exit.*

Scene III. [*The forest.*]

[Enter] *Silvia, Outlaws.*

1. Out. Come, come,
Be patient! We must bring you to our captain.
Sil. A thousand more mischances than this one
Have learn'd me how to brook this patiently.
2. Out. Come, bring her away! 5
1. Out. Where is the gentleman that was with her?
3. Out. Being nimble-footed, he hath outrun us,
But Moyses and Valerius follow him.
Go thou with her to the west end of the wood.
There is our captain. We'll follow him that's fled. 10
The thicket is beset; he cannot scape.
1. Out. Come, I must bring you to our captain's cave.
Fear not. He bears an honourable mind
And will not use a woman lawlessly.
Sil. O Valentine, this I endure for thee! 15
Exeunt.

Scene IV. [*Another part of the forest.*]

Enter *Valentine.*

Val. How use doth breed a habit in a man!
This shadowy desert, unfrequented woods,
I better brook than flourishing peopled towns.
Here can I sit alone, unseen of any,
And to the nightingale's complaining notes 5
Tune my distresses and record my woes.
O thou that dost inhabit in my breast,
Leave not the mansion so long tenantless,
Lest, growing ruinous, the building fall
And leave no memory of what it was! 10
Repair me with thy presence, Silvia.
Thou gentle nymph, cherish thy forlorn swain!
[*Noise within.*]
What halloaing and what stir is this to-day?
These are my mates, that make their wills their law,
Have some unhappy passenger in chase. 15
They love me well; yet I have much to do
To keep them from uncivil outrages.
Withdraw thee, Valentine. Who's this comes here? [*Retires.*]

[Enter *Proteus, Silvia,* and *Julia* as *Sebastian.*]

Pro. Madam, this service I have done for you
(Though you respect not aught your servant doth), 20
To hazard life, and rescue you from him
That would have forc'd your honour and your love.
Vouchsafe me, for my meed, but one fair look!
A smaller boon than this I cannot beg,
And less than this, I am sure you cannot give.
Val. [*aside*] How like a dream is this I see and hear! 26
Love, lend me patience to forbear awhile.
Sil. O miserable, unhappy that I am!
Pro. Unhappy were you, madam, ere I came;
But by my coming I have made you happy. 30
Sil. By thy approach thou mak'st me most unhappy.
Jul. [*aside*] And me, when he approacheth to your presence.
Sil. Had I been seized by a hungry lion,
I would have been a breakfast to the beast
Rather than have false Proteus rescue me. 35
O, heaven be judge how I love Valentine,
Whose life's as tender to me as my soul!
And full as much (for more there cannot be)
I do detest false perjur'd Proteus.
Therefore be gone! solicit me no more! 40
Pro. What dangerous action, stood it next to death,
Would I not undergo for one calm look?
O, 'tis the curse in love, and still approv'd,
When women cannot love where they're belov'd!
Sil. When Proteus cannot love where he's belov'd! 45
Read over Julia's heart, thy first best love,
For whose dear sake thou didst then rend thy faith
Into a thousand oaths; and all those oaths
Descended into perjury, to love me.
Thou hast no faith left now, unless thou'dst two; 50
And that's far worse than none. Better have none
Than plural faith, which is too much by one.
Thou counterfeit to thy true friend!
Pro.   In love
Who respects friend?
Sil.   All men but Proteus.
Pro. Nay, if the gentle spirit of moving words
Can no way change you to a milder form, 56
I'll woo you like a soldier, at arms' end,
And love you 'gainst the nature of love—
force ye.
Sil. O heaven!
Pro.   I'll force thee yield to my desire.

Val. Ruffian! let go that rude uncivil touch
Thou friend of an ill fashion!
Pro.   Valentine! 61
Val. Thou common friend, that's without
    faith or love —
For such is a friend now! — Treacherous man,
Thou hast beguil'd my hopes. Naught but
    mine eye
Could have persuaded me. Now I dare not say
I have one friend alive: thou wouldst disprove
    me.   66
Who should be trusted when one's own right
    hand
Is perjured to the bosom? Proteus,
I am sorry I must never trust thee more
But count the world a stranger for thy sake. 70
The private wound is deepest. O time accurst,
'Mongst all foes that a friend should be the
    worst!
Pro. My shame and guilt confounds me.
Forgive me, Valentine. If hearty sorrow
Be a sufficient ransom for offence,   75
I tender't here. I do as truly suffer
As e'er I did commit.
Val.   Then I am paid;
And once again I do receive thee honest.
Who by repentance is not satisfied
Is nor of heaven nor earth; for these are
    pleas'd;   80
By penitence th' Eternal's wrath 's appeas'd.
And, that my love may appear plain and free,
All that was mine in Silvia I give thee.
Jul. O me unhappy!   [*Swoons.*]
Pro. Look to the boy!   85
Val. Why, boy! why, wag! How now?
    What is the matter?
Look up! speak!
Jul.   O good sir, my master charg'd me
To deliver a ring to Madam Silvia,
Which, out of my neglect, was never done.   90
Pro. Where is that ring, boy?
Jul.   Here 'tis; this is it. [*Gives a ring.*]
Pro. How? Let me see.
Why, this is the ring I gave to Julia!
Jul. O, cry you mercy, sir! I have mis-
    took.
This is the ring you sent to Silvia.   95
                    [*Shows another ring.*]
Pro. But how cam'st thou by this ring?
At my depart I gave this unto Julia.
Jul. And Julia herself did give it me,
And Julia herself hath brought it hither.
Pro. How? Julia?   100
Jul. Behold her that gave aim to all thy
    oaths

And entertain'd 'em deeply in her heart.
How oft hast thou with perjury cleft the
    root!
O Proteus, let this habit make thee blush!
Be thou asham'd that I have took upon me 105
Such an immodest raiment — if shame live
In a disguise of love!
It is the lesser blot, modesty finds,
Women to change their shapes than men their
    minds.
Pro. Than men their minds? 'Tis true. O
    heaven, were man   110
But constant, he were perfect! That one error
Fills him with faults, makes him run through
    all th' sins.
Inconstancy falls off ere it begins.
What is in Silvia's face but I may spy
More fresh in Julia's with a constant eye? 115
Val. Come, come, a hand from either!
Let me be blest to make this happy close.
'Twere pity two such friends should be long
    foes.
Pro. Bear witness, heaven, I have my wish
    for ever!
Jul. And I mine.   120

[*Enter* Outlaws, *with* Duke *and* Thurio.]

Outlaws.   A prize, a prize, a prize!
Val.   Forbear!
Forbear, I say! It is my lord the Duke.
Your Grace is welcome to a man disgrac'd,
Banished Valentine.
Duke.   Sir Valentine?
Thu. Yonder is Silvia; and Silvia's mine!
Val. Thurio, give back, or else embrace thy
    death!   126
Come not within the measure of my wrath.
Do not name Silvia thine! If once again,
Milano shall not hold thee. Here she stands.
Take but possession of her with a touch!   130
I dare thee but to breathe upon my love.
Thu. Sir Valentine, I care not for her, I.
I hold him but a fool that will endanger
His body for a girl that loves him not.
I claim her not, and therefore she is thine. 135
Duke. The more degenerate and base art
    thou
To make such means for her as thou hast done
And leave her on such slight conditions.
Now, by the honour of my ancestry,
I do applaud thy spirit, Valentine,   140
And think thee worthy of an empress' love.
Know then, I here forget all former griefs,
Cancel all grudge, repeal thee home again.
Plead a new state in thy unrivall'd merit,

To which I thus subscribe: Sir Valentine, 145
Thou art a gentleman and well deriv'd;
Take thou thy Silvia, for thou hast deserv'd
   her.
  Val. I thank your Grace. The gift hath made
   me happy.
I now beseech you, for your daughter's sake,
To grant one boon that I shall ask of you. 150
  Duke. I grant it, for thine own, whate'er it be.
  Val. These banish'd men that I have kept
   withal
Are men endu'd with worthy qualities.
Forgive them what they have committed here
And let them be recall'd from their exile. 155
They are reformed, civil, full of good,
And fit for great employment, worthy lord.
  Duke. Thou hast prevail'd. I pardon them
   and thee.

Dispose of them as thou know'st their deserts.
Come, let us go. We will include all jars 160
With triumphs, mirth, and rare solemnity.
  Val. And as we walk along, I dare be bold
With our discourse to make your Grace to smile.
What think you of this page, my lord?
  Duke. I think the boy hath grace in him;
   he blushes. 165
  Val. I warrant you, my lord — more grace
   than boy.
  Duke. What mean you by that saying?
  Val. Please you, I'll tell you as we pass along,
That you will wonder what hath fortuned.
Come, Proteus. 'Tis your penance but to hear
The story of your loves discovered. 171
That done, our day of marriage shall be yours;
One feast, one house, one mutual happiness.
                     Exeunt.

'An excellent and pleasant conceited commedie of Sir John Faulstof and the merry wyves of Windesor' was entered in the Stationers' Register on January 18, 1602, and the First Quarto appeared in the same year. The Second Quarto (1619) is a mere reprint of the First. The Quartos afford a badly mangled form of the play — manifestly 'reported' by one of the actors, chiefly from memory, though possibly to some extent from fragments of manuscript. The reporter is thought to have been the player who represented the Host. The First Folio, on the other hand, was printed from an authoritative manuscript and may be accepted as a substantially correct copy of what Shakespeare wrote, though there are traces of adaptation in some details. The stage directions, however, are arranged in the annoying fashion described in the introduction to *The Two Gentlemen of Verona* (p. 33, above). The First Quarto, bad as it is, gives some assistance in this matter and now and then in the text. Ingenious attempts have been made to trace a process of revision between Shakespeare's original text and the Folio version, but without any substantial result. Perhaps the horse-stealing episode (iv, 3; iv, 5, 64–95; iv, 6, 1–5) has been cut down, but there is no proof that it ever had more than a rather casual place in the plot.

One line in the Quarto version of iv, 2 ('What is the reason that you use me thus?') is word for word the same as a line in *Hamlet* (v, 1, 312). This suggests that the play is later than *Hamlet* and would fix the date as 1600 or 1601; but the expression is so natural and commonplace that it need not be regarded as a quotation. The earliest possible date is 1598, since there can be no question that THE MERRY WIVES is later than *Henry IV*. Whether it is later than *Henry V* is not quite certain. The appearance of Nym with his title of 'Corporal' indicates an affirmative answer. Sentimentally one may be disposed to a negative, on the ground that Shakespeare would not have revived Falstaff as a wildly comic character after the marvellously pathetic description of his death in *Henry V*. But this is no very substantial argument. At all events, the incidents in THE MERRY WIVES fit the biographical interval between his repudiation by the King at the end of *2 Henry IV* and the onset of the 'burning quotidian tertian' that the Hostess describes in *Henry V*. If later than *Henry V*, the play would have to be assigned to 1599 at the earliest. On the whole, we must accept 1600 as a reasonable date, with 1601 as a possibility.

There is a tradition that Shakespeare wrote THE MERRY WIVES by order of Queen Elizabeth. Its earliest recorder is John Dennis, who, in 1702, in the Epistle prefixed to *The Comicall Gallant*, remarks: 'I knew very well, that it had pleas'd one of the greatest Queens that ever was in the World. . . . This Comedy was written at her Command, and by her direction, and she was so eager to see it Acted, that she commanded it to be finished in fourteen days.' Rowe, in his *Life of Shakespeare* (1709), adds an amusing detail. The Queen, he tells us, 'was so well pleas'd with that admirable Character of *Falstaff*, in the two Parts of *Henry* the Fourth, that she commanded him to continue it for one Play more, and to shew him in Love.' The tradition may well be true in substance, though one is not bound to accept the fourteen days.

In Tarlton's *Newes out of Purgatorie*, 1590 (*The Tale of the Two Lovers of Pisa*), Margaret hides her lover successively in 'a great driefatte [tub or cask] full of Feathers,' in a secret place 'between two seelings,' and in 'an olde rotten chest full of writinges,' covering him 'with old papers and euidences.' Tarlton is adapting a story in *Le Tredeci Piacevoli Notti* of Straparola (iv, 4 : 1550–1553), in which the concealment is behind bed curtains, in a chest which the lady covered with garments, and in a chest which, she says, contains documents concerning her dowry. In *Il Pecorone* of Giovanni Fiorentino (1558), the lady hides her lover 'under a great pile of clothes washed but not yet dried.' These are all versions of an old and widely current popular tale, in which the lady's object is to conceal her intrigue, not to play a trick on a despised suitor. In another group of stories, common in both Orient and Occident, the wife is loyal to her husband and wishes to discomfit her would-be seducer. One English specimen of this class is *The Wright's Chaste Wife* by Adam of Cobsam; another is the ballad of *The Friar in the Well* (Child, No. 276), which is mentioned (either as tale or ballad) by Anthony Munday in his play entitled *The Downfall of Robert Earl of Huntington* (1598), iv, 2, and by Skelton in his *Colyn Cloute* (before 1522), vv. 879–881. No definite source for Shakespeare's plot can be determined, since tales of these two groups were manifestly in oral as well as written and printed circulation in England and elsewhere throughout the Elizabethan period.

The episode of the German horse-thieves may be topical. It is thought to have been suggested by the visit of Frederick Count of Mömpelgart to England in 1592. The Count did not steal any horses, but he had posthorses furnished him without payment; and in 1595 one Breuning von Buchenbach, an ambassador of his, had some disagreeable experiences, not discreditable to him, with English horse-dealers. In the Quarto version Sir Hugh Evans, apropos of the horse-trick, warns the Host of the Garter Inn :

> Now my Host, I would desire you looke you now,
> To haue a care of your entertainments,
> For there is three sorts of cosen garmombles,
> Is cosen all the Host of Maidenhead & Readings.

This passage appears in the Folio text (iv, 5, 77–81) as follows :

> Have a care of your entertainments. There is a friend of mine come to town, tells me there is three cozen-germans that has cozen'd all the hosts of Readins, of Maidenhead, of Colebrook, of horses and money.

'Garmombles' certainly sounds like a distortion of 'Mömpelgart.'

That Nym with his favourite jargon about humours was intended as a caricature of Ben Jonson is very improbable.

THE MERRY WIVES
OF WINDSOR

[Dramatis Personæ.

Sir John Falstaff.
Fenton, a young gentleman.
Shallow, a country justice.
Slender, cousin to Shallow.
Ford, } gentlemen of Windsor.
Page, }
William Page, a boy, son to Page.
Sir Hugh Evans, a Welsh parson.
Doctor Caius, a French physician.
Host of the Garter Inn.
Bardolph, ⎫
Pistol, ⎬ followers of Falstaff.
Nym, ⎭

Robin, page to Falstaff.
Simple, servant to Slender.
John Rugby, servant to Doctor Caius.

Mistress Ford.
Mistress Page.
Anne Page, her daughter.
Mistress Quickly, servant to Doctor Caius.

Servants to Page, Ford, &c.

THE SCENE. — Windsor, and the neighbourhood.]

ACT I. Scene I. [Windsor. Before Master Page's house.]

Enter *Justice Shallow, Slender, Sir Hugh Evans.*

Shal. Sir Hugh, persuade me not. I will make a Star Chamber matter of it. If he were twenty Sir John Falstaffs, he shall not abuse Robert Shallow, Esquire.

Slen. In the county of Gloucester, Justice of Peace and Coram. 6

Shal. Ay, cousin Slender, and Cust-alorum.

Slen. Ay, and Rato-lorum too; and a gentleman born, Master Parson, who writes himself 'Armigero' — in any bill, warrant, quittance, or obligation, 'Armigero.' 11

Shal. Ay, that I do, and have done any time these three hundred years.

Slen. All his successors (gone before him) hath done't; and all his ancestors (that come after him) may. They may give the dozen white luces in their coat. 16

Shal. It is an old coat.

Evans. The dozen white louses do become an old coat well. It agrees well passant. It is a familiar beast to man and signifies love. 21

Shal. The luce is the fresh fish. The salt fish is an old coat.

Slen. I may quarter, coz.

Shal. You may, by marrying. 25

Evans. It is marring indeed, if he quarter it.

Shal. Not a whit.

Evans. Yes, py'r lady! If he has a quarter of your coat, there is but three skirts for yourself, in my simple conjectures. But that is all one. If Sir John Falstaff have committed disparagements unto you, I am of the Church and will be glad to do my benevolence to make atonements and comprimises between you.

Shal. The Council shall hear it. It is a riot.

Evans. It is not meet the Council hear a riot. There is no fear of Got in a riot. The Council, look you, shall desire to hear the fear of Got, and not to hear a riot. Take your vizaments in that.

Shal. Ha! o' my life, if I were young again, the sword should end it. 41

Evans. It is petter that friends is the sword and end it. And there is also another device in my prain, which peradventure prings goot discretions with it. There is Anne Page, which is daughter to Master George Page, which is pretty virginity. 47

Slen. Mistress Anne Page? She has brown hair and speaks small like a woman.

Evans. It is that fery person for all the orld, as just as you will desire; and seven hundred pounds of moneys, and gold, and silver, is her grandsire upon his death's-bed (Got deliver to a joyful resurrections!) give when she is able to overtake seventeen years old.

65

It were a goot motion if we leave our pribbles and prabbles and desire a marriage between Master Abraham and Mistress Anne Page.

Shal. Did her grandsire leave her seven hundred pound? 60

Evans. Ay, and her father is make her a petter penny.

Shal. I know the young gentlewoman. She has good gifts.

Evans. Seven hundred pounds, and possibilities, is goot gifts. 66

Shal. Well, let us see honest Master Page. Is Falstaff there?

Evans. Shall I tell you a lie? I do despise a liar as I do despise one that is false, or as I despise one that is not true. The knight Sir John is there; and I beseech you be ruled by your well-willers. I will peat the door for Master Page. [*Knocks.*] What, ho! Got pless your house here!

Page. [*within*] Who's there? 75

[*Enter Master Page.*]

Evans. Here is Got's plessing, and your friend, and Justice Shallow, and here young Master Slender, that peradventures shall tell you another tale, if matters grow to your likings.

Page. I am glad to see your worships well. I thank you for my venison, Master Shallow. 81

Shal. Master Page, I am glad to see you. Much good do it your good heart! I wish'd your venison better; it was ill kill'd. How doth good Mistress Page? And I thank you always with my heart, la; with my heart. 86

Page. Sir, I thank you.

Shal. Sir, I thank you; by yea and no, I do.

Page. I am glad to see you, good Master Slender. 90

Slen. How does your fallow greyhound, sir? I heard say he was outrun on Cotsall.

Page. It could not be judg'd, sir.

Slen. You'll not confess! you'll not confess!

Shal. That he will not. 'Tis your fault! 'tis your fault! 'Tis a good dog. 96

Page. A cur, sir.

Shal. Sir, he's a good dog and a fair dog. Can there be more said? He is good and fair. Is Sir John Falstaff here? 100

Page. Sir, he is within; and I would I could do a good office between you.

Evans. It is spoke as a Christians ought to speak.

Shal. He hath wrong'd me, Master Page. 105

Page. Sir, he doth in some sort confess it.

Shal. If it be confessed, it is not redressed. Is not that so, Master Page? He hath wrong'd me; indeed he hath; at a word, he hath. Believe me! Robert Shallow, Esquire, saith he is wronged. 110

Page. Here comes Sir John.

[*Enter Sir John Falstaff, Bardolph, Nym, and Pistol.*]

Fal. Now, Master Shallow, you'll complain of me to the King?

Shal. Knight, you have beaten my men, kill'd my deer, and broke open my lodge. 115

Fal. But not kiss'd your keeper's daughter?

Shal. Tut, a pin! This shall be answer'd.

Fal. I will answer it straight. I have done all this. That is now answer'd.

Shal. The Council shall know this. 120

Fal. 'Twere better for you if it were known in counsel. You'll be laugh'd at.

Evans. Pauca verba, Sir John; goot worts.

Fal. Good worts? Good cabbage! Slender, I broke your head. What matter have you against me? 126

Slen. Marry, sir, I have matter in my head against you, and against your cony-catching rascals, Bardolph, Nym, and Pistol. They carried me to the tavern and made me drunk, and afterward picked my pocket.

Bard. You Banbury cheese! 130

Slen. Ay, it is no matter.

Pist. How now, Mephostophilus?

Slen. Ay, it is no matter.

Nym. Slice, I say! Pauca, pauca! Slice! That's my humour. 135

Slen. Where's Simple, my man? Can you tell, cousin?

Evans. Peace, I pray you. Now let us understand. There is three umpires in this matter, as I understand: that is, Master Page (fidelicet Master Page) and there is myself (fidelicet myself) and the three party is (lastly and finally) mine host of the Garter.

Page. We three to hear it and end it between them. 145

Evans. Fery goot. I will make a prief of it in my notebook, and we will afterwards ork upon the cause with as great discreetly as we can.

Fal. Pistol!

Pist. He hears with ears. 150

Evans. The tevil and his tam! What phrase is this? 'He hears with ear'? Why, it is affectations.

Fal. Pistol, did you pick Master Slender's purse? 155

Slen. Ay, by these gloves, did he, or I would I might never come in mine own great chamber again else! of seven groats in mill-sixpences, and two Edward shovelboards that cost me two shilling and two pence apiece of Yead Miller, by these gloves!   161

Fal. Is this true, Pistol?

Evans. No; it is false, if it is a pickpurse.

Pist. Ha, thou mountain foreigner! Sir John and master mine,
I combat challenge of this latten bilbo.   165
Word of denial in thy labras here!
Word of denial! Froth and scum, thou liest'

Slen. By these gloves, then 'twas he.

Nym. Be avis'd, sir, and pass good humours. I will say 'marry trap' with you if you run the nuthook's humour on me. That is the very note of it.   172

Slen. By this hat, then he in the red face had it; for though I cannot remember what I did when you made me drunk, yet I am not altogether an ass.   176

Fal. What say you, Scarlet and John?

Bard. Why, sir, for my part, I say the gentleman had drunk himself out of his five sentences —   180

Evans. It is his five senses. Fie, what the ignorance is!

Bard. And being fap, sir, was, as they say, cashier'd.

Nym. And so conclusions pass'd the careers.

Slen. Ay, you spake in Latin then too. But 'tis no matter. I'll ne'er be drunk whilst I live again but in honest, civil, godly company, for this trick. If I be drunk, I'll be drunk with those that have the fear of God, and not with drunken knaves.   190

Evans. So Got udge me, that is a virtuous mind.

Fal. You hear all these matters denied, gentlemen; you hear it.

[*Enter Anne Page, with wine; Mistress Ford and Mistress Page.*]

Page. Nay, daughter, carry the wine in; we'll drink within.   [*Exit Anne Page.*]

Slen. O heaven! this is Mistress Anne Page.

Page. How now, Mistress Ford?   198

Fal. Mistress Ford, by my troth, you are very well met. By your leave, good mistress.
                                    [*Kisses her.*]

Page. Wife, bid these gentlemen welcome. Come, we have a hot venison pasty to dinner. Come, gentlemen; I hope we shall drink down all unkindness.

[*Exeunt all but Shallow, Slender, and Evans.*]

Slen. I had rather than forty shillings I had my Book of Songs and Sonnets here.   206

[*Enter Simple.*]

How now, Simple? Where have you been? I must wait on myself, must I? You have not the Book of Riddles about you, have you?

Sim. Book of Riddles? Why, did you not lend it to Alice Shortcake upon Allhallowmas last, a fortnight afore Michaelmas?   212

Shal. Come, coz; come, coz! We stay for you. A word with you, coz; marry, this, coz: there is, as 'twere, a tender, a kind of tender, made afar off by Sir Hugh here. Do you understand me?   216

Slen. Ay, sir, you shall find me reasonable. If it be so, I shall do that that is reason.

Shal. Nay, but understand me.

Slen. So I do, sir.   220

Evans. Give ear to his motions, Master Slender. I will description the matter to you, if you be capacity of it.

Slen. Nay, I will do as my cousin Shallow says. I pray you pardon me; he's a justice of peace in his country, simple though I stand here.

Evans. But that is not the question. The question is concerning your marriage.

Shal. Ay, there's the point, sir.

Evans. Marry is it; the very point of it! to Mistress Anne Page.   23,

Slen. Why, if it be so, I will marry her upon any reasonable demands.

Evans. But can you affection the oman? Let us command to know that of your mouth, or of your lips; for divers philosophers hold that the lips is parcel of the mouth. Therefore, precisely, can you carry your goot will to the maid?

Shal. Cousin Abraham Slender, can you love her?   240

Slen. I hope, sir, I will do as it shall become one that would do reason.

Evans. Nay, Got's lords and his ladies! you must speak possitable, if you can carry her your desires towards her.   245

Shal. That you must. Will you, upon good dowry, marry her?

Slen. I will do a greater thing than that upon your request, cousin, in any reason.

Shal. Nay, conceive me, conceive me, sweet coz! What I do is to pleasure you, coz. Can you love the maid?   252

Slen. I will marry her, sir, at your request; but if there be no great love in the beginning, yet heaven may decrease it upon better acquaintance, when we are married and have more occasion to know one another. I hope upon familiarity will grow more content. But if you say, 'Marry her,' I will marry her. That I am freely dissolved, and dissolutely.   260

Evans. It is a fery discretion answer, save the fall is in the ord 'dissolutely.' The ort is, according to our meaning, 'resolutely.' His meaning is good.

Shal. Ay, I think my cousin meant well. 265

Slen. Ay, or else I would I might be hang'd, la.

[*Enter Anne Page.*]

Shal. Here comes fair Mistress Anne. Would I were young for your sake, Mistress Anne!

Anne. The dinner is on the table. My father desires your worships' company.   271

Shal. I will wait on him, fair Mistress Anne.

Evans. Od's plessed will! I will not be absence at the grace.

[*Exeunt Shallow and Evans.*]

Anne. Will't please your worship to come in, sir?   276

Slen. No, I thank you, forsooth, heartily. I am very well.

Anne. The dinner attends you, sir.

Slen. I am not ahungry, I thank you, forsooth. — Go, sirrah! For all you are my man, go wait upon my cousin Shallow. [*Exit Simple.*] A justice of peace sometime may be beholding to his friend for a man. I keep but three men and a boy yet, till my mother be dead; but what though? Yet I live like a poor gentleman born.

Anne. I may not go in without your worship. They will not sit till you come.

Slen. I' faith, I'll eat nothing. I thank you as much as though I did.   291

Anne. I pray you, sir, walk in.

Slen. I had rather walk here, I thank you. I bruis'd my shin th' other day with playing at sword and dagger with a master of fence (three veneys for a dish of stew'd prunes) and, by my troth, I cannot abide the smell of hot meat since. Why do your dogs bark so? Be there bears i' th' town?

Anne. I think there are, sir. I heard them talk'd of.   301

Slen. I love the sport well, but I shall as soon quarrel at it as any man in England. You are afraid if you see the bear loose, are you not?

Anne. Ay indeed, sir.   305

Slen. That's meat and drink to me now. I have seen Sackerson loose twenty times, and have taken him by the chain; but, I warrant you, the women have so cried and shriek'd at it

that it pass'd. But women, indeed, cannot abide 'em. They are very ill-favour'd rough things.

[*Enter Master Page.*]

Page. Come, gentle Master Slender, come. We stay for you.

Slen. I'll eat nothing, I thank you, sir. 315

Page. By cock and pie, you shall not choose, sir! Come, come.

Slen. Nay, pray you lead the way.

Page. Come on, sir.

Slen. Mistress Anne, yourself shall go first.

Anne. Not I, sir! Pray you keep on.   321

Slen. Truly I will not go first; truly, la! I will not do you that wrong.

Anne. I pray you, sir.

Slen. I'll rather be unmannerly than troublesome. You do yourself wrong indeed, la! 326

Exeunt.

Scene II. [*Before* Master Page's *house.*]

Enter *Evans* and *Simple*.

Evans. Go your ways, and ask of Doctor Caius' house which is the way; and there dwells one Mistress Quickly, which is in the manner of his nurse, or his try nurse, or his cook, or his laundry, his washer and his wringer.   5

Sim. Well, sir.

Evans. Nay, it is petter yet. Give her this letter; for it is a oman that altogethers acquaintance with Mistress Anne Page; and the letter is to desire and require her to solicit your master's desires to Mistress Anne Page. I pray you be gone. I will make an end of my dinner. There's pippins and cheese to come.   *Exeunt.*

Scene III. [*The Garter Inn.*]

Enter *Falstaff, Host, Bardolph, Nym, Pistol,* [*Robin (Falstaff's) Page*).

Fal. Mine host of the Garter!

Host. What says my bully rook? Speak scholarly and wisely.

Fal. Truly, mine host, I must turn away some of my followers.   5

Host. Discard, bully Hercules! cashier! Let them wag! trot, trot!

Fal. I sit at ten pounds a week.

Host. Thou'rt an emperor — Cæsar, Keiser, and Pheazar. I will entertain Bardolph: he shall draw, he shall tap. Said I well, bully Hector? 11

Fal. Do so, good mine host.

Host. I have spoke. Let him follow. [*To Bardolph*] Let me see thee froth and lime. I am at a word! Follow.   *Exit.*

Fal. Bardolph, follow him. A tapster is a good trade. An old cloak makes a new jerkin; a wither'd servingman a fresh tapster. Go, adieu.

Bard. It is a life that I have desir'd. I will thrive.

Pist. O base Hungarian wight! wilt thou the spigot wield?   [*Exit Bardolph.*]

Nym. He was gotten in drink. Is not the humour conceited?   26

Fal. I am glad I am so acquit of this tinder box. His thefts were too open; his filching was like an unskilful singer — he kept not time.

Nym. The good humour is to steal at a minim's rest.   31

Pist. 'Convey' the wise it call. 'Steal'? foh! a fico for the phrase!

Fal. Well, sirs, I am almost out at heels.

Pist. Why then, let kibes ensue!   35

Fal. There is no remedy; I must cony-catch, I must shift.

Pist. Young ravens must have food.

Fal. Which of you know Ford of this town?

Pist. I ken the wight. He is of substance good.   41

Fal. My honest lads, I will tell you what I am about.

Pist. Two yards, and more.

Fal. No quips now, Pistol! Indeed I am in the waist two yards about; but I am now about no waste: I am about thrift. Briefly, I do mean to make love to Ford's wife. I spy entertainment in her: she discourses, she carves, she gives the leer of invitation. I can construe the action of her familiar style, and the hardest voice of her behaviour (to be English'd rightly) is 'I am Sir John Falstaff's.'

Pist. He hath studied her well and translated her will — out of honesty into English.   55

Nym. The anchor is deep. Will that humour pass?

Fal. Now the report goes she has all the rule of her husband's purse. He hath a legion of angels.   60

Pist. As many devils entertain! and 'To her, boy!' say I.

Nym. The humour rises. It is good. Humour me the angels.   64

Fal. I have writ me here a letter to her; and here another to Page's wife, who even now gave me good eyes too, examin'd my parts with most judicious illiads. Sometimes the beam of her view gilded my foot, sometimes my portly belly.

Pist. [*aside*] Then did the sun on dunghill shine.   70

Nym. [*aside*] I thank thee for that humour.

Fal. O, she did so course o'er my exteriors with such a greedy intention that the appetite of her eye did seem to scorch me up like a burning glass! Here's another letter to her. She bears the purse too. She is a region in Guiana, all gold and bounty. I will be cheaters to them both, and they shall be exchequers to me. They shall be my East and West Indies, and I will trade to them both. [*To Pistol*] Go bear thou this letter to Mistress Page; [*to Nym*] and thou this to Mistress Ford. We will thrive, lads, we will thrive.   82

Pist. Shall I Sir Pandarus of Troy become, And by my side wear steel? Then Lucifer take all!

Nym. I will run no base humour. Here, take the humour-letter. I will keep the haviour of reputation.   87

Fal. [*to Robin*] Hold, sirrah, bear you these letters tightly. Sail like my pinnace to these golden shores.

                                             [*Exit Robin.*]

Rogues, hence, avaunt! vanish like hailstones, go!   90

Trudge, plod away o' th' hoof! seek shelter, pack!

Falstaff will learn the humour of the age, French thrift, you rogues — myself and skirted page.   [*Exit.*]

Pist. Let vultures gripe thy guts! for gourd and fullam holds,   94

And high and low beguiles the rich and poor. Tester I'll have in pouch when thou shalt lack, Base Phrygian Turk!

Nym. I have operations in my head which be humours of revenge.

Pist. Wilt thou revenge?   100

Nym. By welkin and her star!

Pist. With wit or steel?

Nym. With both the humours, I! I will discuss the humour of this love to Page.

Pist. And I to Ford shall eke unfold   105
      How Falstaff, varlet vile,
      His dove will prove, his gold will hold,
         And his soft couch defile.

Nym. My humour shall not cool. I will incense Page to deal with poison. I will possess him with yellowness, for this revolt of mine is dangerous. That is my true humour.   112

Pist. Thou art the Mars of malecontents. I second thee. Troop on!   *Exeunt·*

Scene IV. [Doctor Caius's *house*.]

Enter *Mistress Quickly, Simple, John Rugby*.

Quick. What, John Rugby! I pray thee go to the casement and see if you can see my master, Master Doctor Caius, coming. If he do, i' faith, and find anybody in the house, here will be an old abusing of God's patience and the king's English.
Rug. I'll go watch. 7
Quick. Go, and we'll have a posset for't soon at night, in faith, at the latter end of a sea-coal fire. [*Exit Rugby*.] An honest, willing, kind fellow as ever servant shall come in house withal; and, I warrant you, no telltale nor no breedbate. His worst fault is that he is given to prayer; he is something peevish that way. But nobody but has his fault. But let that pass. Peter Simple you say your name is? 16
Sim. Ay, for fault of a better.
Quick. And Master Slender's your master?
Sim. Ay, forsooth.
Quick. Does he not wear a great round beard, like a glover's paring knife? 21
Sim. No, forsooth. He hath but a little wee face, with a little yellow beard, a Cain-colour'd beard.
Quick. A softly-sprighted man, is he not?
Sim. Ay, forsooth; but he is as tall a man of his hands as any is between this and his head. He hath fought with a warrener.
Quick. How say you? O, I should remember him! Does he not hold up his head, as it were, and strut in his gait? 31
Sim. Yes indeed does he.
Quick. Well, heaven send Anne Page no worse fortune! Tell Master Parson Evans I will do what I can for your master. Anne is a good girl, and I wish — 36

[Enter *Rugby*.]

Rug. Out alas! here comes my master.
Quick. We shall all be shent. Run in here, good young man. Go into this closet. He will not stay long. [*Shuts Simple in the closet*.] What, John Rugby! John! what, John, I say! Go, John, go enquire for my master. I doubt he be not well that he comes not home. [*Sings*.]

And down, down, adown-a, &c.

[Enter *Doctor Caius*.]

Caius. Vat is you sing? I do not like des toys. Pray you go and vetch me in my closset un boitier vert — a box, a green-a box. Do intend vat I speak? A green-a box. 48

Quick. Ay, forsooth, I'll fetch it you. [*Aside* I am glad he went not in himself. If he had found the young man, he would have been horn-mad. 52
Caius. Fe, fe, fe, fe! ma foi, il fait fort chaud. Je m'en vais à la cour — la grande affaire.
Quick. Is it this, sir?
Caius. Oui. Mette le au mon pocket: depeech quickly. Vere is dat knave Rugby? 57
Quick. What, John Rugby! John!
Rug. Here, sir.
Caius. You are John Rugby, and you are Jack Rugby. Come, take-a your rapier and come after my heel to de court. 62
Rug. 'Tis ready, sir, here in the porch.
Caius. By my trot, I tarry too long. Od's me! Qu'ai-j'oublié! Dere is some simples in my closset dat I vill not for de varld I shall leave behind. 67
Quick. Ay me! he'll find the young man there and be mad.
Caius. O diable, diable! Vat is in my closset? Villany! larron! [*Pulls Simple out*.] Rugby, my rapier! 72
Quick. Good master, be content.
Caius. Verefore shall I be content-a?
Quick. The young man is an honest man.
Caius. Vat shall de honest man do in my closset? Dere is no honest man dat shall come in my closset.
Quick. I beseech you be not so phlegmatic. Hear the truth of it. He came of an errand to me from Parson Hugh. 81
Caius. Vell.
Sim. Ay, forsooth! to desire her to —
Quick. Peace, I pray you.
Caius. Peace-a your tongue. Speak-a your tale. 86
Sim. To desire this honest gentlewoman, your maid, to speak a good word to Mistress Anne Page for my master in the way of marriage.
Quick. This is all, indeed, la! but I'll ne'er put my finger in the fire, and need not. 91
Caius. Sir Hugh send-a you? Rugby, baille me some paper. Tarry you a littel-a-while.
[*Writes*.]
Quick. I am glad he is so quiet. If he had been throughly moved, you should have heard him so loud and so melancholy! But notwithstanding, man, I'll do your master what good I can; and the very yea and the no is, the French doctor, my master — I may call him my master, look you, for I keep his house; and I wash, wring, brew, bake, scour, dress meat and drink, make the beds, and do all myself — 102

70

Sim. 'Tis a great charge to come under one ody's hand.

Quick. Are you avis'd o' that? You shall find t a great charge. And to be up early and down te! But notwithstanding (to tell you in your ar; I would have no words of it) my master imself is in love with Mistress Anne Page — ut notwithstanding that, I know Anne's mind. .hat's neither here nor there. 112

Caius. You, jack'nape! give-a dis letter to ir Hugh. By gar, it is a shallenge! I vill cut is troat in de Park; and I vill teach a scurvy ack-a-napc priest to meddle or make! You .ay be gone; it is not good you tarry here. *Exit Simple.*] By gar, I vill cut all his two tones. By gar, he shall not have a stone to row at his dog. 119

Quick. Alas, he speaks but for his friend.

Caius. It is no matter-a ver dat. Do not you ell-a me dat I shall have Anne Page for my- elf? By gar, I vill kill de Jack priest; and I ave appointed mine host of de Jarteer to meas- re our weapon. By gar, I vill myself have nne Page. 126

Quick. Sir, the maid loves you, and all shall e well. We must give folks leave to prate. Vhat the good-jer! 129

Caius. Rugby, come to de court vit me. By ar, if I have not Anne Page, I shall turn your ead out of my door. Follow my heels, Rugby. [*Exeunt Caius and Rugby.*]

Quick. You shall have An fool's-head of your wn! No, I know Anne's mind for that. Never woman in Windsor knows more of Anne's nind than I do, nor can do more than I do with er, I thank heaven.

Fen. [*within*] Who's within there, ho?

Quick. Who's there, I trow? Come near the ouse, I pray you. 141

[Enter *Fenton.*]

Fen. How now, good woman? How dost thou?

Quick. The better that it pleases your good worship to ask. 145

Fen. What news? How does pretty Mistress Anne?

Quick. In truth, sir, and she is pretty, and honest, and gentle, and one that is your friend. I can tell you that by the way, I praise heaven for it. 151

Fen. Shall I do any good, think'st thou? Shall I not lose my suit?

Quick. Troth, sir, all is in his hands above. But notwithstanding, Master Fenton, I'll be sworn on a book she loves you. Have not your worship a wart above your eye? 157

Fen. Yes, marry, have I. What of that?

Quick. Well, thereby hangs a tale. Good faith, it is such another Nan! but, I detest, an honest maid as ever broke bread. We had an hour's talk of that wart. I shall never laugh but in that maid's company! But, indeed, she is given too much to allicholy and musing. But for you — well — go to. 165

Fen. Well, I shall see her to-day. Hold, there's money for thee. Let me have thy voice in my behalf. If thou seest her before me, com- mend me. 169

Quick. Will I? I' faith, that we will! and I will tell your worship more of the wart the next time we have confidence, and of other wooers.

Fen. Well, farewell. I am in great haste now.

Quick. Farewell to your worship. [*Exit Fenton.*] Truly, an honest gentleman; but Anne loves him not, for I know Anne's mind as well as another does. Out upon't! What have I forgot? *Exit.*

ACT II. Scene I. [*Before* Master Page's *house.*]

Enter *Mistress Page* [with a letter].

Mrs. Page. What, have I scap'd love letters n the holiday time of my beauty, and am I now subject for them? Let me see. [*Reads.*] 'Ask me no reason why I love you; for, hough Love use Reason for his physician, he dmits him not for his counsellor. You are not oung, no more am I. Go to then, there's sym- athy. You are merry, so am I. Ha, ha! then here's more sympathy. You love sack, and so lo I. Would you desire better sympathy? Let

it suffice thee, Mistress Page — at the least, if the love of soldier can suffice — that I love thee. I will not say, pity me, — 'tis not a soldier-like phrase; but I say, love me. By me,

Thine own true knight, 15
By day or night,
Or any kind of light,
With all his might
For thee to fight,   John Falstaff.'

What a Herod of Jewry is this! O wicked. wicked world! One that is well-nigh worn to

pieces with age to show himself a young gallant!
What unweighed behaviour hath this Flemish
drunkard pick'd (with the devil's name!) out of
my conversation that he dares in this manner
assay me? Why, he hath not been thrice in my
company! What should I say to him? I was
then frugal of my mirth. Heaven forgive me!
Why, I'll exhibit a bill in the parliament for the
putting down of men! How shall I be reveng'd
on him? for reveng'd I will be, as sure as his
guts are made of puddings.   32

[*Enter Mistress Ford.*]

Mrs. Ford. Mistress Page, trust me, I was
going to your house.
Mrs. Page. And trust me, I was coming to
you. You look very ill.   36
Mrs. Ford. Nay, I'll ne'er believe that. I
have to show to the contrary.
Mrs. Page. Faith, but you do, in my mind.
Mrs. Ford. Well, I do then. Yet I say I could
show you to the contrary. O Mistress Page,
give me some counsel!   42
Mrs. Page. What's the matter, woman?
Mrs. Ford. O woman! if it were not for one
trifling respect, I could come to such honour!
Mrs. Page. Hang the trifle, woman; take
the honour! What is it? Dispense with trifles.
What is it?
Mrs. Ford. If I would but go to hell for an
eternal moment or so, I could be knighted.   50
Mrs. Page. What? Thou liest! Sir Alice
Ford? These knights will hack, and so thou
shouldst not alter the article of thy gentry.
Mrs. Ford. We burn daylight. Here, read,
read! Perceive how I might be knighted. I
shall think the worse of fat men as long as I
have an eye to make difference of men's liking.
And yet he would not swear; prais'd women's
modesty, and gave such orderly and well-
behaved reproof to all uncomeliness that I
would have sworn his disposition would have
gone to the truth of his words. But they do no
more adhere and keep place together than the
Hundred Psalm to the tune of 'Greensleeves.'
What tempest, I trow, threw this whale, with
so many tuns of oil in his belly, ashore at
Windsor? How shall I be revenged on him?
I think the best way were to entertain him with
hope till the wicked fire of lust have melted him
in his own grease. Did you ever hear the like?
Mrs. Page. Letter for letter, but that the
name of Page and Ford differs! To thy great
comfort in this mystery of ill opinions, here's
the twin brother of thy letter. But let thine

inherit first, for I protest mine never shall. I
warrant he hath a thousand of these letters,
writ with blank space for different names —
sure, more! — and these are of the second edition. He will print them, out of doubt; for he
cares not what he puts into the press, when he
would put us two. I had rather be a giantess
and lie under Mount Pelion. Well, I will find
you twenty lascivious turtles ere one chaste man.
Mrs. Ford. Why, this is the very same! the
very hand! the very words! What doth he
think of us?   86
Mrs. Page. Nay, I know not. It makes me
almost ready to wrangle with mine own honesty. I'll entertain myself like one that I am
not acquainted withal; for sure, unless he know
some strain in me that I know not myself, he
would never have boarded me in this fury.
Mrs. Ford. Boarding call you it? I'll be
sure to keep him above deck.   94
Mrs. Page. So will I. If he come under my
hatches, I'll never to sea again. Let's be reveng'd on him. Let's appoint him a meeting,
give him a show of comfort in his suit, and lead
him on with a fine-baited delay till he hath
pawn'd his horses to mine host of the Garter.
Mrs. Ford. Nay, I will consent to act any
villany against him that may not sully the
chariness of our honesty. O that my husband
saw this letter! It would give eternal food to
his jealousy.   105
Mrs. Page. Why, look where he comes! and
my good man too! He's as far from jealousy as
I am from giving him cause, and that, I hope,
is an unmeasurable distance.   109
Mrs. Ford. You are the happier woman.
Mrs. Page. Let's consult together against
this greasy knight. Come hither. [*They retire.*]

[*Enter Ford, with Pistol; and Page, with Nym.*]

Ford. Well, I hope it be not so.
Pist. Hope is a curtal dog in some affairs.
Sir John affects thy wife.   115
Ford. Why, sir, my wife is not young.
Pist. He wooes both high and low, both rich
     and poor,
Both young and old, one with another, Ford.
He loves the gallimaufry. Ford, perpend.
Ford. Love my wife?   120
Pist. With liver burning hot. Prevent; or go
     thou,
Like Sir Actæon he, with Ringwood at thy
     heels.
O, odious is the name!
Ford. What name, sir?

Pist. The horn, I say. Farewell.   125
Take heed, have open eye; for thieves do foot
    by night.
Take heed, ere summer comes or cuckoo birds
    do sing.
Away, Sir Corporal Nym!
Believe it, Page; he speaks sense.   [*Exit.*]
Ford. [*aside*] I will be patient; I will find
out this.   131
Nym. [*to Page*] And this is true. I like not
the humour of lying. He hath wronged me in
some humours. I should have borne the hu-
mour'd letter to her. But I have a sword; and
it shall bite upon my necessity. He loves your
wife: there's the short and the long.
My name is Corporal Nym; I speak, and I
    avouch;
'Tis true. My name is Nym, and Falstaff loves
    your wife.   139
Adieu. I love not the humour of bread and
cheese; and there's the humour of it. Adieu.
    Exit.
Page. [*aside*] 'The humour of it,' quoth 'a?
Here's a fellow frights English out of his
wits.
Ford. [*aside*] I will seek out Falstaff.
Page. [*aside*] I never heard such a drawling,
affecting rogue.   146
Ford. [*aside*] If I do find it — well!
Page. [*aside*] I will not believe such a Ca-
taian, though the priest o' th' town commended
him for a true man.   150
Ford. [*aside*] 'Twas a good sensible fellow.
Well!
    [*Mistress Page and Mistress Ford come for-
    ward.*]
Page. How now, Meg?
Mrs. Page. Whither go you, George? Hark
you.
Mrs. Ford. How now, sweet Frank? Why
art thou melancholy?   156
Ford. I melancholy? I am not melancholy.
Get you home, go.
Mrs. Ford. Faith, thou hast some crotchets
in thy head now. Will you go, Mistress Page?
Mrs. Page. Have with you. — You'll come
to dinner, George?

[*Enter Mistress Quickly.*]

[*Aside to Mrs. Ford*] Look who comes yonder.
She shall be our messenger to this paltry knight.
Mrs. Ford. [*aside to Mrs. Page*] Trust me, I
thought on her. She'll fit it.   166
Mrs. Page. You are come to see my daughter
Anne?

Quick. Ay, forsooth; and I pray, how does
good Mistress Anne?   170
Mrs. Page. Go in with us and see. We have
an hour's talk with you.
    [*Exeunt Mistress Page, Mistress Ford, and
    Mistress Quickly.*]
Page. How now, Master Ford?
Ford. You heard what this knave told me,
did you not?   175
Page. Yes, and you heard what the other
told me?
Ford. Do you think there is truth in them?
Page. Hang 'em, slaves! I do not think the
knight would offer it. But these that accuse
him in his intent towards our wives are a yoke
of his discarded men; very rogues, now they
be out of service.
Ford. Were they his men?
Page. Marry were they.   185
Ford. I like it never the better for that. Does
he lie at the Garter?
Page. Ay, marry does he. If he should intend
this voyage toward my wife, I would turn her
loose to him; and what he gets more of her than
sharp words, let it lie on my head.   191
Ford. I do not misdoubt my wife; but I
would be loath to turn them together. A man
may be too confident. I would have nothing
lie on my head. I cannot be thus satisfied.   195

[*Enter Host.*]

Page. Look where my ranting host of the
Garter comes. There is either liquor in his pate
or money in his purse when he looks so merrily.
How now, mine host?
Host. How now, bully rook? Thou'rt a gen-
tleman. Cavaleiro Justice, I say!   201

[*Enter Shallow.*]

Shal. I follow, mine host, I follow. Good
even and twenty, good Master Page! Master
Page, will you go with us? We have sport in
hand.   205
Host. Tell him, Cavaleiro Justice! Tell him,
bully rook.
Shal. Sir, there is a fray to be fought between
Sir Hugh the Welsh priest and Caius the French
doctor.   210
Ford. Good mine host o' th' Garter, a word
with you.
Host. What say'st thou, my bully rook?
    [*They go aside.*]
Shal. [*to Page*] Will you go with us to behold
it? My merry host hath had the measuring of

their weapons and, I think, hath appointed them contrary places; for, believe me, I hear the parson is no jester. Hark, I will tell you what our sport shall be. [*They go aside.*]

Host. Hast thou no suit against my knight, my guest-cavaleiro? 221

Ford. None, I protest. But I'll give you a pottle of burnt sack to give me recourse to him and tell him my name is Brook — only for a jest.

Host. My hand, bully! Thou shalt have egress and regress (said I well?) and thy name shall be Brook. It is a merry knight. Will you go, cavaleiros?

Shal. Have with you, mine host.

Page. I have heard the Frenchman hath good skill in his rapier. 231

Shal. Tut, sir! I could have told you more. In these times you stand on distance: your passes, stoccadoes, and I know not what. 'Tis the heart, Master Page; 'tis here, 'tis here! I have seen the time with my long sword I would have made you four tall fellows skip like rats.

Host. Here, boys! here, here! Shall we wag?

Page. Have with you. I had rather hear them scold than fight. 240
[*Exeunt Host, Shallow, and Page.*]

Ford. Though Page be a secure fool and stands so firmly on his wife's frailty, yet I cannot put off my opinion so easily. She was in his company at Page's house, and what they made there I know not. Well, I will look further into't, and I have a disguise to sound Falstaff. If I find her honest, I lose not my labour; if she be otherwise, 'tis labour well bestowed. *Exit.*

Scene II. [*The Garter Inn.*]

Enter *Falstaff, Pistol.*

Pist. I will retort the sum in equipage.

Fal. I will not lend thee a penny.

Pist. Why, then the world's mine oyster, Which I with sword will open.

Fal. Not a penny. I have been content, sir, you should lay my countenance to pawn. I have grated upon my good friends for three reprieves for you and your coach-fellow Nym; or else you had look'd through the grate, like a geminy of baboons. I am damn'd in hell for swearing to gentlemen my friends you were good soldiers and tall fellows; and when Mistress Bridget lost the handle of her fan, I took't upon mine honour thou hadst it not.

Pist. Didst not thou share? Hadst thou not fifteen pence? 14

Fal. Reason, you rogue, reason! Think'st thou I'll endanger my soul gratis? At a word, hang no more about me; I am no gibbet for you. Go! a short knife and a throng! To your manor of Pickt-hatch! Go. You'll not bear a letter for me, you rogue? You stand upon your honour! Why, thou unconfinable baseness, it is as much as I can do to keep the terms of my honour precise. I, I, I myself sometimes, leaving the fear of God on the left hand and hiding mine honour in my necessity, am fain to shuffle, to hedge, and to lurch; and yet you, rogue, will ensconce your rags, your cat-a-mountain looks, your red-lattice phrases, and your bold-beating oaths under the shelter of your honour? You will not do it? you? 30

Pist. I do relent. What would thou more of man?

[Enter *Robin.*]

Robin. Sir, here's a woman would speak with you.

Fal. Let her approach.

[Enter *Mistress Quickly.*]

Quick. Give your worship good morrow.

Fal. Good morrow, goodwife. 35

Quick. Not so, an't please your worship.

Fal. Good maid then.

Quick. I'll be sworn, As my mother was the first hour I was born.

Fal. I do believe the swearer. What with me?

Quick. Shall I vouchsafe your worship a word or two? 42

Fal. Two thousand, fair woman, and I'll vouchsafe thee the hearing.

Quick. There is one Mistress Ford, sir — I pray come a little nearer this ways. I myself dwell with Master Doctor Caius —

Fal. Well, on! Mistress Ford, you say —

Quick. Your worship says very true. I pray your worship come a little nearer this ways. 50

Fal. I warrant thee, nobody hears. Mine own people, mine own people.

Quick. Are they so? God bless them and make them his servants!

Fal. Well, Mistress Ford — what of her? 55

Quick. Why, sir, she's a good creature. Lord, Lord! your worship's a wanton! Well, heaven forgive you, and all of us, I pray!

Fal. Mistress Ford — come, Mistress Ford —

Quick. Marry, this is the short and the long of it. You have brought her into such a canaries as 'tis wonderful. The best courtier of them all, when the court lay at Windsor, could never

The merry wives: Peggy Ashcroft as Mistress Page and Ursula Jeans as Mistress Ford

THE MERRY WIVES OF WINDSOR

PHOTOGRAPHS BY JOHN VICKERS
PRODUCED BY THE OLD VIC COMPANY

The sprightly Mistress Page, unwilling object of Falstaff's redoubtable affection

Alec Clunes as Ford, troubled by Falstaff's allegations against his wife's integrity

Nuna Davey as Mistress Quickley, housekeeper of Caius, comic French physician

Roger Livesey in the role of Sir John Falstaff, tavern knight and would-be amorist

The flighty Slender (Robert Eddison) is interrogated by Justice Shallow (William Devlin) and Sir Hugh Evans (Mark Dignam) regarding his proposed marriage with Anne Page (*Act I, Scene I*)

Left: "Mistress Anne, my cousin loves you." Justice Shallow speaks for his bashful protégé, Slender, as the boy presents Anne Page (Dorothy Tutin) with a nosegay (*Act III, Scene IV*)

Below: " 'tis the very riches of thyself that now I aim at." Fenton (Paul Hansard), the favored suitor, avows his love (*Act III, Scene IV*)

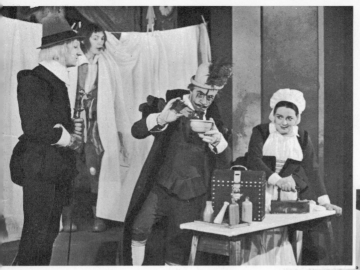

Above: Doctor Caius (Paul Rogers) prepares a potion while Mistress Quickly looks on apprehensively, fearing he will discover Simple (Richard Pasco), with whom she is conspiring to aid Slender's suit (*Act I, Scene IV*)

Right: Mistress Quickly attempts to soothe Doctor Caius, who is enraged to find Simple concealed in his house (*Act I, Scene IV*)

Below: "I warrant thee, nobody hears: mine own people." Falstaff vouches for the discretion of his followers as Mistress Quickly brings him a confidential message from Mistress Ford (*Act II, Scene II*)

Caius has challenged Sir Hugh Evans because of the parson's meddling in the affair of Anne Page and Slender. Here he berates the parson for not meeting him for the duel (Act III, Scene I)

"You shall have her, Master Brook." Falstaff promises to arrange a romance with Mistress Ford, not knowing that he is dealing with the husband himself
(Act II, Scene I)

"What made me love thee? let that persuade thee there's something extraordinary in thee." Falstaff's brusque, vigorous wooing of Mistress Ford
(Act III, Scene III)

"This 'tis to be married: this 'tis to have linen and buck-baskets!" Ford has just heard from the rogue knight that he escaped from his clandestine rendezvous by hiding himself in a basket of soiled linen. His anger is no whit appeased by the discomfort suffered by Falstaff (Act III, Scene V)

"I cannot find him: may be the knave bragged of that he could not compass." Ford is furious to find that Falstaff has escaped him (Act III, Scene III)

"Go fetch me a quart of sack; put a toast in't." Having escaped from Ford at the cost of a ducking in the Thames, Falstaff resorts to the consolations of the bottle and calls for sack to warm him (Act III, Scene V)

Disguised as Mother Prat, the Fat Woman of Brainford, Falstaff makes his second escape from Ford, suffering this time only a minor cudgeling (Act IV, Scene II)

"My belly's as cold as if I had swallowed snowballs for pills to cool the rains." The aftermath of Falstaff's chilly ducking (Act III, Scene V)

The merry wives devise a final plan for the discomfiture of Falstaff
(Act IV, Scene IV)

Mistress Page and Mistress Ford celebrating the success of their ruse against the conniving Falstaff (Act III, Scene III)

have brought her to such a canary. Yet there
has been knights, and lords, and gentlemen,
with their coaches; I warrant you coach after
coach, letter after letter, gift after gift; smelling so sweetly — all musk — and so rushling, I
warrant you, in silk and gold; and in such alligant terms; and in such wine and sugar of the
best, and the fairest, that would have won any
woman's heart; and I warrant you they could
never get an eye-wink of her. I had myself
twenty angels given me this morning; but I
defy all angels (in any such sort, as they say)
but in the way of honesty; and I warrant
you they could never get her so much as sip
on a cup with the proudest of them all; and
yet there has been earls — nay (which is more)
pensioners; but I warrant you all is one with
her.   80
Fal. But what says she to me? Be brief, my
good she-Mercury.
Quick. Marry, she hath receiv'd your letter;
for the which she thanks you a thousand times;
and she gives you to notify that her husband
will be absence from his house between ten and
eleven.   87
Fal. Ten and eleven.
Quick. Ay, forsooth; and then you may
come and see the picture, she says, that you
wot of. Master Ford her husband will be from
home. Alas, the sweet woman leads an ill life
with him! He's a very jealousy man. She leads
a very frampold life with him, good heart!
Fal. Ten and eleven. Woman, commend me
to her. I will not fail her.   96
Quick. Why, you say well. But I have an-
other messenger to your worship. Mistress
Page hath her hearty commendations to you,
too; and let me tell you in your ear, she's as
fartuous a civil modest wife, and one (I tell you)
that will not miss you morning nor evening
prayer, as any is in Windsor, whoe'er be the
other; and she bade me tell your worship that
her husband is seldom from home, but she hopes
there will come a time. I never knew a woman
so dote upon a man. Surely I think you have
charms, la! Yes, in truth.
Fal. Not I, I assure thee. Setting the attraction of my good parts aside, I have no other
charms.   111
Quick. Blessing on your heart for't!
Fal. But I pray thee tell me this: has Ford's
wife and Page's wife acquainted each other how
they love me?   115
Quick. That were a jest indeed! They have
not so little grace, I hope. That were a trick in-

deed! But Mistress Page would desire you to
send her your little page, of all loves. Her husband has a marvellous infection to the little
page. And truly Master Page is an honest man.
Never a wife in Windsor leads a better life than
she does. Do what she will, say what she will,
take all, pay all, go to bed when she list, rise
when she list, all is as she will. And truly she
deserves it; for if there be a kind woman in
Windsor, she is one. You must send her your
page; no remedy.
Fal. Why, I will.   128
Quick. Nay, but do so then; and look you,
he may come and go between you both; and in
any case have a nay-word, that you may know
one another's mind, and the boy never need to
understand anything; for 'tis not good that
children should know any wickedness. Old
folks, you know, have discretion, as they say,
and know the world.   136
Fal. Fare thee well. Commend me to them
both. There's my purse. I am yet thy debtor.
Boy, go along with this woman. [*Exeunt Mistress Quickly and Robin.*] This news distracts
me!   140
Pist. [*aside*] This punk is one of Cupid's
carriers.
Clap on more sails! pursue! up with your
fights!
Give fire! She is my prize, or ocean whelm
them all!   [*Exit.*]
Fal. Say'st thou so, old Jack? Go thy ways.
I'll make more of thy old body than I have done.
Will they yet look after thee? Wilt thou, after
the expense of so much money, be now a gainer?
Good body, I thank thee. Let them say 'tis
grossly done; so it be fairly done, no matter.

[Enter *Bardolph* with a cup of sack.]

Bard. Sir John, there's one Master Brook
below would fain speak with you and be acquainted with you; and hath sent your worship
a morning's draught of sack.
Fal. Brook is his name?
Bard. Ay, sir.   155
Fal. Call him in. [*Exit Bardolph.*] Such
Brooks are welcome to me, that o'erflow such
liquor. Aha! Mistress Ford and Mistress Page,
have I encompass'd you? Go to! via!

[Enter *Bardolph,* with *Ford* disguised.]

Ford. Bless you, sir!   160
Fal. And you, sir! Would you speak with me?
Ford. I make bold to press with so little
preparation upon you.

Fal. You're welcome. What's your will? — Give us leave, drawer. [*Exit Bardolph.*]

Ford. Sir, I am a gentleman that have spent much. My name is Brook.

Fal. Good Master Brook, I desire more acquaintance of you. 169

Ford. Good Sir John, I sue for yours: not to charge you, for I must let you understand I think myself in better plight for a lender than you are; the which hath something embold'ned me to this unseason'd intrusion; for they say, if money go before, all ways do lie open. 175

Fal. Money is a good soldier, sir, and will on.

Ford. Troth, and I have a bag of money here troubles me. If you will help to bear it, Sir John, take all, or half, for easing me of the carriage.

Fal. Sir, I know not how I may deserve to be your porter. 181

Ford. I will tell you, sir, if you will give me the hearing.

Fal. Speak, good Master Brook. I shall be glad to be your servant.

Ford. Sir, I hear you are a scholar (I will be brief with you) and you have been a man long known to me, though I had never so good means as desire to make myself acquainted with you. I shall discover a thing to you wherein I must very much lay open mine own imperfection; but, good Sir John, as you have one eye upon my follies, as you hear them unfolded, turn another into the register of your own, that I may pass with a reproof the easier, sith you yourself know how easy it is to be such an offender. 196

Fal. Very well, sir; proceed.

Ford. There is a gentlewoman in this town, her husband's name is Ford.

Fal. Well, sir. 200

Ford. I have long lov'd her and, I protest to you, bestowed much on her, followed her with a doting observance, engross'd opportunities to meet her, feed every slight occasion that could but niggardly give me sight of her; not only bought many presents to give her, but have given largely to many to know what she would have given. Briefly, I have pursu'd her as love hath pursued me, which hath been on the wing of all occasions. But whatsoever I have merited, either in my mind or in my means, meed, I am sure, I have received none, unless experience be a jewel. That I have purchased at an infinite rate, and that hath taught me to say this:

'Love like a shadow flies when substance love pursues, 215
Pursuing that that flies, and flying what pursues.'

Fal. Have you receiv'd no promise of satisfaction at her hands?

Ford. Never.

Fal. Have you importun'd her to such a purpose? 221

Ford. Never.

Fal. Of what quality was your love then?

Ford. Like a fair house built on another man's ground, so that I have lost my edifice by mistaking the place where I erected it. 226

Fal. To what purpose have you unfolded this to me?

Ford. When I have told you that, I have told you all. Some say that, though she appear honest to me, yet in other places she enlargeth her mirth so far that there is shrewd construction made of her. Now, Sir John, here is the heart of my purpose: you are a gentleman of excellent breeding, admirable discourse, of great admittance, authentic in your place and person, generally allow'd for your many warlike, courtlike, and learned preparations. 238

Fal. O, sir!

Ford. Believe it, for you know it. There is money. Spend it, spend it! spend more! spend all I have! Only give me so much of your time in exchange of it as to lay an amiable siege to the honesty of this Ford's wife. Use your art of wooing; win her to consent to you. If any man may, you may as soon as any. 246

Fal. Would it apply well to the vehemency of your affection that I should win what you would enjoy? Methinks you prescribe to yourself very preposterously. 250

Ford. O, understand my drift. She dwells so securely on the excellency of her honour that the folly of my soul dares not present itself. She is too bright to be look'd against. Now, could I come to her with any detection in my hand, my desires had instance and argument to commend themselves. I could drive her then from the ward of her purity, her reputation, her marriage vow, and a thousand other her defences, which now are too too strongly embattled against me. What say you to 't, Sir John? 261

Fal. Master Brook, I will first make bold with your money; next, give me your hand: and last, as I am a gentleman, you shall, if you will, enjoy Ford's wife. 265

Ford. O good sir!

Fal. I say you shall.

Ford. Want no money, Sir John. You shall want none. 269

Fal. Want no Mistress Ford, Master Brook. You shall want none. I shall be with her (I may tell you) by her own appointment. Even as you came in to me, her assistant or go-between parted from me. I say I shall be with her between ten and eleven; for at that time the jealous rascally knave her husband will be forth. Come you to me at night; you shall know how I speed.

Ford. I am blest in your acquaintance. Do you know Ford, sir?   280

Fal. Hang him, poor cuckoldly knave! I know him not. Yet I wrong him to call him poor. They say the jealous wittolly knave hath masses of money, for the which his wife seems to me well-favour'd. I will use her as the key of the cuckoldly rogue's coffer, and there's my harvest home.   287

Ford. I would you knew Ford, sir, that you might avoid him if you saw him.

Fal. Hang him, mechanical salt-butter rogue! I will stare him out of his wits. I will awe him with my cudgel. It shall hang like a meteor o'er the cuckold's horns. Master Brook, thou shalt know I will predominate over the peasant, and thou shalt lie with his wife. Come to me soon at night. Ford 's a knave, and I will aggravate his style. Thou, Master Brook, shalt know him for knave and cuckold. Come to me soon at night.   *Exit.*

Ford. What a damn'd Epicurian rascal is this! My heart is ready to crack with impatience. Who says this is improvident jealousy? My wife hath sent to him, the hour is fix'd, the match is made. Would any man have thought this? See the hell of having a false woman! My bed shall be abus'd, my coffers ransack'd, my reputation gnawn at; and I shall not only receive this villanous wrong, but stand under the adoption of abominable terms, and by him that does me this wrong. Terms! names! Amaimon sounds well; Lucifer, well; Barbason, well; yet they are devils' additions, the names of fiends. But cuckold! wittol! Cuckold! the devil himself hath not such a name. Page is an ass, a secure ass. He will trust his wife; he will not be jealous. I will rather trust a Fleming with my butter, Parson Hugh the Welshman with my cheese, an Irishman with my aquavitæ bottle, or a thief to walk my ambling gelding, than my wife with herself. Then she plots, then she ruminates, then she devises; and what they think in their hearts they may effect, they will break their hearts but they will effect. God be prais'd for my jealousy! Eleven o'clock the hour. I will prevent this, detect my wife, be reveng'd on Falstaff, and laugh at Page. I will

about it. Better three hours too soon than a minute too late. Fie, fie, fie! Cuckold, cuckold, cuckold!   *Exit.*

Scene III. [*A field near Windsor.*]

Enter *Caius, Rugby.*

Caius. Jack Rugby!

Rug. Sir?

Caius. Vat is de clock, Jack?

Rug. 'Tis past the hour, sir, that Sir Hugh promis'd to meet.   5

Caius. By gar, he has save his soul dat he is no-come; he has pray his Pible vell dat he is no-come. By gar, Jack Rugby, he is dead already if he be come.

Rug. He is wise, sir. He knew your worship would kill him if he came.   11

Caius. By gar, de herring is no dead so as I vill kill him. Take your rapier, Jack, I vill tell you how I vill kill him.

Rug. Alas, sir, I cannot fence.   15

Caius. Villany, take your rapier!

Rug. Forbear! Here's company.

[*Enter Host, Shallow, Slender, and Page.*]

Host. Bless thee, bully Doctor!

Shal. Save you, Master Doctor Caius!

Page. Now, good Master Doctor!   20

Slen. Give you good morrow, sir.

Caius. Vat be all you, one, two, tree, four, come for?

Host. To see thee fight, to see thee foin, to see thee traverse; to see thee here, to see thee there; to see thee pass thy punto, thy stock, thy reverse, thy distance, thy montant. Is he dead, my Ethiopian? Is he dead, my Francisco? Ha, bully! What says my Æsculapius? my Galien? my heart of elder? Ha! is he dead, bully Stale? is he dead?   31

Caius. By gar, he is de coward-Jack-priest of de vorld. He is not show his face.

Host. Thou art a Castalion-King-Urinal! Hector of Greece, my boy!   35

Caius. I pray you bear vitness dat me have stay six or seven, two tree hours for him, and he is no-come.

Shal. He is the wiser man, Master Doctor. He is a curer of souls, and you a curer of bodies. If you should fight, you go against the hair of your professions. Is it not true, Master Page?

Page. Master Shallow, you have yourself been a great fighter, though now a man of peace.

Shal. Bodykins, Master Page, though I now be old, and of the peace, if I see a sword out, my finger itches to make one. Though we are justices, and doctors, and churchmen, Master Page, we have some salt of our youth in us; we are the sons of women, Master Page. 51

Page. 'Tis true, Master Shallow.

Shal. It will be found so, Master Page. Master Doctor Caius, I am come to fetch you home. I am sworn of the peace. You have show'd yourself a wise physician, and Sir Hugh hath shown himself a wise and patient churchman. You must go with me, Master Doctor.

Host. Pardon, Guest Justice. A word, Mounseur Mock-water. 60

Caius. Mock-vater? Vat is dat?

Host. Mock-water in our English tongue is valour, bully.

Caius. By gar, den I have as much mock-vater as de Englishman. Scurvy jack-dog-priest! By gar, me vill cut his ears. 66

Host. He will clapperclaw thee tightly, bully.

Caius. Clapper-de-claw? Vat is dat?

Host. That is, he will make thee amends. 70

Caius. By gar, me do look he shall clapper-de-claw me; for, by gar, me vill have it.

Host. And I will provoke him to't, or let him wag.

Caius. Me tanck you vor dat. 75

Host. And moreover, bully — But first, Master Guest, and Master Page, and eke Cavaleiro Slender, go you through the town to Frogmore. [*Aside to them.*]

Page. Sir Hugh is there, is he? 79

Host. He is there. See what humour he is in. And I will bring the doctor about by the fields. Will it do well?

Shal. We will do it.

All. Adieu, good Master Doctor. 84

[*Exeunt Page, Shallow, and Slender.*]

Caius. By gar, me vill kill de priest, for he speak for a jack-an-ape to Anne Page.

Host. Let him die. But first sheathe thy impatience; throw cold water on thy choler. Go about the fields with me through Frogmore. I will bring thee where Mistress Anne Page is, at a farmhouse a-feasting; and thou shalt woo her. Cried I aim? Said I well? 93

Caius. By gar, me danck you vor dat. By gar, I love you; and I shall procure-a you de good guest — de earl, de knight, de lords, de gentlemen, my patients.

Host. For the which I will be thy adversary toward Anne Page. Said I well?

Caius. By gar, 'tis good. Vell said! 100

Host. Let us wag then.

Caius. Come at my heels, Jack Rugby.

Exeunt.

ACT III. Scene I. [*A field near Frogmore.*]

Enter *Evans, Simple.*

Evans. I pray you now, good Master Slender's servingman, and friend Simple by your name, which way have you look'd for Master Caius, that calls himself Doctor of Physic?

Sim. Marry, sir, the pittie-ward, the Park-ward; every way; old Windsor way, and every way but the town way.

Evans. I most fehemently desire you you will also look that way. 9

Sim. I will, sir. [*Exit.*]

Evans. Pless my soul, how full of chollors I am, and trempling of mind! I shall be glad if he have deceived me. How melancholies I am! I will knog his urinals about his knave's costard when I have good oportunities for the ork. Pless my soul! [*Sings.*]

To shallow rivers, to whose falls
Melodious birds sings madrigals;
There will we make our peds of roses
And a thousand fragrant posies. 20
To shallow —

Mercy on me! I have a great dispositions to cry. [*Sings.*]

Melodious birds sing madrigals —
When as I sat in Pabylon —
And a thousand vagram posies. 25
To shallow, &c.

[Enter *Simple.*]

Sim. Yonder he is coming, this way, Sir Hugh.

Evans. He's welcome. [*Sings.*]

To shallow rivers, to whose falls — 29

Heaven prosper the right! What weapons is he?

Sim. No weapons, sir. There comes my master, Master Shallow, and another gentleman, from Frogmore, over the stile, this way.

Evans. Pray you give me my gown, or else keep it in your arms. [*Reads in a book.*]

Enter *Page, Shallow,* and *Slender.*

Shal. How now, Master Parson? Good morrow, good Sir Hugh. Keep a gamester from the

dice and a good studient from his book, and it
is wonderful.

Slen. [*aside*] Ah, sweet Anne Page!   40
Page. Save you, good Sir Hugh!
Evans. Pless you from his mercy sake, all of
you!
Shal. What, the sword and the word? Do
you study them both, Master Parson?   45
Page. And youthful still, in your doublet and
hose this raw rheumatic day?
Evans. There is reasons and causes for it.
Page. We are come to you to do a good office,
Master Parson.   50
Evans. Fery well. What is it?
Page. Yonder is a most reverend gentleman
who, belike having received wrong by some per-
son, is at most odds with his own gravity and
patience that ever you saw.   55
Shal. I have lived fourscore years and up-
ward. I never heard a man of his place, gravity,
and learning so wide of his own respect.
Evans. What is he?
Page. I think you know him — Master Doc-
tor Caius, the renowned French physician.   61
Evans. Got's will and his passion of my heart!
I had as lief you would tell me of a mess of
porridge.
Page. Why?   65
Evans. He has no more knowledge in Hibo-
crates and Galen, and he is a knave besides —
a cowardly knave as you would desires to be
acquainted withal.
Page. I warrant you he's the man should
fight with him.   71
Slen. [*aside*] O sweet Anne Page!
Shal. It appears so by his weapons.

[Enter *Host, Caius,* and *Rugby.*]

Keep them asunder! Here comes Doctor Caius.
Page. Nay, good Master Parson, keep in
your weapon.
Shal. So do you, good Master Doctor.
Host. Disarm them and let them question.
Let them keep their limbs whole and hack our
English.   80
Caius. I pray you let-a me speak a vord vit
your ear. Verefore vill you not meet-a me?
Evans. [*aside to Caius*] Pray you use your
patience. In goot time.   84
Caius. By gar, you are de coward, de Jack
dog, John ape!
Evans. [*aside to Caius*] Pray you let us not
be laughing-stogs to other men's humours. I
desire you in friendship, and I will one way or

other make you amends. [*Aloud*] I will knog
your urinals about your knave's cogscomb for
missing your meetings and appointments.
Caius. Diable! Jack Rugby! Mine host de
Jarteer! Have I not stay for him to kill him?
Have I not, at de place I did appoint?   95
Evans. As I am a Christians soul now, look
you, this is the place appointed. I'll be judg-
ment by mine host of the Garter.
Host. Peace, I say, Gallia and Gawlia,
French and Welsh, soul-curer and body-curer!
Caius. Ay, dat is very good, excellant!   101
Host. Peace, I say! Hear mine host of the
Garter. Am I politic? Am I subtle? Am I a
Machivel? Shall I lose my doctor? No! he
gives me the potions and the motions. Shall
I lose my parson, my priest, my Sir Hugh? No!
he gives me the proverbs and the no-verbs.
Give me thy hand, terrestrial! so. Give me
thy hand, celestial! so. Boys of art, I have de-
ceiv'd you both; I have directed you to wrong
places. Your hearts are mighty, your skins are
whole, and let burnt sack be the issue. Come,
lay their swords to pawn. Follow me, lads of
peace; follow, follow, follow!
Shal. Trust me, a mad host. Follow, gentlemen, follow.   116
Slen. [*aside*] O sweet Anne Page!
[*Exeunt all but Caius and Evans.*]
Caius. Ha, do I perceive dat? Have you
make-a de sot of us, ha, ha?   119
Evans. This is well. He has made us his
vlouting-stog. I desire you that we may be
friends; and let us knog our prains together to
be revenge on this same scall scurvy cogging
companion, the host of the Garter.
Caius. By gar, vit all my heart! He promise
to bring me vere is Anne Page. By gar, he deceive me too.   127
Evans. Well, I will smite his noddles. Pray
you follow.   [*Exeunt.*]

Scene II. [*Windsor. The street.*]

Enter *Mistress Page, Robin.*

Mrs. Page. Nay, keep your way, little gallant. You were wont to be a follower, but now
you are a leader. Whether had you rather lead
mine eyes, or eye your master's heels?
Rob. I had rather, forsooth, go before you
like a man than follow him like a dwarf.   6
Mrs. Page. O, you are a flattering boy! Now
I see you'll be a courtier.

[Enter *Ford*.]

Ford. Well met, Mistress Page. Whither go you? 10

Mrs. Page. Truly, sir, to see your wife. Is she at home?

Ford. Ay, and as idle as she may hang together, for want of company. I think, if your husbands were dead, you two would marry.

Mrs. Page. Be sure of that — two other husbands. 17

Ford. Where had you this pretty weathercock?

Mrs. Page. I cannot tell what the dickens his name is my husband had him of. — What do you call your knight's name, sirrah? 21

Rob. Sir John Falstaff.

Ford. Sir John Falstaff?

Mrs. Page. He, he! I can never hit on's name. There is such a league between my goodman and he! Is your wife at home indeed? 26

Ford. Indeed she is.

Mrs. Page. By your leave, sir. I am sick till I see her. [*Exeunt Mrs. Page and Robin*.]

Ford. Has Page any brains? Hath he any eyes? Hath he any thinking? Sure they sleep; he hath no use of them. Why, this boy will carry a letter twenty mile as easy as a cannon will shoot point-blank twelve score. He pieces out his wive's inclination; he gives her folly motion and advantage; and now she's going to my wife, and Falstaff's boy with her. A man may hear this show'r sing in the wind! And Falstaff's boy with her! Good plots! They are laid, and our revolted wives share damnation together. Well, I will take him, then torture my wife, pluck the borrowed veil of modesty from the so-seeming Mistress Page, divulge Page himself for a secure and wilful Actæon, and to these violent proceedings all my neighbours shall cry aim. [*Clock strikes*.] The clock gives me my cue, and my assurance bids me search. There I shall find Falstaff. I shall be rather prais'd for this than mock'd; for it is as positive as the earth is firm that Falstaff is there. I will go. 50

[Enter *Page, Shallow, Slender, Host, Evans, Caius*, and *Rugby*.]

Shal., Page, &c. Well met, Master Ford.

Ford. Trust me, a good knot! I have good cheer at home, and I pray you all go with me.

Shal. I must excuse myself, Master Ford

Slen. And so must I, sir. We have appointed to dine with Mistress Anne, and I would not break with her for more money than I'll speak of.

Shal. We have linger'd about a match between Anne Page and my cousin Slender, and this day we shall have our answer. 60

Slen. I hope I have your good will, father Page.

Page. You have, Master Slender. I stand wholly for you. But my wife, Master Doctor, is for you altogether.

Caius. Ay, be gar! and de maid is love-a me. My nursh-a Quickly tell me so mush. 66

Host. What say you to young Master Fenton? He capers, he dances, he has eyes of youth; he writes verses, he speaks holiday, he smells April and May. He will carry't, he will carry't! 'Tis in his buttons; he will carry't!

Page. Not by my consent, I promise you. The gentleman is of no having. He kept company with the wild Prince and Poins. He is of too high a region; he knows too much. No, he shall not knit a knot in his fortunes with the finger of my substance. If he take her, let him take her simply. The wealth I have waits on my consent, and my consent goes not that way.

Ford. I beseech you heartily, some of you go home with me to dinner. Besides your cheer, you shall have sport; I will show you a monster. Master Doctor, you shall go. So shall you, Master Page, and you, Sir Hugh.

Shal. Well, fare you well. We shall have the freer wooing at Master Page's. 86

Exeunt Shallow and Slender.

Caius. Go home, John Rugby; I come anon. [*Exit Rugby*.]

Host. Farewell, my hearts. I will to my honest knight Falstaff and drink canary with him. *Exit*.

Ford. [*aside*] I think I shall drink in pipewine first with him; I'll make him dance. — Will you go, gentles? 92

All. Have with you to see this monster. *Exeunt*.

Scene III. [*Ford's house*.]

Enter *Mistress Ford, Mistress Page*.

Mrs. Ford. What, John! What, Robert!

Mrs. Page. Quickly, quickly! Is the buckbasket —

Mrs. Ford. I warrant. What, Robin, I say!

[Enter two *Servants*] with a great buck-basket.

Mrs. Page. Come, come, come! 5

Mrs. Ford. Here, set it down.

Mrs. Page. Give your men the charge. We must be brief.

Mrs. Ford. Marry, as I told you before, John and Robert, be ready here hard by in the brew-house; and when I suddenly call you, come forth and, without any pause or staggering, take this basket on your shoulders. That done, trudge with it in all haste and carry it among the whitsters in Datchet Mead, and there empty it in the muddy ditch close by the Thames side.   16
Mrs. Page. You will do it?
Mrs. Ford. I ha' told them over and over; they lack no direction. Be gone, and come when you are call'd.   [*Exeunt Servants.*]

[*Enter Robin.*]

Mrs. Page. Here comes little Robin.   21
Mrs. Ford. How now, my eyas-musket? What news with you?
Rob. My master, Sir John, is come in at your back door, Mistress Ford, and requests your company.   26
Mrs. Page. You little Jack-a-Lent, have you been true to us?
Rob. Ay, I'll be sworn. My master knows not of your being here, and hath threat'ned to put me into everlasting liberty if I tell you of it; for he swears he'll turn me away.   32
Mrs. Page. Thou'rt a good boy. This secrecy of thine shall be a tailor to thee and shall make thee a new doublet and hose. I'll go hide me.
Mrs. Ford. Do so. — Go tell thy master I am alone. [*Exit Robin.*] Mistress Page, remember you your cue.   39
Mrs. Page. I warrant thee. If I do not act it, hiss me.   [*Exit.*]
Mrs. Ford. Go to, then! We'll use this unwholesome humidity, this gross wat'ry pumpion; we'll teach him to know turtles from jays.

[*Enter Falstaff.*]

Fal. 'Have I caught my heavenly jewel?' Why, now let me die, for I have liv'd long enough. This is the period of my ambition. O this blessed hour!
Mrs. Ford. O sweet Sir John !   49
Fal. Mistress Ford, I cannot cog, I cannot prate, Mistress Ford. Now shall I sin in my wish. I would thy husband were dead. I'll speak it before the best lord, I would make thee my lady.
Mrs. Ford. I your lady, Sir John? Alas, I should be a pitiful lady!   56
Fal. Let the court of France show me such another! I see how thine eye would emulate the diamond. Thou hast the right arched beauty of the brow that becomes the ship-tire, the tire-valiant, or any tire of Venetian admittance.
Mrs. Ford. A plain kerchief, Sir John. My brows become nothing else, nor that well neither.   64
Fal. By the Lord, thou art a tyrant to say so! Thou wouldst make an absolute courtier, and the firm fixture of thy foot would give an excellent motion to thy gait in a semicircled farthingale. I see what thou wert, if Fortune thy foe were not, Nature thy friend. Come, thou canst not hide it.   71
Mrs. Ford. Believe me, there's no such thing in me.
Fal. What made me love thee? Let that persuade thee. There's something extraordinary in thee. Come, I cannot cog, and say thou art this and that, like a many of these lisping hawthorn buds that come like women in men's apparel and smell like Bucklersbury in simpletime. I cannot. But I love thee, none but thee; and thou deserv'st it.   81
Mrs. Ford. Do not betray me, sir. I fear you love Mistress Page.
Fal. Thou mightst as well say I love to walk by the Counter gate, which is as hateful to me as the reek of a limekiln.   86
Mrs. Ford. Well, heaven knows how I love you, and you shall one day find it.
Fal. Keep in that mind. I'll deserve it.
Mrs. Ford. Nay, I must tell you, so you do; or else I could not be in that mind.   91

[*Enter Robin.*]

Rob. Mistress Ford, Mistress Ford! here's Mistress Page at the door sweating and blowing and looking wildly, and would needs speak with you presently.   95
Fal. She shall not see me; I will ensconce me behind the arras.
Mrs. Ford. Pray you, do so! She's a very tattling woman.

Falstaff stands behind the arras.

[*Enter Mistress Page.*]

What's the matter? How now?   100
Mrs. Page. O Mistress Ford, what have you done? You're sham'd, y'are overthrown, y'are undone for ever!
Mrs. Ford. What's the matter, good Mistress Page?   105
Mrs. Page. O well-a-day, Mistress Ford, having an honest man to your husband, to give him such cause of suspicion!
Mrs. Ford. What cause of suspicion?

Mrs. Page. What cause of suspicion? Out upon you! How am I mistook in you!   111

Mrs. Ford. Why, alas! what's the matter?

Mrs. Page. Your husband's coming hither, woman, with all the officers in Windsor, to search for a gentleman that he says is here now in the house by your consent to take an ill advantage of his absence. You are undone!   117

Mrs. Ford. 'Tis not so, I hope.

Mrs. Page. Pray heaven it be not so that you have such a man here! But 'tis most certain your husband's coming, with half Windsor at his heels, to search for such a one. I come before to tell you. If you know yourself clear, why, I am glad of it; but if you have a friend here, convey, convey him out! Be not amaz'd, call all your senses to you, defend your reputation — or bid farewell to your good life for ever.

Mrs. Ford. What shall I do? There is a gentleman, my dear friend; and I fear not mine own shame so much as his peril. I had rather than a thousand pound he were out of the house.

Mrs. Page. For shame! Never stand 'you had rather' and 'you had rather'! Your husband's here at hand; bethink you of some conveyance. In the house you cannot hide him. O, how have you deceiv'd me! Look, here is a basket. If he be of any reasonable stature, he may creep in here; and throw foul linen upon him, as if it were going to bucking; or it is whiting time — send him by your two men to Datchet Mead.   141

Mrs. Ford. He's too big to go in there. What shall I do?

[*Falstaff comes from behind the arras.*]

Fal. Let me see't, let me see't, O, let me see't! — I'll in, I'll in! Follow your friend's counsel. — I'll in!   146

Mrs. Page. What, Sir John Falstaff? Are these your letters, knight?

Fal. I love thee and none but thee. Help me away! Let me creep in here. I'll never —   150
Goes into the basket. They put clothes over him.

Mrs. Page. Help to cover your master, boy. Call your men, Mistress Ford. You dissembling knight!

Mrs. Ford. What, John! Robert! John!   [*Exit Robin.*]

[Enter *Servants.*]

Go take up these clothes here, quickly. Where's the cowl-staff? Look how you drumble! Carry them to the laundress in Datchet Mead. Quickly, come·

[Enter *Ford, Page, Caius,* and *Evans.*]

Ford. Pray you come near. If I suspect without cause, why then make sport at me, then let me be your jest; I deserve it. — How now? Whither bear you this?   162

Servant. To the laundress forsooth.

Mrs. Ford. Why, what have you to do whither they bear it? You were best meddle with buck-washing!   166

Ford. Buck? I would I could wash myself of the buck! Buck, buck, buck! Ay, buck! I warrant you, buck! and of the season too. It shall appear. [*Exeunt Servants with the basket.*] Gentlemen, I have dream'd to-night; I'll tell you my dream. Here, here, here be my keys. Ascend my chambers; search, seek, find out! I'll warrant we'll unkennel the fox. Let me stop this way first. [*Locks the door.*] So, now uncape.

Page. Good Master Ford, be contented. You wrong yourself too much.   178

Ford. True, Master Page. Up, gentlemen; you shall see sport anon. Follow me, gentlemen.   [*Exit.*]

Evans. This is fery fantastical humours and jealousies.

Caius. By gar, 'tis no de fashion of France. It is not jealous in France.

Page. Nay, follow him, gentlemen. See the issue of his search.   186
[*Exeunt Page, Caius, and Evans.*]

Mrs. Page. Is there not a double excellency in this?

Mrs. Ford. I know not which pleases me better, that my husband is deceived, or Sir John.

Mrs. Page. What a taking was he in when your husband ask'd what was in the basket!

Mrs. Ford. I am half afraid he will have need of washing; so throwing him into the water will do him a benefit.   195

Mrs. Page. Hang him, dishonest rascal! I would all of the same strain were in the same distress.

Mrs. Ford. I think my husband hath some special suspicion of Falstaff's being here; for I never saw him so gross in his jealousy till now.

Mrs. Page. I will lay a plot to try that, and we will yet have more tricks with Falstaff. His dissolute disease will scarce obey this medicine.

Mrs. Ford. Shall we send that foolish carrion, Mistress Quickly, to him and excuse his throwing into the water, and give him another hope, to betray him to another punishment?   208

Mrs. Page. We will do it. Let him be sent for to-morrow eight o'clock to have amends.

Enter [*Ford, Page, Caius,* and *Evans*].

Ford. I cannot find him. May be the knave bragg'd of that he could not compass.

Mrs. Page. [*aside to Mrs. Ford*] Heard you that?

Mrs. Ford. [*aside to Mrs. Page*] Ay, ay, peace. — You use me well, Master Ford, do you?　216

Ford. Ay, I do so.

Mrs. Ford. Heaven make you better than your thoughts!

Ford. Amen.　220

Mrs. Page. You do yourself mighty wrong, Master Ford.

Ford. Ay, ay! I must bear it.

Evans. If there be anypody in the house, and in the chambers, and in the coffers, and in the presses, heaven forgive my sins at the day of judgment!　227

Caius. Be gar, nor I too! Dere is nobodies.

Page. Fie, fie, Master Ford! are you not asham'd? What spirit, what devil suggests this imagination? I would not ha' your distemper in this kind for the wealth of Windsor Castle.　232

Ford. 'Tis my fault, Master Page. I suffer for it.

Evans. You suffer for a pad conscience. Your wife is as honest a omans as I will desires among five thousand, and five hundred too.

Caius. By gar, I see 'tis an honest woman.

Ford. Well, I promis'd you a dinner. Come, come, walk in the Park. I pray you pardon me. I will hereafter make known to you why I have done this. — Come, wife. Come, Mistress Page. — I pray you pardon me. Pray heartly pardon me.

Page. Let's go in, gentlemen; but, trust me, we'll mock him. I do invite you to-morrow morning to my house to breakfast. After, we'll a-birding together; I have a fine hawk for the bush. Shall it be so?

Ford. Anything.

Evans. If there is one, I shall make two in the company.　251

Caius. If dere be one or two, I shall make-a de turd.

Ford. Pray you go, Master Page.

Evans. I pray you now, remembrance tomorrow on the lousy knave, mine host.　256

Caius. Dat is good, by gar, vit all my heart.

Evans. A lousy knave, to have his gibes and his mockeries!　*Exeunt.*

Scene IV. [*Before Page's house.*]

Enter *Fenton, Anne Page.*

Fen. I see I cannot get thy father's love. Therefore no more turn me to him, sweet Nan.

Anne. Alas, how then?

Fen.　　　　　Why, thou must be thyself. He doth object I am too great of birth, And that, my state being gall'd with my expense,　5 I seek to heal it only by his wealth. Besides these, other bars he lays before me, My riots past, my wild societies, And tells me 'tis a thing impossible I should love thee, but as a property.　10

Anne. May be he tells you true.

Fen. No, heaven so speed me in my time to come! Albeit I will confess thy father's wealth Was the first motive that I woo'd thee, Anne; Yet, wooing thee, I found thee of more value Than stamps in gold or sums in sealed bags; And 'tis the very riches of thyself That now I aim at.

Anne.　　　　　Gentle Master Fenton, Yet seek my father's love; still seek it, sir. If opportunity and humblest suit　20 Cannot attain it, why then, hark you hither.　[*They converse apart.*]

[Enter *Shallow, Slender,* and *Mistress Quickly.*]

Shal. Break their talk, Mistress Quickly. My kinsman shall speak for himself.

Slen. I'll make a shaft or a bolt on't. 'Slid, 'tis but venturing.　25

Shal. Be not dismay'd.

Slen. No, she shall not dismay me. I care not for that, but that I am afeard.

Quick. Hark ye, Master Slender would speak a word with you.　30

Anne. I come to him. [*Aside*] This is my father's choice. O, what a world of vile ill-favour'd faults Looks handsome in three hundred pounds a year!

Quick. And how does good Master Fenton? Pray you a word with you.　35

Shal. She's coming. To her, coz. O boy, thou hadst a father!

Slen. I had a father, Mistress Anne. My uncle can tell you good jests of him. Pray you, uncle, tell Mistress Anne the jest how my father stole two geese out of a pen, good uncle.　41

Shal. Mistress Anne, my cousin loves you.

83

Slen. Ay, that I do, as well as I love any woman in Gloucestershire!

Shal. He will maintain you like a gentle-woman. 46

Slen. Ay, that I will, come cut and long-tail, under the degree of a squire!

Shal. He will make you a hundred and fifty pounds jointure. 50

Anne. Good Master Shallow, let him woo for himself.

Shal. Marry, I thank you for it. I thank you for that good comfort. She calls you, coz. I'll leave you. 55

Anne. Now, Master Slender —

Slen. Now, good Mistress Anne —

Anne. What is your will?

Slen. My will? Od's heartlings, that's a pretty jest indeed! I ne'er made my will yet, I thank heaven. I am not such a sickly creature, I give heaven praise. 62

Anne. I mean, Master Slender, what would you with me?

Slen. Truly, for mine own part, I would little or nothing with you. Your father and my uncle hath made motions. If it be my luck, so; if not, happy man be his dole! They can tell you how things go better than I can. You may ask your father; here he comes. 70

[*Enter Page and Mistress Page.*]

Page. Now, Master Slender. Love him, daughter Anne.
Why, how now? What does Master Fenton here?
You wrong me, sir, thus still to haunt my house.
I told you, sir, my daughter is dispos'd of.

Fen. Nay, Master Page, be not impatient.

Mrs. Page. Good Master Fenton, come not to my child. 76

Page. She is no match for you.

Fen. Sir, will you hear me?

Page. No, good Master Fenton.
Come, Master Shallow; come, son Slender; in.
Knowing my mind, you wrong me, Master Fenton. 80

[*Exeunt Page, Shallow, and Slender.*]

Quick. Speak to Mistress Page.

Fen. Good Mistress Page, for that I love your daughter
In such a righteous fashion as I do,
Perforce, against all checks, rebukes, and manners,
I must advance the colours of my love 85
And not retire. Let me have your good will.

Anne. Good mother, do not marry me to yond fool.

Mrs. Page. I mean it not; I seek you a better husband.

Quick. That's my master, Master Doctor.

Anne. Alas, I had rather be set quick i' th' earth 90
And bowl'd to death with turnips!

Mrs. Page. Come, trouble not yourself. Good Master Fenton,
I will not be your friend nor enemy.
My daughter will I question how she loves you,
And as I find her, so am I affected. 95
Till then farewell, sir; she must needs go in,
Her father will be angry.

Fen. Farewell, gentle mistress. — Farewell, Nan.

[*Exeunt Mrs. Page and Anne.*]

Quick. This is my doing now. 'Nay,' said I, 'will you cast away your child on a fool and a physician? Look on Master Fenton.' This is my doing. 102

Fen. I thank thee; and I pray thee, once to-night
Give my sweet Nan this ring. There's for thy pains.

Quick. Now heaven send thee good fortune! [*Exit Fenton.*] A kind heart he hath. A woman would run through fire and water for such a kind heart. But yet I would my master had Mistress Anne; or I would Master Slender had her; or, in sooth, I would Master Fenton had her. I will do what I can for them all three; for so I have promis'd, and I'll be as good as my word; but speciously for Master Fenton. Well, I must of another errand to Sir John Falstaff from my two mistresses. What a beast am I to slack it! *Exit.*

Scene V. [*The Garter Inn.*]

Enter *Falstaff.*

Fal. Bardolph, I say!

Enter *Bardolph.*

Bard. Here, sir.

Fal. Go fetch me a quart of sack; put a toast in't. [*Exit Bardolph.*] Have I liv'd to be carried in a basket like a barrow of butcher's offal? and to be thrown in the Thames? Well, if I be serv'd such another trick, I'll have my brains ta'en out and butter'd, and give them to a dog for a new-year's gift. 'Sblood! The rogues slighted me into the river with as little remorse

as they would have drown'd a blind bitch's
puppies, fifteen i' th' litter. And you may know
by my size that I have a kind of alacrity in sinking. If the bottom were as deep as hell, I should
down. I had been drown'd but that the shore
was shelvy and shallow — a death that I abhor;
for the water swells a man, and what a thing
should I have been when I had been swell'd!
I should have been a mountain of mummy.

[Enter *Bardolph* with sack.]

Bard. Here's Mistress Quickly, sir, to speak
with you.   21
Fal. Come, let me pour in some sack to the
Thames water; for my belly's as cold as if I
had swallow'd snowballs for pills to cool the
reins. Call her in.   25
Bard. Come in, woman.

[Enter *Mistress Quickly*.]

Quick. By your leave. I cry you mercy.
Give your worship good morrow.
Fal. Take away these chalices. Go, brew me
a pottle of sack finely.   30
Bard. With eggs, sir?
Fal. Simple of itself. I'll no pullet-sperm in
my brewage. [*Exit Bardolph.*] How now?
Quick. Marry, sir, I come to your worship
from Mistress Ford.   35
Fal. Mistress Ford? I have had ford enough.
I was thrown into the ford; I have my belly
full of ford.
Quick. Alas the day! Good heart, that was
not her fault. She does so take on with her
men! They mistook their erection.   41
Fal. So did I mine, to build upon a foolish
woman's promise.
Quick. Well, she laments, sir, for it, that it
would yearn your heart to see it. Her husband
goes this morning a-birding. She desires you
once more to come to her, between eight and
nine. I must carry her word quickly. She'll
make you amends, I warrant you.   49
Fal. Well, I will visit her; tell her so. And
bid her think what a man is. Let her consider
his frailty, and then judge of my merit.
Quick. I will tell her.
Fal. Do so. Between nine and ten, say'st
thou?
Quick. Eight and nine, sir.   55
Fal. Well, be gone. I will not miss her.
Quick. Peace be with you, sir!   *Exit.*
Fal. I marvel I hear not of Master Brook.
He sent me word to stay within. I like his
money well.

[Enter *Ford* disguised.]

O, here he comes.   60
Ford. Bless you, sir!
Fal. Now, Master Brook, you come to know
what hath pass'd between me and Ford's wife.
Ford. That indeed, Sir John, is my business.
Fal. Master Brook, I will not lie to you; I
was at her house the hour she appointed me. 66
Ford. And sped you, sir?
Fal. Very ill-favouredly, Master Brook.
Ford. How so, sir? Did she change her determination?   70
Fal. No, Master Brook; but the peaking
cornuto her husband, Master Brook, dwelling
in a continual 'larum of jealousy, comes me in
the instant of our encounter, after we had embrac'd, kiss'd, protested, and (as it were) spoke
the prologue of our comedy; and at his heels a
rabble of his companions, thither provoked and
instigated by his distemper, and (forsooth) to
search his house for his wive's love.
Ford. What, while you were there?   80
Fal. While I was there.
Ford. And did he search for you and could
not find you?
Fal. You shall hear. As good luck would
have it, comes in one Mistress Page, gives intelligence of Ford's approach, and, in her invention and Ford's wive's distraction, they convey'd me into a buck-basket.
Ford. A buck-basket?
Fal. By the Lord, a buck-basket! — ramm'd
me in with foul shirts and smocks, socks, foul
stockings, greasy napkins, that, Master Brook,
there was the rankest compound of villanous
smell that ever offended nostril.
Ford. And how long lay you there?   95
Fal. Nay, you shall hear, Master Brook,
what I have suffer'd to bring this woman to evil
for your good. Being thus cramm'd in the basket, a couple of Ford's knaves, his hinds, were
call'd forth by their mistress to carry me in the
name of foul clothes to Datchet Lane. They
took me on their shoulders; met the jealous
knave their master in the door, who ask'd them
once or twice what they had in their basket. I
quak'd for fear lest the lunatic knave would
have search'd it; but fate, ordaining he should
be a cuckold, held his hand. Well, on went he
for a search, and away went I for foul clothes.
But mark the sequel, Master Brook. I suffered
the pangs of three several deaths: first, an intolerable fright, to be detected with a jealous
rotten bell-wether; next, to be compass'd like a

good bilbo in the circumference of a peck, hilt to point, heel to head; and then, to be stopp'd in, like a strong distillation, with stinking clothes that fretted in their own grease. Think of that — a man of my kidney! — think of that! — that am as subject to heat as butter; a man of continual dissolution and thaw. It was a miracle to scape suffocation. And in the height of this bath, when I was more than half stew'd in grease (like a Dutch dish), to be thrown into the Thames and cool'd, glowing hot, in that surge, like a horseshoe! Think of that! hissing hot! Think of that, Master Brook!

Ford. In good sadness, sir, I am sorry for that for my sake you have suffer'd all this. My suit then is desperate. You'll undertake her no more?

Fal. Master Brook, I will be thrown into Ætna, as I have been into Thames, ere I will leave her thus. Her husband is this morning gone a-birding. I have received from her another embassy of meeting. 'Twixt eight and nine is the hour, Master Brook.

Ford. 'Tis past eight already, sir.   134

Fal. Is it? I will then address me to my appointment. Come to me at your convenient leisure, and you shall know how I speed; and the conclusion shall be crowned with your enjoying her. Adieu. You shall have her, Master Brook. Master Brook, you shall cuckold Ford. [*Exit.*]

Ford. Hum, ha! Is this a vision? Is this a dream? Do I sleep? Master Ford, awake! Awake, Master Ford! There's a hole made in your best coat, Master Ford. This 'tis to be married! This 'tis to have linen and buck-baskets! Well, I will proclaim myself what I am. I will now take the lecher. He is at my house. He cannot scape me. 'Tis impossible he should. He cannot creep into a halfpenny purse nor into a pepperbox: but, lest the devil that guides him should aid him, I will search impossible places. Though what I am I cannot avoid, yet to be what I would not shall not make me tame. If I have horns to make one mad, let the proverb go with me — I'll be horn-mad.   *Exit.*

ACT IV. Scene I. [*Windsor. The street.*]

Enter *Mistress Page, Quickly, William.*

Mrs. Page. Is he at Master Ford's already, think'st thou?

Quick. Sure he is by this, or will be presently. But truly he is very courageous mad about his throwing into the water. Mistress Ford desires you to come suddenly.   6

Mrs. Page. I'll be with her by-and-by. I'll but bring my young man here to school. Look where his master comes; 'tis a playing day, I see.

[Enter *Evans.*]

How now, Sir Hugh? No school to-day?   10

Evans. No. Master Slender is let the boys leave to play.

Quick. Blessing of his heart!

Mrs. Page. Sir Hugh, my husband says my son profits nothing in the world at his book. I pray you ask him some questions in his accidence.   16

Evans. Come hither, William; hold up your head; come.

Mrs. Page. Come on, sirrah; hold up your head; answer your master, be not afraid.   20

Evans. William, how many numbers is in nouns?

Will. Two.

Quick. Truly, I thought there had been one number more, because they say 'Od's nouns.'

Evans. Peace your tattlings. What is 'fair,' William?

Will. Pulcher.

Quick. Polecats? There are fairer things than polecats, sure.   30

Evans. You are a very simplicity oman. I pray you peace. What is *lapis*, William?

Will. A stone.

Evans. And what is 'a stone,' William?

Will. A pebble.   35

Evans. No, it is *lapis*. I pray you remember in your prain.

Will. Lapis.

Evans. That is a good William. What is he, William, that does lend articles?   40

Will. Articles are borrowed of the pronoun, and be thus declined: *Singulariter, nominativo, hic, haec, hoc.*

Evans. Nominativo, *hig, hag, hog.* Pray you mark: *genitivo, huius.* Well, what is your accusative case?   46

Will. Accusativo, *hinc.*

Evans. I pray you have your remembrance, child. *Accusativo, hung, hang, hog.*

Quick. Hang-hog is Latin for bacon, I warrant you.   51

Evans. Leave your prabbles, oman. What is the focative case, William?
Will. O, *vocativo*, O.
Evans. Remember, William : focative is *caret*.
Quick. And that's a good root.   56
Evans. Oman, forbear.
Mrs. Page. Peace!
Evans. What is your genitive case plural, William?   60
Will. Genitive case?
Evans. Ay.
Will. *Genitivo, horum, harum, horum.*
Quick. Vengeance of Jinny's case! Fie on her! Never name her, child, if she be a whore.
Evans. For shame, oman!   66
Quick. You do ill to teach the child such words. He teaches him to hick and to hack, which they'll do fast enough of themselves, and to call *horum*. Fie upon you!   70
Evans. Oman, art thou lunatics? Hast thou no understandings for thy cases, and the numbers of the genders? Thou art as foolish Christian creatures as I would desires.
Mrs. Page. Prithee hold thy peace.   75
Evans. Show me now, William, some declensions of your pronouns.
Will. Forsooth, I have forgot.
Evans. It is *qui, quae, quod.* If you forget your *qui*'s, your *quae*'s, and your *quod*'s, you must be preeches. Go your ways and play, go.
Mrs. Page. He is a better scholar than I thought he was.
Evans. He is a good sprag memory. Farewell, Mistress Page.   85
Mrs. Page. Adieu, good Sir Hugh. [*Exit Sir Hugh.*] Get you home, boy. — Come, we stay too long.   *Exeunt.*

Scene II. [Ford's *house*.]

Enter *Falstaff, Mistress Ford.*

Fal. Mistress Ford, your sorrow hath eaten up my sufferance. I see you are obsequious in your love, and I profess requital to a hair's breadth, not only, Mistress Ford, in the simple office of love, but in all the accustrement, complement, and ceremony of it. But are you sure of your husband now?   7
Mrs. Ford. He's a-birding, sweet Sir John.
Mrs. Page. [*within*] What ho, gossip Ford! what ho!   10
Mrs. Ford. Step into th' chamber, Sir John.
                   [*Exit Falstaff.*]

[Enter *Mistress Page.*]

Mrs. Page. How now, sweetheart? Who's at home besides yourself?
Mrs. Ford. Why, none but mine own people.
Mrs. Page. Indeed?   15
Mrs. Ford. No, certainly. [*Aside to her*] Speak louder.
Mrs. Page. Truly, I am so glad you have nobody here.
Mrs. Ford. Why?   20
Mrs. Page. Why, woman, your husband is in his old lunes again. He so takes on yonder with my husband, so rails against all married mankind, so curses all Eve's daughters, of what complexion soever, and so buffets himself on the forehead, crying 'Peer out, peer out!' that any madness I ever yet beheld seem'd but tameness, civility, and patience to this his distemper he is in now. I am glad the fat knight is not here.
Mrs. Ford. Why, does he talk of him?   30
Mrs. Page. Of none but him ; and swears he was carried out, the last time he search'd for him, in a basket ; protests to my husband he is now here, and hath drawn him and the rest of their company from their sport to make another experiment of his suspicion. But I am glad the knight is not here. Now he shall see his own foolery.
Mrs. Ford. How near is he, Mistress Page?
Mrs. Page. Hard by, at street end ; he will be here anon.   41
Mrs. Ford. I am undone! The knight is here.
Mrs. Page. Why then, you are utterly sham'd, and he's but a dead man. What a woman are you! Away with him, away with him! Better shame than murther.   46
Mrs. Ford. Which way should he go? How should I bestow him? Shall I put him into the basket again?

[Enter *Falstaff.*]

Fal. No, I'll come no more i' th' basket. May I not go out ere he come?   51
Mrs. Page. Alas! three of Master Ford's brothers watch the door with pistols, that none shall issue out ; otherwise you might slip away ere he came. But what make you here?   55
Fal. What shall I do? I'll creep up into the chimney.
Mrs. Ford. There they always use to discharge their birding pieces.
Mrs. Page. Creep into the kiln-hole.
Fal. Where is it?   60
Mrs. Ford. He will seek there, on my word. Neither press, coffer, chest, trunk, well, vault,

but he hath an abstract for the remembrance of such places and goes to them by his note. There is no hiding you in the house. 65

Fal. I'll go out then.

Mrs. Page. If you go out in your own semblance, you die, Sir John. Unless you go out disguis'd —

Mrs. Ford. How might we disguise him? 70

Mrs. Page. Alas the day, I know not! There is no woman's gown big enough for him. Otherwise he might put on a hat, a muffler, and a kerchief, and so escape.

Fal. Good hearts, devise something. Any extremity rather than a mischief! 76

Mrs. Ford. My maid's aunt, the fat woman of Brainford, has a gown above.

Mrs. Page. On my word, it will serve him. She's as big as he is. And there's her thrumm'd hat, and her muffler too! Run up, Sir John.

Mrs. Ford. Go, go, sweet Sir John! Mistress Page and I will look some linen for your head.

Mrs. Page. Quick, quick! We'll come dress you straight. Put on the gown the while. 85

[*Exit Falstaff.*]

Mrs. Ford. I would my husband would meet him in this shape. He cannot abide the old woman of Brainford; he swears she's a witch, forbade her my house, and hath threat'ned to beat her. 89

Mrs. Page. Heaven guide him to thy husband's cudgel! and the devil guide his cudgel afterwards!

Mrs. Ford. But is my husband coming?

Mrs. Page. Ay, in good sadness is he, and talks of the basket too, howsoever he hath had intelligence. 95

Mrs. Ford. We'll try that; for I'll appoint my men to carry the basket again, to meet him at the door with it, as they did last time.

Mrs. Page. Nay, but he'll be here presently. Let's go dress him like the witch of Brainford.

Mrs. Ford. I'll first direct my men what they shall do with the basket. Go up; I'll bring linen for him straight. [*Exit.*]

Mrs. Page. Hang him, dishonest varlet! We cannot misuse him enough. 105

We'll leave a proof by that which we will do, Wives may be merry, and yet honest too. We do not act that often jest and laugh; 'Tis old but true: Still swine eats all the draff. [*Exit.*]

[*Enter Mistress Ford with two Servants.*]

Mrs. Ford. Go, sirs, take the basket again on your shoulders. Your master is hard at door.

If he bid you set it down, obey him. Quickly, dispatch! [*Exit.*]

1. Serv. Come, come, take it up.

2. Serv. Pray heaven it be not full of knight again. 116

1. Serv. I hope not; I had as lief bear so much lead.

[*Enter Ford, Page, Shallow, Caius, and Evans.*]

Ford. Ay, but if it prove true, Master Page, have you any way then to unfool me again? Set down the basket, villains! Somebody call my wife. Youth in a basket! O you panderly rascals! There's a knot, a ging, a pack, a conspiracy against me! Now shall the devil be sham'd. What, wife, I say! Come, come forth! Behold what honest clothes you send forth to bleaching!

Page. Why, this passes, Master Ford! You are not to go loose any longer; you must be pinion'd.

Evans. Why, this is lunatics! This is mad as a mad dog! 131

Shal. Indeed, Master Ford, this is not well, indeed.

Ford. So say I too, sir.

[*Enter Mistress Ford.*]

Come hither, Mistress Ford! Mistress Ford, the honest woman, the modest wife, the virtuous creature, that hath the jealous fool to her husband! I suspect without cause, mistress, do I?

Mrs. Ford. Heaven be my witness you do, if you suspect me in any dishonesty. 140

Ford. Well said, brazen-face! hold it out. — Come forth, sirrah! [*Pulls clothes out of the basket.*]

Page. This passes!

Mrs. Ford. Are you not asham'd? Let the clothes alone. 145

Ford. I shall find you anon.

Evans. 'Tis unreasonable. Will you take up your wife's clothes? Come away!

Ford. Empty the basket, I say!

Mrs. Ford. Why, man, why? 150

Ford. Master Page, as I am a man, there was one convey'd out of my house yesterday in this basket. Why may not he be there again? In my house I am sure he is. My intelligence is true, my jealousy is reasonable. Pluck me out all the linen. 156

Mrs. Ford. If you find a man there, he shall die a flea's death.

Page. Here's no man.

Shal. By my fidelity, this is not well, Master Ford. This wrongs you. 161

Evans. Master Ford, you must pray, and not follow the imaginations of your own heart. This is jealousies.

Ford. Well, he's not here I seek for. 165

Page. No, nor nowhere else but in your brain.

Ford. Help to search my house this one time. If I find not what I seek, show no colour for my extremity. Let me for ever be your table sport. Let them say of me, 'As jealous as Ford, that search'd a hollow walnut for his wife's leman.' Satisfy me once more; once more search with me.

Mrs. Ford. What, ho, Mistress Page! Come you and the old woman down. My husband will come into the chamber. 176

Ford. Old woman? What old woman's that?

Mrs. Ford. Why, it is my maid's aunt of Brainford.

Ford. A witch, a quean, an old cozening quean! Have I not forbid her my house? She comes of errands, does she? We are simple men; we do not know what's brought to pass under the profession of fortune-telling. She works by charms, by spells, by th' figure, and such daub'ry as this is, beyond our element: we know nothing. Come down, you witch, you hag you! come down, I say! 188

Mrs. Ford. Nay, good sweet husband! Good gentlemen, let him not strike the old woman.

Enter Falstaff disguised like an old woman, and Mistress Page with him.

Mrs. Page. Come, Mother Prat. Come, give me your hand.

Ford. I'll prat her! (*Beats him.*) Out of my door, you witch, you hag, you baggage, you polecat, you runnion! out, out! I'll conjure you, I'll fortune-teil you! 196
Falstaff runs away.

Mrs. Page. Are you not asham'd? I think you have kill'd the poor woman.

Mrs. Ford. Nay, he will do it. 'Tis a goodly credit for you. 200

Ford. Hang her, witch!

Evans. By Jeshu, I think the oman is a witch indeed. I like not when a oman has a great peard. I spy a great peard under his muffler. 205

Ford. Will you follow, gentlemen? I beseech you follow. See but the issue of my jealousy. If I cry out thus upon no trail, never trust me when I open again. 209

Page. Let's obey his humour a little further. Come, gentlemen.

[Exeunt all but Mrs. Page and Mrs. Ford.]

Mrs. Page. Trust me, he beat him most pitifully.

Mrs. Ford. Nay, by th' mass, that he did not! He beat him most unpitifully, methought.

Mrs. Page. I'll have the cudgel hallow'd and hung o'er the altar. It hath done meritorious service. 218

Mrs. Ford. What think you? May we with the warrant of womanhood and the witness of a good conscience pursue him with any further revenge? 222

Mrs. Page. The spirit of wantonness is sure scar'd out of him. If the devil have him not in fee simple, with fine and recovery, he will never, I think, in the way of waste, attempt us again.

Mrs. Ford. Shall we tell our husbands how we have serv'd him? 229

Mrs. Page. Yes, by all means; if it be but to scrape the figures out of your husband's brains. If they can find in their hearts the poor unvirtuous fat knight shall be any further afflicted, two will still be the ministers. 234

Mrs. Ford. I'll warrant they'll have him publicly sham'd; and methinks there would be no period to the jest, should he not be publicly sham'd.

Mrs. Page. Come, to the forge with it then; shape it. I would not have things cool. 240
Exeunt.

Scene III. [*The Garter Inn.*]

Enter Host and Bardolph.

Bard. Sir, the Germans desire to have three of your horses. The Duke himself will be tomorrow at court, and they are going to meet him.

Host. What duke should that be comes so secretly? I hear not of him in the court. Let me speak with the gentlemen. They speak English?

Bard. Ay, sir. I'll call them to you. 9

Host. They shall have my horses; but I'll make them pay, I'll sauce them. They have had my house a week at command. I have turn'd away my other guests. They must come off; I'll sauce them! Come. *Exeunt.*

Scene IV. [*Ford's house.*]

Enter Page, Ford, Mistress Page, Mistress Ford, and Evans.

Evans. 'Tis one of the pest discretions of a oman as ever I did look upon.

Page. And did he send you both these letters at an instant?

Mrs. Page. Within a quarter of an hour. 5

Ford. Pardon me, wife. Henceforth do what thou wilt.
I rather will suspect the sun with cold
Than thee with wantonness. Now doth thy honour stand,
In him that was of late an heretic,
As firm as faith.

Page. 'Tis well, 'tis well; no more! 10
Be not as extreme in submission as in offence.
But let our plot go forward. Let our wives
Yet once again, to make us public sport,
Appoint a meeting with this old fat fellow
Where we may take him and disgrace him for it.

Ford. There is no better way than that they spoke of. 16

Page. How? to send him word they'll meet him in the Park at midnight? Fie, fie! he'll never come.

Evans. You say he has bin thrown in the rivers, and has bin grievously peaten as an old oman. Methinks there should be terrors in him, that he should not come. Methinks his flesh is punish'd; he shall have no desires.

Page. So think I too. 25

Mrs. Ford. Devise but how you'll use him when he comes,
And let us two devise to bring him thither.

Mrs. Page. There is an old tale goes that Herne the Hunter,
Sometime a keeper here in Windsor Forest,
Doth all the winter time, at still midnight, 30
Walk round about an oak, with great ragg'd horns;
And there he blasts the trees, and takes the cattle,
And makes milch kine yield blood, and shakes a chain
In a most hideous and dreadful manner.
You have heard of such a spirit, and well you know 35
The superstitious idle-headed eld
Receiv'd and did deliver to our age
This tale of Herne the Hunter for a truth.

Page. Why, yet there want not many that do fear 39
In deep of night to walk by this Herne's Oak.
But what of this?

Mrs. Ford. Marry, this is our device,
That Falstaff at that oak shall meet with us,
Disguis'd like Herne, with huge horns on his head.

Page. Well, let it not be doubted but he'll come;
And in this shape when you have brought him thither, 45
What shall be done with him? What is your plot?

Mrs. Page. That likewise have we thought upon, and thus:
Nan Page (my daughter) and my little son
And three or four more of their growth we'll dress
Like urchins, ouphs, and fairies, green and white, 50
With rounds of waxen tapers on their heads
And rattles in their hands. Upon a sudden,
As Falstaff, she, and I are newly met,
Let them from forth a sawpit rush at once
With some diffused song. Upon their sight,
We two in great amazedness will fly. 56
Then let them all encircle him about
And fairy-like to pinch the unclean knight,
And ask him why, that hour of fairy revel,
In their so sacred paths he dares to tread 60
In shape profane.

Mrs. Ford. And till he tell the truth
Let the supposed fairies pinch him, sound,
And burn him with their tapers.

Mrs. Page. The truth being known,
We'll all present ourselves, dis-horn the spirit,
And mock him home to Windsor.

Ford. The children must 65
Be practis'd well to this, or they'll nev'r do't.

Evans. I will teach the children their behaviours; and I will be like a jack-an-apes also, to burn the knight with my taber.

Ford. That will be excellent. I'll go buy them vizards. 70

Mrs. Page. My Nan shall be the Queen of all the Fairies,
Finely attired in a robe of white.

Page. That silk will I go buy, [*aside*] and in that tire
Shall Master Slender steal my Nan away
And marry her at Eton. — Go, send to Falstaff straight. 75

Ford. Nay, I'll to him again in name of Brook.
He'll tell me all his purpose. Sure he'll come.

Mrs. Page. Fear not you that. Go get us properties
And tricking for our fairies.

Evans. Let us about it. It is admirable pleasures and fery honest knaveries. 81

[*Exeunt Page, Ford, and Evans.*]

Mrs. Page. Go, Mistress Ford,
Send Quickly to Sir John to know his mind.
                              [*Exit Mrs. Ford.*]
I'll to the doctor. He hath my good will,
And none but he, to marry with Nan Page. 85
That Slender, though well landed, is an idiot;
And he my husband best of all affects.
The doctor is well money'd, and his friends
Potent at court. He, none but he, shall have
    her,   89
Though twenty thousand worthier come to
    crave her.   [*Exit.*]

Scene V. [*The Garter Inn.*]

Enter *Host, Simple.*

Host. What wouldst thou have, boor? what,
thick-skin? Speak, breathe, discuss; brief,
short, quick, snap!
Sim. Marry, sir, I come to speak with Sir
John Falstaff from Master Slender.   5
Host. There's his chamber, his house, his
castle, his standing bed and truckle-bed. 'Tis
painted about with the story of the Prodigal,
fresh and new. Go, knock and call. He'll speak
like an Anthropophaginian unto thee. Knock,
I say!   11
Sim. There's an old woman, a fat woman,
gone up into his chamber. I'll be so bold as
stay, sir, till she come down. I come to speak
with her indeed.   15
Host. Ha? a fat woman? The knight may
be robb'd. I'll call. Bully knight! bully Sir
John! speak from thy lungs military. Art
thou there? It is thine host, thine Ephesian,
calls.
Fal. [*above*] How now, mine host?   20
Host. Here's a Bohemian Tartar tarries the
coming down of thy fat woman. Let her descend, bully, let her descend. My chambers are
honourable. Fie! privacy? fie!

[Enter *Falstaff.*]

Fal. There was, mine host, an old fat woman
even now with me, but she's gone.   26
Sim. Pray you, sir, was't not the wise
woman of Brainford?
Fal. Ay, marry was it, mussel-shell. What
would you with her?   30
Sim. My master, sir, Master Slender, sent
to her, seeing her go thorough the streets, to
know, sir, whether one Nym, sir, that beguil'd
him of a chain, had the chain or no.
Fal. I spake with the old woman about it. 35

Sim. And what says she, I pray, sir?
Fal. Marry, she says that the very same man
that beguil'd Master Slender of his chain
cozen'd him of it.   39
Sim. I would I could have spoken with the
woman herself. I had other things to have
spoken with her too from him.
Fal. What are they? Let us know.
Host. Ay, come! quick!
Sim. I may not conceal them, sir.   45
Host. Conceal them, or thou diest.
Sim. Why, sir, they were nothing but about
Mistress Anne Page, to know if it were my
master's fortune to have her, or no.
Fal. 'Tis; 'tis his fortune.   50
Sim. What, sir?
Fal. To have her, or no. Go; say the
woman told me so.
Sim. May I be bold to say so, sir?
Fal. Ay, Sir Tyke. Who more bold?   55
Sim. I thank your worship. I shall make my
master glad with these tidings.   [*Exit.*]
Host. Thou art clerkly, thou art clerkly, Sir
John. Was there a wise woman with thee?
Fal. Ay, that there was, mine host; one
that hath taught me more wit than ever I
learn'd before in my life; and I paid nothing
for it neither, but was paid for my learning.

Enter *Bardolph.*

Bard. Out, alas, sir! cozenage, mere cozenage!
Host. Where be my horses? Speak well of
them, varletto.   66
Bard. Run away with the cozeners; for so
soon as I came beyond Eton, they threw me off,
from behind one of them, in a slough of mire;
and set spurs and away, like three German
devils, three Doctor Faustuses.   71
Host. They are gone but to meet the Duke,
villain. Do not say they be fled. Germans are
honest men.

[Enter *Evans.*]

Evans. Where is mine host?   75
Host. What is the matter, sir?
Evans. Have a care of your entertainments.
There is a friend of mine come to town, tells me
there is three cozen-germans that has cozen'd
all the hosts of Readins, of Maidenhead, of
Colebrook, of horses and money. I tell you for
good will, look you. You are wise, and full of
gibes and vlouting-stogs, and 'tis not convenient you should be cozened. Fare you well.
                                      Exit

[Enter *Caius*.]

Caius. Vere is mine host de Jarteer?   85
Host. Here, Master Doctor, in perplexity and doubtful dilemma.
Caius. I cannot tell vat is dat; but it is tell-a me dat you make grand preparation for a Duke de Jarmanie. By my trot, dere is no duke dat de court is know to come. I tell you for good vill. Adieu.   *Exit.*
Host. Hue and cry, villain, go! — Assist me, knight. — I am undone! — Fly, run! hue and cry, villain! — I am undone!   95
          Exeunt [Host and Bardolph].
Fal. I would all the world might be cozen'd, for I have been cozen'd and beaten too. If it should come to the ear of the court how I have been transformed, and how my transformation hath been wash'd and cudgell'd, they would melt me out of my fat drop by drop and liquor fishermen's boots with me. I warrant they would whip me with their fine wits till I were as crestfall'n as a dried pear. I never prosper'd since I forswore myself at primero. Well, if my wind were but long enough to say my prayers, I would repent.   106

Enter *Mistress Quickly.*

Now? Whence come you?
Quick. From the two parties forsooth.
Fal. The devil take one party and his dam the other! and so they shall be both bestowed. I have suffer'd more for their sakes, more than the villanous inconstancy of man's disposition is able to bear.
Quick And have not they suffer'd? Yes, I warrant; speciously one of them. Mistress Ford, good heart, is beaten black and blue, that you cannot see a white spot about her.   117
Fal. What tell'st thou me of black and blue? I was beaten myself into all the colours of the rainbow; and I was like to be apprehended for the witch of Brainford. But that my admirable dexterity of wit, my counterfeiting the action of an old woman, deliver'd me, the knave constable had set me i' th' stocks, i' th' common stocks, for a witch.   125
Quick. Sir, let me speak with you in your chamber. You shall hear how things go, and (I warrant) to your content. Here is a letter will say somewhat. Good hearts, what ado here is to bring you together! Sure, one of you does not serve heaven well, that you are so cross'd.
Fal. Come up into my chamber.   *Exeunt.*

Scene VI. [*Another room in the Garter Inn.*]

Enter *Fenton, Host.*

Host. Master Fenton, talk not to me; my mind is heavy. I will give over all.
Fen. Yet hear me speak. Assist me in my purpose,
And, as I am a gentleman, I'll give thee   4
A hundred pound in gold more than your loss.
Host. I will hear you, Master Fenton, and I will at the least keep your counsel.
Fen. From time to time I have acquainted you
With the dear love I bear to fair Anne Page,
Who, mutually, hath answer'd my affection   10
(So far forth as herself might be her chooser)
Even to my wish. I have a letter from her
Of such contents as you will wonder at;
The mirth whereof so larded with my matter
That neither, singly, can be manifested   15
Without the show of both; wherein fat Falstaff
Hath a great scene. The image of the jest
I'll show you here at large. Hark, good mine host.
To-night at Herne's Oak, just 'twixt twelve and one,
Must my sweet Nan present the Fairy Queen —
The purpose why, is here — [*Shows a letter.*] in which disguise,   21
While other jests are something rank on foot,
Her father hath commanded her to slip
Away with Slender, and with him at Eton
Immediately to marry. She hath consented.
Now, sir,   26
Her mother (even strong against that match
And firm for Doctor Caius) hath appointed
That he shall likewise shuffle her away
While other sports are tasking of their minds,
And at the dean'ry, where a priest attends,   31
Straight marry her. To this her mother's plot
She seemingly obedient likewise hath
Made promise to the doctor. Now thus it rests:
Her father means she shall be all in white,   35
And in that habit, when Slender sees his time
To take her by the hand and bid her go,
She shall go with him. Her mother hath intended
(The better to denote her to the doctor,
For they must all be mask'd and vizarded)   40
That quaint in green she shall be loose enrob'd,
With ribands-pendent flaring 'bout her head;
And when the doctor spies his vantage ripe,
To pinch her by the hand, and on that token
The maid hath given consent to go with him.
Host. Which means she to deceive, father or mother?   46

Fen. Both, my good host, to go along with
me.
And here it rests, that you'll procure the vicar
To stay for me at church 'twixt twelve and one,
And in the lawful name of marrying   50
To give our hearts united ceremony.

Host. Well, husband your device. I'll to the
vicar.
Bring you the maid, you shall not lack a priest.
Fen. So shall I evermore be bound to thee.
Besides, I'll make a present recompense.   55
Exeunt.

ACT V. Scene I. [*The Garter Inn.*]

Enter *Falstaff, Quickly.*

Fal. Prithee no more prattling! Go; I'll
hold. This is the third time; I hope good luck
lies in odd numbers. Away, go! They say there
is divinity in odd numbers, either in nativity,
chance, or death. Away!   5
Quick. I'll provide you a chain, and I'll do
what I can to get you a pair of horns.
Fal. Away, I say! time wears. Hold up your
head and mince.   [*Exit Mrs. Quickly.*]

[Enter *Ford* disguised.]
How now, Master Brook? Master Brook, the
matter will be known to-night, or never. Be you
in the Park about midnight at Herne's Oak and
you shall see wonders.
Ford. Went you not to her yesterday, sir, as
you told me you had appointed?   15
Fal. I went to her, Master Brook, as you
see, like a poor old man; but I came from her,
Master Brook, like a poor old woman. That
same knave (Ford, her husband) hath the finest
mad devil of jealousy in him, Master Brook,
that ever govern'd frenzy. I will tell you, he
beat me grievously in the shape of a woman;
for in the shape of man, Master Brook, I fear
not Goliah with a weaver's beam, because I
know also life is a shuttle. I am in haste. Go
along with me; I'll tell you all, Master Brook.
Since I pluck'd geese, play'd truant, and
whipp'd top, I knew not what 'twas to be
beaten till lately. Follow me. I'll tell you
strange things of this knave Ford, on whom
to-night I will be revenged, and I will deliver
his wife into your hand. Follow! Strange things
in hand, Master Brook! Follow.   *Exeunt.*

Scene II. [*Windsor Park.*]

Enter *Page, Shallow, Slender.*

Page. Come, come! We'll couch i' th' Castle
ditch till we see the light of our fairies. Remember, son Slender, my daughter.
Slen. Ay, forsooth. I have spoke with her,
and we have a nay-word how to know one another. I come to her in white and cry 'mum';
she cries 'budget'; and by that we know one
another.   8
Shal. That's good too. But what needs
either your 'mum' or her 'budget'? The white
will decipher her well enough. It hath struck
ten o'clock.   12
Page. The night is dark. Light and spirits
will become it well. Heaven prosper our sport!
No man means evil but the devil, and we shall
know him by his horns. Let's away. Follow
me.   *Exeunt.*

Scene III. [*Near the Park.*]

Enter *Mistress Page, Mistress Ford, Caius.*

Mrs. Page. Master Doctor, my daughter is
in green. When you see your time, take her by
the hand, away with her to the deanery, and
dispatch it quickly. Go before into the Park.
We two must go together.   5
Caius. I know vat I have to do. Adieu.
Mrs. Page. Fare you well, sir. [*Exit Caius.*]
My husband will not rejoice so much at the
abuse of Falstaff as he will chafe at the doctor's
marrying my daughter. But 'tis no matter.
Better a little chiding than a great deal of
heartbreak.   11
Mrs. Ford. Where is Nan now? and her
troop of fairies? and the Welsh devil Hugh?
Mrs. Page. They are all couch'd in a pit hard
by Herne's Oak, with obscur'd lights, which at
the very instant of Falstaff's and our meeting
they will at once display to the night.   17
Mrs. Ford. That cannot choose but amaze
him.
Mrs. Page. If he be not amaz'd, he will be
mock'd. If he be amaz'd, he will every way be
mock'd.   21
Mrs. Ford. We'll betray him finely.
Mrs. Page. Against such lewdsters and their
lechery
Those that betray them do no treachery.
Mrs. Ford. The hour draws on. To the oak,
to the oak!   *Exeunt.*

Scene IV. [*Windsor Park.*]

Enter *Evans* [like a *Satyr*] and [others as] *Fairies.*

Evans. Trib, trib, fairies. Come, and remember your parts. Be pold, I pray you. Follow me into the pit; and when I give the watch-ords, do as I pid you. Come, come; trib, trib.
Exeunt.

Scene V. [*Another part of Windsor Park.*]

Enter *Falstaff* [disguised as *Herne*,] with a buck's head upon him.

Fal. The Windsor bell hath stroke twelve; the minute draws on. Now the hot-blooded gods assist me! Remember, Jove, thou wast a bull for thy Europa; love set on thy horns. O powerful love, that in some respects makes a beast a man; in some other, a man a beast! You were also, Jupiter, a swan for the love of Leda. O omnipotent love! how near the god drew to the complexion of a goose! A fault done first in the form of a beast (O Jove, a beastly fault!) and then another fault in the semblance of a fowl — think on't, Jove; a foul fault! When gods have hot backs, what shall poor men do? For me, I am here a Windsor stag, and the fattest, I think, i' th' forest. Send me a cool rut-time, Jove, or who can blame me to piss my tallow? Who comes here? my doe?   17

[Enter *Mistress Ford* and *Mistress Page*.]

Mrs. Ford. Sir John! art thou there, my deer, my male deer?
Fal. My doe with the black scut! Let the sky rain potatoes; let it thunder to the tune of 'Greensleeves,' hail kissing comfits, and snow eringoes. Let there come a tempest of provocation, I will shelter me here.   [*Embraces her.*]
Mrs. Ford. Mistress Page is come with me, sweetheart.   26
Fal. Divide me like a brib'd buck, each a haunch. I will keep my sides to myself, my shoulders for the fellow of this walk, and my horns I bequeath your husbands. Am I a woodman, ha? Speak I like Herne the Hunter? Why, now is Cupid a child of conscience; he makes restitution. As I am a true spirit, welcome!   *A noise of horns.*
Mrs. Page. Alas, what noise?
Mrs. Ford. Heaven forgive our sins!   35
Fal. What should this be?

Mrs. Ford, Mrs. Page. Away, away!
They run away.
Fal. I think the devil will not have me damn'd, lest the oil that's in me should set hell on fire. He would never else cross me thus.   40

Enter [*Evans* like a *Satyr*; *Pistol* like *Hobgoblin*; *Anne Page* (the *Fairy Queen*), and others, as] *Fairies.*

Queen. Fairies black, gray, green, and white,
You moonshine revellers and shades of night,
You orphan heirs of fixed destiny,
Attend your office and your quality.
Crier Hobgoblin, make the fairy oyes.   45
Pist. Elves, list your names. Silence, you airy toys.
Cricket, to Windsor chimneys shalt thou leap.
Where fires thou find'st unrak'd and hearths unswept,
There pinch the maids as blue as bilberry.
Our radiant queen hates sluts and sluttery.   50
Fal. They are fairies. He that speaks to them shall die.
I'll wink and couch. No man their works must eye.   [*Lies down upon his face.*]
Evans. Where's Bead? Go you, and where you find a maid
That ere she sleep has thrice her prayers said,
Raise up the organs of her fantasy,   55
Sleep she as sound as careless infancy;
But those as sleep and think not on their sins,
Pinch them, arms, legs, backs, shoulders, sides, and shins.
Queen. About, about!   59
Search Windsor Castle, elves, within and out,
Strew good luck, ouphs, on every sacred room;
That it may stand till the perpetual doom
In state as wholesome as in state 'tis fit,
Worthy the owner, and the owner it.
The several chairs of order look you scour   65
With juice of balm and every precious flow'r.
Each fair instalment, coat, and sev'ral crest,
With loyal blazon, evermore be blest!
And nightly meadow-fairies, look you sing,
Like to the Garter's compass, in a ring.   70
Th' expressure that it bears, green let it be,
More fertile-fresh than all the field to see;
And *Honi soit qui mal y pense* write
In em'rald tufts, flow'rs purple, blue, and white,
Like sapphire, pearl, and rich embroidery,   75
Buckled below fair knighthood's bending knee.
Fairies use flow'rs for their charactery.
Away, disperse! But till 'tis one o'clock,
Our dance of custom round about the Oak
Of Herne the Hunter let us not forget.   80

Evans. Pray you lock hand in hand; yourselves in order set;
And twenty glowworms shall our lanthorns be
To guide our measure round about the tree.
But, stay! I smell a man of middle earth.

Fal. Heavens defend me from that Welsh fairy, lest he transform me to a piece of cheese!

Pist. Vile worm, thou wast o'erlook'd even in thy birth.

Queen. With trial-fire touch me his finger end.
If he be chaste, the flame will back descend
And turn him to no pain; but if he start,   90
It is the flesh of a corrupted heart.

Pist. A trial, come!

Evans.   Come! Will this wood take fire?
They put the tapers to his fingers, and he starts.

Fal. O, O, O!

Queen. Corrupt, corrupt, and tainted in desire!
About him, fairies; sing a scornful rhyme;   95
And as you trip, still pinch him to your time.

The Song.

Fie on sinful fantasy!
Fie on lust and luxury!
Lust is but a bloody fire,
Kindled with unchaste desire,   100
Fed in heart, whose flames aspire
As thoughts do blow them, higher and higher.
Pinch him, fairies, mutually;
Pinch him for his villany;   104
Pinch him and burn him and turn him about
Till candles and starlight and moonshine be out.

[During this song] they pinch him; and the Doctor comes one way and steals away a Fairy in green, and Slender another way, and takes a Fairy in white; and Fenton steals Mistress Anne Page. And a noise of hunting is made within; and all the Fairies run away. Falstaff pulls off his buck's head and rises up.

[Enter Page, Ford, Mistress Page, and Mistress Ford.]

Page. Nay, do not fly. I think we have watch'd you now.
Will none but Herne the Hunter serve your turn?

Mrs. Page. I pray you, come; hold up the jest no higher.
Now, good Sir John, how like you Windsor wives?   110
See you these, husband? Do not these fair yokes
Become the forest better than the town?

Ford. Now, sir, who's a cuckold now? Master Brook, Falstaff's a knave, a cuckoldly knave; here are his horns, Master Brook. And, Master Brook, he hath enjoyed nothing of Ford's but his buck-basket, his cudgel, and twenty pounds of money, which must be paid to Master Brook. His horses are arrested for it, Master Brook.   119

Mrs. Ford. Sir John, we have had ill luck; we could never meet. I will never take you for my love again, but I will always count you my deer.

Fal. I do begin to perceive that I am made an ass.   125

Ford. Ay, and an ox too. Both the proofs are extant.

Fal. And these are not fairies? I was three or four times in the thought they were not fairies; and yet the guiltiness of my mind, the sudden surprise of my powers, drove the grossness of the foppery into a receiv'd belief, in despite of the teeth of all rhyme and reason, that they were fairies. See now how wit may be made a Jack-a-Lent, when 'tis upon ill employment!   135

Evans. Sir John Falstaff, serve Got and leave your desires, and fairies will not pinse you.

Ford. Well said, fairy Hugh.

Evans. And leave you your jealousies too, I pray you.   140

Ford. I will never mistrust my wife again till thou art able to woo her in good English.

Fal. Have I laid my brain in the sun, and dried it, that it wants matter to prevent so gross o'erreaching as this? Am I ridden with a Welsh goat too? Shall I have a coxcomb of frize? 'Tis time I were chok'd with a piece of toasted cheese.

Evans. Seese is not goot to give putter. Your pelly is all putter.   149

Fal. 'Seese,' and 'putter'? Have I liv'd to stand at the taunt of one that makes fritters of English? This is enough to be the decay of lust and late-walking through the realm.   153

Mrs. Page. Why, Sir John, do you think, though we would have thrust virtue out of our hearts by the head and shoulders and have given ourselves without scruple to hell, that ever the devil could have made you our delight?

Ford. What, a hodge-pudding? a bag of flax?

Mrs. Page. A puff'd man?   160

Page. Old, cold, wither'd, and of intolerable entrails?

Ford. And one that is as slanderous as Satan?

Page. And as poor as Job?

95

Ford. And as wicked as his wife? 165
Evans. And given to fornications and to taverns and sack and wine and metheglins, and to drinkings and swearings and starings, pribbles and prabbles? 169
Fal. Well, I am your theme. You have the start of me; I am dejected. I am not able to answer the Welsh flannel. Ignorance itself is a plummet o'er me. Use me as you will. 173
Ford. Marry, sir, we'll bring you to Windsor to one Master Brook that you have cozen'd of money, to whom you should have been a pander. Over and above that you have suffer'd, I think to repay that money will be a biting affliction. 178
Page. Yet be cheerful, knight. Thou shalt eat a posset to-night at my house, where I will desire thee to laugh at my wife, that now laughs at thee. Tell her Master Slender hath married her daughter.
Mrs. Page. [*aside*] Doctors doubt that. If Anne Page be my daughter, she is, by this, Doctor Caius' wife. 186

[Enter *Slender.*]

Slen. Whoa, ho, ho, father Page!
Page. Son, how now? How now, son? Have you dispatch'd?
Slen. Dispatch'd? I'll make the best in Gloucestershire know on't. Would I were hang'd, la, else! 192
Page. Of what, son?
Slen. I came yonder at Eton to marry Mistress Anne Page, and she's a great lubberly boy. If it had not been i' th' church, I would have swing'd him or he should have swing'd me. If I did not think it had been Anne Page, would I might never stir! and 'tis a postmaster's boy.
Page. Upon my life, then, you took the wrong. 201
Slen. What need you tell me that? I think so, when I took a boy for a girl. If I had been married to him, for all he was in woman's apparel, I would not have had him. 205
Page. Why, this is your own folly. Did not I tell you how you should know my daughter by her garments?
Slen. I went to her in white, and cried 'mum,' and she cried 'budget,' as Anne and I had appointed; and yet it was not Anne, but a postmaster's boy. 212
Mrs. Page. Good George, be not angry. I knew of your purpose, turn'd my daughter into green, and indeed she is now with the doctor at the dean'ry, and there married. 216

[Enter *Caius.*]

Caius. Vere is Mistress Page? By gar, I am cozened! I ha' married oon garsoon, a boy; oon pesant, by gar. A boy! It is not Anne Page. By gar, I am cozened. 220
Mrs. Page. Why, did you take her in green?
Caius. Ay, be gar, and 'tis a boy! Be gar, I'll raise all Windsor! [*Exit.*]
Ford. This is strange. Who hath got the right Anne? 225
Page. My heart misgives me. Here comes Master Fenton.

[Enter *Fenton* and *Anne Page.*]

How now, Master Fenton?
Anne. Pardon, good father! Good my mother, pardon!
Page. Now, mistress! How chance you went not with Master Slender? 231
Mrs. Page. Why went you not with Master Doctor, maid?
Fen. You do amaze her. Hear the truth of it. You would have married her most shamefully, Where there was no proportion held in love. 235
The truth is, she and I (long since contracted) Are now so sure that nothing can dissolve us. Th' offence is holy that she hath committed, And this deceit loses the name of craft, Of disobedience, or unduteous title, 240
Since therein she doth evitate and shun A thousand irreligious cursed hours Which forced marriage would have brought upon her.
Ford. Stand not amaz'd. Here is no remedy. In love the heavens themselves do guide the state; 245
Money buys lands, and wives are sold by fate.
Fal. I am glad, though you have ta'en a special stand to strike at me, that your arrow hath glanc'd.
Page. Well, what remedy? Fenton, heaven give thee joy! 250
What cannot be eschew'd must be embrac'd.
Fal. When night-dogs run, all sorts of deer are chas'd.
Mrs. Page. Well, I will muse no further. Master Fenton,
Heaven give you many, many merry days! Good husband, let us every one go home 255
And laugh this sport o'er by a country fire, Sir John and all.
Ford. Let it be so. Sir John, To Master Brook you yet shall hold your word, For he to-night shall lie with Mistress Ford.
Exeunt.

MEASURE FOR MEASURE

MEASURE FOR MEASURE appears to have been presented at court by Shakespeare's company on St. Stephen's night (December 26), 1604. Probably it was a new play, for it accords in style and temper with Shakespeare's other work at about this time. At all events, 1604 is a reasonable date for its composition. Our only authority for the text is the First Folio, which must have been set up from a rather confused copy, certainly not from an autograph manuscript.

Here and there one may detect possible cuts in the Folio text, but there is no good reason for ascribing any part of the play to another hand than Shakespeare's, except, perhaps, the Duke's rhyming speech at the end of Act iii, and this hardly deserves the harsh language which some critics have bestowed upon it. As marking the interval between two strongly contrasted scenes and introducing, prologue-like, the business of the Moated Grange, this moralizing chorus is neither out of place nor structurally inappropriate. It emphasizes the principle of 'measure for measure' and, at the end, justifies (to the audience) the Duke's use of 'craft against vice,' and it sums up his plan. The style is good enough for the purpose — better, indeed, from that point of view, than if it were better poetically.

The plot of MEASURE FOR MEASURE is mainly derived from George Whetstone's two-part play *Promos and Cassandra*, published in 1578, which, in turn, is founded on the fifth novel in the eighth decade of the *Hecatommithi* of Giovanni Battista Giraldi (surnamed Cinthio or Cintio), first printed in 1565. Whetstone cannot have known Cinthio's *Epitia*, a tragicomedy on the same theme as the novel. He remarks that he 'deuided the whole history into two Commedies for that, *Decorum* vsed, it would not be conuayde in one.' He repeated his plot, as a narrative, in a story book entitled *An Heptameron of Civill Discourses* (1582), noting incidentally that his play had never been acted. The substance of the tale was current on the Continent in several variants before Cinthio wrote and was reported in 1547 as a recent occurrence. Something similar is told by Saint Augustine in his *De Sermone Domini in Monte* (i, 16, 50).

In Cinthio's novel, Juriste the Governor (Shakespeare's Angelo) promises Epitia (Shakespeare's Isabella) to release her brother, who is under sentence of death, and assures her of his own hand in marriage, though without a definite promise. On these terms she yields. Juriste has the brother beheaded and sends the body to her, with the head at its feet. In Cinthio's drama, however, the keeper of the prison, without the Governor's knowledge, substitutes a condemned criminal for the brother; and this important modification of the plot is also made by Whetstone. In both Cinthio and Whetstone the sovereign decrees that the Governor shall marry the heroine and then shall be executed, but after the marriage he spares his life at her entreaty.

Neither Cinthio nor Whetstone has any character that corresponds to Mariana. By bringing her into the story Shakespeare has transformed the plot and rescued Isabella from a really intolerable situation. She does not yield to Angelo, and it is the new character, Mariana, whom he must marry. Thus Isabella's honour is preserved and she is relieved of the necessity of marrying her worst enemy. The concluding speech shows that the Duke means to reward her with his own hand, if she 'a willing ear incline.' This arrangement, which comes as something of a shock to modern readers, was doubtless quite acceptable to the Elizabethans, always eager for Jack to have his Jill. We may infer that Isabella gives up her purpose of becoming a votaress of Saint Clare (i, 4), but this is not stated, and the conclusion of the play leaves the audience guessing — as was doubtless Shakespeare's intent.

In *Promos and Cassandra* Whetstone has sought to enliven the scene and make a strange plot more real by bringing in a good deal of low comedy. His object was also, in part, to illustrate the corruption of society in the city over which Promos rules. Thus we have Lamia, a lively courtesan, and her servant Rosko. Gripax and Rapax are two 'promoters,' whose function is to act as informers in the service of Promos's corrupt officer, Phallax. They attempt to arrest a rustic called John Adroynes. In the fight that ensues, John gets the better. Phallax stops the fray and informs John that he must die for an affair with a maidservant, but lets him off for a bribe — 'ten shillings and thirteen pence.' In one scene, a Hangman enters 'with a great many ropes about his neck.' He is followed by six prisoners on the way to execution, accompanied by a Preacher. Two of them are 'hacksters,' one is a woman, one a Gypsy fortune-teller, the rest are 'poor rogues,' one of whom says pitifully, 'Jesus save me! I am cast for a purse with three halfpence.' All this is poor stuff, no doubt; but it is not without life, and one may profitably consider it in its relation to Shakespeare's low characters in this and other plays.

Rosko is certainly a foreshadowing of Pompey in MEASURE FOR MEASURE; and there is an odd suggestion of this title in one of his moral reflections:

Who others doth deceive
Deserves himself like measure to receive.

The rôle of the Duke is much enlarged in Shakespeare. In Whetstone and Cinthio the sovereign (in Whetstone, the King; in Cinthio, the Emperor) is active only at the outset (to appoint and instruct the Governor) and at the end (to pass judgment). In MEASURE FOR MEASURE he keeps constant watch over Angelo's proceedings, prevents the execution of Claudio, and arranges the final solution of all the problems in advance.

What sounds like a prophecy of Shakespeare's play may be read in *3 Henry VI* (ii, 6, 52 ff.):

From off the gates of York fetch down the head,
Your father's head, which Clifford placed there;
Instead whereof let this supply the room.
Measure for measure must be answered.

MEASURE FOR MEASURE

The Names of all the Actors.

Vincentio, the Duke [of Vienna].
Angelo, the Deputy.
Escalus, an ancient Lord.
Claudio, a young gentleman.
Lucio, a fantastic.
Two other like Gentlemen.
Provost.
Thomas, } two friars.
Peter, }
[A Justice.]
[*Varrius*.]
Elbow, a simple constable.

Froth, a foolish gentleman.
[*Pompey*, a] clown, [servant to *Mistress Overdone*].
Abhorson, an executioner.
Barnardine, a dissolute prisoner.

Isabella, sister to *Claudio*.
Mariana, betrothed to *Angelo*.
Juliet, beloved of *Claudio*.
Francisca, a nun.
Mistress Overdone, a bawd.

[Lords, Officers, Citizens, Boy, and Attendants.]

THE SCENE. — *Vienna.*

ACT I. Scene I. [*Vienna. The* Duke's *Palace.*]

Enter *Duke, Escalus, Lords,* [and *Attendants*].

Duke. Escalus.
Escal. My lord.
Duke. Of government the properties to unfold
Would seem in me t' affect speech and discourse,
Since I am put to know that your own science
Exceeds, in that, the lists of all advice   6
My strength can give you. Then no more remains
But that to your sufficiency, as your worth is able,
. . . .
And let them work. The nature of our people,
Our city's institutions, and the terms   11
For common justice, y'are as pregnant in
As art and practice hath enriched any
That we remember. There is our commission,
                              [*Gives it.*]
From which we would not have you warp.
Call hither,   15
I say, bid come before us Angelo.
                    [*Exit an Attendant.*]
What figure of us think you he will bear?
For you must know we have with special soul
Elected him our absence to supply,
Lent him our terror, dress'd him with our love,
And given his deputation all the organs   21
Of our own power. What think you of it?
Escal. If any in Vienna be of worth
To undergo such ample grace and honour,
It is Lord Angelo.

Enter *Angelo.*

Duke.   Look where he comes.   25
Ang. Always obedient to your Grace's will,
I come to know your pleasure.
Duke.   Angelo,
There is a kind of character in thy life
That to th' observer doth thy history
Fully unfold. Thyself and thy belongings   30
Are not thine own so proper as to waste
Thyself upon thy virtues, they on thee.
Heaven doth with us as we with torches do,
Not light them for themselves; for if our virtues
Did not go forth of us, 'twere all alike   35
As if we had them not. Spirits are not finely touch'd
But to fine issues; nor Nature never lends
The smallest scruple of her excellence
But, like a thrifty goddess, she determines
Herself the glory of a creditor,   40
Both thanks and use. But I do bend my speech
To one that can my part in him advertise.
Hold, therefore, Angelo.
In our remove be thou at full ourself.
Mortality and mercy in Vienna   45
Live in thy tongue and heart. Old Escalus,
Though first in question, is thy secondary.
Take thy commission.
Ang.   Now, good my lord,
Let there be some more test made of my metal
Before so noble and so great a figure   50
Be stamp'd upon it.

99

Duke. No more evasion!
We have with a leaven'd and prepared choice
Proceeded to you. Therefore take your hon-
ours. [*Gives the commission.*]
Our haste from hence is of so quick condition
That it prefers itself, and leaves unquestion'd
Matters of needful value. We shall write to you,
As time and our concernings shall importune,
How it goes with us, and do look to know
What doth befall you here. So fare you well!
To th' hopeful execution do I leave you 60
Of your commissions.
Ang. Yet give leave, my lord,
That we may bring you something on the way.
Duke. My haste may not admit it;
Nor need you, on mine honour, have to do
With any scruple: your scope is as mine own,
So to enforce or qualify the laws 66
As to your soul seems good. Give me your hand.
I'll privily away. I love the people,
But do not like to stage me to their eyes.
Though it do well, I do not relish well 70
Their loud applause and ave's vehement;
Nor do I think the man of safe discretion
That does affect it. Once more fare you well.
Ang. The heavens give safety to your pur-
poses!
Escal. Lead forth and bring you back in
happiness! 75
Duke. I thank you. Fare you well. *Exit.*
Escal. I shall desire you, sir, to give me leave
To have free speech with you; and it concerns
me
To look into the bottom of my place.
A pow'r I have, but of what strength and na-
ture 80
I am not yet instructed.
Ang. 'Tis so with me. Let us withdraw to-
gether,
And we may soon our satisfaction have
Touching that point.
Escal. I'll wait upon your honour.
Exeunt.

Scene II. [*A street in Vienna.*]

Enter *Lucio* and two other *Gentlemen.*

Lucio. If the Duke, with the other dukes,
come not to composition with the King of Hungary, why then, all the dukes fall upon the King.
1. Gent. Heaven grant us its peace, but not
the King of Hungary's! 5
2. Gent. Amen.

Lucio. Thou conclud'st like the sanctimonious pirate, that went to sea with the Ten Com-
mandments, but scrap'd one out of the table.
2. Gent. 'Thou shalt not steal'? 10
Lucio. Ay, that he raz'd.
1. Gent. Why, 'twas a commandment to
command the captain and all the rest from
their functions: they put forth to steal. There's
not a soldier of us all that, in the thanksgiving
before meat, do relish the petition well that
prays for peace. 17
2. Gent. I never heard any soldier dislike it.
Lucio. I believe thee; for I think thou never
wast where grace was said. 20
2. Gent. No? A dozen times at least.
1. Gent. What? in metre?
Lucio. In any proportion or in any language.
1. Gent. I think, or in any religion. 24
Lucio. Ay, why not? Grace is grace, despite
of all controversy: as, for example, thou thyself art a wicked villain, despite of all grace.
1. Gent. Well, there went but a pair of shears
between us.
Lucio. I grant; as there may between the
lists and the velvet. Thou art the list. 31
1. Gent. And thou the velvet. Thou art good
velvet; thou'rt a three-pil'd piece, I warrant
thee. I had as lief be a list of an English kersey
as be pil'd, as thou art pil'd, for a French velvet.
Do I speak feelingly now? 36
Lucio. I think thou dost, and indeed with
most painful feeling of thy speech. I will, out of
thine own confession, learn to begin thy health,
but, whilst I live, forget to drink after thee. 40
1. Gent. I think I have done myself wrong,
have I not?
2. Gent. Yes, that thou hast, whether thou
art tainted or free.

Enter [*Mistress Overdone, the*] *Bawd.*

Lucio. Behold, behold, where Madam Mitigation comes! 45
1. Gent. I have purchas'd as many diseases
under her roof as come to —
2. Gent. To what, I pray?
Lucio. Judge.
2. Gent. To three thousand dolours a year.
1. Gent. Ay, and more. 51
Lucio. A French crown more.
1. Gent. Thou art always figuring diseases in
me; but thou art full of error — I am sound.
Lucio. Nay, not (as one would say) healthy,
but so sound as things that are hollow. Thy
bones are hollow; impiety has made a feast of
thee. 57

100

1. Gent. [*to Bawd*] How now? Which of your hips has the most profound sciatica?
Bawd. Well, well! there's one yonder arrested and carried to prison was worth five thousand of you all.   62
2. Gent. Who's that, I pray thee?
Bawd. Marry, sir, that's Claudio, Signior Claudio.   65
1. Gent. Claudio to prison? 'Tis not so.
Bawd. Nay, but I know 'tis so. I saw him arrested; saw him carried away; and, which is more, within these three days his head to be chopp'd off.   70
Lucio. But, after all this fooling, I would not have it so. Art thou sure of this?
Bawd. I am too sure of it; and it is for getting Madam Julietta with child.
Lucio. Believe me, this may be. He promis'd to meet me two hours since, and he was ever precise in promise-keeping.   77
2. Gent. Besides, you know, it draws something near to the speech we had to such a purpose.
1. Gent. But most of all, agreeing with the proclamation.   81
Lucio. Away! let's go learn the truth of it.
                          Exeunt [*Lucio and Gentlemen*].
Bawd. Thus, what with the war, what with the sweat, what with the gallows, and what with poverty, I am custom-shrunk.   85

Enter [*Pompey, the*] *Clown.*

How now? What's the news with you?
Pom. Yonder man is carried to prison.
Bawd. Well, what has he done?
Pom. A woman.
Bawd. But what's his offence?   90
Pom. Groping for trouts in a peculiar river.
Bawd. What, is there a maid with child by him?
Pom. No, but there's a woman with maid by him. You have not heard of the proclamation, have you?   96
Bawd. What proclamation, man?
Pom. All houses in the suburbs of Vienna must be pluck'd down.
Bawd. And what shall become of those in the city?   101
Pom. They shall stand for seed. They had gone down too but that a wise burgher put in for them.
Bawd. But shall all our houses of resort in the suburbs be pull'd down?   105
Pom. To the ground, mistress.

Bawd. Why, here's a change indeed in the commonwealth! What shall become of me?
Pom. Come, fear not you! Good counsellors lack no clients. Though you change your place, you need not change your trade. I'll be your tapster still. Courage! there will be pity taken on you. You that have worn your eyes almost out in the service, you will be considered.
Bawd. What's to do here, Thomas Tapster? Let's withdraw.   116
Pom. Here comes Signior Claudio, led by the provost to prison; and there's Madam Juliet.
                                      Exeunt.

Enter *Provost, Claudio, Juliet,* and *Officers.*
    Lucio and two *Gentlemen* [follow].

Claud. Fellow, why dost thou show me thus
    to th' world?   120
Bear me to prison, where I am committed.
Prov. I do it not in evil disposition,
But from Lord Angelo by special charge.
Claud. Thus can the demigod, Authority,
Make us pay down for our offence by weight
The words of heaven, on whom it will, it will;
On whom it will not, so; yet still 'tis just.
Lucio. Why, how now, Claudio? Whence
    comes this restraint?
Claud. From too much liberty, my Lucio,
    liberty.
As surfeit is the father of much fast,   130
So every scope by the immoderate use
Turns to restraint. Our natures do pursue,
Like rats that ravin down their proper bane,
A thirsty evil, and when we drink we die.   134
Lucio. If I could speak so wisely under an arrest, I would send for certain of my creditors. And yet, to say the truth, I had as lief have the foppery of freedom as the morality of imprisonment. What's thy offence, Claudio?
Claud. What but to speak of would offend
    again.   140
Lucio. What, is't murder?
Claud. No.
Lucio. Lechery?
Claud. Call it so.
Prov. Away, sir! you must go.   145
Claud. One word, good friend. — Lucio, a
    word with you.
Lucio. A hundred, if they'll do you any good.
Is lechery so look'd after?
Claud. Thus stands it with me: upon a true
    contract
I got possession of Julietta's bed.   150
You know the lady. She is fast my wife,
Save that we do the denunciation lack

Of outward order. This we came not to,
Only for propagation of a dow'r
Remaining in the coffer of her friends,   155
From whom we thought it meet to hide our
love
Till time had made them for us. But it
chances
The stealth of our most mutual entertainment
With character too gross is writ on Juliet.   159
  Lucio. With child, perhaps?
  Claud.   Unhappily, even so.
And the new deputy now for the Duke —
Whether it be the fault and glimpse of newness,
Or whether that the body public be
A horse whereon the governor doth ride,
Who, newly in the seat, that it may know   165
He can command, lets it straight feel the spur;
Whether the tyranny be in his place
Or in his eminence that fills it up,   ✳
I stagger in — but this new governor
Awakes me all the enrolled penalties   170
Which have, like unscour'd armour, hung by
th' wall
So long that nineteen zodiacs have gone round
And none of them been worn; and for a name
Now puts the drowsy and neglected act
Freshly on me. 'Tis surely for a name.   175
  Lucio. I warrant it is! and thy head stands
so tickle on thy shoulders that a milkmaid, if
she be in love, may sigh it off. Send after the
Duke and appeal to him.
  Claud. I have done so, but he's not to be
found.   180
I prithee, Lucio, do me this kind service:
This day my sister should the cloister enter
And there receive her approbation;
Acquaint her with the danger of my state;   184
Implore her, in my voice, that she make friends
To the strict deputy; bid herself assay him.
I have great hope in that; for in her youth
There is a prone and speechless dialect,
Such as move men. Beside, she hath prosperous
art   189
When she will play with reason and discourse,
And well she can persuade.
  Lucio. I pray she may; as well for the en-
couragement of the like, which else would stand
under grievous imposition, as for the enjoying
of thy life, who I would be sorry should be
thus foolishly lost at a game of tick-tack. I'll
to her.   196
  Claud. I thank you, good friend Lucio.
  Lucio. Within two hours.
  Claud.   Come, officer, away!
                                    Exeunt.

Scene III. [*A monastery.*]

Enter *Duke* and *Friar Thomas.*

  Duke. No, holy father! throw away that
thought.
Believe not that the dribbling dart of love
Can pierce a complete bosom. Why I desire
thee
To give me secret harbour hath a purpose
More grave and wrinkled than the aims and
ends   5
Of burning youth.
  Friar.   May your Grace speak of it?
  Duke. My holy sir, none better knows than
you
How I have ever lov'd the life removed
And held in idle price to haunt assemblies
Where youth and cost and witless bravery
keeps.   10
I have deliver'd to Lord Angelo
(A man of stricture and firm abstinence)
My absolute power and place here in Vienna,
And he supposes me travell'd to Poland;
For so I have strew'd it in the common ear   15
And so it is receiv'd. Now, pious sir,
You will demand of me why I do this.
  Friar. Gladly, my lord.
  Duke. We have strict statutes and most bit-
ing laws
(The needful bits and curbs to headstrong
steeds),   20
Which for this fourteen years we have let sleep,
Even like an o'ergrown lion in a cave,
That goes not out to prey. Now, as fond
fathers,
Having bound up the threat'ning twigs of birch,
Only to stick it in their children's sight   25
For terror, not to use, in time the rod
Becomes more mock'd than fear'd; so our de-
crees,
Dead to infliction, to themselves are dead,
And liberty plucks justice by the nose;
The baby beats the nurse, and quite athwart
Goes all decorum.
  Friar.   It rested in your Grace   31
To unloose this tied-up justice when you
pleas'd;
And it in you more dreadful would have seem'd
Than in Lord Angelo.
  Duke.   I do fear, too dreadful.
Sith 'twas my fault to give the people scope,
'Twould be my tyranny to strike and gall them
For what I bid them do. For we bid this be done
When evil deeds have their permissive pass

And not the punishment. Therefore, indeed,
  my father,
I have on Angelo impos'd the office,   40
Who may in th' ambush of my name strike
  home,
And yet my nature never in the fight
To do it slander. And to behold his sway,
I will, as 'twere a brother of your order,
Visit both prince and people. Therefore I
  prithee   45
Supply me with the habit, and instruct me
How I may formally in person bear
Like a true friar. Moe reasons for this action
At our more leisure shall I render you;
Only, this one: Lord Angelo is precise,   50
Stands at a guard with envy, scarce confesses
That his blood flows or that his appetite
Is more to bread than stone; hence shall we see,
If power change purpose, what our seemers be.
                             Exeunt.

Scene IV. [*A nunnery.*]

Enter Isabella and Francisca (a Nun).

Isab. And have you nuns no farther privi-
  leges?
Nun. Are not these large enough?
Isab. Yes, truly; I speak not as desiring more,
But rather wishing a more strict restraint
Upon the sisterhood, the votarists of Saint
  Clare.   5
Lucio. (*within*) Ho! Peace be in this place!
Isab. Who's that which calls?
Nun. It is a man's voice. Gentle Isabella,
Turn you the key and know his business of him.
You may; I may not. You are yet unsworn.
When you have vow'd, you must not speak with
  men   10
But in the presence of the prioress;
Then if you speak, you must not show your face,
Or if you show your face, you must not speak.
He calls again. I pray you answer him. [*Exit.*]
Isab. Peace and prosperity! Who is't that
  calls?   15

        [*Enter Lucio.*]

Lucio. Hail, virgin, if you be — as those
  cheek-roses
Proclaim you are no less. Can you so stead me
As bring me to the sight of Isabella,
A novice of this place, and the fair sister
To her unhappy brother Claudio?   20
Isab. Why 'her unhappy brother'? Let me
  ask,

The rather for I now must make you know
I am that Isabella, and his sister.
Lucio. Gentle and fair, your brother kindly
  greets you.
Not to be weary with you, he's in prison.   25
Isab. Woe me! for what?
Lucio. For that which, if myself might be
  his judge,
He should receive his punishment in thanks.
He hath got his friend with child.
Isab. Sir, make me not your story.
Lucio.   It is true.   30
I would not — though 'tis my familiar sin
With maids to seem the lapwing, and to jest,
Tongue far from heart — play with all virgins
  so.
I hold you as a thing enskied and sainted
By your renouncement, an immortal spirit,   35
And to be talk'd with in sincerity,
As with a saint.
Isab. You do blaspheme the good in mocking
  me.
Lucio. Do not believe it. Fewness and truth,
'tis thus:
Your brother and his lover have embrac'd.   40
As those that feed grow full; as blossoming
  time,
That from the seedness the bare fallow brings
To teeming foison — even so her plenteous
  womb
Expresseth his full tilth and husbandry.
Isab. Some one with child by him? my
  cousin Juliet?   45
Lucio. Is she your cousin?
Isab. Adoptedly, as school-maids change
  their names
By vain though apt affection.
Lucio.   She it is.
Isab. O, let him marry her!
Lucio.   This is the point.
The Duke is very strangely gone from hence;
Bore many gentlemen (myself being one)   51
In hand, and hope of action; but we do learn
By those that know the very nerves of state,
His givings-out were of an infinite distance
From his true-meant design. Upon his place,   56
And with full line of his authority,
Governs Lord Angelo — a man whose blood
Is very snow-broth; one who never feels
The wanton stings and motions of the sense,   60
But doth rebate and blunt his natural edge
With profits of the mind, study and fast.
He (to give fear to use and liberty,
Which have for long run by the hideous law,
As mice by lions) hath pick'd out an act

Under whose heavy sense your brother's life
Falls into forfeit. He arrests him on it,   66
And follows close the rigour of the statute
To make him an example. All hope is gone,
Unless you have the grace by your fair
    prayer
To soften Angelo. And that's my pith of busi-
    ness   70
'Twixt you and your poor brother.
  Isab. Doth he so seek his life?
  Lucio.   Has censur'd him
Already, and, as I hear, the provost hath
A warrant for his execution.
  Isab. Alas, what poor ability 's in me   75
To do him good?
  Lucio.   Assay the pow'r you have.
  Isab. My power? Alas, I doubt —

  Lucio.   Our doubts are traitors
And make us lose the good we oft might win
By fearing to attempt. Go to Lord Angelo
And let him learn to know, when maidens sue
Men give like gods; but when they weep and
    kneel,   81
All their petitions are as freely theirs
As they themselves would owe them.
  Isab. I'll see what I can do.
  Lucio.   But speedily!
  Isab. I will about it straight,   85
No longer staying but to give the Mother
Notice of my affair. I humbly thank you.
Commend me to my brother. Soon at night
I'll send him certain word of my success.
  Lucio. I take my leave of you.
  Isab.   Good sir, adieu. *Exeunt.*

ACT II. Scene I. [*A hall in* Angelo's *house.*]

Enter *Angelo, Escalus,* and *Servants*; *Justice.*

  Ang. We must not make a scarecrow of the
    law,
Setting it up to fear the birds of prey,
And let it keep one shape till custom make it
Their perch, and not their terror.
  Escal.   Ay, but yet
Let us be keen, and rather cut a little   5
Than fall and bruise to death. Alas, this gentle-
    man
Whom I would save had a most noble father!
Let but your honour know
(Whom I believe to be most strait in virtue)
That, in the working of your own affections —
Had time coher'd with place, or place with
    wishing,   11
Or that the resolute acting of your blood
Could have attain'd th' effect of your own pur-
    pose,
Whether you had not sometime in your life
Err'd in this point which now you censure him
And pull'd the law upon you.   16
  Ang. 'Tis one thing to be tempted, Escalus,
Another thing to fall. I not deny
The jury, passing on the prisoner's life,
May in the sworn twelve have a thief or two
Guiltier than him they try. What's open made
    to justice,   21
That justice seizes. What knows the law
That thieves do pass on thieves? 'Tis very
    pregnant,
The jewel that we find, we stoop and take't,
Because we see it; but what we do not see   25

We tread upon and never think of it.
You may not so extenuate his offence
For I have had such faults; but rather tell me,
When I that censure him do so offend,   29
Let mine own judgment pattern out my death,
And nothing come in partial. Sir, he must die.
  Escal. Be it as your wisdom will.

Enter *Provost.*

  Ang.   Where is the provost?
  Prov. Here, if it like your honour.
  Ang.   See that Claudio
Be executed by nine to-morrow morning.
Bring him his confessor, let him be prepar'd;
For that's the utmost of his pilgrimage.   36
                  [*Exit Provost.*]
  Escal. Well, heaven forgive him! and for-
    give us all!
Some rise by sin, and some by virtue fall.
Some run from brakes of vice, and answer none;
And some condemned for a fault alone.   40

Enter *Elbow, Froth,* [*Pompey, the*] *Clown,*
              Officers.

  Elb. Come, bring them away. If these be
good people in a commonweal that do nothing
but use their abuses in common houses, I know
no law. Bring them away.
  Ang. How now, sir! What's your name?
and what's the matter?   46
  Elb. If it please your honour, I am the poor
Duke's constable, and my name is Elbow. I do
lean upon justice, sir, and do bring in here before your good honour two notorious benefactors.

Ang. Benefactors? Well, what benefactors are they? Are they not malefactors? 52

Elb. If it please your honour, I know not well what they are; but precise villains they are, that I am sure of, and void of all profanation in the world that good Christians ought to have.

Escal. This comes off well. Here's a wise officer.

Ang. Go to. What quality are they of? Elbow is your name? Why dost thou not speak, Elbow? 60

Pom. He cannot, sir. He's out at elbow.

Ang. What are you, sir?

Elb. He, sir? A tapster, sir; parcel-bawd; one that serves a bad woman, whose house, sir, was, as they say, pluck'd down in the suburbs; and now she professes a hothouse, which, I think, is a very ill house too.

Escal. How know you that?

Elb. My wife, sir, whom I detest before heaven and your honour — 70

Escal. How? thy wife?

Elb. Ay, sir; whom I thank heaven is an honest woman.

Escal. Dost thou detest her therefore? 74

Elb. I say, sir, I will detest myself also, as well as she, that this house, if it be not a bawd's house, it is pity of her life, for it is a naughty house.

Escal. How dost thou know that, constable?

Elb. Marry, sir, by my wife, who, if she had been a woman cardinally given, might have been accus'd in fornication, adultery, and all uncleanliness there.

Escal. By the woman's means? 84

Elb. Ay, sir, by Mistress Overdone's means. But as she spit in his face, so she defied him.

Pom. Sir, if it please your honour, this is not so.

Elb. Prove it before these varlets here, thou honourable man; prove it.

Escal. [to Angelo] Do you hear how he misplaces? 90

Pom. Sir, she came in great with child; and longing (saving your honour's reverence) for stew'd prunes. Sir, we had but two in the house, which at that very distant time stood, as it were, in a fruit dish — a dish of some threepence. Your honours have seen such dishes; they are not China dishes, but very good dishes. 97

Escal. Go to, go to! No matter for the dish, sir.

Pom. No, indeed, sir, not of a pin! You are therein in the right. But to the point. As I say, this Mistress Elbow, being (as I say) with child, and being great-bellied, and longing (as I said) for prunes; and having but two in the dish (as I said), Master Froth here, this very man, having eaten the rest (as I said) and (as I say) paying for them very honestly; for, as you know, Master Froth, I could not give you three-pence again — 107

Froth. No indeed.

Pom. Very well. You being then (if you be remember'red) cracking the stones of the foresaid prunes — 111

Froth. Ay, so I did indeed.

Pom. Why, very well. I telling you then (if you be remember'red) that such a one and such a one were past cure of the thing you wot of, unless they kept very good diet, as I told you —

Froth. All this is true. 117

Pom. Why, very well, then.

Escal. Come, you are a tedious fool. To the purpose! What was done to Elbow's wife that he hath cause to complain of? Come me to what was done to her. 122

Pom. Sir, your honour cannot come to that yet.

Escal. No, sir, nor I mean it not.

Pom. Sir, but you shall come to it, by your honour's leave. And I beseech you, look into Master Froth here, sir, a man of fourscore pound a year, whose father died at Hallowmas. Was't not at Hallowmas, Master Froth?

Froth. All-hallond eve. 130

Pom. Why, very well. I hope here be truths. He, sir, sitting (as I say) in a lower chair, sir — 'twas in the Bunch of Grapes, where, indeed, you have a delight to sit, have you not?

Froth. I have so, because it is an open room, and good for winter. 136

Pom. Why, very well then. I hope here be truths.

Ang. This will last out a night in Russia When nights are longest there. I'll take my leave 140 And leave you to the hearing of the cause, Hoping you'll find good cause to whip them all.

Escal. I think no less. Good morrow to your lordship.   *Exit [Angelo].*
Now, sir, come on. What was done to Elbow's wife, once more? 145

Pom. Once, sir? There was nothing done to her once.

Elb. I beseech you, sir, ask him what this man did to my wife.

Pom. I beseech your honour, ask me. 150

Escal. Well, sir, what did this gentleman to her?

Pom. I beseech you, sir, look in this gentleman's face. Good Master Froth, look upon his honour; 'tis for a good purpose. Doth your honour mark his face? 156

Escal. Ay, sir, very well.

Pom. Nay, I beseech you mark it well.

Escal. Well, I do so.

Pom. Doth your honour see any harm in his face? 161

Escal. Why, no.

Pom. I'll be suppos'd upon a book his face is the worst thing about him. Good then. If his face be the worst thing about him, how could Master Froth do the constable's wife any harm? I would know that of your honour. 167

Escal. He's in the right, constable. What say you to it?

Elb. First, an it like you, the house is a respected house; next, this is a respected fellow; and his mistress is a respected woman. 172

Pom. By this hand, sir, his wife is a more respected person than any of us all.

Elb. Varlet, thou liest! Thou liest, wicked varlet! The time is yet to come that she was ever respected with man, woman, or child.

Pom. Sir, she was respected with him before he married with her.

Escal. Which is the wiser here, Justice or Iniquity? Is this true? 181

Elb. O thou caitiff! O thou varlet! O thou wicked Hannibal! I respected with her before I was married to her? If ever I was respected with her, or she with me, let not your worship think me the poor Duke's officer. Prove this, thou wicked Hannibal, or I'll have mine action of batt'ry on thee.

Escal. If he took you a box o' th' ear, you might have your action of slander too. 190

Elb. Marry, I thank your good worship for it. What is't your worship's pleasure I shall do with this wicked caitiff?

Escal. Truly, officer, because he hath some offences in him that thou wouldst discover if thou couldst, let him continue in his courses till thou know'st what they are. 197

Elb. Marry, I thank your worship for it. Thou seest, thou wicked varlet now, what's come upon thee! Thou art to continue now, thou varlet; thou art to continue. 201

Escal. [to *Froth*] Where were you born, friend?

Froth. Here in Vienna, sir.

Escal. Are you of fourscore pounds a year?

Froth. Yes, an't please you, sir. 205

Escal. So. — [*To Pompey*] What trade are you of, sir?

Pom. A tapster, a poor widow's tapster.

Escal. Your mistress' name?

Pom. Mistress Overdone.

Escal. Hath she had any more than one husband? 211

Pom. Nine, sir. Overdone by the last.

Escal. Nine? Come hither to me, Master Froth. Master Froth, I would not have you acquainted with tapsters. They will draw you, Master Froth, and you will hang them. Get you gone, and let me hear no more of you.

Froth. I thank your worship. For mine own part, I never come into any room in a taphouse but I am drawn in. 220

Escal. Well, no more of it, Master Froth! Farewell. [*Exit Froth.*] Come you hither to me, Master Tapster. What's your name, Master Tapster?

Pom. Pompey. 225

Escal. What else?

Pom. Bum, sir.

Escal. Troth, and your bum is the greatest thing about you, so that, in the beastliest sense, you are Pompey the Great. Pompey, you are partly a bawd, Pompey, howsoever you colour it in being a tapster, are you not? Come, tell me true; it shall be the better for you.

Pom. Truly, sir, I am a poor fellow that would live. 235

Escal. How would you live, Pompey? By being a bawd? What do you think of the trade, Pompey? Is it a lawful trade?

Pom. If the law would allow it, sir.

Escal. But the law will not allow it, Pompey; nor it shall not be allowed in Vienna. 241

Pom. Does your worship mean to geld and splay all the youth of the city?

Escal. No, Pompey.

Pom. Truly, sir, in my poor opinion, they will to 't then. If your worship will take order for the drabs and the knaves, you need not to fear the bawds.

Escal. There is pretty orders beginning, I can tell you. It is but heading and hanging. 250

Pom. If you head and hang all that offend that way but for ten year together, you'll be glad to give out a commission for more heads. If this law hold in Vienna ten year, I'll rent the fairest house in it after threepence a bay. If you live to see this come to pass, say Pompey told you so. 257

Escal. Thank you, good Pompey; and in requital of your prophecy, hark you: I advise you let me not find you before me again upon any complaint whatsoever; no, not for dwelling

Vincentio (Harry Andrews), the eccentric duke of
Vienna, in his disguise as a monk

MEASURE
FOR
MEASURE

John Gielgud as the duke's lieutenant, Angelo,
who learns that justice must be meted out with
mercy—"measure for measure"

PHOTOGRAPHS BY ANGUS MC BEAN
PRODUCED BY MEMORIAL THEATRE COMPANY
STRATFORD-UPON-AVON

"In our remove be thou at full ourself." Supposedly about to absent himself from Vienna, the duke empowers Angelo to serve as his agent (*Act I, Scene I*)

"Most dangerous is that temptation that doth goad us on to sin in loving virtue." Angelo's soliloquy on his motives in dealing with Isabella (*Act II, Scene II*)

"Shall all our houses of resort in the suburbs be pulled down?" The bawd, Mistress Overdone (Rosalind Atkinson), asks her tapster, Pompey (George Rose), for details about the new proclamation (*Act I, Scene II*)

"I am the poor duke's constable." Elbow (Michael Bates), a simple-minded arm of the law, calls his prisoners Froth (Geoffrey Bayldon) and Pompey "notorious benefactors" (Act II, Scene 1)

Left: "Why, very well: I hope here be truths." Affecting candor, Pompey delays the interrogation by Escalus (Harold Kasket), who shares power with Angelo as the duke's deputy (Act II, Scene I)

Below: Juliet (Hazel Penwarden) and her lover, Claudio (Alan Badel), both charged with immorality, meet before the prison (Act I, Scene II)

"Supply me with the habit, and instruct me how I may formally in person bear me like a true friar." Wishing to look into Angelo's ways, the duke asks Friar Thomas (Cyril Conway) to disguise him (Act I, Scene III)

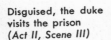

Disguised, the duke visits the prison (Act II, Scene III)

"A very superficial, ignorant, unweighing fellow." Not recognizing Vincentio in his disguise, Lucio (Leon Quartermaine) pretends to be on intimate terms with the duke and proceeds to pick his character to pieces (Act III, Scene II)

"Love you the man th[at]
wrong'd you?" On h[is]
way to visit Claudio [in]
his cell, Vincentio mee[ts]
the youth's mistress, th[e]
lovely Juliet
(Act II, Scene III)

"Be absolute for death; either death or life
shall thereby be the sweeter." The duke tries
to persuade Claudio to accept his fate and to
expect the worst (Act III, Scene I)

"Spare him, spare him! He's not prepar'd for
death." Isabella (Barbara Jefford) begs
Angelo for her brother's life (Act II, Scene II)

Above: "Be ready, Claudio, for your death to-morrow." Isabella tells her brother that his life would cost her her virtue, a condition she cannot accept. The duke listens undetected (*Act III, Scene I*)

"His head is off and sent to Angelo." To intensify the dénouement, the duke lets Isabella believe that Claudio is dead (*Act IV, Scene III*)

The duke comes upon Mariana (Maxine Audley), the woman whom Angelo abandoned long ago (*Act IV, Scene I*)

"This other doth command a little door which from the vineyard to the garden leads." Isabella instructs Mariana on her rendezvous with the fickle Angelo, her former lover (Act IV, Scene I)

"I will not consent to die this day, that's certain." Barnardine (Paul Hardwick), an extraordinary tosspot, declares he is still too drunk to be hanged (Act IV, Scene III)

"O heavens! what stuff is here?" The duke is shocked to behold the misery and vice of his subjects (Act III, Scene II)

"O my dear lord! I crave no other, nor no better man." Mariana will accept no substitute for Angelo, though he once abandoned her because her dowry was too small (Act V, Scene 1)

Through the efforts of the duke, Mariana and Angelo are reconciled (Act V, Scene 1)

where you do. If I do, Pompey, I shall beat you
to your tent and prove a shrewd Cæsar to you:
in plain dealing, Pompey, I shall have you
whipt. So, for this time, Pompey, fare you well.
Pom. I thank your worship for your good
counsel. [*Aside*] But I shall follow it as the flesh
and fortune shall better determine.
Whip me? No, no! Let carman whip his jade;
The valiant heart's not whipt out of his trade.
Exit.
Escal. Come hither to me, Master Elbow.
Come hither, Master Constable. How long
have you been in this place of constable?
Elb. Seven year and a half, sir. 274
Escal. I thought, by your readiness in the
office, you had continued in it some time. You
say seven years together?
Elb. And a half, sir.
Escal. Alas, it hath been great pains to you!
They do you wrong to put you so oft upon't.
Are there not men in your ward sufficient to
serve it? 281
Elb. Faith, sir, few of any wit in such mat-
ters. As they are chosen, they are glad to choose
me for them. I do it for some piece of money,
and go through with all. 285
Escal. Look you bring me in the names of
some six or seven, the most sufficient of your
parish.
Elb. To your worship's house, sir?
Escal. To my house. Fare you well.
[*Exit Elbow.*]
What's o'clock, think you? 290
Justice. Eleven, sir.
Escal. I pray you home to dinner with me.
Justice. I humbly thank you.
Escal. It grieves me for the death of Claudio;
But there's no remedy. 295
Justice. Lord Angelo is severe.
Escal. It is but needful.
Mercy is not itself that oft looks so.
Pardon is still the nurse of second woe.
But yet — poor Claudio! There is no remedy.
Come, sir. *Exeunt.*

Scene II. [*Another room in* Angelo's *house.*]

Enter *Provost, Servant.*

Serv. He's hearing of a cause. He will come
straight.
I'll tell him of you.
Prov. Pray you do. [*Exit Servant.*]
I'll know

His pleasure. May be he will relent. Alas,
He hath but as offended in a dream! 4
All sects, all ages smack of this vice — and he
To die for't!

Enter *Angelo.*

Ang. Now, what's the matter, provost?
Prov. Is it your will Claudio shall die to-
morrow?
Ang. Did not I tell thee yea? Hadst thou
not order?
Why dost thou ask again?
Prov. Lest I might be too rash.
Under your good correction, I have seen 10
When, after execution, judgment hath
Repented o'er his doom.
Ang. Go to! let that be mine.
Do you your office, or give up your place,
And you shall well be spar'd.
Prov. I crave your honour's pardon.
What shall be done, sir, with the groaning
Juliet? 15
She's very near her hour.
Ang. Dispose of her
To some more fitter place, and that with speed.

[Enter *Servant.*]

Serv. Here is the sister of the man condemn'd
Desires access to you.
Ang. Hath he a sister?
Prov. Ay, my good lord, a very virtuous
maid, 20
And to be shortly of a sisterhood,
If not already.
Ang. Well, let her be admitted.
[*Exit Servant.*]
See you the fornicatress be remov'd.
Let her have needful but not lavish means;
There shall be order for't.

Enter *Lucio* and *Isabella.*

Prov. God save your honour! 25
[*Going.*]
Ang. Stay a little while. — [*To Isabella*]
Y'are welcome. What's your will?
Isab. I am a woful suitor to your honour,
Please but your honour hear me.
Ang. Well, what's your suit?
Isab. There is a vice that most I do abhor
And most desire should meet the blow of jus-
tice; 30
For which I would not plead, but that I must;
For which I must not plead, but that I am
At war 'twixt will and will not.
Ang. Well, the matter?

Isab. I have a brother is condemn'd to die.
I do beseech you, let it be his fault, 35
And not my brother.
Prov. [*aside*]   Heaven give thee moving
graces!
Ang. Condemn the fault, and not the actor
of it?
Why, every fault's condemn'd ere it be done.
Mine were the very cipher of a function, 39
To fine the faults whose fine stands in record,
And let go by the actor.
Isab.   O just but severe law!
I had a brother, then. — Heaven keep your
honour!   [*Going.*]
Lucio. [*aside to Isabella*] Give't not o'er so.
To him again! entreat him,
Kneel down before him, hang upon his gown!
You are too cold. If you should need a pin, 45
You could not with more tame a tongue desire
it.
To him, I say!
Isab. Must he needs die?
Ang.   Maiden, no remedy.
Isab. Yes; I do think that you might par-
don him
And neither heaven nor man grieve at the
mercy. 50
Ang. I will not do't.
Isab.   But can you, if you would?
Ang. Look, what I will not, that I cannot do.
Isab. But might you do't, and do the world
no wrong,
If so your heart were touch'd with that remorse
As mine is to him?
Ang.   He's sentenc'd; 'tis too late. 55
Lucio. [*aside to Isabella*] You are too cold.
Isab. Too late? Why, no! I, that do speak
a word,
May call it back again. Well, believe this:
No ceremony that to great ones 'longs,
Not the king's crown nor the deputed sword, 60
The marshal's truncheon nor the judge's robe,
Become them with one half so good a grace
As mercy does.
If he had been as you, and you as he,
You would have slipp'd like him, but he like
you 65
Would not have been so stern.
Ang.   Pray you be gone.
Isab. I would to heaven I had your potency
And you were Isabel! Should it then be thus?
No! I would tell what 'twere to be a judge,
And what a prisoner.
Lucio. [*aside to Isabella*] Ay, touch him!
There's the vein. 70

Ang. Your brother is a forfeit of the law,
And you but waste your words.
Isab.   Alas, alas!
Why, all the souls that were were forfeit once,
And he that might the vantage best have took
Found out the remedy. How would you be 75
If he which is the top of judgment should
But judge you as you are? O, think on that!
And mercy then will breathe within your lips
Like man new made.
Ang.   Be you content, fair maid.
It is the law, not I, condemn your brother. 80
Were he my kinsman, brother, or my son,
It should be thus with him. He must die to-
morrow.
Isab. To-morrow? O, that's sudden! Spare
him, spare him!
He's not prepar'd for death. Even for oun
kitchens
We kill the fowl of season. Shall we serve
heaven 85
With less respect than we ao minister
To our gross selves? Good, good my lord, be-
think you!
Who is it that hath died for this offence?
There's many have committed it.
Lucio. [*aside*]   Ay, well said.
Ang. The law hath not been dead, though it
hath slept. 90
Those many had not dar'd to do that evil
If that the first that did th' edict infringe
Had answer'd for his deed. Now 'tis awake,
Takes note of what is done, and like a prophet
Looks in a glass that shows what future evils —
Either new, or by remissness new conceiv'd, 96
And so in progress to be hatch'd and born —
Are now to have no successive degrees,
But, ere they live, to end.
Isab.   Yet show some pity.
Ang. I show it most of all when I show jus-
tice; 100
For then I pity those I do not know,
Which a dismiss'd offence would after gall,
And do him right that, answering one foul
wrong,
Lives not to act another. Be satisfied.
Your brother dies to-morrow. Be content. 105
Isab. So you must be the first that gives this
sentence,
And he, that suffers. O, it is excellent
To have a giant's strength; but it is tyrannous
To use it like a giant.
Lucio. [*aside*]   That's well said.
Isab. Could great men thunder 110
As Jove himself does, Jove would ne'er be quiet,

For every pelting petty officer
Would use his heaven for thunder — nothing
  but thunder!
Merciful heaven,
Thou rather with thy sharp and sulphurous bolt
Split'st the unwedgeable and gnarled oak   116
Than the soft myrtle. But man, proud man,
Drest in a little brief authority,
Most ignorant of what he's most assur'd
(His glassy essence), like an angry ape,   120
Plays such fantastic tricks before high heaven
As make the angels weep; who, with our
  spleens,
Would all themselves laugh mortal.
Lucio. [*aside to Isabella*] O, to him, to him,
  wench! He will relent;
He's coming. I perceive't.
Prov. [*aside*]   Pray heaven she win him
Isab. We cannot weigh our brother with
  ourself.   126
Great men may jest with saints. 'Tis wit in
  them,
But in the less, foul profanation.
Lucio. [*aside to Isabella*] Thou'rt i' th' right,
  girl. More o' that!
Isab. That in the captain's but a choleric
  word   130
Which in the soldier is flat blasphemy.
Lucio. [*aside to Isabella*] Art avis'd o' that?
  More on't!
Ang. Why do you put these sayings upon me?
Isab. Because authority, though it err like
  others,
Hath yet a kind of medicine in itself   135
That skins the vice o' th' top. Go to your
  bosom,
Knock there, and ask your heart what it doth
  know
That's like my brother's fault. If it confess
A natural guiltiness such as is his,   139
Let it not sound a thought upon your tongue
Against my brother's life.
Ang. [*aside*]   She speaks, and 'tis
Such sense that my sense breeds with it. —
  Fare you well.
Isab. Gentle my lord, turn back.
Ang. I will bethink me. Come again to-
  morrow.
Isab. Hark how I'll bribe you! Good my
  lord, turn back.   145
Ang. How? bribe me?
Isab. Ay, with such gifts that heaven shall
  share with you.
Lucio. [*aside to Isabella*] You had marr'd all
  else.

Isab. Not with fond sicles of the tested gold,
Or stones whose rates are either rich or poor 150
As fancy values them; but with true prayers,
That shall be up at heaven and enter there
Ere sunrise — prayers from preserved souls,
From fasting maids whose minds are dedicate
To nothing temporal.
Ang.   Well, come to me to-morrow.
Lucio. [*aside to Isabella*] Go to! 'Tis well;
  away!   156
Isab. Heaven keep your honour safe!
Ang. [*aside*]   Amen; for I
Am that way going to temptation
Where prayers cross.
Isab.   At what hour to-morrow
Shall I attend your lordship?   160
Ang. At any time fore noon.
Isab.   God save your honour!
                    [*Exeunt all but Angelo.*]
Ang. From thee! even from thy virtue!
What's this? what's this? Is this her fault, or
  mine?
The tempter, or the tempted, who sins most,
  ha?
Not she. Nor doth she tempt. But it is I 165
That, lying with the violet in the sun,
Do as the carrion does, not as the flow'r,
Corrupt with virtuous season. Can it be
That modesty may more betray our sense
Than woman's lightness? Having waste ground
  enough,   170
Shall we desire to raze the sanctuary,
And pitch our evils there? O, fie, fie, fie!
What dost thou? or what art thou, Angelo?
Dost thou desire her foully for those things
That make her good? O, let her brother
  live!
Thieves for their robbery have authority 176
When judges steal themselves. What, do I love
  her,
That I desire to hear her speak again?
And feast upon her eyes? What is't I dream
  on?
O cunning enemy, that, to catch a saint,   180
With saints dost bait thy hook! Most danger-
  ous
Is that temptation that doth goad us on
To sin in loving virtue. Never could the
  strumpet,
With all her double vigour — art and na-
  ture —
Once stir my temper; but this virtuous maid
Subdues me quite. Ever till now,   186
When men were fond, I smil'd, and wond'red
  how.   *Exit.*

Scene III. [*A prison.*]

Enter *Duke* [disguised as a *friar,*] and *Provost.*

Duke. Hail to you, provost! So I think you are.
Prov. I am the provost. What's your will,
good friar?
Duke. Bound by my charity and my blest
order,
I come to visit the afflicted spirits
Here in the prison. Do me the common right 5
To let me see them, and to make me know
The nature of their crimes, that I may minister
To them accordingly.
Prov. I would do more than that, if more
were needful. 9

Enter *Juliet.*

Look, here comes one — a gentlewoman of mine,
Who, falling in the flaws of her own youth,
Hath blister'd her report. She is with child,
And he that got it, sentenc'd — a young man
More fit to do another such offence
Than die for this. 15
Duke. When must he die?
Prov. As I do think, to-morrow.
[*To Juliet*] I have provided for you. Stay awhile,
And you shall be conducted.
Duke. Repent you, fair one, of the sin you
carry?
Jul. I do, and bear the shame most pa-
tiently. 20
Duke. I'll teach you how you shall arraign
your conscience,
And try your penitence, if it be sound
Or hollowly put on.
Jul. I'll gladly learn.
Duke. Love you the man that wrong'd you?
Jul. Yes, as I love the woman that wrong'd
him. 25
Duke. So then it seems your most offenceful
act
Was mutually committed.
Jul. Mutually.
Duke. Then was your sin of heavier kind
than his.
Jul. I do confess it and repent it, father.
Duke. 'Tis meet so, daughter; but lest you
do repent 30
As that the sin hath brought you to this
shame —
Which sorrow is always toward ourselves, not
heaven,
Showing we would not spare heaven as we love it,
But as we stand in fear —

Jul. I do repent me as it is an evil, 35
And take the shame with joy.
Duke. There rest.
Your partner, as I hear, must die to-morrow,
And I am going with instruction to him.
Grace go with you! Benedicite! *Exit.*
Jul. Must die to-morrow? O injurious law,
That respites me a life whose very comfort 41
Is still a dying horror!
Prov. 'Tis pity of him. *Exeunt.*

Scene IV. [Angelo's *house.*]

Enter *Angelo.*

Ang. When I would pray and think, I think
and pray
To several subjects. Heaven hath my empty
words,
Whilst my invention, hearing not my tongue,
Anchors on Isabel. Heaven in my mouth,
As if I did but only chew his name, 5
And in my heart the strong and swelling evil
Of my conception! The state, whereon I
studied,
Is, like a good thing being often read,
Grown sere and tedious. Yea, my gravity,
Wherein (let no man hear me) I take pride, 10
Could I, with boot, change for an idle plume
Which the air beats for vain. O place, O form,
How often dost thou with thy case, thy habit,
Wrench awe from fools, and tie the wiser souls
To thy false seeming! Blood, thou art blood!
Let's write 'good angel' on the devil's horn, 16
'Tis not the devil's crest.

Enter *Servant.*

How now? Who's there?
Serv. One Isabel, a sister, desires access to
you.
Ang. Teach her the way. [*Exit Servant.*]
O heavens!
Why does my blood thus muster to my heart,
Making both it unable for itself 21
And dispossessing all my other parts
Of necessary fitness?
So play the foolish throngs with one that
swounds —
Come all to help him, and so stop the air 25
By which he should revive; and even so
The general, subject to a well-wish'd king,
Quit their own part, and in obsequious fondness
Crowd to his presence, where their untaught love
Must needs appear offence.

110

Enter *Isabella*.

How now, fair maid?

Isab. I am come to know your pleasure. 31

Ang. That you might know it, would much
  better please me
Than to demand what 'tis. Your brother cannot live.

Isab. Even so. — Heaven keep your honour!
  [*Going.*]

Ang. Yet may he live awhile; and, it may
  be, 35
As long as you or I. Yet he must die.

Isab. Under your sentence?

Ang. Yea.

Isab. When, I beseech you? that in his re-
  prieve,
Longer or shorter, he may be so fitted 40
That his soul sicken not.

Ang. Ha! fie, these filthy vices! It were as
  good
To pardon him that hath from nature stol'n
A man already made, as to remit
Their saucy sweetness that do coin heaven's
  image 45
In stamps that are forbid. 'Tis all as easy
Falsely to take away a life true made
As to put metal in restrained means
To make a false one.

Isab. 'Tis set down so in heaven, but not in
  earth. 50

Ang. Say you so? Then I shall pose you
  quickly.
Which had you rather — that the most just law
Now took your brother's life or, to redeem him,
Give up your body to such sweet uncleanness
As she that he hath stain'd?

Isab.   Sir, believe this:
I had rather give my body than my soul. 56

Ang. I talk not of your soul. Our compell'd
  sins
Stand more for number than for accompt.

Isab.   How say you?

Ang. Nay, I'll not warrant that; for I can
  speak
Against the thing I say. Answer to this: 60
I (now the voice of the recorded law)
Pronounce a sentence on your brother's life:
Might there not be a charity in sin
To save this brother's life?

Isab.   Please you to do't,
I'll take it as a peril to my soul, 65
It is no sin at all, but charity.

Ang. Pleas'd you to do't at peril of your soul,
Were equal poise of sin and charity.

Isab. That I do beg his life, if it be sin,
Heaven let me bear it! You granting of my suit,
If that be sin, I'll make it my morn prayer 71
To have it added to the faults of mine
And nothing of your answer.

Ang.   Nay, but hear me.
Your sense pursues not mine. Either you are
  ignorant,
Or seem so, craftily; and that's not good. 75

Isab. Let me be ignorant, and in nothing good
But graciously to know I am no better.

Ang. Thus wisdom wishes to appear most
  bright
When it doth tax itself; as these black masks
Proclaim enshielded beauty ten times louder 80
Than beauty could, display'd. But mark me:
To be received plain, I'll speak more gross.
Your brother is to die.

Isab. So.

Ang. And his offence is so as it appears 85
Accountant to the law upon that pain.

Isab. True.

Ang. Admit no other way to save his life
(As I subscribe not that, nor any other,
But in the loose of question) that you, his sister,
Finding yourself desir'd of such a person 91
Whose credit with the judge, or own great
  place,
Could fetch your brother from the manacles
Of the all-binding law, and that there were
No earthly mean to save him but that either 95
You must lay down the treasures of your body
To this suppos'd, or else to let him suffer:
What would you do?

Isab. As much for my poor brother as myself.
That is, were I under the terms of death, 100
Th' impression of keen whips I'ld wear as
  rubies,
And strip myself to death as to a bed
That longings have been sick for, ere I'ld yield
My body up to shame.

Ang.   Then must
Your brother die.

Isab.   And 'twere the cheaper way.
Better it were a brother died at once 106
Than that a sister, by redeeming him,
Should die for ever.

Ang. Were not you then as cruel as the sentence
That you have slander'd so? 110

Isab. Ignomy in ransom and free pardon
Are of two houses. Lawful mercy
Is nothing kin to foul redemption.

Ang. You seem'd of late to make the law a
  tyrant,

And rather prov'd the sliding of your brother
A merriment than a vice.   116
Isab. O, pardon me, my lord! It oft falls out
To have what we would have, we speak not
what we mean.
I something do excuse the thing I hate
For his advantage that I dearly love.   120
Ang. We are all frail.
Isab.   Else let my brother die,
If not a fedary but only he
Owe and succeed thy weakness.
Ang. Nay, women are frail too.
Isab. Ay, as the glasses where they view
themselves,   125
Which are as easy broke as they make forms.
Women? Help heaven! Men their creation mar
In profiting by them. Nay, call us ten times frail;
For we are soft as our complexions are,
And credulous to false prints.
Ang.   I think it well;
And from this testimony of your own sex   131
(Since I suppose we are made to be no stronger
Than faults may shake our frames) let me be bold.
I do arrest your words. Be that you are;
That is, a woman. If you be more, you're none.
If you be one (as you are well express'd   136
By all external warrants), show it now
By putting on the destin'd livery.
Isab. I have no tongue but one. Gentle my
lord,
Let me entreat you speak the former language.
Ang. Plainly conceive I love you.   141
Isab. My brother did love Juliet, and you
tell me
That he shall die for't.
Ang. He shall not, Isabel, if you give me love.
Isab. I know your virtue hath a license in't,
Which seems a little fouler than it is   146
To pluck on others.
Ang.   Believe me on mine honour;
My words express my purpose.
Isab. Ha! little honour to be much believ'd,
And most pernicious purpose! Seeming, seeming!

I will proclaim thee, Angelo; look for't.   151
Sign me a present pardon for my brother,
Or with an outstretch'd throat I'll tell the
world aloud
What man thou art.
Ang.   Who will believe thee, Isabel?
My unsoil'd name, th' austereness of my life,
My vouch against you, and my place i' th' state
Will so your accusation overweigh   157
That you shall stifle in your own report
And smell of calumny. I have begun,
And now I give my sensual race the rein.   160
Fit thy consent to my sharp appetite;
Lay by all nicety and prolixious blushes
That banish what they sue for. Redeem thy
brother
By yielding up thy body to my will,
Or else he must not only die the death,   165
But thy unkindness shall his death draw out
To ling'ring sufferance. Answer me to-morrow,
Or, by the affection that now guides me most,
I'll prove a tyrant to him! As for you,
Say what you can; my false o'erweighs your
true.   *Exit.*
Isab. To whom should I complain? Did I
tell this,   171
Who would believe me? O perilous mouths
That bear in them one and the selfsame tongue,
Either of condemnation or approof,
Bidding the law make curtsy to their will, 175
Hooking both right and wrong to th' appetite,
To follow as it draws! I'll to my brother.
Though he hath fall'n by prompture of the blood,
Yet hath he in him such a mind of honour
That, had he twenty heads to tender down 180
On twenty bloody blocks, he'ld yield them up
Before his sister should her body stoop
To such abhorr'd pollution.
Then, Isabel, live chaste; and, brother, die!
More than our brother is our chastity.   185
I'll tell him yet of Angelo's request,
And fit his mind to death for his soul's rest.
                                             Exit.

ACT III. Scene I. [*The prison.*]

Enter *Duke*, [disguised as a *friar*,] *Claudio*,
          and *Provost*.

Duke. So then, you hope of pardon from
Lord Angelo?
Claud. The miserable have no other medicine
But only hope.
I have hope to live, and am prepar'd to die.

Duke. Be absolute for death. Either death
or life   5
Shall thereby be the sweeter. Reason thus with
life:
If I do lose thee, I do lose a thing
That none but fools would keep. A breath
thou art,
Servile to all the skyey influences

That do this habitation where thou keep'st 10
Hourly afflict. Merely thou art death's fool;
For him thou labour'st by thy flight to shun,
And yet runn'st toward him still. Thou art not
noble;
For all th' accommodations that thou bear'st
Are nurs'd by baseness. Thou'rt by no means
valiant; 15
For thou dost fear the soft and tender fork
Of a poor worm. Thy best of rest is sleep,
And that thou oft provok'st; yet grossly fear'st
Thy death, which is no more. Thou art not
thyself;
For thou exist'st on many a thousand grains 20
That issue out of dust. Happy thou art not;
For what thou hast not, still thou striv'st to get,
And what thou hast, forget'st. Thou art not
certain;
For thy complexion shifts to strange effects, 24
After the moon. If thou art rich, thou'rt poor;
For, like an ass whose back with ingots bows,
Thou bear'st thy heavy riches but a journey,
And death unloads thee. Friend hast thou
none;
For thine own bowels which do call thee sire,
The mere effusion of thy proper loins, 30
Do curse the gout, serpigo, and the rheum
For ending thee no sooner. Thou hast nor
youth nor age,
But as it were an after-dinner's sleep,
Dreaming on both; for all thy blessed youth
Becomes as aged, and doth beg the alms 35
Of palsied eld; and when thou art old and rich,
Thou hast neither heat, affection, limb, nor
beauty
To make thy riches pleasant. What's yet in this
That bears the name of life? Yet in this life
Lie hid moe thousand deaths; yet death we fear,
That makes these odds all even.
Claud.   I humbly thank you.
To sue to live, I find I seek to die; 42
And seeking death, find life. Let it come on.

Enter *Isabella.*

Isab. What, ho! Peace here! Grace and
good company!
Prov. Who's there? Come in! the wish de-
serves a welcome. 45
Duke. Dear son, ere long I'll visit you again.
Claud. Most holy sir, I thank you.
Isab. My business is a word or two with
Claudio.
Prov. And very welcome. Look, signior,
here's your sister.
Duke. Provost, a word with you. 50

Prov. As many as you please.
Duke. Bring me to hear them speak, where
I may be conceal'd.
              [*Exeunt Duke and Provost.*]
Claud. Now, sister, what's the comfort?
Isab. Why, 55
As all comforts are; most good, most good
indeed.
Lord Angelo, having affairs to heaven,
Intends you for his swift ambassador,
Where you shall be an everlasting leiger.
Therefore your best appointment make with
speed; 60
To-morrow you set on.
Claud.   Is there no remedy?
Isab. None, but such remedy as, to save a
head,
To cleave a heart in twain.
Claud.   But is there any?
Isab. Yes, brother, you may live.
There is a devilish mercy in the judge, 65
If you'll implore it, that will free your life,
But fetter you till death.
Claud.   Perpetual durance?
Isab. Ay, just! perpetual durance — a re-
straint,
Though all the world's vastidity you had,
To a determin'd scope.
Claud.   But in what nature? 70
Isab. In such a one as, you consenting to't,
Would bark your honour from that trunk you
bear
And leave you naked.
Claud.   Let me know the point.
Isab. O, I do fear thee, Claudio, and I quake,
Lest thou a feverous life shouldst entertain, 75
And six or seven winters more respect
Than a perpetual honour. Dar'st thou die?
The sense of death is most in apprehension,
And the poor beetle that we tread upon,
In corporal sufferance finds a pang as great 80
As when a giant dies.
Claud.   Why give you me this shame?
Think you I can a resolution fetch
From flow'ry tenderness? If I must die,
I will encounter darkness as a bride
And hug it in mine arms. 85
Isab. There spake my brother! There my
father's grave
Did utter forth a voice! Yes, thou must die.
Thou art too noble to conserve a life
In base appliances. This outward-sainted dep-
uty —
Whose settled visage and deliberate word 90
Nips youth i' th' head, and follies doth enew

113

As falcon doth the fowl — is yet a devil.
His filth within being cast, he would appear
A pond as deep as hell.
Claud.   The prenzie Angelo?
Isab. O, 'tis the cunning livery of hell   95
The damned'st body to invest and cover
In prenzie guards! Dost thou think, Claudio?
If I would yield him my virginity,
Thou mightst be freed!
Claud.   O heavens! it cannot be!
Isab. Yes, he would give't thee, from this
rank offence,   100
So to offend him still. This night's the time
That I should do what I abhor to name,
Or else thou diest to-morrow.
Claud.   Thou shalt not do't.
Isab. O, were it but my life,
I'd throw it down for your deliverance   105
As frankly as a pin.
Claud.   Thanks, dear Isabel.
Isab. Be ready, Claudio, for your death to-
morrow.
Claud. Yes. Has he affections in him
That thus can make him bite the law by th'
nose
When he would force it? Sure it is no sin, 110
Or of the deadly seven it is the least.
Isab. Which is the least?
Claud. If it were damnable, he being so
wise,
Why would he for the momentary trick
Be perdurably fin'd? O Isabel!   115
Isab. What says my brother?
Claud.   Death is a fearful thing.
Isab. And shamed life a hateful.
Claud. Ay, but to die, and go we know not
where;
To lie in cold obstruction and to rot;
This sensible warm motion to become   120
A kneaded clod; and the delighted spirit
To bathe in fiery floods, or to reside
In thrilling region of thick-ribbed ice,
To be imprison'd in the viewless winds   124
And blown with restless violence round about
The pendent world; or to be worse than
worst
Of those that lawless and incertain thought
Imagines howling! 'Tis too horrible!
The weariest and most loathed worldly life
That age, ache, penury, and imprisonment 130
Can lay on nature is a paradise
To what we fear of death.
Isab. Alas, alas!
Claud.   Sweet sister, let me live!
What sin you do to save a brother's life,

Nature dispenses with the deed so far   135
That it becomes a virtue.
Isab.   O you beast!
O faithless coward! O dishonest wretch!
Wilt thou be made a man out of my vice?
Is't not a kind of incest to take life
From thine own sister's shame? What should
I think?   140
Heaven shield my mother play'd my father fair!
For such a warped slip of wilderness
Ne'er issu'd from his blood. Take my defiance!
Die, perish! Might but my bending down
Reprieve thee from thy fate, it should proceed.
I'll pray a thousand prayers for thy death, 146
No word to save thee.
Claud. Nay, hear me, Isabel.
Isab.   O, fie, fie, fie!
Thy sin's not accidental, but a trade.
Mercy to thee would prove itself a bawd. 150
'Tis best that thou diest quickly.
Claud.   O, hear me, Isabella!

[Enter *Duke*.]

Duke. Vouchsafe a word, young sister, but
one word.
Isab. What is your will?
Duke. Might you dispense with your leisure,
I would by-and-by have some speech with you.
The satisfaction I would require is likewise your
own benefit.   157
Isab. I have no superfluous leisure; my stay
must be stolen out of other affairs; but I will
attend you awhile.   [*Walks aside*.]
Duke. Son, I have overheard what hath
pass'd between you and your sister. Angelo
had never the purpose to corrupt her; only he
hath made an assay of her virtue to practise his
judgment with the disposition of natures. She,
having the truth of honour in her, hath made
him that gracious denial which he is most glad
to receive. I am confessor to Angelo and I know
this to be true. Therefore prepare yourself to
death. Do not satisfy your resolution with
hopes that are fallible. To-morrow you must
die. Go to your knees and make ready.
Claud. Let me ask my sister pardon. I am so
out of love with life that I will sue to be rid of it.
Duke. Hold you there. Farewell.   176
[*Exit Claudio*.]
Provost, a word with you!

[Enter *Provost*.]

Prov. What's your will, father?
Duke. That now you are come, you will be
gone. Leave me awhile with the maid. My

114

mind promises with my habit no loss shall touch her by my company.   182

Prov. In good time.   *Exit.*

Duke. The hand that hath made you fair hath made you good. The goodness that is cheap in beauty makes beauty brief in goodness; but grace, being the soul of your complexion, shall keep the body of it ever fair. The assault that Angelo hath made to you, fortune hath convey'd to my understanding; and, but that frailty hath examples for his falling, I should wonder at Angelo. How will you do to content this substitute and to save your brother?   193

Isab. I am now going to resolve him. I had rather my brother die by the law than my son should be unlawfully born. But, O, how much is the good Duke deceiv'd in Angelo! If ever he return and I can speak to him, I will open my lips in vain, or discover his government.   199

Duke. That shall not be much amiss. Yet, as the matter now stands, he will avoid your accusation: he made trial of you only. Therefore fasten your ear on my advisings. To the love I have in doing good a remedy presents itself. I do make myself believe that you may most uprighteously do a poor wronged lady a merited benefit; redeem your brother from the angry law; do no stain to your own gracious person; and much please the absent Duke, if peradventure he shall ever return to have hearing of this business.   211

Isab. Let me hear you speak farther. I have spirit to do anything that appears not foul in the truth of my spirit.

Duke. Virtue is bold, and goodness never fearful. Have you not heard speak of Mariana, the sister of Frederick, the great soldier who miscarried at sea?

Isab. I have heard of the lady and good words went with her name.   220

Duke. She should this Angelo have married; was affianced to her by oath, and the nuptial appointed; between which time of the contract and limit of the solemnity, her brother Frederick was wrack'd at sea, having in that perished vessel the dowry of his sister. But mark how heavily this befell to the poor gentlewoman. There she lost a noble and renowned brother, in his love toward her ever most kind and natural; with him the portion and sinew of her fortune, her marriage dowry; with both, her combinate husband, this wellseeming Angelo.   232

Isab. Can this be so? Did Angelo so leave her?

Duke. Left her in her tears and dried not one of them with his comfort; swallowed his vows whole, pretending in her discoveries of dishonour; in few, bestow'd her on her own lamentation, which she yet wears for his sake; and he, a marble to her tears, is washed with them but relents not.   239

Isab. What a merit were it in death to take this poor maid from the world! What corruption in this life, that it will let this man live! But how out of this can she avail?

Duke. It is a rupture that you may easily heal; and the cure of it not only saves your brother but keeps you from dishonour in doing it.   246

Isab. Show me how, good father.

Duke. This forenamed maid hath yet in her the continuance of her first affection. His unjust unkindness, that in all reason should have quenched her love, hath, like an impediment in the current, made it more violent and unruly. Go you to Angelo; answer his requiring with a plausible obedience; agree with his demands to the point: only refer yourself to this advantage — first, that your stay with him may not be long; that the time may have all shadow and silence in it, and the place answer to convenience. This being granted in course, and now follows all: we shall advise this wronged maid to stead up your appointment, go in your place. If the encounter acknowledge itself hereafter, it may compel him to her recompense; and here, by this, is your brother saved, your honour untainted, the poor Mariana advantaged, and the corrupt deputy scaled. The maid will I frame, and make fit for his attempt. If you think well to carry this as you may, the doubleness of the benefit defends the deceit from reproof. What think you of it?

Isab. The image of it gives me content already, and I trust it will grow to a most prosperous perfection.   272

Duke. It lies much in your holding up. Haste you speedily to Angelo. If for this night he entreat you to his bed, give him promise of satisfaction. I will presently to Saint Luke's. There at the moated grange resides this dejected Mariana. At that place call upon me; and dispatch with Angelo, that it may be quickly.

Isab. I thank you for this comfort. Fare you well, good father.   281

Exeunt [severally].

115

[Scene II. *The street before the prison.*]

Enter, [at one door, *Duke,* disguised as before; at the other,] *Elbow,* [*Pompey the*] *Clown, Officers.*

Elb. Nay, if there be no remedy for it, but that you will needs buy and sell men and women like beasts, we shall have all the world drink brown and white bastard.

Duke. O heavens! what stuff is here?   5

Pom. 'Twas never merry world since, of two usuries, the merriest was put down and the worser allow'd by order of law a furr'd gown to keep him warm — and furr'd with fox on lambskins too, to signify that craft, being richer than innocency, stands for the facing.   11

Elb. Come your way, sir. — Bless you, good father friar.

Duke. And you, good brother father. What offence
Hath this man made you, sir?   15

Elb. Marry, sir, he hath offended the law; and, sir, we take him to be a thief too, sir; for we have found upon him, sir, a strange picklock, which we have sent to the deputy.

Duke. Fie, sirrah! a bawd, a wicked bawd!
The evil that thou causest to be done,   21
That is thy means to live. Do thou but think
What 'tis to cram a maw or clothe a back
From such a filthy vice. Say to thyself,
'From their abominable and beastly touches
I drink, I eat, array myself, and live.'   26
Canst thou believe thy living is a life,
So stinkingly depending? Go mend, go mend!

Pom. Indeed, it does stink in some sort, sir.
But yet, sir, I would prove —   30

Duke. Nay, if the devil have given thee proofs for sin,
Thou wilt prove his. Take him to prison, officer.
Correction and instruction must both work
Ere this rude beast will profit.   34

Elb. He must before the deputy, sir; he has given him warning. The deputy cannot abide a whoremaster. If he be a whoremonger, and comes before him, he were as good go a mile on his errand.

Duke. That we were all, as some would seem to be,   40
Free from our faults, as from faults seeming free!

Enter *Lucio.*

Elb. His neck will come to your waist — a cord, sir.

Pom. I spy comfort; I cry bail! Here's a gentleman and a friend of mine.   44

Lucio. How now, noble Pompey? What, at the wheels of Cæsar? Art thou led in triumph? What, is there none of Pygmalion's images newly made woman to be had now for putting the hand in the pocket and extracting it clutch'd? What reply? Ha? What say'st thou to this tune, matter, and method? Is't not drown'd i' th' last rain? Ha? What say'st thou, trot? Is the world as it was, man? Which is the way? Is it sad, and few words? Or how? The trick of it?

Duke. Still thus, and thus! still worse!   55

Lucio. How doth my dear morsel, thy mistress? Procures she still? Ha?

Pom. Troth, sir, she hath eaten up all her beef, and she is herself in the tub.   59

Lucio. Why, 'tis good. It is the right of it. It must be so. Ever your fresh whore and your powder'd bawd! An unshunn'd consequence; it must be so. Art going to prison, Pompey?

Pom. Yes, faith, sir.   64

Lucio. Why, 'tis not amiss, Pompey. Farewell. Go, say I sent thee thither. For debt, Pompey? or how?

Elb. For being a bawd; for being a bawd.

Lucio. Well, then imprison him. If imprisonment be the due of a bawd, why, 'tis his right. Bawd is he doubtless, and of antiquity too; bawd-born. Farewell, good Pompey. Commend me to the prison, Pompey. You will turn good husband now, Pompey; you will keep the house.

Pom. I hope, sir, your good worship will be my bail?   76

Lucio. No indeed will I not, Pompey; it is not the wear. I will pray, Pompey, to increase your bondage. If you take it not patiently, why, your mettle is the more! Adieu, trusty Pompey. Bless you, friar.   81

Duke. And you.

Lucio. Does Bridget paint still, Pompey? Ha?

Elb. Come your ways, sir, come.

Pom. You will not bail me then, sir?

Lucio. Then, Pompey, nor now. — What news abroad, friar? what news?

Elb. Come your ways, sir; come.

Lucio. Go to kennel, Pompey, go. [*Exeunt Elbow and Officers with Pompey.*] What news, friar, of the Duke?   91

Duke. I know none. Can you tell me of any?

Lucio. Some say he is with the Emperor of Russia; other some, he is in Rome. But where is he, think you?   95

Duke. I know not where; but wheresoever, I wish him well.

Lucio. It was a mad fantastical trick of him to steal from the state and usurp the beggary he was never born to. Lord Angelo dukes it well in his absence; he puts transgression to't. 101

Duke. He does well in't.

Lucio. A little more lenity to lechery would do no harm in him. Something too crabbed that way, friar. 105

Duke. It is too general a vice, and severity must cure it.

Lucio. Yes, in good sooth, the vice is of a great kindred — it is well allied; but it is impossible to extirp it quite, friar, till eating and drinking be put down. They say this Angelo was not made by man and woman after the downright way of creation. Is it true, think you?

Duke. How should he be made then? 114

Lucio. Some report a sea-maid spawn'd him; some, that he was begot between two stockfishes. But it is certain that, when he makes water, his urine is congeal'd ice; that I know to be true. And he is a motion generative; that's infallible. 119

Duke. You are pleasant, sir, and speak apace.

Lucio. Why, what a ruthless thing is this in him, for the rebellion of a codpiece to take away the life of a man! Would the Duke that is absent have done this? Ere he would have hang'd a man for the getting a hundred bastards, he would have paid for the nursing a thousand. He had some feeling of the sport; he knew the service, and that instructed him to mercy.

Duke. I never heard the absent Duke much detected for women. He was not inclin'd that way. 130

Lucio. O, sir, you are deceiv'd.

Duke. 'Tis not possible.

Lucio. Who? not the Duke? Yes, your beggar of fifty! and his use was to put a ducat in her clack-dish. The Duke had crotchets in him. He would be drunk too; that let me inform you. 136

Duke. You do him wrong, surely.

Lucio. Sir, I was an inward of his. A shy fellow was the Duke; and I believe I know the cause of his withdrawing. 140

Duke. What, I prithee, might be the cause?

Lucio. No, pardon! 'Tis a secret must be lock'd within the teeth and the lips. But this I can let you understand — the greater file of the subject held the Duke to be wise. 145

Duke. Wise? Why, no question but he was.

Lucio. A very superficial, ignorant, unweighing fellow.

Duke. Either this is envy in you, folly, or mistaking. The very stream of his life and the business he hath helmed must, upon a warranted need, give him a better proclamation. Let him be but testimonied in his own bringings-forth, and he shall appear to the envious a scholar, a statesman, and a soldier. Therefore you speak unskilfully; or, if your knowledge be more, it is much dark'ned in your malice. 157

Lucio. Sir, I know him and I love him.

Duke. Love talks with better knowledge, and knowledge with dearer love. 160

Lucio. Come, sir, I know what I know.

Duke. I can hardly believe that, since you know not what you speak. But if ever the Duke return, as our prayers are he may, let me desire you to make your answer before him. If it be honest you have spoke, you have courage to maintain it. I am bound to call upon you, and I pray you your name?

Lucio. Sir, my name is Lucio, well known to the Duke. 170

Duke. He shall know you better, sir, if I may live to report you.

Lucio. I fear you not.

Duke. O, you hope the Duke will return no more; or you imagine me too unhurtful an opposite. But indeed I can do you little harm. You'll forswear this again. 177

Lucio. I'll be hang'd first. Thou art deceiv'd in me, friar. But no more of this. Canst thou tell if Claudio die to-morrow or no? 180

Duke. Why should he die, sir?

Lucio. Why? For filling a bottle with a tundish. I would the Duke we talk of were repeal'd again. This ungenitur'd agent will unpeople the province with continency. Sparrows must not build in his house-eaves, because they are lecherous. The Duke yet would have dark deeds darkly answered; he would never bring them to light. Would he were return'd! Marry, this Claudio is condemned for untrussing. Farewell, good friar; I prithee pray for me. The Duke, I say to thee again, would eat mutton on Fridays. He's not past it yet; and I say to thee, he would mouth with a beggar, though she smelt brown bread and garlic. Say that I said so. Farewell. *Exit.*

Duke. No might nor greatness in mortality Can censure scape. Back-wounding calumny The whitest virtue strikes. What king so strong Can tie the gall up in the slanderous tongue? But who comes here? 200

117

Enter *Escalus, Provost*, and [*Mistress Overdone, the*] *Bawd*, [with *Officers*].

Escal. Go, away with her to prison!

Bawd. Good my lord, be good to me! Your honour is accounted a merciful man. Good my lord!   204

Escal. Double and treble admonition, and still forfeit in the same kind? This would make mercy swear and play the tyrant.

Prov. A bawd of eleven years' continuance, may it please your honour.   209

Bawd. My lord, this is one Lucio's information against me. Mistress Kate Keepdown was with child by him in the Duke's time; he promis'd her marriage. His child is a year and a quarter old, come Philip and Jacob. I have kept it myself; and see how he goes about to abuse me!

Escal. That fellow is a fellow of much license. Let him be call'd before us. Away with her to prison! Go to, no more words! [*Exeunt Officers with Mistress Overdone.*] Provost, my brother Angelo will not be alter'd; Claudio must die to-morrow. Let him be furnish'd with divines and have all charitable preparation. If my brother wrought by my pity, it should not be so with him.   223

Prov. So please you, this friar hath been with him and advis'd him for th' entertainment of death.   226

Escal. Good even, good father.

Duke. Bliss and goodness on you!

Escal. Of whence are you?

Duke. Not of this country, though my chance is now   230
To use it for my time. I am a brother
Of gracious order, late come from the See
In special business from his Holiness.

Escal. What news abroad i' th' world?   234

Duke. None, but that there is so great a fever on goodness that the dissolution of it must cure it. Novelty is only in request, and it is as dangerous to be aged in any kind of course as it is virtuous to be constant in any undertaking. There is scarce truth enough alive to make societies secure, but security enough to make fellowships accurst. Much upon this riddle runs the wisdom of the world. This news is old enough, yet it is every day's news. I pray you, sir, of what disposition was the Duke?   245

Escal. One that, above all other strifes, contended especially to know himself.

Duke. What pleasure was he given to?

Escal. Rather rejoicing to see another merry than merry at anything which profess'd to make him rejoice; a gentleman of all temperance. But leave we him to his events, and let me desire to know how you find Claudio prepar'd. I am made to understand that you have lent him visitation.   255

Duke. He professes to have received no sinister measure from his judge, but most willingly humbles himself to the determination of justice. Yet had he framed to himself, by the instruction of his frailty, many deceiving promises of life, which I, by my good leisure, have discredited to him, and now is he resolv'd to die. 262

Escal. You have paid the heavens your function and the prisoner the very debt of your calling. I have labour'd for the poor gentleman to the extremest shore of my modesty; but my brother justice have I found so severe that he hath forc'd me to tell him he is indeed Justice.

Duke. If his own life answer the straitness of his proceeding, it shall become him well; wherein if he chance to fail, he hath sentenc'd himself.   271

Escal. I am going to visit the prisoner. Fare you well.

Duke. Peace be with you!
                [*Exeunt Escalus and Provost.*]
He who the sword of heaven will bear   275
Should be as holy as severe;
Pattern in himself to know,
Grace to stand, and virtue go;
More nor less to others paying
Than by self-offences weighing.   280
Shame to him whose cruel striking
Kills for faults of his own liking!
Twice treble shame on Angelo
To weed my vice and let his grow!
O, what may man within him hide,   285
Though angel on the outward side!
How may likeness made in crimes,
Mocking, practice on the times
To draw with idle spiders' strings
Most ponderous and substantial things!   290
Craft against vice I must apply.
With Angelo to-night shall lie
His old betrothed (but despised).
So disguise shall, by th' disguised,
Pay with falsehood false exacting   295
And perform an old contracting.   *Exit.*

ACT IV. Scene I. [*The Moated Grange at Saint Luke's.*]

Enter *Mariana*; and *Boy* singing.

Song.

Take, O, take those lips away
  That so sweetly were forsworn;
And those eyes, the break of day,
  Lights that do mislead the morn;
But my kisses bring again, bring again;   5
Seals of love, but seal'd in vain, seal'd in vain.

Enter *Duke*, [disguised as before].

Mar. Break off thy song and haste thee
  quick away.   [*Exit Boy.*]
Here comes a man of comfort, whose advice
Hath often still'd my brawling discontent.
I cry you mercy, sir, and well could wish   10
You had not found me here so musical.
Let me excuse me, and believe me so,
My mirth it much displeas'd, but pleas'd my
  woe.
Duke. 'Tis good; though music oft hath
  such a charm   14
To make bad good, and good provoke to harm.
I pray you tell me, hath anybody enquir'd for
me here to-day? Much upon this time have I
promis'd here to meet.
Mar. You have not been enquir'd after. I
have sat here all day.   20

Enter *Isabella.*

Duke. I do constantly believe you. The
time is come even now. I shall crave your for-
bearance a little. May be I will call upon you
anon for some advantage to yourself.
Mar. I am always bound to you.   *Exit.*
Duke. Very well met, and well come! 26
What is the news from this good deputy?
Isab. He hath a garden circummur'd with
  brick,
Whose western side is with a vineyard back'd;
And to that vineyard is a planched gate 30
That makes his opening with this bigger key.
This other doth command a little door
Which from the vineyard to the garden leads.
There have I made my promise
Upon the heavy middle of the night   35
To call upon him.
Duke. But shall you on your knowledge find
  this way?
Isab. I have ta'en a due and wary note upon't.
With whispering and most guilty diligence,
In action all of precept, he did show me 40
The way twice o'er.

Duke.   Are there no other tokens
Between you 'greed concerning her observance?
Isab. No; none but only a repair i' th' dark,
And that I have possess'd him my most stay
Can be but brief; for I have made him know
I have a servant comes with me along 46
That stays upon me, whose persuasion is
I come about my brother.
Duke.   'Tis well borne up.
I have not yet made known to Mariana
A word of this. — What, ho, within! Come
  forth!   50

Enter *Mariana.*

I pray you be acquainted with this maid.
She comes to do you good.
Isab.   I do desire the like.
Duke. Do you persuade yourself that I re-
  spect you?
Mar. Good friar, I know you do, and I have
  found it.
Duke. Take then this your companion by
  the hand,   55
Who hath a story ready for your ear.
I shall attend your leisure; but make haste;
The vaporous night approaches.
Mar. Will't please you walk aside?
            Exeunt [*Mariana and Isabella*].
Duke. O place and greatness! millions of
  false eyes   60
Are stuck upon thee; volumes of report
Run with these false and most contrarious
  quests
Upon thy doings; thousand escapes of wit
Make thee the father of their idle dreams
And rack thee in their fancies.

Enter *Mariana* and *Isabella.*

            Welcome! How agreed? 65
Isab. She'll take the enterprise upon her,
  father,
If you advise it.
Duke.   It is not my consent,
But my entreaty too.
Isab.   Little have you to say
When you depart from him but, soft and low,
'Remember now my brother.'
Mar.   Fear me not. 70
Duke. Nor, gentle daughter, fear you not
  at all.
He is your husband on a precontract.
To bring you thus together 'tis no sin,

119

Sith that the justice of your title to him
Doth flourish the deceit. Come, let us go.   75
Our corn's to reap, for yet our tithe's to sow.
                                    Exeunt.

Scene II. [*The prison.*]

Enter Provost and [Pompey the] Clown.

Prov. Come hither, sirrah. Can you cut off
a man's head?
Pom. If the man be a bachelor, sir, I can;
but if he be a married man, he's his wive's
head, and I can never cut off a woman's head.
Prov. Come, sir, leave me your snatches and
yield me a direct answer. To-morrow morning
are to die Claudio and Barnardine. Here is in
our prison a common executioner, who in his
office lacks a helper. If you will take it on you
to assist him, it shall redeem you from your
gyves. If not, you shall have your full time of
imprisonment, and your deliverance with an
unpitied whipping, for you have been a notorious bawd.   15
Pom. Sir, I have been an unlawful bawd
time out of mind, but yet I will be content to
be a lawful hangman. I would be glad to receive some instruction from my fellow partner.
Prov. What, ho, Abhorson! Where's Abhorson there?   21

Enter Abhorson.

Abhor. Do you call, sir?
Prov. Sirrah, here's a fellow will help you
to-morrow in your execution. If you think it
meet, compound with him by the year, and let
him abide here with you. If not, use him for
the present and dismiss him. He cannot plead
his estimation with you; he hath been a bawd.
Abhor. A bawd, sir? Fie upon him! he will
discredit our mystery.   30
Prov. Go to, sir! You weigh equally; a
feather will turn the scale.   *Exit.*
Pom. Pray, sir, by your good favour — for
surely, sir, a good favour you have but that you
have a hanging look — do you call, sir, your
occupation a mystery?   36
Abhor. Ay, sir, a mystery.
Pom. Painting, sir, I have heard say, is a
mystery; and your whores, sir, being members
of my occupation, using painting, do prove my
occupation a mystery; but what mystery there
should be in hanging, if I should be hang'd I
cannot imagine.
Abhor. Sir, it is a mystery

Pom. Proof.   45
Abhor. Every true man's apparel fits your
thief. If it be too little for your thief, your true
man thinks it big enough. If it be too big for
your thief, your thief thinks it little enough.
So every true man's apparel fits your thief. 50

Enter Provost.

Prov. Are you agreed?
Pom. Sir, I will serve him. For I do find
your hangman is a more penitent trade than
your bawd; he doth oftener ask forgiveness.
Prov. You, sirrah, provide your block and
your axe to-morrow, four o'clock.   56
Abhor. Come on, bawd. I will instruct thee
in my trade; follow.
Pom. I do desire to learn, sir; and I hope,
if you have occasion to use me for your own
turn, you shall find me yare; for truly, sir, for
your kindness I owe you a good turn.   62
Prov. Call hither Barnardine and Claudio.
                Exeunt [Pompey and Abhorson].
Th' one has my pity; not a jot the other,
Being a murtherer, though he were my brother.

Enter Claudio.

Look, here's the warrant, Claudio, for thy
                                death.   66
'Tis now dead midnight, and by eight to-
                                morrow
Thou must be made immortal. Where's Bar-
                                nardine?
Claud. As fast lock'd up in sleep as guiltless
                                labour
When it lies starkly in the traveller's bones. 70
He will not wake.
Prov.   Who can do good on him?
Well, go, prepare yourself. [*Knocking within.*]
But hark! What noise?
Heaven give your spirits comfort! [*Exit Clau-
                dio. Knocking continues.*] By-and-by!
I hope it is some pardon or reprieve
For the most gentle Claudio.

Enter Duke, [disguised as before].

                        Welcome, father.   75
Duke. The best and wholesom'st spirits of
                the night
Envelop you, good provost! Who call'd here
                of late?
Prov. None since the curfew rung.
Duke. Not Isabel?
Prov. No.
Duke.   They will then, ere't be long.
Prov. What comfort is for Claudio?   80

120

Duke. There's some in hope.
Prov. It is a bitter deputy.
Duke. Not so, not so! His life is parallel'd
Even with the stroke and line of his great
justice.
He doth with holy abstinence subdue
That in himself which he spurs on his pow'r 85
To qualify in others. Were he meal'd with that
Which he corrects, then were he tyrannous;
But this being so, he's just. [*Knocking within.*]
Now are they come.
[*Exit Provost.*]
This is a gentle provost. Seldom when
The steeled jailer is the friend of men. 90
[*Knocking within.*]
How now? What noise? That spirit's possess'd
with haste
That wounds th' unsisting postern with these
strokes.

[*Enter Provost.*]

Prov. There he must stay until the officer
Arise to let him in. He is call'd up.
Duke. Have you no countermand for Claudio
yet 95
But he must die to-morrow?
Prov. None, sir, none.
Duke. As near the dawning, provost, as it is,
You shall hear more ere morning.
Prov. Happily
You something know. Yet I believe there
comes
No countermand. No such example have we.
Besides, upon the very siege of justice 101
Lord Angelo hath to the public ear
Profess'd the contrary.

Enter a *Messenger.*
This is his lordship's man.
Duke. And here comes Claudio's pardon.
Mes. [*gives a paper*] My lord hath sent you
this note, and by me this further charge — that
you swerve not from the smallest article of it,
neither in time, matter, or other circumstance.
Good morrow; for, as I take it, it is almost day.
Prov. I shall obey him. [*Exit Messenger.*]
Duke. [*aside*] This is his pardon, purchas'd
by such sin 111
For which the pardoner himself is in.
Hence hath offence his quick celerity,
When it is borne in high authority. 114
When vice makes mercy, mercy's so extended
That for the fault's love is th' offender friended.
Now, sir, what news?
Prov. I told you. Lord Angelo, belike think-
ing me remiss in mine office, awakens me with

this unwonted putting-on; methinks strangely,
for he hath not us'd it before. 121
Duke. Pray you let's hear.
Prov. [*reads*] *the letter.*
'Whatsoever you may hear to the contrary, let
Claudio be executed by four of the clock, and in
the afternoon Barnardine. For my better satisfaction, let me have Claudio's head sent me by
five. Let this be duly performed, with a thought
that more depends on it than we must yet deliver.
Thus fail not to do your office, as you will answer
it at your peril.' 130

What say you to this, sir?
Duke. What is that Barnardine who is to be
executed in th' afternoon?
Prov. A Bohemian born, but here nurs'd up
and bred; one that is a prisoner nine years old.
Duke. How came it that the absent Duke
had not either deliver'd him to his liberty or
executed him? I have heard it was ever his
manner to do so. 139
Prov. His friends still wrought reprieves for
him; and indeed his fact, till now in the government of Lord Angelo, came not to an un-
doubtful proof.
Duke. It is now apparent?
Prov. Most manifest, and not denied by
himself. 146
Duke. Hath he borne himself penitently in
prison? How seems he to be touch'd?
Prov. A man that apprehends death no more
dreadfully but as a drunken sleep; careless,
reckless, and fearless of what's past, present,
or to come; insensible of mortality and desper-
ately mortal.
Duke. He wants advice. 154
Prov. He will hear none. He hath evermore
had the liberty of the prison. Give him leave
to escape hence, he would not. Drunk many
times a day, if not many days entirely drunk.
We have very oft awak'd him, as if to carry
him to execution, and show'd him a seeming
warrant for it. It hath not moved him at all.
Duke. More of him anon. There is written
in your brow, provost, honesty and constancy.
If I read it not truly, my ancient skill beguiles
me; but in the boldness of my cunning I will
lay myself in hazard. Claudio, whom here you
have warrant to execute, is no greater forfeit to
the law than Angelo who hath sentenc'd him.
To make you understand in a manifested
effect I crave but four days' respite, for the
which you are to do me both a present and a
dangerous courtesy.
Prov. Pray, sir, in what?

121

Duke. In the delaying death.   174

Prov. Alack, how may I do it, having the hour limited and an express command, under penalty, to deliver his head in the view of Angelo? I may make my case as Claudio's, to cross this in the smallest.   179

Duke. By the vow of mine order I warrant you, if my instructions may be your guide. Let this Barnardine be this morning executed and his head borne to Angelo.

Prov. Angelo hath seen them both and will discover the favour.   185

Duke. O, death's a great disguiser, and you may add to it. Shave the head and trim the beard, and say it was the desire of the penitent to be so bar'd before his death. You know the course is common. If anything fall to you upon this more than thanks and good fortune, by the Saint whom I profess, I will plead against it with my life.

Prov. Pardon me, good father, it is against my oath.   195

Duke. Were you sworn to the Duke or to the deputy?

Prov. To him and to his substitutes.

Duke. You will think you have made no offence if the Duke avouch the justice of your dealing?   201

Prov. But what likelihood is in that?

Duke. Not a resemblance, but a certainty. Yet since I see you fearful, that neither my coat, integrity, nor persuasion can with ease attempt you, I will go further than I meant, to pluck all fears out of you. Look you, sir, here is the hand and seal of the Duke. You know the character, I doubt not, and the signet is not strange to you?

Prov. I know them both.   210

Duke. The contents of this is the return of the Duke. You shall anon overread it at your pleasure, where you shall find within these two days he will be here. This is a thing that Angelo knows not; for he this very day receives letters of strange tenour, perchance of the Duke's death, perchance entering into some monastery, but by chance nothing of what is writ. Look, th' unfolding star calls up the shepherd. Put not yourself into amazement how these things should be. All difficulties are but easy when they are known. Call your executioner, and off with Barnardine's head. I will give him a present shrift and advise him for a better place. Yet you are amaz'd, but this shall absolutely resolve you. Come away; it is almost clear dawn.   *Exeunt.*

Scene III. [*Another room in the prison.*]

Enter [*Pompey the*] *Clown.*

Pom. I am as well acquainted here as I was in our house of profession. One would think it were Mistress Overdone's own house, for here be many of her old customers. First, here's young Master Rash: he's in for a commodity of brown paper and old ginger, ninescore and seventeen pounds, of which he made five marks ready money. Marry, then ginger was not much in request, for the old women were all dead. Then is there here one Master Caper, at the suit of Master Threepile the mercer, for some four suits of peach-colour'd satin, which now peaches him a beggar. Then have we here young Dizie, and young Master Deepvow, and Master Copperspur, and Master Starvelackey the rapier-and-dagger man, and young Dropheir that kill'd lusty Pudding, and Master Forthright the tilter, and brave Master Shoetie the great traveller, and wild Halfcan that stabb'd Pots, and I think forty more — all great doers in our trade, and are now 'for the Lord's sake.'

Enter *Abhorson.*

Abhor. Sirrah, bring Barnardine hither.

Pom. Master Barnardine, you must rise and be hang'd! Master Barnardine!

Abhor. What ho, Barnardine!   25

Bar. (*within*) A pox o' your throats! Who makes that noise there? What are you?

Pom. Your friends, sir; the hangman. You must be so good, sir, to rise and be put to death.

Bar. (*within*) Away, you rogue, away! I am sleepy.   31

Abhor. Tell him he must awake, and that quickly too.

Pom. Pray, Master Barnardine, awake till you are executed, and sleep afterwards.   35

Abhor. Go in to him and fetch him out.

Pom. He is coming, sir, he is coming. I hear his straw rustle.

Enter *Barnardine.*

Abhor. Is the axe upon the block, sirrah?

Pom. Very ready, sir.   40

Bar. How now, Abhorson? What's the news with you?

Abhor. Truly, sir, I would desire you to clap into your prayers; for look you, the warrant's come.   45

Bar. You rogue, I have been drinking all night. I am not fitted for't.

Pom. O, the better, sir! for he that drinks all night, and is hanged betimes in the morning, may sleep the sounder all the next day.   50

Enter *Duke*, [disguised as before].

Abhor. Look you, sir, here comes your ghostly father. Do we jest now, think you?

Duke. Sir, induced by my charity, and hearing how hastily you are to depart, I am come to advise you, comfort you, and pray with you.

Bar. Friar, not I! I have been drinking hard all night, and I will have more time to prepare me, or they shall beat out my brains with billets. I will not consent to die this day, that's certain.

Duke. O, sir, you must! and therefore I beseech you   60
Look forward on the journey you shall go.

Bar. I swear I will not die to-day for any man's persuasion.

Duke. But hear you —

Bar. Not a word! If you have anything to say to me, come to my ward; for thence will not I to-day.   *Exit.*

Enter *Provost*.

Duke. Unfit to live or die! O gravel heart! After him, fellows! bring him to the block.
                    [*Exeunt Abhorson and Pompey.*]

Prov. Now, sir, how do you find the prisoner?

Duke. A creature unprepar'd, unmeet for death;   71
And to transport him in the mind he is
Were damnable.

Prov.   Here in the prison, father,
There died this morning of a cruel fever
One Ragozine, a most notorious pirate,   75
A man of Claudio's years; his beard and head
Just of his colour. What if we do omit
This reprobate till he were well inclin'd,
And satisfy the deputy with the visage
Of Ragozine, more like to Claudio?   80

Duke. O, 'tis an accident that heaven provides!
Dispatch it presently; the hour draws on
Prefix'd by Angelo. See this be done,
And sent according to command, whiles I
Persuade this rude wretch willingly to die.   85

Prov. This shall be done, good father, presently.
But Barnardine must die this afternoon;
And how shall we continue Claudio,
To save me from the danger that might come
If he were known alive?

Duke.   Let this be done.   90
Put them in secret holds, both Barnardine and Claudio.
Ere twice the sun hath made his journal greeting
To th' under generation, you shall find
Your safety manifested.

Prov. I am your free dependant.

Duke.   Quick, dispatch,   95
And send the head to Angelo.   *Exit [Provost].*
Now will I write letters to Angelo
(The provost, he shall bear them) whose contents
Shall witness to him I am near at home,
And that by great injunctions I am bound   100
To enter publicly. Him I'll desire
To meet me at the consecrated fount,
A league below the city; and from thence,
By cold gradation and well-balanc'd form,
We shall proceed with Angelo.   105

Enter *Provost*, [with *Ragozine's* head].

Prov. Here is the head. I'll carry it myself.

Duke. Convenient is it. Make a swift return;
For I would commune with you of such things
That want no ear but yours.

Prov.   I'll make all speed.   *Exit.*

Isab. (*within*) Peace, ho, be here!   110

Duke. The tongue of Isabel. She's come to know
If yet her brother's pardon be come hither;
But I will keep her ignorant of her good,
To make her heavenly comforts of despair
When it is least expected.

Enter *Isabella*.

Isab.   Ho, by your leave!

Duke. Good morning to you, fair and gracious daughter.   116

Isab. The better, given me by so holy a man.
Hath yet the deputy sent my brother's pardon?

Duke. He hath releas'd him, Isabel, from the world.
His head is off, and sent to Angelo.   120

Isab. Nay, but it is not so!

Duke. It is no other. Show your wisdom, daughter,
In your close patience.

Isab. O, I will to him and pluck out his eyes!

Duke. You shall not be admitted to his sight.

Isab. Unhappy Claudio! wretched Isabel!
Injurious world! most damned Angelo!

Duke. This nor hurts him nor profits you a jot;
Forbear it therefore; give your cause to heaven.
Mark what I say, which you shall find   130
By every syllable a faithful verity.

123

The Duke comes home to-morrow — Nay, dry
    your eyes!
One of our covent, and his confessor,
Gives me this instance. Already he hath carried
Notice to Escalus and Angelo,   135
Who do prepare to meet him at the gates,
There to give up their pow'r. If you can, pace
    your wisdom
In that good path that I would wish it go;
And you shall have your bosom on this wretch,
Grace of the Duke, revenges to your heart, 140
And general honour.
   Isab.   I am directed by you.
   Duke. This letter, then, to Friar Peter give.
'Tis that he sent me of the Duke's return.
Say, by this token I desire his company   144
At Mariana's house to-night. Her cause and yours
I'll perfect him withal, and he shall bring you
Before the Duke; and to the head of Angelo
Accuse him home and home. For my poor self,
I am combined by a sacred vow   149
And shall be absent. Wend you with this letter.
Command these fretting waters from your eyes
With a light heart. Trust not my holy order
If I pervert your course. — Who's here?

             Enter *Lucio.*

   Lucio. Good even. Friar, where's the provost?   155
   Duke. Not within, sir.
   Lucio. O pretty Isabella, I am pale at mine
heart to see thine eyes so red! Thou must be
patient. I am fain to dine and sup with water
and bran; I dare not for my head fill my belly;
one fruitful meal would set me to't. But they
say the Duke will be here to-morrow. By my
troth, Isabel, I lov'd thy brother. If the old
fantastical Duke of dark corners had been at
home, he had lived.   *[Exit Isabella.]*
   Duke. Sir, the Duke is marvellous little beholding to your reports; but the best is, he
lives not in them.
   Lucio. Friar, thou knowest not the Duke so
well as I do. He's a better woodman than thou
tak'st him for.   171
   Duke. Well, you'll answer this one day.
Fare ye well.
   Lucio. Nay, tarry; I'll go along with thee.
I can tell thee pretty tales of the Duke.   175
   Duke. You have told me too many of him
already, sir, if they be true; if not true, none
were enough.
   Lucio. I was once before him for getting a
wench with child.   180
   Duke. Did you such a thing?

   Lucio. Yes, marry, did I; but I was fain to
forswear it. They would else have married me
to the rotten medlar.
   Duke. Sir, your company is fairer than
honest. Rest you well.   186
   Lucio. By my troth, I'll go with thee to the
lane's end. If bawdy talk offend you, we'll have
very little of it. Nay, friar, I am a kind of burr;
I shall stick.   *Exeunt.*

       Scene IV. [*Angelo's house.*]

      Enter *Angelo* and *Escalus.*

   Escal. Every letter he hath writ hath disvouch'd other.
   Ang. In most uneven and distracted manner.
His actions show much like to madness; pray
heaven his wisdom be not tainted! And why
meet him at the gates and redeliver our authorities there?   7
   Escal. I guess not.
   Ang. And why should we proclaim it in an
hour before his ent'ring, that if any crave redress
of injustice, they should exhibit their petitions
in the street?   12
   Escal. He shows his reason for that: to
have a dispatch of complaints, and to deliver
us from devices hereafter, which shall then
have no power to stand against us.   16
   Ang. Well, I beseech you let it be proclaim'd.
Betimes i' th' morn I'll call you at your house.
Give notice to such men of sort and suit
As are to meet him.
   Escal.   I shall, sir. Fare you well.
   Ang. Good night.   *Exit [Escalus].*
This deed unshapes me quite, makes me un-
    pregnant
And dull to all proceedings. A deflow'red maid!
And by an eminent body that enforc'd
The law against it! But that her tender shame
Will not proclaim against her maiden loss,   26
How might she tongue me! Yet reason dares
    her no;
For my authority bears so credent bulk
That no particular scandal once can touch
But it confounds the breather. He should have
    liv'd,   30
Save that his riotous youth, with dangerous
    sense,
Might in the times to come have ta'en revenge
By so receiving a dishonour'd life
With ransom of such shame. Would yet he had
    liv'd!
Alack, when once our grace we have forgot,   35

Nothing goes right! we would, and we would
 not!   *Exit.*

Scene V. [*Fields without the City.*]

Enter Duke, [in his own habit,] and Friar Peter.

Duke. These letters at fit time deliver me.
                                    [*Gives letters.*]
The provost knows our purpose and our plot.
The matter being afoot, keep your instruction
And hold you ever to our special drift,
Though sometimes you do blench from this to
        that,   5
As cause doth minister. Go call at Flavius'
        house
And tell him where I stay. Give the like notice
To Valentinus, Rowland, and to Crassus,
And bid them bring the trumpets to the gate.
But send me Flavius first.
Peter.   It shall be speeded well. [*Exit.*]

Enter Varrius.

Duke. I thank thee, Varrius; thou hast made
        good haste.   11
Come, we will walk. There's other of our friends
Will greet us here anon. My gentle Varrius!
                                    Exeunt.

Scene VI. [*Street near the City gate.*]

Enter Isabella and Mariana.

Isab. To speak so indirectly I am loath.
I would say the truth; but to accuse him so,
That is your part; yet I am advis'd to do
it;
He says, to veil full purpose.
Mar.   Be rul'd by him.
Isab. Besides, he tells me that, if peradven-
        ture   5
He speak against me on the adverse side,
I should not think it strange, for 'tis a physic
That's bitter to sweet end.

Enter [Friar] Peter.

Mar. I would Friar Peter —
Isab.   O, peace! the friar is come.
Peter. Come, I have found you out a stand
        most fit,   10
Where you may have such vantage on the Duke
He shall not pass you. Twice have the trumpets
        sounded.
The generous and gravest citizens
Have hent the gates, and very near upon   14
The Duke is ent'ring. Therefore, hence, away!
                                    Exeunt.

ACT V. Scene I. [*The City gate.*]

*Enter Duke [in his own habit], Varrius, Lords;
Angelo, Escalus, Lucio, [Provost, Officers, and]
        Citizens: at several doors.*

Duke. My very worthy cousin, fairly met.
Our old and faithful friend, we are glad to see you.
Ang., Escal. Happy return be to your royal
        Grace!
Duke. Many and hearty thankings to you both!
We have made enquiry of you, and we hear
Such goodness of your justice that our soul
Cannot but yield you forth to public thanks,
Forerunning more requital.
Ang.   You make my bonds still greater.
Duke. O, your desert speaks loud, and I
        should wrong it
To lock it in the wards of covert bosom   10
When it deserves, with characters of brass,
A forted residence 'gainst the tooth of time
And razure of oblivion. Give me your hand,
And let the subject see, to make them know
That outward courtesies would fain proclaim 15
Favours that keep within. Come, Escalus,

You must walk by us on our other hand;
And good supporters are you.

Enter Peter and Isabella.

Peter. Now is your time. Speak loud, and
        kneel before him.
Isab. Justice, O royal Duke! Vail your
        regard   20
Upon a wrong'd — I would fain have said, a maid!
O worthy prince, dishonour not your eye
By throwing it on any other object
Till you have heard me in my true complaint
And given me justice, justice, justice, justice!
Duke. Relate your wrongs. In what? by
        whom? Be brief.   26
Here is Lord Angelo shall give you justice.
Reveal yourself to him.
Isab.   O worthy Duke,
You bid me seek redemption of the devil!
Hear me yourself; for that which I must speak
Must either punish me, not being believ'd,   31
Or wring redress from you. Hear me! O, hear
me, hear!

125

Ang. My lord, her wits I fear me are not firm.
She hath been a suitor to me for her brother
Cut off by course of justice —
Isab.   By course of justice! 35
Ang. And she will speak most bitterly and
strange.
Isab. Most strange! but yet most truly will
I speak.
That Angelo's forsworn, is it not strange?
That Angelo's a murtherer, is't not strange?
That Angelo is an adulterous thief,   40
An hypocrite, a virgin-violator —
Is it not strange? and strange?
   Duke.   Nay, it is ten times strange!
Isab. It is not truer he is Angelo
Than this is all as true as it is strange.
Nay, it is ten times true, for truth is truth   45
To th' end of reck'ning.
   Duke.   Away with her! Poor soul!
She speaks this in th' infirmity of sense.
   Isab. O prince, I conjure thee, as thou
believ'st
There is another comfort than this world,
That thou neglect me not with that opinion 50
That I am touch'd with madness! Make not
impossible
That which but seems unlike. 'Tis not im-
possible
But one, the wicked'st caitiff on the ground,
May seem as shy, as grave, as just, as abso-
lute
As Angelo. Even so may Angelo,   55
In all his dressings, characts, titles, forms,
Be an arch-villain. Believe it, royal prince!
If he be less, he's nothing; but he's more,
Had I more name for badness.
   Duke.   By mine honesty,
If she be mad, as I believe no other,   60
Her madness hath the oddest frame of sense,
Such a dependency of thing on thing,
As e'er I heard in madness.
   Isab.   O gracious Duke,
Harp not on that! nor do not banish reason
For inequality, but let your reason serve   65
To make the truth appear where it seems hid
And hide the false seems true!
   Duke.   Many that are not mad
Have sure more lack of reason. What would
you say?
   Isab. I am the sister of one Claudio,
Condemn'd upon the act of fornication   70
To lose his head, condemn'd by Angelo.
I, in probation of a sisterhood,
Was sent to by my brother, one Lucio
As then the messenger.

Lucio.   That's I, an't like your Grace.
I came to her from Claudio and desir'd her   75
To try her gracious fortune with Lord Angelo
For her poor brother's pardon.
   Isab.   That's he indeed.
   Duke. You were not bid to speak.
   Lucio.   No, my good lord,
Nor wish'd to hold my peace.
   Duke.   I wish you now then.
Pray you take note of it. And when you have
A business for yourself, pray heaven you then
Be perfect.
   Lucio. I warrant your honour.
   Duke. The warrant's for yourself. Take heed
to it.
   Isab. This gentleman told somewhat of my
tale.
   Lucio. Right.   85
   Duke. It may be right, but you are i' the
wrong
To speak before your time. — Proceed.
   Isab.   I went
To this pernicious caitiff deputy.
   Duke. That's somewhat madly spoken.
   Isab.   Pardon it.
The phrase is to the matter.   90
   Duke. Mended again. The matter! Proceed.
   Isab. In brief — to set the needless process by,
How I pray'd and kneel'd,
How he refell'd me and how I replied
(For this was of much length) — the vile con-
clusion   95
I now begin with grief and shame to utter.
He would not, but by gift of my chaste body
To his concupiscible intemperate lust,
Release my brother; and after much debate-
ment,
My sisterly remorse confutes mine honour,   100
And I did yield to him. But the next morn be-
times,
His purpose surfeiting, he sends a warrant
For my poor brother's head.
   Duke.   This is most likely!
   Isab. O that it were as like as it is true!
   Duke. By heaven, fond wretch, thou know'st
not what thou speak'st,   105
Or else thou art suborn'd against his honour
In hateful practice. First, his integrity
Stands without blemish. Next, it imports no
reason
That with such vehemency he should pursue
Faults proper to himself. If he had so offended,
He would have weigh'd thy brother by himself
And not have cut him off. Some one hath set
you on.

Confess the truth, and say by whose advice
Thou cam'st here to complain.
   Isab.   And is this all?
Then, O you blessed ministers above,   115
Keep me in patience, and with ripened time
Unfold the evil which is here wrapt up
In countenance! Heaven shield your Grace
   from woe,
As I, thus wrong'd, hence unbelieved go!
   Duke. I know you'ld fain be gone. — An
   officer!   120
To prison with her! Shall we thus permit
A blasting and a scandalous breath to fall
On him so near us? This needs must be a prac-
   tice.
Who knew of your intent and coming hither?
   Isab. One that I would were here, Friar
   Lodowick.   125
   Duke. A ghostly father, belike. Who knows
   that Lodowick?
   Lucio. My lord, I know him. 'Tis a meddling
   friar.
I do not like the man. Had he been lay, my lord,
For certain words he spake against your Grace
In your retirement, I had swing'd him soundly.
   Duke. Words against me! This' a good friar
   belike!   131
And to set on this wretched woman here
Against our substitute! Let this friar be found.
   Lucio. But yesternight, my lord, she and that
   friar,
I saw them at the prison — a saucy friar,   135
A very scurvy fellow.
   Peter. Blessed be your royal Grace!
I have stood by, my lord, and I have heard
Your royal ear abus'd. First, hath this woman
Most wrongfully accus'd your substitute,   140
Who is as free from touch or soil with her
As she from one ungot.
   Duke.   We did believe no less.
Know you that Friar Lodowick that she speaks
   of?
   Peter. I know him for a man divine and holy;
Not scurvy, nor a temporary meddler,   145
As he's reported by this gentleman;
And, on my trust, a man that never yet
Did, as he vouches, misreport your Grace.
   Lucio. My lord, most villanously! Believe it!
   Peter. Well, he in time may come to clear
   himself;   150
But at this instant he is sick, my lord,
Of a strange fever. Upon his mere request,
Being come to knowledge that there was com-
   plaint
Intended 'gainst Lord Angelo, came I hither

To speak, as from his mouth, what he doth know
Is true and false; and what he with his oath
And all probation will make up full clear,
Whensoever he's convented. First, for this
   woman —
To justify this worthy nobleman,
So vulgarly and personally accus'd,   160
Her shall you hear disproved to her eyes
Till she herself confess it.
   Duke.   Good friar, let's hear it.
                    [*Exit Isabella, guarded.*]
Do you not smile at this, Lord Angelo?
O heaven, the vanity of wretched fools!
Give us some seats. Come, cousin Angelo;   165
In this I'll be impartial; be you judge
Of your own cause.

             Enter *Mariana,* [veiled].
                    Is this the witness, friar?
First let her show her face, and after speak.
   Mar. Pardon, my lord. I will not show my face
Until my husband bid me.   170
   Duke. What, are you married?
   Mar. No, my lord.
   Duke. Are you a maid?
   Mar. No, my lord.
   Duke. A widow then?   175
   Mar. Neither, my lord.
   Duke. Why, you are nothing then — neither
maid, widow, nor wife?
   Lucio. My lord, she may be a punk; for
many of them are neither maid, widow, nor wife.
   Duke. Silence that fellow! I would he had
   some cause   181
To prattle for himself.
   Lucio. Well, my lord.
   Mar. My lord, I do confess I ne'er was
   married,
And I confess, besides, I am no maid.   185
I have known my husband; yet my husband
   knows not
That ever he knew me.
   Lucio. He was drunk then, my lord. It can
be no better.
   Duke. For the benefit of silence, would thou
wert so too! | 191
   Lucio. Well, my lord.
   Duke. This is no witness for Lord Angelo.
   Mar. Now I come to 't, my lord.
She that accuses him of fornication,   195
In selfsame manner doth accuse my husband,
And charges him, my lord, with such a time
When I'll depose I had him in mine arms
With all th' effect of love.
   Ang. Charges she moe than me?

127

Mar.   Not that I know. 200
Duke. No? You say your husband.
Mar. Why, just, my lord, and that is Angelo,
Who thinks he knows that he ne'er knew my
    body,
But knows he thinks that he knows Isabel's.
Ang. This is a strange abuse. Let's see thy
    face.   205
Mar. My husband bids me; now I will un-
    mask.   [*Unveils.*]
This is that face, thou cruel Angelo,
Which once thou swor'st was worth the looking
    on.
This is the hand which with a vow'd contract
Was fast belock'd in thine. This is the body 210
That took away the match from Isabel
And did supply thee at thy garden house
In her imagin'd person.
Duke.   Know you this woman?
Lucio. Carnally, she says.
Duke.   Sirrah, no more!
Lucio. Enough, my lord.   215
Ang. My lord, I must confess I know this
    woman,
And five years since there was some speech of
    marriage
Betwixt myself and her; which was broke off,
Partly for that her promised proportions
Came short of composition, but in chief   220
For that her reputation was disvalued
In levity; since which time of five years
I never spake with her, saw her, nor heard from
    her,
Upon my faith and honour.
Mar.   Noble prince,
As there comes light from heaven and words
    from breath,   225
As there is sense in truth and truth in virtue,
I am affianc'd this man's wife as strongly
As words could make up vows; and, my good lord,
But Tuesday night last gone, in's garden house,
He knew me as a wife. As this is true,   230
Let me in safety raise me from my knees,
Or else for ever be confixed here
A marble monument!
Ang.   I did but smile till now.
Now, good my lord, give me the scope of justice;
My patience here is touch'd. I do perceive
These poor informal women are no more   236
But instruments of some more mightier member
That sets them on. Let me have way, my lord,
To find this practice out.
Duke.   Ay, with my heart,
And punish them unto your height of pleasure.
Thou foolish friar, and thou pernicious woman,

Compact with her that's gone, think'st thou
    thy oaths,
Though they would swear down each particular
    saint,
Were testimonies 'gainst his worth and credit
That's seal'd in approbation? You, Lord Es-
    calus,   245
Sit with my cousin. Lend him your kind pains
To find out this abuse, whence 'tis deriv'd.
There is another friar that set them on.
Let him be sent for.
Peter. Would he were here, my lord! for he
    indeed   250
Hath set the women on to this complaint.
Your provost knows the place where he abides,
And he may fetch him.
Duke.   Go, do it instantly.
                                [*Exit Provost.*]
And you, my noble and well-warranted cousin,
Whom it concerns to hear this matter forth,
Do with your injuries as seems you best   256
In any chastisement. I for a while will leave you;
But stir not you till you have well determin'd
Upon these slanderers.
Escal.   My lord, we'll do it throughly.
                                Exit [*Duke*].
Signior Lucio, did not you say you knew that
Friar Lodowick to be a dishonest person? 262
Lucio. 'Cucullus non facit monachum.'
Honest in nothing but in his clothes, and one
that hath spoke most villanous speeches of the
Duke.   265
Escal. We shall entreat you to abide here till
he come, and enforce them against him. We
shall find this friar a notable fellow.
Lucio. As any in Vienna, on my word.   269
Escal. Call that same Isabel here once again.
I would speak with her. [*Exit an Attendant.*]
Pray you, my lord, give me leave to question.
You shall see how I'll handle her.
Lucio. Not better than he, by her own report.
Escal. Say you?   275
Lucio. Marry, sir, I think, if you handled her
privately, she would sooner confess; perchance,
publicly, she'll be asham'd.

Enter *Duke* [in his Friar's habit], *Provost*;
    [*Officers with*] *Isabella.*

Escal. I will go darkly to work with her.
Lucio. That's the way: for women are
light at midnight.   281
Escal. [*to Isabella*] Come on, mistress. Here's
a gentlewoman denies all that you have said.
Lucio. My lord, here comes the rascal I spoke
of — here, with the provost.   285

Escal. In very good time. Speak not you to
him till we call upon you.
Lucio. Mum.
Escal. Come, sir, did you set these women on
to slander Lord Angelo? They have confess'd
you did.   291
Duke. 'Tis false.
Escal. How! Know you where you are?
Duke. Respect to your great place! and let
the devil
Be sometime honour'd for his burning throne!
Where is the Duke? 'Tis he should hear me speak.
Escal. The Duke's in us, and we will hear
you speak.   297
Look you speak justly.
Duke. Boldly, at least. But, O, poor souls,
Come you to seek the lamb here of the fox?
Good night to your redress! Is the Duke gone?
Then is your cause gone too. The Duke's unjust
Thus to retort your manifest appeal
And put your trial in the villain's mouth
Which here you come to accuse.   305
Lucio. This is the rascal. This is he I spoke of.
Escal. Why, thou unreverend and unhal-
lowed friar,
Is't not enough thou hast suborn'd these women
To accuse this worthy man, but, in foul mouth,
And in the witness of his proper ear,   310
To call him villain? and then to glance from him
To th' Duke himself, to tax him with injustice?
Take him hence! To th' rack with him! We'll
touse you
Joint by joint but we will know his purpose.
What? 'unjust'?
Duke.   Be not so hot. The Duke 315
Dare no more stretch this finger of mine than he
Dare rack his own. His subject am I not,
Nor here provincial. My business in this state
Made me a looker-on here in Vienna,
Where I have seen corruption boil and bubble
Till it o'errun the stew; laws for all faults, 321
But faults so countenanc'd that the strong
statutes
Stand like the forfeits in a barber's shop,
As much in mock as mark.
Escal. Slander to th' state! Away with him
to prison!   325
Ang. What can you vouch against him,
Signior Lucio?
Is this the man that you did tell us of?
Lucio. 'Tis he, my lord. Come hither, good-
man baldpate. Do you know me?
Duke. I remember you, sir, by the sound of
your voice. I met you at the prison in the ab-
sence of the Duke.   332

Lucio. O, did you so? And do you remember
what you said of the Duke?
Duke. Most notedly, sir.   335
Lucio. Do you so, sir? And was the Duke a
fleshmonger, a fool, and a coward, as you then
reported him to be?
Duke. You must, sir, change persons with me
ere you make that my report. You indeed spoke
so of him, and much more, much worse.   341
Lucio. O thou damnable fellow! Did not I
pluck thee by the nose for thy speeches?
Duke. I protest I love the Duke as I love
myself.   345
Ang. Hark how the villain would close now,
after his treasonable abuses!
Escal. Such a fellow is not to be talk'd withal.
Away with him to prison! Where is the provost? Away with him to prison! Lay bolts
enough upon him. Let him speak no more.
Away with those giglets too, and with the other
confederate companion!
Duke. [*to Provost*] Stay, sir; stay awhile.
Ang. What, resists he? Help him, Lucio. 355
Lucio. Come, sir; come, sir; come, sir! Foh,
sir! Why, you bald-pated lying rascal, you
must be hooded, must you? Show your knave's
visage, with a pox to you! Show your sheep-
biting face and be hang'd an hour! Will't not
off?   360
[*Plucks off the friar's hood and discovers the Duke.*]
Duke. Thou art the first knave that e'er
mad'st a duke.
First, provost, let me bail these gentle three.
[*To Lucio*] Sneak not away, sir; for the friar and
you
Must have a word anon. — Lay hold on him!
Lucio. This may prove worse than hanging.
Duke. [*to Escalus*] What you have spoke I
pardon. Sit you down.   366
We'll borrow place of him. [*To Angelo*] Sir, by
your leave.
Hast thou or word, or wit, or impudence
That yet can do thee office? If thou hast,
Rely upon it till my tale be heard   370
And hold no longer out.
Ang.   O my dread lord,
I should be guiltier than my guiltiness
To think I can be undiscernible
When I perceive your Grace, like pow'r divine,
Hath look'd upon my passes! Then, good
prince,   375
No longer session hold upon my shame,
But let my trial be mine own confession.
Immediate sentence then, and sequent death,
Is all the grace I beg.

129

Duke.   Come hither, Mariana.
Say, wast thou e'er contracted to this woman?
Ang. I was, my lord.   381
Duke. Go take her hence and marry her
          instantly.
Do you the office, friar; which consummate,
Return him here again. Go with him, provost.
          *Exeunt [Angelo, Mariana, Friar Peter, and
                    Provost].*
Escal. My lord, I am more amaz'd at his
          dishonour   385
Than at the strangeness of it.
Duke.   Come hither, Isabel.
Your friar is now your prince. As I was then
Advertising and holy to your business,
Not changing heart with habit, I am still   389
Attorney'd at your service.
Isab.   O, give me pardon
That I, your vassal, have employ'd and pain'd
Your unknown sovereignty!
Duke.   You are pardon'd, Isabel;
And now, dear maid, be you as free to us.
Your brother's death I know sits at your heart;
And you may marvel why I obscur'd myself,
Labouring to save his life, and would not rather
Make rash remonstrance of my hidden pow'r
Than let him so be lost. O most kind maid,
It was the swift celerity of his death,
Which I did think with slower foot came on,
That brain'd my purpose. But peace be with
          him!   401
That life is better life, past fearing death,
Than that which lives to fear. Make it your
          comfort,
So happy is your brother.
Isab.   I do, my lord.

Enter *Angelo, Mariana, [Friar] Peter, Provost.*

Duke. For this new-married man approach-
          ing here,   405
Whose salt imagination yet hath wrong'd
Your well-defended honour, you must pardon
For Mariana's sake. But as he adjudg'd your
          brother —
Being criminal in double violation
Of sacred chastity, and of promise-breach   410
Thereon dependent for your brother's life —
The very mercy of the law cries out
Most audible, even from his proper tongue,
'An Angelo for Claudio! death for death!'
Haste still pays haste, and leisure answers
          leisure;   415
Like doth quit like, and Measure still for
          Measure.
Then, Angelo, thy fault's thus manifested,

Which, though thou wouldst deny, denies thee
          vantage.
We do condemn thee to the very block
Where Claudio stoop'd to death, and with like
          haste.   420
Away with him!
Mar.   O my most gracious lord,
I hope you will not mock me with a husband!
Duke. It is your husband mock'd you with a
          husband.
Consenting to the safeguard of your honour,
I thought your marriage fit. Else imputation,
For that he knew you, might reproach your life
And choke your good to come. For his posses-
          sions,
Although by confiscation they are ours,
We do enstate and widow you withal,   429
To buy you a better husband.
Mar.   O my dear lord!
I crave no other, nor no better man.
Duke. Never crave him. We are definitive.
Mar. Gentle my liege —   [Kneels.]
Duke.   You do but lose your labour.
Away with him to death! — [To Lucio] Now,
          sir, to you!
Mar. O my good lord! Sweet Isabel, take
          my part;   435
Lend me your knees, and all my life to come
I'll lend you all my life to do you service.
Duke. Against all sense you do importune her.
Should she kneel down in mercy of this fact,
Her brother's ghost his paved bed would break
And take her hence in horror.
Mar.   Isabel!   441
Sweet Isabel, do yet but kneel by me,
Hold up your hands, say nothing! I'll speak all.
They say best men are moulded out of faults,
And, for the most, become much more the better
For being a little bad. So may my husband.   446
O Isabel, will you not lend a knee?
Duke. He dies for Claudio's death.
Isab.   Most bounteous sir, [Kneels.]
Look, if it please you, on this man condemn'd
As if my brother liv'd. I partly think   450
A due sincerity governed his deeds
Till he did look on me. Since it is so,
Let him not die. My brother had but justice
In that he did the thing for which he died.
For Angelo,   455
His act did not o'ertake his bad intent,
And must be buried but as an intent
That perish'd by the way. Thoughts are no sub-
          jects,
Intents but merely thoughts.
Mar.   Merely, my lord.

Duke. Your suit's unprofitable. Stand up, I
   say.   [*They rise.*]
I have bethought me of another fault.   461
Provost, how came it Claudio was beheaded
At an unusual hour?
   Prov.   It was commanded so.
Duke. Had you a special warrant for the deed?
Prov. No, my good lord. It was by private
   message.   465
Duke. For which I do discharge you of your
office.
Give up your keys.
   Prov.   Pardon me, noble lord.
I thought it was a fault, but knew it not;
Yet did repent me after more advice;
For testimony whereof, one in the prison,   470
That should by private order else have died,
I have reserv'd alive.
   Duke.   What's he?
   Prov.   His name is Barnardine.
Duke. I would thou hadst done so by Claudio.
Go fetch him hither; let me look upon him.
                              [*Exit Provost.*]
   Escal. I am sorry one so learned and so wise
As you, Lord Angelo, have still appear'd,   476
Should slip so grossly, both in the heat of blood
And lack of temper'd judgment afterward.
   Ang. I am sorry that such sorrow I procure;
And so deep sticks it in my penitent heart 480
That I crave death more willingly than mercy.
'Tis my deserving, and I do entreat it.

   Enter *Barnardine* and *Provost, Claudio*
   [muffled], *Juliet.*

Duke. Which is that Barnardine?
Prov.   This, my lord.
Duke. There was a friar told me of this man.
Sirrah, thou art said to have a stubborn soul
That apprehends no further than this world,
And squar'st thy life according. Thou'rt con-
demn'd.   487
But, for those earthly faults, I quit them all,
And pray thee take this mercy to provide
For better times to come. Friar, advise him;
I leave him to your hand. What muffled fellow's
that?   491
Prov. This is another prisoner that I sav'd,
Who should have died when Claudio lost his
head,
As like almost to Claudio as himself.
                          [*Unmuffles Claudio.*]
Duke. [*to Isabella*] If he be like your brother,
   for his sake   495
Is he pardoned; and, for your lovely sake,
Give me your hand and say you will be mine.

He is my brother too. But fitter time for that!
By this Lord Angelo perceives he's safe;
Methinks I see a quick'ning in his eye.   500
Well, Angelo, your evil quits you well.
Look that you love your wife, her worth worth
   yours.
I find an apt remission in myself;
And yet here's one in place I cannot pardon.
[*To Lucio*] You, sirrah, that knew me for a fool,
One all of luxury, an ass, a madman!   505
Wherein have I deserved so of you
That you extol me thus?
   Lucio. Faith, my lord, I spoke it but accord-
ing to the trick. If you will hang me for it, you
may; but I had rather it would please you I
might be whipt.   512
   Duke. Whipt first, sir, and hang'd after.
Proclaim it, provost, round about the city,
If any woman's wrong'd by this lewd fellow 515
(As I have heard him swear himself there's one
Whom he begot with child) let her appear,
And he shall marry her. The nuptial finish'd,
Let him be whipt and hang'd.   519
   Lucio. I beseech your Highness do not marry
me to a whore! Your Highness said even now I
made you a duke. Good my lord, do not recom-
pense me in making me a cuckold.
   Duke. Upon mine honour, thou shalt marry
her.
Thy slanders I forgive, and therewithal   525
Remit thy other forfeits. Take him to prison,
And see our pleasure herein executed.
   Lucio. Marrying a punk, my lord, is pressing
to death, whipping, and hanging.
   Duke. Slandering a prince deserves it.   530
                    [*Exeunt Officers with Lucio.*]
She, Claudio, that you wrong'd, look you restore.
Joy to you, Mariana! Love her, Angelo.
I have confess'd her, and I know her virtue.
Thanks, good friend Escalus, for thy much
   goodness;   534
There's more behind that is more gratulate.
Thanks, provost, for thy care and secrecy:
We shall employ thee in a worthier place.
Forgive him, Angelo, that brought you home
The head of Ragozine for Claudio's;
Th' offence pardons itself. Dear Isabel,   540
I have a motion much imports your good,
Whereto if you'll a willing ear incline,
What's mine is yours, and what is yours is mine.
So bring us to our palace, where we'll show
What's yet behind that's meet you all should
   know.   545
                                        [*Exeunt.*]

131

THE COMEDY OF ERRORS

THE COMEDY OF ERRORS was first printed in the Folio of 1623, which affords a reasonably accurate text. There may be a cut here and there; but, if so, nothing of any consequence has been lost. It was performed at Gray's Inn on December 28, 1594. The punning reference to France as 'arm'd and reverted, making war against her heir' (iii, 2, 126) may carry the date of composition back to 1593, for the war in question came to an end in July of that year. But this evidence is not conclusive, for Dromio's jest would still be pertinent in 1594, when the rebellion was fresh in everybody's memory. A date as early as 1592 has been suggested on the basis of a possible quotation ('heart and good will, but neuer a ragge of money') by Nashe in his *Foure Letters Confuted*, registered on January 12, 1593. Compare Dromio of Ephesus (iv, 4, 88–89):

> Money by me? Heart and good will you might,
> But surely, master, not a rag of money.

The coincidence is striking and may be significant; but the phrase was obviously proverbial. Another parallel passage, from *Arden of Feversham* (registered on April 3, 1592, and printed in the same year), is too trivial to deserve attention. In any case, THE COMEDY OF ERRORS is one of Shakespeare's earliest works. 1592 or 1593 is a reasonable date, but neither 1591 nor 1594 is out of the question.

The plot comes in the main from the *Menaechmi* of Plautus, but there is also substantial borrowing from his *Amphitruo*. This is most obvious in the first scene of the third act, but it appears in details of thought, phrase, or situation in almost every part of the play. The farcical substance of the Plautine plot is framed in a new romantic setting which dignifies it and raises the interest above the level of merely comic entertainment: the play opens with the tragic plight of the distressed Ægeon and closes with his happy reunion with his long-lost wife. For this setting Shakespeare had recourse to the old and vastly popular romance of *Apollonius of Tyre*, probably in the version which he found in Gower's *Confessio Amantis* and afterwards elaborated in his *Pericles*. Besides this tragicomical envelopment he has interwoven the romantic episode of the loves of Luciana and the Syracusan Antipholus. In thus raising the tone of the play above that of the *Menaechmi*, Shakespeare was influenced by the *Amphitruo*, which is really a tragicomedy. Thus the *Amphitruo*, besides contributing to the plot, exercised a pervasively dignifying effect, even in those scenes which are original. No English translation of the *Menaechmi* is recorded before 1594, when that of a certain W[illiam] W[arner] was registered; no English version of the *Amphitruo* is known before the late seventeenth century. That Shakespeare was familiar with both plays in the original may be taken for granted. Of course he learned to read Latin if he had any education at all. Ben Jonson's famous remark about 'small Latin and less Greek' meant something very different in those days from what it suggests to a modern reader. It should be read in its context. Jonson is exalting Shakespeare above all preceding dramatists, modern or classical. He is not describing him as an ignoramus but is emphasizing his originality by insisting that he owed little to the dramatists of Greece and Rome.

Many passages might be quoted to show that Shakespeare, though not translating, had the details of the Latin phraseology constantly in mind. The transformation is interesting. Compare the words of Antipholus of Syracuse in i, 2, 33–40, with the following speech of Messenio in the *Menaechmi* (ii, 1):

'What limit will there be to your search? This is the sixth year since we began to give our whole attention to this enterprise. We have traversed the land of the Istrians, of the Spaniards, of the Massilians, of the Illyrians, the whole Adriatic and the Ionian sea, Lower Italy and all the Italian coast. If you were hunting for a needle, I think you would have found it long ago, if it were to be found at all. We are seeking a dead man among the living; for if he were alive, we should have found him long ago.'

There is no likelihood that *The Historie of Error*, a lost play given by the St. Paul's boy actors at Hampton Court on January 1, 1577, had anything to do with Shakespeare's comedy, though scholars have dallied with the conjecture that he may have utilized it as a source. We know nothing about the contents of this *Historie*. The title suggests rather a morality (with personified abstractions for its personages) than a Plautine adaptation.

A curious question is raised by the stage directions in the Folio. Antipholus of Syracuse is styled 'Antipholis Erotes' in the first stage direction of i, 2, and 'Antipholis Errotis' in that of ii, 2; Antipholus of Ephesus is styled 'Antipholis Sereptus' in the first stage direction in Act ii. *Sereptus* is doubtless a misprint for *Surreptus* ('stolen'), which the Plautine Prologue used (as well as *surrepticius*) with reference to the twin who corresponds to the Ephesian Antipholus. *Errotis* and *Erotes* may be misprints for *Erraticus* or *Errans*, an appropriate adjective for Antipholus of Syracuse:

> I to the world am like a drop of water
> That in the ocean seeks another drop.
> . . . .
> So I, to find a mother and a brother,
> In quest of them (unhappy) lose myself.

The natural inference from these terms is that Shakespeare used Plautus in the original.

The variety in metre is noteworthy. We have blank verse, decasyllabic couplets, decasyllabic verses rhyming alternately, and much rhyme doggerel in long irregular lines. This variety, which has been sometimes taken as evidence that the COMEDY is an old play worked over, rather indicates Shakespeare's wish to imitate the variety that he found in Plautus. The form used by him always fits the mood, the speaker, and the situation. The alternate rhymes have a lyrical effect and are appropriate in the love scene (iii, 2), which is original. The doggerel, which has given particular offence to the fastidious, is used by the Dromios, or by others in conversing with them in farcical dialogue (as in iii, 1); and it was certainly a happy thought to make Dromio of Ephesus adopt it when he closes the play by going off the stage with his brother of Syracuse:

> We came into the world like brother and brother;
> And now let's go hand in hand, not one before another.

THE COMEDY OF ERRORS

[Dramatis Personæ.

Solinus, Duke of Ephesus.
Ægeon, a merchant of Syracuse.
Antipholus of Ephesus, } twin brothers, and sons
Antipholus of Syracuse, } to Ægeon and Æmilia.
Dromio of Ephesus, } twin brothers, and attend-
Dromio of Syracuse, } ants on the two Antiph-
oluses.
Balthazar, a merchant.
Angelo, a goldsmith.
A Merchant of Ephesus, friend to Antipholus of
Syracuse.

Another Merchant, to whom Angelo is a debtor.
Pinch, a schoolmaster.

Æmilia, wife to Ægeon, an abbess at Ephesus.
Adriana, wife to Antipholus of Ephesus.
Luciana, her sister.
Luce, servant to Adriana.
A Courtesan.
Jailer, Officers, and Attendants.

SCENE. — Ephesus.]

ACT I. Scene I. [A hall of judgment in the Duke's Palace.]

Enter the Duke of Ephesus, with the Merchant
of Syracusa, [Ægeon,] Jailer, and other Attendants.

Æge. Proceed, Solinus, to procure my fall,
And by the doom of death end woes and all.
Duke. Merchant of Syracusa, plead no more;
I am not partial to infringe our laws.
The enmity and discord which of late   5
Sprung from the rancorous outrage of your duke
To merchants our well-dealing countrymen,
Who, wanting guilders to redeem their lives,
Have seal'd his rigorous statutes with their
blood,
Excludes all pity from our threat'ning looks. 10
For, since the mortal and intestine jars
'Twixt thy seditious countrymen and us,
It hath in solemn synods been decreed,
Both by the Syracusians and ourselves,
To admit no traffic to our adverse towns.   15
Nay more, if any born at Ephesus
Be seen at Syracusian marts and fairs —
Again, if any Syracusian born
Come to the bay of Ephesus — he dies,
His goods confiscate to the Duke's dispose,   20
Unless a thousand marks be levied
To quit the penalty and to ransom him.
Thy substance, valued at the highest rate,
Cannot amount unto a hundred marks.
Therefore by law thou art condemn'd to die.
Æge. Yet this my comfort: when your
words are done,   26
My woes end likewise with the evening sun.

Duke. Well, Syracusian, say in brief the
cause
Why thou departed'st from thy native home,
And for what cause thou cam'st to Ephesus.
Æge. A heavier task could not have been
impos'd   31
Than I to speak my griefs unspeakable.
Yet, that the world may witness that my end
Was wrought by nature, not by vile offence,
I'll utter what my sorrow gives me leave.   35
In Syracusa was I born, and wed
Unto a woman, happy but for me,
And by me too, had not our hap been bad.
With her I liv'd in joy, our wealth increas'd
By prosperous voyages I often made   40
To Epidamnum, till my factor's death
And the great care of goods at randon left
Drew me from kind embracements of my
spouse;
From whom my absence was not six months old
Before herself (almost at fainting under   45
The pleasing punishment that women bear)
Had made provision for her following me,
And soon and safe arrived where I was.
There had she not been long but she became
A joyful mother of two goodly sons,   50
And, which was strange, the one so like the other
As could not be distinguish'd but by names.
That very hour, and in the selfsame inn,
A meaner woman was delivered
Of such a burthen, male twins, both alike.   55
Those, for their parents were exceeding poor,
I bought, and brought up to attend my sons.

135

My wife, not meanly proud of two such boys,
Made daily motions for our home return.
Unwilling I agreed — alas, too soon!   60
We came aboard.
A league from Epidamnum had we sail'd
Before the always-wind-obeying deep
Gave any tragic instance of our harm.
But longer did we not retain much hope;   65
For what obscured light the heavens did grant
Did but convey unto our fearful minds
A doubtful warrant of immediate death;
Which though myself would gladly have embrac'd,
Yet the incessant weepings of my wife,   70
Weeping before for what she saw must come,
And piteous plainings of the pretty babes,
That mourn'd for fashion, ignorant what to fear,
Forc'd me to seek delays for them and me.
And this it was, for other means was none: 75
The sailors sought for safety by our boat
And left the ship, then sinking ripe, to us;
My wife, more careful for the latter-born,
Had fast'ned him unto a small spare mast,
Such as seafaring men provide for storms;   80
To him one of the other twins was bound,
Whilst I had been like heedful of the other;
The children thus dispos'd, my wife and I,
Fixing our eyes on whom our care was fix'd,
Fast'ned ourselves at either end the mast   85
And, floating straight, obedient to the stream,
Were carried towards Corinth, as we thought.
At length the sun, gazing upon the earth,
Dispers'd those vapours that offended us;
And by the benefit of his wished light   90
The seas wax'd calm, and we discovered
Two ships from far making amain to us —
Of Corinth that, of Epidaurus this.
But ere they came — O, let me say no more!
Gather the sequel by that went before.   95
   Duke. Nay, forward, old man! do not break off so,
For we may pity though not pardon thee.
   Æge. O, had the gods done so, I had not now
Worthily term'd them merciless to us!
For, ere the ships could meet by twice five leagues,   100
We were encount'red by a mighty rock,
Which being violently borne upon,
Our helpful ship was splitted in the midst;
So that, in this unjust divorce of us,
Fortune had left to both of us alike   105
What to delight in, what to sorrow for.
Her part, poor soul, seeming as burdened
With lesser weight but not with lesser woe,
Was carried with more speed before the wind,

And in our sight they three were taken up   110
By fishermen of Corinth, as we thought.
At length, another ship had seiz'd on us,
And, knowing whom it was their hap to save,
Gave healthful welcome to their shipwrack'd guests,
And would have reft the fishers of their prey,
Had not their bark been very slow of sail;   116
And therefore homeward did they bend their course.
Thus have you heard me sever'd from my bliss,
That by misfortunes was my life prolong'd
To tell sad stories of my own mishaps.   120
   Duke. And, for the sake of them thou sorrowest for,
Do me the favour to dilate at full
What hath befall'n of them and thee till now.
   Æge. My youngest boy, and yet my eldest care,
At eighteen years became inquisitive   125
After his brother; and importun'd me
That his attendant — so his case was like,
Reft of his brother, but retain'd his name —
Might bear him company in the quest of him;
Whom whilst I laboured of a love to see,   130
I hazarded the loss of whom I lov'd.
Five summers have I spent in farthest Greece,
Roaming clean through the bounds of Asia,
And, coasting homeward, came to Ephesus;
Hopeless to find, yet loath to leave unsought
Or that, or any place that harbours men.   136
But here must end the story of my life;
And happy were I in my timely death,
Could all my travels warrant me they live.
   Duke. Hapless Ægeon, whom the fates have mark'd   140
To bear the extremity of dire mishap!
Now trust me, were it not against our laws,
Against my crown, my oath, my dignity,
Which princes, would they, may not disannul,
My soul should sue as advocate for thee.   145
But, though thou art adjudged to the death,
And passed sentence may not be recall'd
But to our honour's great disparagement,
Yet will I favour thee in what I can.
Therefore, merchant, I'll limit thee this day   151
To seek thy life by beneficial help.
Try all the friends thou hast in Ephesus;
Beg thou or borrow to make up the sum,
And live; if no, then thou art doom'd to die.
Jailer, take him to thy custody.   155
   Jail. I will, my lord.
   Æge. Hopeless and helpless doth Ægeon wend,
But to procrastinate his liveless end.
                                         Exeunt.

[Scene II. *Ephesus. The Mart.*]

Enter *Antipholus Erotes* [*of Syracuse*], a *Merchant* [of Ephesus], and *Dromio* [*of Syracuse*].

Eph. Mer. Therefore give out you are of
    Epidamnum,
Lest that your goods too soon be confiscate.
This very day a Syracusian merchant
Is apprehended for arrival here,
And, not being able to buy out his life,   5
According to the statute of the town,
Dies ere the weary sun set in the west.
There is your money that I had to keep.
S. Ant. Go bear it to the Centaur, where we
    host,
And stay there, Dromio, till I come to thee.
Within this hour it will be dinner time;   11
Till that I'll view the manners of the town,
Peruse the traders, gaze upon the buildings,
And then return, and sleep within mine inn,
For with long travel I am stiff and weary.   15
Get thee away.
    S. Dro. Many a man would take you at your
    word
And go indeed, having so good a mean.   *Exit.*
    S. Ant. A trusty villain, sir, that very
    oft,
When I am dull with care and melancholy,   20
Lightens my humour with his merry jests.
What, will you walk with me about the
    town,
And then go to my inn and dine with me?
Eph. Mer. I am invited, sir, to certain mer-
    chants,
Of whom I hope to make much benefit.   25
I crave your pardon. Soon at five o'clock,
Please you, I'll meet with you upon the
    mart,
And afterward consort you till bedtime.
My present business calls me from you now.
    S. Ant. Farewell till then. I will go lose
    myself   30
And wander up and down to view the city.
Eph. Mer. Sir, I commend you to your own
    content.   *Exit.*
S. Ant. He that commends me to mine own
    content
Commends me to the thing I cannot get.
I to the world am like a drop of water   35
That in the ocean seeks another drop,
Who, falling there to find his fellow forth
(Unseen, inquisitive), confounds himself.
So I, to find a mother and a brother,
In quest of them (unhappy) lose myself.   40

Enter *Dromio of Ephesus.*

Here comes the almanac of my true date.
What now? How chance thou art return'd so
    soon?
E. Dro. Return'd so soon? Rather ap-
    proach'd too late!
The capon burns, the pig falls from the spit;
The clock hath strucken twelve upon the bell —
My mistress made it one upon my cheek;   46
She is so hot, because the meat is cold;
The meat is cold, because you come not home;
You come not home, because you have no
    stomach;   49
You have no stomach, having broke your fast;
But we, that know what 'tis to fast and pray,
Are penitent for your default to-day.
    S. Ant. Stop in your wind, sir! Tell me this,
    I pray,
Where have you left the money that I gave you?
E. Dro. O, sixpence that I had a Wednesday
    last   55
To pay the saddler for my mistress' crupper.
The saddler had it, sir; I kept it not.
    S. Ant. I am not in a sportive humour now.
Tell me, and dally not, where is the money?
We being strangers here, how dar'st thou trust
So great a charge from thine own custody?   61
E. Dro. I pray you jest, sir, as you sit at
    dinner.
I from my mistress come to you in post.
If I return, I shall be post indeed,
For she will score your fault upon my pate.   65
Methinks your maw, like mine, should be your
    clock
And strike you home without a messenger.
    S. Ant. Come, Dromio, come! These jests
    are out of season;
Reserve them till a merrier hour than this.
Where is the gold I gave in charge to thee?   70
E. Dro. To me, sir? Why, you gave no gold
    to me!
    S. Ant. Come on, sir knave! Have done your
    foolishness
And tell me how thou hast dispos'd thy charge.
    E. Dro. My charge was but to fetch you
    from the mart
Home to your house, the Phœnix, sir, to dinner.
My mistress and her sister stays for you.   76
    S. Ant. Now, as I am a Christian, answer me
In what safe place you have bestow'd my
    money,
Or I shall break that merry sconce of yours
That stands on tricks when I am undispos'd.   80
Where is the thousand marks thou hadst of me?

137

E. Dro. I have some marks of yours upon my
pate,
Some of my mistress' marks upon my shoulders;
But not a thousand marks between you both.
If I should pay your worship those again, 85
Perchance you will not bear them patiently.
S. Ant. Thy mistress' marks? What mistress, slave, hast thou?
E. Dro. Your worship's wife, my mistress at
the Phœnix;
She that doth fast till you come home to dinner
And prays that you will hie you home to dinner.
S. Ant. What, wilt thou flout me thus unto
my face, 91
Being forbid? There, take you that, sir knave!
[*Beats him.*]

E. Dro. What mean you, sir? For God sake
hold your hands!
Nay, an you will not, sir, I'll take my heels.
Exit.
S. Ant. Upon my life, by some device or
other 95
The villain is o'erraught of all my money!
They say this town is full of cozenage;
As, nimble jugglers that deceive the eye,
Dark-working sorcerers that change the mind,
Soul-killing witches that deform the body, 100
Disguised cheaters, prating mountebanks,
And many such-like liberties of sin.
If it prove so, I will be gone the sooner.
I'll to the Centaur to go seek this slave.
I greatly fear my money is not safe. *Exit.*

ACT II. [Scene I. *The house of* Antipholus of Ephesus.]

Enter *Adriana*, Wife to *Antipholus Sereptus* [*of
Ephesus*], with *Luciana*, her Sister.

Adr. Neither my husband nor the slave
return'd
That in such haste I sent to seek his master?
Sure, Luciana, it is two o'clock.
Luc. Perhaps some merchant hath invited
him,
And from the mart he's somewhere gone to
dinner. 5
Good sister, let us dine, and never fret.
A man is master of his liberty.
Time is their master; and when they see time,
They'll go or come. If so, be patient, sister.
Adr. Why should their liberty than ours be
more? 10
Luc. Because their business still lies out-o'-door.
Adr. Look, when I serve him so, he takes it
ill.
Luc. O, know he is the bridle of your will.
Adr. There's none but asses will be bridled so.
Luc. Why, headstrong liberty is lash'd with
woe. 15
There's nothing situate under heaven's eye
But hath his bound in earth, in sea, in sky.
The beasts, the fishes, and the winged fowls
Are their males' subjects and at their controls.
Men, more divine, the masters all of these, 20
Lords of the wide world and wild wat'ry seas,
Indu'd with intellectual sense and souls,
Of more preëminence than fish and fowls,
Are masters to their females, and their lords.
Then let your will attend on their accords. 25

Adr. This servitude makes you to keep unwed.
Luc. Not this, but troubles of the marriage
bed.
Adr. But, were you wedded, you would bear
some sway.
Luc. Ere I learn love, I'll practise to obey.
Adr. How if your husband start some otherwhere? 30
Luc. Till he come home again, I would forbear.
Adr. Patience unmov'd, no marvel though
she pause;
They can be meek that have no other cause.
A wretched soul bruis'd with adversity
We bid be quiet when we hear it cry; 35
But were we burd'ned with like weight of pain,
As much, or more, we should ourselves complain.
So thou, that hast no unkind mate to grieve
thee,
With urging helpless patience wouldst relieve
me;
But if thou live to see like right bereft, 40
This fool-begg'd patience in thee will be left.
Luc. Well, I will marry one day, but to try.
Here comes your man. Now is your husband
nigh.

Enter *Dromio* [*of*] *Ephesus.*

Adr. Say, is your tardy master now at hand?
E. Dro. Nay, he's at two hands with me, and
that my two ears can witness. 46
Adr. Say, didst thou speak with him?
Know'st thou his mind?

138

Donald Pleasance as Dromio of Syracuse and Maurice Whittaker as a citizen
of Ephesus in Shakespeare's tale of the tangled affairs of two pairs of twins

THE COMEDY OF ERRORS

PHOTOGRAPHS BY LISEL HAAS
PRODUCED BY THE BIRMINGHAM REPERTORY COMPANY

Ninian Brodie as Solinus, Duke of Ephesus, who decreed that any citizen of Syracuse found in his city be sentenced to death unless he pay the state a princely ransom

Having dispatched his man Dromio to await him at an inn, Antipholus of Syracuse (Gordon Davies) asks the merchant (Tony Steedman) who befriended him to dine with him, but the merchant, with a leer at the ladies of the town, pleads prior appointments and promises to meet Antipholus later at the market of Ephesus (Act I, Scene II)

"What! wilt thou flout me thus unto my face, being forbid? There, take you that, sir knave." Mistaking Dromio of Ephesus (James Ottaway) for his own servant, Antipholus of Syracuse beats him when he denies knowledge of the money supposedly left in his charge (Act I, Scene II)

"Come, I will fasten on this sleeve of thine; thou art an elm, my husband, I a vine."
Adriana (Elizabeth Clifford) mistakes Antipholus of Syracuse for her husband, to the
great dismay of his servant (Act II, Scene II)

"If thou art chang'd to
aught, 'tis to an ass."
Luciana (Patricia Russell)
mistakes Dromio of Syra-
cuse for his twin and
teases him when, in his
bewilderment, he thinks
he has been transformed
(Act II, Scene II)

"Why call you me love? call my sister so."
Believing Antipholus of Syracuse is her brother-
in-law, Luciana rebukes him for making love to
her (Act III, Scene II)

"Come, come, Antipholus; we dine too late."
Mistaking the twin from Syracuse for her
husband, Adriana urges Antipholus to come
in with her to dinner (*Act II, Scene II*)

"What art thou that keep'st me out from the
house I owe?" Antipholus of Ephesus returns
home to find his door is locked against him
and an armed man on watch within
(*Act III, Scene I*)

"Come, where's the chain? I pray you, let me see it." Antipholus of Ephesus demands of the goldsmith Angelo (Bruce Fisk) the chain which was already given his twin (*Act IV, Scene I*)

"Is that the chain you promis'd me to-day?" The Courtezan (Betty Linton) happens to encounter Antipholus of Syracuse wearing the gold chain he has just received from Angelo. Taking him for his brother, she reminds him of his promise to give her such a chain (*Act IV, Scene III*)

"Five hundred ducats, villain, for a rope?" Antipholus of Ephesus (Eric Porter) beats his Dromio for bringing him a coil of rope whereas he had sent him (actually the other twin) for money for bail (*Act IV, Scene IV*)

"Mistress, both man and master is possess'd." The schoolmaster Pinch (Tony Steedman) tells Adriana and Luciana that Antipholus of Ephesus and his man are mad (*Act IV, Scene IV*)

"If any friend will pay the sum for him, he shall not die; so much we tender him."
The duke announces he will pardon Aegeon (Peter Bentley), the father of the twins
from Syracuse, if anyone will stand surety for the ransom due (*Act V, Scene I*)

"Be quiet, people. Wherefore throng you hither?" The Abbess (Barbara Cavan) inquires why
Adriana and Luciana are pursuing Antipholus of Syracuse and his Dromio (*Act V, Scene I*)

E. *Dro.* Ay, ay, he told his mind upon mine
ear.
Beshrew his hand, I scarce could understand
it!
Luc. Spake he so doubtfully thou couldst not
feel his meaning?   51
E. *Dro.* Nay, he struck so plainly I could too
well feel his blows; and withal so doubtfully
that I could scarce understand them.
Adr. But say, I prithee, is he coming home?
It seems he hath great care to please his wife.
E. *Dro.* Why, mistress, sure my master is
horn-mad.   57
Adr. Horn-mad, thou villain?
E. *Dro.*   I mean not cuckold-mad;
But sure he is stark mad.
When I desir'd him to come home to dinner,
He ask'd me for a thousand marks in gold. 61
*'Tis dinner time,' quoth I. 'My gold!' quoth
he.
*Your meat doth burn,' quoth I. 'My gold!'
quoth he.
*Will you come home?' quoth I. 'My gold!'
quoth he.
*Where is the thousand marks I gave thee,
villain?'   65
*The pig,' quoth I, 'is burn'd.' 'My gold!'
quoth he.
*My mistress, sir —' quoth I. 'Hang up thy
mistress!
I know not thy mistress. Out on thy mistress!'
Luc. Quoth who?
E. *Dro.* Quoth my master.   70
*I know,' quoth he, 'no house, no wife, no mis-
tress.'
So that my arrant, due unto my tongue,
I thank him, I bare home upon my shoulders;
For, in conclusion, he did beat me there.
Adr. Go back again, thou slave, and fetch
him home!   75
E. *Dro.* Go back again, and be new beaten
home?
For God's sake send some other messenger.
Adr. Back, slave, or I will break thy pate
across!
E. *Dro.* And he will bless that cross with
other beating.
Between you I shall have a holy head.   80
Adr. Hence, prating peasant! Fetch thy
master home.
E. *Dro.* Am I so round with you, as you with
me,
That like a football you do spurn me thus?
You spurn me hence, and he will spurn me
hether.   84

If I last in this service, you must case me in
leather.   [*Exit.*]
Luc. Fie, how impatience low'reth in your
face!
Adr. His company must do his minions grace
Whilst I at home starve for a merry look.
Hath homely age th' alluring beauty took
From my poor cheek? Then he hath wasted it.
Are my discourses dull? barren my wit?   91
If voluble and sharp discourse be marr'd,
Unkindness blunts it, more than marble hard.
Do their gay vestments his affections bait?
That's not my fault — he's master of my state.
What ruins are in me that can be found   96
By him not ruin'd? Then is the ground
Of my defeatures. My decayed fair
A sunny look of his would soon repair.
But, too unruly deer, he breaks the pale   100
And feeds from home. Poor I am but his stale.
Luc. Self-harming jealousy — fie, beat it
hence!
Adr. Unfeeling fools can with such wrongs
dispense.
I know his eye doth homage otherwhere,
Or else what lets it but he would be here?   105
Sister, you know he promis'd me a chain.
Would that alone alone he would detain,
So he would keep fair quarter with his bed!
I see the jewel best enamelled
Will lose his beauty; and though gold bides
still   110
That others touch, yet often touching will
Wear gold; and no man that hath a name,
But falsehood and corruption doth it shame.
Since that my beauty cannot please his eye,
I'll weep what's left away, and weeping die.
Luc. How many fond fools serve mad
jealousy!   *Exeunt.*

[Scene II. *The Mart.*]

Enter *Antipholus Erotes* [*of Syracuse*].

S. Ant. The gold I gave to Dromio is laid up
Safe at the Centaur, and the heedful slave
Is wand'red forth in care to seek me out.
By computation and mine host's report,
I could not speak with Dromio since at first 5
I sent him from the mart. See, here he comes.

Enter *Dromio of Syracuse.*

How now, sir? Is your merry humour alter'd?
As you love strokes, so jest with me again.
You know no Centaur? You receiv'd no gold?

Your mistress sent to have me home to dinner?
My house was at the Phœnix? Wast thou mad
That thus so madly thou didst answer me?
  S. Dro. What answer, sir? When spake I
    such a word?
  S. Ant. Even now, even here, not half an
    hour since.
  S. Dro. I did not see you since you sent me
    hence   15
Home to the Centaur with the gold you gave me.
  S. Ant. Villain, thou didst deny the gold's
    receipt
And told'st me of a mistress and a dinner,
For which I hope thou felt'st I was displeas'd.
  S. Dro. I am glad to see you in this merry
    vein.   20
What means this jest? I pray you, master, tell
me.
  S. Ant. Yea, dost thou jeer and flout me in
    the teeth?
Think'st thou I jest? Hold, take thou that, and
    that!   *Beats Dromio.*
  S. Dro. Hold, sir, for God's sake! Now your
    jest is earnest.
Upon what bargain do you give it me?   25
  S. Ant. Because that I familiarly sometimes
Do use you for my fool and chat with you,
Your sauciness will jest upon my love
And make a common of my serious hours.
When the sun shines let foolish gnats make
    sport,   30
But creep in crannies when he hides his beams.
If you will jest with me, know my aspect
And fashion your demeanour to my looks,
Or I will beat this method in your sconce. 34
  S. Dro. Sconce call you it? So you would
leave battering, I had rather have it a head.
An you use these blows long, I must get a sconce
for my head, and insconce it too, or else I shall
seek my wit in my shoulders. But I pray, sir,
why am I beaten?   40
  S. Ant. Dost thou not know?
  S. Dro. Nothing, sir, but that I am beaten.
  S. Ant. Shall I tell you why?
  S. Dro. Ay, sir, and wherefore. For they say
every why hath a wherefore.   45
  S. Ant. Why first — for flouting me; and
    then wherefore —
For urging it the second time to me.
  S. Dro. Was there ever any man thus beaten
    out of season,
When in the why and the wherefore is neither
    rhyme nor reason?
Well, sir, I thank you.   50
  S. Ant. Thank me, sir? For what?

  S. Dro. Marry, sir, for this something that
you gave me for nothing.
  S. Ant. I'll make you amends next, to give
you nothing for something. But say, sir, is it
dinner time?   5
  S. Dro. No, sir. I think the meat wants that
    I have.
  S. Ant. In good time, sir! What's that?
  S. Dro. Basting.
  S. Ant. Well, sir, then 'twill be dry.   60
  S. Dro. If it be, sir, I pray you eat none of it.
  S. Ant. Your reason?
  S. Dro. Lest it make you choleric and pur-
chase me another dry basting.
  S. Ant. Well, sir, learn to jest in good time.
There's a time for all things.   65
  S. Dro. I durst have denied that before you
were so choleric.
  S. Ant. By what rule, sir?
  S. Dro. Marry, sir, by a rule as plain as the
plain bald pate of Father Time himself.   70
  S. Ant. Let's hear it.
  S. Dro. There's no time for a man to recover
his hair that grows bald by nature.
  S. Ant. May he not do it by fine and re-
covery?   75
  S. Dro. Yes, to pay a fine for a periwig and
recover the lost hair of another man.
  S. Ant. Why is Time such a niggard of hair,
being, as it is, so plentiful an excrement?   79
  S. Dro. Because it is a blessing that he
bestows on beasts; and what he hath scanted
men in hair, he hath given them in wit.
  S. Ant. Why, but there's many a man hath
more hair than wit.
  S. Dro. Not a man of those but he hath the
wit to lose his hair.   86
  S. Ant. Why, thou didst conclude hairy men
plain dealers without wit.
  S. Dro. The plainer dealer, the sooner lost.
Yet he loseth it in a kind of policy.   90
  S. Ant. For what reason?
  S. Dro. For two, and sound ones too.
  S. Ant. Nay, not sound, I pray you!
  S. Dro. Sure ones then.
  S. Ant. Nay, not sure, in a thing falsing. 95
  S. Dro. Certain ones then.
  S. Ant. Name them.
  S. Dro. The one, to save the money that he
spends in trimming; the other, that at dinner
they should not drop in his porridge.   100
  S. Ant. You would all this time have prov'd
there is no time for all things.
  S. Dro. Marry, and did, sir! namely, no
time to recover hair lost by nature.

S. Ant. But your reason was not substantial,
why there is no time to recover.   106
S. Dro. Thus I mend it: Time himself is
bald, and therefore to the world's end will have
bald followers.
S. Ant. I knew 'twould be a bald conclusion.
But, soft! Who wafts us yonder?   111

Enter *Adriana* and *Luciana*.

Adr. Ay, ay, Antipholus! look strange and
frown!
Some other mistress hath thy sweet aspects.
I am not Adriana nor thy wife.
The time was once when thou unurg'd wouldst
vow   115
That never words were music to thine ear,
That never object pleasing in thine eye,
That never touch well welcome to thy hand,
That never meat sweet-savour'd in thy taste,
Unless I spake or look'd or touch'd or carv'd to
thee.   120
How comes it now, my husband, O, how comes
it,
That thou art then estranged from thyself?
Thyself I call it, being strange to me,
That, undividable incorporate,
Am better than thy dear self's better part.   125
Ah, do not tear away thyself from me!
For know, my love, as easy mayst thou fall
A drop of water in the breaking gulf
And take unmingled thence that drop again
Without addition or diminishing   130
As take from me thyself, and not me too.
How dearly would it touch thee to the quick,
Shouldst thou but hear I were licentious
And that this body, consecrate to thee,
By ruffian lust should be contaminate!   135
Wouldst thou not spit at me and spurn at me,
And hurl the name of husband in my face,
And tear the stain'd skin off my harlot brow,
And from my false hand cut the wedding ring
And break it with a deep-divorcing vow?   140
I know thou canst; and therefore see thou do it.
I am possess'd with an adulterate blot,
My blood is mingled with the crime of lust;
For, if we two be one, and thou play false,
I do digest the poison of thy flesh,   145
Being strumpeted by thy contagion.
Keep then fair league and truce with thy true
bed,
I live unstain'd, thou undishonoured.
S. Ant. Plead you to me, fair dame? I
know you not.
In Ephesus I am but two hours old,   150
As strange unto your town as to your talk,
Who, every word by all my wit being scann'd,
Want wit in all one word to understand.
Luc. Fie, brother! how the world is chang'd
with you!   154
When were you wont to use my sister thus?
She sent for you by Dromio home to dinner.
S. Ant. By Dromio?
S. Dro. By me?
Adr. By thee, and this thou didst return
from him:
That he did buffet thee, and in his blows   160
Denied my house for his, me for his wife.
S. Ant. Did you converse, sir, with this
gentlewoman?
What is the course and drift of your compact?
S. Dro. I, sir? I never saw her till this time.
S. Ant. Villain, thou liest! for even her very
words   165
Didst thou deliver to me on the mart.
S. Dro. I never spake with her in all my life.
S. Ant. How can she thus then call us by our
names,
Unless it be by inspiration?
Adr. How ill agrees it with your gravity 170
To counterfeit thus grossly with your slave,
Abetting him to thwart me in my mood!
Be it my wrong you are from me exempt,
But wrong not that wrong with a more con-
tempt.
Come, I will fasten on this sleeve of thine.   175
Thou art an elm, my husband; I a vine,
Whose weakness, married to thy stronger state,
Makes me with thy strength to communicate.
If aught possess thee from me, it is dross,
Usurping ivy, brier, or idle moss,   180
Who all, for want of pruning, with intrusion
Infect thy sap and live on thy confusion.
S. Ant. [*aside*] To me she speaks. She moves
me for her theme.
What, was I married to her in my dream?
Or sleep I now, and think I hear all this?   185
What error drives our eyes and ears amiss?
Until I know this sure uncertainty,
I'll entertain the offer'd fallacy.
Luc. Dromio, go bid the servants spread for
dinner.
S. Dro. O for my beads! I cross me for a
sinner.   190
This is the fairy land. O spite of spites!
We talk with goblins, owls, and sprites.
If we obey them not, this will ensue:
They'll suck our breath or pinch us black and
blue.
Luc. Why prat'st thou to thyself and an-
swer'st not?   195

Dromio, thou drone, thou snail, thou slug, thou sot!

S. Dro. I am transformed, master, am not I?

S. Ant. I think thou art in mind, and so am I.

S. Dro. Nay, master, both in mind and in my shape.

S. Ant. Thou hast thine own form.

S. Dro. No, I am an ape.

Luc. If thou art chang'd to aught, 'tis to an ass. 201

S. Dro. 'Tis true! She rides me, and I long for grass.

'Tis so, I am an ass; else it could never be

But I should know her as well as she knows me.

Adr. Come, come, no longer will I be a fool,

To put the finger in the eye and weep 206

Whilst man and master laughs my woes to scorn.

Come, sir, to dinner. Dromio, keep the gate.

Husband, I'll dine above with you to-day

And shrive you of a thousand idle pranks. 210

Sirrah, if any ask you for your master,

Say he dines forth, and let no creature enter.

Come, sister. Dromio, play the porter well.

S. Ant. [*aside*] Am I in earth, in heaven, or in hell?

Sleeping or waking? mad or well-advis'd? 215

Known unto these, and to myself disguis'd!

I'll say as they say, and persever so,

And in this mist at all adventures go.

S. Dro. Master, shall I be porter at the gate?

Adr. Ay, and let none enter, lest I break your pate. 220

Luc. Come, come, Antipholus, we dine too late. [*Exeunt.*]

ACT III. Scene I. [*Before the house of* Antipholus of Ephesus.]

Enter *Antipholus of Ephesus*, his Man *Dromio*, *Angelo* the Goldsmith, and *Balthazar* the Merchant.

E. Ant. Good Signior Angelo, you must excuse us all.

My wife is shrewish when I keep not hours.

Say that I linger'd with you at your shop

To see the making of her carcanet,

And that to-morrow you will bring it home. 5

But here's a villain that would face me down

He met me on the mart, and that I beat him

And charg'd him with a thousand marks in gold,

And that I did deny my wife and house.

Thou drunkard thou! what didst thou mean by this? 10

E. Dro. Say what you will, sir, but I know what I know.

That you beat me at the mart, I have your hand to show.

If the skin were parchment, and the blows you gave were ink,

Your own handwriting would tell you what I think. 14

E. Ant. I think thou art an ass.

E. Dro. Marry, so it doth appear

By the wrongs I suffer and the blows I bear.

I should kick, being kick'd; and being at that pass,

You would keep from my heels and beware of an ass.

E. Ant. Y' are sad, Signior Balthazar. Pray God our cheer

May answer my good will and your good welcome here! 20

Bal. I hold your dainties cheap, sir, and your welcome dear.

E. Ant. O, Signior Balthazar, either at flesh or fish,

A table full of welcome makes scarce one dainty dish.

Bal. Good meat, sir, is common. That every churl affords.

E. Ant. And welcome more common, for that's nothing but words. 25

Bal. Small cheer and great welcome makes a merry feast.

E. Ant. Ay, to a niggardly host and more sparing guest.

But though my cates be mean, take them in good part;

Better cheer may you have, but not with better heart.

But, soft! my door is lock'd. — Go bid them let us in. 30

E. Dro. Maud, Bridget, Marian, Cisley, Gillian, Ginn!

S. Dro. [*within*] Mome, malthorse, capon, coxcomb, idiot, patch!

Either get thee from the door, or sit down at the hatch.

Dost thou conjure for wenches, that thou call'st for such store

When one is one too many? Go get thee from the door. 35

E. Dro. What patch is made our porter? My master stays in the street.

S. Dro. [*within*] Let him walk from whence
he came, lest he catch cold on's feet.

E. Ant. Who talks within there? Ho, open
the door!

S. Dro. [*within*] Right, sir! I'll tell you when,
an you'll tell me wherefore.

E. Ant. Wherefore? For my dinner! I have
not din'd to-day.   40

S. Dro. [*within*] Nor to-day here you must
not, come again when you may.

E. Ant. What art thou that keep'st me out
from the house I owe?

S. Dro. [*within*] The porter for this time, sir,
and my name is Dromio.

E. Dro. O villain, thou hast stol'n both mine
office and my name!
The one ne'er got me credit, the other mickle
blame.   45
If thou hadst been Dromio to-day in my place,
Thou wouldst have chang'd thy face for a name,
or thy name for an ass.

Enter *Luce* [above].

Luce. What a coil is there! Dromio, who
are those at the gate?

E. Dro. Let my master in, Luce.

Luce.   Faith, no! he comes too late;
And so tell your master.

E. Dro.   O Lord, I must laugh!
Have at you with a proverb: Shall I set in my
staff?   51

Luce. Have at you with another; that's —
When? can you tell?

S. Dro. [*within*] If thy name be call'd Luce —
Luce, thou hast answer'd him well.

E. Ant. Do you hear, you minion? You'll
let us in, I hope?

Luce. I thought to have ask'd you.

S. Dro. [*within*]   And you said no.

E. Dro. So, come help! Well struck! There
was blow for blow.   56

E. Ant. Thou baggage, let me in.

Luce.   Can you tell for whose sake?

E. Dro. Master, knock the door hard.

Luce.   Let him knock till it ache.

E. Ant. You'll cry for this, minion, if I beat
the door down.

Luce. What needs all that, and a pair of
stocks in the town?   60

Enter *Adriana* [above].

Adr. Who is that at the door that keeps all
this noise?

S. Dro. [*within*] By my troth, your town is
troubled with unruly boys.

E. Ant. Are you there, wife? You might
have come before.

Adr. Your wife, sir knave? Go get you from
the door.   [*Exit with Luce.*]

E. Dro. If you went in pain, master, this
knave would go sore.   65

Ang. Here is neither cheer, sir, nor welcome. We would fain have either.

Bal. In debating which was best, we shall
part with neither.

E. Dro. They stand at the door, master. Bid
them welcome hither.

E. Ant. There is something in the wind, that
we cannot get in.

E. Dro. You would say so, master, if your
garments were thin.   70
Your cake is warm within; you stand here in
the cold.
It would make a man mad as a buck to be so
bought and sold.

E. Ant. Go fetch me something. I'll break
ope the gate.

S. Dro. [*within*] Break any breaking here,
and I'll break your knave's pate.

E. Dro. A man may break a word with you,
sir; and words are but wind;   75
Ay, and break it in your face, so he break it not
behind.

S. Dro. [*within*] It seems thou want'st breaking. Out upon thee, hind!

E. Dro. Here's too much 'out upon thee!' I
pray thee let me in.

S. Dro. [*within*] Ay, when fowls have no
feathers and fish have no fin.

E. Ant. Well, I'll break in. Go borrow me a
crow.   80

E. Dro. A crow without feather? Master,
mean you so?
For a fish without a fin there's a fowl without a
feather!
If a crow help us in, sirrah, we'll pluck a crow
together.

E. Ant. Go, get thee gone; fetch me an iron
crow.

Bal. Have patience, sir. O, let it not be so!
Herein you war against your reputation   86
And draw within the compass of suspect
Th' unviolated honour of your wife.
Once this — your long experience of her wisdom,
Her sober virtue, years, and modesty,   90
Plead on her part some cause to you unknown;
And doubt not, sir, but she will well excuse
Why at this time the doors are made against
you.
Be rul'd by me. Depart in patience,

And let us to the Tiger all to dinner,   95
And about evening come yourself alone
To know the reason of this strange restraint.
If by strong hand you offer to break in
Now in the stirring passage of the day,
A vulgar comment will be made of it,   100
And that supposed by the common rout
Against your yet ungalled estimation
That may with foul intrusion enter in
And dwell upon your grave when you are dead;
For slander lives upon succession,   105
For ever housed where it gets possession.

E. Ant. You have prevail'd. I will depart in
  quiet,
And in despite of mirth mean to be merry.
I know a wench of excellent discourse,
Pretty and witty; wild, and yet too gentle. 110
There will we dine. This woman that I mean,
My wife (but, I protest, without desert)
Hath oftentimes upbraided me withal.
To her will we to dinner. [*To Angelo*] Get you
  home
And fetch the chain; by this I know 'tis made.
Bring it, I pray you, to the Porpentine,   116
For there's the house. That chain will I bestow
(Be it for nothing but to spite my wife)
Upon mine hostess there. Good sir, make haste.
Since mine own doors refuse to entertain me,
I'll knock elsewhere, to see if they'll disdain me.

Ang. I'll meet you at that place some hour
  hence.

E. Ant. Do so. This jest shall cost me some
  expense.   *Exeunt.*

[Scene II. *Before the house of* Antipholus
    of Ephesus.]

Enter, [as from the house,] *Luciana* with
    Antipholus of Syracuse.

Luc. And may it be that you have quite forgot
A husband's office? Shall, Antipholus,
Even in the spring of love, thy love-springs rot?
Shall love, in building, grow so ruinous?
If you did wed my sister for her wealth,   5
Then for her wealth's sake use her with more
  kindness.
Or, if you like elsewhere, do it by stealth,
Muffle your false love with some show of
  blindness:
Let not my sister read it in your eye;
Be not thy tongue thy own shame's orator:
Look sweet, speak fair, become disloyalty; 11
Apparel vice like virtue's harbinger;

Bear a fair presence, though your heart be
  tainted;
Teach sin the carriage of a holy saint;   14
Be secret-false. What need she be acquainted?
What simple thief brags of his own attaint?
'Tis double wrong to truant with your bed
And let her read it in thy looks at board.
Shame hath a bastard fame, well managed;
Ill deed is doubled with an evil word.   20
Alas, poor women! make us but believe
(Being compact of credit) that you love us;
Though others have the arm, show us the
  sleeve:
We in your motion turn, and you may move
  us.
Then, gentle brother, get you in again;   25
Comfort my sister, cheer her, call her wife.
'Tis holy sport to be a little vain
When the sweet breath of flattery conquers
  strife.

S. Ant. Sweet mistress (what your name is
  else, I know not,
Nor by what wonder you do hit of mine),   30
Less in your knowledge and your grace you
  show not
Than our earth's wonder, more than earth
  divine.
Teach me, dear creature, how to think and speak.
Lay open to my earthy gross conceit,
Smoth'red in errors, feeble, shallow, weak, 35
The folded meaning of your words' deceit.
Against my soul's pure truth why labour you,
To make it wander in an unknown field?
Are you a god? Would you create me new?
Transform me then, and to your pow'r I'll
  yield.   40
But if that I am I, then well I know
Your weeping sister is no wife of mine,
Nor to her bed no homage do I owe.
Far more, far more to you do I decline!
O, train me not, sweet mermaid, with thy note,
To drown me in thy sister's flood of tears. 46
Sing, siren, for thyself, and I will dote.
Spread o'er the silver waves thy golden hairs,
And as a bed I'll take them, and there lie
And in that glorious supposition think   50
He gains by death that hath such means to die.
Let Love, being light, be drowned if she sink!

Luc. What, are you mad, that you do reason
  so?

S. Ant. Not mad, but mated! how, I do not
  know.

Luc. It is a fault that springeth from your eye.

S. Ant. For gazing on your beams, fair sun,
  being by.   56

Luc. Gaze where you should, and that will clear your sight.

S. Ant. As good to wink, sweet love, as look on night.

Luc. Why call you me love? Call my sister so.

S. Ant. Thy sister's sister!

Luc.   That's my sister.

S. Ant.   No!
It is thyself, mine own self's better part,   61
Mine eye's clear eye, my dear heart's dearer heart,
My food, my fortune, and my sweet hope's aim,
My sole earth's heaven, and my heaven's claim.

Luc. All this my sister is, or else should be.

S. Ant. Call thyself sister, sweet, for I am thee.   66
Thee will I love and with thee lead my life;
Thou hast no husband yet, nor I no wife.
Give me thy hand.

Luc.   O, soft, sir! hold you still!
I'll fetch my sister to get her good will.   *Exit.*

Enter, [from the house,] *Dromio of Syracuse,*
[running].

S. Ant. Why, how now, Dromio? Where run'st thou so fast?   72

S. Dro. Do you know me, sir? Am I Dromio? Am I your man? Am I myself?

S. Ant. Thou art Dromio; thou art my man; thou art thyself.   76

S. Dro. I am an ass, I am a woman's man, and besides myself.

S. Ant. What woman's man? and how besides thyself?   80

S. Dro. Marry, sir, besides myself, I am due to a woman — one that claims me, one that haunts me, one that will have me.

S. Ant. What claim lays she to thee?   84

S. Dro. Marry, sir, such claim as you would lay to your horse; and she would have me as a beast: not that, I being a beast, she would have me; but that she, being a very beastly creature, lays claim to me.

S. Ant. What is she?   90

S. Dro. A very reverent body. Ay, such a one as a man may not speak of without he say 'sir-reverence.' I have but lean luck in the match, and yet is she a wondrous fat marriage.

S. Ant. How dost thou mean a fat marriage?

S. Dro. Marry, sir, she's the kitchen wench, and all grease; and I know not what use to put her to but to make a lamp of her and run from her by her own light. I warrant, her rags and the tallow in them will burn a Poland winter.

If she lives till doomsday, she'll burn a week longer than the whole world.   102

S. Ant. What complexion is she of?

S. Dro. Swart like my shoe, but her face nothing like so clean kept. For why? She sweats a man may go over shoes in the grime of it.   106

S. Ant. That's a fault that water will mend.

S. Dro. No, sir, 'tis in grain. Noah's flood could not do it.

S. Ant. What's her name?   110

S. Dro. Nell, sir. But her name and three quarters — that's an ell and three quarters — will not measure her from hip to hip.

S. Ant. Then she bears some breadth?   114

S. Dro. No longer from head to foot than from hip to hip. She is spherical, like a globe. I could find out countries in her.

S. Ant. In what part of her body stands Ireland?

S. Dro. Marry, sir, in her buttocks. I found it out by the bogs.   121

S. Ant. Where Scotland?

S. Dro. I found it by the barrenness, hard in the palm of the hand.

S. Ant. Where France?   125

S. Dro. In her forehead; arm'd and reverted, making war against her heir.

S. Ant. Where England?

S. Dro. I look'd for the chalky cliffs, but I could find no whiteness in them. But I guess it stood in her chin by the salt rheum that ran between France and it.   132

S. Ant. Where Spain?

S. Dro. Faith, I saw it not; but I felt it hot in her breath.   135

S. Ant. Where America, the Indies?

S. Dro. O, sir, upon her nose, all o'er embellished with rubies, carbuncles, sapphires, declining their rich aspect to the hot breath of Spain, who sent whole armadoes of carrects to be ballast at her nose.   141

S. Ant. Where stood Belgia, the Netherlands?

S. Dro. O, sir, I did not look so low. To conclude, this drudge or diviner laid claim to me; call'd me Dromio; swore I was assur'd to her; told me what privy marks I had about me, as, the mark of my shoulder, the mole in my neck, the great wart on my left arm, that I, amaz'd, ran from her as a witch.
And I think, if my breast had not been made of faith and my heart of steel,   150
She had transform'd me to a curtal dog and made me turn i' th' wheel.

S. Ant. Go hie thee presently post to the road.
An if the wind blow any way from shore,
I will not harbour in this town to-night.
If any bark put forth, come to the mart, 155
Where I will walk till thou return to me.
If every one knows us, and we know none,
'Tis time, I think, to trudge, pack, and be gone.
S. Dro. As from a bear a man would run for life,
So fly I from her that would be my wife. 160
Exit.
S. Ant. There's none but witches do inhabit here,
And therefore 'tis high time that I were hence.
She that doth call me husband, even my soul
Doth for a wife abhor. But her fair sister, 164
Possess'd with such a gentle sovereign grace,
Of such enchanting presence and discourse,
Hath almost made me traitor to myself.
But, lest myself be guilty to self-wrong,
I'll stop mine ears against the mermaid's song.

Enter *Angelo* with the chain.

Ang. Master Antipholus!
S. Ant. Ay, that's my name. 170

Ang. I know it well, sir. Lo, here is the chain.
I thought to have ta'en you at the Porpentine;
The chain unfinish'd made me stay thus long.
S. Ant. What is your will that I shall do with this?
Ang. What please yourself, sir. I have made it for you. 175
S. Ant. Made it for me, sir? I bespoke it not.
Ang. Not once, nor twice, but twenty times you have.
Go home with it and please your wife withal;
And soon at supper time I'll visit you
And then receive my money for the chain. 180
S. Ant. I pray you, sir, receive the money now,
For fear you ne'er see chain nor money more.
Ang. You are a merry man, sir. Fare you well. *Exit.*
S. Ant. What I should think of this I cannot tell;
But this I think, there's no man is so vain 185
That would refuse so fair an offer'd chain.
I see a man here needs not live by shifts
When in the streets he meets such golden gifts.
I'll to the mart and there for Dromio stay;
If any ship put out, then straight away! *Exit.*

ACT IV. Scene I. [*A public place.*]

Enter a *Merchant,* [*Angelo* the] Goldsmith, and an *Officer.*

Mer. You know since Pentecost the sum is due,
And since I have not much importun'd you;
Nor now I had not but that I am bound
To Persia and want guilders for my voyage.
Therefore make present satisfaction, 5
Or I'll attach you by this officer.
Ang. Even just the sum that I do owe to you
Is growing to me by Antipholus,
And in the instant that I met with you
He had of me a chain. At five o'clock 10
I shall receive the money for the same.
Pleaseth you walk with me down to his house,
I will discharge my bond and thank you too.

Enter *Antipholus* [*of*] *Ephesus* [and] *Dromio* [*of Ephesus*] from the *Courtesan's.*

Off. That labour may you save. See where he comes.
E. Ant. While I go to the goldsmith's house, go thou 15
And buy a rope's-end. That will I bestow

Among my wife and her confederates
For locking me out of my doors by day.
But, soft! I see the goldsmith. Get thee gone;
Buy thou a rope and bring it home to me. 20
E. Dro. I buy a thousand pound a year! I buy a rope! *Exit.*
E. Ant. A man is well holp up that trusts to you!
I promised your presence and the chain,
But neither chain nor goldsmith came to me.
Belike you thought our love would last too long
If it were chain'd together, and therefore came not. 26
Ang. Saving your merry humour, here's the note
How much your chain weighs to the utmost charect,
The fineness of the gold, and chargeful fashion,
Which doth amount to three odd ducats more 30
Than I stand debted to this gentleman.
I pray you see him presently discharg'd,
For he is bound to sea and stays but for it.
E. Ant. I am not furnish'd with the present money;
Besides, I have some business in the town. 35

146

Good signior, take the stranger to my house,
And with you take the chain, and bid my wife
Disburse the sum on the receipt thereof.
Perchance I will be there as soon as you.

Ang. Then you will bring the chain to her
yourself?   40

E. Ant. No. Bear it with you, lest I come
not time enough.

Ang. Well, sir, I will. Have you the chain
about you?

E. Ant. An if I have not, sir, I hope you have;
Or else you may return without your money.

Ang. Nay, come, I pray you, sir, give me the
chain!   45
Both wind and tide stays for this gentleman,
And I, to blame, have held him here too long.

E. Ant. Good Lord! you use this dalliance
to excuse
Your breach of promise to the Porpentine.
I should have chid you for not bringing it,   50
But like a shrew you first begin to brawl.

Mer. The hour steals on. I pray you, sir,
dispatch.

Ang. You hear how he importunes me. The
chain!

E. Ant. Why, give it to my wife, and fetch
your money.

Ang. Come, come, you know I gave it you
even now!   55
Either send the chain or send me by some token.

E. Ant. Fie, now you run this humour out of
breath!
Come, where's the chain? I pray you let me
see it.

Mer. My business cannot brook this dal-
liance.
Good sir, say whe'r you'll answer me or no. 60
If not, I'll leave him to the officer.

E. Ant. I answer you? What should I
answer you?

Ang. The money that you owe me for the
chain.

E. Ant. I owe you none till I receive the chain.

Ang. You know I gave it you half an hour
since.   65

E. Ant. You gave me none. You wrong me
much to say so.

Ang. You wrong me more, sir, in denying it.
Consider how it stands upon my credit.

Mer. Well, officer, arrest him at my suit.

Off. I do, and charge you in the Duke's name
to obey me.   70

Ang. This touches me in reputation.
Either consent to pay this sum for me,
Or I attach you by this officer.

E. Ant. Consent to pay thee that I never
had?
Arrest me, foolish fellow, if thou dar'st.   75

Ang. Here is thy fee; arrest him, officer.
I would not spare my brother in this case
If he should scorn me so apparently.

Off. I do arrest you, sir. You hear the
suit.

E. Ant. I do obey thee till I give thee
bail.
But, sirrah, you shall buy this sport as dear 81
As all the metal in your shop will answer.

Ang. Sir, sir, I shall have law in Ephesus
To your notorious shame, I doubt it not.

Enter *Dromio of Syracuse* from the Bay.

S. Dro. Master, there is a bark of Epidam-
num   85
That stays but till her owner comes aboard,
And then she bears away. Our fraughtage,
sir,
I have convey'd aboard, and I have bought
The oil, the balsamum, and aqua-vitæ.
The ship is in her trim; the merry wind   90
Blows fair from land. They stay for naught at
all
But for their owner, master, and yourself.

E. Ant. How now? a madman? Why, thou
peevish sheep,
What ship of Epidamnum stays for me?

S. Dro. A ship you sent me to, to hire waftage.   95

E. Ant. Thou drunken slave, I sent thee for
a rope,
And told thee to what purpose and what end.

S. Dro. You sent me, sir, for a rope's-end as
soon!
You sent me to the bay, sir, for a bark.

E. Ant. I will debate this matter at more
leisure   100
And teach your ears to list me with more heed.
To Adriana, villain, hie thee straight.
Give her this key, and tell her in the desk
That's cover'd o'er with Turkish tapestry
There is a purse of ducats. Let her send it. 105
Tell her I am arrested in the street,
And that shall bail me. Hie thee, slave, be gone!
On, officer, to prison till it come.
                           Exeunt [*all but Dromio*].

S. Dro. To Adriana? That is where we din'd,
Where Dowsabel did claim me for her husband.
She is too big, I hope, for me to compass.   111
Thither I must, although against my will,
For servants must their masters' minds fulfil.
                                              Exit.

147

[Scene II. *The house of* Antipholus
of Ephesus]

Enter *Adriana* and *Luciana*.

Adr. Ah, Luciana, did he tempt thee so?
Mightst thou perceive austerely in his eye
That he did plead in earnest? yea or no?
Look'd he or red or pale, or sad or merrily?
What observation mad'st thou in this case   5
Of his heart's meteors tilting in his face?

Luc. First he denied you had in him no right.

Adr. He meant he did me none. The more
my spite!

Luc. Then swore he that he was a stranger
here.

Adr. And true he swore, though yet forsworn he were.   10

Luc. Then pleaded I for you.

Adr.   And what said he?

Luc. That love I begg'd for you he begg'd of
me.

Adr. With what persuasion did he tempt thy
love?

Luc. With words that in an honest suit might
move.   14
First he did praise my beauty, then my speech.

Adr. Didst speak him fair?

Luc.   Have patience, I beseech.

Adr. I cannot nor I will not hold me still;
My tongue, though not my heart, shall have his
will.
He is deformed, crooked, old, and sere,
Ill-fac'd, worse bodied, shapeless everywhere;
Vicious, ungentle, foolish, blunt, unkind;   21
Stigmatical in making, worse in mind.

Luc. Who would be jealous then of such a one?
No evil lost is wail'd when it is gone.

Adr. Ah, but I think him better than I say,   25
And yet would herein others' eyes were worse.
Far from her nest the lapwing cries away;
My heart prays for him, though my tongue
do curse.

Enter *Dromio of Syracuse*.

S. Dro. Here, go! the desk, the purse!
Sweet now, make haste.

Luc. How hast thou lost thy breath?

S. Dro.   By running fast.

Adr. Where is thy master, Dromio? Is he
well?   31

S. Dro. No, he's in Tartar limbo, worse than
hell.
A devil in an everlasting garment hath him;
One whose hard heart is button'd up with steel;

A fiend, a fury, pitiless and rough;   35
A wolf; nay, worse — a fellow all in buff;
A back-friend, a shoulder-clapper, one that
countermands
The passages of alleys, creeks, and narrow lands;
A hound that runs counter, and yet draws dry-
foot well;
One that before the Judgment carries poor souls
to hell.   40

Adr. Why, man, what is the matter?

S. Dro. I do not know the matter. He is
'rested on the case.

Adr. What, is he arrested? Tell me at whose
suit.

S. Dro. I know not at whose suit he is
arrested well;
But he's in a suit of buff which 'rested him, that
can I tell.   45
Will you send him, Mistress Redemption, the
money in his desk?

Adr. Go fetch it, sister. (*Exit Luciana*.) This
I wonder at,
Thus he, unknown to me, should be in debt.
Tell me, was he arrested on a band?

S. Dro. Not on a band, but on a stronger
thing —   50
A chain, a chain! Do you not hear it ring?

Adr. What, the chain?

S. Dro. No, no, the bell! 'Tis time that I
were gone.
It was two ere I left him, and now the clock
strikes one.

Adr. The hours come back? That did I
never hear.   55

S. Dro. O, yes! If any hour meet a sergeant,
'a turns back for very fear.

Adr. As if Time were in debt! How fondly
dost thou reason!

S. Dro. Time is a very bankrout and owes
more than he's worth to season.
Nay, he's a thief too. Have you not heard men
say
That Time comes stealing on by night and day?
If he be in debt and theft, and a sergeant in the
way,   61
Hath he not reason to turn back an hour in a
day?

Enter *Luciana* [with the purse].

Adr. Go, Dromio. There's the money, bear it
straight;
And bring thy master home immediately.
Come, sister. I am press'd down with conceit —
Conceit, my comfort and my injury.   66
                Exeunt.

[Scene III.   *The Mart.*]

Enter *Antipholus of Syracuse.*

S. Ant. There's not a man I meet but doth
  salute me
As if I were their well-acquainted friend,
And every one doth call me by my name.
Some tender money to me; some invite me;
Some other give me thanks for kindnesses;   5
Some offer me commodities to buy.
Even now a tailor call'd me in his shop
And show'd me silks that he had bought for
  me
And therewithal took measure of my body.
Sure these are but imaginary wiles,   10
And Lapland sorcerers inhabit here.

Enter *Dromio of Syracuse.*

S. Dro. Master, here's the gold you sent me
for. What, have you got the picture of old
Adam new-apparell'd?
S. Ant. What gold is this? What Adam dost
thou mean?   15
S. Dro. Not that Adam that kept the Paradise, but that Adam that keeps the prison; he
that goes in the calve's skin that was kill'd for
the Prodigal; he that came behind you, sir,
like an evil angel, and bid you forsake your
liberty.   20
S. Ant. I understand thee not.
S. Dro. No? Why, 'tis a plain case. He that
went, like a bass-viol, in a case of leather; the
man, sir, that, when gentlemen are tired, gives
them a sob and rests them; he, sir, that
takes pity on decayed men and gives them
suits of durance; he that sets up his rest to
do more exploits with his mace than a morris-
pike.
S. Ant. What, thou mean'st an officer?   29
S. Dro. Ay, sir, the sergeant of the band; he
that brings any man to answer it that breaks
his band; one that thinks a man always going
to bed, and says 'God give you good rest!'
S. Ant. Well, sir, there rest in your foolery.
Is there any ship puts forth to-night? May we
be gone?   36
S. Dro. Why, sir, I brought you word an hour
since that the bark Expedition put forth to-
night; and then were you hind'red by the sergeant, to tarry for the hoy Delay. Here are the
angels that you sent for to deliver you.   41
S. Ant. The fellow is distract, and so am I,
And here we wander in illusions.
Some blessed power deliver us from hence!

Enter a *Courtesan.*

Court. Well met, well met, Master Antiph-
  olus!   45
I see, sir, you have found the goldsmith now.
Is that the chain you promis'd me to-day?
S. Ant. Sathan, avoid! I charge thee tempt
  me not.
S. Dro. Master, is this Mistress Sathan?
S. Ant. It is the devil.   50
S. Dro. Nay, she is worse, she is the devil's
dam! And here she comes in the habit of a light
wench; and thereof comes that the wenches say
'God damn me!' That's as much to say, 'God
make me a light wench!' It is written, 'They
appear to men like angels of light.' Light is an
effect of fire, and fire will burn; ergo, light
wenches will burn. Come not near her!
Court. Your man and you are marvellous
  merry, sir.
Will you go with me? We'll mend our dinner
  here.   60
S. Dro. Master, if you do, expect spoon-
meat, or bespeak a long spoon.
S. Ant. Why, Dromio?
S. Dro. Marry, he must have a long spoon
that must eat with the devil.   65
S. Ant. Avoid, thou fiend! What tell'st thou
  me of supping?
Thou art, as you are all, a sorceress.
I conjure thee to leave me and be gone.
Court. Give me the ring of mine you had at
  dinner
Or, for my diamond, the chain you promis'd,
And I'll be gone, sir, and not trouble you. 71
S. Dro. Some devils ask but the parings of
one's nail,
A rush, a hair, a drop of blood, a pin,
A nut, a cherry stone;
But she, more covetous, would have a chain.
Master, be wise! An if you give it her,   76
The devil will shake her chain and fright us
  with it.
Court. I pray you, sir, my ring, or else the
  chain.
I hope you do not mean to cheat me so.
S. Ant. Avaunt, thou witch! Come, Dromio,
let us go.   80
S. Dro. 'Fly pride,' says the peacock. Mis-
tress, that you know.
          Exeunt [*S. Ant. and S. Dro.*].
Court. Now out of doubt Antipholus is mad.
Else would he never so demean himself.
A ring he hath of mine worth forty ducats,
And for the same he promis'd me a chain.   85

Both one and other he denies me now.
The reason that I gather he is mad,
Besides this present instance of his rage,
Is a mad tale he told to-day at dinner
Of his own doors being shut against his entrance.
Belike his wife, acquainted with his fits,   91
On purpose shut the doors against his way.
My way is now to hie home to his house
And tell his wife that, being lunatic,
He rush'd into my house and took perforce   95
My ring away. This course I fittest choose,
For forty ducats is too much to lose.   [*Exit.*]

[Scene IV. *A street.*]

Enter *Antipholus of Ephesus* with the *Officer.*

E. Ant. Fear me not, man; I will not break
away.
I'll give thee, ere I leave thee, so much money,
To warrant thee, as I am 'rested for.
My wife is in a wayward mood to-day
And will not lightly trust the messenger.   5
That I should be attach'd in Ephesus,
I tell you 'twill sound harshly in her ears.

Enter *Dromio of Ephesus* with a rope's-end.

Here comes my man. I think he brings the
money.
How now, sir? Have you that I sent you for?
E. Dro. Here's that I warrant you will pay
them all.   10
E. Ant. But where's the money?
E. Dro. Why, sir, I gave the money for the
rope.
E. Ant. Five hundred ducats, villain, for a
rope?
E. Dro. I'll serve you, sir, five hundred at the
rate.
E. Ant. To what end did I bid thee hie thee
home?   15
E. Dro. To a rope's end, sir, and to that
end am I return'd.
E. Ant. And to that end, sir, I will welcome
you.   [*Beats him.*]
Off. Good sir, be patient.
E. Dro. Nay, 'tis for me to be patient! I am
in adversity.   21
Off. Good now, hold thy tongue.
E. Dro. Nay, rather persuade him to hold
his hands.
E. Ant. Thou whoreson senseless villain! 25
E. Dro. I would I were senseless, sir, that I
might not feel your blows.

E. Ant. Thou art sensible in nothing but
blows, and so is an ass.   29
E. Dro. I am an ass indeed! You may prove
it by my long ears. I have served him from the
hour of my nativity to this instant, and have
nothing at his hands for my service but blows.
When I am cold, he heats me with beating;
when I am warm, he cools me with beating. I
am wak'd with it when I sleep; rais'd with it
when I sit; driven out of doors with it when I
go from home; welcom'd home with it when I
return. Nay, I bear it on my shoulders, as a
beggar wont her brat; and I think, when he
hath lam'd me, I shall beg with it from door to
door.   42

Enter *Adriana, Luciana, Courtesan,* and a
Schoolmaster call'd *Pinch.*

E. Ant. Come, go along! My wife is coming
yonder.
E. Dro. Mistress, *respice finem,* respect your
end; or rather, to prophesy like the parrot, 'be-
ware the rope's end.'   46
E. Ant. Wilt thou still talk? *Beats Dromio.*
Court. How say you now? Is not your hus-
band mad?
Adr. His incivility confirms no less.
Good Doctor Pinch, you are a conjurer;   50
Establish him in his true sense again,
And I will please you what you will demand.
Luc. Alas, how fiery and how sharp he looks!
Court. Mark how he trembles in his ecstasy!
Pinch. Give me your hand and let me feel
your pulse.   55
E. Ant. There is my hand, and let it feel your
ear.   [*Strikes him.*]
Pinch. I charge thee, Sathan, hous'd within
this man,
To yield possession to my holy prayers,
And to thy state of darkness hie thee straight.
I conjure thee by all the saints in heaven.   60
E. Ant. Peace, doting wizard, peace! I am
not mad.
Adr. O that thou wert not, poor distressed
soul!
E. Ant. You minion you, are these your
customers?
Did this companion with the saffron face
Revel and feast it at my house to-day,   65
Whilst upon me the guilty doors were shut
And I denied to enter in my house?
Adr. O husband, God doth know you din'd
at home!
Where would you had remain'd until this time,
Free from these slanders and this open shame!

E. Ant. Din'd at home? — Thou, villain,
what sayest thou? 71
E. Dro. Sir, sooth to say, you did not dine at
home.
E. Ant. Were not my doors lock'd up, and
I shut out?
E. Dro. Perdie, your doors were lock'd, and
you shut out.
E. Ant. And did not she herself revile me
there? 75
E. Dro. Sans fable, she herself revil'd you
there.
E. Ant. Did not her kitchen maid rail, taunt,
and scorn me?
E. Dro. Certes she did. The kitchen vestal
scorn'd you.
E. Ant. And did not I in rage depart from
thence?
E. Dro. In verity you did. My bones bear
witness, 80
That since have felt the vigour of his rage.
Adr. Is't good to soothe him in these con-
traries?
Pinch. It is no shame. The fellow finds his
vein
And, yielding to him, humours well his frenzy.
E. Ant. Thou hast suborn'd the goldsmith
to arrest me. 85
Adr. Alas, I sent you money to redeem you
By Dromio here, who came in haste for it.
E. Dro. Money by me? Heart and good will
you might,
But surely, master, not a rag of money.
E. Ant. Went'st not thou to her for a purse
of ducats? 90
Adr. He came to me, and I deliver'd it.
Luc. And I am witness with her that she did.
E. Dro. God and the rope-maker bear me
witness
That I was sent for nothing but a rope!
Pinch. Mistress, both man and master is
possess'd. 95
I know it by their pale and deadly looks.
They must be bound and laid in some dark
room.
E. Ant. Say, wherefore didst thou lock me
forth to-day?
And why dost thou deny the bag of gold?
Adr. I did not, gentle husband, lock thee
forth. 100
E. Dro. And, gentle master, I receiv'd no
gold;
But I confess, sir, that we were lock'd out.
Adr. Dissembling villain, thou speak'st
false in both.

E. Ant. Dissembling harlot, thou art false
in all,
And art confederate with a damned pack 105
To make a loathsome abject scorn of me;
But with these nails I'll pluck out these false
eyes
That would behold in me this shameful sport.
Adr. O, bind him, bind him! Let him not
come near me.
Pinch. More company! The fiend is strong
within him. 110

Enter *three or four* and offer to bind him.
He strives.

Luc. Ay me, poor man! how pale and wan
he looks!
E. Ant. What, will you murther me? Thou
jailer thou,
I am thy prisoner. Wilt thou suffer them
To make a rescue?
Off. Masters, let him go.
He is my prisoner, and you shall not have
him. 115
Pinch. Go bind this man, for he is frantic too.
[*Dromio is bound.*]
Adr. What wilt thou do, thou peevish of-
ficer?
Hast thou delight to see a wretched man
Do outrage and displeasure to himself?
Off. He is my prisoner. If I let him go, 120
The debt he owes will be requir'd of me.
Adr. I will discharge thee ere I go from
thee.
Bear me forthwith unto his creditor,
And, knowing how the debt grows, I will pay it.
Good Master Doctor, see him safe convey'd 125
Home to my house. O most unhappy day!
E. Ant. O most unhappy strumpet!
E. Dro. Master, I am here ent'red in bond for
you.
E. Ant. Out on thee, villain! Wherefore
dost thou mad me?
E. Dro. Will you be bound for nothing? Be
mad, good master. Cry 'The devil!' 131
Luc. God help poor souls! How idly do
they talk!
Adr. Go bear him hence. — Sister, go you
with me.
*Exeunt. Manent Officer, Adriana, Luciana,
Courtesan.*
Say now, whose suit is he arrested at?
Off. One Angelo, a goldsmith. Do you
know him? 135
Adr. I know the man. What is the sum he
owes?

Off. Two hundred ducats.

Adr.   Say, how grows it due?

Off. Due for a chain your husband had of
him.

Adr. He did bespeak a chain for me, but
had it not.

Court. When as your husband, all in rage,
to-day   140
Came to my house and took away my ring —
The ring I saw upon his finger now —
Straight after did I meet him with a chain.

Adr. It may be so, but I did never see it.
Come, jailer, bring me where the goldsmith is.
I long to know the truth hereof at large.   146

Enter *Antipholus of Syracuse*, with his rapier
drawn, and *Dromio of Syracuse*.

Luc. God for thy mercy! They are loose
again.

Adr. And come with naked swords. Let's
call more help
To have them bound again.

Off.   Away! they'll kill us!

*Exeunt omnes [except Antipholus of Syra-
cuse and Dromio of Syracuse] as fast as
may be, frighted.*

S. Ant. I see these witches are afraid of
swords.   150

S. Dro. She that would be your wife now ran
from you.

S. Ant. Come to the Centaur; fetch our
stuff from thence.
I long that we were safe and sound aboard.

S. Dro. Faith, stay here this night. They
will surely do us no harm. You saw they
speak us fair, give us gold. Methinks they are
such a gentle nation that, but for the mountain
of mad flesh that claims marriage of me, I could
find in my heart to stay here still, and turn
witch.   160

S. Ant. I will not stay to-night for all the
town.
Therefore away, to get our stuff aboard!
                                          Exeunt.

ACT V. Scene I. [*A street before a Priory.*]

Enter the [*Second*] *Merchant* and [*Angelo*]
the Goldsmith.

Ang. I am sorry, sir, that I have hind'red you;
But I protest he had the chain of me,
Though most dishonestly he doth deny it.

Mer. How is the man esteem'd here in the
city?

Ang. Of very reverent reputation, sir,   5
Of credit infinite, highly belov'd,
Second to none that lives here in the city.
His word might bear my wealth at any time.

Mer. Speak softly. Yonder, as I think, he
walks.

Enter *Antipholus* [*of Syracuse*] and *Dromio*
[*of Syracuse*] again.

Ang. 'Tis so! and that self chain about his
neck   10
Which he forswore most monstrously to have.
Good sir, draw near with me, I'll speak to him.
Signior Antipholus, I wonder much
That you would put me to this shame and
trouble,
And not without some scandal to yourself,   15
With circumstance and oaths so to deny
This chain which now you wear so openly.
Beside the charge, the shame, imprisonment,
You have done wrong to this my honest friend,

Who, but for staying on our controversy,   20
Had hoisted sail and put to sea to-day.
This chain you had of me. Can you deny it?

S. Ant. I think I had. I never did deny it.

Mer. Yes, that you did, sir, and forswore it
too.

S. Ant. Who heard me to deny it or forswear it?   25

Mer. These ears of mine thou know'st did
hear thee.
Fie on thee, wretch! 'Tis pity that thou liv'st
To walk where any honest men resort.

S. Ant. Thou art a villain to impeach me
thus.
I'll prove mine honour and mine honesty   30
Against thee presently, if thou dar'st stand.

Mer. I dare, and do defy thee for a villain.

They draw. Enter *Adriana, Luciana,
Courtesan*, and others.

Adr. Hold, hurt him not for God's sake! He
is mad.
Some get within him, take his sword away.
Bind Dromio too, and bear them to my house.

S. Dro. Run, master, run! for God's sake
take a house!   36
This is some priory. In, or we are spoil'd!

*Exeunt [Antipholus of Syracuse and Dromio
of Syracuse] to the Priory.*

Enter *Lady Abbess.*

Abb. Be quiet, people. Wherefore throng you hither?

Adr. To fetch my poor distracted husband hence.
Let us come in, that we may bind him fast   40
And bear him home for his recovery.

Ang. I knew he was not in his perfect wits.

Mer. I am sorry now that I did draw on him.

Abb. How long hath this possession held the man?

Adr. This week he hath been heavy, sour, sad,   45
And much much different from the man he was;
But till this afternoon his passion
Ne'er brake into extremity of rage.

Abb. Hath he not lost much wealth by wrack of sea?
Buried some dear friend? Hath not else his eye
Stray'd his affection in unlawful love?   51
A sin prevailing much in youthful men,
Who give their eyes the liberty of gazing.
Which of these sorrows is he subject to?

Adr. To none of these, except it be the last,
Namely, some love that drew him oft from home.   56

Abb. You should for that have reprehended him.

Adr. Why, so I did.

Abb.   Ay, but not rough enough.

Adr. As roughly as my modesty would let me.

Abb. Haply in private.

Adr.   And in assemblies too.   60

Abb. Ay, but not enough.

Adr. It was the copy of our conference.
In bed he slept not for my urging it;
At board he fed not for my urging it;
Alone, it was the subject of my theme;   65
In company I often glanced it:
Still did I tell him it was vile and bad.

Abb. And thereof came it that the man was mad.
The venom clamours of a jealous woman
Poisons more deadly than a mad dog's tooth.   70
It seems his sleeps were hind'red by thy railing,
And thereof comes it that his head is light.
Thou say'st his meat was sauc'd with thy up-braidings:
Unquiet meals make ill digestions;
Thereof the raging fire of fever bred,   75
And what's a fever but a fit of madness?
Thou say'st his sports were hind'red by thy brawls:
Sweet recreation barr'd, what doth ensue
But moody and dull melancholy,
Kinsman to grim and comfortless despair,   80
And at her heels a huge infectious troop
Of pale distemperatures and foes to life?
In food, in sport, and life-preserving rest
To be disturb'd would mad or man or beast.
The consequence is, then, thy jealous fits   85
Have scar'd thy husband from the use of wits.

Luc. She never reprehended him but mildly,
When he demean'd himself rough, rude, and wildly.
Why bear you these rebukes and answer not?

Adr. She did betray me to my own reproof.
Good people, enter and lay hold on him!   91

Abb. No, not a creature enters in my house.

Adr. Then let your servants bring my husband forth.

Abb. Neither. He took this place for sanctuary,
And it shall privilege him from your hands   95
Till I have brought him to his wits again,
Or lose my labour in assaying it.

Adr. I will attend my husband, be his nurse,
Diet his sickness, for it is my office,
And will have no attorney but myself;   100
And therefore let me have him home with me.

Abb. Be patient; for I will not let him stir
Till I have us'd the approved means I have,
With wholesome syrups, drugs, and holy prayers
To make of him a formal man again.   105
It is a branch and parcel of mine oath,
A charitable duty of my order.
Therefore depart and leave him here with me.

Adr. I will not hence and leave my husband here;
And ill it doth beseem your holiness   110
To separate the husband and the wife.

Abb. Be quiet and depart. Thou shalt not have him.   [*Exit.*]

Luc. Complain unto the Duke of this indignity.

Adr. Come, go. I will fall prostrate at his feet
And never rise until my tears and prayers   115
Have won his Grace to come in person hither
And take perforce my husband from the Abbess.

Mer. By this, I think, the dial points at five.
Anon I'm sure the Duke himself in person
Comes this way to the melancholy vale,   120
The place of death and sorry execution,
Behind the ditches of the abbey here.

Ang. Upon what cause?

Mer. To see a reverent Syracusian merchant,
Who put unluckily into this bay   125

Against the laws and statutes of this town,
Beheaded publicly for his offence.
Ang. See where they come. We will behold
his death.
Luc. Kneel to the Duke before he pass the
abbey.

Enter the *Duke of Ephesus*; and [*Ægeon,*] the
Merchant of Syracuse, bareheaded; with the
Headsman and other *Officers*.

Duke. Yet once again proclaim it publicly,
If any friend will pay the sum for him,   131
He shall not die, so much we tender him.
Adr. Justice, most sacred Duke, against the
Abbess!
Duke. She is a virtuous and a reverend lady.
It cannot be that she hath done thee wrong.
Adr. May it please your Grace, Antipholus
my husband —   136
Who I made lord of me and all I had
At your important letters — this ill day
A most outrageous fit of madness took him;
That desp'rately he hurried through the street —
With him his bondman, all as mad as he —   141
Doing displeasure to the citizens
By rushing in their houses, bearing thence
Rings, jewels, anything his rage did like.   144
Once did I get him bound and sent him home,
Whilst to take order for the wrongs I went
That here and there his fury had committed.
Anon, I wot not by what strong escape,
He broke from those that had the guard of
him,
And with his mad attendant and himself,   150
Each one with ireful passion, with drawn
swords,
Met us again and, madly bent on us,
Chas'd us away, till, raising of more aid,
We came again to bind them. Then they fled
Into this abbey, whither we pursu'd them;   155
And here the Abbess shuts the gates on us
And will not suffer us to fetch him out,
Nor send him forth that we may bear him hence.
Therefore, most gracious Duke, with thy com-
mand
Let him be brought forth and borne hence for
help.   160
Duke. Long since thy husband serv'd me in
my wars,
And I to thee engag'd a prince's word,
When thou didst make him master of thy bed,
To do him all the grace and good I could.
Go, some of you, knock at the abbey gate   165
And bid the Lady Abbess come to me.
I will determine this before I stir.

Enter a *Messenger.*

Mess. O mistress, mistress, shift and save
yourself!
My master and his man are both broke loose,
Beaten the maids arow, and bound the doctor,
Whose beard they have sing'd off with brands
of fire;   171
And ever as it blaz'd, they threw on him
Great pails of puddled mire to quench the hair
My master preaches patience to him, and the
while
His man with scissors nicks him like a fool; 175
And sure, unless you send some present help,
Between them they will kill the conjurer.
Adr. Peace, fool! thy master and his man
are here,
And that is false thou dost report to us.
Mess. Mistress, upon my life I tell you true;
I have not breath'd almost since I did see it. 181
He cries for you and vows, if he can take you,
To scorch your face and to disfigure you.
                                Cry within.
Hark, hark! I hear him, mistress. Fly, be gone!
Duke. Come stand by me! fear nothing.—
Guard with halberds!   185
Adr. Ay me, it is my husband! Witness you
That he is borne about invisible.
Even now we hous'd him in the abbey here,
And now he's there, past thought of human
reason.

Enter *Antipholus* [*of Ephesus*] and *Dromio
of Ephesus.*

E. Ant. Justice, most gracious Duke! O,
grant me justice!   190
Even for the service that long since I did thee
When I bestrid thee in the wars and took
Deep scars to save thy life; even for the blood
That then I lost for thee, now grant me justice!
Æge. Unless the fear of death doth make me
dote,   195
I see my son Antipholus and Dromio.
E. Ant. Justice, sweet prince, against that
woman there!
She whom thou gav'st to me to be my wife,
That hath abused and dishonoured me
Even in the strength and height of injury.   200
Beyond imagination is the wrong
That she this day hath shameless thrown on me.
Duke. Discover how, and thou shalt find me
just.
E. Ant. This day, great Duke, she shut the
doors upon me,
While she with harlots feasted in my house. 205

Duke. A grievous fault. Say, woman, didst
  thou so?
Adr. No, my good lord. Myself, he, and my
  sister
To-day did dine together. So befall my soul
As this is false he burthens me withal!
Luc. Ne'er may I look on day nor sleep on
  night   210
But she tells to your Highness simple truth!
Ang. O perjur'd woman! They are both
  forsworn.
In this the madman justly chargeth them.
E. Ant. My liege, I am advised what I say,
Neither disturbed with the effect of wine   215
Nor heady-rash, provok'd with raging ire,
Albeit my wrongs might make one wiser mad.
This woman lock'd me out this day from dinner.
That goldsmith there, were he not pack'd with
  her,
Could witness it, for he was with me then,   220
Who parted with me to go fetch a chain,
Promising to bring it to the Porpentine,
Where Balthazar and I did dine together.
Our dinner done, and he not coming thither,
I went to seek him. In the street I met him,
And in his company that gentleman.   226
There did this perjur'd goldsmith swear me
  down
That I this day of him receiv'd the chain,
Which, God he knows, I saw not; for the which
He did arrest me with an officer.   230
I did obey, and sent my peasant home
For certain ducats. He with none return'd.
Then fairly I bespoke the officer
To go in person with me to my house. By th'
  way
We met my wife, her sister, and a rabble more
Of vile confederates. Along with them   236
They brought one Pinch, a hungry lean-fac'd
  villain,
A mere anatomy, a mountebank,
A threadbare juggler and a fortune-teller,
A needy, hollow-ey'd, sharp-looking wretch,
A living dead man. This pernicious slave 241
Forsooth took on him as a conjurer;
And, gazing in mine eyes, feeling my pulse,
And with no-face, as 'twere, outfacing me,
Cries out I was possess'd. Then all together 245
They fell upon me, bound me, bore me thence,
And in a dark and dankish vault at home
There left me and my man, both bound to-
  gether,
Till, gnawing with my teeth my bonds in sunder,
I gain'd my freedom and immediately   250
Ran hither to your Grace. whom I beseech

To give me ample satisfaction
For these deep shames and great indignities.
Ang. My lord, in truth, thus far I witness
  with him,
That he din'd not at home, but was lock'd out.
Duke. But had he such a chain of thee, or
  no?   256
Ang. He had, my lord; and when he ran
  in here,
These people saw the chain about his neck.
Mer. Besides, I will be sworn these ears of
  mine
Heard you confess you had the chain of him 260
After you first forswore it on the mart;
And thereupon I drew my sword on you;
And then you fled into this abbey here,
From whence I think you are come by miracle.
E. Ant. I never came within these abbey
  walls,   265
Nor ever didst thou draw thy sword on me.
I never saw the chain, so help me heaven!
And this is false you burthen me withal!
Duke. Why, what an intricate impeach is
  this!
I think you all have drunk of Circe's cup. 270
If here you hous'd him, here he would have been.
If he were mad, he would not plead so coldly.
You say he din'd at home. The goldsmith here
Denies that saying. Sirrah, what say you?
E. Dro. Sir, he din'd with her there, at the
  Porpentine.   275
Court. He did, and from my finger snatch'd
  that ring.
E. Ant. 'Tis true, my liege. This ring I had
  of her.
Duke. Saw'st thou him enter at the abbey
  here?
Court. As sure, my liege, as I do see your
  Grace.
Duke. Why, this is strange. Go call the
  Abbess hither.   280
I think you are all mated or stark mad.
                    Exit one to the Abbess.
Æge. Most mighty Duke, vouchsafe me
  speak a word.
Haply I see a friend will save my life
And pay the sum that may deliver me.
Duke. Speak freely, Syracusian, what thou
  wilt.   285
Æge. Is not your name, sir, call'd Antipholus?
And is not that your bondman Dromio?
E. Dro. Within this hour I was his bondman,
  sir,
But he, I thank him, gnaw'd in two my cords.
Now am I Dromio, and his man unbound.   290

Æge. I am sure you both of you remember me.

E. Dro. Ourselves we do remember, sir, by you;
For lately we were bound as you are now.
You are not Pinch's patient, are you, sir?

Æge. Why look you strange on me? You know me well.   295

E. Ant. I never saw you in my life till now.

Æge. O, grief hath chang'd me since you saw me last,
And careful hours with Time's deformed hand
Have written strange defeatures in my face.
But tell me yet, dost thou not know my voice?

E. Ant. Neither.   301

Æge. Dromio, nor thou?

E. Dro.   No, trust me, sir, nor I.

Æge. I am sure thou dost.

E. Dro. Ay, sir, but I am sure I do not; and whatsoever a man denies, you are now bound to believe him.   306

Æge. Not know my voice? O time's extremity,
Hast thou so crack'd and splitted my poor tongue
In seven short years that here my only son
Knows not my feeble key of untun'd cares?
Though now this grained face of mine be hid
In sap-consuming winter's drizzled snow
And all the conduits of my blood froze up,
Yet hath my night of life some memory,
My wasting lamps some fading glimmer left,
My dull deaf ears a little use to hear.   316
All these old witnesses I cannot err
Tell me thou art my son Antipholus.

E. Ant. I never saw my father in my life.

Æge. But seven years since, in Syracusa, boy,
Thou know'st we parted. But perhaps, my son,
Thou sham'st to acknowledge me in misery.

E. Ant. The Duke and all that know me in the city
Can witness with me that it is not so.
I ne'er saw Syracusa in my life.   325

Duke. I tell thee, Syracusian, twenty years
Have I been patron to Antipholus,
During which time he ne'er saw Syracusa.
I see thy age and dangers make thee dote.

Enter the *Abbess*, with *Antipholus of Syracuse* and *Dromio of Syracuse*.

Abb. Most mighty Duke, behold a man much wrong'd.   *All gather to see them.*

Adr. I see two husbands, or mine eyes deceive me.

Duke. One of these men is genius to the other;

And so of these. Which is the natural man
And which the spirit? Who deciphers them?

S. Dro. I, sir, am Dromio. Command him away.   335

E. Dro. I, sir, am Dromio. Pray let me stay.

S. Ant. Ægeon art thou not? or else his ghost.

S. Dro. O, my old master! Who hath bound him here?

Abb. Whoever bound him, I will loose his bonds
And gain a husband by his liberty.   340
Speak, old Ægeon, if thou be'st the man
That hadst a wife once call'd Æmilia,
That bore thee at a burthen two fair sons.
O, if thou be'st the same Ægeon, speak,
And speak unto the same Æmilia!   34F

Æge. If I dream not, thou art Æmilia.
If thou art she, tell me, where is that son
That floated with thee on the fatal raft?

Abb. By men of Epidamnum he and I
And the twin Dromio, all were taken up;   350
But by-and-by rude fishermen of Corinth
By force took Dromio and my son from them,
And me they left with those of Epidamnum.
What then became of them I cannot tell;
I to this fortune that you see me in.   355

Duke. Why, here begins his morning story right.
These two Antipholus', these two so like,
And these two Dromios, one in semblance —
Besides her urging of her wrack at sea —
These are the parents to these children,   360
Which accidentally are met together.
Antipholus, thou cam'st from Corinth first.

S. Ant. No, sir, not I! I came from Syracuse.

Duke. Stay, stand apart. I know not which is which.

E. Ant. I came from Corinth, my most gracious lord —   365

E. Dro. And I with him.

E. Ant. Brought to this town by that most famous warrior,
Duke Menaphon, your most renowned uncle.

Adr. Which of you two did dine with me to-day?

S. Ant. I, gentle mistress.

Adr.   And are not you my husband? 370

E. Ant. No; I say nay to that.

S. Ant. And so do I. Yet did she call me so,
And this fair gentlewoman, her sister here,
Did call me brother. [*To Luciana*] What I told you then
I hope I shall have leisure to make good,   375
If this be not a dream I see and hear.

156

Ang. That is the chain, sir, which you had of me.

S. Ant. I think it be, sir. I deny it not.

E. Ant. And you, sir, for this chain arrested me.

Ang. I think I did, sir. I deny it not.　380

Adr. I sent you money, sir, to be your bail
By Dromio; but I think he brought it not.

E. Dro. No, none by me.

S. Ant. This purse of ducats I receiv'd from you,
And Dromio my man did bring them me.　385
I see we still did meet each other's man,
And I was ta'en for him, and he for me,
And thereupon these errors are arose.

E. Ant. These ducats pawn I for my father here.

Duke. It shall not need. Thy father hath his life.　390

Court. Sir, I must have that diamond from you.

E. Ant. There, take it, and much thanks for my good cheer!

Abb. Renowned Duke, vouchsafe to take the pains
To go with us into the abbey here　394
And hear at large discoursed all our fortunes.
And all that are assembled in this place
That by this sympathized one day's error
Have suffer'd wrong, go keep us company,
And we shall make full satisfaction.　399
Thirty-three years have I but gone in travail
Of you, my sons, and till this present hour
My heavy burthen ne'er delivered.
The Duke, my husband, and my children both,
And you, the calendars of their nativity,
Go to a gossips' feast, and joy with me,　405
After so long grief, such nativity!

Duke. With all my heart I'll gossip at this feast.

Exeunt. Manent the two Dromios and two Brothers [Antipholus].

S. Dro. Master, shall I fetch your stuff from shipboard?

E. Ant. Dromio, what stuff of mine hast thou embark'd?

S. Dro. Your goods that lay at host, sir, in the Centaur.　410

S. Ant. He speaks to me. I am your master, Dromio.
Come, go with us; we'll look to that anon.
Embrace thy brother there; rejoice with him.

Exeunt [the two brothers Antipholus].

S. Dro. There is a fat friend at your master's house
That kitchen'd me for you to-day at dinner.
She now shall be my sister, not my wife.　416

E. Dro. Methinks you are my glass, and not my brother.
I see by you I am a sweet-fac'd youth.
Will you walk in to see their gossiping?

S. Dro. Not I, sir. You are my elder.　420

E. Dro. That's a question. How shall we try it?

S. Dro. We'll draw cuts for the senior. Till then lead thou first.

E. Dro. Nay then, thus!
We came into the world like brother and brother;
And now let's go hand in hand, not one before another.　*Exeunt.*

157

MUCH ADO ABOUT NOTHING

On August 4, 1600, the Stationers' Register records that 'The Commedie of muche A doo about nothing' (along with 'As you like yt,' 'Henry the ffift,' and 'Euery man in his humour') is 'to be staied.' The meaning of this note is far from clear. Perhaps the actors, in accordance with their usual policy, were attempting to block publication. On August 23, however, MUCH ADO ABOUT NOTHING was regularly entered in the Register by Andrew Wyse and William Aspley. Their edition (in quarto) came out before the end of the year. On this Quarto of 1600 is based the text of the present edition. In setting up the First Folio — which is less accurate than the Quarto, but supplies a number of corrections — the printers must have used a copy of the Quarto that had served as a prompt book and contained some manuscript changes, mostly in stage directions and speech headings.

Meres,[1] in the list of Shakespeare's comedies which he gives in his *Palladis Tamia* (1598), does not mention MUCH ADO, but when the Quarto appeared, in 1600, the play had been 'sundrie times publikely acted' by the Lord Chamberlain's players, as the title-page informs us. The part of Dogberry was taken by Will Kemp. This is proved by speech headings in the Quarto (iv, 2). Kemp left the Lord Chamberlain's Company early in 1599. Thus we may confidently fix the date of the play as the winter of 1598–99. Style and metre accord with this date.

The main plot comes from the twenty-second story in Matteo Bandello's *Novelle* (1554), which Shakespeare may have read in the original or in the translation in Volume III of Belleforest's *Histoires Tragiques* (1569). Bandello goes back, somehow, to the Greek romance of *Chæreas and Callirrhoë*, by one Chariton, who lived about the late fourth or early fifth century; but all this is prehistoric, so far as Shakespeare is concerned.

Bandello's *novella* may be summarized as follows:

King Piero of Aragon, having conquered Sicily, is holding court at Messina. One of his nobles, Timbreo di Cardone, is in love with Fenicia, the daughter of Messer Lionato de' Lionati, a gentleman of that city. A marriage is arranged. A cavalier, one Girondo Olerio Valenziano, a friend of Timbreo's, also loves Fenicia, and plots with an acquaintance, a young courtier 'more fond of evil than of good' (compare Shakespeare's Don John), to break off the match and win Fenicia for himself. This accomplice informs Timbreo that Fenicia is carrying on an intrigue with a certain gentleman and offers to give him ocular proof. That night he posts Timbreo in Lionato's garden. Girondo clothes a servant in fine attire and he and his accomplice go with the servant to the garden, accompanied by an attendant with a ladder on his shoulder. The family live on the other side of the palace, so that Girondo's servant can enter the house on the garden side without disturbing them. Timbreo sees him climb the ladder and go in at a window. Convinced of Fenicia's guilt, he leaves the garden without waiting to see the supposed lover come out. He has not recognized Girondo in the darkness and has no suspicion of his perfidy.

Next day Timbreo sends word to Lionato that he refuses to marry his daughter because of her unchastity. The messenger denounces Fenicia in the presence of her father and mother. Lionato accepts the breaking off of the match, but affirms his daughter's innocence and expresses the hope that God, the just judge, will bring the truth to light. Fenicia is overcome and lies cold and lifeless. A physician pronounces her dead, but she revives. Lionato decides to conceal the fact of her recovery. Funeral rites are performed, a coffin is buried, and a tomb is built, on which is set

---

[1] There is no likelihood that the mysterious *Love Labour's Won*, mentioned by Meres as one of Shakespeare's comedies, is MUCH ADO. It is much more likely to be *All's Well that Ends Well*, if indeed, it is still in existence.

up an epitaph in verse declaring her innocence (compare MUCH ADO, v, 3). She is sent in secret to the country house of her uncle Girolamo. All Messina mourns her death.

Timbreo soon comes to his senses and begins to analyze the evidence, which, on consideration, he finds far from convincing. Girondo, thinking Fenicia dead, goes almost mad with remorse. He takes Timbreo to the tomb, gives him a dagger, and begs him to kill him 'as a sacrifice to the guiltless Fenicia.' He makes a full confession; but Timbreo refuses to strike: 'I should lose my friend,' he says, and 'Fenicia would not be restored to life.' They go to the house of Lionato, and Timbreo tells the whole story in the presence of Fenicia's father and mother and others of her kindred. They are forgiven, and Timbreo promises to take no wife except such a one as Lionato shall propose.

A year later Lionato tells Timbreo that he has in mind a wife he thinks suitable. They visit the villa where Fenicia (now called Lucilla) has taken refuge. She has grown so fast in the interval — she was only sixteen when the match was broken off — that she is unrecognizable; but she looks so much like Fenicia that Timbreo falls in love with her on the spot. She pardons him and they are married. That everything may be rounded off symmetrically, her sister, Belfiore, marries the repentant Girondo.

Before Bandello wrote, Ariosto had worked the ancient story into his *Orlando Furioso* (cantos iv–vi), attaching it to the adventures of Rinaldo in Scotland. He calls the lady Ginevra; her suitor is Ariodante. From Ariosto either in the original or in Sir John Harington's translation (1591), Shakespeare derived the incident of the maid's guilelessly attiring herself as her mistress at the request of her villanous lover. Spenser repeats the tale (condensed and altered) in *The Faerie Queene* (ii, 4, 17–36), adapting it from Ariosto (compare stanza 26 with *Orlando Furioso*, v, 24–25, for a significant detail in this regard). Doubtless Shakespeare knew Spenser's version, which includes the maid's disguise; but that he had his eye on Ariosto seems certain. His Claudio is challenged to mortal combat by Leonato and Antonio, and again by Benedick. There is nothing of the kind in either Bandello or Spenser, whereas in Ariosto the wager of battle (to determine the guilt or innocence of the heroine) is the very top of the narrative climax. Harington mentions a verse translation of the episode by George Turbervile, of which nothing more is known.

In 1583 *A historie of Ariodante and Geneuora* was played at court by Richard Mulcaster's pupils, the boys of the Merchant Taylors' School. Nothing more is known of it. That another lost play recorded as *Panecia* in 1574 was really *Fenicia* (and based on Bandello) is an idle guess. *Panacia* (Πανάκεια) is quite as likely, and neither is probable. Jacob Ayrer's German comedy of *Die Schöne Phänicia* and Starter's Dutch *Timbre de Cardone ende Fenicie van Messine* both go back to Bandello, but neither throws any light on Shakespeare or his sources. Bandello and Ariosto suffice. There is no sound basis for the conjecture that our MUCH ADO is a reworking of an older play.

The merry war of Benedick and Beatrice, as well as the contortions of Dogberry and Verges, is Shakespeare's own.

MUCH ADO ABOUT NOTHING

[Dramatis Personæ.

Don Pedro, Prince of Arragon.
Don John, his bastard brother.
Claudio, a young lord of Florence.
Benedick, a young lord of Padua.
Leonato, Governor of Messina.
Antonio, an old man, his brother.
Balthasar, attendant on *Don Pedro*.
Borachio, }
Conrade, } followers of *Don John*.
Friar Francis

Dogberry, a Constable.
Verges, a Headborough.
A Sexton.
A Boy.

Hero, daughter to *Leonato*.
Beatrice, niece to *Leonato*.
Margaret, } waiting gentlewomen attending on
Ursula, } Hero.

Messengers, Watch, Attendants, &c.

SCENE. — *Messina.*]

ACT I. Scene I. [*An orchard before* Leonato's *house*.]

Enter *Leonato* (Governor of Messina), *Hero* (his Daughter), and *Beatrice* (his Niece), with a *Messenger*.

Leon. I learn in this letter that Don Pedro of Arragon comes this night to Messina.

Mess. He is very near by this. He was not three leagues off when I left him.

Leon. How many gentlemen have you lost in this action? 6

Mess. But few of any sort, and none of name.

Leon. A victory is twice itself when the achiever brings home full numbers. I find here that Don Pedro hath bestowed much honour on a young Florentine called Claudio. 11

Mess. Much deserv'd on his part, and equally remember'd by Don Pedro. He hath borne himself beyond the promise of his age, doing in the figure of a lamb the feats of a lion. He hath indeed better bett'red expectation than you must expect of me to tell you how. 17

Leon. He hath an uncle here in Messina will be very much glad of it.

Mess. I have already delivered him letters, and there appears much joy in him; even so much that joy could not show itself modest enough without a badge of bitterness.

Leon. Did he break out into tears?

Mess. In great measure. 25

Leon. A kind overflow of kindness. There are no faces truer than those that are so wash'd. How much better is it to weep at joy than to joy at weeping!

Beat. I pray you, is Signior Mountanto return'd from the wars or no? 31

Mess. I know none of that name, lady. There was none such in the army of any sort.

Leon. What is he that you ask for, niece?

Hero. My cousin means Signior Benedick of Padua. 36

Mess. O, he's return'd, and as pleasant as ever he was.

Beat. He set up his bills here in Messina and challeng'd Cupid at the flight, and my uncle's fool, reading the challenge, subscrib'd for Cupid and challeng'd him at the burbolt. I pray you, how many hath he kill'd and eaten in these wars? But how many hath he kill'd? For indeed I promised to eat all of his killing. 45

Leon. Faith, niece, you tax Signior Benedick too much; but he'll be meet with you, I doubt it not.

Mess. He hath done good service, lady, in these wars.

Beat. You had musty victual, and he hath holp to eat it. He is a very valiant trencherman; he hath an excellent stomach. 52

Mess. And a good soldier too, lady.

Beat. And a good soldier to a lady; but what is he to a lord? 55

Mess. A lord to a lord, a man to a man; stuff'd with all honourable virtues.

Beat. It is so indeed. He is no less than a stuff'd man; but for the stuffing — well, we are all mortal. 60

Leon. You must not, sir, mistake my niece. There is a kind of merry war betwixt Signior Benedick and her. They never meet but there's a skirmish of wit between them. 64

Beat. Alas, he gets nothing by that! In our last conflict four of his five wits went halting off, and now is the whole man govern'd with one; so that if he have wit enough to keep himself warm, let him bear it for a difference between himself and his horse; for it is all the wealth that he hath left to be known a reasonable creature. Who is his companion now? He hath every month a new sworn brother.   73

Mess. Is't possible?

Beat. Very easily possible. He wears his faith but as the fashion of his hat; it ever changes with the next block.   77

Mess. I see, lady, the gentleman is not in your books.

Beat. No. An he were, I would burn my study. But I pray you, who is his companion? Is there no young squarer now that will make a voyage with him to the devil?

Mess. He is most in the company of the right noble Claudio.   85

Beat. O Lord, he will hang upon him like a disease! He is sooner caught than the pestilence, and the taker runs presently mad. God help the noble Claudio! If he have caught the Benedick, it will cost him a thousand pound ere 'a be cured.   90

Mess. I will hold friends with you, lady.

Beat. Do, good friend.

Leon. You will never run mad, niece.

Beat. No, not till a hot January.

Mess. Don Pedro is approach'd.   95

Enter *Don Pedro, Claudio, Benedick, Balthasar.* and *John the Bastard.*

Pedro. Good Signior Leonato, are you come to meet your trouble? The fashion of the world is to avoid cost, and you encounter it.   98

Leon. Never came trouble to my house in the likeness of your Grace; for trouble being gone, comfort should remain; but when you depart from me, sorrow abides and happiness takes his leave.

Pedro. You embrace your charge too willingly. I think this is your daughter.

Leon. Her mother hath many times told me so.   105

Bene. Were you in doubt, sir, that you ask'd her?

Leon. Signior Benedick, no; for then were you a child.

Pedro. You have it full, Benedick. We may guess by this what you are, being a man. Truly the lady fathers herself. Be happy, lady; for you are like an honourable father.

Bene. If Signior Leonato be her father, she would not have his head on her shoulders for all Messina, as like him as she is.   116

Beat. I wonder that you will still be talking, Signior Benedick. Nobody marks you.

Bene. What, my dear Lady Disdain! are you yet living?   120

Beat. Is it possible Disdain should die while she hath such meet food to feed it as Signior Benedick? Courtesy itself must convert to disdain if you come in her presence.   124

Bene. Then is courtesy a turncoat. But it is certain I am loved of all ladies, only you excepted; and I would I could find in my heart that I had not a hard heart, for truly I love none.

Beat. A dear happiness to women! They would else have been troubled with a pernicious suitor. I thank God and my cold blood, I am of your humour for that. I had rather hear my dog bark at a crow than a man swear he loves me.   133

Bene. God keep your ladyship still in that mind! So some gentleman or other shall scape a predestinate scratch'd face.

Beat. Scratching could not make it worse an 'twere such a face as yours were.   138

Bene. Well, you are a rare parrot-teacher.

Beat. A bird of my tongue is better than a beast of yours.   141

Bene. I would my horse had the speed of your tongue, and so good a continuer. But keep your way, a God's name! I have done.

Beat. You always end with a jade's trick. I know you of old.   146

Pedro. That is the sum of all, Leonato. Signior Claudio and Signior Benedick, my dear friend Leonato hath invited you all. I tell him we shall stay here at the least a month, and he heartily prays some occasion may detain us longer. I dare swear he is no hypocrite, but prays from his heart.   153

Leon. If you swear, my lord, you shall not be forsworn. [*To Don John*] Let me bid you welcome, my lord. Being reconciled to the Prince your brother, I owe you all duty.   157

John. I thank you. I am not of many words, but I thank you.

Leon. Please it your Grace lead on?   160

Pedro. Your hand, Leonato. We will go together.

Exeunt. Manent Benedick and Claudio.

Claud. Benedick, didst thou note the daughter of Signior Leonato?   165

Bene. I noted her not, but I look'd on her.

Claud. Is she not a modest young lady?

Bene. Do you question me, as an honest man should do, for my simple true judgment? or would you have me speak after my custom, as being a professed tyrant to their sex? 170

Claud. No. I pray thee speak in sober judgment.

Bene. Why, i' faith, methinks she's too low for a high praise, too brown for a fair praise, and too little for a great praise. Only this commendation I can afford her, that were she other than she is, she were unhandsome, and being no other but as she is, I do not like her.

Claud. Thou thinkest I am in sport. I pray thee tell me truly how thou lik'st her. 180

Bene. Would you buy her, that you enquire after her?

Claud. Can the world buy such a jewel?

Bene. Yea, and a case to put it into. But speak you this with a sad brow? or do you play the flouting Jack, to tell us Cupid is a good hare-finder and Vulcan a rare carpenter? Come, in what key shall a man take you to go in the song?

Claud. In mine eye she is the sweetest lady that ever I look'd on. 190

Bene. I can see yet without spectacles, and I see no such matter. There's her cousin, an she were not possess'd with a fury, exceeds her as much in beauty as the first of May doth the last of December. But I hope you have no intent to turn husband, have you? 196

Claud. I would scarce trust myself, though I had sworn the contrary, if Hero would be my wife.

Bene. Is't come to this? In faith, hath not the world one man but he will wear his cap with suspicion? Shall I never see a bachelor of threescore again? Go to, i' faith! An thou wilt needs thrust thy neck into a yoke, wear the print of it and sigh away Sundays. 204

Enter *Don Pedro.*

Look! Don Pedro is returned to seek you.

Pedro. What secret hath held you here, that you followed not to Leonato's?

Bene. I would your Grace would constrain me to tell.

Pedro. I charge thee on thy allegiance. 210

Bene. You hear, Count Claudio. I can be secret as a dumb man, I would have you think so; but, on my allegiance — mark you this — on my allegiance! he is in love. With who? Now that is your Grace's part. Mark how short his answer is: With Hero, Leonato's short daughter.

Claud. If this were so, so were it utt'red.

Bene. Like the old tale, my lord: 'It is not so, nor 'twas not so; but indeed, God forbid it should be so!' 220

Claud. If my passion change not shortly, God forbid it should be otherwise.

Pedro. Amen, if you love her; for the lady is very well worthy. 224

Claud. You speak this to fetch me in, my lord.

Pedro. By my troth, I speak my thought.

Claud. And, in faith, my lord, I spoke mine.

Bene. And, by my two faiths and troths, my lord, I spoke mine.

Claud. That I love her, I feel. 230

Pedro. That she is worthy, I know.

Bene. That I neither feel how she should be loved, nor know how she should be worthy, is the opinion that fire cannot melt out of me. I will die in it at the stake. 235

Pedro. Thou wast ever an obstinate heretic in the despite of beauty.

Claud. And never could maintain his part but in the force of his will. 239

Bene. That a woman conceived me, I thank her; that she brought me up, I likewise give her most humble thanks; but that I will have a rechate winded in my forehead, or hang my bugle in an invisible baldrick, all women shall pardon me. Because I will not do them the wrong to mistrust any, I will do myself the right to trust none; and the fine is (for the which I may go the finer), I will live a bachelor.

Pedro. I shall see thee, ere I die, look pale with love. 250

Bene. With anger, with sickness, or with hunger, my lord; not with love. Prove that ever I lose more blood with love than I will get again with drinking, pick out mine eyes with a ballad-maker's pen and hang me up at the door of a brothel house for the sign of blind Cupid. 256

Pedro. Well, if ever thou dost fall from this faith, thou wilt prove a notable argument.

Bene. If I do, hang me in a bottle like a cat and shoot at me; and he that hits me, let him be clapp'd on the shoulder and call'd Adam.

Pedro. Well, as time shall try. 262
'In time the savage bull doth bear the yoke.'

Bene. The savage bull may; but if ever the sensible Benedick bear it, pluck off the bull's horns and set them in my forehead, and let me be vilely painted, and in such great letters as they write 'Here is good horse to hire,' let them signify under my sign 'Here you may see Benedick the married man.' 270

Claud. If this should ever happen, thou wouldst be horn-mad.

Pedro. Nay, if Cupid have not spent all his quiver in Venice, thou wilt quake for this shortly.

Bene. I look for an earthquake too then. 275

Pedro. Well, you will temporize with the hours. In the meantime, good Signior Benedick, repair to Leonato's, commend me to him and tell him I will not fail him at supper; for indeed he hath made great preparation. 280

Bene. I have almost matter enough in me for such an embassage; and so I commit you —

Claud. To the tuition of God. From my house — if I had it —

Pedro. The sixth of July. Your loving friend, Benedick. 286

Bene. Nay, mock not, mock not. The body of your discourse is sometime guarded with fragments, and the guards are but slightly basted on neither. Ere you flout old ends any further, examine your conscience. And so I leave you. *Exit.*

Claud. My liege, your Highness now may do me good. 292

Pedro. My love is thine to teach. Teach it but how,
And thou shalt see how apt it is to learn
Any hard lesson that may do thee good. 295

Claud. Hath Leonato any son, my lord?

Pedro. No child but Hero; she's his only heir.
Dost thou affect her, Claudio?

Claud. O my lord,
When you went onward on this ended action,
I look'd upon her with a soldier's eye, 300
That lik'd, but had a rougher task in hand
Than to drive liking to the name of love;
But now I am return'd and that war-thoughts
Have left their places vacant, in their rooms
Come thronging soft and delicate desires, 305
All prompting me how fair young Hero is,
Saying I lik'd her ere I went to wars.

Pedro. Thou wilt be like a lover presently
And tire the hearer with a book of words.
If thou dost love fair Hero, cherish it, 310
And I will break with her and with her father,
And thou shalt have her. Was't not to this end
That thou began'st to twist so fine a story?

Claud. How sweetly you do minister to love,
That know love's grief by his complexion! 315
But lest my liking might too sudden seem,
I would have salv'd it with a longer treatise.

Pedro. What need the bridge much broader than the flood?
The fairest grant is the necessity.
Look, what will serve is fit. 'Tis once, thou lovest, 320
And I will fit thee with the remedy.
I know we shall have revelling to-night.
I will assume thy part in some disguise
And tell fair Hero I am Claudio,
And in her bosom I'll unclasp my heart 325
And take her hearing prisoner with the force
And strong encounter of my amorous tale.
Then after to her father will I break,
And the conclusion is, she shall be thine.
In practice let us put it presently. *Exeunt.*

[Scene II. *A room in* Leonato's *house.*]

Enter [at one door] *Leonato* and [at another door, *Antonio,*] an old man, brother to *Leonato.*

Leon. How now, brother? Where is my cousin your son? Hath he provided this music?

Ant. He is very busy about it. But, brother, I can tell you strange news that you yet dreamt not of. 5

Leon. Are they good?

Ant. As the event stamps them; but they have a good cover, they show well outward. The Prince and Count Claudio, walking in a thick-pleached alley in mine orchard, were thus much overheard by a man of mine: the Prince discovered to Claudio that he loved my niece your daughter and meant to acknowledge it this night in a dance, and if he found her accordant, he meant to take the present time by the top and instantly break with you of it. 16

Leon. Hath the fellow any wit that told you this?

Ant. A good sharp fellow. I will send for him, and question him yourself. 20

Leon. No, no. We will hold it as a dream till it appear itself; but I will acquaint my daughter withal, that she may be the better prepared for an answer, if peradventure this be true. Go you and tell her of it. *[Exit Antonio.]*

[Enter *Antonio's Son* with a *Musician,* and others.]

[*To the Son*] Cousin, you know what you have to do. — [*To the Musician*] O, I cry you mercy, friend. Go you with me, and I will use your skill. — Good cousin, have a care this busy time. *Exeunt.*

[Scene III. *Another room in* Leonato's
house.]

Enter *Sir John the Bastard* and *Conrade*,
his companion.

Con. What the goodyear, my lord! Why are
you thus out of measure sad?

John. There is no measure in the occasion that
breeds; therefore the sadness is without limit.

Con. You should hear reason.

John. And when I have heard it, what blessing brings it?

Con. If not a present remedy, at least a patient sufferance.   10

John. I wonder that thou (being, as thou
say'st thou art, born under Saturn) goest about
to apply a moral medicine to a mortifying mischief. I cannot hide what I am: I must be sad
when I have cause, and smile at no man's jests;
eat when I have stomach, and wait for no man's
leisure; sleep when I am drowsy, and tend on
no man's business; laugh when I am merry, and
claw no man in his humour.   19

Con. Yea, but you must not make the full
show of this till you may do it without control-
ment. You have of late stood out against your
brother, and he hath ta'en you newly into his
grace where it is impossible you should take
true root but by the fair weather that you make
yourself. It is needful that you frame the season for your own harvest.   27

John. I had rather be a canker in a hedge
than a rose in his grace, and it better fits my
blood to be disdain'd of all than to fashion a
carriage to rob love from any. In this, though
I cannot be said to be a flattering honest man,
it must not be denied but I am a plain-dealing
villain. I am trusted with a muzzle and enfranchis'd with a clog; therefore I have decreed
not to sing in my cage. If I had my mouth, I
would bite; if I had my liberty, I would do my

liking. In the meantime let me be that I am,
and seek not to alter me.

Con. Can you make no use of your discontent?

John. I make all use of it, for I use it only.

Enter *Borachio.*

Who comes here? What news, Borachio?   42

Bora. I came yonder from a great supper.
The Prince your brother is royally entertain'd
by Leonato, and I can give you intelligence of
an intended marriage.

John. Will it serve for any model to build
mischief on? What is he for a fool that be-
troths himself to unquietness?   50

Bora. Marry, it is your brother's right hand.

John. Who? the most exquisite Claudio?

Bora. Even he.

John. A proper squire! And who? and who?
which way looks he?   55

Bora. Marry, on Hero, the daughter and heir
of Leonato.

John. A very forward March-chick! How
came you to this?   59

Bora. Being entertain'd for a perfumer, as I
was smoking a musty room, comes me the
Prince and Claudio, hand in hand in sad conference. I whipt me behind the arras and there
heard it agreed upon that the Prince should woo
Hero for himself, and having obtain'd her, give
her to Count Claudio.   66

John. Come, come, let us thither. This may
prove food to my displeasure. That young
start-up hath all the glory of my overthrow. If
I can cross him any way, I bless myself every
way. You are both sure, and will assist me? 71

Con. To the death, my lord.

John. Let us to the great supper. Their
cheer is the greater that I am subdued. Would
the cook were o' my mind! Shall we go prove
what's to be done?   76

Bora. We'll wait upon your lordship.

Exeunt.

Act II. [Scene I. *A hall in* Leonato's *house.*]

Enter *Leonato*, [*Antonio*] his Brother, *Hero* his
Daughter, and *Beatrice* his Niece, and a *Kinsman*; [also *Margaret* and *Ursula*].

Leon. Was not Count John here at supper?

Ant. I saw him not.

Beat. How tartly that gentleman looks! I
never can see him but I am heart-burn'd an
hour after.   5

Hero. He is of a very melancholy disposition.

Beat. He were an excellent man that were
made just in the midway between him and
Benedick. The one is too like an image and
says nothing, and the other too like my lady's
eldest son, evermore tattling.   11

Leon. Then half Signior Benedick's tongue
in Count John's mouth, and half Count John's
melancholy in Signior Benedick's face —   14

165

Beat. With a good leg and a good foot, uncle, and money enough in his purse, such a man would win any woman in the world — if 'a could get her good will.

Leon. By my troth, niece, thou wilt never get thee a husband if thou be so shrewd of thy tongue.   21

Ant. In faith, she's too curst.

Beat. Too curst is more than curst. I shall lessen God's sending that way, for it is said, 'God sends a curst cow short horns,' but to a cow too curst he sends none.   26

Leon. So, by being too curst, God will send you no horns.

Beat. Just, if he send me no husband; for the which blessing I am at him upon my knees every morning and evening. Lord, I could not endure a husband with a beard on his face. I had rather lie in the woollen!

Leon. You may light on a husband that hath no beard.   35

Beat. What should I do with him? dress him in my apparel and make him my waiting gentle-woman? He that hath a beard is more than a youth, and he that hath no beard is less than a man; and he that is more than a youth is not for me; and he that is less than a man, I am not for him. Therefore I will even take sixpence in earnest of the berrord and lead his apes into hell.

Leon. Well then, go you into hell?   44

Beat. No; but to the gate, and there will the devil meet me like an old cuckold with horns on his head, and say 'Get you to heaven, Beatrice, get you to heaven. Here's no place for you maids.' So deliver I up my apes, and away to Saint Peter — for the heavens. He shows me where the bachelors sit, and there live we as merry as the day is long.

Ant. [*to Hero*] Well, niece, I trust you will be rul'd by your father.   54

Beat. Yes faith. It is my cousin's duty to make cursy and say, 'Father, as it please you.' But yet for all that, cousin, let him be a hand-some fellow, or else make another cursy, and say, 'Father, as it please me.'

Leon. Well, niece, I hope to see you one day fitted with a husband.   61

Beat. Not till God make men of some other metal than earth. Would it not grieve a woman to be overmaster'd with a piece of val-iant dust? to make an account of her life to a clod of wayward marl? No, uncle, I'll none. Adam's sons are my brethren, and truly I hold it a sin to match in my kinred.

Leon. Daughter, remember what I told you If the Prince do solicit you in that kind, you know your answer.   71

Beat. The fault will be in the music, cousin if you be not wooed in good time. If the Prince be too important, tell him there is measure in everything, and so dance out the answer. For hear me, Hero: wooing, wedding, and repent ing is as a Scotch jig, a measure, and a cinque pace: the first suit is hot and hasty like a Scotch jig — and full as fantastical; the wed-ding, mannerly modest, as a measure, full o. state and ancientry; and then comes Repent ance and with his bad legs falls into the cinque pace faster and faster, till he sink into his grave

Leon. Cousin, you apprehend passing shrewdly.

Beat. I have a good eye, uncle; I can see a church by daylight.   86

Leon. The revellers are ent'ring, brother. Make good room.

                                        [*Exit Antonio.*]

Enter, [masked,] *Don Pedro, Claudio, Benedick* and *Balthasar.* [With them enter *Antonio,* also masked. After them enter] *Don John* [and *Borachio* (without masks), who stand aside and look on during the dance].

Pedro. Lady, will you walk a bout with your friend?   90

Hero. So you walk softly and look sweetly and say nothing, I am yours for the walk; and especially when I walk away.

Pedro. With me in your company?

Hero. I may say so when I please.   95

Pedro. And when please you to say so?

Hero. When I like your favour, for God defend the lute should be like the case!

Pedro. My visor is Philemon's roof; within the house is Jove.   100

Hero. Why then, your visor should be thatch'd.

Pedro. Speak low if you speak love.

                                        [*Takes her aside.*]

Balth. Well, I would you did like me.

Marg. So would not I for your own sake, for I have many ill qualities.   106

Balth. Which is one?

Marg. I say my prayers aloud.

Balth. I love you the better. The hearers may cry Amen.   110

Marg. God match me with a good dancer!

Balth. Amen.

Marg. And God keep him out of my sight when the dance is done! Answer, clerk.

Balth. No more words. The clerk is an-
swered.   [*Takes her aside.*]
Urs. I know you well enough. You are
Signior Antonio.
Ant. At a word, I am not.   118
Urs. I know you by the waggling of your head.
Ant. To tell you true, I counterfeit him.
Urs. You could never do him so ill-well
unless you were the very man. Here's his dry
hand up and down. You are he, you are he!
Ant. At a word, I am not.   125
Urs. Come, come, do you think I do not
know you by your excellent wit? Can virtue
hide itself? Go to, mum, you are he. Graces
will appear, and there's an end.
                                 [*They step aside.*]
Beat. Will you not tell me who told you so?
Bene. No, you shall pardon me.   131
Beat. Nor will you not tell me who you are?
Bene. Not now.
Beat. That I was disdainful, and that I had
my good wit out of the 'Hundred Merry
Tales.' Well, this was Signior Benedick that
said so.   136
Bene. What's he?
Beat. I am sure you know him well enough.
Bene. Not I, believe me.
Beat. Did he never make you laugh?   140
Bene. I pray you, what is he?
Beat. Why, he is the Prince's jester, a very
dull fool. Only his gift is in devising impossible
slanders. None but libertines delight in him;
and the commendation is not in his wit, but in
his villany; for he both pleases men and angers
them, and then they laugh at him and beat
him. I am sure he is in the fleet. I would he
had boarded me.
Bene. When I know the gentleman, I'll tell
him what you say.   151
Beat. Do, do. He'll but break a comparison or two on me; which peradventure, not
marked or not laugh'd at, strikes him into
melancholy; and then there's a partridge wing
saved, for the fool will eat no supper that night.
                                            [*Music.*]
We must follow the leaders.
Bene. In every good thing.
Beat. Nay, if they lead to any ill, I will
leave them at the next turning.   160
Dance. Exeunt [*all but Don John, Borachio,
                              and Claudio*].
John. Sure my brother is amorous on Hero
and hath withdrawn her father to break with
him about it. The ladies follow her and but
one visor remains.

Bora. And that is Claudio. I know him by
his bearing.   166
John. Are you not Signior Benedick?
Claud. You know me well. I am he.
John. Signior, you are very near my brother
in his love. He is enamour'd on Hero. I pray
you dissuade him from her; she is no equal
for his birth. You may do the part of an honest
man in it.   173
Claud. How know you he loves her?
John. I heard him swear his affection.   175
Bora. So did I too, and he swore he would
marry her to-night.
John. Come, let us to the banquet.
                          Exeunt. Manet Claudio.
Claud. Thus answer I in name of Benedick
But hear these ill news with the ears of Claudio.
                                       [*Unmasks.*]
'Tis certain so. The Prince wooes for himself.
Friendship is constant in all other things   182
Save in the office and affairs of love.
Therefore all hearts in love use their own
      tongues;
Let every eye negotiate for itself   185
And trust no agent; for beauty is a witch
Against whose charms faith melteth into blood.
This is an accident of hourly proof,
Which I mistrusted not. Farewell therefore
      Hero!

          Enter *Benedick* [unmasked].

Bene. Count Claudio?   190
Claud. Yea, the same.
Bene. Come, will you go with me?
Claud. Whither?
Bene. Even to the next willow, about your
own business, County. What fashion will you
wear the garland of? about your neck, like an
usurer's chain? or under your arm, like a
lieutenant's scarf? You must wear it one way,
for the Prince hath got your Hero.
Claud. I wish him joy of her.   200
Bene. Why, that's spoken like an honest
drovier. So they sell bullocks. But did you
think the Prince would have served you thus?
Claud. I pray you leave me.
Bene. Ho! now you strike like the blind
man! 'Twas the boy that stole your meat, and
you'll beat the post.   207
Claud. If it will not be, I'll leave you.
                                            Exit.
Bene. Alas, poor hurt fowl! now will he
creep into sedges. But, that my Lady Beatrice
should know me, and not know me! The
Prince's fool! Ha! it may be I go under that

title because I am merry. Yea, but so I am apt to do myself wrong. I am not so reputed. It is the base (though bitter) disposition of Beatrice that puts the world into her person and so gives me out. Well, I'll be revenged as I may. 217

Enter *Don Pedro*

Pedro. Now, signior, where's the Count? Did you see him?

Bene. Troth, my lord, I have played the part of Lady Fame. I found him here as melancholy as a lodge in a warren. I told him, and I think I told him true, that your Grace had got the good will of this young lady, and I off'red him my company to a willow tree, either to make him a garland, as being forsaken, or to bind him up a rod, as being worthy to be whipt.

Pedro. To be whipt? What's his fault?

Bene. The flat transgression of a schoolboy who, being overjoyed with finding a bird's nest, shows it his companion, and he steals it. 231

Pedro. Wilt thou make a trust a transgression? The transgression is in the stealer.

Bene. Yet it had not been amiss the rod had been made, and the garland too; for the garland he might have worn himself, and the rod he might have bestowed on you, who, as I take it, have stol'n his bird's nest.

Pedro. I will but teach them to sing and restore them to the owner. 240

Bene. If their singing answer your saying, by my faith you say honestly.

Pedro. The Lady Beatrice hath a quarrel to you. The gentleman that danc'd with her told her she is much wrong'd by you. 245

Bene. O, she misus'd me past the endurance of a block! An oak but with one green leaf on it would have answered her; my very visor began to assume life and scold with her. She told me, not thinking I had been myself, that I was the Prince's jester, that I was duller than a great thaw; huddling jest upon jest with such impossible conveyance upon me that I stood like a man at a mark, with a whole army shooting at me. She speaks poniards, and every word stabs. If her breath were as terrible as her terminations, there were no living near her; she would infect to the North Star. I would not marry her though she were endowed with all that Adam had left him before he transgress'd. She would have made Hercules have turn'd spit, yea, and have cleft his club to make the fire too. Come, talk not of her. You shall find her the infernal Ate in good

apparel. I would to God some scholar would conjure her, for certainly, while she is here, a man may live as quiet in hell as in a sanctuary; and people sin upon purpose, because they would go thither; so indeed all disquiet, horror, and perturbation follows her.

Enter *Claudio* and *Beatrice, Leonato, Hero.*

Pedro. Look, here she comes. 270

Bene. Will your Grace command me any service to the world's end? I will go on the slightest errand now to the Antipodes that you can devise to send me on; I will fetch you a toothpicker now from the furthest inch of Asia; bring you the length of Prester John's foot; fetch you a hair off the great Cham's beard; do you any embassage to the Pygmies—rather than hold three words' conference with this harpy. You have no employment for me? 280

Pedro. None, but to desire your good company.

Bene. O God, sir, here's a dish I love not! I cannot endure my Lady Tongue. *Exit.*

Pedro. Come, lady, come; you have lost the heart of Signior Benedick. 286

Beat. Indeed, my lord, he lent it me awhile, and I gave him use for it — a double heart for his single one. Marry, once before he won it of me with false dice; therefore your Grace may well say I have lost it. 291

Pedro. You have put him down, lady; you have put him down.

Beat. So I would not he should do me, my lord, lest I should prove the mother of fools. I have brought Count Claudio, whom you sent me to seek. 297

Pedro. Why, how now, Count? Wherefore are you sad?

Claud. Not sad, my lord. 300

Pedro. How then? sick?

Claud. Neither, my lord.

Beat. The Count is neither sad, nor sick, nor merry, nor well; but civil count — civil as an orange, and something of that jealous complexion. 306

Pedro. I' faith, lady, I think your blazon to be true; though I'll be sworn, if he be so, his conceit is false. Here, Claudio, I have wooed in thy name, and fair Hero is won. I have broke with her father, and his good will obtained. Name the day of marriage, and God give thee joy! 312

Leon. Count, take of me my daughter, and with her my fortunes. His Grace hath made the match, and all grace say Amen to it! 315

Beat. Speak, Count, 'tis your cue.

Claud. Silence is the perfectest herald of joy. I were but little happy if I could say how much. Lady, as you are mine, I am yours. I give away myself for you and dote upon the exchange. 320

Beat. Speak, cousin; or, if you cannot, stop his mouth with a kiss and let not him speak neither.

Pedro. In faith, lady, you have a merry heart.

Beat. Yea, my lord; I thank it, poor fool, it keeps on the windy side of care. My cousin tells him in his ear that he is in her heart.

Claud. And so she doth, cousin. 329

Beat. Good Lord, for alliance! Thus goes every one to the world but I, and I am sunburnt. I may sit in a corner and cry 'Heigh-ho for a husband!'

Pedro. Lady Beatrice, I will get you one.

Beat. I would rather have one of your father's getting. Hath your Grace ne'er a brother like you? Your father got excellent husbands, if a maid could come by them. 338

Pedro. Will you have me, lady?

Beat. No, my lord, unless I might have another for working days: your Grace is too costly to wear every day. But I beseech your Grace pardon me. I was born to speak all mirth and no matter. 344

Pedro. Your silence most offends me, and to be merry best becomes you, for out o' question you were born in a merry hour.

Beat. No, sure, my lord, my mother cried; but then there was a star danc'd, and under that was I born. Cousins, God give you joy!

Leon. Niece, will you look to those things I told you of? 352

Beat. I cry you mercy, uncle. By your Grace's pardon. *Exit.*

Pedro. By my troth, a pleasant-spirited lady.

Leon. There's little of the melancholy element in her, my lord. She is never sad but when she sleeps, and not ever sad then; for I have heard my daughter say she hath often dreamt of unhappiness and wak'd herself with laughing.

Pedro. She cannot endure to hear tell of a husband.

Leon. O, by no means! She mocks all her wooers out of suit. 365

Pedro. She were an excellent wife for Benedick.

Leon. O Lord, my lord! if they were but a week married, they would talk themselves mad.

Pedro. County Claudio, when mean you to go to church? 371

Claud. To-morrow, my lord. Time goes on crutches till love have all his rites.

Leon. Not till Monday, my dear son, which is hence a just sevennight; and a time too brief too, to have all things answer my mind. 376

Pedro. Come, you shake the head at so long a breathing; but I warrant thee, Claudio, the time shall not go dully by us. I will in the interim undertake one of Hercules' labours, which is, to bring Signior Benedick and the Lady Beatrice into a mountain of affection th' one with th' other. I would fain have it a match, and I doubt not but to fashion it if you three will but minister such assistance as I shall give you direction. 386

Leon. My lord, I am for you, though it cost me ten nights' watchings.

Claud. And I, my lord.

Pedro. And you too, gentle Hero? 390

Hero. I will do any modest office, my lord, to help my cousin to a good husband.

Pedro. And Benedick is not the unhopefullest husband that I know. Thus far can I praise him: he is of a noble strain, of approved valour, and confirm'd honesty. I will teach you how to humour your cousin, that she shall fall in love with Benedick; and I, [*to Leonato and Claudio*] with your two helps, will so practise on Benedick that in despite of his quick wit and his queasy stomach, he shall fall in love with Beatrice. If we can do this, Cupid is no longer an archer; his glory shall be ours, for we are the only love-gods. Go in with me, and I will tell you my drift. *Exeunt.*

[Scene II. *A hall in* Leonato's *house.*]

Enter [*Don*] *John* and *Borachio.*

John. It is so. The Count Claudio shall marry the daughter of Leonato.

Bora. Yea, my lord; but I can cross it.

John. Any bar, any cross, any impediment will be med'cinable to me. I am sick in displeasure to him, and whatsoever comes athwart his affection ranges evenly with mine. How canst thou cross this marriage?

Bora. Not honestly, my lord, but so covertly that no dishonesty shall appear in me. 10

John. Show me briefly how.

Bora. I think I told your lordship, a year since, how much I am in the favour of Margaret, the waiting gentlewoman to Hero.

John. I remember. 15

169

Bora. I can, at any unseasonable instant of the night, appoint her to look out at her lady's chamber window.

John. What life is in that to be the death of this marriage? 20

Bora. The poison of that lies in you to temper. Go you to the Prince your brother; spare not to tell him that he hath wronged his honour in marrying the renowned Claudio (whose estimation do you mightily hold up) to a contaminated stale, such a one as Hero. 26

John. What proof shall I make of that?

Bora. Proof enough to misuse the Prince, to vex Claudio, to undo Hero, and kill Leonato. Look you for any other issue? 30

John. Only to despite them I will endeavour anything.

Bora. Go then; find me a meet hour to draw Don Pedro and the Count Claudio alone; tell them that you know that Hero loves me; intend a kind of zeal both to the Prince and Claudio, as — in love of your brother's honour, who hath made this match, and his friend's reputation. who is thus like to be cozen'd with the semblance of a maid — that you have discover'd thus. They will scarcely believe this without trial. Offer them instances; which shall bear no less likelihood than to see me at her chamber window, hear me call Margaret Hero, hear Margaret term me Claudio; and bring them to see this the very night before the intended wedding (for in the meantime I will so fashion the matter that Hero shall be absent) and there shall appear such seeming truth of Hero's disloyalty that jealousy shall be call'd assurance and all the preparation overthrown. 51

John. Grow this to what adverse issue it can, I will put it in practice. Be cunning in the working this, and thy fee is a thousand ducats.

Bora. Be you constant in the accusation, and my cunning shall not shame me. 56

John. I will presently go learn their day of marriage. *Exeunt.*

[Scene III. Leonato's *orchard*.]

Enter *Benedick* alone.

Bene. Boy!

[Enter *Boy*.]

Boy. Signior?

Bene. In my chamber window lies a book. Bring it hither to me in the orchard.

Boy. I am here already, sir. 5

Bene. I know that, but I would have thee hence and here again. (*Exit Boy.*) I do much wonder that one man, seeing how much another man is a fool when he dedicates his behaviours to love, will, after he hath laugh'd at such shallow follies in others, become the argument of his own scorn by falling in love; and such a man is Claudio. I have known when there was no music with him but the drum and the fife; and now had he rather hear the tabor and the pipe. I have known when he would have walk'd ten mile afoot to see a good armour; and now will he lie ten nights awake carving the fashion of a new doublet. He was wont to speak plain and to the purpose, like an honest man and a soldier; and now is he turn'd orthography; his words are a very fantastical banquet — just so many strange dishes. May I be so converted and see with these eyes? I cannot tell; I think not. I will not be sworn but love may transform me to an oyster; but I'll take my oath on it, till he have made an oyster of me he shall never make me such a fool. One woman is fair, yet I am well; another is wise, yet I am well; another virtuous, yet I am well; but till all graces be in one woman, one woman shall not come in my grace. Rich she shall be, that's certain; wise, or I'll none; virtuous, or I'll never cheapen her; fair, or I'll never look on her; mild, or come not near me; noble, or not I for an angel; of good discourse, an excellent musician, and her hair shall be of what colour it please God. Ha, the Prince and Monsieur Love! I will hide me in the arbour. [*Hides.*]

Enter *Don Pedro, Leonato, Claudio.*
Music [within].

Pedro. Come, shall we hear this music?

Claud. Yea, my good lord. How still the evening is, 40
As hush'd on purpose to grace harmony!

Pedro. See you where Benedick hath hid himself?

Claud. O, very well, my lord. The music ended,
We'll fit the kid-fox with a pennyworth.

Enter *Balthasar* with *Music*.

Pedro. Come, Balthasar, we'll hear that song again. 45

Balth. O, good my lord, tax not so bad a voice
To slander music any more than once.

Pedro. It is the witness still of excellency
To put a strange face on his own perfection.
I pray thee sing, and let me woo no more. 50

Benedick and Beatrice are confronted with the documentary evidence of their love (*Act V, Scene IV*)

MUCH ADO
ABOUT NOTHING

PHOTOGRAPH BY HOUSTON ROGERS
PRODUCED BY TENNENT PRODUCTIONS. LTD.

Diana Wynyard in the role of the pert and witty heroine, Beatrice

Dorothy Tutin as Hero, beloved of the foppish gallant, Claudio

Benedick, the reluctant lover of Beatrice, played by John Gielgud

Paul Scofield in the role of the meddling Don Pedro of Arragon

"I will assume thy part in some disguise, and tell fair Hero I am Claudio." Don Pedro tells Claudio (Robert Hardy) he will court Hero for him (Act I, Scene 1)

The "plain dealing villain," Don John (Michael Goodliffe)

Left: Lewis Casson as Leonato

Right: Brewster Mason as Borachio

Left: Dogberry (George Rose)

Right: The Friar (George Howe)

Right: Leonato learns that Don Pedro has arrived in Messina (*Act I, Scene I*)

Left: "I could not endure a husband with a beard on his face." Beatrice expresses her distaste for Don John (*Act II, Scene I*)

"Hath she made her affection known to Benedick?" Don Pedro and Claudio tease Benedick by telling him Beatrice is in love with him (*Act II, Scene III*)

The revelers' masquerade in the hall of Leonato's house (*Act II, Scene I*)

Left: "Lady, will you walk about with your friend?" Don Pedro accosts Hero at the revel in her father's house (*Act II, Scene I*)

Right: "Against my will I am sent to bid you come into dinner." Beatrice's message is cold and perfunctory, but Benedick reads love into her words (*Act II, Scene III*)

"You always end with a jade's trick." Beatrice and Benedick at odds (*Act I, Scene I*)

Don John plots with Borachio and Conrade (Paul Hardwick) to dupe Claudio (*Act I, Scene III*)

Constable Dogberry instructs his watchmen (*Act III, Scene III*)

Left: " 'tis almost five o'clock, cousin."
Beatrice calls to Hero to prepare for
her wedding (Act III, Scene IV)

Margaret (Penelope Munday) assists Hero in preparing
for her marriage to Claudio (Act III, Scene IV)

Claudio interrupts his nuptials with Hero, denouncing her as unchaste (Act IV, Scene I)

Above: Beatrice and Friar Francis seek to revive Hero, who has fallen into a swoon after Claudio's denunciation of her (Act IV, Scene I)

Right: Dogberry arrests Conrade, who has been heard plotting against Claudio (Act IV, Scene II)

Left: "By this hand, Claudio shall render me a dear account." Benedick promises Beatrice that he will challenge Claudio (Act IV, Scene I)

Below: "When I liv'd, I was your other wife." Claudio and Hero reunited (Act V, Scene IV)

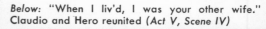

Balth. Because you talk of wooing, I will
  sing,
Since many a wooer doth commence his suit
To her he thinks not worthy, yet he wooes,
Yet will he swear he loves.
  Pedro.   Nay, pray thee come;
Or if thou wilt hold longer argument,   55
Do it in notes.
  Balth.   Note this before my notes:
There's not a note of mine that's worth the
  noting.
  Pedro. Why, these are very crotchets that
  he speaks!
Note notes, forsooth, and nothing!   [*Music.*]
  Bene. [*aside*] Now divine air! Now is his
soul ravish'd! Is it not strange that sheep's
guts should hale souls out of men's bodies?
Well, a horn for my money, when all's done.
                              [*Balthasar sings.*]

The Song.

Sigh no more, ladies, sigh no more!
  Men were deceivers ever,   65
One foot in sea, and one on shore;
  To one thing constant never.
    Then sigh not so,
    But let them go,
  And be you blithe and bonny,
Converting all your sounds of woe   70
  Into Hey nonny, nonny.

Sing no more ditties, sing no moe,
  Of dumps so dull and heavy!
The fraud of men was ever so,
  Since summer first was leavy   75
    Then sigh not so, &c.

  Pedro. By my troth, a good song.
  Balth. And an ill singer, my lord.
  Pedro. Ha, no, no, faith! Thou sing'st well
enough for a shift.   80
  Bene. [*aside*] An he had been a dog that
should have howl'd thus, they would have
hang'd him; and I pray God his bad voice bode
no mischief. I had as live have heard the night
raven, come what plague could have come
after it.   85
  Pedro. Yea, marry. Dost thou hear, Balthasar? I pray thee get us some excellent music; for to-morrow night we would have it at the
Lady Hero's chamber window.
  Balth. The best I can, my lord.   90
  Pedro. Do so. Farewell.
        Exit Balthasar [*with Musicians*].
Come hither, Leonato. What was it you told
me of to-day? that your niece Beatrice was in
love with Signior Benedick?   94

  Claud. O, ay! — [*Aside to Pedro*] Stalk on,
stalk on; the fowl sits. — I did never think that
lady would have loved any man.
  Leon. No, nor I neither; but most wonderful
that she should so dote on Signior Benedick,
whom she hath in all outward behaviours seem'd
ever to abhor.   101
  Bene. [*aside*] Is't possible? Sits the wind in
that corner?
  Leon. By my troth, my lord, I cannot tell
what to think of it, but that she loves him with
an enraged affection. It is past the infinite of
thought.   106
  Pedro. May be she doth but counterfeit.
  Claud. Faith, like enough.
  Leon. O God, counterfeit? There was never
counterfeit of passion came so near the life of
passion as she discovers it.   111
  Pedro. Why, what effects of passion shows
she?
  Claud. [*aside*] Bait the hook well! This
fish will bite.
  Leon. What effects, my lord? She will sit
you — you heard my daughter tell you how. 116
  Claud. She did indeed.
  Pedro. How, how, I pray you? You amaze
me. I would have thought her spirit had been
invincible against all assaults of affection. 120
  Leon. I would have sworn it had, my lord —
especially against Benedick.
  Bene. [*aside*] I should think this a gull but
that the white-bearded fellow speaks it. Knavery cannot, sure, hide himself in such reverence.
  Claud. [*aside*] He hath ta'en th' infection.
Hold it up.
  Pedro. Hath she made her affection known
to Benedick?
  Leon. No, and swears she never will. That's
her torment.   130
  Claud. 'Tis true indeed. So your daughter
says. 'Shall I,' says she, 'that have so oft
encount'red him with scorn, write to him that
I love him?'   134
  Leon. This says she now when she is begin-
ning to write to him; for she'll be up twenty
times a night, and there will she sit in her
smock till she have writ a sheet of paper. My
daughter tells us all.   139
  Claud. Now you talk of a sheet of paper,
I remember a pretty jest your daughter told
us of.
  Leon. O, when she had writ it, and was
reading it over, she found 'Benedick' and
'Beatrice' between the sheet?
  Claud. That.   145

171

Leon. O, she tore the letter into a thousand halfpence, rail'd at herself that she should be so immodest to write to one that she knew would flout her. 'I measure him,' says she, 'by my own spirit; for I should flout him if he writ to me. Yea, though I love him, I should.'

Claud. Then down upon her knees she falls, weeps, sobs, beats her heart, tears her hair, prays, curses — 'O sweet Benedick! God give me patience!' 155

Leon. She doth indeed; my daughter says so. And the ecstasy hath so much overborne her that my daughter is sometime afeard she will do a desperate outrage to herself. It is very true.

Pedro. It were good that Benedick knew of it by some other, if she will not discover it. 161

Claud. To what end? He would make but a sport of it and torment the poor lady worse.

Pedro. An he should, it were an alms to hang him! She's an excellent sweet lady, and (out of all suspicion) she is virtuous. 166

Claud. And she is exceeding wise.

Pedro. In everything but in loving Benedick.

Leon. O, my lord, wisdom and blood combating in so tender a body, we have ten proofs to one that blood hath the victory. I am sorry for her, as I have just cause, being her uncle and her guardian. 174

Pedro. I would she had bestowed this dotage on me. I would have daff'd all other respects and made her half myself. I pray you tell Benedick of it and hear what 'a will say. 178

Leon. Were it good, think you?

Claud. Hero thinks surely she will die; for she says she will die if he love her not, and she will die ere she make her love known, and she will die, if he woo her, rather than she will bate one breath of her accustomed crossness.

Pedro. She doth well. If she should make tender of her love, 'tis very possible he'll scorn it; for the man (as you know all) hath a contemptible spirit.

Claud. He is a very proper man.

Pedro. He hath indeed a good outward happiness. 191

Claud. Before God! and in my mind, very wise.

Pedro. He doth indeed show some sparks that are like wit.

Claud. And I take him to be valiant.

Pedro. As Hector, I assure you; and in the managing of quarrels you may say he is wise, for either he avoids them with great discretion, or undertakes them with a most Christianlike fear.

Leon. If he do fear God, 'a must necessarily keep peace. If he break the peace, he ought to enter into a quarrel with fear and trembling.

Pedro. And so will he do; for the man doth fear God, howsoever it seems not in him by some large jests he will make. Well, I am sorry for your niece. Shall we go seek Benedick and tell him of her love?

Claud. Never tell him, my lord. Let her wear it out with good counsel. 210

Leon. Nay, that's impossible; she may wear her heart out first.

Pedro. Well, we will hear further of it by your daughter. Let it cool the while. I love Benedick well, and I could wish he would modestly examine himself to see how much he is unworthy so good a lady.

Leon. My lord, will you walk? Dinner is ready. [*They walk away.*]

Claud. If he do not dote on her upon this, I will never trust my expectation. 220

Pedro. Let there be the same net spread for her, and that must your daughter and her gentlewomen carry. The sport will be, when they hold one an opinion of another's dotage, and no such matter. That's the scene that I would see, which will be merely a dumb show. Let us send her to call him in to dinner. 227

Exeunt [*Don Pedro, Claudio, and Leonato*].

[*Benedick* advances from the arbour.]

Bene. This can be no trick. The conference was sadly borne; they have the truth of this from Hero; they seem to pity the lady. It seems her affections have their full bent. Love me? Why, it must be requited. I hear how I am censur'd. They say I will bear myself proudly if I perceive the love come from her. They say too that she will rather die than give any sign of affection. I did never think to marry. I must not seem proud. Happy are they that hear their detractions and can put them to mending. They say the lady is fair — 'tis a truth, I can bear them witness; and virtuous — 'tis so, I cannot reprove it; and wise, but for loving me — by my troth, it is no addition to her wit, nor no great argument of her folly, for I will be horribly in love with her. I may chance have some odd quirks and remnants of wit broken on me because I have railed so long against marriage. But doth not the appetite alter? A man loves the meat in his youth that he cannot endure in his age. Shal' quips and sentences and these paper bullets o the brain awe a man from the career of hi

172

umour? No, the world must be peopled.
When I said I would die a bachelor, I did not
think I should live till I were married.   253

Enter *Beatrice.*

Here comes Beatrice. By this day, she's a fair
ady! I do spy some marks of love in her.
Beat. Against my will I am sent to bid you
ome in to dinner.   257
Bene. Fair Beatrice, I thank you for your
pains.
Beat. I took no more pains for those thanks
han you take pains to thank me. If it had been
painful, I would not have come.   261

Bene. You take pleasure then in the message?
Beat. Yea, just so much as you may take
upon a knive's point, and choke a daw withal.
You have no stomach, signior. Fare you well.
Exit.
Bene. Ha! 'Against my will I am sent to
bid you come in to dinner.' There's a double
meaning in that. 'I took no more pains for
those thanks than you took pains to thank me.'
That's as much as to say, 'Any pains that I
take for you is as easy as thanks.' If I do not
take pity of her, I am a villain; if I do not love
her, I am a Jew. I will go get her picture.   273
Exit.

ACT III. [Scene I. Leonato's *orchard.*]

Enter *Hero* and two *Gentlewomen, Margaret* and
Ursula.

Hero. Good Margaret, run thee to the par-
lour.
There shalt thou find my cousin Beatrice
Proposing with the Prince and Claudio.
Whisper her ear and tell her, I and Ursley
Walk in the orchard, and our whole discourse 5
Is all of her. Say that thou overheard'st us;
And bid her steal into the pleached bower,
Where honeysuckles, ripened by the sun,
Forbid the sun to enter — like favourites,
Made proud by princes, that advance their
pride   10
Against that power that bred it. There will
she hide her
To listen our propose. This is thy office.
Bear thee well in it and leave us alone.
Marg. I'll make her come, I warrant you,
presently.   [*Exit.*]
Hero. Now, Ursula, when Beatrice doth
come,   15
As we do trace this alley up and down,
Our talk must only be of Benedick.
When I do name him, let it be thy part
To praise him more than ever man did merit.
My talk to thee must be how Benedick   20
Is sick in love with Beatrice. Of this matter
Is little Cupid's crafty arrow made,
That only wounds by hearsay.

Enter *Beatrice.*

Now begin;
For look where Beatrice like a lapwing runs
Close by the ground, to hear our conference. 25
[*Beatrice hides in the arbour.*]

Urs. The pleasant'st angling is to see the fish
Cut with her golden oars the silver stream
And greedily devour the treacherous bait.
So angle we for Beatrice, who even now
Is couched in the woodbine coverture.   30
Fear you not my part of the dialogue.
Hero. Then go we near her, that her ear lose
nothing
Of the false sweet bait that we lay for it.
[*They approach the arbour.*]
No, truly, Ursula, she is too disdainful.
I know her spirits are as coy and wild
As haggards of the rock.
Urs.   But are you sure   36
That Benedick loves Beatrice so entirely?
Hero. So says the Prince, and my new-
trothed lord.
Urs. And did they bid you tell her of it,
madam?
Hero. They did entreat me to acquaint her
of it;   40
But I persuaded them, if they lov'd Benedick,
To wish him wrestle with affection
And never to let Beatrice know of it.
Urs. Why did you so? Doth not the gen-
tleman
Deserve as full, as fortunate a bed   45
As ever Beatrice shall couch upon?
Hero. O god of love! I know he doth de-
serve
As much as may be yielded to a man;
But Nature never fram'd a woman's heart
Of prouder stuff than that of Beatrice.   50
Disdain and scorn ride sparkling in her eyes,
Misprizing what they look on; and her wit
Values itself so highly that to her
All matter else seems weak. She cannot love,

Nor take no shape nor project of affection,   55
She is so self-endeared.
   Urs.   Sure I think so;
And therefore certainly it were not good
She knew his love, lest she'll make sport at it.
   Hero. Why, you speak truth. I never yet
     saw man,
How wise, how noble, young, how rarely
     featur'd,   60
But she would spell him backward. If fair-fac'd,
She would swear the gentleman should be her
     sister;
If black, why, Nature, drawing of an antic,
Made a foul blot; if tall, a lance ill-headed;
If low, an agate very vilely cut;   65
If speaking, why, a vane blown with all winds;
If silent, why, a block moved with none.
So turns she every man the wrong side out
And never gives to truth and virtue that
Which simpleness and merit purchaseth.   70
   Urs. Sure, sure, such carping is not commendable.
   Hero. No, not to be so odd, and from all
     fashions,
As Beatrice is, cannot be commendable.
But who dare tell her so? If I should speak,
She would mock me into air; O, she would
     laugh me   75
Out of myself, press me to death with wit!
Therefore let Benedick, like cover'd fire,
Consume away in sighs, waste inwardly.
It were a better death than die with mocks,
Which is as bad as die with tickling.   80
   Urs. Yet tell her of it. Hear what she will say.
   Hero. No; rather I will go to Benedick
And counsel him to fight against his passion.
And truly, I'll devise some honest slanders
To stain my cousin with. One doth not know
How much an ill word may empoison liking.
   Urs. O, do not do your cousin such a wrong!
She cannot be so much without true judgment
(Having so swift and excellent a wit
As she is priz'd to have) as to refuse   90
So rare a gentleman as Signior Benedick.
   Hero. He is the only man of Italy,
Always excepted my dear Claudio.
   Urs. I pray you be not angry with me, madam,
Speaking my fancy: Signior Benedick,   95
For shape, for bearing, argument, and valour,
Goes foremost in report through Italy.
   Hero. Indeed he hath an excellent good name.
   Urs. His excellence did earn it ere he had it.
When are you married, madam?   100
   Hero. Why, every day to-morrow! Come,
    go in.

I'll show thee some attires, and have thy counsel
Which is the best to furnish me to-morrow.
                 [They walk away.]
   Urs. She's lim'd, I warrant you! We have
     caught her, madam.
   Hero. If it prove so, then loving goes by haps;
Some Cupid kills with arrows, some with traps.
              Exeunt [Hero and Ursula].

[Beatrice advances from the arbour.]

   Beat. What fire is in mine ears? Can this be
     true?
Stand I condemn'd for pride and scorn so
     much?
Contempt, farewell! and maiden pride, adieu!
No glory lives behind the back of such.   110
And, Benedick, love on; I will requite thee,
Taming my wild heart to thy loving hand.
If thou dost love, my kindness shall incite thee
To bind our loves up in a holy band;
For others say thou dost deserve, and I   115
Believe it better than reportingly.   *Exit.*

[Scene II. *A room in* Leonato's house.]

Enter *Don Pedro, Claudio, Benedick,*
and *Leonato.*

   Pedro. I do but stay till your marriage be
consummate, and then go I toward Arragon.
   Claud. I'll bring you thither, my lord, if
you'll vouchsafe me.   4
   Pedro. Nay, that would be as great a soil in
the new gloss of your marriage as to show a
child his new coat and forbid him to wear it. I
will only be bold with Benedick for his company; for, from the crown of his head to the
sole of his foot, he is all mirth. He hath twice or
thrice cut Cupid's bowstring, and the little hangman dare not shoot at him. He hath a heart as
sound as a bell; and his tongue is the clapper,
for what his heart thinks, his tongue speaks.
   Bene. Gallants, I am not as I have been.   15
   Leon. So say I. Methinks you are sadder.
   Claud. I hope he be in love.
   Pedro. Hang him, truant! There's no true
drop of blood in him to be truly touch'd with
love. If he be sad, he wants money.   20
   Bene. I have the toothache.
   Pedro. Draw it.
   Bene. Hang it!
   Claud. You must hang it first and draw it
afterwards.   25
   Pedro. What? sigh for the toothache?
   Leon. Where is but a humour or a worm.

Bene. Well, every one can master a grief but he that has it.

Claud. Yet say I he is in love.   30

Pedro. There is no appearance of fancy in him, unless it be a fancy that he hath to strange disguises; as to be a Dutchman to-day, a Frenchman to-morrow; or in the shape of two countries at once, as a German from the waist downward, all slops, and a Spaniard from the hip upward, no doublet. Unless he have a fancy to this foolery, as it appears he hath, he is no fool for fancy, as you would have it appear he is.

Claud. If he be not in love with some woman, there is no believing old signs. 'A brushes his hat o' mornings. What should that bode?   42

Pedro. Hath any man seen him at the barber's?

Claud. No, but the barber's man hath been seen with him, and the old ornament of his cheek hath already stuff'd tennis balls.   47

Leon. Indeed he looks younger than he did, by the loss of a beard.

Pedro. Nay, 'a rubs himself with civet. Can you smell him out by that?   51

Claud. That's as much as to say, the sweet youth's in love.

Pedro. The greatest note of it is his melancholy.   55

Claud. And when was he wont to wash his face?

Pedro. Yea, or to paint himself? for the which I hear what they say of him.

Claud. Nay, but his jesting spirit, which is new-crept into a lutestring, and now govern'd by stops.   62

Pedro. Indeed that tells a heavy tale for him. Conclude, conclude, he is in love.

Claud. Nay, but I know who loves him.   65

Pedro. That would I know too. I warrant, one that knows him not.

Claud. Yes, and his ill conditions; and in despite of all, dies for him.

Pedro. She shall be buried with her face upwards.   71

Bene. Yet is this no charm for the toothache. Old signior, walk aside with me. I have studied eight or nine wise words to speak to you, which these hobby-horses must not hear.

[*Exeunt Benedick and Leonato.*]

Pedro. For my life, to break with him about Beatrice!

Claud. 'Tis even so. Hero and Margaret have by this played their parts with Beatrice, and then the two bears will not bite one another when they meet.   81

Enter *John the Bastard.*

John. My lord and brother, God save you.

Pedro. Good den, brother.

John. If your leisure serv'd, I would speak with you.   85

Pedro. In private?

John. If it please you. Yet Count Claudio may hear, for what I would speak of concerns him.

Pedro. What's the matter?   90

John. [*to Claudio*] Means your lordship to be married to-morrow?

Pedro. You know he does.

John. I know not that, when he knows what I know.   95

Claud. If there be any impediment, I pray you discover it.

John. You may think I love you not. Let that appear hereafter, and aim better at me by that I now will manifest. For my brother, I think he holds you well and in dearness of heart hath help to effect your ensuing marriage — surely suit ill spent and labour ill bestowed!

Pedro. Why, what's the matter?   104

John. I came hither to tell you, and, circumstances short'ned (for she has been too long a-talking of), the lady is disloyal.

Claud. Who? Hero?

John. Even she — Leonato's Hero, your Hero, every man's Hero.   110

Claud. Disloyal?

John. The word is too good to paint out her wickedness. I could say she were worse; think you of a worse title, and I will fit her to it. Wonder not till further warrant. Go but with me to-night, you shall see her chamber window ent'red, even the night before her wedding day. If you love her then, to-morrow wed her. But it would better fit your honour to change your mind.

Claud. May this be so?   120

Pedro. I will not think it.

John. If you dare not trust that you see, confess not that you know. If you will follow me, I will show you enough; and when you have seen more and heard more, proceed accordingly.   125

Claud. If I see anything to-night why I should not marry her to-morrow, in the congregation where I should wed, there will I shame her.

Pedro. And, as I wooed for thee to obtain her, I will join with thee to disgrace her.   130

John. I will disparage her no farther till you are my witnesses. Bear it coldly but till midnight, and let the issue show itself.

Pedro. O day untowardly turned!

Claud. O mischief strangely thwarting! 135

John. O plague right well prevented! So will you say when you have seen the sequel.

Exeunt.

[Scene III. *A street.*]

Enter *Dogberry* and his *compartner* [*Verges*], with the *Watch.*

Dog. Are you good men and true?

Verg. Yea, or else it were pity but they should suffer salvation, body and soul.

Dog. Nay, that were a punishment too good for them if they should have any allegiance in them, being chosen for the Prince's watch.

Verg. Well, give them their charge, neighbour Dogberry.

Dog. First, who think you the most desartless man to be constable? 10

1. Watch. Hugh Oatcake, sir, or George Seacoal; for they can write and read.

Dog. Come hither, neighbour Seacoal. God hath bless'd you with a good name. To be a well-favoured man is the gift of fortune, but to write and read comes by nature. 16

2. Watch. Both which, Master Constable —

Dog. You have. I knew it would be your answer. Well, for your favour, sir, why, give God thanks and make no boast of it; and for your writing and reading, let that appear when there is no need of such vanity. You are thought here to be the most senseless and fit man for the constable of the watch. Therefore bear you the lanthorn. This is your charge: you shall comprehend all vagrom men; you are to bid any man stand, in the Prince's name.

2. Watch. How if 'a will not stand? 28

Dog. Why then, take no note of him, but let him go, and presently call the rest of the watch together and thank God you are rid of a knave.

Verg. If he will not stand when he is bidden, he is none of the Prince's subjects. 33

Dog. True, and they are to meddle with none but the Prince's subjects. You shall also make no noise in the streets; for for the watch to babble and to talk is most tolerable, and not to be endured.

2. Watch. We will rather sleep than talk. We know what belongs to a watch. 40

Dog. Why, you speak like an ancient and most quiet watchman, for I cannot see how sleeping should offend. Only have a care that your bills be not stol'n. Well, you are to call at all the alehouses and bid those that are drunk get them to bed. 46

2. Watch. How if they will not?

Dog. Why then, let them alone till they are sober. If they make you not then the better answer, you may say they are not the men you took them for. 51

2. Watch. Well, sir.

Dog. If you meet a thief, you may suspect him, by virtue of your office, to be no true man; and for such kind of men, the less you meddle or make with them, why, the more is for your honesty. 56

2. Watch. If we know him to be a thief, shall we not lay hands on him?

Dog. Truly, by your office you may; but I think they that touch pitch will be defil'd. The most peaceable way for you, if you do take a thief, is to let him show himself what he is, and steal out of your company.

Verg. You have been always called a merciful man, partner. 65

Dog. Truly, I would not hang a dog by my will, much more a man who hath any honesty in him.

Verg. If you hear a child cry in the night, you must call to the nurse and bid her still it.

2. Watch. How if the nurse be asleep and will not hear us? 72

Dog. Why then, depart in peace and let the child wake her with crying; for the ewe that will not hear her lamb when it baes will never answer a calf when he bleats. 76

Verg. 'Tis very true.

Dog. This is the end of the charge: you, constable, are to present the Prince's own person. If you meet the Prince in the night, you may stay him. 81

Verg. Nay, by'r lady, that I think 'a cannot.

Dog. Five shillings to one on't with any man that knows the statutes, he may stay him! Marry, not without the Prince be willing; for indeed the watch ought to offend no man, and it is an offence to stay a man against his will.

Verg. By'r lady, I think it be so. 89

Dog. Ha, ah, ha! Well, masters, good night. An there be any matter of weight chances, call up me. Keep your fellows' counsels and your own, and good night. Come, neighbour.

2. Watch. Well, masters, we hear our charge. Let us go sit here upon the church bench till two, and then all to bed. 96

Dog. One word more, honest neighbours. I pray you watch about Signior Leonato's door; for the wedding being there to-morrow, there is a great coil to-night. Adieu. Be vigitant, I beseech you.   *Exeunt [Dogberry and Verges].*

Enter *Borachio* and *Conrade.*

Bora. What, Conrade!   102
2. Watch. [*aside*] Peace! stir not!
Bora. Conrade, I say!
Con. Here, man. I am at thy elbow.   105
Bora. Mass, and my elbow itch'd! I thought there would a scab follow.
Con. I will owe thee an answer for that; and now forward with thy tale.   109
Bora. Stand thee close then under this penthouse, for it drizzles rain, and I will, like a true drunkard, utter all to thee.
2. Watch. [*aside*] Some treason, masters. Yet stand close.
Bora. Therefore know I have earned of Don John a thousand ducats.   116
Con. Is it possible that any villany should be so dear?
Bora. Thou shouldst rather ask if it were possible any villany should be so rich; for when rich villains have need of poor ones, poor ones may make what price they will.   122
Con. I wonder at it.
Bora. That shows thou art unconfirm'd. Thou knowest that the fashion of a doublet, or a hat, or a cloak, is nothing to a man.   126
Con. Yes, it is apparel.
Bora. I mean the fashion.
Con. Yes, the fashion is the fashion.
Bora. Tush! I may as well say the fool's the fool. But seest thou not what a deformed thief this fashion is?   132
2. Watch. [*aside*] I know that Deformed. 'A has been a vile thief this seven year; 'a goes up and down like a gentleman. I remember his name.   136
Bora. Didst thou not hear somebody?
Con. No; 'twas the vane on the house.
Bora. Seest thou not, I say, what a deformed thief this fashion is? how giddily 'a turns about all the hot-bloods between fourteen and five-and-thirty? sometimes fashioning them like Pharaoh's soldiers in the reechy painting, sometime like god Bel's priests in the old church window, sometime like the shaven Hercules in the smirch'd worm-eaten tapestry, where his codpiece seems as massy as his club?   147
Con. All this I see; and I see that the fashion wears out more apparel than the man. But art not thou thyself giddy with the fashion too, that thou hast shifted out of thy tale into telling me of the fashion?   152
Bora. Not so neither. But know that I have to-night wooed Margaret, the Lady Hero's gentlewoman, by the name of Hero. She leans me out at her mistress' chamber window, bids me a thousand times good night — I tell this tale vilely; I should first tell thee how the Prince, Claudio, and my master, planted and placed and possessed by my master Don John, saw afar off in the orchard this amiable encounter.   161
Con. And thought they Margaret was Hero?
Bora. Two of them did, the Prince and Claudio; but the devil my master knew she was Margaret; and partly by his oaths, which first possess'd them, partly by the dark night, which did deceive them, but chiefly by my villany, which did confirm any slander that Don John had made, away went Claudio enrag'd; swore he would meet her, as he was appointed, next morning at the temple, and there, before the whole congregation, shame her with what he saw o'ernight and send her home again without a husband.   175
2. Watch. We charge you in the Prince's name stand!
1. Watch. Call up the right Master Constable. We have here recover'd the most dangerous piece of lechery that ever was known in the commonwealth.   181
2. Watch. And one Deformed is one of them. I know him; 'a wears a lock.
Con. Masters, masters —
1. Watch. You'll be made bring Deformed forth, I warrant you.   186
Con. Masters —
2. Watch. Never speak, we charge you. Let us obey you to go with us.
Bora. We are like to prove a goodly commodity, being taken up of these men's bills.   191
Con. A commodity in question, I warrant you. Come, we'll obey you.   *Exeunt.*

[Scene IV. *A room in* Leonato's *house.*]

Enter *Hero,* and *Margaret* and *Ursula.*

Hero. Good Ursula, wake my cousin Beatrice and desire her to rise.
Urs. I will, lady.
Hero. And bid her come hither.
Urs. Well.   [*Exit.*]
Marg. Troth, I think your other rebato were better.

Much Ado about Nothing

Hero. No, pray thee, good Meg, I'll wear this.
Marg. By my troth 's not so good, and I warrant your cousin will say so. 10
Hero. My cousin's a fool, and thou art another. I'll wear none but this.
Marg. I like the new tire within excellently, if the hair were a thought browner; and your gown's a most rare fashion, i' faith. I saw the Duchess of Milan's gown that they praise so.
Hero. O, that exceeds, they say. 17
Marg. By my troth, 's but a nightgown in respect of yours — cloth-o'-gold and cuts, and lac'd with silver, set with pearls down sleeves, side-sleeves, and skirts, round underborne with a bluish tinsel. But for a fine, quaint, graceful, and excellent fashion, yours is worth ten on't.
Hero. God give me joy to wear it! for my heart is exceeding heavy. 25
Marg. 'Twill be heavier soon by the weight of a man.
Hero. Fie upon thee! art not ashamed?
Marg. Of what, lady? of speaking honourably? Is not marriage honourable in a beggar? Is not your lord honourable without marriage? I think you would have me say, 'saving your reverence, a husband.' An bad thinking do not wrest true speaking, I'll offend nobody. Is there any harm in 'the heavier for a husband'? None, I think, an it be the right husband and the right wife. Otherwise 'tis light, and not heavy. Ask my Lady Beatrice else. Here she comes.

Enter Beatrice.

Hero. Good morrow, coz.
Beat. Good morrow, sweet Hero. 40
Hero. Why, how now? Do you speak in the sick tune?
Beat. I am out of all other tune, methinks.
Marg. Clap's into 'Light o' love.' That goes without a burden. Do you sing it, and I'll dance it. 46
Beat. Yea, 'Light o' love' with your heels! then, if your husband have stables enough, you'll see he shall lack no barnes.
Marg. O illegitimate construction! I scorn that with my heels. 51
Beat. 'Tis almost five o'clock, cousin; 'tis time you were ready. By my troth, I am exceeding ill. Hey-ho!
Marg. For a hawk, a horse, or a husband?
Beat. For the letter that begins them all, H.
Marg. Well, an you be not turn'd Turk, there's no more sailing by the star.
Beat. What means the fool, trow?

Marg. Nothing I; but God send every one their heart's desire! 61
Hero. These gloves the Count sent me, they are an excellent perfume.
Beat. I am stuff'd, cousin; I cannot smell.
Marg. A maid, and stuff'd! There's goodly catching of cold. 66
Beat. O, God help me! God help me! How long have you profess'd apprehension?
Marg. Ever since you left it. Doth not my wit become me rarely? 70
Beat. It is not seen enough. You should wear it in your cap. By my troth, I am sick.
Marg. Get you some of this distill'd carduus benedictus and lay it to your heart. It is the only thing for a qualm. 75
Hero. There thou prick'st her with a thistle.
Beat. Benedictus? why benedictus? You have some moral in this 'benedictus.'
Marg. Moral? No, by my troth, I have no moral meaning; I meant plain holy thistle. You may think perchance that I think you are in love. Nay, by'r lady, I am not such a fool to think what I list; nor I list not to think what I can; nor indeed I cannot think, if I would think my heart out of thinking, that you are in love, or that you will be in love, or that you can be in love. Yet Benedick was such another, and now is he become a man. He swore he would never marry; and yet now in despite of his heart he eats his meat without grudging; and how you may be converted I know not, but methinks you look with your eyes as other women do. 92
Beat. What pace is this that thy tongue keeps?
Marg. Not a false gallop.

Enter Ursula.

Urs. Madam, withdraw. The Prince, the Count, Signior Benedick, Don John, and all the gallants of the town are come to fetch you to church.
Hero. Help to dress me, good coz, good Meg, good Ursula. [*Exeunt.*]

[Scene V. *The hall in* Leonato's *house.*]

Enter Leonato and the Constable [Dogberry] and the Headborough [Verges].

Leon. What would you with me, honest neighbour?
Dog. Marry, sir, I would have some confidence with you that decerns you nearly.

Leon. Brief, I pray you; for you see it is a busy time with me.   6
Dog. Marry, this it is, sir.
Verg. Yes, in truth it is, sir.
Leon. What is it, my good friends?
Dog. Goodman Verges, sir, speaks a little off the matter — an old man, sir, and his wits are not so blunt as, God help, I would desire they were; but, in faith, honest as the skin between his brows.   14
Verg. Yes, I thank God I am as honest as any man living that is an old man and no honester than I.
Dog. Comparisons are odorous. Palabras, neighbour Verges.
Leon. Neighbours, you are tedious.   20
Dog. It pleases your worhsip to say so, but we are the poor Duke's officers; but truly, for mine own part, if I were as tedious as a king, I could find in my heart to bestow it all of your worship.   25
Leon. All thy tediousness on me, ah?
Dog. Yea, an 'twere a thousand pound more than 'tis; for I hear as good exclamation on your worship as of any man in the city; and though I be but a poor man, I am glad to hear it.
Verg. And so am I.   31
Leon. I would fain know what you have to say.
Verg. Marry, sir, our watch to-night, excepting your worship's presence, ha' ta'en a couple of as arrant knaves as any in Messina.
Dog. A good old man, sir; he will be talking. As they say, 'When the age is in, the wit is out.' God help us! it is a world to see! Well said, i' faith, neighbour Verges. Well, God 's a good man. An two men ride of a horse, one must ride behind. An honest soul, i' faith, sir, by my troth he is, as ever broke bread; but God is to be worshipp'd; all men are not alike, alas, good neighbour!
Leon. Indeed, neighbour, he comes too short of you.   46
Dog. Gifts that God gives.
Leon. I must leave you.
Dog. One word, sir. Our watch, sir, have indeed comprehended two aspicious persons, and we would have them this morning examined before your worship.   52
Leon. Take their examination yourself and bring it me. I am now in great haste, as it may appear unto you.   55
Dog. It shall be suffigance.
Leon. Drink some wine ere you go. Fare you well.

[Enter a *Messenger*.]

Mess. My lord, they stay for you to give your daughter to her husband.   60
Leon. I'll wait upon them. I am ready.
                 [*Exeunt Leonato and Messenger.*]
Dog. Go, good partner, go get you to Francis Seacoal; bid him bring his pen and inkhorn to the jail. We are now to examination these men.
Verg. And we must do it wisely.   65
Dog. We will spare for no wit, I warrant you. Here's that shall drive some of them to a noncome. Only get the learned writer to set down our excommunication, and meet me at the jail.
                                              Exeunt.

ACT IV. [Scene I. *A church.*]

Enter *Don Pedro*, [*John the*] *Bastard, Leonato, Friar* [*Francis*], *Claudio, Benedick, Hero, Beatrice,* [*and Attendants*].

Leon. Come, Friar Francis, be brief. Only to the plain form of marriage, and you shall recount their particular duties afterwards.
Friar. You come hither, my lord, to marry this lady?   5
Claud. No.
Leon. To be married to her. Friar, you come to marry her.
Friar. Lady, you come hither to be married to this count?   10
Hero. I do.
Friar. If either of you know any inward impediment why you should not be conjoined, I charge you on your souls to utter it.
Claud. Know you any, Hero?   15
Hero. None, my lord.
Friar. Know you any, Count?
Leon. I dare make his answer — none.
Claud. O, what men dare do! what men may do! what men daily do, not knowing what they do!   21
Bene. How now? interjections? Why then, some be of laughing, as, ah, ha, he!
Claud. Stand thee by, friar. Father, by
      your leave:
Will you with free and unconstrained soul 25
Give me this maid your daughter?
Leon. As freely, son, as God did give her me.

Claud. And what have I to give you back whose worth
May counterpoise this rich and precious gift?
Pedro. Nothing, unless you render her again.
Claud. Sweet Prince, you learn me noble thankfulness.   31
There, Leonato, take her back again.
Give not this rotten orange to your friend.
She's but the sign and semblance of her honour.
Behold how like a maid she blushes here!   35
O, what authority and show of truth
Can cunning sin cover itself withal!
Comes not that blood as modest evidence
To witness simple virtue? Would you not swear,
All you that see her, that she were a maid   40
By these exterior shows? But she is none:
She knows the heat of a luxurious bed;
Her blush is guiltiness, not modesty.
Leon. What do you mean, my lord?
Claud.   Not to be married,
Not to knit my soul to an approved wanton.   45
Leon. Dear my lord, if you, in your own proof,
Have vanquish'd the resistance of her youth
And made defeat of her virginity —
Claud. I know what you would say. If I have known her,
You will say she did embrace me as a husband,
And so extenuate the forehand sin.   51
No, Leonato,
I never tempted her with word too large,
But, as a brother to his sister, show'd
Bashful sincerity and comely love.   55
Hero. And seem'd I ever otherwise to you?
Claud. Out on the seeming! I will write against it.
You seem to me as Dian in her orb,
As chaste as is the bud ere it be blown;
But you are more intemperate in your blood   60
Than Venus, or those pamp'red animals
That rage in savage sensuality.
Hero. Is my lord well that he doth speak so wide?
Leon. Sweet Prince, why speak not you?
Pedro.   What should I speak?
I stand dishonour'd that have gone about   65
To link my dear friend to a common stale.
Leon. Are these things spoken, or do I but dream?
John. Sir, they are spoken, and these things are true.
Bene. This looks not like a nuptial.
Hero.   'True!' O God!

Claud. Leonato, stand I here?   70
Is this the Prince? Is this the Prince's brother?
Is this face Hero's? Are our eyes our own?
Leon. All this is so; but what of this, my lord?
Claud. Let me but move one question to your daughter,
And by that fatherly and kindly power   75
That you have in her, bid her answer truly.
Leon. I charge thee do so, as thou art my child.
Hero. O, God defend me! How am I beset!
What kind of catechising call you this?
Claud. To make you answer truly to your name.   80
Hero. Is it not Hero? Who can blot that name
With any just reproach?
Claud.   Marry, that can Hero!
Hero itself can blot out Hero's virtue.
What man was he talk'd with you yesternight,
Out at your window betwixt twelve and one?
Now, if you are a maid, answer to this.   86
Hero. I talk'd with no man at that hour, my lord.
Pedro. Why, then are you no maiden. Leonato,
I am sorry you must hear. Upon mine honour,
Myself, my brother, and this grieved Count   90
Did see her, hear her, at that hour last night
Talk with a ruffian at her chamber window,
Who hath indeed, most like a liberal villain,
Confess'd the vile encounters they have had
A thousand times in secret.   95
John. Fie, fie! they are not to be nam'd, my lord —
Not to be spoke of;
There is not chastity enough in language
Without offence to utter them. Thus, pretty lady,
I am sorry for thy much misgovernment.   100
Claud. O Hero! what a Hero hadst thou been
If half thy outward graces had been plac'd
About thy thoughts and counsels of thy heart!
But fare thee well, most foul, most fair! Farewell,
Thou pure impiety and impious purity!   105
For thee I'll lock up all the gates of love,
And on my eyelids shall conjecture hang,
To turn all beauty into thoughts of harm,
And never shall it more be gracious.
Leon. Hath no man's dagger here a point for me?   *[Hero swoons.]*
Beat. Why, how now, cousin? Wherefore sink you down?   111

John. Come let us go. These things, come
thus to light,
Smother her spirits up.
[*Exeunt Don Pedro, Don Juan, and Clau-
dio.*]
Bene. How doth the lady?
Beat.   Dead, I think. Help, uncle!
Hero! why, Hero! Uncle! Signior Benedick!
Friar!   115
Leon. O Fate, take not away thy heavy
hand!
Death is the fairest cover for her shame
That may be wish'd for.
Beat.   How now, cousin Hero?
Friar. Have comfort, lady.
Leon. Dost thou look up?
Friar.   Yea, wherefore should she not?
Leon. Wherefore? Why, doth not every
earthly thing   121
Cry shame upon her? Could she here deny
The story that is printed in her blood?
Do not live, Hero; do not ope thine eyes;
For, did I think thou wouldst not quickly die,
Thought I thy spirits were stronger than thy
shames,   126
Myself would on the rearward of reproaches
Strike at thy life. Griev'd I, I had but one?
Chid I for that at frugal nature's frame?
O, one too much by thee! Why had I one? 130
Why ever wast thou lovely in my eyes?
Why had I not with charitable hand
Took up a beggar's issue at my gates,
Who smirched thus and mir'd with infamy,
I might have said, 'No part of it is mine; 135
This shame derives itself from unknown loins'?
But mine, and mine I lov'd, and mine I prais'd,
And mine that I was proud on — mine so much
That I myself was to myself not mine,
Valuing of her — why, she, O, she is fall'n 140
Into a pit of ink, that the wide sea
Hath drops too few to wash her clean again,
And salt too little which may season give
To her foul tainted flesh!
Bene.   Sir, sir, be patient.
For my part, I am so attir'd in wonder, 145
I know not what to say.
Beat. O, on my soul, my cousin is belied!
Bene. Lady, were you her bedfellow last
night?
Beat. No, truly, not; although, until last
night,
I have this twelvemonth been her bedfellow.
Leon. Confirm'd, confirm'd! O, that is
stronger made   151
Which was before barr'd up with ribs of iron!

Would the two princes lie? and Claudio lie,
Who lov'd her so that, speaking of her foulness,
Wash'd it with tears? Hence from her! let
her die.   155
Friar. Hear me a little;
For I have only been silent so long,
And given way unto this course of fortune,
By noting of the lady. I have mark'd
A thousand blushing apparitions   160
To start into her face, a thousand innocent
shames
In angel whiteness beat away those blushes,
And in her eye there hath appear'd a fire
To burn the errors that these princes hold
Against her maiden truth. Call me a fool; 165
Trust not my reading nor my observation,
Which with experimental seal doth warrant
The tenure of my book; trust not my age,
My reverence, calling, nor my divinity,
If this sweet lady lie not guiltless here   170
Under some biting error.
Leon.   Friar, it cannot be.
Thou seest that all the grace that she hath left
Is that she will not add to her damnation
A sin of perjury: she not denies it.
Why seek'st thou then to cover with excuse 175
That which appears in proper nakedness?
Friar. Lady, what man is he you are accus'd
of?
Hero. They know that do accuse me; I know
none.
If I know more of any man alive
Than that which maiden modesty doth war-
rant,   180
Let all my sins lack mercy! O my father,
Prove you that any man with me convers'd
At hours unmeet, or that I yesternight
Maintain'd the change of words with any
creature,
Refuse me, hate me, torture me to death! 185
Friar. There is some strange misprision in
the princes.
Bene. Two of them have the very bent of
honour;
And if their wisdoms be misled in this,
The practice of it lives in John the bastard,
Whose spirits toil in frame of villanies.   190
Leon. I know not. If they speak but truth
of her,
These hands shall tear her. If they wrong her
honour,
The proudest of them shall well hear of it.
Time hath not yet so dried this blood of mine,
Nor age so eat up my invention,   195
Nor fortune made such havoc of my means,

Nor my bad life reft me so much of friends,
But they shall find awak'd in such a kind
Both strength of limb and policy of mind,
Ability in means, and choice of friends,   200
To quit me of them throughly.
    Friar.   Pause awhile
And let my counsel sway you in this case.
Your daughter here the princes left for dead,
Let her awhile be secretly kept in,
And publish it that she is dead indeed;   205
Maintain a mourning ostentation,
And on your family's old monument
Hang mournful epitaphs, and do all rites
That appertain unto a burial.
    Leon. What shall become of this? What will
        this do?   210
    Friar. Marry, this well carried shall on her
        behalf
Change slander to remorse. That is some good.
But not for that dream I on this strange course,
But on this travail look for greater birth.
She dying, as it must be so maintain'd,   215
Upon the instant that she was accus'd,
Shall be lamented, pitied, and excus'd
Of every hearer; for it so falls out
That what we have we prize not to the worth
Whiles we enjoy it, but being lack'd and lost,
Why, then we rack the value, then we find
The virtue that possession would not show us
Whiles it was ours. So will it fare with Claudio.
When he shall hear she died upon his words,
Th' idea of her life shall sweetly creep   225
Into his study of imagination,
And every lovely organ of her life
Shall come apparell'd in more precious habit,
More moving, delicate, and full of life,
Into the eye and prospect of his soul   230
Than when she liv'd indeed. Then shall he
        mourn
(If ever love had interest in his liver)
And wish he had not so accused her —
No, though he thought his accusation true.
Let this be so, and doubt not but success   235
Will fashion the event in better shape
Than I can lay it down in likelihood.
But if all aim but this be levell'd false,
The supposition of the lady's death
Will quench the wonder of her infamy.   240
And if it sort not well, you may conceal her,
As best befits her wounded reputation,
In some reclusive and religious life,
Out of all eyes, tongues, minds, and injuries.
    Bene. Signior Leonato, let the friar advise
        you;   245
And though you know my inwardness and love

Is very much unto the Prince and Claudio,
Yet, by mine honour, I will deal in this
As secretly and justly as your soul
Should with your body.
    Leon.   Being that I flow in grief,   250
The smallest twine may lead me.
    Friar. 'Tis well consented. Presently away;
For to strange sores strangely they strain the
        cure.
Come, lady, die to live. This wedding day
Perhaps is but prolong'd. Have patience and
        endure.   255
        Exeunt [all but Benedick and Beatrice].
    Bene. Lady Beatrice, have you wept all this
while?
    Beat. Yea, and I will weep a while longer.
    Bene. I will not desire that.
    Beat. You have no reason. I do it freely.   260
    Bene. Surely I do believe your fair cousin is
wronged.
    Beat. Ah, how much might the man deserve
of me that would right her!
    Bene. Is there any way to show such friend-
ship?   265
    Beat. A very even way, but no such friend.
    Bene. May a man do it?
    Beat. It is a man's office, but not yours.
    Bene. I do love nothing in the world so well
as you. Is not that strange?   270
    Beat. As strange as the thing I know not. It
were as possible for me to say I loved nothing so
well as you. But believe me not; and yet I lie
not. I confess nothing, nor I deny nothing. I
am sorry for my cousin.   275
    Bene. By my sword, Beatrice, thou lovest me.
    Beat. Do not swear, and eat it.
    Bene. I will swear by it that you love me, and
I will make him eat it that says I love not you.
    Beat. Will you not eat your word?   280
    Bene. With no sauce that can be devised to
it. I protest I love thee.
    Beat. Why then, God forgive me!
    Bene. What offence, sweet Beatrice?
    Beat. You have stayed me in a happy hour.
I was about to protest I loved you.   286
    Bene. And do it with all thy heart.
    Beat. I love you with so much of my heart
that none is left to protest.
    Bene. Come, bid me do anything for thee.
    Beat. Kill Claudio.   291
    Bene. Ha! not for the wide world!
    Beat. You kill me to deny it. Farewell.
    Bene. Tarry, sweet Beatrice.
    Beat. I am gone, though I am here. There is
no love in you. Nay, I pray you let me go.   296

182

Bene. Beatrice —
Beat. In faith, I will go.
Bene. We'll be friends first.
Beat. You dare easier be friends with me than fight with mine enemy.   301
Bene. Is Claudio thine enemy?
Beat. Is 'a not approved in the height a villain, that hath slandered, scorned, dishonoured my kinswoman? O that I were a man! What? bear her in hand until they come to take hands, and then with public accusation, uncover'd slander, unmitigated rancour — O God, that I were a man! I would eat his heart in the market place.
Bene. Hear me, Beatrice!   310
Beat. Talk with a man out at a window! — a proper saying!
Bene. Nay, but Beatrice —
Beat. Sweet Hero! she is wrong'd, she is sland'red, she is undone.   315
Bene. Beat —
Beat. Princes and Counties! Surely a princely testimony, a goodly count, Count Comfect, a sweet gallant surely! O that I were a man for his sake! or that I had any friend would be a man for my sake! But manhood is melted into cursies, valour into compliment, and men are only turn'd into tongue, and trim ones too. He is now as valiant as Hercules that only tells a lie, and swears it. I cannot be a man with wishing; therefore I will die a woman with grieving.   326
Bene. Tarry, good Beatrice. By this hand, I love thee.
Beat. Use it for my love some other way than swearing by it.   330
Bene. Think you in your soul the Count Claudio hath wrong'd Hero?
Beat. Yea, as sure as I have a thought or a soul.   334
Bene. Enough, I am engag'd, I will challenge him. I will kiss your hand, and so I leave you. By this hand, Claudio shall render me a dear account. As you hear of me, so think of me. Go comfort your cousin. I must say she is dead — and so farewell.   [*Exeunt.*]

[Scene II. *A prison.*]

Enter the Constables [*Dogberry* and *Verges*] and the *Sexton,* in gowns, [and the *Watch,* with *Conrade* and] *Borachio.*

Dog. Is our whole dissembly appear'd?
Verg. O, a stool and a cushion for the sexton.
Sex. Which be the malefactors?

Dog. Marry, that am I and my partner.
Verg. Nay, that's certain. We have the exhibition to examine.   6
Sex. But which are the offenders that are to be examined? let them come before Master Constable.   9
Dog. Yea, marry, let them come before me. What is your name, friend?
Bora. Borachio.
Dog. Pray write down Borachio. Yours, sirrah?
Con. I am a gentleman, sir, and my name is Conrade.   16
Dog. Write down Master Gentleman Conrade. Masters, do you serve God?
Both. Yea, sir, we hope.
Dog. Write down that they hope they serve God; and write God first, for God defend but God should go before such villains! Masters, it is proved already that you are little better than false knaves, and it will go near to be thought so shortly. How answer you for yourselves?   25
Con. Marry, sir, we say we are none.
Dog. A marvellous witty fellow, I assure you; but I will go about with him. Come you hither, sirrah. A word in your ear. Sir, I say to you, it is thought you are false knaves.   30
Bora. Sir, I say to you we are none.
Dog. Well, stand aside. Fore God, they are both in a tale. Have you writ down that they are none?   34
Sex. Master Constable, you go not the way to examine. You must call forth the watch that are their accusers.
Dog. Yea, marry, that's the eftest way. Let the watch come forth. Masters, I charge you in the Prince's name accuse these men.   40
1. Watch. This man said, sir, that Don John the Prince's brother was a villain.
Dog. Write down Prince John a villain. Why, this is flat perjury, to call a prince's brother villain.
Bora. Master Constable —   45
Dog. Pray thee, fellow, peace. I do not like thy look, I promise thee.
Sex. What heard you him say else?
2. Watch. Marry, that he had received a thousand ducats of Don John for accusing the Lady Hero wrongfully.   51
Dog. Flat burglary as ever was committed.
Verg. Yea, by th' mass, that it is.
Sex. What else, fellow?
1. Watch. And that Count Claudio did mean, upon his words, to disgrace Hero before the whole assembly, and not marry her.

Dog. O villain! thou wilt be condemn'd into everlasting redemption for this.

Sex. What else? 60

Watchmen. This is all.

Sex. And this is more, masters, than you can deny. Prince John is this morning secretly stol'n away. Hero was in this manner accus'd, in this very manner refus'd, and upon the grief of this suddenly died. Master Constable, let these men be bound and brought to Leonato's. I will go before and show him their examination. [*Exit.*]

Dog. Come, let them be opinion'd.

Verg. Let them be in the hands — 70

Con. Off, coxcomb!

Dog. God's my life, where's the sexton? Let him write down the Prince's officer coxcomb. Come, bind them. — Thou naughty varlet! 74

Con. Away! you are an ass, you are an ass.

Dog. Dost thou not suspect my place? Dost thou not suspect my years? O that he were here to write me down an ass! But, masters, remember that I am an ass. Though it be not written down, yet forget not that I am an ass. No, thou villain, thou art full of piety, as shall be prov'd upon thee by good witness. I am a wise fellow; and which is more, an officer; and which is more, a householder; and which is more, as pretty a piece of flesh as any is in Messina, and one that knows the law, go to! and a rich fellow enough, go to! and a fellow that hath had losses; and one that hath two gowns and everything handsome about him. Bring him away. O that I had been writ down an ass! *Exeunt.*

ACT V. [Scene I. *The street, near* Leonato's *house.*]

Enter *Leonato* and his brother [*Antonio*].

Ant. If you go on thus, you will kill yourself,
And 'tis not wisdom thus to second grief
Against yourself.

Leon. I pray thee cease thy counsel,
Which falls into mine ears as profitless
As water in a sieve. Give not me counsel, 5
Nor let no comforter delight mine ear
But such a one whose wrongs do suit with mine.
Bring me a father that so lov'd his child,
Whose joy of her is overwhelm'd like mine,
And bid him speak to me of patience. 10
Measure his woe the length and breadth of mine,
And let it answer every strain for strain,
As thus for thus, and such a grief for such,
In every lineament, branch, shape, and form.
If such a one will smile and stroke his beard, 15
Bid sorrow wag, cry 'hem' when he should groan,
Patch grief with proverbs, make misfortune drunk
With candle-wasters — bring him yet to me,
And I of him will gather patience.
But there is no such man; for, brother, men 20
Can counsel and speak comfort to that grief
Which they themselves not feel; but, tasting it,
Their counsel turns to passion, which before
Would give preceptial medicine to rage,
Fetter strong madness in a silken thread, 25
Charm ache with air and agony with words.
No, no! 'Tis all men's office to speak patience

To those that wring under the load of sorrow,
But no man's virtue nor sufficiency
To be so moral when he shall endure 30
The like himself. Therefore give me no counsel.
My griefs cry louder than advertisement.

Ant. Therein do men from children nothing differ.

Leon. I pray thee peace. I will be flesh and blood;
For there was never yet philosopher 35
That could endure the toothache patiently,
However they have writ the style of gods
And made a push at chance and sufferance.

Ant. Yet bend not all the harm upon yourself.
Make those that do offend you suffer too. 40

Leon. There thou speak'st reason. Nay, I will do so.
My soul doth tell me Hero is belied;
And that shall Claudio know; so shall the Prince,
And all of them that thus dishonour her.

Enter *Don Pedro* and *Claudio*.

Ant. Here comes the Prince and Claudio hastily. 45

Pedro. Good den, good den.

Claud. Good day to both of you.

Leon. Hear you, my lords!

Pedro. We have some haste, Leonato.

Leon. Some haste, my lord! well, fare you well, my lord.
Are you so hasty now? Well, all is one.

Pedro. Nay, do not quarrel with us, good old man. 50
Ant. If he could right himself with quarrelling,
Some of us would lie low.
Claud.   Who wrongs him?
Leon. Marry, thou dost wrong me, thou dissembler, thou!
Nay, never lay thy hand upon thy sword;
I fear thee not.
Claud.   Marry, beshrew my hand 55
If it should give your age such cause of fear.
In faith, my hand meant nothing to my sword.
Leon. Tush, tush, man! never fleer and jest at me.
I speak not like a dotard nor a fool,
As under privilege of age to brag 60
What I have done being young, or what would do,
Were I not old. Know, Claudio, to thy head,
Thou hast so wrong'd mine innocent child and me
That I am forc'd to lay my reverence by
And, with grey hairs and bruise of many days,
Do challenge thee to trial of a man. 66
I say thou hast belied mine innocent child;
Thy slander hath gone through and through her heart,
And she lies buried with her ancestors —
O, in a tomb where never scandal slept, 70
Save this of hers, fram'd by thy villany!
Claud. My villany?
Leon. Thine, Claudio; thine I say.
Pedro. You say not right, old man.
Leon.   My lord, my lord,
I'll prove it on his body if he dare,
Despite his nice fence and his active practice,
His May of youth and bloom of lustihood. 76
Claud. Away! I will not have to do with you.
Leon. Canst thou so daff me? Thou hast kill'd my child.
If thou kill'st me, boy, thou shalt kill a man.
Ant. He shall kill two of us, and men indeed.
But that's no matter; let him kill one first. 81
Win me and wear me! Let him answer me.
Come, follow me, boy. Come, sir boy, come follow me.
Sir boy, I'll whip you from your foining fence!
Nay, as I am a gentleman, I will. 85
Leon. Brother —
Ant. Content yourself. God knows I lov'd my niece,
And she is dead, slander'd to death by villains,
That dare as well answer a man indeed
As I dare take a serpent by the tongue. 90
Boys, apes, braggarts, Jacks, milksops!

Leon.   Brother Anthony —
Ant. Hold you content. What, man! I know them, yea,
And what they weigh, even to the utmost scruple,
Scambling, outfacing, fashion-monging boys,
That lie and cog and flout, deprave and slander,
Go anticly, show outward hideousness, 96
And speak off half a dozen dang'rous words,
How they might hurt their enemies, if they durst;
And this is all.
Leon. But, brother Anthony —
Ant.   Come, 'tis no matter. 100
Do not you meddle; let me deal in this.
Pedro. Gentlemen both, we will not wake your patience.
My heart is sorry for your daughter's death;
But, on my honour, she was charg'd with nothing
But what was true, and very full of proof. 105
Leon. My lord, my lord —
Pedro. I will not hear you.
Leon. No? Come, brother, away! — I will be heard.
Ant. And shall, or some of us will smart for it.   *Exeunt ambo.*

Enter *Benedick.*

Pedro. See, see! Here comes the man we went to seek. 110
Claud. Now, signior, what news?
Bene. Good day, my lord.
Pedro. Welcome, signior. You are almost come to part almost a fray. 114
Claud. We had lik'd to have had our two noses snapp'd off with two old men without teeth.
Pedro. Leonato and his brother. What think'st thou? Had we fought, I doubt we should have been too young for them.
Bene. In a false quarrel there is no true valour. I came to seek you both. 121
Claud. We have been up and down to seek thee; for we are high-proof melancholy, and would fain have it beaten away. Wilt thou use thy wit?
Bene. It is in my scabbard. Shall I draw it?
Pedro. Dost thou wear thy wit by thy side?
Claud. Never any did so, though very many have been beside their wit. I will bid thee draw, as we do the minstrels — draw to pleasure us.
Pedro. As I am an honest man, he looks pale. Art thou sick or angry? 131

185

Claud. What, courage, man! What though care kill'd a cat, thou hast mettle enough in thee to kill care.

Bene. Sir, I shall meet your wit in the career an you charge it against me. I pray you choose another subject. 137

Claud. Nay then, give him another staff; this last was broke cross.

Pedro. By this light, he changes more and more. I think he be angry indeed. 141

Claud. If he be, he knows how to turn his girdle.

Bene. Shall I speak a word in your ear?

Claud. God bless me from a challenge! 145

Bene. [*aside to Claudio*] You are a villain. I jest not; I will make it good how you dare, with what you dare, and when you dare. Do me right, or I will protest your cowardice. You have kill'd a sweet lady, and her death shall fall heavy on you. Let me hear from you. 151

Claud. Well, I will meet you, so I may have good cheer.

Pedro. What, a feast? a feast?

Claud. I' faith, I thank him, he hath bid me to a calve's head and a capon, the which if I do not carve most curiously, say my knife's naught. Shall I not find a woodcock too? 153

Bene. Sir, your wit ambles well; it goes easily.

Pedro. I'll tell thee how Beatrice prais'd thy wit the other day. I said thou hadst a fine wit: 'True,' said she, 'a fine little one.' 'No,' said I, 'a great wit.' 'Right,' says she, 'a great gross one.' 'Nay,' said I, 'a good wit.' 'Just,' said she, 'it hurts nobody.' 'Nay,' said I, 'the gentleman is wise.' 'Certain,' said she, 'a wise gentleman.' 'Nay,' said I, 'he hath two tongues.' 'That I believe,' said she, 'for he swore a thing to me on Monday night which he forswore on Tuesday morning. There's a double tongue; there's two tongues.' Thus did she an hour together transshape thy particular virtues. Yet at last she concluded with a sigh, thou wast the proper'st man in Italy.

Claud. For the which she wept heartily and said she cared not. 176

Pedro. Yea, that she did; but yet, for all that, an if she did not hate him deadly, she would love him dearly. The old man's daughter told us all. 180

Claud. All, all! and moreover, God saw him when he was hid in the garden.

Pedro. But when shall we set the savage bull's horns on the sensible Benedick's head?

Claud. Yea, and text underneath, 'Here dwells Benedick, the married man'? 186

Bene. Fare you well, boy; you know my mind. I will leave you now to your gossiplike humour. You break jests as braggards do their blades, which God be thanked hurt not. My lord, for your many courtesies I thank you. I must discontinue your company. Your brother the bastard is fled from Messina. You have among you kill'd a sweet and innocent lady. For my Lord Lackbeard there, he and I shall meet; and till then peace be with him. [*Exit.*]

Pedro. He is in earnest.

Claud. In most profound earnest; and, I'll warrant you, for the love of Beatrice.

Pedro. And hath challeng'd thee. 200

Claud. Most sincerely.

Pedro. What a pretty thing man is when he goes in his doublet and hose and leaves off his wit!

Enter *Constables* [*Dogberry* and *Verges*, with the Watch, leading] *Conrade* and *Borachio*.

Claud. He is then a giant to an ape; but then is an ape a doctor to such a man. 206

Pedro. But, soft you, let me be! Pluck up, my heart, and be sad! Did he not say my brother was fled?

Dog. Come you, sir. If justice cannot tame you, she shall ne'er weigh more reasons in her balance. Nay, an you be a cursing hypocrite once, you must be look'd to.

Pedro. How now? two of my brother's men bound? Borachio one. 215

Claud. Hearken after their offence, my lord.

Pedro. Officers, what offence have these men done?

Dog. Marry, sir, they have committed false report; moreover, they have spoken untruths; secondarily, they are slanders; sixth and lastly, they have belied a lady; thirdly, they have verified unjust things; and, to conclude, they are lying knaves. 224

Pedro. First, I ask thee what they have done; thirdly, I ask thee what's their offence; sixth and lastly, why they are committed; and to conclude, what you lay to their charge.

Claud. Rightly reasoned, and in his own division; and by my troth there's one meaning well suited. 231

Pedro. Who have you offended, masters, that you are thus bound to your answer? This learned constable is too cunning to be understood. What's your offence? 235

186

Bora. Sweet Prince, let me go no farther to mine answer. Do you hear me, and let this Count kill me. I have deceived even your very eyes. What your wisdoms could not discover, these shallow fools have brought to light, who in the night overheard me confessing to this man, how Don John your brother incensed me to slander the Lady Hero; how you were brought into the orchard and saw me court Margaret in Hero's garments; how you disgrac'd her when you should marry her. My villany they have upon record, which I had rather seal with my death than repeat over to my shame. The lady is dead upon mine and my master's false accusation; and briefly, I desire nothing but the reward of a villain. 251

Pedro. Runs not this speech like iron through your blood?

Claud. I have drunk poison whiles he utter'd it.

Pedro. But did my brother set thee on to this?

Bora. Yea, and paid me richly for the practice of it. 256

Pedro. He is compos'd and fram'd of treachery,
And fled he is upon this villany.

Claud. Sweet Hero, now thy image doth appear
In the rare semblance that I lov'd it first. 260

Dog. Come, bring away the plaintiffs. By this time our sexton hath reformed Signior Leonato of the matter. And, masters, do not forget to specify, when time and place shall serve, that I am an ass. 265

Verg. Here, here comes Master Signior Leonato, and the sexton too.

Enter *Leonato*, his brother [*Antonio*], and the *Sexton*.

Leon. Which is the villain? Let me see his eyes,
That, when I note another man like him,
I may avoid him. Which of these is he? 270

Bora. If you would know your wronger, look on me.

Leon. Art thou the slave that with thy breath hast kill'd
Mine innocent child?

Bora.   Yea, even I alone.

Leon. No, not so, villain! thou beliest thyself.
Here stand a pair of honourable men —   275
A third is fled — that had a hand in it.

I thank you princes for my daughter's death.
Record it with your high and worthy deeds.
'Twas bravely done, if you bethink you of it.

Claud. I know not how to pray your patience;   280
Yet I must speak. Choose your revenge yourself;
Impose me to what penance your invention
Can lay upon my sin. Yet sinn'd I not
But in mistaking.

Pedro.   By my soul, nor I!   285
And yet, to satisfy this good old man,
I would bend under any heavy weight
That he'll enjoin me to.

Leon. I cannot bid you bid my daughter live —
That were impossible; but I pray you both,
Possess the people in Messina here   290
How innocent she died; and if your love
Can labour aught in sad invention,
Hang her an epitaph upon her tomb,
And sing it to her bones — sing it to-night.
To-morrow morning come you to my house, 295
And since you could not be my son-in-law,
Be yet my nephew. My brother hath a daughter,
Almost the copy of my child that's dead,
And she alone is heir to both of us.
Give her the right you should have giv'n her cousin,   300
And so dies my revenge.

Claud.   O noble sir!
Your over-kindness doth wring tears from me.
I do embrace your offer; and dispose
For henceforth of poor Claudio.

Leon. To-morrow then I will expect your coming;   305
To-night I take my leave. This naughty man
Shall face to face be brought to Margaret,
Who I believe was pack'd in all this wrong,
Hir'd to it by your brother.

Bora.   No, by my soul, she was not;
Nor knew not what she did when she spoke to me;   310
But always hath been just and virtuous
In anything that I do know by her.

Dog. Moreover, sir, which indeed is not under white and black, this plaintiff here, the offender, did call me ass. I beseech you let it be rememb'red in his punishment. And also the watch heard them talk of one Deformed. They say he wears a key in his ear, and a lock hanging by it, and borrows money in God's name, the which he hath us'd so long and never paid that

now men grow hard-hearted and will lend nothing for God's sake. Pray you examine him
upon that point.　　　　　　　　　　322
　Leon. I thank thee for thy care and honest
pains.
　Dog. Your worship speaks like a most thankful and reverent youth, and I praise God for
you.
　Leon. There's for thy pains. [*Gives money.*]
　Dog. God save the foundation!
　Leon. Go, I discharge thee of thy prisoner,
and I thank thee.　　　　　　　　　329
　Dog. I leave an arrant knave with your worship, which I beseech your worship to correct
yourself, for the example of others. God keep
your worship! I wish your worship well. God
restore you to health! I humbly give you leave
to depart; and if a merry meeting may be
wish'd, God prohibit it! Come, neighbour. 336
　　　　　　Exeunt [*Dogberry and Verges*].
　Leon. Until to-morrow morning, lords, farewell.
　Ant. Farewell, my lords. We look for you
to-morrow.
　Pedro. We will not fail.
　Claud.　　　To-night I'll mourn with Hero.
　　　　　　　[*Exeunt Don Pedro and Claudio.*]
　Leon. [*to the Watch*] Bring you these fellows
on. — We'll talk with Margaret,　　340
How her acquaintance grew with this lewd
fellow.　　　　　　　　　　　　*Exeunt.*

[Scene II. Leonato's *orchard*.]

Enter Benedick and Margaret [*meeting*].

　Bene. Pray thee, sweet Mistress Margaret,
deserve well at my hands by helping me to the
speech of Beatrice.
　Marg. Will you then write me a sonnet in
praise of my beauty?　　　　　　　5
　Bene. In so high a style, Margaret, that no
man living shall come over it; for in most
comely truth thou deservest it.
　Marg. To have no man come over me? Why,
shall I always keep below stairs?　　10
　Bene. Thy wit is as quick as the greyhound's
mouth — it catches.
　Marg. And yours as blunt as the fencer's
foils, which hit but hurt not.
　Bene. A most manly wit, Margaret: it will
not hurt a woman. And so I pray thee call
Beatrice. I give thee the bucklers.
　Marg. Give us the swords; we have bucklers of our own.　　　　　　　　19

　Bene. If you use them, Margaret, you must
put in the pikes with a vice, and they are dan-
gerous weapons for maids.
　Marg. Well, I will call Beatrice to you, who
I think hath legs.
　Bene. And therefore will come.　　25
　　　　　　　　　　　Exit Margaret.

　　[*Sings.*] The god of love,
　　　　　　That sits above
　　　And knows me, and knows me,
　　　　　　How pitiful I deserve —　　29

I mean in singing; but in loving Leander the
good swimmer, Troilus the first employer of
panders, and a whole book full of these quondam carpet-mongers, whose names yet run
smoothly in the even road of a blank verse —
why, they were never so truly turn'd over and
over as my poor self in love. Marry, I cannot
show it in rhyme. I have tried. I can find out
no rhyme to 'lady' but 'baby' — an innocent
rhyme; for 'scorn,' 'horn' — a hard rhyme;
for 'school,' 'fool' — a babbling rhyme: very
ominous endings! No, I was not born under
a rhyming planet, nor I cannot woo in festival
terms.　　　　　　　　　　　41

Enter *Beatrice.*

Sweet Beatrice, wouldst thou come when I
call'd thee?
　Beat. Yea, signior, and depart when you bid
me.
　Bene. O, stay but till then!　　45
　Beat. 'Then' is spoken. Fare you well now.
And yet, ere I go, let me go with that I came
for, which is, with knowing what hath pass'd
between you and Claudio.
　Bene. Only foul words; and thereupon I will
kiss thee.　　　　　　　　　51
　Beat. Foul words is but foul wind, and foul
wind is but foul breath, and foul breath is noi-
some. Therefore I will depart unkiss'd.
　Bene. Thou hast frighted the word out of
his right sense, so forcible is thy wit. But I
must tell thee plainly, Claudio undergoes my
challenge; and either I must shortly hear from
him or I will subscribe him a coward. And I
pray thee now tell me, for which of my bad parts
didst thou first fall in love with me?　　61
　Beat. For them all together, which maintain'd so politic a state of evil that they will
not admit any good part to intermingle with
them. But for which of my good parts did you
first suffer love for me?　　　　66
　Bene. Suffer love! — a good epithet. I do suffer love indeed, for I love thee against my will.

188

Beat. In spite of your heart, I think. Alas, poor heart! If you spite it for my sake, I will spite it for yours, for I will never love that which my friend hates.   72

Bene. Thou and I are too wise to woo peaceably.

Beat. It appears not in this confession. There's not one wise man among twenty that will praise himself.   77

Bene. An old, an old instance, Beatrice, that liv'd in the time of good neighbours. If a man do not erect in this age his own tomb ere he dies, he shall live no longer in monument than the bell rings and the widow weeps.   82

Beat. And how long is that, think you?

Bene. Question: why, an hour in clamour and a quarter in rheum. Therefore is it most expedient for the wise, if Don Worm (his conscience) find no impediment to the contrary, to be the trumpet of his own virtues, as I am, to myself. So much for praising myself, who, I myself will bear witness, is praiseworthy. And now tell me, how doth your cousin?   91

Beat. Very ill.

Bene. And how do you?

Beat. Very ill too.

Bene. Serve God, love me, and mend. There will I leave you too, for here comes one in haste.

Enter Ursula.

Urs. Madam, you must come to your uncle. Yonder's old coil at home. It is proved my Lady Hero hath been falsely accus'd, the Prince and Claudio mightily abus'd, and Don John is the author of all, who is fled and gone. Will you come presently?   102

Beat. Will you go hear this news, signior?

Bene. I will live in thy heart, die in thy lap, and be buried in thy eyes; and moreover, I will go with thee to thy uncle's.   *Exeunt.*

[Scene III. *A churchyard.*]

Enter *Claudio, Don Pedro*, and three or four with tapers, [followed by *Musicians*].

Claud. Is this the monument of Leonato?

Lord. It is, my lord.

Claud. [*reads from a scroll*]

Epitaph.

Done to death by slanderous tongues
  Was the Hero that here lies.
Death, in guerdon of her wrongs,   5
  Gives her fame which never dies.

So the life that died with shame
Lives in death with glorious fame.

Hang thou there upon the tomb,
                    [*Hangs up the scroll.*]
Praising her when I am dumb.   10
Now, music, sound, and sing your solemn hymn.

Song.

Pardon, goddess of the night,
Those that slew thy virgin knight;
For the which, with songs of woe,
Round about her tomb they go.   15
  Midnight, assist our moan,
  Help us to sigh and groan
    Heavily, heavily.
Graves, yawn and yield your dead,
Till death be uttered   20
    Heavily, heavily.

Claud. Now unto thy bones good night!
  Yearly will I do this rite.

Pedro. Good morrow, masters. Put your torches out.
The wolves have prey'd, and look, the gentle day,   25
Before the wheels of Phœbus, round about
Dapples the drowsy east with spots of grey.
Thanks to you all, and leave us. Fare you well.

Claud. Good morrow, masters. Each his several way.

Pedro. Come, let us hence and put on other weeds,   30
And then to Leonato's we will go.

Claud. And Hymen now with luckier issue speeds
Than this for whom we rend'red up this woe.
                                    Exeunt.

[Scene IV. *The hall in* Leonato's *house.*]

Enter *Leonato, Benedick, [Beatrice,] Margaret, Ursula, Antonio, Friar [Francis], Hero.*

Friar. Did I not tell you she was innocent?

Leon. So are the Prince and Claudio, who accus'd her
Upon the error that you heard debated.
But Margaret was in some fault for this,
Although against her will, as it appears   5
In the true course of all the question.

Ant. Well, I am glad that all things sort so well.

Bene. And so am I, being else by faith enforc'd
To call young Claudio to a reckoning for it.

Leon. Well, daughter, and you gentlewomen all, 10
Withdraw into a chamber by yourselves,
And when I send for you, come hither mask'd.
Exeunt Ladies.
The Prince and Claudio promis'd by this hour
To visit me. You know your office, brother:
You must be father to your brother's daughter,
And give her to young Claudio. 16
Ant. Which I will do with confirm'd countenance.
Bene. Friar, I must entreat your pains, I think.
Friar. To do what, signior?
Bene. To bind me, or undo me — one of them. 20
Signior Leonato, truth it is, good signior,
Your niece regards me with an eye of favour.
Leon. That eye my daughter lent her. 'Tis most true.
Bene. And I do with an eye of love requite her.
Leon. The sight whereof I think you had from me, 25
From Claudio, and the Prince; but what's your will?
Bene. Your answer, sir, is enigmatical;
But, for my will, my will is, your good will
May stand with ours, this day to be conjoin'd
In the state of honourable marriage; 30
In which, good friar, I shall desire your help.
Leon. My heart is with your liking.
Friar. And my help.

Enter *Don Pedro* and *Claudio* and
two or three other.

Here comes the Prince and Claudio.
Pedro. Good morrow to this fair assembly.
Leon. Good morrow, Prince; good morrow, Claudio. 35
We here attend you. Are you yet determin'd
To-day to marry with my brother's daughter?
Claud. I'll hold my mind, were she an Ethiope.
Leon. Call her forth, brother. Here's the friar ready.

[*Exit Antonio.*]

Pedro. Good morrow, Benedick. Why, what's the matter 40
That you have such a February face,
So full of frost, of storm, and cloudiness?
Claud. I think he thinks upon the savage bull.
Tush, fear not, man! We'll tip thy horns with gold,

And all Europa shall rejoice at thee, 45
As once Europa did at lusty Jove
When he would play the noble beast in love.
Bene. Bull Jove, sir, had an amiable low,
And some such strange bull leap'd your father's cow
And got a calf in that same noble feat 50
Much like to you, for you have just his bleat.

Enter [*Leonato's*] brother [*Antonio*], *Hero,
Beatrice, Margaret, Ursula,* [the ladies wearing masks].

Claud. For this I owe you. Here comes other reck'nings.
Which is the lady I must seize upon?
Ant. This same is she, and I do give you her.
Claud. Why then, she's mine. Sweet, let me see your face. 55
Leon. No, that you shall not till you take her hand
Before this friar and swear to marry her.
Claud. Give me your hand before this holy friar.
I am your husband if you like of me.
Hero. And when I liv'd I was your other wife; [*Unmasks.*]
And when you lov'd you were my other husband. 61
Claud. Another Hero!
Hero. Nothing certainer.
One Hero died defil'd; but I do live,
And surely as I live, I am a maid.
Pedro. The former Hero! Hero that is dead!
Leon. She died, my lord, but whiles her slander liv'd. 66
Friar. All this amazement can I qualify,
When, after that the holy rites are ended,
I'll tell you largely of fair Hero's death.
Meantime let wonder seem familiar, 70
And to the chapel let us presently.
Bene. Soft and fair, friar. Which is Beatrice?
Beat. [*unmasks*] I answer to that name. What is your will?
Bene. Do not you love me?
Beat. Why, no; no more than reason.
Bene. Why, then your uncle, and the Prince, and Claudio 75
Have been deceived; for they swore you did.
Beat. Do not you love me?
Bene. Troth, no; no more than reason.
Beat. Why, then my cousin, Margaret, and Ursula
Are much deceiv'd; for they did swear you did.
Bene. They swore that you were almost sick for me. 80

190

Beat. They swore that you were well-nigh dead for me.

Bene. 'Tis no such matter. Then you do not love me?

Beat. No, truly, but in friendly recompense.

Leon. Come, cousin, I am sure you love the gentleman.

Claud. And I'll be sworn upon't that he loves her;   85
For here's a paper written in his hand,
A halting sonnet of his own pure brain,
Fashion'd to Beatrice.

Hero.   And here's another,
Writ in my cousin's hand, stol'n from her pocket,
Containing her affection unto Benedick.   90

Bene. A miracle! Here's our own hands against our hearts. Come, I will have thee; but, by this light, I take thee for pity.

Beat. I would not deny you; but, by this good day, I yield upon great persuasion, and partly to save your life, for I was told you were in a consumption.   97

Bene. Peace! I will stop your mouth.
                              [*Kisses her.*]

Pedro. How dost thou, Benedick, the married man?

Bene. I'll tell thee what, Prince: a college of wit-crackers cannot flout me out of my humour. Dost thou think I care for a satire or an epigram? No. If a man will be beaten with brains, 'a shall wear nothing handsome about him. In brief, since I do purpose to marry, I will think nothing to any purpose that the world can say against it; and therefore never flout at me for what I have said against it; for man is a giddy thing, and this is my conclusion. For thy part, Claudio, I did think to have beaten thee; but in that thou art like to be my kinsman, live unbruis'd, and love my cousin.   113

Claud. I had well hop'd thou wouldst have denied Beatrice, that I might have cudgell'd thee out of thy single life, to make thee a double-dealer, which out of question thou wilt be if my cousin do not look exceeding narrowly to thee.

Bene. Come, come, we are friends. Let's have a dance ere we are married, that we may lighten our own hearts and our wives' heels. 121

Leon. We'll have dancing afterward.

Bene. First, of my word! Therefore play, music. Prince, thou art sad. Get thee a wife, get thee a wife! There is no staff more reverent than one tipp'd with horn.   126

Enter *Messenger.*

Mess. My lord, your brother John is ta'en in flight,
And brought with armed men back to Messina.

Bene. Think not on him till to-morrow. I'll devise thee brave punishments for him. Strike up, pipers!   *Dance.* [*Exeunt.*]

LOVE'S LABOUR'S LOST

For the text of LOVE'S LABOUR'S LOST the Quarto of 1598 (carelessly printed from an autograph manuscript) is our only real authority. The Folio compositor used it as copy, correcting many obvious errors, but perpetrating many new misprints. The Quarto has no division into acts and scenes; the Folio marks the acts (misprinting *Quartus* for *Quintus*), but not the scenes.

Doubtless the play was written for performance at court or at some great house. The Quarto records that it 'was presented before her Highnes' Queen Elizabeth 'this last Christmas,' that is, apparently, in 1597. There was doubtless a considerable interval between composition and this performance at court. Meres's list (p. 33, above) shows that *A Midsummer Night's Dream* and *The Merchant of Venice* were known to him before October 19, 1598. Both of them seem later than LOVE'S LABOUR'S LOST. He also mentions a *Love's Labour's Won*. What this was, we do not know, possibly the first form of *All's Well* (see p. 361). In any event, it can hardly have come before LOVE'S LABOUR'S LOST if its title means anything. LOVE'S LABOUR'S LOST, then, should in all probability be put back to 1594 or 1595. There is no good reason for regarding it as the earliest of Shakespeare's comedies and dating it 1591. The plot seems to be original, though a hint for the visit of the Princess and her ladies has been detected in a picturesque incident of 1578 — the visit of Queen Catherine of France and Marguerite de Valois to the court of Navarre. Though slight, the plot suffices to keep things moving. Our interest centres not in the action but in the delightfully whimsical situation; and the eccentricities of that situation are managed with consummate skill, set forth vividly in ironic characterization, and illuminated by polished wit in dialogue and soliloquy. The farcical personages who bring this courtly fairyland into contact with the working-day world are, to be sure, conventional figures; but they are so robustly individualized that one is ready to accept them as original creations.

Meres's catalogue of Shakespeare's comedies may well coincide with chronology in mentioning *The Two Gentlemen* and *The Comedy of Errors* before LOVE'S LABOUR'S LOST. Style and versification accord with 1594 or 1595. The blank verse is not that of a tyro. The rhyming speeches and the interspersed lyrics show masterly skill in a variety of metres. The song at the end is one of the best in the world. The Euphuistic prose is as good of its kind as anything achieved by Lyly, whom Shakespeare was obviously emulating, and the 'tender juvenal,' Moth (that is, *Mote*), is quite as amusing as the wittiest of Lyly's clever youngsters. However, there is enough pleasant parody of Euphuism and other stylistic extravagances to show that Shakespeare was no blind disciple of any rhetorical master.

The 1598 title-page contains the words 'Newly corrected and augmented.' This may mean that the play had been printed before in a shorter form, or it may be a mere advertising formula to assure the customer that he was purchasing a complete and accurate text. Whether there was or was not an earlier issue, we cannot accept the title-page as evidence that the Quarto represents a rewriting by Shakespeare (for the Christmas performance) of a drama which he originally composed in or about 1593. Certain confusions and odd features of the Quarto text have been adduced in support of this theory, but they are otherwise explicable. The most striking is the repetition in Berowne's long oration (iv, 3, 289 ff.). To reduce this speech to order, something must be cut out. In the present edition lines 298–319 are italicized. If these are omitted, Berowne's discourse becomes orderly enough. The repetition seems to be due to the printer's carelessness in setting up a passage which stood in his copy, but with marks for deletion. Perhaps Shakespeare changed his mind while writing the speech and crossed out certain lines, but not so drastically as to render them illegible. The same explanation will account for lines 826–831 in Act v, scene 2 (also italicized in the present edition). These major errors and other cases of confusion or inconsistency in minor matters certainly do not prove that there were ever two distinct versions of Shakespeare's play. There may have been some revision for the Christmas performance, but we need not assume that this was either extensive or thoroughgoing.

The influence of the Italian *commedia dell' arte* is visible throughout the play. Several of the characters correspond to standard figures of the Italian convention: Armado to the bragging soldier (a lineal descendant of Pyrgopolynices of the *Miles Gloriosus* of Plautus); Moth to the *zanni* who regularly accompanies the braggart; Holofernes to the pedant; Nathaniel to the parasite; Costard to the rustic. Armado is styled 'Braggart' and Holofernes 'Pedant' in stage directions. But these similarities must not be pushed to the extreme. There were Costards enough in Shakespeare's England and the breed is not extinct. Armado is quite as much a pedant as a boaster: he is pedantic in his boasting and boastful in his pedantry.

It is merely whimsical to identify Holofernes with Florio, the translator of Montaigne, or with Chapman (even if Chapman was, as is very doubtful, the rival poet of the *Sonnets*), or with Gabriel Harvey, or to find the original of Armado in Philip of Spain or Sir Walter Raleigh, or the prototype of Moth in Thomas Nashe. No Elizabethan could have recognized Harvey, the eminent college don, as latent in a schoolmaster who 'teaches boys the hornbook.' Boyet describes Armado as 'a Monarcho' (iv, 1, 101). The real Monarcho was an Italian, a harmless and amusing madman who frequented the English court and was dead by 1580. His resemblance to Armado must have been merely generic.

A favourite literary exercise for Elizabethan wits was the paradox, and this too emerges in the rich abundance of LOVE'S LABOUR'S LOST. See, for example, Berowne's praise of the black-browed Rosaline (iv, 3, 248 ff.), which leads up to his argument that he and his associates are not bound by their rash vow. The King styles his defence a paradox in the same speech in which he calls black 'the school of night.'

This last phrase (though 'school' may be a misprint) has led to ingenious theorizing. Taken in connection with Chapman's *Shadow of Night* (1594), it has been held to indicate that there actually was a coterie called or nicknamed 'The School of Night,' which devoted itself to the study of the new astronomy; and this has been identified with the group of philosophical speculators patronized by Raleigh and regarded by their contemporaries as atheists. However this may be, there is no reason whatever for interpreting the 'Academe' of Shakespeare's play as a satire on these scientific innovators.

LOVE'S LABOUR'S LOST

[Dramatis Personæ.

Ferdinand, King of Navarre.
Berowne, ⎫
Longaville, ⎬ lords attending on the King.
Dumain, ⎭
Boyet, ⎫ lords attending on the Princess of
Marcade, ⎭ France.
Don Adriano de Armado, a Spaniard.
Sir Nathaniel, a curate.
Holofernes, a schoolmaster.
Dull, a constable.

Costard, a clown.
Moth, page to Don Armado.
A Forester.

The Princess of France.
Rosaline, ⎫
Maria, ⎬ ladies attending on the Princess.
Katherine, ⎭
Jaquenetta, a country wench.

Lords, Attendants, &c.

SCENE. — Navarre.]

ACT I. [Scene I. Navarre. The King's Park.]

Enter *Ferdinand, King of Navarre, Berowne,
Longaville,* and *Dumain.*

Ferd. Let fame, that all hunt after in their
lives,
Live regist'red upon our brazen tombs
And then grace us, in the disgrace of death,
When, spite of cormorant devouring Time,
Th' endeavour of this present breath may buy 5
That honour which shall bate his scythe's keen
edge
And make us heirs of all eternity.
Therefore, brave conquerors — for so you are
That war against your own affections
And the huge army of the world's desires — 10
Our late edict shall strongly stand in force:
Navarre shall be the wonder of the world;
Our court shall be a little Academe,
Still and contemplative in living art.
You three, Berowne, Dumain, and Longaville,
Have sworn for three years' term to live with
me, 16
My fellow scholars, and to keep those statutes
That are recorded in this schedule here.
Your oaths are pass'd; and now subscribe
your names,
That his own hand may strike his honour down
That violates the smallest branch herein. 21
If you are arm'd to do as sworn to do,
Subscribe to your deep oaths, and keep it too.
Long. I am resolv'd. 'Tis but a three years'
fast. 24
The mind shall banquet, though the body pine.

Fat paunches have lean pates, and dainty bits
Make rich the ribs but bankrout quite the wits.
Dum. My loving lord, Dumain is mortified.
The grosser manner of these world's delights
He throws upon the gross world's baser slaves.
To love, to wealth, to pomp, I pine and die, 31
With all these living in philosophy.
Ber. I can but say their protestation over,
So much, dear liege, I have already sworn,
That is, to live and study here three years. 35
But there are other strict observances:
As, not to see a woman in that term,
Which I hope well is not enrolled there;
And one day in a week to touch no food,
And but one meal on every day beside, 40
The which I hope is not enrolled there;
And then to sleep but three hours in the night
And not be seen to wink of all the day
(When I was wont to think no harm all night
And make a dark night too of half the day), 45
Which I hope well is not enrolled there.
O, these are barren tasks, too hard to keep —
Not to see ladies, study, fast, not sleep!
Ferd. Your oath is pass'd, to pass away from
these.
Ber. Let me say no, my liege, an if you please.
I only swore to study with your Grace 51
And stay here in your court for three years'
space.
Long. You swore to that, Berowne, and to
the rest.
Ber. By yea and nay, sir, then I swore in jest.
What is the end of study? Let me know. 55

195

Ferd. Why, that to know which else we
  should not know.
Ber. Things hid and barr'd (you mean) from
  common sense.
Ferd. Ay, that is study's godlike recompense.
Ber. Com' on then! I will swear to study so,
To know the thing I am forbid to know: 60
As thus — to study where I well may dine
  When I to feast expressly am forbid;
Or study where to meet some mistress fine
  When mistresses from common sense are hid;
Or, having sworn too hard-a-keeping oath, 65
Study to break it and not break my troth.
If study's gain be thus, and this be so,
Study knows that which yet it doth not know.
Swear me to this, and I will ne'er say no.
Ferd. These be the stops that hinder study
  quite 70
And train our intellects to vain delight.
Ber. Why, all delights are vain, but that
  most vain
Which, with pain purchas'd, doth inherit pain:
As, painfully to pore upon a book 74
  To seek the light of truth while truth the while
Doth falsely blind the eyesight of his look.
Light, seeking light, doth light of light be-
  guile.
So, ere you find where light in darkness lies,
Your light grows dark by losing of your eyes.
Study me how to please the eye indeed 80
  By fixing it upon a fairer eye,
Who dazzling so, that eye shall be his heed
  And give him light that it was blinded by.
Study is like the heaven's glorious sun,
  That will not be deep search'd with saucy
  looks. 85
Small have continual plodders ever won
Save base authority from others' books.
These earthly godfathers of heaven's lights
  That give a name to every fixed star
Have no more profit of their shining nights 90
  Than those that walk and wot not what they
  are.
Too much to know is to know naught but fame;
And every godfather can give a name.
Ferd. How well he's read, to reason against
  reading!
Dum. Proceeded well, to stop all good pro-
  ceeding! 95
Long. He weeds the corn and still lets grow
  the weeding.
Ber. The spring is near when green geese
  are a-breeding.
Dum. How follows that?
Ber.   Fit in his place and time.

Dum. In reason nothing.
Ber.   Something then in rhyme.
Ferd. Berowne is like an envious sneaping
  frost 100
That bites the first-born infants of the spring.
Ber. Well, say I am! Why should proud sum-
  mer boast
Before the birds have any cause to sing?
Why should I joy in any abortive birth?
At Christmas I no more desire a rose 105
Than wish a snow in May's newfangled shows,
But like of each thing that in season grows.
So you — to study now it is too late —
Climb o'er the house to unlock the little gate.
Ferd. Well, sit you out. Go home, Berowne.
  Adieu. 110
Ber. No, my good lord. I have sworn to
  stay with you;
And though I have for barbarism spoke more
  Than for that angel knowledge you can say,
Yet confident I'll keep what I have swore
  And bide the penance of each three years'
  day. 115
Give me the paper; let me read the same,
And to the strictest decrees I'll write my name.
Ferd. How well this yielding rescues thee
  from shame!
Ber. [*reads*] 'Item. That no woman shall
come within a mile of my court' — Hath this
been proclaimed? 121
Long. Four days ago.
Ber. Let's see the penalty: '— on pain of
losing her tongue.' Who devis'd this penalty?
Long. Marry, that did I. 126
Ber. Sweet lord, and why?
Long. To fright them hence with that dread
penalty.
Ber. A dangerous law against gentility!
[*Reads.*] 'Item. If any man be seen to talk with
a woman within the term of three years, he shall
endure such public shame as the rest of the court
can devise.'
This article, my liege, yourself must break;
For well you know here comes in embassy 135
The French king's daughter with yourself to
  speak,
A maid of grace and complete majesty,
About surrender-up of Aquitaine
To her decrepit, sick, and bedrid father.
Therefore this article is made in vain, 140
  Or vainly comes th' admired princess hither.
Ferd. What say you, lords? Why, this was
  quite forgot.
Ber. So study evermore is overshot.
While it doth study to have what it would,

It doth forget to do the thing it should;   145
And when it hath the thing it hunteth most,
'Tis won as towns with fire — so won, so lost.
Ferd. We must of force dispense with this
    decree.
She must lie here on mere necessity.
Ber. Necessity will make us all forsworn   150
Three thousand times within this three years'
    space;
For every man with his affects is born,
    Not by might mast'red, but by special grace.
If I break faith, this word shall speak for me,
I am forsworn on mere necessity.   155
So to the laws at large I write my name;
                              [*Subscribes.*]
And he that breaks them in the least degree
Stands in attainder of eternal shame.
Suggestions are to other as to me;
But I believe, although I seem so loath,   160
I am the last that will last keep his oath.
But is there no quick recreation granted?
Ferd. Ay, that there is. Our court you know
    is haunted
With a refined traveller of Spain,
A man in all the world's new fashion planted,
    That hath a mint of phrases in his brain; 166
One whom the music of his own vain tongue
Doth ravish like enchanting harmony;
A man of complements, whom right and wrong
Have chose as umpire of their mutiny.   170
This child of fancy, that Armado hight,
    For interim to our studies shall relate
In high-born words the worth of many a knight
From tawny Spain lost in the world's debate.
How you delight, my lords, I know not, I;   175
But I protest I love to hear him lie,
And I will use him for my minstrelsy.
Ber. Armado is a most illustrious wight,
A man of fire-new words, fashion's own knight.
Long. Costard the swain and he shall be our
    sport,   180
And so to study three years is but short.

Enter [*Dull,*] a Constable, with *Costard,*
    [a Clown,] with a letter.

Dull. Which is the Duke's own person?
Ber. This, fellow. What wouldst?
Dull. I myself reprehend his own person, for
I am his Grace's farborough. But I would see
his own person in flesh and blood.   186
Ber. This is he.
Dull. Signior Arme — Arme — commends
you. There's villany abroad. This letter will
tell you more.   190

Cost. Sir, the contempts thereof are as touch-
ing me.
Ferd. A letter from the magnificent Armado.
Ber. How low soever the matter, I hope in
God for high words.   195
Long. A high hope for a low heaven. God
grant us patience!
Ber. To hear? or forbear hearing?
Long. To hear meekly, sir, and to laugh mod-
erately, or to forbear both.   200
Ber. Well, sir, be it as the style shall give us
cause to climb in the merriness.
Cost. The matter is to me, sir, as concerning
Jaquenetta. The manner of it is, I was taken
with the manner.   205
Ber. In what manner?
Cost. In manner and form following, sir —
all those three. I was seen with her in the
manor house, sitting with her upon the form,
and taken following her into the park; which
put together is in manner and form following.
Now, sir, for the manner — it is the manner
of a man to speak to a woman; for the form —
in some form.
Ber. For the following, sir?
Cost. As it shall follow in my correction —
and God defend the right!   216
Ferd. Will you hear this letter with attention?
Ber. As we would hear an oracle.
Cost. Such is the simplicity of man to hearken
after the flesh.   220
Ferd. [*reads*] 'Great deputy, the welkin's vice-
gerent, and sole dominator of Navarre, my soul's
earth's god and body's fost'ring patron' —
Cost. Not a word of Costard yet.
Ferd. 'So it is' —   225
Cost. It may be so; but if he say it is so, he
is, in telling true, but so.
Ferd. Peace!
Cost. Be to me, and every man that dares
not fight!   230
Ferd. No words!
Cost. Of other men's secrets, I beseech you.
Ferd. 'So it is, besieged with sable-coloured
melancholy, I did commend the black oppressing
humour to the most wholesome physic of thy
health-giving air; and, as I am a gentleman, be-
took myself to walk. The time When? About the
sixth hour, when beasts most graze, birds best
peck, and men sit down to that nourishment which
is called supper. So much for the time When.
Now for the ground Which? which, I mean, I
walk'd upon. It is ycliped thy park. Then for the
place Where? where, I mean, I did encounter that
obscene and most prepost'rous event that draweth

from my snow-white pen the ebon-coloured ink which here thou viewest, beholdest, surveyest, or seest. But to the place Where? It standeth north-north-east and by east from the west corner of thy curious-knotted garden. There did I see that low-spirited swain, that base minnow of thy mirth' —
Cost. Me!
Ferd. 'that unlettered small-knowing soul' —
Cost. Me!   255
Ferd. 'that shallow vassal' —
Cost. Still me!
Ferd. 'which, as I remember, hight Costard' —
Cost. O, me!   260
Ferd. 'sorted and consorted, contrary to thy established proclaimed edict and continent canon, with — with — O, with — but with this I passion to say wherewith' —
Cost. With a wench.   265
Ferd. 'with a child of our grandmother Eve, a female, or, for thy more sweet understanding, a woman. Him I (as my ever-esteemed duty pricks me on) have sent to thee, to receive the meed of punishment, by thy sweet Grace's officer, Anthony Dull, a man of good repute, carriage, bearing, and estimation.'   272
Dull. Me, an't shall please you. I am Anthony Dull.
Ferd. 'For Jaquenetta (so is the weaker vessel called), which I apprehended with the aforesaid swain, I keep her as a vessel of thy law's fury, and shall, at the least of thy sweet notice, bring her to trial.
'Thine, in all complements of devoted and heart-burning heat of duty,

'DON ADRIANO DE ARMADO.'   280

Ber. This is not so well as I looked for, but the best that ever I heard.
Ferd. Ay, the best for the worst. But, sirrah, what say you to this?
Cost. Sir, I confess the wench.   285
Ferd. Did you hear the proclamation?
Cost. I do confess much of the hearing it, but little of the marking of it.
Ferd. It was proclaimed a year's imprisonment to be taken with a wench.   290
Cost. I was taken with none, sir. I was taken with a damsel.
Ferd. Well, it was proclaimed 'damsel.'
Cost. This was no damsel neither, sir. She was a virgin.   295
Ferd. It is so varied too, for it was proclaimed 'virgin.'
Cost. If it were, I deny her virginity. I was taken with a maid.
Ferd. This 'maid' will not serve your turn, sir.   300

Cost. This maid will serve my turn, sir.
Ferd. Sir, I will pronounce your sentence: you shall fast a week with bran and water.
Cost. I had rather pray a month with mutton and porridge.   305
Ferd. And Don Armado shall be your keeper. My Lord Berowne, see him delivered o'er, And go we, lords, to put in practice that Which each to other hath so strongly sworn.
                    [*Exeunt King Ferdinand, Longaville, and Dumain.*]

Ber. I'll lay my head to any good man's hat These oaths and laws will prove an idle scorn. Sirrah, come on.   312
Cost. I suffer for the truth, sir; for true it is I was taken with Jaquenetta, and Jaquenetta is a true girl, and therefore welcome the sour cup of prosperity! Affliction may one day smile again, and till then, sit thee down, sorrow!
                                                                        Exeunt.

[Scene II. *The park.*]

Enter *Armado* and *Moth*, his page.

Arm. Boy, what sign is it when a man of great spirit grows melancholy?
Moth. A great sign, sir, that he will look sad.
Arm. Why, sadness is one and the selfsame thing, dear imp.   5
Moth. No, no! O Lord, sir, no!
Arm. How canst thou part sadness and melancholy, my tender juvenal?
Moth. By a familiar demonstration of the working, my tough signior.   10
Arm. Why tough signior? Why tough signior?
Moth. Why tender juvenal? Why tender juvenal?
Arm. I spoke it tender juvenal as a congruent epitheton appertaining to thy young days, which we may nominate tender.   16
Moth. And I tough signior as an appertinent title to your old time, which we may name tough.
Arm. Pretty and apt.
Moth. How mean you, sir? I pretty, and my saying apt? or I apt, and my saying pretty?
Arm. Thou pretty, because little.
Moth. Little pretty, because little. Wherefore apt?
Arm. And therefore apt, because quick.   25
Moth. Speak you this in my praise, master?
Arm. In thy condign praise.
Moth. I will praise an eel with the same praise.

Arm. What? that an eel is ingenious?
Moth. That an eel is quick.   30
Arm. I do say thou art quick in answers.
Thou heat'st my blood.
Moth. I am answer'd, sir.
Arm. I love not to be cross'd.
Moth. [*aside*] He speaks the mere contrary
— crosses love not him.   36
Arm. I have promised to study three years
with the Duke.
Moth. You may do it in an hour, sir.
Arm. Impossible.   40
Moth. How many is one thrice told?
Arm. I am ill at reck'ning; it fitteth the
spirit of a tapster.
Moth. You are a gentleman and a gamester,
sir.   45
Arm. I confess both; they are both the var-
nish of a complete man.
Moth. Then I am sure you know how much
the gross sum of deuce-ace amounts to.
Arm. It doth amount to one more than two.
Moth. Which the base vulgar do call three.
Arm. True.   52
Moth. Why, sir, is this such a piece of study?
Now here is three studied ere ye'll thrice wink;
and how easy it is to put 'years' to the word
'three,' and study three years in two words, the
dancing horse will tell you.
Arm. A most fine figure!
Moth. [*aside*] To prove you a cipher.   59
Arm. I will hereupon confess I am in love;
and as it is base for a soldier to love, so am I in
love with a base wench. If drawing my sword
against the humour of affection would deliver
me from the reprobate thought of it, I would
take Desire prisoner and ransom him to any
French courtier for a new-devis'd cursy. I think
scorn to sigh; methinks I should outswear
Cupid. Comfort me, boy. What great men
have been in love?
Moth. Hercules, master.   69
Arm. Most sweet Hercules! More authority,
dear boy, name more; and, sweet my child, let
them be men of good repute and carriage.
Moth. Samson, master. He was a man of
good carriage, great carriage, for he carried the
town gates on his back like a porter; and he
was in love.   76
Arm. O well-knit Samson! strong-jointed
Samson! I do excel thee in my rapier as much
as thou didst me in carrying gates. I am in love
too. Who was Samson's love, my dear Moth?
Moth. A woman, master.   81
Arm. Of what complexion?

Moth. Of all the four, or the three, or the
two, or one of the four.
Arm. Tell me precisely of what complexion.
Moth. Of the sea-water green, sir.   86
Arm. Is that one of the four complexions?
Moth. As I have read, sir, and the best of
them too.   89
Arm. Green indeed is the colour of lovers;
but to have a love of that colour, methinks
Samson had small reason for it. He surely
affected her for her wit.
Moth. It was so, sir, for she had a green wit.
Arm. My love is most immaculate white and
red.   96
Moth. Most maculate thoughts, master, are
mask'd under such colours.
Arm. Define, define, well-educated infant.
Moth. My father's wit and my mother's
tongue assist me!   101
Arm. Sweet invocation of a child! most
pretty and pathetical!
Moth. If she be made of white and red,
     Her faults will ne'er be known;
     For blushing cheeks by faults are bred
     And fears by pale white shown.
     Then if she fear, or be to blame,
     By this you shall not know;
     For still her cheeks possess the same
     Which native she doth owe.   111
A dangerous rhyme, master, against the reason
of white and red.
Arm. Is there not a ballet, boy, of The King
and the Beggar?   115
Moth. The world was very guilty of such a
ballet some three ages since, but I think now
'tis not to be found; or if it were, it would
neither serve for the writing nor the tune.   119
Arm. I will have that subject newly writ o'er,
that I may example my digression by some
mighty precedent. Boy, I do love that country
girl that I took in the park with the rational
hind Costard. She deserves well.   124
Moth. [*aside*] To be whipp'd — and yet a
better love than my master.
Arm. Sing, boy. My spirit grows heavy in
love.
Moth. And that's great marvel, loving a
light wench.
Arm. I say sing.   130
Moth. Forbear till this company be past.

Enter Clown [*Costard*], Constable [*Dull*], and
                    Wench [*Jaquenetta*.]

Dull. Sir, the Duke's pleasure is that you
keep Costard safe, and you must suffer him to

take no delight nor no penance, but 'a must fast three days a week. For this damsel, I must keep her at the park ; she is allow'd for the day-woman. Fare you well.

Arm. I do betray myself with blushing. Maid.

Jaq. Man.

Arm. I will visit thee at the lodge.   140

Jaq. That's hereby.

Arm. I know where it is situate.

Jaq. Lord, how wise you are!

Arm. I will tell thee wonders.

Jaq. With that face?   145

Arm. I love thee.

Jaq. So I heard you say.

Arm. And so farewell.

Jaq. Fair weather after you!

Dull. Come, Jaquenetta, away!   150

Exeunt [Dull and Jaquenetta].

Arm. Villain, thou shalt fast for thy offences ere thou be pardoned.

Cost. Well, sir, I hope when I do it I shall do it on a full stomach.

Arm. Thou shalt be heavily punished.   155

Cost. I am more bound to you than your fellows, for they are but lightly rewarded.

Arm. Take away this villain ; shut him up.

Moth. Come, you transgressing slave, away!

Cost. Let me not be pent up, sir. I will fast, being loose.   161

Moth. No, sir ; that were fast and loose. Thou shalt to prison.

Cost. Well, if ever I do see the merry days of desolation that I have seen, some shall see.   165

Moth. What shall some see?

Cost. Nay, nothing, Master Moth, but what they look upon. It is not for prisoners to be too silent in their words, and therefore I will say nothing. I thank God I have as little patience as another man, and therefore I can be quiet.

Exeunt [Moth and Costard].

Arm. I do affect the very ground (which is base) where her shoe (which is baser) guided by her foot (which is basest) doth tread. I shall be forsworn (which is a great argument of falsehood) if I love. And how can that be true love which is falsely attempted? Love is a familiar ; Love is a devil. There is no evil angel but Love. Yet was Samson so tempted, and he had an excellent strength. Yet was Salomon so seduced, and he had a very good wit. Cupid's buttshaft is too hard for Hercules' club, and therefore too much odds for a Spaniard's rapier. The first and second cause will not serve my turn ; the passado he respects not, the duello he regards not. His disgrace is to be called boy ; but his glory is to subdue men. Adieu, valour! rust, rapier! be still, drum! for your manager is in love ; yea, he loveth. Assist me some extemporal god of rhyme, for I am sure I shall turn sonnet. Devise, wit! write, pen! for I am for whole volumes in folio.   *Exit.*

ACT II. [Scene I. *The park.*]

Enter the *Princess of France* with three attending Ladies, [*Maria, Katherine, Rosaline,*] and three Lords, [one named *Boyet*].

Boyet. Now, madam, summon up your dearest spirits.

Consider who the King your father sends,
To whom he sends, and what's his embassy :
Yourself, held precious in the world's esteem,
To parley with the sole inheritor   5
Of all perfections that a man may owe,
Matchless Navarre ; the plea of no less weight
Than Aquitaine, a dowry for a queen.
Be now as prodigal of all dear grace
As Nature was in making graces dear   10
When she did starve the general world beside
And prodigally gave them all to you.

Prin. Good Lord Boyet, my beauty, though but mean,

Needs not the painted flourish of your praise.
Beauty is bought by judgment of the eye,   15
Not utt'red by base sale of chapmen's tongues.
I am less proud to hear you tell my worth
Than you much willing to be counted wise
In spending your wit in the praise of mine.
But now to task the tasker : — good Boyet,   20
You are not ignorant all-telling fame
Doth noise abroad Navarre hath made a vow,
Till painful study shall outwear three years,
No woman may approach his silent court.
Therefore to 's seemeth it a needful course,   25
Before we enter his forbidden gates,
To know his pleasure ; and in that behalf,
Bold of your worthiness, we single you
As our best-moving fair solicitor.
Tell him the daughter of the King of France   30
On serious business, craving quick dispatch,
Importunes personal conference with his Grace.

200

Haste, signify so much while we attend,
Like humble-visag'd suitors, his high will.
  Boyet. Proud of employment, willingly I go.
                             Exit Boyet.
  Prin. All pride is willing pride, and yours
    is so.   36
Who are the votaries, my loving lords,
That are vow-fellows with this virtuous duke?
  Lord. Lord Longaville is one.
  Prin.   Know you the man?
  Mar. 1 know him, madam. At a marriage
    feast,   40
Between Lord Perigort and the beauteous heir
Of Jaques Falconbridge solemnized,
In Normandy saw I this Longaville.
A man of sovereign parts he is esteem'd;
Well fitted in arts, glorious in arms.   45
Nothing becomes him ill that he would well.
The only soil of his fair virtue's gloss —
If virtue's gloss will stain with any soil —
Is a sharp wit match'd with too blunt a will,
Whose edge hath power to cut, whose will still
    wills   50
It should none spare that come within his power.
  Prin. Some merry mocking lord belike —
    is't so?
  Mar. They say so most that most his hu-
    mours know.
  Prin. Such short-liv'd wits do wither as they
    grow.
Who are the rest?   55
  Kath. The young Dumain, a well-accom-
    plish'd youth,
Of all that virtue love for virtue lov'd;
Most power to do most harm, least knowing ill;
For he hath wit to make an ill shape good,
And shape to win grace though he had no wit.
I saw him at the Duke Alençon's once,   61
And much too little of that good I saw
Is my report to his great worthiness.
  Ros. Another of these students at that time
Was there with him, if I have heard a truth.   65
Berowne they call him; but a merrier man,
Within the limit of becoming mirth,
I never spent an hour's talk withal.
His eye begets occasion for his wit;
For every object that the one doth catch   70
The other turns to a mirth-moving jest,
Which his fair tongue (conceit's expositor)
Delivers in such apt and gracious words
That aged ears play truant at his tales
And younger hearings are quite ravished,   75
So sweet and voluble is his discourse.
  Prin. God bless my ladies! Are they all in
  love,

That every one her own hath garnished
With such bedecking ornaments of praise?

              Enter *Boyet.*

  Lord. Here comes Boyet.
  Prin.   Now, what admittance, lord? 80
  Boyet. Navarre had notice of your fair ap-
    proach,
And he and his competitors in oath
Were all address'd to meet you, gentle lady,
Before I came. Marry, thus much I have learnt,
He rather means to lodge you in the field,   85
Like one that comes here to besiege his court,
Than seek a dispensation for his oath,
To let you enter his unpeopled house.
                   [*The Ladies mask.*]

Enter *Navarre, Longaville, Dumain,* and
    Berowne, [with *Attendants*].

Here comes Navarre.
  Ferd. Fair Princess, welcome to the court of
    Navarre.   90
  Prin. 'Fair' I give you back again, and wel-
come I have not yet. The roof of this court is
too high to be yours, and welcome to the wide
fields too base to be mine.
  Ferd. You shall be welcome, madam, to my
    court.   95
  Prin. I will be welcome, then. Conduct me
    thither.
  Ferd. Hear me, dear lady — I have sworn an
    oath —
  Prin. Our Lady help my lord! He'll be for-
    sworn.
  Ferd. Not for the world, fair madam, by my
    will.
  Prin. Why, will shall break it; will, and
    nothing else.   100
  Ferd. Your ladyship is ignorant what it is.
  Prin. Were my lord so, his ignorance were
    wise,
Where now his knowledge must prove ignorance.
I hear your Grace hath sworn out housekeeping.
'Tis deadly sin to keep that oath, my lord,   103
And sin to break it.
But pardon me, I am too sudden-bold;
To teach a teacher ill beseemeth me.
Vouchsafe to read the purpose of my coming,
And suddenly resolve me in my suit.   110
                 [*Gives a paper.*]
  Ferd. Madam, I will, if suddenly I may.
  Prin. You will the sooner that I were away,
For you'll prove perjur'd if you make me stay.
  Ber. Did not I dance with you in Brabant
    once?

Kath. Did not I dance with you in Brabant
once? 115
Ber. I know you did.
Kath. How needless was it then to ask the
question!
Ber. You must not be so quick.
Kath. 'Tis long of you that spur me with
such questions.
Ber. Your wit's too hot, it speeds too fast,
'twill tire. 120
Kath. Not till it leave the rider in the mire.
Ber. What time o' day?
Kath. The hour that fools should ask.
Ber. Now fair befall your mask!
Kath. Fair fall the face it covers! 125
Ber. And send you many lovers!
Kath. Amen, so you be none.
Ber. Nay, then will I be gone.
Ferd. Madam, your father here doth intimate
The payment of a hundred thousand crowns,
Being but the one half of an entire sum 131
Disbursed by my father in his wars.
But say that he or we — as neither have —
Receiv'd that sum, yet there remains unpaid
A hundred thousand more, in surety of the which
One part of Aquitaine is bound to us, 136
Although not valued to the money's worth.
If then the King your father will restore
But that one half which is unsatisfied,
We will give up our right in Aquitaine 140
And hold fair friendship with his Majesty.
But that, it seems, he little purposeth;
For here he doth demand to have repaid
A hundred thousand crowns; and not demands,
On payment of a hundred thousand crowns,
To have his title live in Aquitaine; 146
Which we much rather had depart withal,
And have the money by our father lent,
Than Aquitaine, so gelded as it is.
Dear Princess, were not his requests so far 150
From reason's yielding, your fair self should make
A yielding 'gainst some reason in my breast,
And go well satisfied to France again.
Prin. You do the King my father too much
wrong,
And wrong the reputation of your name, 155
In so unseeming to confess receipt
Of that which hath so faithfully been paid.
Ferd. I do protest I never heard of it;
And if you prove it, I'll repay it back
Or yield up Aquitaine.
Prin. We arrest your word. 160
Boyet, you can produce acquittances
For such a sum from special officers
Of Charles his father.

Ferd. Satisfy me so.
Boyet. So please your Grace, the packet is
not come
Where that and other specialties are bound. 165
To-morrow you shall have a sight of them.
Ferd. It shall suffice me; at which interview
All liberal reason I will yield unto.
Meantime receive such welcome at my hand
As honour (without breach of honour) may 170
Make tender of to thy true worthiness.
You may not come, fair Princess, in my gates;
But here without you shall be so receiv'd
As you shall deem yourself lodg'd in my heart,
Though so denied fair harbour in my house.
Your own good thoughts excuse me, and farewell.
To-morrow shall we visit you again. 177
Prin. Sweet health and fair desires consort
your Grace.
Ferd. Thy own wish wish I thee in every
place. *Exeunt [King and his Train].*
Ber. Lady, I will commend you to mine own
heart. 180
Ros. Pray you, do my commendations. I
would be glad to see it.
Ber. I would you heard it groan.
Ros. Is the fool sick?
Ber. Sick at the heart. 185
Ros. Alack, let it blood!
Ber. Would that do it good?
Ros. My physic says ay.
Ber. Will you prick't with your eye?
Ros. No point, with my knife. 190
Ber. Now God save thy life!
Ros. And yours from long living!
Ber. I cannot stay thanks-giving. *Exit.*

Enter *Dumain.*

Dum. Sir, I pray you a word. What lady is
that same?
Boyet. The heir of Alençon, Katherine her
name. 195
Dum. A gallant lady. Monsieur, fare you well.
Exit.

[Enter *Longaville.*]

Long. I beseech you a word. What is she in
the white?
Boyet. A woman sometimes, an you saw her
in the light.
Long. Perchance light in the light. I desire
her name.
Boyet. She hath but one for herself. To de-
sire that were a shame. 200
Long. Pray you, sir, whose daughter?
Boyet. Her mother's, I have heard.

202

LOVE'S LABOUR'S LOST

Above: The opening scene, in which the King of Navarre and his nobles bind themselves to live a monastic life for three years

Left: Angela Baddeley as the Princess of France and Michael Aldridge as the King of Navarre

Below left: Diana Churchill as Rosaline

Below right: Michael Redgrave as Berowne, lover of the witty and brilliant Rosaline

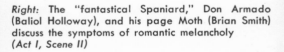

Above: "There's villainy abroad: this letter will tell you more." Constable Dull (Paul Rogers) brings the Clown Costard (George Benson) before the king and presents Don Armado's letter charging Costard with consorting with a woman, a violation of the king's monastic rule *(Act I, Scene I)*

Right: The "fantastical Spaniard," Don Armado (Baliol Holloway), and his page Moth (Brian Smith) discuss the symptoms of romantic melancholy *(Act I, Scene II)*

Left: "Who are the votaries, my loving lords." The Princess of France, on an embassy to Navarre, seeks information on the king's vows, which prevent all women from entering his court *(Act II, Scene I)*

Above: "You may not come, fair princess, in my gates." Holding to his vow respecting women, the king is forced to refuse entry to the princess (*Act II, Scene I*)

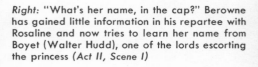

Left: "Did I not dance with you in Brabant once?" Berowne tries to strike up an acquaintance with Rosaline (*Act II, Scene I*)

Right: "What's her name, in the cap?" Berowne has gained little information in his repartee with Rosaline and now tries to learn her name from Boyet (Walter Hudd), one of the lords escorting the princess (*Act II, Scene I*)

Right: "Gardon, O sweet gardon! better than remuneration; a 'levenpence farthing better. Most sweet gardon." Given a shilling by Berowne as a "guerdon" (reward) for carrying a letter, Costard esteems it above the "remuneration" Armado offered him
(Act III, Scene I)

Left: "Thou hast no feeling of it, Moth: I will speak that l'envoy." Costard tells Moth to let him take the final lines of the pun they have been developing for the bafflement of Don Armado
(Act III, Scene I)

The princess and her retinue hunt in the King of Navarre's park (Act IV, Scene I)

Left: A forester points out to the princess an advantageous stand for her to shoot from (*Act IV, Scene I*)

The king gives Berowne his love letter to Rosaline and tells him to read it aloud (*Act IV, Scene III*)

Below: "Advance your standards, and upon them, lords." Berowne rallies his companions, who have determined to renounce their vows of seclusion and are eager to begin wooing their loves (*Act IV, Scene III*)

Above: "Sir, I praise the Lord for you." Sir Nathaniel (Miles Malleson), the curate, is impressed by the spurious learning of Holofernes (Mark Dignam), the schoolmaster *(Act IV, Scene III)*

Left: Armado asks his friends to aid in presenting an entertainment for the Princess of France *(Act V, Scene I)*

Holofernes suggests a masque of the Nine Worthies (ancient heroes), with Nathaniel as Joshua and Moth, the page, as Hercules *(Act V, Scene I)*

Above: In the masque, Armado represents Hector and Moth appears as the infant Hercules (*Act V, Scene II*)

Right: "We have had pastime here and pleasant game. A mess of Russians left us but of late." The princess pretends not to have recognized the king and his friends when they were disguised as Russians (*Act V, Scene II*)

Below: "When in the world I liv'd, I was the world's commander." Sir Nathaniel plays Alexander in the masque presented for the princess (*Act V, Scene II*)

"Look you what I have from the loving king." The Princess of France and her ladies admire the gifts sent to them by the King of Navarre and his companions (*Act V, Scene II*)

"I am sorry, madam; for the news I bring is heavy in my tongue." The masque is interrupted by the news that the King of France is dead (*Act V, Scene II*)

Long. God's blessing on your beard!
Boyet. Good sir, be not offended.
She is an heir of Falconbridge.   205
Long. Nay, my choler is ended.
She is a most sweet lady.
Boyet. Not unlike, sir; that may be.

Exit Longaville.

Enter *Berowne.*

Ber. What's her name in the cap?
Boyet. Rosaline, by good hap.   210
Ber. Is she wedded or no?
Boyet. To her will, sir, or so.
Ber. O, you are welcome, sir! Adieu.
Boyet. Farewell to me, sir, and welcome to
you.

Exit Berowne.

Mar. That last is Berowne, the merry mad-
cap lord.   215
Not a word with him but a jest.
Boyet.   And every jest but a word.
Prin. It was well done of you to take him
at his word.
Boyet. I was as willing to grapple as he was
to board.
Kath. Two hot sheeps, marry!
Boyet.   And wherefore not ships?
No sheep, sweet lamb, unless we feed on your lips.
Kath. You sheep, and I pasture? Shall that
finish the jest?   221
Boyet. So you grant pasture for me.

[Offers to kiss her.]

Kath.   Not so, gentle beast.
My lips are no common, though several they be.
Boyet. Belonging to whom?
Kath.   To my fortunes and me.
Prin. Good wits will be jangling; but,
gentles, agree.   225
This civil war of wits were much better used
On Navarre and his bookmen, for here 'tis
abused.
Boyet. If my observation (which very sel-
dom lies),

By the heart's still rhetoric, disclosed with eyes,
Deceive me not now, Navarre is infected.   230
Prin. With what?
Boyet. With that which we lovers entitle
'affected.'
Prin. Your reason?
Boyet. Why, all his behaviours did make
their repair
To the court of his eye, peeping thorough desire.
His heart, like an agate with your print im-
pressed,   236
Proud with his form, in his eye pride expressed.
His tongue, all impatient to speak and not see,
Did stumble with haste in his eyesight to be;
All senses to that sense did make their repair,
To feel only looking on fairest of fair.   241
Methought all his senses were lock'd in his eye,
As jewels in crystal for some prince to buy,
Who, tend'ring their own worth from where
they were glass'd,
Did point you to buy them along as you pass'd.
His face's own margent did quote such amazes
That all eyes saw his eyes enchanted with gazes.
I'll give you Aquitaine and all that is his
An you give him for my sake but one loving kiss.
Prin. Come, to our pavilion. Boyet is dis-
pos'd.   250
Boyet. But to speak that in words which his
eye hath disclos'd.
I only have made a mouth of his eye
By adding a tongue which I know will not lie.
Mar. Thou art an old love-monger and
speakest skilfully.
Kath. He is Cupid's grandfather and learns
news of him.   255
Ros. Then was Venus like her mother, for
her father is but grim.
Boyet. Do you hear, my mad wenches?
Mar.   No.
Boyet.   What then? do you see?
Mar. Ay, our way to be gone.
Boyet.   You are too hard for me.

Exeunt omnes.

ACT III. [Scene I. *The park.*]

Enter [*Armado* the] Braggart and
his Boy [*Moth*].

Arm. Warble, child; make passionate my
sense of hearing.
Moth. [*sings*] Concolinel.
Arm. Sweet air! Go, tenderness of years,
take this key, give enlargement to the swain,
bring him festinately hither. I must employ
him in a letter to my love.   7
Moth. Master, will you win your love with a
French brawl?
Arm. How meanest thou? Brawling in
French?   10
Moth. No, my complete master; but to jig
off a tune at the tongue's end, canary to it

203

with your feet, humour it with turning up your
eyelids; sigh a note and sing a note, sometime
through the throat, as if you swallowed love
with singing love, sometime through the nose,
as if you snuff'd up love by smelling love, with
your hat penthouse-like o'er the shop of your
eyes, with your arms cross'd on your thin-belly
doublet, like a rabbit on a spit, or your hands in
your pocket, like a man after the old painting;
and keep not too long in one tune, but a snip
and away. These are complements; these are
humours; these betray nice wenches that
would be betrayed without these, and make
them men of note — do you note me? — that
most are affected to these.   26
Arm. How hast thou purchased this experience?
Moth. By my penny of observation.
Arm. But O — but O —
Moth. 'The hobby-horse is forgot.'   30
Arm. Call'st thou my love hobby-horse?
Moth. No, master. The hobby-horse is but
a colt, [*aside*] and your love perhaps a hackney.
But have you forgot your love?
Arm. Almost I had.   35
Moth. Negligent student! learn her by heart.
Arm. By heart and in heart, boy.
Moth. And out of heart, master. All those
three I will prove.
Arm. What wilt thou prove?   40
Moth. A man, if I live; and this, by, in, and
without, upon the instant. By heart you love
her, because your heart cannot come by her;
in heart you love her, because your heart is
in love with her; and out of heart you love
her, being out of heart that you cannot enjoy
her.
Arm. I am all these three.   47
Moth. [*aside*] And three times as much more,
and yet nothing at all.
Arm. Fetch hither the swain; he must carry
me a letter.   51
Moth. A message well sympathiz'd — a horse
to be ambassador for an ass!
Arm. Ha, ha! what sayest thou?   54
Moth. Marry, sir, you must send the ass
upon the horse, for he is very slow-gaited. But
I go.
Arm. The way is but short. Away!
Moth. As swift as lead, sir.
Arm. Thy meaning, pretty ingenious?
Is not lead a metal heavy, dull, and slow?   60
Moth. *Minime*, honest master; or rather,
master, no.
Arm. I say lead is slow.

Moth.   You are too swift, sir, to say so
Is that lead slow which is fir'd from a gun?
Arm. Sweet smoke of rhetoric!
He reputes me a cannon; and the bullet, that's
he.   65
I shoot thee at the swain.
Moth.   Thump then, and I flee. [*Exit.*]
Arm. A most acute juvenal, voluble and free
of grace!
By thy favour, sweet welkin, I must sigh in
thy face.
Most rude melancholy, valour gives thee
place.
My herald is return'd.   70

Enter Page [*Moth*] and Clown [*Costard*].

Moth. A wonder, master! Here's a costard
broken in a shin.
Arm. Some enigma, some riddle. Come,
thy l'envoy; begin.
Cost. No egma, no riddle, no l'envoy; no
salve in the mail, sir. O sir, plantain, a plain
plantain! No l'envoy, no l'envoy, no salve, sir,
but a plantain!   75
Arm. By virtue, thou enforcest laughter;
thy silly thought, my spleen; the heaving of
my lungs provokes me to ridiculous smiling.
O, pardon me, my stars! Doth the inconsiderate take salve for l'envoy, and the word
'l'envoy' for a salve?   80
Moth. Do the wise think them other? Is
not l'envoy a salve?
Arm. No, page; it is an epilogue or discourse to make plain
Some obscure precedence that hath tofore been
sain.
I will example it: 84
          The fox, the ape, and the humblebee
          Were still at odds, being but three.
There's the moral. Now the l'envoy.
Moth. I will add the l'envoy. Say the moral
again.   89
Arm.   The fox, the ape, and the humblebee
          Were still at odds, being but three.
Moth. Until the goose came out of door
          And stay'd the odds by adding four.
Now will I begin your moral, and do you fol-
low with my l'envoy.   95
          The fox, the ape, and the humblebee
          Were still at odds, being but three.
Arm. Until the goose came out of door,
          Staying the odds by adding four.
Moth. A good l'envoy, ending in the goose.
Would you desire more?   101

Cost. The boy hath sold him a bargain — a
goose, that's flat.

Sir, your pennyworth is good an your goose be
fat.

To sell a bargain well is as cunning as fast and
loose.

Let me see: a fat l'envoy — ay, that's a fat
goose. 105

Arm. Come hither, come hither. How did
this argument begin?

Moth. By saying that a costard was broken
in a shin.

Then call'd you for the l'envoy.

Cost. True, and I for a plantain. Thus came
your argument in;

Then the boy's fat l'envoy, the goose that you
bought, 110

And he ended the market.

Arm. But tell me! How was there a costard
broken in a shin?

Moth. I will tell you sensibly.

Cost. Thou hast no feeling of it, Moth. I
will speak that l'envoy: 116

I, Costard, running out, that was safely
within,

Fell over the threshold and broke my shin.

Arm. We will talk no more of this matter.

Cost. Till there be more matter in the
shin. 120

Arm. Sirrah Costard, I will enfranchise thee.

Cost. O, marry me to one Frances! I smell
some l'envoy, some goose, in this.

Arm. By my sweet soul, I mean setting thee
at liberty, enfreedoming thy person. Thou wert
immured, restrained, captivated, bound. 126

Cost. True, true! and now you will be my
purgation and let me loose.

Arm. I give thee thy liberty, set thee from
durance, and, in lieu thereof, impose on thee
nothing but this: bear this significant [*gives a
letter*] to the country maid Jaquenetta. There
is remuneration [*gives money*]; for the best
ward of mine honour is rewarding my depend-
ents. Moth, follow.

Moth. Like the sequel, I. Signior Costard,
adieu. 135

Exit [*Armado, followed by Moth*].

Cost. My sweet ounce of man's flesh! my
incony Jew! —

Now will I look to his remuneration. Remuneration — O, that's the Latin word for three
farthings. Three farthings — remuneration.
'What's the price of this inkle?' 'One penny.'
'No, I'll give you a remuneration.' Why, it
carries it! Remuneration. Why, it is a fairer
name than French crown. I will never buy and
sell out of this word.

Enter Berowne.

Ber. O my good knave Costard, exceedingly
well met! 145

Cost. Pray you, sir, how much carnation
ribbon may a man buy for a remuneration?

Ber. O, what is a remuneration?

Cost. Marry, sir, halfpenny farthing.

Ber. O, why then, three-farthing worth of
silk. 150

Cost. I thank your worship. God be wi' you!

Ber. O, stay, slave; I must employ thee.
As thou wilt win my favour, good my knave,
Do one thing for me that I shall entreat.

Cost. When would you have it done, sir? 155

Ber. O, this afternoon.

Cost. Well, I will do it, sir. Fare you well.

Ber. O, thou knowest not what it is.

Cost. I shall know, sir, when I have done it.

Ber. Why, villain, thou must know first. 160

Cost. I will come to your worship to-morrow
morning.

Ber. It must be done this afternoon. Hark,
slave, it is but this:
The Princess comes to hunt here in the park,
And in her train there is a gentle lady. 166
When tongues speak sweetly, then they name
her name,
And Rosaline they call her. Ask for her,
And to her white hand see thou do commend
This seal'd-up counsel. There's thy guerdon.
Go. [*Gives him a shilling.*]

Cost. Gardon — O sweet gardon! better
than remuneration! a 'levenpence-farthing better. Most sweet gardon! I will do it, sir, in
print. Gardon — remuneration. *Exit.*

Ber. O — and I, forsooth, in love? I that
have been love's whip, 176
A very beadle to a humorous sigh,
A critic, nay, a night-watch constable,
A domineering pedant o'er the boy,
Than whom no mortal so magnificent! 180
This wimpled, whining, purblind, wayward
boy;
This senior junior, giant dwarf, Dan Cupid,
Regent of love-rhymes, lord of folded arms,
Th' anointed sovereign of sighs and groans,
Liege of all loiterers and malecontents, 185
Dread prince of plackets, king of codpieces,
Sole emperator and great general
Of trotting paritors (O my little heart!) —
And I to be a corporal of his field
And wear his colours like a tumbler's hoop!

What, I? I love? I sue? I seek a wife?   191
A woman, that is like a German clock,
Still a-repairing, ever out of frame,
And never going aright, being a watch,
But being watch'd that it may still go right!
Nay, to be perjur'd, which is worst of all;   196
And, among three, to love the worst of all,
A whitely wanton, with a velvet brow,
With two pitch-balls stuck in her face for eyes;
Ay, and, by heaven, one that will do the deed

Though Argus were her eunuch and her guard!
And I to sigh for her! to watch for her!   202
To pray for her! Go to! it is a plague
That Cupid will impose for my neglect
Of his almighty dreadful little might.   205
Well, I will love, write, sigh, pray, sue, and
groan.
Some men must love my lady, and some Joan.
[*Exit.*]

ACT IV. [Scene I. *The park.*]

Enter the *Princess*, a *Forester*, her *Ladies*,
and her *Lords*.

Prin. Was that the King that spurr'd his
horse so hard
Against the steep uprising of the hill?
Boyet. I know not, but I think it was not he.
Prin. Whoe'er 'a was, 'a show'd a mounting
mind.
Well, lords, to-day we shall have our dispatch;
On Saturday we will return to France.   6
Then, forester my friend, where is the bush
That we must stand and play the murtherer in?
For. Hereby upon the edge of yonder cop-
pice,   9
A stand where you may make the fairest shoot.
Prin. I thank my beauty, I am fair that
shoot,
And thereupon thou speak'st the fairest shoot.
For. Pardon me, madam, for I meant not so.
Prin. What, what? first praise me, and
again say no?   14
O short-liv'd pride! Not fair? Alack for woe!
For. Yes, madam, fair.
Prin.   Nay, never paint me now!
Where fair is not, praise cannot mend the brow.
Here (good my glass) take this for telling true.
[*Gives money.*]
Fair payment for foul words is more than due.
For. Nothing but fair is that which you
inherit.   20
Prin. See, see, my beauty will be sav'd by
merit!
O heresy in fair, fit for these days!
A giving hand, though foul, shall have fair
praise.
But come, the bow! Now mercy goes to kill,
And shooting well is then accounted ill.   25
Thus will I save my credit in the shoot.
Not wounding, pity would not let me do't;
If wounding, then it was to show my skill,

That more for praise than purpose meant to
kill.
And, out of question, so it is sometimes: 30
Glory grows guilty of detested crimes
When for fame's sake, for praise, an outward
part,
We bend to that the working of the heart;
As I for praise alone now seek to spill
The poor deer's blood that my heart means no
ill.   35
Boyet. Do not curst wives hold that self
sovereignty
Only for praise sake when they strive to be
Lords o'er their lords?
Prin. Only for praise; and praise we may
afford
To any lady that subdues a lord.   40

Enter [*Costard, the*] *Clown.*

Boyet. Here comes a member of the common-
wealth.
Cost. God dig-you-den all! Pray you which
is the head lady?
Prin. Thou shalt know her, fellow, by the
rest that have no heads.   45
Cost. Which is the greatest lady, the highest?
Prin. The thickest and the tallest.
Cost. The thickest and the tallest. It is so;
truth is truth.
An your waist, mistress, were as slender as my
wit,
One o' these maids' girdles for your waist should
be fit.   50
Are not you the chief woman? You are the
thickest here.
Prin. What's your will, sir? What's your
will?
Cost. I have a letter from Monsieur Berowne
to one Lady Rosaline.
Prin. O, thy letter, thy letter! He's a good
friend of mine.

Stand aside, good bearer. Boyet, you can
    carve;   55
Break up this capon.
    Boyet.   I am bound to serve.
This letter is mistook; it importeth none here.
It is writ to Jaquenetta.
    Prin.   We will read it, I swear.
Break the neck of the wax, and every one give
    ear.   59
    Boyet reads. 'By heaven, that thou art fair
is most infallible; true that thou art beauteous;
truth itself that thou art lovely. More fairer than
fair, beautiful than beauteous, truer than truth
itself, have commiseration on thy heroical vassal!
The magnanimous and most illustrate king
Cophetua set eye upon the pernicious and indubitate beggar Zenelophon; and he it was that
might rightly say, "Veni, vidi, vici"; which to annothanize in the vulgar (O base and obscure vulgar!), videlicet, He came, saw, and overcame. He
came, one; saw, two; overcame, three. Who
came? The king. Why did he come? To see.
Why did he see? To overcome. To whom came
he? To the beggar. What saw he? The beggar.
Who overcame he? The beggar. The conclusion
is victory. On whose side? The king's. The captive is enrich'd. On whose side? The beggar's.
The catastrophe is a nuptial. On whose side? The
king's. No, on both in one, or one in both. I am
the king, for so stands the comparison; thou the
beggar, for so witnesseth thy lowliness. Shall I
command thy love? I may. Shall I enforce thy
love? I could. Shall I entreat thy love? I will.
What shalt thou exchange for rags? Robes. For
tittles? Titles. For thyself? Me. Thus, expecting thy reply, I profane my lips on thy foot, my
eyes on thy picture, and my heart on thy every
part.
    'Thine, in the dearest design of industry,
                'DON ADRIANO DE ARMADO.'

'Thus dost thou hear the Nemean lion roar   90
'Gainst thee, thou lamb, that standest as his
    prey.
Submissive fall his princely feet before,
    And he from forage will incline to play.
But if thou strive, poor soul, what art thou then?
Food for his rage, repasture for his den.'   95

    Prin. What plume of feathers is he that in-
    dited this letter?
What vane? what weathercock? Did you ever
    hear better?
    Boyet. I am much deceived but I remember
    the style.
    Prin. Else your memory is bad, going o'er it
    erewhile.
    Boyet. This Armado is a Spaniard that keeps
    here in court;   100

A phantasime, a Monarcho, and one that makes
    sport
To the Prince and his bookmates.
    Prin.   Thou fellow, a word.
Who gave thee this letter?
    Cost.   I told you; my lord.
    Prin. To whom shouldst thou give it?
    Cost.   From my lord to my lady.
    Prin. From which lord to which lady?   105
    Cost. From my Lord Berowne, a good master
    of mine,
To a lady of France that he call'd Rosaline.
    Prin. Thou hast mistaken his letter. Come,
    lords, away.
[*To Rosaline*] Here, sweet, put up this; 'twill
    be thine another day.   109
    Exeunt [Princess and Lords except Boyet].
    Boyet. Who is the suitor? Who is the suitor?
    Ros.   Shall I teach you to know?
    Boyet. Ay, my continent of beauty.
    Ros.   Why, she that bears the bow.
Finely put off!
    Boyet. My lady goes to kill horns; but if
    thou marry,
Hang me by the neck if horns that year mis-
    carry.
Finely put on!   115
    Ros. Well then, I am the shooter.
    Boyet.   And who is your deer?
    Ros. If we choose by the horns, yourself.
    Come not near.
Finely put on indeed!
    Mar. You still wrangle with her, Boyet, and
    she strikes at the brow.
    Boyet. But she herself is hit lower. Have I
    hit her now?   120
    Ros. Shall I come upon thee with an old
saying, that was a man when King Pippen of
France was a little boy, as touching the hit it?
    Boyet. So I may answer thee with one as old,
that was a woman when Queen Guinover of
Britain was a little wench, as touching the hit it.
    Ros.
    'Thou canst not hit it, hit it, hit it,   127
    Thou canst not hit it, my good man.'
    Boyet.
    'An I cannot, cannot, cannot,
    An I cannot, another can.'   130
                Exeunt [Rosaline and Katherine].
    Cost. By my troth, most pleasant. How both
    did fit it!
    Mar. A mark marvellous well shot, for they
    both did hit it.
    Boyet. A mark! O, mark but that mark!
    'A mark,' says my lady!

Let the mark have a prick in't, to mete at, if
  it may be.
Mar. Wide o' the bow-hand! I' faith, your
  hand is out. 135
Cost. Indeed 'a must shoot nearer, or he'll
  ne'er hit the clout.
Boyet. An if my hand be out, then belike
  your hand is in.
Cost. Then will she get the upshoot by cleav-
  ing the pin.
Mar. Come, come, you talk greasily; your
  lips grow foul.
Cost. She's too hard for you at pricks, sir.
  Challenge her to bowl. 140
Boyet. I fear too much rubbing. Good night,
  my good owl. [*Exeunt Boyet and Maria.*]
Cost. By my soul, a swain! a most simple
  clown!
Lord, Lord, how the ladies and I have put him
  down!
O' my troth, most sweet jests, most incony
  vulgar wit,
When it comes so smoothly off, so obscenely, as
  it were, so fit! 145
Armado o' th' t'one side — O, a most dainty
  man!
To see him walk before a lady and to bear her
  fan!
To see him kiss his hand! and how most
  sweetly 'a will swear!
And his page o' t'other side, that handful of
  wit!
Ah, heavens, it is a most pathetical nit! 150
      Shout within.
Sowla, sowla!   *Exit.*

[Scene II. *The park.*]

Enter *Dull, Holofernes the Pedant,* and
    Nathaniel.

Nath. Very reverent sport truly, and done in
the testimony of a good conscience.
Hol. The deer was, as you know, *sanguis,* in
blood; ripe as the pomwater, who now hangeth
like a jewel in the ear of *coelo,* the sky, the
welkin, the heaven, and anon falleth like a crab
on the face of *terra,* the soil, the land, the earth.
Nath. Truly, Master Holofernes, the epithets
are sweetly varied, like a scholar at the least;
but, sir, I assure ye it was a buck of the first
head. 10
Hol. Sir Nathaniel, haud credo.
Dull. 'Twas not a haud credo; 'twas a
pricket.

Hol. Most barbarous intimation! yet a kind
of insinuation, as it were, *in via,* in way, of
explication; *facere,* as it were, replication, or
rather, *ostentare,* to show, as it were, his inclination, after his undressed, unpolished, un-
educated, unpruned, untrained, or rather, unlettered, or ratherest, unconfirmed fashion, to
insert again my 'haud credo' for a deer. 20
Dull. I said the deer was not a haud credo,
'twas a pricket.
Hol. Twice-sod simplicity, bis coctus!
O thou monster ignorance, how deformed dost
  thou look!
Nath. Sir, he hath never fed of the dainties
  that are bred in a book. 25
He hath not eat paper, as it were; he hath not
drunk ink. His intellect is not replenished; he
is only an animal, only sensible in the duller
parts;
And such barren plants are set before us that
  we thankful should be —
Which we of taste and feeling are — for those
  parts that do fructify in us more than he.
For as it would ill become me to be vain, indis-
  creet, or a fool, 31
So, were there a patch set on learning, to see
  him in a school.
But, omne bene, say I, being of an old father's
  mind —
Many can brook the weather that love not
  the wind.
Dull. You two are bookmen. Can you tell
  me by your wit 35
What was a month old at Cain's birth that's
  not five weeks old as yet?
Hol. Dictynna, goodman Dull; Dictynna,
  goodman Dull.
Dull. What is Dictynna?
Nath. A title to Phœbe, to Luna, to the
  moon.
Hol. The moon was a month old when Adam
  was no more, 40
And raught not to five weeks when he came to
  five-score.
Th' allusion holds in the exchange.
Dull. 'Tis true indeed; the collusion holds
in the exchange.
Hol. God comfort thy capacity! I say th'
allusion holds in the exchange. 46
Dull. And I say the polusion holds in the
exchange, for the moon is never but a month
old; and I say beside that, 'twas a pricket
that the Princess kill'd. 50
Hol. Sir Nathaniel, will you hear an extemporal epitaph on the death of the deer?

And, to humour the ignorant, call I the deer the
Princess kill'd a pricket.   54
Nath. Perge, good Master Holofernes, perge,
so it shall please you to abrogate squirility.
Hol. I will something affect the letter, for it
argues facility.

The preyful princess pierc'd and prick'd a pretty
    pleasing pricket;
Some say a sore; but not a sore till now made
    sore with shooting.
The dogs did yell: put el to sore, then sorel jumps
    from thicket,   60
Or pricket sore, or else sorel. The people fall
    a-hooting.
If sore be sore, then L to sore makes fifty sores one
    sorel.
Of one sore I an hundred make by adding but one
    more L.

Nath. A rare talent!
Dull. [*aside*] If a talent be a claw, look how
he claws him with a talent.   66
Hol. This is a gift that I have, simple, simple;
a foolish extravagant spirit, full of forms, figures, shapes, objects, ideas, apprehensions, motions, revolutions. These are begot in the
ventricle of memory, nourish'd in the womb of
pia mater, and delivered upon the mellowing
of occasion. But the gift is good in those in
whom it is acute, and I am thankful for it.   74
Nath. Sir, I praise the Lord for you, and so
may my parishioners, for their sons are well
tutor'd by you, and their daughters profit very
greatly under you. You are a good member of
the commonwealth.   79
Hol. *Mehercle*, if their sons be ingenuous,
they shall want no instruction; if their daughters be capable, I will put it to them. But vir
sapit qui pauca loquitur. A soul feminine
saluteth us.

Enter *Jaquenetta* and [*Costard*] the Clown.

Jaq. God give you good morrow, Master
Person.   84
Hol. Master Person, quasi pers-one. And if
one should be pierc'd, which is the one?
Cost. Marry, Master Schoolmaster, he that
is likest to a hogshead.
Hol. Of piercing a hogshead! A good lustre
of conceit in a turf of earth; fire enough for a
flint, pearl enough for a swine. 'Tis pretty;
it is well.   91
Jaq. Good Master Person, be so good as
read me this letter. It was given me by Costard and sent me from Don Armado. I be-
seech you read it.   94

Hol. Fauste, precor, gelida quando pecus
omne sub umbra Ruminat, and so forth. Ah,
good old Mantuan! I may speak of thee as the
traveller doth of Venice:
    Venetia, Venetia,
      Chi non ti vede, non ti pretia.   100
Old Mantuan! old Mantuan! Who under-
standeth thee not, loves thee not. Ut, re, sol,
la, mi, fa. Under pardon, sir, what are the
contents? or rather, as Horace says in his —
What, my soul, verses?   105
Nath. Ay, sir, and very learned.
Hol. Let me hear a staff, a stanze, a verse.
Lege, domine.
Nath. [*reads*]

'If love make me forsworn, how shall I swear to
    love?
Ah, never faith could hold, if not to beauty
    vowed!   110
Though to myself forsworn, to thee I'll faithful
    prove;
Those thoughts to me were oaks, to thee like
    osiers bowed.
Study his bias leaves and makes his book thine
    eyes,
Where all those pleasures live that art would
    comprehend.
If knowledge be the mark, to know thee shall
    suffice;   115
Well learned is that tongue that well can thee
    commend,
All ignorant that soul that sees thee without
    wonder;
Which is to me some praise that I thy parts
    admire.
Thy eye Jove's lightning bears, thy voice his dread-
    ful thunder,
Which, not to anger bent, is music and sweet
    fire.   120
Celestial as thou art, O, pardon love this wrong,
That singes heaven's praise with such an earthly
    tongue.'

Hol. You find not the apostrophas, and so
miss the accent. Let me supervise the canzonet. Here are only numbers ratified; but
for the elegancy, facility, and golden cadence
of poesy, caret. Ovidius Naso was the man.
And why indeed 'Naso,' but for smelling out
the odoriferous flowers of fancy, the jerks of
invention? Imitari is nothing. So doth the
hound his master, the ape his keeper, the tired
horse his rider. But, damosella virgin, was this
directed to you?   132
Jaq. Ay, sir, from one Monsieur Berowne,
one of the strange queen's lords.
Hol. I will overglance the superscript. 'To
the snow-white hand of the most beauteous

Lady Rosaline.' I will look again on the intellect of the letter, for the nomination of the party writing to the person written unto. 'Your ladyship's in all desired employment, Berowne.' Sir Nathaniel, this Berowne is one of the votaries with the King; and here he hath framed a letter to a sequent of the stranger queen's, which accidentally, or by the way of progression, hath miscarried. Trip and go, my sweet; deliver this paper into the royal hand of the King; it may concern much. Stay not thy compliment; I forgive thy duty. Adieu.

Jaq. Good Costard, go with me. — Sir, God save your life!   150

Cost. Have with thee, my girl.

Exeunt [Costard and Jaquenetta].

Nath. Sir, you have done this in the fear of God, very religiously; and, as a certain father saith —   154

Hol. Sir, tell not me of the father; I do fear colourable colours. But to return to the verses: did they please you, Sir Nathaniel?

Nath. Marvellous well for the pen.   158

Hol. I do dine to-day at the father's of a certain pupil of mine, where, if (before repast) it shall please you to gratify the table with a grace, I will, on my privilege I have with the parents of the foresaid child or pupil, undertake your *ben venuto,* where I will prove those verses to be very unlearned, neither savouring of poetry, wit, nor invention. I beseech your society.   166

Nath. And thank you too; for society (saith the text) is the happiness of life.

Hol. And certes the text most infallibly concludes it. [*To Dull*] Sir, I do invite you too; you shall not say me nay. *Pauca verba.* Away! the gentles are at their game, and we will to our recreation.   *Exeunt.*

[Scene III. *The park.*]

Enter Berowne, with a paper in his hand, alone.

Ber. The King he is hunting the deer; I am coursing myself. They have pitch'd a toil; I am toiling in a pitch — pitch that defiles. Defile! a foul word. Well, 'set thee down, sorrow!' for so they say the fool said, and so say I, and I the fool. Well proved, wit. By the Lord, this love is as mad as Ajax: it kills sheep; it kills me — I a sheep. Well proved again o' my side. I will not love; if I do, hang me. I' faith. I will not. O, but her eye! By

this light, but for her eye, I would not love her; yes, for her two eyes. Well, I do nothing in the world but lie, and lie in my throat. By heaven, I do love, and it hath taught me to rhyme and to be mallicholy; and here is part of my rhyme, and here my mallicholy. Well, she hath one o' my sonnets already. The clown bore it, the fool sent it, and the lady hath it. Sweet clown, sweeter fool, sweetest lady! By the world, I would not care a pin if the other three were in. Here comes one with a paper. God give him grace to groan!

He stands aside. The King ent'reth [with a paper].

King. Ay me!   22

Ber. [*aside*] Shot, by heaven! Proceed, sweet Cupid. Thou hast thump'd him with thy birdbolt under the left pap. In faith, secrets!   25

King. [*reads*]

'So sweet a kiss the golden sun gives not
    To those fresh morning drops upon the rose
As thy eyebeams when their fresh rays have smot
    The night of dew that on my cheeks down flows;
Nor shines the silver moon one half so bright   30
    Through the transparent bosom of the deep
As doth thy face through tears of mine give light.
Thou shin'st in every tear that I do weep;
No drop but as a coach doth carry thee.
So ridest thou triumphing in my woe.   35
Do but behold the tears that swell in me,
    And they thy glory through my grief will show.
But do not love thyself; then thou wilt keep
My tears for glasses, and still make me weep.
O queen of queens, how far dost thou excel   40
No thought can think nor tongue of mortal tell.'

How shall she know my griefs? I'll drop the paper.
Sweet leaves, shade folly. Who is he comes here?

Enter Longaville [with a paper].
The King steps aside.

What, Longaville! and reading! Listen, ear.

Ber. [*aside*] Now, in thy likeness, one more fool appear!   45

Long. Ay me! I am forsworn.

Ber. [*aside*] Why, he comes in like a perjure, wearing papers.

King. [*aside*] In love, I hope — sweet fellowship in shame.

Ber. [*aside*] One drunkard loves another of the name.   50

Long. Am I the first that have been perjur'd so?

Ber. [*aside*] I could put thee in comfort —
not by two that I know!
Thou makest the triumviry, the corner-cap of
society,
The shape of Love's Tyburn, that hangs up
simplicity.
Long. I fear these stubborn lines lack power
to move.   55
O sweet Maria, empress of my love,
These numbers will I tear, and write in prose!
Ber. [*aside*] O, rhymes are guards on wanton
Cupid's hose.
Disfigure not his slop.
Long.   This same shall go.

He reads the Sonnet.

'Did not the heavenly rhetoric of thine eye,   60
 'Gainst whom the world cannot hold argument,
Persuade my heart to this false perjury?
Vows for thee broke deserve not punishment.
A woman I forswore; but I will prove,
 Thou being a goddess, I forswore not thee.   65
My vow was earthly, thou a heavenly love.
 Thy grace being gain'd cures all disgrace in me.
Vows are but breath, and breath a vapour is.
 Then thou, fair sun, which on my earth dost
shine,
Exhal'st this vapour-vow; in thee it is.   70
 If broken then, it is no fault of mine;
If by me broke, what fool is not so wise
To lose an oath to win a paradise?'

Ber. [*aside*] This is the liver vein, which
makes flesh a deity,
A green goose a goddess — pure, pure idolatry.
God amend us, God amend! we are much out
o' th' way.   76

Enter *Dumain* [with a paper].

Long. By whom shall I send this? — Com-
pany? Stay.   [*Steps aside.*]
Ber. [*aside*] All hid, all hid — an old infant
play.
Like a demigod here sit I in the sky
And wretched fools' secrets heedfully o'er-eye.
More sacks to the mill. O heavens, I have my
wish!   81
Dumain transform'd! Four woodcocks in a
dish!
Dum. O most divine Kate!
Ber. [*aside*] O most profane coxcomb!
Dum. By heaven, the wonder in a mortal eye!
Ber. [*aside*] By earth, she is not, Corporal.
There you lie.   86
Dum. Her amber hairs for foul hath amber
quoted.

Ber. [*aside*] An amber-colour'd raven was
well noted.
Dum. As upright as the cedar.
Ber. [*aside*]   Stoop, I say;
Her shoulder is with child.
Dum.   As fair as day.   90
Ber. [*aside*] Ay, as some days; but then no
sun must shine.
Dum. O that I had my wish!
Long. [*aside*]   And I had mine!
King. [*aside*] And I mine too, good Lord!
Ber. [*aside*] Amen, so I had mine! Is not
that a good word?
Dum. I would forget her, but a fever she   95
Reigns in my blood and will rememb'red be.
Ber. [*aside*] A fever in your blood? Why,
then incision
Would let her out in saucers. Sweet misprision!
Dum. Once more I'll read the ode that I have
writ.
Ber. [*aside*] Once more I'll mark how love
can vary wit.   100

Dumain reads his Sonnet.

'On a day — alack the day! —
Love, whose month is ever May,
Spied a blossom passing fair
Playing in the wanton air.
Through the velvet leaves the wind,   105
All unseen, can passage find;
That the lover, sick to death,
Wish'd himself the heaven's breath.
"Air," quoth he, "thy cheeks may blow.
Air, would I might triumph so!   110
But, alack, my hand is sworn
Ne'er to pluck thee from thy thorn:
Vow, alack, for youth unmeet,
Youth so apt to pluck a sweet!
Do not call it sin in me   115
That I am forsworn for thee;
Thou for whom Jove would swear
Juno but an Æthiop were,
And deny himself for Jove,
Turning mortal for thy love."   120

This will I send, and something else more plain
That shall express my true love's fasting pain.
O, would the King, Berowne, and Longaville
Were lovers too! Ill, to example ill,
Would from my forehead wipe a perjur'd note;
For none offend where all alike do dote.   126
Long. [*advances*] Dumain, thy love is far
from charity,
That in love's grief desir'st society.
You may look pale, but I should blush, I know,
To be o'erheard and taken napping so.   130
King. [*advances*] Come, sir, you blush! As
his your case is such.

You chide at him, offending twice as much.
You do not love Maria! Longavile
Did never sonnet for her sake compile,
Nor never lay his wreathed arms athwart 135
His loving bosom to keep down his heart.
I have been closely shrouded in this bush,
And mark'd you both and for you both did blush.
I heard your guilty rhymes, observ'd your fashion,
Saw sighs reek from you, noted well your passion. 140
'Ay me!' says one. 'O Jove!' the other cries.
One, her hairs were gold; crystal the other's eyes.
You would for paradise break faith and troth,
[*To Longaville.*]
And Jove for your love would infringe an oath.
[*To Dumain.*]
What will Berowne say when that he shall hear
Faith infringed, which such zeal did swear? 146
How will he scorn! How will he spend his wit!
How will he triumph, leap, and laugh at it!
For all the wealth that ever I did see,
I would not have him know so much by me.
  Ber. [*advances*] Now step I forth to whip hypocrisy. 151
Ah, good my liege, I pray thee pardon me!
Good heart, what grace hast thou thus to reprove
These worms for loving, that art most in love?
Your eyes do make no coaches; in your tears
There is no certain princess that appears. 156
You'll not be perjur'd; 'tis a hateful thing.
Tush, none but minstrels like of sonneting!
But are you not asham'd? Nay, are you not,
All three of you, to be thus much o'ershot? 160
You found his mote, the King your mote did see;
But I a beam do find in each of three.
O, what a scene of fool'ry have I seen —
Of sighs, of groans, of sorrow, and of teen!
O me, with what strict patience have I sat 165
To see a king transformed to a gnat!
To see great Hercules whipping a gig,
And profound Salomon to tune a jig,
And Nestor play at push-pin with the boys,
And critic Timon laugh at idle toys! 170
Where lies thy grief, O, tell me, good Dumain?
And, gentle Longaville, where lies thy pain?
And where my liege's? All about the breast.
A caudle ho!
  King.   Too bitter is thy jest.
Are we betray'd thus to thy over-view? 175

  Ber. Not you to me, but I betray'd by you:
I that am honest; I that hold it sin
To break the vow I am engaged in.
I am betray'd by keeping company
With men like you, men of inconstancy. 180
When shall you see me write a thing in rhyme?
Or groan for love? or spend a minute's time
In pruning me? When shall you hear that I
Will praise a hand, a foot, a face, an eye,
A gait, a state, a brow, a breast, a waist, 185
A leg, a limb?
  King.   Soft! Whither away so fast?
A true man, or a thief, that gallops so?
  Ber. I post from love. Good lover, let me go.

Enter Jaquenetta *and [*Costard*] the Clown.*

  Jaq. God bless the King!
  King.   What present hast thou there?
  Cost. Some certain treason.
  King.   What makes treason here?
  Cost. Nay, it makes nothing, sir.
  King.   If it mar nothing neither,
The treason and you go in peace away together.
  Jaq. I beseech your Grace let this letter be read.
Our person misdoubts it; 'twas treason, he said.
  King. Berowne, read it over. 195
      He reads the letter.
Where hadst thou it?
  Jaq. Of Costard.
  King. Where hadst thou it?
  Cost. Of Dun Adramadio, Dun Adramadio.
      [*Berowne tears the letter.*]
  King. How now? What is in you? Why dost thou tear it? 200
  Ber. A toy, my liege, a toy! Your Grace needs not fear it.
  Long. It did move him to passion, and therefore let's hear it.
  Dum. It is Berowne's writing, and here is his name.   [*Picks up the pieces.*]
  Ber. [*to Costard*] Ah, you whoreson loggerhead! you were born to do me shame.
Guilty, my lord, guilty! I confess, I confess.
  King. What? 206
  Ber. That you three fools lack'd me fool to make up the mess.
He, he, and you — and you, my liege — and I
Are pickpurses in love, and we deserve to die.
O, dismiss this audience, and I shall tell you more. 210
  Dum. Now the number is even.
  Ber.   True, true! We are four.
Will these turtles be gone?

King.   Hence, sirs! away!
Cost. Walk aside the true folk, and let the
traitors stay.
           [Exeunt Costard and Jaquenetta.]
Ber. Sweet lords, sweet lovers, O, let us
embrace!
As true we are as flesh and blood can be. 215
The sea will ebb and flow, heaven show his
face;
Young blood doth not obey an old decree.
We cannot cross the cause why we were born;
Therefore of all hands must we be forsworn.
  King. What, did these rent lines show some
love of thine?   220
  Ber. 'Did they?' quoth you? Who sees the
heavenly Rosaline
That, like a rude and savage man of Inde
At the first op'ning of the gorgeous East,
Bows not his vassal head and, strucken blind,
Kisses the base ground with obedient breast?
What peremptory eagle-sighted eye   226
Dares look upon the heaven of her brow
That is not blinded by her majesty?
  King. What zeal, what fury hath inspir'd
thee now?
My love (her mistress) is a gracious moon; 230
She (an attending star) scarce seen a light.
  Ber. My eyes are then no eyes, nor I
Berowne.
O, but for my love, day would turn to night!
Of all complexions the cull'd sovereignty
Do meet, as at a fair, in her fair cheek,   235
Where several worthies make one dignity,
Where nothing wants that want itself doth
seek.
Lend me the flourish of all gentle tongues —
Fie! painted rhetoric — O, she needs it not!
To things of sale a seller's praise belongs: 240
She passes praise; then praise too short doth
blot.
A wither'd hermit, fivescore winters worn,
Might shake off fifty, looking in her eye.
Beauty doth varnish age, as if new-born,
And gives the crutch the cradle's infancy. 245
O, 'tis the sun that maketh all things shine.
  King. By heaven, thy love is black as ebony!
  Ber. Is ebony like her? O wood divine!
A wife of such wood were felicity.
O, who can give an oath? Where is a book? 250
That I may swear beauty doth beauty lack
If that she learn not of her eye to look.
No face is fair that is not full so black.
  King. O paradox! Black is the badge of hell,
The hue of dungeons, and the school of night;
And beauty's crest becomes the heavens well.

  Ber. Devils soonest tempt, resembling spirits
of light.
O, if in black my lady's brows be deckt,
It mourns that painting and usurping hair
Should ravish doters with a false aspect;   260
And therefore is she born to make black fair.
Her favour turns the fashion of the days,
For native blood is counted painting now;
And therefore red that would avoid dispraise
Paints itself black to imitate her brow.   265
  Dum. To look like her are chimney-sweepers
black.
  Long. And since her time are colliers counted
bright.
  King. And Æthiops of their sweet complexion
crack.
  Dum. Dark needs no candles now, for dark
is light.   269
  Ber. Your mistresses dare never come in rain
For fear their colours should be wash'd away.
  King. 'Twere good yours did; for, sir, to tell
you plain,
I'll find a fairer face not wash'd to-day.
  Ber. I'll prove her fair, or talk till doomsday
here.
  King. No devil will fright thee then so much
as she.   275
  Dum. I never knew man hold vile stuff so
dear.
  Long. Look, here's thy love; my foot and
her face see.   *[Shows his shoe.]*
  Ber. O, if the streets were paved with thine
eyes,
Her feet were much too dainty for such tread!
  Dum. O vile! Then, as she goes, what up-
ward lies   280
The street should see as she walk'd overhead.
  King. But what of this? Are we not all in
love?
  Ber. Nothing so sure, and thereby all for-
sworn.
  King. Then leave this chat; and, good
Berowne, now prove
Our loving lawful and our faith not torn. 285
  Dum. Ay marry, there, some flattery for this
evil!
  Long. O, some authority how to proceed!
Some tricks, some quillets, how to cheat the
devil!
  Dum. Some salve for perjury.
  Ber.   O, 'tis more than need!
Have at you, then, affection's men-at-arms. 290
Consider what you first did swear unto:
To fast, to study, and to see no woman —
Flat treason 'gainst the kingly state of youth.

Say, can you fast? Your stomachs are too
  young,
And abstinence engenders maladies.   295
And where that you have vow'd to study, lords,
In that each of you have forsworn his book;
Can you still dream, and pore, and thereon look?
For when would you, my lord, or you, or you,
Have found the ground of study's excellence 300
Without the beauty of a woman's face?
From women's eyes this doctrine I derive:
They are the ground, the books, the academes,
From whence doth spring the true Promethean fire.
Why, universal plodding prisons up   305
The nimble spirits in the arteries,
As motion and long-during action tires
The sinewy vigour of the traveller.
Now for not looking on a woman's face,
You have in that forsworn the use of eyes,   310
And study too, the causer of your vow;
For where is any author in the world
Teaches such beauty as a woman's eye?
Learning is but an adjunct to ourself,
And where we are our learning likewise is.   315
Then when ourselves we see in ladies' eyes,
Do we not likewise see our learning there?
O, we have made a vow to study, lords,
And in that vow we have forsworn our books;
For when would you, my liege, or you, or you,
In leaden contemplation, have found out   321
Such fiery numbers as the prompting eyes
Of beauty's tutors have enrich'd you with?
Other slow arts entirely keep the brain,
And therefore finding barren practisers,   325
Scarce show a harvest of their heavy toil;
But love, first learned in a lady's eyes,
Lives not alone immured in the brain,
But with the motion of all elements
Courses as swift as thought in every power,   330
And gives to every power a double power
Above their functions and their offices.
It adds a precious seeing to the eye:
A lover's eyes will gaze an eagle blind.
A lover's ear will hear the lowest sound   335
When the suspicious head of theft is stopp'd.
Love's feeling is more soft and sensible
Than are the tender horns of cockled snails.
Love's tongue proves dainty Bacchus gross in
  taste.
For valour, is not Love a Hercules,   340
Still climbing trees in the Hesperides?
Subtle as Sphinx; as sweet and musical
As bright Apollo's lute, strung with his hair.
And when Love speaks, the voice of all the gods

Make heaven drowsy with the harmony.   345
Never durst poet touch a pen to write
Until his ink were temp'red with Love's sighs.
O, then his lines would ravish savage ears
And plant in tyrants mild humility.
From women's eyes this doctrine I derive.   350
They sparkle still the right Promethean fire;
They are the books, the arts, the academes,
That show, contain, and nourish all the world,
Else none at all in aught proves excellent.   354
Then fools you were these women to forswear;
Or keeping what is sworn, you will prove fools.
For wisdom's sake, a word that all men love;
Or for love's sake, a word that loves all men;
Or for men's sake, the authors of these women;
Or women's sake, by whom we men are men —
Let us once lose our oaths to find ourselves,
Or else we lose ourselves to keep our oaths.
It is religion to be thus forsworn;
For charity itself fulfils the law,
And who can sever love from charity?   365
    King. Saint Cupid then! and, soldiers, to
      the field!
    Ber. Advance your standards, and upon
      them, lords!
Pell-mell, down with them! But be first ad-
  vis'd,
In conflict that you get the sun of them.
    Long. Now to plain-dealing. Lay these
      glozes by.   370
Shall we resolve to woo these girls of France?
    King. And win them too! Therefore let us
      devise
Some entertainment for them in their tents.
    Ber. First from the park let us conduct them
      thither;
Then homeward every man attach the hand   375
Of his fair mistress. In the afternoon
We will with some strange pastime solace them,
Such as the shortness of the time can shape,
For revels, dances, masques, and merry hours
Forerun fair Love, strewing her way with flow-
  ers.   380
    King. Away, away! No time shall be
      omitted
That will be time and may by us be fitted.
    Ber. Allons! allons! Sow'd cockle reap'd no
      corn,
And justice always whirls in equal measure.
Light wenches may prove plagues to men for-
  sworn: 385
    If so, our copper buys no better treasure.
                                    Exeunt.

ACT V. [Scene I. *The park.*]

Enter [*Holofernes*] the Pedant, [*Sir Nathaniel*]
the Curate, and *Dull.*

Hol. Satis quod sufficit.

Nath. I praise God for you, sir. Your reasons
at dinner have been sharp and sententious;
pleasant without scurrility, witty without affection, audacious without impudency, learned
without opinion, and strange without heresy.
I did converse this quondam day with a companion of the King's, who is intituled, nominated, or called Don Adriano de Armado. 9

Hol. Novi hominem tanquam te. His humour is lofty, his discourse peremptory, his
tongue filed, his eye ambitious, his gait majestical, and his general behaviour vain, ridiculous,
and thrasonical. He is too picked, too spruce,
too affected, too odd, as it were, too peregrinate,
as I may call it. 16

Nath. A most singular and choice epithet.

Draws out his table-book.

Hol. He draweth out the thread of his ver-
bosity finer than the staple of his argument.
I abhor such fanatical phantasims, such insociable and point-devise companions; such
rackers of orthography as to speak 'dout' fine
when he should say 'doubt,' 'det' when he
should pronounce 'debt' — d, e, b, t, not d, e, t.
He clepeth a calf 'cauf,' 'half' 'hauf,' neighbour
vocatur 'nebour,' 'neigh' abbreviated 'ne.'
This is abhominable, which he would call
'abbominable': it insinuateth me of insanie.
Ne intelligis, domine? to make frantic, lunatic.

Nath. Laus Deo, bone intelligo. 30

Hol. 'Bone'? — 'bone' for 'bene.' Priscian
a little scratch'd; 'twill serve.

Enter [*Armado* the] Braggart, [*Moth* the] Boy,
[and *Costard*].

Nath. Videsne quis venit?

Hol. Video et gaudeo.

Arm. [*to Moth*] Chirrah! 35

Hol. Quare 'chirrah,' not 'sirrah'?

Arm. Men of peace, well encount'red.

Hol. Most military sir, salutation.

Moth. [*aside to Costard*] They have been at
a great feast of languages and stol'n the scraps.

Cost. O, they have liv'd long on the alms-
basket of words. I marvel thy master hath not
eaten thee for a word; for thou art not so long
by the head as honorificabilitudinitatibus; thou
art easier swallowed than a flapdragon. 45

Moth. Peace! the peal begins.

Arm. [*to Holofernes*] Monsieur, are you not
lett'red?

Moth. Yes, yes! he teaches boys the hornbook. What is a, b, spell'd backward with the
horn on his head? 51

Hol. Ba, pueritia, with a horn added.

Moth. Ba, most seely sheep, with a horn! —
You hear his learning.

Hol. Quis, quis, thou consonant? 55

Moth. The last of the five vowels, if You
repeat them; or the fifth, if I.

Hol. I will repeat them: — a, e, I —

Moth. The sheep: the other two concludes
it — O, U. 60

Arm. Now by the salt wave of the Mediter-
raneum, a sweet touch, a quick venew of wit!
Snip, snap, quick and home! It rejoiceth my
intellect. True wit!

Moth. Offer'd by a child to an old man;
which is wit-old. 66

Hol. What is the figure? What is the figure?

Moth. Horns.

Hol. Thou disputes like an infant. Go whip
thy gig. 70

Moth. Lend me your horn to make one, and
I will whip about your infamy circum circa —
a gig of a cuckold's horn.

Cost. An I had but one penny in the world,
thou shouldst have it to buy gingerbread. Hold,
there is the very remuneration I had of thy
master, thou halfpenny purse of wit, thou
pigeon egg of discretion. O, an the heavens
were so pleased that thou wert but my bastard,
what a joyful father wouldest thou make me!
Go to; thou hast it ad dunghill, at the fingers'
ends, as they say. 82

Hol. O, I smell false Latin! 'dunghill' for
unguem.

Arm. Arts-man, preambulate. We will be
singuled from the barbarous. Do you not edu-
cate youth at the charge-house on the top of the
mountain?

Hol. Or mons, the hill.

Arm. At your sweet pleasure, for the mountain. 90

Hol. I do, sans question.

Arm. Sir, it is the King's most sweet pleasure and affection to congratulate the Princess
at her pavilion in the posteriors of this day,
which the rude multitude call the afternoon. 95

Hol. The posterior of the day, most generous
sir, is liable, congruent, and measurable for the

215

afternoon. The word is well cull'd, chose, sweet, and apt, I do assure you, sir, I do assure. 99

Arm. Sir, the King is a noble gentleman, and my familiar, I do assure ye, very good friend. For what is inward between us, let it pass. I do beseech thee remember thy courtesy. I beseech thee apparel thy head. And among other importunate and most serious designs, and of great import indeed, too — but let that pass; for I must tell thee it will please his Grace (by the world) sometime to lean upon my poor shoulder, and with his royal finger thus dally with my excrement, with my mustachio — but, sweet heart, let that pass. By the world, I recount no fable! Some certain special honours it pleaseth his greatness to impart to Armado, a soldier, a man of travel, that hath seen the world — but let that pass. The very all of all is — but, sweet heart, I do implore secrecy — that the King would have me present the Princess (sweet chuck) with some delightful ostentation, or show, or pageant, or antic, or firework. Now, understanding that the curate and your sweet self are good at such eruptions and sudden breaking-out of mirth, as it were, I have acquainted you withal, to the end to crave your assistance. 123

Hol. Sir, you shall present before her the Nine Worthies. Sir Nathaniel, as concerning some entertainment of time, some show in the posterior of this day, to be rend'red by our assistance at the King's command, and this most gallant, illustrate, and learned gentleman, before the Princess — I say none so fit as to present the Nine Worthies. 130

Nath. Where will you find men worthy enough to present them?

Hol. Joshua, yourself; myself, or this gallant gentleman, Judas Maccabæus; this swain, because of his great limb or joint, shall pass Pompey the Great; the page, Hercules — 136

Arm. Pardon, sir; error! He is not quantity enough for that Worthy's thumb; he is not so big as the end of his club.

Hol. Shall I have audience? He shall present Hercules in minority. His enter and exit shall be strangling a snake; and I will have an apology for that purpose. 143

Moth. An excellent device! So, if any of the audience hiss, you may cry 'Well done, Hercules! Now thou crushest the snake!' That is the way to make an offence gracious, though few have the grace to do it.

Arm. For the rest of the Worthies?

Hol. I will play three myself. 150

Moth. Thrice-worthy gentleman!

Arm. Shall I tell you a thing?

Hol. We attend.

Arm. We will have, if this fadge not, an antic. I beseech you follow. 155

Hol. Via, goodman Dull! Thou hast spoken no word all this while.

Dull. Nor understood none neither, sir.

Hol. Allons! we will employ thee. .

Dull. I'll make one in a dance, or so; or I will play 160
On the tabor to the Worthies, and let them dance the hay.

Hol. Most dull, honest Dull! To our sport, away! *Exeunt.*

[Scene II. *The park.*]

Enter the Ladies: [the *Princess, Maria, Katherine*, and *Rosaline*].

Prin. Sweet hearts, we shall be rich ere we depart
If fairings come thus plentifully in.
A lady wall'd about with diamonds!
Look you, what I have from the loving King.

Ros. Madam, came nothing else along with that? 5

Prin. Nothing but this? Yes, as much love in rhyme
As would be cramm'd up in a sheet of paper
Writ o' both sides the leaf, margent and all,
That he was fain to seal on Cupid's name.

Ros. That was the way to make his godhead wax, 10
For he hath been five thousand years a boy.

Kath. Ay, and a shrowd unhappy gallows too.

Ros. You'll ne'er be friends with him; 'a kill'd your sister.

Kath. He made her melancholy, sad, and heavy,
And so she died. Had she been light like you,
Of such a merry, nimble, stirring spirit, 16
She might 'a' been a grandam ere she died.
And so may you; for a light heart lives long.

Ros. What's your dark meaning, mouse, of this light word?

Kath. A light condition in a beauty dark.

Ros. We need more light to find your meaning out. 21

Kath. You'll mar the light by taking it in snuff.
Therefore I'll darkly end the argument.

Ros. Look, what you do, you do it still i' th'
dark.

Kath. So do not you, for you are a light
wench. 25

Ros. Indeed I weigh not you, and therefore
light.

Kath. You weigh me not? O, that's you
care not for me.

Ros. Great reason; for past cure is still past
care.

Prin. Well bandied both! a set of wit well
play'd.

But, Rosaline, you have a favour too? 30
Who sent it? and what is it?

Ros. I would you knew.
An if my face were but as fair as yours,
My favour were as great. Be witness this.
Nay, I have verses too, I thank Berowne;
The numbers true; and, were the numb'ring
too, 35
I were the fairest goddess on the ground.
I am compar'd to twenty thousand fairs.
O, he hath drawn my picture in his letter!

Prin. Anything like?

Ros. Much in the letters, nothing in the
praise. 40

Prin. Beauteous as ink — a good conclusion.

Kath. Fair as a text B in a copy-book.

Ros. Ware pencils, ho! Let me not die your
debtor,
My red dominical, my golden letter.
O, that your face were not so full of O's! 45

Kath. A pox of that jest, and I beshrow all
shrows!

Prin. But, Katherine, what was sent to you
from fair Dumain?

Kath. Madam, this glove.

Prin. Did he not send you twain?

Kath. Yes, madam; and moreover,
Some thousand verses of a faithful lover, 50
A huge translation of hypocrisy,
Vilely compil'd, profound simplicity.

Mar. This, and these pearl, to me sent
Longavile.
The letter is too long by half a mile.

Prin. I think no less. Dost thou not wish
in heart 55
The chain were longer and the letter short?

Mar. Ay, or I would these hands might never
part.

Prin. We are wise girls to mock our lovers so.

Ros. They are worse fools to purchase mock-
ing so.
That same Berowne I'll torture ere I go. 60
O that I knew he were but in by th' week!

How I would make him fawn, and beg, and seek,
And wait the season, and observe the times,
And spend his prodigal wits in bootless rhymes,
And shape his service wholly to my hests, 65
And make him proud to make me proud that
jests!
So pertaunt-like would I o'ersway his state
That he should be my fool, and I his fate.

Prin. None are so surely caught, when they
are catch'd, 69
As wit turn'd fool. Folly, in wisdom hatch'd,
Hath wisdom's warrant, and the help of school,
And wit's own grace to grace a learned fool.

Ros. The blood of youth burns not with such
excess
As gravity's revolt to wantonness.

Mar. Folly in fools bears not so strong a note
As fool'ry in the wise when wit doth dote; 76
Since all the power thereof it doth apply
To prove, by wit, worth in simplicity.

Enter Boyet.

Prin. Here comes Boyet, and mirth is in his
face.

Boyet. O, I am stabb'd with laughter!
Where's her Grace? 80

Prin. Thy news, Boyet?

Boyet. Prepare, madam, prepare!
Arm, wenches, arm! Encounters mounted are
Against your peace; Love doth approach dis-
guis'd,
Armed in arguments; you'll be surpris'd. 84
Muster your wits; stand in your own defence,
Or hide your heads like cowards and fly hence.

Prin. Saint Denis to Saint Cupid! What are
they
That charge their breath against us? Say,
scout, say.

Boyet. Under the cool shade of a sycamore
I thought to close mine eyes some half an hour;
When, lo! to interrupt my purpos'd rest, 91
Toward that shade I might behold addrest
The King and his companions! Warily
I stole into a neighbour thicket by
And overheard what you shall overhear — 95
That by-and-by disguis'd they will be here.
Their herald is a pretty knavish page
That well by heart hath conn'd his embassage.
Action and accent did they teach him there:
'Thus must thou speak,' and 'thus thy body
bear.' 100
And ever and anon they made a doubt
Presence majestical would put him out;
'For,' quoth the King, 'an angel shalt thou see;
Yet fear not thou, but speak audaciously.'

The boy replied, 'An angel is not evil.   105
I should have fear'd her had she been a devil.'
With that all laugh'd and clapp'd him on the
   shoulder,
Making the bold wag by their praises bolder.
One rubb'd his elbow thus, and fleer'd, and
   swore
A better speech was never spoke before.   110
Another with his finger and his thumb
Cried, 'Via! we will do't, come what will
   come!'
The third he caper'd and cried 'All goes well.'
The fourth turn'd on the toe and down he fell.
With that they all did tumble on the ground
With such a zealous laughter, so profound, 116
That in this spleen ridiculous appears,
To check their folly, passion's solemn tears.
  Prin. But what? but what? Come they to
   visit us?
  Boyet. They do, they do! and are apparell'd
   thus —   120
Like Muscovites or Russians, as I guess.
Their purpose is, to parley, court, and dance;
And every one his love-feat will advance
Unto his several mistress; which they'll know
By favours several which they did bestow. 125
  Prin. And will they so? The gallants shall
   be task'd;
For, ladies, we will every one be mask'd;
And not a man of them shall have the grace,
Despite of suit, to see a lady's face.
Hold, Rosaline, this favour thou shalt wear, 130
And then the King will court thee for his dear.
Hold, take thou this, my sweet, and give me
   thine;
So shall Berowne take me for Rosaline.
And change you favours too. So shall your loves
Woo contrary, deceiv'd by these removes. 135
  Ros. Come on, then. Wear the favours most
   in sight.
  Kath. But in this changing what is your
   intent?
  Prin. The effect of my intent is to cross
   theirs.
They do it but in mocking merriment,
And mock for mock is only my intent.   140
Their several counsels they unbosom shall
To loves mistook, and so be mock'd withal
Upon the next occasion that we meet
With visages display'd to talk and greet.
  Ros. But shall we dance if they desire us to't?
  Prin. No, to the death we will not move a
   foot;   146
Nor to their penn'd speech render we no grace,
But while 'tis spoke each turn away her face.

  Boyet. Why, that contempt will kill the
   speaker's heart   149
And quite divorce his memory from his part.
  Prin. Therefore I do it; and I make no doubt
The rest will ne'er come in if he be out.
There's no such sport as sport by sport o'er-
   thrown —
To make theirs ours, and ours none but our
   own.
So shall we stay, mocking intended game, 155
And they, well mock'd, depart away with
   shame.   *Sound trumpet* [*within*].
  Boyet. The trumpet sounds. Be mask'd;
   the maskers come.

                  [*The Ladies mask.*]

Enter *Blackmoors* with music; the Boy [*Moth*]
with a speech, and [the *King* and] the rest of
the *Lords*, disguised [like *Russians* and masked].

  Moth. 'All hail, the richest beauties on the
   earth!'
  Boyet. Beauties no richer than rich taffeta.
  Moth. 'A holy parcel of the fairest dames 160
     The Ladies turn their backs to him.
That ever turn'd their backs to mortal views!'
  Ber. 'Their eyes,' villain! 'their eyes!'
  Moth. 'That ever turn'd their eyes to mortal
   views!
Out' —
  Boyet. True! Out indeed!   165
  Moth. 'Out of your favours, heavenly spirits,
   vouchsafe
Not to behold' —
  Ber. 'Once to behold,' rogue!
  Moth. 'Once to behold with your sun-beamed
   eyes,
— with your sun-beamed eyes' —   169
  Boyet. They will not answer to that epithet.
You were best call it 'daughter-beamed eyes.'
  Moth. They do not mark me, and that brings
   me out.
  Ber. Is this your perfectness? Be gone, you
   rogue!

                  [*Exit Moth.*]

  Ros. What would these strangers? Know
   their minds, Boyet.
If they do speak our language, 'tis our will 175
That some plain man recount their purposes.
Know what they would.
  Boyet. What would you with the Princess?
  Ber. Nothing but peace and gentle visitation.
  Ros. What would they, say they?   180
  Boyet. Nothing but peace and gentle visi-
   tation.
  Ros. Why, that they have, and bid them so
   be gone.

Boyet. She says, you have it and you may
    be gone.
King. Say to her we have measur'd many
    miles
To tread a measure with her on this grass. 185
Boyet. They say that they have measur'd
    many a mile
To tread a measure with you on this grass.
Ros. It is not so. Ask them how many inches
Is in one mile. If they have measur'd many,
The measure then of one is eas'ly told.   190
Boyet. If to come hither you have measur'd
    miles,
And many miles, the Princess bids you tell
How many inches doth fill up one mile.
Ber. Tell her we measure them by weary
    steps.
Boyet. She hears herself.
Ros.   How many weary steps
Of many weary miles you have o'ergone   196
Are numb'red in the travel of one mile?
Ber. We number nothing that we spend for
    you.
Our duty is so rich, so infinite,
That we may do it still without accompt.   200
Vouchsafe to show the sunshine of your face,
That we (like savages) may worship it.
Ros. My face is but a moon, and clouded too.
King. Blessed are clouds, to do as such clouds
    do.
Vouchsafe, bright moon, and these thy stars, to
    shine   205
(Those clouds remov'd) upon our watery eyne.
Ros. O vain petitioner, beg a greater matter!
Thou now requests but moonshine in the water.
King. Then in our measure do but vouchsafe
    one change.
Thou bid'st me beg; this begging is not strange.
Ros. Play music then. Nay, you must do
    it soon.   211
Not yet? No dance! Thus change I like the
    moon.
King. Will you not dance? How come you
    thus estranged?
Ros. You took the moon at full, but now
    she's changed.
King. Yet still she is the Moon, and I the
    Man.   215
The music plays; vouchsafe some motion to it.
Ros. Our ears vouchsafe it.
King.   But your legs should do it.
Ros. Since you are strangers, and come here
    by chance,
We'll not be nice. Take hands. We will not
    dance.

King. Why take we hands then?
Ros.   Only to part friends. 220
Curtsy, sweet hearts — and so the measure
    ends.
King. More measure of this measure! Be
    not nice.
Ros. We can afford no more at such a price.
King. Price you yourselves. What buys your
    company?
Ros. Your absence only.
King.   That can never be. 225
Ros. Then cannot we be bought; and so
    adieu —
Twice to your visor, and half once to you.
King. If you deny to dance, let's hold more
    chat.
Ros. In private then.
King.   I am best pleas'd with that.
                [*They converse apart.*]
Ber. White-handed mistress, one sweet word
    with thee.   230
Prin. Honey, and milk, and sugar: there is
    three.
Ber. Nay, then, two treys, an if you grow
    so nice —
Metheglin, wort, and malmsey. Well run, dice!
There's half a dozen sweets.
Prin.   Seventh sweet, adieu.
Since you can cog, I'll play no more with you.
Ber. One word in secret.
Prin.   Let it not be sweet. 236
Ber. Thou grievest my gall.
Prin.   Gall! bitter.
Ber.   Therefore meet.
                [*They converse apart.*]
Dum. Will you vouchsafe with me to change
    a word?
Mar. Name it.
Dum.   Fair lady —
Mar.   Say you so? Fair lord.
Take that for your 'fair lady.'
Dum.   Please it you, 240
As much in private, and I'll bid adieu.
                [*They converse apart.*]
Kath. What, was your vizard made without
    a tongue?
Long. I know the reason, lady, why you ask.
Kath. O for your reason! Quickly, sir; I
    long!
Long. You have a double tongue within your
    mask   245
And would afford my speechless vizard half.
Kath. 'Veal,' quoth the Dutchman. Is not
    veal a calf?
Long. A calf, fair lady?

Kath. No, a fair lord calf.
Long. Let's part the word.
Kath. No, I'll not be your half.
Take all and wean it, it may prove an ox. 250
Long. Look how you butt yourself in these
sharp mocks!
Will you give horns, chaste lady? Do not so.
Kath. Then die a calf before your horns do
grow.
Long. One word in private with you ere I die.
Kath. Bleat softly then. The butcher hears
you cry. 255
[*They converse apart.*]
Boyet. The tongues of mocking wenches are
as keen
As is the razor's edge invisible,
Cutting a smaller hair than may be seen,
Above the sense of sense: so sensible
Seemeth their conference; their conceits have
wings, 260
Fleeter than arrows, bullets, wind, thought,
swifter things.
Ros. Not one word more, my maids! Break
off, break off.
Ber. By heaven, all dry-beaten with pure
scoff!
King. Farewell, mad wenches. You have
simple wits.
Exeunt [*King, Lords, and Blackamoors*].
Prin. Twenty adieus, my frozen Muscovits.
Are these the breed of wits so wondered at? 266
Boyet. Tapers they are, with your sweet
breaths puff'd out.
Ros. Well-liking wits they have; gross,
gross; fat, fat.
Prin. O poverty in wit, kingly poor flout!
Will they not (think you) hang themselves
to-night? 270
Or ever but in vizards show their faces?
This pert Berowne was out of count'nance
quite.
Ros. O, they were all in lamentable cases.
The King was weeping-ripe for a good word.
Prin. Berowne did swear himself out of all
suit. 275
Mar. Dumain was at my service, and his
sword:
'No point,' quoth I. My servant straight
was mute.
Kath. Lord Longaville said I came o'er his
heart;
And trow you what he call'd me?
Prin. Qualm, perhaps.
Kath. Yes, in good faith.
Prin. Go, sickness as thou art! 280

Ros. Well, better wits have worn plain stat-
ute caps.
But will you hear? The King is my love sworn.
Prin. And quick Berowne hath plighted
faith to me.
Kath. And Longaville was for my service
born.
Mar. Dumain is mine as sure as bark on
tree. 285
Boyet. Madam, and pretty mistresses, give
ear.
Immediately they will again be here
In their own shapes; for it can never be
They will digest this harsh indignity.
Prin. Will they return?
Boyet. They will, they will, God knows,
And leap for joy, though they are lame with
blows. 291
Therefore change favours, and when they re-
pair,
Blow like sweet roses in this summer air.
Prin. How blow? how blow? Speak to be
understood.
Boyet. Fair ladies mask'd are roses in their
bud; 295
Dismask'd, their damask sweet commixture
shown,
Are angels vailing clouds, or roses blown.
Prin. Avaunt perplexity! What shall we do
If they return in their own shapes to woo?
Ros. Good madam, if by me you'll be ad-
vis'd, 300
Let's mock them still, as well known as dis-
guis'd.
Let us complain to them what fools were here,
Disguis'd like Muscovites in shapeless gear;
And wonder what they were, and to what end
Their shallow shows, and prologue vilely
penn'd, 305
And their rough carriage so ridiculous,
Should be presented at our tent to us.
Boyet. Ladies, withdraw. The gallants are
at hand.
Prin. Whip to our tents, as roes run o'er
the land.
Exeunt [*Princess, Rosaline, Katherine, and
Maria*].

Enter the *King* and the rest, [*Berowne, Longaville, and Dumain, in their proper habits*].

King. Fair sir, God save you! Where is the
Princess? 310
Boyet. Gone to her tent. Please it your
Majesty
Command me any service to her thither?

King. That she vouchsafe me audience for
    one word.
Boyet. I will; and so will she, I know, my
    lord.   *Exit.*
Ber. This fellow pecks up wit as pigeons
    pease,   315
And utters it again when God doth please.
He is wit's pedlar, and retails his wares
At wakes and wassails, meetings, markets,
    fairs;
And we that sell by gross, the Lord doth know,
Have not the grace to grace it with such show.
This gallant pins the wenches on his sleeve. 321
Had he been Adam, he had tempted Eve.
'A can carve too, and lisp. Why, this is he
That kiss'd his hand away in courtesy.
This is the ape of form, Monsieur the Nice, 325
That, when he plays at tables, chides the dice
In honourable terms. Nay, he can sing
A mean most meanly; and in ushering
Mend him who can. The ladies call him sweet.
The stairs, as he treads on them, kiss his feet.
This is the flow'r that smiles on every one 331
To show his teeth as white as whalës-bone;
And consciences that will not die in debt
Pay him the due of 'honey-tongu'd Boyet.'
    King. A blister on his sweet tongue with my
    heart,   335
That put Armado's page out of his part!

    Enter the *Ladies* [and *Boyet*].

Ber. See where it comes! Behaviour, what
    wert thou
Till this man show'd thee? and what art thou
    now?
King. All hail, sweet madam, and fair time
    of day!
Prin. 'Fair' in 'all hail' is foul, as I con-
    ceive.   340
King. Construe my speeches better, if you
    may.
Prin. Then wish me better; I will give you
    leave.
King. We came to visit you, and purpose
    now
To lead you to our court. Vouchsafe it then.
Prin. This field shall hold me, and so hold
    your vow.   345
Nor God nor I delights in perjur'd men.
King. Rebuke me not for that which you
    provoke.
The virtue of your eye must break my oath.
Prin. You nickname virtue. 'Vice' you
    should have spoke;
For virtue's office never breaks men's troth.

Now, by my maiden honour, yet as pure 351
    As the unsullied lily, I protest,
A world of torments though I should endure,
    I would not yield to be your house's guest;
So much I hate a breaking cause to be 355
Of heavenly oaths, vow'd with integrity.
King. O, you have liv'd in desolation here,
Unseen, unvisited, much to our shame.
Prin. Not so, my lord. It is not so, I swear.
We have had pastimes here and pleasant
    game;   360
A mess of Russians left us but of late.
King. How, madam? Russians?
Prin.   Ay, in truth, my lord;
Trim gallants, full of courtship and of state.
Ros. Madam, speak true. — It is not so, my
    lord.
My lady (to the manner of the days)   365
In courtesy gives undeserving praise.
We four indeed confronted were with four
In Russian habit. Here they stay'd an hour
And talk'd apace; and in that hour, my lord,
They did not bless us with one happy word. 370
I dare not call them fools; but this I think,
When they are thirsty, fools would fain have
    drink.
Ber. This jest is dry to me. Fair gentle
    sweet,
Your wit makes wise things foolish. When we
    greet,
With eyes best seeing, heaven's fiery eye, 375
By light we lose light. Your capacity
Is of that nature that to your huge store
Wise things seem foolish and rich things but
    poor.
Ros. This proves you wise and rich; for in
    my eye —
Ber. I am a fool, and full of poverty.   380
Ros. But that you take what doth to you
    belong,
It were a fault to snatch words from my
    tongue.
Ber. O, I am yours, and all that I possess!
Ros. All the fool mine?
Ber.   I cannot give you less.
Ros. Which of the vizards was it that you
    wore?   385
Ber. Where? when? what vizard? Why de-
    mand you this?
Ros. There, then, that vizard; that super-
    fluous case
That hid the worse and show'd the better face.
King. We were descried. They'll mock us
    now downright.
Dum. Let us confess and turn it to a jest. 390

221

Prin. Amaz'd, my lord? Why looks your Highness sad?
Ros. Help! hold his brows! He'll sound! Why look you pale?
Seasick, I think, coming from Muscovy.
Ber. Thus pour the stars down plagues for perjury.
Can any face of brass hold longer out? 395
Here stand I, lady. Dart thy skill at me,
Bruise me with scorn, confound me with a flout,
Thrust thy sharp wit quite through my ignorance,
Cut me to pieces with thy keen conceit;
And I will wish thee never more to dance, 400
Nor never more in Russian habit wait.
O, never will I trust to speeches penn'd
Nor to the motion of a schoolboy's tongue,
Nor never come in vizard to my friend,
Nor woo in rhyme like a blind harper's song!
Taffeta phrases, silken terms precise, 406
Three-pil'd hyperboles, spruce affectation,
Figures pedantical — these summer flies
Have blown me full of maggot ostentation.
I do forswear them; and I here protest, 410
By this white glove (how white the hand, God knows!),
Henceforth my wooing mind shall be express'd
In russet yea's and honest kersey no's.
And to begin: wench, so God help me, law!
My love to thee is sound, sans crack or flaw. 415
Ros. Sans 'sans,' I pray you!
Ber.   Yet I have a trick
Of the old rage. Bear with me, I am sick.
I'll leave it by degrees. Soft, let us see!
Write 'Lord have mercy on us' on those three.
They are infected, in their hearts it lies; 420
They have the plague, and caught it of your eyes.
These lords are visited; you are not free,
For the Lord's tokens on you do I see.
Prin. No, they are free that gave these tokens to us.
Ber. Our states are forfeit. Seek not to undo us. 425
Ros. It is not so; for how can this be true,
That you stand forfeit, being those that sue?
Ber. Peace! for I will not have to do with you.
Ros. Nor shall not, if I do as I intend.
Ber. Speak for yourselves. My wit is at an end. 430
King. Teach us. sweet madam, for our rude transgression
Some fair excuse.

Prin.   The fairest is confession.
Were not you here but even now, disguis'd?
King. Madam, I was.
Prin.   And were you well advis'd?
King. I was, fair madam.
Prin.   When you then were here,
What did you whisper in your lady's ear? 436
King. That more than all the world I did respect her.
Prin. When she shall challenge this, you will reject her.
King. Upon mine honour, no.
Prin.   Peace, peace! forbear.
Your oath once broke, you force not to forswear.
King. Despise me when I break this oath of mine! 441
Prin. I will, and therefore keep it. — Rosaline,
What did the Russian whisper in your ear?
Ros. Madam, he swore that he did hold me dear
As precious eyesight and did value me 445
Above this world; adding thereto moreover,
That he would wed me or else die my lover.
Prin. God give thee joy of him! The noble lord
Most honourably doth uphold his word.
King. What mean you, madam? By my life, my troth, 450
I never swore this lady such an oath.
Ros. By heaven, you did! and to confirm it plain,
You gave me this; but take it, sir, again.
King. My faith and this the Princess I did give.
I knew her by this jewel on her sleeve. 455
Prin. Pardon me, sir, this jewel did she wear,
And Lord Berowne (I thank him) is my dear.
What? will you have me, or your pearl again?
Ber. Neither of either; I remit both twain.
I see the trick on't. Here was a consent, 460
Knowing aforehand of our merriment,
To dash it like a Christmas comedy.
Some carry-tale, some please-man, some slight zany,
Some mumble-news, some trencher knight, some Dick
That smiles his cheek in years and knows the trick 465
To make my lady laugh when she's dispos'd,
Told our intents before; which once disclos'd,
The ladies did change favours; and then we,
Following the signs, woo'd but the sign of She.
Now, to our perjury to add more terror, 470
We are again forsworn in will and error.

Much upon this it is. And might not you
                                [*To Boyet.*]
Forestall our sport, to make us thus untrue?
Do not you know my lady's foot by th' squier?
And laugh upon the apple of her eye?   475
And stand between her back, sir, and the fire,
  Holding a trencher, jesting merrily?
You put our page out. Go, you are allow'd.
Die when you will, a smock shall be your
  shroud.
You leer upon me, do you? There's an eye 480
Wounds like a leaden sword.
    Boyet.   Full merrily
Hath this brave manage, this career, been run.
    Ber. Lo, he is tilting straight! Peace! I
  have done.

            Enter [*Costard the*] *Clown.*

Welcome, pure wit! Thou part'st a fair fray.
    Cost. O Lord, sir, they would know   485
Whether the three Worthies shall come in or no.
    Ber. What, are there but three?
    Cost.   No, sir; but it is vara fine,
For every one pursents three.
    Ber.   And three times thrice is nine.
    Cost. Not so, sir, under correction, sir; I
  hope it is not so.
You cannot beg us, sir, I can assure you, sir;
  we know what we know.   490
I hope, sir, three times thrice, sir —
    Ber. Is not nine?
    Cost. Under correction, sir, we know where-
until it doth amount.
    Ber. By Jove, I always took three threes for
  nine.   496
    Cost. O Lord, sir, it were pity you should get
your living by reck'ning, sir.
    Ber. How much is it?
    Cost. O Lord, sir, the parties themselves, the
actors, sir, will show whereuntil it doth amount.
For mine own part, I am, as they say, but to
parfect one man in one poor man — Pompion
the Great, sir.
    Ber. Art thou one of the Worthies?   505
    Cost. It pleased them to think me worthy of
Pompey the Great. For mine own part, I know
not the degree of the Worthy, but I am to
stand for him.
    Ber. Go bid them prepare.   510
    Cost. We will turn it finely off, sir; we will
  take some care.   *Exit.*
    King. Berowne, they will shame us. Let
  them not approach.
    Ber. We are shame-proof, my lord; and 'tis
  some policy

To have one show worse than the King's and
  his company.
    King. I say they shall not come.   515
    Prin. Nay, my good lord, let me o'errule
  you now.
That sport best pleases that doth least know
  how:
Where zeal strives to content, and the contents
Dies in the zeal of that which it presents.
Their form confounded makes most form in
  mirth   520
When great things labouring perish in their
  birth.
    Ber. A right description of our sport, my
  lord.

            Enter [*Armado the*] *Braggart.*

    Arm. Anointed, I implore so much expense
of thy royal sweet breath as will utter a brace
of words.   525
    [*Converses apart with the King and delivers
                                  a paper.*]
    Prin. Doth this man serve God?
    Ber. Why ask you?
    Prin. 'A speaks not like a man of God
his making.   529
    Arm. That is all one, my fair, sweet, honey
monarch; for, I protest, the schoolmaster is
exceeding fantastical; too too vain, too too
vain. But we will put it, as they say, to for-
tuna della guerra. I wish you the peace of
mind, most royal couplement.   *Exit.*
    King. Here is like to be a good presence of
Worthies. He presents Hector of Troy; the
swain, Pompey the Great; the parish curate,
Alexander; Armado's page, Hercules; the
pedant, Judas Maccabæus;   540
And if these four Worthies in their first show
  thrive,
These four will change habits and present the
  other five.
    Ber. There is five in the first show.
    King. You are deceived; 'tis not so.
    Ber. The pedant, the braggart, the hedge-
priest, the fool, and the boy: 546
Abate throw at novum, and the whole world
  again
Cannot pick out five such, take each one in his
  vein.
    King. The ship is under sail, and here she
  comes amain.

            Enter [*Costard, for*] *Pompey.*

    Cost. I Pompey am —
    Ber.   You lie! you are not he. 550

Cost. I Pompey am —
Boyet.   With libbard's head on
knee.
Ber. Well said, old mocker. I must needs be
friends with thee.
Cost. I Pompey am, Pompey surnam'd the
Big —
Dum. 'The Great.'
Cost. It is 'Great,' sir.
               Pompey surnam'd the Great,   555
That oft in field with targe and shield did make my
foe to sweat,
And travelling along this coast, I here am come
by chance,
And lay my arms before the legs of this sweet lass
of France.
If your ladyship would say 'Thanks, Pompey,'
I had done.
Prin. Great thanks, great Pompey.   560
Cost. 'Tis not so much worth. But I hope I
was perfect. I made a little fault in 'Great.'
Ber. My hat to a halfpenny, Pompey proves
the best Worthy.

Enter *Curate,* [*Sir Nathaniel,*] for *Alexander.*

Nath. When in the world I liv'd, I was the
world's commander;   565
By east, west, north, and south I spread my con-
quering might;
My scutcheon plain declares that I am Alisander.
Boyet. Your nose says, no, you are not; for
it stands too right.
Ber. Your nose smells 'no' in this, most
tender-smelling knight.
Prin. The conqueror is dismay'd. Proceed,
good Alexander.   570
Nath. When in the world I liv'd, I was the
world's commander —
Boyet. Most true, 'tis right! You were so,
Alisander.
Ber. Pompey the Great!
Cost. Your servant, and Costard.
Ber. Take away the conqueror, take away
Alisander.   576
Cost. [*to Sir Nathaniel*] O, sir, you have overthrown Alisander the conqueror! You will be
scrap'd out of the painted cloth for this. Your
lion that holds his poleaxe sitting on a close-
stool, will be given to Ajax. He will be the
ninth Worthy. A conqueror, and afeard to
speak? Run away for shame, Alisander. [*Sir
Nathaniel stands aside.*] There, an't shall please
you! a foolish mild man; an honest man, look
you, and soon dash'd. He is a marvellous good
neighbour. faith, and a very good bowler; but
for Alisander — alas! you see how 'tis — a little o'erparted. But there are Worthies a-coming
will speak their mind in some other sort.   590
Prin. Stand aside, good Pompey.
               [*Costard stands aside.*]

Enter [*Holofernes the*] *Pedant* for *Judas*; and
     the Boy [*Moth*] for *Hercules.*

Hol. Great Hercules is presented by this imp,
     Whose club kill'd Cerberus, that three-
          headed canus;
     And when he was a babe, a child, a shrimp,
     Thus did he strangle serpents in his
          manus.   595
     Quoniam he seemeth in minority,
     Ergo I come with this apology.
Keep some state in thy exit, and vanish.
               Boy [*stands back*].
Judas I am —
Dum. A Judas?   600
Hol. Not Iscariot, sir.
Judas I am, ycliped Maccabæus.
Dum. Judas Maccabæus clipt is plain Judas.
Ber. A kissing traitor. How art thou prov'd
Judas?
Hol. Judas I am —   605
Dum. The more shame for you, Judas!
Hol. What mean you, sir?
Boyet. To make Judas hang himself.
Hol. Begin, sir; you are my elder.
Ber. Well followed: Judas was hanged on
an elder.   610
Hol. I will not be put out of countenance.
Ber. Because thou hast no face.
Hol. What is this?
Boyet. A cittern-head.
Dum. The head of a bodkin.   615
Ber. A death's face in a ring.
Long. The face of an old Roman coin, scarce
seen.
Boyet. The pommel of Cæsar's falchion.
Dum. The carv'd-bone face on a flask.
Ber. Saint George's half-cheek in a brooch.
Dum. Ay, and in a brooch of lead.   621
Ber. Ay, and worn in the cap of a tooth-
drawer. And now forward, for we have put
thee in countenance.
Hol. You have put me out of counte-
nance.
Ber. False! We have given thee faces.   625
Hol. But you have outfac'd them all.
Ber. An thou wert a lion, we would do
so.
Boyet. Therefore, as he is — an ass, let him
go.
And so adieu, sweet Jude! Nay, why dost thou
stay?

Dum. For the latter end of his name.   630
Ber. For the ass to the Jude. Give it him. Jud-as, away!
Hol. This is not generous, not gentle, not humble.   [*Stands aside.*]
Boyet. A light for Monsieur Judas! It grows dark; he may stumble.
Prin. Alas, poor Maccabæus, how hath he been baited!

Enter *Braggart,* [*Armado,* for Hector].

Ber. Hide thy head, Achilles! Here comes Hector in arms.   636
Dum. Though my mocks come home by me, I will now be merry.
King. Hector was but a Troyan in respect of this.   640
Boyet. But is this Hector?
King. I think Hector was not so clean-timber'd.
Long. His leg is too big for Hector's.
Dum. More calf, certain.   645
Boyet. No; he is best indued in the small.
Ber. This cannot be Hector.
Dum. He's a god or a painter; for he makes faces.
Arm. The armipotent Mars, of lances the almighty,   650
Gave Hector a gift —
Dum. A gilt nutmeg.
Ber. A lemon.
Long. Stuck with cloves.
Dum. No, cloven.   655
Arm. Peace!
The armipotent Mars, of lances the almighty,
Gave Hector a gift, the heir of Ilion;
A man so breathed that certain he would fight; yea,
From morn till night out of his pavilion.   660
I am that flower —
Dum.   That mint.
Long.   That columbine.
Arm. Sweet Lord Longaville, rein thy tongue.
Long. I must rather give it the rein; for it runs against Hector.
Dum. Ay, and Hector's a greyhound.   665
Arm. The sweet war-man is dead and rotten. Sweet chucks, beat not the bones of the buried: when he breathed, he was a man. But I will forward with my device. [*To the Princess*] Sweet royalty, bestow on me the sense of hearing.   670
Berowne steps forth [*to Costard, whispers him, and returns to his place*].
Prin. Speak, brave Hector. We are much delighted.

Arm. I do adore thy sweet Grace's slipper.
Boyet. [*aside to Dumain*] Loves her by the foot.
Dum. [*aside to Boyet*] He may not by the yard.   676
Arm. This Hector far surmounted Hannibal —
Cost. [*suddenly comes from behind*] The party is gone. Fellow Hector, she is gone. She is two months on her way.
Arm. What meanest thou?   680
Cost. Faith, unless you play the honest Troyan, the poor wench is cast away. She's quick; the child brags in her belly already. 'Tis yours.
Arm. Dost thou infamonize me among potentates? Thou shalt die.   685
Cost. Then shall Hector be whipp'd for Jaquenetta that is quick by him, and hang'd for Pompey that is dead by him.
Dum. Most rare Pompey!
Boyet. Renowned Pompey!   690
Ber. Greater than Great! Great, great, great Pompey! Pompey the Huge!
Dum. Hector trembles.
Ber. Pompey is moved. More Ates, more Ates! Stir them on! stir them on!   695
Dum. Hector will challenge him.
Ber. Ay, if 'a have no more man's blood in his belly than will sup a flea.
Arm. By the North Pole, I do challenge thee.   699
Cost. I will not fight with a pole, like a Northren man. I'll slash; I'll do it by the sword. I bepray you let me borrow my arms again.
Dum. Room for the incensed Worthies!
Cost. I'll do it in my shirt.
Dum. Most resolute Pompey!   705
Moth. Master, let me take you a button-hole lower. Do you not see Pompey is uncasing for the combat? What mean you? You will lose your reputation.
Arm. Gentlemen and soldiers, pardon me. I will not combat in my shirt.   711
Dum. You may not deny it. Pompey hath made the challenge.
Arm. Sweet bloods, I both may and will.
Ber. What reason have you for't?   715
Arm. The naked truth of it is, I have no shirt; I go woolward for penance.
Moth. True, and it was enjoined him in Rome for want of linen; since when, I'll be sworn he wore none but a dishclout of Jaquenetta's, and that 'a wears next his heart for a favour.   722

Enter a Messenger, *Monsieur Marcade.*

Mar. God save you, madam!

Prin.   Welcome, Marcade,
But that thou interruptest our merriment. 725

Mar. I am sorry, madam, for the news I bring
Is heavy in my tongue. The King your father—

Prin. Dead, for my life!

Mar.   Even so. My tale is told.

Ber. Worthies, away! The scene begins to cloud. 730

Arm. For mine own part, I breathe free breath. I have seen the day of wrong through the little hole of discretion, and I will right myself like a soldier. *Exeunt Worthies.*

King. How fares your Majesty? 735

Prin. Boyet, prepare. I will away to-night.

King. Madam, not so. I do beseech you stay.

Prin. Prepare, I say. I thank you, gracious lords,
For all your fair endeavours, and entreat,
Out of a new-sad soul, that you vouchsafe 740
In your rich wisdom to excuse, or hide,
The liberal opposition of our spirits
If over-boldly we have borne ourselves
In the converse of breath. Your gentleness
Was guilty of it. Farewell, worthy lord. 745
A heavy heart bears not a nimble tongue.
Excuse me so, coming too short of thanks
For my great suit, so easily obtain'd.

King. The extreme parts of time extremely forms
All causes to the purpose of his speed; 750
And often at his very loose decides
That which long process could not arbitrate.
And though the mourning brow of progeny
Forbid the smiling courtesy of love
The holy suit which fain it would convince, 755
Yet, since love's argument was first on foot,
Let not the cloud of sorrow justle it
From what it purpos'd; since to wail friends lost
Is not by much so wholesome profitable
As to rejoice at friends but newly found. 760

Prin. I understand you not. My griefs are double.

Ber. Honest plain words best pierce the ear of grief,
And by these badges understand the King.
For your fair sakes have we neglected time,
Play'd foul play with our oaths. Your beauty, ladies, 765
Hath much deform'd us, fashioning our humours
Even to the opposed end of our intents;

And what in us hath seem'd ridiculous —
As love is full of unbefitting strains,
All wanton as a child, skipping and vain, 770
Form'd by the eye and therefore, like the eye,
Full of strange shapes, of habits, and of forms,
Varying in subjects as the eye doth roll
To every varied object in his glance;
Which parti-coated presence of loose love 775
Put on by us, if, in your heavenly eyes,
Have misbecom'd our oaths and gravities,
Those heavenly eyes that look into these faults
Suggested us to make them. Therefore, ladies,
Our love being yours, the error that love makes
Is likewise yours. We to ourselves prove false,
By being once false for ever to be true
To those that make us both — fair ladies, you;
And even that falsehood, in itself a sin,
Thus purifies itself and turns to grace. 785

Prin. We have receiv'd your letters, full of love;
Your favours, the ambassadors of love;
And in our maiden council rated them
At courtship, pleasant jest, and courtesy,
As bombast and as lining to the time; 790
But more devout than this in our respects
Have we not been, and therefore met your loves
In their own fashion, like a merriment.

Dum. Our letters, madam, show'd much more than jest.

Long. So did our looks.

Ros.   We did not quote them so. 795

King. Now at the latest minute of the hour
Grant us your loves.

Prin.   A time methinks too short
To make a world-without-end bargain in.
No, no, my lord! Your Grace is perjur'd much,
Full of dear guiltiness; and therefore this : —
If for my love (as there is no such cause) 801
You will do aught, this shall you do for me :
Your oath I will not trust, but go with speed
To some forlorn and naked hermitage,
Remote from all the pleasures of the world; 805
There stay until the twelve celestial signs
Have brought about the annual reckoning.
If this austere insociable life
Change not your offer made in heat of blood —
If frosts and fasts, hard lodging and thin weeds
Nip not the gaudy blossoms of your love, 811
But that it bear this trial, and last love —
Then, at the expiration of the year,
Come challenge me, challenge me by these deserts,
And, by this virgin palm now kissing thine, 815
I will be thine; and till that instant, shut
My woeful self up in a mourning house,

Raining the tears of lamentation
For the remembrance of my father's death.
If this thou do deny, let our hands part,   820
Neither intitled in the other's heart.
    King. If this, or more than this, I would
    deny,
To flatter up these powers of mine with rest,
The sudden hand of death close up mine eye!
Hence hermit then — my heart is in thy
    breast.   825
    *Ber. And what to me, my love? and what
    to me?*
    *Ros. You must be purged too, your sins are
    rack'd,*
You are attaint with faults and perjury;
Therefore, if you my favour mean to get,   829
A twelvemonth shall you spend, and never rest,
But seek the weary beds of people sick.
    Dum. But what to me, my love? but what
    to me?
A wife?
    Kath.   A beard, fair health, and honesty.
With threefold love I wish you all these three.
    Dum. O, shall I say 'I thank you, gentle
    wife'?   835
    Kath. Not so, my lord. A twelvemonth and
    a day
I'll mark no words that smooth-fac'd wooers say.
Come when the King doth to my lady come;
Then, if I have much love, I'll give you some.
    Dum. I'll serve thee true and faithfully till
    then.   840
    Kath. Yet swear not, lest ye be forsworn
    again.
    Long. What says Maria?
    Mar.   At the twelvemonth's end
I'll change my black gown for a faithful friend.
    Long. I'll stay with patience; but the time
    is long.
    Mar. The liker you! Few taller are so
    young.   845
    Ber. Studies my lady? Mistress, look on me;
Behold the window of my heart, mine eye,
What humble suit attends thy answer there.
Impose some service on me for thy love.
    Ros. Oft have I heard of you, my Lord
    Berowne,   850
Before I saw you; and the world's large tongue
Proclaims you for a man replete with mocks,
Full of comparisons and wounding flouts,
Which you on all estates will execute
That lie within the mercy of your wit.   855
To weed this wormwood from your fructful
    brain,
And therewithal to win me, if you please,

Without the which I am not to be won,
You shall this twelvemonth term from day to
    day
Visit the speechless sick and still converse   860
With groaning wretches; and your task shall be,
With all the fierce endeavour of your wit
To enforce the pained impotent to smile.
    Ber. To move wild laughter in the throat of
    death?
It cannot be; it is impossible.   865
Mirth cannot move a soul in agony.
    Ros. Why, that's the way to choke a gibing
    spirit,
Whose influence is begot of that loose grace
Which shallow laughing hearers give to fools.
A jest's prosperity lies in the ear   870
Of him that hears it, never in the tongue
Of him that makes it. Then, if sickly ears,
Deaf'd with the clamours of their own dear
    groans,
Will hear your idle scorns, continue them,
And I will have you, and that fault withal; 875
But if they will not, throw away that spirit,
And I shall find you empty of that fault,
Right joyful of your reformation.
    Ber. A twelvemonth? Well, befall what will
    befall,
I'll jest a twelvemonth in an hospital.   880
    Prin. [*to the King*] Ay, sweet my lord, and
    so I take my leave.
    King. No, madam; we will bring you on
    your way.
    Ber. Our wooing doth not end like an old
    play:
Jack hath not Gill. These ladies' courtesy
Might well have made our sport a comedy. 885
    King. Come, sir, it wants a twelvemonth
    and a day,
And then 'twill end.
    Ber.   That's too long for a play.

    Enter *Braggart* [*Armado*].

    Arm. Sweet Majesty, vouchsafe me.
    Prin. Was not that Hector?
    Dum. The worthy knight of Troy.   890
    Arm. I will kiss thy royal finger, and take
leave. I am a votary: I have vow'd to Jaquenetta to hold the plough for her sweet love
three year. But, most esteemed greatness, will
you hear the Dialogue that the two learned
men have compiled in praise of the Owl and the
Cuckoo? It should have followed in the end of
our show.
    King. Call them forth quickly; we will do so.
    Arm. Holla! approach.   900

227

Enter *all* [*the rest*].

This side is Hiems, Winter; this Ver, the Spring: the one maintained by the Owl, th' other by the Cuckoo. Ver, begin.

The Song.

Spring. When daisies pied and violets blue
    And lady-smocks all silver-white 905
And cuckoo-buds of yellow hue
    Do paint the meadows with delight,
The cuckoo then on every tree,
Mocks married men; for thus sings he,
        'Cuckoo! 910
Cuckoo, cuckoo!' O word of fear,
Unpleasing to a married ear!

When shepherds pipe on oaten straws,
    And merry larks are ploughmen's
      clocks;
When turtles tread and rooks and daws,
    And maidens bleach their summer
      smocks, 916
The cuckoo then on every tree,
Mocks married men; for thus sings he:
       'Cuckoo!

Cuckoo, cuckoo!' O word of fear, 920
Unpleasing to a married ear!

Winter. When icicles hang by the wall,
    And Dick the shepherd blows his nail,
And Tom bears logs into the hall,
    And milk comes frozen home in pail,
When blood is nipp'd, and ways be foul,
Then nightly sings the staring owl: 927
      'Tu-who!
Tu-whit, tu-who!' a merry note,
While greasy Joan doth keel the pot. 930

When all aloud the wind doth blow,
    And coughing drowns the parson's saw,
And birds sit brooding in the snow,
    And Marian's nose looks red and raw;
When roasted crabs hiss in the bowl, 935
Then nightly sings the staring owl:
      'Tu-who!
Tu-whit, tu-who!' a merry note,
While greasy Joan doth keel the pot.

Arm. The words of Mercury are harsh after the songs of Apollo. You that way, we this way. 942
    Exeunt omnes.

A MIDSUMMER NIGHT'S DREAM

A MIDSUMMER NIGHT'S DREAM was entered in the Stationers' Register on October 8, 1600, by Thomas Fisher, and the First Quarto appeared before the end of the year. Though not very carefully printed, it furnishes an authoritative text. Probably the copy used was a manuscript prompt book, which may have been in Shakespeare's own handwriting. The Second Quarto (1619, fraudulently dated 1600) reprints the First, and the text in the First Folio comes from the Second Quarto.

In the Quartos there is no division into acts and scenes. Acts, but not scenes, are marked in the Folio. At the end of Act iii, the Folio adds the stage direction 'They sleepe all the Act,' which indicates that the four lovers remain on the stage, sleeping, until they are roused by the shouts and horn-blowing after iv, 1, 141.

The date of the play cannot be exactly determined. It may have been specially composed for some wedding festivity in high life. Ingenious scholars have suggested six different marriages, ranging all the way from 1590 to 1600, as possibilities. The first of these is certainly too early; the last is certainly too late. So far as style and metre testify, the play might be dated anywhere from 1594 to 1596. An allusion to the death of Robert Greene (in 1592) has been detected in v, 1, 52–55:

> ' The thrice three Muses mourning for the death
> Of Learning, late deceas'd in beggary.'
> That is some satire keen and critical,
> Not sorting with a nuptial ceremony.

Nothing could be less likely. Not the death of any particular person, but that of Learning in general, must have been the subject of this satirical show. This consideration likewise rules out the death of Tasso (1595). Of the other topical allusions suggested the only one that has any probability is Titania's account of the horrible weather and consequent distress that Oberon's brawls have caused (ii, 1, 81–117). This fits the actual condition of things in 1594, 1595, and 1596. Titania declares that spring, summer, autumn, and winter so 'change their wonted liveries' that one cannot tell 'which is which.' This suggests that at least a year has passed since the onset of bad weather and that no relief is in sight. The best choice among the three years, then, appears to be 1595.

The plot seems to be of Shakespeare's own design. The materials he drew from his general reading. He knew Chaucer's *Knight's Tale*, of course, which summarizes the main facts about Theseus and Hippolyta and mentions 'the feast' at their wedding. Plutarch's life of Theseus was accessible to him in Sir Thomas North's translation (1579), a work which he afterwards used extensively and minutely for his Roman plays. For Pyramus and Thisbe he had only to recall the Ovid that he had read at school.

The fairy lore goes back to tales that he had heard in childhood — 'Old Wives Fables,' Ady calls them, writing forty years after Shakespeare's death, told as they sit 'chatting of many false old Stories of Witches, and Fairies, and *Robin Good-fellow*, and walking Spirits, and the Dead walking again; all of which lying fancies people are more naturally inclined to listen after than to the Scriptures.' Bishop Corbet, not yet a bishop, was lost in a forest in the North about 1620. His man William was sure that Puck was 'busy in these oakes' and, when they met a forester, thought it was 'Robin, or some sprite that walkes about.' John Gadbury, as late as 1660, found it necessary to maintain that the *ignis fatuus* is a natural phenomenon and not an imp that leads one astray. Puck, as a name, goes back to Anglo-Saxon times. Shakespeare was not obliged to consult Reginald Scot's *Discoverie of Witchcraft* (1584) for information on English folklore, though he doubtless read the book with interest if it fell into his hands.

Bottom and his ass's head need not derive from either Lukios of Patræ or Apuleius; but, anyhow, Apuleius was accessible in Adlington's translation. Oberon and Titania, to be sure, were not names known in English folklore. Titania is a name for Circe in Ovid. Oberon had already been brought upon the stage as the fairy king in Robert Greene's *James IV*. His name occurs for the first time, so far as we know, in the Old French *chanson de geste* of *Huon de Bordeaux*, in which he is a woodland dwarf with magic powers who first embarrasses the hero but afterwards befriends him. The romance was well known in Shakespeare's time in Berners's translation. In 1593 and 1594 Henslow records in his *Diary* performances of an old play on the subject: he calls it *Hewen of Burdoche (Burdockes)*. Fairy plays and pageants had long been favourite entertainments with all ranks of society, and A MIDSUMMER NIGHT's DREAM did nothing to lessen their popularity. In Ben Jonson's masque of *Oberon*, performed at court on New Year's Day, 1611, the fairy prince enters in a chariot drawn by two white bears (see p. 431, below).

The most famous of all tributes to Queen Elizabeth is that of Oberon (in ii, 1, 155–164) to the 'fair Vestal throned by the West.'

A MIDSUMMER NIGHT'S DREAM

[Dramatis Personæ.

Theseus, Duke of Athens.
Egeus, father to *Hermia*.
Lysander, beloved of *Hermia*.
Demetrius, suitor to *Hermia*, approved by *Egeus*.
Philostrate, Master of the Revels to *Theseus*.

Peter Quince, a carpenter; *Prologue* in the interlude.
Nick Bottom, a weaver; *Pyramus* in the same.
Francis Flute, a bellows-mender; *Thisby* in the same.
Tom Snout, a tinker; *Wall* in the same.
Snug, a joiner; *Lion* in the same.
Robin Starveling, a tailor; *Moonshine* in the same.

Hippolyta, Queen of the Amazons, betrothed to *Theseus*.
Hermia, daughter to *Egeus*, in love with *Lysander*.
Helena, in love with *Demetrius*.

Oberon, King of the Fairies.
Titania, Queen of the Fairies.
Puck, or *Robin Goodfellow*.
Peaseblossom,
Cobweb,
Moth, } fairies.
Mustardseed,
Other Fairies attending *Oberon* and *Titania*. Attendants on *Theseus* and *Hippolyta*.

SCENE. *Athens, and a wood near by.*]

ACT I. [Scene I. *Athens. The Palace of* Theseus.]

Enter *Theseus, Hippolyta,* [*Philostrate,*]
with others.

The. Now, fair Hippolyta, our nuptial hour
Draws on apace. Four happy days bring in
Another moon; but, O, methinks, how slow
This old moon wanes! She lingers my desires,
Like to a stepdame or a dowager,   5
Long withering out a young man's revenue.
Hip. Four days will quickly steep themselves
in night;
Four nights will quickly dream away the time;
And then the moon, like to a silver bow
New-bent in heaven, shall behold the night 10
Of our solemnities.
The.   Go, Philostrate,
Stir up the Athenian youth to merriments,
Awake the pert and nimble spirit of mirth,
Turn melancholy forth to funerals;
The pale companion is not for our pomp. 15
              [*Exit Philostrate.*]
Hippolyta, I woo'd thee with my sword,
And won thy love doing thee injuries;
But I will wed thee in another key,
With pomp, with triumph, and with revelling.

Enter *Egeus* and his Daughter *Hermia*, and
Lysander and *Demetrius*.

Ege. Happy be Theseus, our renowned Duke!
The. Thanks, good Egeus. What's the news
with thee? 21
Ege. Full of vexation come I, with complaint
Against my child, my daughter Hermia.
Stand forth, Demetrius. My noble lord,
This man hath my consent to marry her. 25
Stand forth, Lysander. And, my gracious Duke,
This man hath bewitch'd the bosom of my child.
Thou, thou, Lysander, thou hast given her
rhymes
And interchang'd love tokens with my child;
Thou hast by moonlight at her window sung 30
With feigning voice verses of feigning love,
And stol'n the impression of her fantasy
With bracelets of thy hair, rings, gauds, conceits,
Knacks, trifles, nosegays, sweetmeats — messengers 34
Of strong prevailment in unharden'd youth.
With cunning hast thou filch'd my daughter's
heart;
Turn'd her obedience, which is due to me,

231

To stubborn harshness. And, my gracious Duke,
Be it so she will not here before your Grace
Consent to marry with Demetrius,   40
I beg the ancient privilege of Athens —
As she is mine, I may dispose of her;
Which shall be either to this gentleman
Or to her death, according to our law
Immediately provided in that case.   45
   The. What say you, Hermia? Be advis'd,
   fair maid.
To you your father should be as a god;
One that compos'd your beauties; yea, and one
To whom you are but as a form in wax,
By him imprinted, and within his power   50
To leave the figure, or disfigure it.
Demetrius is a worthy gentleman.
   Her. So is Lysander.
   The.   In himself he is;
But in this kind, wanting your father's voice,
The other must be held the worthier.   55
   Her. I would my father look'd but with my
   eyes.
   The. Rather your eyes must with his judg-
   ment look.
   Her. I do entreat your Grace to pardon me.
I know not by what power I am made bold,
Nor how it may concern my modesty   60
In such a presence here to plead my thoughts;
But I beseech your Grace that I may know
The worst that may befall me in this case
If I refuse to wed Demetrius.
   The. Either to die the death, or to abjure 65
For ever the society of men.
Therefore, fair Hermia, question your desires,
Know of your youth, examine well your blood,
Whether, if you yield not to your father's
   choice,
You can endure the livery of a nun,   70
For aye to be in shady cloister mew'd,
To live a barren sister all your life,
Chaunting faint hymns to the cold fruitless
   moon.
Thrice blessed they that master so their blood
To undergo such maiden pilgrimage;   75
But earthlier happy is the rose distill'd
Than that which, withering on the virgin thorn,
Grows, lives, and dies in single blessedness.
   Her. So will I grow, so live, so die, my lord,
Ere I will yield my virgin patent up   80
Unto his lordship whose unwished yoke
My soul consents not to give sovereignty.
   The. Take time to pause; and by the next
   new moon —
The sealing day betwixt my love and me
For everlasting bond of fellowship —   85

Upon that day either prepare to die
For disobedience to your father's will,
Or else to wed Demetrius, as he would,
Or on Diana's altar to protest
For aye austerity and single life.   90
   Dem. Relent, sweet Hermia; and, Lysander,
   yield
Thy crazed title to my certain right.
   Lys. You have her father's love, Demetrius;
Let me have Hermia's. Do you marry him.
   Ege. Scornful Lysander, true, he hath my
   love;   95
And what is mine my love shall render him;
And she is mine, and all my right of her
I do estate unto Demetrius.
   Lys. I am, my lord, as well deriv'd as he,
As well possess'd; my love is more than his;
My fortunes every way as fairly rank'd   101
(If not with vantage) as Demetrius';
And (which is more than all these boasts can be)
I am belov'd of beauteous Hermia.
Why should not I then prosecute my right? 105
Demetrius, I'll avouch it to his head,
Made love to Nedar's daughter, Helena,
And won her soul; and she (sweet lady) dotes,
Devoutly dotes, dotes in idolatry,
Upon this spotted and inconstant man.   110
   The. I must confess that I have heard so
   much,
And with Demetrius thought to have spoke
   thereof;
But, being over-full of self-affairs,
My mind did lose it. But, Demetrius, come;
And come, Egeus. You shall go with me;   115
I have some private schooling for you both.
For you, fair Hermia, look you arm yourself
To fit your fancies to your father's will;
Or else the law of Athens yields you up
(Which by no means we may extenuate)   120
To death or to a vow of single life.
Come, my Hippolyta. What cheer, my love?
Demetrius and Egeus, go along.
I must employ you in some business
Against our nuptial and confer with you   125
Of something nearly that concerns yourselves.
   Ege. With duty and desire we follow you.
       Exeunt. Manent Lysander and Hermia.
   Lys. How now, my love? Why is your cheek
   so pale?
How chance the roses there do fade so fast?
   Her. Belike for want of rain, which I could
   well   130
Beteem them from the tempest of my eyes.
   Lys. Ay me! for aught that I could ever read,
Could ever hear by tale or history,

The course of true love never did run smooth;
But, either it was different in blood — 135
Her. O cross! too high to be enthrall'd to low!
Lys. Or else misgraffed in respect of years —
Her. O spite! too old to be engag'd to young!
Lys. Or else it stood upon the choice of friends —
Her. O hell! to choose love by another's eyes! 140
Lys. Or, if there were a sympathy in choice,
War, death, or sickness did lay siege to it,
Making it momentany as a sound,
Swift as a shadow, short as any dream,
Brief as the lightning in the collied night, 145
That, in a spleen, unfolds both heaven and earth,
And ere a man hath power to say 'Behold!'
The jaws of darkness do devour it up:
So quick bright things come to confusion.
Her. If then true lovers have been ever cross'd, 150
It stands as an edict in destiny.
Then let us teach cur trial patience,
Because it is a customary cross,
As due to love as thoughts and dreams and sighs,
Wishes and tears, poor Fancy's followers. 155
Lys. A good persuasion. Therefore hear me, Hermia.
I have a widow aunt, a dowager,
Of great revenue, and she hath no child.
From Athens is her house remote seven leagues;
And she respects me as her only son. 160
There, gentle Hermia, may I marry thee;
And to that place the sharp Athenian law
Cannot pursue us. If thou lovest me then,
Steal forth thy father's house to-morrow night;
And in the wood, a league without the town, 165
Where I did meet thee once with Helena
To do observance to a morn of May,
There will I stay for thee.
Her.   My good Lysander!
I swear to thee by Cupid's strongest bow,
By his best arrow, with the golden head, 170
By the simplicity of Venus' doves,
By that which knitteth souls and prospers loves,
And by that fire which burn'd the Carthage queen
When the false Troyan under sail was seen,
By all the vows that ever men have broke 175
(In number more than ever women spoke),
In that same place thou hast appointed me
To-morrow truly will I meet with thee.
Lys. Keep promise, love. Look, here comes Helena.

Enter *Helena*.

Her. God speed fair Helena! Whither away?
Hel. Call you me fair? That fair again unsay. 181
Demetrius loves your fair. O happy fair!
Your eyes are lodestars, and your tongue's sweet air
More tuneable than lark to shepherd's ear
When wheat is green, when hawthorn buds appear. 185
Sickness is catching. O, were favour so,
Yours would I catch, fair Hermia, ere I go!
My ear should catch your voice, my eye your eye,
My tongue should catch your tongue's sweet melody. 189
Were the world mine, Demetrius being bated,
The rest I'ld give to be to you translated.
O, teach me how you look, and with what art
You sway the motion of Demetrius' heart!
Her. I frown upon him; yet he loves me still.
Hel. O that your frowns would teach my smiles such skill! 195
Her. I give him curses; yet he gives me love.
Hel. O that my prayers could such affection move!
Her. The more I hate, the more he follows me.
Hel. The more I love, the more he hateth me.
Her. His folly, Helena, is no fault of mine.
Hel. None but your beauty. Would that fault were mine! 201
Her. Take comfort. He no more shall see my face;
Lysander and myself will fly this place.
Before the time I did Lysander see,
Seem'd Athens as a paradise to me. 205
O, then, what graces in my love do dwell
That he hath turn'd a heaven unto a hell!
Lys. Helen, to you our minds we will unfold.
To-morrow night, when Phœbe doth behold
Her silver visage in the wat'ry glass, 210
Decking with liquid pearl the bladed grass
(A time that lovers' flights doth still conceal),
Through Athens gates have we devis'd to steal.
Her. And in the wood where often you and I 215
Upon faint primrose beds were wont to lie,
Emptying our bosoms of their counsel sweet,
There my Lysander and myself shall meet,
And thence from Athens turn away our eyes
To seek new friends and stranger companies.
Farewell, sweet playfellow. Pray thou for us:
And good luck grant thee thy Demetrius! 221

233

Keep word, Lysander. We must starve our sight
From lovers' food till morrow deep midnight.
Lys. I will, my Hermia.   *Exit Hermia.*
                Helena, adieu.
As you on him, Demetrius dote on you! *Exit.*
  Hel. How happy some o'er other some can be!
Through Athens I am thought as fair as she.
But what of that? Demetrius thinks not so,
He will not know what all but he do know.
And as he errs, doting on Hermia's eyes,   230
So I, admiring of his qualities.
Things base and vile, holding no quantity,
Love can transpose to form and dignity.
Love looks not with the eyes, but with the mind;
And therefore is wing'd Cupid painted blind. 235
Nor hath Love's mind of any judgment taste;
Wings, and no eyes, figure unheedy haste.
And therefore is Love said to be a child,
Because in choice he is so oft beguil'd.
As waggish boys in game themselves forswear,
So the boy Love is perjur'd everywhere;   241
For ere Demetrius look'd on Hermia's eyne,
He hail'd down oaths that he was only mine;
And when this hail some heat from Hermia felt,
So he dissolv'd, and show'rs of oaths did melt.
I will go tell him of fair Hermia's flight.   246
Then to the wood will he to-morrow night
Pursue her; and for this intelligence
If I have thanks, it is a dear expense;
But herein mean I to enrich my pain,   250
To have his sight thither and back again. *Exit.*

[Scene II. *Athens.* Quince's *house.*]

Enter *Quince* the Carpenter, and *Snug* the
Joiner, and *Bottom* the Weaver, and *Flute* the
Bellows-mender, and *Snout* the Tinker, and
Starveling the Tailor.

Quince. Is all our company here?
Bot. You were best to call them generally,
man by man, according to the scrip.
Quince. Here is the scroll of every man's
name which is thought fit, through all Athens,
to play in our enterlude before the Duke and
the Duchess on his wedding day at night.   7
Bot. First, good Peter Quince, say what the
play treats on; then read the names of the actors; and so grow to a point.   10
Quince. Marry, our play is 'The most Lamentable Comedy and most Cruel Death of
Pyramus and Thisby.'
Bot. A very good piece of work, I assure
you, and a merry. Now, good Peter Quince,
call forth your actors by the scroll. Masters,
spread yourselves.   17
Quince. Answer as I call you. Nick Bottom
the weaver.
Bot. Ready. Name what part I am for, and
proceed.   21
Quince. You, Nick Bottom, are set down for
Pyramus.
Bot. What is Pyramus? a lover, or a tyrant?
Quince. A lover that kills himself, most gallant, for love.   26
Bot. That will ask some tears in the true
performing of it. If I do it, let the audience
look to their eyes! I will move storms; I will
condole in some measure. To the rest. Yet my
chief humour is for a tyrant. I could play
Ercles rarely, or a part to tear a cat in, to make
all split.   32

      'The raging rocks
      And shivering shocks
      Shall break the locks   35
         Of prison gates;
      And Phibbus' car
      Shall shine from far
      And make and mar
         The foolish Fates.'   40

This was lofty! Now name the rest of the play-
ers. This is Ercles' vein, a tyrant's vein. A
lover is more condoling.
Quince. Francis Flute the bellows-mender.
Flute. Here, Peter Quince.   45
Quince. Flute, you must take Thisby on you.
Flute. What is Thisby? a wand'ring knight?
Quince. It is the lady that Pyramus must
love.
Flute. Nay, faith, let not me play a woman.
I have a beard coming.   50
Quince. That's all one. You shall play it in
a mask, and you may speak as small as you will.
Bot. An I may hide my face, let me play
Thisby too. I'll speak in a monstrous little
voice: — 'Thisne, Thisne!' 'Ah, Pyramus, my
lover dear! thy Thisby dear, and lady dear!'
Quince. No, no! you must play Pyramus;
and, Flute, you Thisby.
Bot. Well, proceed.
Quince. Robin Starveling the tailor.   60
Starv. Here, Peter Quince.
Quince. Robin Starveling, you must play
Thisby's mother. Tom Snout the tinker.
Snout. Here, Peter Quince.   64
Quince. You, Pyramus' father; myself,
Thisby's father; Snug, the joiner, you the
lion's part. And I hope here is a play fitted.

Robert Helpmann as Oberon, king of the fairies, and Moira Shearer as his queen, Titania

A MIDSUMMER-NIGHT'S DREAM

Philip Guard as Oberon's mischievous helper, Puck, whose pranks and antics twist the fates of both human and fairy lovers on a midsummer night

PHOTOGRAPHS BY HOUSTON ROGERS
PRODUCED BY THE OLD VIC COMPANY

Right: King Oberon. At odds with his queen, Titania, over her interest in Theseus and the possession of a changeling boy, he sends Puck to fetch a magic herb whose juice, placed in the eyes of the sleeping queen, will make her love the first thing she sees on waking

Below: The fairy king surrounded by a band of henchmen

Right: Titania, Oberon's beautiful but capricious wife

Below: Titania asleep in the forest, "Lull'd in these flowers with dances and delight" (*Act II, Scene I*)

Left: Margaret Courtenay as Hippolyta, the queen of the Amazons, betrothed of Theseus

Right: Theseus, Duke of Athens, played by Anthony Nicholls

Left: Joan Benham as Helena and Patrick MacNee as Demetrius

Right: Ann Walford as Hermia and Terence Longdon as Lysander

Left: Bottom (Stanley Holloway) in his role as the lover, Pyramus

Right: Eliot Makeham as Quince, the carpenter

"And maidens call it, Love-in-idleness. Fetch me that flower: the herb I show'd thee once." Oberon sends Puck for the magic herb with which he intends to revenge himself on Titania (*Act II, Scene I*)

"What thou seest when thou dost wake do it for thy true-love take." While Titania is sleeping, Oberon drops the juice of the magic herb into her eyes, casting a spell (*Act II, Scene II*)

Puck with the fairy Pease-Blossom (Jocelyn Britton), one of the four fairies assigned by Titania as Bottom's attendants (*Act III, Scene I*)

Puck, who has made himself invisible, annoys the Athenian craftsmen as they rehearse their play in the forest. Philip Locke in the role of Flute and Norman Rossington playing Snout (*Act III, Scene I*)

The craftsmen of Athens rehearse the play they intend to give to celebrate the nuptials of Duke Theseus (*Act III, Scene I*)

"If I were fair, Thisby, I were only thine." Changed into an ass, Bottom startles Flute (*Act III, Scene I*)

"Be kind and courteous to this gentleman." Infatuated with the donkey-headed Bottom through Oberon's spell, Titania orders her fairies to deck him in flowers (*Act III, Scene I*)

Titania dotes on the enraptured donkey head, Bottom (*Act III, Scene I*)

Lysander and Demetrius, both in love with Helena through the power of Oberon's drug, prevent Hermia from attacking her rival (*Act III, Scene II*)

Hunting in the forest, Theseus and Hippolyta find the sleeping lovers and waken them
(*Act IV, Scene I*)

Left: Bottom and his companions present their play to the duke (*Act V, Scene I*)

Below: Snug the Joiner (Michael Redington) as the Lion and Starveling the Tailor (Daniel Thorndike) as the Moon in the masque presented to celebrate the nuptials of Duke Theseus
(*Act V, Scene I*)

Below: Bottom and Flute in the nonsensical pantomime of Pyramus and Thisby. Snout portrays the wall through which the ill-fated couple whisper their love
(*Act V, Scene I*)

With the two pairs of lovers reunited before the throne, Theseus and his bride, Hippolyta watch
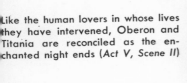 Bottom and his craftsmen players present the drama of Pyramus and Thisby (Act V, Scene I)

Like the human lovers in whose lives they have intervened, Oberon and Titania are reconciled as the en-chanted night ends (Act V, Scene II)

Snug. Have you the lion's part written? Pray you, if it be, give it me, for I am slow of study.

Quince. You may do it extempore, for it is nothing but roaring.   71

Bot. Let me play the lion too. I will roar that I will do any man's heart good to hear me. I will roar that I will make the Duke say 'Let him roar again; let him roar again.'   75

Quince. An you should do it too terribly, you would fright the Duchess and the ladies, that they would shrike; and that were enough to hang us all.   79

All. That would hang us, every mother's son.

Bot. I grant you, friends, if you should fright the ladies out of their wits, they would have no more discretion but to hang us; but I will aggravate my voice so that I will roar you as gently as any sucking dove; I will roar you an 'twere any nightingale.   86

Quince. You can play no part but Pyramus; for Pyramus is a sweet-fac'd man; a proper man as one shall see in a summer's day; a most lovely gentlemanlike man. Therefore you must needs play Pyramus.   91

Bot. Well, I will undertake it. What beard were I best to play it in?

Quince. Why, what you will.   94

Bot. I will discharge it in either your straw-colour beard, your orange-tawny beard, your purple-in-grain beard, or your French-crown-colour beard, your perfit yellow.   98

Quince. Some of your French crowns have no hair at all, and then you will play barefac'd. But, masters, here are your parts; and I am to entreat you, request you, and desire you to con them by to-morrow night; and meet me in the palace wood, a mile without the town, by moonlight. There will we rehearse; for if we meet in the city, we shall be dogg'd with company, and our devices known. In the meantime I will draw a bill of properties, such as our play wants. I pray you fail me not.   109

Bot. We will meet; and there we may rehearse most obscenely and courageously. Take pains; be perfit. Adieu.

Quince. At the Duke's Oak we meet.

Bot. Enough. Hold, or cut bowstrings.

Exeunt.

ACT II. [Scene I. *A wood near Athens.*]

Enter a *Fairy* at one door, and *Robin Goodfellow* at another.

Rob. How now, spirit? Whither wander you?

Fai. Over hill, over dale,
    Thorough bush, thorough brier,
Over park, over pale,
    Thorough flood, thorough fire;   5
I do wander everywhere,
Swifter than the moonës sphere;
And I serve the Fairy Queen,
To dew her orbs upon the green.
The cowslips tall her pensioners be;   10
In their gold coats 'spots you see.
Those be rubies, fairy favours;
In those freckles live their savours.
I must go seek some dewdrops here,
And hang a pearl in every cowslip's ear.   15
Farewell, thou lob of spirits; I'll be gone.
Our Queen and all her elves come here anon.

Rob. The King doth keep his revels here to-night.
Take heed the Queen come not within his sight.
For Oberon is passing fell and wrath,   20
Because that she, as her attendant, hath
A lovely boy, stolen from an Indian king;

She never had so sweet a changeling.
And jealous Oberon would have the child
Knight of his train, to trace the forests wild;   25
But she perforce withholds the loved boy,
Crowns him with flowers, and makes him all her joy.
And now they never meet in grove or green,
By fountain clear or spangled starlight sheen,
But they do square, that all their elves, for fear,
Creep into acorn cups and hide them there.   31

Fai. Either I mistake your shape and making quite,
Or else you are that shrewd and knavish sprite
Call'd Robin Goodfellow. Are not you he
That frights the maidens of the villagery;   35
Skim milk, and sometimes labour in the quern,
And bootless make the breathless housewife churn;
And sometime make the drink to bear no barm;
Mislead night-wanderers, laughing at their harm?
Those that Hobgoblin call you, and sweet Puck,
You do their work, and they shall have good luck.   41
Are not you he?

Rob.   Thou speakest aright;
I am that merry wanderer of the night.
I jest to Oberon, and make him smile
When I a fat and bean-fed horse beguile, 45
Neighing in likeness of a filly foal;
And sometime lurk I in a gossip's bowl
In very likeness of a roasted crab,
And when she drinks, against her lips I bob
And on her withered dewlap pour the ale. 50
The wisest aunt, telling the saddest tale,
Sometime for three-foot stool mistaketh me;
Then slip I from her bum, down topples she,
And 'tailor' cries, and falls into a cough;
And then the whole quire hold their hips and
    loffe, 55
And waxen in their mirth, and neeze, and swear
A merrier hour was never wasted there.
But room, fairy! Here comes Oberon.
    Fai. And here my mistress. Would that he
      were gone!

Enter [*Oberon*] *the* King of Fairies, *at one door,*
with his Train; *and the* Queen, [*Titania,*] *at*
another, with hers.

    Ob. Ill met by moonlight, proud Titania. 60
    Queen. What, jealous Oberon? Fairies, skip
    hence.
I have forsworn his bed and company.
    Ob. Tarry, rash wanton. Am not I thy lord?
    Queen. Then I must be thy lady; but I know
When thou hast stolen away from fairyland, 65
And in the shape of Corin sat all day,
Playing on pipes of corn, and versing love
To amorous Phillida. Why art thou here,
Come from the farthest steep of India,
But that, forsooth, the bouncing Amazon, 70
Your buskin'd mistress and your warrior love,
To Theseus must be wedded, and you come
To give their bed joy and prosperity?
    Ob. How canst thou thus, for shame, Titania,
Glance at my credit with Hippolyta, 75
Knowing I know thy love to Theseus?
Didst thou not lead him through the glimmer-
    ing night
From Perigouna, whom he ravished?
And make him with fair Ægles break his faith,
With Ariadne, and Antiopa? 80
    Queen. These are the forgeries of jealousy;
And never, since the middle summer's spring,
Met we on hill, in dale, forest, or mead,
By paved fountain or by rushy brook,
Or in the beached margent of the sea, 85
To dance our ringlets to the whistling wind,
But with thy brawls thou hast disturb'd our
    sport.

Therefore the winds, piping to us in vain,
As in revenge, have suck'd up from the sea
Contagious fogs; which falling in the land 90
Hath every pelting river made so proud
That they have overborne their continents.
The ox hath therefore stretch'd his yoke in vain,
The ploughman lost his sweat, and the green
    corn
Hath rotted ere his youth attain'd a beard; 95
The fold stands empty in the drowned field,
And crows are fatted with the murrion flock;
The nine men's morris is fill'd up with mud;
And the quaint mazes in the wanton green
For lack of tread are undistinguishable. 100
The human mortals want their winter cheer;
No night is now with hymn or carol blest.
Therefore the moon, the governess of floods,
Pale in her anger, washes all the air,
That rheumatic diseases do abound. 105
And thorough this distemperature we see
The seasons alter. Hoary-headed frosts
Fall in the fresh lap of the crimson rose;
And on old Hiems' thin and icy crown
An odorous chaplet of sweet summer buds 110
Is, as in mockery, set. The spring, the summer,
The childing autumn, angry winter change
Their wonted liveries; and the mazed world,
By their increase, now knows not which is which.
And this same progeny of evils comes 115
From our debate, from our dissension;
We are their parents and original.
    Ob. Do you amend it then; it lies in you.
Why should Titania cross her Oberon?
I do but beg a little changeling boy 120
To be my henchman.
    Queen.   Set your heart at rest.
The fairyland buys not the child of me.
His mother was a vot'ress of my order;
And in the spiced Indian air, by night,
Full often hath she gossip'd by my side, 125
And sat with me on Neptune's yellow sands,
Marking th' embarked traders on the flood;
When we have laugh'd to see the sails conceive
And grow big-bellied with the wanton wind;
Which she, with pretty and with swimming gait
Following (her womb then rich with my young
    squire) 131
Would imitate, and sail upon the land
To fetch me trifles, and return again,
As from a voyage, rich with merchandise.
But she, being mortal, of that boy did die, 135
And for her sake do I rear up her boy;
And for her sake I will not part with him.
    Ob. How long within this wood intend you
    stay?

Queen. Perchance till after Theseus' wedding
  day.
If you will patiently dance in our round   140
And see our moonlight revels, go with us.
If not, shun me, and I will spare your haunts.
  Ob. Give me that boy, and I will go with
    thee.
  Queen. Not for thy fairy kingdom. Fairies,
    away!
We shall chide downright if I longer stay.   145
          Exeunt [*Titania and her Train*].
  Ob. Well, go thy way. Thou shalt not from
    this grove
Till I torment thee for this injury.
My gentle Puck, come hither. Thou remem-
  b'rest
Since once I sat upon a promontory   149
And heard a mermaid, on a dolphin's back,
Uttering such dulcet and harmonious breath
That the rude sea grew civil at her song,
And certain stars shot madly from their spheres
To hear the sea-maid's music.
    Puck.   I remember.
  Ob. That very time I saw (but thou couldst
    not)   155
Flying between the cold moon and the earth
Cupid, all arm'd. A certain aim he took
At a fair Vestal, throned by the West,
And loos'd his love-shaft smartly from his bow,
As it should pierce a hundred thousand hearts.
But I might see young Cupid's fiery shaft   161
Quench'd in the chaste beams of the wat'ry
  moon,
And the imperial vot'ress passed on,
In maiden meditation, fancy-free.
Yet mark'd I where the bolt of Cupid fell.   165
It fell upon a little Western flower,
Before milk-white, now purple with love's
  wound,
And maidens call it love-in-idleness.
Fetch me that flow'r; the herb I show'd thee
  once.
The juice of it, on sleeping eyelids laid,   170
Will make or man or woman madly dote
Upon the next live creature that it sees.
Fetch me this herb, and be thou here again
Ere the Leviathan can swim a league.   174
  Puck. I'll put a girdle round about the earth
In forty minutes.   [*Exit*.]
  Ob.   Having once this juice,
I'll watch Titania when she is asleep
And drop the liquor of it in her eyes.
The next thing then she, waking, looks upon
(Be it on lion, bear, or wolf, or bull,   180
On meddling monkey, or on busy ape)

She shall pursue it with the soul of love.
And ere I take this charm from off her sight
(As I can take it with another herb)
I'll make her render up her page to me.   185
But who comes here? I am invisible,
And I will overhear their conference.

    Enter *Demetrius, Helena* following him.

  Dem. I love thee not; therefore pursue me
    not.
Where is Lysander and fair Hermia?
The one I'll slay, the other slayeth me.   190
Thou told'st me they were stol'n unto this
  wood;
And here am I, and wood within this wood
Because I cannot meet my Hermia.
Hence, get thee gone, and follow me no more!
  Hel. You draw me, you hard-hearted ada-
    mant!   195
But yet you draw not iron, for my heart
Is true as steel. Leave you your power to draw,
And I shall have no power to follow you.
  Dem. Do I entice you? Do I speak you fair?
Or rather do I not in plainest truth   200
Tell you I do not nor I cannot love you?
  Hel. And even for that do I love you the
    more.
I am your spaniel; and, Demetrius,
The more you beat me, I will fawn on you.
Use me but as your spaniel — spurn me, strike
  me,   205
Neglect me, lose me; only give me leave
(Unworthy as I am) to follow you.
What worser place can I beg in your love
(And yet a place of high respect with me)
Than to be used as you use your dog?   210
  Dem. Tempt not too much the hatred of my
    spirit;
For I am sick when I do look on thee.
  Hel. And I am sick when I look not on
    you.
  Dem. You do impeach your modesty too
    much
To leave the city and commit yourself   215
Into the hands of one that loves you not;
To trust the opportunity of night
And the ill counsel of a desert place
With the rich worth of your virginity.
  Hel. Your virtue is my privilege. For that
It is not night when I do see your face,   221
Therefore I think I am not in the night;
Nor doth this wood lack worlds of company,
For you, in my respect, are all the world.
Then how can it be said I am alone   225
When all the world is here to look on me?

Dem. I'll run from thee and hide me in the brakes
And leave thee to the mercy of wild beasts.
Hel. The wildest hath not such a heart as you.
Run when you will. The story shall be chang'd:
Apollo flies, and Daphne holds the chase;   231
The dove pursues the griffon; the mild hind
Makes speed to catch the tiger — bootless speed,
When cowardice pursues, and valour flies!
Dem. I will not stay thy questions. Let me go!   235
Or if thou follow me, do not believe
But I shall do thee mischief in the wood.
Hel. Ay, in the temple, in the town, the field
You do me mischief. Fie, Demetrius!
Your wrongs do set a scandal on my sex.   240
We cannot fight for love, as men may do;
We should be woo'd, and were not made to woo.
                              [*Exit Demetrius.*]
I'll follow thee, and make a heaven of hell,
To die upon the hand I love so well.   *Exit.*
Ob. Fare thee well, nymph. Ere he do leave this grove,   245
Thou shalt fly him, and he shall seek thy love.

Enter *Puck.*

Hast thou the flower there? Welcome, wanderer.
Puck. Ay, there it is.
Ob.   I pray thee give it me.
I know a bank where the wild thyme blows,
Where oxlips and the nodding violet grows;
Quite over-canopied with luscious woodbine,
With sweet musk-roses, and with eglantine.
There sleeps Titania sometime of the night,
Lull'd in these flowers with dances and delight;
And there the snake throws her enamell'd skin,
Weed wide enough to wrap a fairy in;   256
And with the juice of this I'll streak her eyes
And make her full of hateful fantasies.
Take thou some of it and seek through this grove.
A sweet Athenian lady is in love   260
With a disdainful youth. Anoint his eyes;
But do it when the next thing he espies
May be the lady. Thou shalt know the man
By the Athenian garments he hath on.
Effect it with some care, that he may prove   265
More fond on her than she upon her love;
And look thou meet me ere the first cock crow.
Puck. Fear not, my lord; your servant shall do so.   *Exeunt.*

[Scene II. *Another part of the wood.*]

Enter *Titania, Queen of Fairies*, with her *Train.*

Queen. Come, now a roundel and a fairy song;
Then, for the third part of a minute, hence —
Some to kill cankers in the musk-rose buds,
Some war with reremice for their leathren wings,
To make my small elves coats, and some keep back   5
The clamorous owl, that nightly hoots and wonders
At our quaint spirits. Sing me now asleep.
Then to your offices, and let me rest.

Fairies sing.

1. Fai. You spotted snakes with double tongue,   9
        Thorny hedgehogs, be not seen;
    Newts and blindworms, do no wrong,
        Come not near our Fairy Queen.

[CHORUS.]

    Philomele, with melody
    Sing in our sweet lullaby;
    Lulla, lulla, lullaby; lulla, lulla, lullaby: 15
        Never harm
        Nor spell nor charm
    Come our lovely lady nigh.
    So good night, with lullaby.

1. Fai. Weaving spiders, come not here;   20
        Hence, you long-legg'd spinners, hence!
    Beetles black, approach not near;
        Worm nor snail, do no offence.

[CHORUS.]

Philomele, with melody, &c.
                              She sleeps.

2. Fai. Hence, away! Now all is well.   25
    One aloof stand sentinel.
                              [*Exeunt Fairies.*]

Enter *Oberon*, [and squeezes the flower on *Titania's* eyelids].

Ob. What thou seest when thou dost wake,
    Do it for thy true-love take;
    Love and languish for his sake.
    Be it ounce or cat or bear,   30
    Pard, or boar with bristled hair
    In thy eye that shall appear
    When thou wak'st, it is thy dear.
    Wake when some vile thing is near.
                              [*Exit.*]

Enter *Lysander* and *Hermia*.

Lys. Fair love, you faint with wand'ring in
  the wood;   35
And to speak troth, I have forgot our way.
We'll rest us, Hermia, if you think it good,
And tarry for the comfort of the day.
Her. Be it so, Lysander. Find you out a
  bed;
For I upon this bank will rest my head.   40
Lys. One turf shall serve as pillow for us
  both;
One heart, one bed, two bosoms, and one troth.
Her. Nay, good Lysander. For my sake,
  my dear,
Lie further off yet; do not lie so near.
Lys. O, take the sense, sweet, of my inno-
  cence!   45
Love takes the meaning in love's conference.
I mean that my heart unto yours is knit,
So that but one heart we can make of it;
Two bosoms interchained with an oath —
So then two bosoms and a single troth.   50
Then by your side no bed-room me deny;
For lying so, Hermia, I do not lie.
Her. Lysander riddles very prettily.
Now much beshrew my manners and my pride
If Hermia meant to say Lysander lied!   55
But, gentle friend, for love and courtesy
Lie further off, in humane modesty;
Such separation as may well be said
Becomes a virtuous bachelor and a maid,
So far be distant; and good night, sweet friend.
Thy love ne'er alter till thy sweet life end!   61
Lys. Amen, amen, to that fair prayer say I,
And then end life when I end loyalty!
Here is my bed. Sleep give thee all his rest!
Her. With half that wish the wisher's eyes
  be press'd!   *They sleep.*

Enter *Puck.*

Puck. Through the forest have I gone,   66
But Athenian found I none
On whose eyes I might approve
This flower's force in stirring love.
Night and silence! Who is here?   70
Weeds of Athens he doth wear.
This is he (my master said)
Despised the Athenian maid;
And here the maiden, sleeping sound
On the dank and dirty ground.   75
Pretty soul! she durst not lie
Near this lack-love, this kill-courtesy.
Churl, upon thy eyes I throw
All the power this charm doth owe.

When thou wak'st, let love forbid   80
Sleep his seat on thy eyelid.
So awake when I am gone;
For I must now to Oberon.   *Exit.*

Enter *Demetrius* and *Helena,* running.

Hel. Stay, though thou kill me, sweet De-
  metrius.
Dem. I charge thee, hence, and do not haunt
  me thus.   85
Hel. O, wilt thou darkling leave me? Do
  not so.
Dem. Stay, on thy peril! I alone will go.
                          Exit.
Hel. O, I am out of breath in this fond chase!
The more my prayer, the lesser is my grace.
Happy is Hermia, wheresoe'er she lies;   90
For she hath blessed and attractive eyes.
How came her eyes so bright? Not with salt
  tears.
If so, my eyes are oft'ner wash'd than hers.
No, no! I am as ugly as a bear;
For beasts that meet me run away for fear.   95
Therefore no marvel though Demetrius
Do, as a monster, fly my presence thus.
What wicked and dissembling glass of mine
Made me compare with Hermia's sphery eyne?
But who is here? Lysander! on the ground?
Dead, or asleep? I see no blood, no wound.
Lysander, if you live, good sir, awake.   102
Lys. [*starts up*] And run through fire I will
  for thy sweet sake.
Transparent Helena! Nature shows art,
That through thy bosom makes me see thy
  heart.   105
Where is Demetrius? O, how fit a word
Is that vile name to perish on my sword!
Hel. Do not say so, Lysander; say not so.
What though he love your Hermia? Lord!
  what though?   109
Yet Hermia still loves you. Then be content.
Lys. Content with Hermia? No! I do repent
The tedious minutes I with her have spent.
Not Hermia, but Helena I love.
Who will not change a raven for a dove?
The will of man is by his reason sway'd;   115
And reason says you are the worthier maid.
Things growing are not ripe until their season;
So I, being young, till now ripe not to reason;
And touching now the point of human skill,
Reason becomes the marshal to my will   120
And leads me to your eyes; where I o'erlook
Love's stories, written in Love's richest book.
Hel. Wherefore was I to this keen mockery
  born?

When at your hands did I deserve this scorn?
Is't not enough, is't not enough, young man,
That I did never, no, nor never can,   126
Deserve a sweet look from Demetrius' eye,
But you must flout my insufficiency?
Good troth, you do me wrong! good sooth,
      you do!
In such disdainful manner me to woo.   130
But fare you well. Perforce I must confess
I thought you lord of more true gentleness.
O, that a lady, of one man refus'd,
Should of another therefore be abus'd!   *Exit.*
  Lys. She sees not Hermia. Hermia, sleep
      thou there,   135
And never mayst thou come Lysander near!
For, as a surfeit of the sweetest things
The deepest loathing to the stomach brings,
Or as the heresies that men do leave
Are hated most of those they did deceive, 140

So thou, my surfeit and my heresy,
Of all be hated, but the most of me!
And, all my powers, address your love and
      might
To honour Helen and to be her knight!   *Exit.*
  Her. [*awakes*] Help me, Lysander, help me!
      Do thy best   145
To pluck this crawling serpent from my breast!
Ay me, for pity! What a dream was here!
Lysander, look how I do quake with fear.
Methought a serpent eat my heart away,
And you sat smiling at his cruel prey.   150
Lysander! What, remov'd? Lysander! lord!
What, out of hearing? gone? No sound, no
      word?
Alack, where are you? Speak, an if you hear.
Speak, of all loves! I swoon almost with fear.
No? Then I well perceive you are not nigh. 155
Either death or you I'll find immediately. *Exit.*

ACT III. [Scene I. *The wood.* Titania *lying asleep.*]

Enter the Clowns — [*Quince, Snug, Bottom,
      Flute, Snout,* and *Starveling*].

  Bot. Are we all met?
  Quince. Pat, pat; and here's a marvaill's
convenient place for our rehearsal. This green
plot shall be our stage, this hawthorn brake
our tiring house, and we will do it in action as
we will do it before the Duke.   6
  Bot. Peter Quince!
  Quince. What sayest thou, bully Bottom?
  Bot. There are things in this Comedy of
Pyramus and Thisby that will never please.
First, Pyramus must draw a sword to kill himself; which the ladies cannot abide. How answer you that?
  Snout. By'r lakin, a parlous fear!
  Starv. I believe we must leave the killing
out, when all is done.   16
  Bot. Not a whit. I have a device to make
all well. Write me a prologue; and let the prologue seem to say, we will do no harm with our
swords, and that Pyramus is not kill'd indeed;
and for the more better assurance, tell them
that I Pyramus am not Pyramus, but Bottom
the weaver. This will put them out of fear.
  Quince. Well, we will have such a prologue,
and it shall be written in eight and six.   25
  Bot. No, make it two more; let it be written
in eight and eight.
  Snout. Will not the ladies be afeard of the
lion?

  Starv. I fear it, I promise you.   29
  Bot. Masters, you ought to consider with
yourselves, to bring in (God shield us!) a lion
among ladies is a most dreadful thing. For
there is not a more fearful wild-fowl than your
lion living; and we ought to look to't.
  Snout. Therefore another prologue must tell
he is not a lion.   36
  Bot. Nay, you must name his name, and
half his face must be seen through the lion's
neck, and he himself must speak through, saying thus, or to the same defect: 'Ladies,' — or
'Fair ladies, — I would wish you' — or 'I
would request you' — or 'I would entreat you
— not to fear, not to tremble. My life for
yours! If you think I come hither as a lion, it
were pity of my life. No! I am no such thing.
I am a man as other men are.' And there, indeed, let him name his name and tell them
plainly he is Snug the joiner.
  Quince. Well, it shall be so. But there is
two hard things: that is, to bring the moonlight
into a chamber; for, you know, Pyramus and
Thisby meet by moonlight.   51
  Snout. Doth the moon shine that night we
play our play?
  Bot. A calendar, a calendar! Look in the almanac. Find out moonshine, find out moonshine!   55
  Quince. Yes, it doth shine that night.
  Bot. Why, then may you leave a casement
of the great chamber window, where we play,

open, and the moon may shine in at the casement. 59

Quince. Ay; or else one must come in with a bush of thorns and a lantern, and say he comes to disfigure, or to present, the person of Moonshine. Then there is another thing. We must have a wall in the great chamber; for Pyramus and Thisby, says the story, did talk through the chink of a wall. 66

Snout. You can never bring in a wall. What say you, Bottom?

Bot. Some man or other must present Wall; and let him have some plaster, or some loam, or some roughcast about him, to signify wall; and let him hold his fingers thus; and through that cranny shall Pyramus and Thisby whisper.

Quince. If that may be, then all is well. Come, sit down every mother's son, and rehearse your parts. Pyramus, you begin. When you have spoken your speech, enter into that brake; and so every one according to his cue.

Enter Robin [Goodfellow].

Rob. What hempen homespuns have we swagg'ring here, So near the cradle of the Fairy Queen? 80 What, a play toward? I'll be an auditor; An actor too perhaps, if I see cause.

Quince. Speak, Pyramus. Thisby, stand forth.

Pyr. Thisby, the flowers of odious savours sweet —

Quince. Odorous! odorous! 85

Pyr. —— odours savours sweet; So hath thy breath, my dearest Thisby dear. But hark, a voice! Stay thou but here awhile, And by-and-by I will to thee appear. *Exit.*

Rob. A stranger Pyramus than e'er play'd here! [*Exit.*]

This. Must I speak now? 91

Quince. Ay, marry, must you; for you must understand he goes but to see a noise that he heard, and is to come again.

This. Most radiant Pyramus, most lily-white of hue, 95 Of colour like the red rose on triumphant brier, Most brisky juvenal, and eke most lovely Jew, As true as truest horse, that yet would never tire, I'll meet thee, Pyramus, at Ninny's tomb. 99

Quince. 'Ninus' tomb,' man! Why, you must not speak that yet. That you answer to Pyramus. You speak all your part at once, cues and all. Pyramus, enter. Your cue is past; it is 'never tire.'

This. O — As true as truest horse, that yet would never tire. 105

[Enter *Robin*, and] *Pyramus* with an ass-head.

Pyr. If I were fair, Thisby, I were only thine.

Quince. O monstrous! O strange! We are haunted. Pray, masters! Fly, masters! Help!

Exeunt all the Clowns [but Bottom].

Rob. I'll follow you; I'll lead you about a round, Through bog, through bush, through brake, through brier. 110 Sometime a horse I'll be, sometime a hound, A hog, a headless bear, sometime a fire; And neigh, and bark, and grunt, and roar, and burn, Like horse, hound, hog, bear, fire, at every turn. *Exit.*

Bot. Why do they run away? This is a knavery of them to make me afeard. 116

Enter Snout.

Snout. O Bottom, thou art chang'd! What do I see on thee?

Bot. What do you see? You see an ass-head of your own, do you? [*Exit Snout.*]

Enter Quince.

Quince. Bless thee, Bottom! bless thee! Thou art translated. *Exit.*

Bot. I see their knavery. This is to make an ass of me; to fright me, if they could. But I will not stir from this place, do what they can. I will walk up and down here, and will sing, that they shall hear I am not afraid. [*Sings.*]

The woosel cock so black of hue, With orange-tawny bill, The throstle with his note so true, 130 The wren with little quill —

Tita. What angel wakes me from my flow'ry bed?

Bot. [*sings*]

The finch, the sparrow, and the lark, The plain-song cuckoo gray, Whose note full many a man doth mark, And dares not answer nay. 136

For, indeed, who would set his wit to so foolish a bird? Who would give a bird the lie, though he cry 'cuckoo' never so?

Tita. I pray thee, gentle mortal, sing again. Mine ear is much enamoured of thy note; 141 So is mine eye enthralled to thy shape; And thy fair virtue's force (perforce) doth move me, On the first view, to say, to swear, I love thee.

Bot. Methinks, mistress, you should have little reason for that. And yet, to say the truth, reason and love keep little company together now-a-days. The more the pity that some honest neighbours will not make them friends. Nay, I can gleek, upon occasion. 150

Tita. Thou art as wise as thou art beautiful.

Bot. Not so, neither; but if I had wit enough to get out of this wood, I have enough to serve mine own turn. 154

Tita. Out of this wood do not desire to go.
Thou shalt remain here, whether thou wilt or no.
I am a spirit of no common rate,
The summer still doth tend upon my state;
And I do love thee. Therefore go with me.
I'll give thee fairies to attend on thee; 160
And they shall fetch thee jewels from the deep,
And sing while thou on pressed flowers dost sleep;
And I will purge thy mortal grossness so
That thou shalt like an airy spirit go.
Peaseblossom! Cobweb! Moth! and Mustard-
seed! 165

Enter four Fairies — [Peaseblossom, Cobweb, Moth, and Mustardseed].

Peas. Ready.
Cob. And I.
Moth.   And I.
Must.   And I.
All.   Where shall we go?

Tita. Be kind and courteous to this gentle-
man.
Hop in his walks and gambol in his eyes;
Feed him with apricocks and dewberries,
With purple grapes, green figs, and mulberries;
The honey-bags steal from the humblebees, 171
And for night tapers crop their waxen thighs,
And light them at the fiery glowworm's eyes,
To have my love to bed and to arise;
And pluck the wings from painted butterflies
To fan the moonbeams from his sleeping eyes.
Nod to him, elves, and do him courtesies.

Peas. Hail, mortal!
Cob. Hail!
Moth. Hail!   180
Must. Hail!

Bot. I cry your worships mercy, heartily. I beseech your worship's name.

Cob. Cobweb.   184

Bot. I shall desire you of more acquaintance, good Master Cobweb. If I cut my finger, I shall make bold with you. Your name, honest gentleman?

Peas. Peaseblossom.   189

Bot. I pray you, commend me to Mistress Squash, your mother, and to Master Peascod, your father. Good Master Peaseblossom, I shall desire you of more acquaintance too. Your name, I beseech you, sir?

Must. Mustardseed.   195

Bot. Good Master Mustardseed, I know your patience well. That same cowardly, giantlike ox-beef hath devour'd many a gentleman of your house. I promise you your kindred hath made my eyes water ere now. I desire you of more acquaintance, good Master Mustardseed.

Tita. Come wait upon him; lead him to my bower.
The moon, methinks, looks with a wat'ry eye;
And when she weeps, weeps every little flower,
Lamenting some enforced chastity. 205
Tie up my love's tongue, bring him silently.
Exeunt.

[Scene II. *Another part of the wood.*]

Enter [Oberon,] King of Fairies.

Ob. I wonder if Titania be awak'd;
Then, what it was that next came in her eye,
Which she must dote on in extremity.

Enter Puck.

Here comes my messenger. How now, mad
spirit? 4
What night-rule now about this haunted grove?

Puck. My mistress with a monster is in love.
Near to her close and consecrated bower,
While she was in her dull and sleeping hour,
A crew of patches, rude mechanicals,
That work for bread upon Athenian stalls, 10
Were met together to rehearse a play,
Intended for great Theseus' nuptial day.
The shallowest thickskin of that barren sort,
Who Pyramus presented in their sport,
Forsook his scene and ent'red in a brake. 15
When I did him at this advantage take,
An ass's nole I fixed on his head.
Anon his Thisby must be answered,
And forth my mimic comes. When they him
spy,
As wild geese that the creeping fowler eye, 20
Or russet-pated choughs, many in sort,
Rising and cawing at the gun's report,
Sever themselves and madly sweep the sky;
So at his sight away his fellows fly; 24
And, at a stump, here o'er and o'er one falls;
He murther cries and help from Athens calls.

Their sense thus weak, lost with their fears thus
   strong,
Made senseless things begin to do them wrong;
For briers and thorns at their apparel snatch;
Some, sleeves — some, hats; from yielders all
   things catch.   30
I led them on in this distracted fear
And left sweet Pyramus translated there;
When in that moment (so it came to pass)
Titania wak'd, and straightway lov'd an ass.
  Ob. This falls out better than I could devise.
But hast thou yet latch'd the Athenian's eyes
With the love-juice, as I did bid thee do?
  Rob. I took him sleeping (that is finish'd too)
And the Athenian woman by his side,   39
That, when he wak'd, of force she must be ey'd.

     Enter *Demetrius* and *Hermia.*

  Ob. Stand close. This is the same Athenian.
  Rob. This is the woman; but not this the
   man.
  Dem. O, why rebuke you him that loves you
   so?
Lay breath so bitter on your bitter foe.
  Her. Now I but chide; but I should use
   thee worse,   45
For thou, I fear, hast given me cause to curse.
If thou hast slain Lysander in his sleep,
Being o'er shoes in blood, plunge in the deep,
And kill me too.
The sun was not so true unto the day   50
As he to me. Would he have stolen away
From sleeping Hermia? I'll believe as soon
This whole earth may be bor'd, and that the
   moon
May through the centre creep, and so displease
Her brother's noontide with th' Antipodes. 55
It cannot be but thou hast murth'red him.
So should a murtherer look — so dead, so grim.
  Dem. So should the murthered look, and so
   should I,
Pierc'd through the heart with your stern
   cruelty.
Yet you, the murtherer, look as bright, as clear,
As yonder Venus in her glimmering sphere.   61
  Her. What's this to my Lysander? Where
   is he?
Ah, good Demetrius, wilt thou give him me?
  Dem. I had rather give his carcass to my
   hounds.
  Her. Out, dog! out, cur! Thou driv'st me
   past the bounds   65
Of maiden's patience. Hast thou slain him
   then?
Henceforth be never numb'red among men!

O, once tell true! tell true, even for my sake!
Durst thou have look'd upon him, being awake?
And hast thou kill'd him sleeping? O brave
   touch!   70
Could not a worm, an adder, do so much?
An adder did it; for with doubler tongue
Than thine (thou serpent!) never adder stung.
  Dem. You spend your passion on a mispris'd
   mood.
I am not guilty of Lysander's blood;   75
Nor is he dead, for aught that I can tell.
  Her. I pray thee, tell me then that he is well.
  Dem. An if I could, what should I get there-
   fore?
  Her. A privilege never to see me more;
And from thy hated presence part I so.   80
See me no more, whether he be dead or no.
                     Exit.
  Dem. There is no following her in this fierce
   vein.
Here therefore for a while I will remain.
So sorrow's heaviness doth heavier grow   84
For debt that bankrout sleep doth sorrow owe;
Which now in some slight measure it will pay,
If for his tender here I make some stay.
              Lie down [*and sleep*].
  Ob. What hast thou done? Thou hast mis-
   taken quite
And laid the love-juice on some true-love's
   sight.
Of thy misprision must perforce ensue   90
Some true-love turn'd, and not a false turn'd
   true.
  Rob. The fate o'errules, that, one man hold-
   ing troth,
A million fail, confounding oath on oath.
  Ob. About the wood! Go swifter than the
   wind,
And Helena of Athens look thou find.   95
All fancy-sick she is, and pale of cheer
With sighs of love, that costs the fresh blood
   dear.
By some illusion see thou bring her here.
I'll charm his eyes against she do appear.
  Rob. I go, I go! Look how I go!   100
Swifter than arrow from the Tartar's bow.
                     Exit.
  Ob.   Flower of this purple dye,
       Hit with Cupid's archery,
       Sink in apple of his eye!
       When his love he doth espy,   105
       Let her shine as gloriously
       As the Venus of the sky.
       When thou wak'st, if she be by,
       Beg of her for remedy.

Enter *Puck*.

Puck. Captain of our fairy band, 110
Helena is here at hand,
And the youth, mistook by me,
Pleading for a lover's fee.
Shall we their fond pageant see?
Lord, what fools these mortals be!
Ob. Stand aside. The noise they make
Will cause Demetrius to awake. 117
Puck. Then will two at once woo one.
That must needs be sport alone;
And those things do best please me
That befall prepost'rously. 121

Enter *Lysander* and *Helena*.

Lys. Why should you think that I should
woo in scorn?
Scorn and derision never come in tears.
Look, when I vow, I weep; and vows so born,
In their nativity all truth appears. 125
How can these things in me seem scorn to you,
Bearing the badge of faith to prove them true?
Hel. You do advance your cunning more and
more.
When truth kills truth, O devilish-holy fray!
Those vows are Hermia's. Will you give her o'er?
Weigh oath with oath, and you will nothing
weigh. 131
Your vows to her and me, put in two scales,
Will even weigh; and both as light as tales.
Lys. I had no judgment when to her I swore.
Hel. Nor none, in my mind, now you give
her o'er. 135
Lys. Demetrius loves her; and he loves not
you.
Dem. (*awakes*) O Helen, goddess, nymph,
perfect, divine!
To what, my love, shall I compare thine eyne?
Crystal is muddy. O, how ripe in show 139
Thy lips, those kissing cherries, tempting grow!
That pure congealed white, high Taurus' snow,
Fann'd with the eastern wind, turns to a crow
When thou hold'st up thy hand. O, let me kiss
This princess of pure white, this seal of bliss!
Hel. O spite! O hell! I see you all are bent
To set against me for your merriment. 146
If you were civil and knew courtesy,
You would not do me thus much injury.
Can you not hate me, as I know you do,
But you must join in souls to mock me too?
If you were men, as men you are in show, 151
You would not use a gentle lady so;
To vow, and swear, and superpraise my parts,
When I am sure you hate me with your hearts.

You both are rivals, and love Hermia; 155
And now both rivals to mock Helena.
A trim exploit, a manly enterprise,
To conjure tears up in a poor maid's eyes
With your derision! None of noble sort
Would so offend a virgin and extort 160
A poor soul's patience, all to make you sport.
Lys. You are unkind, Demetrius. Be not so!
For you love Hermia. This you know I know;
And here, with all good will, with all my heart,
In Hermia's love I yield you up my part; 165
And yours of Helena to me bequeath,
Whom I do love, and will do to my death.
Hel. Never did mockers waste more idle
breath.
Dem. Lysander, keep thy Hermia. I will
none.
If e'er I lov'd her, all that love is gone. 170
My heart to her but as guestwise sojourn'd,
And now to Helen is it home return'd,
There to remain.
Lys.   Helen, it is not so.
Dem. Disparage not the faith thou dost not
know,
Lest, to thy peril, thou aby it dear. 175
Look where thy love comes. Yonder is thy dear.

Enter *Hermia*.

Her. Dark night, that from the eye his func-
tion takes,
The ear more quick of apprehension makes.
Wherein it doth impair the seeing sense,
It pays the hearing double recompense. 180
Thou art not by mine eye, Lysander, found;
Mine ear, I thank it, brought me to thy sound.
But why unkindly didst thou leave me so?
Lys. Why should he stay whom love doth
press to go?
Her. What love could press Lysander from
my side? 185
Lys. Lysander's love, that would not let
him bide —
Fair Helena; who more engilds the night
Than all yon fiery oes and eyes of light.
Why seek'st thou me? Could not this make
thee know,
The hate I bare thee made me leave thee so?
Her. You speak not as you think. It can-
not be. 191
Hel. Lo, she is one of this confederacy!
Now I perceive they have conjoin'd all three
To fashion this false sport in spite of me.
Injurious Hermia! most ungrateful maid! 195
Have you conspir'd, have you with these
contriv'd

To bait me with this foul derision?
Is all the counsel that we two have shar'd,
The sister's vows, the hours that we have spent
When we have chid the hasty-footed time   200
For parting us — O, is all forgot?
All schooldays friendship, childhood innocence?
We, Hermia, like two artificial gods,
Have with our needles created both one flower,
Both on one sampler, sitting on one cushion,
Both warbling of one song, both in one key;
As if our hands, our sides, voices, and minds
Had been incorporate. So we grew together,
Like to a double cherry, seeming parted,
But yet an union in partition —   210
Two lovely berries moulded on one stem;
So, with two seeming bodies, but one heart;
Two of the first, like coats in heraldry,
Due but to one, and crowned with one crest.
And will you rent our ancient love asunder,   215
To join with men in scorning your poor friend?
It is not friendly, 'tis not maidenly!
Our sex, as well as I, may chide you for it,
Though I alone do feel the injury.   219
  Her. I am amazed at your passionate words.
I scorn you not. It seems that you scorn me.
  Hel. Have you not set Lysander, as in scorn,
To follow me and praise my eyes and face?
And made your other love, Demetrius
(Who even but now did spurn me with his
  foot),   225
To call me goddess, nymph, divine, and rare,
Precious, celestial? Wherefore speaks he this
To her he hates? And wherefore doth Lysander
Deny your love (so rich within his soul)
And tender me (forsooth) affection,   230
But by your setting on, by your consent?
What though I be not so in grace as you,
So hung upon with love, so fortunate;
But miserable most, to love unlov'd?
This you should pity rather than despise.   235
  Her. I understand not what you mean by
  this.
  Hel. Ay, do! persever, counterfeit sad looks;
Make mouths upon me when I turn my back;
Wink each at other; hold the sweet jest up.
This sport, well carried, shall be chronicled.   240
If you have any pity, grace, or manners,
You would not make me such an argument.
But fare ye well. 'Tis partly my own fault;
Which death or absence soon shall remedy.
  Lys. Stay, gentle Helena; hear my excuse,
My love, my life, my soul, fair Helena!   246
  Hel. O excellent!
  Her.   Sweet, do not scorn her so.
  Dem. If she cannot entreat, I can compel.

  Lys. Thou canst compel no more than she
  entreat.
Thy threats have no more strength than her
  weak prayers.   250
Helen, I love thee; by my life, I do!
I swear by that which I will lose for thee
To prove him false that says I love thee not.
  Dem. I say I love thee more than he can do.
  Lys. If thou say so, withdraw and prove it
  too.   255
  Dem. Quick, come!
  Her.   Lysander, whereto tends all this?
  Lys. Away, you Ethiope!
  Dem.   No, no, sir! You
Seem to break loose, take on as you would
  follow,
But yet come not. You are a tame man, go!
  Lys. Hang off, thou cat, thou burr! Vile
  thing, let loose,   260
Or I will shake thee from me like a serpent!
  Her. Why are you grown so rude? What
  change is this,
Sweet love?
  Lys.   Thy love? Out, tawny Tartar, out!
Out, loathed med'cine! O hated potion, hence!
  Her. Do you not jest?
  Hel.   Yes, sooth! and so do you.
  Lys. Demetrius, I will keep my word with
  thee.   266
  Dem. I would I had your bond; for I perceive
A weak bond holds you. I'll not trust your
  word.
  Lys. What, should I hurt her, strike her, kill
  her dead?
Although I hate her, I'll not harm her so.   270
  Her. What, can you do me greater harm than
  hate?
Hate me? Wherefore? O me! what news, my
  love?
Am not I Hermia? Are not you Lysander?
I am as fair now as I was erewhile.
Since night you lov'd me; yet since night you
  left me.   275
Why then, you left me (O, the gods forbid!)
In earnest, shall I say?
  Lys.   Ay, by my life!
And never did desire to see thee more.
Therefore be out of hope, of question, doubt;
Be certain! Nothing truer. 'Tis no jest   280
That I do hate thee, and love Helena.
  Her. O me! you juggler! you canker blos-
  som!
You thief of love! What, have you come by
  night
And stol'n my love's heart from him?

245

Hel. Fine, i' faith!
Have you no modesty, no maiden shame, 285
No touch of bashfulness? What, will you tear
Impatient answers from my gentle tongue?
Fie, fie! you counterfeit, you puppet you!
Her. Puppet? Why, so! Ay, that way goes
the game.
Now I perceive that she hath made compare
Between our statures; she hath urg'd her
height, 291
And with her personage, her tall personage,
Her height (forsooth), she hath prevail'd with
him.
And are you grown so high in his esteem
Because I am so dwarfish and so low? 295
How low am I, thou painted maypole? Speak!
How low am I? I am not yet so low
But that my nails can reach unto thine eyes.
Hel. I pray you, though you mock me,
gentlemen,
Let her not hurt me. I was never curst; 300
I have no gift at all in shrewishness;
I am a right maid for my cowardice.
Let her not strike me. You perhaps may think,
Because she is something lower than myself,
That I can match her.
Her. Lower? Hark again! 305
Hel. Good Hermia, do not be so bitter with
me.
I evermore did love you, Hermia,
Did ever keep your counsels, never wrong'd you;
Save that, in love unto Demetrius,
I told him of your stealth unto this wood. 310
He followed you; for love I followed him;
But he hath chid me hence, and threat'ned me
To strike me, spurn me; nay, to kill me too.
And now, so you will let me quiet go,
To Athens will I bear my folly back 315
And follow you no further. Let me go.
You see how simple and how fond I am.
Her. Why, get you gone! Who is't that hinders you?
Hel. A foolish heart, that I leave here behind.
Her. What, with Lysander?
Hel. With Demetrius.
Lys. Be not afraid. She shall not harm thee,
Helena. 321
Dem. No, sir, she shall not, though you take
her part.
Hel. O, when she is angry, she is keen and
shrewd!
She was a vixen when she went to school;
And though she be but little, she is fierce. 325
Her. 'Little' again? nothing but 'low' and
'little'?

Why will you suffer her to flout me thus?
Let me come to her.
Lys. Get you gone, you dwarf!
You minimus, of hind'ring knotgrass made!
You bead, you acorn!
Dem. You are too officious 330
In her behalf that scorns your services.
Let her alone. Speak not of Helena;
Take not her part; for if thou dost intend
Never so little show of love to her,
Thou shalt aby it.
Lys. Now she holds me not. 335
Now follow, if thou dar'st, to try whose right,
Of thine or mine, is most in Helena.
Dem. Follow? Nay, I'll go with thee, cheek
by jowl.

Exeunt Lysander and Demetrius.

Her. You, mistress, all this coil is long of you.
Nay, go not back.
Hel. I will not trust you, I, 340
Nor longer stay in your curst company.
Your hands than mine are quicker for a fray;
My legs are longer though, to run away. [*Exit.*]
Her. I am amaz'd, and know not what to say.

Exit.

Ob. This is thy negligence. Still thou mistak'st, 345
Or else committ'st thy knaveries wilfully.
Puck. Believe me, king of shadows, I mistook.
Did not you tell me I should know the man
By the Athenian garments he had on?
And so far blameless proves my enterprise 350
That I have 'nointed an Athenian's eyes;
And so far am I glad it so did sort
As this their jangling I esteem a sport.
Ob. Thou seest these lovers seek a place to
fight.
Hie therefore, Robin, overcast the night. 355
The starry welkin cover thou anon
With drooping fog as black as Acheron,
And lead these testy rivals so astray
As one come not within another's way.
Like to Lysander sometime frame thy tongue,
Then stir Demetrius up with bitter wrong; 361
And sometime rail thou like Demetrius.
And from each other look thou lead them thus
Till o'er their brows death-counterfeiting sleep
With leaden legs and batty wings doth creep.
Then crush this herb into Lysander's eye; 366
Whose liquor hath this virtuous property,
To take from thence all error with his might
And make his eyeballs roll with wonted sight.
When they next wake, all this derision 370
Shall seem a dream and fruitless vision;

And back to Athens shall the lovers wend
With league whose date till death shall never end.
Whiles I in this affair do thee employ,
I'll to my queen and beg her Indian boy;   375
And then I will her charmed eye release
From monster's view, and all things shall be
    peace.
Puck. My fairy lord, this must be done with
    haste,
For night's swift dragons cut the clouds full fast,
And yonder shines Aurora's harbinger;   380
At whose approach ghosts, wand'ring here and
    there,
Troop home to churchyards; damned spirits all,
That in crossways and floods have burial,
Already to their wormy beds are gone.
For fear lest day should look their shames upon,
They wilfully themselves exile from light,   386
And must for aye consort with black-brow'd
    night.
Ob. But we are spirits of another sort.
I with the Morning's love have oft made sport;
And, like a forester, the groves may tread   390
Even till the eastern gate, all fiery red,
Opening on Neptune, with fair blessed beams
Turns into yellow gold his salt green streams.
But notwithstanding, haste; make no delay.
We may effect this business yet ere day. [*Exit.*]
Puck. Up and down, up and down,   396
    I will lead them up and down.
    I am fear'd in field and town.
    Goblin, lead them up and down.
Here comes one.   400

        Enter *Lysander.*

Lys. Where art thou, proud Demetrius?
    Speak thou now.
Rob. Here, villain, drawn and ready. Where
    art thou?
Lys. I will be with thee straight.
Rob.   Follow me then
To plainer ground.

            [*Exit Lysander.*]

        Enter *Demetrius.*

Dem.   Lysander, speak again!
Thou runaway, thou coward, art thou fled?   405
Speak! In some bush? Where dost thou hide
    thy head?
Rob. Thou coward, art thou bragging to the
    stars,
Telling the bushes that thou look'st for wars,
And wilt not come? Come, recreant! come,
    thou child!
I'll whip thee with a rod. He is defil'd   410

That draws a sword on thee.
Dem.   Yea, art thou there?
Rob. Follow my voice. We'll try no man-
    hood here.   *Exeunt.*

        [Enter *Lysander.*]
Lys. He goes before me and still dares me on;
When I come where he calls, then he is gone.
The villain is much lighter-heel'd than I.   415
I followed fast, but faster he did fly,
That fallen am I in dark uneven way,
And here will rest me. (*Lie down.*) Come, thou
    gentle day!
For if but once thou show me thy grey light,
I'll find Demetrius and revenge this spite.   420
            [*Sleeps.*]

      Enter *Robin* and *Demetrius.*

Rob. Ho, ho, ho! Coward, why com'st thou
    not?
Dem. Abide me, if thou dar'st; for well I wot
Thou run'st before me, shifting every place,
And dar'st not stand nor look me in the face.
Where art thou now?
Rob.   Come hither. I am here.
Dem. Nay then, thou mock'st me. Thou
    shalt buy this dear   426
If ever I thy face by daylight see.
Now, go thy way. Faintness constraineth me
To measure out my length on this cold bed.
By day's approach look to be visited.   430
        [*Lies down and sleeps.*]

         Enter *Helena.*

Hel. O weary night, O long and tedious night,
    Abate thy hours! Shine comforts from the
    East,
That I may back to Athens by daylight
From these that my poor company detest;
And sleep, that sometimes shuts up sorrow's eye,
Steal me awhile from mine own company.   436
             Sleep.
Rob. Yet but three? Come one more.
    Two of both kinds makes up four.
    Here she comes, curst and sad.
    Cupid is a knavish lad   440
    Thus to make poor females mad.

         Enter *Hermia.*

Her. Never so weary, never so in woe;
Bedabbled with the dew, and torn with briers;
I can no further crawl, no further go;
    My legs can keep no pace with my desires.
Here will I rest me till the break of day.   446
Heavens shield Lysander, if they mean a fray!
        [*Lies down and sleeps.*]

Rob. On the ground
Sleep sound.
I'll apply   450
To your eye,
Gentle lover, remedy.
[*Squeezes the herb on Lysander's eyelids.*]
When thou wak'st,
Thou tak'st
True delight   455
In the sight

Of thy former lady's eye;
And the country proverb known,
That every man should take his own,
In your waking shall be shown :   460
Jack shall have Jill;
Naught shall go ill;
The man shall have his mare again, and all
shall be well.   [*Exit.*]

ACT IV. [Scene I. *The wood.* Lysander, Demetrius, Helena, *and* Hermia,
all lying asleep.]

Enter [*Titania,*] Queen of Fairies, and [*Bottom the*] Clown and Fairies, [*Peaseblossom, Cobweb, Moth, Mustardseed,* and others]; and the King, [*Oberon,*] behind them.

Tita. Come, sit thee down upon this flow'ry bed,
While I thy amiable cheeks do coy,
And stick musk-roses in thy sleek smooth head,
And kiss thy fair large ears, my gentle joy.
Bot. Where's Peaseblossom?   5
Peas. Ready.
Bot. Scratch my head, Peaseblossom. Where's Mounsieur Cobweb?
Cob. Ready.   9
Bot. Mounsieur Cobweb, good mounsieur, get you your weapons in your hand, and kill me a red-hipp'd humblebee on the top of a thistle; and, good mounsieur, bring me the honey-bag. Do not fret yourself too much in the action, mounsieur; and, good mounsieur, have a care the honey-bag break not. I would be loath to have you overflowen with a honey-bag, signior. Where's Mounsieur Mustardseed?   18
Mus. Ready.
Bot. Give me your neaf, Mounsieur Mustardseed. Pray you, leave your curtsy, good mounsieur.   22
Mus. What's your will?
Bot. Nothing, good mounsieur, but to help Cavalery Peaseblossom to scratch. I must to the barber's, mounsieur; for methinks I am marvail's hairy about the face; and I am such a tender ass, if my hair do but tickle me, I must scratch.
Tita. What, wilt thou hear some music, my sweet love?
Bot. I have a reasonable good ear in music. Let's have the tongs and the bones.   31
Tita. Or say, sweet love, what thou desirest to eat.

Bot. Truly, a peck of provender. I could munch your good dry oats. Methinks I have a great desire to a bottle of hay. Good hay, sweet hay, hath no fellow.   36
Tita. I have a venturous fairy that shall seek The squirrel's hoard, and fetch thee thence new nuts.
Bot. I had rather have a handful or two of dried pease. But I pray you, let none of your people stir me. I have an exposition of sleep come upon me.   42
Tita. Sleep thou, and I will wind thee in my arms.
Fairies, be gone, and be all ways away.
[*Exeunt Fairies.*]
So doth the woodbine the sweet honeysuckle 45
Gently entwist; the female ivy so
Enrings the barky fingers of the elm.
O, how I love thee! how I dote on thee!
[*They sleep.*]

Enter *Robin Goodfellow.*

Ob. [*advances*] Welcome, good Robin. Seest thou this sweet sight?
Her dotage now I do begin to pity;   50
For, meeting her of late behind the wood,
Seeking sweet favours for this hateful fool,
I did upbraid her and fall out with her.
For she his hairy temples then had rounded
With coronet of fresh and fragrant flowers; 55
And that same dew which sometime on the buds
Was wont to swell like round and orient pearls
Stood now within the pretty flouriets' eyes,
Like tears that did their own disgrace bewail.
When I had at my pleasure taunted her,   60
And she in mild terms begg'd my patience,
I then did ask of her her changeling child;
Which straight she gave me, and her fairy sent
To bear him to my bower in fairyland.
And now I have the boy, I will undo   65

This hateful imperfection of her eyes.
And, gentle Puck, take this transformed scalp
From off the head of this Athenian swain;
That, he awaking when the other do,
May all to Athens back again repair,   70
And think no more of this night's accidents
But as the fierce vexation of a dream.
But first I will release the Fairy Queen.
        Be as thou wast wont to be;
        See as thou wast wont to see.   75
        Dian's bud o'er Cupid's flower
        Hath such force and blessed power.
Now, my Titania! Wake you, my sweet queen.
  Tita. My Oberon, what visions have I seen!
Methought I was enamour'd of an ass.   80
  Ob. There lies your love.
  Tita.   How came these things to pass?
O, how mine eyes do loathe his visage now!
  Ob. Silence awhile. Robin. take off this head.
Titania, music call; and strike more dead
Than common sleep of all these five the sense.
  Tita. Music, ho, music! such as charmeth
        sleep!   86
  Rob. Now, when thou wak'st, with thine
        own fool's eyes peep.
  Ob. Sound, music!   [*Music.*]
        Come, my queen, take hands with me.
And rock the ground whereon these sleepers be.
                                         [*Dance.*]
Now thou and I are new in amity,   90
And will to-morrow midnight solemnly
Dance in Duke Theseus' house triumphantly
And bless it to all fair prosperity.
There shall the pairs of faithful lovers be
Wedded, with Theseus, all in jollity.   95
  Rob. Fairy King, attend and mark.
I do hear the morning lark.
  Ob. Then, my queen, in silence sad
        Trip we after night's shade.
        We the globe can compass soon,   100
        Swifter than the wand'ring moon.
  Tita. Come, my lord, and in our flight
        Tell me how it came this night
        That I sleeping here was found
        With these mortals on the ground. 105
                                         Exeunt.

        Wind horn.

Enter *Theseus* and all his *Train*; [*Hippolyta,*
        Egeus].

  The. Go, one of you, find out the forester;
For now our observation is perform'd;
And since we have the vaward of the day,
My love shall hear the music of my hounds.
Uncouple in the western valley; let them go.

Dispatch, I say, and find the forester.   111
                         [*Exit an Attendant.*]
We will, fair Queen, up to the mountain's top
And mark the musical confusion
Of hounds and echo in conjunction.   114
  Hip. I was with Hercules and Cadmus once
When in a wood of Crete they bay'd the bear
With hounds of Sparta. Never did I hear
Such gallant chiding; for, besides the groves,
The skies, the fountains, every region near
Seem'd all one mutual cry. I never heard   120
So musical a discord, such sweet thunder.
  The. My hounds are bred out of the Spartan
        kind;
So flew'd, so sanded; and their heads are hung
With ears that sweep away the morning dew;
Crook-knee'd, and dew-lapp'd like Thessalian
        bulls;   125
Slow in pursuit, but match'd in mouth like bells,
Each under each. A cry more tuneable
Was never holloa'd to nor cheer'd with horn
In Crete, in Sparta, nor in Thessaly.
Judge when you hear. But, soft! What nymphs
        are these?   130
  Ege. My lord, this is my daughter here
        asleep;
And this, Lysander; this Demetrius is;
This Helena, old Nedar's Helena.
I wonder of their being here together.
  The. No doubt they rose up early to observe
The rite of May; and, hearing our intent,   136
Came here in grace of our solemnity.
But speak, Egeus. Is not this the day
That Hermia should give answer of her choice?
  Ege. It is, my lord.   140
  The. Go, bid the huntsmen wake them with
        their horns.
        [*Exit an Attendant.*] *Shout within. Wind*
                horns. They all start up.
Good morrow, friends. Saint Valentine is past.
Begin these woodbirds but to couple now?
  Lys. Pardon, my lord.   [*They kneel.*]
  The.   I pray you all, stand up.
I know you two are rival enemies.   145
How comes this gentle concord in the world
That hatred is so far from jealousy
To sleep by hate and fear no enmity?
  Lys. My lord, I shall reply amazedly,
Half sleep, half waking; but as yet, I swear,
I cannot truly say how I came here;   151
But, as I think (for truly would I speak).
And now I do bethink me, so it is —
I came with Hermia hither. Our intent
Was to be gone from Athens, where we might.
Without the peril of the Athenian law —   156

Ege. Enough, enough, my lord! you have
enough.
I beg the law, the law, upon his head.
They would have stol'n away; they would,
Demetrius!
Thereby to have defeated you and me — 160
You of your wife, and me of my consent,
Of my consent that she should be your wife.
Dem. My lord, fair Helen told me of their
stealth,
Of this their purpose hither, to this wood;
And I in fury hither followed them, 165
Fair Helena in fancy following me.
But, my good lord, I wot not by what power
(But by some power it is) my love to Hermia,
Melted as the snow, seems to me now
As the remembrance of an idle gaud 170
Which in my childhood I did dote upon;
And all the faith, the virtue of my heart,
The object and the pleasure of mine eye,
Is only Helena. To her, my lord,
Was I betroth'd ere I saw Hermia; 175
But, like a sickness, did I loathe this food;
But, as in health, come to my natural taste,
Now I do wish it, love it, long for it,
And will for evermore be true to it.
The. Fair lovers, you are fortunately met.
Of this discourse we more will hear anon. 181
Egeus, I will overbear your will;
For in the temple, by-and-by, with us,
These couples shall eternally be knit;
And, for the morning now is something worn,
Our purpos'd hunting shall be set aside. 186
Away, with us to Athens! Three and three,
We'll hold a feast in great solemnity.
Come, Hippolyta.
*Exeunt Duke [Theseus, Hippolyta, Egeus,]
and Lords.*
Dem. These things seem small and undis-
tinguishable, 190
Like far-off mountains turned into clouds.
Her. Methinks I see these things with parted
eye,
When everything seems double.
Hel.   So methinks;
And I have found Demetrius like a jewel,
Mine own, and not mine own.
Dem.   Are you sure 195
That we are awake? It seems to me
That yet we sleep, we dream. Do not you think
The Duke was here, and bid us follow him?
Her. Yea, and my father.
Hel.   And Hippolyta.
Lys. And he did bid us follow to the
temple.

Dem. Why then, we are awake. Let's follow him, 201
And by the way let us recount our dreams.
Exeunt.
Bot. (*wakes*) When my cue comes, call me,
and I will answer. My next is 'Most fair Pyramus.' Hey-ho! Peter Quince! Flute the bellows-
mender! Snout the tinker! Starveling! God's
my life! Stol'n hence, and left me asleep! I have
had a most rare vision. I have had a dream,
past the wit of man to say what dream it was.
Man is but an ass if he go about to expound this
dream. Methought I was — there is no man
can tell what. Methought I was, and methought
I had — But man is but a patch'd fool if he
will offer to say what methought I had. The
eye of man hath not heard, the ear of man hath
not seen, man's hand is not able to taste, his
tongue to conceive, nor his heart to report what
my dream was. I will get Peter Quince to write a
ballet of this dream. It shall be call'd 'Bottom's
Dream,' because it hath no bottom; and I will
sing it in the latter end of our play, before the
Duke. Peradventure, to make it the more gracious, I shall sing it at her death. *Exit.*

[Scene II. *Athens.* Quince's *house.*]

Enter *Quince, Flute, Snout,* and *Starveling.*

Quince. Have you sent to Bottom's house?
Is he come home yet?
Starv. He cannot be heard of. Out of doubt
he is transported.
Flute. If he come not, then the play is
marr'd; it goes not forward, doth it? 6
Quince. It is not possible. You have not a
man in all Athens able to discharge Pyramus
but he.
Flute. No, he hath simply the best wit of any
handicraft man in Athens. 10
Quince. Yea, and the best person too, and
he is a very paramour for a sweet voice.
Flute. You must say 'paragon.' A paramour
is (God bless us!) a thing of naught. 14

Enter *Snug the Joiner.*

Snug. Masters, the Duke is coming from the
temple, and there is two or three lords and
ladies more married. If our sport had gone forward, we had all been made men. 18
Flute. O sweet bully Bottom! Thus hath he
lost sixpence a day during his life. He could not
have scaped sixpence a day. An the Duke had
not given him sixpence a day for playing Pyra-

mus, I'll be hanged! He would have deserved it. Sixpence a day in Pyramus, or nothing!

Enter *Bottom.*

Bot. Where are these lads? Where are these hearts?   26
Quince. Bottom! O most courageous day! O most happy hour!
Bot. Masters, I am to discourse wonders; but ask me not what. For if I tell you, I am no true Athenian. I will tell you everything, right as it fell out.   32
Quince. Let us hear, sweet Bottom.

Bot. Not a word of me. All that I will tell you is, that the Duke hath dined. Get your apparel together, good strings to your beards, new ribbands to your pumps; meet presently at the palace; every man look o'er his part; for the short and the long is, our play is preferr'd. In any case, let Thisby have clean linen; and let not him that plays the lion pare his nails, for they shall hang out for the lion's claws. And, most dear actors, eat no onions nor garlic, for we are to utter sweet breath; and I do not doubt but to hear them say it is a sweet comedy. No more words. Away! go, away!   *Exeunt.*

ACT V. [Scene I. *Athens. The Palace of* Theseus.]

Enter *Theseus, Hippolyta,* and *Philostrate,*
      [with *Lords* and *Attendants*].

Hip. 'Tis strange, my Theseus, that these
      lovers speak of.
The. More strange than true. I never may
      believe
These antique fables nor these fairy toys.
Lovers and madmen have such seething brains,
Such shaping fantasies, that apprehend   5
More than cool reason ever comprehends.
The lunatic, the lover, and the poet
Are of imagination all compact.
One sees more devils than vast hell can hold:
That is the madman. The lover, all as frantic,
Sees Helen's beauty in a brow of Egypt.   11
The poet's eye, in a fine frenzy rolling,
Doth glance from heaven to earth, from earth
      to heaven;
And as imagination bodies forth
The forms of things unknown, the poet's pen 15
Turns them to shapes, and gives to airy nothing
A local habitation and a name.
Such tricks hath strong imagination
That, if it would but apprehend some joy,
It comprehends some bringer of that joy;   20
Or in the night, imagining some fear,
How easy is a bush suppos'd a bear!
Hip. But all the story of the night told over,
And all their minds transfigur'd so together,
More witnesseth than fancy's images   25
And grows to something of great constancy;
But howsoever, strange and admirable.

Enter Lovers — *Lysander, Demetrius, Hermia,*
      and *Helena.*

The. Here come the lovers, full of joy and
      mirth.

Joy, gentle friends, joy and fresh days of love
Accompany your hearts!
Lys.   More than to us   30
Wait in your royal walks, your board, your bed!
The. Come now, what masques, what dances
      shall we have,
To wear away this long age of three hours
Between our after-supper and bedtime?
Where is our usual manager of mirth?   35
What revels are in hand? Is there no play
To ease the anguish of a torturing hour?
Call Philostrate.
Phil.   Here, mighty Theseus.
The. Say, what abridgment have you for this
      evening?
What masque? what music? How shall we
      beguile   40
The lazy time, if not with some delight?
Phil. There is a brief how many sports are
      ripe.
Make choice of which your Highness will see
      first.   [*Gives a paper.*]
The. 'The battle with the Centaurs, to be
      sung
By an Athenian eunuch to the harp.'   45
We'll none of that. That have I told my love
In glory of my kinsman Hercules.
'The riot of the tipsy Bacchanals,
Tearing the Thracian singer in their rage.'
That is an old device; and it was play'd   50
When I from Thebes came last a conqueror.
'The thrice three Muses mourning for the death
Of Learning, late deceas'd in beggary.'
That is some satire keen and critical,
Not sorting with a nuptial ceremony.   55
'A tedious brief scene of young Pyramus
And his love Thisby; very tragical mirth.'
Merry and tragical? tedious and brief?

That is hot ice and wondrous strange snow. 59
How shall we find the concord of this discord?
Phil. A play there is, my lord, some ten
  words long,
Which is as brief as I have known a play;
But by ten words, my lord, it is too long,
Which makes it tedious; for in all the play
There is not one word apt, one player fitted. 65
And tragical, my noble lord, it is;
For Pyramus therein doth kill himself.
Which when I saw rehears'd, I must confess,
Made mine eyes water; but more merry tears
The passion of loud laughter never shed.   70
The. What are they that do play it?
Phil. Hard-handed men that work in Athens
  here,
Which never labour'd in their minds till now;
And now have toil'd their unbreathed memories
With this same play, against your nuptial. 75
The. And we will hear it.
Phil.   No, my noble lord;
It is not for you. I have heard it over,
And it is nothing, nothing in the world;
Unless you can find sport in their intents, 79
Extremely stretch'd and conn'd with cruel pain,
To do you service.
The.   I will hear that play;
For never anything can be amiss
When simpleness and duty tender it.
Go bring them in; and take your places, ladies.
                    [*Exit Philostrate.*]
Hip. I love not to see wretchedness o'er-
  charg'd,   85
And duty in his service perishing.
The. Why, gentle sweet, you shall see no
  such thing.
Hip. He says they can do nothing in this kind.
The. The kinder we, to give them thanks for
  nothing.   89
Our sport shall be to take what they mistake;
And what poor duty cannot do, noble respect
Takes it in might, not merit.
Where I have come, great clerks have purposed
To greet me with premeditated welcomes;
Where I have seen them shiver and look pale,
Make periods in the midst of sentences,   96
Throttle their practis'd accent in their fears,
And, in conclusion, dumbly have broke off,
Not paying me a welcome. Trust me, sweet,
Out of this silence yet I pick'd a welcome; 100
And in the modesty of fearful duty
I read as much as from the rattling tongue
Of saucy and audacious eloquence.
Love, therefore, and tongue-tied simplicity
In least speak most, to my capacity.   105

[Enter *Philostrate.*]

Phil. So please your Grace, the Prologue is
address'd.
The. Let him approach.

Flourish trumpets. Enter the *Prologue* (*Quince*).

Pro. If we offend, it is with our good will.
  That you should think, we come not to offend,
But with good will. To show our simple skill, 110
  That is the true beginning of our end.
Consider then, we come but in despite.
  We do not come, as minding to content you,
Our true intent is. All for your delight,   114
  We are not here. That you should here repent you,
The actors are at hand: and, by their show,
You shall know all, that you are like to know.
The. This fellow doth not stand upon points.
Lys. He hath rid his prologue like a rough
colt; he knows not the stop. A good moral, my
lord: it is not enough to speak, but to speak
true.   121
Hip. Indeed he hath play'd on his prologue
like a child on a recorder — a sound, but not in
government.
The. His speech was like a tangled chain;
nothing impaired, but all disordered. Who is
next?   127

Enter *Pyramus* and *Thisby*, and *Wall* and *Moonshine* and *Lion.*

Pro. Gentles, perchance you wonder at this
  show;
But wonder on, till truth make all things plain.
This man is Pyramus, if you would know;   130
  This beauteous lady Thisby is certain.
This man, with lime and roughcast, doth present
  Wall, that vile Wall which did these lovers
  sunder;
And through Wall's chink, poor souls, they are
  content   134
To whisper. At the which let no man wonder.
This man, with lantern, dog, and bush of thorn,
  Presenteth Moonshine. For, if you will know,
By moonshine did these lovers think no scorn
  To meet at Ninus' tomb, there, there to woo.
This grisly beast, which Lion hight by name, 140
  The trusty Thisby, coming first by night,
Did scare away, or rather did affright;
  And as she fled, her mantle she did fall,
Which Lion vile with bloody mouth did stain.
Anon comes Pyramus, sweet youth and tall, 145
  And finds his trusty Thisby's mantle slain;
Whereat, with blade, with bloody blameful blade,
  He bravely broach'd his boiling bloody breast.
And Thisby, tarrying in mulberry shade,
  His dagger drew, and died. For all the rest, 150
Let Lion, Moonshine, Wall, and lovers twain
At large discourse while here they do remain.

The. I wonder if the lion be to speak.

Dem. No wonder, my lord. One lion may, when many asses do.   155

    Exeunt [Prologue, Pyramus,] Lion, Thisby,
                    and Moonshine.

Wall. In this same enterlude it doth befall
That I, one Snout by name, present a wall;
And such a wall, as I would have you think,
That had in it a crannied hole or chink;   159
Through which the lovers, Pyramus and Thisby,
Did whisper often, very secretly.
This loam, this roughcast, and this stone doth show
That I am that same wall. The truth is so.
And this the cranny is, right and sinister,   164
Through which the fearful lovers are to whisper.

The. Would you desire lime and hair to speak better?

Dem. It is the wittiest partition that ever I heard discourse, my lord.

Enter *Pyramus.*

The. Pyramus draws near the wall. Silence!

Pyr. O grim-look'd night! O night with hue so black!   171
O night, which ever art when day is not!
O night, O night! alack, alack, alack,
  I fear my Thisby's promise is forgot!
And thou, O wall, O sweet, O lovely wall,   175
  That stand'st between her father's ground and mine!
Thou wall, O wall, O sweet and lovely wall,
  Show me thy chink, to blink through with mine eyne!

    [Wall holds up his fingers.]
Thanks, courteous wall. Jove shield thee well for this!
But what see I? No Thisby do I see.   180
O wicked wall, through whom I see no bliss,
Curs'd be thy stones for thus deceiving me!

The. The wall, methinks, being sensible, should curse again.   184

Pyr. No, in truth, sir, he should not. 'Deceiving me' is Thisby's cue. She is to enter now, and I am to spy her through the wall. You shall see it will fall pat as I told you. Yonder she comes.

Enter *Thisby.*

This. O Wall, full often hast thou heard my moans   190
For parting my fair Pyramus and me!
My cherry lips have often kiss'd thy stones,
Thy stones with lime and hair knit up in thee.

Pyr. I see a voice. Now will I to the chink,
To spy an I can hear my Thisby's face.   195
Thisby!

This. My love! thou art my love, I think.

Pyr. Think what thou wilt, I am thy lover's grace;
And, like Limander, am I trusty still.   199

This. And I, like Helen, till the Fates me kill.

Pyr. Not Shafalus to Procrus was so true.

This. As Shafalus to Procrus, I to you.

Pyr. O, kiss me through the hole of this vile wall!

This. I kiss the wall's hole, not your lips at all.

Pyr. Wilt thou at Ninny's tomb meet me straightway?   205

This. Tide life, tide death, I come without delay.

    [Exeunt Pyramus and Thisby.]

Wall. Thus have I, Wall, my part discharged so;
And, being done, thus Wall away doth go.

                     Exit.

The. Now is the mural down between the two neighbours.

Dem. No remedy, my lord, when walls are so wilful to hear without warning.   212

Hip. This is the silliest stuff that ever I heard.

The. The best in this kind are but shadows; and the worst are no worse, if imagination amend them.   216

Hip. It must be your imagination then, and not theirs.

The. If we imagine no worse of them than they of themselves, they may pass for excellent men. Here come two noble beasts in, a man and a lion.   221

Enter *Lion* and *Moonshine.*

Lion. You, ladies, you, whose gentle hearts do fear
The smallest monstrous mouse that creeps on floor,
May now perchance both quake and tremble here,
  When lion rough in wildest rage doth roar.   225
Then know that I one Snug the joiner am,
A lion fell, nor else no lion's dam;
For, if I should as lion come in strife
Into this place, 'twere pity on my life.

The. A very gentle beast, and of a good conscience.   231

Dem. The very best at a beast, my lord, that e'er I saw.

Lys. This lion is a very fox for his valour.

The. True; and a goose for his discretion. 235

Dem. Not so, my lord; for his valour cannot carry his discretion, and the fox carries the goose.

The. His discretion, I am sure, cannot carry his valour; for the goose carries not the fox. It is well. Leave it to his discretion, and let us listen to the moon.

Moon. This lanthorn doth the horned moon present —

Dem. He should have worn the horns on his head.   245

The. He is no crescent, and his horns are invisible within the circumference.

Moon. This lanthorn doth the horned moon present.
Myself the man i' th' moon do seem to be. 249

The. This is the greatest error of all the rest. The man should be put into the lanthorn. How is it else the man i' th' moon?

Dem. He dares not come there for the candle; for, you see, it is already in snuff.

Hip. I am aweary of this moon. Would he would change! 256

The. It appears, by his small light of discretion, that he is in the wane; but yet, in courtesy, in all reason, we must stay the time.

Lys. Proceed, Moon. 260

Moon. All that I have to say is to tell you that the lanthorn is the moon; I, the man i' th' moon; this thornbush, my thornbush; and this dog, my dog. 264

Dem. Why, all these should be in the lanthorn; for all these are in the moon. But silence! Here comes Thisby.

Enter *Thisby.*

This. This is old Ninny's tomb. Where is my love?

Lion. O! *The Lion roars. Thisby runs off.*

Dem. Well roar'd, Lion! 270

The. Well run, Thisby!

Hip. Well shone, Moon! Truly, the moon shines with a good grace.

[*The Lion tears Thisby's mantle, and exit.*]

The. Well mous'd, Lion!

Dem. And then came Pyramus. 275

Lys. And so the lion vanish'd.

Enter *Pyramus.*

Pyr. Sweet moon, I thank thee for thy sunny beams;
I thank thee, moon, for shining now so bright;
For, by thy gracious, golden, glittering gleams,
I trust to take of truest Thisby sight. 280
But stay! O spite!
But mark, poor knight!
What dreadful dole is here?
Eyes, do you see?
How can it be? 285
O dainty duck! O dear!
Thy mantle good,
What, stain'd with blood?
Approach, ye Furies fell!
O Fates, come, come! 290
Cut thread and thrum;
Quail, crush, conclude, and quell!

The. This passion, and the death of a dear friend, would go near to make a man look sad.

Hip. Beshrew my heart but I pity the man.

Pyr. O, wherefore, Nature, didst thou lions frame?
Since lion vile hath here deflow'r'd my dear;
Which is — no, no! — which was the fairest dame
That liv'd, that lov'd, that lik'd, that look'd with cheer.
Come, tears, confound! 300
Out, sword, and wound
The pap of Pyramus!
Ay, that left pap
Where heart doth hop.

[*Stabs himself.*]
Thus die I, thus, thus, thus. 305
Now am I dead,
Now am I fled;
My soul is in the sky.
Tongue, lose thy light;
Moon, take thy flight. 310

[*Exit Moonshine.*]
Now die, die, die, die, die! [*Dies.*]

Dem. No die, but an ace, for him! for he is but one.

Lys. Less than an ace, man; for he is dead, he is nothing. 315

The. With the help of a surgeon he might yet recover, and yet prove an ass.

Hip. How chance Moonshine is gone before Thisby comes back and finds her lover?

Enter *Thisby.*

The. She will find him by starlight. Here she comes; and her passion ends the play. 321

Hip. Methinks she should not use a long one for such a Pyramus. I hope she will be brief.

Dem. A mote will turn the balance, which Pyramus, which Thisby, is the better; he for a man, God warr'nd us! — she for a woman, God bless us!

Lys. She hath spied him already with those sweet eyes.

Dem. And thus she means, videlicet: 330

This. Asleep, my love?
What, dead, my dove?
O Pyramus, arise!
Speak, speak! Quite dumb?
Dead, dead? A tomb 335
Must cover thy sweet eyes.
These lily lips,
This cherry nose,
These yellow cowslip cheeks,
Are gone, are gone. 340
Lovers, make moan!
His eyes were green as leeks.
O Sisters Three,
Come, come to me,
With hands as pale as milk; 345
Lay them in gore,
Since you have shore

With shears his thread of silk.
  Tongue, not a word!
  Come, trusty sword;   350
  Come, blade, my breast imbrue!
                          [*Stabs herself.*]
  And farewell, friends.
  Thus Thisby ends.
  Adieu, adieu, adieu!   [*Dies.*]
The. Moonshine and Lion are left to bury
the dead.   356
Dem. Ay, and Wall too.
Bot. [*starts up*] No, I assure you; the wall is
down that parted their fathers. Will it please
you to see the Epilogue, or to hear a Bergomask
dance between two of our company?   361
  The. No epilogue, I pray you; for your play
needs no excuse. Never excuse; for when the
players are all dead, there need none to be
blamed. Marry, if he that writ it had played
Pyramus and hang'd himself in Thisby's garter,
it would have been a fine tragedy; and so it is
truly, and very notably discharg'd. But, come,
your Bergomask! Let your epilogue alone.
                                 [*A dance.*]
The iron tongue of midnight hath told twelve.
Lovers, to bed; 'tis almost fairy time. 371
I fear we shall outsleep the coming morn
As much as we this night have overwatch'd.
This palpable gross play hath well beguil'd
The heavy gait of night. Sweet friends, to bed.
A fortnight hold we this solemnity   376
In nightly revels and new jollity.   *Exeunt.*

  Enter *Puck*, [with a broom].

Puck. Now the hungry lion roars,
    And the wolf behowls the moon;
  Whilst the heavy ploughman snores,
    All with weary task fordone.   381
  Now the wasted brands do glow,
    Whilst the screech owl, screeching
        loud,
  Puts the wretch that lies in woe
    In remembrance of a shroud.   385
  Now it is the time of night
    That the graves, all gaping wide,
  Every one lets forth his sprite,
    In the churchway paths to glide;
  And we fairies, that do run   390
    By the triple Hecate's team
  From the presence of the sun,
    Following darkness like a dream,
  Now are frolic. Not a mouse
  Shall disturb this hallowed house.   395
  I am sent, with broom, before,
  To sweep the dust behind the door.

Enter *King* and *Queen of Fairies*, with all their
                    Train.
Ob. Through the house give glimmering
            light,
    By the dead and drowsy fire;
  Every elf and fairy sprite   400
    Hop as light as bird from brier;
  And this ditty, after me,
  Sing, and dance it trippingly.
Tita. First rehearse your song by rote,
    To each word a warbling note.   405
  Hand in hand, with fairy grace,
  Will we sing, and bless this place.
                        [*Song and dance.*]
Ob. Now, until the break of day,
  Through this house each fairy stray.
  To the best bride-bed will we,   410
  Which by us shall blessed be;
  And the issue there create
  Ever shall be fortunate.
  So shall all the couples three
  Ever true in loving be;   415
  And the blots of Nature's hand
  Shall not in their issue stand;
  Never mole, harelip, nor scar,
  Nor mark prodigious, such as are
  Despised in nativity,   420
  Shall upon their children be.
  With this field-dew consecrate,
  Every fairy take his gait,
  And each several chamber bless,
  Through this palace, with sweet peace.
  And the owner of it blest   426
  Ever shall in safety rest.
  Trip away; make no stay;
  Meet me all by break of day.
          Exeunt [*all but Robin Goodfellow*].
Rob. If we shadows have offended,   430
  Think but this, and all is mended —
  That you have but slumb'red here
  While these visions did appear.
  And this weak and idle theme,
  No more yielding but a dream,   435
  Gentles, do not reprehend.
  If you pardon, we will mend.
  And, as I am an honest Puck,
  If we have unearned luck
  Now to scape the serpent's tongue,
  We will make amends ere long;   441
  Else the Puck a liar call.
  So, good night unto you all.
  Give me your hands, if we be friends,
  And Robin shall restore amends.   445
                              [*Exit.*]

THE MERCHANT OF VENICE

THE MERCHANT OF VENICE was entered in the Stationers' Register on July 22, 1598 ('a booke of the Marchaunt of Venyce, or otherwise called the Jewe of Venyce'), and again (without the alternative title) on October 28, 1600. In 1600 the First Quarto appeared. It furnishes a good text, on which the present edition is based. The Second Quarto (1619, fraudulently misdated 1600) and the First Folio go back to the First Quarto. For the composition of the play a reasonable date is 1596. Meres mentions it in 1598 (see p. 33, above).

Most of the plot comes in some fashion from the story of Giannetto, in *Il Pecorone* of Ser Giovanni Fiorentino (iv, 1), which dates from the last quarter of the fourteenth century but was not printed until 1558. Here we have the name Belmonte and the whole plot except for two features — The Choice of a Casket and the episode of Jessica. There are no caskets; to win the lady one must avoid a craftily administered sleeping potion. The twelfth-century *Dolopathos* by Joannes de Alta Silva affords a version like that in *Il Pecorone*, except for the concluding episode of the rings. Sleep is caused by an enchanted feather of an owl, laid under the suitor's pillow. From the *Dolopathos* comes the version in the Latin *Gesta Romanorum* (cap. 195; No. 40 in the English *Gesta* in the fifteenth-century Harleian MS. 7333).

The wooing story (without The Pound of Flesh) represents an ancient and wide-spread theme — The Winning of an Otherworld Wife — of which the tale of Ulysses and Circe is a variant. The ballad of *The Broomfield Hill* (Child, No. 43) and the Old French *Lai de Doon* belong in this same group.

The Pound of Flesh (without the wooing) is also old and has circulated extensively. In the Middle English *Cursor Mundi* it is worked into the legend of the discovery of the True Cross. It occurs in *Les Divers Propos Memorables* of Gilles Corrozet (1556), in the ballad of *The Crueltie of Gernutus* (earlier, probably, than 1590), and in *The Orator*, 'Englished by L. P.' (Lazarus Piot) from the *Histoires Tragiques* of Alexandre van den Busche (*alias* Sylvain) and published in 1596. There are striking resemblances between the language of Gernutus and Shylock's words in ii, 1, 139–152; and Shylock's argument in court has points in common with the Jew's oration in Piot.

The Choice of the Casket comes from the Orient. It had originally nothing to do with winning a wife but was used to illustrate the perverse judgment that prefers show to substance. From the legend of *Barlaam and Joasaph* it was taken in the thirteenth century by Vincent of Beauvais into his *Speculum Historiale* (xv, 10) and by Jacobus de Voragine into his *Legenda Aurea* (cap. 176). In several variants it found a place in mediæval collections of *exempla* (including the *Gesta Romanorum*), and Gower's *Confessio Amantis* repeats it in two forms (v, 2273–2434), neither of which agrees with that in the *Decameron* (x, 1). The *Speculum*, the *Golden Legend*, the *Decameron*, and the *Confessio Amantis* were all accessible to Shakespeare. So was at least one of the versions in the *Gesta* — that which appears in the English translation edited by Richard Robinson (1577). This is particularly interesting since the choice is applied to the winning of a husband and there are details that remind one of Shakespeare's play.

At this point we are confronted by one of those phantom plays that haunt the literary history of the Elizabethan age. Stephen Gosson, in his famous diatribe against the stage *The School of Abuse* (1579), describes a drama called *The Jew*, 'showne at the Bull,' as 'representing the greedinesse of worldly chusers, and bloody mindes of Usurers.' These phrases suggest that the plot anticipated Shakespeare in combining The Choice of the Casket with The Pound of Flesh. If he owed anything to *The Jew*, his indebtedness was doubtless limited to the substitution of the caskets for the dramatically unmanageable sleeping potion. Some scholars maintain, however, that THE MERCHANT OF VENICE is a rifacimento of *The Jew* (or of some derivative) worked up by Shakespeare in 1594 and revised by him a few years later. This is very improbable. William Wager's 'interlude of the Cruell Detter,' licensed in 1565 or 1566, is not likely to have been *The Jew*.

Anthony Munday combines the bond story with the winning of the usurer's daughter in Part III of his *Zelauto* (1580), but the episode is not very similar to that of Jessica. There is a story much like Jessica's in the 14th tale in *Le Cinquanta Novelle* (1541) of Masuccio Salernitano, who died *ca.* 1477. The girl (Charmosina) is the daughter of an avaricious old merchant (not a Jew). Perhaps no source for the Jessica episode need be sought beyond the rôle of Marlowe's Abigail in *The Jew of Malta*. That Shakespeare knew Marlowe's tragedy was a matter of course. Its influence is pervasively discernible and there are several points of special contact — in particular, the scene in which the daughter throws the treasure out of the window. But Jessica is not Abigail, and Shylock is not, like Barabas, a Machiavellian villain.

The name *Shylock* is thought to be the Hebrew *shalach*, translated by 'cormorant' in *Leviticus*, xi, 17, and *Deuteronomy*, xiv, 17. 'Away, thou money-mong'ring cormorant!' says Eutrapelus to the usurer Philargurus in the anonymous play of *Timon* (v, 5), which may date from 1590 or earlier. In *Coriolanus* (i, 1, 125) 'the cormorant belly' typifies the patricians who 'make edicts for usury, to support usurers.' *Jessica* seems to come from *Jesca* (*Iescha* in the Vulgate), a form of *Iscah*, the name of the daughter of Haran (*Genesis*, xi, 29), interpreted as 'she that looketh out.' This would fit ii, 5, 29 ff., where Shylock forbids Jessica to 'clamber up to the casements' and 'thrust her head into the public street to gaze on Christian fools,' and Launcelot prompts her to 'look out at a window, for all this.' Roderigo Lopez, Queen Elizabeth's physician, a converted Jew, was accused of plotting to poison her. Though probably innocent, he was executed for high treason on June 7, 1594. It is hard to see what this affair has to do with Shakespeare's play. *Lopez*, to be sure, resembles *lupus*, and Gratiano imagines Shylock's 'currish spirit' to be that of a wolf 'hang'd for human slaughter' since his 'desires are wolvish, bloody, starv'd and ravenous.' The character of Shylock fascinates critics and has lured them into endless mazes of debate. One thing is clear, however: THE MERCHANT OF VENICE is no anti-Semitic document; Shakespeare was not attacking the Jewish people when he gave Shylock the villain's rôle. If so, he was attacking the Moors in *Titus Andronicus*, the Spaniards in *Much Ado*, the Italians in *Cymbeline*, the Viennese in *Measure for Measure*, the Danes in *Hamlet*, the Britons in *King Lear*, the Scots in *Macbeth*, and the English in *Richard the Third*.

THE MERCHANT OF VENICE

[Dramatis Personæ.

The Duke of Venice.
The Prince of Morocco, } suitors to *Portia*.
The Prince of Arragon, }
Antonio, a Venetian merchant.
Bassanio, his friend, suitor to *Portia*.
Solanio, }
Salerio, } friends to *Antonio* and *Bassanio*.
Gratiano, }
Lorenzo, in love with *Jessica*.
Shylock, a Jew.
Tubal, a Jew, his friend.

Launcelot Gobbo, a clown, servant to *Shylock*.
Old Gobbo, father to *Launcelot*.
Leonardo, servant to *Bassanio*.
Balthasar, } servants to *Portia*.
Stephano, }

Portia, an heiress.
Nerissa, her waiting gentlewoman.
Jessica, daughter to *Shylock*.

Magnificoes, Officers, Jailer, Servants, and other Attendants.

SCENE. — *Partly at Venice and partly at Belmont, Portia's estate.*]

ACT I. [Scene I. *Venice. A street.*]

Enter *Antonio, Salerio,* and *Solanio.*

Ant. In sooth, I know not why I am so sad.
It wearies me; you say it wearies you;
But how I caught it, found it, or came by it,
What stuff 'tis made of, whereof it is born,
I am to learn; 5
And such a want-wit sadness makes of me
That I have much ado to know myself.
Saler. Your mind is tossing on the ocean;
There where your argosies with portly sail —
Like signiors and rich burghers on the flood, 10
Or, as it were, the pageants of the sea —
Do overpeer the petty traffickers,
That cursy to them, do them reverence,
As they fly by them with their woven wings.
Solan. Believe me, sir, had I such venture forth, 15
The better part of my affections would
Be with my hopes abroad. I should be still
Plucking the grass to know where sits the wind,
Piring in maps for ports, and piers, and roads;
And every object that might make me fear 20
Misfortune to my ventures, out of doubt
Would make me sad.
Saler. My wind, cooling my broth,
Would blow me to an ague when I thought
What harm a wind too great might do at sea.
I should not see the sandy hourglass run 25
But I should think of shallows and of flats,
And see my wealthy Andrew dock'd in sand,
Vailing her high top lower than her ribs
To kiss her burial. Should I go to church
And see the holy edifice of stone 30
And not bethink me straight of dangerous rocks,
Which, touching but my gentle vessel's side,
Would scatter all her spices on the stream,
Enrobe the roaring waters with my silks,
And, in a word, but even now worth this, 35
And now worth nothing? Shall I have the thought
To think on this, and shall I lack the thought
That such a thing bechanc'd would make me sad?
But tell not me! I know Antonio
Is sad to think upon his merchandise. 40
Ant. Believe me, no. I thank my fortune for it,
My ventures are not in one bottom trusted,
Nor to one place; nor is my whole estate
Upon the fortune of this present year. 44
Therefore my merchandise makes me not sad.
Solan. Why, then you are in love.
Ant. Fie, fie!
Solan. Not in love neither? Then let us say you are sad
Because you are not merry; and 'twere as easy
For you to laugh, and leap, and say you are merry
Because you are not sad. Now, by two-headed Janus, 50
Nature hath fram'd strange fellows in her time:
Some that will evermore peep through their eyes,
And laugh like parrots at a bagpiper;
And other of such vinegar aspect

259

That they'll not show their teeth in way of smile, 55
Though Nestor swear the jest be laughable.

Enter *Bassanio, Lorenzo,* and *Gratiano.*

Here comes Bassanio, your most noble kinsman,
Gratiano, and Lorenzo. Fare ye well.
We leave you now with better company.

Saler. I would have stay'd till I had made you merry, 60
If worthier friends had not prevented me.

Ant. Your worth is very dear in my regard.
I take it your own business calls on you,
And you embrace th' occasion to depart.

Saler. Good morrow, my good lords. 65

Bass. Good signiors both, when shall we laugh? Say, when?
You grow exceeding strange. Must it be so?

Saler. We'll make our leisures to attend on yours. *Exeunt Salerio and Solanio.*

Lor. My Lord Bassanio, since you have found Antonio,
We two will leave you; but at dinner time 70
I pray you have in mind where we must meet.

Bass. I will not fail you.

Gra. You look not well, Signior Antonio.
You have too much respect upon the world;
They lose it that do buy it with much care. 75
Believe me, you are marvellously chang'd.

Ant. I hold the world but as the world, Gratiano —
A stage, where every man must play a part,
And mine a sad one.

Gra. Let me play the fool.
With mirth and laughter let old wrinkles come,
And let my liver rather heat with wine 81
Than my heart cool with mortifying groans.
Why should a man whose blood is warm within
Sit like his grandsire cut in alablaster?
Sleep when he wakes? and creep into the jaundice 85
By being peevish? I tell thee what, Antonio —
I love thee, and it is my love that speaks —
There are a sort of men whose visages
Do cream and mantle like a standing pond,
And do a wilful stillness entertain 90
With purpose to be dress'd in an opinion
Of wisdom, gravity, profound conceit;
As who should say, 'I am Sir Oracle,
And when I ope my lips, let no dog bark!'
O my Antonio, I do know of these 95
That therefore only are reputed wise
For saying nothing; when, I am very sure,
If they should speak, would almost damn those ears

Which, hearing them, would call their brothers fools.
I'll tell thee more of this another time. 100
But fish not with this melancholy bait
For this fool gudgeon, this opinion.
Come, good Lorenzo. Fare ye well awhile.
I'll end my exhortation after dinner.

Lor. Well, we will leave you then till dinner time. 105
I must be one of these same dumb wise men,
For Gratiano never lets me speak.

Gra. Well, keep me company but two years moe,
Thou shalt not know the sound of thine own tongue.

Ant. Fare you well. I'll grow a talker for this gear. 110

Gra. Thanks, i' faith; for silence is only commendable
In a neat's tongue dried and a maid not vendible. *Exeunt [Gratiano and Lorenzo].*

Ant. Is that anything now?

Bass. Gratiano speaks an infinite deal of nothing, more than any man in all Venice. His reasons are as two grains of wheat hid in two bushels of chaff. You shall seek all day ere you find them; and when you have them, they are not worth the search.

Ant. Well, tell me now, what lady is the same
To whom you swore a secret pilgrimage 120
That you to-day promis'd to tell me of?

Bass. 'Tis not unknown to you, Antonio,
How much I have disabled mine estate
By something showing a more swelling port
Than my faint means would grant continuance;
Nor do I now make moan to be abridg'd 126
From such a noble rate; but my chief care
Is to come fairly off from the great debts
Wherein my time, something too prodigal,
Hath left me gag'd. To you, Antonio, 130
I owe the most, in money and in love;
And from your love I have a warranty
To unburthen all my plots and purposes
How to get clear of all the debts I owe.

Ant. I pray you, good Bassanio, let me know it; 135
And if it stand, as you yourself still do,
Within the eye of honour, be assur'd
My purse, my person, my extremest means
Lie all unlock'd to your occasions.

Bass. In my schooldays, when I had lost one shaft, 140
I shot his fellow of the selfsame flight
The selfsame way with more advised watch,
To find the other forth; and by adventuring both

I oft found both. I urge this childhood proof
Because what follows is pure innocence. 145
I owe you much, and, like a wilful youth,
That which I owe is lost; but if you please
To shoot another arrow that self way
Which you did shoot the first, I do not doubt,
As I will watch the aim, or to find both, 150
Or bring your latter hazard back again
And thankfully rest debtor for the first.
  Ant. You know me well, and herein spend
      but time
To wind about my love with circumstance;
And out of doubt you do me now more wrong
In making question of my uttermost 156
Than if you had made waste of all I have.
Then do but say to me what I should do
That in your knowledge may by me be done,
And I am prest unto it. Therefore speak. 160
  Bass. In Belmont is a lady richly left;
And she is fair, and, fairer than that word,
Of wondrous virtues. Sometimes from her eyes
I did receive fair speechless messages.
Her name is Portia — nothing undervalu'd 165
To Cato's daughter, Brutus' Portia.
Nor is the wide world ignorant of her worth;
For the four winds blow in from every coast
Renowned suitors, and her sunny locks
Hang on her temples like a golden fleece, 170
Which makes her seat of Belmont Colchos'
      strond,
And many Jasons come in quest of her.
O my Antonio, had I but the means
To hold a rival place with one of them,
I have a mind presages me such thrift 175
That I should questionless be fortunate!
  Ant. Thou know'st that all my fortunes are
      at sea;
Neither have I money, nor commodity
To raise a present sum. Therefore go forth;
Try what my credit can in Venice do. 180
That shall be rack'd, even to the uttermost,
To furnish thee to Belmont to fair Portia.
Go presently enquire, and so will I,
Where money is; and I no question make
To have it of my trust, or for my sake. *Exeunt.*

[Scene II. *Belmont.* Portia's *house.*]

Enter *Portia* with her waiting woman, *Nerissa.*

  Por. By my troth, Nerissa, my little body is
aweary of this great world.
  Ner. You would be, sweet madam, if your
miseries were in the same abundance as your
good fortunes are; and yet, for aught I see,
they are as sick that surfeit with too much as
they that starve with nothing. It is no mean
happiness, therefore, to be seated in the mean.
Superfluity comes sooner by white hairs, but
competency lives longer. 10
  Por. Good sentences, and well pronounc'd.
  Ner. They would be better if well followed.
  Por. If to do were as easy as to know what
were good to do, chapels had been churches,
and poor men's cottages princes' palaces. It is
a good divine that follows his own instructions.
I can easier teach twenty what were good to be
done than be one of the twenty to follow mine
own teaching. The brain may devise laws for
the blood, but a hot temper leaps o'er a cold
decree: such a hare is madness the youth, to
skip o'er the meshes of good counsel the crip-
ple. But this reasoning is not in the fashion
to choose me a husband. O me, the word
'choose'! I may neither choose who I would
nor refuse who I dislike, so is the will of a living
daughter curb'd by the will of a dead father.
Is it not hard, Nerissa, that I cannot choose
one nor refuse none? 29
  Ner. Your father was ever virtuous; and
holy men at their death have good inspirations.
Therefore the lott'ry that he hath devised in
these three chests of gold, silver, and lead,
whereof who chooses his meaning chooses you,
will no doubt never be chosen by any rightly
but one who you shall rightly love. But what
warmth is there in your affection towards any
of these princely suitors that are already come?
  Por. I pray thee overname them; and as
thou namest them, I will describe them; and according to my description level at my affection.
  Ner. First, there is the Neapolitan prince.
  Por. Ay, that's a colt indeed, for he doth
nothing but talk of his horse; and he makes it
a great appropriation to his own good parts that
he can shoe him himself. I am much afeard my
lady his mother play'd false with a smith. 48
  Ner. Then is there the County Palatine.
  Por. He doth nothing but frown; as who
should say, 'An you will not have me, choose!'
He hears merry tales and smiles not. I fear he
will prove the weeping philosopher when he
grows old, being so full of unmannerly sadness
in his youth. I had rather be married to a
death's-head with a bone in his mouth than to
either of these. God defend me from these two!
  Ner. How say you by the French lord, Monsieur Le Bon? 59
  Por. God made him, and therefore let him
pass for a man. In truth, I know it is a sin to

261

be a mocker; but he — why, he hath a horse better than the Neapolitan's, a better bad habit of frowning than the Count Palatine. He is every man in no man. If a throstle sing, he falls straight a-cap'ring; he will fence with his own shadow. If I should marry him, I should marry twenty husbands. If he would despise me, I would forgive him; for if he love me to madness, I shall never requite him.   70

Ner. What say you then to Falconbridge, the young baron of England?

Por. You know I say nothing to him; for he understands not me, nor I him. He hath neither Latin, French, nor Italian; and you will come into the court and swear that I have a poor pennyworth in the English. He is a proper man's picture; but alas! who can converse with a dumb-show? How oddly he is suited! I think he bought his doublet in Italy, his round hose in France, his bonnet in Germany, and his behaviour everywhere.   82

Ner. What think you of the Scottish lord, his neighbour?

Por. That he hath a neighbourly charity in him; for he borrowed a box of the ear of the Englishman, and swore he would pay him again when he was able. I think the Frenchman became his surety and seal'd under for another.

Ner. How like you the young German, the Duke of Saxony's nephew?   91

Por. Very vilely in the morning, when he is sober, and most vilely in the afternoon, when he is drunk. When he is best, he is a little worse than a man; and when he is worst, he is little better than a beast. An the worst fall that ever fell, I hope I shall make shift to go without him.

Ner. If he should offer to choose, and choose the right casket, you should refuse to perform your father's will if you should refuse to accept him.   102

Por. Therefore, for fear of the worst, I pray thee set a deep glass of Rhenish wine on the contrary casket; for, if the devil be within and that temptation without, I know he will choose it. I will do anything, Nerissa, ere I will be married to a sponge.   108

Ner. You need not fear, lady, the having any of these lords. They have acquainted me with their determinations; which is indeed to return to their home, and to trouble you with no more suit, unless you may be won by some other sort than your father's imposition, depending on the caskets.   115

Por. If I live to be as old as Sibylla, I will die as chaste as Diana unless I be obtained by the manner of my father's will. I am glad this parcel of wooers are so reasonable, for there is not one among them but I dote on his very absence; and I pray God grant them a fair departure.

Ner. Do you not remember, lady, in your father's time, a Venetian, a scholar and a soldier, that came hither in company of the Marquis of Montferrat?   126

Por. Yes, yes, it was Bassanio. As I think, so was he call'd.

Ner. True, madam. He, of all the men that ever my foolish eyes look'd upon, was the best deserving a fair lady.   131

Por. I remember him well, and I remember him worthy of thy praise.

Enter a Servingman.

How now? What news?

Serv. The four strangers seek for you, madam, to take their leave; and there is a forerunner come from a fifth, the Prince of Morocco, who brings word the Prince his master will be here to-night.   139

Por. If I could bid the fifth welcome with so good heart as I can bid the other four farewell, I should be glad of his approach. If he have the condition of a saint and the complexion of a devil, I had rather he should shrive me than wive me.   145

Come, Nerissa. Sirrah, go before.
Whiles we shut the gate upon one wooer, another knocks at the door.   *Exeunt.*

[Scene III. *Venice. A public place.*]

Enter Bassanio with Shylock the Jew.

Shy. Three thousand ducats — well.

Bass. Ay, sir, for three months.

Shy. For three months — well.

Bass. For the which, as I told you, Antonio shall be bound.   5

Shy. Antonio shall become bound — well.

Bass. May you stead me? Will you pleasure me? Shall I know your answer?

Shy. Three thousand ducats for three months, and Antonio bound.   10

Bass. Your answer to that.

Shy. Antonio is a good man.

Bass. Have you heard any imputation to the contrary?   14

Shy. Ho, no, no, no, no! My meaning in saying he is a good man is to have you understand me that he is sufficient. Yet his means are in supposition. He hath an argosy bound to

Tripolis, another to the Indies. I understand,
moreover, upon the Rialto, he hath a third at
Mexico, a fourth for England, and other ventures he hath, squand'red abroad. But ships
are but boards, sailors but men; there be land
rats and water rats, land thieves and water
thieves — I mean pirates; and then there is
the peril of waters, winds, and rocks. The man
is, notwithstanding, sufficient. Three thousand
ducats. I think I may take his bond.   28

Bass. Be assur'd you may.

Shy. I will be assur'd I may; and, that I
may be assured, I will bethink me. May I
speak with Antonio?   32

Bass. If it please you to dine with us.

Shy. Yes, to smell pork, to eat of the habitation which your prophet the Nazarite con-
jured the devil into! I will buy with you, sell
with you, talk with you, walk with you, and so
following; but I will not eat with you, drink
with you, nor pray with you. What news on
the Rialto? Who is he comes here?   40

Enter *Antonio.*

Bass. This is Signior Antonio.

Shy. [*aside*] How like a fawning publican he
looks!
I hate him for he is a Christian;
But more for that in low simplicity
He lends out money gratis and brings down   45
The rate of usance here with us in Venice.
If I can catch him once upon the hip,
I will feed fat the ancient grudge I bear him.
He hates our sacred nation, and he rails,
Even there where merchants most do congregate,
On me, my bargains, and my well-won thrift,
Which he calls interest. Cursed be my tribe
If I forgive him!

Bass.   Shylock, do you hear?

Shy. I am debating of my present store,
And by the near guess of my memory   55
I cannot instantly raise up the gross
Of full three thousand ducats. What of that?
Tubal, a wealthy Hebrew of my tribe,
Will furnish me. But soft! How many months
Do you desire? — [*To Antonio*] Rest you fair,
good signior!   60
Your worship was the last man in our mouths.

Ant. Shylock, albeit I neither lend nor borrow
By taking nor by giving of excess,
Yet, to supply the ripe wants of my friend,
I'll break a custom. [*To Bassanio*] Is he yet
possess'd   65
How much ye would?

Shy.   Ay, ay, three thousand ducats.

Ant. And for three months.

Shy. I had forgot — three months, you told
me so.
Well then, your bond. And let me see — but
hear you:
Methoughts you said you neither lend nor borrow
Upon advantage.

Ant.   I do never use it.   71

Shy. When Jacob graz'd his uncle Laban's
sheep —
This Jacob from our holy Abram was
(As his wise mother wrought in his behalf)
The third possessor; ay, he was the third —   75

Ant. And what of him? Did he take interest?

Shy. No, not take interest; not, as you
would say,
Directly int'rest. Mark what Jacob did.
When Laban and himself were compremis'd
That all the eanlings which were streak'd and
pied   80
Should fall as Jacob's hire, the ewes, being rank,
In end of autumn turned to the rams;
And when the work of generation was
Between these woolly breeders in the act,
The skilful shepherd pill'd me certain wands,   85
And, in the doing of the deed of kind,
He stuck them up before the fulsome ewes,
Who then conceiving, did in eaning time
Fall parti-colour'd lambs, and those were
Jacob's.
This was a way to thrive, and he was blest;   90
And thrift is blessing, if men steal it not.

Ant. This was a venture, sir, that Jacob
serv'd for;
A thing not in his power to bring to pass,
But sway'd and fashion'd by the hand of heaven.
Was this inserted to make interest good?   95
Or is your gold and silver ewes and rams?

Shy. I cannot tell; I make it breed as fast.
But note me, signior.

Ant. [*aside*]   Mark you this, Bassanio,
The devil can cite Scripture for his purpose.
An evil soul, producing holy witness,   100
Is like a villain with a smiling cheek,
A goodly apple rotten at the heart.
O, what a goodly outside falsehood hath!

Shy. Three thousand ducats — 'tis a good
round sum.
Three months from twelve — then, let me see,
the rate —   105

Ant. Well, Shylock, shall we be beholding
to you?

Shy. Signior Antonio, many a time and oft
In the Rialto you have rated me
About my moneys and my usances.

Still have I borne it with a patient shrug; 110
For suff'rance is the badge of all our tribe.
You call me misbeliever, cutthroat dog,
And spet upon my Jewish gaberdine,
And all for use of that which is mine own.
Well then, it now appears you need my help. 115
Go to then, you come to me and you say,
'Shylock, we would have moneys.' You say so—
You that did void your rheum upon my beard
And foot me as you spurn a stranger cur
Over your threshold. Moneys is your suit. 120
What should I say to you? Should I not say
'Hath a dog money? Is it possible
A cur can lend three thousand ducats?' or
Shall I bend low, and in a bondman's key,
With bated breath and whisp'ring humbleness,
Say this: 126
'Fair sir, you spet on me on Wednesday last;
You spurn'd me such a day; another time
You call'd me dog; and for these courtesies
I'll lend you thus much moneys'? 130
Ant. I am as like to call thee so again,
To spet on thee again, to spurn thee too.
If thou wilt lend this money, lend it not
As to thy friends — for when did friendship take
A breed for barren metal of his friend? 135
But lend it rather to thine enemy,
Who if he break, thou mayst with better face
Exact the penalty.
Shy. Why, look you, how you storm!
I would be friends with you and have your love,
Forget the shames that you have stain'd me
with, 140
Supply your present wants, and take no doit
Of usance for my moneys,
And you'll not hear me. This is kind I offer.
Bass. This were kindness.
Shy. This kindness will I show.
Go with me to a notary, seal me there 145
Your single bond; and, in a merry sport,
If you repay me not on such a day,
In such a place, such sum or sums as are
Express'd in the condition, let the forfeit

Be nominated for an equal pound 150
Of your fair flesh, to be cut off and taken
In what part of your body pleaseth me.
Ant. Content, in faith. I'll seal to such a
bond,
And say there is much kindness in the Jew.
Bass. You shall not seal to such a bond for
me! 155
I'll rather dwell in my necessity.
Ant. Why, fear not, man! I will not for-
feit it.
Within these two months — that's a month
before
This bond expires — I do expect return
Of thrice three times the value of this bond. 160
Shy. O father Abram, what these Christians
are,
Whose own hard dealing teaches them suspect
The thoughts of others! Pray you tell me this:
If he should break his day, what should I gain
By the exaction of the forfeiture? 165
A pound of man's flesh taken from a man
Is not so estimable, profitable neither,
As flesh of muttons, beefs, or goats. I say,
To buy his favour I extend this friendship.
If he will take it, so; if not, adieu; 170
And for my love I pray you wrong me not.
Ant. Yes, Shylock, I will seal unto this bond.
Shy. Then meet me forthwith at the no-
tary's;
Give him direction for this merry bond,
And I will go and purse the ducats straight, 175
See to my house, left in the fearful guard
Of an unthrifty knave, and presently
I will be with you.
Ant. Hie thee, gentle Jew. *Exit [Shylock].*
The Hebrew will turn Christian; he grows kind.
Bass. I like not fair terms and a villain's
mind. 180
Ant. Come on. In this there can be no
dismay;
My ships come home a month before the day.
Exeunt.

ACT II. [Scene I. *Belmont.* Portia's *house.*]

Enter [the *Prince of*] *Morocco*, a tawny Moor,
all in white, and three or four *Followers* accordingly, with *Portia, Nerissa*, and their *Train*.

Mor. Mislike me not for my complexion,
The shadowed livery of the burnish'd sun,
To whom I am a neighbour and near bred.
Bring me the fairest creature northward born,
Where Phœbus' fire scarce thaws the icicles, 5
And let us make incision for your love
To prove whose blood is reddest, his or mine.
I tell thee, lady, this aspect of mine
Hath fear'd the valiant. By my love I swear,
The best-regarded virgins of our clime 10
Have lov'd it too. I would not change this hue,
Except to steal your thoughts, my gentle queen.

Por. In terms of choice I am not solely led
By nice direction of a maiden's eyes.
Besides, the lott'ry of my destiny   15
Bars me the right of voluntary choosing.
But, if my father had not scanted me,
And hedg'd me by his wit to yield myself
His wife who wins me by that means I told you,
Yourself, renowned Prince, then stood as fair
As any comer I have look'd on yet   21
For my affection.
    Mor.   Even for that I thank you.
Therefore I pray you lead me to the caskets
To try my fortune. By this scimitar,
That slew the Sophy and a Persian prince   25
That won three fields of Sultan Solyman,
I would o'erstare the sternest eyes that look,
Outbrave the heart most daring on the earth,
Pluck the young sucking cubs from the she-bear,
Yea, mock the lion when 'a roars for prey,   30
To win thee, lady. But, alas the while!
If Hercules and Lichas play at dice
Which is the better man, the greater throw
May turn by fortune from the weaker hand:
So is Alcides beaten by his page,   35
And so may I, blind Fortune leading me,
Miss that which one unworthier may attain,
And die with grieving.
    Por.   You must take your chance;
And either not attempt to choose at all,
Or swear before you choose, if you choose wrong,
Never to speak to lady afterward   41
In way of marriage. Therefore be advis'd.
    Mor. Nor will not. Come, bring me unto
my chance.
    Por. First, forward to the temple; after
dinner
Your hazard shall be made.
    Mor.   Good fortune then! 45
To make me blest or cursed'st among men.
                                        Exeunt.

[Scene II. *Venice. A street.*]

Enter [*Launcelot*] *the Clown,* alone.

Laun. Certainly my conscience will serve me
to run from this Jew my master. The fiend is
at mine elbow and tempts me, saying to me,
'Gobbo, Launcelot Gobbo, good Launcelot,' or
'good Gobbo,' or 'good Launcelot Gobbo, use
your legs, take the start, run away.' My conscience says, 'No. Take heed, honest Launcelot; take heed, honest Gobbo,' or, as aforesaid,
'honest Launcelot Gobbo, do not run; scorn
running with thy heels.' Well, the most courageous fiend bids me pack. 'Via!' says the fiend.
'Away!' says the fiend. 'For the heavens,
rouse up a brave mind,' says the fiend, 'and
run.' Well, my conscience, hanging about the
neck of my heart, says very wisely to me, 'My
honest friend Launcelot, being an honest man's
son' — or rather an honest woman's son; for
indeed my father did something smack, something grow to, he had a kind of taste —Well,
my conscience says, 'Launcelot, budge not.'
'Budge,' says the fiend. 'Budge not,' says my
conscience. 'Conscience,' say I, 'you counsel
well.' 'Fiend,' say I, 'you counsel well.' To be
rul'd by my conscience, I should stay with the
Jew my master, who (God bless the mark!) is
a kind of devil; and, to run away from the
Jew, I should be ruled by the fiend, who (saving your reverence) is the devil himself. Certainly the Jew is the very devil incarnation;
and, in my conscience, my conscience is but a
kind of hard conscience to offer to counsel me
to stay with the Jew. The fiend gives the more
friendly counsel. I will run, fiend; my heels
are at your commandment; I will run.

Enter *Old Gobbo,* with a basket.

    Gob. Master young man, you, I pray you,
which is the way to Master Jew's?   35
    Laun. [*aside*] O heavens, this is my true-
begotten father! who, being more than sand-
blind, high-gravel-blind, knows me not. I will
try confusions with him.
    Gob. Master young gentleman, I pray you
which is the way to Master Jew's?   41
    Laun. Turn up on your right hand at the
next turning, but, at the next turning of all,
on your left; marry, at the very next turning,
turn of no hand, but turn down indirectly to
the Jew's house.   46
    Gob. Be God's sonties, 'twill be a hard way
to hit! Can you tell me whether one Launcelot
that dwells with him, dwell with him or no?
    Laun. Talk you of young Master Launcelot?
[*Aside*] Mark me now! Now will I raise the
waters. — Talk you of young Master Launcelot?
    Gob. No master, sir, but a poor man's son.
His father, though I say't, is an honest exceeding poor man, and, God be thanked, well
to live.   55
    Laun. Well, let his father be what 'a will,
we talk of young Master Launcelot.
    Gob. Your worship's friend, and Launcelot, sir.
    Laun. But, I pray you, ergo, old man, ergo,
I beseech you, talk you of young Master
Launcelot?   60

265

Gob. Of Launcelot, an't please your mastership.

Laun. Ergo Master Launcelot. Talk not of Master Launcelot, father; for the young gentleman, according to Fates and Destinies and such odd sayings, the Sisters Three and such branches of learning, is indeed deceased, or, as you would say in plain terms, gone to heaven.

Gob. Marry, God forbid! The boy was the very staff of my age, my very prop. 70

Laun. [*aside*] Do I look like a cudgel or a hovel-post, a staff, or a prop? — Do you know me, father?

Gob. Alack the day, I know you not, young gentleman! but I pray you tell me, is my boy (God rest his soul!) alive or dead? 75

Laun. Do you not know me, father?

Gob. Alack, sir, I am sand-blind! I know you not.

Laun. Nay, indeed, if you had your eyes, you might fail of the knowing me. It is a wise father that knows his own child. Well, old man, I will tell you news of your son. [*Kneels.*] Give me your blessing. Truth will come to light; murder cannot be hid long — a man's son may, but in the end truth will out. 85

Gob. Pray you, sir, stand up. I am sure you are not Launcelot, my boy.

Laun. Pray you let's have no more fooling about it, but give me your blessing. I am Launcelot — your boy that was, your son that is, your child that shall be. 91

Gob. I cannot think you are my son.

Laun. I know not what I shall think of that; but I am Launcelot, the Jew's man, and I am sure Margery your wife is my mother. 95

Gob. Her name is Margery indeed. I'll be sworn, if thou be Launcelot, thou art mine own flesh and blood. Lord worshipp'd might he be! What a beard hast thou got! Thou hast got more hair on thy chin than Dobbin my fill-horse has on his tail. 101

Laun. [*rises*] It should seem then that Dobbin's tail grows backward. I am sure he had more hair of his tail than I have of my face when I last saw him. 105

Gob. Lord, how art thou chang'd! How dost thou and thy master agree? I have brought him a present. How 'gree you now?

Laun. Well, well; but, for mine own part, as I have set up my rest to run away, so I will not rest till I have run some ground. My master's a very Jew. Give him a present? Give him a halter! I am famish'd in his service. You may tell every finger I have with my ribs.

Father, I am glad you are come. Give me your present to one Master Bassanio, who indeed gives rare new liveries. If I serve not him, I will run as far as God has any ground. O rare fortune! here comes the man. To him, father; for I am a Jew if I serve the Jew any longer.

Enter Bassanio, with [Leonardo and] a
Follower or two.

Bass. You may do so; but let it be so hasted that supper be ready at the farthest by five of the clock. See these letters delivered, put the liveries to making, and desire Gratiano to come anon to my lodging. 125

Exit one of his men.

Laun. To him, father.

Gob. God bless your worship!

Bass. Gramercy. Wouldst thou aught with me?

Gob. Here's my son, sir, a poor boy — 129

Laun. Not a poor boy, sir, but the rich Jew's man, that would, sir, as my father shall specify —

Gob. He hath a great infection, sir, as one would say, to serve — 134

Laun. Indeed, the short and the long is, I serve the Jew, and have a desire, as my father shall specify —

Gob. His master and he (saving your worship's reverence) are scarce cater-cousins. 139

Laun. To be brief, the very truth is, that the Jew having done me wrong, doth cause me, as my father, being, I hope, an old man, shall frutify unto you —

Gob. I have here a dish of doves that I would bestow upon your worship; and my suit is —

Laun. In very brief, the suit is impertinent to myself, as your worship shall know by this honest old man; and, though I say it, though old man, yet poor man, my father. 149

Bass. One speak for both. What would you?

Laun. Serve you, sir.

Gob. That is the very defect of the matter, sir.

Bass. I know thee well; thou hast obtain'd thy suit.
Shylock thy master spoke with me this day
And hath preferr'd thee, if it be preferment 155
To leave a rich Jew's service to become
The follower of so poor a gentleman.

Laun. The old proverb is very well parted between my master Shylock and you, sir. You have the grace of God, sir, and he hath enough.

Bass. Thou speak'st it well. Go, father, with thy son. 161
Take leave of thy old master and enquire

Paul Rogers in the role of the crafty, vindictive Shylock. Claire Bloom as dark-eyed Jessica, his daughter

THE MERCHANT
of VENICE

Left: The lovely Portia (Irene Worth), as wise as she is beautiful

Right: Robert Urquhart in the role of Bassanio, Portia's suitor

Left: Jane Wenham as Nerissa, Portia's maid

Right: Nerissa's lover, Gratiano (William Squire)

Left: Richard Gale in the role of Lorenzo, the lover of Jessica

Right: Douglas Campbell as the Merchant of Venice, Antonio

Right: "I would have stay'd till I had made you merry, if worthier friends had not prevented me." Having vainly attempted to cheer up the dispirited Antonio, Salarino (Tony van Bridge) and Salanio (Patrick Wymark) depart as his young friends arrive *(Act I, Scene I)*

Left: "He will fence with his own shadow: if I should marry him, I should marry twenty husbands." Portia mimics one of her suitors *(Act I, Scene II)*

Right: The Prince of Morocco (George Murcell), Portia's suitor; constrained by love to put aside his scimitar and take his chances in the lottery which Portia imposes on all who court her affection

Left: Misguided by outward show, the Prince of Morocco chooses the golden casket and is forced to withdraw his suit for the fair Portia (Act II, Scene VII)

Right: The Prince of Arragon (John Warner) departs after choosing the silver casket and finding in it "the portrait of a blinking idiot" (Act II, Scene IX)

Below: "Master young man, you; I pray you, which is the way to Master Jew's." Not recognizing his son Launcelot (Kenneth Connor), Old Gobbo (Newton Blick) asks him the way to his master's house (Act II, Scene II)

Shylock's daughter Jessica, whose dusky beauty captures the heart of young Lorenzo

"Give him this letter; do it secretly." Jessica entrusts Launcelot with a letter for Lorenzo (Act II, Scene III)

Left: "The villainy you teach me I will execute, and it shall go hard but I will better the instruction." Shylock broods upon his vengeance (Act III, Scene I)

Below: Disguised as revelers, Lorenzo and his friends come to help Jessica escape from Shylock (Act II, Scene VI)

"Why, this bond is forfeit; and lawfully by this the Jew may claim a pound of flesh to be by him cut off nearest the merchant's heart." Disguised as a lawyer, Portia leads Shylock on by confirming the validity of his bond (Act IV, Scene I)

"Most learned judge! A sentence! come, prepare!" Unaware of the trap laid for him, Shylock praises the lawyer's decision (Act IV, Scene I)

"Tarry a little, there is something else." As Shylock prepares to collect his pound of flesh, Portia points out that his lands and goods will be forfeit if he sheds a single drop of Antonio's blood (*Act IV, Scene I*)

Left: "Well, while I live I'll fear no other thing so sore as keeping safe Nerissa's ring." Nerissa returns to Gratiano the ring which he gave her when she was disguised as a law clerk (*Act V, Scene I*)

Right: "Let us go in; and charge us there upon inter'gatories, and we will answer all things faithfully." Bassiano and Portia are united in the final scene of the play (*Act V, Scene I*)

The last scene of the play finds Antonio absolved of his debt and the six young lovers blissfully paired (Act V, Scene 1)

My lodging out. [*To a Servant*] Give him a livery
More guarded than his fellows'. See it done.
   Laun. Father, in. I cannot get a service, no!
I have ne'er a tongue in my head! Well, [*looks on his palm*] if any man in Italy have a fairer table which doth offer to swear upon a book —!
I shall have good fortune. Go to, here's a simple line of life! Here's a small trifle of wives!
Alas, fifteen wives is nothing! a 'leven widows and nine maids is a simple coming-in for one man; and then to scape drowning thrice, and to be in peril of my life with the edge of a featherbed! Here are simple scapes. Well, if Fortune be a woman, she's a good wench for this gear.
Father, come. I'll take my leave of the Jew in the twinkling.   *Exit* [*with Old Gobbo*].
   Bass. I pray thee, good Leonardo, think on this:
These things being bought and orderly bestow'd
Return in haste, for I do feast to-night   180
My best-esteem'd acquaintance. Hie thee, go.
   Leon. My best endeavours shall be done herein.

                    Enter *Gratiano*.

   Gra. Where 's your master?
   Leon.   Yonder, sir, he walks. *Exit.*
   Gra. Signior Bassanio!
   Bass. Gratiano!   185
   Gra. I have a suit to you.
   Bass.   You have obtain'd it.
   Gra. You must not deny me. I must go with you
To Belmont.
   Bass. Why, then you must. But hear thee, Gratiano.   189
Thou art too wild, too rude, and bold of voice—
Parts that become thee happily enough
And in such eyes as ours appear not faults;
But where thou art not known, why, there they show
Something too liberal. Pray thee take pain
To allay with some cold drops of modesty   195
Thy skipping spirit, lest through thy wild behaviour
I be misconst'red in the place I go to
And lose my hopes.
   Gra.   Signior Bassanio, hear me.
If I do not put on a sober habit,   199
Talk with respect, and swear but now and then,
Wear prayer books in my pocket, look demurely,
Nay more, while grace is saying hood mine eyes
Thus with my hat, and sigh, and say amen,
Use all the observance of civility

Like one well studied in a sad ostent   205
To please his grandam, never trust me more.
   Bass. Well, we shall see your bearing.
   Gra. Nay, but I bar to-night. You shall not gauge me
By what we do to-night.
   Bass.   No, that were pity.
I would entreat you rather to put on   210
Your boldest suit of mirth, for we have friends
That purpose merriment. But fare you well.
I have some business.
   Gra. And I must to Lorenzo and the rest;
But we will visit you at supper time. *Exeunt.*

[Scene III. *Venice. Shylock's house.*]

Enter *Jessica* and [*Launcelot*] *the Clown.*

   Jes. I am sorry thou wilt leave my father so.
Our house is hell; and thou, a merry devil,
Didst rob it of some taste of tediousness.
But fare thee well. There is a ducat for thee;
And, Launcelot, soon at supper shalt thou see 5
Lorenzo, who is thy new master's guest.
Give him this letter; do it secretly;
And so farewell. I would not have my father
See me in talk with thee.   9
   Laun. Adieu! Tears exhibit my tongue.
Most beautiful pagan, most sweet Jew! if a Christian did not play the knave and get thee,
I am much deceived. But adieu! These foolish drops do something drown my manly spirit. Adieu!
   Jes. Farewell, good Launcelot.   15
                              Exit [*Launcelot*].
Alack, what heinous sin is it in me
To be asham'd to be my father's child!
But though I am a daughter to his blood,
I am not to his manners. O Lorenzo,   19
If thou keep promise, I shall end this strife,
Become a Christian and thy loving wife. *Exit.*

[Scene IV. *Venice. A street.*]

Enter *Gratiano, Lorenzo, Salerio,* and *Solanio.*

   Lor. Nay, we will slink away in supper time,
Disguise us at my lodging, and return
All in an hour.
   Gra. We have not made good preparation.
   Saler. We have not spoke us yet of torchbearers.   5
   Solan. 'Tis vile, unless it may be quaintly ordered,
And better in my mind not undertook.

Lor. 'Tis now but four o'clock. We have two hours
To furnish us.

Enter *Launcelot*, with a letter.

Friend Launcelot, what's the news?
Laun. An it shall please you to break up this, it shall seem to signify.   11
Lor. I know the hand. In faith, 'tis a fair hand,
And whiter than the paper it writ on
Is the fair hand that writ.
Gra.   Love-news, in faith!
Laun. By your leave, sir.   15
Lor. Whither goest thou?
Laun. Marry, sir, to bid my old master the Jew to sup to-night with my new master the Christian.
Lor. Hold here, take this [*gives money*]. Tell gentle Jessica   20
I will not fail her. Speak it privately.
Go. [*Exit Launcelot.*] Gentlemen,
Will you prepare you for this masque to-night?
I am provided of a torchbearer.
Saler. Ay, marry, I'll be gone about it straight.   25
Solan. And so will I.
Lor.   Meet me and Gratiano
At Gratiano's lodging some hour hence.
Saler. 'Tis good we do so.
                                Exeunt [*Salerio and Solanio*].
Gra. Was not that letter from fair Jessica?
Lor. I must needs tell thee all. She hath directed   30
How I shall take her from her father's house;
What gold and jewels she is furnish'd with;
What page's suit she hath in readiness.
If e'er the Jew her father come to heaven,
It will be for his gentle daughter's sake;   35
And never dare misfortune cross her foot,
Unless she do it under this excuse,
That she is issue to a faithless Jew.
Come, go with me; peruse this as thou goest.
Fair Jessica shall be my torchbearer. *Exeunt.*

[Scene V. *Venice. Before* Shylock's *house.*]

Enter [*the*] *Jew* [*Shylock*] and [*Launcelot,*] his man that was the *Clown.*

Shy. Well, thou shalt see, thy eyes shall be thy judge,
The difference of old Shylock and Bassanio. —
What, Jessica! — Thou shalt not gormandize
As thou hast done with me — What, Jessica! —

And sleep, and snore, and rend apparel out. —
Why, Jessica, I say!
Laun.   Why, Jessica!
Shy. Who bids thee call? I do not bid thee call.   7
Laun. Your worship was wont to tell me I could do nothing without bidding.

Enter *Jessica.*

Jes. Call you? What is your will?   10
Shy. I am bid forth to supper, Jessica.
There are my keys. But wherefore should I go?
I am not bid for love; they flatter me.
But yet I'll go in hate, to feed upon
The prodigal Christian. Jessica, my girl,   15
Look to my house. I am right loath to go.
There is some ill a-brewing towards my rest,
For I did dream of money bags to-night.
Laun. I beseech you, sir, go. My young master doth expect your reproach.   20
Shy. So do I his.
Laun. And they have conspired together. I will not say you shall see a masque; but if you do, then it was not for nothing that my nose fell a-bleeding on Black Monday last at six o'clock i' th' morning, falling out that year on Ash Wednesday was four year in th' afternoon.
Shy. What, are there masques? Hear you me, Jessica.
Lock up my doors; and when you hear the drum
And the vile squealing of the wry-neck'd fife,   30
Clamber not you up to the casements then,
Nor thrust your head into the public street
To gaze on Christian fools with varnish'd faces;
But stop my house's ears — I mean my casements.
Let not the sound of shallow fopp'ry enter   35
My sober house. By Jacob's staff I swear
I have no mind of feasting forth to-night;
But I will go. Go you before me, sirrah.
Say I will come.
Laun. I will go before, sir. Mistress, look out at window for all this.   41
There will come a Christian by
Will be worth a Jewess' eye.   [*Exit.*]
Shy. What says that fool of Hagar's offspring? ha?
Jes. His words were 'Farewell, mistress' — nothing else.   45
Shy. The patch is kind enough, but a huge feeder,
Snail-slow in profit, and he sleeps by day
More than the wildcat. Drones hive not with me;

Therefore I part with him, and part with him
To one that I would have him help to waste　50
His borrowed purse. Well, Jessica, go in.
Perhaps I will return immediately.
Do as I bid you; shut doors after you.
Fast bind, fast find —
A proverb never stale in thrifty mind.　*Exit.*

   Jes. Farewell; and if my fortune be not
crost,　56
I have a father, you a daughter, lost.　*Exit.*

[Scene VI. *Venice. Near* Shylock's *house.*]

Enter the Maskers, *Gratiano* and *Salerio.*

   Gra. This is the penthouse under which
Lorenzo
Desir'd us to make stand.
   Saler.　　　　His hour is almost past.
   Gra. And it is marvel he outdwells his hour,
For lovers ever run before the clock.　4
   Saler. O, ten times faster Venus' pigeons fly
To seal love's bonds new-made than they are
wont
To keep obliged faith unforfeited!
   Gra. That ever holds. Who riseth from a
feast
With that keen appetite that he sits down?
Where is the horse that doth untread again　10
His tedious measures with the unbated fire
That he did pace them first? All things that are
Are with more spirit chased than enjoy'd.
How like a younker or a prodigal
The scarfed bark puts from her native bay,　15
Hugg'd and embraced by the strumpet wind!
How like the Prodigal doth she return,
With over-weather'd ribs and ragged sails,
Lean, rent, and beggar'd by the strumpet wind!

Enter *Lorenzo.*

   Saler. Here comes Lorenzo. More of this
hereafter.　20
   Lor. Sweet friends, your patience for my long
abode.
Not I, but my affairs, have made you wait.
When you shall please to play the thieves for
wives,
I'll watch as long for you then. Approach.　24
Here dwells my father Jew. Ho! who's within?

[Enter] *Jessica*, above, [in boy's clothes].

   Jes. Who are you? Tell me for more cer-
tainty,
Albeit I'll swear that I do know your tongue.
   Lor. Lorenzo, and thy love.

   Jes. Lorenzo certain, and my love indeed,
For who love I so much? And now who knows
But you, Lorenzo, whether I am yours?　31
   Lor. Heaven and thy thoughts are witness
that thou art.
   Jes. Here, catch this casket; it is worth the
pains.
I am glad 'tis night, you do not look on me,
For I am much asham'd of my exchange.　35
But love is blind, and lovers cannot see
The pretty follies that themselves commit;
For if they could, Cupid himself would blush
To see me thus transformed to a boy.
   Lor. Descend, for you must be my torch-
bearer.　40
   Jes. What, must I hold a candle to my
shames?
They in themselves, good sooth, are too too
light.
Why, 'tis an office of discovery, love,
And I should be obscur'd.
   Lor.　　　　　　So are you, sweet,
Even in the lovely garnish of a boy.　45
But come at once;
For the close night doth play the runaway,
And we are stay'd for at Bassanio's feast.
   Jes. I will make fast the doors, and gild
myself　49
With some moe ducats, and be with you
straight.　[*Exit above.*]
   Gra. Now, by my hood, a gentle, and no
Jew!
   Lor. Beshrow me but I love her heartily;
For she is wise, if I can judge of her;
And fair she is, if that mine eyes be true;
And true she is, as she hath prov'd herself;　55
And therefore, like herself, wise, fair, and true,
Shall she be placed in my constant soul.

Enter *Jessica*, [below].

What, art thou come? On, gentlemen! away!
Our masquing mates by this time for us stay.
   Exit [*with Jessica and Salerio*].

Enter *Antonio.*

   Ant. Who's there?　60
   Gra. Signior Antonio?
   Ant. Fie, fie, Gratiano! Where are all the
rest?
'Tis nine o'clock; our friends all stay for you.
No masque to-night. The wind is come about;
Bassanio presently will go aboard.　65
I have sent twenty out to seek for you.
   Gra. I am glad on't. I desire no more delight
Than to be under sail and gone to-night. *Exeunt.*

[Scene VII. *Belmont*. Portia's *house.*]

Enter *Portia*, with *Morocco*, and
both their *Trains*.

Por. Go, draw aside the curtains and dis-
cover
The several caskets to this noble Prince.
Now make your choice.
                    [*The curtains are drawn aside.*]
Mor. The first, of gold, which this inscrip-
tion bears,
'Who chooseth me shall gain what many men
desire.'   5
The second, silver, which this promise carries,
'Who chooseth me shall get as much as he
deserves.'
This third, dull lead, with warning all as blunt,
'Who chooseth me must give and hazard all
he hath.'
How shall I know if I do choose the right?   10
Por. The one of them contains my picture,
Prince.
If you choose that, then I am yours withal.
Mor. Some god direct my judgment! Let
me see.
I will survey th' inscriptions back again.
What says this leaden casket?   15
'Who chooseth me must give and hazard all he
hath.'
Must give — for what? for lead! hazard for
lead?
This casket threatens. Men that hazard all
Do it in hope of fair advantages.
A golden mind stoops not to shows of dross. 20
I'll then nor give nor hazard aught for lead.
What says the silver, with her virgin hue?
'Who chooseth me shall get as much as he
deserves.'
As much as he deserves? Pause there, Morocco,
And weigh thy value with an even hand.   25
If thou beest rated by thy estimation,
Thou dost deserve enough; and yet enough
May not extend so far as to the lady;
And yet to be afeard of my deserving
Were but a weak disabling of myself.   30
As much as I deserve? Why, that's the lady!
I do in birth deserve her, and in fortunes,
In graces, and in qualities of breeding;
But more than these, in love I do deserve.
What if I stray'd no farther, but chose here? 35
Let's see once more this saying grav'd in gold:
'Who chooseth me shall gain what many men
desire.'
Why, that's the lady! All the world desires her.

From the four corners of the earth they come
To kiss this shrine, this mortal breathing saint.
The Hyrcanian deserts and the vasty wilds   41
Of wide Arabia are as throughfares now
For princes to come view fair Portia.
The watery kingdom, whose ambitious head
Spets in the face of heaven, is no bar   45
To stop the foreign spirits; but they come,
As o'er a brook, to see fair Portia.
One of these three contains her heavenly picture.
Is't like that lead contains her? 'Twere dam-
nation
To think so base a thought. It were too gross
To rib her cerecloth in the obscure grave.   51
Or shall I think in silver she's immur'd,
Being ten times undervalued to tried gold?
O sinful thought! Never so rich a gem
Was set in worse than gold. They have in
England   55
A coin that bears the figure of an angel
Stamped in gold — but that's insculp'd upon;
But here an angel in a golden bed
Lies all within. Deliver me the key.
Here do I choose, and thrive I as I may!   60
Por. There, take it, Prince; and if my form
lie there,
Then I am yours. [*He opens the golden casket.*]
Mor.   O hell! what have we here?
A carrion Death, within whose empty eye
There is a written scroll! I'll read the writing.

'All that glisters is not gold —   65
Often have you heard that told.
Many a man his life hath sold
But my outside to behold.
Gilded tombs do worms infold.
Had you been as wise as bold,   70
Young in limbs, in judgment old,
Your answer had not been inscroll'd.
Fare you well; your suit is cold.'

Cold indeed, and labour lost.
Then farewell heat, and welcome frost!   75
Portia, adieu. I have too griev'd a heart
To take a tedious leave. Thus losers part.
                              Exit [*with his Train*].
Por. A gentle riddance. Draw the curtains,
go.
Let all of his complexion choose me so. *Exeunt.*

[Scene VIII. *Venice. A street.*]

Enter *Salerio* and *Solanio*.

Saler. Why, man, I saw Bassanio under sail;
With him is Gratiano gone along;
And in their ship I am sure Lorenzo is not.

Solan. The villain Jew with outcries rais'd the Duke,
Who went with him to search Bassanio's ship. 5
Saler. He came too late, the ship was under sail;
But there the Duke was given to understand
That in a gondilo were seen together
Lorenzo and his amorous Jessica.
Besides, Antonio certified the Duke   10
They were not with Bassanio in his ship.
Solan. I never heard a passion so confus'd,
So strange, outrageous, and so variable,
As the dog Jew did utter in the streets.   14
'My daughter! O my ducats! O my daughter!
Fled with a Christian! O my Christian ducats!
Justice! the law! My ducats, and my daughter!
A sealed bag, two sealed bags of ducats,
Of double ducats, stol'n from me by my daughter!
And jewels — two stones, two rich and precious stones,   20
Stol'n by my daughter! Justice! Find the girl!
She hath the stones upon her, and the ducats!'
Saler. Why, all the boys in Venice follow him,
Crying his stones, his daughter, and his ducats.
Solan. Let good Antonio look he keep his day,
Or he shall pay for this.
Saler.   Marry, well remem'bred.
I reason'd with a Frenchman yesterday,   27
Who told me, in the narrow seas that part
The French and English there miscarried
A vessel of our country richly fraught.   30
I thought upon Antonio when he told me,
And wish'd in silence that it were not his.
Solan. You were best to tell Antonio what you hear.
Yet do not suddenly, for it may grieve him.
Saler. A kinder gentleman treads not the earth.   35
I saw Bassanio and Antonio part.
Bassanio told him he would make some speed
Of his return; he answered, 'Do not so.
Slubber not business for my sake, Bassanio,
But stay the very riping of the time;   40
And for the Jew's bond which he hath of me,
Let it not enter in your mind of love.
Be merry, and employ your chiefest thoughts
To courtship, and such fair ostents of love
As shall conveniently become you there.'   45
And even there, his eye being big with tears,
Turning his face, he put his hand behind him,
And with affection wondrous sensible
He wrung Bassanio's hand; and so they parted.
Solan. I think he only loves the world for him.   50

I pray thee let us go and find him out,
And quicken his embraced heaviness
With some delight or other.
Saler.   Do we so. *Exeunt.*

[Scene IX. *Belmont. Portia's house.*]

Enter *Nerissa* and a *Servitor.*

Ner. Quick, quick, I pray thee; draw the curtain straight.
The Prince of Arragon hath ta'en his oath
And comes to his election presently.

Enter *Arragon,* his *Train,* and *Portia* [with her *Train*].

Por. Behold, there stand the caskets, noble Prince.
If you choose that wherein I am contain'd, 5
Straight shall our nuptial rites be solemniz'd;
But if you fail, without more speech, my lord,
You must be gone from hence immediately.
Ar. I am enjoin'd by oath to observe three things:
First, never to unfold to any one   10
Which casket 'twas I chose; next, if I fail
Of the right casket, never in my life
To woo a maid in way of marriage;
Lastly,
If I do fail in fortune of my choice,   15
Immediately to leave you and be gone.
Por. To these injunctions every one doth swear
That comes to hazard for my worthless self.
Ar. And so have I address'd me. Fortune now
To my heart's hope! Gold, silver, and base lead.
'Who chooseth me must give and hazard all he hath.'   21
You shall look fairer ere I give or hazard.
What says the golden chest? Ha, let me see!
'Who chooseth me shall gain what many men desire.'
What many men desire! That 'many' may be meant   25
By the fool multitude, that choose by show,
Not learning more than the fond eye doth teach;
Which pries not to th' interior, but, like the martlet,
Builds in the weather on the outward wall,
Even in the force and road of casualty.   30
I will not choose what many men desire,
Because I will not jump with common spirits

And rank me with the barbarous multitude,
Why then, to thee, thou silver treasure house!
Tell me once more what title thou dost bear. 35
'Who chooseth me shall get as much as he
    deserves.'
And well said too; for who shall go about
To cozen fortune, and be honourable
Without the stamp of merit? Let none presume
To wear an undeserved dignity. 40
O that estates, degrees, and offices
Were not deriv'd corruptly, and that clear
    honour
Were purchas'd by the merit of the wearer!
How many then should cover that stand bare!
How many be commanded that command! 45
How much low peasantry would then be gleaned
From the true seed of honour! and how much
    honour
Pick'd from the chaff and ruin of the times
To be new varnish'd! Well, but to my choice.
'Who chooseth me shall get as much as he
    deserves.' 50
I will assume desert. Give me a key for this,
And instantly unlock my fortunes here.
           [*He opens the silver casket.*]
  Por. [*aside*] Too long a pause for that
    which you find there.
  Ar. What's here? The portrait of a blinking
    idiot,
Presenting me a schedule! I will read it. 55
How much unlike art thou to Portia!
How much unlike my hopes and my deservings!
'Who chooseth me shall have as much as he
    deserves.'
Did I deserve no more than a fool's head?
Is that my prize? Are my deserts no better? 60
  Por. To offend and judge are distinct offices
And of opposed natures.
  Ar.   What is here?

  'The fire seven times tried this.
  Seven times tried that judgment is
  That did never choose amiss. 65

Some there be that shadows kiss;
Such have but a shadow's bliss.
There be fools alive iwis
Silver'd o'er, and so was this.
Take what wife you will to bed, 70
I will ever be your head.
So be gone; you are sped.'

Still more fool I shall appear
By the time I linger here.
With one fool's head I came to woo, 75
But I go away with two.
Sweet, adieu. I'll keep my oath,
Patiently to bear my wroth.
           [*Exit with his Train.*]
  Por. Thus hath the candle sing'd the moth.
O, these deliberate fools! When they do choose,
They have the wisdom by their wit to lose. 81
  Ner. The ancient saying is no heresy,
Hanging and wiving goes by destiny.
  Por. Come draw the curtain, Nerissa.

        Enter *Messenger.*

  Mess. Where is my lady?
  Por.   Here. What would my lord? 85
  Mess. Madam, there is alighted at your gate
A young Venetian, one that comes before
To signify th' approaching of his lord;
From whom he bringeth sensible regreets,
To wit, besides commends and courteous breath,
Gifts of rich value. Yet I have not seen 91
So likely an ambassador of love.
A day in April never came so sweet
To show how costly summer was at hand
As this fore-spurrer comes before his lord. 95
  Por. No more, I pray thee. I am half afeard
Thou wilt say anon he is some kin to thee,
Thou spend'st such high-day wit in praising
    him.
Come, come, Nerissa; for I long to see
Quick Cupid's post that comes so mannerly. 100
  Ner. Bassanio, Lord Love, if thy will it be!
           Exeunt.

    ACT III. [Scene I. *Venice. A street.*]

      Enter *Solanio* and *Salerio.*

  Solan. Now what news on the Rialto?
  Saler. Why, yet it lives there uncheck'd that
Antonio hath a ship of rich lading wrack'd on
the narrow seas — the Goodwins I think they
call the place — a very dangerous flat, and
fatal, where the carcases of many a tall ship lie

buried, as they say, if my gossip Report be an
honest woman of her word. 8
  Solan. I would she were as lying a gossip in
that as ever knapp'd ginger or made her neighbours believe she wept for the death of a third
husband. But it is true, without any slips of
prolixity or crossing the plain highway of talk,
that the good Antonio, the honest Antonio — O

that I had a title good enough to keep his name company! — 16

Saler. Come, the full stop.

Solan. Ha, what sayest thou? Why, the end is, he hath lost a ship.

Saler. I would it might prove the end of his losses. 21

Solan. Let me say amen betimes, lest the devil cross my prayer, for here he comes in the likeness of a Jew.

Enter *Shylock.*

How now, Shylock? What news among the merchants? 26

Shy. You knew, none so well, none so well as you, of my daughter's flight.

Saler. That's certain. I, for my part, knew the tailor that made the wings she flew withal.

Solan. And Shylock, for his own part, knew the bird was fledge; and then it is the complexion of them all to leave the dam.

Shy. She is damn'd for it.

Saler. That's certain, if the devil may be her judge. 36

Shy. My own flesh and blood to rebel!

Solan. Out upon it, old carrion! Rebels it at these years?

Shy. I say my daughter is my flesh and my blood. 40

Saler. There is more difference between thy flesh and hers than between jet and ivory; more between your bloods than there is between red wine and Rhenish. But tell us, do you hear whether Antonio have had any loss at sea or no? 45

Shy. There I have another bad match! A bankrout, a prodigal, who dare scarce show his head on the Rialto! a beggar, that was us'd to come so smug upon the mart! Let him look to his bond. He was wont to call me usurer. Let nim look to his bond. He was wont to lend money for a Christian cursy. Let him look to his bond.

Saler. Why, I am sure, if he forfeit, thou wilt not take his flesh. What's that good for? 54

Shy. To bait fish withal. If it will feed nothing else, it will feed my revenge. He hath disgrac'd me, and hind'red me half a million; laugh'd at my losses, mock'd at my gains, scorned my nation, thwarted my bargains, cooled my friends, heated mine enemies — and what's his reason? I am a Jew. Hath not a Jew eyes? Hath not a Jew hands, organs, dimensions, senses, affections, passions? fed with the same food, hurt with the same weapons, subject to the same diseases, healed by the same means, warmed and cooled by the same winter and summer as a Christian is? If you prick us, do we not bleed? If you tickle us, do we not laugh? If you poison us, do we not die? And if you wrong us, shall we not revenge? If we are like you in the rest, we will resemble you in that. If a Jew wrong a Christian, what is his humility? Revenge. If a Christian wrong a Jew, what should his sufferance be by Christian example? Why, revenge. The villany you teach me I will execute, and it shall go hard but I will better the instruction. 76

Enter a *Man* from *Antonio.*

Man. Gentlemen, my master Antonio is at his house, and desires to speak with you both.

Saler. We have been up and down to seek him.

Enter *Tubal.*

Solan. Here comes another of the tribe. A third cannot be match'd, unless the devil himself turn Jew. 82

Exeunt [Solanio, Salerio, and Man].

Shy. How now, Tubal? What news from Genoa? Hast thou found my daughter?

Tub. I often came where I did hear of her, but cannot find her. 86

Shy. Why, there, there, there, there! A diamond gone cost me two thousand ducats in Frankford! The curse never fell upon our nation till now; I never felt it till now. Two thousand ducats in that, and other precious, precious jewels. I would my daughter were dead at my foot, and the jewels in her ear! Would she were hears'd at my foot, and the ducats in her coffin! No news of them? Why, so — and I know not what's spent in the search. Why, thou loss upon loss! the thief gone with so much, and so much to find the thief; and no satisfaction, no revenge! nor no ill luck stirring but what lights o' my shoulders; no sighs but o' my breathing; no tears but o' my shedding. 101

Tub. Yes, other men have ill luck too. Antonio, as I heard in Genoa —

Shy. What, what, what? Ill luck, ill luck?

Tub. Hath an argosy cast away coming from Tripolis. 106

Shy. I thank God, I thank God! Is it true? is it true?

Tub. I spoke with some of the sailors that escaped the wrack. 110

Shy. I thank thee, good Tubal. Good news, good news! Ha, ha! Where? in Genoa?

Tub. Your daughter spent in Genoa, as I heard, one night fourscore ducats.

Shy. Thou stick'st a dagger in me. I shall never see my gold again. Fourscore ducats at a sitting! fourscore ducats! 117

Tub. There came divers of Antonio's creditors in my company to Venice that swear he cannot choose but break. 120

Shy. I am very glad of it. I'll plague him; I'll torture him. I am glad of it.

Tub. One of them showed me a ring that he had of your daughter for a monkey. 124

Shy. Out upon her! Thou torturest me, Tubal. It was my turquoise; I had it of Leah when I was a bachelor. I would not have given it for a wilderness of monkeys.

Tub. But Antonio is certainly undone. 129

Shy. Nay, that's true, that's very true. Go, Tubal, fee me an officer; bespeak him a fortnight before. I will have the heart of him if he forfeit; for, were he out of Venice, I can make what merchandise I will. Go, Tubal, and meet me at our synagogue; go, good Tubal; at our synagogue, Tubal. *Exeunt.*

[Scene II. *Belmont.* Portia's *house.*]

Enter *Bassanio, Portia, Gratiano,* and all their *Trains*; [*Nerissa*].

Por. I pray you tarry; pause a day or two
Before you hazard; for in choosing wrong
I lose your company. Therefore forbear awhile.
There's something tells me (but it is not love)
I would not lose you; and you know yourself 5
Hate counsels not in such a quality.
But lest you should not understand me well —
And yet a maiden hath no tongue but thought—
I would detain you here some month or two 9
Before you venture for me. I could teach you
How to choose right, but then I am forsworn.
So will I never be; so may you miss me;
But if you do, you'll make me wish a sin —
That I had been forsworn. Beshrow your eyes!
They have o'erlook'd me and divided me; 15
One half of me is yours, the other half yours —
Mine own, I would say; but if mine, then yours,
And so all yours! O, these naughty times
Puts bars between the owners and their rights!
And so, though yours, not yours. Prove it so,
Let fortune go to hell for it, not I. 21
I speak too long; but 'tis to peize the time,
To eche it, and to draw it out in length,
To stay you from election.

Bass.   Let me choose;
For as I am, I live upon the rack. 25

Por. Upon the rack, Bassanio? Then confess
What treason there is mingled with your love.

Bass. None but that ugly treason of mistrust,
Which makes me fear th' enjoying of my love.
There may as well be amity and life 30
'Tween snow and fire as treason and my love.

Por. Ay, but I fear you speak upon the rack,
Where men enforced do speak anything.

Bass. Promise me life, and I'll confess the truth.

Por. Well then, confess and live.

Bass.   'Confess' and 'love' 35
Had been the very sum of my confession.
O happy torment, when my torturer
Doth teach me answers for deliverance!
But let me to my fortune and the caskets.

Por. Away then! I am lock'd in one of them.
If you do love me, you will find me out. 41
Nerissa and the rest, stand all aloof.
Let music sound while he doth make his choice;
Then, if he lose, he makes a swanlike end,
Fading in music. That the comparison 45
May stand more proper, my eye shall be the stream
And wat'ry deathbed for him. He may win;
And what is music then? Then music is
Even as the flourish when true subjects bow
To a new-crowned monarch. Such it is 50
As are those dulcet sounds in break of day
That creep into the dreaming bridegroom's ear
And summon him to marriage. Now he goes
With no less presence, but with much more love,
Than young Alcides when he did redeem 55
The virgin tribute paid by howling Troy
To the sea monster. I stand for sacrifice;
The rest aloof are the Dardanian wives,
With bleared visages come forth to view
The issue of th' exploit. Go, Hercules! 60
Live thou, I live. With much much more dismay
I view the fight than thou that mak'st the fray.

A Song, the whilst Bassanio comments on the caskets to himself.

Tell me, where is fancy bred,
Or in the heart, or in the head?
How begot, how nourished? 65
    Reply, reply.
It is engend'red in the eyes,
With gazing fed; and fancy dies
In the cradle where it lies.
    Let us all ring fancy's knell. 70
    I'll begin it — Ding, dong, bell.

All.   Ding, dong, bell.

Bass. So may the outward shows be least
  themselves;
The world is still deceiv'd with ornament.
In law, what plea so tainted and corrupt   75
But, being season'd with a gracious voice,
Obscures the show of evil? In religion,
What damned error but some sober brow
Will bless it, and approve it with a text,
Hiding the grossness with fair ornament?   80
There is no vice so simple but assumes
Some mark of virtue on his outward parts.
How many cowards, whose hearts are all as false
As stairs of sand, wear yet upon their chins
The beards of Hercules and frowning Mars; 85
Who, inward search'd, have livers white as
  milk!
And these assume but valour's excrement
To render them redoubted. Look on beauty,
And you shall see 'tis purchas'd by the weight,
Which therein works a miracle in nature,   90
Making them lightest that wear most of it.
So are those crisped snaky golden locks
Which make such wanton gambols with the
  wind
Upon supposed fairness often known
To be the dowry of a second head,   95
The skull that bred them in the sepulchre.
Thus ornament is but the guiled shore
To a most dangerous sea; the beauteous scarf
Veiling an Indian beauty; in a word,   99
The seeming truth which cunning times put on
To entrap the wisest. Therefore, thou gaudy
  gold,
Hard food for Midas, I will none of thee;
Nor none of thee, thou pale and common drudge
'Tween man and man: but thou, thou meagre
  lead,
Which rather threaten'st than dost promise
  aught,   105
Thy plainness moves me more than eloquence;
And here choose I. Joy be the consequence!
  Por. [*aside*] How all the other passions fleet
  to air,
As doubtful thoughts, and rash-embrac'd de-
  spair,   109
And shudd'ring fear, and green-e,'d jealousy!
O love, be moderate; allay thy ecstasy;
In measure rain thy joy; scant this excess!
I feel too much thy blessing. Make it less
For fear I surfeit!
  Bass. [*opening the leaden casket*] What find
  I here?
Fair Portia's counterfeit! What demigod   115
Hath come so near creation? Move these eyes?
Or whether, riding on the balls of mine,

Seem they in motion? Here are sever'd lips,
Parted with sugar breath. So sweet a bar
Should sunder such sweet friends. Here in her
  hairs   120
The painter plays the spider; and hath woven
A golden mesh t' entrap the hearts of men
Faster than gnats in cobwebs. But her eyes —
How could he see to do them? Having made
  one,   124
Methinks it should have power to steal both his
And leave itself unfurnish'd. Yet look, how far
The substance of my praise doth wrong this
  shadow
In underprizing it, so far this shadow
Doth limp behind the substance. Here's the
  scroll,   129
The continent and summary of my fortune.

   'You that choose not by the view
   Chance as fair and choose as true.
   Since this fortune falls to you,
   Be content and seek no new.
   If you be well pleas'd with this   135
   And hold your fortune for your bliss,
   Turn you where your lady is
   And claim her with a loving kiss.'

A gentle scroll. Fair lady, by your leave;
                   [*Kisses her.*]
I come by note, to give and to receive.   140
Like one of two contending in a prize,
That thinks he hath done well in people's eyes,
Hearing applause and universal shout,
Giddy in spirit, still gazing in a doubt
Whether those peals of praise be his or no;   145
So, thrice-fair lady, stand I, even so,
As doubtful whether what I see be true,
Until confirm'd, sign'd, ratified by you.
  Por. You see me, Lord Bassanio, where I
  stand,
Such as I am. Though for myself alone   150
I would not be ambitious in my wish
To wish myself much better, yet for you
I would be trebled twenty times myself,
A thousand times more fair, ten thousand times
  more rich,
That, only to stand high in your account,   155
I might in virtues, beauties, livings, friends,
Exceed account. But the full sum of me
Is sum of nothing, which, to term in gross,
Is an unlesson'd girl, unschool'd, unpractis'd;
Happy in this, she is not yet so old   160
But she may learn; happier than this,
She is not bred so dull but she can learn;
Happiest of all is that her gentle spirit
Commits itself to yours to be directed,
As from her lord, her governor, her king. **165**

Myself and what is mine to you and yours
Is now converted. But now I was the lord
Of this fair mansion, master of my servants,
Queen o'er myself; and even now, but now,
This house, these servants, and this same my-
    self   170
Are yours, my lord's. I give them with this ring;
Which when you part from, lose, or give away,
Let it presage the ruin of your love
And be my vantage to exclaim on you.
   Bass. Madam, you have bereft me of all
    words,   175
Only my blood speaks to you in my veins;
And there is such confusion in my powers
As, after some oration fairly spoke
By a beloved prince, there doth appear
Among the buzzing pleased multitude,   180
Where every something, being blent together,
Turns to a wild of nothing, save of joy,
Express'd and not express'd. But when this
   ring
Parts from this finger, then parts life from
   hence!
O, then be bold to say Bassanio's dead!   185
   Ner. My lord and lady, it is now our time
That have stood by and seen our wishes prosper
To cry 'good joy.' Good joy, my lord and lady!
   Gra. My Lord Bassanio, and my gentle lady,
I wish you all the joy that you can wish;   190
For I am sure you can wish none from me;
And when your honours mean to solemnize
The bargain of your faith, I do beseech you
Even at that time I may be married too.
   Bass. With all my heart, so thou canst get a
   wife.   195
   Gra. I thank your lordship, you have got me
   one.
My eyes, my lord, can look as swift as yours.
You saw the mistress, I beheld the maid;
You lov'd, I lov'd; for intermission
No more pertains to me, my lord, than you.   200
Your fortune stood upon the caskets there,
And so did mine too, as the matter falls;
For wooing here until I sweat again,
And swearing till my very roof was dry
With oaths of love, at last — if promise last —
I got a promise of this fair one here   206
To have her love, provided that your fortune
Achiev'd her mistress.
   Por.   Is this true, Nerissa?
   Ner. Madam, it is, so you stand pleas'd
   withal.
   Bass. And do you, Gratiano, mean good
   faith?   210
   Gra. Yes, faith, my lord.

   Bass. C_. feast shall be much honoured in
   your marriage.
   Gra. We'll play with them the first boy for a
   thousand ducats.
   Ner. What, and stake down?   215
   Gra. No, we shall ne'er win at that sport, and
stake down.
But who comes here? Lorenzo and his infidel?
What, and my old Venetian friend Salerio?

    Enter *Lorenzo, Jessica*, and *Salerio*
    (a *Messenger* from Venice).

   Bass. Lorenzo and Salerio, welcome hither,
If that the youth of my new int'rest here   221
Have power to bid you welcome. By your leave,
I bid my very friends and countrymen,
Sweet Portia, welcome.
   Por.   So do I, my lord.
They are entirely welcome.   225
   Lor. I thank your honour. For my part, my
   lord,
My purpose was not to have seen you here;
But meeting with Salerio by the way,
He did entreat me, past all saying nay,
To come with him along.
   Saler.   I did, my lord,   230
And I have reason for it. Signior Antonio
Commends him to you.
             [*Gives Bassanio a letter.*]
   Bass.   Ere I ope his letter,
I pray you tell me how my good friend doth.
   Saler. Not sick, my lord, unless it be in
   mind;
Nor well, unless in mind. His letter there   235
Will show you his estate.
                  Open the letter.
   Gra. Nerissa, cheer yond stranger; bid her
welcome.
Your hand, Salerio. What's the news from
   Venice?
How doth that royal merchant, good Antonio?
I know he will be glad of our success.   240
We are the Jasons, we have won the Fleece.
   Saler. I would you had won the fleece that
   he hath lost!
   Por. There are some shrowd contents in yond
   same paper
That steals the colour from Bassanio's cheek:
Some dear friend dead; else nothing in the
   world   245
Could turn so much the constitution
Of any constant man. What, worse and worse?
With leave, Bassanio — I am half yourself,
And I must freely have the half of anything
That this same paper brings you.

Bass.   O sweet Portia,
Here are a few of the unpleasant'st words 251
That ever blotted paper! Gentle lady,
When I did first impart my love to you,
I freely told you all the wealth I had
Ran in my veins — I was a gentleman; 255
And then I told you true; and yet, dear lady,
Rating myself at nothing, you shall see
How much I was a braggart. When I told you
My state was nothing, I should then have told
    you   259
That I was worse than nothing; for indeed
I have engag'd myself to a dear friend,
Engag'd my friend to his mere enemy
To feed my means. Here is a letter, lady —
The paper as the body of my friend,
And every word in it a gaping wound 265
Issuing lifeblood. But is it true, Salerio?
Have all his ventures fail'd? What, not one
    hit?
From Tripolis, from Mexico, and England,
From Lisbon, Barbary, and India?
And not one vessel scape the dreadful touch 270
Of merchant-marring rocks?
Saler.   Not one, my lord.
Besides, it should appear that, if he had
The present money to discharge the Jew,
He would not take it. Never did I know
A creature that did bear the shape of man 275
So keen and greedy to confound a man.
He plies the Duke at morning and at night,
And doth impeach the freedom of the state
If they deny him justice. Twenty merchants,
The Duke himself, and the magnificoes 280
Of greatest port have all persuaded with him;
But none can drive him from the envious plea
Of forfeiture, of justice, and his bond.
Jes. When I was with him, I have heard him
    swear
To Tubal and to Chus, his countrymen, 285
That he would rather have Antonio's flesh
Than twenty times the value of the sum
That he did owe him; and I know, my lord,
If law, authority, and power deny not,
It will go hard with poor Antonio. 290
Por. Is it your dear friend that is thus in
    trouble?
Bass. The dearest friend to me, the kindest
    man,
The best-condition'd and unwearied spirit
In doing courtesies, and one in whom
The ancient Roman honour more appears 295
Than any that draws breath in Italy.
Por. What sum owes he the Jew?
Bass. For me three thousand ducats.

Por.   What, no more?
Pay him six thousand, and deface the bond.
Double six thousand and then treble that 300
Before a friend of this description
Shall lose a hair through Bassanio's fault.
First go with me to church and call me wife,
And then away to Venice to your friend!
For never shall you lie by Portia's side 305
With an unquiet soul! You shall have gold
To pay the petty debt twenty times over.
When it is paid, bring your true friend along.
My maid Nerissa and myself meantime
Will live as maids and widows. Come, away!
For you shall hence upon your wedding day. 311
Bid your friends welcome, show a merry cheer;
Since you are dear bought, I will love you dear.
But let me hear the letter of your friend. 314
Bass. 'Sweet Bassanio, my ships have all mis-
carried, my creditors grow cruel, my estate is very
low, my bond to the Jew is forfeit; and since in
paying it, it is impossible I should live, all debts are
clear'd between you and I if I might but see you at
my death. Notwithstanding, use your pleasure. If
your love do not persuade you to come, let not my
letter.'   322
Por. O love, dispatch all business and be
    gone!
Bass. Since I have your good leave to go
    away,
I will make haste; but till I come again, 325
No bed shall e'er be guilty of my stay,
Nor rest be interposer 'twixt us twain.
                                    Exeunt.

[Scene III. *Venice. The street before*
        Shylock's *house.*]

Enter [*Shylock*] *the Jew* and *Solanio*
        and *Antonio* and the *Jailer.*

Shy. Jailer, look to him. Tell not me of
    mercy.
This is the fool that lent out money gratis.
Jailer, look to him.
Ant.   Hear me yet, good Shylock.
Shy. I'll have my bond! Speak not against
    my bond!   4
I have sworn an oath that I will have my bond.
Thou call'dst me dog before thou hadst a cause;
But, since I am a dog, beware my fangs.
The Duke shall grant me justice. I do wonder,
Thou naughty jailer, that thou art so fond
To come abroad with him at his request. 10
Ant. I pray thee hear me speak.
Shy. I'll have my bond. I will not hear thee
    speak.

I'll have my bond, and therefore speak no more.
I'll not be made a soft and dull-ey'd fool,
To shake the head, relent, and sigh, and yield
To Christian intercessors. Follow not. 16
I'll have no speaking; I will have my bond.
Exit.
Solan. It is the most impenetrable cur
That ever kept with men.
Ant.   Let him alone.
I'll follow him no more with bootless prayers.
He seeks my life. His reason well I know: 21
I oft deliver'd from his forfeitures
Many that have at times made moan to me.
Therefore he hates me.
Solan.   I am sure the Duke
Will never grant this forfeiture to hold. 25
Ant. The Duke cannot deny the course of
law;
For the commodity that strangers have
With us in Venice, if it be denied,
Will much impeach the justice of the state,
Since that the trade and profit of the city 30
Consisteth of all nations. Therefore go.
These griefs and losses have so bated me
That I shall hardly spare a pound of flesh
To-morrow to my bloody creditor.
Well, jailer, on. Pray God Bassanio come 35
To see me pay his debt, and then I care not!
Exeunt.

[Scene IV. *Belmont.* Portia's *house.*]

Enter *Portia, Nerissa, Lorenzo, Jessica,* and
[*Balthasar,*] a Man of *Portia's.*

Lor. Madam, although I speak it in your
presence,
You have a noble and a true conceit
Of godlike amity, which appears most strongly
In bearing thus the absence of your lord.
But if you knew to whom you show this hon-
our, 5
How true a gentleman you send relief,
How dear a lover of my lord your husband,
I know you would be prouder of the work
Than customary bounty can enforce you.
Por. I never did repent for doing good, 10
Nor shall not now; for in companions
That do converse and waste the time together,
Whose souls do bear an egal yoke of love,
There must be needs a like proportion
Of lineaments, of manners, and of spirit; 15
Which makes me think that this Antonio,
Being the bosom lover of my lord,

Must needs be like my lord. If it be so,
How little is the cost I have bestow'd
In purchasing the semblance of my soul 20
From out the state of hellish cruelty!
This comes too near the praising of myself.
Therefore no more of it. Hear other things.
Lorenzo, I commit into your hands
The husbandry and manage of my house 25
Until my lord's return. For mine own part,
I have toward heaven breath'd a secret vow
To live in prayer and contemplation,
Only attended by Nerissa here,
Until her husband and my lord's return. 30
There is a monastery two miles off,
And there we will abide. I do desire you
Not to deny this imposition,
The which my love and some necessity
Now lays upon you.
Lor.   Madam, with all my heart. 35
I shall obey you in all fair commands.
Por. My people do already know my mind
And will acknowledge you and Jessica
In place of Lord Bassanio and myself.
So fare you well till we shall meet again. 40
Lor. Fair thoughts and happy hours attend
on you!
Jes. I wish your ladyship all heart's content.
Por. I thank you for your wish, and am well
pleas'd
To wish it back on you. Fare you well, Jessica.
Exeunt [*Jessica and Lorenzo*].
Now, Balthasar, 45
As I have ever found thee honest-true,
So let me find thee still. Take this same letter,
And use thou all th' endeavour of a man
In speed to Padua. See thou render this
Into my cousin's hand, Doctor Bellario; 50
And look, what notes and garments he doth
give thee,
Bring them, I pray thee, with imagin'd speed
Unto the Tranect, to the common ferry
Which trades to Venice. Waste no time in
words 54
But get thee gone. I shall be there before thee.
Balth. Madam, I go with all convenient
speed.   *Exit.*
Por. Come on, Nerissa. I have work in hand
That you yet know not of. We'll see our hus-
bands
Before they think of us.
Ner.   Shall they see us? 59
Por. They shall, Nerissa, but in such a habit
That they shall think we are accomplished
With that we lack. I'll hold thee any wager,
When we are both accoutered like young men,

I'll prove the prettier fellow of the two,
And wear my dagger with the braver grace, 65
And speak between the change of man and boy
With a reed voice, and turn two mincing steps
Into a manly stride; and speak of fra
Like a fine bragging youth; and tell qu—nt lies,
How honourable ladies sought my love,   70
Which I denying, they fell sick and died —
I could not do withal! Then I'll repent,
And wish, for all that, that I had not kill'd
   them.
And twenty of these puny lies I'll tell,
That men shall swear I have discontinued
   school   75
Above a twelvemonth. I have within my mind
A thousand raw tricks of these bragging Jacks,
Which I will practise.
  Ner.   Why, shall we turn to men?
  Por. Fie, what a question 's that,
If thou wert near a lewd interpreter!   80
But come, I'll tell thee all my whole device
When I am in my coach, which stays for us
At the park gate; and therefore haste away,
For we must measure twenty miles to-day.
                              Exeunt.

[Scene V. *Belmont. A garden.*]

Enter [*Launcelot the*] *Clown* and *Jessica.*

  Laun. Yes, truly; for look you, the sins of
the father are to be laid upon the children.
Therefore, I promise you, I fear you. I was
always plain with you, and so now I speak my
agitation of the matter. Therefore be o' good
cheer, for truly I think you are damn'd. There
is but one hope in it that can do you any good,
and that is but a kind of bastard hope neither.
  Jes. And what hope is that, I pray thee? 10
  Laun. Marry, you may partly hope that
your father got you not — that you are not the
Jew's daughter.
  Jes. That were a kind of bastard hope indeed! So the sins of my mother should be visited upon me.   16
  Laun. Truly then I fear you are damn'd both
by father and mother. Thus when I shun
Scylla, your father, I fall into Charybdis, your
mother. Well, you are gone both ways.   20
  Jes. I shall be sav'd by my husband. He
hath made me a Christian.
  Laun. Truly, the more to blame he! We
were Christians enow before, e'en as many as
could well live one by another. This making of

Christians will raise the price of hogs. If we
grow all to be pork-eaters, we shall not shortly
have a rasher on the coals for money.

Enter *Lorenzo.*

  Jes. I'll tell my husband, Launcelot, what
you say. Here he comes.   30
  Lor. I shall grow jealous of you shortly,
Launcelot, if you thus get my wife into corners.
  Jes. Nay, you need not fear us, Lorenzo.
Launcelot and I are out. He tells me flatly
there's no mercy for me in heaven because I am
a Jew's daughter; and he says you are no good
member of the commonwealth, for in converting
Jews to Christians you raise the price of pork.
  Lor. I shall answer that better to the com-
monwealth than you can the getting up of the
Negro's belly. The Moor is with child by you,
Launcelot.   43
  Laun. It is much that the Moor should be
more than reason; but if she be less than an
honest woman, she is indeed more than I took
her for.   47
  Lor. How every fool can play upon the word!
I think the best grace of wit will shortly turn
into silence, and discourse grow commendable
in none only but parrots. Go in, sirrah; bid
them prepare for dinner.   52
  Laun. That is done, sir. They have all
stomachs.
  Lor. Goodly Lord, what a wit-snapper are
you! Then bid them prepare dinner.   56
  Laun. That is done too, sir. Only 'cover' is
the word.
  Lor. Will you cover then, sir?
  Laun. Not so, sir, neither! I know my duty.
  Lor. Yet more quarrelling with occasion?
Wilt thou show the whole wealth of thy wit in
an instant? I pray thee understand a plain man
in his plain meaning. Go to thy fellows, bid
them cover the table, serve in the meat, and we
will come in to dinner.   65
  Laun. For the table, sir, it shall be serv'd in;
for the meat, sir, it shall be cover'd; for your
coming in to dinner, sir, why, let it be as hu-
mours and conceits shall govern.   *Exit.*
  Lor. O dear discretion, how his words are
   suited!   70
The fool hath planted in his memory
An army of good words; and I do kno v
A many fools, that stand in better place,
Garnish'd like him, that for a tricksy word 74
Defy the matter. How cheer'st thou, Jessica?
And now, good sweet, say thy opinion —
How dost thou like the Lord Bassanio's wife?

Jes. Past all expressing. It is very meet
The Lord Bassanio live an upright life;
For, having such a blessing in his lady,   80
He finds the joys of heaven here on earth;
And if on earth he do not merit it,
In reason he should never come to heaven.
Why, if two gods should play some heavenly match,
And on the wager lay two earthly women,   85
And Portia one, there must be something else
Pawn'd with the other; for the poor rude world
Hath not her fellow.

Lor.   Even such a husband
Hast thou of me as she is for a wife.   89
Jes. Nay, but ask my opinion too of that!
Lor. I will anon. First let us go to dinner.
Jes. Nay, let me praise you while I have a stomach.
Lor. No, pray thee, let it serve for table-talk;
Then, howsome'er thou speak'st, 'mong other things
I shall disgest it.
Jes.   Well, I'll set you forth.   95
Exeunt.

ACT IV. [Scene I. *Venice. A court of justice.*]

Enter the *Duke*, the *Magnificoes*, *Antonio*, *Bassanio*, *Gratiano*, [*Solanio*, and others].

Duke. What, is Antonio here?
Ant. Ready, so please your Grace.
Duke. I am sorry for thee. Thou art come to answer
A stony adversary, an inhuman wretch,
Uncapable of pity, void and empty   5
From any dram of mercy.
Ant.   I have heard
Your Grace hath ta'en great pains to qualify
His rigorous course; but since he stands obdurate,
And that no lawful means can carry me
Out of his envy's reach, I do oppose   10
My patience to his fury, and am arm'd
To suffer with a quietness of spirit
The very tyranny and rage of his.
Duke. Go one, and call the Jew into the court.
Solan. He is ready at the door; he comes, my lord.   15

Enter *Shylock*.

Duke. Make room, and let him stand before our face.
Shylock, the world thinks, and I think so too,
That thou but leadest this fashion of thy malice
To the last hour of act; and then 'tis thought
Thou'lt show thy mercy and remorse more strange   20
Than is thy strange apparent cruelty;
And where thou now exacts the penalty,
Which is a pound of this poor merchant's flesh,
Thou wilt not only loose the forfeiture,
But, touch'd with humane gentleness and love,
Forgive a moiety of the principal,   26
Glancing an eye of pity on his losses,
That have of late so huddled on his back —

Enow to press a royal merchant down
And pluck commiseration of his state   30
From brassy bosoms and rough hearts of flint,
From stubborn Turks and Tartars, never train'd
To offices of tender courtesy.
We all expect a gentle answer, Jew.
Shy. I have possess'd your Grace of what I purpose,   35
And by our holy Sabbath have I sworn
To have the due and forfeit of my bond.
If you deny it, let the danger light
Upon your charter and your city's freedom!
You'll ask me why I rather choose to have   40
A weight of carrion flesh than to receive
Three thousand ducats. I'll not answer that!
But say it is my humour, is it answer'd?
What if my house be troubled with a rat,   44
And I be pleas'd to give ten thousand ducats
To have it ban'd? What, are you answer'd yet?
Some men there are love not a gaping pig,
Some that are mad if they behold a cat,
And others, when the bagpipe sings i' th' nose,
Cannot contain their urine; for affection,   50
Mistress of passion, sways it to the mood
Of what it likes or loathes. Now for your answer:
As there is no firm reason to be rend'red
Why he cannot abide a gaping pig,
Why he a harmless necessary cat,   55
Why he a woollen bagpipe — but of force
Must yield to such inevitable shame
As to offend himself, being offended;
So can I give no reason, nor I will not,
More than a lodg'd hate and a certain loathing
I bear Antonio, that I follow thus   61
A losing suit against him. Are you answer'd?
Bass. This is no answer, thou unfeeling man,
To excuse the current of thy cruelty!

280

Shy. I am not bound to please thee with my
answers. 65
Bass. Do all men kill the things they do not
love?
Shy. Hates any man the thing he would not
kill?
Bass. Every offence is not a hate at first.
Shy. What, wouldst thou have a serpent
sting thee twice?
Ant. I pray you think you question with the
Jew. 70
You may as well go stand upon the beach
And bid the main flood bate his usual height;
You may as well use question with the wolf,
Why he hath made the ewe bleat for the lamb;
You may as well forbid the mountain pines 75
To wag their high tops and to make no noise
When they are fretten with the gusts of heaven;
You may as well do anything most hard
As seek to soften that — than which what's
harder? —
His Jewish heart. Therefore I do beseech you
Make no moe offers, use no farther means, 81
But with all brief and plain conveniency
Let me have judgment, and the Jew his will.
Bass. For thy three thousand ducats here is
six. 84
Shy. If every ducat in six thousand ducats
Were in six parts, and every part a ducat,
I would not draw them, I would have my bond.
Duke. How shalt thou hope for mercy, ren-
d'ring none?
Shy. What judgment shall I dread, doing
no wrong? 89
You have among you many a purchas'd slave,
Which, like your asses and your dogs and mules,
You use in abject and in slavish parts,
Because you bought them. Shall I say to you,
'Let them be free, marry them to your heirs!
Why sweat they under burthens? Let their beds
Be made as soft as yours, and let their palates
Be season'd with such viands'? You will an-
swer, 97
'The slaves are ours.' So do I answer you.
The pound of flesh which I demand of him
Is dearly bought, 'tis mine, and I will have it.
If you deny me, fie upon your law! 101
There is no force in the decrees of Venice.
I stand for judgment. Answer. Shall I have it?
Duke. Upon my power I may dismiss this
court
Unless Bellario, a learned doctor, 105
Whom I have sent for to determine this,
Come here to-day.
Solan. My lord, here stays without

A messenger with letters from the doctor,
New come from Padua.
Duke. Bring us the letters. Call the messenger.
Bass. Good cheer, Antonio! What, man,
courage yet! 111
The Jew shall have my flesh, blood, bones,
and all,
Ere thou shalt lose for me one drop of blood.
Ant. I am a tainted wether of the flock,
Meetest for death. The weakest kind of fruit
Drops earliest to the ground, and so let me. 116
You cannot better be employ'd, Bassanio,
Than to live still, and write mine epitaph.

Enter *Nerissa*, [dressed like a *Lawyer's Clerk*].

Duke. Came you from Padua from Bellario?
Ner. From both, my lord. Bellario greets
your Grace.   [*Presents a letter.*]
Bass. Why dost thou whet thy knife so
earnestly? 121
Shy. To cut the forfeiture from that bank-
rout there.
Gra. Not on thy sole, but on thy soul, harsh
Jew,
Thou mak'st thy knife keen; but no metal can—
No, not the hangman's axe — bear half the
keenness 125
Of thy sharp envy. Can no prayers pierce thee?
Shy. No, none that thou hast wit enough to
make.
Gra. O, be thou damn'd, inexorable dog,
And for thy life let justice be accus'd!
Thou almost mak'st me waver in my faith, 130
To hold opinion with Pythagoras,
That souls of animals infuse themselves
Into the trunks of men. Thy currish spirit
Govern'd a wolf, who, hang'd for human
slaughter,
Even from the gallows did his fell soul fleet, 135
And, whilst thou layest in thy unhallowed dam,
Infus'd itself in thee; for thy desires
Are wolvish, bloody, starv'd, and ravenous.
Shy. Till thou canst rail the seal from off my
bond,
Thou but offend'st thy lungs to speak so loud.
Repair thy wit, good youth, or it will fall 141
To cureless ruin. I stand here for law.
Duke. This letter from Bellario doth com-
mend
A young and learned doctor to our court.
Where is he?
Ner. He attendeth here hard by 145
To know your answer whether you'll admit him.
Duke. With all my heart. Some three or
four of you

281

Go give him courteous conduct to this place.
Meantime the court shall hear Bellario's letter.
[*Clerk reads.*] 'Your Grace shall understand
that at the receipt of your letter I am very sick;
but in the instant that your messenger came, in
loving visitation was with me a young doctor of
Rome — his name is Balthasar. I acquainted him
with the cause in controversy between the Jew and
Antonio the merchant. We turn'd o'er many books
together. He is furnished with my opinion, which,
bettered with his own learning (the greatness
whereof I cannot enough commend), comes with
him at my importunity to fill up your Grace's request in my stead. I beseech you let his lack of
years be no impediment to let him lack a reverend
estimation; for I never knew so young a body with
so old a head. I leave him to your gracious acceptance, whose trial shall better publish his
commendation.'   166

Enter *Portia* for *Balthasar*, [dressed like a
Doctor of Laws].

Duke. You hear the learn'd Bellario what
he writes;
And here, I take it, is the doctor come.
Give me your hand. Come you from old Bel-
lario?
Por. I did, my lord.
Duke.   You are welcome; take your place.
Are you acquainted with the difference   171
That holds this present question in the court?
Por. I am informed throughly of the cause.
Which is the merchant here? and which the Jew?
Duke. Antonio and old Shylock, both stand
forth.   175
Por. Is your name Shylock?
Shy.   Shylock is my name.
Por. Of a strange nature is the suit you follow;
Yet in such rule that the Venetian law
Cannot impugn you as you do proceed. —
You stand within his danger, do you not?   180
Ant. Ay, so he says.
Por.   Do you confess the bond?
Ant. I do.
Por.   Then must the Jew be merciful.
Shy. On what compulsion must I? Tell me
that.
Por. The quality of mercy is not strain'd;
It droppeth as the gentle rain from heaven   185
Upon the place beneath. It is twice blest —
It blesseth him that gives, and him that takes.
'Tis mightiest in the mightiest. It becomes
The throned monarch better than his crown.
His sceptre shows the force of temporal power,
The attribute to awe and majesty,   191
Wherein doth sit the dread and fear of kings;
But mercy is above this sceptred sway;

It is enthroned in the hearts of kings,
It is an attribute to God himself;   195
And earthly power doth then show likest God's
When mercy seasons justice. Therefore, Jew,
Though justice be thy plea, consider this —
That, in the course of justice, none of us   199
Should see salvation. We do pray for mercy,
And that same prayer doth teach us all to render
The deeds of mercy. I have spoke thus much
To mitigate the justice of thy plea;
Which if thou follow, this strict court of Venice
Must needs give sentence 'gainst the merchant
there.   205
Shy. My deeds upon my head! I crave the
law,
The penalty and forfeit of my bond.
Por. Is he not able to discharge the money?
Bass. Yes, here I tender it for him in the
court;
Yea, thrice the sum. If that will not suffice,
I will be bound to pay it ten times o'er   211
On forfeit of my hands, my head, my heart.
If this will not suffice, it must appear
That malice bears down truth. And I beseech
you,
Wrest once the law to your authority.   215
To do a great right, do a little wrong,
And curb this cruel devil of his will.
Por. It must not be. There is no power in
Venice
Can alter a decree established.
'Twill be recorded for a precedent;   220
And many an error by the same example
Will rush into the state. It cannot be.
Shy. A Daniel come to judgment! yea, a
Daniel!
O wise young judge, how I do honour thee!
Por. I pray you let me look upon the bond.
Shy. Here 'tis, most reverend Doctor, here it
is.   226
Por. Shylock, there's thrice thy money of-
f'red thee.
Shy. An oath, an oath, I have an oath in
heaven!
Shall I lay perjury upon my soul?
No, not for Venice.
Por.   Why, this bond is forfeit;
And lawfully by this the Jew may claim   231
A pound of flesh, to be by him cut off
Nearest the merchant's heart. Be merciful.
Take thrice thy money; bid me tear the bond.
Shy. When it is paid, according to the tenure.
It doth appear you are a worthy judge;   236
You know the law, your exposition
Hath been most sound. I charge you by the law,

Whereof you are a well-deserving pillar,
Proceed to judgment. By my soul I swear   240
There is no power in the tongue of man
To alter me. I stay here on my bond.
   Ant. Most heartily I do beseech the court
To give the judgment.
   Por.   Why then, thus it is :
You must prepare your bosom for his knife.   245
   Shy. O noble judge! O excellent young man!
   Por. For the intent and purpose of the law
Hath full relation to the penalty,
Which here appeareth due upon the bond.
   Shy. 'Tis very true. O wise and upright
      judge!   250
How much more elder art thou than thy looks!
   Por. Therefore lay bare your bosom.
   Shy.   Ay, his breast —
So says the bond; doth it not, noble judge?
Nearest his heart. Those are the very words.
   Por. It is so. Are there balance here to weigh
The flesh?
   Shy.   I have them ready.   256
   Por. Have by some surgeon, Shylock, on
      your charge,
To stop his wounds, lest he do bleed to death.
   Shy. Is it so nominated in the bond?
   Por. It is not so express'd; but what of that?
'Twere good you do so much for charity.   261
   Shy. I cannot find it; 'tis not in the bond.
   Por. You, merchant, have you anything to
      say?
   Ant. But little. I am arm'd and well pre-
      par'd.
Give me your hand, Bassanio. Fare you well!
Grieve not that I am fall'n to this for you;   266
For herein Fortune shows herself more kind
Than is her custom. It is still her use
To let the wretched man outlive his wealth
To view with hollow eye and wrinkled brow
An age of poverty; from which ling'ring
      penance   271
Of such misery doth she cut me off.
Commend me to your honourable wife;
Tell her the process of Antonio's end;
Say how I lov'd you, speak me fair in death;   275
And when the tale is told, bid her be judge
Whether Bassanio had not once a love.
Repent but you that you shall lose your friend,
And he repents not that he pays your debt;
For if the Jew do cut but deep enough,   280
I'll pay it instantly with all my heart.
   Bass. Antonio, I am married to a wife
Which is as dear to me as life itself;
But life itself, my wife, and all the world
Are not with me esteem'd above thy life.   285

I would lose all, ay, sacrifice them all
Here to this devil, to deliver you.
   Por. Your wife would give you little thanks
      for that
If she were by to hear you make the offer.
   Gra. I have a wife who I protest I love.   290
I would she were in heaven, so she could
Entreat some power to change this currish Jew.
   Ner. 'Tis well you offer it behind her back.
The wish would make else an unquiet house.
   Shy. [*aside*] These be the Christian hus-
      bands! I have a daughter —   295
Would any of the stock of Barrabas
Had been her husband rather than a Chris-
      tian! —
We trifle time. I pray thee pursue sentence.
   Por. A pound of that same merchant's flesh
      is thine.   299
The court awards it, and the law doth give it.
   Shy. Most rightful judge!
   Por. And you must cut this flesh from off his
      breast.
The law allows it, and the court awards it.
   Shy. Most learned judge! A sentence!
      Come, prepare!   304
   Por. Tarry a little; there is something else.
This bond doth give thee here no jot of blood;
The words expressly are 'a pound of flesh.'
Take then thy bond, take thou thy pound of
      flesh;
But in the cutting it if thou dost shed
One drop of Christian blood, thy lands and goods
Are, by the laws of Venice, confiscate   311
Unto the state of Venice.
   Gra. O upright judge! Mark, Jew. O learned
      judge!
   Shy. Is that the law?
   Por.   Thyself shalt see the act;
For, as thou urgest justice, be assur'd   315
Thou shalt have justice more than thou desir'st.
   Gra. O learned judge! Mark, Jew. A learned
      judge!
   Shy. I take this offer then. Pay the bond
      thrice,
And let the Christian go.
   Bass.   Here is the money.
   Por. Soft!   320
The Jew shall have all justice. Soft! no haste.
He shall have nothing but the penalty.
   Gra. O Jew! an upright judge! a learned
      judge!
   Por. Therefore prepare thee to cut off the
      flesh.   324
Shed thou no blood, nor cut thou less nor more
But just a pound of flesh. If thou tak'st more

Or less than a just pound — be it but so much
As makes it light or heavy in the substance
Or the division of the twentieth part
Of one poor scruple; nay, if the scale do turn
But in the estimation of a hair —   331
Thou diest, and all thy goods are confiscate.
 Gra. A second Daniel! a Daniel, Jew!
Now, infidel, I have you on the hip.
 Por. Why doth the Jew pause? Take thy
  forfeiture.   335
 Shy. Give me my principal, and let me go.
 Bass. I have it ready for thee; here it is.
 Por. He hath refus'd it in the open court.
He shall have merely justice and his bond.
 Gra. A Daniel still say I, a second Daniel! 340
I thank thee, Jew, for teaching me that word.
 Shy. Shall I not have barely my principal?
 Por. Thou shalt have nothing but the forfei-
  ture,
To be so taken at thy peril, Jew.   344
 Shy. Why, then the devil give him good of it!
I'll stay no longer question.
 Por.   Tarry, Jew.
The law hath yet another hold on you.
It is enacted in the laws of Venice,
If it be prov'd against an alien
That by direct or indirect attempts   350
He seek the life of any citizen,
The party 'gainst the which he doth contrive
Shall seize one half his goods; the other half
Comes to the privy coffer of the state;
And the offender's life lies in the mercy   355
Of the Duke only, 'gainst all other voice.
In which predicament I say thou stand'st;
For it appears by manifest proceeding
That indirectly, and directly too,
Thou hast contriv'd against the very life   360
Of the defendant, and thou hast incurr'd
The danger formerly by me rehears'd.
Down, therefore, and beg mercy of the Duke.
 Gra. Beg that thou mayst have leave to hang
  thyself!
And yet, thy wealth being forfeit to the state,
Thou hast not left the value of a cord;   366
Therefore thou must be hang'd at the state's
  charge.
 Duke. That thou shalt see the difference of
  our spirit,
I pardon thee thy life before thou ask it.
For half thy wealth, it is Antonio's;   370
The other half comes to the general state,
Which humbleness may drive unto a fine.
 Por. Ay, for the state, not for Antonio.
 Shy. Nay, take my life and all! Pardon not
  that!   374

You take my house when you do take the prop
That doth sustain my house. You take my life
When you do take the means whereby I live.
 Por. What mercy can you render him, An-
  tonio?
 Gra. A halter gratis. Nothing else, for God's
  sake!
 Ant. So please my lord the Duke and all the
  court   380
To quit the fine for one half of his goods,
I am content; so he will let me have
The other half in use, to render it
Upon his death unto the gentleman
That lately stole his daughter —   385
Two things provided more: that, for this favour,
He presently become a Christian;
The other, that he do record a gift
Here in the court of all he dies possess'd
Unto his son Lorenzo and his daughter.   390
 Duke. He shall do this, or else I do recant
The pardon that I late pronounced here.
 Por. Art thou contented, Jew? What dost
  thou say?
 Shy. I am content.
 Por.   Clerk, draw a deed of gift.
 Shy. I pray you give me leave to go from
  hence.   395
I am not well. Send the deed after me,
And I will sign it.
 Duke.   Get thee gone, but do it.
 Gra. In christ'ning shalt thou have two god-
  fathers.
Had I been judge, thou shouldst have had ten
  more,
To bring thee to the gallows, not the font. 400
        Exit [*Shylock*].
 Duke. Sir, I entreat you home with me to
  dinner.
 Por. I humbly do desire your Grace of par-
  don.
I must away this night toward Padua,
And it is meet I presently set forth.
 Duke. I am sorry that your leisure serves
  you not.   405
Antonio, gratify this gentleman,
For in my mind you are much bound to him.
     Exeunt Duke and his Train.
 Bass. Most worthy gentleman, I and my
  friend
Have by your wisdom been this day acquitted
Of grievous penalties, in lieu whereof,   410
Three thousand ducats, due unto the Jew,
We freely cope your courteous pains withal.
 Ant. And stand indebted, over and above,
In love and service to you evermore.

Por. He is well paid that is well satisfied; 415
And I, delivering you, am satisfied,
And therein do account myself well paid.
My mind was never yet more mercenary.
I pray you know me when we meet again.
I wish you well, and so I take my leave.   420
   Bass. Dear sir, of force I must attempt you
      further.
Take some remembrance of us as a tribute,
Not as a fee. Grant me two things, I pray you—
Not to deny me, and to pardon me.
   Por. You press me far, and therefore I will
      yield.   425
Give me your gloves, I'll wear them for your
   sake;   [*Bassanio takes off his gloves.*]
And for your love I'll take this ring from you.
Do not draw back your hand. I'll take no more;
And you in love shall not deny me this.
   Bass. This ring, good sir? Alas, it is a trifle!
I will not shame myself to give you this.   431
   Por. I will have nothing else but only this;
And now methinks I have a mind to it.
   Bass. There's more depends on this than on
      the value.
The dearest ring in Venice will I give you,   435
And find it out by proclamation.
Only for this, I pray you pardon me.
   Por. I see, sir, you are liberal in offers.
You taught me first to beg, and now methinks
You teach me how a beggar should be answer'd.
   Bass. Good sir, this ring was given me by
      my wife;   441
And when she put it on, she made me vow
That I should neither sell nor give nor lose it.
   Por. That 'scuse serves many men to save
      their gifts.
And if your wife be not a madwoman,   445
And know how well I have deserv'd this ring,
She would not hold out enemy for ever
For giving it to me. Well, peace be with you!
      Exeunt [*Portia and Nerissa*].
   Ant. My Lord Bassanio, let him have the ring.

Let his deservings, and my love withal,   450
Be valued 'gainst your wive's commandëment.
   Bass. Go, Gratiano, run and overtake him.
Give him the ring and bring him, if thou canst,
Unto Antonio's house. Away! make haste.
      Exit Gratiano.
Come, you and I will thither presently,   455
And in the morning early will we both
Fly toward Belmont. Come, Antonio. *Exeunt.*

[Scene II. *Venice. A street.*]

Enter *Portia* and *Nerissa*, [disguised as before].

   Por. Enquire the Jew's house out, give him
      this deed,
And let him sign it. We'll away to-night
And be a day before our husbands home.
This deed will be well welcome to Lorenzo.

      Enter *Gratiano.*

   Gra. Fair sir, you are well o'erta'en.   5
My Lord Bassanio, upon more advice,
Hath sent you here this ring, and doth entreat
Your company at dinner.
   Por.   That cannot be.
His ring I do accept most thankfully,
And so I pray you tell him. Furthermore,   10
I pray you show my youth old Shylock's house.
   Gra. That will I do.
   Ner.   Sir, I would speak with you.
[*Aside to Portia*] I'll see if I can get my hus-
      band's ring,
Which I did make him swear to keep for ever.
   Por. [*aside to Nerissa*] Thou mayst, I war-
      rant. We shall have old swearing   15
That they did give the rings away to men;
But we'll outface them, and outswear them too.
[*Aloud*] Away! make haste. Thou know'st
      where I will tarry.
   Ner. Come, good sir, will you show me to
      this house?   *Exeunt.*

ACT V. [Scene I. *Belmont. Grounds of* Portia's *house.*]

      Enter *Lorenzo* and *Jessica*.

   Lor. The moon shines bright. In such a
      night as this,
When the sweet wind did gently kiss the trees
And they did make no noise — in such a night
Troilus methinks mounted the Troyan walls
And sigh'd his soul toward the Grecian tents, 5
Where Cressid lay that night.

   Jes.   In such a night
Did Thisbe fearfully o'ertrip the dew,
And saw the lion's shadow ere himself,
And ran dismay'd away.
   Lor.   In such a night
Stood Dido with a willow in her hand   10
Upon the wild sea-banks, and waft her love
To come again to Carthage.
   Jes.   In such a night

285

Medea gathered the enchanted herbs
That did renew old Æson.
Lor.   In such a night
Did Jessica steal from the wealthy Jew,   15
And with an unthrift love did run from Venice
As far as Belmont.
Jes.   In such a night
Did young Lorenzo swear he lov'd her well,
Stealing her soul with many vows of faith,
And ne'er a true one.
Lor.   In such a night
Did pretty Jessica (like a little shrow)   21
Slander her love, and he forgave it her.
Jes. I would out-night you, did no body
    come ;
But, hark, I hear the footing of a man.

Enter [*Stephano,*] a *Messenger.*

Lor. Who comes so fast in silence of the
    night ?   25
Mess. A friend.
Lor. A friend ? What friend ? Your name,
    I pray you, friend ?
Mess. Stephano is my name, and I bring word
My mistress will before the break of day
Be here at Belmont. She doth stray about   30
By holy crosses, where she kneels and prays
For happy wedlock hours.
Lor.   Who comes with her ?
Mess. None but a holy hermit and her maid.
I pray you, is my master yet return'd ?
Lor. He is not, nor we have not heard from
    him.   35
But go we in, I pray thee, Jessica,
And ceremoniously let us prepare
Some welcome for the mistress of the house.

Enter [*Launcelot, the*] *Clown.*

Laun. Sola, sola ! wo ha, ho ! sola, sola !
Lor. Who calls ?   40
Laun. Sola ! Did you see Master Lorenzo
and Mistress Lorenzo ? Sola, sola !
Lor. Leave holloaing, man ! Here.
Laun. Sola ! Where ? where ?
Lor. Here !   45
Laun. Tell him there's a post come from my
master, with his horn full of good news. My
master will be here ere morning.   [*Exit.*]
Lor. Sweet soul, let's in, and there expect
    their coming.
And yet no matter. Why should we go in ?   50
My friend Stephano, signify, I pray you,
Within the house, your mistress is at hand
And bring your music forth into the air.
                                   [*Exit Stephano.*]

How sweet the moonlight sleeps upon this bank !
Here will we sit and let the sounds of music 55
Creep in our ears. Soft stillness and the night
Become the touches of sweet harmony.
Sit, Jessica. Look how the floor of heaven
Is thick inlaid with patens of bright gold.
There's not the smallest orb which thou be-
    hold'st   60
But in his motion like an angel sings,
Still quiring to the young-ey'd cherubins ;
Such harmony is in immortal souls ;
But whilst this muddy vesture of decay
Doth grossly close it in, we cannot hear it. 65

[Enter *Musicians.*]

Come, ho, and wake Diana with a hymn !
With sweetest touches pierce your mistress' ear
And draw her home with music.   *Play music.*
Jes. I am never merry when I hear sweet
    music.
Lor. The reason is, your spirits are attentive.
For do but note a wild and wanton herd,   71
Or race of youthful and unhandled colts,
Fetching mad bounds, bellowing and neighing
    loud,
Which is the hot condition of their blood :
If they but hear perchance a trumpet sound, 75
Or any air of music touch their ears,
You shall perceive them make a mutual stand,
Their savage eyes turn'd to a modest gaze
By the sweet power of music. Therefore the
    poet
Did feign that Orpheus drew trees, stones, and
    floods,   80
Since naught so stockish, hard, and full of rage
But music for the time doth change his nature.
The man that hath no music in himself,
Nor is not mov'd with concord of sweet sounds,
Is fit for treasons, stratagems, and spoils ; 85
The motions of his spirit are dull as night,
And his affections dark as Erebus.
Let no such man be trusted. Mark the music.

Enter *Portia* and *Nerissa.*

Por. That light we see is burning in my hall.
How far that little candle throws his beams ! 90
So shines a good deed in a naughty world.
Ner. When the moon shone, we did not see
    the candle.
Por. So doth the greater glory dim the less.
A substitute shines brightly as a king
Until a king be by ; and then his state   95
Empties itself, as doth an inland brook
Into the main of waters. Music ! hark !
Ner. It is your music, madam, of the house.

Por. Nothing is good, I see, without respect.
Methinks it sounds much sweeter than by day.
Ner. Silence bestows that virtue on it,
madam. 101
Por. The crow doth sing as sweetly as the lark
When neither is attended; and I think
The nightingale, if she should sing by day
When every goose is cackling, would be thought
No better a musician than the wren. 106
How many things by season season'd are
To their right praise and true perfection!
Peace, ho! The moon sleeps with Endymion,
And would not be awak'd. *Music ceases.*
Lor. That is the voice,
Or I am much deceiv'd, of Portia. 111
Por. He knows me as the blind man knows
the cuckoo,
By the bad voice.
Lor. Dear lady, welcome home.
Por. We have been praying for our husbands'
welfare, 114
Which speed, we hope, the better for our words.
Are they return'd?
Lor. Madam, they are not yet;
But there is come a messenger before
To signify their coming.
Por. Go in, Nerissa.
Give order to my servants that they take
No note at all of our being absent hence— 120
Nor you, Lorenzo — Jessica, nor you.
A tucket sounds.
Lor. Your husband is at hand; I hear his
trumpet.
We are no telltales, madam; fear you not.
Por. This night methinks is but the daylight
sick;
It looks a little paler. 'Tis a day 125
Such as the day is when the sun is hid.

Enter *Bassanio, Antonio, Gratiano,* and their
Followers.

Bass. We should hold day with the Antipodes
If you would walk in absence of the sun.
Por. Let me give light, but let me not be light;
For a light wife doth make a heavy husband,
And never be Bassanio so for me. 131
But God sort all! You are welcome home, my
lord.
Bass. I thank you, madam. Give welcome
to my friend.
This is the man, this is Antonio,
To whom I am so infinitely bound. 135
Por. You should in all sense be much bound
to him,
For, as I hear, he was much bound for you.

Ant. No more than I am well acquitted of.
Por. Sir, you are very welcome to our house.
It must appear in other ways than words, 140
Therefore I scant this breathing courtesy.
Gra. [*to Nerissa*] By yonder moon I swear
you do me wrong!
In faith, I gave it to the judge's clerk.
Would he were gelt that had it, for my part,
Since you do take it, love, so much at heart.
Por. A quarrel, ho, already! What's the
matter? 146
Gra. About a hoop of gold, a paltry ring
That she did give to me, whose posy was
For all the world like cutler's poetry
Upon a knife, 'Love me, and leave me not.'
Ner. What talk you of the posy or the value?
You swore to me, when I did give it you, 152
That you would wear it till your hour of death,
And that it should lie with you in your grave.
Though not for me, yet for your vehement oaths,
You should have been respective and have kept
it. 156
Gave it a judge's clerk! No, God's my judge,
The clerk will ne'er wear hair on's face that
had it.
Gra. He will, an if he live to be a man.
Ner. Ay, if a woman live to be a man. 160
Gra. Now, by this hand, I gave it to a youth,
A kind of boy, a little scrubbed boy,
No higher than thyself, the judge's clerk,
A prating boy that begg'd it as a fee.
I could not for my heart deny it him. 165
Por. You were to blame — I must be plain
with you —
To part so slightly with your wive's first gift,
A thing stuck on with oaths upon your finger
And so riveted with faith unto your flesh.
I gave my love a ring, and made him swear
Never to part with it; and here he stands. 171
I dare be sworn for him he would not leave it
Nor pluck it from his finger for the wealth
That the world masters. Now, in faith, Gra-
tiano,
You give your wife too unkind a cause of grief,
An 'twere to me, I should be mad at it. 176
Bass. [*aside*] Why, I were best to cut my
left hand off
And swear I lost the ring defending it.
Gra. My Lord Bassanio gave his ring away
Unto the judge that begg'd it, and indeed 180
Deserv'd it too; and then the boy, his clerk,
That took some pains in writing, he begg'd
mine;
And neither man nor master would take aught
But the two rings.

287

Por.   What ring gave you, my lord?
Not that, I hope, which you receiv'd of me.   185
  Bass. If I could add a lie unto a fault,
I would deny it; but you see my finger
Hath not the ring upon it — it is gone.
  Por. Even so void is your false heart of truth.
By heaven, I will ne'er come in your bed   190
Until I see the ring!
  Ner.   Nor I in yours
Till I again see mine!
  Bass.   Sweet Portia,
If you did know to whom I gave the ring,
If you did know for whom I gave the ring,
And would conceive for what I gave the ring,
And how unwillingly I left the ring   196
When naught would be accepted but the ring,
You would abate the strength of your dis-
  pleasure.
  Por. If you had known the virtue of the ring,
Or half her worthiness that gave the ring,   200
Or your own honour to contain the ring,
You would not then have parted with the ring.
What man is there so much unreasonable,
If you had pleas'd to have defended it
With any terms of zeal, wanted the modesty
To urge the thing held as a ceremony?   206
Nerissa teaches me what to believe.
I'll die for't but some woman had the ring!
  Bass. No, by my honour, madam, by my
  soul,
No woman had it, but a civil doctor,   210
Which did refuse three thousand ducats of me
And begg'd the ring; the which I did deny him,
And suffer'd him to go displeas'd away,
Even he that had held up the very life
Of my dear friend. What should I say, sweet
  lady?   215
I was enforc'd to send it after him.
I was beset with shame and courtesy.
My honour would not let ingratitude
So much besmear it. Pardon me, good lady;
For, by these blessed candles of the night,   220
Had you been there, I think you would have
  begg'd
The ring of me to give the worthy doctor.
  Por. Let not that doctor e'er come near my
  house.
Since he hath got the jewel that I lov'd,
And that which you did swear to keep for me,
I will become as liberal as you;   226
I'll not deny him anything I have,
No, not my body, nor my husband's bed.
Know him I shall, I am well sure of it.
Lie not a night from home; watch me like
  Argus.   230

If you do not, if I be left alone,
Now, by mine honour, which is yet mine own,
I'll have that doctor for my bedfellow.
  Ner. And I his clerk. Therefore be well
  advis'd   234
How you do leave me to mine own protection.
  Gra. Well, do you so. Let not me take him
  then;
For if I do, I'll mar the young clerk's pen.
  Ant. I am th' unhappy subject of these
  quarrels.
  Por. Sir, grieve not you. You are welcome
  notwithstanding.   239
  Bass. Portia, forgive me this enforced wrong,
And in the hearing of these many friends
I swear to thee, even by thine own fair eyes,
Wherein I see myself —
  Por.   Mark you but that?
In both my eyes he doubly sees himself;   244
In each eye one. Swear by your double self,
And there's an oath of credit.
  Bass.   Nay, but hear me.
Pardon this fault, and by my soul I swear
I never more will break an oath with thee.
  Ant. I once did lend my body for his wealth,
Which, but for him that had your husband's
  ring,   250
Had quite miscarried. I dare be bound again,
My soul upon the forfeit, that your lord
Will never more break faith advisedly.
  Por. Then you shall be his surety. Give him
  this,
And bid him keep it better than the other.   255
  Ant. Here, Lord Bassanio. Swear to keep
  this ring.
  Bass. By heaven, it is the same I gave the
  doctor!
  Por. I had it of him. Pardon me, Bassanio;
For, by this ring, the doctor lay with me.   259
  Ner. And pardon me, my gentle Gratiano;
For that same scrubbed boy, the doctor's clerk,
In lieu of this, last night did lie with me.
  Gra. Why, this is like the mending of high-
  ways
In summer, where the ways are fair enough.
What, are we cuckolds ere we have deserv'd
  it?
  Por. Speak not so grossly. You are all
  amaz'd.   266
Here is a letter, read it at your leisure;
It comes from Padua from Bellario.
There you shall find that Portia was the doctor,
Nerissa there her clerk. Lorenzo here   270
Shall witness I set forth as soon as you,
And even but now return'd. I have not yet

Enter'd my house. Antonio, you are welcome,
And I have better news in store for you
Than you expect. Unseal this letter soon. 275
There you shall find three of your argosies
Are richly come to harbour suddenly.
You shall not know by what strange accident
I chanced on this letter.
　Ant. 　　　　I am dumb.
　Bass. Were you the doctor, and I knew you
　　not? 280
　Gra. Were you the clerk that is to make me
　　cuckold?
　Ner. Ay, but the clerk that never means to
　　do it,
Unless he live until he be a man.
　Bass. Sweet Doctor, you shall be my bed-
　　fellow.
When I am absent, then lie with my wife. 285
　Ant. Sweet lady, you have given me life and
　　living;
For here I read for certain that my ships
Are safely come to road.

　Por. 　　　　How now, Lorenzo?
My clerk hath some good comforts too for you.
　Ner. Ay, and I'll give them him without
　　a fee. 290
There do I give to you and Jessica,
From the rich Jew, a special deed of gift,
After his death, of all he dies possess'd of.
　Lor. Fair ladies, you drop manna in the way
Of starved people.
　Por. 　　　　It is almost morning, 295
And yet I am sure you are not satisfied
Of these events at full. Let us go in;
And charge us there upon inter'gatories,
And we will answer all things faithfully.
　Gra. Let it be so. The first inter'gatory 300
That my Nerissa shall be sworn on is,
Whether till the next night she had rather stay,
Or go to bed now, being two hours to day.
But were the day come, I should wish it dark
Till I were couching with the doctor's clerk. 305
Well, while I live I'll fear no other thing
So sore as keeping safe Nerissa's ring. *Exeunt.*

As You Like It

As You Like It was first published, so far as we know, in the Folio of 1623, which affords a reasonably good text. For the date of composition 1599 may be confidently accepted. Meres, writing in 1598 (before October 19), does not record the play, but it is mentioned in the Stationers' Register on August 4, 1600. Marlowe's Hero and Leander, first printed in 1598, is quoted in iii, 5, 81–82:

> Dead shepherd, now I find thy saw of might:
> 'Who ever lov'd that lov'd not at first sight?'

There is no good ground for the theory that Shakespeare wrote As You Like It in 1593 and drastically revised it some years later. This conjecture depends in part on the detection of blank-verse lines embedded in prose passages. These 'fossils,' it is argued, are an indication that verse has been turned into prose. The evidence is fallacious. Such lines abound in works which certainly never existed in verse form: in North's Plutarch, for example, and Milton's *Doctrine and Discipline of Divorce*. English prose runs easily into occasional blank-verse rhythm.

The speeches of Hymen and the nuptial song (v, 4) have often been regarded as un-Shakespearean — that is, as not good enough for Shakespeare, and therefore, in all probability, an insertion by some dramatic journeyman. But Hymen is no interloper. An actual marriage could not be brought upon the stage; some kind of symbolism was needed; Hymen makes an appropriate master of ceremonies, and his speeches are every bit as good as they need be. In real life, no one expects formalities to soar.

The plot is taken from Thomas Lodge's novel *Rosalynde*. *Euphues golden legacie: found after his death in his Cell at Silexedra* (1590). Lodge informs us in his dedication that he 'writ this booke' to 'beguile the time' on his voyage to the islands of 'Terceras and the Canaries' with Captain Clarke. This would have been about 1588. In his address 'To the Gentlemen Readers' he says that he wrote it 'in the Ocean, when euerie line was wet with a surge, and euerie humorous passion countercheckt with a storme.'

Shakespeare follows Lodge's story closely, but softens some of the more violent incidents.

In Lodge, the quarrel with which the play begins is terrific. Saladyne (Shakespeare's Oliver) bids his servants lay hold on Rosader (Orlando) and bind him. Rosader, 'half mad' with wrath, though 'of a mild and courteous nature,' belabours them with a great rake and forces Saladyne to take refuge in a loft adjoining the garden. They make peace, Saladyne promising to reinstate Rosader in his proper rank in the family. After the wrestling match, in which the champion is killed, Rosader goes home with a troop of gentlemen. The door is shut against him, but he breaks it down, enters the hall, sword in hand, and feasts his companions royally. As soon as they are gone, Rosader draws his sword, resolved to be revenged on Saladyne, but peace is made once more, this time by the mediation of Adam Spencer. Shortly after, however, Saladyne surprises Rosader in his sleep and has him chained to a post. He is released by Adam, who tells him that Saladyne has informed their kindred and allies that he is insane and has invited them to breakfast next morning to see him chained up as a desperate madman. Adam fastens him once more to the post, but leaves the fetters unlocked. The guests are convinced that Rosader is mad indeed, and after dinner, heated with wine, they begin to rail at him. Adam gives a sign, Rosader breaks loose, and armed with poleaxes, they attack the guests, hurting many, killing some, and driving the rest out of the house. The sheriff of the county is summoned and vows to arrest Rosader. He and

Adam break through the sheriff's posse and make their way to the Forest of Arden. There is no plot on Saladyne's part (as there is in Shakespeare) to murder his brother by burning down his lodging (ii, 3).

From this point the novel proceeds like the play. In the love story Shakespeare follows Lodge closely. Le Beau, Jaques, Touchstone, Audrey, William, and Sir Oliver Martext are Shakespeare's own. All the other important characters have their representatives in Lodge. The conclusion of the play is like that of the novel, except that Lodge's usurper, instead of being 'converted both from his enterprise' against his brother (Shakespeare's Duke Senior) 'and from the world' (v, 4, 167–168), is killed in battle.

The novel is intensely Euphuistic in style and tells its tale in a leisurely fashion, but it has considerable merit. Like the play, it contains a number of love poems. The only character who is at all humorous is Coridon, and his humour is very mild indeed. The leisurely mode gives the novelist one advantage over the playwright. The sudden conversion of the wicked brother seems less precipitate in Lodge than in Shakespeare.

Lodge's source is the anonymous *Tale of Gamelyn*, which dates from about the middle of the fourteenth century. It occurs in manuscripts of *The Canterbury Tales* and once passed as Chaucer's work. Lodge must have had access to a manuscript, for *Gamelyn* was not printed until 1721, when Urry included it in his edition of Chaucer. In the violent features of his novel (summarized above), Lodge follows *Gamelyn* pretty closely. On reaching the woods, Gamelyn and Adam encounter certain banished men, who conduct them to their 'master, king of outlaws.' He makes Gamelyn second in command. Soon after, the leader has tidings that he can return home, since his peace is made, and Gamelyn is crowned as outlaw king. For the rest of the story Lodge varies considerably from the old tale. In the upshot, Gamelyn makes his peace with the king of the country and becomes Chief Justice of the royal forest. His companions are pardoned and the wicked brother is hanged. There is no love story in the old tale. All such matter in the novel is Lodge's own contribution. The poem ends with Gamelyn's marriage and death, but there are no details as to his wife. Not even her name is mentioned. The conclusion is simply:

> And siththen wedded Gamelyn a wyf both good and feyr.
> They lyueden to-gidere whil that Crist wolde,
> And sithen was Gamelyn grauen vnder molde;
> And so schal we alle; may ther no man fle.
> God bringe vs to the Ioye that euer schal be!

It is just possible that Shakespeare had recourse to the *Tale of Gamelyn* for a few details, but the balance of probabilities is against it.

The famous song 'It was a lover and his lass' (v, 3) is contained, with music, in Thomas Morley's *First Booke of Ayres* (1600). The order of stanzas in the present text follows Morley. In the Folio the fourth stanza comes second. The first line of the last stanza runs in Morley 'Then prettie louers take the time.' In line 19 Morley reads 'corne fields,' in line 25 'Countrie fooles.'

AS YOU LIKE IT

[Dramatis Personæ.

Duke Senior, living in banishment.
Duke Frederick, his brother, and usurper of his dukedom.
Amiens, } lords attending on the banished Duke.
Jaques,
Le Beau, a courtier attending on Duke Frederick.
Charles, wrestler to Duke Frederick.
Oliver,
Jaques de Boys, } sons of Sir Rowland de Boys.
Orlando,
Adam, } servants to Oliver.
Dennis,

Touchstone, a clown.
Sir Oliver Martext, a vicar.
Corin, } shepherds.
Silvius,
William, a country fellow, in love with Audrey.
Hymen.

Rosalind, daughter to the banished Duke.
Celia, daughter to Duke Frederick.
Phebe, a shepherdess.
Audrey, a country wench.

Lords, pages, and attendants, &c.

SCENE — Oliver's orchard; Duke Frederick's court; the Forest of Arden.]

ACT I. Scene I. [Oliver's orchard.]

Enter Orlando and Adam.

Orl. As I remember, Adam, it was upon this fashion: he bequeathed me by will but poor a thousand crowns, and, as thou say'st, charged my brother on his blessing to breed me well; and there begins my sadness. My brother Jaques he keeps at school, and report speaks goldenly of his profit. For my part, he keeps me rustically at home or, to speak more properly, stays me here at home unkept; for call you that keeping for a gentleman of my birth that differs not from the stalling of an ox? His horses are bred better; for, besides that they are fair with their feeding, they are taught their manage, and to that end riders dearly hir'd; but I, his brother, gain nothing under him but growth, for the which his animals on his dunghills are as much bound to him as I. Besides this nothing that he so plentifully gives me, the something that nature gave me his countenance seems to take from me. He lets me feed with his hinds, bars me the place of a brother, and, as much as in him lies, mines my gentility with my education. This is it, Adam, that grieves me; and the spirit of my father, which I think is within me, begins to mutiny against this servitude. I will no longer endure it, though yet I know no wise remedy how to avoid it.

Enter Oliver.

Adam. Yonder comes my master, your brother.

Orl. Go apart, Adam, and thou shalt hear how he will shake me up.   30
                              [*Adam retires.*]
Oli. Now, sir, what make you here?
Orl. Nothing. I am not taught to make anything.
Oli. What mar you then, sir?   34
Orl. Marry, sir, I am helping you to mar that which God made, a poor unworthy brother of yours, with idleness.
Oli. Marry, sir, be better employed, and be naught awhile!   39
Orl. Shall I keep your hogs and eat husks with them? What prodigal portion have I spent that I should come to such penury?
Oli. Know you where you are, sir?
Orl. O, sir, very well. Here in your orchard.
Oli. Know you before whom, sir?   45
Orl. Ay, better than him I am before knows me. I know you are my eldest brother, and in the gentle condition of blood you should so know me. The courtesy of nations allows you my better in that you are the first born; but the same tradition takes not away my blood, were there twenty brothers betwixt us. I have as much of my father in me as you, albeit I confess your coming before me is nearer to his reverence.   54
Oli. What, boy!   [*Strikes him.*]
Orl. Come, come, elder brother, you are too young in this.   [*Seizes him.*]
Oli. Wilt thou lay hands on me, villain?

Orl. I am no villain. I am the youngest son of Sir Rowland de Boys; he was my father, and he is thrice a villain that says such a father begot villains. Wert thou not my brother, I would not take this hand from thy throat till this other had pull'd out thy tongue for saying so. Thou hast rail'd on thyself.   65

Adam. [*comes forward*] Sweet masters, be patient! For your father's remembrance, be at accord!

Oli. Let me go, I say.   68

Orl. I will not till I please. You shall hear me. My father charg'd you in his will to give me good education. You have train'd me like a peasant, obscuring and hiding from me all gentlemanlike qualities. The spirit of my father grows strong in me, and I will no longer endure it. Therefore allow me such exercises as may become a gentleman, or give me the poor allottery my father left me by testament. With that I will go buy my fortunes.   78

[*Releases him.*]

Oli. And what wilt thou do? beg when that is spent? Well, sir, get you in. I will not long be troubled with you. You shall have some part of your will. I pray you leave me.

Orl. I will no further offend you than becomes me for my good.

Oli. Get you with him, you old dog!   85

Adam. Is 'old dog' my reward? Most true, I have lost my teeth in your service. God be with my old master! he would not have spoke such a word.   89

Exeunt Orlando, Adam.

Oli. Is it even so? Begin you to grow upon me? I will physic your rankness, and yet give no thousand crowns neither. Holla, Dennis!

Enter *Dennis*.

Den. Calls your worship?

Oli. Was not Charles the Duke's wrestler here to speak with me?   95

Den. So please you, he is here at the door and importunes access to you.

Oli. Call him in. [*Exit Dennis.*] 'Twill be a good way; and to-morrow the wrestling is.

Enter *Charles*.

Cha. Good morrow to your worship.   100

Oli. Good Monsieur Charles! What's the new news at the new court?

Cha. There's no news at the court, sir, but the old news. That is, the old Duke is banished by his younger brother the new Duke, and three or four loving lords have put themselves into voluntary exile with him, whose lands and revenues enrich the new Duke; therefore he gives them good leave to wander.   109

Oli. Can you tell if Rosalind, the Duke's daughter, be banished with her father?

Cha. O, no! for the Duke's daughter her cousin so loves her, being ever from their cradles bred together, that she would have followed her exile, or have died to stay behind her. She is at the court, and no less beloved of her uncle than his own daughter, and never two ladies loved as they do.

Oli. Where will the old Duke live?   119

Cha. They say he is already in the Forest of Arden, and a many merry men with him; and there they live like the old Robin Hood of England. They say many young gentlemen flock to him every day, and fleet the time carelessly as they did in the golden world.   125

Oli. What, you wrestle to-morrow before the new Duke?

Cha. Marry do I, sir; and I came to acquaint you with a matter. I am given, sir, secretly to understand that your younger brother, Orlando, hath a disposition to come in disguis'd against me to try a fall. To-morrow, sir, I wrestle for my credit, and he that escapes me without some broken limb shall acquit him well. Your brother is but young and tender, and for your love I would be loath to foil him, as I must for my own honour if he come in. Therefore, out of my love to you, I came hither to acquaint you withal, that either you might stay him from his intendment, or brook such disgrace well as he shall run into, in that it is a thing of his own search and altogether against my will.   142

Oli. Charles, I thank thee for thy love to me, which thou shalt find I will most kindly requite. I had myself notice of my brother's purpose herein and have by underhand means laboured to dissuade him from it; but he is resolute. I'll tell thee, Charles it is the stubbornest young fellow of France; full of ambition, an envious emulator of every man's good parts, a secret and villanous contriver against me his natural brother. Therefore use thy discretion. I had as lief thou didst break his neck as his finger. And thou wert best look to 't; for if thou dost him any slight disgrace, or if he do not mightily grace himself on thee, he will practise against thee by poison, entrap thee by some treacherous device, and never leave thee till he hath ta'en thy life by some indirect means or other; for I

294

assure thee (and almost with tears I speak it)
there is not one so young and so villanous this
day living. I speak but brotherly of him; but
should I anatomize him to thee as he is, I must
blush and weep, and thou must look pale and
wonder.   164
Cha. I am heartily glad I came hither to you.
If he come to-morrow, I'll give him his payment. If ever he go alone again, I'll never
wrestle for prize more. And so God keep your
worship!   168
Oli. Farewell, good Charles. *Exit [Charles].*
Now will I stir this gamester. I hope I shall see
an end of him; for my soul (yet I know not
why) hates nothing more than he. Yet he's
gentle; never school'd and yet learned; full of
noble device; of all sorts enchantingly beloved,
and indeed so much in the heart of the world,
and especially of my own people, who best know
him, that I am altogether misprised. But it
shall not be so long; this wrestler shall clear
all. Nothing remains but that I kindle the boy
thither, which now I'll go about.   *Exit.*

Scene II. [*A lawn before* Duke Frederick's
Palace.*]

Enter *Rosalind and Celia.*

Cel. I pray thee, Rosalind, sweet my coz, be
merry.
Ros. Dear Celia, I show more mirth than I
am mistress of, and would you yet I were merrier? Unless you could teach me to forget a
banished father, you must not learn me how to
remember any extraordinary pleasure.   7
Cel. Herein I see thou lov'st me not with the
full weight that I love thee. If my uncle, thy
banished father, had banished thy uncle, the
Duke my father, so thou hadst been still with
me, I could have taught my love to take thy
father for mine. So wouldst thou, if the truth
of thy love to me were so righteously temper'd
as mine is to thee.   15
Ros. Well, I will forget the condition of my
estate to rejoice in yours.
Cel. You know my father hath no child but
I, nor none is like to have; and truly, when he
dies, thou shalt be his heir; for what he hath
taken away from thy father perforce, I will
render thee again in affection. By mine honour,
I will! and when I break that oath, let me turn
monster. Therefore, my sweet Rose, my dear
Rose, be merry.   25

Ros. From henceforth I will, coz, and devise
sports. Let me see. What think you of falling
in love?   28
Cel. Marry, I prithee do, to make sport
withal! But love no man in good earnest, nor
no further in sport neither than with safety of a
pure blush thou mayst in honour come off again.
Ros. What shall be our sport then?   33
Cel. Let us sit and mock the good housewife
Fortune from her wheel, that her gifts may
henceforth be bestowed equally.   36
Ros. I would we could do so; for her benefits
are mightily misplaced, and the bountiful blind
woman doth most mistake in her gifts to women.
Cel. 'Tis true; for those that she makes fair
she scarce makes honest, and those that she
makes honest she makes very ill-favouredly. 42
Ros. Nay, now thou goest from Fortune's
office to Nature's. Fortune reigns in gifts of the
world, not in the lineaments of Nature.   45

Enter [*Touchstone, the*] Clown.

Cel. No? When Nature hath made a fair
creature, may she not by Fortune fall into the
fire? Though Nature hath given us wit to flout
at Fortune, hath not Fortune sent in this fool
to cut off the argument?   50
Ros. Indeed, there is Fortune too hard for
Nature when Fortune makes Nature's natural
the cutter-off of Nature's wit.
Cel. Peradventure this is not Fortune's work
neither, but Nature's; who perceiveth our natural wits too dull to reason of such goddesses
and hath sent this natural for our whetstone,
for always the dulness of the fool is the whetstone of the wits. How now, wit? Whither
wander you?
Touch. Mistress, you must come away to
your father.   61
Cel. Were you made the messenger?
Touch. No, by mine honour; but I was bid
to come for you.
Ros. Where learned you that oath, fool?   65
Touch. Of a certain knight that swore by his
honour they were good pancakes, and swore by
his honour the mustard was naught. Now I'll
stand to it, the pancakes were naught, and the
mustard was good, and yet was not the knight
forsworn.   71
Cel. How prove you that in the great heap of
your knowledge?
Ros. Ay, marry, now unmuzzle your wisdom.
Touch. Stand you both forth now. Stroke
your chins, and swear by your beards that I am
a knave.   77

Cel. By our beards (if we had them), thou art.

Touch. By my knavery (if I had it), then I were. But if you swear by that that is not, you are not forsworn. No more was this knight, swearing by his honour, for he never had any; or if he had, he had sworn it away before ever he saw those pancakes or that mustard. 85

Cel. Prithee, who is't that thou mean'st?

Touch. One that old Frederick, your father, loves.

Cel. My father's love is enough to honour him. Enough! Speak no more of him. You'll be whipp'd for taxation one of these days. 91

Touch. The more pity that fools may not speak wisely what wise men do foolishly.

Cel. By my troth, thou sayest true; for, since the little wit that fools have was silenced, the little foolery that wise men have makes a great show. Here comes Monsieur Le Beau. 97

Enter *Le Beau.*

Ros. With his mouth full of news.

Cel. Which he will put on us as pigeons feed their young. 100

Ros. Then shall we be news-cramm'd.

Cel. All the better! We shall be the more marketable. — Bon jour, Monsieur Le Beau. What's the news?

Le Beau. Fair princess, you have lost much good sport. 106

Cel. Sport? of what colour?

Le Beau. What colour, madam? How shall ' answer you?

Ros. As wit and fortune will. 110

Touch. Or as the Destinies decree.

Cel. Well said! That was laid on with a trowel.

Touch. Nay, if I keep not my rank —

Ros. Thou losest thy old smell.

Le Beau. You amaze me, ladies. I would have told you of good wrestling, which you have lost the sight of. 117

Ros. Yet tell us the manner of the wrestling.

Le Beau. I will tell you the beginning; and if it please your ladyships, you may see the end; for the best is yet to do; and here, where you are, they are coming to perform it. 122

Cel. Well, the beginning that is dead and buried.

Le Beau. There comes an old man and his three sons — 126

Cel. I could match this beginning with an old tale.

Le Beau. Three proper young men, of excellent growth and presence. 130

Ros. With bills on their necks, 'Be it known unto all men by these presents' —

Le Beau. The eldest of the three wrestled with Charles, the Duke's wrestler; which Charles in a moment threw him and broke three of his ribs, that there is little hope of life in him. So he serv'd the second, and so the third. Yonder they lie, the poor old man, their father, making such pitiful dole over them that all the beholders take his part with weeping.

Ros. Alas! 141

Touch. But what is the sport, monsieur, that the ladies have lost?

Le Beau. Why, this that I speak of.

Touch. Thus men may grow wiser every day. It is the first time that ever I heard breaking of ribs was sport for ladies. 147

Cel. Or I, I promise thee.

Ros. But is there any else longs to see this broken music in his sides? Is there yet another dotes upon rib-breaking? Shall we see this wrestling, cousin? 152

Le Beau. You must, if you stay here; for here is the place appointed for the wrestling, and they are ready to perform it. 155

Cel. Yonder sure they are coming. Let us now stay and see it.

Flourish. Enter *Duke [Frederick], Lords, Orlando, Charles,* and *Attendants.*

Duke. Come on. Since the youth will not be entreated, his own peril on his forwardness!

Ros. Is yonder the man? 160

Le Beau. Even he, madam.

Cel. Alas, he is too young! Yet he looks successfully.

Duke. How now, daughter, and cousin! Are you crept hither to see the wrestling? 165

Ros. Ay, my liege, so please you give us leave.

Duke. You will take little delight in it, I can tell you, there is such odds in the men. In pity of the challenger's youth I would fain dissuade him, but he will not be entreated. Speak to him, ladies; see if you can move him. 172

Cel. Call him hither, good Monsieur Le Beau.

Duke. Do so. I'll not be by. [*Steps aside.*]

Le Beau. Monsieur the challenger, the princess calls for you. 176

Orl. I attend them with all respect and duty.

Ros. Young man, have you challeng'd Charles the wrestler?

Orl. No, fair princess. He is the general

challenger; I come but in as others do, to try with him the strength of my youth.   182

Cel. Young gentleman, your spirits are too bold for your years. You have seen cruel proof of this man's strength. If you saw yourself with your eyes, or knew yourself with your judgment, the fear of your adventure would counsel you to a more equal enterprise. We pray you for your own sake to embrace your own safety and give over this attempt.   190

Ros. Do, young sir. Your reputation shall not therefore be misprised. We will make it our suit to the Duke that the wrestling might not go forward.   194

Orl. I beseech you, punish me not with your hard thoughts, wherein I confess me much guilty to deny so fair and excellent ladies anything. But let your fair eyes and gentle wishes go with me to my trial; wherein if I be foil'd, there is but one sham'd that was never gracious; if kill'd, but one dead that is willing to be so. I shall do my friends no wrong, for I have none to lament me; the world no injury, for in it I have nothing. Only in the world I fill up a place, which may be better supplied when I have made it empty.   205

Ros. The little strength that I have, I would it were with you.

Cel. And mine, to eke out hers.

Ros. Fare you well. Pray heaven I be deceiv'd in you!   210

Cel. Your heart's desires be with you!

Cha. Come, where is this young gallant that is so desirous to lie with his mother earth?

Orl. Ready, sir; but his will hath in it a more modest working.   215

Duke. You shall try but one fall.

Cha. No, I warrant your Grace you shall not entreat him to a second that have so mightily persuaded him from a first.   219

Orl. You mean to mock me after. You should not have mock'd me before. But come your ways!

Ros. Now Hercules be thy speed, young man!

Cel. I would I were invisible, to catch the strong fellow by the leg.   *Wrestle.*

Ros. O excellent young man!   225

Cel. If I had a thunderbolt in mine eye, I can tell who should down.

                    [*Charles is thrown.*] *Shout.*

Duke. No more, no more!

Orl. Yes, I beseech your Grace. I am not yet well breath'd.   230

Duke. How dost thou, Charles?

Le Beau.   He cannot speak, my lord.

Duke. Bear him away.   [*Charles is borne out.*]
                    What is thy name, young man?

Orl. Orlando, my liege, the youngest son of Sir Rowland de Boys.

Duke. I would thou hadst been son to some man else!   235
The world esteem'd thy father honourable,
But I did find him still mine enemy.
Thou shouldst have better pleas'd me with this deed,
Hadst thou descended from another house.   239
But fare thee well; thou art a gallant youth;
I would thou hadst told me of another father.
                    Exeunt Duke, [*Train, and Le Beau*].

Cel. Were I my father, coz, would I do this?

Orl. I am more proud to be Sir Rowland's son,
His youngest son, and would not change that calling
To be adopted heir to Frederick.   245

Ros. My father lov'd Sir Rowland as his soul,
And all the world was of my father's mind.
Had I before known this young man his son,
I should have given him tears unto entreaties
Ere he should thus have ventur'd.

Cel.   Gentle cousin,
Let us go thank him and encourage him.   251
My father's rough and envious disposition
Sticks me at heart. Sir, you have well deserv'd.
If you do keep your promises in love
But justly as you have exceeded all promise,
Your mistress shall be happy.

Ros.   Gentleman,   256
                    [*Gives him a chain from her neck.*]
Wear this for me, one out of suits with fortune,
That could give more but that her hand lacks means.
Shall we go, coz?

Cel.   Ay. Fare you well, fair gentleman.

Orl. Can I not say 'I thank you'? My better parts   260
Are all thrown down, and that which here stands up
Is but a quintain, a mere liveless block.

Ros. He calls us back. My pride fell with my fortunes;
I'll ask him what he would. Did you call, sir?
Sir, you have wrestled well, and overthrown
More than your enemies.

Cel.   Will you go, coz?   **266**

Ros. Have with you. Fare you well.

          Exeunt [Rosalind and Celia].

Orl. What passion hangs these weights upon my tongue?
I cannot speak to her, yet she urg'd conference.

      Enter *Le Beau.*

O poor Orlando, thou art overthrown!   270
Or Charles or something weaker masters thee.

Le Beau. Good sir, I do in friendship counsel you
To leave this place. Albeit you have deserv'd
High commendation, true applause, and love,
Yet such is now the Duke's condition   275
That he misconsters all that you have done.
The Duke is humorous. What he is, indeed,
More suits you to conceive than I to speak of.

Orl. I thank you, sir: and pray you tell me this —
Which of the two was daughter of the Duke,
That here was at the wrestling?   281

Le Beau. Neither his daughter, if we judge by manners;
But yet indeed the smaller is his daughter;
The other is daughter to the banish'd Duke,
And here detain'd by her usurping uncle   285
To keep his daughter company, whose loves
Are dearer than the natural bond of sisters.
But I can tell you that of late this Duke
Hath ta'en displeasure 'gainst his gentle niece,
Grounded upon no other argument   290
But that the people praise her for her virtues
And pity her for her good father's sake;
And, on my life, his malice 'gainst the lady
Will suddenly break forth. Sir, fare you well.
Hereafter, in a better world than this,   295
I shall desire more love and knowledge of you.

Orl. I rest much bounden to you. Fare you well.

          [Exit Le Beau.]

Thus must I from the smoke into the smother,
From tyrant Duke unto a tyrant brother.   299
But heavenly Rosalind!   *Exit.*

Scene III. [*A room in the* Duke's *Palace.*]

      Enter *Celia* and *Rosalind.*

Cel. Why, cousin! why, Rosalind! Cupid have mercy! not a word?

Ros. Not one to throw at a dog.

Cel. No, thy words are too precious to be cast away upon curs; throw some of them at me. Come, lame me with reasons.   6

Ros. Then there were two cousins laid up, when the one should be lam'd with reasons, and the other mad without any.

Cel. But is all this for your father?   10

Ros. No, some of it is for my child's father. O, how full of briers is this working-day world!

Cel. They are but burrs, cousin, thrown upon thee in holiday foolery. If we walk not in the trodden paths, our very petticoats will catch them.   15

Ros. I could shake them off my coat. These burrs are in my heart.

Cel. Hem them away.

Ros. I would try, if I could cry 'hem!' and have him.   20

Cel. Come, come, wrestle with thy affections.

Ros. O, they take the part of a better wrestler than myself!

Cel. O, a good wish upon you! You will try in time, in despite of a fall. But, turning these jests out of service, let us talk in good earnest. Is it possible on such a sudden you should fall into so strong a liking with old Sir Rowland's youngest son?

Ros. The Duke my father lov'd his father dearly.   31

Cel. Doth it therefore ensue that you should love his son dearly? By this kind of chase, I should hate him, for my father hated his father dearly; yet I hate not Orlando.   35

Ros. No, faith, hate him not, for my sake!

Cel. Why should I not? Doth he not deserve well?

   Enter *Duke [Frederick]*, with *Lords.*

Ros. Let me love him for that; and do you love him because I do. Look, here comes the Duke.   41

Cel. With his eyes full of anger.

Duke. Mistress, dispatch you with your safest haste
And get you from our court!

Ros.   Me, uncle?

Duke.   You, cousin.
Within these ten days if that thou beest found
So near our public court as twenty miles,   46
Thou diest for it.

Ros.   I do beseech your Grace
Let me the knowledge of my fault bear with me.
If with myself I hold intelligence
Or have acquaintance with mine own desires;
If that I do not dream or be not frantic,   51

AS YOU LIKE IT

The mock marriage in the Forest of Arden (*Act IV, Scene I*). Gwen Cherrell as Celia, John Neville as Orlando, and Virginia McKenna as Rosalind, daughter of the banished duke

Paul Rogers in the role of Touchstone, the clown, master of dry, caustic humor

PHOTOGRAPHS BY HOUSTON ROGERS
PRODUCED BY THE OLD VIC COMPANY

Orlando in his wrestling bout with Charles (Kerrigan Prescott), the bully of the usurping duke. Here seen at a disadvantage, he eventually triumphs over the champion (*Act I, Scene II*)

"Wear this for me, one out of suits with fortune." Victor in the wrestling match with Charles, Orlando receives a locket from Rosalind as his reward (*Act I, Scene II*)

"I cannot live out of her company."
Celia beseeches her father, Duke
Frederick (Charles Gray), the
usurper, not to banish her cousin
Rosalind (*Act I, Scene III*)

Touchstone comforts Celia when they are
lost in the forest (*Act II, Scene IV*)

Celia tells Rosalind she has found Orlando in
the forest (*Act III, Scene II*)

"Forbear, and eat no more." Seeking food in the Forest of Arden, the famished Orlando comes upon the banished duke (John Woodvine) and his followers at their supper (*Act II, Scene VII*)

"Sweet are the uses of adversity." The banished duke exhorts his men (Act II, Scene I)

"All the world's a stage, and all the men and women merely players." Jaques (Eric Porter) delivers his celebrated monologue, developing a remark made by the duke (Act II, Scene VII)

"I would cure you, if you would but call me Rosalind." Disguised as a boy, Rosalind leads the unwitting Orlando to expound on the sweet anguish of his love for her (*Act III, Scene II*)

"And how like you this shepherd's life, Master Touchstone?" Corin (Paul Daneman) introduces a debate on city versus country living (*Act III, Scene II*)

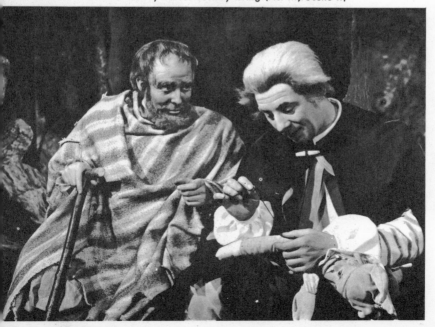

"I will kill thee a hundred and fifty ways." Touchstone disposes of his rival, William (Job Stewart), while Audrey (Rachel Roberts) watches (*Act V, Scene I*)

"Say that you love me not, but say not so in bitterness." The wooing of Phebe (Eleanore Bryan) by Silvius (Alan Dobie) becomes a model for Orlando in his courting of Rosalind (*Act III, Scene V*)

Disguised as a shepherd, Rosalind rests in the Forest of Arden and dreams of her sweetheart, Orlando

The final scene: the formal betrothal of Orlando and Rosalind (Act. V, Scene I\ )

As I do trust I am not — then, dear uncle,
Never so much as in a thought unborn
Did I offend your Highness.
Duke.   Thus do all traitors.
If their purgation did consist in words,   55
They are as innocent as grace itself.
Let it suffice thee that I trust thee not.
  Ros. Yet your mistrust cannot make me a
    traitor.
Tell me whereon the likelihood depends.
  Duke. Thou art thy father's daughter.
    There's enough!   60
  Ros. So was I when your Highness took his
    dukedom;
So was I when your Highness banish'd him.
Treason is not inherited, my lord;
Or if we did derive it from our friends,   64
What's that to me? My father was no traitor.
Then, good my liege, mistake me not so much
To think my poverty is treacherous.
  Cel. Dear sovereign, hear me speak.
  Duke. Ay, Celia. We stay'd her for your
    sake,
Else had she with her father rang'd along.   70
  Cel. I did not then entreat to have her stay;
It was your pleasure and your own remorse.
I was too young that time to value her;
But now I know her. If she be a traitor,
Why, so am I! We still have slept together,   75
Rose at an instant, learn'd, play'd, eat together;
And wheresoe'er we went, like Juno's swans,
Still we went coupled and inseparable.
  Duke. She is too subtile for thee; and her
    smoothness,
Her very silence and her patience,   80
Speak to the people, and they pity her.
Thou art a fool. She robs thee of thy name,
And thou wilt show more bright and seem more
    virtuous
When she is gone. Then open not thy lips,
Firm and irrevocable is my doom   85
Which I have pass'd upon her. She is banish'd.
  Cel. Pronounce that sentence then on me,
    my liege!
I cannot live out of her company.
  Duke. You are a fool. You, niece, provide
    yourself.
If you outstay the time, upon mine honour,   90
And in the greatness of my word, you die.
                              Exeunt Duke &c.
  Cel. O my poor Rosalind! whither wilt
    thou go?
Wilt thou change fathers? I will give thee mine.
I charge thee be not thou more griev'd than
    I am.   94

  Ros. I have more cause.
  Cel.   Thou hast not, cousin.
Prithee be cheerful. Know'st thou not the Duke
Hath banish'd me, his daughter?
  Ros.   That he hath not!
  Cel. No? hath not? Rosalind lacks then
    the love
Which teacheth me that thou and I am one.
Shall we be sund'red? shall we part, sweet girl?
No! let my father seek another heir.   101
Therefore devise with me how we may fly,
Whither to go, and what to bear with us.
And do not seek to take your charge upon you,
To bear your griefs yourself and leave me out;
For, by this heaven, now at our sorrows pale,
Say what thou canst, I'll go along with thee!
  Ros. Why, whither shall we go?
  Cel. To seek my uncle in the Forest of Arden.
  Ros. Alas, what danger will it be to us,   110
Maids as we are, to travel forth so far!
Beauty provoketh thieves sooner than gold.
  Cel. I'll put myself in poor and mean attire
And with a kind of umber smirch my face;
The like do you. So shall we pass along   115
And never stir assailants.
  Ros.   Were it not better,
Because that I am more than common tall,
That I did suit me all points like a man?
A gallant curtleaxe upon my thigh,   119
A boar-spear in my hand, and — in my heart
Lie there what hidden woman's fear there will —
We'll have a swashing and a martial outside,
As many other mannish cowards have
That do outface it with their semblances.
  Cel. What shall I call thee when thou art a
    man?   125
  Ros. I'll have no worse a name than Jove's
    own page,
And therefore look you call me Ganymede.
But what will you be call'd?
  Cel. Something that hath a reference to my
    state —
No longer Celia, but Aliena.   130
  Ros. But, cousin, what if we assay'd to
    steal
The clownish fool out of your father's court?
Would he not be a comfort to our travel?
  Cel. He'll go along o'er the wide world with
    me.
Leave me alone to woo him. Let's away   135
And get our jewels and our wealth together,
Devise the fittest time and safest way
To hide us from pursuit that will be made
After my flight. Now go we in content
To liberty, and not to banishment.   *Exeunt.*

Act II. Scene I. [*The Forest of Arden. Before* Duke Senior's *cave.*]

Enter *Duke Senior, Amiens,* and two or three
    Lords, like *Foresters.*

  Duke S. Now, my co-mates and brothers in
    exile,
Hath not old custom made this life more sweet
Than that of painted pomp? Are not these
    woods
More free from peril than the envious court?
Here feel we but the penalty of Adam,   5
The seasons' difference; as, the icy fang
And churlish chiding of the winter's wind,
Which, when it bites and blows upon my body
Even till I shrink with cold, I smile, and say
'This is no flattery; these are counsellors   10
That feelingly persuade me what I am.'
Sweet are the uses of adversity,
Which, like the toad, ugly and venomous,
Wears yet a precious jewel in his head;
And this our life, exempt from public haunt,   15
Finds tongues in trees, books in the running
    brooks,
Sermons in stones, and good in everything:
I would not change it.
  Ami.   Happy is your Grace
That can translate the stubbornness of fortune
Into so quiet and so sweet a style.   20
  Duke S. Come, shall we go and kill us
    venison?
And yet it irks me the poor dappled fools,
Being native burghers of this desert city,
Should, in their own confines, with forked heads
Have their round haunches gor'd.
  1. Lord.   Indeed, my lord,
The melancholy Jaques grieves at that,   26
And in that kind swears you do more usurp
Than doth your brother that hath banish'd you.
To-day my Lord of Amiens and myself
Did steal behind him as he lay along   30
Under an oak, whose antique root peeps out
Upon the brook that brawls along this wood;
To the which place a poor sequest'red stag,
That from the hunter's aim had ta'en a hurt,
Did come to languish; and indeed, my lord,
The wretched animal heav'd forth such groans
That their discharge did stretch his leathern
    coat
Almost to bursting, and the big round tears
Cours'd one another down his innocent nose
In piteous chase; and thus the hairy fool,   40
Much marked of the melancholy Jaques,

Stood on th' extremest verge of the swift brook,
Augmenting it with tears.
  Duke S.   But what said Jaques?
Did he not moralize this spectacle?
  1. Lord. O, yes, into a thousand similes.   45
First, for his weeping into the needless stream:
'Poor deer,' quoth he, 'thou mak'st a testament
As worldlings do, giving thy sum of more
To that which had too much.' Then, being
    alone,
Left and abandoned of his velvet friends: 50
''Tis right!' quoth he, 'thus misery doth part
The flux of company.' Anon a careless herd,
Full of the pasture, jumps along by him
And never stays to greet him: 'Ay,' quoth
    Jaques,
'Sweep on, you fat and greasy citizens!   55
'Tis just the fashion! Wherefore do you look
Upon that poor and broken bankrupt there?'
Thus most invectively he pierceth through
The body of the country, city, court;
Yea, and of this our life, swearing that we   60
Are mere usurpers, tyrants, and what's worse,
To fright the animals and to kill them up
In their assign'd and native dwelling place.
  Duke S. And did you leave him in this con-
    templation?
  2. Lord. We did, my lord, weeping and com-
    menting   65
Upon the sobbing deer.
  Duke S.   Show me the place.
I love to cope him in these sullen fits,
For then he's full of matter.
  1. Lord. I'll bring you to him straight.
                              Exeunt.

Scene II. [*A room in* Duke Frederick's
    Palace.]

Enter *Duke* [*Frederick*], with *Lords.*

  Duke. Can it be possible that no man saw
    them?
It cannot be. Some villains of my court
Are of consent and sufferance in this.
  1. Lord. I cannot hear of any that did see her.
The ladies her attendants of her chamber   5
Saw her abed, and in the morning early
They found the bed untreasur'd of their mis-
    tress.

300

2. *Lord.* My lord, the roynish clown at whom
    so oft
Your Grace was wont to laugh is also missing.
Hisperia, the princess' gentlewoman,   10
Confesses that she secretly o'erheard
Your daughter and her cousin much commend
The parts and graces of the wrestler
That did but lately foil the sinewy Charles;
And she believes, wherever they are gone,   15
That youth is surely in their company.
    Duke. Send to his brother, fetch that gallant
    hither.
If he be absent, bring his brother to me;
I'll make him find him. Do this suddenly,
And let not search and inquisition quail   20
To bring again these foolish runaways. *Exeunt.*

Scene III. [*Before* Oliver's *house.*]

    Enter *Orlando* and *Adam,* [meeting].
    Orl. Who's there?
    Adam. What, my young master! O my
gentle master!
O my sweet master! O you memory
Of old Sir Rowland! Why, what make you
here?
Why are you virtuous? Why do people love
you?   5
And wherefore are you gentle, strong, and
valiant?
Why would you be so fond to overcome
The bonny prizer of the humorous Duke?
Your praise is come too swiftly home before
you.
Know you not, master, to some kind of men 10
Their graces serve them but as enemies?
No more do yours. Your virtues, gentle master,
Are sanctified and holy traitors to you.
O, what a world is this, when what is comely
Envenoms him that bears it!   15
    Orl. Why, what's the matter?
    Adam.   O unhappy youth,
Come not within these doors! Within this roof
The enemy of all your graces lives.
Your brother (no, no brother! yet the son —
Yet not the son — I will not call him son   20
Of him I was about to call his father)
Hath heard your praises, and this night he
means
To burn the lodging where you use to lie
And you within it. If he fail of that,
He will have other means to cut you off.   25
I overheard him and his practices.

This is no place, this house is but a butchery.
Abhor it, fear it, do not enter it!
    Orl. Why, whither, Adam, wouldst thou
have me go?
    Adam. No matter whither, so you come not
here.   30
    Orl. What, wouldst thou have me go and
beg my food,
Or with a base and boist'rous sword enforce
A thievish living on the common road?
This I must do, or know not what to do.
Yet this I will not do, do how I can.   35
I rather will subject me to the malice
Of a diverted blood and bloody brother.
    Adam. But do not so. I have five hundred
crowns,
The thrifty hire I sav'd under your father,
Which I did store to be my foster nurse   40
When service should in my old limbs lie lame
And unregarded age in corners thrown.
Take that, and he that doth the ravens feed,
Yea, providently caters for the sparrow,
Be comfort to my age! Here is the gold;   45
All this I give you. Let me be your servant.
Though I look old, yet I am strong and lusty;
For in my youth I never did apply
Hot and rebellious liquors in my blood,
Nor did not with unbashful forehead woo   50
The means of weakness and debility;
Therefore my age is as a lusty winter,
Frosty, but kindly. Let me go with you;
I'll do the service of a younger man
In all your business and necessities.   55
    Orl. O good old man, how well in thee appears
The constant service of the antique world,
When service sweat for duty, not for meed!
Thou art not for the fashion of these times,
Where none will sweat but for promotion,   60
And having that, do choke their service up
Even with the having. It is not so with thee.
But, poor old man, thou prun'st a rotten tree
That cannot so much as a blossom yield
In lieu of all thy pains and husbandry.   65
But come thy ways! We'll go along together,
And ere we have thy youthful wages spent,
We'll light upon some settled low content.
    Adam. Master, go on, and I will follow thee
To the last gasp with truth and loyalty!   70
From seventeen years till now almost fourscore
Here lived I, but now live here no more.
At seventeen years many their fortunes seek,
But at fourscore it is too late a week;
Yet fortune cannot recompense me better   75
Than to die well and not my master's debtor.
                                        Exeunt.

Scene IV. [*The Forest of Arden.*
Near a sheepcote.]

Enter *Rosalind* for *Ganymede, Celia* for *Aliena,*
and *Clown,* alias *Touchstone.*

Ros. O Jupiter, how weary are my spirits!
Touch. I care not for my spirits if my legs
were not weary.
Ros. I could find in my heart to disgrace my
man's apparel and to cry like a woman; but I
must comfort the weaker vessel, as doublet and
hose ought to show itself courageous to petticoat. Therefore, courage, good Aliena!
Cel. I pray you bear with me; I cannot go
no further.   10
Touch. For my part, I had rather bear with
you than bear you. Yet I should bear no cross
if I did bear you, for I think you have no money
in your purse.
Ros. Well, this is the Forest of Arden.   15
Touch. Ay, now am I in Arden, the more fool
I! When I was at home, I was in a better place;
but travellers must be content.

Enter *Corin* and *Silvius.*

Ros. Ay, be so, good Touchstone. — Look
you, who comes here,
A young man and an old in solemn talk.   20
Cor. That is the way to make her scorn you
still.
Sil. O Corin, that thou knew'st how I do
love her!
Cor. I partly guess; for I have lov'd ere now.
Sil. No, Corin, being old, thou canst not
guess,
Though in thy youth thou wast as true a
lover
As ever sigh'd upon a midnight pillow.   26
But if thy love were ever like to mine
(As sure I think did never man love so),
How many actions most ridiculous
Hast thou been drawn to by thy fantasy!   30
Cor. Into a thousand that I have forgotten.
Sil. O, thou didst then never love so heartily!
If thou rememb'rest not the slightest folly
That ever love did make thee run into,
Thou hast not lov'd.   35
Or if thou hast not sat as I do now,
Wearing thy hearer in thy mistress' praise,
Thou hast not lov'd.
Or if thou hast not broke from company
Abruptly, as my passion now makes me,   40
Thou hast not lov'd. O Phebe, Phebe, Phebe!
                                                    Exit.

Ros. Alas, poor shepherd! Searching of thy
wound,
I have by hard adventure found mine own.
Touch. And I mine. I remember, when I was
in love I broke my sword upon a stone and bid
him take that for coming a-night to Jane Smile;
and I remember the kissing of her batlet, and
the cow's dugs that her pretty chopt hands had
milk'd; and I remember the wooing of a peascod instead of her, from whom I took two cods,
and giving her them again, said with weeping
tears, 'Wear these for my sake.' We that are
true lovers run into strange capers; but as all is
mortal in nature, so is all nature in love mortal
in folly.   56
Ros. Thou speak'st wiser than thou art
ware of.
Touch. Nay, I shall ne'er be ware of mine
own wit till I break my shins against it.   60
Ros. Jove, Jove! this shepherd's passion
    Is much upon my fashion.
Touch. And mine, but it grows something
    stale with me.
Cel. I pray you, one of you question yond
    man
If he for gold will give us any food.   65
I faint almost to death.
Touch.   Holla, you clown!
Ros. Peace, fool! he's not thy kinsman.
Cor. Who calls?
Touch.   Your betters, sir.
Cor.   Else are they very wretched.
Ros. Peace, I say! — Good even to you,
    friend.   69
Cor. And to you, gentle sir, and to you all.
Ros. I prithee, shepherd, if that love or gold
Can in this desert place buy entertainment,
Bring us where we may rest ourselves and feed.
Here's a young maid with travel much op-
    press'd,
And faints for succour.
Cor.   Fair sir, I pity her   75
And wish, for her sake more than for mine own,
My fortunes were more able to relieve her;
But I am shepherd to another man
And do not shear the fleeces that I graze.
My master is of churlish disposition   80
And little recks to find the way to heaven
By doing deeds of hospitality.
Besides, his cote, his flocks, and bounds of feed
Are now on sale, and at our sheepcote now,
By reason of his absence, there is nothing   85
That you will feed on; but what is, come
    see,
And in my voice most welcome shall you be.

302

Ros. What is he that shall buy his flock and
pasture?
Cor. That young swain that you saw here
but erewhile,
That little cares for buying anything.   90
Ros. I pray thee, if it stand with honesty,
Buy thou the cottage, pasture, and the flock,
And thou shalt have to pay for it of us.
Cel. And we will mend thy wages. I like
this place
And willingly could waste my time in it.   95
Cor. Assuredly the thing is to be sold.
Go with me. If you like, upon report,
The soil, the profit, and this kind of life,
I will your very faithful feeder be
And buy it with your gold right suddenly.   100
                              Exeunt.

Scene V. [*The Forest. Before Duke Senior's cave.*]

Enter Amiens, Jaques, and others.

Song.

Ami. Under the greenwood tree
Who loves to lie with me,
And turn his merry note
Unto the sweet bird's throat,
Come hither, come hither, come hither!   5
    Here shall he see
    No enemy
But winter and rough weather.

Jaq. More, more, I prithee more!
Ami. It will make you melancholy, Monsieur Jaques.   11
Jaq. I thank it. More, I prithee more! I can
suck melancholy out of a song as a weasel sucks
eggs. More, I prithee more!
Ami. My voice is ragged. I know I cannot
please you.   16
Jaq. I do not desire you to please me; I do
desire you to sing. Come, more! another
stanzo! Call you 'em stanzos?
Ami. What you will, Monsieur Jaques.   20
Jaq. Nay, I care not for their names; they
owe me nothing. Will you sing?
Ami. More at your request than to please
myself.   24
Jaq. Well then, if ever I thank any man, I'll
thank you. But that they call compliment is
like th' encounter of two dog-apes; and when a
man thanks me heartily, methinks I have given
him a penny, and he renders me the beggarly

thanks. Come, sing! and you that will not,
hold your tongues.   31
Ami. Well, I'll end the song. Sirs, cover the
while; the Duke will drink under this tree. He
hath been all this day to look you.   34
Jaq. And I have been all this day to avoid
him. He is too disputable for my company. I
think of as many matters as he; but I give
heaven thanks and make no boast of them.
Come, warble, come.

Song.
All together here.

Who doth ambition shun   40
And loves to live i' th' sun,
Seeking the food he eats,
And pleas'd with what he gets,
Come hither, come hither, come hither!
    Here shall he see   45
    No enemy
But winter and rough weather.

Jaq. I'll give you a verse to this note that I
made yesterday in despite of my invention.
Ami. And I'll sing it.   50
Jaq. Thus it goes:

If it do come to pass
That any man turn ass,
Leaving his wealth and ease
A stubborn will to please,   55
Ducdame, ducdame, ducdame!
    Here shall he see
    Gross fools as he,
An if he will come to me.

Ami. What's that 'ducdame'?   60
Jaq. 'Tis a Greek invocation to call fools into
a circle. I'll go sleep, if I can; if I cannot, I'll
rail against all the first-born of Egypt.
Ami. And I'll go seek the Duke. His banquet is prepar'd.   *Exeunt [severally]*

Scene VI. [*The Forest.*]

Enter Orlando and Adam.

Adam. Dear master, I can go no further. O,
I die for food! Here lie I down and measure out
my grave. Farewell, kind master.
Orl. Why, how now, Adam? no greater
heart in thee? Live a little, comfort a little.
cheer thyself a little. If this uncouth forest
yield anything savage, I will either be food for
it or bring it for food to thee. Thy conceit is
nearer death than thy powers. For my sake be
comfortable; hold death awhile at the arm's

end. I will here be with thee presently; and if
I bring thee not something to eat, I will give
thee leave to die; but if thou diest before I
come, thou art a mocker of my labour. Well
said! thou look'st cheerly, and I'll be with thee
quickly. Yet thou liest in the bleak air. Come,
I will bear thee to some shelter, and thou shalt
not die for lack of a dinner if there live anything
in this desert. Cheerly, good Adam! *Exeunt.*

Scene VII. [*The Forest. Before the Cave.*]

[A table set out.] Enter *Duke Senior,*
[*Amiens,*] and *Lords,* like *Outlaws.*

Duke S. I think he be transform'd into a
beast,
For I can nowhere find him like a man.
1. Lord. My lord, he is but even now gone
hence.
Here was he merry, hearing of a song.
Duke S. If he, compact of jars, grow musical,
We shall have shortly discord in the spheres. 6
Go seek him; tell him I would speak with him.

Enter *Jaques.*

1. Lord. He saves my labour by his own
approach.
Duke S. Why, how now, monsieur! what a
life is this,
That your poor friends must woo your company!
What, you look merrily. 11
Jaq. A fool, a fool! I met a fool i' th' forest,
A motley fool! — a miserable world! —
As I do live by food, I met a fool,
Who laid him down and bask'd him in the sun
And rail'd on Lady Fortune in good terms, 16
In good set terms — and yet a motley fool.
'Good morrow, fool,' quoth I. 'No, sir,' quoth
he,
'Call me not fool till heaven hath sent me
fortune.'
And then he drew a dial from his poke, 20
And looking on it with lack-lustre eye,
Says very wisely, 'It is ten o'clock.
Thus we may see,' quoth he, 'how the world
wags.
'Tis but an hour ago since it was nine,
And after one hour more 'twill be eleven; 25
And so, from hour to hour, we ripe and ripe,
And then, from hour to hour, we rot and rot;
And thereby hangs a tale.' When I did hear
The motley fool thus moral on the time,
My lungs began to crow like chanticleer 30

That fools should be so deep contemplative;
And I did laugh sans intermission
An hour by his dial. O noble fool!
A worthy fool! Motley's the only wear!
Duke S. What fool is this? 35
Jaq. O worthy fool! One that hath been a
courtier,
And says, if ladies be but young and fair,
They have the gift to know it. And in his brain,
Which is as dry as the remainder biscuit
After a voyage, he hath strange places
cramm'd 40
With observation, the which he vents
In mangled forms. O that I were a fool!
I am ambitious for a motley coat.
Duke S. Thou shalt have one.
Jaq. It is my only suit,
Provided that you weed your better judgments
Of all opinion that grows rank in them 45
That I am wise. I must have liberty
Withal, as large a charter as the wind,
To blow on whom I please; for so fools have.
And they that are most galled with my folly, 50
They most must laugh. And why, sir, must
they so?
The why is plain as way to parish church:
He that a fool doth very wisely hit
Doth very foolishly, although he smart,
Not to seem senseless of the bob. If not, 55
The wise man's folly is anatomiz'd
Even by the squand'ring glances of the fool.
Invest me in my motley. Give me leave
To speak my mind, and I will through and
through
Cleanse the foul body of th' infected world, 60
If they will patiently receive my medicine.
Duke S. Fie on thee! I can tell what thou
wouldst do.
Jaq. What, for a counter, would I do but
good?
Duke S. Most mischievous foul sin, in chid-
ing sin.
For thou thyself hast been a libertine, 65
As sensual as the brutish sting itself;
And all th' embossed sores and headed evils
That thou with license of free foot hast caught,
Wouldst thou disgorge into the general world.
Jaq. Why, who cries out on pride 70
That can therein tax any private party?
Doth it not flow as hugely as the sea
Till that the wearer's very means do ebb?
What woman in the city do I name
When that I say the city woman bears 75
The cost of princes on unworthy shoulders?
Who can come in and say that I mean her,

When such a one as she, such is her neighbour?
Or what is he of basest function
That says his bravery is not on my cost,   80
Thinking that I mean him, but therein suits
His folly to the mettle of my speech?
There then! how then? what then? Let me
    see wherein
My tongue hath wrong'd him. If it do him right,
Then he hath wrong'd himself. If he be free,
Why, then my taxing like a wild goose flies,   86
Unclaim'd of any man. But who comes here?

Enter *Orlando* [with his sword drawn].

Orl. Forbear, and eat no more!
Jaq.   Why, I have eat none yet.
Orl. Nor shalt not, till necessity be serv'd.
Jaq. Of what kind should this cock come of?
Duke S. Art thou thus bolden'd, man, by
    thy distress,   91
Or else a rude despiser of good manners,
That in civility thou seem'st so empty?
Orl. You touch'd my vein at first. The
    thorny point
Of bare distress hath ta'en from me the show
Of smooth civility; yet am I inland bred   96
And know some nurture. But forbear, I say!
He dies that touches any of this fruit
Till I and my affairs are answered.
Jaq. An you will not be answer'd with rea-
son, I must die.   101
Duke S. What would you have? Your gen-
tleness shall force
More than your force move us to gentleness.
Orl. I almost die for food, and let me have it!
Duke S. Sit down and feed, and welcome to
    our table.   105
Orl. Speak you so gently? Pardon me, I
    pray you.
I thought that all things had been savage here,
And therefore put I on the countenance
Of stern commandment. But whate'er you are
That in this desert inaccessible,   110
Under the shade of melancholy boughs,
Lose and neglect the creeping hours of time —
If ever you have look'd on better days,
If ever been where bells have knoll'd to church,
If ever sat at any good man's feast,   115
If ever from your eyelids wip'd a tear
And know what 'tis to pity and be pitied,
Let gentleness my strong enforcement be;
In the which hope I blush, and hide my sword.
Duke S. True is it that we have seen better
    days,   120
And have with holy bell been knoll'd to church,
And sat at good men's feasts, and wip'd our eyes

Of drops that sacred pity hath engend'red;
And therefore sit you down in gentleness,
And take upon command what help we have
That to your wanting may be minist'red.   126
Orl. Then but forbear your food a little while,
Whiles, like a doe, I go to find my fawn
And give it food. There is an old poor man
Who after me hath many a weary step   130
Limp'd in pure love. Till he be first suffic'd,
Oppress'd with two weak evils, age and hunger,
I will not touch a bit.
Duke S.   Go find him out,
And we will nothing waste till you return.
Orl. I thank ye, and be blest for your good
    comfort!   [*Exit.*]
Duke S. Thou seest we are not all alone un-
    happy.   136
This wide and universal theatre
Presents more woful pageants than the scene
Wherein we play in.
Jaq.   All the world's a stage,
And all the men and women merely players.
They have their exits and their entrances,   141
And one man in his time plays many parts,
His acts being seven ages. At first, the infant,
Mewling and puking in the nurse's arms.
Then the whining schoolboy, with his satchel
And shining morning face, creeping like snail
Unwillingly to school. And then the lover,
Sighing like furnace, with a woful ballad   148
Made to his mistress' eyebrow. Then a soldier,
Full of strange oaths and bearded like the pard.
Jealous in honour, sudden and quick in quarrel.
Seeking the bubble reputation
Even in the cannon's mouth. And then the
    justice,
In fair round belly with good capon lin'd,
With eyes severe and beard of formal cut,   155
Full of wise saws and modern instances;
And so he plays his part. The sixth age shifts
Into the lean and slipper'd pantaloon,
With spectacles on nose and pouch on side;
His youthful hose, well sav'd, a world too wide
For his shrunk shank, and his big manly voice,
Turning again toward childish treble, pipes
And whistles in his sound. Last scene of all,
That ends this strange eventful history,
Is second childishness and mere oblivion,   165
Sans teeth, sans eyes, sans taste, sans every-
    thing.

Enter *Orlando*, with *Adam*.

Duke S. Welcome. Set down your venerable
    burthen
And let him feed.

Orl. I thank you most for him.

Adam.   So had you
need.

I scarce can speak to thank you for myself. 170

Duke S. Welcome, fall to. I will not trouble
you,

As yet to question you about your fortunes.

Give us some music; and, good cousin, sing.

Song.

Ami. Blow, blow, thou winter wind,
  Thou art not so unkind   175
    As man's ingratitude.
  Thy tooth is not so keen,
  Because thou art not seen,
    Although thy breath be rude.
  Heigh-ho, sing heigh-ho, unto the green
    holly!   180
  Most friendship is feigning, most loving
    mere folly:
    Then, heigh-ho, the holly!
  This life is most jolly.

  Freeze, freeze, thou bitter sky,
  That dost not bite so nigh   185
    As benefits forgot.
  Though thou the waters warp,
  Thy sting is not so sharp
    As friend rememb'red not.
  Heigh-ho! sing, &c.   190

Duke S. If that you were the good Sir
  Rowland's son —

As you have whisper'd faithfully you were,

And as mine eye doth his effigies witness

Most truly limn'd and living in your face —

Be truly welcome hither. I am the Duke   195

That lov'd your father. The residue of your
  fortune,

Go to my cave and tell me. Good old man,

Thou art right welcome, as thy master is.

Support him by the arm. Give me your
  hand,

And let me all your fortunes understand.   200

                                    Exeunt.

ACT III. Scene I. [*A room in the Palace.*]

Enter *Duke* [*Frederick*], *Lords*, and *Oliver.*

Duke. Not see him since? Sir, sir, that cannot be!

But were I not the better part made mercy,

I should not seek an absent argument

Of my revenge, thou present. But look to
it!

Find out thy brother, wheresoe'er he is;   5

Seek him with candle; bring him dead or living

Within this twelvemonth, or turn thou no
more

To seek a living in our territory.

Thy lands, and all things that thou dost call
thine

Worth seizure, do we seize into our hands   10

Till thou canst quit thee by thy brother's
mouth

Of what we think against thee.

Oli. O that your Highness knew my heart
in this!

I never lov'd my brother in my life.

Duke. More villain thou! Well, push him
out of doors,   15

And let my officers of such a nature

Make an extent upon his house and lands.

Do this expediently and turn him going.

                                    Exeunt.

Scene II. [*The Forest. Near the sheepcote.*]

Enter *Orlando*, [with a paper, which he
  hangs on a tree].

Orl. Hang there, my verse, in witness of my
  love;

And thou, thrice-crowned Queen of Night,
  survey

With thy chaste eye, from thy pale sphere
  above,

  Thy huntress' name that my full life doth
  sway.

O Rosalind! these trees shall be my books,   5

And in their barks my thoughts I'll character,

That every eye which in this forest looks

  Shall see thy virtue witness'd everywhere.

Run, run, Orlando! carve on every tree

The fair, the chaste, and unexpressive she. 10

                                    Exit.

Enter *Corin* and [*Touchstone the*] *Clown.*

Cor. And how like you this shepherd's life,
Master Touchstone?

Touch. Truly, shepherd, in respect of itself,
it is a good life; but in respect that it is a shepherd's life, it is naught. In respect that it is
solitary, I like it very well; but in respect that

it is private, it is a very vile life. Now in respect it is in the fields, it pleaseth me well; but in respect it is not in the court, it is tedious. As it is a spare life, look you, it fits my humour well; but as there is no more plenty in it, it goes much against my stomach. Hast any philosophy in thee, shepherd?   23

Cor. No more but that I know the more one sickens, the worse at ease he is; and that he that wants money, means, and content is without three good friends; that the property of rain is to wet and fire to burn; that good pasture makes fat sheep, and that a great cause of the night is lack of the sun; that he that hath learned no wit by nature nor art may complain of good breeding, or comes of a very dull kindred.   32

Touch. Such a one is a natural philosopher. Wast ever in court, shepherd?

Cor. No, truly.   35

Touch. Then thou art damn'd.

Cor. Nay, I hope.

Touch. Truly thou art damn'd, like an ill-roasted egg, all on one side.   39

Cor. For not being at court? Your reason.

Touch. Why, if thou never wast at court, thou never saw'st good manners; if thou never saw'st good manners, then thy manners must be wicked; and wickedness is sin, and sin is damnation. Thou art in a parlous state, shepherd.   45

Cor. Not a whit, Touchstone. Those that are good manners at the court are as ridiculous in the country as the behaviour of the country is most mockable at the court. You told me you salute not at the court but you kiss your hands. That courtesy would be uncleanly if courtiers were shepherds.   52

Touch. Instance, briefly. Come, instance.

Cor. Why, we are still handling our ewes, and their fells you know are greasy.   55

Touch. Why, do not your courtier's hands sweat? and is not the grease of a mutton as wholesome as the sweat of a man? Shallow, shallow! A better instance, I say. Come.

Cor. Besides, our hands are hard.   60

Touch. Your lips will feel them the sooner. Shallow again! A more sounder instance, come.

Cor. And they are often tarr'd over with the surgery of our sheep, and would you have us kiss tar? The courtier's hands are perfum'd with civet.   66

Touch. Most shallow man! Thou worm's meat in respect of a good piece of flesh indeed! Learn of the wise, and perpend. Civet is of a

baser birth than tar — the very uncleanly flux of a cat. Mend the instance, shepherd.   71

Cor. You have too courtly a wit for me. I'll rest.

Touch. Wilt thou rest damn'd? God help thee, shallow man! God make incision in thee, thou art raw!   76

Cor. Sir, I am a true labourer; I earn that I eat, get that I wear; owe no man hate, envy no man's happiness; glad of other men's good, content with my harm; and the greatest of my pride is to see my ewes graze and my lambs suck.   81

Touch. That is another simple sin in you: to bring the ewes and the rams together and to offer to get your living by the copulation of cattle; to be bawd to a bell-wether, and to betray a she-lamb of a twelvemonth to a crooked-pated old cuckoldly ram, out of all reasonable match. If thou beest not damn'd for this, the devil himself will have no shepherds; I cannot see else how thou shouldst scape.   90

Cor. Here comes young Master Ganymede, my new mistress's brother.

Enter *Rosalind*, [reading a paper].

Ros. 'From the east to western Inde,
No jewel is like Rosalinde.   94
Her worth, being mounted on the wind,
Through all the world bears Rosalinde.
All the pictures fairest lin'd
Are but black to Rosalinde.
Let no face be kept in mind
But the fair of Rosalinde.'   100

Touch. I'll rhyme you so eight years together, dinners and suppers and sleeping hours excepted. It is the right butter-women's rank to market.

Ros. Out, fool!   105

Touch. For a taste:

If a hart do lack a hind,
Let him seek out Rosalinde.
If the cat will after kind,
So be sure will Rosalinde.   110
Winter garments must be lin'd,
So must slender Rosalinde.
They that reap must sheaf and bind,
Then to cart with Rosalinde.
Sweetest nut hath sourest rind,   115
Such a nut is Rosalinde.
He that sweetest rose will find
Must find love's prick, and Rosalinde.

This is the very false gallop of verses! Why do you infect yourself with them?   120

Ros. Peace, you dull fool! I found them on a tree.

307

Touch. Truly the tree yields bad fruit.

Ros. I'll graff it with you, and then I shall graff it with a medlar. Then it will be the earliest fruit i' th' country; for you'll be rotten ere you be half ripe, and that's the right virtue of the medlar.

Touch. You have said; but whether wisely or no, let the forest judge.   130

     Enter *Celia*, with a writing.

Ros. Peace!
Here comes my sister reading. Stand aside.

Cel. 'Why should this a desert be,
    For it is unpeopled? No!
Tongues I'll hang on every tree   135
    That shall civil sayings show:
Some, how brief the life of man
    Runs his erring pilgrimage,
That the stretching of a span
    Buckles in his sum of age;   140
Some, of violated vows
    'Twixt the souls of friend and friend;
But upon the fairest boughs,
    Or at every sentence end,
Will I "Rosalinda" write,   145
    Teaching all that read to know
The quintessence of every sprite
    Heaven would in little show.
Therefore heaven Nature charg'd
    That one body should be fill'd   150
With all graces wide-enlarg'd.
    Nature presently distill'd
Helen's cheek, but not her heart,
    Cleopatra's majesty,
Atalanta's better part,   155
    Sad Lucretia's modesty.
Thus Rosalinde of many parts
    By heavenly synod was devis'd,
Of many faces, eyes, and hearts,
    To have the touches dearest priz'd.   160
Heaven would that she these gifts should have,
And I to live and die her slave.'

Ros. O most gentle pulpiter! what tedious homily of love have you wearied your parishioners withal, and never cried, 'Have patience, good people'!   166

Cel. How now? Back, friends. Shepherd, go off a little. Go with him, sirrah.

Touch. Come, shepherd, let us make an honourable retreat; though not with bag and baggage, yet with scrip and scrippage.   171
     Exeunt [Corin and Touchstone].

Cel. Didst thou hear these verses?

Ros. O, yes, I heard them all, and more too; for some of them had in them more feet than the verses would bear.   175

Cel. That's no matter. The feet might bear the verses.

Ros. Ay, but the feet were lame, and could not bear themselves without the verse, and therefore stood lamely in the verse.   180

Cel. But didst thou hear without wondering how thy name should be hang'd and carved upon these trees?

Ros. I was seven of the nine days out of the wonder before you came; for look here what I found on a palm tree. I was never so berhym'd since Pythagoras' time that I was an Irish rat, which I can hardly remember.

Cel. Trow you who hath done this?

Ros. Is it a man?   190

Cel. And a chain that you once wore, about his neck. Change you colour?

Ros. I prithee who?

Cel. O Lord, Lord! it is a hard matter for friends to meet; but mountains may be remov'd with earthquakes, and so encounter. 196

Ros. Nay, but who is it?

Cel. Is it possible?

Ros. Nay, I prithee now with most petitionary vehemence, tell me who it is.   200

Cel. O wonderful, wonderful, and most wonderful wonderful! and yet again wonderful, and after that, out of all hooping!

Ros. Good my complexion! Dost thou think, though I am caparison'd like a man, I have a doublet and hose in my disposition? One inch of delay more is a South Sea of discovery. I prithee tell me who is it quickly, and speak apace. I would thou couldst stammer, that thou mightst pour this conceal'd man out of thy mouth as wine comes out of a narrow-mouth'd bottle — either too much at once, or none at all. I prithee take the cork out of thy mouth, that I may drink thy tidings.   214

Cel. So you may put a man in your belly.

Ros. Is he of God's making? What manner of man? Is his head worth a hat? or his chin worth a beard?

Cel. Nay, he hath but a little beard.   219

Ros. Why, God will send more, if the man will be thankful! Let me stay the growth of his beard, if thou delay me not the knowledge of his chin.

Cel. It is young Orlando, that tripp'd up the wrestler's heels and your heart both in an instant.   225

Ros. Nay, but the devil take mocking! Speak sad brow and true maid.

Cel. I' faith, coz, 'tis he.

Ros. Orlando?

Cel. Orlando. 230
Ros. Alas the day! what shall I do with my doublet and hose? What did he when thou saw'st him? What said he? How look'd he? Wherein went he? What makes he here? Did he ask for me? Where remains he? How parted he with thee? and when shalt thou see him again? Answer me in one word. 237
Cel. You must borrow me Gargantua's mouth first; 'tis a word too great for any mouth of this age's size. To say ay and no to these particulars is more than to answer in a catechism. 241
Ros. But doth he know that I am in this forest, and in man's apparel? Looks he as freshly as he did the day he wrestled? 244
Cel. It is as easy to count atomies as to resolve the propositions of a lover; but take a taste of my finding him, and relish it with good observance. I found him under a tree, like a dropp'd acorn.
Ros. It may well be called Jove's tree when it drops forth such fruit. 250
Cel. Give me audience, good madam.
Ros. Proceed.
Cel. There lay he stretch'd along like a wounded knight. 254
Ros. Though it be pity to see such a sight, it well becomes the ground.
Cel. Cry 'holla' to thy tongue, I prithee. It curvets unseasonably. He was furnish'd like a hunter. 259
Ros. O, ominous! he comes to kill my heart.
Cel. I would sing my song without a burthen. Thou bring'st me out of tune.
Ros. Do you not know I am a woman? When I think, I must speak. Sweet, say on.
Cel. You bring me out. 265

Enter *Orlando* and *Jaques.*

Soft! comes he not here?
Ros. 'Tis he! Slink by, and note him.
[*They step aside.*]
Jaq. I thank you for your company; but, good faith, I had as lief have been myself alone. 270
Orl. And so had I; but yet for fashion sake I thank you too for your society.
Jaq. God b'wi' you! Let's meet as little as we can. 274
Orl. I do desire we may be better strangers.
Jaq. I pray you mar no more trees with writing love songs in their barks.
Orl. I pray you mar no moe of my verses with reading them ill-favouredly.
Jaq. Rosalind is your love's name? 280

Orl. Yes, just.
Jaq. I do not like her name.
Orl. There was no thought of pleasing you when she was christen'd.
Jaq. What stature is she of? 285
Orl. Just as high as my heart.
Jaq. You are full of pretty answers. Have you not been acquainted with goldsmiths' wives, and conn'd them out of rings?
Orl. Not so; but I answer you right painted cloth, from whence you have studied your questions. 292
Jaq. You have a nimble wit; I think 'twas made of Atalanta's heels. Will you sit down with me? and we two will rail against our mistress the world and all our misery. 296
Orl. I will chide no breather in the world but myself, against whom I know most faults.
Jaq. The worst fault you have is to be in love.
Orl. 'Tis a fault I will not change for your best virtue. I am weary of you. 302
Jaq. By my troth, I was seeking for a fool when I found you.
Orl. He is drown'd in the brook. Look but in and you shall see him. 306
Jaq. There I shall see mine own figure.
Orl. Which I take to be either a fool or a cipher.
Jaq. I'll tarry no longer with you. Farewell, good Signior Love. 310
Orl. I am glad of your departure. Adieu, good Monsieur Melancholy.
[*Exit Jaques. Celia and Rosalind come forward.*]
Ros. [*aside to Celia*] I will speak to him like a saucy lackey, and under that habit play the knave with him.— Do you hear, forester? 315
Orl. Very well. What would you?
Ros. I pray you, what is't o'clock?
Orl. You should ask me, what time o' day. There's no clock in the forest. 319
Ros. Then there is no true lover in the forest; else sighing every minute and groaning every hour would detect the lazy foot of Time as well as a clock.
Orl. And why not the swift foot of Time? Had not that been as proper? 325
Ros. By no means, sir. Time travels in divers paces with divers persons. I'll tell you who Time ambles withal, who Time trots withal, who Time gallops withal, and who he stands still withal. 329
Orl. I prithee, who doth he trot withal?
Ros. Marry, he trots hard with a young maid between the contract of her marriage and the

day it is solemniz'd. If the interim be but a se'nnight, Time's pace is so hard that it seems the length of seven year. 335

Orl. Who ambles Time withal?

Ros. With a priest that lacks Latin and a rich man that hath not the gout; for the one sleeps easily because he cannot study, and the other lives merrily because he feels no pain; the one lacking the burthen of lean and wasteful learning, the other knowing no burthen of heavy tedious penury. These Time ambles withal.

Orl. Who doth he gallop withal? 344

Ros. With a thief to the gallows; for though he go as softly as foot can fall, he thinks himself too soon there.

Orl. Who stays it still withal?

Ros. With lawyers in the vacation; for they sleep between term and term, and then they perceive not how time moves. 351

Orl. Where dwell you, pretty youth?

Ros. With this shepherdess, my sister; here in the skirts of the forest, like fringe upon a petticoat. 355

Orl. Are you native of this place?

Ros. As the cony that you see dwell where she is kindled.

Orl. Your accent is something finer than you could purchase in so removed a dwelling. 360

Ros. I have been told so of many. But indeed an old religious uncle of mine taught me to speak, who was in his youth an inland man; one that knew courtship too well, for there he fell in love. I have heard him read many lectures against it; and I thank God I am not a woman, to be touch'd with so many giddy offences as he hath generally tax'd their whole sex withal.

Orl. Can you remember any of the principal evils that he laid to the charge of women? 370

Ros. There were none principal. They were all like one another as halfpence are, every one fault seeming monstrous till his fellow-fault came to match it.

Orl. I prithee recount some of them. 375

Ros. No, I will not cast away my physic but on those that are sick. There is a man haunts the forest that abuses our young plants with carving 'Rosalind' on their barks; hangs odes upon hawthorns, and elegies on brambles; all, forsooth, deifying the name of Rosalind. If I could meet that fancy-monger, I would give him some good counsel, for he seems to have the quotidian of love upon him. 384

Orl. I am he that is so love-shak'd. I pray you tell me your remedy.

Ros. There is none of my uncle's marks upon you. He taught me how to know a man in love; in which cage of rushes I am sure you are not prisoner. 390

Orl. What were his marks?

Ros. A lean cheek, which you have not; a blue eye and sunken, which you have not; an unquestionable spirit, which you have not; a beard neglected, which you have not. But I pardon you for that, for simply your having in beard is a younger brother's revenue. Then your hose should be ungarter'd, your bonnet unbanded, your sleeve unbutton'd, your shoe untied, and everything about you demonstrating a careless desolation. But you are no such man: you are rather point-device in your accoustrements, as loving yourself, than seeming the lover of any other.

Orl. Fair youth, I would I could make thee believe I love. 405

Ros. Me believe it? You may as soon make her that you love believe it, which I warrant she is apter to do than to confess she does. That is one of the points in the which women still give the lie to their consciences. But in good sooth, are you he that hangs the verses on the trees wherein Rosalind is so admired? 412

Orl. I swear to thee, youth, by the white hand of Rosalind, I am that he, that unfortunate he. 415

Ros. But are you so much in love as your rhymes speak?

Orl. Neither rhyme nor reason can express how much. 419

Ros. Love is merely a madness, and, I tell you, deserves as well a dark house and a whip as madmen do; and the reason why they are not so punish'd and cured is that the lunacy is so ordinary that the whippers are in love too. Yet I profess curing it by counsel. 425

Orl. Did you ever cure any so?

Ros. Yes, one, and in this manner. He was to imagine me his love, his mistress; and I set him every day to woo me. At which time would I, being but a moonish youth, grieve, be effeminate, changeable, longing, and liking, proud, fantastical, apish, shallow, inconstant, full of tears, full of smiles; for every passion something and for no passion truly anything, as boys and women are for the most part cattle of this colour; would now like him, now loathe him; then entertain him, then forswear him; now weep for him, then spit at him; that I drave my suitor from his mad humour of love to a living humour of madness, which was, to forswear the full stream of the world and to live in a nook merely monastic. And thus I cur'd him; and this way will I take upon me to wash your liver as clean as a sound sheep's heart, that there shall not be one spot of love in't.✳   445

Orl. I would not be cured, youth.

Ros. I would cure you, if you would but call me Rosalind and come every day to my cote and woo me.

Orl. Now, by the faith of my love, I will! Tell me where it is.   451

Ros. Go with me to it, and I'll show it you; and by the way you shall tell me where in the forest you live. Will you go?

Orl. With all my heart, good youth.   455

Ros. Nay, you must call me Rosalind. Come, sister, will you go?   *Exeunt.*

Scene III. [*The Forest. Near the sheepcote.*]

Enter [*Touchstone the*] *Clown, Audrey*; and *Jaques* [behind].

Touch. Come apace, good Audrey. I will fetch up your goats, Audrey. And how, Audrey, am I the man yet? Doth my simple feature content you?

Aud. Your features? Lord warrant us! What features?   6

Touch. I am here with thee and thy goats, as the most capricious poet, honest Ovid, was among the Goths.

Jaq. [*aside*] O knowledge ill-inhabited, worse than Jove in a thatch'd house!   11

Touch. When a man's verses cannot be understood, nor a man's good wit seconded with the forward child, understanding, it strikes a man more dead than a great reckoning in a little room. Truly, I would the gods had made thee poetical.   16

Aud. I do not know what poetical is. Is it honest in deed and word? Is it a true thing?

Touch. No, truly; for the truest poetry is the most feigning, and lovers are given to poetry; and what they swear in poetry may be said, as lovers, they do feign.   22

Aud. Do you wish then that the gods had made me poetical?

Touch. I do truly. For thou swear'st to me thou art honest. Now if thou wert a poet, I might have some hope thou didst feign.   27

Aud. Would you not have me honest?

Touch. No, truly, unless thou wert hard-favour'd; for honesty coupled to beauty is to have honey a sauce to sugar.   31

Jaq. [*aside*] A material fool!

Aud. Well, I am not fair; and therefore I pray the gods make me honest.

Touch. Truly, and to cast away honesty upon a foul slut were to put good meat into an unclean dish.   37

Aud. I am not a slut, though I thank the gods I am foul.

Touch. Well, praised be the gods for thy foulness! Sluttishness may come hereafter. But be it as it may be, I will marry thee; and to that end I have been with Sir Oliver Martext, the vicar of the next village, who hath promis'd to meet me in this place of the forest and to couple us.   45

Jaq. [*aside*] I would fain see this meeting.

Aud. Well, the gods give us joy!

Touch. Amen. A man may, if he were of a fearful heart, stagger in this attempt; for here we have no temple but the wood, no assembly but horn-beasts. But what though? Courage! As horns are odious, they are necessary. It is said, 'Many a man knows no end of his goods.' Right! Many a man has good horns and knows no end of them. Well, that is the dowry of his wife; 'tis none of his own getting. Horns? Even so. Poor men alone? No, no! the noblest deer hath them as huge as the rascal. Is the single man therefore blessed? No; as a wall'd town is more worthier than a village, so is the forehead of a married man more honourable than the bare brow of a bachelor; and by how much defence is better than no skill, by so much is a horn more precious than to want.   64

Enter *Sir Oliver Martext.*

Here comes Sir Oliver. Sir Oliver Martext, you are well met. Will you dispatch us here under this tree, or shall we go with you to your chapel?

Oli. Is there none here to give the woman?

Touch. I will not take her on gift of any man.

Oli. Truly, she must be given, or the marriage is not lawful.   71

Jaq. [*comes forward*] Proceed, proceed! I'll give her.

Touch. Good even, good Master What-ye-call't. How do you, sir? You are very well met. Goddild you for your last company. I am very glad to see you. Even a toy in hand here, sir. Nay, pray be cover'd.

Jaq. Will you be married, motley?   79

Touch. As the ox hath his bow, sir, the horse his curb, and the falcon her bells, so man hath his desires; and as pigeons bill, so wedlock would be nibbling.   83

311

Jaq. And will you, being a man of your breeding, be married under a bush like a beggar? Get you to church, and have a good priest that can tell you what marriage is. This fellow will but join you together as they join wainscot; then one of you will prove a shrunk panel, and like green timber warp, warp. 90

Touch. [*aside*] I am not in the mind but I were better to be married of him than of another; for he is not like to marry me well; and not being well married, it will be a good excuse for me hereafter to leave my wife. 95

Jaq. Go thou with me and let me counsel thee.

Touch. Come, sweet Audrey.
We must be married, or we must live in bawdry. Farewell, good Master Oliver: not 100

    O sweet Oliver,
    O brave Oliver,
    Leave me not behind thee!
but
    Wind away, 105
    Be gone, I say!
    I will not to wedding with thee.

[*Exeunt Jaques, Touchstone, and Audrey.*]
Oli. 'Tis no matter. Ne'er a fantastical knave of them all shall flout me out of my calling. *Exit.*

Scene IV. [*The Forest. Near the sheepcote.*]

Enter *Rosalind* and *Celia.*

Ros. Never talk to me! I will weep.

Cel. Do, I prithee; but yet have the grace to consider that tears do not become a man.

Ros. But have I not cause to weep?

Cel. As good cause as one would desire. Therefore weep. 6

Ros. His very hair is of the dissembling colour.

Cel. Something browner than Judas's. Marry, his kisses are Judas's own children. 10

Ros. I' faith, his hair is of a good colour.

Cel. An excellent colour. Your chestnut was ever the only colour.

Ros. And his kissing is as full of sanctity as the touch of holy bread. 15

Cel. He hath bought a pair of cast lips of Diana. A nun of winter's sisterhood kisses not more religiously; the very ice of chastity is in them.

Ros. But why did he swear he would come this morning, and comes not? 21

Cel. Nay, certainly there is no truth in him.

Ros. Do you think so?

Cel. Yes. I think he is not a pickpurse nor a horse-stealer; but for his verity in love, I do think him as concave as a covered goblet or a worm-eaten nut. 27

Ros. Not true in love?

Cel. Yes, when he is in; but I think he is not in. 30

Ros. You have heard him swear downright he was.

Cel. 'Was' is not 'is.' Besides, the oath of a lover is no stronger than the word of a tapster: they are both the confirmer of false reckonings. He attends here in the forest on the Duke your father. 37

Ros. I met the Duke yesterday and had much question with him. He ask'd me of what parentage I was. I told him, of as good as he. So he laugh'd and let me go. But what talk we of fathers when there is such a man as Orlando?

Cel. O, that's a brave man! He writes brave verses, speaks brave words, swears brave oaths, and breaks them bravely — quite traverse, athwart the heart of his lover; as a puisny tilter, that spurs his horse but on one side, breaks his staff like a noble goose. But all's brave that youth mounts and folly guides. Who comes here?

Enter *Corin.*

Cor. Mistress and master, you have oft enquir'd 50
After the shepherd that complain'd of love,
Who you saw sitting by me on the turf,
Praising the proud disdainful shepherdess
That was his mistress.

Cel.   Well, and what of him?

Cor. If you will see a pageant truly play'd 56
Between the pale complexion of true love
And the red glow of scorn and proud disdain,
Go hence a little, and I shall conduct you,
If you will mark it.

Ros.   O, come, let us remove!
The sight of lovers feedeth those in love. 60
Bring us to this sight, and you shall say
I'll prove a busy actor in their play. *Exeunt.*

Scene V. [*Another part of the Forest.*]

Enter *Silvius* and *Phebe.*

Sil. Sweet Phebe, do not scorn me; do not, Phebe!
Say that you love me not, but say not so
In bitterness. The common executioner,

312

Whose heart th' accustom'd sight of death
  makes hard,
Falls not the axe upon the humbled neck   5
But first begs pardon. Will you sterner be
Than he that dies and lives by bloody drops?

Enter Rosalind, Celia, and Corin, [behind].

  Phe. I would not be thy executioner.
I fly thee, for I would not injure thee.
Thou tell'st me there is murder in mine eye: 10
'Tis pretty, sure, and very probable
That eyes, that are the frail'st and softest things,
Who shut their coward gates on atomies,
Should be call'd tyrants, butchers, murtherers!
Now I do frown on thee with all my heart; 15
And if mine eyes can wound, now let them kill
  thee!
Now counterfeit to swound; why, now fall
  down;
Or if thou canst not, O, for shame, for shame,
Lie not, to say mine eyes are murtherers!
Now show the wound mine eye hath made in
  thee.   20
Scratch thee but with a pin, and there remains
Some scar of it; lean but upon a rush,
The cicatrice and capable impressure
Thy palm some moment keeps; but now mine
  eyes,
Which I have darted at thee, hurt thee not, 25
Nor I am sure there is no force in eyes
That can do hurt.
  Sil.   O dear Phebe,
If ever (as that ever may be near)
You meet in some fresh cheek the power of
  fancy,
Then shall you know the wounds invisible 30
That love's keen arrows make.
  Phe.   But till that time
Come not thou near me; and when that time
  comes,
Afflict me with thy mocks, pity me not,
As till that time I shall not pity thee.
  Ros. And why, I pray you? Who might be
  your mother,   35
That you insult, exult, and all at once,
Over the wretched? What though you have no
  beauty —
As, by my faith, I see no more in you
Than without candle may go dark to bed! —
Must you be therefore proud and pitiless? 40
Why, what means this? Why do you look on
  me?
I see no more in you than in the ordinary
Of nature's sale-work. 'Od's my little life,
I think she means to tangle my eyes too!

No, faith, proud mistress, hope not after it. 45
'Tis not your inky brows, your black silk hair,
Your bugle eyeballs, nor your cheek of cream
That can entame my spirits to your worship.
You foolish shepherd, wherefore do you follow
  her,
Like foggy south, puffing with wind and rain?
You are a thousand times a properer man 51
Than she a woman. 'Tis such fools as you
That makes the world full of ill-favour'd chil-
  dren.
'Tis not her glass, but you, that flatters her,
And out of you she sees herself more proper 55
Than any of her lineaments can show her.
But, mistress, know yourself. Down on your
  knees,
And thank heaven, fasting, for a good man's
  love;
For I must tell you friendly in your ear, 59
Sell when you can! you are not for all markets.
Cry the man mercy, love him, take his offer.
Foul is most foul, being foul to be a scoffer.
So take her to thee, shepherd. Fare you well.
  Phe. Sweet youth, I pray you chide a year
  together.   64
I had rather hear you chide than this man woo.
  Ros. [*to Phebe*] He's fall'n in love with your
foulness, [*to Silvius*] and she'll fall in love with
my anger. If it be so, as fast as she answers
thee with frowning looks, I'll sauce her with
bitter words. — Why look you so upon me? 70
  Phe. For no ill will I bear you.
  Ros. I pray you do not fall in love with me,
For I am falser than vows made in wine.
Besides, I like you not. If you will know my
  house,
'Tis at the tuft of olives, here hard by. — 75
Will you go, sister? — Shepherd, ply her hard.—
Come, sister. — Shepherdess, look on him better
And be not proud. Though all the world could
  see,
None could be so abus'd in sight as he. —
Come, to our flock.   80
        Exeunt [Rosalind, Celia, and Corin].
  Phe. Dead shepherd, now I find thy saw of
  might,
'Who ever lov'd that lov'd not at first sight?'
  Sil. Sweet Phebe —
  Phe.   Ha! what say'st thou, Silvius?
  Sil. Sweet Phebe, pity me.
  Phe. Why, I am sorry for thee, gentle Silvius.
  Sil. Wherever sorrow is, relief would be. 86
If you do sorrow at my grief in love,
By giving love your sorrow and my grief
Were both extermin'd.

Phe. Thou hast my love. Is not that neigh-
bourly? 90
Sil. I would have you.
Phe. Why, that were covetousness.
Silvius, the time was that I hated thee,
And yet it is not that I bear thee love;
But since that thou canst talk of love so well,
Thy company, which erst was irksome to me,
I will endure; and I'll employ thee too. 96
But do not look for further recompense
Than thine own gladness that thou art em-
ploy'd.
Sil. So holy and so perfect is my love,
And I in such a poverty of grace, 100
That I shall think it a most plenteous crop
To glean the broken ears after the man
That the main harvest reaps. Loose now and
then
A scatt'red smile, and that I'll live upon.
Phe. Know'st thou the youth that spoke to
me erewhile? 105
Sil. Not very well, but I have met him oft,
And he hath bought the cottage and the bounds
That the old Carlot once was master of.
Phe. Think not I love him, though I ask for
him.
'Tis but a peevish boy; yet he talks well. 110
But what care I for words? Yet words do well
When he that speaks them pleases those that hear.
It is a pretty youth — not very pretty —

But sure he's proud; and yet his pride becomes
him. 114
He'll make a proper man. The best thing in him
Is his complexion; and faster than his tongue
Did make offence, his eye did heal it up.
He is not very tall; yet for his years he's tall.
His leg is but so so; and yet 'tis well.
There was a pretty redness in his lip, 120
A little riper and more lusty red
Than that mix'd in his cheek; 'twas just the
difference
Betwixt the constant red and mingled damask.
There be some women, Silvius, had they mark'd
him
In parcels as I did, would have gone near 125
To fall in love with him; but, for my part,
I love him not nor hate him not; and yet
I have more cause to hate him than to love him;
For what had he to do to chide at me? 129
He said mine eyes were black and my hair black;
And, now I am remember'd, scorn'd at me.
I marvel why I answer'd not again.
But that's all one: omittance is no quittance.
I'll write to him a very taunting letter,
And thou shalt bear it. Wilt thou, Silvius? 135
Sil. Phebe, with all my heart.
Phe. I'll write it straight;
The matter's in my head and in my heart.
I will be bitter with him and passing short.
Go with me, Silvius. *Exeunt.*

ACT IV. Scene I. [*The Forest. Near the sheepcote.*]

Enter *Rosalind* and *Celia* and *Jaques.*

Jaq. I prithee, pretty youth, let me be better
acquainted with thee.
Ros. They say you are a melancholy fellow.
Jaq. I am so. I do love it better than
laughing. 4
Ros. Those that are in extremity of either are
abominable fellows, and betray themselves to
every modern censure worse than drunkards.
Jaq. Why, 'tis good to be sad and say nothing.
Ros. Why then, 'tis good to be a post. 9
Jaq. I have neither the scholar's melancholy,
which is emulation; nor the musician's, which
is fantastical; nor the courtier's, which is
proud; nor the soldier's, which is ambitious;
nor the lawyer's, which is politic; nor the
lady's, which is nice; nor the lover's, which is
all these: but it is a melancholy of mine own,
compounded of many simples, extracted from
many objects, and indeed the sundry contem-

plation of my travels, in which my often rumi-
nation wraps me in a most humorous sadness.
Ros. A traveller! By my faith, you have
great reason to be sad. I fear you have sold
your own lands to see other men's. Then to
have seen much and to have nothing is to have
rich eyes and poor hands. 25
Jaq. Yes, I have gain'd my experience.

Enter *Orlando.*

Ros. And your experience makes you sad. I
had rather have a fool to make me merry than
experience to make me sad — and to travel for
it too! 29
Orl. Good day and happiness, dear Rosalind!
Jaq. Nay then, God b'wi' you, an you talk
in blank verse!
Ros. Farewell, Monsieur Traveller. Look
you lisp and wear strange suits, disable all the
benefits of your own country, be out of love
with your nativity and almost chide God for

making you that countenance you are; or I will scarce think you have swam in a gundello. [*Exit Jaques.*] Why, how now, Orlando? Where have you been all this while? You a lover? An you serve me such another trick, never come in my sight more.   41

Orl. My fair Rosalind, I come within an hour of my promise.

Ros. Break an hour's promise in love? He that will divide a minute into a thousand parts and break but a part of the thousand part of a minute in the affairs of love, it may be said of him that Cupid hath clapp'd him o' th' shoulder, but I'll warrant him heart-whole.

Orl. Pardon me, dear Rosalind.   50

Ros. Nay, an you be so tardy, come no more in my sight. I had as lief be woo'd of a snail.

Orl. Of a snail?

Ros. Ay, of a snail; for though he comes slowly, he carries his house on his head — a better jointure, I think, than you make a woman. Besides, he brings his destiny with him.   57

Orl. What's that?

Ros. Why, horns! which such as you are fain to be beholding to your wives for; but he comes armed in his fortune and prevents the slander of his wife.   62

Orl. Virtue is no horn-maker; and my Rosalind is virtuous.

Ros. And I am your Rosalind.   65

Cel. It pleases him to call you so; but he hath a Rosalind of a better leer than you.

Ros. Come, woo me, woo me! for now I am in a holiday humour and like enough to consent. What would you say to me now, an I were your very very Rosalind?   71

Orl. I would kiss before I spoke.

Ros. Nay, you were better speak first; and when you were gravell'd for lack of matter, you might take occasion to kiss. Very good orators, when they are out, they will spit; and for lovers, lacking (God warn us!) matter, the cleanliest shift is to kiss.

Orl. How if the kiss be denied?

Ros. Then she puts you to entreaty, and there begins new matter.   81

Orl. Who could be out, being before his beloved mistress?

Ros. Marry, that should you, if I were your mistress, or I should think my honesty ranker than my wit.   86

Orl. What, of my suit?

Ros. Not out of your apparel, and yet out of your suit. Am not I your Rosalind?

Orl. I take some joy to say you are, because I would be talking of her.   91

Ros. Well, in her person, I say I will not have you.

Orl. Then, in mine own person, I die.

Ros. No, faith, die by attorney. The poor world is almost six thousand years old, and in all this time there was not any man died in his own person, videlicet, in a love cause. Troilus had his brains dash'd out with a Grecian club; yet he did what he could to die before, and he is one of the patterns of love. Leander, he would have liv'd many a fair year though Hero had turn'd nun, if it had not been for a hot midsummer night; for (good youth) he went but forth to wash him in the Hellespont, and being taken with the cramp, was drown'd; and the foolish chroniclers of that age found it was 'Hero of Sestos.' But these are all lies. Men have died from time to time, and worms have eaten them, but not for love.   108

Orl. I would not have my right Rosalind of this mind, for I protest her frown might kill me.

Ros. By this hand, it will not kill a fly! But come, now I will be your Rosalind in a more coming-on disposition; and ask me what you will, I will grant it.

Orl. Then love me, Rosalind.   115

Ros. Yes, faith, will I, Fridays and Saturdays and all.

Orl. And wilt thou have me?

Ros. Ay, and twenty such.

Orl. What sayest thou?   120

Orl. Are you not good?

Orl. I hope so.

Ros. Why then, can one desire too much of a good thing? Come, sister, you shall be the priest and marry us. Give me your hand, Orlando. What do you say, sister?   126

Orl. Pray thee marry us.

Cel. I cannot say the words.

Ros. You must begin, 'Will you, Orlando' —

Cel. Go to. Will you, Orlando, have to wife this Rosalind?   131

Orl. I will.

Ros. Ay, but when?

Orl. Why now, as fast as she can marry us.

Ros. Then you must say, 'I take thee, Rosalind, for wife.'   136

Orl. I take thee, Rosalind, for wife.

Ros. I might ask you for your commission; but I do take thee, Orlando, for my husband. There's a girl goes before the priest, and certainly a woman's thought runs before her actions.   141

315

Orl. So do all thoughts; they are wing'd.

Ros. Now tell me how long you would have her after you have possess'd her.

Orl. For ever and a day. 145

Ros. Say 'a day,' without the 'ever.' No, no, Orlando! Men are April when they woo, December when they wed. Maids are May when they are maids, but the sky changes when they are wives. I will be more jealous of thee than a Barbary cock-pigeon over his hen, more clamorous than a parrot against rain, more newfangled than an ape, more giddy in my desires than a monkey. I will weep for nothing, like Diana in the fountain, and I will do that when you are dispos'd to be merry; I will laugh like a hyen, and that when thou art inclin'd to sleep. 157

Orl. But will my Rosalind do so?

Ros. By my life, she will do as I do.

Orl. O, but she is wise! 160

Ros. Or else she could not have the wit to do this. The wiser, the waywarder. Make the doors upon a woman's wit, and it will out at the casement; shut that, and 'twill out at the keyhole; stop that, 'twill fly with the smoke out at the chimney. 166

Orl. A man that had a wife with such a wit, he might say, 'Wit, whither wilt?'

Ros. Nay, you might keep that check for it till you met your wive's wit going to your neighbour's bed. 171

Orl. And what wit could wit have to excuse that?

Ros. Marry, to say she came to seek you there. You shall never take her without her answer unless you take her without her tongue. O, that woman that cannot make her fault her husband's occasion, let her never nurse her child herself, for she will breed it like a fool!

Orl. For these two hours, Rosalind, I will leave thee. 181

Ros. Alas, dear love, I cannot lack thee two hours!

Orl. I must attend the Duke at dinner. By two o'clock I will be with thee again. 185

Ros. Ay, go your ways, go your ways! I knew what you would prove. My friends told me as much, and I thought no less. That flattering tongue of yours won me. 'Tis but one cast away, and so, come death! Two o'clock is your hour? 190

Orl. Ay, sweet Rosalind.

Ros. By my troth, and in good earnest, and so God mend me, and by all pretty oaths that are not dangerous, if you break one jot of your promise or come one minute behind your hour, I will think you the most pathetical break-promise, and the most hollow lover, and the most unworthy of her you call Rosalind, that may be chosen out of the gross band of the unfaithful. Therefore beware my censure and keep your promise. 200

Orl. With no less religion than if thou wert indeed my Rosalind. So adieu.

Ros. Well, Time is the old justice that examines all such offenders, and let Time try. Adieu.
Exit [Orlando].

Cel. You have simply misus'd our sex in your love-prate. We must have your doublet and hose pluck'd over your head, and show the world what the bird hath done to her own nest.

Ros. O coz, coz, coz, my pretty little coz, that thou didst know how many fathom deep I am in love! But it cannot be sounded. My affection hath an unknown bottom, like the Bay of Portugal.

Cel. Or rather, bottomless, that as fast as you pour affection in, it runs out. 215

Ros. No, that same wicked bastard of Venus that was begot of thought, conceiv'd of spleen, and born of madness, that blind rascally boy that abuses every one's eyes because his own are out — let him be judge how deep I am in love. I'll tell thee, Aliena, I cannot be out of the sight of Orlando. I'll go find a shadow, and sigh till he come. 223

Cel. And I'll sleep. *Exeunt.*

Scene II. [*The Forest. Before* Duke Senior's *cave.*]

Enter *Jaques,* and *Lords* ([like] *Foresters*) [with a dead deer].

Jaq. Which is he that killed the deer?

Lord. Sir, it was I.

Jaq. Let's present him to the Duke like a Roman conqueror; and it would do well to set the deer's horns upon his head for a branch of victory. Have you no song, forester, for this purpose? 7

Lord. Yes, sir.

Jaq. Sing it. 'Tis no matter how it be in tune, so it make noise enough. *Music.*

Song.

What shall he have that kill'd the deer?
His leather skin and horns to wear.
　　Then sing him home.
　　(The rest shall bear this burthen.)

Take thou no scorn to wear the horn;
It was a crest ere thou wast born: 15
 Thy father's father wore it,
 And thy father bore it.
The horn, the horn, the lusty horn,
Is not a thing to laugh to scorn.
           Exeunt.

Scene III. [*The Forest. Near the sheepcote.*]

   Enter *Rosalind* and *Celia.*

Ros. How say you now? Is it not past two
o'clock? and here much Orlando!
 Cel. I warrant you, with pure love and
troubled brain, he hath ta'en his bow and arrows, and is gone forth to sleep.

    Enter *Silvius.*

Look who comes here.   5
 Sil. My errand is to you, fair youth.
My gentle Phebe bid me give you this.
       [*Gives a letter.*]
I know not the contents; but, as I guess
By the stern brow and waspish action
Which she did use as she was writing of it,   10
It bears an angry tenure. Pardon me;
I am but as a guiltless messenger.
 Ros. Patience herself would startle at this
letter
And play the swaggerer. Bear this, bear all!
She says I am not fair, that I lack manners; 15
She calls me proud, and that she could not love
me,
Were man as rare as phœnix. 'Od's my will!
Her love is not the hare that I do hunt.
Why writes she so to me? Well, shepherd, well,
This is a letter of your own device.   20
 Sil. No, I protest, I know not the contents.
Phebe did write it.
 Ros.   Come, come, you are a fool,
And turn'd into the extremity of love.
I saw her hand. She has a leathern hand,
A freestone-coloured hand. I verily did think
That her old gloves were on, but 'twas her
hands.   26
She has a housewive's hand; but that's no
matter.
I say she never did invent this letter;
This is a man's invention and his hand.
 Sil. Sure it is hers.   30
 Ros. Why, 'tis a boisterous and a cruel style,
A style for challengers. Why, she defies me
Like Turk to Christian! Women's gentle brain
Could not drop forth such giant-rude invention,

Such Ethiop words, blacker in their effect   35
Than in their countenance. Will you hear the
letter?
 Sil. So please you, for I never heard it yet —
Yet heard too much of Phebe's cruelty.
 Ros. She Phebes me. Mark how the tyrant
writes.   *Read.*

 'Art thou god to shepherd turn'd,   40
 That a maiden's heart hath burn'd?'

Can a woman rail thus?
 Sil. Call you this railing?
 Ros.

 'Why, thy godhead laid apart,   *Read.*
 Warr'st thou with a woman's heart?'   45

Did you ever hear such railing?

 'Whiles the eye of man did woo me,
 That could do no vengeance to me.'

Meaning me a beast.

 'If the scorn of your bright eyne   50
 Have power to raise such love in mine,
 Alack, in me what strange effect
 Would they work in mild aspect!
 Whiles you chid me, I did love;
 How then might your prayers move!   55
 He that brings this love to thee
 Little knows this love in me;
 And by him seal up thy mind,
 Whether that thy youth and kind
 Will the faithful offer take   60
 Of me and all that I can make,
 Or else by him my love deny,
 And then I'll study how to die.'

 Sil. Call you this chiding?
 Cel. Alas, poor shepherd!   65
 Ros. Do you pity him? No, he deserves no
pity. Wilt thou love such a woman? What, to
make thee an instrument, and play false strains
upon thee? Not to be endur'd! Well, go your
way to her (for I see love hath made thee a tame
snake) and say this to her: that if she love me,
I charge her to love thee; if she will not, I will
never have her unless thou entreat for her. If
you be a true lover, hence, and not a word; for
here comes more company.   75
         Exit Silvius.

    Enter *Oliver.*

 Oli. Good morrow, fair ones. Pray you, if
you know,
Where in the purlieus of this forest stands
A sheepcote, fenc'd about with olive trees?
 Cel. West of this place, down in the neigh-
bour bottom.

The rank of osiers by the murmuring stream 80
Left on your right hand brings you to the place.
But at this hour the house doth keep itself;
There's none within.
   Oli. If that an eye may profit by a tongue,
Then should I know you by description — 85
Such garments and such years: 'The boy is fair,
Of female favour, and bestows himself
Like a ripe sister; the woman low,
And browner than her brother.' Are not you
The owner of the house I did enquire for? 90
   Cel. It is no boast, being ask'd, to say we are.
   Oli. Orlando doth commend him to you both,
And to that youth he calls his Rosalind
He sends this bloody napkin. Are you he?
   Ros. I am. What must we understand by
this? 95
   Oli. Some of my shame, if you will know of
me
What man I am, and how, and why, and where
This handkercher was stain'd.
   Cel.   I pray you tell it.
   Oli. When last the young Orlando parted
from you,
He left a promise to return again 100
Within an hour; and pacing through the forest,
Chewing the food of sweet and bitter fancy,
Lo, what befell! He threw his eye aside,
And mark what object did present itself.
Under an oak, whose boughs were moss'd with
age 105
And high top bald with dry antiquity,
A wretched ragged man, o'ergrown with hair,
Lay sleeping on his back. About his neck
A green and gilded snake had wreath'd itself,
Who with her head, nimble in threats, ap-
proach'd 110
The opening of his mouth; but suddenly,
Seeing Orlando, it unlink'd itself
And with indented glides did slip away
Into a bush, under which bush's shade
A lioness, with udders all drawn dry, 115
Lay couching, head on ground, with catlike
watch
When that the sleeping man should stir; for 'tis
The royal disposition of that beast
To prey on nothing that doth seem as dead.
This seen, Orlando did approach the man 120
And found it was his brother, his elder brother.
   Cel. O, I have heard him speak of that same
brother,
And he did render him the most unnatural
That liv'd amongst men.
   Oli.   And well he might so do,
For well I know he was unnatural. 125

   Ros. But, to Orlando! Did he leave him
there,
Food to the suck'd and hungry lioness?
   Oli. Twice did he turn his back and pur-
pos'd so;
But kindness, nobler ever than revenge,
And nature, stronger than his just occasion, 130
Made him give battle to the lioness,
Who quickly fell before him; in which hurtling
From miserable slumber I awak'd.
   Cel. Are you his brother?
   Ros.   Was it you he rescu'd?
   Cel. Was't you that did so oft contrive to
kill him? 135
   Oli. 'Twas I. But 'tis not I! I do not shame
To tell you what I was, since my conversion
So sweetly tastes, being the thing I am.
   Ros. But, for the bloody napkin?
   Oli.   By-and-by.
When from the first to last, betwixt us two, 140
Tears our recountments had most kindly bath'd,
As how I came into that desert place —
In brief, he led me to the gentle Duke,
Who gave me fresh array and entertainment,
Committing me unto my brother's love, 145
Who led me instantly unto his cave,
There stripp'd himself, and here upon his arm
The lioness had torn some flesh away,
Which all this while had bled; and now he
fainted,
And cried, in fainting, upon Rosalind. 150
Brief, I recover'd him, bound up his wound;
And after some small space, being strong at
heart,
He sent me hither, stranger as I am,
To tell this story, that you might excuse 154
His broken promise, and to give this napkin,
Dy'd in his blood, unto the shepherd youth
That he in sport doth call his Rosalind.
                     [*Rosalind swoons.*]
   Cel. Why, how now, Ganymede? sweet
Ganymede!
   Oli. Many will swoon when they do look on
blood.
   Cel. There is more in it. Cousin Ganymede!
   Oli. Look, he recovers. 161
   Ros. I would I were at home.
   Cel.   We'll lead you thither.
I pray you, will you take him by the arm?
   Oli. Be of good cheer, youth. You a man?
You lack a man's heart. 165
   Ros. I do so, I confess it. Ah, sirrah, a body
would think this was well counterfeited! I pray
you tell your brother how well I counterfeited.
Heigh-ho! 169

Oli. This was not counterfeit. There is too great testimony in your complexion that it was a passion of earnest.

Ros. Counterfeit, I assure you.

Oli. Well then, take a good heart and counterfeit to be a man. 175

Ros. So I do; but, i' faith, I should have been a woman by right.

Cel. Come, you look paler and paler. Pray you draw homewards. Good sir, go with us.

Oli. That will I; for I must bear answer back How you excuse my brother, Rosalind. 181

Ros. I shall devise something. But I pray you commend my counterfeiting to him. Will you go? *Exeunt.*

ACT V. Scene I. [*The Forest. Near the sheepcote.*]

Enter [*Touchstone the*] *Clown* and *Audrey.*

Touch. We shall find a time, Audrey. Patience, gentle Audrey.

Aud. Faith, the priest was good enough, for all the old gentleman's saying.

Touch. A most wicked Sir Oliver, Audrey, a most vile Martext! But, Audrey, there is a youth here in the forest, lays claim to you. 7

Aud. Ay, I know who 'tis. He hath no interest in me in the world. Here comes the man you mean. 10

Enter *William.*

Touch. It is meat and drink to me to see a clown. By my troth, we that have good wits have much to answer for. We shall be flouting; we cannot hold.

Will. Good ev'n, Audrey. 15

Aud. God ye good ev'n, William.

Will. And good ev'n to you, sir.

Touch. Good ev'n, gentle friend. Cover thy head, cover thy head. Nay, prithee be cover'd. How old are you, friend? 20

Will. Five-and-twenty, sir.

Touch. A ripe age. Is thy name William?

Will. William, sir.

Touch. A fair name. Wast born i' th' forest here? 25

Will. Ay, sir, I thank God.

Touch. 'Thank God.' A good answer. Art rich?

Will. Faith, sir, so so.

Touch. 'So so' is good, very good, very excellent good; and yet it is not, it is but so so. Art thou wise? 31

Will. Ay, sir, I have a pretty wit.

Touch. Why, thou say'st well. I do now remember a saying, 'The fool doth think he is wise, but the wise man knows himself to be a fool.' The heathen philosopher, when he had a desire to eat a grape, would open his lips when he put it into his mouth, meaning thereby that grapes were made to eat and lips to open. You do love this maid? 40

Will. I do, sir.

Touch. Give me your hand. Art thou learned?

Will. No, sir.

Touch. Then learn this of me: to have is to have; for it is a figure in rhetoric that drink, being pour'd out of a cup into a glass, by filling the one doth empty the other; for all your writers do consent that *ipse* is he. Now, you are not *ipse*, for I am he.

Will. Which he, sir? 50

Touch. He, sir, that must marry this woman. Therefore, you clown, abandon (which is in the vulgar, leave) the society (which in the boorish is, company) of this female (which in the common is, woman); which together is, abandon the society of this female, or, clown, thou perishest; or, to thy better understanding, diest; or, to wit, I kill thee, make thee away, translate thy life into death, thy liberty into bondage. I will deal in poison with thee, or in bastinado, or in steel. I will bandy with thee in faction; I will o'errun thee with policy; I will kill thee a hundred and fifty ways. Therefore tremble and depart.

Aud. Do, good William. 64

Will. God rest you merry, sir. *Exit.*

Enter *Corin.*

Cor. Our master and mistress seeks you. Come away, away!

Touch. Trip, Audrey! trip, Audrey! I attend, I attend. *Exeunt.*

Scene II. [*The Forest. Near the sheepcote.*]

Enter *Orlando* and *Oliver.*

Orl. Is't possible that on so little acquaintance you should like her? that but seeing, you should love her? and loving, woo? and wooing,

319

she should grant? And will you persever to enjoy her? 5

Oli. Neither call the giddiness of it in question, the poverty of her, the small acquaintance, my sudden wooing, nor her sudden consenting; but say with me, I love Aliena; say with her that she loves me; consent with both that we may enjoy each other. It shall be to your good; for my father's house, and all the revenue that was old Sir Rowland's, will I estate upon you, and here live and die a shepherd. 14

Enter *Rosalind.*

Orl. You have my consent. Let your wedding be to-morrow. Thither will I invite the Duke and all's contented followers. Go you and prepare Aliena; for look you, here comes my Rosalind.

Ros. God save you, brother. 20

Oli. And you, fair sister. [*Exit.*]

Ros. O my dear Orlando, how it grieves me to see thee wear thy heart in a scarf!

Orl. It is my arm.

Ros. I thought thy heart had been wounded with the claws of a lion. 26

Orl. Wounded it is, but with the eyes of a lady.

Ros. Did your brother tell you how I counterfeited to sound when he show'd me your handkercher? 30

Orl. Ay, and greater wonders than that.

Ros. O, I know where you are! Nay, 'tis true. There was never anything so sudden but the fight of two rams and Cæsar's thrasonical brag of 'I came, saw, and overcame.' For your brother and my sister no sooner met but they look'd; no sooner look'd but they lov'd; no sooner lov'd but they sigh'd; no sooner sigh'd but they ask'd one another the reason; no sooner knew the reason but they sought the remedy: and in these degrees have they made a pair of stairs to marriage, which they will climb incontinent, or else be incontinent before marriage. They are in the very wrath of love, and they will together. Clubs cannot part them. 45

Orl. They shall be married to-morrow, and I will bid the Duke to the nuptial. But, O, how bitter a thing it is to look into happiness through another man's eyes! By so much the more shall I to-morrow be at the height of heart-heaviness, by how much I shall think my brother happy in having what he wishes for.

Ros. Why then, to-morrow I cannot serve your turn for Rosalind?

Orl. I can live no longer by thinking. 55

Ros. I will weary you then no longer with idle talking. Know of me then (for now I speak to some purpose) that I know you are a gentleman of good conceit. I speak not this that you should bear a good opinion of my knowledge, insomuch I say I know you are; neither do I labour for a greater esteem than may in some little measure draw a belief from you, to do yourself good, and not to grace me. Believe then, if you please, that I can do strange things. I have, since I was three year old, convers'd with a magician, most profound in his art and yet not damnable. If you do love Rosalind so near the heart as your gesture cries it out, when your brother marries Aliena shall you marry her. I know into what straits of fortune she is driven; and it is not impossible to me, if it appear not inconvenient to you, to set her before your eyes to-morrow human as she is, and without any danger. 75

Orl. Speak'st thou in sober meanings?

Ros. By my life, I do! which I tender dearly, though I say I am a magician. Therefore put you in your best array, bid your friends; for if you will be married to-morrow, you shall; and to Rosalind, if you will. 81

Enter *Silvius* and *Phebe.*

Look, here comes a lover of mine and a lover of hers.

Phe. Youth, you have done me much ungentleness
To show the letter that I writ to you.

Ros. I care not if I have. It is my study 85
To seem despiteful and ungentle to you.
You are there followed by a faithful shepherd.
Look upon him, love him; he worships you.

Phe. Good shepherd, tell this youth what 'tis to love.

Sil. It is to be all made of sighs and tears;
And so am I for Phebe. 91

Phe. And I for Ganymede.

Orl. And I for Rosalind.

Ros. And I for no woman.

Sil. It is to be all made of faith and service;
And so am I for Phebe. 96

Phe. And I for Ganymede.

Orl. And I for Rosalind.

Ros. And I for no woman.

Sil. It is to be all made of fantasy, 100
All made of passion, and all made of wishes,
All adoration, duty, and observance,
All humbleness, all patience, and impatience,
All purity, all trial, all obedience;
And so am I for Phebe. 105

Phe. And so am I for Ganymede.
Orl. And so am I for Rosalind.
Ros. And so am I for no woman.
Phe. [*to Rosalind*] If this be so, why blame
you me to love you?   110
Sil. [*to Phebe*] If this be so, why blame you
me to love you?
Orl. If this be so, why blame you me to
love you?
Ros. Who do you speak to, 'Why blame you
me to love you?'   116
Orl. To her that is not here, nor doth not
hear.
Ros. Pray you, no more of this; 'tis like the
howling of Irish wolves against the moon. [*To
Silvius*] I will help you if I can. — [*To Phebe*]
I would love you if I could . — To-morrow meet
me all together. — [*To Phebe*] I will marry you
if ever I marry woman, and I'll be married to-
morrow. — [*To Orlando*] I will satisfy you if
ever I satisfied man, and you shall be married
to-morrow. — [*To Silvius*] I will content you if
what pleases you contents you, and you shall be
married to-morrow. — [*To Orlando*] As you
love Rosalind, meet. — [*To Silvius*] As you love
Phebe, meet. — And as I love no woman, I'll
meet. So fare you well. I have left you commands.   131
Sil. I'll not fail if I live.
Phe. Nor I.
Orl. Nor I.   *Exeunt.*

Scene III. [*The Forest. Near the sheepcote.*]

Enter [*Touchstone the*] *Clown* and *Audrey.*

Touch. To-morrow is the joyful day, Audrey;
to-morrow will we be married.
Aud. I do desire it with all my heart; and I
hope it is no dishonest desire to desire to be a
woman of the world. Here come two of the
banish'd Duke's pages.   6

Enter two *Pages.*

1. Page. Well met, honest gentleman.
Touch. By my troth, well met. Come, sit,
sit, and a song!   9
2. Page. We are for you. Sit i' th' middle.
1. Page. Shall we clap into't roundly, without hawking or spitting or saying we are hoarse,
which are the only prologues to a bad voice?
2. Page. I' faith, i' faith! and both in a tune,
like two gypsies on a horse.   16

Song.

It was a lover and his lass —
  With a hey, and a ho, and a hey nonino —
That o'er the green cornfield did pass
  In springtime, the only pretty ring-time,   20
When birds do sing, hey ding a ding, ding.
Sweet lovers love the spring.

Between the acres of the rye —
  With a hey, and a ho, and a hey nonino —
These pretty country folks would lie   25
  In springtime, &c.

This carol they began that hour —
  With a hey, and a ho, and a hey nonino —
How that a life was but a flower
  In springtime, &c.   30

And therefore take the present time —
  With a hey, and a ho, and a hey nonino —
For love is crowned with the prime
  In springtime, &c.   34

Touch. Truly, young gentlemen, though
there was no great matter in the ditty, yet the
note was very untuneable.
1. Page. You are deceiv'd, sir. We kept
time, we lost not our time.   39
Touch. By my troth, yes! I count it but
time lost to hear such a foolish song. God b'wi'
you, and God mend your voices! Come, Audrey.
                               Exeunt.

Scene IV. [*The Forest. Near the sheepcote.*]

Enter *Duke Senior, Amiens, Jaques, Orlando,
Oliver, Celia.*

Duke S. Dost thou believe, Orlando, that
the boy
Can do all this that he hath promised?
Orl. I sometimes do believe, and sometimes
do not,
As those that fear they hope, and know they
fear.

Enter *Rosalind, Silvius,* and *Phebe.*

Ros. Patience once more, whiles our compact
is urg'd.   5
You say, if I bring in your Rosalind,
You will bestow her on Orlando here?
Duke. S. That would I, had I kingdoms to
give with her.
Ros. And you say you will have her when I
bring her?
Orl. That would I, were I of all kingdoms
king.   10

Ros. You say you'll marry me, if I be willing?

Phe. That will I, should I die the hour after.

Ros. But if you do refuse to marry me,
You'll give yourself to this most faithful shepherd?

Phe. So is the bargain. 15

Ros. You say that you'll have Phebe, if she will?

Sil. Though to have her and death were both one thing.

Ros. I have promis'd to make all this matter even.
Keep you your word, O Duke, to give your daughter; 19
You yours, Orlando, to receive his daughter;
Keep your word, Phebe, that you'll marry me,
Or else, refusing me, to wed this shepherd;
Keep your word, Silvius, that you'll marry her
If she refuse me; and from hence I go,
To make these doubts all even. 25
                  Exeunt Rosalind and Celia.

Duke S. I do remember in this shepherd boy
Some lively touches of my daughter's favour.

Orl. My lord, the first time that I ever saw him
Methought he was a brother to your daughter.
But, my good lord, this boy is forest-born, 30
And hath been tutor'd in the rudiments
Of many desperate studies by his uncle,
Whom he reports to be a great magician,
Obscured in the circle of this forest. 34

Enter [*Touchstone the*] *Clown* and *Audrey.*

Jaq. There is, sure, another flood toward, and these couples are coming to the ark. Here comes a pair of very strange beasts, which in all tongues are call'd fools.

Touch. Salutation and greeting to you all! 39

Jaq. Good my lord, bid him welcome. This is the motley-minded gentleman that I have so often met in the forest. He hath been a courtier, he swears. 43

Touch. If any man doubt that, let him put me to my purgation. I have trod a measure; I have flatt'red a lady; I have been politic with my friend, smooth with mine enemy; I have undone three tailors; I have had four quarrels, and like to have fought one.

Jaq. And how was that ta'en up? 50

Touch. Faith, we met, and found the quarrel was upon the seventh cause.

Jaq. How seventh cause? Good my lord, like this fellow.

Duke S. I like him very well. 55

Touch. God 'ild you, sir; I desire you of the like. I press in here, sir, amongst the rest of the country copulatives, to swear and to forswear, according as marriage binds and blood breaks. A poor virgin, sir, an ill-favour'd thing, sir, but mine own. A poor humour of mine, sir, to take that that no man else will. Rich honesty dwells like a miser, sir, in a poor house, as your pearl in your foul oyster. 64

Duke S. By my faith, he is very swift and sententious.

Touch. According to the fool's bolt, sir, and such dulcet diseases.

Jaq. But, for the seventh cause. How did you find the quarrel on the seventh cause? 70

Touch. Upon a lie seven times removed (bear your body more seeming, Audrey): as thus, sir. I did dislike the cut of a certain courtier's beard. He sent me word, if I said his beard was not cut well, he was in the mind it was. This is call'd the Retort Courteous. If I sent him word again it was not well cut, he would send me word he cut it to please himself. This is call'd the Quip Modest. If again, it was not well cut, he disabled my judgment. This is call'd the Reply Churlish. If again, it was not well cut, he would answer I spake not true. This is call'd the Reproof Valiant. If again, it was not well cut, he would say I lie. This is call'd the Countercheck Quarrelsome; and so to the Lie Circumstantial and the Lie Direct. 86

Jaq. And how oft did you say his beard was not well cut?

Touch. I durst go no further than the Lie Circumstantial, nor he durst not give me the Lie Direct; and so we measur'd swords and parted. 91

Jaq. Can you nominate in order now the degrees of the lie?

Touch. O sir, we quarrel in print, by the book, as you have books for good manners. I will name you the degrees. The first, the Retort Courteous; the second, the Quip Modest; the third, the Reply Churlish; the fourth, the Reproof Valiant; the fifth, the Countercheck Quarrelsome; the sixth, the Lie with Circumstance; the seventh, the Lie Direct. All these you may avoid but the Lie Direct, and you may avoid that too, with an If. I knew when seven justices could not take up a quarrel, but when the parties were met themselves, one of them thought but of an If: as, 'If you said so, then I said so'; and they shook

322

hands and swore brothers. Your If is the only
peacemaker. Much virtue in If.

Jaq. Is not this a rare fellow, my lord? He's
as good at anything, and yet a fool.   110

Duke S. He uses his folly like a stalking
horse, and under the presentation of that he
shoots his wit.

Enter *Hymen, Rosalind,* and *Celia.* Still music.

Hym. Then is there mirth in heaven
  When earthly things made even   115
  Atone together.
  Good Duke, receive thy daughter;
  Hymen from heaven brought her,
  Yea, brought her hether,
  That thou mightst join her hand with
   his   120
  Whose heart within his bosom is.

Ros. To you I give myself, for I am yours.
        [To Duke.]
To you I give myself, for I am yours.
        [To Orlando.]

Duke S. If there be truth in sight, you are
my daughter.

Orl. If there be truth in shape, you are my
Rosalind.   125

Phe. If sight and shape be true,
Why then, my love adieu!

Ros. I'll have no father, if you be not he.
        [To Duke.]
I'll have no husband, if you be not he.
        [To Orlando.]
Nor ne'er wed woman, if you be not she.   130
        [To Phebe.]

Hym. Peace ho! I bar confusion.
  'Tis I must make conclusion
  Of these most strange events.
  Here's eight that must take hands
  To join in Hymen's bands,   135
  If truth holds true contents.
  You and you no cross shall part.
    [To Orlando and Rosalind.]
  You and you are heart in heart.
    [To Oliver and Celia.]
  You to his love must accord,
       [To Phebe.]
  Or have a woman to your lord.   140
  You and you are sure together
    [To Touchstone and Audrey.]
  As the winter to foul weather.
  Whiles a wedlock hymn we sing,
  Feed yourselves with questioning,
  That reason wonder may diminish 145
  How thus we met, and these things
  finish.

Song.

  Wedding is great Juno's crown —
   O blessed bond of board and bed!
  'Tis Hymen peoples every town;
   High wedlock then be honoured.   150
  Honour, high honour, and renown
  To Hymen, god of every town!

Duke S. O my dear niece, welcome thou art
  to me,
Even daughter, welcome, in no less degree!

Phe. *[to Silvius]* I will not eat my word, now
  thou art mine;   155
Thy faith my fancy to thee doth combine.

Enter *Second Brother,* *[Jaques de Boys].*

2. Bro. Let me have audience for a word or
two.
I am the second son of old Sir Rowland
That bring these tidings to this fair assembly.
Duke Frederick, hearing how that every day
Men of great worth resorted to this forest, 161
Address'd a mighty power, which were on foot
In his own conduct, purposely to take
His brother here and put him to the sword;
And to the skirts of this wild wood he came, 165
Where, meeting with an old religious man,
After some question with him, was converted
Both from his enterprise and from the world,
His crown bequeathing to his banish'd brother,
And all their lands restor'd to them again   170
That were with him exil'd. This to be true
I do engage my life.

Duke S.   Welcome, young man.
Thou offer'st fairly to thy brothers' wedding:
To one, his lands withheld; and to the other,
A land itself at large, a potent dukedom.   175
First, in this forest let us do those ends
That here were well begun and well begot;
And after, every of this happy number
That have endur'd shrewd days and nights
  with us
Shall share the good of our returned fortune,
According to the measure of their states.   181
Meantime forget this new-fall'n dignity
And fall into our rustic revelry.
Play, music, and you brides and bridegrooms
  all,
With measure heap'd in joy, to th' measures
  fall.   185

Jaq. Sir, by your patience. If I heard you
  rightly,
The Duke hath put on a religious life
And thrown into neglect the pompous court.

2. Bro. He hath.   189

Jaq. To him will I. Out of these convert-
ites
There is much matter to be heard and learn'd.
[*To Duke*] You to your former honour I be-
queath;
Your patience and your virtue well deserves
it.
[*To Orlando*] You to a love that your true faith
doth merit;
[*To Oliver*] You to your land and love and great
allies;   195
[*To Silvius*] You to a long and well-deserved
bed;
[*To Touchstone*] And you to wrangling, for thy
loving voyage
Is but for two months victuall'd. — So, to your
pleasures!
I am for other than for dancing measures.
Duke S. Stay, Jaques, stay.   200
Jaq. To see no pastime I! What you would
have
I'll stay to know at your abandon'd cave.
Exit.
Duke S. Proceed, proceed. We will begin
these rites,
As we do trust they'll end, in true delights.
[*A dance.*]

[EPILOGUE.]

Ros. It is not the fashion to see the lady the
epilogue; but it is no more unhandsome than
to see the lord the prologue. If it be true that
good wine needs no bush, 'tis true that a good
play needs no epilogue. Yet to good wine
they do use good bushes, and good plays prove
the better by the help of good epilogues. What
a case am I in then, that am neither a good
epilogue, nor cannot insinuate with you in the
behalf of a good play! I am not furnish'd like
a beggar; therefore to beg will not become me.
My way is to conjure you, and I'll begin with
the women. I charge you, O women, for the
love you bear to men, to like as much of this
play as please you; and I charge you, O men,
for the love you bear to women (as I perceive
by your simp'ring none of you hates them),
that between you and the women the play may
please. If I were a woman, I would kiss as
many of you as had beards that pleas'd me,
complexions that lik'd me, and breaths that I
defied not; and I am sure, as many as have
good beards, or good faces, or sweet breaths,
will, for my kind offer, when I make curtsy, bid
me farewell.   *Exeunt.*

THE TAMING OF THE SHREW

For THE TAMING OF THE SHREW the Folio of 1623 is our sole authority. The date of the play is uncertain. The extreme possibilities appear to be 1594 (which seems too early) and 1598 (which seems rather late). It is not mentioned by Meres in 1598 (see p. 33), for surely it cannot be the mysterious *Love Labour's Won*.

The main source is *The Taming of a Shrew*, an anonymous play printed in 1594 but obviously written some years earlier. This combines the taming story with much of the plot of Ariosto's *I Suppositi*, which had been translated by George Gascoigne as *The Supposes* (1566; printed 1573, 1575).

For the taming story no exact original has been found. It handles a theme widely current in the folklore of Orient and Occident and has points of contact with a large variety of tales and proverbs. 'The tongue can no man tame,' St. James avers. 'It is an unruly evil, full of deadly poison'; and the Abbess in *The Comedy of Errors* echoes his words (v, 1, 69–70):

> The venom clamours of a jealous woman
> Poisons more deadly than a mad dog's tooth.

The tale of the Shrewish Wife who is a Terror to Demons, an ancient anecdote in the East, is well represented in English by the ballad of *The Farmer's Curst Wife* (Child, No. 278): she is carried off to hell, but the devil is glad to take her back to her husband. The cucking stool is not the only corrective for shrews. Witness a savage old story in verse (printed before 1575) — *A merry Ieste of a shrewde and curste Wyfe lapped in Morrelles skin* (see Child, No. 277). Petruchio's declaration in iii, 2, 232–234,

> She is my goods, my chattels; she is my house,
> My household stuff, my field, my barn,
> My horse, my dog, my ass, my anything!

sounds like an echo from other folk-tales. Thus in *El Conde Lucanor* by Juan Manuel (1282–1347; first printed in 1575) a bridegroom tames his shrew by killing his dog, his cat, and his horse when they disregard his call for water to wash his hands. In another tale in the same collection an obedient wife agrees with her husband that certain cows are mares (cf. iv, 5). A folk-tale from Jutland combines the two and includes a test of obedience like that at the end of the play. Perhaps the Elizabethans knew a similar complex.

In reworking the material of *A Shrew* Shakespeare is commonly thought to have had a collaborator, to whom is ascribed the subplot of Bianca and her suitors. Everybody is ready to credit the Induction and the main plot (Katherine and Petruchio) to the master's hand. However, the differences in style and metre are hardly sufficient to establish dual authorship. The technical excellence in construction is a good argument on the conservative side. The author of *A Shrew* did good work in combining two stories, but THE SHREW, which increases the complexity of the Bianca plot, goes far beyond its source in ingenious unification.

When *I Suppositi* begins, Polinesta has been carrying on an intrigue for two years with Erostrato, who came to the city to study, fell in love with her,

325

exchanged identities with his man Dulipo, and took service with her father. Cleandro, an elderly lawyer, is now suing for her hand. To thwart him, Dulipo, in the character of Erostrato, is posing as a rival suitor. In THE TAMING OF THE SHREW we have a similar situation. Lucentio, who came to the city to study, falls in love with Bianca, exchanges identities with his man Tranio, and takes service with her father as a tutor in polite letters. There are two avowed rivals for her hand — young Hortensio and old Gremio. Hortensio, disguised, is engaged by her father as instructor in music. In *The Taming of a Shrew* things are simpler, except for the fusion with the taming story. The student (Aurelius), who is a duke's son, neither exchanges identities with his man nor enters the service of the girl's father (Alfonso). He conceals his high rank, passes as the son of a merchant, and is acceptable to Alfonso as a suitor for his second daughter. Polidor, a friend of Aurelius, is equally acceptable as a suitor for the youngest daughter. The only obstacle is Alfonso's determination that his eldest daughter, the shrew, must be married before either of her sisters. There is no rival, old or young, in either case. Neither Aurelius nor Polidor disguises himself as a tutor. Aurelius does cause his man Valerio to take service with Alfonso as an instructor in music, but this is merely to enable the two younger girls to meet their lovers while the eldest is busy with her lessons on the lute, for otherwise she would keep them at work in the house. There is no Latin tutor in *A Shrew*, nor does either lover enter the father's house as a servant.

This comparison shows that Shakespeare, though utilizing the old play, has had recourse to *I Suppositi* as well. Such recourse is obvious elsewhere — in iv, 2, 59–121, for example, and in v, 1. In one passage, indeed, THE SHREW may be said to acknowledge its indebtedness to Gascoigne's translation: 'While counterfeit supposes blear'd thine eyne' (v, 1, 120).

The Induction dramatizes an old tale, best known to modern readers from 'The Sleeper Wakes' in the *Arabian Nights*, but current in Western Europe as a supposedly historical anecdote in the sixteenth and seventeenth centuries.

The Induction of *A Shrew* has been completely rewritten for THE SHREW; but the plan is retained in detail and there are many echoes of the old phrases. In THE SHREW, however, nothing is heard of Sly and the rest after i, 1, 259, whereas in *A Shrew* the Sly *motif* persists, emerging at appropriate intervals. Sly falls asleep. Stripped of his fine clothes and dressed 'in his own apparel,' he is left near the alehouse door. He tells the tapster, who rouses him, that he has had a fine dream which has taught him 'how to tame a shrew' and that he will straightway go home and tame his wife. The tapster declares that he will accompany him and hear the rest of the dream. Thus the old tale is brought to its appropriate and traditional conclusion. One suspects that the absence of this material in THE SHREW is due to a cut in the Folio text.

The names *Tranio* and *Grumio* come from the *Mostellaria* of Plautus.

Fletcher capped THE TAMING OF THE SHREW by *The Woman's Prize; or, The Tamer Tamed*. Petruchio weds Maria after his first wife's death. His friends pity her for marrying 'this dragon,' but she soon reduces him to submissive decorum.

THE TAMING OF THE SHREW

[Dramatis Personæ.

A Lord.
Christopher Sly, a tinker.
Hostess, Page, Players, Huntsmen, and Servants.
} Persons in the Induction.

Baptista Minola, a gentleman of Padua.
Vincentio, a merchant of Pisa.
Lucentio, son to Vincentio, in love with Bianca.
Petruchio, a gentleman of Verona, suitor to Katherina.
Gremio,
Hortensio,
} suitors to Bianca.

Tranio,
Biondello,
} servants to Lucentio.

Grumio,
Curtis, &c.
} servants to Petruchio.

A Pedant.

Katherina, the shrew,
Bianca,
} daughters to Baptista.

A Widow.

Tailor, Haberdasher, and Servants.

SCENE. — Padua, and Petruchio's house in the country.]

[INDUCTION.] [Scene I. Before an alehouse on a heath.]

Enter *Beggar* (*Christopher Sly*) and *Hostess*.

Beg. I'll pheeze you, in faith!

Host. A pair of stocks, you rogue!

Beg. Y'are a baggage! The Slys are no rogues. Look in the chronicles: we came in with Richard Conqueror. Therefore paucas pallabris; let the world slide. Sessa! 6

Host. You will not pay for the glasses you have burst?

Beg. No, not a denier. Go by, Saint Jeronimy! Go to thy cold bed and warm thee. 10

Host. I know my remedy; I must go fetch the thirdborough. [*Exit.*]

Beg. Third or fourth or fifth borough, I'll answer him by law. I'll not budge an inch, boy. Let him come, and kindly. 15

Falls asleep [*on the ground*].

Wind horns. Enter a *Lord* from hunting, with his *Train* [of *Huntsmen* and *Servants*].

Lord. Huntsman, I charge thee, tender well my hounds:
Broach Merriman, the poor cur is emboss'd;
And couple Clowder with the deep-mouth'd brach.
Saw'st thou not, boy, how Silver made it good
At the hedge corner, in the coldest fault? 20
I would not lose the dog for twenty pound.

1. Hunt. Why, Belman is as good as he, my lord.
He cried upon it at the merest loss
And twice to-day pick'd out the dullest scent.
Trust me, I take him for the better dog. 25

Lord. Thou art a fool. If Echo were as fleet,
I would esteem him worth a dozen such.
But sup them well and look unto them all.
To-morrow I intend to hunt again.

1. Hunt. I will, my lord. 30

Lord. What's here? One dead, or drunk? See, doth he breathe?

2. Hunt. He breathes, my lord. Were he not warm'd with ale,
This were a bed but cold to sleep so soundly.

Lord. O monstrous beast! how like a swine he lies!
Grim death, how foul and loathsome is thine image! 35
Sirs, I will practise on this drunken man.
What think you? If he were convey'd to bed,
Wrapp'd in sweet clothes, rings put upon his fingers,
A most delicious banquet by his bed,
And brave attendants near him when he wakes,
Would not the beggar then forget himself? 41

1. Hunt. Believe me, lord, I think he cannot choose.

2. Hunt. It would seem strange unto him when he wak'd.

Lord. Even as a flatt'ring dream or worthless fancy.
Then take him up and manage well the jest. 45
Carry him gently to my fairest chamber
And hang it round with all my wanton pictures.
Balm his foul head in warm distilled waters
And burn sweet wood to make the lodging sweet.
Procure me music ready when he wakes 50
To make a dulcet and a heavenly sound;

327

And if he chance to speak, be ready straight
And with a low submissive reverence
Say 'What is it your honour will command?'
Let one attend him with a silver basin   55
Full of rosewater and bestrew'd with flowers;
Another bear the ewer, the third a diaper,
And say 'Will't please your lordship cool your
  hands?'
Some one be ready with a costly suit
And ask him what apparel he will wear.   60
Another tell him of his hounds and horse,
And that his lady mourns at his disease.
Persuade him that he hath been lunatic;
And when he says he is — say that he dreams,
For he is nothing but a mighty lord.   65
This do, and do it kindly, gentle sirs.
It will be pastime passing excellent,
If it be husbanded with modesty.
    1. Hunt. My lord, I warrant you we will
    play our part
As he shall think, by our true diligence,   70
He is no less than what we say he is.
    Lord. Take him up gently and to bed with
    him,
And each one to his office when he wakes.
        [*Sly is borne out.*] *Sound trumpet.*
Sirrah, go see what trumpet 'tis that sounds.
        [*Exit Servingman.*]
Belike some noble gentleman that means,   75
Travelling some journey, to repose him here.

    Enter *Servingman.*

How now? Who is it?
    Serv.   An't please your honour, players,
That offer service to your lordship.
    Lord. Bid them come near.

    Enter *Players.*

            Now, fellows, you are welcome.
    Players. We thank your honour.   80
    Lord. Do you intend to stay with me to-
    night?
    Player. So please your lordship to accept our
    duty.
    Lord. With all my heart. This fellow I re-
    member
Since once he play'd a farmer's eldest son.
'Twas where you woo'd the gentlewoman so
  well.   85
I have forgot your name; but sure that part
Was aptly fitted and naturally perform'd.
    Player. I think 'twas Soto that your honour
    means.
    Lord. 'Tis very true. Thou didst it excellent.
Well, you are come to me in happy time,   90

The rather for I have some sport in hand
Wherein your cunning can assist me much.
There is a lord will hear you play to-night;
But I am doubtful of your modesties,
Lest, over-eying of his odd behaviour   95
(For yet his honour never heard a play),
You break into some merry passion
And so offend him; for I tell you, sirs,
If you should smile, he grows impatient.
    Player. Fear not, my lord. We can contain
    ourselves,   100
Were he the veriest antic in the world.
    Lord. Go, sirrah, take them to the buttery
And give them friendly welcome every one.
Let them want nothing that my house affords.
            Exit one with the Players.
Sirrah, go you to Barthol'mew my page,   105
And see him dress'd in all suits like a lady.
That done, conduct him to the drunkard's
  chamber,
And call him 'madam,' do him obeisance.
Tell him from me, as he will win my love,
He bear himself with honourable action,   110
Such as he hath observ'd in noble ladies
Unto their lords by them accomplished.
Such duty to the drunkard let him do
With soft low tongue and lowly courtesy,
And say 'What is't your honour will command
Wherein your lady and your humble wife   116
May show her duty and make known her love?'
And then with kind embracements, tempting
  kisses,
And with declining head into his bosom,
Bid him shed tears, as being overjoy'd   120
To see her noble lord restor'd to health,
Who for this seven years hath esteemed him
No better than a poor and loathsome beggar.
And if the boy have not a woman's gift
To rain a shower of commanded tears,   125
An onion will do well for such a shift,
Which, in a napkin being close convey'd,
Shall in despite enforce a watery eye.
See this dispatch'd with all the haste thou canst.
Anon I'll give thee more instructions.   130
            Exit a Servingman.
I know the boy will well usurp the grace,
Voice, gait, and action of a gentlewoman.
I long to hear him call the drunkard husband,
And how my men will stay themselves from
  laughter
When they do homage to this simple peasant.
I'll in to counsel them. Haply my presence 136
May well abate the over-merry spleen,
Which otherwise would grow into extremes.
            [*Exeunt.*]

[Scene II. *A bedchamber in the Lord's house.*]

Enter aloft *the Drunkard*, [*Sly the Beggar*,] with *Attendants*, some with apparel, basin and ewer, and other appurtenances; and *Lord*.

Beg. For God's sake, a pot of small ale!

1. Serv. Will't please your lordship drink a cup of sack?

2. Serv. Will't please your honour taste of these conserves?

3. Serv. What raiment will your honour wear to-day?   4

Beg. I am Christophero Sly. Call not me 'honour' nor 'lordship.' I ne'er drank sack in my life; and if you give me any conserves, give me conserves of beef. Ne'er ask me what raiment I'll wear; for I have no more doublets than backs, no more stockings than legs, nor no more shoes than feet; nay, sometime more feet than shoes, or such shoes as my toes look through the overleather.

Lord. Heaven cease this idle humour in your honour!

O that a mighty man of such descent,   15
Of such possessions and so high esteem,
Should be infused with so foul a spirit!

Beg. What, would you make me mad? Am not I Christopher Sly, old Sly's son of Burton Heath; by birth a pedlar, by education a cardmaker, by transmutation a bearherd, and now by present profession a tinker? Ask Marian Hacket, the fat alewife of Wincot, if she know me not. If she say I am not fourteen pence on the score for sheer ale, score me up for the lying'st knave in Christendom. What! I am not bestraught. Here's —   27

3. Man. O, this it is that makes your lady mourn!

2. Man. O, this is it that makes your servants droop!

Lord. Hence comes it that your kindred shuns your house,   30
As beaten hence by your strange lunacy.
O noble lord, bethink thee of thy birth,
Call home thy ancient thoughts from banishment
And banish hence these abject lowly dreams!
Look how thy servants do attend on thee,   35
Each in his office ready at thy beck.
Wilt thou have music? Hark! Apollo plays,
                                                    Music.
And twenty caged nightingales do sing.
Or wilt thou sleep? We'll have thee to a couch
Softer and sweeter than the lustful bed   40

On purpose trimm'd up for Semiramis.
Say thou wilt walk. We will bestrow the ground.
Or wilt thou ride? Thy horses shall be trapp'd,
Their harness studded all with gold and pearl.
Dost thou love hawking? Thou hast hawks will soar   45
Above the morning lark. Or wilt thou hunt?
Thy hounds shall make the welkin answer them
And fetch shrill echoes from the hollow earth.

1. Man. Say thou wilt course. Thy greyhounds are as swift
As breathed stags; ay, fleeter than the roe.   50

2. Man. Dost thou love pictures? We will fetch thee straight
Adonis painted by a running brook,
And Cytherea all in sedges hid,
Which seem to move and wanton with her breath,
Even as the waving sedges play with wind.   55

Lord. We'll show thee Io as she was a maid,
And how she was beguiled and surpris'd,
As lively painted as the deed was done.

3. Man. Or Daphne roaming through a thorny wood,
Scratching her legs that one shall swear she bleeds,   60
And at that sight shall sad Apollo weep,
So workmanly the blood and tears are drawn.

Lord. Thou art a lord, and nothing but a lord.
Thou hast a lady far more beautiful
Than any woman in this waning age.   65

1. Man. And, till the tears that she hath shed for thee
Like envious floods o'errun her lovely face,
She was the fairest creature in the world;
And yet she is inferior to none.   69

Beg. Am I a lord? and have I such a lady?
Or do I dream? or have I dream'd till now?
I do not sleep: I see, I hear, I speak;
I smell sweet savours and I feel soft things.
Upon my life, I am a lord indeed,
And not a tinker, nor Christophero Sly.   75
Well, bring our lady hither to our sight,
And once again a pot o' th' smallest ale.

2. Man. Will't please your Mightiness to wash your hands?
O, how we joy to see your wit restor'd!   79
O that once more you knew but what you are!
These fifteen years you have been in a dream,
Or when you wak'd, so wak'd as if you slept.

Beg. These fifteen years! by my fay, a goodly nap.
But did I never speak of all that time?

1. Man. O, yes, my lord! but very idle words;   85

329

For though you lay here in this goodly chamber,
Yet would you say ye were beaten out of door,
And rail upon the hostess of the house,
And say you would present her at the leet
Because she brought stone jugs and no seal'd
    quarts. 90
Sometimes you would call out for Cicely Hacket.
Beg. Ay, the woman's maid of the house.
3 Man. Why, sir, you know no house nor
   no such maid,
Nor no such men as you have reckon'd up —
As Stephen Sly, and old John Naps of Greece,
And Peter Turph, and Henry Pimpernell, 96
And twenty more such names and men as these,
Which never were nor no man ever saw.
Beg. Now, Lord be thanked for my good
   amends!
All. Amen. 100

Enter [*the Page as*] *Lady*, with *Attendants*.

Beg. I thank thee. Thou shalt not lose by it.
Lady. How fares my noble lord?
Beg. Marry, I fare well, for here is cheer
   enough.
Where is my wife?
Lady. Here, noble lord. What is thy will
   with her? 105
Beg. Are you my wife, and will not call me
   husband?
My men should call me 'lord'; I am your
   goodman.
Lady. My husband and my lord, my lord
   and husband,
I am your wife in all obedience.
Beg. I know it well. What must I call her?
Lord. Madam. 111
Beg. Al'ce madam, or Joan madam?
Lord. Madam, and nothing else. So lords
   call ladies.
Beg. Madam wife, they say that I have
   dream'd,
And slept above some fifteen year or more. 115

Lady. Ay, and the time seems thirty unto
   me,
Being all this time abandon'd from your bed.
Beg. 'Tis much. Servants, leave me and her
   alone. [*Exeunt Servants.*]
Madam, undress you and come now to bed.
Lady. Thrice-noble lord, let me entreat of
   you 120
To pardon me yet for a night or two,
Or if not so, until the sun be set,
For your physicians have expressly charg'd,
In peril to incur your former malady,
That I should yet absent me from your bed.
I hope this reason stands for my excuse. 126
Beg. Ay, it stands so that I may hardly tarry
so long. But I would be loath to fall into my
dreams again. I will therefore tarry in despite
of the flesh and the blood. 130

Enter a *Messenger*.

Mess. Your honour's players, hearing your
   amendment,
Are come to play a pleasant comedy;
For so your doctors hold it very meet,
Seeing too much sadness hath congeal'd your
   blood
And melancholy is the nurse of frenzy. 135
Therefore they thought it good you hear a
   play
And frame your mind to mirth and merriment,
Which bars a thousand harms and lengthens
   life.
Beg. Marry, I will; let them play it. Is not
a comonty a Christmas gambold or a tumbling
trick? 141
Lady. No, my good lord; it is more pleasing
   stuff.
Beg. What, household stuff?
Lady. It is a kind of history. 144
Beg. Well, we'll see't. Come, madam wife,
sit by my side and let the world slip. We shall
ne'er be younger.

[ACT I. Scene I. *Padua. A public place before* Baptista's *house.*]

Flourish. Enter *Lucentio* and his man *Tranio*.

Luc. Tranio, since, for the great desire I had
To see fair Padua, nursery of arts,
I am arriv'd for fruitful Lombardy,
The pleasant garden of great Italy,
And by my father's love and leave am arm'd 5
With his good will and thy good company,
My trusty servant, well approv'd in all —

Here let us breathe, and haply institute
A course of learning and ingenious studies.
Pisa, renowned for grave citizens, 10
Gave me my being and my father first,
A merchant of great traffic through the world,
Vincentio, come of the Bentivolii.
Vincentio's son, brought up in Florence,
It shall become to serve all hopes conceiv'd, 15
To deck his fortune with his virtuous deeds;

THE TAMING
OF
THE SHREW

PHOTOGRAPHS BY HOUSTON ROGERS
PRODUCED BY THE OLD VIC COMPANY

Above: The hot-tempered Katharina (Ann Todd), "as curst and shrewd as Socrates' Xantippe"

Right: Paul Rogers portraying Petruchio, who tamed the shrew by killing her with kindness

Below: "I know not what to say; but give me your hands. God send you joy, Petruchio! 'tis a match." Baptista (Laurence Hardy) rejoices at Petruchio's request to marry the fiery Katharina, who revolts at the prospect (*Act II, Scene I*)

Left: Paul Rogers as the patient Petruchio

Right: Katharina demands that her sister Bianca (Gwen Cherrell) name her favored suitor
(Act II, Scene I)

Left: Tranio (Alan Dobie) outbids Gremio for Bianca's hand
(Act II, Scene I)

Right: Lucentio (Paul Daneman) and Tranio try to explain to Biondello (Job Stewart) the reasons for their exchanging identities
(Act I, Scene I)

Left: "I find you passing gentle." Petruchio defends himself against Katharina during their first meeting
(Act II, Scene I)

Right: "I am he am born to tame you, Kate." Petruchio tells Katharina of his plans for her
(Act II, Scene I)

"Come, come, you wasp; i' faith you are too angry." Petruchio drubs Katharina at the first stormy encounter (*Act II, Scene I*)

Below: "If you strike me, you are no gentleman." The shrew turns petulant as Petruchio gives her blow for blow and treats her like a stubborn young child (*Act II, Scene I*)

Below: "Master, master! news! Biondello tells the wedding guests that Petruchio is coming to his marriage wearing shabby old clothes and mounted on a spavined and staggering sway-backed nag (*Act III, Scene II*)

Petruchio takes his bride away immediately after the wedding, giving her no chance to enjoy the banquet (Act III, Scene II)

Petruchio infuriates his famished spouse by asking a blessing before the frugal meal (Act IV, Scene I)

"Where is the rascal cook?" Petruchio finds fault with all the food so that Katharina goes to bed hungry (Act IV, Scene I)

"Here, love; thou seest how diligent I am to dress thy meat myself." Petruchio continues his experiment in tantalizing the starving Katharina (Act IV, Scene III)

Gremio (Meredith Edwards) also teases his master's wife (Act IV, Scene III)

Tranio and Biondello arrange for an old pedant (Aubrey Morris) to pass himself off as the father of Lucentio (Act IV, Scene IV)

"And happily I have arriv'd at last unto the wished haven of my bliss." The arrival of his real father forces Lucentio to acknowledge his ruse and confess that he and Bianca have been married (Act V, Scene I)

"Why, what, i' the devil's name, tailor, call'st thou this?" Petruchio criticizes the new gown he has ordered for his wife (Act IV, Scene III)

Petruchio and his wife on their way back to her house (Act IV, Scene V)

"Young budding virgin, fair and fresh and sweet." Accepting Petruchio's caprice, Katharina pretends to think Vincentio (John Woodvine) is a girl (Act IV, Scene V)

At Lucentio's wedding feast, Vincentio and Gremio witness the proof Petruchio has tamed his shrew (Act V, Scene II)

"I would your duty were as foolish too." Jesting with his wife at the wedding feast, Lucentio compares her obedience with that of the unquestioning Katharina (Act V, Scene II)

Above: "My hand is ready; may it do him ease." At the wedding feast, Petruchio wins his wager when Katharina confesses her complete submission to her husband (Act V, Scene II)

Right: "Why, there's a wench! Come on, and kiss me, Kate." Petruchio rewards the shrew's profession of loyalty (Act V, Scene II)

Below: Katharina kneels in token of her submission to Petruchio (Act V, Scene II)

And therefore, Tranio, for the time I study,
Virtue and that part of philosophy
Will I apply that treats of happiness
By virtue specially to be achiev'd.   20
Tell me thy mind; for I have Pisa left
And am to Padua come as he that leaves
A shallow plash to plunge him in the deep,
And with satiety seeks to quench his thirst.
    Tra. *Mi perdonato*, gentle master mine.   25
I am in all affected as yourself;
Glad that you thus continue your resolve
To suck the sweets of sweet philosophy.
Only, good master, while we do admire
This virtue and this moral discipline,   30
Let's be no Stoics nor no stocks, I pray,
Or so devote to Aristotle's checks
As Ovid be an outcast quite abjur'd.
Balk logic with acquaintance that you have,
And practise rhetoric in your common talk;
Music and poesy use to quicken you;   36
The mathematics and the metaphysics,
Fall to them as you find your stomach serves you.
No profit grows where is no pleasure ta'en.
In brief, sir, study what you most affect.   40
    Luc. Gramercies, Tranio, well dost thou
        advise.
If, Biondello, thou wert come ashore,
We could at once put us in readiness
And take a lodging fit to entertain
Such friends as time in Padua shall beget.   45

*Enter Baptista, with his two daughters Kath-
erina and Bianca; Gremio, a pantaloon; Hortensio, suitor to Bianca. Lucentio, Tranio
stand by.*

But stay awhile. What company is this?
    Tra. Master, some show to welcome us to
        town.
    Bap. Gentlemen, importune me no farther,
For how I firmly am resolv'd you know;
That is, not to bestow my youngest daughter
Before I have a husband for the elder.   51
If either of you both love Katherina,
Because I know you well and love you well,
Leave shall you have to court her at your pleas-
    ure.
    Gre. To cart her rather. She's too rough
        for me.   55
There, there, Hortensio, will you any wife?
    Kath. [*to Baptista*] I pray you, sir, is it your
        will
To make a stale of me amongst these mates?
    Hor. Mates, maid? How mean you that?
        No mates for you,
Unless you were of gentler, milder mould.   60

    Kath. I' faith, sir, you shall never need to
        fear.
Iwis it is not halfway to her heart;
But if it were, doubt not her care should be
To comb your noddle with a three-legg'd stool
And paint your face and use you like a fool.   65
    Hor. From all such devils good Lord de
        liver us!
    Gre. And me too, good Lord!
    Tra. [*aside to Lucentio*] Husht, master!
        Here's some good pastime toward.
That wench is stark mad or wonderful froward.
    Luc. [*aside to Tranio*] But in the other's
        silence do I see   70
Maid's mild behaviour and sobriety.
Peace, Tranio!
    Tra. [*aside to Lucentio*] Well said, master.
        Mum! and gaze your fill.
    Bap. Gentlemen, that I may soon make good
What I have said — Bianca, get you in;   75
And let it not displease thee, good Bianca,
For I will love thee ne'er the less, my girl.
    Kath. A pretty peat! it is best
Put finger in the eye, an she knew why.
    Bian. Sister, content you in my discontent.
Sir, to your pleasure humbly I subscribe.   81
My books and instruments shall be my com-
    pany,
On them to look and practise by myself.
    Luc. [*aside to Tranio*] Hark, Tranio! thou
        mayst hear Minerva speak.
    Hor. Signior Baptista, will you be so strange?
Sorry am I that our good will effects   86
Bianca's grief.
    Gre.   Why will you mew her up,
Signior Baptista, for this fiend of hell,
And make her bear the penance of her tongue?
    Bap. Gentlemen, content ye. I am resolv'd.
Go in, Bianca.   91
                                        [*Exit Bianca.*]
And for I know she taketh most delight
In music, instruments, and poetry,
Schoolmasters will I keep within my house
Fit to instruct her youth. If you, Hortensio —
Or, Signior Gremio, you — know any such —   96
Prefer them hither; for to cunning men
I will be very kind, and liberal
To mine own children in good bringing-up.
And so farewell. Katherina, you may stay, 100
For I have more to commune with Biancà.
                                                  Exit.
    Kath. Why, and I trust I may go too, may
        I not?
What, shall I be appointed hours, as though,
    belike,

331

I knew not what to take, and what to leave?
Ha! *Exit.*

Gre. You may go to the devil's dam! Your
gifts are so good here's none will hold you. Our
love is not so great, Hortensio, but we may blow
our nails together and fast it fairly out. Our
cake's dough on both sides. Farewell. Yet, for
the love I bear my sweet Bianca, if I can by any
means light on a fit man to teach her that
wherein she delights, I will wish him to her
father. 114

Hor. So will I, Signior Gremio. But a word,
I pray. Though the nature of our quarrel yet
never brook'd parle, know now, upon advice, it
toucheth us both — that we may yet again have
access to our fair mistress, and be happy rivals
in Bianca's love — to labour and effect one
thing specially. 121

Gre. What's that, I pray?

Hor. Marry, sir, to get a husband for her
sister.

Gre. A husband? a devil! 125

Hor. I say a husband.

Gre. I say a devil. Think'st thou, Hortensio,
though her father be very rich, any man is so
very a fool to be married to hell? 129

Hor. Tush, Gremio! Though it pass your
patience and mine to endure her loud alarums,
why, man, there be good fellows in the world,
an a man could light on them, would take her
with all faults, and money enough. 134

Gre. I cannot tell; but I had as lief take her
dowry with this condition — to be whipp'd at
the high cross every morning.

Hor. Faith, as you say, there's small choice
in rotten apples. But come; since this bar in
law makes us friends, it shall be so far forth
friendly maintain'd till by helping Baptista's
eldest daughter to a husband we set his youngest free for a husband; and then have to't
afresh! Sweet Bianca! Happy man be his
dole! He that runs fastest gets the ring. How
say you, Signior Gremio? 146

Gre. I am agreed; and would I had given
him the best horse in Padua to begin his wooing
that would thoroughly woo her, wed her, and
bed her, and rid the house of her! Come on. 150

Exeunt ambo. Manent Tranio and Lucentio.

Tra. I pray, sir, tell me, is it possible
That love should of a sudden take such hold?

Luc. O Tranio, till I found it to be true,
I never thought it possible or likely.
But, see! while idly I stood looking on, 155
I found the effect of love in idleness;
And now in plainness do confess to thee —

That art to me as secret and as dear
As Anna to the Queen of Carthage was —
Tranio, I burn, I pine; I perish, Tranio, 160
If I achieve not this young modest girl.
Counsel me, Tranio, for I know thou canst;
Assist me, Tranio, for I know thou wilt.

Tra. Master, it is no time to chide you now;
Affection is not rated from the heart. 165
If love have touch'd you, naught remains but
so:
Redime te captum quam queas minimo.

Luc. Gramercies, lad. Go forward; this
contents;
The rest will comfort, for thy counsel's sound.

Tra. Master, you look'd so longly on the
maid 170
Perhaps you mark'd not what's the pith of all.

Luc. O, yes, I saw sweet beauty in her face,
Such as the daughter of Agenor had,
That made great Jove to humble him to her
hand
When with his knees he kiss'd the Cretan strand.

Tra. Saw you no more? Mark'd you not how
her sister 176
Began to scold and raise up such a storm
That mortal ears might hardly endure the din?

Luc. Tranio, I saw her coral lips to move,
And with her breath she did perfume the air.
Sacred and sweet was all I saw in her. 181

Tra. Nay, then 'tis time to stir him from
his trance.
I pray, awake, sir. If you love the maid,
Bend thoughts and wits to achieve her. Thus
it stands:
Her elder sister is so curst and shrewd 185
That, till the father rid his hands of her,
Master, your love must live a maid at home;
And therefore has he closely mew'd her up,
Because he will not be annoy'd with suitors.

Luc. Ah, Tranio, what a cruel father's he!
But art thou not advis'd he took some care 191
To get her cunning schoolmasters to instruct
her?

Tra. Ay, marry, am I, sir; and now 'tis
plotted.

Luc. I have it, Tranio.

Tra. Master, for my hand,
Both our inventions meet and jump in one. 195

Luc. Tell me thine first.

Tra. You will be schoolmaster
And undertake the teaching of the maid.
That's your device.

Luc. It is. May it be done?

Tra. Not possible; for who shall bear your
part

And be in Padua here Vincentio's son;   200
Keep house and ply his book, welcome his
    friends,
Visit his countrymen and banquet them?
    Luc. Basta! content thee! for I have it full.
We have not yet been seen in any house,
Nor can we be distinguish'd by our faces   205
For man or master. Then it follows thus:
Thou shalt be master, Tranio, in my stead,
Keep house and port and servants as I should;
I will some other be — some Florentine,
Some Neapolitan, or meaner man of Pisa.   210
'Tis hatch'd, and shall be so! Tranio, at once
Uncase thee; take my colour'd hat and cloak.
When Biondello comes, he waits on thee,
But I will charm him first to keep his tongue.
    Tra. So had you need.   215
In brief, sir, sith it your pleasure is,
And I am tied to be obedient,
For so your father charg'd me at our parting:
'Be serviceable to my son,' quoth he,
Although I think 'twas in another sense —   220
I am content to be Lucentio,
Because so well I love Lucentio.
                    [*They exchange habits.*]
    Luc. Tranio, be so because Lucentio loves;
And let me be a slave t' achieve that maid
Whose sudden sight hath thrall'd my wounded
    eye.   225

            Enter *Biondello.*

Here comes the rogue. Sirrah, where have you
    been?
    Bion. Where have I been? Nay, how now?
    where are you?
Master, has my fellow Tranio stol'n your
    clothes?
Or you stol'n his? or both? Pray what's the
    news?   230
    Luc. Sirrah, come hither. 'Tis no time to
    jest,
And therefore frame your manners to the time.
Your fellow Tranio here, to save my life,
Puts my apparel and my count'nance on,
And I for my escape have put on his;   235
For in a quarrel since I came ashore
I kill'd a man, and fear I was descried.
Wait you on him, I charge you, as becomes,
While I make way from hence to save my life.
You understand me?
    Bion.   I, sir? Ne'er a whit!   240
    Luc. And not a jot of Tranio in your mouth!
Tranio is chang'd into Lucentio.
    Bion. The better for him. Would I were so
    too!

    Tra. So could I, faith, boy, to have the next
    wish after,
That Lucentio indeed had Baptista's youngest
    daughter.   245
But, sirrah, not for my sake but your master's,
    I advise
You use your manners discreetly in all kind of
    companies.
When I am alone, why, then I am Tranio;
But in all places else, your master Lucentio.
    Luc. Tranio, let's go.   250
One thing more rests, that thyself execute —
To make one among these wooers. If thou ask
    me why,
Sufficeth my reasons are both good and weighty.
                            Exeunt.

            The Presenters above speak.

    1. Man. My lord, you nod; you do not mind
    the play.
    Beg. Yes, by Saint Anne, do I! A good mat-
ter, surely. Comes there any more of it?   256
    Lady. My lord, 'tis but begun.
    Beg. 'Tis a very excellent piece of work,
madam lady. Would 'twere done!   259
                            They sit and mark.

[Scene II. *Padua. Before* Hortensio's
                    house.]

        Enter *Petruchio* and his man *Grumio.*

    Pet. Verona, for a while I take my leave,
To see my friends in Padua; but of all
My best beloved and approved friend,
Hortensio; and I trow this is his house.
Here, sirrah Grumio; knock, I say.   5
    Gru. Knock, sir? Whom should I knock?
Is there any man has rebus'd your worship?
    Pet. Villain, I say knock me here soundly.
    Gru. Knock you here, sir? Why, sir, what
am I, sir, that I should knock you here, sir? 10
    Pet. Villain, I say knock me at this gate,
And rap me well or I'll knock your knave's pate.
    Gru. My master is grown quarrelsome. I
    should knock you first,
And then I know after who comes by the worst.
    Pet. Will it not be?   15
Faith, sirrah, an you'll not knock, I'll ring it;
I'll try how you can *sol, fa,* and sing it.
                    He wrings him by the ears.
    Gru. Help, masters, help! My master is mad.
    Pet. Now knock when I bid you, sirrah
villain!   19

Enter *Hortensio*.

Hor. How now? what's the matter? My old friend Grumio, and my good friend Petruchio? How do you all at Verona?   22

Pet. Signior Hortensio, come you to part the fray?

Con tutto il core ben trovato, may I say.

Hor. Alla nostra casa ben venuto, molto honorato signor mio Petrucio.   26

Rise, Grumio, rise. We will compound this quarrel.

Gru. Nay, 'tis no matter, sir, what he 'leges in Latin. If this be not a lawful cause for me to leave his service, look you, sir. He bid me knock him and rap him soundly, sir. Well, was it fit for a servant to use his master so, being perhaps (for aught I see) two-and-thirty, a peep out?

Whom would to God I had well knock'd at first!

Then had not Grumio come by the worst.   35

Pet. A senseless villain! Good Hortensio, I bade the rascal knock upon your gate And could not get him for my heart to do it.

Gru. Knock at the gate? O heavens! Spake you not these words plain, 'Sirrah, knock me here; rap me here; knock me well, and knock me soundly'? And come you now with 'knocking at the gate'?

Pet. Sirrah, be gone; or talk not, I advise you.

Hor. Petruchio, patience; I am Grumio's pledge.   45

Why, this' a heavy chance 'twixt him and you,

Your ancient, trusty, pleasant servant Grumio.

And tell me now, sweet friend, what happy gale

Blows you to Padua here from old Verona?

Pet. Such wind as scatters young men through the world   50

To seek their fortunes farther than at home,

Where small experience grows. But in a few,

Signior Hortensio, thus it stands with me:

Antonio, my father, is deceas'd,

And I have thrust myself into this maze,   55

Happily to wive and thrive as best I may.

Crowns in my purse I have, and goods at home,

And so am come abroad to see the world.

Hor. Petruchio, shall I then come roundly to thee

And wish thee to a shrewd ill-favour'd wife?   60

Thou'dst thank me but a little for my counsel;

And yet I'll promise thee she shall be rich,

And very rich. But th'art too much my friend,

And I'll not wish thee to her.

Pet. Signior Hortensio, 'twixt such friends as we   65

Few words suffice; and therefore, if thou know

One rich enough to be Petruchio's wife

(As wealth is burthen of my wooing dance),

Be she as foul as was Florentius' love,

As old as Sibyl, and as curst and shrowd   70

As Socrates' Xantippe or a worse,

She moves me not, or not removes, at least,

Affection's edge in me, were she as rough

As are the swelling Adriatic seas.

I come to wive it wealthily in Padua;   75

If wealthily, then happily in Padua.

Gru. Nay, look you, sir, he tells you flatly what his mind is. Why, give him gold enough and marry him to a puppet or an aglet-baby, or an old trot with ne'er a tooth in her head, though she have as many diseases as two-and-fifty horses. Why, nothing comes amiss, so money comes withal.

Hor. Petruchio, since we are stepp'd thus far in,

I will continue that I broach'd in jest.

I can, Petruchio, help thee to a wife   85

With wealth enough and young and beauteous,

Brought up as best becomes a gentlewoman.

Her only fault (and that is faults enough)

Is that she is intolerable curst,

And shrowd and froward so beyond all measure

That, were my state far worser than it is,   91

I would not wed her for a mine of gold.

Pet. Hortensio, peace! thou know'st not gold's effect.

Tell me her father's name, and 'tis enough;

For I will board her, though she chide as loud

As thunder when the clouds in autumn crack.

Hor. Her father is Baptista Minola,

An affable and courteous gentleman.

Her name is Katherina Minola,   99

Renown'd in Padua for her scolding tongue.

Pet. I know her father, though I know not her,

And he knew my deceased father well.

I will not sleep, Hortensio, till I see her;

And therefore let me be thus bold with you,

To give you over at this first encounter,   105

Unless you will accompany me thither.

Gru. I pray you, sir, let him go while the humour lasts. O' my word, an she knew him as well as I do, she would think scolding would do little good upon him. She may perhaps call him half a score knaves, or so. Why, that's nothing! An he begin once, he'll rail in his rope-

tricks. I'll tell you what, sir, an she stand him
but a little, he will throw a figure in her face,
and so disfigure her with it that she shall have
no more eyes to see withal than a cat. You
know him not, sir.   116

Hor. Tarry, Petruchio, I must go with thee,
For in Baptista's keep my treasure is.
He hath the jewel of my life in hold,
His youngest daughter, beautiful Bianca,   120
And her withholds from me and other more,
Suitors to her and rivals in my love,
Supposing it a thing impossible,
For those defects I have before rehears'd,
That ever Katherina will be woo'd.   125
Therefore this order hath Baptista ta'en,
That none shall have access unto Bianca
Till Katherine the curst have got a husband.

Gru. Katherine the curst!
A title for a maid of all titles the worst.   130

Hor. Now shall my friend Petruchio do me
grace,
And offer me, disguis'd in sober robes,
To old Baptista as a schoolmaster
Well seen in music, to instruct Bianca,
That so I may by this device at least   135
Have leave and leisure to make love to her
And unsuspected court her by herself.

Gru. [*aside*] Here's no knavery! See, to beguile the old folks, how the young folks lay
their heads together!   140

Enter *Gremio*; and *Lucentio* disguised [as
Cambio, with books under his arm*].

Master, master, look about you! Who goes
there? Ha!

Hor. Peace, Grumio! It is the rival of my
love.
Petruchio, stand by awhile.

Gru. A proper stripling and an amorous!
                        [*They stand aside.*]

Gre. O, very well, I have perus'd the note.
Hark you, sir; I'll have them very fairly
bound —   146
All books of love, see that at any hand;
And see you read no other lectures to her.
You understand me. Over and beside
Signior Baptista's liberality,   150
I'll mend it with a largess. Take your paper
too;
And let me have them very well perfum'd,
For she is sweeter than perfume itself
To whom they go to. What will you read to
her?

Luc. Whate'er I read to her, I'll plead for
you   155

As for my patron — stand you so assur'd —
As firmly as yourself were still in place;
Yea, and perhaps with more successful words
Than you, unless you were a scholar, sir.

Gre. O this learning, what a thing it is!   160
Gru. O this woodcock, what an ass it is!
Pet. Peace, sirrah!
Hor. Grumio, mum! [*Comes forward.*] God
save you, Signior Gremio!
Gre. And you are well met, Signior Hortensio.
Trow you whither I am going? To Baptista
Minola.   165
I promis'd to enquire carefully
About a schoolmaster for the fair Bianca;
And by good fortune I have lighted well
On this young man, for learning and behaviour
Fit for her turn, well read in poetry   170
And other books — good ones, I warrant ye.

Hor. 'Tis well; and I have met a gentle-
man
Hath promis'd me to help me to another,
A fine musician to instruct our mistress.
So shall I no whit be behind in duty   175
To fair Bianca, so belov'd of me.

Gre. Belov'd of me, and that my deeds shall
prove.
Gru. [*aside*] And that his bags shall prove.
Hor. Gremio, 'tis now no time to vent our
love.
Listen to me, and if you speak me fair,   180
I'll tell you news indifferent good for either.
Here is a gentleman whom by chance I met,
Upon agreement from us to his liking,
Will undertake to woo curst Katherine,
Yea, and to marry her, if her dowry please.   185

Gre. So said, so done, is well.
Hortensio, have you told him all her faults?

Pet. I know she is an irksome brawling scold.
If that be all, masters, I hear no harm.

Gre. No, say'st me so, friend? What countryman?   190

Pet. Born in Verona, old Antonio's son.
My father dead, my fortune lives for me,
And I do hope good days and long to see.

Gre. O sir, such a life with such a wife were
strange.
But if you have a stomach, to't a God's name!
You shall have me assisting you in all.   196
But will you woo this wildcat?

Pet.   Will I live?

Gru. [*aside*] Will he woo her? Ay, or I'll
hang her.

Pet. Why came I hither but to that intent?
Think you a little din can daunt mine ears?   200
Have I not in my time heard lions roar?

Have I not heard the sea, puff'd up with winds,
Rage like an angry boar chafed with sweat?
Have I not heard great ordnance in the field,
And heaven's artillery thunder in the skies? 205
Have I not in a pitched battle heard
Loud 'larums, neighing steeds, and trumpets'
    clang?
And do you tell me of a woman's tongue,
That gives not half so great a blow to th' ear
As will a chestnut in a farmer's fire?   210
Tush, tush! Fear boys with bugs!
    Gru. [*aside*]   For he fears none.
    Gre. Hortensio, hark.
This gentleman is happily arriv'd,
My mind presumes, for his own good and ours.
    Hor. I promis'd we would be contributors
And bear his charge of wooing, whatsoe'er. 216
    Gre. And so we will, provided that he win
her.
    Gru. [*aside*] I would I were as sure of a good
dinner.

    Enter *Tranio* brave, [as *Lucentio*,] and
              Biondello.

    Tra. Gentlemen, God save you! If I may
be bold,
Tell me, I beseech you, which is the readiest
way
To the house of Signior Baptista Minola?   221
    Bion. He that has the two fair daughters,
is't he you mean?
    Tra. Even he, Biondello.
    Gre. Hark you, sir; you mean not her too?
    Tra. Perhaps him and her, sir. What have
you to do?   226
    Pet. Not her that chides, sir, at any hand,
I pray.
    Tra. I love no chiders, sir. Biondello, let's
away.
    Luc. [*aside*] Well begun, Tranio.
    Hor.   Sir, a word ere you go.
Are you a suitor to the maid you talk of, yea
or no?   230
    Tra. And if I be, sir, is it any offence?
    Gre. No, if without more words you will get
you hence.
    Tra. Why, sir, I pray, are not the streets as
free
For me as for you?
    Gre.   But so is not she.
    Tra. For what reason, I beseech you?
    Gre.   For this reason, if you'll know,
That she's the choice love of Signior Gremio.
    Hor. That she's the chosen of Signior Hor-
tensio.

    Tra. Softly, my masters! If you be gentle-
men,
Do me this right — hear me with patience.
Baptista is a noble gentleman,   240
To whom my father is not all unknown,
And, were his daughter fairer than she is,
She may more suitors have, and me for one.
Fair Leda's daughter had a thousand wooers;
Then well one more may fair Bianca have; 245
And so she shall: Lucentio shall make one,
Though Paris came in hope to speed alone.
    Gre. What, this gentleman will outtalk us
all!
    Luc. Sir, give him head; I know he'll prove
a jade.
    Pet. Hortensio, to what end are all these
words?   250
    Hor. Sir, let me be so bold as ask you,
Did you yet ever see Baptista's daughter?
    Tra. No, sir, but hear I do that he hath
two;
The one as famous for a scolding tongue
As is the other for beauteous modesty.   255
    Pet. Sir, sir, the first's for me! let her go
by.
    Gre. Yea, leave that labour to great Hercules,
And let it be more than Alcides' twelve.
    Pet. Sir, understand you this of me, in sooth:
The youngest daughter, whom you hearken for,
Her father keeps from all access of suitors, 261
And will not promise her to any man
Until the elder sister first be wed.
The younger then is free, and not before.
    Tra. If it be so, sir, that you are the man 265
Must stead us all, and me amongst the rest;
And if you break the ice and do this feat,
Achieve the elder, set the younger free
For our access — whose hap shall be to have
her
Will not so graceless be to be ingrate.   270
    Hor. Sir, you say well, and well you do
conceive;
And since you do profess to be a suitor,
You must, as we do, gratify this gentleman,
To whom we all rest generally beholding.
    Tra. Sir, I shall not be slack; in sign where-
of,
Please ye we may contrive this afternoon, 276
And quaff carouses to our mistress' health,
And do as adversaries do in law —
Strive mightily, but eat and drink as friends.
    Gru., Bion. O excellent motion! Fellows,
let's be gone.   280
    Hor. The motion's good indeed, and be it so.
Petruchio, I shall be your ben venuto. *Exeunt.*

[ACT II. Scene I. *Padua.* Baptista's *house.*]

Enter *Katherina,* and *Bianca* [with her
hands bound].

Bian. Good sister, wrong me not, nor wrong
yourself,
To make a bondmaid and a slave of me.
That I disdain; but for these other gauds,
Unbind my hands, I'll pull them off myself,
Yea, all my raiment, to my petticoat;   5
Or what you will command me will I do,
So well I know my duty to my elders.
Kath. Of all thy suitors here I charge thee
tell
Whom thou lov'st best. See thou dissemble not.
Bian. Believe me, sister, of all the men alive
I never yet beheld that special face   11
Which I could fancy more than any other.
Kath. Minion, thou liest. Is't not Hortensio?
Bian. If you affect him, sister, here I swear
I'll plead for you myself but you shall have him.
Kath. O, then belike you fancy riches more;
You will have Gremio to keep you fair.
Bian. Is it for him you do envy me so?
Nay then, you jest, and now I well perceive
You have but jested with me all this while.   20
I prithee, sister Kate, untie my hands.
Kath. (*strikes her*) If that be jest, then all the
rest was so.

Enter *Baptista.*

Bap. Why, how now, dame? Whence grows
this insolence?
Bianca, stand aside. Poor girl! she weeps.
                              [*Unbinds her.*]
Go ply thy needle; meddle not with her.   25
For shame, thou hilding of a devilish spirit!
Why dost thou wrong her that did ne'er wrong
thee?
When did she cross thee with a bitter word?
Kath. Her silence flouts me, and I'll be re-
veng'd.   *Flies after Bianca.*
Bap. [*holds her back*] What, in my sight?
Bianca, get thee in.   30
                              Exit [*Bianca*].
Kath. What, will you not suffer me? Nay,
now I see
She is your treasure, she must have a husband;
I must dance barefoot on her wedding day
And for your love to her lead apes in hell.
Talk not to me! I will go sit and weep   35
Till I can find occasion of revenge.   [*Exit.*]

Bap. Was ever gentleman thus griev'd as I?
But who comes here?

Enter *Gremio; Lucentio* in the habit of a mean
man; *Petruchio,* [with *Hortensio* as a musician];
Tranio [as *Lucentio*], with his boy [*Biondello*]
bearing a lute and books.

Gre. Good morrow, neighbour Baptista.
Bap. Good morrow, neighbour Gremio. God
save you, gentlemen.   41
Pet. And you, good sir. Pray have you not
a daughter
Call'd Katherina, fair and virtuous?
Bap. I have a daughter, sir, call'd Katherina.
Gre. You are too blunt. Go to it orderly. 45
Pet. You wrong me, Signior Gremio; give
me leave.
I am a gentleman of Verona, sir,
That, hearing of her beauty and her wit,
Her affability and bashful modesty,
Her wondrous qualities and mild behaviour, 50
Am bold to show myself a forward guest
Within your house, to make mine eye the
witness
Of that report which I so oft have heard.
And for an entrance to my entertainment,
I do present you with a man of mine,   55
                          [*Presents Hortensio.*]
Cunning in music and the mathematics,
To instruct her fully in those sciences,
Whereof I know she is not ignorant.
Accept of him, or else you do me wrong.
His name is Licio, born in Mantua.   60
Bap. Y'are welcome, sir, and he for your
good sake.
But for my daughter Katherine, this I know,
She is not for your turn, the more my grief.
Pet. I see you do not mean to part with her,
Or else you like not of my company.   65
Bap. Mistake me not; I speak but as I find.
Whence are you, sir? What may I call your
name?
Pet. Petruchio is my name, Antonio's son,
A man well known throughout all Italy.
Bap. I know him well; you are welcome for
his sake.   70
Gre. Saving your tale, Petruchio, I pray
Let us that are poor petitioners speak too.
Bacare! you are marvellous forward.
Pet. O, pardon me, Signior Gremio! I would
fain be doing.   74

337

Gre. I doubt it not, sir, but you will curse your wooing.
Neighbour, this is a gift very grateful, I am sure of it. To express the like kindness, myself, that have been more kindly beholding to you than any, freely give unto you this young scholar [*presents Lucentio*], that hath been long studying at Rheims, as cunning in Greek, Latin, and other languages as the other in music and mathematics. His name is Cambio. Pray accept his service. 84

Bap. A thousand thanks, Signior Gremio! Welcome, good Cambio. [*To Tranio*] But, gentle sir, methinks you walk like a stranger. May I be so bold to know the cause of your coming?

Tra. Pardon me, sir, the boldness is mine own
That, being a stranger in this city here, 90
Do make myself a suitor to your daughter,
Unto Bianca, fair and virtuous.
Nor is your firm resolve unknown to me
In the preferment of the eldest sister.
This liberty is all that I request, 95
That, upon knowledge of my parentage,
I may have welcome 'mongst the rest that woo
And free access and favour as the rest.
And toward the education of your daughters
I here bestow a simple instrument, 100
[*Offers the lute.*]
And this small packet of Greek and Latin books.
If you accept them, then their worth is great.

Bap. Lucentio is your name — of whence, I pray?

Tra. Of Pisa, sir, son to Vincentio.

Bap. A mighty man of Pisa; by report 105
I know him well. You are very welcome, sir.
Take you [*to Hortensio*] the lute, and you [*to Lucentio*] the set of books.
You shall go see your pupils presently.
Holla, within!

Enter a *Servant*.

Sirrah, lead these gentlemen
To my two daughters, and tell them both 110
These are their tutors. Bid them use them well.
[*Exit Servant, with Hortensio, Lucentio, and Biondello.*]
We will go walk a little in the orchard,
And then to dinner. You are passing welcome,
And so I pray you all to think yourselves.

Pet. Signior Baptista, my business asketh haste, 115
And every day I cannot come to woo.
You knew my father well, and in him me,

Left solely heir to all his lands and goods,
Which I have bettered rather than decreas'd.
Then tell me, if I get your daughter's love, 120
What dowry shall I have with her to wife?

Bap. After my death the one half of my lands,
And in possession twenty thousand crowns.

Pet. And, for that dowry, I'll assure her of
Her widowhood, be it that she survive me, 125
In all my lands and leases whatsoever.
Let specialties be therefore drawn between us,
That covenants may be kept on either hand.

Bap. Ay, when the special thing is well obtain'd,
That is, her love; for that is all in all. 130

Pet. Why, that is nothing! for I tell you, father,
I am as peremptory as she proud-minded;
And where two raging fires meet together,
They do consume the thing that feeds their fury.
Though little fire grows great with little wind,
Yet extreme gusts will blow out fire and all.
So I to her, and so she yields to me,
For I am rough and woo not like a babe.

Bap. Well mayst thou woo and happy be thy speed!
But be thou arm'd for some unhappy words.

Pet. Ay, to the proof, as mountains are for winds, 141
That shake not, though they blow perpetually.

Enter *Hortensio*, with his head broke.

Bap. How now, my friend? Why dost thou look so pale?

Hor. For fear, I promise you, if I look pale.

Bap. What, will my daughter prove a good musician? 145

Hor. I think she'll sooner prove a soldier.
Iron may hold with her, but never lutes.

Bap. Why, then thou canst not break her to the lute?

Hor. Why, no! for she hath broke the lute to me.
I did but tell her she mistook her frets, 150
And bow'd her hand to teach her fingering,
When, with a most impatient devilish spirit,
'Frets call you these?' quoth she. 'I'll fume with them!'
And with that word she stroke me on the head,
And through the instrument my pate made way,
And there I stood amazed for a while, 156
As on a pillory, looking through the lute,
While she did call me rascal fiddler
And twangling Jack, with twenty such vile terms,
As had she studied to misuse me so. 160

Pet. Now, by the world, it is a lusty wench!
I love her ten times more than e'er I did.
O, how I long to have some chat with her!
Bap. Well, go with me, and be not so dis-
comfited. 164
Proceed in practice with my younger daughter;
She's apt to learn and thankful for good turns.
Signior Petruchio, will you go with us,
Or shall I send my daughter Kate to you?
Pet. I pray you do; I will attend her here,
Exeunt. Manet Petruchio.
And woo her with some spirit when she comes.
Say that she rail; why, then I'll tell her plain 172
She sings as sweetly as a nightingale.
Say that she frown; I'll say she looks as clear
As morning roses newly wash'd with dew.
Say she be mute and will not speak a word; 175
Then I'll commend her volubility
And say she uttereth piercing eloquence.
If she do bid me pack, I'll give her thanks,
As though she bid me stay by her a week.
If she deny to wed, I'll crave the day 180
When I shall ask the banes, and when be
married.
But here she comes; and now, Petruchio, speak.

Enter *Katherina.*

Good morrow, Kate; for that's your name, I
hear.
Kath. Well have you heard, but something
hard of hearing.
They call me Katherine that do talk of me. 185
Pet. You lie, in faith! for you are call'd
plain Kate,
And bonny Kate, and sometimes Kate the
curst;
But, Kate, the prettiest Kate in Christendom,
Kate of Kate Hall, my super-dainty Kate,
For dainties are all Kates — and therefore,
Kate, 190
Take this of me, Kate of my consolation:
Hearing thy mildness prais'd in every town,
Thy virtues spoke of, and thy beauty sounded,
Yet not so deeply as to thee belongs,
Myself am mov'd to woo thee for my wife.
Kath. Mov'd? In good time! Let him that
mov'd you hither 196
Remove you hence. I knew you at the first
You were a moveable.
Pet. Why, what's a moveable?
Kath. A join'd-stool.
Pet. Thou hast hit it! Come sit on me.
Kath. Asses are made to bear, and so are you.
Pet. Women are made to bear, and so are you.
Kath. No such jade as you, if me you mean.

Pet. Alas, good Kate, I will not burthen
thee!
For, knowing thee to be but young and light —
Kath. Too light for such a swain as you to
catch, 205
And yet as heavy as my weight should be.
Pet. Should be! should — buzz!
Kath. Well ta'en, and like a buzzard.
Pet. O slow-wing'd turtle! shall a buzzard
take thee?
Kath. Ay, for a turtle, as he takes a buzzard.
Pet. Come, come, you wasp! i' faith, you
are too angry. 210
Kath. If I be waspish, best beware my sting.
Pet. My remedy is then to pluck it out.
Kath. Ay, if the fool could find it where it lies.
Pet. Who knows not where a wasp does wear
his sting?
In his tail. 215
Kath. In his tongue.
Pet. Whose tongue?
Kath. Yours, if you talk of tales. And so
farewell.
Pet. What, with my tongue in your tail?
Nay, come again!
Good Kate, I am a gentleman.
Kath. That I'll try. 220
She strikes him.
Pet. I swear I'll cuff you if you strike again.
Kath. So may you lose your arms.
If you strike me, you are no gentleman;
And if no gentleman, why then no arms.
Pet. A herald, Kate? O, put me in thy
books! 225
Kath. What is your crest? a coxcomb?
Pet. A combless cock, so Kate will be my hen.
Kath. No cock of mine; you crow too like a
craven.
Pet. Nay, come, Kate, come! you must not
look so sour.
Kath. It is my fashion when I see a crab.
Pet. Why, here's no crab, and therefore look
not sour. 231
Kath. There is, there is!
Pet. Then show it me.
Kath. Had I a glass, I would.
Pet. What, you mean my face?
Kath. Well aim'd of such a young one.
Pet. Now, by Saint George, I am too young
for you.
Kath. Yet you are wither'd.
Pet. 'Tis with cares.
Kath. I care not.
Pet. Nay, hear you, Kate. In sooth you
scape not so!

Kath. I chafe you if I tarry. Let me go.

Pet. No, not a whit; I find you passing gentle.

'Twas told me you were rough and coy and sullen, 245
And now I find report a very liar;
For thou art pleasant, gamesome, passing courteous,
But slow in speech, yet sweet as springtime flowers.
Thou canst not frown, thou canst not look askance,
Nor bite the lip, as angry wenches will, 250
Nor hast thou pleasure to be cross in talk;
But thou with mildness entertain'st thy wooers,
With gentle conference, soft and affable.
Why does the world report that Kate doth limp?
O sland'rous world! Kate like the hazel twig 256
Is straight and slender, and as brown in hue
As hazelnuts, and sweeter than the kernels.
O, let me see thee walk: thou dost not halt.

Kath. Go, fool! and whom thou keep'st command.

Pet. Did ever Dian so become a grove 260
As Kate this chamber with her princely gait?
O, be thou Dian, and let her be Kate;
And then let Kate be chaste, and Dian sportful!

Kath. Where did you study all this goodly speech? 264

Pet. It is extempore, from my mother wit.

Kath. A witty mother! witless else her son.

Pet. Am I not wise?

Kath. Yes; keep you warm.

Pet. Marry, so I mean, sweet Katherine, in thy bed.
And therefore, setting all this chat aside, 270
Thus in plain terms: your father hath consented
That you shall be my wife, your dowry 'greed on;
And, will you, nill you, I will marry you.
Now, Kate, I am a husband for your turn; 274
For, by this light, whereby I see thy beauty,
Thy beauty, that doth make me like thee well,
Thou must be married to no man but me;
For I am he am born to tame you, Kate,
And bring you from a wild Kate to a Kate
Conformable as other household Kates. 280

Enter *Baptista, Gremio, Tranio.*

Here comes your father. Never make denial.
I must and will have Katherine to my wife.

Bap. Now, Signior Petruchio, how speed you with my daughter?

Pet. How but well, sir? how but well?
It were impossible I should speed amiss. 285

Bap. Why, how now, daughter Katherine? in your dumps?

Kath. Call you me daughter? Now I promise you
You have show'd a tender fatherly regard
To wish me wed to one half lunatic,
A madcap ruffian and a swearing Jack,
That thinks with oaths to face the matter out.

Pet. Father, 'tis thus: yourself and all the world
That talk'd of her have talk'd amiss of her.
If she be curst, it is for policy, 294
For she's not froward, but modest as the dove;
She is not hot, but temperate as the morn;
For patience she will prove a second Grissel,
And Roman Lucrece for her chastity;
And to conclude, we have 'greed so well together
That upon Sunday is the wedding day. 300

Kath. I'll see thee hang'd on Sunday first.

Gre. Hark, Petruchio; she says she'll see thee hang'd first.

Tra. Is this your speeding? Nay then, good night our part!

Pet. Be patient, gentlemen; I choose her for myself.
If she and I be pleas'd, what's that to you? 305
'Tis bargain'd 'twixt us twain, being alone,
That she shall still be curst in company.
I tell you 'tis incredible to believe
How much she loves me. O, the kindest Kate!
She hung about my neck, and kiss on kiss 310
She vied so fast, protesting oath on oath,
That in a twink she won me to her love.
O, you are novices! 'Tis a world to see
How tame, when men and women are alone,
A meacock wretch can make the curstest shrew.
Give me thy hand, Kate; I will unto Venice
To buy apparel 'gainst the wedding day. 317
Provide the feast, father, and bid the guests;
I will be sure my Katherine shall be fine.

Bap. I know not what to say — but give me your hands; 320
God send you joy, Petruchio! 'tis a match.

Gre., Tra. Amen say we; we will be witnesses.

Pet. Father, and wife, and gentlemen, adieu.
I will to Venice; Sunday comes apace.
We will have rings and things and fine array;
And kiss me, Kate! We will be married a Sunday. 326

Exeunt Petruchio and Katherine [severally].

Gre. Was ever match clapp'd up so suddenly?

Bap. Faith, gentlemen, now I play a merchant's part
And venture madly on a desperate mart.

Tra. 'Twas a commodity lay fretting by you.
'Twill bring you gain, or perish on the seas. 331

Bap. The gain I seek is, quiet in the match.

Gre. No doubt but he hath got a quiet catch.
But now, Baptista, to your younger daughter:
Now is the day we long have looked for; 335
I am your neighbour and was suitor first.

Tra. And I am one that love Bianca more
Than words can witness or your thoughts can guess.

Gre. Youngling, thou canst not love so dear as I.

Tra. Greybeard, thy love doth freeze.

Gre.   But thine doth fry. 340
Skipper, stand back! 'tis age that nourisheth.

Tra. But youth in ladies' eyes that flourisheth.

Bap. Content you, gentlemen; I will compound this strife.
'Tis deeds must win the prize, and he of both
That can assure my daughter greatest dower
Shall have my Bianca's love. 346
Say, Signior Gremio, what can you assure her?

Gre. First, as you know, my house within the city
Is richly furnished with plate and gold,
Basins and ewers to lave her dainty hands; 350
My hangings all of Tyrian tapestry;
In ivory coffers I have stuff'd my crowns;
In cypress chests my arras counterpoints,
Costly apparel, tents, and canopies,
Fine linen, Turkey cushions boss'd with pearl,
Valance of Venice gold in needlework; 356
Pewter and brass and all things that belong
To house or housekeeping. Then at my farm
I have a hundred milch kine to the pail,
Sixscore fat oxen standing in my stalls, 360
And all things answerable to this portion.
Myself am struck in years, I must confess;
And if I die to-morrow, this is hers,
If whilst I live she will be only mine.

Tra. That 'only' came well in. Sir, list to me. 365
I am my father's heir and only son.
If I may have your daughter to my wife,
I'll leave her houses three or four as good
Within rich Pisa walls as any one
Old Signior Gremio has in Padua; 370
Besides, two thousand ducats by the year
Of fruitful land, all which shall be her jointure.
What, have I pinch'd you, Signior Gremio?

Gre. [*aside*] Two thousand ducats by the year of land!
My land amounts not to so much in all. — 375
That she shall have, besides an argosy
That now is lying in Marseilles road.
What, have I chok'd you with an argosy?

Tra. Gremio, 'tis known my father hath no less
Than three great argosies, besides two galliasses
And twelve tight galleys. These I will assure her, 381
And twice as much whate'er thou off'rest next.

Gre. Nay, I have off'red all! I have no more;
And she can have no more than all I have.
If you like me, she shall have me and mine. 385

Tra. Why, then the maid is mine from all the world
By your firm promise; Gremio is outvied.

Bap. I must confess your offer is the best;
And, let your father make her the assurance,
She is your own; else you must pardon me. 390
If you should die before him, where's her dower?

Tra. That's but a cavil. He is old, I young.

Gre. And may not young men die as well as old?

Bap. Well, gentlemen, 394
I am thus resolv'd: on Sunday next you know
My daughter Katherine is to be married;
Now on the Sunday following shall Bianca
Be bride to you, if you make this assurance;
If not, to Signior Gremio.
And so I take my leave, and thank you both.
Exit.

Gre. Adieu, good neighbour. — Now I fear thee not. 401
Sirrah, young gamester, your father were a fool
To give thee all, and in his waning age
Set foot under thy table. Tut, a toy!
An old Italian fox is not so kind, my boy. 405
Exit.

Tra. A vengeance on your crafty withered hide!
Yet I have fac'd it with a card of ten.
'Tis in my head to do my master good.
I see no reason but suppos'd Lucentio
Must get a father, call'd suppos'd Vincentio;
And that's a wonder: fathers commonly 411
Do get their children; but in this case of wooing,
A child shall get a sire, if I fail not of my cunning.
Exit.

Enter *Lucentio* [as *Cambio*], *Hortensio* [as
   Licio], and *Bianca*.

Luc. Fiddler, forbear! you grow too for-
   ward, sir.
Have you so soon forgot the entertainment
Her sister Katherine welcom'd you withal?
  Hor. But, wrangling pedant, this is
The patroness of heavenly harmony.   5
Then give me leave to have prerogative;
And when in music we have spent an hour,
Your lecture shall have leisure for as much.
  Luc. Preposterous ass, that never read so
   far
To know the cause why music was ordain'd! 10
Was it not to refresh the mind of man
After his studies or his usual pain?
Then give me leave to read philosophy,
And while I pause, serve in your harmony.
  Hor. Sirrah, I will not bear these braves of
   thine.   15
  Bian. Why, gentlemen, you do me double
   wrong
To strive for that which resteth in my choice.
I am no breeching scholar in the schools;
I'll not be tied to hours, nor 'pointed times,
But learn my lessons as I please myself.   20
And, to cut off all strife, here sit we down:
Take you your instrument, play you the whiles;
His lecture will be done ere you have tun'd.
  Hor. You'll leave his lecture when I am in
   tune.
  Luc. That will be never. Tune your instru-
   ment.   [*Hortensio steps aside.*]
  Bian. Where left we last?   26
  Luc. Here, madam: [*Reads.*]

'Hic ibat Simois, hic est Sigeia tellus,
  Hic steterat Priami regia celsa senis.'

  Bian. Conster them.   30
  Luc. *Hic ibat*, as I told you before; *Simois*,
I am Lucentio; *hic est*, son unto Vincentio of
Pisa; *Sigeia tellus*, disguised thus to get your
love; *Hic steterat*, and that Lucentio that comes
a-wooing; *Priami*, is my man Tranio; *regia*,
bearing my port; *celsa senis*, that we might be-
guile the old pantaloon.
  Hor. Madam, my instrument's in tune.
  Bian.   Let's hear.
                        [*He plays.*]
O, fie! the treble jars.

  Luc.   Spit in the hole, man,
And tune again.   40
  Bian. Now let me see if I can conster it:
Hic ibat Simois, I know you not; *hic est Sigeia
tellus*, I trust you not; *Hic steterat Priami*, take
heed he hear us not; *regia*, presume not; *celsa
senis*, despair not.   45
  Hor. Madam, 'tis now in tune. [*He plays.*]
  Luc.   All but the bass.
  Hor. The bass is right; 'tis the base knave
   that jars.
[*Aside*] How fiery and forward our pedant is!
Now, for my life, the knave doth court my love.
Pedascule, I'll watch you better yet.   50
  Bian. In time I may believe, yet I mistrust.
  Luc. Mistrust it not; for, sure, Æacides
Was Ajax, call'd so from his grandfather.
  Bian. I must believe my master; else, I
   promise you,
I should be arguing still upon that doubt; 55
But let it rest. Now, Licio, to you.
Good master, take it not unkindly, pray,
That I have been thus pleasant with you both.
  Hor. [*to Lucentio*] You may go walk and give
   me leave awhile;
My lessons make no music in three parts. 60
  Luc. Are you so formal, sir? Well, I must
   wait,
[*Aside*] And watch withal; for, but I be de-
   ceiv'd,
Our fine musician groweth amorous.
  Hor. Madam, before you touch the instrument
To learn the order of my fingering,   65
I must begin with rudiments of art,
To teach you gamouth in a briefer sort,
More pleasant, pithy, and effectual,
Than hath been taught by any of my trade;
And there it is in writing fairly drawn.   70
  Bian. Why, I am past my gamouth long ago!
  Hor. Yet read the gamouth of Hortensio.
  Bian. [*reads*]

'*Gamouth* I am, the ground of all accord,
   A re, to plead Hortensio's passion.
B mi, Bianca, take him for thy lord,   75
   C fa ut, that loves with all affection.
D sol re, one cliff, two notes have I;
   E la mi, show pity, or I die.'

Call you this gamouth? Tut, I like it not!
Old fashions please me best; I am not so nice
To change true rules for odd inventions.   81

Enter a *Messenger*.

Mess. Mistress, your father prays you leave
your books
And help to dress your sister's chamber up.
You know to-morrow is the wedding day.

Bian. Farewell, sweet masters both; I must
be gone.   85
        [*Exeunt Bianca and Messenger.*]

Luc. Faith, mistress, then I have no cause
to stay.   [*Exit.*]

Hor. But I have cause to pry into this
pedant;
Methinks he looks as though he were in love.
Yet if thy thoughts, Bianca, be so humble
To cast thy wand'ring eyes on every stale, 90
Seize thee that list! If once I find thee ranging,
Hortensio will be quit with thee by changing.
                                               Exit.

[Scene II. *Padua. Before* Baptista's
        house.]

Enter *Baptista, Gremio, Tranio* [(as *Lucentio*)],
Katherina, Bianca, [*Lucentio* (as *Cambio*),] and
        others, *Attendants.*

Bap. [*to Tranio*] Signior Lucentio, this is the
'pointed day
That Katherine and Petruchio should be
married,
And yet we hear not of our son-in-law.
What will be said? What mockery will it be
To want the bridegroom when the priest at-
tends   5
To speak the ceremonial rites of marriage!
What says Lucentio to this shame of ours?

Kath. No shame but mine! I must forsooth
be forc'd
To give my hand, oppos'd against my heart,
Unto a mad-brain rudesby, full of spleen,   10
Who woo'd in haste and means to wed at
leisure.
I told you, I, he was a frantic fool,
Hiding his bitter jests in blunt behaviour;
And, to be noted for a merry man,
He'll woo a thousand, 'point the day of mar-
riage,   15
Make feast, invite friends, and proclaim the
banes;
Yet never means to wed where he hath woo'd.
Now must the world point at poor Katherine
And say, 'Lo, there is mad Petruchio's wife,
If it would please him come and marry her!'

Tra. Patience, good Katherine, and Bap-
tista too!   21
Upon my life, Petruchio means but well,
Whatever fortune stays him from his word.
Though be he blunt, I know him passing wise;
Though he be merry, yet withal he's honest. 25

Kath. Would Katherine had never seen him
though!
        Exit weeping [*followed by Bianca and others*].

Bap. Go, girl. I cannot blame thee now to
weep;
For such an injury would vex a saint,
Much more a shrew of thy impatient humour.

Enter *Biondello.*

Bion. Master, master! News! and such old
news as you never heard of!   31

Bap. Is it new and old too? How may that
be?

Bion. Why, is it not news to hear of Petruchio's coming?

Bap. Is he come?   35

Bion. Why, no, sir.

Bap. What then?

Bion. He is coming.

Bap. When will he be here?

Bion. When he stands where I am and sees
you there.   41

Tra. But say, what to thine old news?

Bion. Why, Petruchio is coming — in a new
hat and an old jerkin; a pair of old breeches
thrice turn'd; a pair of boots that have been
candle-cases, one buckled, another lac'd; an old
rusty sword ta'en out of the town armoury,
with a broken hilt, and chapeless; with two
broken points; his horse hipp'd, with an old
mothy saddle and stirrups of no kindred; besides possess'd with the glanders and like to
mose in the chine, troubled with the lampass,
infected with the fashions, full of windgalls,
sped with spavins, rayed with the yellows, past
cure of the fives, stark spoil'd with the staggers,
begnawn with the bots, sway'd in the back and
shoulder-shotten, near-legg'd before, and with
a half-cheek'd bit, and a headstall of sheep's
leather which, being restrain'd to keep him from
stumbling, hath been often burst, and now re-
paired with knots; one girth six times piec'd,
and a woman's crupper of velure, which hath
two letters for her name fairly set down in studs,
and here and there piec'd with packthread.

Bap. Who comes with him?   65

Bion. O, sir, his lackey, for all the world
caparison'd like the horse — with a linen stock
on one leg and a kersey boothose on the other,

gart'red with a red and blue list; an old hat,
and 'The Humour of Forty Fancies' prick'd
in't for a feather; a monster, a very monster in
apparel, and not like a Christian footboy or a
gentleman's lackey.

Tra. 'Tis some odd humour pricks him to
this fashion.
Yet oftentimes he goes but mean-apparell'd. 75

Bap. I am glad he's come, howsoe'er he
comes.

Bion. Why, sir, he comes not.

Bap. Didst thou not say he comes?

Bion. Who? that Petruchio came?

Bap. Ay, that Petruchio came. 80

Bion. No, sir. I say his horse comes with
him on his back.

Bap. Why, that's all one.

Bion. Nay, by Saint Jamy,
I hold you a penny, 85
A horse and a man
Is more than one,
And yet not many.

Enter *Petruchio* and *Grumio.*

Pet. Come, where be these gallants? Who's
at home? 89

Bap. You are welcome, sir.

Pet.   And yet I come not well.

Bap. And yet you halt not.

Tra.   Not so well apparell'd
As I wish you were.

Pet. Were it better, I should rush in thus.
But where is Kate? Where is my lovely bride?
How does my father? Gentles, methinks you
frown; 95
And wherefore gaze this goodly company,
As if they saw some wondrous monument,
Some comet or unusual prodigy?

Bap. Why, sir, you know this is your wed-
ding day.
First were we sad, fearing you would not come;
Now sadder that you come so unprovided. 101
Fie! doff this habit, shame to your estate,
An eyesore to our solemn festival.

Tra. And tell us what occasion of import
Hath all so long detain'd you from your wife
And sent you hither so unlike yourself. 106

Pet. Tedious it were to tell, and harsh to
hear.
Sufficeth I am come to keep my word,
Though in some part enforced to digress;
Which at more leisure I will so excuse 110
As you shall well be satisfied withal.
But where is Kate? I stay too long from
her;

The morning wears; 'tis time we were at
church.

Tra. See not your bride in these unrevent
robes. 114
Go to my chamber; put on clothes of mine.

Pet. Not I, believe me! Thus I'll visit her.

Bap. But thus I trust you will not marry her.

Pet. Good sooth, even thus. Therefore ha'
done with words!
To me she's married, not unto my clothes.
Could I repair what she will wear in me 120
As I can change these poor accoutrements,
'Twere well for Kate and better for myself.
But what a fool am I to chat with you
When I should bid good morrow to my bride
And seal the title with a lovely kiss! 125
                    Exit [with Grumio].

Tra. He hath some meaning in his mad
attire.
We will persuade him, be it possible,
To put on better ere he go to church.

Bap. I'll after him and see the event of this.
                    Exeunt [Baptista, Gremio, and Attendants].

Tra. But to her love concerneth us to add
Her father's liking; which to bring to pass, 131
As I before imparted to your worship,
I am to get a man, whate'er he be —
It skills not much, we'll fit him to our turn —
And he shall be Vincentio of Pisa 135
And make assurance, here in Padua,
Of greater sums than I have promised.
So shall you quietly enjoy your hope
And marry sweet Bianca with consent.

Luc. Were it not that my fellow school-
master 140
Doth watch Bianca's steps so narrowly,
'Twere good, methinks, to steal our marriage;
Which once perform'd, let all the world say no,
I'll keep mine own despite of all the world.

Tra. That by degrees we mean to look into
And watch our vantage in this business. 146
We'll overreach the greybeard, Gremio,
The narrow-prying father, Minola,
The quaint musician, amorous Licio —
All for my master's sake, Lucentio. 150

Enter *Gremio.*

Signior Gremio, came you from the church?

Gre. As willingly as e'er I came from school.

Tra. And is the bride and bridegroom coming home?

Gre. A bridegroom say you? 'Tis a groom
indeed, 154
A grumbling groom, and that the girl shall find.

Tra. Curster than she? Why, 'tis impossible.

Gre. Why, he's a devil, a devil, a very fiend.
Tra. Why, she's a devil, a devil, the devil's dam.
Gre. Tut, she's a lamb, a dove, a fool to him!
I'll tell you, Sir Lucentio — when the priest
Should ask if Katherine should be his wife, 161
'Ay, by gogs-woons!' quoth he, and swore so loud
That, all amaz'd, the priest let fall the book;
And as he stoop'd again to take it up,
This mad-brain'd bridegroom took him such a cuff   165
That down fell priest and book, and book and priest.
'Now take them up,' quoth he, 'if any list!'
Tra. What said the wench when he arose again?
Gre. Trembled and shook; for-why he stamp'd and swore
As if the vicar meant to cozen him.   170
But after many ceremonies done,
He calls for wine. 'A health!' quoth he, as if
He had been aboard, carousing to his mates
After a storm; quaff'd off the muscadel
And threw the sops all in the sexton's face:
Having no other reason   176
But that his beard grew thin and hungerly
And seem'd to ask him sops as he was drinking.
This done, he took the bride about the neck
And kiss'd her lips with such a clamorous smack
That at the parting all the church did echo.   181
And I, seeing this, came thence for very shame,
And after me I know the rout is coming.
Such a mad marriage never was before.
Hark, hark! I hear the minstrels play.   185

Music plays.

Enter *Petruchio, Kate, Bianca, Hortensio,*
Baptista, [*Grumio, and* Train].

Pet. Gentlemen and friends, I thank you for your pains.
I know you think to dine with me to-day,
And have prepar'd great store of wedding cheer;
But so it is, my haste doth call me hence, 189
And therefore here I mean to take my leave.
Bap. Is't possible you will away to-night?
Pet. I must away to-day before night come.
Make it no wonder. If you knew my business,
You would entreat me rather go than stay.
And, honest company, I thank you all   195
That have beheld me give away myself
To this most patient, sweet, and virtuous wife.
Dine with my father, drink a health to me;
For I must hence — and farewell to you all.
Tra. Let us entreat you stay till after dinner.

Pet. It may not be.
Gre.   Let me entreat you. 201
Pet. It cannot be.
Kath.   Let me entreat you.
Pet. I am content.
Kath.   Are you content to stay?
Pet. I am content you shall entreat me stay;
But yet not stay, entreat me how you can. 205
Kath. Now if you love me, stay!
Pet.   Grumio, my horse!
Gru. Ay, sir, they be ready. The oats have eaten the horses.
Kath. Nay then,
Do what thou canst, I will not go to-day! 210
No, nor to-morrow! not till I please myself.
The door is open, sir; there lies your way;
You may be jogging whiles your boots are green.
For me, I'll not be gone till I please myself.
'Tis like you'll prove a jolly surly groom 215
That take it on you at the first so roundly.
Pet. O, Kate, content thee; prithee be not angry.
Kath. I will be angry. What hast thou to do?
Father, be quiet! He shall stay my leisure.
Gre. Ay, marry, sir, now it begins to work.
Kath. Gentlemen, forward to the bridal dinner.   221
I see a woman may be made a fool
If she had not a spirit to resist.
Pet. They shall go forward, Kate, at thy command.
Obey the bride, you that attend on her.   225
Go to the feast, revel and domineer,
Carouse full measure to her maidenhead,
Be mad and merry, or go hang yourselves!
But for my bonny Kate, she must with me.
Nay, look not big nor stamp nor stare nor fret!
I will be master of what is mine own.   231
She is my goods, my chattels; she is my house,
My household stuff, my field, my barn,
My horse, my ox, my ass, my anything!
And here she stands, touch her whoever dare.
I'll bring mine action on the proudest he   236
That stops my way in Padua. Grumio,
Draw forth thy weapon, we are beset with thieves!
Rescue thy mistress if thou be a man.
Fear not, sweet wench; they shall not touch thee, Kate!   240
I'll buckler thee against a million.

Exeunt Petruchio, Katherina. [*and Grumio*].
Bap. Nay, let them go! a couple of quiet ones.
Gre. Went they not quickly. I should die with laughing.

Tra. Of all mad matches never was the like.

Luc. Mistress, what's your opinion of your sister? 245

Bian. That, being mad herself, she's madly mated.

Gre. I warrant him, Petruchio is Kated.

Bap. Neighbours and friends, though bride and bridegroom wants For to supply the places at the table, You know there wants no junkets at the feast. Lucentio, you shall supply the bridegroom's place, 251 And let Bianca take her sister's room.

Tra. Shall sweet Bianca practise how to bride it?

Bap. She shall, Lucentio. Come, gentlemen, let's go. *Exeunt.*

[ACT IV. Scene I. Petruchio's *country house.*]

Enter *Grumio.*

Gru. Fie, fie on all tired jades, on all mad masters, and all foul ways! Was ever man so beaten? Was ever man so ray'd? Was ever man so weary? I am sent before to make a fire, and they are coming after to warm them. Now were not I a little pot and soon hot, my very lips might freeze to my teeth, my tongue to the roof of my mouth, my heart in my belly, ere I should come by a fire to thaw me. But I with blowing the fire shall warm myself; for, considering the weather, a taller man than I will take cold. Holla, ho! Curtis! 12

Enter *Curtis.*

Curt. Who is that calls so coldly?

Gru. A piece of ice. If thou doubt it, thou mayst slide from my shoulder to my heel with no greater a run but my head and my neck. A fire, good Curtis! 17

Curt. Is my master and his wife coming, Grumio?

Gru. O, ay, Curtis, ay! and therefore fire, fire! Cast on no water. 21

Curt. Is she so hot a shrew as she's reported?

Gru. She was, good Curtis, before this frost; but thou know'st winter tames man, woman, and beast; for it hath tam'd my old master, and my new mistress, and myself, fellow Curtis.

Curt. Away, you three-inch fool! I am no beast. 28

Gru. Am I but three inches? Why, thy horn is a foot, and so long am I at the least. But wilt thou make a fire, or shall I complain on thee to our mistress? whose hand (she being now at hand) thou shalt soon feel, to thy cold comfort, for being slow in thy hot office. 34

Curt. I prithee, good Grumio, tell me, how goes the world?

Gru. A cold world, Curtis, in every office but thine; and therefore fire! Do thy duty, and have thy duty; for my master and mistress are almost frozen to death. 40

Curt. There's fire ready; and therefore, good Grumio, the news!

Gru. Why, 'Jack, boy! ho, boy!' and as much news as wilt thou. 44

Curt. Come, you are so full of cony-catching!

Gru. Why, therefore fire! for I have caught extreme cold. Where's the cook? Is supper ready, the house trimm'd, rushes strew'd, cobwebs swept, the servingmen in their new fustian, their white stockings, and every officer his wedding garment on? Be the Jacks fair within, the Gills fair without, the carpets laid, and everything in order?

Curt. All ready; and therefore, I pray thee, news! 55

Gru. First, know my horse is tired, my master and mistress fall'n out.

Curt. How?

Gru. Out of their saddles into the dirt, and thereby hangs a tale. 60

Curt. Let's ha't, good Grumio.

Gru. Lend thine ear.

Curt. Here.

Gru. There! [*Cuffs him.*] 64

Curt. This is to feel a tale, not to hear a tale.

Gru. And therefore 'tis call'd a sensible tale, and this cuff was but to knock at your ear and beseech list'ning. Now I begin: Inprimis, we came down a foul hill, my master riding behind my mistress — 70

Curt. Both of one horse?

Gru. What's that to thee?

Curt. Why, a horse!

Gru. Tell thou the tale! But hadst thou not cross'd me, thou shouldst have heard how her horse fell, and she under her horse; thou shouldst have heard in how miry a place, how she was bemoil'd, how he left her with the horse upon her, how he beat me because her horse stumbled, how she waded through the dirt to pluck him off me; how he swore, how she pray'd that never pray'd before; how I cried, how the horses ran away, how her bridle was burst; how I lost my crupper — with many things of worthy memory, which now shall die in oblivion, and thou return unexperienc'd to thy grave.   86

Curt. By this reck'ning, he is more shrew than she.

Gru. Ay! and that thou and the proudest of you all shall find when he comes home. But what talk I of this? Call forth Nathaniel, Joseph, Nicholas, Philip, Walter, Sugarsop, and the rest. Let their heads be slickly comb'd, their blue coats brush'd, and their garters of an indifferent knit. Let them curtsy with their left legs, and not presume to touch a hair of my master's horse-tail till they kiss their hands. Are they all ready?   97

Curt. They are.

Gru. Call them forth.

Curt. Do you hear, ho? You must meet my master, to countenance my mistress!   101

Gru. Why, she hath a face of her own.

Curt. Who knows not that?

Gru. Thou, it seems, that calls for company to countenance her.   105

Curt. I call them forth to credit her.

Gru. Why, she comes to borrow nothing of them.

Enter four or five *Servingmen.*

Nathaniel. Welcome home, Grumio!

Philip. How now, Grumio?   110

Joseph. What, Grumio?

Nick. Fellow Grumio!

Nathaniel. How now, old lad?

Gru. Welcome, you! — How now, you! — What, you! — Fellow, you! — and thus much for greeting. Now, my spruce companions, is all ready, and all things neat?   117

Nathaniel. All things is ready. How near is our master?

Gru. E'en at hand, alighted by this; and therefore be not — Cock's passion, silence! I hear my master.   122

Enter *Petruchio* and *Kate.*

Pet. Where be these knaves? What, no man at door
To hold my stirrup nor to take my horse?
Where is Nathaniel, Gregory, Philip?   125

All Serv. Here! here, sir! here, sir!

Pet. Here, sir! here, sir! here, sir! here, sir! You loggerheaded and unpolish'd grooms!

What, no attendance? no regard? no duty?
Where is the foolish knave I sent before?   130

Gru. Here, sir, as foolish as I was before.

Pet. You peasant swain! you whoreson malt-horse drudge!
Did I not bid thee meet me in the park
And bring along these rascal knaves with thee?

Gru. Nathaniel's coat, sir, was not fully made,   135
And Gabriel's pumps were all unpink'd i' th' heel;
There was no link to colour Peter's hat,
And Walter's dagger was not come from sheathing.
There were none fine but Adam, Ralph, and Gregory;
The rest were ragged, old, and beggarly.   140
Yet, as they are, here are they come to meet you.

Pet. Go, rascals, go, and fetch my supper in.
Exeunt [some of the] Servants. *[Petruchio sings.]*

Where is the life that late I led?
Where are those —

Sit down, Kate, and welcome. Soud, soud, soud, soud!   145

Enter *Servants* with supper.

Why, when, I say! Nay, good sweet Kate, be merry.
Off with my boots, you rogues! you villains, when?   *[Sings.]*

It was the friar of orders grey,
As he forth walked on his way.

Out, you rogue! you pluck my foot awry.   150
Take that, and mend the plucking off the other.
[Strikes him.]
Be merry, Kate. Some water, here! what, ho!

Enter *one with water.*

Where's my spaniel Troilus? Sirrah, get you hence
And bid my cousin Ferdinand come hither.
[Exit Servant.]
One, Kate, that you must kiss and be acquainted with.   155
Where are my slippers? Shall I have some water?
Come, Kate, and wash, and welcome heartily.
You whoreson villain! will you let it fall?
[Strikes him.]

Kath. Patience, I pray you. 'Twas a fault unwilling.

Pet. A whoreson, beetle-headed, flap-ear'd
knave! 160
Come, Kate, sit down; I know you have a
stomach.
Will you give thanks, sweet Kate, or else shall I?
What's this? mutton?
1. Serv. Ay.
Pet. Who brought it?
Peter. I.
Pet. 'Tis burnt, and so is all the meat. 164
What dogs are these! Where is the rascal cook?
How durst you villains bring it from the dresser
And serve it thus to me that love it not?
There, take it to you — trenchers, cups, and all.
[*Throws the meat &c. at them.*]
You heedless joltheads and unmanner'd slaves!
What, do you grumble? I'll be with you
straight. 170
[*Exeunt Servants.*]
Kath. I pray you, husband, be not so dis-
quiet.
The meat was well, if you were so contented.
Pet. I tell thee, Kate, 'twas burnt and dried
away,
And I expressly am forbid to touch it;
For it engenders choler, planteth anger, 175
And better 'twere that both of us did fast,
Since, of ourselves, ourselves are choleric,
Than feed it with such over-roasted flesh.
Be patient. To-morrow 't shall be mended,
And for this night we'll fast for company. 180
Come, I will bring thee to thy bridal chamber.
Exeunt.

Enter *Servants* severally.

Nathaniel. Peter, didst ever see the like?
Peter. He kills her in her own humour.

Enter *Curtis, a Servant.*

Gru. Where is he?
Curt. In her chamber, making a sermon of
continency to her; 186
And rails and swears and rates, that she, poor
soul,
Knows not which way to stand, to look, to
speak,
And sits as one new risen from a dream. 189
Away, away! for he is coming hither. [*Exeunt.*]

Enter *Petruchio.*

Pet. Thus have I politicly begun my reign,
And 'tis my hope to end successfully.
My falcon now is sharp, and passing empty,
And till she stoop she must not be full-gorg'd,
For then she never looks upon her lure. 195

Another way I have to man my haggard,
To make her come, and know her keeper's call:
That is, to watch her, as we watch these kites
That bate and beat and will not be obedient.
She eat no meat to-day, nor none shall eat; 200
Last night she slept not, nor to-night she shall
not.
As with the meat, some undeserved fault
I'll find about the making of the bed;
And here I'll fling the pillow, there the bolster,
This way the coverlet, another way the sheets.
Ay, and amid this hurly I intend 206
That all is done in reverend care of her;
And in conclusion, she shall watch all night;
And if she chance to nod, I'll rail and brawl
And with the clamour keep her still awake. 210
This is a way to kill a wife with kindness,
And thus I'll curb her mad and headstrong
humour.
He that knows better how to tame a shrew,
Now let him speak: 'tis charity to shew. *Exit.*

[Scene II. *Padua. Before* Baptista's
house.]

Enter *Tranio* [as *Lucentio*] and *Hortensio*
[as *Licio*].

Tra. Is't possible, friend Licio, that Mistress
Bianca
Doth fancy any other but Lucentio?
I tell you, sir, she bears me fair in hand.
Hor. Sir, to satisfy you in what I have said,
Stand by and mark the manner of his teaching.
[*They stand aside.*]

Enter *Bianca* [and *Lucentio* as *Cambio*].

Luc. Now, mistress, profit you in what you
read? 6
Bian. What, master, read you? First resolve
me that.
Luc. I read that I profess, 'The Art to Love.'
Bian. And may you prove, sir, master of
your art!
Luc. While you, sweet dear, prove mistress
of my heart! 10
[*They step aside.*]
Hor. Quick proceeders, marry! Now tell
me, I pray,
You that durst swear that your mistress Bianca
Lov'd none in the world so well as Lucentio!
Tra. O despiteful love! unconstant woman-
kind!
I tell thee, Licio, this is wonderful. 15

Hor. Mistake no more. I am not Licio,
Nor a musician, as I seem to be,
But one that scorn to live in this disguise
For such a one as leaves a gentleman
And makes a god of such a cullion.   20
Know, sir, that I am call'd Hortensio.
  Tra. Signior Hortensio, I have often heard
Of your entire affection to Bianca;
And since mine eyes are witness of her light-
    ness,
I will with you, if you be so contented,   25
Forswear Bianca and her love for ever.
  Hor. See how they kiss and court! Signior
    Lucentio,
Here is my hand, and here I firmly vow
Never to woo her more, but do forswear her,
As one unworthy all the former favours   30
That I have fondly flatter'd her withal.
  Tra. And here I take the like unfeigned oath,
Never to marry with her though she would
    entreat.
Fie on her! See how beastly she doth court him!
  Hor. Would all the world but he had quite
    forsworn!   35
For me, that I may surely keep mine oath,
I will be married to a wealthy widow,
Ere three days pass, which hath as long lov'd me
As I have lov'd this proud disdainful haggard.
And so farewell, Signior Lucentio.   40
Kindness in women, not their beauteous looks,
Shall win my love. And so I take my leave,
In resolution as I swore before.   [*Exit.*]
  Tra. Mistress Bianca, bless you with such
    grace
As 'longeth to a lover's blessed case!   45
Nay, I have ta'en you napping, gentle love,
And have forsworn you with Hortensio.
  Bian. Tranio, you jest, But have you both
    forsworn me?
  Tra. Mistress, we have.
  Luc.   Then we are rid of Licio.
  Tra. I' faith, he'll have a lusty widow now
That shall be woo'd and wedded in a day.   51
  Bian. God give him joy!
  Tra. Ay, and he'll tame her.
  Bian.   He says so, Tranio.
  Tra. Faith, he is gone unto the taming
    school.
  Bian. The taming school? What, is there
    such a place?   55
  Tra. Ay, mistress, and Petruchio is the
    master,
That teacheth tricks eleven-and-twenty long,
To tame a shrew and charm her chattering
    tongue.

Enter *Biondello.*

  Bion. O master, master, I have watch'd so
    long   60
That I am dog-weary! but at last I spied
An ancient angel coming down the hill
Will serve the turn.
  Tra.   What is he, Biondello?
  Bion. Master, a mercatante, or a pedant —
I know not what; but formal in apparel,
In gait and countenance surely like a father. 65
  Luc. And what of him, Tranio?
  Tra. If he be credulous and trust my tale,
I'll make him glad to seem Vincentio
And give assurance to Baptista Minola,
As if he were the right Vincentio.   70
Take in your love, and then let me alone.
    [*Exeunt Lucentio and Bianca.*]

Enter a *Pedant.*

  Ped. God save you, sir.
  Tra.   And you, sir. You are welcome.
Travel you far on, or are you at the farthest?
  Ped. Sir, at the farthest for a week or two;
But then up farther, and as far as Rome;   75
And so to Tripoli, if God lend me life.
  Tra. What countryman, I pray?
  Ped.   Of Mantua.
  Tra. Of Mantua, sir? Marry, God forbid,
And come to Padua, careless of your life!
  Ped. My life, sir? How, I pray? For that
    goes hard.   80
  Tra. 'Tis death for any one in Mantua
To come to Padua. Know you not the cause?
Your ships are stay'd at Venice; and the Duke,
For private quarrel 'twixt your Duke and him,
Hath publish'd and proclaim'd it openly.   85
'Tis marvel, but that you are but newly come;
You might have heard it else proclaim'd about.
  Ped. Alas, sir, it is worse for me than so!
For I have bills for money by exchange
From Florence, and must here deliver them. 90
  Tra. Well, sir, to do you courtesy,
This will I do, and this I will advise you:
First tell me, have you ever been at Pisa?
  Ped. Ay, sir, in Pisa have I often been,
Pisa, renowned for grave citizens.   95
  Tra. Among them know you one Vincentio?
  Ped. I know him not, but I have heard of
    him;
A merchant of incomparable wealth.
  Tra. He is my father, sir; and, sooth to say,
In count'nance somewhat doth resemble you.
  Bion. [*aside*] As much as an apple doth an
oyster, and all one!   101

349

Tra. To save your life in this extremity,
This favour will I do you for his sake;
And think it not the worst of all your fortunes
That you are like to Sir Vincentio. 105
His name and credit shall you undertake,
And in my house you shall be friendly lodg'd.
Look that you take upon you as you should.
You understand me, sir. So shall you stay
Till you have done your business in the city.
If this be court'sy, sir, accept of it. 111

Ped. O, sir, I do! and will repute you ever
The patron of my life and liberty.

Tra. Then go with me to make the matter
good.
This by the way I let you understand: 115
My father is here look'd for every day
To pass assurance of a dow'r in marriage
'Twixt me and one Baptista's daughter here.
In all these circumstances I'll instruct you.
Go with me, sir, to clothe you as becomes you.
Exeunt.

[Scene III. Petruchio's *house.*]

Enter *Katherina* and *Grumio.*

Gru. No, no, forsooth! I dare not for my life.
Kath. The more my wrong, the more his
spite appears.
What, did he marry me to famish me?
Beggars that come unto my father's door
Upon entreaty have a present alms; 5
If not, elsewhere they meet with charity;
But I, who never knew how to entreat,
Nor never needed that I should entreat,
Am starv'd for meat, giddy for lack of sleep;
With oaths kept waking, and with brawling fed.
And that which spites me more than all these
wants — 11
He does it under name of perfect love;
As who should say, if I should sleep or eat,
'Twere deadly sickness or else present death.
I prithee go and get me some repast; 15
I care not what, so it be wholesome food.
Gru. What say you to a neat's foot?
Kath. 'Tis passing good. I prithee let me
have it.
Gru. I fear it is too choleric a meat.
How say you to a fat tripe finely broil'd? 20
Kath. I like it well. Good Grumio, fetch it
me.
Gru. I cannot tell. I fear 'tis choleric.
What say you to a piece of beef and mustard?
Kath. A dish that I do love to feed upon.

Gru. Ay, but the mustard is too hot a little.
Kath. Why then, the beef! and let the mus-
tard rest. 26
Gru. Nay then, I will not. You shall have
the mustard,
Or else you get no beef of Grumio.
Kath. Then both, or one, or anything thou
wilt.
Gru. Why then, the mustard without the
beef. 30
Kath. Go, get thee gone, thou false deluding
slave, *Beats him.*
That feed'st me with the very name of meat.
Sorrow on thee and all the pack of you
That triumph thus upon my misery!
Go, get thee gone, I say! 35

Enter *Petruchio* and *Hortensio* with meat.

Pet. How fares my Kate? What, sweeting,
all amort?
Hor. Mistress, what cheer?
Kath. Faith, as cold as can be.
Pet. Pluck up thy spirits; look cheerfully
upon me.
Here, love; thou seest how diligent I am,
To dress thy meat myself and bring it thee. 40
I am sure, sweet Kate, this kindness merits
thanks.
What, not a word? Nay then, thou lov'st it
not,
And all my pains is sorted to no proof.
Here, take away this dish.
Kath. I pray you let it stand.
Pet. The poorest service is repaid with
thanks; 45
And so shall mine before you touch the meat.
Kath. I thank you, sir.
Hor. Signior Petruchio, fie! you are to blame.
Come, Mistress Kate, I'll bear you company.
Pet. [*aside to Hortensio*] Eat it up all, Hor-
tensio, if thou lovest me. 50
[*To Katherine*] Much good do it unto thy gentle
heart!
Kate, eat apace. And now, my honey love,
Will we return unto thy father's house,
And revel it as bravely as the best 54
With silken coats and caps, and golden rings,
With ruffs and cuffs and fardingales and things,
With scarfs and fans and double change of
brav'ry,
With amber bracelets, beads, and all this
knav'ry.
What, hast thou din'd? The tailor stays thy
leisure,
To deck thy body with his ruffling treasure. 60

350

Enter *Tailor*.

Come, tailor, let us see these ornaments.
Lay forth the gown.

Enter *Haberdasher*.

What news with you, sir?

Hab. Here is the cap your worship did bespeak.

Pet. Why, this was moulded on a porringer!
A velvet dish! Fie, fie, 'tis lewd and filthy! 65
Why, 'tis a cockle or a walnut shell,
A knack, a toy, a trick, a baby's cap.
Away with it! Come, let me have a bigger.

Kath. I'll have no bigger. This doth fit the time,
And gentlewomen wear such caps as these. 70

Pet. When you are gentle, you shall have one too,
And not till then.

Hor. [*aside*] That will not be in haste.

Kath. Why, sir, I trust I may have leave to speak,
And speak I will! I am no child, no babe.
Your betters have endur'd me say my mind, 75
And if you cannot, best you stop your ears.
My tongue will tell the anger of my heart,
Or else my heart, concealing it, will break;
And rather than it shall, I will be free
Even to the uttermost, as I please, in words. 80

Pet. Why, thou say'st true. It is a paltry cap,
A custard coffin, a bauble, a silken pie.
I love thee well in that thou lik'st it not.

Kath. Love me or love me not, I like the cap;
And it I will have, or I will have none. 85
[*Exit Haberdasher.*]

Pet. Thy gown? Why, ay. Come, tailor, let us see't.
O mercy, God! what masquing stuff is here?
What's this? a sleeve? 'Tis like a demi-cannon!
What, up and down carv'd like an apple tart?
Here's snip and nip and cut, and slish and slash,
Like to a censer in a barber's shop. 91
Why, what a devil's name, tailor, call'st thou this?

Hor. [*aside*] I see she's like to have neither cap nor gown.

Tai. You bid me make it orderly and well,
According to the fashion and the time. 95

Pet. Marry, and did; but if you be remem-b'red,
I did not bid you mar it to the time.
Go hop me over every kennel home,

For you shall hop without my custom, sir. 99
I'll none of it. Hence! make your best of it.

Kath. I never saw a better-fashion'd gown,
More quaint, more pleasing, nor more commendable.
Belike you mean to make a puppet of me.

Pet. Why, true! he means to make a puppet of thee.

Tai. She says your worship means to make a puppet of her. 106

Pet. O monstrous arrogance! Thou liest, thou thread, thou thimble,
Thou yard, three-quarters, half-yard, quarter, nail!
Thou flea, thou nit, thou winter cricket thou!
Brav'd in mine own house with a skein of thread? 111
Away, thou rag, thou quantity, thou remnant,
Or I shall so bemete thee with thy yard
As thou shalt think on prating whilst thou liv'st!
I tell thee, I, that thou hast marr'd her gown.

Tai. Your worship is deceiv'd. The gown is made 116
Just as my master had direction.
Grumio gave order how it should be done.

Gru. I gave him no order. I gave him the stuff.

Tai. But how did you desire it should be made? 120

Gru. Marry, sir, with needle and thread.

Tai. But did you not request to have it cut?

Gru. Thou hast fac'd many things.

Tai. I have. 124

Gru. Face not me. Thou hast brav'd many men; brave not me. I will neither be fac'd nor brav'd. I say unto thee, I bid thy master cut out the gown, but I did not bid him cut it to pieces. Ergo, thou liest.

Tai. Why, here is the note of the fashion to testify. 131

Pet. Read it.

Gru. The note lies in 's throat if he say I said so.

Tai. [*reads*] 'Inprimis, a loose-bodied gown' — 135

Gru. Master, if ever I said loose-bodied gown, sew me in the skirts of it and beat me to death with a bottom of brown thread. I said a gown.

Pet. Proceed.

Tai. [*reads*] 'With a small compass'd cape'—

Gru. I confess the cape. 141

Tai. [*reads*] 'With a trunk sleeve' —

Gru. I confess two sleeves.

Tai. [*reads*] 'The sleeves curiously cut.'

Pet. Ay, there's the villany! 145

Gru. Error i' th' bill, sir! error i' th' bill! I commanded the sleeves should be cut out and sew'd up again; and that I'll prove upon thee, though thy little finger be armed in a thimble.

Tai. This is true that I say. An I had thee in place where, thou shouldst know it. 151

Gru. I am for thee straight. Take thou the bill, give me thy mete-yard, and spare not me.

Hor. God-a-mercy, Grumio! Then he shall have no odds. 155

Pet. Well, sir, in brief, the gown is not for me.

Gru. You are i' th' right, sir. 'Tis for my mistress.

Pet. [*to Tailor*] Go take it up unto thy master's use. 159

Gru. Villain, not for thy life! Take up my mistress' gown for thy master's use?

Pet. Why, sir, what's your conceit in that?

Gru. O, sir, the conceit is deeper than you think for.

Take up my mistress' gown to his master's use?

O, fie, fie, fie! 165

Pet. [*aside to Hortensio*] Hortensio, say thou wilt see the tailor paid.

[*To Tailor*] Go take it hence. Be gone, and say no more.

Hor. Tailor, I'll pay thee for thy gown tomorrow.

Take no unkindness of his hasty words.

Away, I say! commend me to thy master. 170

Exit Tailor.

Pet. Well, come, my Kate. We will unto your father's

Even in these honest mean habiliments.

Our purses shall be proud, our garments poor;

For 'tis the mind that makes the body rich;

And as the sun breaks through the darkest clouds, 175

So honour peereth in the meanest habit.

What, is the jay more precious than the lark

Because his feathers are more beautiful?

Or is the adder better than the eel

Because his painted skin contents the eye? 180

O, no, good Kate! Neither art thou the worse

For this poor furniture and mean array.

If thou account'st it shame, lay it on me.

And therefore frolic! We will hence forthwith

To feast and sport us at thy father's house. 185

Go call my men, and let us straight to him,

And bring our horses unto Long Lane end;

There will we mount, and thither walk on foot.

Let's see; I think 'tis now some seven o'clock,

And well we may come there by dinner time.

Kath. I dare assure you, sir, 'tis almost two,

And 'twill be supper time ere you come there.

Pet. It shall be seven ere I go to horse.

Look, what I speak, or do, or think to do,

You are still crossing it. Sirs, let 't alone. 195

I will not go to-day; and ere I do,

It shall be what o'clock I say it is.

Hor. Why, so! this gallant will command the sun! [*Exeunt.*]

[Scene IV. *Padua. Before* Baptista's *house.*]

Enter *Tranio* [as *Lucentio*]; and the *Pedant* dress'd like *Vincentio*, booted.

Tra. Sir, this is the house. Please it you that I call?

Ped. Ay, what else? and, but I be deceiv'd,

Signior Baptista may remember me

Near twenty years ago in Genoa,

Where we were lodgers at the Pegasus. 5

Tra. 'Tis well; and hold your own, in any case,

With such austerity as longeth to a father.

Enter *Biondello.*

Ped. I warrant you. But, sir, here comes your boy.

'Twere good he were school'd.

Tra. Fear you not him. Sirrah Biondello,

Now do your duty throughly, I advise you. 11

Imagine 'twere the right Vincentio.

Bion. Tut, fear not me.

Tra. But hast thou done thy errand to Baptista?

Bion. I told him that your father was at Venice, 15

And that you look'd for him this day in Padua.

Tra. Th'art a tall fellow. Hold thee that to drink. [*Gives money.*]

Enter *Baptista* and *Lucentio* [as *Cambio*].

Here comes Baptista. Set your countenance, sir.

Signior Baptista, you are happily met.

[*To the Pedant*] Sir, this is the gentleman I told you of. 20

I pray you stand good father to me now;

Give me Bianca for my patrimony.

Ped. Soft, son!

Sir, by your leave. Having come to Padua

To gather in some debts, my son Lucentio 25

Made me acquainted with a weighty cause

Of love between your daughter and himself
And, for the good report I hear of you,
And for the love he beareth to your daughter,
And she to him — to stay him not too long —
I am content, in a good father's care,   31
To have him match'd; and, if you please to
    like
No worse than I, upon some agreement
Me shall you find most ready and most willing
With one consent to have her so bestow'd; 35
For curious I cannot be with you,
Signior Baptista, of whom I hear so well.
  Bap. Sir, pardon me in what I have to say.
Your plainness and your shortness please me
    well.
Right true it is your son Lucentio here   40
Doth love my daughter, and she loveth him,
Or both dissemble deeply their affections;
And therefore, if you say no more than this,
That like a father you will deal with him,
And pass my daughter a sufficient dower, 45
The match is made, and all is done:
Your son shall have my daughter with consent.
  Tra. I thank you, sir. Where then do you
    know best
We be affied, and such assurance ta'en
As shall with either part's agreement stand? 50
  Bap. Not in my house, Lucentio; for you
    know
Pitchers have ears, and I have many servants;
Besides, old Gremio is heark'ning still,
And happily we might be interrupted.   54
  Tra. Then at my lodging, an it like you, sir.
There doth my father lie; and there this night
We'll pass the business privately and well.
Send for your daughter by your servant here;
My boy shall fetch the scrivener presently.
The worst is this, that at so slender warning 60
You are like to have a thin and slender pittance.
  Bap. It likes me well. Cambio, hie you home,
And bid Bianca make her ready straight;
And, if you will, tell what hath happened:
Lucentio's father is arriv'd in Padua,   65
And how she's like to be Lucentio's wife.
                      [*Exit Lucentio.*]
  Bion. I pray the gods she may with all my
    heart!
  Tra. Dally not with the gods, but get thee
    gone.
                      Exit [Biondello].
Signior Baptista, shall I lead the way?
Welcome! One mess is like to be your cheer;
Come, sir; we will better it in Pisa.   71
  Bap. I follow you.
        Exeunt [Tranio, Pedant, and Baptista].

Enter *Lucentio* and *Biondello.*

  Bion. Cambio.
  Luc. What say'st thou, Biondello?
  Bion. You saw my master wink and laugh
    upon you?   76
  Luc. Biondello, what of that?
  Bion. Faith, nothing; but has left me here
behind to expound the meaning or moral of his
signs and tokens.   80
  Luc. I pray thee moralize them.
  Bion. Then thus: Baptista is safe, talking
with the deceiving father of a deceitful son.
  Luc. And what of him?
  Bion. His daughter is to be brought by you
to the supper.   86
  Luc. And then?
  Bion. The old priest at Saint Luke's Church
is at your command at all hours.
  Luc. And what of all this?   90
  Bion. I cannot tell, except they are busied
about a counterfeit assurance. Take you as-
surance of her *cum privilegio ad imprimendum
solum.* To th' church! Take the priest, clerk,
and some sufficient honest witnesses.   95
If this be not that you look for, I have no more
    to say,
But bid Bianca farewell for ever and a day.
                      [*Going.*]
  Luc. Hear'st thou, Biondello?
  Bion. I cannot tarry. I knew a wench married in an afternoon as she went to the garden
for parsley to stuff a rabbit; and so may you,
sir; and so, adieu, sir. My master hath appointed me to go to Saint Luke's to bid the
priest be ready to come against you come with
your appendix.   *Exit.*
  Luc. I may and will, if she be so contented.
She will be pleas'd; then wherefore should I
    doubt?   108
Hap what hap may, I'll roundly go about her;
It shall go hard if Cambio go without her. *Exit.*

[Scene V. *A public road.*]

Enter *Petruchio, Kate, Hortensio,* [with
        Servants].

  Pet. Come on, a God's name! once more
    toward our father's.
Good Lord, how bright and goodly shines the
    moon!
  Kath. The moon? the sun. It is not moon-
light now.

Pet. I say it is the moon that shines so bright.

Kath. I know it is the sun that shines so bright. 5

Pet. Now by my mother's son, and that's myself,
It shall be moon, or star, or what I list,
Or ere I journey to your father's house.

[*To Servants*] Go on, and fetch our horses back again. —
Evermore cross'd and cross'd! nothing but cross'd! 10

Hor. [*aside to Katherina*] Say as he says, or we shall never go.

Kath. Forward, I pray, since we have come so far,
And be it moon, or sun, or what you please.
And if you please to call it a rush candle,
Henceforth I vow it shall be so for me. 15

Pet. I say it is the moon.

Kath. I know it is the moon.

Pet. Nay then, you lie! it is the blessed sun.

Kath. Then God be bless'd, it is the blessed sun!
But sun it is not when you say it is not,
And the moon changes even as your mind. 20
What you will have it nam'd, even that it is,
And so it shall be so for Katherine.

Hor. [*aside*] Petruchio, go thy ways; the field is won.

Pet. Well, forward, forward! thus the bowl should run,
And not unluckily against the bias. 25
But, soft! what company is coming here?

Enter *Vincentio.*

[*To Vincentio*] Good morrow, gentle mistress, where away?
Tell me, sweet Kate, and tell me truly too,
Hast thou beheld a fresher gentlewoman? 29
Such war of white and red within her cheeks!
What stars do spangle heaven with such beauty
As those two eyes become that heavenly face?
Fair lovely maid, once more good day to thee.
Sweet Kate, embrace her for her beauty's sake.

Hor. [*aside*] 'A will make the man mad to make a woman of him. 36

Kath. Young budding virgin, fair and fresh and sweet,
Whither away? or where is thy abode?
Happy the parents of so fair a child!
Happier the man whom favourable stars 40
Allot thee for his lovely bedfellow!

Pet. Why, how now, Kate? I hope thou art not mad.
This is a man, old, wrinkled, faded, withered,
And not a maiden, as thou say'st he is.

Kath. Pardon, old father, my mistaking eyes,
That have been so bedazzled with the sun 46
That everything I look on seemeth green.
Now I perceive thou art a reverent father.
Pardon, I pray thee, for my mad mistaking!

Pet. Do, good old grandsire, and withal make known 50
Which way thou travellest; if along with us,
We shall be joyful of thy company.

Vin. Fair sir, and you, my merry mistress,
That with your strange encounter much amaz'd me,
My name is call'd Vincentio, my dwelling Pisa,
And bound I am to Padua, there to visit 56
A son of mine, which long I have not seen.

Pet. What is his name?

Vin. Lucentio, gentle sir.

Pet. Happily met; the happier for thy son.
And now by law, as well as reverent age, 60
I may entitle thee my loving father:
The sister to my wife, this gentlewoman,
Thy son by this hath married. Wonder not,
Nor be not griev'd. She is of good esteem,
Her dowry wealthy, and of worthy birth; 65
Beside, so qualified as may beseem
The spouse of any noble gentleman.
Let me embrace with old Vincentio;
And wander we to see thy honest son,
Who will of thy arrival be full joyous. 70

Vin. But is this true? or is it else your pleasure,
Like pleasant travellers, to break a jest
Upon the company you overtake?

Hor. I do assure thee, father, so it is.

Pet. Come, go along, and see the truth hereof; 75
For our first merriment hath made thee jealous.

Exeunt [*Petruchio, Katherina, and Vincentio, with Servants*].

Hor. Well, Petruchio, this has put me in heart.
Have to my widow! and if she be froward,
Then hast thou taught Hortensio to be untoward. *Exit.*

Enter *Biondello, Lucentio,* and *Bianca.*
Gremio is out before.

Bion. Softly and swiftly, sir, for the priest is ready.

Luc. I fly, Biondello. But they may chance to need thee at home; therefore leave us.

Bion. Nay, faith, I'll see the church a your back and then come back to my master's as soon as I can. 7

Exeunt [*Lucentio, Bianca, and Biondello*].

Gre. I marvel Cambio comes not all this while.

Enter *Petruchio, Kate, Vincentio, Grumio,* with *Attendants.*

Pet. Sir, here's the door; this is Lucentio's house;
My father's bears more toward the market place. 10
Thither must I, and here I leave you, sir.

Vin. You shall not choose but drink before you go.
I think I shall command your welcome here,
And by all likelihood some cheer is toward. *Knock.*

Gre. They're busy within. You were best knock louder. 16

Pedant looks out of the window.

Ped. What's he that knocks as he would beat down the gate?

Vin. Is Signior Lucentio within, sir?

Ped. He's within, sir, but not to be spoken withal. 21

Vin. What if a man bring him a hundred pound or two to make merry withal?

Ped. Keep your hundred pounds to yourself. He shall need none so long as I live. 25

Pet. Nay, I told you your son was well beloved in Padua. Do you hear, sir? To leave frivolous circumstances, I pray you tell Signior Lucentio that his father is come from Pisa and is here at the door to speak with him. 30

Ped. Thou liest. His father is come from Padua and here looking out at the window.

Vin. Art thou his father?

Ped. Ay, sir. So his mother says, if I may believe her. 35

Pet. [*to Vincentio*] Why, how now, gentleman? Why, this is flat knavery to take upon you another man's name.

Ped. Lay hands on the villain. I believe 'a means to cozen somebody in this city under my countenance. 41

Enter *Biondello.*

Bion. I have seen them in the church together, God send 'em good shipping! But who is here? Mine old master, Vincentio! Now we are undone and brought to nothing. 45

Vin. Come hither, crackhemp.

Bion. I hope I may choose, sir.

Vin. Come hither, you rogue. What, have you forgot me? 50

Bion. Forgot you? No, sir. I could not forget you, for I never saw you before in all my life.

Vin. What, you notorious villain, didst thou never see thy master's father, Vincentio? 55

Bion. What, my old worshipful old master? Yes, marry, sir! See where he looks out of the window.

Vin. Is't so indeed? *He beats Biondello.*

Bion. Help, help, help! Here's a madman will murder me. [*Exit.*]

Ped. Help, son! help, Signior Baptista! 62 [*Exit above.*]

Pet. Prithee, Kate, let's stand aside and see the end of this controversy. [*They stand aside.*]

Enter *Pedant* with *Servants; Baptista, Tranio.*

Tra. Sir, what are you that offer to beat my servant? 66

Vin. What am I, sir? Nay, what are you, sir? O immortal gods! O fine villain! A silken doublet, a velvet hose, a scarlet cloak, and a copatain hat! O, I am undone, I am undone! While I play the good husband at home, my son and my servant spend all at the university.

Tra. How now? What's the matter?

Bap. What, is the man lunatic? 74

Tra. Sir, you seem a sober ancient gentleman by your habit, but your words show you a madman. Why, sir, what 'cerns it you if I wear pearl and gold? I thank my good father, I am able to maintain it.

Vin. Thy father? O villain! he is a sailmaker in Bergamo. 81

Bap. You mistake, sir; you mistake, sir. Pray what do you think is his name?

Vin. His name? As if I knew not his name! I have brought him up ever since he was three years old, and his name is Tranio. 86

Péd. Away, away, mad ass! His name is Lucentio; and he is mine only son, and heir to the lands of me, Signior Vincentio.   89

Vin. Lucentio? O, he hath murd'red his master! Lay hold on him, I charge you in the Duke's name. O my son, my son! Tell me, thou villain, where is my son Lucentio?

Tra. Call forth an officer.

[Enter one with an *Officer.*]

Carry this mad knave to the jail. Father Baptista, I charge you see that he be forthcoming.   96

Vin. Carry me to the jail?

Gre. Stay, officer! He shall not go to prison.

Bap. Talk not, Signior Gremio. I say he shall go to prison.   100

Gre. Take heed, Signior Baptista, lest you be cony-catch'd in this business. I dare swear this is the right Vincentio.

Ped. Swear if thou dar'st!

Gre. Nay, I dare not swear it.   105

Tra. Then thou wert best say that I am not Lucentio.

Gre. Yes, I know thee to be Signior Lucentio.

Bap. Away with the dotard! To the jail with him!   110

Vin. Thus strangers may be haled and abus'd.

O monstrous villain!

Enter *Biondello, Lucentio,* and *Bianca.*

Bion. O, we are spoil'd, and yonder he is! Deny him, forswear him, or else we are all undone.

Luc. Pardon, sweet father.   *Kneel.*

Vin.   Lives my sweet son? 115

Exeunt Biondello, Tranio, and Pedant, as fast as may be.

Bian. Pardon, dear father.

Bap.   How hast thou offended? Where is Lucentio?

Luc.   Here's Lucentio,

Right son unto the right Vincentio,

That have by marriage made thy daughter mine

While counterfeit supposes blear'd thine eyne.

Gre. Here's packing, with a witness, to deceive us all!   122

Vin. Where is that damned villain Tranio

That fac'd and brav'd me in this matter so?

Bap. Why, tell me, is not this my Cambio?

Bian. Cambio is chang'd into Lucentio. 126

Luc. Love wrought these miracles. Bianca's love

Made me exchange my state with Tranio,

While he did bear my countenance in the town;

And happily I have arriv'd at last   130

Unto the wished haven of my bliss.

What Tranio did, myself enforc'd him to.

Then pardon him, sweet father, for my sake.

Vin. I'll slit the villain's nose that would have sent me to the jail.   135

Bap. [*to Lucentio*] But do you hear, sir? Have you married my daughter without asking my good will?

Vin. Fear not, Baptista. We will content you; go to. But I will in, to be reveng'd for this villany.   *Exit.*

Bap. And I, to sound the depth of this knavery.   *Exit.*

Luc. Look not pale, Bianca. Thy father will not frown.   *Exeunt* [*Lucentio and Bianca*].

Gre. My cake is dough. But I'll in among the rest,   145

Out of hope of all but my share of the feast.

[*Exit.*]

Kath. Husband, let's follow, to see the end of this ado.

Pet. First kiss me, Kate, and we will.

Kath. What, in the midst of the street?

Pet. What, art thou asham'd of me?   150

Kath. No, sir, God forbid! but asham'd to kiss.

Pet. Why then, let's home again. Come, sirrah, let's away.

Kath. Nay, I will give thee a kiss [*kisses him*]. Now pray thee, love, stay.

Pet. Is not this well? Come, my sweet Kate. Better once than never, for never too late.

Exeunt.

[Scene II. Lucentio's *house.*]

Enter *Baptista, Vincentio, Gremio, the Pedant, Lucentio* and *Bianca,* [*Petruchio and Katherina, Hortensio*] and *Widow, Tranio, Biondello, Grumio;* the *Servingmen,* with *Tranio,* bringing in a banquet.

Luc. At last, though long, our jarring notes agree;

And time it is, when raging war is done,

To smile at scapes and perils overblown.

My fair Bianca, bid my father welcome,   4

While I with selfsame kindness welcome thine.

Brother Petruchio, sister Katherina,

And thou, Hortensio, with thy loving widow,

Feast with the best, and welcome to my house.

My banquet is to close our stomachs up   9
After our great good cheer. Pray you sit down;
For now we sit to chat as well as eat.
                              [*They sit.*]
Pet. Nothing but sit and sit, and eat and
  eat!
Bap. Padua affords this kindness, son
  Petruchio.
Pet. Padua affords nothing but what is kind.
Hor. For both our sakes I would that word
  were true.   15
Pet. Now, for my life, Hortensio fears his
  widow.
Wid. Then never trust me if I be afeard.
Pet. You are very sensible, and yet you miss
  my sense.
I mean Hortensio is afeard of you.
Wid. He that is giddy thinks the world turns
  round.   20
Pet. Roundly replied.
Kath.   Mistress, how mean you that?
Wid. Thus I conceive by him.
Pet. Conceives by me? How likes Hortensio
  that?
Hor. My widow says, thus she conceives her
  tale.
Pet. Very well mended. Kiss him for that,
  good widow.   25
Kath. 'He that is giddy thinks the world
  turns round' —
I pray you tell me what you meant by that.
Wid. Your husband, being troubled with a
  shrow,
Measures my husband's sorrow by his woe.
And now you know my meaning.   30
Kath. A very mean meaning.
Wid.   Right, I mean you.
Kath. And I am mean indeed, respecting you.
Pet. To her, Kate!
Hor. To her, widow!
Pet. A hundred marks, my Kate does put
  her down!   35
Hor. That's my office.
Pet. Spoke like an officer. Ha' to thee, lad!
                    Drinks to Hortensio.
Bap. How likes Gremio these quick-witted
  folks?
Gre. Believe me, sir, they butt together well.
Bian. Head and butt! An hasty-witted body
Would say your head and butt were head and
  horn.   41
Vin. Ay, mistress bride, hath that awakened
  you?
Bian. Ay, but not frighted me; therefore
  I'll sleep again.

Pet. Nay, that you shall not. Since you
  have begun,
Have at you for a bitter jest or two!   45
Bian. Am I your bird? I mean to shift my
  bush;
And then pursue me as you draw your bow.
You are welcome all.
        Exeunt Bianca, [Katherina, and Widow].
Pet She hath prevented me. Here, Signior
  Tranio,   49
This bird you aim'd at, though you hit her not.
Therefore a health to all that shot and miss'd!
Tra. O sir, Lucentio slipp'd me like his grey-
  hound,
Which runs himself, and catches for his master.
Pet. A good swift simile, but something
  currish.
Tra. 'Tis well, sir, that you hunted for your-
  self.   55
'Tis thought your deer does hold you at a bay.
Bap. O, O, Petruchio! Tranio hits you now.
Luc. I thank thee for that gird, good Tranio.
Hor. Confess, confess! Hath he not hit you
  here?
Pet. 'A has a little gall'd me, I confess;   60
And, as the jest did glance away from me,
'Tis ten to one it maim'd you two outright.
Bap. Now in good sadness, son Petruchio,
I think thou hast the veriest shrew of all.
Pet. Well, I say no; and therefore, for as-
  surance,   65
Let's each one send unto his wife,
And he whose wife is most obedient,
To come at first when he doth send for her,
Shall win the wager which we will propose.
Hor. Content. What is the wager?
Luc.   Twenty crowns.
Pet. Twenty crowns!   71
I'll venture so much of my hawk or hound,
But twenty times so much upon my wife.
Luc. A hundred then.
Hor.   Content.
Pet.   A match! 'tis done. 74
Hor. Who shall begin?
Luc.   That will I. Go, Biondello,
Bid your mistress come to me.
Bion.   I go.   *Exit.*
Bap. Son, I will be your half, Bianca comes.
Luc. I'll have no halves. I'll bear it all
  myself.

              Enter Biondello.

How now? what news?
Bion. Sir, my mistress sends you word   80
That she is busy and she cannot come.

357

Pet. How? She is busy, and she cannot come!
Is that an answer?
Gre. Ay, and a kind one too.
Pray God, sir, your wife send you not a worse.
Pet. I hope better. 85
Hor. Sirrah Biondello, go and entreat my wife
To come to me forthwith.
Exit Biondello.
Pet. O, ho! entreat her?
Nay, then she must needs come.
Hor. I am afraid, sir,
Do what you can, yours will not be entreated.

Enter *Biondello.*

Now where's my wife? 90
Bion. She says you have some goodly jest in hand.
She will not come; she bids you come to her.
Pet. Worse and worse! She will not come?
O vile,
Intolerable, not to be endur'd!
Sirrah Grumio, go to your mistress; 95
Say I command her come to me.
Exit [Grumio].
Hor. I know her answer.
Pet. What?
Hor. She will not.
Pet. The fouler fortune mine, and there an end.

Enter *Katherina.*

Bap. Now, by my holidam, here comes Katherina!
Kath. What is your will, sir, that you send for me? 100
Pet. Where is your sister, and Hortensio's wife?
Kath. They sit conferring by the parlour fire.
Pet. Go fetch them hither. If they deny to come,
Swinge me them soundly forth unto their husbands.
Away, I say, and bring them hither straight.
[Exit Katherina.]
Luc. Here is a wonder, if you talk of a wonder. 106
Hor. And so it is. I wonder what it bodes.
Pet. Marry, peace it bodes, and love, and quiet life,
An awful rule, and right supremacy,
And, to be short, what not that's sweet and happy. 110

Bap. Now, fair befall thee, good Petruchio!
The wager thou hast won; and I will add
Unto their losses twenty thousand crowns,
Another dowry to another daughter,
For she is chang'd, as she had never been. 115
Pet. Nay, I will win my wager better yet
And show more sign of her obedience,
Her new-built virtue and obedience.

Enter *Kate,* *Bianca,* and *Widow.*

See where she comes, and brings your froward wives
As prisoners to her womanly persuasion. 120
Katherine, that cap of yours becomes you not.
Off with that bauble, throw it under foot.
[She obeys.]
Wid. Lord let me never have a cause to sigh
Till I be brought to such a silly pass! 124
Bian. Fie, what a foolish duty call you this?
Luc. I would your duty were as foolish too.
The wisdom of your duty, fair Bianca,
Hath cost me a hundred crowns since supper time.
Bian. The more fool you for laying on my duty!
Pet. Katherine, I charge thee tell these head-strong women 130
What duty they do owe their lords and husbands.
Wid. Come, come, you're mocking! We will have no telling.
Pet. Come on, I say! and first begin with her.
Wid. She shall not.
Pet. I say she shall. And first begin with her.
Kath. Fie, fie! unknit that threat'ning unkind brow, 136
And dart not scornful glances from those eyes
To wound thy lord, thy king, thy governor!
It blots thy beauty as frosts do bite the meads,
Confounds thy fame as whirlwinds shake fair buds, 140
And in no sense is meet or amiable.
A woman mov'd is like a fountain troubled,
Muddy, ill-seeming, thick, bereft of beauty;
And while it is so, none so dry or thirsty
Will deign to sip or touch one drop of it. 145
Thy husband is thy lord, thy life, thy keeper,
Thy head, thy sovereign; one that cares for thee
And for thy maintenance; commits his body
To painful labour both by sea and land, 149
To watch the night in storms, the day in cold,
Whilst thou li'st warm at home, secure and safe;
And craves no other tribute at thy hands
But love, fair looks, and true obedience —

358

Too little payment for so great a debt.
Such duty as the subject owes the prince, 155
Even such a woman oweth to her husband;
And when she is froward, peevish, sullen, sour,
And not obedient to his honest will,
What is she but a foul contending rebel
And graceless traitor to her loving lord? 160
I am asham'd that women are so simple
To offer war where they should kneel for peace;
Or seek for rule, supremacy, and sway
When they are bound to serve, love, and obey.
Why are our bodies soft and weak and smooth,
Unapt to toil and trouble in the world, 166
But that our soft conditions and our hearts
Should well agree with our external parts?
Come, come, you froward and unable worms!
My mind hath been as big as one of yours, 170
My heart as great, my reason haply more,
To bandy word for word and frown for frown;
But now I see our lances are but straws,
Our strength as weak, our weakness past com-
   pare,
That seeming to be most which we indeed
   least are.   175

Then vail your stomachs, for it is no boot,
And place your hands below your husband's
   foot;
In token of which duty, if he please,
My hand is ready, may it do him ease.
  Pet. Why, there's a wench! Come on and
   kiss me, Kate.   180
  Luc. Well, go thy ways, old lad; for thou
   shalt ha't.
  Vin. 'Tis a good hearing when children are
   toward.
  Luc. But a harsh hearing when women are
   froward.
  Pet. Come, Kate, we'll to bed.
We three are married, but you two are sped.
[*To Lucentio*] 'Twas I won the wager, though
   you hit the white;   186
And being a winner, God give you good night!
                  Exit Petruchio [*with Katherina*].
  Hor. Now go thy ways. Thou hast tam'd a
   curst shrow.
  Luc. 'Tis a wonder, by your leave, she will
   be tam'd so.   [*Exeunt.*]

ALL'S WELL THAT ENDS WELL

For the text of ALL'S WELL THAT ENDS WELL the First Folio is our only authority. The date of composition is very uncertain. Much of the blank verse suggests a time much later than one would infer from the rhyming passages. Probably Shakespeare revised, and in part rewrote, an earlier play of his own. There is slight ground for the conjecture that the earlier play was from some other hand.

In its present form the play may be safely dated about 1602. In its earlier form it may have been the *Love Labour's Won* mentioned by Meres in 1598. That would be an appropriate title for it. On the other hand, one would expect *Love Labour's Won* to be more in the tone and temper of *Love's Labour's Lost*.

External evidence as to date is almost *nil*. In *The Weakest Goeth to the Wall* (printed in 1600), there is a Dutchman whose pet ejaculation is 'lustick,' and some regard Lafew's 'Lustick! as the Dutchman says' (ii, 3, 47), as an allusion to this character. But the article 'the' is probably generic, and Shakespeare must have been personally acquainted with many Dutchmen, to say nothing of his familiarity with stage Dutch or German. The Clown's mention of an earthquake (i, 3, 91), if read in the context, does not sound like anything that must needs have been suggested by the earthquake actually felt in England on December 24, 1601. However, even if these points are of no significance, they at least do not conflict with what is in any case a reasonable date.

The plot comes in the main from the *novella* of Beltramo de Rossiglione and Giglietta di Nerbone in Boccaccio's *Decameron* (iii, 9), as translated in Painter's *Palace of Pleasure* (1566). There are important changes, however. In the source, the king disappears from the story immediately after the marriage, and the girl corresponding to Diana (nameless) drops out as soon as she has played her part in the deception of Beltramo. She remains at Rome or Florence, having received a good *dot* from Giglietta (Helena). Giglietta stays away from home until she has borne twin sons. Then she returns to Rossiglione, presents herself to Count Beltramo with the infants in her arms, and shows him the ring. The occasion is a great feast that he is giving at his palace on All Saints' Day. He recognizes the ring, acknowledges the children as his own ('they were so like him'), and accepts Giglietta as his wife without demur, though with no great enthusiasm. The king is not present. There is no imbroglio about rings and no suggestion of a second marriage. The dowager Countess, one of Shakespeare's most delightful characters, is new. So are Lafew, Parolles, and the Clown.

To the Elizabethan theatre-goer ALL'S WELL was undoubtedly a romantic play with a happy ending. To some serious-minded moderns it appears to be ironic or even cynical, for they cannot accept the ending as happy. We sometimes forget that we are just as conventional as the Elizabethans, though with a different set of conventions, and that to Shakespeare, the practical playwright, the conventions of his age were rules of the game. We are not obliged to defend Bertram — we may detest and despise him if we like — but Helena was in love with him, and to Shakespeare's audience she was doubly fortunate, in winning the man of her choice and in making a brilliant marriage. If they had bothered their minds about the further history of the couple, they would doubtless have felt confident that Bertram had learned his lesson and would behave himself in the future. We are not obliged to enjoy the plot as a plot, but we can take comfort in the character of the Countess; we can enjoy the cleverness of Lavatch, who, though he is not a philosopher (like Touchstone) or a tragic chorus individualized (like Lear's fool), is as witty as any humourist has a right to be; we can associate with a genial gentleman in the person of Lafew; we can luxuriate in the magnificent new language, a veritable esperanto, which the poet has created to satisfy his own fondness for 'words, words, words' and to take the downfall of Parolles out of the sternly moral realm into the wonderland of fantastic comedy.

Parolles is one of Shakespeare's masterpieces. He has been called a fore-runner of Falstaff, but that description misses the mark. Falstaff is disinclined to underrate his own exploits, but he is not a braggart, for he is always a humourist in his boasting; in fact, he is an experienced professional soldier. Parolles is more like Pistol in high life. Like Pistol, he lacks a sense of humour. He has seen military service, but we are left dubious as to his previous record. That he is a coward is certain. He is a bit of a fop, and may pass (for analysis' sake) as a cross between the *miles gloriosus* and the parasite. When exposed and disgraced — shamed out of the army like the cudgelled Pistol in *Henry V* (v, 1, 92–94) — he resembles that 'ancient swaggerer' in refusing to be despondent. 'To England,' says Pistol,

> ' To England will I steal, and there I'll steal;
> And patches will I get unto these cudgell'd scars,
> And swear I got them in the Gallia wars.'

And note the rebound of Parolles (iv, 3, 373–375) — less spirited, but equally sanguine :

> ' Rust, sword! cool, blushes! and, Parolles, live
> Safest in shame! Being fool'd, by fool'ry thrive!
> There's place and means for every man alive.'

Joyce Redman in the role of Helena, whose quest
for her errant husband is the subject of the play

ALL'S WELL
THAT ENDS WELL

PHOTOGRAPHS BY ANGUS MCBEAN
PRODUCED BY MEMORIAL THEATRE COMPANY, STRATFORD-UPON-AVON

"Be thou blest, Bertram; and succeed thy father in manners, as in shape." The Countess of Rousillon (Rosalind Atkinson) bids farewell to her son Bertram (Michael Denison) as he departs for court (Act I, Scene I)

Below left: Asking advice of Parolles (Keith Mitchell), Bertram's rakehell comrade, who is to accompany him to the French court, Helena is rewarded with a barrage of cynical, scurrilous witticisms (Act I, Scene I)

Below right: "Then, I confess, here on my knee, before high heaven and you, that before you, and next unto high heaven, I love your son." Helena tells the gentle countess of her affection for Bertram (Act I, Scene III)

Above: "Youth, thou bearest thy father's face; frank nature, rather curious than in haste, hath well compos'd thee." The king (Alan Webb) welcomes Bertram de Rousillon as the youth arrives at court (*Act I, Scene II*)

Above: "An thy mind stand to 't, boy, steal away bravely." As Bertram's companions leave for the wars in Italy, Parolles suggests that he leave the court and join them (*Act II, Scene I*)

Left: "I am driven on by the flesh; and he must needs go that the devil drives." The clown, Lavache (Edward Atienza), explains to the Countess of Rousillon that he wishes to wed one of her serving women. Rinaldo, the steward (Geoffrey Bayldon) and the countess are amused by Lavache's avowal of love (*Act I, Scene III*)

"This is his Majesty, say your mind to him: a traitor you do look like; but such traitors his Majesty seldom fears." The king's confidant, Lafeu (Ralph Michael), presents Helena, who has claimed that a remedy she received from her deceased father, a physician, will cure the king's illness (Act II, Scene I)

Left: "But if I help, what do you promise me?" Helena makes a pact with the king whereby if she cannot cure him she will die, but if she is successful, he will give her in marriage to any man she shall choose among his courtiers (Act II, Scene I)

Right: "Sit, my preserver, by thy patient's side." Restored to health by Helena's remedy, the king expresses his gratitude and invites her to choose among his courtiers the husband he promised her if her medicine proved to be successful (Act II, Scene III)

Above: "I dare not say I take you; but I give me and my service, ever whilst I live, into your guiding power." Helena chooses Bertram from amongst the suitors assembled for her (*Act II, Scene III*)

Above: "Till I have no wife, I have nothing in France." Helena reads a bitter letter from Bertram, who has left for the wars in Italy and swears never to return while she still claims to be his wife. Lavache and the countess share her dismay (*Act III, Scene II*)

Right: "Come, pilgrim, I will bring you where you shall host." Disguised as a pilgrim, Helena has followed Bertram to Florence, where a widow (Nancye Stewart) and her daughter, Diana (Jill Dixon) offer her hospitality (*Act III, Scene IV*)

"By the hand of a soldier, I will undertake it." Eager to perform some feat of valor, Parolles promises to recover from the enemy a drum lost in battle *(Act III, Scene VI)*

To prove the cowardice of Parolles, Bertram and his companions trick him into believing that he has been captured by the enemy *(Act IV, Scene I)*

Above: Continuing their sport with Parolles, Bertram and his friends lead him to denounce his fellow officers *(Act IV, Scene III)*

Left: Lavache greets Parolles quizzically as the bedraggled warrior returns to Rousillon *(Act V, Scene II)*

Left: "This exceeding posting, day and nig must wear your spirits low." Pausing Marseille during the trip back to Franc Helena tries to cheer the weary wido whom she is bringing back as her serva *(Act V, Scene I)*

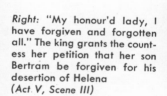

Right: "My honour'd lady, I have forgiven and forgotten all." The king grants the countess her petition that her son Bertram be forgiven for his desertion of Helena *(Act V, Scene III)*

Below: "He's guilty, and he's not guilty. He knows I am no maid, and he'll swear to 't." Diana's speech becomes cryptic as she tries to explain the romantic imbroglio to the angry monarch *(Act V, Scene III)*

"There is your ring." Helena proves that she is wife in fact as well as name (Act V, Scene III)

"If she, my liege, can make me know this clearly, I'll love her dearly, ever, ever dearly." All ends well as the elusive Bertram and Helena are finally united (Act V, Scene III)

ALL'S WELL THAT ENDS WELL

[Dramatis Personæ.

The *King of France*.
The *Duke of Florence*.
Bertram, Count of Rossillion.
Lafew, an old lord.
Parolles, a follower of *Bertram*.
Two French Lords in the Florentine service.
Rinaldo, steward to the *Countess*.
Lavatch, a clown, servant to the *Countess*.
A Page.

The *Dowager Countess of Rossillion*, mother to *Bertram*.
Helena, a gentlewoman, protected by the *Countess*.
A Widow of Florence.
Diana, her daughter.
Violenta, } neighbours and friends to the Widow.
Mariana, }
Lords, Soldiers, etc.

SCENE. — *Rossillion; Paris; Florence; Marseilles*.]

ACT I. Scene I. [*Rossillion. The* Count's *Palace*.]

Enter young *Bertram, Count of Rossillion*, his
Mother [the *Dowager Countess*], and *Helena*;
   Lord *Lafew* — all in black.

Countess. In delivering my son from me I
bury a second husband.

Ber. And I in going, madam, weep o'er my
father's death anew; but I must attend his
Majesty's command, to whom I am now in
ward, evermore in subjection.   6

Laf. You shall find of the King a husband,
madam; you, sir, a father. He that so generally is at all times good must of necessity hold
his virtue to you, whose worthiness would stir
it up where it wanted, rather than lack it where
there is such abundance.

Countess. What hope is there of his Majesty's
amendment?   14

Laf. He hath abandon'd his physicians,
madam; under whose practices he hath persecuted time with hope, and finds no other advantage in the process but only the losing of hope
by time.   18

Countess. This young gentlewoman had a
father — O, that 'had,' how sad a passage 'tis!
— whose skill was almost as great as his honesty; had it stretch'd so far, would have made
nature immortal, and death should have play
for lack of work. Would for the King's sake he
were living! I think it would be the death of
the King's disease.   26

Laf. How call'd you the man you speak of,
madam?

Countess. He was famous, sir, in his profession, and it was his great right to be so —
Gerard de Narbon.   31

Laf. He was excellent indeed, madam. The
King very lately spoke of him admiringly and
mourningly. He was skilful enough to have
liv'd still, if knowledge could be set up against
mortality.   36

Ber. What is it, my good lord, the King
languishes of?

Laf. A fistula, my lord.

Ber. I heard not of it before.   40

Laf. I would it were not notorious. Was this
gentlewoman the daughter of Gerard de Narbon?

Countess. His sole child, my lord, and bequeathed to my overlooking. I have those
hopes of her good that her education promises.
Her dispositions she inherits, which makes fair
gifts fairer; for where an unclean mind carries
virtuous qualities, their commendations go with
pity — they are virtues and traitors too. In her
they are the better for their simpleness. She
derives her honesty and achieves her goodness.

Laf. Your commendations, madam, get from
her tears.   54

Countess. 'Tis the best brine a maiden can
season her praise in. The remembrance of her
father never approaches her heart but the

tyranny of her sorrows takes all livelihood from
her cheek. No more of this, Helena. Go to, no
more! lest it be rather thought you affect a
sorrow than to have. 61
Hel. [*aside*] I do affect a sorrow indeed, but
I have it too.
Laf. Moderate lamentation is the right of the
dead; excessive grief the enemy to the living.
Countess. If the living be enemy to the grief,
the excess makes it soon mortal.
Laf. How understand we that?
Ber. Madam, I desire your holy wishes.
Countess. Be thou blest, Bertram, and suc-
ceed thy father 70
In manners, as in shape! Thy blood and virtue
Contend for empire in thee, and thy goodness
Share with thy birthright! Love all, trust a few,
Do wrong to none. Be able for thine enemy
Rather in power than use, and keep thy friend
Under thy own life's key. Be check'd for silence,
But never tax'd for speech. What heaven more
will,
That thee may furnish, and my prayers pluck
down,
Fall on thy head! — Farewell, my lord.
'Tis an unseason'd courtier; good my lord, 80
Advise him.
Laf. He cannot want the best
That shall attend his love.
Countess. Heaven bless him! Farewell, Ber-
tram. [*Exit.*]
Ber. [*to Helena*] The best wishes that can be
forg'd in your thoughts be servants to you! Be
comfortable to my mother, your mistress, and
make much of her. 87
Laf. Farewell, pretty lady. You must hold
the credit of your father.
[*Exeunt Bertram and Lafew.*]
Hel. O, were that all! I think not on my
father, 90
And these great tears grace his remembrance
more
Than those I shed for him. What was he like?
I have forgot him. My imagination
Carries no favour in't but Bertram's.
I am undone! There is no living, none, 95
If Bertram be away. 'Twere all one
That I should love a bright particular star
And think to wed it, he is so above me.
In his bright radiance and collateral light
Must I be comforted, not in his sphere. 100
Th' ambition in my love thus plagues itself.
The hind that would be mated by the lion
Must die for love. 'Twas pretty, though a
plague,

To see him every hour; to sit and draw
His arched brows, his hawking eye, his curls,
In our heart's table — heart too capable 106
Of every line and trick of his sweet favour.
But now he's gone, and my idolatrous fancy
Must sanctify his relics. Who comes here?

Enter Parolles.

One that goes with him. I love him for his
sake; 110
And yet I know him a notorious liar,
Think him a great way fool, solely a coward.
Yet these fix'd evils sit so fit in him
That they take place when virtue's steely bones
Look bleak i' th' cold wind. Withal, full oft
we see 115
Cold wisdom waiting on superfluous folly.
Par. Save you, fair queen!
Hel. And you, monarch!
Par. No.
Hel. And no. 120
Par. Are you meditating on virginity?
Hel. Ay. You have some stain of soldier in
you: let me ask you a question. Man is enemy
to virginity; how may we barricado it against
him?
Par. Keep him out. 125
Hel. But he assails, and our virginity, though
valiant in the defence, yet is weak. Unfold to us
some warlike resistance.
Par. There is none. Man, setting down before you, will undermine you and blow you up.
Hel. Bless our poor virginity from under-
miners and blowers-up! Is there no military
policy how virgins might blow up men? 133
Par. Virginity being blown down, man will
quicklier be blown up. Marry, in blowing him
down again, with the breach yourselves made
you lose your city. It is not politic in the commonwealth of nature to preserve virginity. Loss
of virginity is rational increase; and there was
never virgin got till virginity was first lost.
That you were made of, is metal to make virgins. Virginity by being once lost may be ten
times found; by being ever kept it is ever lost.
'Tis too cold a companion. Away with't!
Hel. I will stand for't a little, though therefore I die a virgin. 146
Par. There's little can be said in't; 'tis
against the rule of nature. To speak on the part
of virginity is to accuse your mothers, which is
most infallible disobedience. He that hangs
himself is a virgin: virginity murthers itself,
and should be buried in highways out of all
sanctified limit, as a desperate offendress against

nature. Virginity breeds mites, much like a cheese; consumes itself to the very paring, and so dies with feeding his own stomach. Besides, virginity is peevish, proud, idle, made of self-love, which is the most inhibited sin in the canon. Keep it not; you cannot choose but lose by't. Out with't! within ten year it will make itself ten, which is a goodly increase, and the principal itself not much the worse. Away with't! 162

Hel. How might one do, sir, to lose it to her own liking?

Par. Let me see. Marry, ill, to like him that ne'er it likes. 'Tis a commodity will lose the gloss with lying; the longer kept, the less worth. Off with't while 'tis vendible; answer the time of request. Virginity, like an old courtier, wears her cap out of fashion; richly suited, but unsuitable: just like the brooch and the toothpick, which wear not now. Your date is better in your pie and your porridge than in your cheek; and your virginity, your old virginity, is like one of our French wither'd pears: it looks ill, it eats drily. Marry, 'tis a wither'd pear; it was formerly better; marry, yet 'tis a wither'd pear! Will you anything with it? 178

Hel. Not my virginity yet. . . .
There shall your master have a thousand loves,
A mother, and a mistress, and a friend, 181
A phoenix, captain, and an enemy,
A guide, a goddess, and a sovereign,
A counsellor, a traitress, and a dear;
His humble ambition, proud humility, 185
His jarring concord, and his discord dulcet,
His faith, his sweet disaster; with a world
Of pretty, fond, adoptious christendoms
That blinking Cupid gossips. Now shall he —
I know not what he shall. God send him well!
The court's a learning place, and he is one —

Par. What one, i' faith?

Hel. That I wish well. 'Tis pity —

Par. What's pity? 194

Hel. That wishing well had not a body in't
Which might be felt; that we, the poorer born,
Whose baser stars do shut us up in wishes,
Might with effects of them follow our friends
And show what we alone must think, which never
Returns us thanks. 200

Enter *Page.*

Page. Monsieur Parolles, my lord calls for you. [*Exit.*]

Par. Little Helen, farewell. If I can remember thee, I will think of thee at court.

Hel. Monsieur Parolles, you were born under a charitable star. 205

Par. Under Mars I.

Hel. I especially think, under Mars.

Par. Why under Mars?

Hel. The wars have so kept you under that you must needs be born under Mars. 210

Par. When he was predominant.

Hel. When he was retrograde, I think rather.

Par. Why think you so?

Hel. You go so much backward when you fight.

Par. That's for advantage. 215

Hel. So is running away when fear proposes the safety. But the composition that your valour and fear makes in you is a virtue of a good wing, and I like the wear well. 219

Par. I am so full of businesses I cannot answer thee acutely. I will return perfect courtier; in the which my instruction shall serve to naturalize thee, so thou wilt be capable of a courtier's counsel and understand what advice shall thrust upon thee; else thou diest in thine unthankfulness, and thine ignorance makes thee away. Farewell. When thou hast leisure, say thy prayers; when thou hast none, remember thy friends. Get thee a good husband, and use him as he uses thee. So, farewell. [*Exit.*]

Hel. Our remedies oft in ourselves do lie, 231
Which we ascribe to heaven. The fated sky
Gives us free scope; only doth backward pull
Our slow designs when we ourselves are dull.
What power is it which mounts my love so high?
That makes me see, and cannot feed mine eye?
The mightiest space in fortune nature brings
To join like likes and kiss like native things.
Impossible be strange attempts to those 239
That weigh their pains in sense, and do suppose
What hath been cannot be. Who ever strove
To show her merit that did miss her love?
The King's disease — my project may deceive me,
But my intents are fix'd and will not leave me.
Exit.

[Scene II. *Paris. The* King's *Palace.*]

Flourish cornets. Enter the *King of France* with letters, and divers *Attendants.*

King. The Florentines and Senoys are by th' ears,
Have fought with equal fortune, and continue
A braving war.

1. Lord. So 'tis reported, sir.

King. Nay, 'tis most credible. We here receive it
A certainty vouch'd from our cousin Austria, 5
With caution, that the Florentine will move us
For speedy aid; wherein our dearest friend
Prejudicates the business, and would seem
To have us make denial.

1. Lord. His love and wisdom,
Approv'd so to your Majesty, may plead 10
For amplest credence.

King. He hath arm'd our answer,
And Florence is denied before he comes.
Yet for our gentlemen that mean to see
The Tuscan service, freely have they leave
To stand on either part.

2. Lord. It well may serve 15
A nursery to our gentry, who are sick
For breathing and exploit.

King. What's he comes here?

Enter *Bertram*, *Lafew*, and *Parolles*.

1. Lord. It is the Count Rossillion, my good
lord,
Young Bertram.

King. Youth, thou bear'st thy father's face.
Frank nature, rather curious than in haste, 20
Hath well compos'd thee. Thy father's moral
parts
Mayst thou inherit too! Welcome to Paris.

Ber. My thanks and duty are your Majesty's.

King. I would I had that corporal soundness
now
As when thy father and myself in friendship 25
First tried our soldiership! He did look far
Into the service of the time, and was
Discipled of the bravest. He lasted long;
But on us both did haggish age steal on,
And wore us out of act. It much repairs me 30
To talk of your good father. In his youth
He had the wit which I can well observe
To-day in our young lords; but they may jest
Till their own scorn return to them unnoted
Ere they can hide their levity in honour 35
So like a courtier. Contempt nor bitterness
Were in his pride or sharpness. If they were,
His equal had awak'd them; and his honour,
Clock to itself, knew the true minute when
Exception bid him speak, and at this time 40
His tongue obey'd his hand. Who were below
him
He us'd as creatures of another place;
And bow'd his eminent top to their low ranks,
Making them proud of his humility,
In their poor praise he humbled. Such a man

Might be a copy to these younger times, 46
Which, followed well, would demonstrate them
now
But goers backward.

Ber. His good remembrance, sir,
Lies richer in your thoughts than on his tomb.
So in approof lives not his epitaph 50
As in your royal speech.

King. Would I were with him! He would
always say —
Methinks I hear him now; his plausive words
He scatter'd not in ears, but grafted them
To grow there and to bear — 'Let me not
live' — 55
Thus his good melancholy oft began,
On the catastrophe and heel of pastime,
When it was out — 'Let me not live,' quoth he,
'After my flame lacks oil, to be the snuff
Of younger spirits, whose apprehensive senses
All but new things disdain; whose judgments
are 61
Mere fathers of their garments; whose constancies
Expire before their fashions.' This he wish'd.
I, after him, do after him wish too,
Since I nor wax nor honey can bring home, 65
I quickly were dissolved from m_ .ive,
To give some labourers room.

2. Lord. You're loved, sir.
They that least lend it you shall lack you first.

King. I fill a place, I know't. How long
is't, Count,
Since the physician at your father's died? 70
He was much fam'd.

Ber. Some six months since, my lord.

King. If he were living, I would try him yet.
Lend me an arm. The rest have worn me out
With several applications. Nature and sickness
Debate it at their leisure. Welcome, Count; 75
My son's no dearer.

Ber. Thank your Majesty.

Exeunt. Flourish.

[Scene III. *Rossillion. The* Count's
Palace.]

Enter *Countess*, *Steward*, and *Clown*.

Count. I will now hear. What say you of
this gentlewoman?

Stew. Madam, the care I have had to even
your content I wish might be found in the calendar of my past endeavours; for then we wound
our modesty, and make foul the clearness of our
deservings, when of ourselves we publish them.

Count. What does this knave here? Get you gone, sirrah. The complaints I have heard of you I do not all believe. 'Tis my slowness that I do not; for I know you lack not folly to commit them and have ability enough to make such knaveries yours.

Clown. 'Tis not unknown to you, madam, I am a poor fellow.   15

Count. Well, sir.

Clown. No, madam. 'Tis not so well that I am poor, though many of the rich are damn'd. But, if I may have your ladyship's good will to go to the world, Isbel the woman and I will do as we may.   21

Count. Wilt thou needs be a beggar?

Clown. I do beg your good will in this case.

Count. In what case?   24

Clown. In Isbel's case and mine own. Service is no heritage; and I think I shall never have the blessing of God till I have issue o' my body; for they say barnes are blessings.

Count. Tell me thy reason why thou wilt marry.   29

Clown. My poor body, madam, requires it. I am driven on by the flesh; and he must needs go that the devil drives.

Count. Is this all your worship's reason?

Clown. Faith, madam, I have other holy reasons, such as they are.   35

Count. May the world know them?

Clown. I have been, madam, a wicked creature, as you and all flesh and blood are, and indeed I do marry that I may repent.

Count. Thy marriage, sooner than thy wickedness.   41

Clown. I am out o' friends, madam, and I hope to have friends for my wive's sake.

Count. Such friends are thine enemies, knave.

Clown. Y'are shallow, madam, in great friends; for the knaves come to do that for me which I am aweary of. He that ears my land spares my team and gives me leave to inn the crop. If I be his cuckold, he's my drudge. He that comforts my wife is the cherisher of my flesh and blood; he that cherishes my flesh and blood loves my flesh and blood; he that loves my flesh and blood is my friend: ergo, he that kisses my wife is my friend. If men could be contented to be what they are, there were no fear in marriage; for young Charbon the Puritan and old Poysam the Papist, howsome'er their hearts are sever'd in religion, their heads are both one — they may jowl horns together like any deer i' th' herd.   59

Count. Wilt thou ever be a foul-mouth'd and calumnious knave?

Clown. A prophet I, madam, and I speak the truth the next way:

> For I the ballad will repeat,
>   Which men full true shall find: 65
> Your marriage comes by destiny,
>   Your cuckoo sings by kind.

Count. Get you gone, sir. I'll talk with you more anon.   69

Stew. May it please you, madam, that he bid Helen come to you. Of her I am to speak.

Count. Sirrah, tell my gentlewoman I would speak with her; Helen I mean.

Clown. 'Was this fair face the cause,' quoth she,
> 'Why the Grecians sacked Troy?   75
> Fond done, done fond!
>   Was this King Priam's joy?'
> With that she sighed as she stood,
> With that she sighed as she stood,
>   And gave this sentence then: 80
> 'Among nine bad if one be good,
> Among nine bad if one be good,
>   There's yet one good in ten.'

Count. What, one good in ten? You corrupt the song, sirrah.   85

Clown. One good woman in ten, madam; which is a purifying o' th' song. Would God would serve the world so all the year! We'd find no fault with the tithe woman, if I were the parson. One in ten, quoth 'a? An we might have a good woman born but for every blazing star, or at an earthquake, 'twould mend the lottery well. A man may draw his heart out ere 'a pluck one.

Count. You'll be gone, sir knave, and do as I command you.   95

Clown. That man should be at woman's command, and yet no hurt done! Though honesty be no Puritan, yet it will do no hurt. It will wear the surplice of humility over the black gown of a big heart. I am going forsooth! The business is for Helen to come hither.   *Exit.*

Count. Well now.

Stew. I know, madam, you love your gentlewoman entirely.   104

Count. Faith, I do. Her father bequeath'd her to me; and she herself, without other advantage, may lawfully make title to as much love as she finds. There is more owing her than is paid, and more shall be paid her than she'll demand.   109

Stew. Madam, I was very late more near her than I think she wish'd me. Alone she was, and did communicate to herself her own words to her own ears. She thought, I dare vow for her, they touch'd not any stranger sense. Her matter was, she loved your son. 'Fortune,' she said, 'was no goddess, that had put such difference betwixt their two estates; Love no god, that would not extend his might, only where qualities were level; Dian no queen of virgins, that would suffer her poor knight surpris'd without rescue in the first assault or ransom afterward.' This she deliver'd in the most bitter touch of sorrow that e'er I heard virgin exclaim in; which I held my duty speedily to acquaint you withal, sithence, in the loss that may happen, it concerns you something to know it. 126

Count. You have discharg'd this honestly. Keep it to yourself. Many likelihoods inform'd me of this before, which hung so tott'ring in the balance that I could neither believe nor misdoubt. Pray you leave me. Stall this in your bosom, and I thank you for your honest care. I will speak with you further anon.

Exit Steward.

Enter *Helen.*

Even so it was with me when I was young!
If ever we are nature's, these are ours. This thorn 135
Doth to our rose of youth rightly belong;
Our blood to us, this to our blood is born.
It is the show and seal of nature's truth
Where love's strong passion is impress'd in youth.
By our remembrances of days foregone, 140
Such were our faults, or then we thought them none.
Her eye is sick on't. I observe her now.

Hel. What is your pleasure, madam?

Count.   You know, Helen,
I am a mother to you. 144

Hel. Mine honourable mistress.

Count.   Nay, a mother.
Why not a mother? When I said 'a mother,'
Methought you saw a serpent. What's in 'mother'
That you start at it? I say I am your mother,
And put you in the catalogue of those
That were enwombed mine. 'Tis often seen 150
Adoption strives with nature, and choice breeds
A native slip to us from foreign seeds.
You ne'er oppress'd me with a mother's groan,
Yet I express to you a mother's care. 154
God's mercy, maiden! does it curd thy blood
To say I am thy mother? What's the matter,
That this distempered messenger of wet,

The many-colour'd Iris, rounds thine eye?
Why? that you are my daughter?

Hel.   That I am not.

Count. I say I am your mother.

Hel.   Pardon, madam. 160
The Count Rossillion cannot be my brother.
I am from humble, he from honoured name;
No note upon my parents, his all noble.
My master, my dear lord he is, and I
His servant live and will his vassal die. 165
He must not be my brother.

Count.   Nor I your mother?

Hel. You are my mother, madam. Would you were
(So that my lord your son were not my brother)
Indeed my mother! or were you both our mothers,
I care no more for than I do for heaven, 170
So I were not his sister! Can't no other,
But, I your daughter, he must be my brother?

Count. Yes, Helen, you might be my daughter-in-law.
God shield you mean it not! 'daughter' and 'mother' 174
So strive upon your pulse. What, pale again?
My fear hath catch'd your fondness. Now I see
The myst'ry of your loneliness and find
Your salt tears' head. Now to all sense 'tis gross —
You love my son. Invention is asham'd, 180
Against the proclamation of thy passion,
To say thou dost not. Therefore tell me true!
But tell me then, 'tis so; for look! thy cheeks
Confess it, th' one to th' other; and thine eyes
See it so grossly shown in thy behaviours
That in their kind they speak it. Only sin 185
And hellish obstinacy tie thy tongue,
That truth should be suspected. Speak, is't so?
If it be so, you have wound a goodly clew;
If it be not, forswear 't. Howe'er, I charge thee,
As heaven shall work in me for thine avail, 190
To tell me truly.

Hel.   Good madam, pardon me!

Count. Do you love my son?

Hel.   Your pardon, noble mistress!

Count. Love you my son?

Hel.   Do not you love him, madam?

Count. Go not about. My love hath in't a bond,
Whereof the world takes note. Come, come, disclose 195
The state of your affection, for your passions
Have to the full appeach'd.

Hel.   Then I confess
Here on my knee before high heaven and you,

368

That before you, and next unto high heaven,
I love your son.   200
My friends were poor but honest ; so's my love.
Be not offended, for it hurts not him
That he is lov'd of me. I follow him not
By any token of presumptuous suit ;
Nor would I have him till I do deserve him, 205
Yet never know how that desert should be.
I know I love in vain, strive against hope ;
Yet in this captious and intenible sieve
I still pour in the waters of my love
And lack not to lose still. Thus, Indian-like,
Religious in mine error, I adore   211
The sun, that looks upon his worshipper
But knows of him no more. My dearest madam,
Let not your hate encounter with my love
For loving where you do ; but if yourself,   215
Whose aged honour cites a virtuous youth,
Did ever in so true a flame of liking
Wish chastely and love dearly that your Dian
Was both herself and Love, O, then give pity
To her whose state is such that cannot choose
But lend and give where she is sure to lose ;
That seeks not to find that her search implies,
But, riddle-like, lives sweetly where she dies !
Count. Had you not lately an intent — speak
truly —   224
To go to Paris?
Hel.   Madam, I had.
Count.   Wherefore? Tell true.
Hel. I will tell truth, by grace itself I swear !
You know my father left me some prescriptions
Of rare and prov'd effects, such as his reading
And manifest experience had collected   229
For general sovereignty ; and that he will'd me
In heedfull'st reservation to bestow them,
As notes whose faculties inclusive were
More than they were in note. Amongst the rest
There is a remedy, approv'd, set down,   234

To cure the desperate languishings whereof
The King is render'd lost.
Count.   This was your motive
For Paris, was it? Speak.
Hel. My lord your son made me to think of
this ;
Else Paris and the medicine and the King
Had from the conversation of my thoughts 240
Happily been absent then.
Count.   But think you, Helen,
If you should tender your supposed aid,
He would receive it? He and his physicians
Are of a mind : he, that they cannot help him :
They, that they cannot help. How shall they
credit   245
A poor unlearned virgin, when the schools,
Embowell'd of their doctrine, have left off
The danger to itself?
Hel.   There's something in 't
More than my father's skill, which was the
great'st
Of his profession, that his good receipt   250
Shall for my legacy be sanctified
By th' luckiest stars in heaven : and, would
your honour
But give me leave to try success, I'd venture
The well-lost life of mine on his Grace's cure
By such a day and hour.
Count.   Dost thou believe 't?
Hel. Ay, madam, knowingly.   256
Count. Why, Helen, thou shalt have my
leave and love,
Means and attendants, and my loving greet-
ings
To those of mine in court. I'll stay at home
And pray God's blessing into thy attempt. 260
Be gone to-morrow ; and be sure of this,
What I can help thee to, thou shalt not miss.
Exeunt.

ACT II. [Scene I. *Paris. The* King's *Palace.*]

Enter the *King* [attended], with divers young
Lords taking leave for the Florentine war ;
[*Bertram*] *Count Rossillion*, and *Parolles.* Flour-
ish cornets.

King. Farewell, young lords ; these warlike
principles
Do not throw from you. And you, my lords,
farewell.
Share the advice betwixt you ; if both gain all,
The gift doth stretch itself as 'tis receiv'd
And is enough for both.

1. Lord.   'Tis our hope, sir·   5
After well-ent'red soldiers, to return
And find your Grace in health.
King. No, no, it cannot be. And yet my
heart
Will not confess he owes the malady
That doth my life besiege. Farewell, young
lords.   10
Whether I live or die, be you the sons
Of worthy Frenchmen. Let higher Italy
(Those bated that inherit but the fall
Of the last monarchy) see that you come

Not to woo honour, but to wed it. When 15
The bravest questant shrinks, find what you seek,
That fame may cry you loud. I say, farewell.

2. Lord. Health at your bidding serve your
  Majesty!

King. Those girls of Italy, take heed of them.
They say our French lack language to deny 20
If they demand. Beware of being captives
Before you serve.

Both.   Our hearts receive your warnings.

King. Farewell. [*To Attendants*] Come
  hither to me. [*Exit, led by Attendants.*]

1. Lord. O my sweet lord, that you will stay
  behind us!

Par. 'Tis not his fault, the spark.

2. Lord.   O, 'tis brave wars!

Par. Most admirable. I have seen those
  wars. 26

Ber. I am commanded here and kept a coil
  with —
'Too young,' and 'The next year,' and ''Tis too
  early.'

Par. An thy mind stand to't, boy, steal
  away bravely.

Ber. I shall stay here the forehorse to a
  smock, 30
Creaking my shoes on the plain masonry,
Till honour be bought up, and no sword worn
But one to dance with. By heaven, I'll steal
  away!

1. Lord. There's honour in the theft.

Par.   Commit it, Count.

2. Lord. I am your accessary; and so farewell. 35

Ber. I grow to you, and our parting is a
  tortur'd body.

1. Lord. Farewell, Captain.

2. Lord. Sweet Monsieur Parolles! 39

Par. Noble heroes, my sword and yours are
kin. Good sparks and lustrous, a word, good
metals: you shall find in the regiment of the
Spinii one Captain Spurio, with his cicatrice, an
emblem of war, here on his sinister cheek. It
was this very sword entrench'd it. Say to him
I live, and observe his reports for me. 46

1. Lord. We shall, noble Captain.

Par. Mars dote on you for his novices!
                    [*Exeunt Lords.*]
What will ye do?

[*Enter the King, led back to his chair by
  Attendants.*]

Ber. Stay — the King! 50

Par. Use a more spacious ceremony to the
noble lords. You have restrain'd yourself

within the list of too cold an adieu. Be more
expressive to them; for they wear themselves
in the cap of the time, there do muster true
gait; eat, speak, and move under the influence
of the most receiv'd star; and though the devil
lead the measure, such are to be followed. After
them! and take a more dilated farewell.

Ber. And I will do so. 60

Par. Worthy fellows! and like to prove most
sinewy swordmen.

        Exeunt [Bertram and Parolles].

        Enter *Lafew.*

Laf. [*kneels*] Pardon, my lord, for me and
  for my tidings!

King. I'll fee thee to stand up.

Laf. [*rises*] Then here's a man stands that
  has brought his pardon. 65
I would you had kneel'd, my lord, to ask me
  mercy,
And that at my bidding you could so stand up.

King. I would I had. So I had broke thy pate
And ask'd thee mercy for't.

Laf. Good faith, across! But, my good lord.
  'tis thus: 70
Will you be cur'd of your infirmity?

King. No.

Laf. O, will you eat no grapes, my royal fox?
Yes, but you will my noble grapes, an if
My royal fox could reach them. I have seen a
  medicine 75
That's able to breathe life into a stone,
Quicken a rock, and make you dance canary
With sprightly fire and motion; whose simple
  touch
Is powerful to araise King Pepin, nay,
To give great Charlemaine a pen in's hand, 80
And write to her a love-line.

King.   What her is this?

Laf. Why, Doctor She! My lord, there's one
  arriv'd,
If you will see her. Now by my faith and
  honour,
If seriously I may convey my thoughts
In this my light deliverance, I have spoke 85
With one that in her sex, her years, profession,
Wisdom and constancy, hath amaz'd me more
Than I dare blame my weakness. Will you see
  her,
For that is her demand, and know her business?
That done, laugh well at me.

King.   Now, good Lafew
Bring in the admiration, that we with thee 91
May spend our wonder too, or take off thine
By wond'ring how thou took'st it.

Laf.   Nay, I'll fit you,
And not be all day neither.   [*Exit.*]
  King. Thus he his special nothing ever pro-
    logues.   95

        Enter [*Lafew*, with] *Helen.*

Laf. Nay, come your ways!
King.   This haste hath wings indeed.
Laf. Nay, come your ways!
This is his Majesty; say your mind to him.
A traitor you do look like, but such traitors 99
His Majesty seldom fears. I am Cressid's uncle,
That dare leave two together. Fare you well.
                           Exit.
  King. Now, fair one, does your business fol-
    low us?
  Hel. Ay, my good lord.
Gerard de Narbon was my father;
In what he did profess, well-found.
  King.   I knew him.
  Hel. The rather will I spare my praises
    towards him;   106
Knowing him is enough. On 's bed of death
Many receipts he gave me; chiefly one,
Which, as the dearest issue of his practice,
And of his old experience th' only darling,   110
He bade me store up as a triple eye,
Safer than mine own two, more dear. I have so;
And hearing him your high Majesty is touch'd
With that malignant cause wherein the honour
Of my dear father's gift stands chief in power,
I come to tender it, and my appliance,   116
With all bound humbleness.
  King.   We thank you, maiden;
But may not be so credulous of cure,
When our most learned doctors leave us, and
The congregated college have concluded   120
That labouring art can never ransom nature
From her inaidable estate. I say, we must not
So stain our judgment or corrupt our hope
To prostitute our past-cure malady
To empirics, or to dissever so   125
Our great self and our credit to esteem
A senseless help, when help past sense we deem.
  Hel. My duty then shall pay me for my pains.
I will no more enforce mine office on you,
Humbly entreating from your royal thoughts
A modest one, to bear me back again.   131
  King. I cannot give thee less, to be call'd
    grateful.
Thou thought'st to help me, and such thanks
    I give
As one near death to those that wish him live.
But what at full I know, thou know'st no part,
I knowing all my peril, thou no art.   136

  Hel. What I can do can do no hurt to try,
Since you set up your rest 'gainst remedy.
He that of greatest works is finisher
Oft does them by the weakest minister.   140
So holy writ in babes hath judgment shown
When judges have been babes; great floods
    have flown
From simple sources, and great seas have dried
When miracles have by the greatest been denied.
Oft expectation fails, and most oft there   145
Where most it promises; and oft it hits
Where hope is coldest and despair most fits.
  King. I must not hear thee. Fare thee well,
    kind maid!
Thy pains, not us'd, must by thyself be paid;
Proffers not took reap thanks for their reward.
  Hel. Inspired merit so by breath is barr'd.
It is not so with him that all things knows
As 'tis with us that square our guess by shows;
But most it is presumption in us when
The help of heaven we count the act of men.
Dear sir, to my endeavours give consent;   156
Of heaven, not me, make an experiment.
I am not an impostor that proclaim
Myself against the level of mine aim;   159
But know I think, and think I know most sure,
My art is not past power, nor you past cure.
  King. Art thou so confident? Within what
    space
Hop'st thou my cure?
  Hel.   The great'st grace lending grace,
Ere twice the horses of the sun shall bring
Their fiery torcher his diurnal ring,   165
Ere twice in murk and occidental damp
Moist Hesperus hath quench'd his sleepy lamp,
Or four-and-twenty times the pilot's glass
Hath told the thievish minutes how they pass,
What is infirm from your sound parts shall fly,
Health shall live free, and sickness freely die.
  King. Upon thy certainty and confidence
What dar'st thou venture?
  Hel.   Tax of impudence,
A strumpet's boldness, a divulged shame
Traduc'd by odious ballads; my maiden's
    name   175
Sear'd otherwise; nay, worst of worst extended,
With vilest torture let my life be ended.
  King. Methinks in thee some blessed spirit
    doth speak
His powerful sound within an organ weak;
And what impossibility would slay   180
In common sense, sense saves another way.
Thy life is dear; for all that life can rate
Worth name of life in thee hath estimate —
Youth, beauty, wisdom, courage, all

That happiness and prime can happy call: 185
Thou this to hazard needs must intimate
Skill infinite, or monstrous desperate.
Sweet practiser, thy physic I will try,
That ministers thine own death if I die. 189
  Hel. If I break time or flinch in property
Of what I spoke, unpitied let me die;
And well deserv'd. Not helping, death's my fee;
But if I help, what do you promise me?
  King. Make thy demand.
  Hel.   But will you make it even?
  King. Ay, by my sceptre and my hopes of
    heaven. 195
  Hel. Then shalt thou give me with thy
    kingly hand
What husband in thy power I will command.
Exempted be from me the arrogance
To choose from forth the royal blood of France,
My low and humble name to propagate 200
With any branch or image of thy state;
But such a one, thy vassal, whom I know
Is free for me to ask, thee to bestow.
  King. Here is my hand. The premises ob-
    serv'd,
Thy will by my performance shall be serv'd.
So make the choice of thy own time; for I, 206
Thy resolv'd patient, on thee still rely.
More should I question thee, and more I must,
Though more to know could not be more to
    trust —
From whence thou cam'st, how tended on.
  But rest 210
Unquestion'd welcome, and undoubted blest.
Give me some help here, ho! — If thou proceed
As high as word, my deed shall match thy deed.
                        Flourish. Exeunt.

[Scene II. *Rossillion. The* Count's
        Palace.]

Enter *Countess* and *Clown.*

  Count. Come on, sir; I shall now put you to
the height of your breeding.
  Clown. I will show myself highly fed and
lowly taught. I know my business is but to
the court.
  Count. To the court? Why, what place
make you special, when you put off that with
such contempt? But to the court? 7
  Clown. Truly, madam, if God have lent a
man any manners, he may easily put it off at
court. He that cannot make a leg, put off's cap,
kiss his hand, and say nothing, has neither leg,
hands, lip, nor cap; and indeed such a fellow,

to say precisely, were not for the court; but for
me, I have an answer will serve all men.
  Count. Marry, that's a bountiful answer that
fits all questions. 16
  Clown. It is like a barber's chair, that fits all
buttocks — the pin buttock, the quatch buttock, the brawn buttock, or any buttock.
  Count. Will your answer serve fit to all
questions? 21
  Clown. As fit as ten groats is for the hand of
an attorney, as your French crown for your
taffety punk, as Tib's rush for Tom's forefinger,
as a pancake for Shrove Tuesday, a morris for
May Day, as the nail to his hole, the cuckold to
his horn, as a scolding quean to a wrangling
knave, as the nun's lip to the friar's mouth, nay,
as the pudding to his skin. 29
  Count. Have you, I say, an answer of such
fitness for all questions?
  Clown. From below your duke to beneath
your constable, it will fit any question.
  Count. It must be an answer of most monstrous size that must fit all demands. 35
  Clown. But a trifle neither, in good faith, if
the learned should speak truth of it. Here it is,
and all that belongs to't. Ask me if I am a
courtier. It shall do you no harm to learn. 39
  Count. To be young again, if we could! I
will be a fool in question, hoping to be the wiser
by your answer. I pray you, sir, are you a
courtier?
  Clown. O Lord, sir! — There's a simple putting off. More, more! a hundred of them!
  Count. Sir, I am a poor friend of yours, that
loves you. 46
  Clown. O Lord, sir! — Thick, thick, spare
not me!
  Count. I think, sir, you can eat none of this
homely meat.
  Clown. O Lord, sir! — Nay, put me to't, I
warrant you. 51
  Count. You were lately whipp'd, sir, as I
think.
  Clown. O Lord, sir! — Spare not me.
  Count. Do you cry, 'O Lord, sir!' at your
whipping, and 'Spare not me'? Indeed, your
'O Lord, sir!' is very sequent to your whipping.
You would answer very well to a whipping, if
you were but bound to't.
  Clown. I ne'er had worse luck in my life in
my 'O Lord, sir!' I see things may serve long,
but not serve ever. 61
  Count. I play the noble housewife with the
    time
To entertain it so merrily with a fool.

Clown. O Lord, sir! — Why, there 't serves
well again.   65
  Count. An end, sir! To your business. Give
  Helen this,
And urge her to a present answer back;
Commend me to my kinsmen and my son.
This is not much.   69
  Clown. Not much commendation to them?
  Count. Not much employment for you. You
understand me?
  Clown. Most fruitfully. I am there before
my legs.
  Count. Haste you again.   *Exeunt.*

[Scene III. *Paris. The* King's *Palace.*]

Enter *Count* [*Bertram*], *Lafew,* and *Parolles.*

  Laf. They say miracles are past, and we have
our philosophical persons, to make modern and
familiar, things supernatural and causeless.
Hence is it that we make trifles of terrors, en-
sconcing ourselves into seeming knowledge
when we should submit ourselves to an un-
known fear.   6
  Par. Why, 'tis the rarest argument of won-
der that hath shot out in our latter times.
  Ber. And so 'tis.
  Laf. To be relinquish'd of the artists —   10
  Par. So I say.
  Laf. Both of Galen and Paracelsus —
  Par. So I say.
  Laf. Of all the learned and authentic fel-
lows —
  Par. Right! So I say.   15
  Laf. That gave him out incurable —
  Par. Why, there 'tis! so say I too.
  Laf. Not to be help'd —
  Par. Right! as 'twere a man assured of a —
  Laf. Uncertain life, and sure death.   20
  Par. Just! you say well. So would I have
said.
  Laf. I may truly say it is a novelty to the
world.
  Par. It is indeed. If you will have it in
showing, you shall read it in What-do-ye-call
there.   26
  Laf. A showing of a heavenly effect in an
earthly actor.
  Par. That's it I would have said, the very
same.   30
  Laf. Why, your dolphin is not lustier. Fore
me, I speak in respect —
  Par. Nay, 'tis strange, 'tis very strange!
that is the brief and the tedious of it; and he's

of a most facinerious spirit that will not ac-
knowledge it to be the —   36
  Laf. Very hand of heaven —
  Par. Ay, so I say.
  Laf. In a most weak —
  Par. And debile minister, great power, great
transcendence; which should, indeed, give us a
further use to be made than alone the recov'ry
of the King, as to be —
  Laf. Generally thankful.

Enter *King, Helen,* and *Attendants.*

  Par. I would have said it! you say well.
Here comes the King.   46
  Laf. Lustick! as the Dutchman says. I'll
like a maid the better whilst I have a tooth in
my head. Why, he's able to lead her a coranto.
  Par. Mort du vinaigre! Is not this Helen?
  Laf. Fore God, I think so.   51
  King. Go call before me all the lords in court.
                            [*Exit an Attendant.*]
Sit, my preserver, by thy patient's side
And with this healthful hand whose banish'd
sense
Thou hast repeal'd, a second time receive   55
The confirmation of my promis'd gift,
Which but attends thy naming.

Enter three or four *Lords.*

Fair maid, send forth thine eye. This youthful
parcel
Of noble bachelors stand at my bestowing,
O'er whom both sovereign power and father's
voice   60
I have to use. Thy frank election make.
Thou hast power to choose, and they none to
forsake.
  Hel. To each of you one fair and virtuous
mistress
Fall, when Love please! Marry, to each but
one!
  Laf. [*aside*] I'd give bay Curtal and his fur-
niture   65
My mouth no more were broken than these
boys'
And writ as little beard.
  King.   Peruse them well.
Not one of those but had a noble father.
  Hel. Gentlemen,
Heaven hath through me restor'd the King to
health.   70
  All. We understand it, and thank heaven
for you.
  Hel. I am a simple maid, and therein
wealthiest

373

That I protest I simply am a maid.
Please it your Majesty, I have done already.
The blushes in my cheeks thus whisper me, 75
'We blush that thou shouldst choose; but be
  refus'd,
Let the white death sit on thy cheek for ever,
We'll ne'er come there again.'
  King.   Make choice and see —
Who shuns thy love shuns all his love in me.
  Hel. Now, Dian, from thy altar do I fly, 80
And to imperial Love, that god most high,
Do my sighs stream.
         She addresses her to a Lord.
         Sir, will you hear my suit?
  1. Lord. And grant it.
  Hel.   Thanks, sir. All the rest is mute.
  Laf. [*aside*] I had rather be in this choice
than throw ames-ace for my life. 85
  Hel. [*to another*] The honour, sir, that flames
  in your fair eyes,
Before I speak, too threat'ningly replies.
Love make your fortunes twenty times above
Her that so wishes and her humble love!
  2. Lord. No better, if you please.
  Hel.   My wish receive,
Which great Love grant! and so I take my
  leave. 91
  Laf. [*aside*] Do all they deny her? An they
were sons of mine, I'd have them whipp'd, or I
would send them to th' Turk to make eunuchs
of.
  Hel. [*to a third*] Be not afraid that I your
  hand should take; 95
I'll never do you wrong for your own sake.
Blessing upon your vows! and in your bed
Find fairer fortune, if you ever wed!
  Laf. [*aside*] These boys are boys of ice;
they'll none have her. Sure they are bastards
to the English; the French ne'er got 'em. 101
  Hel. [*to a fourth*] You are too young, too
  happy, and too good
To make yourself a son out of my blood.
  4. Lord. Fair one, I think not so.
  Laf. [*aside*] There's one grape yet; I am
sure thy father drunk wine. But if thou be'st
not an ass, I am a youth of fourteen. I have
known thee already.
  Hel. [*to Bertram*] I dare not say I take you;
but I give
Me and my service, ever whilst I live, 110
Into your guiding power. — This is the man.
  King. Why then, young Bertram, take her;
  she's thy wife.
  Ber. My wife, my liege? I shall beseech
  your Highness,

In such a business give me leave to use 114
The help of mine own eyes.
  King.   Know'st thou not, Bertram,
What she has done for me?
  Ber.   Yes, my good lord;
But never hope to know why I should marry
  her.
  King. Thou know'st she has rais'd me from
  my sickly bed.
  Ber. But follows it, my lord, to bring me
  down 119
Must answer for your raising? I know her well.
She had her breeding at my father's charge.
A poor physician's daughter my wife? Disdain
Rather corrupt me ever!
  King.   'Tis only title thou disdain'st in her,
  the which 124
I can build up. Strange is it that our bloods,
Of colour, weight, and heat, pour'd all together,
Would quite confound distinction, yet stand off
In differences so mighty. If she be
All that is virtuous — save what thou dislik'st,
A poor physician's daughter — thou dislik'st
Of virtue for the name. But do not so. 131
From lowest place when virtuous things pro-
  ceed,
The place is dignified by th' doer's deed.
Where great additions swell 's, and virtue none,
It is a dropsied honour. Good alone 135
Is good without a name; vileness is so:
The property by what it is should go,
Not by the title. She is young, wise, fair;
In these to nature she's immediate heir;
And these breed honour. That is honour's scorn
Which challenges itself as honour's born 141
And is not like the sire. Honours thrive
When rather from our acts we them derive
Than our foregoers. The mere word 's a slave,
Debosh'd on every tomb, on every grave 145
A lying trophy; and as oft is dumb
Where dust and damn'd oblivion is the tomb
Of honour'd bones indeed. What should be
  said?
If thou canst like this creature as a maid,
I can create the rest. Virtue and she 150
Is her own dower; honour and wealth from me.
  Ber. I cannot love her, nor will strive to do't.
  King. Thou wrong'st thyself if thou shouldst
  strive to choose.
  Hel. That you are well restor'd, my lord,
  I'm glad.
Let the rest go. 155
  King. My honour 's at the stake; which to
  defeat,
I must produce my power. Here, take her hand.

Proud scornful boy, unworthy this good gift,
That dost in vile misprision shackle up
My love and her desert; that canst not dream
We, poising us in her defective scale,   161
Shall weigh thee to the beam; that wilt not
  know,
It is in us to plant thine honour where
We please to have it grow. Check thy contempt.
Obey our will, which travails in thy good.   165
Believe not thy disdain, but presently
Do thine own fortunes that obedient right
Which both thy duty owes and our power
  claims;
Or I will throw thee from my care for ever
Into the staggers and the careless lapse   170
Of youth and ignorance; both my revenge and
  hate
Loosing upon thee in the name of justice,
Without all terms of pity. Speak! thine
  answer!
  Ber. Pardon, my gracious lord! for I submit
My fancy to your eyes. When I consider   175
What great creation and what dole of honour
Flies where you bid it, I find that she which
  late
Was in my nobler thoughts most base, is now
The praised of the King, who, so ennobled,
Is as 'twere born so.
  King.   Take her by the hand,   180
And tell her she is thine; to whom I promise
A counterpoise, if not to thy estate
A balance more replete.
  Ber.   I take her hand.
  King. Good fortune and the favour of the
  King
Smile upon this contract, whose ceremony   185
Shall seem expedient on the now-born brief
And be perform'd to-night. The solemn feast
Shall more attend upon the coming space,
Expecting absent friends. As thou lov'st her,
Thy love's to me religious; else, does err.   190
                                                Exeunt.

  *Parolles and Lafew stay behind, commenting
                              of this wedding.*
  Laf. Do you hear, monsieur? A word with
you.
  Par. Your pleasure, sir?
  Laf. Your lord and master did well to make
his recantation.   195
  Par. Recantation? My lord? my master?
  Laf. Ay. Is it not a language I speak?
  Par. A most harsh one, and not to be under-
stood without bloody succeeding. My master?
  Laf. Are you companion to the Count
Rossillion?   201

  Par. To any count! to all counts! to what
is man!
  Laf. To what is count's man; count's master is of another style.   205
  Par. You are too old, sir. Let it satisfy you,
you are too old.
  Laf. I must tell thee, sirrah, I write Man;
to which title age cannot bring thee.   209
  Par. What I dare too well do, I dare not do.
  Laf. I did think thee, for two ordinaries, to
be a pretty wise fellow; thou didst make tolerable vent of thy travel, it might pass. Yet the
scarfs and the bannerets about thee did mani-
foldly dissuade me from believing thee a vessel
of too great a burthen. I have now found thee;
when I lose thee again, I care not. Yet art thou
good for nothing but taking up; and that
thou'rt scarce worth.
  Par. Hadst thou not the privilege of antiquity upon thee —   221
  Laf. Do not plunge thyself too far in anger,
lest thou hasten thy trial; which if — Lord
have mercy on thee for a hen! So, my good
window of lattice, fare thee well. Thy casement
I need not open, for I look through thee. Give
me thy hand.   227
  Par. My lord, you give me most egregious
indignity.
  Laf. Ay, with all my heart! and thou art
worthy of it.   231
  Par. I have not, my lord, deserv'd it.
  Laf. Yes, good faith, ev'ry dram of it, and I
will not bate thee a scruple.
  Par. Well, I shall be wiser.   235
  Laf. Ev'n as soon as thou canst, for thou hast
to pull at a smack o' th' contrary. If ever thou
be'st bound in thy scarf and beaten, thou shalt
find what it is to be proud of thy bondage. I
have a desire to hold my acquaintance with
thee, or rather my knowledge, that I may say
in the default, 'He is a man I know.'
  Par. My lord, you do me most insupportable
vexation.   244
  Laf. I would it were hell pains for thy sake,
and my poor doing eternal; for doing I am
past, as I will by thee, in what motion age will
give me leave.   *Exit.*
  Par. Well, thou hast a son shall take this disgrace off me, scurvy, old, filthy, scurvy lord!
Well, I must be patient; there is no fettering
of authority. I'll beat him, by my life, if I can
meet him with any convenience, an he were
double and double a lord. I'll have no more
pity of his age than I would have of — I'll beat
him, an if I could but meet him again.   256

Enter *Lafew.*

Laf. Sirrah, your lord and master's married;
there's news for you. You have a new mistress.

Par. I most unfeignedly beseech your lordship to make some reservation of your wrongs.
He is my good lord; whom I serve above is my
master.   261

Laf. Who? God?

Par. Ay, sir.

Laf. The devil it is that's thy master. Why
dost thou garter up thy arms o' this fashion?
Dost make hose of thy sleeves? Do other servants so? Thou wert best set thy lower part
where thy nose stands. By mine honour, if I
were but two hours younger, I'd beat thee.
Methink'st thou art a general offence, and every
man should beat thee. I think thou wast created for men to breathe themselves upon thee.

Par. This is hard and undeserved measure,
my lord.   274

Laf. Go to, sir! You were beaten in Italy for
picking a kernel out of a pomegranate. You are
a vagabond, and no true traveller. You are
more saucy with lords and honourable personages than the commission of your birth and
virtue gives you heraldry. You are not worth
another word, else I'd call you knave. I leave
you.   *Exit.*

Enter *[Bertram] Count Rossillion.*

Par. Good, very good! It is so then. Good,
very good! Let it be conceal'd awhile.

Ber. Undone, and forfeited to cares for ever!

Par. What's the matter, sweetheart?   285

Ber. Although before the solemn priest I
have sworn,
I will not bed her.

Par. What? what, sweetheart?

Ber. O my Parolles, they have married me!
I'll to the Tuscan wars, and never bed her.   290

Par. France is a dog-hole, and it no more
merits
The tread of a man's foot. To th' wars!

Ber. There's letters from my mother. What
th' import is,
I know not yet.

Par. Ay, that would be known. To th' wars,
my boy, to th' wars!   295
He wears his honour in a box unseen
That hugs his kicky-wicky here at home,
Spending his manly marrow in her arms,
Which should sustain the bound and high curvet
Of Mars's fiery steed. To other regions!   300
France is a stable; we that dwell in't jades.
Therefore. to th' wars!

Ber. It shall be so. I'll send her to my house,
Acquaint my mother with my hate to her,   304
And wherefore I am fled; write to the King
That which I durst not speak. His present gift
Shall furnish me to those Italian fields
Where noble fellows strike. War is no strife
To the dark house and the detested wife.

Par. Will this caprichio hold in thee? art
sure?   310

Ber. Go with me to my chamber and advise
me.
I'll send her straight away. To-morrow
I'll to the wars, she to her single sorrow.

Par. Why, these balls bound! there's noise
in it! 'Tis hard:
A young man married is a man that's marr'd.
Therefore away, and leave her bravely, go!   316
The King has done you wrong; but hush! 'tis
so.   *Exeunt.*

[Scene IV. *Paris. The* King's *Palace.*]

Enter *Helena* and *Clown.*

Hel. My mother greets me kindly. Is she
well?

Clown. She is not well, but yet she has her
health. She's very merry, but yet she is not
well. But thanks be given, she's very well and
wants nothing i' th' world. But yet she is not
well.   5

Hel. If she be very well, what does she ail
that she's not very well?

Clown. Truly she's very well indeed, but for
two things.

Hel. What two things?   10

Clown. One, that she's not in heaven, whither
God send her quickly! the other, that she's in
earth, from whence God send her quickly!

Enter *Parolles.*

Par. Bless you, my fortunate lady!

Hel. I hope, sir, I have your good will to have
mine own good fortunes.   16

Par. You had my prayers to lead them on;
and to keep them on, have them still. O my
knave, how does my old lady?

Clown. So that you had her wrinkles and I
her money, I would she did as you say.   21

Par. Why, I say nothing.

Clown. Marry, you are the wiser man; for
many a man's tongue shakes out his master's
undoing. To say nothing, to do nothing, to
know nothing, and to have nothing, is to be a

376

great part of your title, which is within a very
little of nothing.

Par. Away! th'art a knave!

Clown. You should have said, sir, 'Before a
knave th'art a knave'; that's 'Before me th'art
a knave.' This had been truth, sir.   31

Par. Go to, thou art a witty fool! I have
found thee.

Clown. Did you find me in yourself, sir, or
were you taught to find me? The search, sir,
was profitable; and much fool may you find in
you, even to the world's pleasure and the increase of laughter.

Par. A good knave, i' faith, and well fed!
Madam, my lord will go away to-night;   40
A very serious business calls on him.
The great prerogative and rite of love,
Which, as your due, time claims, he does ac-
     knowledge;
But puts it off to a compell'd restraint;
Whose want, and whose delay, is strew'd with
     sweets,   45
Which they distil now in the curbed time,
To make the coming hour o'erflow with joy
And pleasure drown the brim.

Hel.   What's his will else?

Par. That you will take your instant leave
     o' th' King
And make this haste as your own good pro-
     ceeding,   50
Strength'ned with what apology you think
May make it probable need.

Hel.   What more commands he?

Par. That, having this obtain'd, you pres-
     ently
Attend his further pleasure.

Hel. In everything I wait upon his will.   55

Par. I shall report it so.

Hel.   I pray you.

Exit Parolles.
Come, sirrah.
Exeunt.

[Scene V. *Paris.* *The* King's *Palace.*]

Enter *Lafew* and *Bertram.*

Laf. But I hope your lordship thinks not him
a soldier.

Ber. Yes, my lord, and of very valiant
approof.

Laf. You have it from his own deliverance.

Ber. And by other warranted testimony.   5

Laf. Then my dial goes not true. I took
this lark for a bunting.

Ber. I do assure you, my lord, he is very
great in knowledge and accordingly valiant.

Laf. I have then sinn'd against his experience and transgress'd against his valour; and
my state that way is dangerous, since I cannot
yet find in my heart to repent.

Enter *Parolles.*

Here he comes. I pray you make us friends;
I will pursue the amity.   15

Par. [*to Bertram*] These things shall be done,
sir.

Laf. Pray you, sir, who's his tailor?

Par. Sir?

Laf. O, I know him well, I, sir. He, sir, 's a
good workman, a very good tailor.   21

Ber. [*aside to Parolles*] Is she gone to the
King?

Par. She is.

Ber. Will she away to-night?

Par. As you'll have her.   25

Ber. I have writ my letters, casketed my
     treasure,
Given order for our horses, and to-night,
When I should take possession of the bride,
End ere I do begin.   29

Laf. A good traveller is something at the latter end of a dinner; but one that lies three
thirds and uses a known truth to pass a thousand nothings with, should be once heard and
thrice beaten. God save you, Captain.

Ber. Is there any unkindness between my
lord and you, monsieur?   36

Par. I know not how I have deserved to run
into my lord's displeasure.

Laf. You have made shift to run into't,
boots and spurs and all, like him that leapt
into the custard; and out of it you'll run
again rather than suffer question for your residence.

Ber. It may be you have mistaken him, my
lord.   44

Laf. And shall do so ever, though I took him
at 's prayers. Fare you well, my lord; and believe this of me, there can be no kernel in this
light nut. The soul of this man is his clothes.
Trust him not in matter of heavy consequence.
I have kept of them tame and know their natures. — Farewell, monsieur. I have spoken
better of you than you have or will to deserve
at my hand; but we must do good against evil.
[Exit.]

Par. An idle lord, I swear.

Ber. I think so.   55

Par. Why, do you not know him?

377

Ber. Yes, I do know him well, and common speech
Gives him a worthy pass.

Enter *Helena.*

Here comes my clog.
Hel. I have, sir, as I was commanded from you,
Spoke with the King, and have procur'd his leave   60
For present parting. Only he desires
Some private speech with you.
Ber.   I shall obey his will.
You must not marvel, Helen, at my course,
Which holds not colour with the time, nor does
The ministration and required office   65
On my particular. Prepar'd I was not
For such a business; therefore am I found
So much unsettled. This drives me to entreat you
That presently you take your way for home,
And rather muse than ask why I entreat you;
For my respects are better than they seem, 71
And my appointments have in them a need
Greater than shows itself at the first view
To you that know them not. This to my mother: [*Gives a letter.*]
'Twill be two days ere I shall see you. So 75
I leave you to your wisdom.
Hel.   Sir, I can nothing say
But that I am your most obedient servant.

Ber. Come, come, no more of that!
Hel.   And ever shall
With true observance seek to eke out that
Wherein toward me my homely stars have fail'd   80
To equal my great fortune.
Ber.   Let that go!
My haste is very great. Farewell, hie home.
Hel. Pray, sir, your pardon.
Ber.   Well, what would you say?
Hel. I am not worthy of the wealth I owe,
Nor dare I say 'tis mine; and yet it is — 85
But, like a timorous thief, most fain would steal
What law does vouch mine own.
Ber.   What would you have?
Hel. Something, and scarce so much; nothing, indeed.
I would not tell you what I would, my lord.
Faith, yes!   90
Strangers and foes do sunder, and not kiss.
Ber. I pray you stay not, but in haste to horse!
Hel. I shall not break your bidding, good my lord.
Ber. Where are my other men, monsieur? Farewell.   94
Go thou toward home —   *Exit* [*Helena*].
                       where I will never come
Whilst I can shake my sword or hear the drum.
Away, and for our flight!
Par.   Bravely, coragio!
                                      [*Exeunt.*]

ACT III. [Scene I. *Florence. The* Duke's *Palace.*]

Flourish. Enter the *Duke of Florence,* the two *Frenchmen,* with a *Troop of Soldiers.*

Duke. So that from point to point now have you heard
The fundamental reasons of this war,
Whose great decision hath much blood let forth,
And more thirsts after.
1. Lord.   Holy seems the quarrel
Upon your Grace's part, black and fearful   5
On the opposer.
Duke. Therefore we marvel much our cousin France
Would in so just a business shut his bosom
Against our borrowing prayers.
2. Lord.   Good my lord,
The reasons of our state I cannot yield   10

But like a common and an outward man
That the great figure of a council frames
By self-unable motion; therefore dare not
Say what I think of it, since I have found
Myself in my incertain grounds to fail   15
As often as I guess'd.
Duke.   Be it his pleasure.
1. Lord. But I am sure the younger of our nature,
That surfeit on their ease, will day by day
Come here for physic.
Duke.   Welcome shall they be,
And all the honours that can fly from us   20
Shall on them settle. You know your places well.
When better fall, for your avails they fell:
To-morrow to th' field.
                    Flourish. [*Exeunt.*]

378

[Scene II. *Rossillion. The* Count's *Palace.*]

Enter *Countess* and *Clown.*

Count. It hath happen'd all as I would have
had it, save that he comes not along with her.
Clown. By my troth, I take my young lord
to be a very melancholy man.
Count. By what observance, I pray you?   5
Clown. Why, he will look upon his boot, and
sing; mend the ruff, and sing; ask questions,
and sing; pick his teeth, and sing. I know a
man that had this trick of melancholy sold a
goodly manor for a song.   10
Count. Let me see what he writes, and when
he means to come.   [*Opens a letter.*]
Clown. I have no mind to Isbel since I was
at court. Our old ling and our Isbels o' th'
country are nothing like your old ling and your
Isbels o' th' court. The brains of my Cupid's
knock'd out, and I begin to love, as an old man
loves money, with no stomach.
Count. What have we here?   19
Clown. E'en that you have there.   *Exit.*

[*Countess reads*] *a letter.* 'I have sent you a
daughter-in-law. She hath recovered the King,
and undone me. I have wedded her, not bedded
her; and sworn to make the "not" eternal. You
shall hear I am run away. Know it before the report come. If there be breadth enough in the
world, I will hold a long distance. My duty to you.
          'Your unfortunate son,
                              'BERTRAM.'

This is not well, rash and unbridled boy,   30
To fly the favours of so good a king,
To pluck his indignation on thy head
By the misprizing of a maid too virtuous
For the contempt of empire.

Enter *Clown.*

Clown. O madam, yonder is heavy news
within between two soldiers and my young lady!
Count. What is the matter?   37
Clown. Nay, there is some comfort in the
news, some comfort. Your son will not be
kill'd so soon as I thought he would.   40
Count. Why should he be kill'd?
Clown. So say I, madam, if he run away, as I
hear he does. The danger is in standing to't;
that's the loss of men, though it be the getting
of children. Here they come will tell you more.
For my part, I only hear your son was run away.
                                         [*Exit.*]

Enter *Helen* and [the] two [French] *Gentlemen.*

2. Lord. Save you, good madam.
Hel. Madam, my lord is gone, for ever gone!
1. Lord. Do not say so.
Count. Think upon patience. Pray you,
gentlemen —   50
I have felt so many quirks of joy and grief
That the first face of neither on the start
Can woman me unto't. Where is my son, I
pray you?
1. Lord. Madam, he's gone to serve the Duke
of Florence.
We met him thitherward; for thence we came,
And, after some dispatch in hand at court,   56
Thither we bend again.
Hel. Look on his letter, madam. Here's my
passport.

[*Reads*] 'When thou canst get the ring upon my
finger which never shall come off, and show me a
child begotten of thy body that I am father to,
then call me husband; but in such a "then" I
write a "never." '

This is a dreadful sentence.   64
Count. Brought you this letter, gentlemen?
1. Lord.   Ay, madam,
And for the contents' sake are sorry for our
pains.
Count. I prithee, lady, have a better cheer.
If thou engrossest all the griefs are thine,
Thou robb'st me of a moiety. He was my son;
But I do wash his name out of my blood,   70
And thou art all my child. Towards Florence
is he?
1. Lord. Ay, madam.
Count.   And to be a soldier?
1. Lord. Such is his noble purpose; and be-
lieve't,
The Duke will lay upon him all the honour
That good convenience claims.
Count.   Return you thither?
2. Lord. Ay, madam, with the swiftest wing
of speed.   76
Hel. [*reads*] 'Till I have no wife, I have
nothing in France.'
'Tis bitter.
Count. Find you that there?
Hel.   Ay, madam.
2. Lord. 'Tis but the boldness of his hand
haply, which his heart was not consenting to. 80
Count. Nothing in France until he have no
wife!
There's nothing here that is too good for him
But only she; and she deserves a lord
That twenty such rude boys might tend upon

And call her hourly mistress. Who was with
him? 85
2. Lord. A servant only, and a gentleman
Which I have sometime known.
 Count.   Parolles, was it not?
 2. Lord. Ay, my good lady, he.
 Count. A very tainted fellow, and full of
wickedness.
My son corrupts a well-derived nature 90
With his inducement.
 2. Lord.   Indeed, good lady,
The fellow has a deal of that too-much
Which holds him much to have.
 Count.   Y'are welcome, gentlemen.
I will entreat you, when you see my son, 95
To tell him that his sword can never win
The honour that he loses. More I'll entreat you
Written to bear along.
 1. Lord.   We serve you, madam,
In that and all your worthiest affairs.
 Count. Not so, but as we change our cour-
tesies. 100
Will you draw near?
       Exit [with the Gentlemen].
 Hel. 'Till I have no wife I have nothing in
France.'
Nothing in France until he has no wife!
Thou shalt have none, Rossillion, none in
France;
Then hast thou all again. Poor lord! is't I 105
That chase thee from thy country and expose
Those tender limbs of thine to the event
Of the none-sparing war? And is it I
That drive thee from the sportive court, where
thou
Wast shot at with fair eyes, to be the mark 110
Of smoky muskets? O you leaden messengers
That ride upon the violent speed of fire,
Fly with false aim; move the still-piecing air,
That sings with piercing! do not touch my lord!
Whoever shoots at him, I set him there; 115
Whoever charges on his forward breast,
I am the caitiff that do hold him to't,
And though I kill him not, I am the cause
His death was so effected. Better 'twere
I met the ravin lion when he roar'd 120
With sharp constraint of hunger; better 'twere
That all the miseries which nature owes
Were mine at once. No! come thou home,
Rossillion,
Whence honour but of danger wins a scar,
As oft it loses all. I will be gone. 125
My being here it is that holds thee hence.
Shall I stay here to do't? No, no, although
The air of paradise did fan the house

And angels offic'd all! I will be gone,
That pitiful rumour may report my flight 130
To consolate thine ear. Come, night! end, day!
For with the dark (poor thief) I'll steal away.
           Exit.

[Scene III.   *Florence.*   *Before the*
Duke's *Palace.*]

Flourish. Enter the *Duke of Florence, Bertram,*
 Drum and *Trumpets, Soldiers, Parolles.*

 Duke. The General of our Horse thou art;
 and we,
Great in our hope, lay our best love and credence
Upon thy promising fortune.
 Ber.   Sir, it is
A charge too heavy for my strength; but yet
We'll strive to bear it for your worthy sake 5
To th' extreme edge of hazard.
 Duke.   Then go thou forth,
And Fortune play upon thy prosperous helm
As thy auspicious mistress!
 Ber.   This very day,
Great Mars, I put myself into thy file.
Make me but like my thoughts, and I shall prove
A lover of thy drum, hater of love.
          Exeunt omnes.

[Scene IV.   *Rossillion.*   *The* Count's
Palace.]

Enter *Countess* and *Steward.*

 Count. Alas! and would you take the letter
of her?
Might you not know she would do as she has
done
By sending me a letter? Read it again.
 [*Steward reads the*] *letter.*

'I am Saint Jaques' pilgrim, thither gone.
 Ambitious love hath so in me offended 5
That barefoot plod I the cold ground upon
 With sainted vow my faults to have amended.
Write, write, that from the bloody course of war
 My dearest master, your dear son, may hie!
Bless him at home in peace, whilst I from far 10
 His name with zealous fervour sanctify.
His taken labours bid him me forgive.
 I, his despiteful Juno, sent him forth
From courtly friends, with camping foes to live,
 Where death and danger dogs the heels of worth.
He is too good and fair for death and me; 16
Whom I myself embrace to set him free.'

Count. Ah, what sharp stings are in her
  mildest words!
Rinaldo, you did never lack advice so much
As letting her pass so. Had I spoke with her,
I could have well diverted her intents,   21
Which thus she hath prevented.
  Stew.   Pardon me, madam.
If I had given you this at overnight,
She might have been o'erta'en; and yet she
  writes
Pursuit would be but vain.
  Count.   What angel shall   25
Bless this unworthy husband? He cannot
  thrive
Unless her prayers, whom heaven delights to
  hear
And loves to grant, reprieve him from the wrath
Of greatest justice. Write, write, Rinaldo,
To this unworthy husband of his wife.   30
Let every word weigh heavy of her worth
That he does weigh too light. My greatest grief,
Though little he do feel it, set down sharply.
Dispatch the most convenient messenger.
When haply he shall hear that she is gone,   35
He will return; and hope I may that she,
Hearing so much, will speed her foot again,
Led hither by pure love. Which of them both
Is dearest to me, I have no skill in sense
To make distinction. Provide this messenger.
My heart is heavy, and mine age is weak.   41
Grief would have tears, and sorrow bids me
  speak.   *Exeunt.*

[Scene V. *Without the walls of Florence.*]

A tucket afar off. Enter old *Widow* of Florence,
her Daughter [*Diana*], *Violenta*, and *Mariana*,
with other *Citizens.*

Wid. Nay, come; for if they do approach
the city, we shall lose all the sight.
  Dia. They say the French count has done
most honourable service.
  Wid. It is reported that he has taken their
great'st commander, and that with his own
hand he slew the Duke's brother. [*Tucket.*] We
have lost our labour; they are gone a contrary
way. Hark! you may know by their trumpets.
  Mar. Come, let's return again and suffice
ourselves with the report of it. Well, Diana,
take heed of this French earl. The honour of a
maid is her name, and no legacy is so rich as
honesty.   14
  Wid. I have told my neighbour how you

have been solicited by a gentleman his companion.
  Mar. I know that knave, hang him! one Parolles. A filthy officer he is in those suggestions
for the young earl. Beware of them, Diana.
Their promises, enticements, oaths, tokens, and
all these engines of lust, are not the things they
go under. Many a maid hath been seduced by
them; and the misery is, example, that so terrible shows in the wrack of maidenhood, cannot
for all that dissuade succession but that they
are limed with the twigs that threaten them. I
hope I need not to advise you further; but I
hope your own grace will keep you where you
are, though there were no further danger known
but the modesty which is so lost.   30
  Dia. You shall not need to fear me.

            Enter *Helen*, [like a pilgrim].

  Wid. I hope so. Look, here comes a pilgrim.
I know she will lie at my house. Thither they
send one another. I'll question her.
God save you, pilgrim! Whither are you
  bound?   36
  Hel. To Saint Jaques le Grand.
Where do the palmers lodge, I do beseech you?
  Wid. At the Saint Francis here, beside the
  port.
  Hel. Is this the way?   40
  Wid. Ay, marry, is't.   *A march afar.*
            Hark you! they come this way.
If you will tarry, holy pilgrim,
But till the troops come by,
I will conduct you where you shall be lodg'd,
The rather for I think I know your hostess   45
As ample as myself.
  Hel.   Is it yourself?
  Wid. If you shall please so, pilgrim.
  Hel. I thank you and will stay upon your
  leisure.
  Wid. You came, I think, from France?
  Hel.   I did so.
  Wid. Here you shall see a countryman of
  yours   50
That has done worthy service.
  Hel.   His name, I pray you?
  Dia. The Count Rossillion. Know you such
a one?
  Hel. But by the ear, that hears most nobly
of him;
His face I know not.
  Dia.   Whatsome'er he is,   54
He's bravely taken here. He stole from France,
As 'tis reported, for the King had married him
Against his liking. Think you it is so?

Hel. Ay, surely, mere the truth. I know his
lady.
Dia. There is a gentleman that serves the
Count   59
Reports but coarsely of her.
Hel.   What's his name?
Dia. Monsieur Parolles.
Hel.   O, I believe with him,
In argument of praise, or to the worth
Of the great Count himself, she is too mean
To have her name repeated. All her deserv-
ing
Is a reserved honesty, and that   65
I have not heard examin'd.
Dia.   Alas, poor lady!
'Tis a hard bondage to become the wife
Of a detesting lord.
Wid. I write, good creature, wheresoe'er she
is,
Her heart weighs sadly. This young maid
might do her   70
A shrewd turn, if she pleas'd.
Hel.   How do you mean?
May be the amorous Count solicits her
In the unlawful purpose.
Wid.   He does indeed!
And brokes with all that can in such a suit
Corrupt the tender honour of a maid;   75
But she is arm'd for him, and keeps her guard
In honestest defence.

Drum and Colours.

Enter [*Bertram*] *Count Rossillion, Parolles*, and
the whole *Army*.

Mar.   The gods forbid else!
Wid. So, now they come.
That is Antonio, the Duke's eldest son;
That, Escalus.
Hel.   Which is the Frenchman?
Dia.   He!
That with the plume. 'Tis a most gallant fel-
low.   81
I would he lov'd his wife. If he were honester,
He were much goodlier. Is't not a handsome
gentleman?
Hel. I like him well.
Dia. 'Tis pity he is not honest. Yond's that
same knave   85
That leads him to these places. Were I his
lady,
I would poison that vile rascal.
Hel.   Which is he?
Dia. That jackanapes with scarfs. Why is
he melancholy?

Hel. Perchance he's hurt i' th' battle.   90
Par. Lose our drum? well.
Mar. He's shrewdly vex'd at something.
Look, he has spied us.
Wid. Marry, hang you!
Mar. And your courtesy, for a ring-carrier!
Exeunt [*Bertram, Parolles, and Army*].
Wid. The troop is past. Come, pilgrim, I
will bring you
Where you shall host. Of enjoin'd penitents
There's four or five, to Great Saint Jaques
bound,
Already at my house.
Hel.   I humbly thank you.
Please it this matron and this gentle maid 100
To eat with us to-night, the charge and thank-
ing
Shall be for me; and, to requite you further,
I will bestow some precepts of this virgin
Worthy the note.
Both.   We'll take your offer kindly.
Exeunt.

[Scene VI. *Camp before Florence.*]

Enter [*Bertram*] *Count Rossillion* and the
Frenchmen, as at first.

2. Lord. Nay, good my lord, put him to't.
Let him have his way.
1. Lord. If your lordship find him not a hilding, hold me no more in your respect.
2. Lord. On my life, my lord, a bubble!   5
Ber. Do you think I am so far deceived in
him?
2. Lord. Believe it, my lord, in mine own direct knowledge, without any malice, but to
speak of him as my kinsman, he's a most notable coward, an infinite and endless liar, an
hourly promise-breaker, the owner of no one
good quality worthy your lordship's entertainment.   13
1. Lord. It were fit you knew him, lest, re-
posing too far in his virtue, which he hath not,
he might at some great and trusty business in a
main danger fail you.
Ber. I would I knew in what particular action to try him.
1. Lord. None better than to let him fetch off
his drum, which you hear him so confidently
undertake to do.   22
2. Lord. I with a troop of Florentines will
suddenly surprise him. Such I will have whom
I am sure he knows not from the enemy. We

382

will bind and hoodwink him so that he shall suppose no other but that he is carried into the leaguer of the adversaries when we bring him to our own tents. Be but your lordship present at his examination. If he do not, for the promise of his life and in the highest compulsion of base fear, offer to betray you and deliver all the intelligence in his power against you, and that with the divine forfeit of his soul upon oath, never trust my judgment in anything.   35

1. Lord. O, for the love of laughter, let him fetch his drum! He says he has a stratagem for't. When your lordship sees the bottom of his success in't, and to what metal this counterfeit lump of ore will be melted, if you give him not John Drum's entertainment, your inclining cannot be removed. Here he comes.   42

Enter *Parolles.*

2. Lord. O, for the love of laughter, hinder not the honour of his design! Let him fetch off his drum in any hand.   45

Ber. How now, monsieur? This drum sticks sorely in your disposition.

1. Lord. A pox on't, let it go! 'tis but a drum.

Par. But a drum? Is't but a drum? A drum so lost! There was excellent command — to charge in with our horse upon our own wings and to rend our own soldiers!

1. Lord. That was not to be blam'd in the command of the service. It was a disaster of war that Cæsar himself could not have prevented, if he had been there to command.

Ber. Well, we cannot greatly condemn our success. Some dishonour we had in the loss of that drum; but it is not to be recovered.   60

Par. It might have been recovered.

Ber. It might, but it is not now.

Par. It is to be recovered. But that the merit of service is seldom attributed to the true and exact performer, I would have that drum or another, or *hic jacet*!   66

Ber. Why, if you have a stomach, to't, monsieur! If you think your mystery in stratagem can bring this instrument of honour again into his native quarter, be magnanimous in the enterprise and go on. I will grace the attempt for a worthy exploit. If you speed well in it, the Duke shall both speak of it and extend to you what further becomes his greatness, even to the utmost syllable of your worthiness.   75

Par. By the hand of a soldier, I will undertake it.

Ber. But you must not now slumber in it.

Par. I'll about it this evening; and I will presently pen down my dilemmas, encourage myself in my certainty, put myself into my mortal preparation; and by midnight look to hear further from me.

Ber. May I be bold to acquaint his Grace you are gone about it?   85

Par. I know not what the success will be, my lord, but the attempt I vow.

Ber. I know th'art valiant, and to the possibility of thy soldiership will subscribe for thee. Farewell.   90

Par. I love not many words.   *Exit.*

2. Lord. No more than a fish loves water. Is not this a strange fellow, my lord, that so confidently seems to undertake this business, which he knows is not to be done; damns himself to do, and dares better be damn'd than to do't?

1. Lord. You do not know him, my lord, as we do. Certain it is that he will steal himself into a man's favour and for a week escape a great deal of discoveries; but when you find him out, you have him ever after.   101

Ber. Why, do you think he will make no deed at all of this that so seriously he does address himself unto?   104

2. Lord. None in the world; but return with an invention, and clap upon you two or three probable lies. But we have almost emboss'd him. You shall see his fall to-night; for indeed he is not for your lordship's respect.   109

1. Lord. We'll make you some sport with the fox ere we case him. He was first smok'd by the old Lord Lafew. When his disguise and he is parted, tell me what a sprat you shall find him; which you shall see this very night.

2. Lord. I must go look my twigs. He shall be caught.   115

Ber. Your brother, he shall go along with me.

2. Lord. As 't please your lordship. I'll leave you.   [*Exit.*]

Ber. Now will I lead you to the house and show you
The lass I spoke of.

1. Lord.   But you say she's honest.

Ber. That's all the fault. I spoke with her but once,   120
And found her wondrous cold; but I sent to her,
By this same coxcomb that we have i' th' wind,
Tokens and letters, which she did resend;
And this is all I have done. She's a fair creature.
Will you go see her?

1. Lord.   With all my heart, my lord.
          Exeunt.

[Scene VII. *Florence. The* Widow's
house.]

Enter *Helen* and *Widow.*

Hel. If you misdoubt me that I am not she,
I know not how I shall assure you further
But I shall lose the grounds I work upon.
Wid. Though my estate be fall'n, I was well
born,
Nothing acquainted with these businesses, 5
And would not put my reputation now
In any staining act.
Hel. Nor would I wish you.
First give me trust the Count he is my husband,
And what to your sworn counsel I have spoken
Is so from word to word; and then you cannot,
By the good aid that I of you shall borrow, 11
Err in bestowing it.
Wid. I should believe you,
For you have show'd me that which well ap-
proves
Y'are great in fortune.
Hel. Take this purse of gold,
And let me buy your friendly help thus far, 15
Which I will overpay and pay again
When I have found it. The Count he wooes
your daughter,
Lays down his wanton siege before her beauty,
Resolv'd to carry her. Let her in fine consent,
As we'll direct her how 'tis best to bear it. 20

Now his important blood will naught deny
That she'll demand. A ring the County wears
That downward hath succeeded in his house
From son to son some four or five descents
Since the first father wore it. This ring he holds
In most rich choice; yet in his idle fire, 26
To buy his will, it would not seem too dear,
Howe'er repented after.
Wid. Now I see
The bottom of your purpose. 29
Hel. You see it lawful then. It is no more
But that your daughter, ere she seems as won,
Desires this ring; appoints him an encounter;
In fine, delivers me to fill the time,
Herself most chastely absent. After this, 34
To marry her, I'll add three thousand crowns
To what is pass'd already.
Wid. I have yielded.
Instruct my daughter how she shall persever,
That time and place with this deceit so lawful
May prove coherent. Every night he comes
With musics of all sorts, and songs compos'd 40
To her unworthiness. It nothing steads us
To chide him from our eaves, for he persists
As if his life lay on't.
Hel. Why then, to-night
Let us assay our plot; which, if it speed,
Is wicked meaning in a lawful deed, 45
And lawful meaning in a wicked act,
Where both not sin, and yet a sinful fact.
But let's about it. [*Exeunt.*]

ACT IV. [Scene I. *Without the Florentine camp.*]

Enter one of the *Frenchmen,* [the *Second Lord,*]
with five or six other *Soldiers,* in ambush.

2. Lord. He can come no other way but by
this hedge corner. When you sally upon him,
speak what terrible language you will. Though
you understand it not yourselves, no matter;
for we must not seem to understand him, unless
some one among us, whom we must produce for
an interpreter.
1. Sold. Good Captain, let me be th' interpreter.
2. Lord. Art not acquainted with him?
Knows he not thy voice? 11
1. Sold. No, sir, I warrant you.
2. Lord. But what linsey-woolsey hast thou
to speak to us again?
1. Sold. E'en such as you speak to me. 15
2. Lord. He must think us some band of
strangers i' th' adversary's entertainment. Now

he hath a smack of all neighbouring languages.
Therefore we must every one be a man of his
own fancy, not to know what we speak one to
another. So we seem to know, is to know
straight our purpose. Choughs' language —
gabble enough, and good enough. As for you,
interpreter, you must seem very politic. But
couch, ho! Here he comes, to beguile two hours
in a sleep, and then to return and swear the lies
he forges. [*They hide.*] 26

Enter *Parolles.*

Par. Ten o'clock. Within these three hours
'twill be time enough to go home. What shall I
say I have done? It must be a very plausive
invention that carries it. They begin to smoke
me, and disgraces have of late knock'd too often
at my door. I find my tongue is too foolhardy;
but my heart hath the fear of Mars before it.

and of his creatures, not daring the reports of my tongue.

2. Lord. This is the first truth that e'er thine own tongue was guilty of.   36

Par. What the devil should move me to undertake the recovery of this drum, being not ignorant of the impossibility, and knowing I had no such purpose? I must give myself some hurts and say I got them in exploit. Yet slight ones will not carry it. They will say, 'Came you off with so little?' And great ones I dare not give. Wherefore, what's the instance? Tongue, I must put you into a butter-woman's mouth, and buy myself another of Bajazet's mule, if you prattle me into these perils.   47

2. Lord. Is it possible he should know what he is, and be that he is?

Par. I would the cutting of my garments would serve the turn, or the breaking of my Spanish sword.   52

2. Lord. We cannot afford you so.

Par. Or the baring of my beard, and to say it was in stratagem.   55

2. Lord. 'Twould not do.

Par. Or to drown my clothes, and say I was stripp'd.

2. Lord. Hardly serve.

Par. Though I swore I leapt from the window of the citadel —   61

2. Lord. How deep?

Par. Thirty fadom.

2. Lord. Three great oaths would scarce make that be believed.   65

Par. I would I had any drum of the enemy's. I would swear I recover'd it.

2. Lord. You shall hear one anon.

Alarum within.

Par. A drum now of the enemy's!   69

2. Lord. *Throca movousus, cargo, cargo, cargo.*

All. Cargo, cargo, cargo, villianda par corbo, cargo.

Par. O, ransom, ransom! Do not hide mine eyes.   *[They hoodwink him.]*

[1. Sold. as] Interpreter. Boskos thromuldo boskos.   75

Par. I know you are the Muskos' regiment,

And I shall lose my life for want of language. If there be here German, or Dane, Low Dutch, Italian, or French, let him speak to me. I'll discover that which shall undo the Florentine.   80

Interp. Boskos vauvado.

I understand thee, and can speak thy tongue. *Kerelybonto.* Sir,

Betake thee to thy faith, for seventeen poniards Are at thy bosom.

Par.   O!

Interp.   O, pray, pray, pray!   85

Manka revania dulche.

2. Lord. Oscorbidulchos volivorco.

Interp. The General is content to spare thee yet,

And, hoodwink'd as thou art, will lead thee on To gather from thee. Haply thou mayst inform Something to save thy life.

Par.   O, let me live!   91

And all the secrets of our camp I'll show, Their force, their purposes. Nay, I'll speak that Which you will wonder at.

Interp.   But wilt thou faithfully?

Par. If I do not, damn me.   95

Interp. Acordo linta.

Come on. Thou art granted space.

Exit [with Parolles]. A short alarum within.

2. Lord. Go tell the Count Rossillion and my brother

We have caught the woodcock and will keep him muffled

Till we do hear from them.

2. Sold.   Captain, I will.   100

2. Lord. 'A will betray us all unto ourselves. Inform on that.

2. Sold.   So I will, sir.

2. Lord. Till then I'll keep him dark and safely lock'd.   *Exeunt.*

[Scene II. *Florence. The* Widow's *house.*]

Enter *Bertram* and the Maid called *Diana.*

Ber. They told me that your name was Fontibell.

Dia. No, my good lord, Diana.

Ber.   Titled goddess!

And worth it with addition! But, fair soul, In your fine frame hath love no quality? If the quick fire of youth light not your mind, You are no maiden, but a monument;   6 When you are dead you should be such a one As you are now; for you are cold and stern, And now you should be as your mother was When your sweet self was got.   10

Dia. She then was honest.

Ber.   So should you be.

Dia.   No.

My mother did but duty; such, my lord, As you owe to your wife.

Ber.   No more o' that!
I prithee do not strive against my vows.
I was compell'd to her, but I love thee   15
By love's own sweet constraint, and will for
     ever
Do thee all rights of service.
Dia.   Ay, so you serve us
Till we serve you; but when you have our
     roses,
You barely leave our thorns to prick ourselves
And mock us with our bareness.
Ber.   How have I sworn!
Dia. 'Tis not the many oaths that makes the
     truth,   21
But the plain single vow that is vow'd true.
What is not holy, that we swear not by,
But take the High'st to witness. Then pray
     you tell me,
If I should swear by Jove's great attributes   25
I lov'd you dearly, would you believe my oaths
When I did love you ill? This has no holding,
To swear by Him whom I protest to love,
That I will work against Him. Therefore your
     oaths
Are words and poor conditions, but unseal'd —
At least, in my opinion.
Ber.   Change it, change it!
Be not so holy-cruel. Love is holy,   32
And my integrity ne'er knew the crafts
That you do charge men with. Stand no more
     off,
But give thyself unto my sick desires,   35
Who then recover. Say thou art mine, and ever
My love, as it begins, shall so persever.
Dia. I see that men make ropes in such a
     scarre,
That we'll forsake ourselves. Give me that ring.
Ber. I'll lend it thee, my dear, but have no
     power   40
To give it from me.
Dia.   Will you not, my lord?
Ber. It is an honour 'longing to our house,
Bequeathed down from many ancestors,
Which were the greatest obloquy i' th' world
In me to lose.
Dia.   Mine honour's such a ring; 45
My chastity's the jewel of our house,
Bequeathed down from many ancestors,
Which were the greatest obloquy i' th' world
In me to lose. Thus your own proper wisdom
Brings in the champion Honour on my part   50
Against your vain assault.
Ber.   Here, take my ring!
My house, mine honour, yea, my life, be thine,
And I'll be bid by thee.

Dia. When midnight comes, knock at my
     chamber window.
I'll order take my mother shall not hear.   55
Now will I charge you in the band of truth,
When you have conquer'd my yet maiden bed,
Remain there but an hour, nor speak to me.
My reasons are most strong, and you shall
     know them
When back again this ring shall be deliver'd.   60
And on your finger in the night I'll put
Another ring, that what in time proceeds
May token to the future our past deeds.
Adieu till then! then fail not. You have won
A wife of me, though there my hope be done.
Ber. A heaven on earth I have won by woo-
     ing thee!   [*Exit.*]
Dia. For which live long to thank both
     heaven and me!
You may so in the end.
My mother told me just how he would woo,
As if she sat in 's heart. She says all men   70
Have the like oaths. He has sworn to marry me
When his wife's dead. Therefore I'll lie with
     him
When I am buried. Since Frenchmen are so
     braid,
Marry that will, I live and die a maid.
Only, in this disguise I think't no sin   75
To cozen him that would unjustly win.   *Exit.*

[Scene III. *The Florentine camp.*]

Enter the two French Captains *and some two
     or three* Soldiers.

2. Lord. You have not given him his mother's letter?
1. Lord. I have deliv'red it an hour since.
There is something in't that stings his nature;
for on the reading it he chang'd almost into
another man.   6
2. Lord. He has much worthy blame laid
upon him for shaking off so good a wife and so
sweet a lady.   9
1. Lord. Especially he hath incurred the everlasting displeasure of the King, who had even
tun'd his bounty to sing happiness to him. I
will tell you a thing, but you shall let it dwell
darkly with you.
2. Lord. When you have spoken it, 'tis dead
and I am the grave of it.   16
1. Lord. He hath perverted a young gentlewoman here in Florence, of a most chaste renown; and this night he fleshes his will in the

spoil of her honour. He hath given her his monumental ring, and thinks himself made in the unchaste composition.

2. Lord. Now God delay our rebellion! As we are ourselves, what things are we!   24

1. Lord. Merely our own traitors. And as, in the common course of all treasons, we still see them reveal themselves till they attain to their abhorr'd ends, so he that in this action contrives against his own nobility, in his proper stream o'erflows himself.   30

2. Lord. Is it not meant damnable in us, to be trumpeters of our unlawful intents? We shall not then have his company to-night?

1. Lord. Not till after midnight, for he is dieted to his hour.   35

2. Lord. That approaches apace. I would gladly have him see his company anatomiz'd, that he might take a measure of his own judgments, wherein so curiously he had set this counterfeit.   40

1. Lord. We will not meddle with him till he come; for his presence must be the whip of the other.

2. Lord. In the meantime, what hear you of these wars?   45

1. Lord. I hear there is an overture of peace.

2. Lord. Nay, I assure you, a peace concluded.

1. Lord. What will Count Rossillion do then? Will he travel higher or return again into France?   51

2. Lord. I perceive by this demand you are not altogether of his council.

1. Lord. Let it be forbid, sir! So should I be a great deal of his act.   55

2. Lord. Sir, his wife some two months since fled from his house. Her pretence is a pilgrimage to Saint Jaques le Grand; which holy undertaking with most austere sanctimony she accomplish'd; and there residing, the tenderness of her nature became as a prey to her grief; in fine, made a groan of her last breath, and now she sings in heaven.

1. Lord. How is this justified?   64

2. Lord. The stronger part of it by her own letters, which makes her story true, even to the point of her death. Her death itself, which could not be her office to say is come, was faithfully confirm'd by the rector of the place.   69

1. Lord. Hath the Count all this intelligence?

2. Lord. Ay, and the particular confirmations, point from point, to the full arming of the verity.

1. Lord. I am heartily sorry that he'll be glad of this.   75

2. Lord. How mightily sometimes we make us comforts of our losses!

1. Lord. And how mightily some other times we drown our gain in tears! The great dignity that his valour hath here acquir'd for him shall at home be encount'red with a shame as ample.

2. Lord. The web of our life is of a mingled yarn, good and ill together. Our virtues would be proud if our faults whipp'd them not, and our crimes would despair if they were not cherish'd by our virtues.   87

Enter a [*Servant* as] *Messenger*.

How now? Where's your master?

Serv. He met the Duke in the street, sir, of whom he hath taken a solemn leave. His lordship will next morning for France. The Duke hath offered him letters of commendations to the King.   [*Exit.*]

2. Lord. They shall be no more than needful there, if they were more than they can commend.

Enter [*Bertram*] *Count Rossillion*.

1. Lord. They cannot be too sweet for the King's tartness. Here's his lordship now. How now, my lord! Is't not after midnight?   97

Ber. I have to-night dispatch'd sixteen businesses, a month's length apiece, by an abstract of success. I have congied with the Duke, done my adieu with his nearest, buried a wife, mourn'd for her, writ to my lady mother I am returning, entertain'd my convoy, and between these main parcels of dispatch effected many nicer needs. The last was the greatest, but that I have not ended yet.   106

2. Lord. If the business be of any difficulty, and this morning your departure hence, it requires haste of your lordship.   109

Ber. I mean the business is not ended, as fearing to hear of it hereafter. But shall we have this dialogue between the Fool and the Soldier? Come, bring forth this counterfeit module has deceiv'd me like a double-meaning prophesier.

2. Lord. Bring him forth. [*Exeunt Soldiers.*] Has sat i' th' stocks all night, poor gallant knave.

Ber. No matter. His heels have deserv'd it, in usurping his spurs so long. How does he carry himself?   120

2. Lord. I have told your lordship already: the stocks carry him. But to answer you as you would be understood, he weeps like a wench that had shed her milk. He hath confess'd himself to Morgan, whom he supposes to be a friar, from the time of his remembrance to this very instant disaster of his setting i' th' stocks. And what think you he hath confess'd?

Ber. Nothing of me, has 'a? 129

2. Lord. His confession is taken, and it shall be read to his face. If your lordship be in't, as I believe you are, you must have the patience to hear it.

Enter *Parolles* with his *Interpreter.*

Ber. A plague upon him! muffled? He can say nothing of me.

1. Lord. Hush, hush! Hoodman comes! *Portotartarossa.* 136

Interp. He calls for the tortures. What will you say without 'em?

Par. I will confess what I know without constraint. If ye pinch me like a pasty, I can say no more. 141

Interp. Bosko chimurcho.

1. Lord. Boblibindo chicurmurco.

Interp. You are a merciful general. Our General bids you answer to what I shall ask you out of a note. 146

Par. And truly, as I hope to live!

Interp. [reads] 'First demand of him how many horse the Duke is strong.' What say you to that? 150

Par. Five or six thousand, but very weak and unserviceable. The troops are all scattered, and the commanders very poor rogues, upon my reputation and credit, and as I hope to live.

Interp. Shall I set down your answer so? 155

Par. Do. I'll take the sacrament on't, how and which way you will.

Ber. All's one to him. What a past-saving slave is this! 159

1. Lord. Y'are deceiv'd, my lord. This is Monsieur Parolles, the gallant militarist (that was his own phrase) that had the whole theoric of war in the knot of his scarf, and the practice in the chape of his dagger. 164

2. Lord. I will never trust a man again for keeping his sword clean, nor believe he can have everything in him by wearing his apparel neatly.

Interp. Well, that's set down. 169

Par. 'Five or six thousand horse,' I said — I will say true — 'or thereabouts' set down, for I'll speak truth.

1. Lord. He's very near the truth in this.

Ber. But I con him no thanks for't, in the nature he delivers it. 175

Par. 'Poor rogues,' I pray you say.

Interp. Well, that's set down.

Par. I humbly thank you, sir. A truth's a truth — the rogues are marvellous poor. 179

Interp. [reads] 'Demand of him of what strength they are afoot.' What say you to that?

Par. By my troth, sir, if I were to live this present hour, I will tell true. Let me see: Spurio, a hundred and fifty; Sebastian, so many; Corambus, so many; Jaques, so many; Guiltian, Cosmo, Lodowick, and Gratii, two hundred fifty each; mine own company, Chitopher, Vaumond, Bentii, two hundred fifty each; so that the muster file, rotten and sound, upon my life, amounts not to fifteen thousand poll, half of the which dare not shake the snow from off their cassocks, lest they shake themselves to pieces. 193

Ber. What shall be done to him?

1. Lord. Nothing, but let him have thanks. Demand of him my condition, and what credit I have with the Duke. 197

Interp. Well, that's set down. [Reads] 'You shall demand of him whether one Captain Dumain be i' th' camp, a Frenchman; what his reputation is with the Duke; what his valour, honesty, and expertness in wars; or whether he thinks it were not possible, with well-weighing sums of gold, to corrupt him to a revolt.' What say you to this? What do you know of it? 205

Par. I beseech you let me answer to the particular of the inter'gatories. Demand them singly. 208

Interp. Do you know this Captain Dumain?

Par. I know him. 'A was a botcher's prentice in Paris, from whence he was whipp'd for getting the shrieve's fool with child — a dumb innocent, that could not say him nay.

[*First Lord makes as if to strike him.*]

Ber. Nay, by your leave, hold your hands, though I know his brains are forfeit to the next tile that falls. 217

Interp. Well, is this captain in the Duke of Florence's camp?

Par. Upon my knowledge he is, and lousy.

1. Lord. Nay, look not so upon me. We shall hear of your lordship anon.

Interp. What is his reputation with the Duke? 224

Par. The Duke knows him for no other but a poor officer of mine, and writ to me this other day to turn him out o' th' band. I think I have his letter in my pocket.

Interp. Marry, we'll search. 229

Par. In good sadness, I do not know. Either it is there, or it is upon a file with the Duke's other letters in my tent.

Interp. Here 'tis; here's a paper. Shall I read it to you?
Par. I do not know if it be it or no.   235
Ber. Our interpreter does it well.
1. Lord. Excellently.
Interp. [*reads*]
'Dian, the Count 's a fool, and full of gold.'
Par. That is not the Duke's letter, sir. That is an advertisement to a proper maid in Florence, one Diana, to take heed of the allurement of one Count Rossillion, a foolish idle boy; but for all that very ruttish. I pray you, sir, put it up again.   243
Interp. Nay, I'll read it first, by your favour.
Par. My meaning in't, I protest, was very honest in the behalf of the maid; for I knew the young Count to be a dangerous and lascivious boy, who is a whale to virginity, and devours up all the fry it finds.   250
Ber. Damnable both-sides rogue!
Interp. [*reads*]
'When he swears oaths, bid him drop gold, and take it:
After he scores, he never pays the score.
Half won is match well made; match, and well make it;
He ne'er pays after-debts, take it before;   255
And say a soldier, Dian, told thee this;
Men are to mell with, boys are not to kiss:
For count of this, the Count 's a fool, I know it,
Who pays before, but not when he does owe it.

'Thine, as he vow'd to thee in thine ear,   260
'PAROLLES.'

Ber. He shall be whipp'd through the army with this rhyme in 's forehead.
2. Lord. This is your devoted friend, sir, the manifold linguist and the armipotent soldier.
Ber. I could endure anything before but a cat, and now he's a cat to me.
Interp. I perceive, sir, by the General's looks, we shall be fain to hang you.   269
Par. My life, sir, in any case! Not that I am afraid to die; but that, my offences being many, I would repent out the remainder of nature. Let me live, sir, in a dungeon, i' th' stocks, or anywhere, so I may live.   274
Interp. We'll see what may be done, so you confess freely. Therefore, once more to this Captain Dumain! You have answer'd to his reputation with the Duke and to his valour. What is his honesty?   279
Par. He will steal, sir, an egg out of a cloister. For rapes and ravishments he parallels Nessus. He professes not keeping of oaths; in breaking 'em he is stronger than Hercules. He will lie,

sir, with such volubility that you would think truth were a fool. Drunkenness is his best virtue, for he will be swine-drunk, and in his sleep he does little harm, save to his bedclothes about him; but they know his conditions and lay him in straw. I have but little more to say, sir, of his honesty. He has everything that an honest man should not have; what an honest man should have, he has nothing.   292
1. Lord. I begin to love him for this.
Ber. For this description of thine honesty? A pox upon him for me! he's more and more a cat.   295
Interp. What say you to his expertness in war?
Par. Faith, sir, has led the drum before the English tragedians. To belie him I will not, and more of his soldiership I know not, except in that country he had the honour to be the officer at a place there called Mile-end, to instruct for the doubling of files. I would do the man what honour I can, but of this I am not certain.
1. Lord. He hath out-villain'd villany so far that the rarity redeems him.   306
Ber. A pox on him! he's a cat still.
Interp. His qualities being at this poor price, I need not to ask you if gold will corrupt him to revolt.   310
Par. Sir, for a cardecue he will sell the fee simple of his salvation, the inheritance of it, and cut th' entail from all remainders, and a perpetual succession for it perpetually.
Interp. What's his brother, the other Captain Dumain?   316
2. Lord. Why does he ask him of me?
Interp. What's he?
Par. E'en a crow o' th' same nest; not altogether so great as the first in goodness, but greater a great deal in evil. He excels his brother for a coward; yet his brother is reputed one of the best that is. In a retreat he outruns any lackey; marry, in coming on he has the cramp.
Interp. If your life be saved, will you undertake to betray the Florentine?   326
Par. Ay, and the Captain of his Horse, Count Rossillion.
Interp. I'll whisper with the General and know his pleasure.   330
Par. [*aside*] I'll no more drumming; a plague of all drums! Only to seem to deserve well, and to beguile the supposition of that lascivious young boy the Count, have I run into this danger. Yet who would have suspected an ambush where I was taken?   336
Interp. There is no remedy, sir, but you must die. The General says, you that have so traitor-

ously discover'd the secrets of your army, and made such pestiferous reports of men very nobly held, can serve the world for no honest use; therefore you must die. Come, headsman, off with his head!

Par. O Lord, sir, let me live, or let me see my death! 345

Interp. That shall you, and take your leave of all your friends. [*Unmuffles him.*] So, look about you. Know you any here?

Ber. Good morrow, noble Captain.

2. Lord. God bless you, Captain Parolles!

1. Lord. God save you, noble Captain! 351

2. Lord. Captain, what greeting will you to my Lord Lafew? I am for France.

1. Lord. Good Captain, will you give me a copy of the sonnet you writ to Diana in behalf of the Count Rossillion? An I were not a very coward, I'd compel it of you. But fare you well.
          Exeunt [Bertram and Lords].

Interp. You are undone, Captain, all but your scarf; that has a knot on't yet.

Par. Who cannot be crush'd with a plot? 360

Interp. If you could find out a country where but women were that had received so much shame, you might begin an impudent nation. Fare ye well, sir. I am for France too. We shall speak of you there. *Exit [with Soldiers].*

Par. Yet am I thankful. If my heart were great, 366
'Twould burst at this. Captain I'll be no more;
But I will eat, and drink, and sleep as soft
As captain shall. Simply the thing I am
Shall make me live. Who knows himself a braggart, 370
Let him fear this; for it will come to pass
That every braggart shall be found an ass.
Rust, sword! cool, blushes! and, Parolles, live
Safest in shame! Being fool'd, by fool'ry thrive!
There's place and means for every man alive.
I'll after them. *Exit.*

[Scene IV. *Florence. The* Widow's *house.*]

Enter *Helen, Widow,* and *Diana.*

Hel. That you may well perceive I have not wrong'd you,
One of the greatest in the Christian world
Shall be my surety; fore whose throne 'tis needful,
Ere I can perfect mine intents, to kneel.
Time was I did him a desired office, 5
Dear almost as his life; which gratitude

Through flinty Tartar's bosom would peep forth
And answer thanks. I duly am inform'd
His Grace is at Marseilles, to which place
We have convenient convoy. You must know
I am supposed dead. The army breaking, 11
My husband hies him home, where, heaven aiding,
And by the leave of my good lord the King,
We'll be before our welcome.

Wid.   Gentle madam,
You never had a servant to whose trust 15
Your business was more welcome.

Hel.   Nor you, mistress,
Ever a friend whose thoughts more truly labour
To recompense your love. Doubt not but heaven
Hath brought me up to be your daughter's dower,
As it hath fated her to be my motive 20
And helper to a husband. But, O strange men!
That can such sweet use make of what they hate,
When saucy trusting of the cozen'd thoughts
Defiles the pitchy night! So lust doth play
With what it loathes, for that which is away.
But more of this hereafter. You, Diana, 26
Under my poor instructions yet must suffer
Something in my behalf.

Dia.   Let death and honesty
Go with your impositions, I am yours
Upon your will to suffer.

Hel.   Yet, I pray you! 30
But with the word the time will bring on summer,
When briers shall have leaves as well as thorns
And be as sweet as sharp. We must away;
Our wagon is prepar'd, and time revives us.
All's well that ends well. Still the fine's the crown. 35
Whate'er the course, the end is the renown.
          Exeunt.

[Scene V. *Rossillion. The* Count's *Palace.*]

Enter *Clown, Old Lady [Countess],* and *Lafew.*

Laf. No, no, no! your son was misled with a snipt-taffeta fellow there, whose villanous saffron would have made all the unbak'd and doughy youth of a nation in his colour. Your daughter-in-law had been alive at this hour, and your son here at home, more advanc'd by the King than by that red-tail'd humblebee I speak of. 7

Count. I would I had not known him! It was

the death of the most virtuous gentlewoman
that ever nature had praise for creating. If she
had partaken of my flesh and cost me the dearest groans of a mother, I could not have owed
her a more rooted love.   13

Laf. 'Twas a good lady, 'twas a good lady.
We may pick a thousand sallets ere we light on
such another herb.   16

Clown. Indeed, sir, she was the sweet marjoram of the sallet, or rather, the herb of grace.

Laf. They are not sallet herbs, you knave;
they are nose herbs.   20

Clown. I am no great Nebuchadnezzar, sir;
I have not much skill in grass.

Laf. Whether dost thou profess thyself — a
knave or a fool?

Clown. A fool, sir, at a woman's service, and
a knave at a man's.   26

Laf. Your distinction?

Clown. I would cozen the man of his wife and
do his service.

Laf. So you were a knave at his service
indeed.   31

Clown. And I would give his wife my bauble,
sir, to do her service.

Laf. I will subscribe for thee, thou art both
knave and fool.   35

Clown. At your service.

Laf. No, no, no!

Clown. Why, sir, if I cannot serve you, I can
serve as great a prince as you are.

Laf. Who's that? a Frenchman?   40

Clown. Faith, sir, 'a has an English name;
but his fisnomy is more hotter in France than
there.

Laf. What prince is that?

Clown. The Black Prince, sir, alias the Prince
of Darkness, alias the devil.   45

Laf. Hold thee, there's my purse. I give
thee not this to suggest thee from thy master
thou talk'st of. Serve him still.

Clown. I am a woodland fellow, sir, that always loved a great fire; and the master I speak
of ever keeps a good fire. But sure he is the
prince of the world; let his nobility remain in 's
court. I am for the house with the narrow gate,
which I take to be too little for pomp to enter.
Some that humble themselves may; but the
many will be too chill and tender, and they'll be
for the flow'ry way that leads to the broad gate
and the great fire.   58

Laf. Go thy ways, I begin to be aweary of
thee; and I tell thee so before, because I would
not fall out with thee. Go thy ways. Let my
horses be well look'd to without any tricks.   62

Clown. If I put any tricks upon 'em, sir, they
shall be jades' tricks, which are their own right
by the law of nature.   *Exit.*

Laf. A shrewd knave and an unhappy.   66

Count. So 'a is. My lord that's gone made
himself much sport out of him. By his authority he remains here, which he thinks is a patent
for his sauciness; and indeed he has no pace,
but runs where he will.   71

Laf. I like him well; 'tis not amiss. And I
was about to tell you, since I heard of the good
lady's death, and that my lord your son was
upon his return home, I moved the King my
master to speak in the behalf of my daughter;
which, in the minority of them both, his Majesty out of a self-gracious remembrance did
first propose. His Highness hath promis'd me
to do it; and to stop up the displeasure he hath
conceived against your son there is no fitter
matter. How does your ladyship like it?   82

Count. With very much content, my lord,
and I wish it happily effected.

Laf. His Highness comes post from Marseilles, of as able body as when he number'd
thirty; 'a will be here to-morrow, or I am deceiv'd by him that in such intelligence hath
seldom fail'd.

Count. It rejoices me that I hope I shall see
him ere I die. I have letters that my son will be
here to-night. I shall beseech your lordship to
remain with me till they meet together.   92

Laf. Madam, I was thinking with what manners I might safely be admitted.

Count. You need but plead your honourable
privilege.   96

Laf. Lady, of that I have made a bold charter; but I thank my God it holds yet.

Enter *Clown.*

Clown. O madam, yonder's my lord your son
with a patch of velvet on 's face. Whether there
be a scar under't or no, the velvet knows; but
'tis a goodly patch of velvet. His left cheek is a
cheek of two pile and a half, but his right cheek
is worn bare.

Laf. A scar nobly got, or a noble scar, is a
good liv'ry of honour. So belike is that.   106

Clown. But it is your carbonado'd face.

Laf. Let us go see your son, I pray you. I
long to talk with the young noble soldier.   109

Clown. Faith, there's a dozen of 'em, with
delicate fine hats, and most courteous feathers,
which bow the head and nod at every man.

Exeunt.

ACT V. [Scene I. *Marseilles. A street.*]

Enter *Helen*, *Widow*, and *Diana*, with two
Attendants.

Hel. But this exceeding posting day and
night
Must wear your spirits low; we cannot help it.
But, since you have made the days and nights
as one,
To wear your gentle limbs in my affairs,
Be bold you do so grow in my requital 5
As nothing can unroot you.

Enter a *Gentleman*, a stranger.

In happy time
This man may help me to his Majesty's ear,
If he would spend his power. God save you, sir.
Gent. And you.
Hel. Sir, I have seen you in the court of
France. 10
Gent. I have been sometimes there.
Hel. I do presume, sir, that you are not fall'n
From the report that goes upon your goodness;
And therefore, goaded with most sharp occa-
sions,
Which lay nice manners by, I put you to 15
The use of your own virtues, for the which
I shall continue thankful.
Gent. What's your will?
Hel. That it will please you
To give this poor petition to the King,
And aid me with that store of power you have
To come into his presence. 21
Gent. The King's not here.
Hel. Not here, sir?
Gent. Not indeed.
He hence remov'd last night, and with more
haste
Than is his use.
Wid. Lord, how we lose our pains!
Hel. All's well that ends well yet, 25
Though time seem so adverse and means unfit.
I do beseech you, whither is he gone?
Gent. Marry, as I take it, to Rossillion,
Whither I am going.
Hel. I do beseech you, sir,
Since you are like to see the King before me, 30
Commend the paper to his gracious hand,
Which I presume shall render you no blame,
But rather make you thank your pains for it.
I will come after you with what good speed
Our means will make us means.

Gent. This I'll do for you.
Hel. And you shall find yourself to be well
thank'd,
Whate'er falls more. — We must to horse again.
Go, go, provide. [*Exeunt.*]

[Scene II. *Rossillion. Before the
Count's Palace.*]

Enter *Clown* and *Parolles*.

Par. Good Monsieur Lavatch, give my Lord
Lafew this letter. I have ere now, sir, been better known to you, when I have held familiarity
with fresher clothes; but I am now, sir, muddied
in Fortune's mood, and smell somewhat strong
of her strong displeasure. 6
Clown. Truly, Fortune's displeasure is but
sluttish if it smell so strongly as thou speak'st
of. I will henceforth eat no fish of Fortune's
butt'ring. Prithee allow the wind! 10
Par. Nay, you need not to stop your nose,
sir. I spake but by a metaphor.
Clown. Indeed, sir, if your metaphor stink, I
will stop my nose, or against any man's metaphor. Prithee get thee further! 15
Par. Pray you, sir, deliver me this paper.
Clown. Foh! prithee stand away! A paper
from Fortune's close-stool to give to a nobleman! Look, here he comes himself. 19

Enter *Lafew*.

Here is a purr of Fortune's, sir, or of Fortune's
cat, but not a musk cat, that has fall'n into the
unclean fishpond of her displeasure and, as he
says, is muddied withal. Pray you, sir, use the
carp as you may; for he looks like a poor decayed, ingenious, foolish, rascally knave. I do
pity his distress in my similes of comfort, and
leave him to your lordship. [*Exit.*]
Par. My lord, I am a man whom Fortune
hath cruelly scratch'd. 29
Laf. And what would you have me to do?
'Tis too late to pare her nails now. Wherein
have you played the knave with Fortune that
she should scratch you, who of herself is a good
lady, and would not have knaves thrive long
under her? There's a cardecue for you. Let the
justices make you and Fortune friends; I am
for other business. 36

Par. I beseech your honour to hear me one single word.

Laf. You beg a single penny more. Come, you shall ha't; save your word.   40

Par. My name, my good lord, is Parolles.

Laf. You beg more than word then. Cox my passion! give me your hand. How does your drum?

Par. O my good lord, you were the first that found me.   46

Laf. Was I, in sooth? And I was the first that lost thee.

Par. It lies in you, my lord, to bring me in some grace, for you did bring me out.   50

Laf. Out upon thee, knave! Dost thou put upon me at once both the office of God and the devil? One brings thee in grace, and the other brings thee out. [*Trumpets sound.*] The King's coming; I know by his trumpets. Sirrah, inquire further after me. I had talk of you last night. Though you are a fool and a knave, you shall eat. Go to, follow.   58

Par. I praise God for you.   [*Exeunt.*]

[Scene III. *Rossillion. The* Count's Palace.]

Flourish. Enter *King, Old Lady* [*Countess*], *Lafew*, the two *French Lords*, with *Attendants.*

King. We lost a jewel of her, and our esteem
Was made much poorer by it; but your son,
As mad in folly, lack'd the sense to know
Her estimation home.

Count.   'Tis past, my liege,
And I beseech your Majesty to make it   5
Natural rebellion, done i' th' blaze of youth,
When oil and fire, too strong for reason's force,
O'erbears it and burns on.

King.   My honour'd lady,
I have forgiven and forgotten all,   9
Though my revenges were high bent upon him
And watch'd the time to shoot.

Laf.   This I must say —
But first I beg my pardon — the young lord
Did to his Majesty, his mother, and his lady,
Offence of mighty note; but to himself
The greatest wrong of all. He lost a wife   15
Whose beauty did astonish the survey
Of richest eyes; whose words all ears took captive;
Whose dear perfection hearts that scorn'd to serve
Humbly call'd mistress

King.   Praising what is lost
Makes the remembrance dear. Well, call him hither.   20
We are reconcil'd, and the first view shall kill
All repetition. Let him not ask our pardon;
The nature of his great offence is dead,
And deeper than oblivion we do bury
Th' incensing relics of it. Let him approach,   25
A stranger, no offender; and inform him
So 'tis our will he should.

Gent.   I shall, my liege.
                                             [*Exit.*]

King. What says he to your daughter? Have you spoke?

Laf. All that he is hath reference to your Highness.

King. Then shall we have a match. I have letters sent me   30
That sets him high in fame.

                    Enter *Count Bertram.*

Laf.   He looks well on't.

King. I am not a day of season,
For thou mayst see a sunshine and a hail
In me at once. But to the brightest beams
Distracted clouds give way. So stand thou forth,   35
The time is fair again.

Ber.   My high-repented blames,
Dear sovereign, pardon to me.

King.   All is whole.
Not one word more of the consumed time!
Let's take the instant by the forward top;
For we are old, and on our quick'st decrees   40
Th' inaudible and noiseless foot of Time
Steals, ere we can effect them. You remember
The daughter of this lord?

Ber. Admiringly, my liege. At first   45
I stuck my choice upon her, ere my heart
Durst make too bold a herald of my tongue;
Where the impression of mine eye infixing,
Contempt his scornful perspective did lend me,
Which warp'd the line of every other favour,
Scorn'd a fair colour or express'd it stol'n,   50
Extended or contracted all proportions
To a most hideous object. Thence it came
That she whom all men prais'd, and whom myself,
Since I have lost, have lov'd, was in mine eye
The dust that did offend it.

King.   Well excus'd!   55
That thou didst love her strikes some scores away
From the great compt But love that comes too late,

393

Like a remorseful pardon slowly carried,
To the great sender turns a sour offence,
Crying, 'That's good that's gone.' Our rash faults   60
Make trivial price of serious things we have,
Not knowing them until we know their grave.
Oft our displeasures, to ourselves unjust,
Destroy our friends, and after weep their dust ;
Our own love, waking, cries to see what's done,
While shameful hate sleeps out the afternoon.
Be this sweet Helen's knell, and now forget her.
Send forth your amorous token for fair Maudlin.
The main consents are had, and here we'll stay
To see our widower's second marriage day.   70

Count. Which better than the first, O dear heaven, bless,
Or, ere they meet, in me, O nature, cesse!

Laf. Come on, my son, in whom my house's name
Must be digested. Give a favour from you
To sparkle in the spirits of my daughter,   75
That she may quickly come.
[*Bertram gives him a ring.*]
By my old beard
And ev'ry hair that's on't, Helen that's dead
Was a sweet creature! Such a ring as this,
The last that e'er I took her leave at court,
I saw upon her finger.

Ber.   Hers it was not.   80

King. Now pray you let me see it; for mine eye,
While I was speaking, oft was fasten'd to't.
[*Takes the ring.*]
This ring was mine; and when I gave it Helen,
I bade her, if her fortunes ever stood
Necessitied to help, that by this token   85
I would relieve her. Had you that craft to reave her
Of what should stead her most?

Ber.   My gracious sovereign
Howe'er it pleases you to take it so,
The ring was never hers.

Count.   Son, on my life,
I have seen her wear it, and she reckon'd it   90
At her live's rate.

Laf.   I am sure I saw her wear it.

Ber. You are deceiv'd, my lord; she never saw it.
In Florence was it from a casement thrown me,
Wrapp'd in a paper, which contain'd the name
Of her that threw it. Noble she was, and thought   95
I stood engag'd; but when I had subscrib'd
To mine own fortune and inform'd her fully
I could not answer in that course of honour

As she had made the overture, she cras'd
In heavy satisfaction, and would never   100
Receive the ring again.

King.   Plutus himself,
That knows the tinct and multiplying med'cine,
Hath not in nature's mystery more science
Than I have in this ring. 'Twas mine, 'twas Helen's,
Whoever gave it you. Then if you know   105
That you are well acquainted with yourself,
Confess 'twas hers, and by what rough enforcement
You got it from her. She call'd the saints to surety
That she would never put it from her finger
Unless she gave it to yourself in bed —   110
Where you have never come — or sent it us
Upon her great disaster.

Ber.   She never saw it.

King. Thou speak'st it falsely, as I love mine honour!
And mak'st conjectural fears to come into me
Which I would fain shut out. If it should prove
That thou art so inhuman — 'Twill not prove so!   116
And yet I know not — thou didst hate her deadly,
And she is dead, which nothing but to close
Her eyes myself could win me to believe
More than to see this ring. Take him away.   120
[*Attendants arrest Bertram.*]
My forepast proofs, howe'er the matter fall,
Shall tax my fears of little vanity,
Having vainly fear'd too little. Away with him!
We'll sift this matter further.

Ber.   If you shall prove
This ring was ever hers, you shall as easy   125
Prove that I husbanded her bed in Florence,
Where yet she never was.   [*Exit, guarded.*]

Enter a *Gentleman.*

King. I am wrapp'd in dismal thinkings.

Gent.   Gracious sovereign,
Whether I have been to blame or no, I know not.
Here's a petition from a Florentine,   130
Who hath for four or five removes come short
To tender it herself. I undertook it,
Vanquish'd thereto by the fair grace and speech
Of the poor suppliant, who by this, I know,
Is here attending. Her business looks in her   135
With an importing visage, and she told me
In a sweet verbal brief it did concern
Your Highness with herself.

[*King reads*] *a letter.* 'Upon his many protestations to marry me when his wife was dead,

394

blush to say it, he won me. Now is the Count
Rossillion a widower, his vows are forfeited to me,
and my honour's paid to him. He stole from Florence, taking no leave, and I follow him to his
country for justice. Grant it me, O King! in you
it best lies; otherwise a seducer flourishes, and a
poor maid is undone.

'DIANA CAPILET.'

Laf. I will buy me a son-in-law in a fair, and
toll for this. I'll none of him.

King. The heavens have thought well on
   thee, Lafew, 150
To bring forth this discov'ry. Seek these
   suitors.
Go speedily and bring again the Count.
   [*Exeunt Gentleman and an Attendant.*]
I am afeard the life of Helen, lady,
Was foully snatch'd.

Count.   Now justice on the doers!

Enter *Bertram*, [guarded].

King. I wonder, sir, sith wives are monsters
   to you, 155
And that you fly them as you swear them lordship,
Yet you desire to marry.

Enter *Widow* [and] *Diana*.

          What woman's that?
Dia. I am, my lord, a wretched Florentine,
Derived from the ancient Capilet.
My suit, as I do understand, you know, 160
And therefore know how far I may be pitied.
Wid. I am her mother, sir, whose age and
   honour
Both suffer under this complaint we bring,
And both shall cease, without your remedy.
King. Come hither, Count. Do you know
   these women? 165
Ber. My lord, I neither can nor will deny
But that I know them. Do they charge me
   further?
Dia. Why do you look so strange upon your
   wife?
Ber. She's none of mine, my lord.
Dia.   If you shall marry,
You give away this hand, and that is mine; 170
You give away heaven's vows, and those are
   mine;
You give away myself, which is known mine,
For I by vow am so embodied yours
That she which marries you must marry me,
Either both or none. 175
Laf. Your reputation comes too short for my
daughter: you are no husband for her.

Ber. My lord, this is a fond and desp'rate
   creature,
Whom sometime I have laugh'd with. Let your
   Highness 179
Lay a more noble thought upon mine honour
Than for to think that I would sink it here.
King. Sir, for my thoughts, you have them
   ill to friend
Till your deeds gain them. Fairer prove your
   honour
Than in my thought it lies!
Dia.   Good my lord,
Ask him upon his oath if he does think 185
He had not my virginity.
King. What say'st thou to her?
Ber.   She's impudent, my lord,
And was a common gamester to the camp.
Dia. He does me wrong, my lord. If I
   were so, 189
He might have bought me at a common price.
Do not believe him. O, behold this ring,
Whose high respect and rich validity
Did lack a parallel. Yet for all that
He gave it to a commoner o' th' camp
If I be one.
Count.   He blushes, and 'tis his. 195
Of six preceding ancestors, that gem,
Conferr'd by testament to th' sequent issue,
Hath it been ow'd and worn. This is his wife.
That ring's a thousand proofs.
King.   Methought you said
You saw one here in court could witness it. 200
Dia. I did, my lord, but loath am to produce
So bad an instrument. His name's Parolles.
Laf. I saw the man to-day, if man he be.
King. Find him and bring him hither.
           [*Exit an Attendant.*]
Ber.   What of him?
He's quoted for a most perfidious slave 205
With all the spots o' th' world tax'd and de-
   bosh'd,
Whose nature sickens but to speak a truth.
Am I or that or this for what he'll utter,
That will speak anything?
King.   She hath that ring of yours.
Ber. I think she has. Certain it is I lik'd her,
And boarded her i' th' wanton way of youth.
She knew her distance and did angle for me,
Madding my eagerness with her restraint,
As all impediments in fancy's course
Are motives of more fancy; and, in fine, 215
Her infinite cunning, with her modern grace,
Subdu'd me to her rate. She got the ring,
And I had that which any inferior might
At market price have bought.

Dia. I must be patient.
You that turn'd off a first so noble wife 220
May justly diet me. I pray you yet
(Since you lack virtue, I will lose a husband)
Send for your ring, I will return it home,
And give me mine again.
Ber. I have it not.
King. What ring was yours, I pray you?
Dia. Sir, much like
The same upon your finger. 226
King. Know you this ring? This ring was
his of late.
Dia. And this was it I gave him, being abed.
King. The story then goes false, you threw
it him
Out of a casement?
Dia. I have spoke the truth. 230

Enter *Parolles.*

Ber. My lord, I do confess the ring was hers.
King. You boggle shrewdly, every feather
starts you.
Is this the man you speak of?
Dia. Ay, my lord.
King. Tell me, sirrah — but tell me true I
charge you,
Not fearing the displeasure of your master, 235
Which, on your just proceeding, I'll keep off —
By him and by this woman here what know
you?
Par. So please your Majesty, my master
hath been an honourable gentleman. Tricks
he hath had in him, which gentlemen have. 240
King. Come, come, to th' purpose! Did he
love this woman?
Par. Faith, sir, he did love her! but how?
King. How, I pray you?
Par. He did love her, sir, as a gentleman
loves a woman. 246
King. How is that?
Par. He lov'd her, sir, and lov'd her not.
King. As thou art a knave, and no knave.
What an equivocal companion is this! 250
Par. I am a poor man, and at your Majesty's
command.
Laf. He's a good drum, my lord, but a
naughty orator. 254
Dia. Do you know he promis'd me marriage?
Par. Faith, I know more than I'll speak.
King. But wilt thou not speak all thou
know'st? 257
Par. Yes, so please your Majesty. I did go
between them as I said; but more than that, he
loved her — for indeed he was mad for her, and
talk'd of Sathan and of Limbo and of Furies and

I know not what. Yet I was in that credit with
them at that time that I knew of their going to
bed, and of other motions, as promising her
marriage, and things which would derive me ill
will to speak of. Therefore I will not speak what
I know. 26
King. Thou hast spoken all already, unless
thou canst say they are married. But thou art
too fine in thy evidence; therefore stand aside.
This ring you say was yours?
Dia. Ay, my good lord.
King. Where did you buy it? or who gave
it you? 27:
Dia. It was not given me, nor I did not buy
it.
King. Who lent it you?
Dia. It was not lent me neither
King. Where did you find it then?
Dia. I found it not
King. If it were yours by none of all these
ways, 27
How could you give it him?
Dia. I never gave it him
Laf. This woman's an easy glove, my lord
she goes off and on at pleasure.
King. This ring was mine. I gave it his firs
wife. 28
Dia. It might be yours or hers for aught
know.
King. Take her away, I do not like her now
To prison with her! and away with him!
Unless thou tell'st me where thou hadst thi
ring, 28
Thou diest within this hour.
Dia. I'll never tell you
King. Take her away!
Dia. I'll put in bail, my liege
King. I think thee now some common cus
tomer.
Dia. [*to Lafew*] By Jove, if ever I knew man
'twas you!
King. Wherefore hast thou accus'd him al
this while? 28
Dia. Because he's guilty, and he is not guilty
He knows I am no maid, and he'll swear to't
I'll swear I am a maid and he knows not.
Great King, I am no strumpet, by my life!
I am either maid, or else this old man's wife
[*Points to Lafew.*
King. She does abuse our ears. To prison
with her! 29
Dia. Good mother, fetch my bail. Stay
royal sir: [*Exit Widow.*
The jeweller that owes the ring is sent for,

And he shall surety me. But for this lord,
Who hath abus'd me, as he knows himself,
Though yet he never harm'd me, here I quit
    him.   300
He knows himself my bed he hath defil'd,
And at that time he got his wife with child.
Dead though she be, she feels her young one
    kick.
So there's my riddle : one that's dead is quick —
And now behold the meaning.

      Enter *Helen* and *Widow.*

   King.   Is there no exorcist
Beguiles the truer office of mine eyes?   306
Is't real that I see?
   Hel.   No, my good lord.
'Tis but the shadow of a wife you see,
The name and not the thing.
   Ber.   Both, both! O, pardon!
   Hel. O my good lord, when I was like this
    maid   310
I found you wondrous kind. There is your ring,
And look you, here's your letter. This it says :
'When from my finger you can get this ring,
And are by me with child,' &c. This is done.
Will you be mine now you are doubly won?   315
   Ber. If she, my liege, can make me know this
    clearly,
I'll love her dearly — ever, ever dearly.
   Hel. If it appear not plain, and prove untrue,
Deadly divorce step between me and you!
O my dear mother, do I see you living?   320

   Laf. Mine eyes smell onions; I shall weep
    anon.
[*To Parolles*] Good Tom Drum, lend me a hand-
    kercher. So,
I thank thee. Wait on me home; I'll make
    sport with thee.
Let thy curtsies alone! they are scurvy ones.
   King. Let us from point to point this story
    know,   325
To make the even truth in pleasure flow.
[*To Diana*] If thou beest yet a fresh uncropped
    flower,
Choose thou thy husband, and I'll pay thy
    dower ;
For I can guess that by thy honest aid
Thou kept'st a wife herself, thyself a maid.
Of that and all the progress more and less 331
Resolvedly more leisure shall express.
All yet seems well ; and if it end so meet,
The bitter past, more welcome is the sweet,
                   Flourish.

           [EPILOGUE.]

The King's a beggar, now the play is done. 335
All is well ended if this suit be won,
That you express content ; which we will pay
With strife to please you, day exceeding day.
Ours be your patience then, and yours our
    parts ;   339
Your gentle hands lend us, and take our hearts.
                 Exeunt omnes.

TWELFTH NIGHT

The text of TWELFTH NIGHT, as printed in the Folio of 1623, is unusually accurate. There is no earlier edition. John Manningham of the Middle Temple saw TWELFTH NIGHT performed on February 2, 1602. 'At our feast,' he notes in his *Diary*, 'wee had a play called Twelue Night, or What You Will, much like the Commedy of Errores, or Menechmi in Plautus, but most like and neere to that in Italian called *Inganni*.' He commends particularly the trick played on Malvolio, which he calls 'a good practise' (i. e., a clever device). 'Twelue' is an old form of the ordinal; the Folio spells it 'twelfe.' Manningham's record fixes one limit for the date of composition. Obviously he had never seen the play before, but that does not prove that it was absolutely new. The title tempts inference that the first production was on the twelfth night (Epiphany) immediately preceding, that is, on January 6, 1602. Anyhow, 1601 (or 1600 at the earliest) may safely be accepted as the date of composition. No circumstantial evidence conflicts with this date. 'The new map with the augmentation of the Indies' (iii, 2, 85) was doubtless that of Emerie Molyneux (*ca.* 1599). The 'pension of thousands to be paid from the Sophy' (ii, 5, 197), that is, the Shah of Persia, may allude to Sir Robert Shirley's return from that country in 1599, with rich gifts from the Shah. Support for the accepted date (1600 or 1601) has been sought in Ben Jonson's *Poetaster* (iii, 4), where Captain Tucca describes a certain 'fat fool' called Mango. The passage has been thought to glance at Sir Toby Belch. *Poetaster* was acted in 1601. The evidence would be welcome if it were trustworthy, but Tucca's Mango never could have played Sir Toby.

The source for the main plot of TWELFTH NIGHT is Barnabe Riche's tale *Of Apolonius and Silla*, the second 'historie' in *Riche his Farewell to Militarie Profession* (1581).

Shakespeare's Viola is Riche's Silla. Viola's romance begins with a shipwreck, which separated her from her brother Sebastian and cast her up on Duke Orsino's Illyrian coast. Silla is likewise shipwrecked, but the first chapter of her love story is staged in Cyprus, at her father's court, where she fell in love with Duke Apolonius, her father's guest, and sought to win him, but in vain. Apolonius returns to his home in Constantinople and Silla determines to follow him. The shipwreck is the end of her journey. Her brother Silvio is not with her, but she is accompanied by a trusty servant (Pedro) who passes for her brother during the voyage. The shipwreck is fortunate, for, though it separates her from Pedro, it saves her from the violent attentions of the shipmaster. She is washed ashore on a chest that contains good store of coin and sundry suits of the captain's clothes. Under the name of her brother Silvio (Shakespeare's Sebastian) she takes service with Apolonius, who of course does not recognize her. He, in the meantime, has succumbed to the charms of an obdurate young widow, Julina (Shakespeare's Olivia), and he employs Silla as his messenger with letters and gifts. Julina falls in love with her while she is pleading her master's cause and interrupts: 'Silvio, it is enough that you have said for your maister; from henceforthe, either speake for your self, or saie nothyng at all.' Shakespeare's Olivia is less blunt, but equally frank (iii, 1, 117-121):

> 'O, by your leave, I pray you!
> I bade you never speak again of him;
> But, would you undertake another suit,
> I had rather hear you to solicit that
> Than music from the spheres.'

In the interval, Silvio has arrived at Constantinople, after wandering through many cities in search of his sister, who he supposes has eloped with Pedro. Julina falls in love with him as he is walking about the city, mistakes him for Silla, whom he resembles closely, and reproves him in gentle terms for his coldness. He apologizes and they are secretly betrothed; but he soon decamps, to continue his quest, leaving Julina with child.

Apolonius calls upon Julina for a final answer. She replies that she is already betrothed. Somewhat later he learns from the gossip of servants that she has received Silvio (Silla) at her house. He infers that it is his own man who has ' thrust his nose so farre out of joynte ' and shuts Silla up in a dungeon. She tries every means, except that of revealing her sex, to induce him to suspend judgment, but to no purpose.

Julina visits Apolonius and begs him to show mercy to her betrothed husband. He draws his rapier and swears that he will kill Silla if she does not consent to marry Julina (cf. v, 1, 128 ff.). Silla takes Julina aside, confesses that she is a woman, and explains how she had come to Constantinople because of her love for Apolonius. Julina repeats the story to Apolonius and goes home in despair.

Apolonius, enraptured, transfers his affections to Silla on the spot, and they are married. The romantic tale of Silla's adventurous love quest spreads throughout Greece and reaches the ears of the wandering Silvio. He hastens back to Constantinople and is joyfully received by his sister and her husband. Apolonius tells him, as a matter of curious interest, how Silla had been claimed by Julina as her betrothed husband. Silvio explains the circumstances and Apolonius escorts him to Julina's house. She recognizes him and they are married. Both couples live happily forever after.

Riche's tale is based on the thirty-sixth story in Part II of Bandello's *Novelle*, which he may have known either directly or through the translation in Belleforest's *Histoires Tragiques*. Bandello seems to have taken his story from *Gl' Ingannati*, a comedy written about 1531 by some member of the Sienese academy of the Intronati, perhaps Alessandro Piccolomini. This is doubtless the play which Manningham miscalls *Inganni*. A Latin version, *Lælia*, was acted at Queen's College, Cambridge, in 1595.

In adapting Bandello's *novella* Riche has made significant changes.

There is no shipwreck in Bandello. The twins have been separated in infancy at the sack of Rome. The boy (Paolo) was captured by a German who took him to Naples and treated him as his son and, at his death, left him all his property. The girl (Nicuola) fell into the hands of two Spaniards. They treated her well and she was recovered by her father (Ambrogio), who bought her for five hundred ducats. He could get no trace of Paolo. The rest of the story takes place at Esi, Ambrogio's native town. Nicuola puts on man's attire, takes the name Romulo, and acts as page and messenger for Lattantio, her own lover, who has transferred his affections to Catella, the daughter of one Gerardo, an elderly citizen of Esi and himself a suitor for Nicuola's hand. Catella falls in love with the disguised messenger. Paolo comes to Esi; she mistakes him for Romulo, and they are betrothed. Meantime Nicuola has revealed her identity to Lattantio and he has repented of his fickleness. They also pledge their troth. The *finale* is at Ambrogio's house. He is overjoyed at the sudden appearance of his long-lost son and accepts Lattantio as son-in-law. Gerardo consents to the match between Catella and Paolo. All are happy except Gerardo, who has lost his chance of winning Nicuola.

The significance of a study of sources lies in the opportunity it gives to see Shakespeare at work. The most casual comparison of Riche's novel with TWELFTH NIGHT reveals what Shakespeare has done in the mere matter of plot. Characterization one does not expect of an Elizabethan writer of short stories. That Riche's men and women are puppets is no discredit to Riche; for that is all they need be: he is telling a tale: he is not bringing men and women before us (on the stage) in their habits as they lived. Viola and Olivia and Duke Orsino have their prototypes in Riche, but are Shakespeare's own delightful creations. Sebastian is lightly sketched, but is quite worthy to be Viola's brother. No plausible suggestion has ever been made as to a source for the underplot ; nor is it profitable to identify its characters with other characters in Shakespeare. Sir Toby is not Falstaff, nor is Sir Andrew our good friend Slender. Somehow, one thinks that poor Yorick must have resembled Feste — the merriest of all Shakespeare's fools.

TWELFTH NIGHT;

OR, WHAT YOU WILL

[Dramatis Personæ.

Orsino, *Duke of Illyria.*
Sebastian, *a young gentleman, brother to* Viola.
Antonio, *a sea captain, friend to* Sebastian.
A Sea Captain, *friend to* Viola.
Valentine, } *gentlemen attending on the* Duke.
Curio,
Sir Toby Belch, *uncle to* Olivia.
Sir Andrew Aguecheek.
Malvolio, *steward to* Olivia.

Fabian, } *servants to* Olivia.
Feste, *a* Clown,

Olivia, *a countess.*
Viola, *sister to* Sebastian.
Maria, *Olivia's woman.*

Lords, a Priest, Sailors, Officers, Musicians, and
Attendants.

SCENE. — *A city in Illyria, and the seacoast near by.*]

ACT I. Scene I. [*The* Duke's *Palace.*]

Enter *Orsino (Duke of Illyria), Curio,* and
other *Lords;* [with *Musicians*].

Duke. If music be the food of love, play on,
Give me excess of it, that, surfeiting,
The appetite may sicken, and so die.
That strain again! It had a dying fall;
O, it came o'er my ear like the sweet sound 5
That breathes upon a bank of violets,
Stealing and giving odour! Enough, no more!
'Tis not so sweet now as it was before.
O spirit of love, how quick and fresh art thou!
That, notwithstanding thy capacity 10
Receiveth as the sea, naught enters there,
Of what validity and pitch soe'er,
But falls into abatement and low price
Even in a minute! So full of shapes is fancy
That it alone is high fantastical. 15
Cur. Will you go hunt, my lord?
Duke. What, Curio?
Cur. The hart.
Duke. Why, so I do, the noblest that I have.
O, when mine eyes did see Olivia first,
Methought she purg'd the air of pestilence! 20
That instant was I turn'd into a hart,
And my desires, like fell and cruel hounds,
E'er since pursue me.

Enter *Valentine.*

How now? What news from her?
Val. So please my lord, I might not be admitted,

But from her handmaid do return this answer:
The element itself, till seven years' heat, 26
Shall not behold her face at ample view;
But like a cloistress she will veiled walk,
And water once a day her chamber round
With eye-offending brine: all this to season 30
A brother's dead love, which she would keep
fresh
And lasting in her sad remembrance.
Duke. O, she that hath a heart of that fine
frame
To pay this debt of love but to a brother,
How will she love when the rich golden shaft
Hath kill'd the flock of all affections else 36
That live in her; when liver, brain, and heart,
These sovereign thrones, are all supplied and
fill'd,
Her sweet perfections, with one self king!
Away before me to sweet beds of flow'rs! 40
Love-thoughts lie rich when canopied with
bow'rs. *Exeunt.*

Scene II. [*The seacoast.*]

Enter *Viola, a Captain,* and *Sailors.*

Vio. What country, friends, is this?
Capt. This is Illyria, lady.
Vio. And what should I do in Illyria?
My brother he is in Elysium.
Perchance he is not drown'd. What think you,
sailors? 5

Capt. It is perchance that you yourself were
sav'd.

Vio. O my poor brother! and so perchance
may he be.

Capt. True, madam; and, to comfort you
with chance,
Assure yourself, after our ship did split,
When you, and those poor number sav'd with
you, 10
Hung on our driving boat, I saw your brother.
Most provident in peril, bind himself
(Courage and hope both teaching him the
practice)
To a strong mast that liv'd upon the sea;
Where, like Arion on the dolphin's back, 15
I saw him hold acquaintance with the waves
So long as I could see.

Vio. For saying so, there's gold.
Mine own escape unfoldeth to my hope,
Whereto thy speech serves for authority, 20
The like of him. Know'st thou this country?

Capt. Ay, madam, well, for I was bred and
born
Not three hours' travel from this very place.

Vio. Who governs here?

Capt. A noble duke, in nature as in name. 25

Vio. What is his name?

Capt. Orsino.

Vio. Orsino! I have heard my father name
him.
He was a bachelor then.

Capt. And so is now, or was so very late; 30
For but a month ago I went from hence,
And then 'twas fresh in murmur (as you know
What great ones do, the less will prattle of)
That he did seek the love of fair Olivia.

Vio. What's she? 35

Capt. A virtuous maid, the daughter of a
count
That died some twelvemonth since; then leav-
ing her
In the protection of his son, her brother,
Who shortly also died; for whose dear love,
They say, she hath abjur'd the company 40
And sight of men.

Vio. O that I serv'd that lady,
And might not be delivered to the world,
Till I had made mine own occasion mellow,
What my estate is!

Capt. That were hard to compass,
Because she will admit no kind of suit; 45
No, not the Duke's.

Vio. There is a fair behaviour in thee,
Captain;
And though that nature with a beauteous wall

Doth oft close in pollution, yet of thee
I will believe thou hast a mind that suits 50
With this thy fair and outward character.
I prithee (and I'll pay thee bounteously)
Conceal me what I am, and be my aid
For such disguise as haply shall become
The form of my intent. I'll serve this duke, 55
Thou shalt present me as an eunuch to him;
It may be worth thy pains. For I can sing,
And speak to him in many sorts of music
That will allow me very worth his service.
What else may hap, to time I will commit; 60
Only shape thou thy silence to my wit.

Capt. Be you his eunuch, and your mute
I'll be.
When my tongue blabs, then let mine eyes
not see.

Vio. I thank thee. Lead me on. *Exeunt.*

Scene III. [Olivia's *house.*]

Enter Sir Toby and Maria.

To. What a plague means my niece to take
the death of her brother thus? I am sure care's
an enemy to life.

Mar. By my troth, Sir Toby, you must come
in earlier o' nights. Your cousin, my lady, takes
great exceptions to your ill hours. 6

To. Why, let her except before excepted!

Mar. Ay, but you must confine yourself
within the modest limits of order. 9

To. Confine? I'll confine myself no finer than
I am. These clothes are good enough to drink
in, and so be these boots too. An they be not,
let them hang themselves in their own straps.

Mar. That quaffing and drinking will undo
you. I heard my lady talk of it yesterday; and
of a foolish knight that you brought in one night
here to be her wooer. 17

To. Who? Sir Andrew Aguecheek?

Mar. Ay, he.

To. He's as tall a man as any's in Illyria.

Mar. What's that to th' purpose? 21

To. Why, he has three thousand ducats a
year.

Mar. Ay, but he'll have but a year in all
these ducats. He's a very fool and a prodigal.

To. Fie that you'll say so! He plays o' th'
viol-de-gamboys, and speaks three or four languages word for word without book, and hath
all the good gifts of nature. 29

Mar. He hath, indeed, almost natural! for,
besides that he's a fool, he's a great quarreller;
and but that he hath the gift of a coward to

allay the gust he hath in quarrelling, 'tis thought
among the prudent he would quickly have the
gift of a grave.   35
To. By this hand, they are scoundrels and
substractors that say so of him. Who are they?
Mar. They that add, moreover, he's drunk
nightly in your company.   39
To. With drinking healths to my niece. I'll
drink to her as long as there is a passage in my
throat and drink in Illyria. He's a coward and
a coystrill that will not drink to my niece till his
brains turn o' th' toe like a parish top. What,
wench! Castiliano vulgo! for here comes Sir
Andrew Agueface.   46

Enter Sir Andrew.

And. Sir Toby Belch! How now, Sir Toby
Belch?
To. Sweet Sir Andrew!
And. Bless you, fair shrew.   50
Mar. And you too, sir.
To. Accost, Sir Andrew, accost.
And. What's that?
To. My niece's chambermaid.
And. Good Mistress Accost, I desire better
acquaintance.   56
Mar. My name is Mary, sir.
And. Good Mistress Mary Accost —
To. You mistake, knight. 'Accost' is front
her, board her, woo her, assail her.   60
And. By my troth, I would not undertake her
in this company. Is that the meaning of 'accost'?
Mar. Fare you well, gentlemen.
To. An thou let part so, Sir Andrew, would
thou mightst never draw sword again!   66
And. An you part so, mistress, I would I
might never draw sword again! Fair lady, do
you think you have fools in hand?
Mar. Sir, I have not you by th' hand.   70
And. Marry, but you shall have! and here's
my hand.
Mar. Now, sir, thought is free. I pray you,
bring your hand to th' butt'ry bar and let it
drink.
And. Wherefore, sweetheart? What's your
metaphor?   76
Mar. It's dry, sir.
And. Why, I think so. I am not such an ass
but I can keep my hand dry. But what's your
jest?   80
Mar. A dry jest, sir.
And. Are you full of them?
Mar. Ay, sir, I have them at my fingers'
ends. Marry, now I let go your hand, I am
barren.   *Exit.*

To. O knight, thou lack'st a cup of canary!
When did I see thee so put down?   86
And. Never in your life, I think, unless you
see canary put me down. Methinks sometimes
I have no more wit than a Christian or an ordi-
nary man has. But I am a great eater of beef,
and I believe that does harm to my wit.   91
To. No question.
And. An I thought that, I'd forswear it. I'll
ride home to-morrow, Sir Toby.
To. Pourquoi, my dear knight?   95
And. What is 'pourquoi'? Do, or not do?
I would I had bestowed that time in the tongues
that I have in fencing, dancing, and bear-
baiting. O, had I but followed the arts!
To. Then hadst thou had an excellent head
of hair.   101
And. Why, would that have mended my hair?
To. Past question, for thou seest it will not
curl by nature.   105
And. But it becomes me well enough, does't
not?
To. Excellent. It hangs like flax on a distaff;
and I hope to see a housewife take thee between
her legs and spin it off.   110
And. Faith, I'll home to-morrow, Sir Toby.
Your niece will not be seen; or if she be, it's
four to one she'll none of me. The Count himself here hard by wooes her.   114
To. She'll none o' th' Count. She'll not
match above her degree, neither in estate,
years, nor wit; I have heard her swear't. Tut,
there's life in't, man.   118
And. I'll stay a month longer. I am a fellow
o' th' strangest mind i' th' world. I delight in
masques and revels sometimes altogether. 121
To. Art thou good at these kickshawses,
knight?
And. As any man in Illyria, whatsoever he
be, under the degree of my betters; and yet I
will not compare with an old man.   126
To. What is thy excellence in a galliard,
knight?
And. Faith, I can cut a caper.
To. And I can cut the mutton to't.   130
And. And I think I have the back-trick
simply as strong as any man in Illyria.
To. Wherefore are these things hid? Wherefore have these gifts a curtain before 'em? Are
they like to take dust, like Mistress Mall's picture? Why dost thou not go to church in a
galliard and come home in a coranto? My very
walk should be a jig. I would not so much as
make water but in a sink-a-pace. What dost
thou mean? Is it a world to hide virtues in? I

403

did think, by the excellent constitution of thy
leg, it was form'd under the star of a galliard.

And. Ay, 'tis strong, and it does indifferent
well in a flame-colour'd stock. Shall we set
about some revels? 145

To. What shall we do else? Were we not
born under Taurus?

And. Taurus? That's sides and heart.

To. No, sir; it is legs and thighs. Let me see
thee caper. [*Sir Andrew dances.*] Ha, higher!
Ha, ha, excellent! *Exeunt.*

Scene IV. [*The* Duke's *Palace.*]

Enter *Valentine*, and *Viola* in man's attire.

Val. If the Duke continue these favours
towards you, Cesario, you are like to be much
advanc'd. He hath known you but three days,
and already you are no stranger. 4

Vio. You either fear his humour or my negligence, that you call in question the continuance
of his love. Is he inconstant, sir, in his favours?

Val. No, believe me.

Enter *Duke, Curio*, and *Attendants.*

Vio. I thank you. Here comes the Count.

Duke. Who saw Cesario, ho? 10

Vio. On your attendance, my lord, here.

Duke. Stand you awhile aloof. — Cesario,
Thou know'st no less but all. I have unclasp'd
To thee the book even of my secret soul.
Therefore, good youth, address thy gait unto
her; 15
Be not denied access, stand at her doors,
And tell them there thy fixed foot shall grow
Till thou have audience.

Vio. Sure, my noble lord,
If she be so abandon'd to her sorrow
As it is spoke, she never will admit me. 20

Duke. Be clamorous and leap all civil bounds
Rather than make unprofited return.

Vio. Say I do speak with her, my lord, what
then?

Duke. O, then unfold the passion of my love;
Surprise her with discourse of my dear faith! 25
It shall become thee well to act my woes.
She will attend it better in thy youth
Than in a nuncio's of more grave aspect.

Vio. I think not so, my lord.

Duke. Dear lad, believe it;
For they shall yet belie thy happy years 30
That say thou art a man. Diana's lip
Is not more smooth and rubious; thy small pipe
Is as the maiden's organ, shrill and sound,

And all is semblative a woman's part.
I know thy constellation is right apt 35
For this affair. Some four or five attend him —
All, if you will; for I myself am best
When least in company. Prosper well in this,
And thou shalt live as freely as thy lord
To call his fortunes thine.

Vio. I'll do my best 40
To woo your lady. [*Aside*] Yet a barful strife!
Whoe'er I woo, myself would be his wife.
Exeunt.

Scene V. [Olivia's *house.*]

Enter *Maria* and *Clown.*

Mar. Nay, either tell me where thou hast
been, or I will not open my lips so wide as a
bristle may enter in way of thy excuse. My lady
will hang thee for thy absence.

Clown. Let her hang me! He that is well
hang'd in this world needs to fear no colours. 6

Mar. Make that good.

Clown. He shall see none to fear.

Mar. A good lenten answer. I can tell thee
where that saying was born, of 'I fear no
colours.' 10

Clown. Where, good Mistress Mary?

Mar. In the wars; and that may you be
bold to say in your foolery.

Clown. Well, God give them wisdom that
have it; and those that are fools, let them use
their talents. 16

Mar. Yet you will be hang'd for being so long
absent, or to be turn'd away — is not that as
good as a hanging to you?

Clown. Many a good hanging prevents a bad
marriage; and for turning away, let summer
bear it out. 22

Mar. You are resolute then?

Clown. Not so, neither; but I am resolv'd
on two points. 25

Mar. That if one break, the other will hold;
or if both break, your gaskins fall.

Clown. Apt, in good faith; very apt. Well,
go thy way! If Sir Toby would leave drinking,
thou wert as witty a piece of Eve's flesh as any
in Illyria. 31

Mar. Peace, you rogue; no more o' that.
Here comes my lady. Make your excuse wisely,
you were best. [*Exit*

Enter *Lady Olivia* with *Malvolio.*

Clown. Wit, an't be thy will, put me into
good fooling! Those wits that think they have

thee do very oft prove fools; and I that am sure
I lack thee may pass for a wise man. For what
says Quinapalus? 'Better a witty fool than a
foolish wit.' — God bless thee, lady!   40

Oli. Take the fool away.

Clown. Do you not hear, fellows? Take
away the lady.

Oli. Go to, y'are a dry fool! I'll no more of
you. Besides, you grow dishonest.   46

Clown. Two faults, madonna, that drink and
good counsel will amend. For give the dry fool
drink, then is the fool not dry. Bid the dishonest man mend himself: if he mend, he is no
longer dishonest; if he cannot, let the botcher
mend him. Anything that's mended is but
patch'd; virtue that transgresses is but patch'd
with sin, and sin that amends is but patch'd
with virtue. If that this simple syllogism will
serve, so; if it will not, what remedy? As there
is no true cuckold but calamity, so beauty's a
flower. The lady bade take away the fool;
therefore, I say again, take her away.

Oli. Sir, I bade them take away you.   60

Clown. Misprision in the highest degree!
Lady, *cucullus non facit monachum*. That's as
much to say as, I wear not motley in my brain.
Good madonna, give me leave to prove you a
fool.

Oli. Can you do it?   65

Clown. Dexteriously, good madonna.

Oli. Make your proof.

Clown. I must catechize you for it, madonna.
Good my mouse of virtue, answer me.

Oli. Well, sir, for want of other idleness, I'll
bide your proof.   71

Clown. Good madonna, why mourn'st thou?

Oli. Good fool, for my brother's death.

Clown. I think his soul is in hell, madonna.

Oli. I know his soul is in heaven, fool.   75

Clown. The more fool, madonna, to mourn
for your brother's soul, being in heaven. Take
away the fool, gentlemen.

Oli. What think you of this fool, Malvolio?
Doth he not mend?   80

Mal. Yes, and shall do till the pangs of death
shake him. Infirmity, that decays the wise,
doth ever make the better fool.

Clown. God send you, sir, a speedy infirmity,
for the better increasing your folly! Sir Toby
will be sworn that I am no fox; but he will not
pass his word for twopence that you are no fool.

Oli. How say you to that, Malvolio?   88

Mal. I marvel your ladyship takes delight in
such a barren rascal. I saw him put down the
other day with an ordinary fool that has no
more brain than a stone. Look you now, he's
out of his guard already. Unless you laugh and
minister occasion to him, he is gagg'd. I protest
I take these wise men that crow so at these set
kind of fools no better than the fools' zanies.

Oli. O, you are sick of self-love, Malvolio,
and taste with a distemper'd appetite. To be
generous, guiltless, and of free disposition, is to
take those things for birdbolts that you deem
cannon bullets. There is no slander in an allow'd fool, though he do nothing but rail; nor
no railing in a known discreet man, though he
do nothing but reprove.

Clown. Now Mercury indue thee with leasing, for thou speak'st well of fools!   106

Enter *Maria*.

Mar. Madam, there is at the gate a young
gentleman much desires to speak with you.

Oli. From the Count Orsino, is it?

Mar. I know not, madam. 'Tis a fair young
man, and well attended.   111

Oli. Who of my people hold him in delay?

Mar. Sir Toby, madam, your kinsman.

Oli. Fetch him off, I pray you. He speaks
nothing but madman. Fie on him! [*Exit
Maria.*] Go you, Malvolio. If it be a suit from
the Count, I am sick, or not at home. What you
will, to dismiss it. (*Exit Malvolio.*) Now you
see, sir, how your fooling grows old, and people
dislike it.   119

Clown. Thou hast spoke for us, madonna, as
if thy eldest son should be a fool; whose skull
Jove cram with brains!

Enter *Sir Toby*.

for — here he comes — one of thy kin has a
most weak pia mater.

Oli. By mine honour, half drunk! What is
he at the gate, cousin?   125

To. A gentleman.

Oli. A gentleman? What gentleman?

To. 'Tis a gentleman here. A plague o' these
pickle-herring! How now, sot?

Clown. Good Sir Toby!   130

Oli. Cousin, cousin, how have you come so
early by this lethargy?

To. Lechery? I defy lechery. There's one
at the gate.

Oli. Ay, marry, what is he?   135

To. Let him be the devil an he will, I care
not! Give me faith, say I. Well, it's all one.
                                              Exit.

Oli. What's a drunken man like, fool?

Clown. Like a drown'd man, a fool, and a madman. One draught above heat makes him a fool, the second mads him, and a third drowns him.   141

Oli. Go thou and seek the crowner, and let him sit o' my coz; for he's in the third degree of drink — he's drown'd. Go look after him.

Clown. He is but mad yet, madonna, and the fool shall look to the madman.   [*Exit.*]

Enter *Malvolio.*

Mal. Madam, yond young fellow swears he will speak with you. I told him you were sick: he takes on him to understand so much, and therefore comes to speak with you. I told him you were asleep: he seems to have a foreknowledge of that too, and therefore comes to speak with you. What is to be said to him, lady? He's fortified against any denial.

Oli. Tell him he shall not speak with me.   155

Mal. Has been told so; and he says he'll stand at your door like a sheriff's post, and be the supporter to a ber, ^h, but he'll speak with you.

Oli. What kind o' man is he?

Mal. Why, of mankind.   160

Oli. What manner of man?

Mal. Of very ill manner. He'll speak with you, will you or no.

Oli. Of what personage and years is he?   164

Mal. Not yet old enough for a man nor young enough for a boy; as a squash is before 'tis a peascod, or a codling when 'tis almost an apple. 'Tis with him in standing water, between boy and man. He is very well-favour'd and he speaks very shrewishly. One would think his mother's milk were scarce out of him.

Oli. Let him approach. Call in my gentlewoman.   173

Mal. Gentlewoman, my lady calls.   *Exit.*

Enter *Maria.*

Oli. Give me my veil; come, throw it o'er
 my face.   175
We'll once more hear Orsino's embassy.

Enter *Viola.*

Vio. The honourable lady of the house, which is she?

Oli. Speak to me; I shall answer for her. Your will?   180

Vio. Most radiant, exquisite, and unmatchable beauty — I pray you tell me if this be the lady of the house, for I never saw her. I would be loath to cast away my speech; for, besides that it is excellently well penn'd, I have taken great pains to con it. Good beauties, let me sustain no scorn. I am very comptible, even to the least sinister usage.

Oli. Whence came you, sir?   189

Vio. I can say little more than I have studied, and that question's out of my part. Good gentle one, give me modest assurance if you be the lady of the house, that I may proceed in my speech.

Oli. Are you a comedian?   194

Vio. No, my profound heart; and yet (by the very fangs of malice I swear) I am not that I play. Are you the lady of the house?

Oli. If I do not usurp myself, I am.   198

Vio. Most certain, if you are she, you do usurp yourself; for what is yours to bestow is not yours to reserve. But this is from my commission. I will on with my speech in your praise and then show you the heart of my message.

Oli. Come to what is important in't. I forgive you the praise.   205

Vio. Alas, I took great pains to study it, and 'tis poetical.

Oli. It is the more like to be feigned; I pray you keep it in. I heard you were saucy at my gates; and allow'd your approach rather to wonder at you than to hear you. If you be not mad, be gone; if you have reason, be brief. 'Tis not that time of moon with me to make one in so skipping a dialogue.

Mar. Will you hoist sail, sir? Here lies your way.   216

Vio. No, good swabber; I am to hull here a little longer. Some mollification for your giant, sweet lady!

Oli. Tell me your mind.

Vio. I am a messenger.   220

Oli. Sure you have some hideous matter to deliver, when the courtesy of it is so fearful. Speak your office.

Vio. It alone concerns your ear. I bring no overture of war, no taxation of homage. I hold the olive in my hand. My words are as full of peace as matter.   227

Oli. Yet you began rudely. What are you? What would you?

Vio. The rudeness that hath appear'd in me have I learn'd from my entertainment. What I am, and what I would, are as secret as maidenhead: to your ears, divinity; to any other's, profanation.   234

Oli. Give us the place alone; we will hear this divinity. [*Exit Maria.*] Now, sir, what is your text?

Vio. Most sweet lady —

Oli. A comfortable doctrine, and much may
be said of it. Where lies your text?   240
Vio. In Orsino's bosom.
Oli. In his bosom? In what chapter of his
bosom?
Vio. To answer by the method, in the first
of his heart.   245
Oli. O, I have read it! it is heresy. Have
you no more to say?
Vio. Good madam, let me see your face.
Oli. Have you any commission from your
lord to negotiate with my face? You are now
out of your text. But we will draw the curtain
and show you the picture. [*Unveils.*] Look you,
sir, such a one I was this present. Is't not well
done?
Vio. Excellently done, if God did all.
Oli. 'Tis in grain, sir; 'twill endure wind and
weather.   256
Vio. 'Tis beauty truly blent, whose red and
white
Nature's own sweet and cunning hand laid on.
Lady, you are the cruell'st she alive
If you will lead these graces to the grave,   260
And leave the world no copy.
Oli. O, sir, I will not be so hard-hearted. I
will give out divers schedules of my beauty. It
shall be inventoried, and every particle and
utensil labell'd to my will: — as, item, two lips,
indifferent red; item, two grey eyes, with lids
to them; item, one neck, one chin, and so forth.
Were you sent hither to praise me?
Vio. I see you what you are — you are too
proud;
But if you were the devil, you are fair.   270
My lord and master loves you. O, such love
Could be but recompens'd though you were
crown'd
The nonpareil of beauty!
Oli.   How does he love me?
Vio. With adorations, with fertile tears,
With groans that thunder love, with sighs of fire.
Oli. Your lord does know my mind; I can-
not love him.   276
Yet I suppose him virtuous, know him noble,
Of great estate, of fresh and stainless youth;
In voices well divulg'd, free, learn'd, and valiant,
And in dimension and the shape of nature 280
A gracious person. But yet I cannot love him.
He might have took his answer long ago.
Vio. If I did love you in my master's flame,
With such a suff'ring, such a deadly life,
In your denial I would find no sense;   285
I would not understand it.
Oli.   Why, what would you?

Vio. Make me a willow cabin at your gate
And call upon my soul within the house;
Write loyal cantons of contemned love
And sing them loud even in the dead of night;
Halloa your name to the reverberate hills 291
And make the babbling gossip of the air
Cry out 'Olivia!' O, you should not rest
Between the elements of air and earth
But you should pity me!   295
Oli. You might do much. What is your
  parentage?
Vio. Above my fortunes, yet my state is well.
I am a gentleman.
Oli.   Get you to your lord.
I cannot love him. Let him send no more,
Unless, perchance, you come to me again 300
To tell me how he takes it. Fare you well.
I thank you for your pains. Spend this for me.
Vio. I am no fee'd post, lady; keep your
  purse;
My master, not myself, lacks recompense.
Love make his heart of flint that you shall love;
And let your fervour, like my master's, be 306
Plac'd in contempt! Farewell, fair cruelty.
                                        Exit.
Oli. 'What is your parentage?'
'Above my fortunes, yet my state is well.
I am a gentleman.' I'll be sworn thou art. 310
Thy tongue, thy face, thy limbs, actions, and
  spirit
Do give thee fivefold blazon. Not too fast!
  soft, soft!
Unless the master were the man. How now?
Even so quickly may one catch the plague?
Methinks I feel this youth's perfections   315
With an invisible and subtle stealth
To creep in at mine eyes. Well, let it be.
What ho, Malvolio!

              Enter *Malvolio.*

Mal.   Here, madam, at your service.
Oli. Run after that same peevish messenger,
The County's man. He left this ring behind
  him,   320
Would I or not. Tell him I'll none of it.
Desire him not to flatter with his lord
Nor hold him up with hopes. I am not for him.
If that the youth will come this way to-morrow,
I'll give him reasons for't. Hie thee, Malvolio.
Mal. Madam, I will.   *Exit.*
Oli. I do I know not what, and fear to find
Mine eye too great a flatterer for my mind.
Fate, show thy force! Ourselves we do not owe.
What is decreed must be — and be this so! 330
                                        [*Exit.*]

407

ACT II. Scene I. [*The seacoast.*]

Enter *Antonio* and *Sebastian*.

Ant. Will you stay no longer? nor will you
not that I go with you?

Seb. By your patience, no. My stars shine
darkly over me; the malignancy of my fate
might perhaps distemper yours. Therefore I
shall crave of you your leave, that I may bear
my evils alone. It were a bad recompense for
your love to lay any of them on you.

Ant. Let me yet know of you whither you
are bound. 10

Seb. No, sooth, sir. My determinate voyage
is mere extravagancy. But I perceive in you so
excellent a touch of modesty that you will not
extort from me what I am willing to keep in;
therefore it charges me in manners the rather to
express myself. You must know of me then,
Antonio, my name is Sebastian, which I call'd
Roderigo. My father was that Sebastian of
Messaline whom I know you have heard of. He
left behind him myself and a sister, both born
in an hour. If the heavens had been pleas'd,
would we had so ended! But you, sir, alter'd
that, for some hour before you took me from the
breach of the sea was my sister drown'd.

Ant. Alas the day! 25

Seb. A lady, sir, though it was said she much
resembled me, was yet of many accounted
beautiful. But though I could not with such
estimable wonder overfar believe that, yet thus
far I will boldly publish her: she bore a mind
that envy could not but call fair. She is
drown'd already, sir, with salt water, though I
seem to drown her remembrance again with
more.

Ant. Pardon me, sir, your bad entertainment.

Seb. O good Antonio, forgive me your
trouble! 35

Ant. If you will not murther me for my love,
let me be your servant.

Seb. If you will not undo what you have
done, that is, kill him whom you have recover'd, desire it not. Fare ye well at once. My
bosom is full of kindness; and I am yet so near
the manners of my mother that, upon the least
occasion more, mine eyes will tell tales of me. Farewell. *Exit.*

Ant. The gentleness of all the gods go with
thee! 45

I have many enemies in Orsino's court,
Else would I very shortly see thee there.
But come what may, I do adore thee so
That danger shall seem sport, and I will go. 49
Exit.

Scene II. [*A street.*]

Enter *Viola* and *Malvolio* at several doors.

Mal. Were not you ev'n now with the
Countess Olivia?

Vio. Even now, sir. On a moderate pace I
have since arriv'd but hither. 4

Mal. She returns this ring to you, sir. You
might have saved me my pains, to have taken
it away yourself. She adds, moreover, that you
should put your lord into a desperate assurance
she will none of him. And one thing more, that
you be never so hardy to come again in his affairs, unless it be to report your lord's taking
of this. Receive it so. 12

Vio. She took the ring of me. I'll none of it.

Mal. Come, sir, you peevishly threw it to
her; and her will is, it should be so return'd. If
it be worth stooping for, there it lies, in your
eye; if not, be it his that finds it. *Exit.*

Vio. I left no ring with her. What means
this lady? 18
Fortune forbid my outside have not charm'd
her!
She made good view of me; indeed, so much
That, as methought, her eyes had lost her
tongue, 21
For she did speak in starts distractedly.
She loves me sure; the cunning of her passion
Invites me in this churlish messenger.
None of my lord's ring? Why, he sent her none!
I am the man. If it be so — as 'tis — 26
Poor lady, she were better love a dream!
Disguise, I see thou art a wickedness
Wherein the pregnant enemy does much.
How easy is it for the proper false 30
In women's waxen hearts to set their forms!
Alas, our frailty is the cause, not we!
For such as we are made of, such we be.
How will this fadge? My master loves her
dearly;
And I (poor monster) fond as much on him; 35
And she (mistaken) seems to dote on me.

What will become of this? As I am man,
My state is desperate for my master's love.
As I am woman (now alas the day!),
What thriftless sighs shall poor Olivia breathe!
O Time, thou must untangle this, not I;   41
It is too hard a knot for me t' untie!   [*Exit.*]

Scene III. [Olivia's *house.*]

Enter *Sir Toby* and *Sir Andrew.*

To. Approach, Sir Andrew. Not to be abed
after midnight is to be up betimes; and 'diluculo surgere,' thou know'st —
And. Nay, by my troth, I know not; but I
know to be up late is to be up late.   5
To. A false conclusion! I hate it as an un-
fill'd can. To be up after midnight, and to go
to bed then, is early; so that to go to bed after
midnight is to go to bed betimes. Does not our
life consist of the four elements?   10
And. Faith, so they say; but I think it
rather consists of eating and drinking.
To. Th'art a scholar! Let us therefore eat
and drink. Marian I say! a stoup of wine!

Enter *Clown.*

And. Here comes the fool, i' faith.   15
Clown. How now, my hearts? Did you never
see the picture of We Three?
To. Welcome, ass. Now let's have a catch.
And. By my troth, the fool has an excellent
breast. I had rather than forty shillings I had
such a leg, and so sweet a breath to sing, as the
fool has. In sooth, thou wast in very gracious
fooling last night, when thou spok'st of Pigro-
gromitus, of the Vapians passing the equinoctial
of Queubus. 'Twas very good, i' faith. I sent
thee sixpence for thy leman. Hadst it?   26
Clown. I did impeticos thy gratillity; for
Malvolio's nose is no whipstock. My lady has a
white hand, and the Myrmidons are no bottle-
ale houses.
And. Excellent! Why, this is the best fooling, when all is done. Now a song!   31
To. Come on! there is sixpence for you.
Let's have a song.
And. There's a testril of me too. If one
knight give a —   35
Clown. Would you have a love song, or a
song of good life?
To. A love song, a love song.
And. Ay, ay! I care not for good life.

Clown sings.

O mistress mine, where are you roaming?   40
O, stay and hear! your true-love 's coming,
   That can sing both high and low.
Trip no further, pretty sweeting;
Journeys end in lovers meeting,
   Every wise man's son doth know.   45
And. Excellent good, i' faith!
To. Good, good!

Clown [sings].

What is love? 'Tis not hereafter;
Present mirth hath present laughter;
   What's to come is still unsure: 50
In delay there lies no plenty;
Then come kiss me, sweet and twenty!
Youth's a stuff will not endure.

And. A mellifluous voice, as I am true knight.
To. A contagious breath.   56
And. Very sweet and contagious, i' faith.
To. To hear by the nose, it is dulcet in contagion. But shall we make the welkin dance
indeed? Shall we rouse the night owl in a catch
that will draw three souls out of one weaver?
Shall we do that?   62
And. An you love me, let's do't! I am dog
at a catch.
Clown. By'r Lady, sir, and some dogs will
catch well.   65
And. Most certain. Let our catch be 'Thou
knave.'
Clown. 'Hold thy peace, thou knave,'
knight? I shall be constrain'd in't to call thee
knave, knight.   70
And. 'Tis not the first time I have constrained one to call me knave. Begin, fool. It
begins, 'Hold thy peace.'
Clown. I shall never begin if I hold my peace.
And. Good, i' faith! Come, begin.   75

Catch sung. Enter Maria.

Mar. What a caterwauling do you keep here!
If my lady have not call'd up her steward
Malvolio and bid him turn you out of doors,
never trust me.   79
To. My lady 's a Catayan, we are politicians,
Malvolio 's a Peg-a-Ramsey, and [*sings*] 'Three
merry men be we.' Am not I consanguineous?
Am I not of her blood? Tilly-vally, lady! [*sings*]
'There dwelt a man in Babylon, lady, lady!'
Clown. Beshrew me, the knight 's in admi-
rable fooling.   86
And. Ay, he does well enough if he be dis-
pos'd, and so do I too. He does it with a better
grace, but I do it more natural.

To. [*sings*] 'O' the twelf day of December' —
Mar. For the love o' God, peace!   92

Enter *Malvolio.*

Mal. My masters, are you mad? or what are
you? Have you no wit, manners, nor honesty,
but to gabble like tinkers at this time of night?
Do ye make an alehouse of my lady's house,
that ye squeak out your coziers' catches without
any mitigation or remorse of voice? Is there no
respect of place, persons, nor time in you?
To. We did keep time, sir, in our catches.
Sneck up!   101
Mal. Sir Toby, I must be round with you.
My lady bade me tell you that, though she harbours you as her kinsman, she's nothing allied
to your disorders. If you can separate yourself
and your misdemeanours, you are welcome to
the house. If not, and it would please you to
take leave of her, she is very willing to bid you
farewell.
To. [*sings*] 'Farewell, dear heart since I
must needs be gone.'   110
Mar. Nay, good Sir Toby!
Clown. [*sings*] 'His eyes do show his days are
almost done.'
Mal. Is't even so?
To. 'But I will never die.'   115
Clown. Sir Toby, there you lie.
Mal. This is much credit to you!
To. 'Shall I bid him go?'
Clown. 'What an if you do?'
To. 'Shall I bid him go, and spare not?'   120
Clown. 'O, no, no, no, no, you dare not!'
To. Out o' tune, sir? Ye lie. Art any more
than a steward? Dost thou think, because thou
art virtuous, there shall be no more cakes and
ale?   125
Clown. Yes, by Saint Anne! and ginger shall
be hot i' th' mouth too.
To. Th'art i' th' right. — Go, sir, rub your
chain with crumbs. A stoup of wine, Maria!
Mal. Mistress Mary, if you priz'd my lady's
favour at anything more than contempt, you
would not give means for this uncivil rule. She
shall know of it, by this hand.   *Exit.*
Mar. Go shake your ears!   134
And. 'Twere as good a deed as to drink when
a man's ahungry, to challenge him the field, and
then to break promise with him and make a
fool of him.   138
To. Do't, knight. I'll write thee a challenge;
or I'll deliver thy indignation to him by word
of mouth.
Mar. Sweet Sir Toby, be patient for to-night.

Since the youth of the Count's was to-day with
my lady, she is much out of quiet. For Monsieur Malvolio, let me alone with him. If I do
not gull him into a nayword, and make him a
common recreation, do not think I have wit
enough to lie straight in my bed. I know I can
do it.
To. Possess us, possess us! Tell us something of him.   150
Mar. Marry, sir, sometimes he is a kind of
Puritan.
And. O, if I thought that, I'd beat him like
a dog!
To. What, for being a Puritan? Thy exquisite reason, dear knight?   156
And. I have no exquisite reason for't, but I
have reason good enough.
Mar. The devil a Puritan that he is, or anything constantly but a time-pleaser; an affection'd ass, that cons state without book and
utters it by great swarths; the best persuaded
of himself; so cramm'd, as he thinks, with ex-
cellencies that it is his grounds of faith that all
that look on him love him; and on that vice in
him will my revenge find notable cause to work.
To. What wilt thou do?   167
Mar. I will drop in his way some obscure
epistles of love, wherein by the colour of his
beard, the shape of his leg, the manner of his
gait, the expressure of his eye, forehead, and
complexion, he shall find himself most feelingly
personated. I can write very like my lady your
niece; on a forgotten matter we can hardly
make distinction of our hands.   175
To. Excellent! I smell a device.
And. I have't in my nose too.
To. He shall think by the letters that thou
wilt drop that they come from my niece, and
that she's in love with him.   180
Mar. My purpose is indeed a horse of that
colour.
And. And your horse now would make him
an ass.
Mar. Ass, I doubt not.   185
And. O, 'twill be admirable!
Mar. Sport royal, I warrant you. I know my
physic will work with him. I will plant you
two, and let the fool make a third, where he
shall find the letter. Observe his construction
of it. For this night, to bed, and dream on the
event. Farewell.   *Exit.*
To. Good night, Penthesilea.
And. Before me, she's a good wench.
To. She's a beagle true-bred, and one that
adores me. What o' that?   196

And. I was ador'd once too.

To. Let's to bed, knight. Thou hadst need send for more money.

And. If I cannot recover your niece, I am a foul way out.   201

To. Send for money, knight. If thou hast her not i' th' end, call me Cut.

And. If I do not, never trust me, take it how you will.   205

To. Come, come; I'll go burn some sack. 'Tis too late to go to bed now. Come, knight; come, knight.   *Exeunt.*

Scene IV. [*The* Duke's *Palace.*]

Enter *Duke, Viola, Curio,* and others.

Duke. Give me some music. Now good morrow, friends.
Now, good Cesario, but that piece of song,
That old and antique song we heard last night.
Methought it did relieve my passion much,
More than light airs and recollected terms   5
Of these most brisk and giddy-paced times.
Come, but one verse.

Cur. He is not here, so please your lordship, that should sing it.

Duke. Who was it?   10

Cur. Feste the jester, my lord, a fool that the Lady Olivia's father took much delight in. He is about the house.

Duke. Seek him out. [*Exit Curio.*] And play
the tune the while.   *Music plays.*
Come hither, boy. If ever thou shalt love,   15
In the sweet pangs of it remember me;
For such as I am all true lovers are,
Unstaid and skittish in all motions else
Save in the constant image of the creature
That is belov'd. How dost thou like this tune?
Vio. It gives a very echo to the seat   21
Where Love is thron'd.
Duke.   Thou dost speak masterly.
My life upon't, young though thou art, thine eye
Hath stay'd upon some favour that it loves.
Hath it not, boy?
Vio.   A little, by your favour.   26
Duke. What kind of woman is't?
Vio.   Of your complexion.
Duke. She is not worth thee then. What years, i' faith?
Vio. About your years, my lord.
Duke. Too old, by heaven! Let still the woman take   30

An elder than herself: so wears she to him,
So sways she level in her husband's heart;
For, boy, however we do praise ourselves,
Our fancies are more giddy and unfirm,
More longing, wavering, sooner lost and won,
Than women's are.
Vio.   I think it well, my lord.   36
Duke. Then let thy love be younger than thyself,
Or thy affection cannot hold the bent;
For women are as roses, whose fair flow'r,   39
Being once display'd, doth fall that very hour.
Vio. And so they are; alas, that they are so!
To die, even when they to perfection grow!

Enter *Curio* and *Clown.*

Duke. O, fellow, come, the song we had last night.
Mark it, Cesario; it is old and plain.
The spinsters and the knitters in the sun,   45
And the free maids that weave their thread with bones,
Do use to chant it. It is silly sooth,
And dallies with the innocence of love
Like the old age.
Clown. Are you ready, sir?   50
Duke. Ay; prithee sing.   *Music.*

The [*Clown's*] *Song.*

Come away, come away, death,
    And in sad cypress let me be laid.
Fly away, fly away, breath;
    I am slain by a fair cruel maid.   55
My shroud of white, stuck all with yew,
    O, prepare it!
My part of death, no one so true
    Did share it.

Not a flower, not a flower sweet,   60
    On my black coffin let there be strown;
Not a friend, not a friend greet
    My poor corpse, where my bones shall be thrown.
A thousand thousand sighs to save,
    Lay me, O, where   65
Sad true lover never find my grave,
    To weep there!

Duke. There's for thy pains.
Clown. No pains, sir. I take pleasure in singing, sir.   70
Duke. I'll pay thy pleasure then.
Clown. Truly, sir, and pleasure will be paid one time or another.
Duke. Give me now leave to leave thee.   74
Clown. Now the melancholy god protect thee, and the tailor make thy doublet of change-

able taffeta, for thy mind is a very opal! I would have men of such constancy put to sea, that their business might be everything, and their intent everywhere; for that's it that always makes a good voyage of nothing. Farewell. 81

Exit.

Duke. Let all the rest give place.

[*Exeunt Curio and Attendants.*]

Once more, Cesario,
Get thee to yond same sovereign cruelty.
Tell her, my love, more noble than the world,
Prizes not quantity of dirty lands. 85
The parts that fortune hath bestow'd upon her,
Tell her I hold as giddily as fortune;
But 'tis that miracle and queen of gems
That nature pranks her in, attracts my soul.

Vio. But if she cannot love you, sir — 90

Duke. I cannot be so answer'd.

Vio. Sooth, but you must.
Say that some lady, as perhaps there is,
Hath for your love as great a pang of heart
As you have for Olivia. You cannot love her.
You tell her so. Must she not then be answer'd? 95

Duke. There is no woman's sides
Can bide the beating of so strong a passion
As love doth give my heart; no woman's heart
So big to hold so much; they lack retention.
Alas, their love may be call'd appetite — 100
No motion of the liver, but the palate —
That suffers surfeit, cloyment, and revolt;
But mine is all as hungry as the sea
And can digest as much. Make no compare
Between that love a woman can bear me 105
And that I owe Olivia.

Vio. Ay, but I know —

Duke. What dost thou know?

Vio. Too well what love women to men may owe.
In faith, they are as true of heart as we.
My father had a daughter lov'd a man 110
As it might be perhaps, were I a woman,
I should your lordship.

Duke. And what's her history?

Vio. A blank, my lord. She never told her love,
But let concealment, like a worm i' th' bud,
Feed on her damask cheek. She pin'd in thought; 115
And, with a green and yellow melancholy,
She sat like Patience on a monument,
Smiling at grief. Was not this love indeed?
We men may say more, swear more; but indeed
Our shows are more than will; for still we prove
Much in our vows but little in our love. 121

Duke. But died thy sister of her love, my boy?

Vio. I am all the daughters of my father's house,
And all the brothers too — and yet I know not.
Sir, shall I to this lady?

Duke. Ay, that's the theme.
To her in haste! Give her this jewel. Say 126
My love can give no place, bide no denay.

Exeunt.

Scene V. [Olivia's *orchard*.]

Enter *Sir Toby, Sir Andrew*, and *Fabian*.

To. Come thy ways, Signior Fabian.

Fab. Nay, I'll come. If I lose a scruple of this sport, let me be boil'd to death with melancholy. 4

To. Wouldst thou not be glad to have the niggardly rascally sheep-biter come by some notable shame?

Fab. I would exult, man. You know he brought me out o' favour with my lady about a bear-baiting here. 10

To. To anger him we'll have the bear again; and we will fool him black and blue. Shall we not, Sir Andrew?

And. An we do not, it is pity of our lives. 14

Enter *Maria*.

To. Here comes the little villain. How now, my metal of India?

Mar. Get ye all three into the box tree. Malvolio's coming down this walk. He has been yonder i' the sun practising behaviour to his own shadow this half hour. Observe him, for the love of mockery; for I know this letter will make a contemplative idiot of him. Close, in the name of jesting! [*The others hide.*] Lie thou there [*Throws down a letter*]; for here comes the trout that must be caught with tickling. *Exit.*

Enter *Malvolio*.

Mal. 'Tis but fortune; all is fortune. Maria once told me she did affect me; and I have heard herself come thus near, that, should she fancy, it should be one of my complexion. Besides, she uses me with a more exalted respect than any one else that follows her. What should I think on't?

To. Here's an overweening rogue! 34

Fab. O, peace! Contemplation makes a rare turkey cock of him. How he jets under his advanc'd plumes!

And. 'Slight, I could so beat the rogue!

Fab. Peace, I say.

Mal. To be Count Malvolio!   40

To. Ah, rogue!

And. Pistol him, pistol him!

Fab. Peace, peace!

Mal. There is example for't. The Lady of the Strachy married the yeoman of the wardrobe.   45

And. Fie on him, Jezebel!

Fab. O, peace! Now he's deeply in. Look how imagination blows him.

Mal. Having been three months married to her, sitting in my state —   50

To. O for a stone-bow, to hit him in the eye!

Mal. Calling my officers about me, in my branch'd velvet gown; having come from a day-bed, where I have left Olivia sleeping — 55

To. Fire and brimstone!

Fab. O, peace, peace!

Mal. And then to have the humour of state; and after a demure travel of regard — telling them I know my place, as I would they should do theirs — to ask for my kinsman Toby —

To. Bolts and shackles!   62

Fab. O, peace, peace, peace! Now, now.

Mal. Seven of my people, with an obedient start, make out for him. I frown the while, and perchance wind up my watch, or play with my — some rich jewel. Toby approaches; curtsies there to me —

To. Shall this fellow live?

Fab. Though our silence be drawn from us by th' ears, yet peace!   71

Mal. I extend my hand to him thus, quenching my familiar smile with an austere regard of control —

To. And does not Toby take you a blow o' the lips then?   76

Mal. Saying, 'Cousin Toby, my fortunes having cast me on your niece, give me this prerogative of speech.'

To. What, what?   80

Mal. 'You must amend your drunkenness.'

To. Out, scab!

Fab. Nay, patience, or we break the sinews of our plot.

Mal. 'Besides, you waste the treasure of your time with a foolish knight' —   86

And. That's me, I warrant you.

Mal. 'One Sir Andrew' —

And. I knew 'twas I, for many do call me fool.

Mal. What employment have we here?
[*Takes up the letter.*]

Fab. Now is the woodcock near the gin.

To. O, peace! and the spirit of humours intimate reading aloud to him!   94

Mal. By my life, this is my lady's hand! These be her very C's, her U's, and her T's; and thus makes she her great P's. It is, in contempt of question, her hand.

And. Her C's, her U's, and her T's? Why that?

Mal. [*reads*] 'To the unknown belov'd, this, and my good wishes.' Her very phrases! By your leave, wax. Soft! and the impressure her Lucrece, with which she uses to seal! 'Tis my lady. To whom should this be?   105

Fab. This wins him, liver and all.

Mal. [*reads*]

'Jove knows I love —
But who?
Lips, do not move;
No man must know.'   110

'No man must know.' What follows? The numbers alter'd! 'No man must know.' If this should be thee, Malvolio?

To. Marry, hang thee, brock!

Mal. [*reads*]

'I may command where I adore;   115
But silence, like a Lucrece knife,
With bloodless stroke my heart doth gore.
M. O. A. I. doth sway my life.'

Fab. A fustian riddle!

To. Excellent wench, say I.   120

Mal. 'M. O. A. I. doth sway my life.' Nay, but first, let me see, let me see, let me see.

Fab. What dish o' poison has she dress'd him!

To. And with what wing the staniel checks at it!   125

Mal. 'I may command where I adore.' Why, she may command me: I serve her; she is my lady. Why, this is evident to any formal capacity. There is no obstruction in this. And the end — what should that alphabetical position portend? If I could make that resemble something in me! Softly! M. O. A. I.   132

To. O, ay, make up that! He is now at a cold scent.

Fab. Sowter will cry upon't for all this, though it be as rank as a fox.   136

Mal. M. — Malvolio. M. — Why, that begins my name!

Fab. Did not I say he would work it out? The cur is excellent at faults.   140

Mal. M. — But then there is no consonancy in the sequel. That suffers under probation. A should follow, but O does.

Fab. And O shall end, I hope.

To. Ay, or I'll cudgel him, and make him cry O!   146

413

Mal. And then I comes behind.'

Fab. Ay, an you had any eye behind you, you might see more detraction at your heels than fortunes before you. 150

Mal. M, O, A, I. This simulation is not as the former; and yet, to crush this a little, it would bow to me, for every one of these letters are in my name. Soft! here follows prose. 154

[*Reads*] 'If this fall into thy hand, revolve. In my stars I am above thee; but be not afraid of greatness. Some are born great, some achieve greatness, and some have greatness thrust upon 'em. Thy Fates open their hands; let thy blood and spirit embrace them; and to inure thyself to what thou art like to be, cast thy humble slough and appear fresh. Be opposite with a kinsman, surly with servants. Let thy tongue tang arguments of state; put thyself into the trick of singularity. She thus advises thee that sighs for thee. Remember who commended thy yellow stockings and wish'd to see thee ever cross-garter'd. I say, remember. Go to, thou art made, if thou desir'st to be so. If not, let me see thee a steward still, the fellow of servants, and not worthy to touch Fortune's fingers. Farewell. She that would alter services with thee,

'THE FORTUNATE UNHAPPY.'

Daylight and champian discovers not more. This is open. I will be proud, I will read politic authors, I will baffle Sir Toby, I will wash off gross acquaintance, I will be point-devise, the very man. I do not now fool myself, to let imagination jade me; for every reason excites to this, that my lady loves me. She did commend my yellow stockings of late, she did praise my leg being cross-garter'd; and in this she manifests herself to my love, and with a kind of injunction drives me to these habits of her liking. I thank my stars, I am happy. I will be strange, stout, in yellow stockings, and cross-garter'd, even with the swiftness of putting on. Jove and my stars be praised! Here is yet a postscript.

'Thou canst not choose but know who I am. If thou entertain'st my love, let it appear in thy smiling. Thy smiles become thee well. Therefore in my presence still smile, dear my sweet, I prithee.'

Jove, I thank thee. I will smile; I will do everything that thou wilt have me. *Exit.*

Fab. I will not give my part of this sport for a pension of thousands to be paid from the Sophy.

To. I could marry this wench for this device —

And. So could I too. 200

To. And ask no other dowry with her but such another jest.

Enter *Maria*.

And. Nor I neither.

Fab. Here comes my noble gull-catcher.

To. Wilt thou set thy foot o' my neck? 205

And. Or o' mine either?

To. Shall I play my freedom at tray-trip and become thy bondslave?

And. I' faith, or I either? 209

To. Why, thou hast put him in such a dream that, when the image of it leaves him, he must run mad.

Mar. Nay, but say true, does it work upon him?

To. Like aqua-vitæ with a midwife. 215

Mar. If you will, then, see the fruits of the sport, mark his first approach before my lady. He will come to her in yellow stockings, and 'tis a colour she abhors, and cross-garter'd, a fashion she detests; and he will smile upon her, which will now be so unsuitable to her disposition, being addicted to a melancholy as she is, that it cannot but turn him into a notable contempt. If you will see it, follow me.

To. To the gates of Tartar, thou most excellent devil of wit! 226

And. I'll make one too. *Exeunt.*

ACT III. Scene I. [Olivia's *orchard.*]

Enter *Viola*, and *Clown* [with a tabor and pipe].

Vio. Save thee, friend, and thy music! Dost thou live by thy tabor?

Clown. No, sir, I live by the church.

Vio. Art thou a churchman? 4

Clown. No such matter, sir. I do live by the church; for I do live at my house, and my house doth stand by the church.

Vio. So thou mayst say, the king lies by a beggar, if a beggar dwell near him; or, the church stands by thy tabor, if thy tabor stand by the church. 11

Clown. You have said, sir. To see this age! A sentence is but a chev'ril glove to a good wit. How quickly the wrong side may be turn'd outward! 15

Vio. Nay, that's certain. They that dally nicely with words may quickly make them wanton.

SCENE I.]

Twelfth Night

Clown. I would therefore my sister had had no name, sir. 20
Vio. Why, man?
Clown. Why, sir, her name's a word, and to dally with that word might make my sister wanton. But indeed words are very rascals since bonds disgrac'd them. 25
Vio. Thy reason, man?
Clown. Troth, sir, I can yield you none without words, and words are grown so false I am loath to prove reason with them.
Vio. I warrant thou art a merry fellow and car'st for nothing. 31
Clown. Not so, sir; I do care for something; but in my conscience, sir, I do not care for you. If that be to care for nothing, sir, I would it would make you invisible. 35
Vio. Art not thou the Lady Olivia's fool?
Clown. No, indeed, sir. The Lady Olivia has no folly. She will keep no fool, sir, till she be married; and fools are as like husbands as pilchers are to herrings — the husband's the bigger. I am indeed not her fool, but her corrupter of words. 41
Vio. I saw thee late at the Count Orsino's.
Clown. Foolery, sir, does walk about the orb like the sun; it shines everywhere. I would be sorry, sir, but the fool should be as oft with your master as with my mistress. I think I saw your wisdom there. 47
Vio. Nay, an thou pass upon me, I'll no more with thee. Hold, there's expenses for thee. [*Gives a piece of money.*]
Clown. Now Jove, in his next commodity of hair, send thee a beard! 51
Vio. By my troth, I'll tell thee, I am almost sick for one, though I would not have it grow on my chin. Is thy lady within?
Clown. Would not a pair of these have bred, sir? 55
Vio. Yes, being kept together and put to use.
Clown. I would play Lord Pandarus of Phrygia, sir, to bring a Cressida to this Troilus.
Vio. I understand you, sir. 'Tis well begg'd. [*Gives another piece.*]
Clown. The matter, I hope, is not great, sir, begging but a beggar : Cressida was a beggar. My lady is within, sir. I will conster to them whence you come. Who you are and what you would are out of my welkin — I might say 'element,' but the word is over-worn. *Exit.*
Vio. This fellow is wise enough to play the fool, 67
And to do that well craves a kind of wit.
He must observe their mood on whom he jests,

The quality of persons, and the time; 70
Not, like the haggard, check at every feather
That comes before his eye. This is a practice
As full of labour as a wise man's art;
For folly that he wisely shows, is fit;
But wise men, folly-fall'n, quite taint their wit.

Enter *Sir Toby* and [*Sir*] *Andrew.*

To. Save you, gentleman! 76
Vio. And you, sir.
And. Dieu vous garde, monsieur.
Vio. Et vous aussi; vostre serviteur.
And. I hope, sir, you are, and I am yours.
To. Will you encounter the house? My niece is desirous you should enter, if your trade be to her.
Vio. I am bound to your niece, sir. I mean, she is the list of my voyage. 86
To. Taste your legs, sir; put them to motion.
Vio. My legs do better understand me, sir, than I understand what you mean by bidding me taste my legs. 91
To. I mean, to go, sir, to enter.
Vio. I will answer you with gait and entrance. But we are prevented.

Enter *Olivia* and *Gentlewoman,* [*Maria*].

Most excellent accomplish'd lady, the heavens rain odours on you! 96
And. [*aside*] That youth's a rare courtier. 'Rain odours' — well!
Vio. My matter hath no voice, lady, but to your own most pregnant and vouchsafed ear.
And. [*aside*] 'Odours,' 'pregnant,' and 'vouchsafed' — I'll get 'em all three all ready.
Oli. Let the garden door be shut, and leave me to my hearing. [*Exeunt Sir Toby, Sir Andrew, and Maria.*] Give me your hand, sir.
Vio. My duty, madam, and most humble service. 106
Oli. What is your name?
Vio. Cesario is your servant's name, fair princess.
Oli. My servant, sir? 'Twas never merry world 109
Since lowly feigning was call'd compliment. Y'are servant to the Count Orsino, youth.
Vio. And he is yours, and his must needs be yours.
Your servant's servant is your servant, madam.
Oli. For him, I think not on him; for his thoughts,
Would they were blanks, rather than fill'd with me! 115

415

Vio. Madam, I come to whet your gentle
thoughts
On his behalf.
Oli.   O, by your leave, I pray you!
I bade you never speak again of him;
But, would you undertake another suit,
I had rather hear you to solicit that   120
Than music from the spheres.
Vio.   Dear lady —
Oli. Give me leave, beseech you. I did send,
After the last enchantment you did here,
A ring in chase of you. So did I abuse
Myself, my servant, and, I fear me, you.   125
Under your hard construction must I sit,
To force that on you in a shameful cunning
Which you knew none of yours. What might
you think?
Have you not set mine honour at the stake
And baited it with all th' unmuzzled thoughts
That tyrannous heart can think? To one of
your receiving   131
Enough is shown; a cypress, not a bosom,
Hides my heart. So, let me hear you speak.
Vio. I pity you.
Oli.   That's a degree to love.
Vio. No, not a grize; for 'tis a vulgar proof
That very oft we pity enemies.   136
Oli. Why then, methinks 'tis time to smile
again.
O world, how apt the poor are to be proud!
If one should be a prey, how much the better
To fall before the lion than the wolf!   140
                    Clock strikes.
The clock upbraids me with the waste of time.
Be not afraid, good youth, I will not have you;
And yet, when wit and youth is come to harvest,
Your wife is like to reap a proper man.
There lies your way, due west.
Vio.   Then westward ho!   146
Grace and good disposition attend your lady-
ship!
You'll nothing, madam, to my lord by me?
Oli. Stay.
I prithee tell me what thou think'st of me.   150
Vio. That you do think you are not what
you are.
Oli. If I think so, I think the same of you.
Vio. Then think you right. I am not what
I am.
Oli. I would you were as I would have you
be!
Vio. Would it be better, madam, than I am?
I wish it might; for now I am your fool.   156
Oli. O, what a deal of scorn looks beautiful
In the contempt and anger of his lip!

A murd'rous guilt shows not itself more soon
Than love that would seem hid: love's night
is noon.   160
Cesario, by the roses of the spring,
By maidhood, honour, truth, and everything,
I love thee so that, maugre all thy pride,
Nor wit nor reason can my passion hide.
Do not extort thy reasons from this clause,   165
For that I woo, thou therefore hast no cause;
But rather reason thus with reason fetter:
Love sought is good, but given unsought is
better.
Vio. By innocence I swear, and by my youth,
I have one heart, one bosom, and one truth,   170
And that no woman has; nor never none
Shall mistress be of it, save I alone.
And so adieu, good madam. Never more
Will I my master's tears to you deplore.
Oli. Yet come again; for thou perhaps
mayst move   175
That heart which now abhors to like his love.
                    Exeunt.

Scene II. [Olivia's *house.*]

Enter *Sir Toby*, *Sir Andrew*, and *Fabian*.

And. No, faith, I'll not stay a jot longer.
To. Thy reason, dear venom; give thy
reason.
Fab. You must needs yield your reason, Sir
Andrew.   5
And. Marry, I saw your niece do more fa-
vours to the Count's servingman than ever she
bestow'd upon me. I saw't i' th' orchard.
To. Did she see thee the while, old boy?
Tell me that.   10
And. As plain as I see you now.
Fab. This was a great argument of love in
her toward you.
And. 'Slight! will you make an ass o' me?
Fab. I will prove it legitimate, sir, upon the
oaths of judgment and reason.   16
To. And they have been grand-jurymen
since before Noah was a sailor.
Fab. She did show favour to the youth in
your sight only to exasperate you, to awake
your dormouse valour, to put fire in your heart
and brimstone in your liver. You should then
have accosted her; and with some excellent
jests, fire-new from the mint, you should have
bang'd the youth into dumbness. This was
look'd for at your hand, and this was balk'd.
The double gilt of this opportunity you let time

wash off, and you are now sail'd into the North
of my lady's opinion, where you will hang like
an icicle on a Dutchman's beard unless you do
redeem it by some laudable attempt either of
valour or policy.   31

And. An't be any way, it must be with valour; for policy I hate. I had as lief be a
Brownist as a politician.   34

To. Why then, build me thy fortunes upon
the basis of valour. Challenge me the Count's
youth to fight with him; hurt him in eleven
places. My niece shall take note of it; and
assure thyself there is no love-broker in the
world can more prevail in man's commendation
with woman than report of valour.   41

Fab. There is no way but this, Sir Andrew.

And. Will either of you bear me a challenge
to him?   44

To. Go, write it in a martial hand. Be curst
and brief; it is no matter how witty, so it be
eloquent and full of invention. Taunt him with
the license of ink. If thou thou'st him some
thrice, it shall not be amiss; and as many lies
as will lie in thy sheet of paper, although the
sheet were big enough for the bed of Ware in
England, set 'em down. Go, about it! Let
there be gall enough in thy ink, though thou
write with a goose-pen, no matter. About it!

And. Where shall I find you?   55

To. We'll call thee at the cubiculo. Go.
                                       Exit Sir Andrew.

Fab. This is a dear manikin to you, Sir Toby.

To. I have been dear to him, lad — some
two thousand strong, or so.

Fab. We shall have a rare letter from him —
but you'll not deliver 't?   61

To. Never trust me then; and by all means
stir on the youth to an answer. I think oxen
and wainropes cannot hale them together. For
Andrew, if he were open'd, and you find so much
blood in his liver as will clog the foot of a flea,
I'll eat the rest of th' anatomy.   67

Fab. And his opposite, the youth, bears in
his visage no great presage of cruelty.

Enter *Maria.*

To. Look where the youngest wren of nine
comes.   71

Mar. If you desire the spleen, and will laugh
yourselves into stitches, follow me. Yond gull
Malvolio is turned heathen, a very renegado;
for there is no Christian that means to be saved
by believing rightly can ever believe such impossible passages of grossness. He's in yellow
stockings!

To. And cross-garter'd?   79

Mar. Most villanously; like a pedant that
keeps a school i' th' church. I have dogg'd him
like his murtherer. He does obey every point
of the letter that I dropp'd to betray him. He
does smile his face into more lines than is in the
new map with the augmentation of the Indies.
You have not seen such a thing as 'tis. I can
hardly forbear hurling things at him. I know
my lady will strike him. If she do, he'll smile,
and take't for a great favour.

To. Come bring us, bring us where he is!   90
                                          Exeunt omnes.

Scene III. [*A street.*]

Enter *Sebastian* and *Antonio.*

Seb. I would not by my will have troubled
     you;
But since you make your pleasure of your pains,
I will no further chide you.

Ant.   I could not stay behind you. My desire,
More sharp than filed steel, did spur me forth;
And not all love to see you (though so much   6
As might have drawn one to a longer voyage)
But jealousy what might befall your travel,
Being skilless in these parts; which to a
     stranger,
Unguided and unfriended, often prove   10
Rough and unhospitable. My willing love,
The rather by these arguments of fear,
Set forth in your pursuit.

Seb.   My kind Antonio,
I can no other answer make but thanks,
And thanks, and ever thanks; and oft good
     turns   15
Are shuffled off with such uncurrent pay.
But, were my worth as is my conscience firm,
You should find better dealing. What's to do?
Shall we go see the relics of this town?

Ant. To-morrow, sir; best first go see your
     lodging.   20

Seb. I am not weary, and 'tis long to night.
I pray you let us satisfy our eyes
With the memorials and the things of fame
That do renown this city.

Ant.   Would you'ld pardon me.
I do not without danger walk these streets.   25
Once in a sea-fight 'gainst the Count his galleys
I did some service; of such note indeed
That, were I ta'en here, it would scarce be
     answer'd.

Seb. Belike you slew great number of his
     people?

Ant. Th' offence is not of such a bloody nature, 30
Albeit the quality of the time and quarrel
Might well have given us bloody argument.
It might have since been answer'd in repaying
What we took from them, which for traffic's sake
Most of our city did. Only myself stood out;
For which, if I be lapsed in this place, 36
I shall pay dear.
Seb. Do not then walk too open.
Ant. It doth not fit me. Hold, sir, here's my purse.
In the south suburbs at the Elephant
Is best to lodge. I will bespeak our diet, 40
Whiles you beguile the time and feed your knowledge
With viewing of the town. There shall you have me.
Seb. Why I your purse?
Ant. Haply your eye shall light upon some toy 44
You have desire to purchase; and your store
I think is not for idle markets, sir.
Seb. I'll be your purse-bearer, and leave you for
An hour.
Ant. To th' Elephant.
Seb. I do remember.
Exeunt.

Scene IV. [Olivia's *orchard*.]

Enter *Olivia* and *Maria.*

Oli. I have sent after him; he says he'll come.
How shall I feast him? what bestow of him?
For youth is bought more oft than begg'd or borrow'd.
I speak too loud.
Where is Malvolio? He is sad and civil, 5
And suits well for a servant with my fortunes.
Where is Malvolio?
Mar. He's coming, madam; but in very strange manner. He is sure possess'd, madam.
Oli. Why, what's the matter? Does he rave?
Mar. No, madam, he does nothing but smile. Your ladyship were best to have some guard about you if he come, for sure the man is tainted in 's wits.
Oli. Go call him hither. [*Exit Maria.*] I am as mad as he, 15
If sad and merry madness equal be.

Enter [*Maria*, with] *Malvolio.*

How now, Malvolio?
Mal. Sweet lady, ho, ho!
Oli. Smil'st thou?
I sent for thee upon a sad occasion. 20
Mal. Sad, lady? I could be sad. This does make some obstruction in the blood, this cross-gartering; but what of that? If it please the eye of one, it is with me as the very true sonnet is, 'Please one, and please all.' 25
Oli. Why, how dost thou, man? What is the matter with thee?
Mal. Not black in my mind, though yellow in my legs. It did come to his hands, and commands shall be executed. I think we do know the sweet Roman hand. 31
Oli. Wilt thou go to bed, Malvolio?
Mal. To bed? Ay, sweetheart; and I'll come to thee.
Oli. God comfort thee! Why dost thou smile so, and kiss thy hand so oft? 36
Mar. How do you, Malvolio?
Mal. At your request? Yes, nightingales answer daws!
Mar. Why appear you with this ridiculous boldness before my lady? 41
Mal. 'Be not afraid of greatness.' 'Twas well writ.
Oli. What mean'st thou by that, Malvolio?
Mal. 'Some are born great' — 45
Oli. Ha?
Mal. 'Some achieve greatness' —
Oli. What say'st thou?
Mal. 'And some have greatness thrust upon them.' 50
Oli. Heaven restore thee!
Mal. 'Remember who commended thy yellow stockings' —
Oli. My yellow stockings? 54
Mal. 'And wish'd to see thee cross-garter'd.'
Oli. Cross-garter'd?
Mal. 'Go to, thou art made, if thou desir'st to be so' —
Oli. Am I made? 59
Mal. 'If not, let me see thee a servant still.'
Oli. Why, this is very midsummer madness.

Enter *Servant.*

Ser. Madam, the young gentleman of the Count Orsino's is return'd. I could hardly entreat him back. He attends your ladyship's pleasure. 65
Oli. I'll come to him. [*Exit Servant.*] Good Maria, let this fellow be look'd to. Where's my

cousin Toby? Let some of my people have a special care of him. I would not have him miscarry for the half of my dowry.   70
Exit [Olivia; then Maria].
Mal. O ho! do you come near me now? No worse man than Sir Toby to look to me! This concurs directly with the letter. She sends him on purpose, that I may appear stubborn to him; for she incites me to that in the letter. 'Cast thy humble slough,' says she; 'be opposite with a kinsman, surly with servants; let thy tongue tang with arguments of state; put thyself into the trick of singularity'; — and consequently sets down the manner how: as, a sad face, a reverend carriage, a slow tongue, in the habit of some sir of note, and so forth. I have lim'd her; but it is Jove's doing, and Jove make me thankful! And when she went away now, 'Let this fellow be look'd to.' 'Fellow!' not 'Malvolio,' nor after my degree, but 'fellow.' Why, everything adheres together, that no dram of a scruple, no scruple of a scruple, no obstacle, no incredulous or unsafe circumstance — What can be said? Nothing that can be can come between me and the full prospect of my hopes. Well, Jove, not I, is the doer of this, and he is to be thanked.   92

Enter [Sir] Toby, Fabian, and Maria.

To. Which way is he, in the name of sanctity? If all the devils of hell be drawn in little, and Legion himself possess'd him, yet I'll speak to him.   96
Fab. Here he is, here he is! How is't with you, sir?
To. How is't with you, man?
Mal. Go off; I discard you. Let me enjoy my private. Go off.   100
Mar. Lo, how hollow the fiend speaks within him! Did not I tell you? Sir Toby, my lady prays you to have a care of him.
Mal. Aha! does she so?   104
To. Go to, go to; peace, peace! We must deal gently with him. Let me alone. How do you, Malvolio? How is't with you? What, man! defy the devil! Consider, he's an enemy to mankind.
Mal. Do you know what you say?   110
Mar. La you, an you speak ill of the devil, how he takes it at heart! Pray God he be not bewitch'd!
Fab. Carry his water to th' wise woman.   114
Mar. Marry, and it shall be done to-morrow morning if I live. My lady would not lose him for more than I'll say.

Mal. How now, mistress?
Mar. O Lord!   119
To. Prithee hold thy peace. This is not the way. Do you not see you move him? Let me alone with him.
Fab. No way but gentleness; gently, gently. The fiend is rough and will not be roughly us'd.
To. Why, how now, my bawcock? How dost thou, chuck?   126
Mal. Sir!
To. Ay, biddy, come with me. What, man! 'tis not for gravity to play at cherry-pit with Satan. Hang him, foul collier!   130
Mar. Get him to say his prayers. Good Sir Toby, get him to pray.
Mal. My prayers, minx?
Mar. No, I warrant you, he will not hear of godliness.   135
Mal. Go hang yourselves all! You are idle shallow things; I am not of your element. You shall know more hereafter.   *Exit.*
To. Is't possible?
Fab. If this were play'd upon a stage now, I could condemn it as an improbable fiction. 141
To. His very genius hath taken the infection of the device, man.
Mar. Nay, pursue him now, lest the device take air and taint.   145
Fab. Why, we shall make him mad indeed.
Mar. The house will be the quieter.
To. Come, we'll have him in a dark room and bound. My niece is already in the belief that he's mad. We may carry it thus, for our pleasure and his penance, till our very pastime, tired out of breath, prompt us to have mercy on him; at which time we will bring the device to the bar and crown thee for a finder of madmen. But see, but see!   155

Enter Sir Andrew.

Fab. More matter for a May morning.
And. Here's the challenge; read it. I warrant there's vinegar and pepper in't.
Fab. Is't so saucy?   159
And. Ay, is't, I warrant him. Do but read.
To. Give me. [*Reads*] 'Youth, whatsoever thou art, thou art but a scurvy fellow.'
Fab. Good, and valiant.
To. [*reads*] 'Wonder not nor admire not in thy mind why I do call thee so, for I will show thee no reason for't.'
Fab. A good note! That keeps you from the blow of the law.   169
To. [*reads*] 'Thou com'st to the Lady Olivia, and in my sight she uses thee kindly. But thou

liest in thy throat; that is not the matter I challenge thee for.'

Fab. Very brief, and to exceeding good sense — less. 175

To. [*reads*] 'I will waylay thee going home; where if it be thy chance to kill me' —

Fab. Good.

To. [*reads*] 'Thou kill'st me like a rogue and a villain.' 180

Fab. Still you keep o' th' windy side of the law. Good.

To. [*reads*] 'Fare thee well, and God have mercy upon one of our souls! He may have mercy upon mine, but my hope is better; and so look to thyself. Thy friend, as thou usest him, and thy sworn enemy,

                          'ANDREW AGUECHEEK.'
If this letter move him not, his legs cannot. I'll give't him. 189

Mar. You may have very fit occasion for't. He is now in some commerce with my lady and will by-and-by depart.

To. Go, Sir Andrew! Scout me for him at the corner of the orchard like a bum-baily. So soon as ever thou seest him, draw; and as thou draw'st, swear horrible; for it comes to pass oft that a terrible oath, with a swaggering accent sharply twang'd off, gives manhood more approbation than ever proof itself would have earn'd him. Away! 200

And. Nay, let me alone for swearing. *Exit.*

To. Now will not I deliver his letter; for the behaviour of the young gentleman gives him out to be of good capacity and breeding; his employment between his lord and my niece confirms no less. Therefore this letter, being so excellently ignorant, will breed no terror in the youth. He will find it comes from a clodpoll. But, sir, I will deliver his challenge by word of mouth, set upon Aguecheek a notable report of valour, and drive the gentleman (as I know his youth will aptly receive it) into a most hideous opinion of his rage, skill, fury, and impetuosity. This will so fright them both that they will kill one another by the look, like cockatrices. 215

Enter *Olivia* and *Viola.*

Fab. Here he comes with your niece. Give them way till he take leave, and presently after him.

To. I will meditate the while upon some horrid message for a challenge. 220

[*Exeunt Sir Toby, Fabian, and Maria.*]

Oli. I have said too much unto a heart of stone

And laid mine honour too unchary out. There's something in me that reproves my fault; But such a headstrong potent fault it is That it but mocks reproof. 225

Vio. With the same haviour that your passion bears Goes on my master's grief.

Oli. Here, wear this jewel for me; 'tis my picture. Refuse it not; it hath no tongue to vex you. And I beseech you come again to-morrow. 230 What shall you ask of me that I'll deny, That honour, sav'd, may upon asking give?

Vio. Nothing but this — your true love for my master.

Oli. How with mine honour may I give him that Which I have given to you?

Vio.   I will acquit you.

Oli. Well, come again to-morrow. Fare thee well. 236 A fiend like thee might bear my soul to hell.

[*Exit.*]

Enter [*Sir*] *Toby* and *Fabian.*

To. Gentleman, God save thee!

Vio. And you, sir. 239

To. That defence thou hast, betake thee to't. Of what nature the wrongs are thou hast done him, I know not; but thy intercepter, full of despite, bloody as the hunter, attends thee at the orchard end. Dismount thy tuck, be yare in thy preparation; for thy assailant is quick, skilful, and deadly. 246

Vio. You mistake, sir. I am sure no man hath any quarrel to me. My remembrance is very free and clear from any image of offence done to any man. 250

To. You'll find it otherwise, I assure you. Therefore, if you hold your life at any price, betake you to your guard; for your opposite hath in him what youth, strength, skill, and wrath can furnish man withal. 255

Vio. I pray you, sir, what is he?

To. He is knight, dubb'd with unhatch'd rapier and on carpet consideration; but he is a devil in private brawl. Souls and bodies hath he divorc'd three; and his incensement at this moment is so implacable that satisfaction can be none but by pangs of death and sepulchre. 'Hob, nob' is his word; 'give't or take't.'

Vio. I will return again into the house and desire some conduct of the lady. I am no fighter. I have heard of some kind of men that put quarrels purposely on others to taste their valour. Belike this is a man of that quirk.

To. Sir, no. His indignation derives itself out of a very competent injury; therefore get you on and give him his desire. Back you shall not to the house, unless you undertake that with me which with as much safety you might answer him. Therefore on! or strip your sword stark naked; for meddle you must, that's certain, or forswear to wear iron about you. 276

Vio. This is as uncivil as strange. I beseech you do me this courteous office, as to know of the knight what my offence to him is. It is something of my negligence, nothing of my purpose. 280

To. I will do so. Signior Fabian, stay you by this gentleman till my return.   *Exit.*

Vio. Pray you, sir, do you know of this matter? 284

Fab. I know the knight is incens'd against you, even to a mortal arbitrement; but nothing of the circumstance more.

Vio. I beseech you, what manner of man is he? 289

Fab. Nothing of that wonderful promise, to read him by his form, as you are like to find him in the proof of his valour. He is indeed, sir, the most skilful, bloody, and fatal opposite that you could possibly have found in any part of Illyria. Will you walk towards him? I will make your peace with him if I can. 296

Vio. I shall be much bound to you for't. I am one that had rather go with sir priest than sir knight. I care not who knows so much of my mettle.   *Exeunt.*

Enter [*Sir*] *Toby* and [*Sir*] *Andrew* [at the orchard end].

To. Why, man, he's a very devil; I have not seen such a firago. I had a pass with him, rapier, scabbard, and all, and he gives me the stuck-in with such a mortal motion that it is inevitable; and on the answer he pays you as surely as your feet hit the ground they step on. They say he has been fencer to the Sophy.

And. Pox on't, I'll not meddle with him.

To. Ay, but he will not now be pacified. Fabian can scarce hold him yonder. 310

And. Plague on't, an I thought he had been valiant, and so cunning in fence, I'd have seen him damn'd ere I'd have challeng'd him. Let him let the matter slip, and I'll give him my horse, grey Capilet. 315

To. I'll make the motion. Stand here; make a good show on't. This shall end without the perdition of souls. [*Aside*] Marry, I'll ride your horse as well as I ride you.

Enter *Fabian* and *Viola.*

I have his horse to take up the quarrel. I have persuaded him the youth's a devil. 321

Fab. He is as horribly conceited of him; and pants and looks pale, as if a bear were at his heels. 324

To. There's no remedy, sir; he will fight with you for 's oath sake. Marry, he hath better bethought him of his quarrel, and he finds that now scarce to be worth talking of. Therefore draw for the supportance of his vow. He protests he will not hurt you. 330

Vio. [*aside*] Pray God defend me! A little thing would make me tell them how much I lack of a man.

Fab. Give ground if you see him furious. 334

To. Come, Sir Andrew, there's no remedy. The gentleman will for his honour's sake have one bout with you; he cannot by the duello avoid it; but he has promised me, as he is a gentleman and a soldier, he will not hurt you. Come on, to't! 340

And. Pray God he keep his oath! [*Draws.*]

Enter *Antonio.*

Vio. I do assure you 'tis against my will.
[*Draws.*]

Ant. Put up your sword. If this young gentleman
Have done offence, I take the fault on me;
If you offend him, I for him defy you. 345

To. You, sir? Why, what are you?

Ant. [*draws*] One, sir, that for his love dares yet do more
Than you have heard him brag to you he will.

To. Nay, if you be an undertaker, I am for you.   [*Draws.*] 350

Enter *Officers.*

Fab. O good Sir Toby, hold! Here come the officers.

To. [*to Antonio*] I'll be with you anon.

Vio. [*to Sir Andrew*] Pray, sir, put your sword up, if you please. 355

And. Marry, will I, sir; and for that I promis'd you, I'll be as good as my word. He will bear you easily, and reins well.

1. Off. This is the man; do thy office.

2. Off. Antonio, I arrest thee at the suit 360
Of Count Orsino.

Ant.   You do mistake me, sir.

1. Off. No, sir, no jot. I know your favour well,

Though now you have no sea-cap on your head.
Take him away. He knows I know him well.
   Ant. I must obey. [*To Viola*] This comes
    with seeking you. 366
But there's no remedy; I shall answer it.
What will you do, now my necessity
Makes me to ask you for my purse? It grieves
   me
Much more for what I cannot do for you 370
Than what befalls myself. You stand amaz'd,
But be of comfort.
   2. Off. Come, sir, away.
   Ant. I must entreat of you some of that
   money.
   Vio. What money, sir? 375
For the fair kindness you have show'd me
   here,
And part being prompted by your present
   trouble,
Out of my lean and low ability
I'll lend you something. My having is not
   much.
I'll make division of my present with you. 380
Hold, there's half my coffer.
   Ant. Will you deny me now?
Is't possible that my deserts to you
Can lack persuasion? Do not tempt my misery,
Lest that it make me so unsound a man
As to upbraid you with those kindnesses 385
That I have done for you.
   Vio. I know of none,
Nor know I you by voice or any feature.
I hate ingratitude more in a man
Than lying, vainness, babbling, drunkenness,
Or any taint of vice whose strong corruption
Inhabits our frail blood.
   Ant. O heavens themselves! 391
   2. Off. Come, sir, I pray you go.
   Ant. Let me speak a little. This youth that
   you see here
I snatch'd one half out of the jaws of death;
Reliev'd him with such sanctity of love, 395

And to his image, which methought did promise
Most venerable worth, did I devotion.
   1. Off. What's that to us? The time goes
    by. Away!
   Ant. But, O, how vile an idol proves this god!
Thou hast, Sebastian, done good feature shame.
In nature there's no blemish but the mind;
None can be call'd deform'd but the unkind.
Virtue is beauty; but the beauteous evil
Are empty trunks, o'erflourish'd by the devil.
   1. Off. The man grows mad. Away with
    him! Come, come, sir. 405
   Ant. Lead me on.   *Exit* [*with Officers*].
   Vio. Methinks his words do from such
    passion fly
That he believes himself; so do not I.
Prove true, imagination, O, prove true,
That I, dear brother, be now ta'en for you! 410
   To. Come hither, knight; come hither,
Fabian. We'll whisper o'er a couplet or two of
most sage saws.
   Vio. He nam'd Sebastian. I my brother
   know
Yet living in my glass. Even such and so 415
In favour was my brother, and he went
Still in this fashion, colour, ornament,
For him I imitate. O, if it prove,
Tempests are kind, and salt waves fresh in love!
      [Exit.]
   To. A very dishonest paltry boy, and more a
coward than a hare. His dishonesty appears in
leaving his friend here in necessity and denying
him; and for his cowardship, ask Fabian.
   Fab. A coward, a most devout coward; re-
ligious in it. 425
   And. 'Slid, I'll after him again and beat him!
   To. Do; cuff him soundly, but never draw
thy sword.
   And. An I do not —   *[Exit.]*
   Fab. Come, let's see the event.
   To. I dare lay any money 'twill be nothing
yet.   *Exeunt.*

ACT IV. Scene I. [*Before* Olivia's *house.*]

Enter Sebastian and Clown.

   Clown. Will you make me believe that I am
not sent for you?
   Seb. Go to, go to, thou art a foolish fellow.
Let me be clear of thee. 4
   Clown. Well held out, i' faith! No, I do not
know you; nor I am not sent to you by my
lady, to bid you come speak with her; nor your

name is not Master Cesario: nor this is not my
nose neither. Nothing that is so is so.
   Seb. I prithee vent thy folly somewhere else.
Thou know'st not me. 11
   Clown. Vent my folly! He has heard that
word of some great man, and now applies it to
a fool. Vent my folly! I am afraid this great
lubber, the world, will prove a cockney. I
prithee now, ungird thy strangeness, and tell me

what I shall vent to my lady. Shall I vent to her that thou art coming?

Seb. I prithee, foolish Greek, depart from me. There's money for thee. If you tarry longer, 20 I shall give worse payment.

Clown. By my troth, thou hast an open hand. These wise men that give fools money get themselves a good report — after fourteen years' purchase. 25

Enter [*Sir*] *Andrew*, [*Sir*] *Toby*, and *Fabian*.

And. Now, sir, have I met you again? There's for you!   [*Strikes Sebastian.*]

Seb. Why, there's for thee, and there, and there!   [*Strikes Sir Andrew.*] Are all the people mad?

To. Hold, sir, or I'll throw your dagger o'er the house.   [*Seizes Sebastian.*]

Clown. This will I tell my lady straight. I would not be in some of your coats for twopence.   [*Exit.*]

To. Come on, sir; hold! 34

And. Nay, let him alone. I'll go another way to work with him. I'll have an action of battery against him, if there be any law in Illyria. Though I stroke him first, yet it's no matter for that.

Seb. Let go thy hand. 40

To. Come, sir, I will not let you go. Come, my young soldier, put up your iron. You are well flesh'd. Come on.

Seb. I will be free from thee. [*Disengages himself.*] What wouldst thou now? If thou dar'st tempt me further, draw thy sword.   [*Draws.*] 45

To. What, what? Nay then, I must have an ounce or two of this malapert blood from you.   [*Draws.*]

Enter *Olivia*.

Oli. Hold, Toby! On thy life I charge thee hold!

To. Madam! 50

Oli. Will it be ever thus? Ungracious wretch, Fit for the mountains and the barbarous caves, Where manners ne'er were preach'd! Out of my sight! Be not offended, dear Cesario. Rudesby, be gone!

[*Exeunt Sir Toby, Sir Andrew, and Fabian.*]   I prithee, gentle friend, 55 Let thy fair wisdom, not thy passion, sway In this uncivil and unjust extent Against thy peace. Go with me to my house, And hear thou there how many fruitless pranks

This ruffian hath botch'd up, that thou thereby Mayst smile at this. Thou shalt not choose but go; 61 Do not deny. Beshrew his soul for me! He started one poor heart of mine, in thee.

Seb. What relish is in this? How runs the stream? Or I am mad, or else this is a dream. 65 Let fancy still my sense in Lethe steep; If it be thus to dream, still let me sleep!

Oli. Nay, come, I prithee. Would thou'dst be rul'd by me!

Seb. Madam, I will.

Oli.   O, say so, and so be!   *Exeunt.*

Scene II. [Olivia's *house.*]

Enter *Maria* and *Clown*.

Mar. Nay, I prithee put on this gown and this beard; make him believe thou art Sir Topas the curate; do it quickly. I'll call Sir Toby the whilst.   [*Exit.*]

Clown. Well, I'll put it on, and I will dissemble myself in't, and I would I were the first that ever dissembled in such a gown. I am not tall enough to become the function well, nor lean enough to be thought a good studient; but to be said an honest man and a good housekeeper goes as fairly as to say a careful man and a great scholar. The competitors enter. 12

Enter [*Sir*] *Toby* [and *Maria*].

To. Jove bless thee, Master Parson.

Clown. Bonos dies, Sir Toby; for, as the old hermit of Prague, that never saw pen and ink, very wittily said to a niece of King Gorboduc, 'That that is is'; so I, being Master Parson, am Master Parson; for what is 'that' but that, and 'is' but is?

To. To him, Sir Topas. 20

Clown. What ho, I say. Peace in this prison!

To. The knave counterfeits well; a good knave.

Malvolio within.

Mal. Who calls there?

Clown. Sir Topas the curate, who comes to visit Malvolio the lunatic. 26

Mal. Sir Topas, Sir Topas, good Sir Topas, go to my lady.

Clown. Out, hyperbolical fiend! How vexest thou this man! Talkest thou nothing but of ladies? 30

To. Well said, Master Parson.

Mal. Sir Topas, never was man thus wronged.
Good Sir Topas, do not think I am mad. They
have laid me here in hideous darkness.   34

Clown. Fie, thou dishonest Satan! I call
thee by the most modest terms; for I am one
of those gentle ones that will use the devil
himself with courtesy. Say'st thou that house
is dark?

Mal. As hell, Sir Topas.   39

Clown. Why, it hath bay windows transparent as barricadoes, and the clerestories
toward the south north are as lustrous as ebony;
and yet complainest thou of obstruction?

Mal. I am not mad, Sir Topas. I say to you
this house is dark.   45

Clown. Madman, thou errest. I say there
is no darkness but ignorance, in which thou
art more puzzled than the Egyptians in their
fog.

Mal. I say this house is as dark as ignorance,
though ignorance were as dark as hell; and I
say there was never man thus abus'd. I am no
more mad than you are. Make the trial of it in
any constant question.

Clown. What is the opinion of Pythagoras
concerning wild fowl?   55

Mal. That the soul of our grandam might
happily inhabit a bird.

Clown. What think'st thou of his opinion?

Mal. I think nobly of the soul and no way
approve his opinion.   60

Clown. Fare thee well. Remain thou still in
darkness. Thou shalt hold th' opinion of
Pythagoras ere I will allow of thy wits, and
fear to kill a woodcock, lest thou dispossess the
soul of thy grandam. Fare thee well.   65

Mal. Sir Topas, Sir Topas!

To. My most exquisite Sir Topas!

Clown. Nay, I am for all waters.

Mar. Thou mightst have done this without
thy beard and gown. He sees thee not.   70

To. To him in thine own voice, and bring me
word how thou find'st him. — [*To Maria*] I
would we were well rid of this knavery. If he
may be conveniently deliver'd, I would he
were; for I am now so far in offence with
my niece that I cannot pursue with any safety
this sport to the upshot. — [*To the Clown*]
Come by-and-by to my chamber.

Exit [*with Maria*].

Clown. [*sings*] 'Hey, Robin, jolly Robin,
                    Tell me how thy lady does.'

Mal. Fool!   80

Clown. 'My lady is unkind, perdie!'

Mal. Fool!

Clown. 'Alas, why is she so?'

Mal. Fool, I say!   84

Clown. 'She loves another' — Who calls, ha?

Mal. Good fool, as ever thou wilt deserve
well at my hand, help me to a candle, and pen,
ink, and paper. As I am a gentleman, I will live
to be thankful to thee for't.

Clown. Master Malvolio?   90

Mal. Ay, good fool.

Clown. Alas, sir, how fell you besides your
five wits?

Mal. Fool, there was never man so notoriously abus'd. I am as well in my wits, fool, as
thou art.   96

Clown. But as well? Then you are mad indeed, if you be no better in your wits than a fool.

Mal. They have here propertied me; keep
me in darkness, send ministers to me, asses, and
do all they can to face me out of my wits.   101

Clown. Advise you what you say. The minister is here. — Malvolio, Malvolio, thy wits
the heavens restore! Endeavour thyself to
sleep and leave thy vain bibble babble.   105

Mal. Sir Topas!

Clown. Maintain no words with him, good
fellow. — Who, I, sir? Not I, sir. God b' wi'
you, good Sir Topas! — Marry, amen. — I will,
sir, I will.

Mal. Fool, fool, fool, I say!   110

Clown. Alas, sir, be patient. What say you,
sir? I am shent for speaking to you.

Mal. Good fool, help me to some light and
some paper. I tell thee, I am as well in my wits
as any man in Illyria.   115

Clown. Well-a-day that you were, sir!

Mal. By this hand, I am. Good fool, some
ink, paper, and light; and convey what I will
set down to my lady. It shall advantage thee
more than ever the bearing of letter did.   120

Clown. I will help you to't. But tell me true,
are you not mad indeed? or do you but
counterfeit?

Mal. Believe me, I am not. I tell thee true.

Clown. Nay, I'll ne'er believe a madman till
I see his brains. I will fetch you light and paper
and ink.   127

Mal. Fool, I'll requite it in the highest degree. I prithee be gone.

Clown. [*sings*] I am gone, sir;   130
                    And anon, sir,
                  I'll be with you again,
                    In a trice,
                  Like to the old Vice,
                  Your need to sustain;   135

Who, with dagger of lath,
In his rage and his wrath,
  Cries 'aha!' to the devil.
Like a mad lad,
  'Pare thy nails, dad.'   140
  Adieu, goodman devil.   *Exit.*

Scene III. [Olivia's *orchard.*]

Enter Sebastian.

Seb. This is the air; that is the glorious sun;
This pearl she gave me, I do feel't and see't;
And though 'tis wonder that enwraps me thus,
Yet 'tis not madness. Where's Antonio then?
I could not find him at the Elephant;   5
Yet there he was; and there I found this credit,
That he did range the town to seek me out.
His counsel now might do me golden service;
For though my soul disputes well with my sense
That this may be some error, but no madness,
Yet doth this accident and flood of fortune 11
So far exceed all instance, all discourse,
That I am ready to distrust mine eyes
And wrangle with my reason, that persuades me
To any other trust but that I am mad,   15
Or else the lady's mad. Yet, if 'twere so,

She could not sway her house, command her
  followers,
Take and give back affairs and their dispatch
With such a smooth, discreet, and stable bearing
As I perceive she does. There's something in't
That is deceivable. But here the lady comes.

Enter Olivia and Priest.

Oli. Blame not this haste of mine. If you
  mean well,
Now go with me and with this holy man
Into the chantry by. There, before him,
And underneath that consecrated roof,   25
Plight me the full assurance of your faith,
That my most jealous and too doubtful soul
May live at peace. He shall conceal it
Whiles you are willing it shall come to note,
What time we will our celebration keep   30
According to my birth. What do you say?
Seb. I'll follow this good man and go with
  you
And having sworn truth, ever will be true.
Oli. Then lead the way, good father; and
  heavens so shine
That they may fairly note this act of mine! 35
                           Exeunt.

ACT V. Scene I. [*Before* Olivia's *house.*]

Enter Clown and Fabian.

Fab. Now as thou lov'st me, let me see his
letter.
Clown. Good Master Fabian, grant me an-
other request.
Fab. Anything.   5
Clown. Do not desire to see this letter.
Fab. This is to give a dog, and in recompense
desire my dog again.

Enter Duke, Viola, Curio, and Lords.

Duke. Belong you to the Lady Olivia,
friends?   9
Clown. Ay, sir, we are some of her trappings.
Duke. I know thee well. How dost thou, my
good fellow?
Clown. Truly, sir, the better for my foes, and
the worse for my friends.
Duke. Just the contrary: the better for thy
friends.   16
Clown. No, sir, the worse.
Duke. How can that be?
Clown. Marry, sir, they praise me and make
an ass of me. Now my foes tell me plainly I am

an ass; so that, by my foes, sir, I profit in the
knowledge of myself, and by my friends I am
abused; so that, conclusions to be as kisses, if
your four negatives make your two affirmatives,
why then, the worse for my friends and the
better for my foes.   26
Duke. Why, this is excellent.
Clown. By my troth, sir, no; though it
please you to be one of my friends.
Duke. Thou shalt not be the worse for me.
There's gold.   31
Clown. But that it would be double-dealing,
sir, I would you could make it another.
Duke. O, you give me ill counsel.
Clown. Put your grace in your pocket, sir,
for this once, and let your flesh and blood
obey it.   36
Duke. Well, I will be so much a sinner to be
a double-dealer. There's another.
Clown. Primo, secundo, tertio is a good play;
and the old saying is 'The third pays for all.'
The triplex, sir, is a good tripping measure; or
the bells of Saint Bennet, sir, may put you in
mind — one, two, three.   43

425

Duke. You can fool no more money out of me
at this throw. If you will let your lady know I
am here to speak with her, and bring her along
with you, it may awake my bounty further.
Clown. Marry, sir, lullaby to your bounty
till I come again! I go, sir; but I would not
have you to think that my desire of having is
the sin of covetousness. But, as you say, sir, let
your bounty take a nap; I will awake it anon.
Exit.

Enter *Antonio* and *Officers.*

Vio. Here comes the man, sir, that did rescue
me.
Duke. That face of his I do remember well;
Yet when I saw it last, it was besmear'd   55
As black as Vulcan in the smoke of war.
A baubling vessel was he captain of,
For shallow draught and bulk unprizable,
With which such scathful grapple did he make
With the most noble bottom of our fleet   60
That very envy and the tongue of loss
Cried fame and honour on him. What's the
matter?
1. Off. Orsino, this is that Antonio
That took the Phœnix and her fraught from
Candy;
And this is he that did the Tiger board   65
When your young nephew Titus lost his leg.
Here in the streets, desperate of shame and
state,
In private brabble did we apprehend him.
Vio. He did me kindness, sir; drew on my
side;
But in conclusion put strange speech upon me.
I know not what 'twas but distraction.   71
Duke. Notable pirate, thou salt-water thief!
What foolish boldness brought thee to their
mercies
Whom thou in terms so bloody and so dear
Hast made thine enemies?
Ant.   Orsino, noble sir,   75
Be pleas'd that I shake off these names you
give me.
Antonio never yet was thief or pirate,
Though I confess, on base and ground enough,
Orsino's enemy. A witchcraft drew me hither.
That most ingrateful boy there by your side
From the rude sea's enrag'd and foamy mouth
Did I redeem. A wrack past hope he was.
His life I gave him, and did thereto add
My love without retention or restraint,
All his in dedication. For his sake   85
Did I expose myself (pure for his love)
Into the danger of this adverse town;

Drew to defend him when he was beset;
Where being apprehended, his false cunning
(Not meaning to partake with me in danger)   90
Taught him to face me out of his acquaintance,
And grew a twenty years removed thing
While one would wink; denied me mine own
purse,
Which I had recommended to his use
Not half an hour before.
Vio.   How can this be?   95
Duke. When came he to this town?
Ant. To-day, my lord; and for three months
before,
No int'rim, not a minute's vacancy,
Both day and night did we keep company.

Enter *Olivia* and *Attendants.*

Duke. Here comes the Countess; now heaven
walks on earth.   100
But for thee, fellow — fellow, thy words are
madness.
Three months this youth hath tended upon me;
But more of that anon. Take him aside.
Oli. What would my lord, but that he may
not have,
Wherein Olivia may seem serviceable?   105
Cesario, you do not keep promise with me.
Vio. Madam!
Duke. Gracious Olivia —
Oli. What do you say, Cesario? — Good my
lord —
Vio. My lord would speak; my duty hushes
me.   110
Oli. If it be aught to the old tune, my lord,
It is as fat and fulsome to mine ear
As howling after music.
Duke.   Still so cruel?
Oli. Still so constant, lord.
Duke. What, to perverseness? You uncivil
lady,   115
To whose ingrate and unauspicious altars
My soul the faithfull'st off'rings hath breath'd
out
That e'er devotion tender'd! What shall I do?
Oli. Even what it please my lord, that shall
become him.
Duke. Why should I not, had I the heart to
do it,   120
Like to th' Egyptian thief at point of death,
Kill what I love? — a savage jealousy
That sometime savours nobly. But hear me this:
Since you to non-regardance cast my faith,
And that I partly know the instrument   125
That screws me from my true place in your
favour,

Vivien Leigh as the winsome heroine, Viola, enamored of Duke Orsino

TWELFTH NIGHT

Attired in her brother's clothes, Viola enters Orsino's service as a page

PHOTOGRAPHS BY ANGUS MCBEAN
PRODUCED BY THE MEMORIAL THEATRE COMPANY
STRATFORD-UPON-AVON

"What country, friends, is this?" Voyaging with her brother, Viola is shipwrecked on the coast of Illyria, in the realm of the melancholy Duke Orsino (*Act I, Scene II*)

"I prithee,—and I'll pay thee bounteously,—conceal me what I am, and be my aid." Viola persuades the captain (Mervyn Blake) to aid her in entering the duke's service and in disguising herself as a man (*Act I, Scene II*)

"So please my lord, I might not be admitted." An attendant, Valentine (Gabriel Woolf), reports to Orsino (Keith Michell) that the Countess Olivia receives his wooing coldly (*Act I, Scene I*)

"Give us the place alone: we will hear this divinity." Olivia (Maxine Audley) is attracted by the handsome page, who comes to her with a love letter from Orsino (*Act I, Scene V*)

"Holla your name to the reverberate hills, and make the babbling gossip of the air cry out, 'Olivia!'" Romantic rhetoric marks Viola's vicarious wooing of the countess (*Act I, Scene V*)

Seeking to ingratiate herself with Orsino's page, Olivia sends her man Malvolio (Laurence Olivier) after Viola to present her with a ring (*Act II, Scene II*)

Alan Webb as the uncle of Olivia, Sir Toby Belch, capricious, light-headed winebibber

Feste (Edward Atienza), the jester of the duke, gives vent to a melancholy madrigal

Right: Michael Denison in the role of Sir Andrew Aguecheek, the senile suitor of Countess Olivia

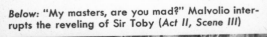

Below: "My masters, are you mad?" Malvolio interrupts the reveling of Sir Toby (*Act II, Scene III*)

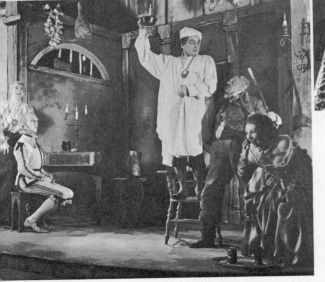

"Come away, come away, death." The jester Feste sings an old love song before the duke and his court (*Act II, Scene IV*)

"My father had a daughter lov'd a man, as it might be, perhaps, were I a woman, I should your lordship." Viola hints at her affection for the duke (*Act II, Scene IV*)

"By my life, this is my lady's hand!" Malvolio finds the letter which the conspirators have forged to lead him to believe that Countess Olivia is in love with him (*Act II, Scene V*)

Above: "How do you, Malvolio? How is 't with you?" Sir Toby baits Malvolio (*Act III, Scene IV*)

Left: Certified as mad by Sir Toby, the lovesick Malvolio is confined in a dark room in the house of the Countess Olivia (*Act IV, Scene II*)

"What is the opinion of Pythagoras concerning wild fowl?" Disguised as Sir Topas, the curate, Feste brings Malvolio cold consolation from an ancient Greek philosopher (*Act IV, Scene II*)

Viola engages in a duel with Sir Andrew Aguecheek, who thinks she is his rival for the love of the countess (*Act III, Scene IV*)

"Put up your sword. If this young gentleman have done offence, I take the fault on me." Mistaking Viola for her brother, Antonio (William Devlin) interrupts the duel and crosses swords with Sir Toby Belch (*Act III, Scene IV*)

Viola and her brother Sebastian (Trader Faulkner) are reunited (*Act V, Scene I*)

Sir Andrew Aguecheek is soundly beaten by Viola's brother (*Act IV, Scene I*)

"One face, one voice, one habit, and two persons." The duke is astonished at the resemblance between Viola and Sebastian (Act V, Scene I)

"Is this the madman?" Malvolio is released from his confinement (Act V, Scene I)

"With hey, ho, the wind and the rain." Feste sings an idle ditty as Viola and the duke embrace in the last scene of the play

Live you the marble-breasted tyrant still.
But this your minion, whom I know you love,
And whom, by heaven I swear, I tender dearly,
Him will I tear out of that cruel eye   130
Where he sits crowned in his master's spite.
Come, boy, with me. My thoughts are ripe in
   mischief.
I'll sacrifice the lamb that I do love
To spite a raven's heart within a dove. [*Going.*]
   Vio. And I, most jocund, apt, and willingly,
To do you rest a thousand deaths would die.
                     [*Following.*]
   Oli. Where goes Cesario?
   Vio.   After him I love
More than I love these eyes, more than my
   life,
More, by all mores, than e'er I shall love wife.
If I do feign, you witnesses above   140
Punish my life for tainting of my love!
   Oli. Ay me detested! how am I beguil'd!
   Vio. Who does beguile you? Who does do
   you wrong?
   Oli. Hast thou forgot thyself? Is it so long?
Call forth the holy father.
              [*Exit an Attendant.*]
   Duke.   [*to Viola*] Come, away! 145
   Oli. Whither, my lord? Cesario, husband,
   stay.
   Duke. Husband?
   Oli.   Ay, husband. Can he that deny?
   Duke. Her husband, sirrah?
   Vio.   No, my lord, not I.
   Oli. Alas, it is the baseness of thy fear
That makes thee strangle thy propriety.   150
Fear not, Cesario; take thy fortunes up;
Be that thou know'st thou art, and then thou
   art
As great as that thou fear'st.

          Enter *Priest.*

            O, welcome, father!
Father, I charge thee by thy reverence
Here to unfold — though lately we intended
To keep in darkness what occasion now   156
Reveals before 'tis ripe — what thou dost know
Hath newly pass'd between this youth and me.
   Priest. A contract of eternal bond of love,
Confirm'd by mutual joinder of your hands,
Attested by the holy close of lips,   161
Strength'ned by interchangement of your rings;
And all the ceremony of this compact
Seal'd in my function, by my testimony;
Since when, my watch hath told me, toward
   my grave   165
I have travell'd but two hours.

   Duke. O thou dissembling cub! What wilt
   thou be
When time hath sow'd a grizzle on thy case?
Or will not else thy craft so quickly grow
That thine own trip shall be thine overthrow?
Farewell, and take her; but direct thy feet 171
Where thou and I, henceforth, may never meet.
   Vio. My lord, I do protest —
   Oli.   O, do not swear!
Hold little faith, though thou hast too much fear.

         Enter *Sir Andrew.*

   And. For the love of God, a surgeon! Send
one presently to Sir Toby.   176
   Oli. What's the matter?
   And. Has broke my head across, and has
given Sir Toby a bloody coxcomb too. For the
love of God, your help! I had rather than forty
pound I were at home.   181
   Oli. Who has done this, Sir Andrew?
   And. The Count's gentleman, one Cesario.
We took him for a coward, but he's the very
devil incardinate.   185
   Duke. My gentleman Cesario?
   And. Od's lifelings, here he is! You broke
my head for nothing; and that that I did, I was
set on to do't by Sir Toby.
   Vio. Why do you speak to me? I never hurt
you.   190
You drew your sword upon me without cause,
But I bespake you fair and hurt you not.

       Enter [*Sir*] *Toby* and *Clown.*

   And. If a bloody coxcomb be a hurt, you
have hurt me. I think you set nothing by a
bloody coxcomb. Here comes Sir Toby halting
— you shall hear more. But if he had not been
in drink, he would have tickled you othergates
than he did.
   Duke. How now, gentleman? How is't with
you?   200
   To. That's all one! Has hurt me, and there's
th' end on't. — Sot, didst see Dick Surgeon,
sot?
   Clown. O, he's drunk, Sir Toby, an hour
agone. His eyes were set at eight i' th' morning.
   To. Then he's a rogue and a passy measures
pavin. I hate a drunken rogue.   207
   Oli. Away with him! Who hath made this
havoc with them?
   And. I'll help you, Sir Toby, because we'll
be dress'd together.   211
   To. Will you help — an ass-head and a coxcomb and a knave — a thin-fac'd knave, a
gull?

Oli. Get him to bed, and let his hurt be
look'd to.   215
[*Exeunt Clown, Fabian, Sir Toby, and Sir
Andrew.*]

Enter *Sebastian.*

Seb. I am sorry, madam, I have hurt your
kinsman;
But had it been the brother of my blood,
I must have done no less with wit and
safety.
You throw a strange regard upon me, and by
that
I do perceive it hath offended you.   220
Pardon me, sweet one, even for the vows
We made each other but so late ago.
Duke. One face, one voice, one habit, and
two persons!
A natural perspective, that is and is not!
Seb. Antonio! O my dear Antonio!   225
How have the hours rack'd and tortur'd me
Since I have lost thee!
Ant.   Sebastian are you?
Seb.   Fear'st thou that, Antonio?
Ant. How have you made division of your-
self?
An apple cleft in two is not more twin   230
Than these two creatures. Which is Sebastian?
Oli. Most wonderful!
Seb. Do I stand there? I never had a
brother;
Nor can there be that deity in my nature
Of here and everywhere. I had a sister,   235
Whom the blind waves and surges have de-
vour'd.
Of charity, what kin are you to me?
What countryman? what name? what par-
entage?
Vio. Of Messaline; Sebastian was my
father —
Such a Sebastian was my brother too;   240
So went he suited to his watery tomb.
If spirits can assume both form and suit,
You come to fright us.
Seb.   A spirit I am indeed,
But am in that dimension grossly clad
Which from the womb I did participate.   245
Were you a woman, as the rest goes even,
I should my tears let fall upon your cheek
And say, 'Thrice welcome, drowned Viola!' —
Vio. My father had a mole upon his brow —
Seb. And so had mine.   250
Vio. And died that day when Viola from her
birth
Had numb'red thirteen years.

Seb. O, that record is lively in my soul!
He finished indeed his mortal act   254
That day that made my sister thirteen years.
Vio. If nothing lets to make us happy
both
But this my masculine usurp'd attire,
Do not embrace me till each circumstance
Of place, time, fortune do cohere and jump
That I am Viola; which to confirm,   260
I'll bring you to a captain in this town,
Where lie my maiden weeds; by whose gentle
help
I was preserv'd to serve this noble Count.
All the occurrence of my fortune since
Hath been between this lady and this lord. 265
Seb. [*to Olivia*] So comes it, lady, you have
been mistook.
But nature to her bias drew in that.
You would have been contracted to a maid;
Nor are you therein, by my life, deceiv'd:
You are betroth'd both to a maid and man.
Duke. Be not amaz'd; right noble is his
blood.   271
If this be so, as yet the glass seems true,
I shall have share in this most happy wrack.
[*To Viola*] Boy, thou hast said to me a thou-
sand times
Thou never shouldst love woman like to me.
Vio. And all those sayings will I over
swear,
And all those swearings keep as true in soul
As doth that orbed continent the fire,
That severs day from night.
Duke.   Give me thy hand,
And let me see thee in thy woman's weeds. 280
Vio. The captain that did bring me first on
shore
Hath my maid's garments. He upon some
action
Is now in durance, at Malvolio's suit,
A gentleman, and follower of my lady's.
Oli. He shall enlarge him. Fetch Malvolio
hither.   285
And yet alas! now I remember me,
They say, poor gentleman, he's much distract.

Enter *Clown* with a letter, and *Fabian.*

A most extracting frenzy of mine own
From my remembrance clearly banish'd his.
How does he, sirrah?   290
Clown. Truly, madam, he holds Belzebub at
the stave's end as well as a man in his case may
do. Has here writ a letter to you; I should
have given't you to-day morning. [*Offers the
letter.*] But as a madman's epistles are no gos-

pels, so it skills not much when they are
deliver'd.   296
Oli. Open't and read it.
Clown. Look then to be well edified, when
the fool delivers the madman. [*Reads in a loud
voice*] 'By the Lord, madam' —   300
Oli. How now? Art thou mad?
Clown. No, madam, I do but read madness.
An your ladyship will have it as it ought to be,
you must allow vox.
Oli. Prithee read i' thy right wits.   305
Clown. So I do, madonna; but to read his
right wits is to read thus. Therefore perpend,
my princess, and give ear.
Oli. [*to Fabian*] Read it you, sirrah.   309
Fab. (*reads*) 'By the Lord, madam, you wrong
me, and the world shall know it. Though you have
put me into darkness, and given your drunken
cousin rule over me, yet have I the benefit of my
senses as well as your ladyship. I have your own
letter that induced me to the semblance I put on;
with the which I doubt not but to do myself much
right, or you much shame. Think of me as you
please. I leave my duty a little unthought of, and
speak out of my injury.
  'THE MADLY US'D MALVOLIO.'
Oli. Did he write this?   320
Clown. Ay, madam.
Duke. This savours not much of distrac-
tion.
Oli. See him deliver'd, Fabian; bring him
hither.
                              [*Exit Fabian.*]
My lord, so please you, these things further
    thought on,
To think me as well a sister as a wife,   325
One day shall crown th' alliance on't, so please
    you,
Here at my house and at my proper cost.
Duke. Madam, I am most apt t' embrace
    your offer.
[*To Viola*] Your master quits you; and for your
    service done him,
So much against the mettle of your sex,   330
So far beneath your soft and tender breed-
    ing,
And since you call'd me master, for so long,
Here is my hand: you shall from this time
    be
Your master's mistress.
Oli.   A sister! you are she.

    Enter [*Fabian*, with] *Malvolio*.

Duke. Is this the madman?
Oli.   Ay, my lord, this same.
How now, Malvolio?

Mal.   Madam, you have done me wrong,
Notorious wrong.
Oli.   Have I, Malvolio? No.
Mal. Lady, you have. Pray you peruse that
    letter.
You must not now deny it is your hand.   339
Write from it if you can, in hand or phrase,
Or say 'tis not your seal, not your invention.
You can say none of this. Well, grant it
    then,
And tell me, in the modesty of honour,
Why you have given me such clear lights of
    favour,
Bade me come smiling and cross-garter'd to
    you,   345
To put on yellow stockings, and to frown
Upon Sir Toby and the lighter people;
And, acting this in an obedient hope,
Why have you suffer'd me to be imprison'd,
Kept in a dark house, visited by the priest,
And made the most notorious geck and gull
That e'er invention play'd on? Tell me why.
Oli. Alas, Malvolio, this is not my writ-
    ing,
Though I confess much like the character;
But, out of question, 'tis Maria's hand.   355
And now I do bethink me, it was she
First told me thou wast mad. Thou cam'st in
    smiling,
And in such forms which here were presup-
    pos'd
Upon thee in the letter. Prithee be content.
This practice hath most shrewdly pass'd upon
    thee;   360
But when we know the grounds and authors
    of it,
Thou shalt be both the plaintiff and the judge
Of thine own cause.
Fab.   Good madam, hear me speak,
And let no quarrel, nor no brawl to come,
Taint the condition of this present hour,   365
Which I have wond'red at. In hope it shall
    not.
Most freely I confess myself and Toby
Set this device against Malvolio here,
Upon some stubborn and uncourteous parts
We had conceiv'd against him. Maria writ 370
The letter, at Sir Toby's great importance,
In recompense whereof he hath married her.
How with a sportful malice it was follow'd
May rather pluck on laughter than revenge,
If that the injuries be justly weigh'd   375
That have on both sides pass'd.
Oli. Alas poor fool, how have they baffled
    thee!

Clown. Why, 'some are born great, some achieve greatness, and some have greatness thrown upon them.' I was one, sir, in this interlude — one Sir Topas, sir; but that's all one. 'By the Lord, fool, I am not mad!' But do you remember — 'Madam, why laugh you at such a barren rascal? An you smile not, he's gagg'd'? And thus the whirligig of time brings in his revenges. 385
Mal. I'll be reveng'd on the whole pack of you! [*Exit.*]
Oli. He hath been most notoriously abus'd.
Duke. Pursue him and entreat him to a peace. He hath not told us of the captain yet. 390 When that is known, and golden time convents, A solemn combination shall be made Of our dear souls. Meantime, sweet sister, We will not part from hence. Cesario, come — For so you shall be while you are a man; 395 But when in other habits you are seen, Orsino's mistress and his fancy's queen.
Exeunt [all but the Clown].

Clown sings.

When that I was and a little tiny boy,
  With hey, ho, the wind and the rain,
A foolish thing was but a toy, 400
  For the rain it raineth every day.

But when I came to man's estate,
  With hey, ho, the wind and the rain,
'Gainst knaves and thieves men shut their gate,
  For the rain it raineth every day. 405

But when I came, alas! to wive,
  With hey, ho, the wind and the rain,
By swaggering could I never thrive,
  For the rain it raineth every day.

But when I came unto my beds, 410
  With hey, ho, the wind and the rain,
With tosspots still had drunken heads,
  For the rain it raineth every day.

A great while ago the world begun,
  With hey, ho, the wind and the rain; 415
But that's all one, our play is done,
  And we'll strive to please you every day.
[Exit.]

430

THE WINTER'S TALE

For the text of THE WINTER'S TALE our sole authority is the First Folio. In style and metre, tone and dramatic method, the play reveals itself as one of Shakespeare's latest works. Perhaps it followed *Cymbeline* and preceded *The Tempest*.

On May 15, 1611, Simon Forman, astrologer and physician, saw THE WINTER'S TALE at the Globe. His summary of the plot, in his own handwriting, is preserved in Ashmole MS. 208. If either the bear (iii, 3, 58) or the dance of satyrs (iv, 4, 352) was suggested by Ben Jonson's masque of *Oberon*, which was exhibited at court on the first day of that same year, the limits of composition are fixed with almost uncanny precision. The bear, however, is not a very trustworthy witness, even if Oberon's chariot is drawn by two white bears. The evidence of the satyrs is more satisfactory, for three of Shakespeare's 'saltiers' had 'danced before the king.' At all events, 1611 is a satisfactory date for THE WINTER'S TALE.

The source of the main plot is Robert Greene's novel *Pandosto. The Triumph of Time*, printed in 1588 and reprinted in 1607 under the title of *Dorastus and Fawnia* (the subtitle in the original edition). Pandosto, King of Bohemia, is Shakespeare's Leontes; his wife Bellaria is his Hermione; their son (Mamillius in the play) is named Garinter. Egistus, King of Sicilia, is Shakespeare's Polixenes. Shakespeare has exchanged the kingdoms.

Greene takes pains to describe the jealousy of Pandosto as to all intents and purposes insane. 'A certaine melancholy passion entring the minde of Pandosto drave him into sundry and doubtfull [i.e. suspicious] thoughts.' These, 'a long time smoothering in his stomacke, beganne at last to kindle in his minde a secret mistrust, which increased by suspition, grewe at last to be a flaming Iealousie, that so tormented him as he could take no rest.' These phrases accord with Shakespeare's account of Leontes. He is not, as a modern critic has called him, 'an irritable, suspicious, jealous-natured tyrant.' The whole atmosphere of the court — which is like a happy family — shows that he is no tyrant, and the perplexity of Hermione and Polixenes proves that he has never shown jealousy before. His paroxysm of jealous fury is virtually a fit of madness. It seizes him in a moment, and it releases him with equal suddenness.

The seacoast of Bohemia, which Shakespeare took from Greene, called forth some remarks from Ben Jonson in his conversations with William Drummond of Hawthornden (1619). All we know of the matter is Drummond's jotting: 'Shakspear in a play brought in a number of men saying they had suffered Shipwrack in Bohemia, wher ther is no Sea neer by some 100 Miles.' Ben's remark has been repeated, in substance, by multitudes who, but for this supposed geographical blunder, would not have known whether Bohemia has, or ever had, a seacoast. With equal persistence for more than a hundred years others have defended Shakespeare by arguing that once upon a time (in the thirteenth century) Bohemian sovereignty actually extended to the ports of Aquileia and Trieste. But it is very prosy to equate Shakespeare's Bohemia with any actual Bohemia. Had Bohemia a seacoast? Yes. When? At some indeterminate date B.C., when Leontes was king of Sicilia — that

431

Leontes who married a daughter of the Emperor of Russia and was a boyhood friend of Polixenes, King of Bohemia.

The Chorus at the beginning of the Fourth Act has for almost two hundred years been under suspicion as the work of an interpolator, but for no good reason. Somebody who knows things must hold forth at this juncture, for the audience needs information and there are no printed programmes. Father Time meets the exigency with admirable precision. He tells us that sixteen years have elapsed; that Leontes is a penitent hermit; that the scene shifts from Sicilia to Bohemia; that the son of Polixenes is named Florizel; that Perdita (who has 'grown in grace equal with wond'ring') passes for the old shepherd's daughter, and that our next concern is with her. And how is Father Time to speak? Shall it be in Shakespeare's best style — with the tragic passion of Lear, the philosophy of Hamlet, the gaiety of Beatrice, the cynicism of Apemantus, the warlike parade of Coriolanus? Of course not. He should speak in character. And that is precisely how he does speak — as old Father Time — a doddering, toothless ancient, halting but fluent, senile but self-assured, ridiculous but triumphant. His verse, his dialect, his jests, his truisms, all are in character. The stumbling emptiness of which the critics complain is Time's own. If the speech were better, it would not be so good.

Shakespeare follows Greene's story for the most part, except at the end, nor does he hesitate to borrow ideas or striking turns of phrase. Perdita's

> I think affliction may subdue the cheek,
> But not take in the mind (iv, 4, 587-588)

is transmuted from Fawnia's 'The body is subiect to victories, but the minde not to be subdued by conquest.' Hermione's ''Tis rigour, and not law' (iii, 2, 115) comes word for word from Greene. Her whole defensive argument, indeed, is Greene's prose turned into poetry.

Some significant variations may be noted.

Apollo is consulted at the request of the queen. The king does not blaspheme when the oracle is read in court; he repents instantly and is making public confession when word is brought that his son is dead. This news is fatal to the queen: 'she fell down presently dead, and could never be revived.' The baby is not left on the shore; it is abandoned at sea (like Prospero and Miranda in *The Tempest*) in a boat without sail or rudder, which comes safe to land by good fortune after a mighty storm. Antigonus and Paulina have no prototypes in the novel and Shakespeare's Camillo combines the rôles of two of Greene's characters.

The old shepherd comes from the novel, but his son and Dorcas and Mopsa and Autolycus are all new characters. Rustic revels are mentioned in the tale, but not described. The trick by which Autolycus picks the young shepherd's pocket agrees well enough with that in an anecdote told for a fact in Greene's *Second Part of Conny-catching* (1592).

The novel has a happy ending, so far as the young people are concerned, but Pandosto (Leontes) is a tragic personage throughout. After years of mourning for his dead wife, he falls in love with Fawnia (Perdita), whom of course he supposes to be the shepherd's daughter. When he learns that she is his own child ' whome he sent to floate in the sea,' he is overjoyed; but after her marriage he is smitten with remorse for all his sins, falls once more ' into a melancholie fit,' and kills himself.

The recognition scene which Shakespeare has substituted for this dismal conclusion, however improbable in fact, has proved superbly effective on the stage. For the suggestion of the statue that comes to life one need not have recourse to Lyly's *Woman in the Moon* (1597) or to Marston's *Pygmalion's Image* (1598). A poet who wrote *Venus and Adonis* in 1593 (or earlier) did not need to ask Lyly or Marston in 1611 to lead him to the story of Pygmalion in Ovid's *Metamorphoses* (x, 243 ff.).

THE WINTER'S TALE

The Names of the Actors.

Leontes, King of Sicilia.
Mamillius, [his son,] young Prince of Sicilia.
Camillo,
Antigonus, ⎱ Four Lords of Sicilia.
Cleomenes,
Dion,
Polixenes, King of Bohemia.
Florizel, [his son,] Prince of Bohemia.
Archidamus, a Lord of Bohemia.
Old Shepherd, reputed father of *Perdita.*
Clown, his son.
Autolycus, a rogue.

[A Mariner.]
[A Jailer.]

Hermione, queen to *Leontes.*
Perdita, daughter to *Leontes* and *Hermione.*
Paulina, wife to *Antigonus.*
Emilia, a lady, ⎱ [attending on the Queen].
[Other Ladies,] ⎰
Mopsa, ⎱ Shepherdesses.]
Dorcas, ⎰

Other Lords and Gentlemen, [Ladies, Officers,] and
Servants, Shepherds and Shepherdesses.
[*Time,* as Chorus.]

[SCENE. — *Sicilia; Bohemia.*]

ACT I. Scene I. [*Sicilia. The Palace of* Leontes.]

Enter *Camillo* and *Archidamus.*

Arch. If you shall chance, Camillo, to visit
Bohemia, on the like occasion whereon my
services are now on foot, you shall see, as I
have said, great difference betwixt our Bohemia
and your Sicilia.   5
Cam. I think this coming summer the King
of Sicilia means to pay Bohemia the visitation
which he justly owes him.
Arch. Wherein our entertainment shall shame
us we will be justified in our loves; for indeed —
Cam. Beseech you —   11
Arch. Verily I speak it in the freedom of my
knowledge: we cannot with such magnificence
— in so rare — I know not what to say. We
will give you sleepy drinks, that your senses
(unintelligent of our insufficience) may, though
they cannot praise us, as little accuse us.
Cam. You pay a great deal too dear for
what's given freely.   19
Arch. Believe me, I speak as my understand-
ing instructs me and as mine honesty puts it to
utterance.
Cam. Sicilia cannot show himself over-kind to
Bohemia. They were train'd together in their
childhoods; and there rooted betwixt them then
such an affection which cannot choose but
branch now. Since their more mature dignities
and royal necessities made separation of their
society, their encounters (though not personal)
have been royally attorneyed with interchange

of gifts, letters, loving embassies; that they
have seem'd to be together, though absent;
shook hands, as over a vast; and embrac'd as it
were from the ends of opposed winds. The
heavens continue their love!   35
Arch. I think there is not in the world either
malice or matter to alter it. You have an unspeakable comfort of your young Prince Mamillius. It is a gentleman of the greatest promise that ever came into my note.   40
Cam. I very well agree with you in the hopes
of him. It is a gallant child; one that, indeed,
physics the subject, makes old hearts fresh.
They that went on crutches ere he was born
desire yet their life, to see him a man.   45
Arch. Would they else be content to die?
Cam. Yes; if there were no other excuse
why they should desire to live.
Arch. If the King had no son, they would
desire to live on crutches till he had one.
                                                                    Exeunt.

Scene II. [*Sicilia. The Palace of* Leontes.]

Enter *Leontes, Hermione, Mamillius, Polixenes,
Camillo,* [and *Attendants*].

Pol. Nine changes of the wat'ry star hath
been
The shepherd's note since we have left our
throne

433

Without a burthen. Time as long again
Would be fill'd up, my brother, with our thanks,
And yet we should, for perpetuity,   5
Go hence in debt. And therefore, like a cipher,
Yet standing in rich place, I multiply
With one 'We thank you' many thousands moe
That go before it.

Leon.   Stay your thanks a while,
And pay them when you part.

Pol.   Sir, that's to-morrow.
I am question'd by my fears, of what may
chance,   11
Or breed upon our absence. That may blow
No sneaping winds at home, to make us say
'This is put forth too truly'! Besides, I have
stay'd
To tire your royalty.

Leon.   We are tougher, brother, 15
Than you can put us to't.

Pol.   No longer stay.

Leon. One sev'nnight longer.

Pol.   Very sooth, to-morrow.

Leon. We'll part the time between 's then;
and in that
I'll no gainsaying.

Pol.   Press me not, beseech you, so.
There is no tongue that moves, none, none i'
th' world,   20
So soon as yours could win me. So it should
now,
Were there necessity in your request, although
'Twere needful I denied it. My affairs
Do even drag me homeward; which to hinder,
Were, in your love, a whip to me; my stay 25
To you a charge and trouble: to save both,
Farewell, our brother.

Leon. Tongue-tied our queen? Speak you.

Her. I had thought, sir, to have held my
peace until
You had drawn oaths from him not to stay.
You, sir,
Charge him too coldly. Tell him you are sure
All in Bohemia's well; this satisfaction   31
The bygone day proclaim'd. Say this to him,
He's beat from his best ward.

Leon.   Well said, Hermione.

Her. To tell he longs to see his son, were
strong.
But let him say so then, and let him go;   35
But let him swear so, and he shall not stay,
We'll thwack him hence with distaffs.

[*To Polixenes*] Yet of your royal presence I'll
adventure
The borrow of a week. When at Bohemia
You take my lord, I'll give him my commission

To let him there a month behind the gest   41
Prefix'd for 's parting.—Yet, good-deed, Leontes,
I love thee not a jar o' th' clock behind
What lady she her lord. — You'll stay?

Pol.   No, madam.

Her. Nay, but you will?

Pol.   I may not, verily.

Her. Verily?
You put me off with limber vows; but I,
Though you would seek t' unsphere the stars
with oaths,
Should yet say, 'Sir, no going.' Verily
You shall not go! a lady's 'verily' is   50
As potent as a lord's. Will you go yet?
Force me to keep you as a prisoner,
Not like a guest: so you shall pay your fees
When you depart, and save your thanks. How
say you?
My prisoner? or my guest? By your dread
'verily,'   55
One of them you shall be.

Pol.   Your guest then, madam.
To be your prisoner should import offending;
Which is for me less easy to commit
Than you to punish.

Her.   Not your jailer then,
But your kind hostess. Come, I'll question you
Of my lord's tricks and yours when you were
boys.   61
You were pretty lordings then?

Pol.   We were, fair queen,
Two lads that thought there was no more behind
But such a day to-morrow as to-day,
And to be boy eternal.

Her.   Was not my lord
The verier wag o' th' two?   66

Pol. We were as twinn'd lambs that did
frisk i' th' sun
And bleat the one at th' other. What we
chang'd
Was innocence for innocence; we knew not
The doctrine of ill-doing, nor dream'd   70
That any did. Had we pursu'd that life,
And our weak spirits ne'er been higher rear'd
With stronger blood, we should have answer'd
heaven
Boldly, 'Not guilty,' the imposition clear'd
Hereditary ours.

Her.   By this we gather   75
You have tripp'd since.

Pol.   O my most sacred lady,
Temptations have since then been born to 's; for
In those unfledg'd days was my wife a girl;
Your precious self had then not cross'd the eyes
Of my young playfellow.

Her.   Grace to boot!   80
Of this make no conclusion, lest you say
Your queen and I are devils. Yet go on.
Th' offences we have made you do, we'll answer,
If you first sinn'd with us, and that with us
You did continue fault, and that you slipp'd not
With any but with us.
  Leon.   Is he won yet?   86
  Her. He'll stay, my lord.
  Leon.   At my request he would not.
Hermione, my dearest, thou never spok'st
To better purpose.
  Her.   Never?
  Leon.   Never, but once.
  Her. What? have I twice said well? When
    was't before?   90
I prithee tell me. Cram 's with praise, and
    make 's
As fat as tame things. One good deed dying
    tongueless
Slaughters a thousand waiting upon that.
Our praises are our wages. You may ride 's
With one soft kiss a thousand furlongs ere   95
With spur we heat an acre. But to th' goal!
My last good deed was to entreat his stay.
What was my first? It has an elder sister,
Or I mistake you. O, would her name were
    Grace!   99
But once before I spoke to th' purpose? When?
Nay, let me have't! I long.
  Leon.   Why, that was when
Three crabbed months had sour'd themselves
    to death
Ere I could make thee open thy white hand
And clap thyself my love. Then didst thou
    utter,
'I am yours for ever.'
  Her.   'Tis Grace indeed.   105
Why, lo you now! I have spoke to th' purpose
    twice.
The one for ever earn'd a royal husband;
Th' other for some while a friend.
    [*Gives her hand to Polixenes.*]
  Leon.   [*aside*] Too hot, too hot!
To mingle friendship far, is mingling bloods.
I have tremor cordis on me; my heart dances,
But not for joy; not joy. This entertainment
May a free face put on; derive a liberty   112
From heartiness, from bounty's fertile bosom,
And well become the agent. 'T may, I grant.
But to be paddling palms and pinching fingers,
As now they are, and making practis'd smiles
As in a looking glass; and then to sigh, as
    'twere
The mort o' th' deer — O, that is entertainment

My bosom likes not, nor my brows. — Ma-
    millius,   119
Art thou my boy?
  Mam.   Ay, my good lord.
  Leon.   I' fecks!
Why, that's my bawcock! What? hast
    smutch'd thy nose?
They say it is a copy out of mine. Come,
    captain,
We must be neat — not neat, but cleanly, cap-
    tain.
And yet the steer, the heifer, and the calf
Are all call'd neat. — Still virginalling   125
Upon his palm? — How now, you wanton calf?
Art thou my calf?
  Mam.   Yes, if you will, my lord.
  Leon. Thou want'st a rough pash and the
    shoots that I have,
To be full like me. Yet they say we are
Almost as like as eggs. Women say so —   130
That will say anything! But were they false
As o'er-dy'd blacks, as wind, as waters — false
As dice are to be wish'd by one that fixes
No bourn 'twixt his and mine; yet were it true
To say this boy were like me. Come, sir page,
Look on me with your welkin eye. Sweet villain!
Most dear'st! my collop! Can thy dam —
    may't be?
Affection! thy intention stabs the centre.
Thou dost make possible things not so held,
Communicat'st with dreams! How can this be?
With what's unreal thou coactive art,   141
And fellow'st nothing. Then 'tis very credent
Thou mayst cojoin with something; and thou
    dost —
And that beyond commission; and I find it,
And that to the infection of my brains   145
And hard'ning of my brows.
  Pol.   What means Sicilia?
  Her. He something seems unsettled.
  Pol.   How, my lord?
What cheer? How is't with you, best brother?
  Her.   You look
As if you held a brow of much distraction.   149
Are you mov'd, my lord?
  Leon.   No, in good earnest.
How sometimes nature will betray its folly,
Its tenderness, and make itself a pastime
To harder bosoms! Looking on the lines
Of my boy's face, methoughts I did recoil   154
Twenty-three years, and saw myself unbreech'd,
In my green velvet coat, my dagger muzzled,
Lest it should bite its master and so prove
(As ornaments oft do) too dangerous.
How like, methought, I then was to this kernel.

This squash, this gentleman. Mine honest friend, 160
Will you take eggs for money?
Mam. No, my lord, I'll fight.
Leon. You will? Why, happy man be's dole!
My brother,
Are you so fond of your young prince as we
Do seem to be of ours? 165
Pol. If at home, sir,
He's all my exercise, my mirth, my matter;
Now my sworn friend, and then mine enemy;
My parasite, my soldier, statesman — all.
He makes a July's day short as December, 170
And with his varying childness cures in me
Thoughts that would thick my blood.
Leon. So stands this squire
Offic'd with me. We two will walk, my lord,
And leave you to your graver steps. Hermione,
How thou lov'st us, show in our brother's welcome.
Let what is dear in Sicily be cheap. 175
Next to thyself and my young rover, he's
Apparent to my heart.
Her. If you would seek us,
We are yours i' th' garden. Shall 's attend you there?
Leon. To your own bents dispose you. You'll be found,
Be you beneath the sky. [*Aside*] I am angling now, 180
Though you perceive me not how I give line.
Go to, go to!
How she holds up the neb, the bill to him!
And arms her with the boldness of a wife
To her allowing husband!
[*Exeunt Polixenes, Hermione, and Attendants.*]
Gone already! 185
Inch-thick, knee-deep, o'er head and ears a fork'd one!
Go play, boy, play. Thy mother plays, and I
Play too; but so disgrac'd a part whose issue
Will hiss me to my grave. Contempt and clamour
Will be my knell. — Go play, boy, play. — 190
There have been
(Or I am much deceiv'd) cuckolds ere now;
And many a man there is (even at this present,
Now, while I speak this) holds his wife by th' arm
That little thinks she has been sluic'd in 's absence 194
And his pond fish'd by his next neighbour — by
Sir Smile, his neighbour. Nay, there's comfort in't

Whiles other men have gates, and those gates open'd
(As mine) against their will. Should all despair
That have revolted wives, the tenth of mankind
Would hang themselves. Physic for't there's none. 200
It is a bawdy planet, that will strike
Where 'tis predominant; and 'tis pow'rful, think it,
From east, west, north, and south. Be it concluded,
No barricado for a belly! Know't,
It will let in and out the enemy 205
With bag and baggage. Many thousand on 's
Have the disease, and feel't not. How now, boy?
Mam. I am like you, they say.
Leon. Why, that's some comfort.
What? Camillo there?
Cam. Ay, my good lord. 210
Leon. Go play, Mamillius. Thou'rt an honest man.
[*Exit Mamillius.*]
Camillo, this great sir will yet stay longer.
Cam. You had much ado to make his anchor hold;
When you cast out, it still came home.
Leon. Didst note it?
Cam. He would not stay at your petitions, made 215
His business more material.
Leon. Didst perceive it?
[*Aside*] They're here with me already; whisp'ring, rounding,
'Sicilia is a so-forth!' 'Tis far gone
When I shall gust it last. — How came't, Camillo, 219
That he did stay?
Cam. At the good Queen's entreaty.
Leon. 'At the Queen's' be't. 'Good' should be pertinent;
But so it is, it is not. Was this taken
By any understanding pate but thine?
For thy conceit is soaking, will draw in 224
More than the common blocks. Not noted, is't,
But of the finer natures? by some severals
Of headpiece extraordinary? Lower messes
Perchance are to this business purblind? Say.
Cam. Business, my lord? I think most understand
Bohemia stays here longer.
Leon. Ha?
Cam. Stays here longer.
Leon. Ay, but why? 231

Cam. To satisfy your Highness, and the entreaties
Of our most gracious mistress.
   Leon.   Satisfy?
Th' entreaties of your mistress? Satisfy? 234
Let that suffice. I have trusted thee, Camillo,
With all the nearest things to my heart, as well
My chamber-councils, wherein (priest-like) thou
Hast cleans'd my bosom, I from thee departed
Thy penitent reform'd. But we have been
Deceiv'd in thy integrity, deceiv'd   240
In that which seems so.
   Cam.   Be it forbid, my lord!
   Leon. To bide upon't: thou art not honest;
     or,
If thou inclin'st that way, thou art a coward,
Which hoxes honesty behind, restraining
From course requir'd; or else thou must be counted   245
A servant grafted in my serious trust
And therein negligent; or else a fool
That seest a game play'd home, the rich stake drawn,
And tak'st it all for jest.
   Cam.   My gracious lord,
I may be negligent, foolish, and fearful: 250
In every one of these no man is free,
But that his negligence, his folly, fear,
Among the infinite doings of the world,
Sometime puts forth. In your affairs, my lord,
If ever I were wilful-negligent,   255
It was my folly; if industriously
I play'd the fool, it was my negligence,
Not weighing well the end; if ever fearful
To do a thing where I the issue doubted,
Whereof the execution did cry out   260
Against the non-performance, 'twas a fear
Which oft infects the wisest. These, my lord,
Are such allow'd infirmities that honesty
Is never free of. But beseech your Grace
Be plainer with me; let me know my trespass
By its own visage. If I then deny it 266
'Tis none of mine.
   Leon. Ha' not you seen, Camillo
(But that's past doubt; you have, or your eye-glass
Is thicker than a cuckold's horn), or heard
(For to a vision so apparent rumour 270
Cannot be mute) or thought (for cogitation
Resides not in that man that does not think)
My wife is slippery? If thou wilt confess —
Or else be impudently negative
To have nor eyes nor ears nor thought — then say 275

My wife's a hobby-horse, deserves a name
As rank as any flax-wench that puts to
Before her troth-plight. Say't, and justify't.
   Cam. I would not be a stander-by to hear
My sovereign mistress clouded so, without 280
My present vengeance taken. Shrew my heart!
You never spoke what did become you less
Than this; which to reiterate were sin
As deep as that, though true.
   Leon.   Is whispering nothing?
Is leaning cheek to cheek? Is meeting noses?
Kissing with inside lip? stopping the career
Of laughter with a sigh? — a note infallible
Of breaking honesty! — horsing foot on foot?
Skulking in corners? wishing clocks more swift?
Hours, minutes? noon, midnight? and all eyes
Blind with the pin and web but theirs — theirs only, 291
That would unseen be wicked? Is this nothing?
Why, then the world and all that's in't is nothing;
The covering sky is nothing; Bohemia nothing;
My wife is nothing; nor nothing have these nothings, 295
If this be nothing.
   Cam.   Good my lord, be cur'd
Of this diseas'd opinion, and betimes;
For 'tis most dangerous.
   Leon.   Say it be, 'tis true.
   Cam. No, no, my lord.
   Leon.   It is! You lie, you lie!
I say thou liest, Camillo, and I hate thee, 300
Pronounce thee a gross lout, a mindless slave,
Or else a hovering temporizer that
Canst with thine eyes at once see good and evil,
Inclining to them both. Were my wive's liver
Infected as her life, she would not live 305
The running of one glass.
   Cam.   Who does infect her?
   Leon. Why, he that wears her like her medal, hanging
About his neck — Bohemia; who — if I
Had servants true about me, that bare eyes
To see alike mine honour as their profits, 310
Their own particular thrifts, they would do that
Which should undo more doing. Ay, and thou,
His cupbearer — whom I from meaner form
Have bench'd, and rear'd to worship; who mayst see,
Plainly as heaven sees earth and earth sees heaven, 315
How I am gall'd — thou mightst bespice a cup
To give mine enemy a lasting wink;
Which draught to me were cordial.

Cam.   Sir, my lord,
I could do this, and that with no rash potion,
But with a ling'ring dram that should not work
Maliciously, like poison. But I cannot   321
Believe this crack to be in my dread mistress,
So sovereignly being honourable.
I have lov'd thee —
    Leon.   Make that thy question, and go rot!
Dost think I am so muddy, so unsettled,   325
To appoint myself in this vexation, sully
The purity and whiteness of my sheets
(Which to preserve is sleep; which being
    spotted
Is goads, thorns, nettles, tails of wasps),   329
Give scandal to the blood o' th' Prince, my son
(Who I do think is mine, and love as mine),
Without ripe moving to't? Would I do this?
Could man so blench?
    Cam.   I must believe you, sir.
I do, and will fetch off Bohemia for't;
Provided that, when he's remov'd, your High-
    ness   335
Will take again your queen as yours at first,
Even for your son's sake, and thereby for sealing
The injury of tongues in courts and kingdoms
Known and allied to yours.
    Leon.   Thou dost advise me
Even so as I mine own course have set down.
I'll give no blemish to her honour, none.   341
    Cam. My lord,
Go then; and with a countenance as clear
As friendship wears at feasts, keep with Bo-
    hemia   344
And with your queen. I am his cupbearer;
If from me he have wholesome beverage,
Account me not your servant.
    Leon.   This is all:
Do't, and thou hast the one half of my heart;
Do't not, thou splitt'st thine own.
    Cam.   I'll do't, my lord.
    Leon. I will seem friendly, as thou hast
    advis'd me.   *Exit.*
    Cam. O miserable lady! But, for me,   351
What case stand I in? I must be the poisoner
Of good Polixenes; and my ground to do't
Is the obedience to a master — one
Who, in rebellion with himself, will have   355
All that are his so too. To do this deed,
Promotion follows. If I could find example
Of thousands that had struck anointed kings
And flourish'd after, I'ld not do't. But since
Nor brass nor stone nor parchment bears not
    one,   360
Let villany itself forswear't. I must
Forsake the court. To do't, or no, is certain

To me a break-neck. Happy star reign now!
Here comes Bohemia.

        Enter *Polixenes.*

    Pol.   This is strange. Methinks
My favour here begins to warp. Not speak?
Good day, Camillo.
    Cam.   Hail, most royal sir.   366
    Pol. What is the news i' th' court?
    Cam.   None rare, my lord.
    Pol. The King hath on him such a coun-
    tenance
As he had lost some province, and a region
Lov'd as he loves himself. Even now I met him
With customary compliment, when he,   371
Wafting his eyes to th' contrary and falling
A lip of much contempt, speeds from me, and
So leaves me to consider what is breeding
That changes thus his manners.   375
    Cam. I dare not know, my lord.
    Pol. How? dare not? do not? Do you
    know, and dare not
Be intelligent to me? 'Tis thereabouts;
For, to yourself, what you do know, you must,
And cannot say you dare not. Good Camillo,
Your chang'd complexions are to me a mirror,
Which shows me mine chang'd too; for I must
    be
A party in this alteration, finding
Myself thus alter'd with't.
    Cam.   There is a sickness'
Which puts some of us in distemper, but   385
I cannot name the disease; and it is caught
Of you, that yet are well.
    Pol.   How? caught of me?
Make me not sighted like the basilisk.
I have look'd on thousands who have sped the
    better   389
By my regard, but kill'd none so. Camillo —
As you are certainly a gentleman; thereto
Clerk-like experienc'd, which no less adorns
Our gentry than our parents' noble names,
In whose success we are gentle — I beseech you,
If you know aught which does behove my
    knowledge   395
Thereof to be inform'd, imprison't not
In ignorant concealment.
    Cam.   I may not answer.
    Pol. A sickness caught of me, and yet I well?
I must be answer'd. Dost thou hear, Camillo?
I conjure thee, by all the parts of man   400
Which honour does acknowledge, whereof the
    least
Is not this suit of mine, that thou declare
What incidency thou dost guess of harm

Is creeping toward me; how far off, how near;
Which way to be prevented, if to be;   405
If not, how best to bear it.
    Cam.   Sir, I will tell you,
Since I am charg'd in honour, and by him
That I think honourable. Therefore mark my
    counsel,
Which must be ev'n as swiftly followed as
I mean to utter it; or both yourself and me 410
Cry lost, and so good night!
    Pol.   On, good Camillo.
    Cam. I am appointed him to murther you.
    Pol. By whom, Camillo?
    Cam.   By the King.
    Pol.   For what?
    Cam. He thinks — nay, with all confidence
    he swears,
As he had seen't, or been an instrument   415
To vice you to't — that you have touch'd his
    queen
Forbiddenly.
    Pol.   O, then my best blood turn
To an infected jelly, and my name
Be yok'd with his that did betray the Best!
Turn then my freshest reputation to   420
A savour that may strike the dullest nostril
Where I arrive, and my approach be shunn'd,
Nay, hated too, worse than the great'st in-
    fection
That e'er was heard or read!
    Cam.   Swear his thought over
By each particular star in heaven and   425
By all their influences, you may as well
Forbid the sea for to obey the moon
As or by oath remove or counsel shake
The fabric of his folly, whose foundation
Is pil'd upon his faith and will continue   430
The standing of his body.
    Pol.   How should this grow?
    Cam. I know not; but I am sure 'tis safer to

Avoid what's grown than question how 'tis born.
If therefore you dare trust my honesty,
That lies enclosed in this trunk, which you 435
Shall bear along impawn'd, away to-night!
Your followers I will whisper to the business,
And will, by twos and threes, at several pos-
    terns,
Clear them o' th' city. For myself, I'll put
My fortunes to your service, which are here 440
By this discovery lost. Be not uncertain,
For, by the honour of my parents, I
Have utt'red truth; which if you seek to prove,
I dare not stand by; nor shall you be safer
Than one condemn'd by the King's own mouth
    — thereon   445
His execution sworn.
    Pol.   I do believe thee.
I saw his heart in 's face. Give me thy hand.
Be pilot to me, and thy places shall
Still neighbour mine. My ships are ready, and
My people did expect my hence departure   450
Two days ago. This jealousy
Is for a precious creature. As she's rare,
Must it be great; and as his person's mighty,
Must it be violent; and as he does conceive
He is dishonour'd by a man which ever   455
Profess'd to him, why, his revenges must
In that be made more bitter. Fear o'ershades
    me.
Good expedition be my friend, and comfort
The gracious Queen, part of his theme, but
    nothing
Of his ill-ta'en suspicion! Come, Camillo.   460
I will respect thee as a father if
Thou bear'st my life off. Hence! Let us avoid.
    Cam. It is in mine authority to command
The keys of all the posterns. Please your
    Highness
To take the urgent hour. Come, sir, away!
                                 Exeunt.

ACT II. Scene I. [*Sicilia. The Palace of* Leontes.]

Enter *Hermione, Mamillius, Ladies.*

    Her. Take the boy to you. He so troubles me
'Tis past enduring.
    1. Lady.   Come, my gracious lord,
Shall I be your playfellow?
    Mam.   No, I'll none of you.
    1. Lady. Why, my sweet lord?
    Mam. You'll kiss me hard, and speak to me
    as if   5
I were a baby still. I love you better.

    2. Lady. And why so, my lord?
    Mam.   Not for because
Your brows are blacker. Yet black brows, they
    say,
Become some women best, so that there be not
Too much hair there, but in a semicircle   10
Or a half-moon made with a pen.
    2. Lady.   Who taught you this?
    Mam. I learn'd it out of women's faces.
    Pray now,
What colour are your eyebrows?

1. Lady.   Blue, my lord.
Mam. Nay, that's a mock. I have seen a
lady's nose
That has been blue, but not her eyebrows.
1. Lady.   Hark ye!   15
The Queen your mother rounds apace. We shall
Present our services to a fine new prince
One of these days, and then you'ld wanton
    with us
If we would have you.
2. Lady.   She is spread of late
Into a goodly bulk. Good time encounter her!
Her. What wisdom stirs amongst you?
Come, sir, now   21
I am for you again. Pray you sit by us
And tell 's a tale.
Mam.   Merry, or sad, shall't be?
Her. As merry as you will.
Mam. A sad tale's best for winter. I have
    one   25
Of sprites and goblins.
Her.   Let's have that, good sir.
Come on, sit down; come on, and do your best
To fright me with your sprites; you're pow'rful
    at it.
Mam. There was a man —
Her.   Nay, come sit down; then on.
Mam. Dwelt by a churchyard. I will tell it
    softly;   30
Yond crickets shall not hear it.
Her.   Come on then,
And give't me in mine ear.

Enter Leontes, Antigonus, Lords, [and others].

Leon. Was he met there? his train? Ca-
    millo with him?
Lord. Behind the tuft of pines I met them.
    Never   34
Saw I men scour so on their way. I ey'd them
Even to their ships.
Leon.   How blest am I
In my just censure, in my true opinion!
Alack for lesser knowledge! how accurs'd   38
In being so blest! There may be in the cup
A spider steep'd, and one may drink, depart,
And yet partake no venom, for his knowledge
Is not infected; but if one present
Th' abhorr'd ingredient to his eye, make known
How he hath drunk, he cracks his gorge, his
    sides,
With violent hefts. I have drunk, and seen
    the spider.   45
Camillo was his help in this, his pander;
There is a plot against my life, my crown;
All's true that is mistrusted. That false villain

Whom I employ'd was pre-employ'd by him.
He has discover'd my design, and I   50
Remain a pinch'd thing; yea, a very trick
For them to play at will. How came the
    posterns
So easily open?
Lord.   By his great authority,
Which often hath no less prevail'd than so
On your command.
Leon.   I know't too well.   55
Give me the boy. I am glad you did not nurse
    him.
Though he does bear some signs of me, yet you
Have too much blood in him.
Her.   What is this? sport?
Leon. Bear the boy hence; he shall not come
    about her.
Away with him! and let her sport herself   60
    [Mamillius is carried out.]
With that she's big with — for 'tis Polixenes
Has made thee swell thus.
Her.   But I'ld say he had not,
And I'll be sworn you would believe my saying,
Howe'er you lean to th' nayward.
Leon.   You, my lords,
Look on her, mark her well. Be but about   65
To say 'She is a goodly lady,' and
The justice of your hearts will thereto add
''Tis pity she's not honest — honourable!'
Praise her but for this her without-door form
(Which on my faith deserves high speech) and
    straight   70
The shrug, the 'hum!' or 'ha!' — these petty
    brands
That calumny doth use — O, I am out!
That mercy does; for calumny will sear
Virtue itself — these shrugs, these hum's and
    ha's,
When you have said she's goodly, come be-
    tween,   75
Ere you can say she's honest. But be't known
(From him that has most cause to grieve it
    should be)
She's an adultress.
Her.   Should a villain say so,
The most replenish'd villain in the world,   79
He were as much more villain. You, my lord,
Do but mistake.
Leon.   You have mistook, my lady,
Polixenes for Leontes. O thou thing!
Which I'll not call a creature of thy place,
Lest barbarism, making me the precedent,
Should a like language use to all degrees   85
And mannerly distinguishment leave out
Betwixt the prince and beggar. I have said

She's an adultress; I have said with whom.
More, she's a traitor, and Camillo is
A federary with her, and one that knows   90
What she should shame to know herself
But with her most vile principal — that she's
A bed-swerver, even as bad as those
That vulgars give bold'st titles; ay, and privy
To this their late escape.

Her.   No, by my life,   95
Privy to none of this! How will this grieve you,
When you shall come to clearer knowledge, that
You thus have publish'd me! Gentle my lord,
You scarce can right me throughly then to say
You did mistake.

Leon.   No! If I mistake   100
In those foundations which I build upon,
The centre is not big enough to bear
A schoolboy's top. Away with her to prison!
He who shall speak for her is afar off guilty
But that he speaks.

Her.   There's some ill planet reigns.
I must be patient till the heavens look   106
With an aspect more favourable. Good my lords,
I am not prone to weeping, as our sex
Commonly are; the want of which vain dew
Perchance shall dry your pities; but I have   110
That honourable grief lodg'd here which burns
Worse than tears drown. Beseech you all, my lords,
With thoughts so qualified as your charities
Shall best instruct you, measure me; and so
The King's will be perform'd!

Leon.   Shall I be heard?
Her. Who is't that goes with me? Beseech
    your Highness   116
My women may be with me; for you see
My plight requires it. Do not weep, good fools;
There is no cause. When you shall know your mistress
Has deserv'd prison, then abound in tears   120
As I come out. This action I now go on
Is for my better grace. Adieu, my lord.
I never wish'd to see you sorry; now
I trust I shall. My women, come; you have leave.

Leon. Go, do our bidding! hence!   125
    [*Exeunt Hermione, guarded, with Ladies.*]
Lord. Beseech your Highness call the Queen again!
Ant. Be certain what you do, sir, lest your justice
Prove violence, in the which three great ones suffer,
Yourself, your queen, your son.

Lord.   For her, my lord,
I dare my life lay down, and will do't, sir,   130
Please you t' accept it, that the Queen is spotless
I' th' eyes of heaven and to you — I mean,
In this which you accuse her.

Ant.   If it prove
She's otherwise, I'll keep my stables where
I lodge my wife; I'll go in couples with her;   135
Than when I feel and see her no farther trust her;
For every inch of woman in the world,
Ay, every dram of woman's flesh is false,
If she be.

Leon.   Hold your peaces!
Lord.   Good my lord —-
Ant. It is for you we speak, not for ourselves.
You are abus'd, and by some putter-on   141
That will be damn'd for't. Would I knew the villain!
I would land-damn him! Be she honour-flaw'd,
I have three daughters: the eldest is eleven;
The second and the third, nine and some five —
If this prove true, they'll pay for't! By mine honour,   146
I'll geld 'em all. Fourteen they shall not see
To bring false generations. They are co-heirs,
And I had rather glib myself than they
Should not produce fair issue.

Leon.   Cease! no more!   150
You smell this business with a sense as cold
As is a dead man's nose; but I do see't and feel't,
As you feel doing thus —   [*Seizes his arm.*]
                    and see withal
The instruments that feel.

Ant.   If it be so,
We need no grave to bury honesty.   155
There's not a grain of it the face to sweeten
Of the whole dungy earth.

Leon.   What? lack I credit?
Lord. I had rather you did lack than I, my lord,
Upon this ground; and more it would content me   159
To have her honour true than your suspicion,
Be blam'd for't how you might.

Leon.   Why, what need we
Commune with you of this, but rather follow
Our forceful instigation? Our prerogative
Calls not your counsels, but our natural goodness
Imparts this; which, if you (or stupefied,   165
Or seeming so in skill) cannot or will not
Relish a truth like us, inform yourselves
We need no more of your advice. The matter,

The loss, the gain, the ord'ring on't, is all
Properly ours.
   Ant.   And I wish, my liege,   170
You had only in your silent judgment tried it,
Without more overture.
   Leon.   How could that be?
Either thou art most ignorant by age
Or thou wert born a fool. Camillo's flight,
Added to their familiarity   175
(Which was as gross as ever touch'd conjecture,
That lack'd sight only, naught for approbation
But only seeing; all other circumstances
Made up to th' deed), doth push on this pro-
ceeding.
Yet, for a greater confirmation   180
(For in an act of this importance 'twere
Most piteous to be wild) I have dispatch'd in
post
To sacred Delphos, to Apollo's temple,
Cleomenes and Dion, whom you know
Of stuff'd sufficiency. Now from the oracle 185
They will bring all, whose spiritual counsel had,
Shall stop or spur me. Have I done well?
   Lord. Well done, my lord.
   Leon.   Though I am satisfied and need no
more
Than what I know, yet shall the oracle   190
Give rest to th' minds of others, such as he
Whose ignorant credulity will not
Come up to th' truth. So have we thought it
good
From our free person she should be confin'd,
Lest that the treachery of the two fled hence
Be left her to perform. Come follow us.   196
We are to speak in public; for this business
Will raise us all.
   Ant. [*aside*] To laughter, as I take it,
If the good truth were known.   *Exeunt.*

Scene II. [*Sicilia. A prison.*]

Enter *Paulina, a Gentleman,* [and *Attendants*].

   Paul. The keeper of the prison — call to him;
Let him have knowledge who I am.
                 [*Exit Gentleman.*]
                 Good lady!
No court in Europe is too good for thee.
What dost thou then in prison?

          Enter *Jailer.*

               Now, good sir,
You know me, do you not?
   Jail.   For a worthy lady, 5
And one who much I honour.

   Paul.   Pray you then,
Conduct me to the Queen.
   Jail. I may not, madam; to the contrary
I have express commandment.
   Paul.   Here's ado
To lock up honesty and honour from   10
Th' access of gentle visitors! Is't lawful, pray
you,
To see her women? any of them? Emilia?
   Jail. So please you, madam,
To put apart these your attendants, I
Shall bring Emilia forth.
   Paul.   I pray now call her. 15
Withdraw yourselves.   [*Exeunt Attendants.*]
   Jail.   And, madam,
I must be present at your conference.
   Paul. Well, be't so. Prithee.
                 [*Exit Jailer.*]
Here's such ado to make no stain a stain
As passes colouring.

      [Enter *Jailer*, with] *Emilia.*

             Dear gentlewoman,   20
How fares our gracious lady?
   Emil. As well as one so great and so forlorn
May hold together. On her frights and griefs
(Which never tender lady hath borne greater)
She is, something before her time, deliver'd.   25
   Paul. A boy?
   Emil.   A daughter, and a goodly babe,
Lusty, and like to live. The Queen receives
Much comfort in't; says 'My poor prisoner,
I am innocent as you.'
   Paul.   I dare be sworn.
These dangerous unsafe lunes i' th' King, be-
shrew them!   30
He must be told on't, and he shall. The office
Becomes a woman best; I'll take't upon me.
If I prove honey-mouth'd, let my tongue blister,
And never to my red-look'd anger be
The trumpet any more. Pray you, Emilia, 35
Commend my best obedience to the Queen.
If she dares trust me with her little babe,
I'll show't the King and undertake to be
Her advocate to th' loud'st. We do not know
How he may soften at the sight o' th' child. 40
The silence often of pure innocence
Persuades when speaking fails.
   Emil.   Most worthy madam,
Your honour and your goodness is so evident
That your free undertaking cannot miss
A thriving issue. There is no lady living   45
So meet for this great errand. Please your
ladyship
To visit the next room, I'll presently

Acquaint the Queen of your most noble offer,
Who but to-day hammered of this design,
But durst not tempt a minister of honour,   50
Lest she should be denied.
  Paul.   Tell her, Emilia,
I'll use that tongue I have. If wit flow from't
As boldness from my bosom, let't not be
    doubted
I shall do good.
  Emil.   Now be you blest for it!
I'll to the Queen. Please you come something
    nearer.   55
  Jail. Madam, if't please the Queen to send
    the babe,
I know not what I shall incur to pass it,
Having no warrant.
  Paul.   You need not fear it, sir.
This child was prisoner to the womb, and is
By law and process of great Nature thence   60
Freed and enfranchis'd — not a party to
The anger of the King, nor guilty of
(If any be) the trespass of the Queen.
  Jail. I do believe it.   64
  Paul. Do not you fear. Upon mine honour, I
Will stand betwixt you and danger.   *Exeunt.*

Scene III. [*Sicilia. The Palace.*]

Enter *Leontes, Servants, Antigonus,* and *Lords.*
  Leon. Nor night nor day no rest! It is but
    weakness
To bear the matter thus — mere weakness. If
The cause were not in being — part o' th' cause,
She, the adultress; for the harlot king
Is quite beyond mine arm, out of the blank 5
And level of my brain, plot-proof; but she
I can hook to me — say that she were gone,
Given to the fire, a moiety of my rest
Might come to me again. Who's there?
  Serv.   My lord?
  Leon. How does the boy?
  Serv.   He took good rest to-night.
'Tis hop'd his sickness is discharg'd.   11
  Leon. To see his nobleness!
Conceiving the dishonour of his mother,
He straight declin'd, droop'd, took it deeply,
Fasten'd and fix'd the shame on't in himself,
Threw off his spirit, his appetite, his sleep, 16
And downright languish'd. Leave me solely.
    Go.
See how he fares. [*Exit Servant.*] Fie, fie, no
    thought of him!
The very thought of my revenges that way

Recoil upon me — in himself too mighty,   20
And in his parties, his alliance. Let him be
Until a time may serve. For present vengeance,
Take it on her. Camillo and Polixenes
Laugh at me, make their pastime at my sorrow.
They should not laugh if I could reach them;
    nor   25
Shall she, within my pow'r.

      Enter *Paulina,* [with a Child].

  Lord.   You must not enter.
  Paul. Nay, rather, good my lords, be second
    to me.
Fear you his tyrannous passion more, alas!
Than the Queen's lie? a gracious innocent soul,
More free than he is jealous.
  Ant.   That's enough. 30
  Serv. Madam, he hath not slept to-night,
    commanded
None should come at him.
  Paul.   Not so hot, good sir!
I come to bring him sleep. 'Tis such as you,
That creep like shadows by him and do sigh
At each his needless heavings — such as you 35
Nourish the cause of his awaking. I
Do come with words as medicinal as true,
Honest as either, to purge him of that humour
That presses him from sleep.
  Leon.   What noise there, ho?
  Paul. No noise, my lord, but needful con-
    ference   40
About some gossips for your Highness.
  Leon.   How?
Away with that audacious lady! Antigonus,
I charg'd thee that she should not come about
    me.
I knew she would.
  Ant.   I told her so, my lord,
On your displeasure's peril and on mine,   45
She should not visit you.
  Leon.   What? canst not rule her?
  Paul. From all dishonesty he can. In this,
Unless he take the course that you have done,
Commit me for committing honour, trust it,
He shall not rule me.
  Ant.   La you now, you hear! 50
When she will take the rein, I let her run;
But she'll not stumble.
  Paul.   Good my liege, I come;
And I beseech you hear me, who professes
Myself your loyal servant, your physician,
Your most obedient counsellor; yet that dares
Less appear so, in comforting your evils,   56
Than such as most seem yours. I say, I come
From your good queen.

443

Leon.   Good queen?
Paul. Good queen, my lord, good queen;
I say, good queen,   59
And would by combat make her good, so were I
A man, the worst about you.
Leon.   Force her hence.
Paul. Let him that makes but trifles of his
  eyes
First hand me. On mine own accord I'll off;
But first I'll do my errand. The good queen
(For she is good) hath brought you forth a
  daughter;   65
Here 'tis — commends it to your blessing.
                          [*Lays down the child.*]
Leon.   Out!
A mankind witch! Hence with her, out o' door!
A most intelligencing bawd!
Paul.   Not so.
I am as ignorant in that as you
In so entitling me; and no less honest   70
Than you are mad; which is enough, I'll
  warrant,
As this world goes, to pass for honest.
Leon.   Traitors!
Will you not push her out? [*To Antigonus*]
  Give her the bastard.
Thou dotard, thou art woman-tir'd; unroosted
By thy Dame Partlet here. Take up the bas-
  tard.   75
Take't up, I say! give't to thy crone.
Paul.   For ever
Unvenerable be thy hands if thou
Tak'st up the Princess by that forced baseness
Which he has put upon't!
Leon.   He dreads his wife.
Paul. So I would you did. Then 'twere past
  all doubt   80
You'ld call your children yours.
Leon.   A nest of traitors!
Ant. I am none, by this good light.
Paul.   Nor I; nor any,
But one, that's here, and that's himself; for he
The sacred honour of himself, his queen's,
His hopeful son's, his babe's, betrays to slander,
Whose sting is sharper than the sword's; and
  will not   86
(For, as the case now stands, it is a curse
He cannot be compell'd to't) once remove
The root of his opinion, which is rotten
As ever oak or stone was sound.
Leon.   A callat   90
Of boundless tongue, who late hath beat her
  husband
And now baits me! This brat is none of mine;
It is the issue of Polixenes.

Hence with it, and together with the dam
Commit them to the fire!
Paul.   It is yours;   95
And, might we lay th' old proverb to your
  charge,
So like you 'tis the worse. Behold, my lords,
Although the print be little, the whole matter
And copy of the father — eye, nose, lip,
The trick of 's frown, his forehead; nay, the
  valley,   100
The pretty dimples of his chin and cheek; his
  smiles;
The very mould and frame of hand, nail, finger.
And thou, good goddess Nature, which hast
  made it
So like to him that got it, if thou hast
The ordering of the mind too, 'mongst all
  colours   105
No yellow in't, lest she suspect, as he does,
Her children not her husband's!
Leon.   A gross hag!
And, lozel, thou art worthy to be hang'd
That wilt not stay her tongue.
Ant.   Hang all the husbands
That cannot do that feat, you'll leave yourself
Hardly one subject.
Leon.   Once more, take her hence.
Paul. A most unworthy and unnatural lord
Can do no more.
Leon.   I'll ha' thee burnt.
Paul.   I care not.
It is an heretic that makes the fire,
Not she which burns in't. I'll not call you
  tyrant;   115
But this most cruel usage of your queen
(Not able to produce more accusation
Than your own weak-hing'd fancy) something
  savours
Of tyranny, and will ignoble make you,   119
Yea, scandalous to the world.
Leon.   On your allegiance,
Out of the chamber with her! Were I a tyrant,
Where were her life? She durst not call me so
If she did know me one. Away with her!
Paul. I pray you do not push me; I'll be
  gone.
Look to your babe, my lord; 'tis yours. Jove
  send her   125
A better guiding spirit! What needs these
  hands?
You that are thus so tender o'er his follies
Will never do him good, not one of you.
So, so. Farewell, we are gone.   *Exit.*
Leon. Thou, traitor, hast set on thy wife to
  this.   130

444

My child? Away with't! Even thou, that hast
A heart so tender o'er it, take it hence
And see it instantly consum'd with fire.
Even thou, and none but thou. Take it up
  straight!
Within this hour bring me word 'tis done,   135
And by good testimony, or I'll seize thy life,
With what thou else call'st thine. If thou re-
  fuse
And wilt encounter with my wrath, say so:
The bastard brains with these my proper
  hands
Shall I dash out. Go, take it to the fire!   140
For thou set'st on thy wife.
  Ant.   I did not, sir.
These lords, my noble fellows, if they please,
Can clear me in't.
  Lords.   We can. My royal liege,
He is not guilty of her coming hither.
  Leon. You're liars all.   145
  Lord. Beseech your Highness, give us better
  credit.
We have always truly serv'd you, and beseech
So to esteem of us; and on our knees we
  beg
(As recompense of our dear services
Past and to come) that you do change this
  purpose,   150
Which being so horrible, so bloody, must
Lead on to some foul issue. We all kneel.
  Leon. I am a feather for each wind that
  blows.
Shall I live on to see this bastard kneel
And call me father? Better burn it now   155
Than curse it then. But be it; let it live.
It shall not neither! [*To Antigonus*] You, sir,
  come you hither.
You that have been so tenderly officious,
With Lady Margery, your midwife there,
To save this bastard's life — for 'tis a bastard,
So sure as this beard's grey — what will you
  adventure   161
To save this brat's life?
  Ant.   Anything, my lord,
That my ability may undergo
And nobleness impose. At least, thus much —
I'll pawn the little blood which I have left 165
To save the innocent. Anything possible.
  Leon. It shall be possible. Swear by this
  sword
Thou wilt perform my bidding.
  Ant.   I will, my lord.
  Leon. Mark, and perform it — seest thou?
  for the fail
Of any point in't shall not only be   170

Death to thyself, but to thy lewd-tongu'd
  wife,
Whom for this time we pardon. We enjoin
  thee,
As thou art liegeman to us, that thou carry
This female bastard hence; and that thou
  bear it   174
To some remote and desert place, quite out
Of our dominions; and that there thou leave
  it
(Without more mercy) to it own protection
And favour of the climate. As by strange
  fortune
It came to us, I do in justice charge thee,
On thy soul's peril and thy body's torture, 180
That thou commend it strangely to some place
Where chance may nurse or end it. Take it
  up.
  Ant. I swear to do this; though a present
  death
Had been more merciful. Come on, poor babe!
Some powerful spirit instruct the kites and
  ravens   185
To be thy nurses! Wolves and bears, they
  say,
Casting their savageness aside, have done
Like offices of pity. Sir, be prosperous
In more than this deed does require! And
  blessing
Against this cruelty fight on thy side,   190
Poor thing, condemn'd to loss!
                      Exit [*with the child*].
  Leon.   No, I'll not rear
Another's issue.

              Enter a *Servant*.

  Serv.   Please your Highness, posts
From those you sent to th' oracle are come
An hour since. Cleomenes and Dion,
Being well arriv'd from Delphos, are both
  landed,   195
Hasting to th' court.
  Lord.   So please you, sir, their speed
Hath been beyond accompt.
  Leon.   Twenty-three days
They have been absent. 'Tis good speed,
  foretells
The great Apollo suddenly will have
The truth of this appear. Prepare you, lords;
Summon a session, that we may arraign   201
Our most disloyal lady; for, as she hath
Been publicly accus'd, so shall she have
A just and open trial. While she lives,
My heart will be a burthen to me. Leave me,
And think upon my bidding.   *Exeunt.*

ACT III. Scene I. [*Sicilia. On the road.*]

Enter Cleomenes and Dion.

Cleo. The climate's delicate, the air most
sweet;
Fertile the isle, the temple much surpassing
The common praise it bears.
 Dion.   I shall report,
For most it caught me, the celestial habits
(Methinks I so should term them) and the
reverence   5
Of the grave wearers. O, the sacrifice!
How ceremonious, solemn, and unearthly
It was i' th' off'ring!
 Cleo.   But of all, the burst
And the ear-deaf'ning voice o' th' oracle,
Kin to Jove's thunder, so surpris'd my sense 10
That I was nothing.
 Dion. If th' event o' th' journey
Prove as successful to the Queen (O, be't so!)
As it hath been to us rare, pleasant, speedy,
The time is worth the use on't.
 Cleo.   Great Apollo
Turn all to th' best! These proclamations, 15
So forcing faults upon Hermione,
I little like.
 Dion. The violent carriage of it
Will clear or end the business. When the oracle
(Thus by Apollo's great divine seal'd up)
Shall the contents discover, something rare 20
Even then will rush to knowledge. Go; fresh
horses!
And gracious be the issue!   *Exeunt.*

Scene II. [*Sicilia. A court of justice.*]

Enter Leontes, Lords, Officers.

Leon. This sessions (to our great grief we
pronounce)
Even pushes 'gainst our heart — the party
tried
The daughter of a king, our wife, and one
Of us too much belov'd. Let us be clear'd
Of being tyrannous, since we so openly 5
Proceed in justice, which shall have due course,
Even to the guilt or the purgation.
Produce the prisoner.
 Officer. It is his Highness' pleasure that the
Queen
Appear in person here in court. Silence! 10

*Enter Hermione, as to her trial, [Paulina,
and] Ladies.*

Leon. Read the indictment.
 Officer. [*reads*] 'Hermione, Queen to the
worthy Leontes, King of Sicilia, thou art here
accused and arraigned of high treason, in committing adultery with Polixenes, King of Bohemia,
and conspiring with Camillo to take away the life
of our sovereign lord the King, thy royal husband;
the pretence whereof being by circumstances
partly laid open, thou, Hermione, contrary to the
faith and allegiance of a true subject, didst counsel
and aid them, for their better safety, to fly away
by night.'
 Her. Since what I am to say must be but that
Which contradicts my accusation, and
The testimony on my part no other   25
But what comes from myself, it shall scarce
boot me
To say 'Not guilty.' Mine integrity,
Being counted falsehood, shall, as I express it,
Be so receiv'd. But thus: — if pow'rs divine
Behold our human actions (as they do), 30
I doubt not then but innocence shall make
False accusation blush and tyranny
Tremble at patience. You, my lord, best know
(Who least will seem to do so) my past life
Hath been as continent, as chaste, as true, 35
As I am now unhappy; which is more
Than history can pattern, though devis'd
And play'd to take spectators. For behold me —
A fellow of the royal bed, which owe   39
A moiety of the throne, a great king's daughter,
The mother to a hopeful prince — here standing
To prate and talk for life and honour fore
Who please to come and hear. For life, I prize it
As I weigh grief, which I would spare. For
honour,
'Tis a derivative from me to mine,   45
And only that I stand for. I appeal
To your own conscience, sir, before Polixenes
Came to your court, how I was in your grace,
How merited to be so; since he came,
With what encounter so uncurrent I 50
Have strain'd t' appear thus; if one jot beyond
The bound of honour, or in act or will
That way inclining, hard'ned be the hearts
Of all that hear me, and my near'st of kin
Cry fie upon my grave!
 Leon.   I ne'er heard yet 55
That any of these bolder vices wanted

446

Less impudence to gainsay what they did
Than to perform it first.
  Her.   That's true enough;
Though 'tis a saying, sir, not due to me.   59
  Leon. You will not own it.
  Her.   More than mistress of
Which comes to me in name of fault, I must not
At all acknowledge. For Polixenes,
With whom I am accus'd, I do confess
I lov'd him as in honour he requir'd;
With such a kind of love as might become   65
A lady like me; with a love even such,
So and no other, as yourself commanded;
Which not to have done, I think had been in me
Both disobedience and ingratitude
To you and toward your friend, whose love
        had spoke,   70
Even since it could speak, from an infant,
        freely,
That it was yours. Now for conspiracy,
I know not how it tastes, though it be dish'd
For me to try how. All I know of it
Is, that Camillo was an honest man;   75
And why he left your court, the gods themselves
(Wotting no more than I) are ignorant.
  Leon. You knew of his departure, as you
        know
What you have underta'en to do in 's absence.
  Her. Sir,   80
You speak a language that I understand not.
My life stands in the level of your dreams,
Which I'll lay down.
  Leon.   Your actions are my dreams.
You had a bastard by Polixenes,
And I but dream'd it. As you were past all
        shame   85
(Those of your fact are so), so past all truth;
Which to deny concerns more than avails;
        for as
Thy brat hath been cast out, like to itself,
No father owning it (which is indeed
More criminal in thee than it), so thou   90
Shalt feel our justice; in whose easiest passage
Look for no less than death.
  Her.   Sir, spare your threats.
The bug which you would fright me with I seek.
To me can life be no commodity.
The crown and comfort of my life, your favour,
I do give lost, for I do feel it gone,   96
But know not how it went. My second joy
And first fruits of my body, from his presence
I am barr'd, like one infectious. My third
        comfort,
Starr'd most unluckily, is from my breast   100
(The innocent milk in it most innocent mouth)

Hal'd out to murther. Myself on every post
Proclaim'd a strumpet. With immodest hatred
The childbed privilege denied, which 'longs
To women of all fashion. Lastly, hurried   105
Here to this place, i' th' open air, before
I have got strength of limit. Now, my liege,
Tell me what blessings I have here alive
That I should fear to die. Therefore proceed.
But yet hear this — mistake me not : for life,
I prize it not a straw; but for mine honour, 111
Which I would free — if I shall be condemn'd
Upon surmises (all proofs sleeping else,
But what your jealousies awake), I tell you,
'Tis rigour, and not law. Your honours all, 115
I do refer me to the oracle.
Apollo be my judge!
  Lord.   This your request
Is altogether just. Therefore bring forth,
And in Apollo's name, his oracle.
                    [*Exeunt certain Officers.*]
  Her. The Emperor of Russia was my father.
O that he were alive, and here beholding   121
His daughter's trial! that he did but see
The flatness of my misery! yet with eyes
Of pity, not revenge.

[Enter *Officers*, with] *Cleomenes* [and] *Dion.*

  Officer. You here shall swear upon this sword
        of justice   125
That you, Cleomenes and Dion, have
Been both at Delphos, and from thence have
        brought
This seal'd-up oracle, by the hand deliver'd
Of great Apollo's priest; and that since then
You have not dar'd to break the holy seal   130
Nor read the secrets in't.
  Cleo., Dion.   All this we swear.
  Leon. Break up the seals and read.
  Officer. [*reads*] 'Hermione is chaste; Polixenes
blameless; Camillo a true subject; Leontes a
jealous tyrant; his innocent babe truly begotten;
and the King shall live without an heir, if that
which is lost be not found.'   137
  Lords. Now blessed be the great Apollo!
  Her.   Praised!
  Leon. Hast thou read truth?
  Officer.   Ay, my lord; even so
As it is here set down.   140
  Leon. There is no truth at all i' th' oracle!
The sessions shall proceed. This is mere false-
        hood!

[Enter a *Servant.*]

  Serv. My lord the King! the King!
  Leon.   What is the business?

447

Serv. O sir, I shall be hated to report it.
The Prince your son, with mere conceit and fear
Of the Queen's speed, is gone.
Leon.   How? gone?
Serv.   Is dead.
Leon. Apollo's angry, and the heavens them-
    selves
Do strike at my injustice. [*Hermione swoons.*]
    How now there?
Paul. This news is mortal to the Queen.
    Look down   149
And see what death is doing.
Leon.   Take her hence.
Her heart is but o'ercharg'd; she will recover.
I have too much believ'd mine own suspicion.
Beseech you tenderly apply to her
Some remedies for life.
[*Exeunt Paulina and Ladies, with Hermione.*]
                    Apollo, pardon
My great profaneness 'gainst thine oracle! 155
I'll reconcile me to Polixenes,
New woo my queen, recall the good Camillo,
Whom I proclaim a man of truth, of mercy;
For, being transported by my jealousies
To bloody thoughts and to revenge, I chose 160
Camillo for the minister to poison
My friend Polixenes; which had been done
But that the good mind of Camillo tardied
My swift command, though I with death and
    with
Reward did threaten and encourage him,   165
Not doing it and being done. He (most hu-
    mane,
And fill'd with honour) to my kingly guest
Unclasp'd my practice, quit his fortunes here,
Which you knew great, and to the certain hazard
Of all incertainties himself commended,   170
No richer than his honour. How he glisters
Thorough my rust! and how his piety
Does my deeds make the blacker!

[*Enter Paulina.*]

Paul.   Woe the while!
O, cut my lace, lest my heart, cracking it,
Break too!
Lord.   What fit is this, good lady?   175
Paul. What studied torments, tyrant, hast
    for me?
What wheels? racks? fires? what flaying?
    boiling
In leads or oils? What old or newer torture
Must I receive, whose every word deserves
To taste of thy most worst? Thy tyranny 180
Together working with thy jealousies
Fancies too weak for boys, too green and idle

For girls of nine) — O, think what they have
    done,
And then run mad indeed, stark mad! for all
Thy bygone fooleries were but spices of it. 185
That thou betray'dst Polixenes, 'twas nothing:
That did but show thee, of a fool, inconstant,
And damnable ingrateful. Nor was't much
Thou wouldst have poison'd good Camillo's
    honour,
To have him kill a king — poor trespasses, 190
More monstrous standing by; whereof I reckon
The casting forth to crows thy baby daughter
To be or none or little, though a devil
Would have shed water out of fire ere done't;
Nor is't directly laid to thee, the death   195
Of the young Prince, whose honourable thoughts
(Thoughts high for one so tender) cleft the
    heart
That could conceive a gross and foolish sire
Blemish'd his gracious dam. This is not, no,
Laid to thy answer; but the last — O lords,
When I have said, cry 'woe!' — the Queen, the
    Queen,   201
The sweet'st, dear'st creature's dead; and ven-
    geance for't
Not dropp'd down yet.
Lord.   The higher pow'rs forbid!
Paul. I say she's dead; I'll swear't. If word
    nor oath
Prevail not, go and see. If you can bring 205
Tincture or lustre in her lip, her eye,
Heat outwardly or breath within, I'll serve you
As I would do the gods. But, O thou tyrant!
Do not repent these things; for they are heavier
Than all thy woes can stir. Therefore betake
    thee   210
To nothing but despair. A thousand knees,
Ten thousand years together, naked, fasting,
Upon a barren mountain, and still winter
In storm perpetual, could not move the gods
To look that way thou wert!
Leon.   Go on, go on.   215
Thou canst not speak too much. I have de-
    serv'd
All tongues to talk their bitt'rest.
Lord.   Say no more.
Howe'er the business goes, you have made fault
I' th' boldness of your speech.
Paul.   I am sorry for't.
All faults I make, when I shall come to know
    them,   220
I do repent. Alas, I have show'd too much
The rashness of a woman! He is touch'd
To th' noble heart. What's gone and what's
    past help

Should be past grief. Do not receive affliction
At my petition. I beseech you, rather   225
Let me be punish'd that have minded you
Of what you should forget. Now, good my
   liege,
Sir, royal sir, forgive a foolish woman.
The love I bore your queen — lo, fool again!
I'll speak of her no more, nor of your children;
I'll not remember you of my own lord,   231
Who is lost too. Take you your patience to you,
And I'll say nothing.
   Leon.   Thou didst speak but well
When most the truth; which I receive much
   better
Than to be pitied of thee. Prithee bring me 235
To the dead bodies of my queen and son.
One grave shall be for both. Upon them shall
The causes of their death appear, unto
Our shame perpetual. Once a day I'll visit
The chapel where they lie, and tears shed there
Shall be my recreation. So long as nature 241
Will bear up with this exercise, so long
I daily vow to use it. Come, and lead me
To these sorrows.   *Exeunt.*

Scene III. [*Bohemia. The seacoast.*]

Enter Antigonus [with the] *Babe, a Mariner.*

   Ant. Thou art perfect then our ship hath
   touch'd upon
The deserts of Bohemia?
   Mar.   Ay, my lord, and fear
We have landed in ill time. The skies look
   grimly
And threaten present blusters. In my con-
   science
The heavens with that we have in hand are
   angry   5
And frown upon 's.
   Ant. Their sacred wills be done! Go get
   aboard;
Look to thy bark. I'll not be long before
I call upon thee.
   Mar. Make your best haste, and go not 10
Too far i' th' land. 'Tis like to be loud weather.
Besides, this place is famous for the creatures
Of prey that keep upon't.
   Ant.   Go thou away;
I'll follow instantly.
   Mar.   I am glad at heart
To be so rid o' th' business.   *Exit.*
   Ant.   Come, poor babe.
I have heard, but not believ'd, the spirits o' th'
   dead   16

May walk again. If such thing be, thy mother
Appear'd to me last night; for ne'er was dream
So like a waking. To me comes a creature,
Sometimes her head on one side, some another;
I never saw a vessel of like sorrow,   21
So fill'd and so becoming. In pure white robes,
Like very sanctity, she did approach
My cabin where I lay; thrice bow'd before me;
And, gasping to begin some speech, her eyes 25
Became two spouts. The fury spent, anon
Did this break from her: 'Good Antigonus,
Since fate, against thy better disposition,
Hath made thy person for the thrower-out
Of my poor babe, according to thine oath, 30
Places remote enough are in Bohemia,
There weep, and leave it crying; and, for the
   babe
Is counted lost for ever, Perdita
I prithee call't. For this ungentle business,
Put on thee by my lord, thou ne'er shalt see 35
Thy wife Paulina more.' And so, with shrieks
She melted into air. Affrighted much,
I did in time collect myself, and thought
This was so and no slumber. Dreams are toys;
Yet for this once, yea, superstitiously,   40
I will be squar'd by this. I do believe
Hermione hath suffer'd death, and that
Apollo would (this being indeed the issue
Of King Polixenes) it should here be laid,
Either for life or death, upon the earth   45
Of its right father. Blossom, speed thee well!
        [*Lays down the Child, with a scroll.*]
There lie, and there thy character; there these,
             [*Lays down a bundle.*]
Which may, if fortune please, both breed thee,
   pretty,
And still rest thine. [*Thunder.*] The storm be-
   gins. Poor wretch,
That for thy mother's fault art thus expos'd 50
To loss and what may follow! Weep I cannot,
But my heart bleeds; and most accurs'd am I
To be by oath enjoin'd to this. Farewell!
The day frowns more and more. Thou'rt like
   to have
A lullaby too rough. I never saw   55
The heavens so dim by day.
        [*Noise of hunters and dogs within.*]
                A savage clamour!
Well may I get aboard. — This is the chase!
I am gone for ever.   *Exit, pursued by a bear.*

Enter *Shepherd.*

   Shep. I would there were no age between ten
and three-and-twenty, or that youth would
sleep out the rest; for there is nothing in the

between but getting wenches with child, wronging the anciently, stealing, fighting — Hark you now! Would any but these boil'd-brains of nineteen and two-and-twenty hunt this weather? They have scar'd away two of my best sheep, which I fear the wolf will sooner find than the master. If anywhere I have them, 'tis by the seaside, browsing of ivy. [*Sees the child.*] Good luck, an't be thy will! What have we here? Mercy on 's, a barne! a very pretty barne! A boy or a child, I wonder? A pretty one; a very pretty one. Sure, some scape! Though I am not bookish, yet I can read waiting gentlewoman in the scape. This has been some stair-work, some trunk-work, some behind-door-work. They were warmer that got this than the poor thing is here. I'll take it up for pity. Yet I'll tarry till my son come. He halloa'd but even now. Whoa-ho-hoa!

Enter *Clown*.

Clown. Hilloa, loa! 80
Shep. What? art so near? If thou'lt see a thing to talk on when thou art dead and rotten, come hither. What ail'st thou, man?
Clown. I have seen two such sights, by sea and by land! But I am not to say it is a sea, for it is now the sky; betwixt the firmament and it you cannot thrust a bodkin's point. 87
Shep. Why, boy, how is it?
Clown. I would you did but see how it chafes, how it rages, how it takes up the shore! But that's not to the point. O, the most piteous cry of the poor souls! Sometimes to see 'em, and not to see 'em! Now the ship boring the moon with her mainmast, and anon swallowed with yeast and froth, as you'ld thrust a cork into a hogshead. And then for the land service — to see how the bear tore out his shoulder bone; how he cried to me for help and said his name was Antigonus, a nobleman! But to make an end of the ship — to see how the sea flap-dragon'd it; but first, how the poor souls

roared, and the sea mock'd them; and how the poor gentleman roared, and the bear mock'd him, both roaring louder than the sea or weather. 104
Shep. Name of mercy, when was this, boy?
Clown. Now, now! I have not wink'd since I saw these sights. The men are not yet cold under water, nor the bear half din'd on the gentleman — he's at it now.
Shep. Would I had been by, to have help'd the old man! 111
Clown. I would you had been by the ship side, to have help'd her! There your charity would have lack'd footing.
Shep. Heavy matters, heavy matters! But look thee here, boy. Now bless thyself! thou met'st with things dying, I with things new-born. Here's a sight for thee. Look thee a bearing cloth for a squire's child! Look thee here; take up, take up, boy; open't. So, let's see. It was told me I should be rich by the fairies. This is some changeling. Open't. What's within, boy?
Clown. You're a made old man. If the sins of your youth are forgiven you, you're well to live. Gold! all gold! 126
Shep. This is fairy gold, boy, and 'twill prove so. Up with't, keep it close. Home, home, the next way! We are lucky, boy, and to be so still requires nothing but secrecy. Let my sheep go. Come, good boy, the next way home! 131
Clown. Go you the next way with your findings. I'll go see if the bear be gone from the gentleman, and how much he hath eaten. They are never curst but when they are hungry. If there be any of him left, I'll bury it. 136
Shep. That's a good deed. If thou mayest discern by that which is left of him what he is, fetch me to th' sight of him.
Clown. Marry, will I; and you shall help to put him i' th' ground. 141
Shep. 'Tis a lucky day, boy, and we'll do good deeds on't. *Exeunt.*

ACT IV. Scene I.

Enter *Time, the Chorus*.

Time. I, that please some, try all, both joy and terror
Of good and bad, that makes and unfolds error,
Now take upon me, in the name of Time,
To use my wings. Impute it not a crime
To me or my swift passage that I slide 5

O'er sixteen years and leave the growth untried
Of that wide gap, since it is in my pow'r
To o'erthrow law, and in one self born hour
To plant and o'erwhelm custom. Let me pass
The same I am, ere ancient'st order was 10
Or what is now receiv'd. I witness to
The times that brought them in; so shall I
do

450

To th' freshest things now reigning, and make
   stale
The glistering of this present, as my tale   14
Now seems to it. Your patience this allowing,
I turn my glass, and give my scene such growing
As you had slept between. Leontes leaving
Th' effects of his fond jealousies so grieving
That he shuts up himself, imagine me,
Gentle spectators, that I now may be   20
In fair Bohemia; and remember well
I mention'd a son o' th' King's, which Florizel
I now name to you; and with speed so pace
To speak of Perdita, now grown in grace
Equal with wond'ring. What of her ensues 25
I list not prophesy; but let Time's news
Be known when 'tis brought forth. A shep-
   herd's daughter
And what to her adheres, which follows after,
Is th' argument of Time. Of this allow,
If ever you have spent time worse ere now; 30
If never, yet that Time himself doth say
He wishes earnestly you never may.   *Exit.*

Scene II. [*Bohemia. The Palace of*
   Polixenes.]

Enter *Polixenes* and *Camillo.*

Pol. I pray thee, good Camillo, be no more
importunate. 'Tis a sickness denying thee anything; a death to grant this.
Cam. It is fifteen years since I saw my country. Though I have for the most part been
aired abroad, I desire to lay my bones there.
Besides, the penitent King, my master, hath
sent for me, to whose feeling sorrows I might be
some allay, or I o'erween to think so, which is
another spur to my departure.   10
Pol. As thou lov'st me, Camillo, wipe not
out the rest of thy services by leaving me now.
The need I have of thee thine own goodness
hath made. Better not to have had thee than
thus to want thee. Thou, having made me businesses which none without thee can sufficiently
manage, must either stay to execute them thyself or take away with thee the very services
thou hast done; which if I have not enough
considered (as too much I cannot), to be more
thankful to thee shall be my study, and my
profit therein the heaping friendships. Of that
fatal country Sicilia prithee speak no more,
whose very naming punishes me with the remembrance of that penitent (as thou call'st
him) and reconciled king, my brother, whose

loss of his most precious queen and children are
even now to be afresh lamented. Say to me,
when saw'st thou the Prince Florizel, my son?
Kings are no less unhappy, their issue not being
gracious, than they are in losing them when
they have approved their virtues.   32
Cam. Sir, it is three days since I saw the
Prince. What his happier affairs may be, are to
me unknown; but I have (missingly) noted he
is of late much retired from court, and is less
frequent to his princely exercises than formerly
he hath appeared.   38
Pol. I have considered so much, Camillo, and
with some care, so far that I have eyes under
my service which look upon his removedness;
from whom I have this intelligence, that he is
seldom from the house of a most homely shepherd; a man, they say, that from very nothing,
and beyond the imagination of his neighbours,
is grown into an unspeakable estate.   46
Cam. I have heard, sir, of such a man, who
hath a daughter of most rare note. The report
of her is extended more than can be thought to
begin from such a cottage.   50
Pol. That's likewise part of my intelligence;
but, I fear, the angle that plucks our son thither.
Thou shalt accompany us to the place, where we
will (not appearing what we are) have some
question with the shepherd; from whose simplicity I think it not uneasy to get the cause of
my son's resort thither. Prithee be my present
partner in this business and lay aside the
thoughts of Sicilia.
Cam. I willingly obey your command.   60
Pol. My best Camillo! We must disguise
ourselves.   *Exeunt.*

Scene III. [*Bohemia. A highway near
the* Shepherd's *house.*

Enter *Autolycus,* singing

When daffodils begin to peer,
   With heigh! the doxy over the dale —
Why, then comes in the sweet o' the year,
   For the red blood reigns in the winter's pale.

The white sheet bleaching on the hedge —   5
   With heigh! the sweet birds, O, how they sing!
Doth set my pugging tooth on edge,
   For a quart of ale is a dish for a king.

The lark, that tirra-lyra chants, —
   With heigh! with heigh! the thrush and the
     jay —   10
Are summer songs for me and my aunts,
   While we lie tumbling in the hay,

I have serv'd Prince Florizel and in my time wore three-pile, but now I am out of service.

But shall I go mourn for that, my dear?　15
　　The pale moon shines by night;
　And when I wander here and there,
　　I then do most go right.

If tinkers may have leave to live
　And bear the sow-skin budget,　20
Then my account I well may give,
　And in the stocks avouch it.

My traffic is sheets. When the kite builds, look to lesser linen. My father nam'd me Autolycus, who being, as I am, litter'd under Mercury, was likewise a snapper-up of unconsidered trifles. With die and drab I purchas'd this caparison, and my revenue is the silly cheat. Gallows and knock are too powerful on the highway. Beating and hanging are terrors to me. For the life to come, I sleep out the thought of it. A prize! a prize!　32

Enter Clown.

Clown. Let me see: every 'leven wether tods; every tod yields pound and odd shilling; fifteen hundred shorn, what comes the wool to?

Aut. [*aside*] If the springe hold, the cock's mine.　37

Clown. I cannot do't without compters. Let me see: what am I to buy for our sheep-shearing feast? Three pound of sugar, five pound of currants, rice — What will this sister of mine do with rice? But my father hath made her mistress of the feast, and she lays it on. She hath made me four-and-twenty nosegays for the shearers — three-man songmen all, and very good ones; but they are most of them means and basses; but one Puritan amongst them, and he sings psalms to hornpipes. I must have saffron to colour the warden pies, mace; dates — none, that's out of my note; nutmegs, seven; a race or two of ginger, but that I may beg; four pound of prunes, and as many of raisins o' th' sun.　52

Aut. O, that ever I was born!
　　　　　　　[*Grovels on the ground.*]

Clown. I' th' name of me!

Aut. O, help me, help me! Pluck but off these rags; and then, death, death!　56

Clown. Alack, poor soul! thou hast need of more rags to lay on thee, rather than have these off.

Aut. O sir, the loathsomeness of them offends me more than the stripes I have received, which are mighty ones and millions.　61

Clown. Alas, poor man! A million of beating may come to a great matter.

Aut. I am robb'd, sir, and beaten; my money and apparel ta'en from me, and these detestable things put upon me.　66

Clown. What, by a horseman or a footman?

Aut. A footman, sweet sir, a footman.

Clown. Indeed, he should be a footman by the garments he has left with thee. If this be a horseman's coat, it hath seen very hot service. Lend me thy hand, I'll help thee. Come, lend me thy hand.　　　　　　　[*Helps him up.*]

Aut. O, good sir, tenderly, O!

Clown. Alas, poor soul!　75

Aut. O, good sir, softly, good sir! I fear, sir, my shoulder blade is out.

Clown. How now? Canst stand?

Aut. Softly, dear sir! good sir, softly! [*Picks his pocket.*] You ha' done me a charitable office.　81

Clown. Dost lack any money? I have a little money for thee.

Aut. No, good sweet sir; no, I beseech you, sir. I have a kinsman not past three quarters of a mile hence, unto whom I was going. I shall there have money or anything I want. Offer me no money, I pray you; that kills my heart.

Clown. What manner of fellow was he that robb'd you?　90

Aut. A fellow, sir, that I have known to go about with troll-my-dames. I knew him once a servant of the Prince. I cannot tell, good sir, for which of his virtues it was, but he was certainly whipp'd out of the court.　95

Clown. His vices, you would say. There's no virtue whipp'd out of the court. They cherish it to make it stay there; and yet it will no more but abide.　99

Aut. Vices I would say, sir. I know this man well. He hath been since an ape-bearer; then a process-server, a bailiff; then he compass'd a motion of the Prodigal Son, and married a tinker's wife within a mile where my land and living lies; and, having flown over many knavish professions, he settled only in rogue. Some call him Autolycus.　107

Clown. Out upon him! prig, for my life, prig! He haunts wakes, fairs, and bear-baitings.

Aut. Very true, sir; he, sir, he. That's the rogue that put me into this apparel.　111

Clown. Not a more cowardly rogue in all Bohemia. If you had but look'd big and spit at him, he'ld have run.　114

452

The Winter's Tale

Aut. I must confess to you, sir, I am no fighter. I am false of heart that way; and that he knew, I warrant him.

Clown. How do you now?

Aut. Sweet sir, much better than I was. I can stand and walk. I will even take my leave of you and pace softly towards my kinsman's.

Clown. Shall I bring thee on the way? 122

Aut. No, good-fac'd sir; no, sweet sir.

Clown. Then fare thee well. I must go buy spices for our sheep-shearing. 125

Aut. Prosper you, sweet sir! *Exit [Clown].* Your purse is not hot enough to purchase your spice. I'll be with you at your sheep-shearing too. If I make not this cheat bring out another and the shearers prove sheep, let me be unroll'd and my name put in the book of virtue! 131

Song.

Jog on, jog on the footpath way,
And merrily hent the stile-a.
A merry heart goes all the day,
Your sad tires in a mile-a. *Exit.*

Scene IV. [*Bohemia. A green before the* Shepherd's *house.*]

Enter *Florizel* [and] *Perdita.*

Flo. These your unusual weeds to each part of you
Do give a life — no shepherdess, but Flora
Peering in April's front! This your sheep-shearing
Is as a meeting of the petty gods,
And you the queen on't.

Per. Sir, my gracious lord, 5
To chide at your extremes it not becomes me;
O, pardon that I name them! Your high self,
The gracious mark o' th' land, you have obscur'd
With a swain's wearing; and me, poor lowly maid,
Most goddess-like prank'd up. But that our feasts 10
In every mess have folly, and the feeders
Digest it with a custom, I should blush
To see you so attir'd — sworn, I think,
To show myself a glass.

Flo. I bless the time
When my good falcon made her flight across 15
Thy father's ground.

Per. Now Jove afford you cause!
To me the difference forges dread; your greatness
Hath not been us'd to fear. Even now I tremble

To think your father, by some accident, 19
Should pass this way, as you did. O, the Fates!
How would he look to see his work, so noble,
Vilely bound up? What would he say? Or how
Should I, in these my borrowed flaunts, behold
The sternness of his presence?

Flo. Apprehend
Nothing but jollity. The gods themselves, 25
Humbling their deities to love, have taken
The shapes of beasts upon them. Jupiter
Became a bull, and bellow'd; the green Neptune
A ram, and bleated; and the fire-rob'd god,
Golden Apollo, a poor humble swain, 30
As I seem now. Their transformations
Were never for a piece of beauty rarer,
Nor in a way so chaste, since my desires
Run not before mine honour, nor my lusts
Burn hotter than my faith.

Per. O, but, sir, 35
Your resolution cannot hold when 'tis
Oppos'd, as it must be, by th' pow'r of the King!
One of these two must be necessities,
Which then will speak — that you must change this purpose,
Or I my life.

Flo. Thou dearest Perdita, 40
With these forc'd thoughts I prithee darken not
The mirth o' th' feast. Or I'll be thine, my fair,
Or not my father's; for I cannot be
Mine own, nor anything to any, if
I be not thine. To this I am most constant, 45
Though destiny say no. Be merry, gentle!
Strangle such thoughts as these with anything
That you behold the while. Your guests are coming.
Lift up your countenance, as it were the day
Of celebration of that nuptial which 50
We two have sworn shall come.

Per. O Lady Fortune,
Stand you auspicious!

Flo. See, your guests approach.
Address yourself to entertain them sprightly,
And let's be red with mirth.

Enter *Shepherd, Clown, Polixenes* [and] *Camillo* [disguised], *Mopsa, Dorcas,* [and others].

Shep. Fie, daughter! When my old wife liv'd, upon 55
This day she was both pantler, butler, cook,
Both dame and servant; welcom'd all; serv'd all;
Would sing her song and dance her turn; now here
At upper end o' th' table, now i' th' middle;

453

On his shoulder, and his; her face o' fire   60
With labour, and the thing she took to quench it
She would to each one sip. You are retir'd,
As if you were a feasted one, and not
The hostess of the meeting. Pray you bid   64
These unknown friends to 's welcome, for it is
A way to make us better friends, more known.
Come, quench your blushes and present yourself
That which you are, mistress o' th' feast.
      Come on,
And bid us welcome to your sheep-shearing,
As your good flock shall prosper.
      Per.   [*to Polixenes*] Sir, welcome.
It is my father's will I should take on me   71
The hostessship o' th' day. [*To Camillo*]
      You're welcome, sir.
Give me those flow'rs there, Dorcas. Reverend
      sirs,
For you there's rosemary and rue; these keep
Seeming and savour all the winter long.   75
Grace and remembrance be to you both,
And welcome to our shearing!
      Pol.   Shepherdess
(A fair one are you), well you fit our ages
With flow'rs of winter.
      Per.   Sir, the year growing ancient,
Not yet on summer's death nor on the birth   80
Of trembling winter, the fairest flow'rs o' th'
      season
Are our carnations and streak'd gillyvors,
Which some call nature's bastards. Of that kind
Our rustic garden's barren, and I care not   84
To get slips of them.
      Pol.   Wherefore, gentle maiden,
Do you neglect them?
      Per.   For I have heard it said
There is an art which in their piedness shares
With great creating nature.
      Pol.   Say there be.
Yet nature is made better by no mean
But nature makes that mean. So, over that art
Which you say adds to nature, is an art   91
That nature makes. You see, sweet maid, we
      marry
A gentler scion to the wildest stock
And make conceive a bark of baser kind
By bud of nobler race. This is an art   95
Which does mend nature — change it rather;
      but
The art itself is nature.
      Per.   So it is.
      Pol. Then make your garden rich in gillyvors,
And do not call them bastards.
      Per.   I'll not put
The dibble in earth to set one slip of them; 100

No more than, were I painted, I would wish
This youth should say 'twere well, and only
      therefore
Desire to breed by me. Here's flow'rs for you:
Hot lavender, mints, savory, marjoram;
The marigold, that goes to bed wi' th' sun 105
And with him rises weeping. These are flow'rs
Of middle summer, and I think they are given
To men of middle age. Y'are very welcome.
      Cam. I should leave grazing, were I of your
      flock,
And only live by gazing.
      Per.   Out, alas!   110
You'ld be so lean that blasts of January
Would blow you through and through. [*To
      Florizel*] Now, my fair'st friend,
I would I had some flow'rs o' th' spring that
      might
Become your time of day; [*to the Girls*] and
      yours, and yours,
That wear upon your virgin branches yet   115
Your maidenheads growing. O Proserpina,
For the flowers now that, frighted, thou let'st
      fall
From Dis's wagon! daffodils,
That come before the swallow dares and take
The winds of March with beauty; violets —
      dim,   120
But sweeter than the lids of Juno's eyes
Or Cytherea's breath; pale primeroses,
That die unmarried ere they can behold
Bright Phœbus in his strength (a malady
Most incident to maids); bold oxlips and 125
The crown imperial; lilies of all kinds,
The flow'r-de-luce being one! O, these I lack
To make you garlands of; and my sweet friend,
To strew him o'er and o'er!
      Flo.   What, like a corse?
      Per. No, like a bank for love to lie and play
      on;   130
Not like a corse; or if — not to be buried,
But quick, and in mine arms. Come, take your
      flow'rs.
Methinks I play as I have seen them do
In Whitsun pastorals. Sure this robe of mine
Does change my disposition.
      Flo.   What you do 135
Still betters what is done. When you speak,
      sweet,
I'ld have you do it ever. When you sing,
I'ld have you buy and sell so; so give alms;
Pray so; and for the ord'ring your affairs,
To sing them too. When you do dance, I wish
      you   140
A wave o' th' sea, that you might ever do

454

Nothing but that; move still, still so,
And own no other function. Each your doing,
So singular in each particular,
Crowns what you are doing in the present deed,   145
That all your acts are queens.
 Per.   O Doricles,
Your praises are too large. But that your youth,
And the true blood which peeps so fairly through't,
Do plainly give you out an unstain'd shepherd,
With wisdom I might fear, my Doricles,   150
You woo'd me the false way.
 Flo.   I think you have
As little skill to fear as I have purpose
To put you to't. But come; our dance, I pray!
Your hand, my Perdita. So turtles pair,
That never mean to part.
 Per.   I'll swear for 'em.   155
 Pol. This is the prettiest low-born lass that ever
Ran on the greensward. Nothing she does or seems
But smacks of something greater than herself,
Too noble for this place.
 Cam.   He tells her something
That makes her blood look out. Good sooth, she is   160
The queen of curds and cream.
 Clown.   Come on, strike up!
 Dor. Mopsa must be your mistress! Marry, garlic,
To mend her kissing with!
 Mop.   Now in good time!
 Clown. Not a word, a word! We stand upon our manners.
Come, strike up!   165
 [*Music.*] *Here a dance of Shepherds and Shepherdesses.*
 Pol. Pray, good shepherd, what fair swain is this
Which dances with your daughter?
 Shep. They call him Doricles, and boasts himself
To have a worthy feeding; but I have it
Upon his own report, and I believe it: 170
He looks like sooth. He says he loves my daughter.
I think so too; for never gaz'd the moon
Upon the water as he'll stand and read,
As 'twere, my daughter's eyes; and to be plain,
I think there is not half a kiss to choose   175
Who loves another best.
 Pol.   She dances featly.

 Shep. So she does anything, though I report it
That should be silent. If young Doricles
Do light upon her, she shall bring him that
Which he not dreams of.   180

    Enter *Servant.*

 Serv. O master! if you did but hear the pedlar at the door, you would never dance again after a tabor and pipe; no, the bagpipe could not move you! He sings several tunes faster than you'll tell money; he utters them as he had eaten ballads, and all men's ears grow to his tunes.   186
 Clown. He could never come better. He shall come in. I love a ballad but even too well, if it be doleful matter merrily set down, or a very pleasant thing indeed and sung lamentably.
 Serv. He hath songs for man or woman, of all sizes. No milliner can so fit his customers with gloves. He has the prettiest love songs for maids; so without bawdry, which is strange; with such delicate burthens of dildo's and fading's, 'jump her and thump her'! and where some stretch-mouth'd rascal would, as it were, mean mischief, and break a foul gap into the matter, he makes the maid to answer 'Whoop, do me no harm, good man!' puts him off, slights him, with 'Whoop, do me no harm, good man!'
 Pol. This is a brave fellow.
 Clown. Believe me, thou talkest of an admirable conceited fellow. Has he any unbraided wares?   204
 Serv. He hath ribbons of all the colours i' th' rainbow; points, more than all the lawyers in Bohemia can learnedly handle, though they come to him by th' gross; inkles, caddisses, cambrics, lawns. Why, he sings 'em over as they were gods or goddesses. You would think a smock were a she-angel, he so chants to the sleeve-hand and the work about the square on't.
 Clown. Prithee bring him in, and let him approach singing.   214
 Per. Forewarn him that he use no scurrilous words in 's tunes.   [*Exit Servant.*]
 Clown. You have of these pedlars that have more in them than you'ld think, sister.
 Per. Ay, good brother, or go about to think.

   Enter *Autolycus,* singing.

  Lawn as white as driven snow;   220
  Cypress black as e'er was crow;
  Gloves as sweet as damask roses;
  Masks for faces and for noses;
  Bugle bracelet, necklace amber,
  Perfume for a lady's chamber;   225

Golden quoifs and stomachers
For my lads to give their dears;
Pins, and poking sticks of steel :
What maids lack from head to heel.
Come buy of me, come! come buy, come buy!
Buy, lads, or else your lasses cry. Come buy!

Clown. If I were not in love with Mopsa,
thou shouldst take no money of me; but being
enthrall'd as I am, it will also be the bondage
of certain ribbons and gloves.   236
Mop. I was promis'd them against the feast,
but they come not too late now.
Dor. He hath promis'd you more than that,
or there be liars.   240
Mop. He hath paid you all he promis'd you.
May be he has paid you more, which will shame
you to give him again.
Clown. Is there no manners left among
maids? Will they wear their plackets where
they should bear their faces? Is there not milk-
ing time, when you are going to bed, or kiln-
hole, to whistle off these secrets, but you must
be tittle-tattling before all our guests? 'Tis
well they are whisp'ring. Charm your tongues,
and not a word more!   251
Mop. I have done. Come, you promis'd me a
tawdry-lace and a pair of sweet gloves.
Clown. Have I not told thee how I was coz-
en'd by the way and lost all my money?   255
Aut. And indeed, sir, there are cozeners
abroad. Therefore it behooves men to be wary.
Clown. Fear not thou, man; thou shalt lose
nothing here.
Aut. I hope so, sir, for I have about me
many parcels of charge.   261
Clown. What hast here? ballads?
Mop. Pray now buy some. I love a ballet in
print a-life, for then we are sure they are true.
Aut. Here's one, to a very doleful tune, how
a usurer's wife was brought to bed of twenty
money bags at a burthen, and how she long'd
to eat adders' heads, and toads carbonado'd.
Mop. Is it true, think you?
Aut. Very true, and but a month old.   270
Dor. Bless me from marrying a usurer!
Aut. Here's the midwive's name to't, one
Mistress Taleporter, and five or six honest wives
that were present. Why should I carry lies
abroad?   275
Mop. Pray you now buy it.
Clown. Come on, lay it by; and let's first see
moe ballads. We'll buy the other things anon.
Aut. Here's another ballad, of a fish that ap-
peared upon the coast on Wednesday the four-
score of April, forty thousand fadom above

water and sung this ballad against the hard
hearts of maids. It was thought she was a
woman, and was turn'd into a cold fish for she
would not exchange flesh with one that lov'd her.
The ballad is very pitiful, and as true.   286
Dor. Is it true too, think you?
Aut. Five justices' hands at it, and witnesses
more than my pack will hold.
Clown. Lay it by too. Another.   290
Aut. This is a merry ballad, but a very pretty
one.
Mop. Let's have some merry ones.
Aut. Why, this is a passing merry one, and
goes to the tune of 'Two maids wooing a man.'
There's scarce a maid westward but she sings it.
'Tis in request, I can tell you.   297
Mop. We can both sing it. If thou'lt bear a
part, thou shalt hear; 'tis in three parts.
Dor. We had the tune on't a month ago. 300
Aut. I can bear my part; you must know
'tis my occupation. Have at it with you!

Song.

Aut. Get you hence, for I must go
Where it fits not you to know.
  Dor. Whither?   *Mop.* O, whither?
  Dor. Whither?   305
Mop. It becomes thee oath full well
Thou to me thy secrets tell.
  Dor. Me too! Let me go thither.

Mop. Or thou goest to th' grange or mill.
Dor. If to either, thou dost ill.   310
  Aut. Neither.   *Dor.* What, neither?
    Aut. Neither.
Dor. Thou hast sworn my love to be.
Mop. Thou hast sworn it more to me.
  Then whither goest? Say, whither?   314

Clown. We'll have this song out anon by ourselves. My father and the gentlemen are in sad
talk, and we'll not trouble them. Come, bring
away your pack after me. Wenches, I'll buy for
you both. Pedlar, let's have the first choice.
Follow me, girls. [*Exit with Dorcas and Mopsa.*]
Aut. And you shall pay well for 'em.   321

Song.

Will you buy any tape,
  Or lace for your cape,
My dainty duck, my dear-a?
  Any silk, any thread,   325
  Any toys for your head
Of the new'st and fin'st, fin'st wear-a?
  Come to the pedlar.
  Money 's a meddler
That doth utter all men's ware-a.   330
                              Exit.

[Enter *Servant.*]

Serv. Master, there is three carters, three shepherds, three neatherds, three swineherds, that have made themselves all men of hair. They call themselves Saltiers; and they have a dance which the wenches say is a gallimaufry of gambols, because they are not in't; but they themselves are o' th' mind (if it be not too rough for some that know little but bowling) it will please plentifully.   339

Shep. Away! We'll none on't. Here has been too much homely foolery already. I know, sir, we weary you.

Pol. You weary those that refresh us. Pray let's see these four threes of herdsmen.   344

Serv. One three of them, by their own report, sir, hath danc'd before the King; and not the worst of the three but jumps twelve foot and a half by th' squire.   348

Shep. Leave your prating. Since these good men are pleas'd, let them come in; but quickly now.

Serv. Why, they stay at door, sir.

Here a Dance of twelve Satyrs.

Pol. [*to Shepherd*] O, father, you'll know more of that hereafter.
[*To Camillo*] Is it not too far gone? 'Tis time to part them.   355
He's simple and tells much. [*To Florizel*] How now, fair shepherd?
Your heart is full of something that does take
Your mind from feasting. Sooth, when I was young,
And handed love as you do, I was wont
To load my she with knacks. I would have ransack'd   360
The pedlar's silken treasury and have pour'd it
To her acceptance. You have let him go
And nothing marted with him. If your lass
Interpretation should abuse and call this
Your lack of love or bounty, you were straited
For a reply, at least if you make a care   366
Of happy holding her.

Flo.   Old sir, I know
She prizes not such trifles as these are.
The gifts she looks from me are pack'd and lock'd   369
Up in my heart, which I have given already,
But not deliver'd. O, hear me breathe my life
Before this ancient sir, who, it should seem,
Hath sometime lov'd! I take thy hand — this hand,
As soft as dove's down and as white as it,

Or Ethiopian's tooth, or the fann'd snow that's bolted   375
By th' northern blasts twice o'er.

Pol.   What follows this?
How prettily the young swain seems to wash
The hand was fair before! I have put you out;
But to your protestation! Let me hear
What you profess.

Flo.   Do, and be witness to't.   380

Pol. And this my neighbour too?

Flo.   And he, and more
Than he, and men — the earth, the heavens, and all!
That, were I crown'd the most imperial monarch —
Thereof most worthy — were I the fairest youth
That ever made eye swerve, had force and knowledge   385
More than was ever man's, I would not prize them
Without her love; for her employ them all;
Commend them and condemn them to her service
Or to their own perdition.

Pol.   Fairly offer'd.

Cam. This shows a sound affection.

Shep.   But, my daughter,
Say you the like to him?

Per.   I cannot speak   391
So well, nothing so well; no, nor mean better.
By th' pattern of mine own thoughts I cut out
The purity of his.

Shep.   Take hands, a bargain!
And, friends unknown, you shall bear witness to't: 395
I give my daughter to him, and will make
Her portion equal his.

Flo.   O, that must be
I' th' virtue of your daughter. One being dead,
I shall have more than you can dream of yet;
Enough then for your wonder. But come on,
Contract us fore these witnesses.

Shep.   Come, your hand;
And, daughter, yours.

Pol.   Soft, swain, awhile, beseech you.
Have you a father?

Flo.   I have; but what of him?

Pol. Knows he of this?

Flo.   He neither does nor shall.

Pol. Methinks a father   405
Is at the nuptial of his son a guest
That best becomes the table. Pray you once more,
Is not your father grown incapable
Of reasonable affairs? Is he not stupid

With age and alt'ring rheums? Can he speak?
hear? 410
Know man from man? dispute his own estate?
Lies he not bedrid? and again does nothing
But what he did being childish?
Flo. No, good sir;
He has his health, and ampler strength indeed
Than most have of his age.
Pol. By my white beard,
You offer him, if this be so, a wrong 416
Something unfilial. Reason my son
Should choose himself a wife; but as good
reason
The father (all whose joy is nothing else
But fair posterity) should hold some counsel
In such a business.
Flo. I yield all this; 421
But for some other reasons, my grave sir,
Which 'tis not fit you know, I not acquaint
My father of this business.
Pol. Let him know't.
Flo. He shall not.
Pol. Prithee let him.
Flo. No, he must not.
Shep. Let him, my son. He shall not need
to grieve 426
At knowing of thy choice.
Flo. Come, come, he must not.
Mark our contract.
Pol. [*Discovers himself.*] Mark your
divorce, young sir!
Whom son I dare not call. Thou art too base
To be acknowledg'd. Thou a sceptre's heir, 430
That thus affects a sheephook? — Thou, old
traitor,
I am sorry that by hanging thee I can but
Shorten thy life one week. — And thou, fresh
piece
Of excellent witchcraft, who of force must know
The royal fool thou cop'st with —
Shep. O, my heart!
Pol. I'll have thy beauty scratch'd with
briers and made 436
More homely than thy state. — For thee, fond
boy,
If I may ever know thou dost but sigh
That thou no more shalt see this knack (as never
I mean thou shalt), we'll bar thee from suc-
cession; 440
Not hold thee of our blood, no, not our kin,
Farre than Deucalion off! Mark thou my
words.
Follow us to the court. — Thou churl, for this
time,
Though full of our displeasure, yet we free thee

From the dead blow of it. — And you, enchant-
ment, 445
Worthy enough a herdsman; yea, him too
That makes himself (but for our honour therein)
Unworthy thee — if ever henceforth thou
These rural latches to his entrance open,
Or hoop his body more with thy embraces, 450
I will devise a death as cruel for thee
As thou art tender to't. *Exit.*
Per. Even here undone!
I was not much afeard; for once or twice
I was about to speak, and tell him plainly
The selfsame sun that shines upon his court 455
Hides not his visage from our cottage, but
Looks on alike. [*To Florizel*] Will't please you,
sir, be gone?
I told you what would come of this. Beseech
you
Of your own state take care. This dream of
mine — 459
Being now awake, I'll queen it no inch farther,
But milk my ewes and weep.
Cam. Why, how now, father?
Speak ere thou diest.
Shep. I cannot speak nor think,
Nor dare to know that which I know. [*To
Florizel*] O sir,
You have undone a man of fourscore three,
That thought to fill his grave in quiet; yea, 465
To die upon the bed my father died,
To lie close by his honest bones; but now
Some hangman must put on my shroud and
lay me
Where no priest shovels-in dust. [*To Perdita*]
O cursed wretch,
That knew'st this was the Prince and wouldst
adventure 470
To mingle faith with him! — Undone! undone!
If I might die within this hour, I have liv'd
To die when I desire. *Exit.*
Flo. Why look you so upon me?
I am but sorry, not afeard; delay'd,
But nothing alt'red. What I was, I am; 475
More straining on for plucking back; not fol-
lowing
My leash unwillingly.
Cam. Gracious my lord,
You know your father's temper. At this time
He will allow no speech (which I do guess
You do not purpose to him) and as hardly 480
Will he endure your sight as yet, I fear.
Then, till the fury of his highness settle,
Come not before him.
Flo. I not purpose it.
I think Camillo?

The song of Autolycus (George Rose), a "snapper-up of unconsidered trifles," introduces the first joyful note in the somber winter's tale (*Act IV, Scene II*)

THE WINTER'S TALE

PHOTOGRAPHS BY ANGUS MCBEAN
PRODUCED BY TENNENT PRODUCTIONS, LTD.

"Verily, you shall not go." At the request of Leontes (John Gielgud), her husband, Hermione (Diana Wynyard) invites Polixenes (Brewster Mason) to extend his already long visit (Act I, Scene II)

Polixenes' innocent conversation with Hermione wakens her husband's jealousy (Act I, Scene II)

Above: Temporizing with Leontes, whom he sees to be mad with jealousy, Lord Camillo (Michael Goodliffe) tells him he will poison Polixenes (Act I, Scene II)

Left: "You, sir, charge him too coldly." Leontes is suspicious of Hermione's warmth in pressing Polixenes to extend his stay as their guest (Act I, Scene II)

John Gielgud as King Leontes of Sicilia, sick with jealousy of his innocent wife, Hermione

"Let us be clear'd of being tyrannous, since we so openly proceed in justice." Leontes himself opens the trial of his wife, Hermione, who is accused of adultery (Act III, Scene II)

Left: Paulina (Flora Robson) promises to bring Hermione's child to its father (Act II, Scene II)

Below: Leontes completely disowns the child born to Hermione while in prison (Act II, Scene III)

The old shepherd (George Howe) and his son (Philip Guard) discover the gold which Leontes left for the care of Hermione's infant (Act III, Scene III)

Virginia McKenna as Hermione's child, Perdita, who has been brought up by the shepherd who found her on the seashore

"I cannot be mine own, nor any thing to any, if I be not thine." Polixenes' son, Prince Florizel (Richard Gale), plights his troth to Perdita at the sheep-shearing festival (Act IV, Scene III)

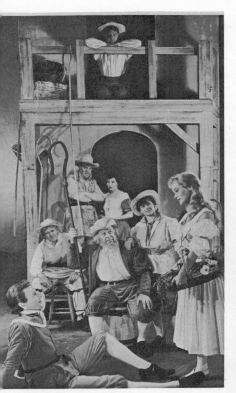

Below: "Reverend sirs, for you there's rosemary and rue; these keep seeming and savour all the winter long." Perdita offers herbs to Polixenes and Camillo, who have disguised themselves as curates and have come to the festival to look for Prince Florizel (*Act IV, Scene III*)

Florizel greets Perdita at the sheep-shearing festival (*Act IV, Scene III*)

Autolycus directs the ballad singing at the festival (*Act IV, Scene III*)

Having eloped with Perdita to Sicilia, Prince Florizel is welcomed by Leontes, who promises to attempt to reconcile Polixenes to the prince's marriage (Act V, Scene I)

Paulina, Antigonus' wife and the confidant of Hermione, devises a strange ruse to reunite the remorseful Leontes and his wife, whom he supposes to have died many years before

Autolycus meets the shepherds on their way to the court of Leontes (Act IV, Scene III)

Asking help of the shepherd, Autolycus skillfully picks his pocket (Act IV, Scene II)

Above: "No longer shall you gaze on't, lest your fancy may think anon it moves." Paulina reveals to Leontes what he thinks is a statue of Hermione by an Italian artist, but is, in fact, Hermione herself (*Act V, Scene III*)

Above: "Tell me, mine own, where hast thou been preserved?" Hermione is reunited with her lost daughter, Perdita. (*Act V, Scene III*)

Left: John Gielgud as Leontes, who paid with years of bitter loneliness for his cruel suspicion and persecution of Hermione

Hermione gently forgives Leontes for his cruelty to her (Act V, Scene III)

Cam.   Even he, my lord.
Per. How often have I told you 'twould be
thus!   485
How often said my dignity would last
But till 'twere known!
Flo.   It cannot fail but by
The violation of my faith; and then
Let nature crush the sides o' th' earth together
And mar the seeds within! Lift up thy looks.
From my succession wipe me, father! I   491
Am heir to my affection.
Cam.   Be advis'd.
Flo. I am, and by my fancy. If my reason
Will thereto be obedient, I have reason;   494
If not, my senses, better pleas'd with madness,
Do bid it welcome.
Cam.   This is desperate, sir.
Flo. So call it; but it does fulfil my vow;
I needs must think it honesty. Camillo,
Not for Bohemia nor the pomp that may
Be thereat glean'd, for all the sun sees or 500
The close earth wombs or the profound sea
hides
In unknown fadoms, will I break my oath
To this my fair belov'd. Therefore, I pray you,
As you have ever been my father's honour'd
friend,
When he shall miss me (as, in faith, I mean
not   505
To see him any more), cast your good counsels
Upon his passion. Let myself and Fortune
Tug for the time to come. This you may know,
And so deliver: I am put to sea
With her who here I cannot hold on shore;   510
And most opportune to our need, I have
A vessel rides fast by, but not prepar'd
For this design. What course I mean to hold
Shall nothing benefit your knowledge nor
Concern me the reporting.
Cam.   O my lord,   515
I would your spirit were easier for advice
Or stronger for your need!
Flo.   Hark, Perdita.
                              [*Takes her aside.*]
[*To Camillo*] I'll hear you by-and-by.
Cam.   He's irremovable,
Resolv'd for flight. Now were I happy if
His going I could frame to serve my turn, 520
Save him from danger, do him love and honour,
Purchase the sight again of dear Sicilia
And that unhappy king my master, whom
I so much thirst to see.
Flo.   Now, good Camillo,
I am so fraught with curious business that 525
I leave out ceremony.

Cam.   Sir, I think
You have heard of my poor services i' th' love
That I have borne your father?
Flo.   Very nobly
Have you deserv'd. It is my father's music
To speak your deeds; not little of his care 530
To have them recompens'd as thought on.
Cam.   Well, my lord,
If you may please to think I love the King
And, through him, what is nearest to him,
which is
Your gracious self, embrace but my direction,
If your more ponderous and settled project 535
May suffer alteration. On mine honour,
I'll point you where you shall have such re-
ceiving
As shall become your Highness, where you may
Enjoy your mistress, — from the whom I see
There's no disjunction to be made but by   540
(As heavens forfend!) your ruin,—marry her;
And with my best endeavours, in your absence,
Your discontenting father strive to qualify
And bring him up to liking.
Flo.   How, Camillo,
May this (almost a miracle) be done?   545
That I may call thee something more than man,
And after that trust to thee.
Cam.   Have you thought on
A place whereto you'll go?
Flo.   Not any yet;
But as th' unthought-on accident is guilty
To what we wildly do, so we profess   550
Ourselves to be the slaves of chance and flies
Of every wind that blows.
Cam.   Then list to me.
This follows, if you will not change your pur-
pose,
But undergo this flight: make for Sicilia,
And there present yourself and your fair
princess   555
(For so I see she must be) fore Leontes.
She shall be habited as it becomes
The partner of your bed. Methinks I see
Leontes opening his free arms and weeping
His welcomes forth; asks thee, the son, for-
giveness,   560
As 'twere i' th' father's person; kisses the
hands
Of your fresh princess; o'er and o'er divides him
'Twixt his unkindness and his kindness: th' one
He chides to hell, and bids the other grow
Faster than thought or time.
Flo.   Worthy Camillo,
What colour for my visitation shall I   566
Hold up before him?

Cam.   Sent by the King your father
To greet him and to give him comforts. Sir,
The manner of your bearing towards him, with
What you (as from your father) shall deliver,
Things known betwixt us three, I'll write you
          down,   571
The which shall point you forth at every sitting
What you must say; that he shall not perceive
But that you have your father's bosom there
And speak his very heart.
Flo.   I am bound to you.
There is some sap in this!
Cam.   A course more promising
Than a wild dedication of yourselves
To unpath'd waters, undream'd shores, most
          certain
To miseries enough; no hope to help you,
But, as you shake off one, to take another; 580
Nothing so certain as your anchors, who
Do their best office if they can but stay you
Where you'll be loath to be. Besides, you know
Prosperity's the very bond of love,
Whose fresh complexion and whose heart to-
          gether   585
Affliction alters.
Per.   One of these is true.
I think affliction may subdue the cheek,
But not take in the mind.
Cam.   Yea? say you so?
There shall not at your father's house these
          seven years
Be born another such.
Flo.   My good Camillo, 590
She is as forward of her breeding as
She is i' th' rear 'our birth.
Cam.   I cannot say 'tis pity
She lacks instructions, for she seems a mistress
To most that teach.
Per.   Your pardon, sir! For this
I'll blush you thanks.
Flo.   My prettiest Perdita! 595
But, O, the thorns we stand upon! Camillo —
Preserver of my father, now of me,
The medicine of our house — how shall we do?
We are not furnish'd like Bohemia's son,
Nor shall appear in Sicilia.
Cam.   My lord, 600
Fear none of this. I think you know my
          fortunes
Do all lie there. It shall be so my care
To have you royally appointed as if
The scene you play were mine. For instance, sir,
That you may know you shall not want — one
          word.   605
          [*They talk aside.*]

Enter *Autolycus.*

Aut. Ha, ha! what a fool Honesty is! and
Trust, his sworn brother, a very simple gentleman! I have sold all my trumpery. Not a
counterfeit stone, not a ribbon, glass, pomander,
brooch, table book, ballad, knife, tape, glove,
shoe-tie, bracelet, horn ring, to keep my pack
from fasting! They throng who should buy
first, as if my trinkets had been hallowed and
brought a benediction to the buyer; by which
means I saw whose purse was best in picture;
and what I saw, to my good use I rememb'red.
My clown (who wants but something to be a
reasonable man) grew so in love with the
wenches' song that he would not stir his pettitoes till he had both tune and words, which so
drew the rest of the herd to me that all their
other senses stuck in ears. You might have
pinch'd a placket, it was senseless; 'twas
nothing to geld a codpiece of a purse; I would
have fil'd keys off that hung in chains. No
hearing, no feeling, but my sir's song, and admiring the nothing of it! So that, in this time
of lethargy, I pick'd and cut most of their
festival purses; and had not the old man come
in with a whoobub against his daughter and the
King's son and scar'd my choughs from the
chaff, I had not left a purse alive in the whole
army.   631
          [*Camillo, Florizel, and Perdita come for-
          ward.*]

Cam. Nay, but my letters, by this means
          being there
So soon as you arrive, shall clear that doubt.
Flo. And those that you'll procure from King
          Leontes?
Cam. Shall satisfy your father.
Per.   Happy be you! 635
All that you speak shows fair.
Cam. [*sees Autolycus*] Who have we here?
We'll make an instrument of this; omit
Nothing may give us aid.
Aut. [*aside*] If they have overheard me now
— why, hanging!   640
Cam. How now, good fellow? Why shak'st
thou so? Fear not, man. Here's no harm in-
tended to thee.
Aut. I am a poor fellow, sir.   644
Cam. Why, be so still. Here's nobody will
steal that from thee. Yet, for the outside of thy
poverty, we must make an exchange. Therefore
discase thee instantly (thou must think there's
a necessity in't) and change garments with this
gentleman. Though the pennyworth (on his

side) be the worst, yet hold thee, there's some
boot.   [*Gives money.*]
Aut. I am a poor fellow, sir. [*Aside*] I know
ye well enough.
Cam. Nay, prithee dispatch! The gentleman
is half flay'd already.   655
Aut. Are you in earnest, sir? [*Aside*] I smell
the trick on't.
Flo. Dispatch, I prithee.
Aut. Indeed I have had earnest, but I cannot
with conscience take it.   660
Cam. Unbuckle, unbuckle.
[*Florizel and Autolycus exchange garments.*]
Fortunate mistress (let my prophecy
Come home to ye!), you must retire yourself
Into some covert; take your sweetheart's hat
And pluck it o'er your brows; muffle your face;
Dismantle you; and (as you can) disliken 666
The truth of your own seeming, that you may
(For I do fear eyes over) to shipboard
Get undescried.
Per.   I see the play so lies
That I must bear a part.
Cam.   No remedy.   670
Have you done there?
Flo.   Should I now meet my father,
He would not call me son.
Cam.   Nay, you shall have no hat.
                              [*Gives it to Perdita.*]
Come, lady, come. Farewell, my friend.
Aut.   Adieu, sir.
Flo. O Perdita, what have we twain forgot!
Pray you a word.   [*They converse apart.*]
Cam. [*aside*] What I do next shall be to tell
the King   676
Of this escape and whither they are bound;
Wherein, my hope is, I shall so prevail
To force him after; in whose company
I shall review Sicilia, for whose sight   680
I have a woman's longing.
Flo.   Fortune speed us!
Thus we set on, Camillo, to the seaside.
Cam. The swifter speed the better.
          Exit [*with Florizel and Perdita*].
Aut. I understand the business, I hear it. To
have an open ear, a quick eye, and a nimble
hand is necessary for a cutpurse; a good nose
is requisite also, to smell out work for th' other
senses. I see this is the time that the unjust
man doth thrive. What an exchange had this
been without boot! What a boot is here with
this exchange! Sure the gods do this year con-
nive at us, and we may do anything extempore.
The Prince himself is about a piece of iniquity
— stealing away from his father with his clog at

his heels. If I thought it were a piece of honesty
to acquaint the King withal, I would not do't.
I hold it the more knavery to conceal it; and
therein am I constant to my profession.   698

Enter Clown and Shepherd.

Aside, aside! Here is more matter for a hot
brain. Every lane's end, every shop, church,
session, hanging, yields a careful man work.
Clown. See, see! What a man you are now!
There is no other way but to tell the King she's
a changeling and none of your flesh and blood.
Shep. Nay, but hear me.   706
Clown. Nay, but hear me.
Shep. Go to, then.
Clown. She being none of your flesh and
blood, your flesh and blood has not offended the
King, and so your flesh and blood is not to be
punish'd by him. Show those things you found
about her — those secret things, all but what
she has with her. This being done, let the law
go whistle; I warrant you.   716
Shep. I will tell the King all, every word!
yea, and his son's pranks too; who, I may say,
is no honest man, neither to his father nor to me,
to go about to make me the King's brother-in-
law.   721
Clown. Indeed, brother-in-law was the farthest off you could have been to him, and
then how your blood had been the dearer by I know
not how much an ounce.   725
Aut. [*aside*] Very wisely, puppies!
Shep. Well, let us to the King. There is that
in this farthel will make him scratch his beard.
Aut. [*aside*] I know not what impediment
this complaint may be to the flight of my
master.   730
Clown. Pray heartily he be at' palace.
Aut. [*aside*] Though I am not naturally honest, I am so sometimes by chance. Let me
pocket up my pedlar's excrement. *Takes off
his false beard.*] How now, rustics? Whither
are you bound?   736
Shep. To th' palace, an it like your worship.
Aut. Your affairs there? what? with whom?
the condition of that farthel? the place of your
dwelling? your names? your ages? of what
having? breeding? and anything that is fitting
to be known, discover.   742
Clown. We are but plain fellows, sir.
Aut. A lie! You are rough and hairy. Let
me have no lying. It becomes none but trades-
men, and they often give us soldiers the lie; but
we pay them for it with stamped coin, not stab-
bing steel; therefore they do not give us the lie.

Clown. Your worship had like to have given us one, if you had not taken yourself with the manner. 752

Shep. Are you a courtier, an't like you, sir?

Aut. Whether it like me or no, I am a courtier. Seest thou not the air of the court in these enfoldings? Hath not my gait in it the measure of the court? Receives not thy nose court odour from me? Reflect I not on thy baseness court contempt? Think'st thou, for that I insinuate, or toaze from thee thy business, I am therefore no courtier? I am courtier cap-a-pe; and one that will either push on or pluck back thy business there. Whereupon I command thee to open thy affair.

Shep. My business, sir, is to the King. 765

Aut. What advocate hast thou to him?

Shep. I know not, an't like you.

Clown. [*aside to Shepherd*] Advocate's the court word for a pheasant. Say you have none.

Shep. None, sir. I have no pheasant, cock nor hen. 771

Aut. How blessed are we that are not simple men!
Yet Nature might have made me as these are;
Therefore I will not disdain.

Clown. [*aside to Shepherd*] This cannot be but a great courtier. 775

Shep. [*aside to Clown*] His garments are rich, but he wears them not handsomely.

Clown. [*aside to Shepherd*] He seems to be the more noble in being fantastical. A great man, I'll warrant; I know by the picking on's teeth. 780

Aut. The farthel there? What's i' th' farthel? Wherefore that box?

Shep. Sir, there lies such secrets in this farthel and box which none must know but the King, and which he shall know within this hour if I may come to th' speech of him. 786

Aut. Age, thou hast lost thy labour.

Shep. Why, sir?

Aut. The King is not at the palace. He is gone aboard a new ship to purge melancholy and air himself; for, if thou be'st capable of things serious, thou must know the King is full of grief. 792

Shep. So 'tis said, sir — about his son, that should have married a shepherd's daughter.

Aut. If that shepherd be not in handfast, let him fly! The curses he shall have, the tortures he shall feel. will break the back of man, the heart of monster.

Clown. Think you so, sir? 799

Aut. Not he alone shall suffer what wit can make heavy and vengeance bitter; but those that are germane to him, though remov'd fifty times, shall all come under the hangman; which, though it be great pity, yet it is necessary. An old sheep-whistling rogue, a ram-tender, to offer to have his daughter come into grace? Some say he shall be ston'd; but that death is too soft for him, say I. Draw our throne into a sheepcote? All deaths are too few, the sharpest too easy. 809

Clown. Has the old man e'er a son, sir, do you hear, an't like you, sir?

Aut. He has a son — who shall be flay'd alive; then, 'nointed over with honey, set on the head of a wasps' nest; then stand till he be tiree quarters and a dram dead; then recover'd again with aqua-vitæ or some other hot infusion; then, raw as he is, and in the hottest day prognostication proclaims, shall he be set against a brick wall, the sun looking with a southward eye upon him, where he is to behold him with flies blown to death. But what talk we of these traitorly rascals, whose miseries are to be smil'd at, their offences being so capital? Tell me (for you seem to be honest plain men) what you have to the King. Being something gently consider'd, I'll bring you where he is aboard, tender your persons to his presence, whisper him in your behalfs; and if it be in man, besides the King, to effect your suits, here is man shall do it. 829

Clown. [*aside to Shepherd*] He seems to be of great authority. Close with him, give him gold; and though Authority be a stubborn bear, yet he is oft led by the nose with gold. Show the inside of your purse to the outside of his hand, and no more ado. Remember — ston'd, and flay'd alive. 835

Shep. An't please you, sir, to undertake the business for us, here is that gold I have. I'll make it as much more, and leave this young man in pawn till I bring it you.

Aut. After I have done what I promised? 840

Shep. Ay, sir.

Aut. Well, give me the moiety. Are you a party in this business?

Clown. In some sort, sir; but though my case be a pitiful one, I hope I shall not be flay'd out of it. 845

Aut. O, that's the case of the shepherd's son! Hang him, he'll be made an example.

Clown. [*aside to Shepherd*] Comfort, good comfort! We must to the King and show our.

strange sights. He must know 'tis none of your
daughter nor my sister: we are gone else. —
Sir, I will give you as much as this old man does
when the business is performed, and remain, as
he says, your pawn till it be brought you.   854
Aut. I will trust you. Walk before toward
the seaside; go on the right hand. I will but
look upon the hedge, and follow you.
                                    [*Steps aside.*]
Clown. We are bless'd in this man, as I may
say; even bless'd.   859
Shep. Let's before, as he bids us. He was
provided to do us good.
                    [*Exeunt Shepherd and Clown.*]

Aut. If I had a mind to be honest, I see Fortune would not suffer me; she drops booties in
my mouth. I am courted now with a double
occasion — gold, and a means to do the Prince
my master good; which who knows how that
may turn back to my advancement? I will
bring these two moles, these blind ones, aboard
him. If he think it fit to shore them again, and
that the complaint they have to the King concerns him nothing, let him call me rogue for
being so far officious; for I am proof against
that title and what shame else belongs to't. To
him will I present them; there may be matter
in it.   *Exit.*

ACT V. Scene I. [*Sicilia. The Palace of* Leontes.]

Enter *Leontes, Cleomenes, Dion, Paulina.*

Cleo. Sir, you have done enough, and have
    perform'd
A saintlike sorrow. No fault could you make
Which you have not redeem'd; indeed, paid
    down
More penitence than done trespass. At the last,
Do as the heavens have done: forget your evil;
With them, forgive yourself.
Leon.   Whilst I remember
Her and her virtues, I cannot forget
My blemishes in them, and so still think of
The wrong I did myself; which was so much
That heirless it hath made my kingdom and 10
Destroy'd the sweet'st companion that e'er man
Bred his hopes out of.
Paul.   True, too true, my lord!
If, one by one, you wedded all the world,
Or from the all that are took something good
To make a perfect woman, she you kill'd   15
Would be unparallel'd.
Leon.   I think so. Kill'd?
She I kill'd? I did so; but thou strik'st me
Sorely to say I did. It is as bitter
Upon thy tongue as in my thought. Now,
    good now,
Say so but seldom.
Cleo.   Not at all, good lady.   20
You might have spoken a thousand things that
    would
Have done the time more benefit and grac'd
Your kindness better.
Paul.   You are one of those
Would have him wed again.
Dion.   If you would not so,
You pity not the state nor the remembrance 25

Of his most sovereign name; consider little
What dangers, by his Highness' fail of issue,
May drop upon his kingdom and devour
Incertain lookers-on. What were more holy
Than to rejoice the former queen is well?   30
What holier than, for royalty's repair,
For present comfort and for future good,
To bless the bed of majesty again
With a sweet fellow to't?
Paul.   There is none worthy,
Respecting her that's gone. Besides, the gods
Will have fulfill'd their secret purposes;   36
For has not the divine Apollo said,
Is't not the tenour of his oracle,
That King Leontes shall not have an heir
Till his lost child be found? Which that it shall
Is all as monstrous to our human reason   41
As my Antigonus to break his grave
And come again to me; who, on my life,
Did perish with the infant. 'Tis your counsel
My lord should to the heavens be contrary, 45
Oppose against their wills. [*To Leontes*] Care
    not for issue;
The crown will find an heir. Great Alexander
Left his to th' worthiest; so his successor
Was like to be the best.
Leon.   Good Paulina,
Who hast the memory of Hermione,   50
I know, in honour, O that ever I
Had squar'd me to thy counsel! Then, even now,
I might have look'd upon my queen's full eyes,
Have taken treasure from her lips —
Paul.   And left them
More rich for what they yielded.
Leon.   Thou speak'st truth.
No more such wives; therefore no wife! One
    worse,   56

463

And better us'd, would make her sainted spirit
Again possess her corpse, and on this stage
Where we offenders now, appear soul-vex'd,
And begin, 'Why to me — ?'
Paul.   Had she such power, 60
She had just cause.
Leon.   She had, and would incense me
To murther her I married.
Paul.   I should so.
Were I the ghost that walk'd, I'ld bid you
     mark
Her eye, and tell me for what dull part in't
You chose her; then I'ld shriek, that even your
     ears   65
Should rift to hear me, and the words that
     follow'd
Should be, 'Remember mine!'
Leon.   Stars, stars!
And all eyes else dead coals. Fear thou no
     wife;
I'll have no wife, Paulina.
Paul.   Will you swear
Never to marry but by my free leave?   70
Leon. Never, Paulina, so be bless'd my
     spirit!
Paul. Then, good my lords, bear witness to
     his oath.
Cleo. You tempt him over-much.
Paul.   Unless another,
As like Hermione as is her picture,
Affront his eye.
Cleo.   Good madam —
Paul.   I have done. 75
Yet, if my lord will marry — if you will, sir,
No remedy but you will — give me the office
To choose you a queen. She shall not be so
     young
As was your former; but she shall be such
As, walk'd your first queen's ghost, it should
     take joy   80
To see her in your arms.
Leon.   My true Paulina,
We shall not marry till thou bid'st us.
Paul.   That
Shall be when your first queen's again in breath;
Never till then.

Enter a *Servant*.

Serv. One that gives out himself Prince
     Florizel,   85
Son of Polixenes, with his princess (she
The fairest I have yet beheld) desires access
To your high presence.
Leon.   What with him? He comes not
Like to his father's greatness. His approach,

So out of circumstance and sudden, tells us 90
'Tis not a visitation fram'd, but forc'd
By need and accident. What train?
Serv.   But few,
And those but mean.
Leon.   His princess, say you, with him?
Serv. Ay, the most peerless piece of earth, I
     think,
That e'er the sun shone bright on.
Paul.   O Hermione,
As every present time doth boast itself   96
Above a better, gone, so must thy grave
Give way to what's seen now! Sir, you your-
     self
Have said and writ so, but your writing now
Is colder than that theme: 'She had not been
Nor was not to be equall'd.' Thus your verse
Flow'd with her beauty once. 'Tis shrewdly
     ebb'd
To say you have seen a better.
Serv.   Pardon, madam.
The one I have almost forgot — your pardon.
The other, when she has obtain'd your eye, 105
Will have your tongue too. This is a creature,
Would she begin a sect, might quench the zeal
Of all professors else, make proselytes
Of who she but bid follow.
Paul.   How? not women?
Serv. Women will love her that she is a
     woman   110
More worth than any man; men, that she is
The rarest of all women.
Leon.   Go, Cleomenes;
Yourself, assisted with your honour'd friends,
Bring them to our embracement.
     Exit [*Cleomenes*].
     Still, 'tis strange
He thus should steal upon us.
Paul.   Had our Prince, 115
Jewel of children, seen this hour, he had pair'd
Well with this lord. There was not full a
     month
Between their births.
Leon. Prithee, no more! cease! Thou know'st
He dies to me again when talk'd of. Sure, 120
When I shall see this gentleman, thy speeches
Will bring me to consider that which may
Unfurnish me of reason.

Enter *Florizel, Perdita, Cleomenes*, and others.

     They are come.
Your mother was most true to wedlock, Prince,
For she did print your royal father off,   125
Conceiving you. Were I but twenty-one,
Your father's image is so hit in you,

464

His very air, that I should call you brother,
As I did him, and speak of something wildly
By us perform'd before. Most dearly welcome!
And your fair princess — goddess! O, alas, 131
I lost a couple that 'twixt heaven and earth
Might thus have stood begetting wonder, as
You, gracious couple, do! and then I lost
(All mine own folly) the society, 135
Amity too, of your brave father, whom,
Though bearing misery, I desire my life
Once more to look on him.
  Flo.   By his command
Have I here touch'd Sicilia, and from him
Give you all greetings that a king, at friend, 140
Can send his brother; and, but infirmity,
Which waits upon worn times, hath something
  seiz'd
His wish'd ability, he had himself
The lands and waters 'twixt your throne and
  his
Measur'd to look upon you; whom he loves 145
(He bade me say so) more than all the sceptres
And those that bear them living.
  Leon.   O my brother,
Good gentleman, the wrongs I have done thee
  stir
Afresh within me; and these thy offices,
So rarely kind, are as interpreters 150
Of my behindhand slackness! Welcome hither
As is the spring to th' earth. And hath he too
Expos'd this paragon to th' fearful usage
(At least ungentle) of the dreadful Neptune,
To greet a man not worth her pains, much less
Th' adventure of her person?
  Flo.   Good my lord, 156
She came from Libya.
  Leon.   Where the warlike Smalus,
That noble honour'd lord, is fear'd and lov'd?
  Flo. Most royal sir, from thence; from him,
  whose daughter
His tears proclaim'd his, parting with her.
  Thence 160
(A prosperous south wind friendly) we have
  cross'd,
To execute the charge my father gave me
For visiting your Highness. My best train
I have from your Sicilian shores dismiss'd;
Who for Bohemia bend, to signify 165
Not only my success in Libya, sir,
But my arrival and my wife's in safety
Here where we are.
  Leon.   The blessed gods
Purge all infection from our air whilst you
Do climate here! You have a holy father, 170
A graceful gentleman, against whose person,

So sacred as it is, I have done sin,
For which the heavens, taking angry note,
Have left me issueless; and your father's
  bless'd,
As he from heaven merits it, with you, 175
Worthy his goodness. What might I have been,
Might I a son and daughter now have look'd
  on,
Such goodly things as you!
            Enter a Lord.
  Lord.   Most noble sir,
That which I shall report will bear no credit,
Were not the proof so nigh. Please you, great
  sir, 180
Bohemia greets you from himself by me;
Desires you to attach his son, who has
(His dignity and duty both cast off)
Fled from his father, from his hopes, and with
A shepherd's daughter.
  Leon.   Where's Bohemia? Speak.
  Lord. Here in your city. I now came from
  him. 186
I speak amazedly, and it becomes
My marvel and my message. To your court
Whiles he was hast'ning (in the chase, it seems,
Of this fair couple), meets he on the way 190
The father of this seeming lady and
Her brother, having both their country quitted
With this young prince.
  Flo.   Camillo has betray'd me,
Whose honour and whose honesty till now
Endur'd all weathers.
  Lord.   Lay't so to his charge. 195
He's with the King your father.
  Leon.   Who? Camillo?
  Lord. Camillo, sir. I spake with him; who
  now
Has these poor men in question. Never saw I
Wretches so quake. They kneel, they kiss the
  earth;
Forswear themselves as often as they speak.
Bohemia stops his ears, and threatens them 201
With divers deaths in death.
  Per.   O my poor father!
The heaven sets spies upon us, will not have
Our contract celebrated.
  Leon.   You are married?
  Flo. We are not, sir, nor are we like to be.
The stars, I see, will kiss the valleys first. 206
The odds for high and low 's alike.
  Leon.   My lord,
Is this the daughter of a king?
  Flo.   She is,
When once she is my wife.

Leon. That 'once,' I see, by your good
father's speed, 210
Will come on very slowly. I am sorry,
Most sorry, you have broken from his liking
Where you were tied in duty; and as sorry
Your choice is not so rich in worth as beauty,
That you might well enjoy her.
Flo. Dear, look up.
Though Fortune, visible an enemy, 216
Should chase us, with my father, pow'r no jot
Hath she to change our loves. Beseech you,
sir,
Remember since you ow'd no more to time
Than I do now. With thought of such affec-
tions, 220
Step forth mine advocate. At your request
My father will grant precious things as trifles.
Leon. Would he do so, I'ld beg your precious
mistress,
Which he counts but a trifle.
Paul. Sir, my liege,
Your eye hath too much youth in't. Not a
month 225
Fore your queen died, she was more worth
such gazes
Than what you look on now.
Leon. I thought of her
Even in these looks I made. [*To Florizel*] But
your petition
Is yet unanswer'd. I will to your father.
Your honour not o'erthrown by your desires,
I am friend to them and you. Upon which
errand 231
I now go toward him; therefore follow me,
And mark what way I make. Come, good my
lord. *Exeunt.*

Scene II. [*Sicilia. Before the Palace
of* Leontes.]

Enter *Autolycus* and a *Gentleman.*

Aut. Beseech you, sir, were you present at
this relation?
1. Gent. I was by at the opening of the farthel,
heard the old shepherd deliver the manner how
he found it; whereupon, after a little amazedness, we were all commanded out of the chamber. Only this, methought, I heard the shepherd
say — he found the child. 8
Aut. I would most gladly know the issue of it.
1. Gent. I make a broken delivery of the business; but the changes I perceived in the King
and Camillo were very notes of admiration.

They seem'd almost, with staring on one another, to tear the cases of their eyes. There was
speech in their dumbness, language in their
very gesture. They look'd as they had heard
of a world ransom'd, or one destroyed. A
notable passion of wonder appeared in them;
but the wisest beholder that knew no more
but seeing, could not say if th' importance were
joy or sorrow; but in the extremity of the
one it must needs be. 21

Enter another *Gentleman.*

Here comes a gentleman that happily knows
more. The news, Rogero?
2. Gent. Nothing but bonfires. The oracle is
fulfill'd; the King's daughter is found. Such a
deal of wonder is broken out within this hour
that ballad-makers cannot be able to express it.

Enter another *Gentleman.*

Here comes the Lady Paulina's steward; he
can deliver you more. How goes it now, sir?
This news, which is call'd true, is so like an old
tale that the verity of it is in strong suspicion.
Has the King found his heir? 32
3. Gent. Most true, if ever truth were pregnant by circumstance. That which you hear
you'll swear you see, there is such unity in the
proofs. The mantle of Queen Hermione's; her
jewel about the neck of it; the letters of Antigonus found with it, which they know to be
his character; the majesty of the creature, in
resemblance of the mother; the affection of
nobleness which nature shows above her breeding, and many other evidences — proclaim her
with all certainty to be the King's daughter.
Did you see the meeting of the two kings?
2. Gent. No. 45
3. Gent. Then have you lost a sight which
was to be seen, cannot be spoken of. There
might you have beheld one joy crown another,
so and in such manner that it seem'd sorrow
wept to take leave of them; for their joy waded
in tears. There was casting up of eyes, holding
up of hands, with countenance of such distraction that they were to be known by garment,
not by favour. Our king, being ready to leap
out of himself for joy of his found daughter, as
if that joy were now become a loss, cries, 'O, thy
mother, thy mother!' then asks Bohemia forgiveness; then embraces his son-in-law; then
again worries he his daughter with clipping her.
Now he thanks the old shepherd, which stands
by like a weather-bitten conduit of many kings'
reigns. I never heard of such another encoun-

ter, which lames report to follow it and undoes description to do it.

2. Gent. What, pray you, became of Antigonus, that carried hence the child?   65

3. Gent. Like an old tale still, which will have matter to rehearse, though credit be asleep and not an ear open. He was torn to pieces with a bear! This avouches the shepherd's son, who has not only his innocence (which seems much) to justify him, but a handkerchief and rings of his that Paulina knows.

1. Gent. What became of his bark and his followers?   74

3. Gent. Wrack'd the same instant of their master's death, and in the view of the shepherd; so that all the instruments which aided to expose the child were even then lost when it was found. But, O, the noble combat that 'twixt joy and sorrow was fought in Paulina! She had one eye declin'd for the loss of her husband, another elevated that the oracle was fulfill'd. She lifted the Princess from the earth, and so locks her in embracing as if she would pin her to her heart, that she might no more be in danger of losing.

1. Gent. The dignity of this act was worth the audience of kings and princes, for by such was it acted.   88

3. Gent. One of the prettiest touches of all, and that which angled for mine eyes (caught the water, though not the fish) was when, at the relation of the Queen's death (with the manner how she came to't bravely confess'd and lamented by the King), how attentiveness wounded his daughter, till, from one sign of dolour to another, she did (with an 'Alas!'), I would fain say, bleed tears; for I am sure my heart wept blood. Who was most marble there changed colour; some swounded, all sorrowed. If all the world could have seen't, the woe had been universal.   100

1. Gent. Are they returned to the court?

3. Gent. No. The Princess hearing of her mother's statue, which is in the keeping of Paulina — a piece many years in doing, and now newly perform'd, by that rare Italian master, Julio Romano, who, had he himself eternity and could put breath into his work, would beguile Nature of her custom, so perfectly he is her ape — he so near to Hermione hath done Hermione that they say one would speak to her and stand in hope of answer. Thither with all greediness of affection are they gone, and there they intend to sup.   112

2. Gent. I thought she had some great matter there in hand; for she hath privately twice or thrice a day, ever since the death of Hermione, visited that removed house. Shall we thither, and with our company piece the rejoicing?   11?

1. Gent. Who would be thence that has the benefit of access? Every wink of an eye, some new grace will be born. Our absence makes us unthrifty to our knowledge. Let's along.   121

Exeunt [Gentlemen].

Aut. Now, had I not the dash of my former life in me, would preferment drop on my head. I brought the old man and his son aboard the Prince; told him I heard them talk of a farthel and I know not what; but he at that time over-fond of the shepherd's daughter (so he then took her to be), who began to be much seasick, and himself little better, extremity of weather continuing, this mystery remained undiscover'd. But 'tis all one to me; for had I been the finder-out of this secret, it would not have relish'd among my other discredits.

Enter Shepherd *and* Clown, [richly dressed].

Here come those I have done good to against my will, and already appearing in the blossoms of their fortune.   136

Shep. Come, boy. I am past moe children, but thy sons and daughters will be all gentlemen born.

Clown. You are well met, sir. You denied to fight with me this other day, because I was no gentleman born. See you these clothes? Say you see them not and think me still no gentleman born. You were best say these robes are not gentlemen born. Give me the lie, do; and try whether I am not now a gentleman born.

Aut. I know you are now, sir, a gentleman born.

Clown. Ay, and have been so any time these four hours.

Shep. And so have I, boy.   149

Clown. So you have. But I was a gentleman born before my father; for the King's son took me by the hand and call'd me brother; and then the two kings call'd my father brother; and then the Prince, my brother, and the Princess, my sister, call'd my father father; and so we wept — and there was the first gentleman-like tears that ever we shed.   156

Shep. We may live, son, to shed many more.

Clown. Ay! or else 'twere hard luck, being in so preposterous estate as we are.   159

Aut. I humbly beseech you, sir, to pardon me all the faults I have committed to your worship, and to give me your good report to the Prince my master.

Shep. Prithee, son, do; for we must be gentle, now we are gentlemen. 165

Clown. Thou wilt amend thy life?

Aut. Ay, an it like your good worship.

Clown. Give me thy hand. I will swear to the Prince thou art as honest a true fellow as any is in Bohemia. 170

Shep. You may say it, but not swear it.

Clown. Not swear it, now I am a gentleman? Let boors and franklins say it; I'll swear it.

Shep. How if it be false, son? 174

Clown. If it be ne'er so false, a true gentleman may swear it in the behalf of his friend. And I'll swear to the Prince thou art a tall fellow of thy hands, and that thou wilt not be drunk; but I know thou art no tall fellow of thy hands, and that thou wilt be drunk. But I'll swear it; and I would thou wouldst be a tall fellow of thy hands. 181

Aut. I will prove so, sir, to my power.

Clown. Ay, by any means prove a tall fellow. If I do not wonder how thou dar'st venture to be drunk, not being a tall fellow, trust me not. Hark! the kings and the princes, our kindred, are going to see the Queen's picture. Come, follow us. We'll be thy good masters. *Exeunt.*

Scene III. [*Sicilia. A chapel in Paulina's house.*]

Enter Leontes, Polixenes, Florizel, Perdita, Camillo, Paulina, Lords, &c.

Leon. O grave and good Paulina, the great comfort
That I have had of thee!

Paul.   What, sovereign sir,
I did not well, I meant well. All my services
You have paid home. But that you have vouchsaf'd,
With your crown'd brother and these your contracted 5
Heirs of your kingdoms, my poor house to visit,
It is a surplus of your grace, which never
My life may last to answer.

Leon.   O Paulina,
We honour you with trouble. But we came
To see the statue of our queen. Your gallery
Have we pass'd through, not without much content 11
In many singularities; but we saw not
That which my daughter came to look upon,
The statue of her mother.

Paul.   As she liv'd peerless,
So her dead likeness I do well believe 15
Excels whatever yet you look'd upon,
Or hand of man hath done. Therefore I keep it
Lonely, apart. But here it is. Prepare
To see the life as lively mock'd as ever
Still sleep mock'd death. Behold, and say 'tis well. 20

[*Paulina draws a curtain and discovers Hermione standing like a statue.*]

I like your silence; it the more shows off
Your wonder. But yet speak; first you, my liege.
Comes it not something near?

Leon.   Her natural posture!
Chide me, dear stone, that I may say indeed
Thou art Hermione; or rather, thou art she 25
In thy not chiding; for she was as tender
As infancy and grace. But yet, Paulina,
Hermione was not so much wrinkled, nothing
So aged as this seems.

Pol.   O, not by much!

Paul. So much the more our carver's excellence, 30
Which lets go by some sixteen years and makes her
As she liv'd now.

Leon.   As now she might have done,
So much to my good comfort as it is
Now piercing to my soul. O, thus she stood,
Even with such life of majesty (warm life, 35
As now it coldly stands), when first I woo'd her!
I am asham'd. Does not the stone rebuke me
For being more stone than it? O royal piece,
There's magic in thy majesty, which has
My evils conjur'd to remembrance, and 40
From thy admiring daughter took the spirits,
Standing like stone with thee!

Per.   And give me leave,
And do not say 'tis superstition that
I kneel, and then implore her blessing. Lady,
Dear queen, that ended when I but began, 45
Give me that hand of yours to kiss.

Paul.   O, patience!
The statue is but newly fix'd; the colour's
Not dry.

Cam. My lord, your sorrow was too sore laid on,
Which sixteen winters cannot blow away, 50
So many summers dry. Scarce any joy
Did ever so long live; no sorrow
But kill'd itself much sooner.

Pol.   Dear my brother,
Let him that was the cause of this have pow'r

To take off so much grief from you as he   55
Will piece up in himself.
Paul.   Indeed, my lord,
If I had thought the sight of my poor image
Would thus have wrought you — for the stone
    is mine —
I'ld not have show'd it.
Leon.   Do not draw the curtain.
Paul. No longer shall you gaze on't, lest
    your fancy   60
May think anon it moves.
Leon.   Let be, let be!
Would I were dead, but that methinks al-
    ready —
What was he that did make it? See, my lord,
Would you not deem it breath'd? and that
    those veins
Did verily bear blood?
Pol.   Masterly done!   65
The very life seems warm upon her lip.
Leon. The fixure of her eye has motion in't,
As we are mock'd with art.
Paul.   I'll draw the curtain.
My lord's almost so far transported that
He'll think anon it lives.
Leon.   O sweet Paulina,   70
Make me to think so twenty years together!
No settled senses of the world can match
The pleasure of that madness. Let't alone.
Paul. I am sorry, sir, I have thus far stirr'd
    you; but
I could afflict you farther.
Leon.   Do, Paulina!   75
For this affliction has a taste as sweet
As any cordial comfort. Still methinks
There is an air comes from her. What fine
    chisel
Could ever yet cut breath? Let no man mock
    me,
For I will kiss her.
Paul.   Good my lord, forbear!   80
The ruddiness upon her lip is wet.
You'll mar it if you kiss it; stain your own
With oily painting. Shall I draw the curtain?
Leon. No, not these twenty years!
Per.   So long could I
Stand by, a looker-on.
Paul.   Either forbear,   85
Quit presently the chapel, or resolve you
For more amazement. If you can behold it,
I'll make the statue move indeed, descend,
And take you by the hand. But then you'll
    think
(Which I protest against) I am assisted   90
By wicked powers.

Leon.   What you can make her do,
I am content to look on; what to speak,
I am content to hear; for 'tis as easy
To make her speak as move.
Paul.   It is requir'd
You do awake your faith. Then all stand still;
Or those that think it is unlawful business   96
I am about, let them depart.
Leon.   Proceed.
No foot shall stir.
Paul.   Music! awake her! strike!
                                    [*Music.*]
'Tis time; descend; be stone no more; ap-
    proach;   99
Strike all that look upon with marvel. Come;
I'll fill your grave up! Stir; nay, come away!
Bequeath to death your numbness, for from
    him
Dear life redeems you. You perceive she stirs:
    [*Hermione comes down from the pedestal.*]
Start not! Her actions shall be holy as
You hear my spell is lawful. Do not shun
    her
Until you see her die again; for then   106
You kill her double. Nay, present your hand.
When she was young, you woo'd her; now, in
    age,
Is she become the suitor?
Leon.   O, she's warm!
If this be magic, let it be an art   110
Lawful as eating.
Pol.   She embraces him.
Cam. She hangs about his neck.
If she pertain to life, let her speak too.
Pol. Ay, and make it manifest where she
    has liv'd,
Or how stol'n from the dead.
Paul.   That she is living,
Were it but told you, should be hooted at   116
Like an old tale; but it appears she lives,
Though yet she speak not. Mark a little while.
Please you to interpose, fair madam; kneel,
And pray your mother's blessing. — Turn, good
    lady;   120
Our Perdita is found.
                            [*Perdita kneels.*]
Her.   You gods, look down,
And from your sacred vials pour your graces
Upon my daughter's head! Tell me, mine own,
Where hast thou been preserv'd? where liv'd?
    how found   124
Thy father's court? For thou shalt hear that I,
Knowing by Paulina that the oracle
Gave hope thou wast in being, have preserv'd
Myself to see the issue.

Paul.   There's time enough for that,
Lest they desire, upon this push, to trouble
Your joys with like relation. Go together, 130
You precious winners all; your exultation
Partake to every one. I, an old turtle,
Will wing me to some wither'd bough, and there
My mate, that's never to be found again,
Lament till I am lost.

Leon.   O, peace, Paulina! 135
Thou should3t a husband take by my consent,
As I by thine a wife. This is a match,
And made between's by vows. Thou hast
found mine;
But how, is to be question'd; for I saw her,
As I thought, dead; and have (in vain) said
many   140
A prayer upon her grave. I'll not seek far
(For him, I partly know his mind) to find
thee

An honourable husband. — Come, Camillo,
And take her by the hand; whose worth and
honesty
Is richly noted, and here justified   145
By us, a pair of kings. — Let's from this
place. —
What! look upon my brother. Both your par-
dons,
That e'er I put between your holy looks
My ill suspicion. This' your son-in-law,
And son unto the King, whom heavens direct-
ing,   150
Is troth-plight to your daughter. — Good
Paulina,
Lead us from hence where we may leisurely
Each one demand, and answer to his part
Perform'd in this wide gap of time since first
We were dissever'd. Hastily lead away.   155

Exeunt.

470

GLOSSARY

a, in, on
'a, he
'a', have
abate, to humble; shorten; dull; reduce the estimate of; omit; cut off
abide, see aby
abject, a servile creature (*Rich. III*, i, 1, 106)
able, to authorize (*Lear*, iv, 6, 172)
abode, to bode, forebode
abodement, bad omen
aborn, auburn
abortive, an unnatural thing, abnormality (*K. John*, iii, 4, 158)
abram, auburn
Abram, Abraham (*M. of V.*, i, 3, 73)
abridgment, pastime; that which cuts short
abroad, away from here; outside one's house; on foot; here and there; in the world; current
abrogate, avoid (*L. L. L.*, iv, 2, 55)
abrook, to brook, endure (*2 Hen. VI*, ii, 4, 10)
abruption, a breaking off
absey book, A B C book, primer
absolute, perfect; accomplished; precise, finical
abstract, a summary, epitome; condensation; a short cut, a means of shortening one's way
abuse, to deceive
abuse, deception; fault
abuser, deceiver
aby (abide), pay for, answer for
abysm, abyss
academe, academy
accept, decision (*Hen. V*, v, 2, 82)
accepted, acceptable
accidence, that part of grammar that treats of inflectional forms
accident, a chance occurrence (good or bad), incident
accite, to summon; incite, prompt (*2 Hen. IV*, iii, 2, 64)
accommodate, to equip, furnish; attire
accomplice, an associate (*1 Hen. VI*, v, 2, 9)
accomplish, to finish off; furnish; obtain, win
accompt, n., account, reckoning
accord, harmony; consent, assent
according, accordingly
accountant, accountable
accoustrement, accoutrement
accuse, accusation
ace, the number one (in dice)
achieve, to obtain, acquire
achievement, acquisition
acknown on (to be), to admit knowledge of
acold, cold, chilly
aconitum, aconite, monkshood
acquit, to pay for (in full); free, absolve; *p.p.*, rid
acquittance, n., a receipt in full; acquittal; *v.*, to acquit, clear
act, action, operation
action-taking, prone to go to law instead of fighting
acture, action (*Compl.*, 185)
adamant, magnet
addiction, inclination

addition, name; title; honour
address, to direct; prepare, make ready
adhere, to be consistent or appropriate; be connected; be attached (in friendship)
admirable, wonderful, strange
admiral, the admiral's ship
admiration, wonder; object of wonder
admire, to wonder, wonder at
admired, admirable; wonderful, strange
admit, to accept, favour; include
admittance, accepted fashion; social prestige
adoor, see in-a-door
adoptious Christendoms, fond nicknames (*All's W.*, i, 1, 188)
adulterate, *v.*, to commit adultery; *adj.*, adulterous
advance, to raise, lift up; display
advantage, *n.*, interest, usury; *v.*, to benefit; increase (by interest)
adventure, *n.*, chance; *v.*, to take the risk
advertise, inform, instruct
advertisement, information; advice, counsel
advice, consideration
advise, to consider; inform
advised, wise, discreet, considerate; carefully considered; (be), consider, take care
advisedly, with due consideration
aery, the nest of a bird of prey, eyrie; brood
affect, *n.*, inclination, liking; *v.*, to care for, love, like; strive for
affected, disposed; in love
affectedly, fancifully (*Compl.*, 48)
affection, disposition, inclination; fancy, thing fancied for the moment; passion; affectation
affectioned, *adj.*, affected
affeered, confirmed, established by authority (*Macb.*, iv, 3, 34)
affiance, trust; loyalty
affined, *adj.*, related; under obligation
affinity, relationship, kindred
affliction, the beating of the storm (*Lear*, iii, 2, 49)
affray, to frighten
affright, to surround with fear (*Per.*, i, 1, 29)
affront, *n.*, an encounter face to face; *v.*, to meet, encounter
affy, to confide, trust; betroth
afoot, in infantry (*All's W.*, iv, 3, 181)
afore, before
Afric, Africa, African
afront, face to face with one
after, according to; at the rate of; afterwards
after-debts, indebtedness for a service already performed (*All's W.*, iv, 3, 255)
after-eye, *v.*, to follow with one's eyes (*Cymb.*, i, 3, 16)
against, in preparation for or expectation of; just before; in anticipation of the time when
agazed, gazing, with their eyes fixed (*1 Hen. VI*, i, 1, 126)

aged, befitting or characteristic of old age
agent, the doer
aglet, the metal tag of a lace
aglet-baby, a girl as small as an aglet (*T. of S.*, i, 2, 79)
agnize, to recognize as one's own (*Oth.*, i, 3, 232)
agued, *adj.*, quaking as with ague
a-height (a-high), on high, aloft
ahold, close to the wind (*Temp.*, i, 1, 52)
ahungry (anhungry), hungry
aidance, aid, help
aidant, helpful
aim, *n.*, *v.*, guess, conjecture. See cry aim
air, the style, fashion
air-drawn, imaginary
alablaster, alabaster
aland, on land, to land
alarm, a call to arms; assault
alarum, *n.*, a call to arms, combat; *v.*, to call to arms or to the combat
albeit, although
alderliefest, dearest of all, very dear (*2 Hen. VI*, i, 1, 28)
ale, ale-drinking
a-life, as much as life (*W. T.*, iv, 4, 264)
alight, to dismount from (*Ven.*, 13)
allay, relief
allayment, mitigation
allegiant, loyal
All-hallond eve, the eve of All Saints' Day
Allhallowmas, All Saints' Day (November 1)
All-hallown summer, summer weather in late autumn, Indian summer (*1 Hen. IV*, i, 2, 178)
all hid, hide and seek
allied, related, kindred
alligant, *for* elegant (*M. W.*, ii, 2, 69)
allottery, allotted portion
allow, to approve
allowance, acknowledgement, approval
all-thing, *adv.*, altogether, in every way (*Macb.* iii, 1, 13)
all-watched, passed without sleep
ally, kinsman
allycholly (allicholly), *for* melancholy
Almain, a German
alms-drink, more than his share (*A. and C.*, ii, 7, 5)
aloft, *prep.*, above
alone, unparalleled, superior to all
along, at one's full length
alter, to exchange
alway, always
amain, strongly, aloud, swiftly
amaze, *v.*, to bring into a maze, confound, confuse utterly; *n.*, confusion
amazedly, with utter confusion, as one in a maze
amazedness, bewilderment; panic
amazement, utter perplexity; panic
ambuscado, ambuscade, ambush
amerce, to punish (with a fine)
ames-ace, two aces (in dice)
amiss, offence, misfortune; astray (in one's mind)

among, *see* ever among
amort, dispirited, in dejection
ample, amply, fully
an, on
an, if; if only; even if, though; as if; (an if), if
anatomize, dissect
anatomy, skeleton
anchor, anchorite, hermit
ancient, *n.*, ensign (flag *or* officer); *adj.*, aged; old, former, bygone
ancientry, the old, aged people; old-fashioned ceremony
an end, on end, upright. *See* still an end
angel, a gold coin, half a pound
angerly, angrily
anguish, excruciating pain (of body or mind)
anhungry, *see* ahungry
annexion, addition
annothanize, to anatomize, interpret (*L. L. L.*, iv, 1, 69)
annoy, *n.*, pain, grief; harm, injury; *v.*, to hurt, molest
annoyance, harm, injury
anon, soon, presently; and then; (ever and), now and then
answer, *n.*, response in action, retaliation; acceptance of a challenge; return attack, return blow or thrust; *v.*, to meet in combat; answer for; atone for
an't, on it, of it
anter, cavern
Anthropophagi, cannibals
Anthropophaginian, cannibal, man-eater
Antiates, the people of Antium
antic, *adj.*, quaint, queer, fantastic; *n.*, odd person, buffoon; a fantastic dance; *v.*, to turn one to a buffoon
ap (*Welsh*), son of (*Rich. III*, iv, 5, 15)
apaid, satisfied, contented
apish, imitative (*Rich II*, ii, 1, 22)
apology, an explanatory address in defence
apoplexed, paralyzed
apostropha, omission of a letter or letters (*L. L. L.*, iv. 2, 123)
appalled, pale, pallid; annulled (*Phœn.*, 37)
apparent, heir apparent (i.e., one whose right is indefeasible)
apparitions, appearances
appeach, inform against, impeach
appeal, *n.*, impeachment, accusation; *v.*, to accuse, impeach
appellant, accuser
apperil, peril, risk
apple-John, a late apple (which shrinks when it ripens)
appliance, medicine, medical treatment, remedy
apply, administer (a medicine or potion); devote one's self
appoint, equip
appointment, equipment, attire
apprehensive, quick-witted, perceptive
approbation, proof
approof, approval; proof, testing
appropriation, special credit (*M. of V.*, i, 2, 46)
approve, test, prove; confirm, justify
approver, one who tests
apricock, apricot
apron-man, mechanic, craftsman
apt, ready; probable
aqua-vitæ, distilled liquor

Aquilon, the north wind
Arabian bird, phœnix
araise, raise from the dead
arbitrement, decision, legal inquiry
arch, *n.*, *adj.*, chief
argal (argo), *for* ergo, therefore
argentine, silver-bright
Argier, Algiers
argosy, a merchant ship of the largest size
argument, theme, subject matter, plot (of a play)
arm, furnish, prepare; embrace
arm-gaunt, slender and spirited in his armour (*A. and C.*, i, 5, 48)
armigero, esquire
armipotent, powerful in war
aroint thee, avaunt, get thee gone
arras, tapestry hangings
arrivance, persons arriving
arrive, arrive at, reach
arrose, besprinkle (*T. N. K.*, v, 4, 104)
Arthur's Show, a company of London archers who called themselves by the names of King Arthur's knights
article (of great), consisting of many items of excellence
articulate, negotiate; itemize
artificial, made by art
artire, sinew, muscle (*Haml.*, i, 4, 82)
artist, learned and skilful man; physician
artless, lacking skill or wisdom
arts-man, scholarly person
asinico, little ass; fool
askaunce, to turn aside (*Lucr.*, 637)
aspect, the action of the planets (by virtue of their astrological positions) upon human affairs; influence
aspersion, sprinkling (as of dew), shower
aspic, asp
aspire, mount up, rise; soar to
assay, *n.*, a trial, test; an attempt; criterion; raid; *v.*, to try, test, make trial of; attempt; tempt; make an attempt upon
assemblance, semblance, appearance
assigns, appurtenances
assist, accompany, attend
assubjugate, degrade, debase
assured, betrothed
astonish, stun, stupefy
a-tilt (run), to tilt, to just
atomy, atom; tiny creature
atone, reconcile; accord with one another
attach, take hold of, seize, attack, arrest
attainder, dishonour, stain, disgrace
attaint, *n.*, stain, disgrace; infection; worn and fatigued appearance; *v.*, to stain, dishonour; convict; deprive of civil rights
attainture, conviction and disgrace
at task, blamed
attent, attentive
attest, testimony, evidence
attribute, good reputation, credit
atwain, in two, asunder
audible, quick of ear
augure, augury
augurer, augur
auld, old (*Oth.*, ii, 3, 99)
aunt, old dame; prostitute
avised, sensible, considerate; informed
avoid, leave; get rid of
aweless, fearless; inspiring no awe

awful, reverential; awe-inspiring
awkward, back-handed; adverse, contrary; irregular or contrary to right

baccare, stand back!
back friend, false friend
backsword man, a single-stick fencer
back-trick, a caper backward in a dance
baffle, degrade from knighthood; treat with contempt
bait, to set dogs upon; attack, harass
baked meats, pies, pasties
balk, to neglect, pass by, overlook
balked, heaped up in ridges
ball, the globe used at coronation, the orb (*Hen. V*, iv, 1, 277)
ballow, cudgel
ban, *n.*, *v.*, curse
band, bond
bandog, dog kept chained, mastiff
bandy, knock to and fro; contend
bane, poison; destruction, ruin
banes, the bans (notice of intended marriage given in church)
bank, to coast along by (*K. John*, v, 2, 104)
bankrout, bankrupt
banquet, a service of fruit and sweetmeats
barbed, armed with a barb (a covering for the breast of a warhorse)
barely, in a bare condition
barful, much impeded
barley-break, a rustic game
barnacle, a kind of wild goose
barne, child
Bartholomew, served at Bartholomew Fair (*2 Hen. IV*, ii, 4, 250)
base, the game of prisoner's base. *See* bid
base court, the lower court of a castle
bases, a skirt attached to an armed horseman's doublet
Basilisco-like, like Basilisco (a braggart knight in the old play of *Soliman and Perseda*)
basilisk, a cockatrice, a fabulous reptile whose eyes were deadly; a large cannon
basta, enough
bastard, a sweet Spanish wine
batch, a baking of bread
bate, *n.*, contention, dispute; *v.*, to flap the wings
bate, abate, diminish, weaken; deduct, remit
bate-breeding, causing strife
bateless, not to be dulled
bat-fowling, bird-catching by night
batlet, a bat used to beat clothes in washing
battalia, army
batten, feed coarsely
battle, battalion, army, troop
bauble, a worthless thing or person; a trifle or toy; a fool's sceptre
bavian, baboon
bavin, *adj.*, like brushwood (*1 Hen. IV*, iii, 2, 61)
bawcock, fine fellow
beadsman, one who prays for another
be-all, all there is to the matter (*Macb.*, i, 7, 5)
bear (a brain), to have a good mind; (hard), bear a grudge against; (in hand), deceive by a course of false pretences, cajole; (it, it away), win, get the victory

Glossary

bearing cloth, mantle in which an infant is carried to the font to be christened

beaver, lower moveable part of a helmet; visor; helmet

becking, n., beckoning

becomed, fitting, becoming

bedlam, n., Bethlehem hospital for lunatics; madhouse; madman; adj., insane

bed-swerver, adulteress

been, are (Per., ii, Gow., 28)

beesom (bisson), blind, purblind

beg us, sue for and obtain guardianship of us as idiotic (L. L. L., v, 2, 490)

begnaw, gnaw at, eat away

beholding, beholden, under obligation

being, n., life, existence; residence; adv., while, since

beldam(e), grandmother; old woman; hag

belee'd, forced into the lee (away from the wind)

belied, falsified (Lucr., 1533)

bellman, watchman (with a bell)

bemadding, maddening

bemet, p.p., met

bemoiled, besmeared with mud

bench, sit on the bench (as judge); raise to a high seat or station

bend, n., look, glance; direction; bow, graceful and reverential attitude; v., to aim, direct; make tense or ready for action

benevolence, a forced loan (as if in gift)

bent, force and direction (as from a bent bow); inclination; look

ben venuto, welcome

berard (berod), bearward

berattle, berate, decry

Bergomask dance, a grotesque dance imitating the natives of Bergamo in Italy

Bermoothes, Bermudas

berod (berard), bearward

beseeming, appearance, guise

beshrew, curse (a light word)

besides, out of (Sonn., 23)

beslubber, smear

besonian (bezonian), a miserable creature, low fellow

besort, v., suit; n., suitability

bespeak, speak to, address

bestead (worse), in a worse plight

bestow, stow, place, dispose of; use, employ; behave

bestraught, distracted (T. of S., Ind., ii, 27)

bestride, defend (a fallen soldier)

beteem, allow

betime, betimes, early

bewray, reveal, disclose

bezonian, see besonian

bias, n., a weight on a bowl which gives it an oblique course; the oblique course; tendency, inclination, propensity; indirect means; adv., awry; adj., swollen, puffed out

bid a (or the) base, to challenge to a race

biddy, chicken

bide, abide, endure, undergo

biding, place of abode

bigamy, marriage with a widow (Rich. III, iii, 7, 189)

biggen, nightcap

big-looked, menacing (T. N. K., i, 1, 215)

bilbo, sword (made at Bilboa, Spain), swordsman

bilboes, a shackled bar

bile, a boil

bill, halberd, pike

bill, written paper, document, order

bird, young bird, nestling

bird-bolt, blunt-headed arrow for shooting birds

birding, fowling

birth-child (Thetis'), child belonging to Thetis because born at sea (Per., iv, 4, 41)

birthdom, native land

bisson, see beesom

bite the thumb, an insulting and contemptuous gesture

bitumed, daubed with bitumen

black, of dark complexion

black-cornered, that darkens corners (hiding places)

Black Monday, Easter Monday

blacks, black or mourning garments

blank, n., the white spot at the centre of a target; line of aim; v., to blanch, make pale

blanks, grants or charters with blank spaces left to be filled in; lottery tickets that win nothing; blank pages

blaze, make public

blazon, n., description; v., to describe

blench, v., to start, flinch; start away, show inconstancy; n., an inconstant action

blend, blended (Compl., 215)

blistered, adorned with puffs

blood-boltered, having the hair matted with blood

blood-sized, daubed with clotted blood

blow, make flyblown

blown, windy, inflated, unsubstantial

blowse, a ruddy, fat-cheeked girl

blue-cap, a Scot

blue eye, one having a dark circle round it

blue-eyed, with eyes surrounded by blue circles

blunt, stupid

blurted at, greeted with scornful 'pooh's'

board, accost, address, woo

bob, v., beat, thrash; cheat, trick; n., a taunting jest

bodkin, stiletto

bodykins (God's bodykins), an oath (by God's body)

boggle, to shy, equivocate

boggler, an inconstant person

boldened, made bold

bolin, bowline

bollen, swollen

bolting hutch, a box or chest into which anything is bolted or sifted

bombard, a big leather bottle

bombast, n., cotton wool; padding; adj., bombastic

bona roba, a showy wanton

bonnet, to doff the hat

bonny, handsome; stalwart

boot, n., booty; profit, gain; avail; (to), for our help; v., to avail; to present (one) over and above

boothose, a heavy stocking to be worn instead of a boot

bore, to cheat, gull

boresprit, bowsprit

bosky, bushy

botch, to patch, mend clumsily

bots, a disease of horses, caused by worms

bottle, a bundle of hay

bottled, swollen unwholesomely

bottom, n., skein or ball (of thread); v., to wind

bottom, a ship; low land by a river

bound, to make to leap (Hen. V, v, 2, 146); p.p., confined, circumscribed (J. C., iv, 3, 221)

bounty, goodness

bourn, boundary; brook

bowels, offspring; compassion, feeling

bow-hand, the (left) hand which holds the bow

bowling, bowline (T. N. K., iv, 1, 148)

boy-queller, boy-killer

brabble, brawl, quarrel

brace, a piece of armour; posture or condition of defence

brach, a bitch-hound

braid, adj., deceitful, tricky

braid, to upbraid (Per. i, 1, 93)

brain, v., comprehend

brainish, insane

brainpan, skull

brainsick, insane

brake, underbrush

brave, adj., fine, splendid, grand (in appearance or character); v., to make fine, adorn; challenge, defy (especially in a swaggering manner); show off, make a display

bravery, splendour, display; finery; ostentation; bravado

brawl, a kind of dance

brawn, muscle; mass of flesh

breach of the sea, breaking waves, surf

breast, voice (in singing)

breath, mild exercise

breathe, speak softly; utter, reveal; take exercise

breathed, well exercised, in good condition as to wind

breed-bate, a stirrer-up of quarrels

breeder, a mare

breese (brize), gadfly

bribed buck, a stolen deer (M. W., v, 5, 27)

bride, to marry

brief, a letter; a short document; a summary; a brief account

briefly, a little while ago; soon; without delay

brinded, brindled, marked with dark streaks

bring out, confuse, put out

Britain, n., Brittany; adj., British Breton

Briton, native of Brittany

Brittany, Britain

brize (breese), gadfly

broach, to stick upon and pierce, spit; tap; bleed; set going, start

brock, badger

brogue, a coarse heavy shoe

broke, act as go-between or agent

broken (music), arranged for various instruments, concerted

broker, one who brokes

brooch, adorn (as with a brooch)

brooded, watchful (as a hen over her brood) (K. John, iii, 3, 52)

Brownist, member of the non-conformist sect founded by Robert Brown about 1581

bubble, worthless fellow

bubukles, red swellings, great pimples

buck, a lot of soiled clothes for the wash

buck-basket, a basket for soiled clothes

buckle, bend, give way; join in hand-to-hand fight, grapple

buckler, to shield, defend

Bucklersbury, a London street in which were many grocers and apothecaries

bug, bugbear

bulk, trunk; huge body; a projecting stal:

bully, fine fellow (common as a friendly form of address: as, 'bully doctor')

bully rook, jovial fellow

bum-baily, a sheriff's officer

bung, cutpurse, pickpocket

burgonet, a kind of helmet

busky, bushy

buss, *n., v.,* kiss

buttery, storeroom for liquor and food

button, a bud

buttons (in his), within his grasp (*M. W.,* iii, 2, 71)

butt-shaft, unbarbed arrow

buzzer, whisperer (of scandal)

by-and-by, immediately

by-dependences, incidental circumstances (*Cymb.,* v, 5, 390)

by-drinkings, drinks between meals

by'r, by our

cabin, to shut up in a cabin; to be confined

cacodemon, evil spirit, devil

cade, a 'barrel' of herrings (720 in number)

cadent, ever-falling

cage, a lock-up

'cagion, occasion, cause

Cain-coloured, of the same colour as Cain's, red, (*M. W.,* i, 4, 23)

caitiff, *n.,* wretch, miserable creature; *adj.,* miserable

caliver, a light musket

calkins, caiks on a horseshoe (*T. N. K.,* v, 4, 55)

callet (callot), low woman

calm, *for* qualm (*2 Hen. IV,* ii, 4, 40)

Cambyses' vein, bombastic style (as in Thomas Preston's tragedy of *Cambyses*)

can (*for* gan), did

can, can do or accomplish, has skill or ability; knows

canakin, little can

canary, a sweet wine from the Canary Islands; a lively Spanish dance; quandary (*M. W.,* ii, 2, 61)

candidatus, clad in white, as a candidate for the consulship

candle mine, vast deposit of tallow

canker, a sore, an ulcer; a worm that eats rosebuds; a wild rose

cankered, ulcerated, malignant; tarnished

canon, rule; law, divine law

canstick, candlestick

cantle, piece cut out, segment

canton, song

canvass, to toss (as in a canvas sheet)

canzonet, a short song

capable, ready to take, to feel, or to understand; ample; susceptible; intelligent; legally qualified as inheritor (*Lear,* ii, 1, 87)

capitulate, draw up an agreement, come to terms

capriccio, caprice, notion

captain, chief commander, general

captious, ready to take (*All's W.,* i, 3, 208)

captivate, to take or keep captive

captive, take captive

car, chariot

carack (careck, carrect), galleon

carbonado, *n.,* piece of meat slashed for broiling; *v.,* to slash

carcanet, jewelled necklace

card, *n.,* the compass card marked with the points of the compass; chart; (by the), with precision, accurately; *v.,* to mix, adulterate

cardecue, quart d'écu, a French coin worth a quarter of a French gold crown

cardinally, *for* carnally (*M. for M.,* ii, 1, 81)

career, a short gallop; a headstrong action or whim

careful, anxious, care-burdened

care-tuned, sorrowful in sound

carl, a rustic, peasant

carnal, flesh-eating, ravenous (*Rich. III,* iv, 4, 56)

carouse, *n.,* a full cup drunk at a draught; *v.,* to drink a toast

carpet consideration, grounds of mere gallantry and courtly service (*T. N.,* iii, 4, 258)

carpet-monger, one who frequents carpeted rooms, a gallant

carrect, *see* carack

carriage, load, burden, purport, tenour

carry, to manage; (out my side), win my game, achieve my object

cart, *n.,* chariot; *v.,* to expose to disgrace by carrying (one) about the streets in a cart

carve, to serve in carving at table; to act and speak with attentive courtesy; (for), to serve (one) in carving; to indulge; (to), to serve (one) at table

case, *n.,* body; skin; socket (of the eye); setting; a full set; *v.,* to mask; skin, flay

cashier, dismiss; slang for 'cleaned out' (by a pickpocket)

cast, *v.,* cashier, dismiss (from office); inspect (for diagnosis); *adj.,* thrown aside, discarded

Cataian, native of Cathay, Chinaman

cataract, waterspout

catastrophe, rump

cater-cousins, intimate friends

catlings, fiddlestrings of catgut

caudle, a warm spiced drink

cautel, deceit, crafty scheme

cautelous, deceitful, deceptive

cavaleiro, cavalier, gallant

cavalery, cavalier

caviary, caviare

cease, *n.,* decease

censure, *n.,* judgment, opinion; *v.,* to judge, pass judgment on

centre, the earth (as the centre of the universe)

cerecloth, waxed cloth for wrapping a corpse

'cern, to concern (*T. of S.,* v, 1, 77)

certes, certainly, assuredly

cess (out of all), beyond all measure

cesse, *n.,* cessation, death; *v.,* to cease, come to an end

cestron, cistern

chafe, *n.,* anger; *v.,* to show anger; make angry

chaffy, worthless (*T. N. K.,* iii, 1, 41)

challenger, claimant

cham, khan (ruler of Tartary)

chamber, a small piece of ordnance

chamber councils, private councils

chamberer, a gallant

chamberlain, a servant in charge of the chambers at an inn

chamblet, a garment made of camlet (a light fabric)

champain (champian), a fertile plain; level country

champion, *v.,* meet in single combat

chance, *v.,* chances

change, to deal in exchange

changeable, of varying colours

changeling, a fickle person

channel, a gutter

chanson, song

chape, metal tip of a sheath

chapel, bury with due rites (*T. N. K.,* i, 1, 50)

chapeless, without a chape

chapfallen, lacking the lower jaw (*with a pun*) (*Haml.,* v, 1, 212)

chapless, without a (lower) jaw

chaps, jaws

character, *n.,* handwriting; a mark, sign; *v.,* to write, inscribe

charactery, writing; what is written or inscribed

chare, *n.,* chore, small job; *v.,* to do (a task)

charect, carat

charge, *n.,* load, burden; importance; expense, cost, value; military command; troop; *v.,* to load

chargeful, costly, expensive

charge house, a boarding school

Charles' wain, the Great Bear

charneco, a kind of Portuguese wine

chase, the first bound of an unreturned tennis ball; a hunting preserve

chaudron, entrails

che, I

cheapen, to bargain for

cheater, escheator

check, *n., v.,* rebuke; check at

checkin, a sequin (an Italian coin)

cherry-pit, a children's game (throwing cherry stones into a small hole or pit)

cheveril (chev'ril, chiverel), kid leather (soft and easily stretched); made of cheveril; yielding, elastic

chewet, a small mince pie; *fig.,* a fat fellow

child, a girl baby

childing, *adj.,* fruitful, fertile

chill, I will (*Lear,* iv, 6, 240)

chipochia (*Ital.* capocchia), simpleton (*T. and C.,* iv, 2, 33)

chirurgeonly, like a surgeon

chiverel, *see* cheveril

choler, bile; anger

chop, to exchange, make an exchange

chopine, a shoe with a thick sole of cork

choplogic, one who argues contentiously

chops, *n.,* fissures, deep lines (*Lucr.,* 1452)

chops, a fat-cheeked fellow

chopt, seamed, wrinkled (*Sonn.,* 62)

choris, *for* chorus (*T. N. K.,* iii, 5 107)

chough, a kind of crow

christen, christened

christom child, infant wearing the chrisom, a white robe put on when

Glossary

he was christened; innocent (*Hen. V*, ii, 3, 12)

chuck, chick (a term of affection)

chud, I would (*Lear*, iv, 6, 243)

chuff, a boor; a miser

Ci.iter, Cirencester

'cide, decide

Cimmerian, native of the Land of Darkness, blackamoor

cinque-pace (sink-a-pace), a lively dance, galliard

cipher, decipher

circummured, walled round

circumstance, circumlocution, elaborate style or phraseology; talk

cital, mention

cite, summon, urge

citizen, *adj.*, city-bred, delicate

cittern, an instrument somewhat like a guitar

civil, civilized, decorous, well-behaved; (doctor), a doctor of civil (Roman) law

clack-dish, a beggar's dish with a cover which he clacked to attract notice

clap hands, to clasp hands (in a bargain or agreement); *hence*, clap, to pledge

clap i' th' clout, hit the bull's eye

clapperclaw, scratch and beat

clean, shapely, well-moulded

clear, pure

clearness, freedom from being suspected (*Macb.*, iii, 1, 133)

cleep (clip), embrace

clepe (clip) to call, style

clerk, a scholar

cliff, clef, key (in music)

climate, *n.*, region, clime; quarter of the sky; *v.*, to sojourn

climature, clime, region

cling, cause (one) to shrivel up

clinquant, glittering (with gold)

clip (cleep), to embrace

clip (clepe), to call, style

clipper, one who clips coins

cloistress, nun

close, *adj.*, secret; secretive

close, enclose; join closely; come together; come to an agreement, agree; come to grips, grapple

closet, private room

closure, enclosure; close, end

clotpoll (i. e., sod-head), blockhead

clothier's yard, an arrow a cloth yard long

cloudy, sad, sullen, gloomy

clout, a piece of cloth; the mark, the bull's eye

clouted, having the soles set with nails or strips of metal

clown, a rustic, boor, clumsy fellow; clownish servant; jester

cloy, to claw (*Cymb.*, v, 4, 118)

coast, to move in a sly or circuitous course (*Hen. VIII*, iii, 2, 38)

clyster pipe, syringe

cobloaf, a small loaf with a round head

cock, cockboat

Cock, a corrupt form of 'God'

cock-a-hoop (set), to carry all before you

cocklight, morning twilight

cockney, one reared in the city and ignorant of all but town life

cockshut time, evening twilight

cod, a peapod

codding, lustful

codling, small unripe apple

codpiece, part of the hose

coffin, a pastry mould for a pie

cog, to cheat; beguile

cognizance, heraldic badge or sign; token; distinguishing mark

cohere, agree

coif (quoif), a close-fitting cap

coign, corner, corner stone, projection

coil, tumult, disturbance (in *Haml.*, iii, 1, 67, with a play on the sense 'entanglement')

Colbrand, a Danish giant slain by Guy of Warwick

cold fault, cold or lost scent (in hunting)

collect, gather (mentally), infer

collection, putting together (mentally), inference

collied, darkened; black

collop, slice of meat, piece of flesh

collusion, *for* allusion (*L. L. L.*, iv, 2, 43)

colour, pretext, excuse

colourable, plausible, specious

colt, to trick

comart, a bargain, agreement (*Haml.*, i, 1, 93)

combinate, betrothed (*M. for M.*, iii, 1, 231)

combustion, tumult, riotous disturbance

come (near), to touch, to hit; (tardy off), not satisfactorily performed

comely, becomingly

comely-distant, at a proper distance

comfect, comfit, sweetmeat

comfort, *n.*, support, assistance; *v.*, to take comfort, cheer up; support, assist

comfortable, helpful, comforting

comfortless, unhelpful

coming-in, income, revenue

coming-on, complaisant, forward

command, to issue with authority; require of

commandment, command, orders

commend, *n.*, recommendation; *pl.*, regards

commend, *v.*, recommend; deliver, present; (me), give my regards

comment, power in observing or scrutinizing (*Haml.*, iii, 2, 84)

commerce, intercourse

commixtion, mixture, composition

commodity, advantage, expediency; convenient opportunity, convenience of intercourse; a lot or quantity (of goods or persons)

commoner, prostitute

comonty, *for* comedy (*T. of S.*, Ind., ii, 140)

compact, composed (of)

companion, bad fellow, knave

comparative, *adj.*, clever in making satirical comparisons; *n.*, one who is or tries to be thus clever (*1 Hen. IV*, iii, 2, 67)

compare, comparison

compassed, rounded

compassed window, bay window

compassionate (to be), to show passionate grief

compeer, to be a peer of, to rank with

competitor, partner, associate

compile, to compose, write

complement, fulness of accomplishments and good qualities (*Hen. V*, ii, 2, 134); *pl.*, abundant accomplishments; accomplishments; stores

complexion, temperament, disposition; appearance

complice, accomplice, associate

compliment, ceremony, courtesy, civility; manners, bearing; appearance

complimental, courteous

comply, use courteous ceremony

compose well, come to an agreement

composture, compost, manure

composure, constitution, temperament; combination, union

compt, account; the last accounting, the Day of Judgment (*Oth.*, v, 2, 273); (in), computed; on deposit

compter, *see* counter

comptible to, sensitive to

comptless, past counting

con (thanks), feel (gratitude)

concealments, secrets; secret arts

conceit, *n.*, conception, idea; thought, imagination; clever or fanciful idea or device; *v.*, to conceive, estimate, judge

conceited, having an idea or opinion (about one); fanciful, imaginative, clever

conceitless, witless

conceptious, prolific

concern, to be of importance, signify; matter to (one)

concernancy, purport, import

concernings, important matters

conclusion, an experiment; a riddle

conclusions passed the careers, the affairs proceeded in due course to the end (*M. W.*, i, 1, 184)

condition, rank, station; character, nature, quality

condole, mourn for

condolement, mourning; *pl.*, *for* doles (*Per.*, ii, 1, 156)

confidence, private conference

confiner, inhabitant

confirmity, *for* infirmity (*2 Hen. IV*, ii, 4, 64)

confound, destroy; (of time), spend, waste

confusion, destruction, ruin

congest, bring together, compound

congree, harmonize

congreet, meet and greet

congrue, agree

congruent, appropriate, fitting

congy, to congee, take formal leave

conjunct, joined, intimate; in conjunction

conscience, consciousness, inmost thought, honest opinion

conscionable, conscientious

consequence, what follows, the future, future events

consider, to reward, remunerate

considered, affording leisure for deliberation

consign, agree

consist, stand firm, insist

consort, company; band of musicians; concert

conspectuity, sense of sight (*Cor.*, ii, 1, 71)

constancy, consistent probability

constant, rational, logical

constringed, drawn together

contemptible, contemptuous

contemptuous, contemptible

contend, to contend with

content, *n.*, happiness; *v.*, to please; *adj.*, calm

continent, container; bank (of a river); sum and substance

475

continue, retain

contraction, the act of making a contract

contrive, wear away, spend (time)

control, refute; rebuke; overpower

convenience, propriety

convent, call together, summon

conversation, intercourse; behaviour

convertite, a convert

convey, bring or carry or manage secretly; palm off as; steal

conveyance, fraud, trickery

conveyer, robber, trickster

convicted, defeated, vanquished

convince, overcome, convict, disprove

convive, feast in company

convoy, means of conveyance

cony, rabbit

cony-catch, to cheat

cooling card, something that disconcerts one

copatain, high in the crown (*T. of S.,* v, 1, 70)

cope, the sky

cope, have to do with, encounter, repay

copesmate, associate, companion

copped, with rounded top

copulative, one wishing to be married (*A. Y. L.,* v, 4, 58)

copy, copyhold tenure (*cf.* 'lease of life')

coram, *for* quorum, certain specially designated justices of the peace (*M. W.,* i, 1, 6)

coranto, a running dance

Corinthian, a sporting character, a sport

corn, wheat

cornuto, cuckold

corollary (a), more than enough

corporal, corporeal, material

correspondent, submissive

corresponsive, well fitted (*T. and C.,* Prol., 18)

corrigible, corrective

corrival, associate

corroborate, *adj., Pistol's word for* broken to pieces (*Hen. V,* ii, 1, 130)

corrosive, irritant; a caustic remedy

corslet, to embrace, clasp

cost, attack, assail (*3 Hen. VI,* i, 1, 268)

costard, an apple; the head

cote, to pass

cot-quean, a man who interferes in housewifely matters

Cotshall (Cotsall, Cotsole), Cotswold

couch, to lie in bed

counsel, secret

countenance, authority, favour

counter (compter), a round piece of metal or bone used in computation; a worthless coin

counter, *adv.,* in a reverse direction

Counter, a prison for debtors

counter-caster, accountant

counterfeit, likeness, portrait

counterpoint, counterpane, bedquilt

counter-reflect, a corresponding reflection (*T. N. K.,* i, 1, 127)

countervail, to equal

county, a count

couplet, a couple, pair; *pl.,* twins

courage, disposition; desire

course, one attack in bear-baiting; a sail

court-cubbert (cupboard), a sideboard for plate

court-hand, style of penmanship used in legal documents

court holy water, flattering words

cousin, a collateral kinsman more distant than brother; nephew, etc.

covent, a convent

cover, to prepare the table for a meal

cowish, cowardly

cowl-staff, a stout pole to which is attached a basket or other burden which two persons carry between them

Cox, *for* God's

coy, to scorn; to stroke

coystrill (custrel), a low fellow

coz, cousin

cozen, to cheat

cozier, a cobbler

crack, *n.,* a lively youngster; *v.,* to brag

crackhemp, one likely to be hanged

crank, *n.,* winding passage; *v.,* to wind

crants, wreaths, garlands (*Haml.,* v, 2, 255)

crare, a small trading vessel

credent, credulous; credible

creek, a narrow passage

crescive, growing, increasing

cresset, an iron fire-basket; a torch

crime, an offence (serious or trivial)

cringe, shrink up, distort

crisp, curly; rippled

Crispin Crispian, the day sacred to Saints Crispinus and Crispianus (Crispinianus), October 25 (*Hen. V,* iv, 3, 57)

cross, *n.,* a coin stamped with a cross; any coin; trouble; *adj.,* perverse; *adv., prep.,* across

cross-row, the alphabet

crow-keeper, a guard against crows; a scarecrow

crowner, coroner

crownet, coronet

crudy, thick and heavy

crusado, a Portuguese coin marked with a cross

crush, quaff (*literally,* squeeze)

cry, a report, rumour; a pack; a troop

cry aim, to encourage, abet

cry on, to cry out, shout

cubiculo, bedroom

cullion, a low fellow

culverin, a long cannon

curiosity, nice care, fussy particularity, scrupulosity, fastidiousness

curious, careful, particular, scrupulous; elegant, choice; elaborate

currance, flow

cursorary, cursory

curst, ill-tempered, cross, shrewish

cursy, *n., v.,* curtsy

curtal, *adj.,* with a docked tail; *v.,* to curtail

curtleaxe, cutlass

cushes, cuisses

Custalorum, Custos Rotulorum, Keeper of the Rolls

custard coffin, *see* coffin

customer, a prostitute

custrel, *see* coystrill

cut, a gelding; a horse; a dock-tailed dog or horse

cuttle, cutpurse, pickpocket

cypress, crape, lawn

daff, doff, put aside or off

Daintry, Daventry (Northamptonshire)

dainty (to make), to object, be reluctant

damask, of a damask-rose colour

Dan Cupid, Sir Cupid

danger, uncompliance; (within his), in his power

Dansker, a Dane

Dardan, Troy, Trojan

dare, to daze, terrify

dareful, in bold defiance

darkling, in the dark

darraign, draw up, array

dash, mark of infamy

date, time, length of time

dateless, everlasting

daub'ry, coarse imposture

day-bed, sofa, lounge

day-woman, dairy-woman

deaf, to deafen

dear (*used to emphasize the sense of a noun*), important, intensive, heartfelt, bitter, grievous, hateful

dearly, intensely

death-practised, whose death is plotted

death tokens, spots on the body of a plague-stricken patient forewarning him of death

debate, *n.,* quarrel, combat, fight; *v.,* to settle by combat

debile, weak, feeble

deboshed, debauched; disgraced

decay, one in misfortune, a wreck

decern, *for* concern (*M. Ado,* iii, 5, 4)

decesse, *n.,* decease (*Ven.,* 1002)

decking, adornment

decline, recite in order

decoct, to heat

deem, idea, notion

deep-fet, deep-fetched (groan)

deer, animals, creatures

deface, destroy; lay waste

defeat, *n.,* destruction; *v.,* to unmake, destroy, mar, disfigure

defeature, damage, disfigurement

defence, fencing

defend, forbid

defensible, able to defend

deformed, deforming

defunct, deadened

defunction, decease

defunctive, funereal

defuse, confuse, make unrecognizable

defused, disordered; deformed, misshapen

delighted, delightful; sensitive to pleasure

deliver, to report

deliverance, utterance

deliverly, skilfully

demand, ask

demerits, deserts, merits, services

demonstrable, apparent, clear

demure, look demurely

denay, *n.,* refusal; *v.,* to deny

denier, a small copper coin

denounce, proclaim, declare

denunciation, announcement

depart, *n.,* departure; *v.,* to part company

depend, to lean; impend; be a dependant

depravation, detraction

deprave, to slander

deprive, take away

deputation, the office of a substitute

deracinate, uproot

dern, *adj.,* secret (*Per.,* iii, Prol., 15)

derogate, *v.,* to fail in honour and dignity; *adj.,* degenerate

Glossary

descant, *n.*, musical variations; a comment (with variations, as in music); *v.*, to dwell (upon)
deserved, meritorious
design, to draw up (a document); mark
designment, an undertaking
despised, contemptible, despicable
detect, uncover, reveal; accuse, discredit
determinate, to terminate, bring to a close
determination, ending
determine, come to an end
detest, *for* protest (*M. W.*, i, 4, 160)
devest, to undress
devoted, devout
dexteriously, dexterously
dexterity, agile speed
diablo, the devil
diaper, a linen napkin
dibble, a tool for making holes for planting
dich, may it do (*Tim.*, i, 2, 73)
diet, to limit, restrict
dieted, fed
difference, a decline in fortune; distinction as to rank; a variation in a coat of arms
diffidence, distrust, suspicion
diffused, confused, uncouth
digress, stray from the right, err
digression, error, transgression
dig-you-den, give you good e'en (*L. L. L.*, iv, 1, 42)
dilated, expressed in full, detailed
dilation, swelling (*or for* delation, information) (*Oth.*, iii, 3, 123)
dildo, burden of a song
diluculo surgere (saluberrimum est), early to rise (to rise at dawn) makes a man healthy (*T. N.*, ii, 3, 2)
dimensions, parts of the frame, limbs
diminitive, *adj.*, diminutive, tiny; *n.*, any very small coin
direct, to assign, depute
directions, truths, facts (*Haml.*, ii, 1, 66)
directitude (in), in a discredited position, under a cloud (*Cor.*, iv, 5, 222)
directive, fit to be managed
Dis, Pluto
disable, belittle, disparage
disanimate, dishearten
disappointed, not fitted out, unprepared
disaster, *n.*, evil astrological sign, portentous appearance; *v.*, to disfigure, mar
disbenched you, made you leave your seat
discandy, melt
discase (one's self), take off the outer garment(s)
discharge, perform (a task), play (a part); pay
disclaims in thee, disowns every part of thee (*Lear*, ii, 2, 59)
disclose, *v.*, to open; hatch; *n.* what is hatched
discontenting, *adj.*, feeling displeasure
discourse, the reason; the reasoning process; (of reason), the process of reasoning; the reasoning faculty; (of thought), the process of thought
discover, lay open, reveal, show; recognize; scout
discoverer, a scout

discovery, disclosure; scouting; that which is discovered (*Temp*,. ii, 1, 243)
disdained, disdainful
disease, discomfort, trouble; *v.*, to disturb
disedge, to have the appetite dulled
disensanity, stupidity (*T. N. K.*, iii, 5, 2)
disfurnish myself, i. e., of ready money
disgest, to digest
disgracious, displeasing, out of favour
disguise, a revel. drinking bout (*A. and C.*, ii, 7, 129)
dishabit, dislodge
dishonest, dishonourable, unchaste
dislike, displease
disliman, obliterate, blur
dismal, ill-omened, ominous
disme, tenth man
dismount, to lower, let fall, cast down (*Compl.*, 281)
disnatured, unnatural
disorbed, unsphered
dispark, throw open
dispatch, deprive, bereave
dispiteous, pitiless, merciless
disponge, pour out
dispose, *n.*, disposal; disposition, temperament; *v.*, to make or come to terms
disposer (my), one who rules me as she will (*T. and C.*, iii, 1, 95)
disposition, mood, state of mind or feeling; mental constitution
disproperty, dispossess (one) of
dispurse, disburse
disputable, fond of discussion, argumentative
disputation, discussion, conference
dispute, argue, discuss
disquantity, reduce in number
disroot, uproot, unseat
disseat, unseat
dissemble, to disguise
dissembly, *for* assembly (*M. Ado*, iv, 2, 1)
dissolve, undo, loose
distain, to stain, defile, pollute
distance, enmity
distaste, to be or make distasteful; dislike
distemper, *n.*, any disorder of body or mind; *v.*, to derange, disorder
distemperature, ailment, disorder, derangement
distilled, dissolved
distinctly, separately; in particular; intelligibly
distinguish, describe as, designate
distract, divide; diversify
distractions, separate and distinct parts
distrain, seize, confiscate
distressful, earned by severe toil
disvouch, disavow, contradict
dive-dapper, didapper, grebe
dividable, separate, different
dividant, separate, distinguishable
dividual, different, distinct
division, modulation
divulged (well), favourably reported, of good reputation
do, *see* withal
document, piece of instruction
dogged, surly, savage, fierce
doit, a coin worth half a farthing
dole, sorrow, lamentation
dole, dealing out, distribution; portion, lot
domine, schoolmaster

doom, *n.*, judgment; *v.*, to judge, decide
dotant, dotard
doubt, *n.*, *v.*, fear
doubtless, without fear or anxiety
doucets, a deer's testes
dout, to put out; abolish
dowlas, a coarse kind of linen
dowle, bit of down
dowln, down (of a feather)
dowlny, downy
down, *prep.*, down along (*M. Ado*, iii, 4, 20)
down-gyved, down and round the ankles like fetters
down-roping, hanging in viscous strings
doxy, mistress, sweetheart
dozy, confuse (*Haml.*, v, 2, 119)
draff, swill
draught, privy
draw, assemble, muster; withdraw; track (in hunting)
drawer, waiter who draws and serves wine
drawn, emptied
dreg, to clog, as with dregs (*T. N. K.*, i, 2, 97)
drench, a dose (for horses)
dress, make ready
dribbling, feeble (of an arrow ill shot)
drift, purpose, intention
drift-winds, strong steady winds
drollery, puppet show; comic picture
dropping, dripping wet (*Per.*, iv, 1, 63)
drouth, drought
drovier, drover
drugs, dull sluggish masses (*Tim.*, iv, 3, 254)
drum, drummer
Drum, *see* John Drum
drumble, move slowly
dry, thirsty; stupid, dull
dry-beat, thrash soundly
dry-foot (draw), to track by the scent of the foot
ducdame, purposely unintelligible formula of invitation (*A. Y. L.*, ii, 5, 56)
dudgeon, hilt of a dagger
due, *n.*, fit ceremony; *v.*, to endow
duello, duelling and its rules
duke, leader (*Hen. V*, iii, 2, 23)
dumb, to silence
dumb show, a dramatic action without words
dump, a doleful song or tune; any song or tune
dun, dark, mouse-coloured; *n.*, a dun horse; (dun's the mouse), *proverbial for* keep quiet or the like; (Dun is in the mire), a Christmas sport in which a heavy log (called by the horse's name) is lifted and carried
dup, do up, open
durance, imprisonment; a kind of stout cloth
duty, homage, respectful ceremony; tribute of respect

each (at), joined in succession
eager, sour, acid; biting, bitter cold
ean, to bring forth offspring
eaning time, time of giving birth
eanling, lamb just born
ear, to plough, till
ear, to give ear to
earl, a count

earnest, a sum paid in advance to bind the bargain

earth, bury, inter

easedropper, eavesdropper

easy, trivial, slight, insignificant

ebon, black as ebony

eche, eke out; draw out, lengthen

ecstasy, state of being beside one's self; passion of joy, terror, sorrow, etc.; fit of excitement; swoon; madness

edify, instruct; be instructed

effect, fulfilment, accomplishment; manifestation, sign; act, action

effectually, to all intents and purposes (*Sonn.*, 113)

effigies, image, likeness

effuse, *n.*, effusion

efvest, most fitting (*M. Ado*, iv, 2, 33)

eftsoons, soon, presently

egal, equal

egally, equally

eggs for money (take), suffer imposition tamely (*W. T.*, i, 2, 161)

egma, *for* enigma (*L. L. L.*, iii, 1, 73)

e'il, *n.*, evil (*Haml.*, i, 4, 36)

'eild, *see* God-dild

elbow, to prod with the elbow; *fig.*, to torment roughly and continually

eld, old age; old times

element, the sky; the air

elf, to tie in tangled knots

elflocks, locks of hair matted by the fairies

eliad (illiad), œillade, languishing look

elvish-marked, marked by elves; ugly and misshapen (*Rich. III*, i, 3, 228)

emballing, the investing with the ball at coronation (*Hen. VIII*, ii, 3, 47). *See* ball

embargement, embargo, hindrance, restraint

embayed, sheltered in a bay or harbour

ember-eve, the eve (vigil) of a fastday (ember-day) (*Per.*, i, Prol., 6)

emboss, to drive (a hunted creature) into a thicket or ambush; to drive to an extremity

embossed, infuriated (like a boar at bay); exhausted

embossed, swollen; corpulent; rising in knobs

embounded, enclosed

embowelled, eviscerated, emptied

embrace, submit to, accept

embrasure, embrace

embrewed, stained with blood (*T. A.*, ii, 3, 222). *See* imbrue

empale (impale), hem in, surround, encircle

emperial, emperor (*T. A.*, iv, 3, 94; iv, 4, 40)

empery, imperial dominion; empire

empiricutic, empirical, quackish (*Cor.*, ii, 1, 128)

emulate pride, pride of rivalry

emulation, envy

emulous, envious

enact, action

enacture, action

encave, hide, conceal

enchantingly, as if by magic

encompassment, roundabout method

encounter, behaviour; social intercourse; assault

encounterer, one ready to meet another halfway; coquette

encumbered, (arms) folded

end, to get in, as a crop at harvest (*Cor.*, v, 6, 36)

end-all, conclusion of the whole matter

endeared, bound, obliged

endite, *see* indite

endue, *see* indue

enew, drive into the water; pursue, chase, prosecute (*M. for M.*, iii, 1, 91)

enfeoff, deliver (as a fief), give up entirely, devote

enforce, to force; attack vigorously; urge

enfranch, enfranchise, set free (*A. and C.*, iii, 13, 149)

enfreedom, set free (*L. L. L.*, iii, 1, 125)

engage, to pledge; pledge as a hostage; hold as prisoner; entangle; involve (in a conflict)

engine, machine, apparatus; instrument; implement of war; contrivance; plot

englut, engulf, swallow

engraffed to, intimately associated with, attached to. *See* ingraffed

engross, fatten; take or purchase in gross (at wholesale or entire); accumulate; monopolize

engrossments, accumulations, store of wealth

enjail, imprison

enlard, fatten grossly

enlarge, set free, liberate

enlargement, liberation, release; liberty; freedom of action

enlighten, make bright or brilliant

enormous, abnormal

enow, enough

enpatron me, are my patron saint (*Compl.*, 224)

enridged, with a surface rising in ridges (*Lear*, iv, 6, 71)

ensconce (one's self into), take refuge in. *See* insconce

enseamed, defiled with sweat

ensear, dry up

enshield, to cover (as with a shield), conceal

ensinewed, closely knit

ensteeped, immersed, lying under water

entertain, *v.*, to receive (as a guest or in general); take into service; treat; spend (time); *n.*, reception, entertainment

entertainment, reception; treatment; polite attention; service

entitled, having a claim

entranced, in a swoon, unconscious

entreat, *v.*, treat; negotiate; *n.*, entreaty, petition

entreatments, negotiations

envious, malicious, ill-willed, malevolent

envy, *n.*, malice, spite, ill will; *v.*, to show ill will

enwheel, encircle

Ephesian, jovial fellow, boon companion

Epicurian, Epicurean

epithet, phrase, term

epitheton, phrase, term

equal, *n.*, one of the same age; *adj.*, impartial; *v.*, to match

equivocation, ambiguity

Ercles, Hercules

erection, *for* direction (*M. W.*, iii, 5, 41)

erewhile, a little while ago, just now

eringo, the candied root of the seaholly

ern (yearn), grieve

errant, wandering; deviating

erring, *adj.*, wandering

error, a defect

erst, formerly

escape, flight; escapade; (of wit), sally, clever and whimsical idea (*M. for M.*, iv, 1, 63)

escapen, escape (*Per.*, ii, Gow., 36)

escoted, supported, maintained

esill, *see* eysell

esperance, hope

espial, a spy

essay, a trial, test. *See* assay

estate, *n.*, state or condition; rank, position; one's affairs; situation; the state (commonweal); *v.*, to settle or bestow (on); (in), settle one in the possession of

estimable, valuable; (wonder), admiring judgment

estimation, opinion, conjecture

estridge, ostrich

eterne, eternal, everlasting

eternize, immortalize

even, *v.*, act on a par with, match by our actions (*Cymb.*, iii, 4, 184)

even-Christen, even-Christian, fellow Christian

evened (I am), I am made even, I have squared accounts (*Oth.*, ii, 1, 308)

even-pleached, smoothly plaited

event, the outcome

ever among, ever and always (*2 Hen. IV*, v, 3, 23)

evil, disease; the king's evil, scrofula

evitate, avoid

examine, call in question

exceed, be preëminent

except, take exception

except before excepted, including all previous exceptions

exception, objection, disapproval, dissatisfaction

exchange, transformation

excite, incite

excitement, incentive; exhortation

exclaim, *n.*, outcry; *pl.*, cries (of grief, anger, etc.)

excrement, outgrowth, hair, beard

executor, executioner

exempt, separated, removed, expelled; remote; estranged

exercise, devout practice, act of devotion; preaching; penance

exhalation, meteor

exhale, breathe out; breathe your last (*Hen. V*, ii, 1, 66); draw out (blood, tears, a meteor)

exhaust, draw forth

exhibition, an allowance (of money)

exigent, exigence, emergency, crisis; end

exion, *for* action (*2 Hen. IV*, ii, 1, 33)

exorciser (exorcist), conjurer

exorcism, conjuration

expect, await

expectancy, hope (*Haml.*, iii, 1, 160)

expedience, speed; expedition

expedient, speedy

expend, spend, waste

expense, the spending; waste; loss

expiate, bring to a close (*Sonn.*, 22); fully come (*Rich. III*, iii, 3, 23)

exploit, a combat

expostulate, discuss, argue

exposure, exposure (*Cor.*, iv. 1, 36)

express, *v.*, to show, manifest; *adj.*,

exactly fitted to its purpose and function
expressive, frank and cordial (*All's W.*, ii, 1, 54)
expressly, clearly
expressure, expression; figure or inscription
expulse, expel, banish
exsufflicate, inflated, unsubstantial (*Oth.*, iii, 3, 182)
extant, *adj.*, present
extend, prolong, increase, magnify; seize upon; show, display
extent, seizure (by legal process); assault; manifestation; courteous greeting
extenuate, diminish; mitigate; palliate; belittle
extermine, banish; put an end to
extern, *adj.*, outward; *n.*, outward appearance
extinct (extincted), extinguished
extincture, extinction
extinguish, to eclipse
extirp, extirpate, clear away
extracting, distracting
extraught, extracted, derived (by birth)
extravagancy, random travel
extravagant, straying from home or out of bounds
eyas, a hawk still in the eyrie (nest), a falcon nestling
eyas-musket, a male sparrow hawk nestling; a lively youngster
eye, *n.*, tinge or slight shade (of colour); immediate presence; *v.*, to look, appear
eye-glass, the crystalline lens of the eye
eyestrings, muscles and tendons of the eye
eyne, eyes
eysell (esill), vinegar

face, *n.*, appearance; bold appearance, effrontery; *v.*, to brave; outface; play the hypocrite; patch, trim
face it with a card of ten, to bluff when one's highest card is a ten; to put a good face on it (*T. of S.*, ii, 1, 407)
facinerious, facinorous, wicked
fact, evil deed, crime
faction, a party, union as a party, party spirit
factionary, strongly partisan
factious, active as a partisan; (be), form a party
factor, agent, representative
faculty, power, authority; strength, vigour; potency; natural quality
fadge, succeed, come off
fading, burden of a song
fadom, fathom
fail, failure
fain, glad, content; forced, obliged; gladly
faint, languid; neglectful
fair, *n.*, fairness, beauty; beautiful person or thing; *v.*, to make beautiful
fairing, gift bought at a fair
faithed, credited, believed
faithless, unbelieving
faitor, rogue, vagabond
fall, *n.*, ebb, low tide; cadence; *v.*, to shrink, grow thin; let fall; give birth to; be born; befall; fail, prove false
fall (a-bleeding, etc.), begin to;

(away), desert; shrink, grow thin; (in with), join, become intimate; (out), quarrel; happen, turn out; (over), desert, revolt
falliable, *for* infallible
falling-from, desertion (*Tim.*, iv, 3, 402)
falling sickness, epilepsy
fallow, of a brownish colour
false, *n.*, falsehood, lying; (fire), a flash in the pan
falsing, deceptive, fallacious
fame, *n.*, rumour, report; reputation; *v.*, to make famous
famed, *p.p.*, reported (by common fame)
familiar, *adj.*, serviceable; *n.*, intimate friend; familiar (serviceable) spirit
famoused, made famous, renowned
fan, to winnow
fancies, song tunes (in impromptu style)
fancy, *n.*, *v.*, love
fang, seize as with fangs
fangled, fantastically minded, given to showy follies (*Cymb.*, v, 4, 134)
fantastic, imaginary; prodigious
fantastical, imaginary; imaginative; fantastic
fantastico, a fantastic coxcomb
fantasy, love
fap, drunk (*M. W.*, i, 1, 183)
far (farre), farther
farborough, thirdborough, constable (*L. L. L.*, i, 1, 185)
farce, to stuff
farced, stuffed; bombastic
fardel (farthel), bundle, parcel, burden
fardingale, *see* farthingale
far-fet, far-fetched, devious
farm, to let (on lease); to hire
farrow, young pigs (a litter)
farthel, *see* fardel
farthingale (fardingale), a hooped petticoat
fartuous, *for* virtuous (*M. W.*, ii, 2, 101)
fashion-monger, follower of every new fashion
fashion-monging, *adj.*, following the fashion
fashions, the farcy (a disease of horses similar to glanders)
fastened, confirmed
fat, vat
fat, *adj.*, gross, stupid; nauseating
fated, invested with the control of men's fate (*All's W.*, i, 1, 232)
fatigate, fatigued
fat-room, vat-room
fatuus, foolish
fault, *n.*, default, lack, want; mistake, loss of scent (in hunting). *See* cold fault
favour, feature, face, countenance; form; likeness; appearance; a posture in dancing
fay, faith
fear, an object of fear, person or thing feared; *v.*, to make (one) afraid, frighten; (for), be anxious about
feared by, an object of anxiety to (one)
fearful, full of fear, afraid; terrible
fear-surprised, seized upon by fear
feast, feast-day, festival; celebration; fête
feasted, *adj.*, fêted (*W. T.*, iv, 4, 63)
feat, deed; wicked deed, crime; skill

feat, *adj.*, neat; clever, dexterous
feated them, showed them how they should look, gave them a model for behaviour (*Cymb.*, i, 1, 49)
feathered, swiftly passing (*Per.*, v, 2, 15)
featly, gracefully and with skill; nimbly
feature, shape, form; likeness, make-up
featured, formed, shaped
featureless, shapeless, misshapen, ugly
fedary (feodary, federary), confederate, accomplice
fee, possession; income; rate, value
feeder, a menial; a parasite
feeding, pasturage
fee-farm (in), in perpetuity (an estate in fee-farm being granted for ever, with reservation of a certain rent)
fee grief, a personal grief
fee simple, absolute ownership
feere, *see* fere
felicitate, made happy
fell, *n.*, skin; (of hair), skin with the hair on it
fell, *adj.*, fierce, cruel, savage
fellies, felloes, segments of the rim of a wheel
fellow, *n.*, associate, comrade, companion; an equal, one's peer, match, like; *v.*, to pair or couple with
fellowly, *adj.*, companionable, sympathetic
fellowship, company, association, partnership, friendly relations, companionship
fence, to protect
feodary, *see* fedary
fere (feere), companion, spouse
ferret, *adj.*, inflamed (like a ferret's eyes); *v.*, to worry, tear, mangle
ferula, ferule
fescue, twig
festinate, speedy
festinately, speedily
fet, fetched
fetch, *n.*, trick, device, stratagem; pretence, pretext
fetch in, take captive, dupe
fettle, settle, make ready, adjust
few (in), in few words, in short
fico (figo), fig. *See* fig
fidiused, trounced (*Cor.*, ii, 1, 144)
fielded, in the battlefield (*Cor.* i, 4, 12)
fifteenth, tax amounting to a fifteenth of one's personal property
fig, *n.*, an insulting gesture made with the thumb between the first and the second finger; *v.*, to insult with this gesture
fights, canvas screens to hide the crew in a sea-fight
figo (fico), *see* fig
figure, *n.*, statue, model, image; a form in the mind or imagination; idea; *v.*, to imagine; symbolize; prefigure
file, *n.*, list, catalogue; number (of persons); position, rank; *v.*, to smooth, polish; perfect; keep pace with
fill, thill, shaft (of cart)
fill-horse, cart-horse
fillip (fillop), to snap (one) with the finger; buffet; send up into the air by a blow on a tilted board (*2 Hen. IV*, i, 2, 255)

479

Glossary

filth, a vile person
find, find out, detect; furnish, provide, fit out. *See* well-found
fine, *n.*, *v.*, end; *v.*, to make fine or specious, adorn; (for), to fix as the price
fineless, endless, infinite
firago, *for* virago, fury (*T. N.*, iii, 4, 302)
fire, to drive out or away by fire
fire-drake, fiery dragon
fire-new, fresh from the forge, brand new
firk, to drub, thrash
fisnomy, physiognomy
fit, canto
fitchew (fitchook), polecat; harlot
fitment, what befits, proper service
fitted, forced by a spasm
five for one, a method of travellers' insurance by which the person insured received five times his stake
fives, a glandular disease of horses
fixure, fixed or stable position
flake, a strand (or lock) of hair
flapdragon, a raisin floating in flaming brandy and to be caught up and swallowed; *v.*, to swallow
flap-mouthed, with broad hanging lips (*Ven.*, 920)
flat, a plain or level region; low marshy ground; a shoal, a shallow
flatlong, with the flat side
flatness, absoluteness
flatter up, indulge, soothe
flaunts, showy attire, finery
flaw, *n.*, crack, breach; fragment; gust of wind, storm; passionate impulse; outbreak, outburst; disaster, ruin; *v.*, to crack, break
flecked, dappled (with light)
fleer, *n.*, *v.*, mock, sneer, gibe (in look or speech)
fleet, float; fade, dissolve; fly away, pass swiftly; while away (time)
fleeting, inconstant
flesh, to give one a first taste of flesh, initiate; to make fierce (as by feeding on raw meat); to satiate, glut
fleshment, stimulation (by a first success)
flewed, having flews (the hanging chaps of a deep-mouthed dog)
flexure, bending, obeisance
flight, a light arrow for long-distance shooting
flighty, flying (away) quickly
flirt-gill, flighty woman (*R. and J.*, ii, 4, 162)
flote, flood, sea (*Temp.*, i, 2, 234)
flourish, *n.*, adornment, ornamentation; flowery language; fanfare (of trumpets); *v.*, to embellish; brandish; show off, swagger; blossom gorgeously; sound a flourish
flower-de-luce (fleur-de-luce), iris; fleur-de-lis
fluent, abundant, copious
flurt, to scoff at, scout
flush, in full bloom or vigour
flushing, redness (*Haml.*, i, 2, 155)
fluxive, flowing (with tears)
fly, to cause a hawk to fly after the game
fob, to cheat, trick; (off), put off with an excuse
foil, *n.*, rapier; swordsman; defeat, discomfice, disgrace; shortcoming; leaf of metal placed under

a gem to set it off; setting; *v.*, to defeat; soil, disgrace
foin, *n.*, *v.*, thrust (with a sword)
foison, abundance, harvest
fold, offspring (*Lear*, iii, 4, 126)
folly, unchastity
folly-fallen, fallen into dotage (*T. N.*, iii, 1, 75)
fond, *adj.*, foolish, trifling; (upon), foolishly partial to; *adv.*, foolishly; *v.*, to dote
fool, *n.*, a term of endearment or compassion; *v.*, to make foolish
fool-begged, so foolish as to deserve a petition for guardianship as an idiot; idiotic (*C. of E.*, ii, 1, 41)
foot, to kick, spurn; seize with the talons (*Cymb.*, v, 4, 116)
footcloth, an ornamented robe on a horse's back hanging down to the ground on both sides
footed, landed
fop, *n.*, a fool; *v.*, to dupe, cheat
foppery, foolishness; deceit
foppish, foolish
for, because; as for
forage, *n.*, preying; *v.*, to glut one's self, to raven
forbid, under a ban (*Macb.*, i, 3, 21)
forbod, *p.p.*, forbidden (*Compl.*, 164)
forbode, forbade (*Lucr.*, 1648)
force (of), of necessity, perforce; of weight
force, to reinforce; enforce; ravish, violate; urge, insist on; value, care for, regard; (not), do not hesitate or scruple
force, to farce, stuff
force perforce, by strong constraint
fordo, undo, destroy
fordone, tired out, exhausted
fore, before
forego, to go through with previously
forehand, *n.*, superior position, the better; the mainstay; *adj.*, anticipatory; (shaft), for straight-forward long-distance shooting
forehorse, leading horse in a team; usher
foresay, to decree (for the future)
forespent, past; previously spent
forestall, prevent by anticipation; deprive
forestalled, refused in advance (*2 Hen. IV*, v, 2, 38)
foreward, vanguard
forfend, forbid
forgery, invention, imagination
forgetive, quick and fertile in ideas, inventive
forked, horned (as a cuckold)
forlorn, lost
formal, in proper form, regular; rational, sane
former, forward
forsake, to refuse, deny
forset-seller, dealer in faucets (taps for casks)
forslow, to delay, linger
forspeak, speak against, oppose
forspent, tired out, exhausted
forted, fortified
forthcoming, ready to appear
forthright, straight course or path
fortune, *v.*, happen, chance; determine one's fortune
forwearied, tired out
foul, not fair, ill-looking, ugly; dirty
fouled, soiled
foulness, ugliness
founder, to exhaust, cause to break down

fox, a sword
foxship, craft, guile
fracted, broken
fraction, separation, dissension
frame, structure, edifice; device, invention
frampold (frampal), ill-tempered, perverse; turbulent
franchise, liberation, restoration; *pl.*, rights and privileges
franchised, free from offence or guilt
frank, free; liberal, free-handed
frank, *n.*, a sty for hogs; *v.*, to shut up in a sty
franklin, freeholder (of rank just below the gentry)
fraught, *n.*, cargo; load; *v.*, to load, burden; *p.p.*, laden, loaded; burdened; freighted; filled
fraughtage, cargo, freight
fraughting souls, persons on board a ship
fray, frighten, terrify
free, *adj.*, free from care, happy; innocent, free from guile; generous, noble-minded; *v.*, to acquit, absolve; *adv.*, freely
freeness, generosity
frequent, intimate; addicted, devoted
fresh, *adj.*, blooming, fair; *n.*, spring of fresh water
freshness, youthful bloom
fret, eat or wear away; variegate; ornament with carving etc.
fretful, gnawing, irritating
frets, bars under the strings of a musical instrument
friend, to befriend, help
frippery, a shop for old clothes
frize, frieze
from, out of accord with, alien to, contrary to; absent from
front, *n.*, forehead, face; forelock; first part; *v.*, to face, confront, oppose; march in front; defend
frontier, outwork
frontlet, a forehead cloth (or band)
froward, refractory, perverse, rebellious
fruitful, bounteous, bountiful
fruitfully, fully, abundantly
fruitless, barren
frush, break up
frutify, explain in full (*M. of V.*, ii, 2, 143)
fub off, put off with excuses
fulfil, fill full; fit close (*T. and C.*, Prol., 18)
fullam, false dice (*M. W.*, i, 3, 94)
fulsome, lustful
fumiter, fumitory
fust, grow musty
fustian, gibberish, especially if bombastic
fustilarian, musty old creature
futurely, in the future

gaberdine, a smock frock
gad, a sharp spike; a stylus; (upon the), on the spur of the moment
gage, *n.*, a pledge (*especially*, a glove as pledge of combat); *v.*, to pledge, risk; entangle, involve
gaingiving, misgiving
gait, act of going, way; going on, proceeding
gall, *v.*, excoriate, scratch, chafe, gnaw; vex, annoy; scoff (at); make bitter; *n.*, an irritant or annoyance; distress; bitterness, resentment

480

Glossary

Gallia, France
Gallian, French
galliard, a kind of lively dance
gallias, a large heavy galley
gallimaufry, a hotchpotch, all sorts
gallow, frighten, terrify
gallowglass, a kind of Irish soldier
gallows, gallows bird, scamp
gambol, *adj.*, sportive; *v.*, to wander incoherently
gamester, a frolicksome fellow; a prostitute
gan, began
garb, fashion, manner
garboil, disturbance, brawl
garden house, arbour, summer house
garnish, attire, equipment
gaskins, loose breeches
gasted, frightened
gastness, terrified expression
gaud, gewgaw, toy
Gawlia, Wales
gaze, object gazed at
gear, attire; stuff; business, state of affairs
geck (geek), a butt, object of ridicule; dupe
geminy, a pair (of twins)
gender, *n.*, kind, species; sort (of people); *v.*, to breed
general, *n.*, the general run of people, the multitude; *adj.*, universal
generally, universally, without exception
generation, offspring, progeny
generative, born of woman, human (*M. for M.*, iii, 2, 119)
generosity, nobility
generous, of noble or gentle birth; of noble nature; gentlemanlike, refined
genius, attendant spirit (good or evil); personification (2 *Hen. IV*, iii, 2, 337)
gennet (jennet), a small Spanish horse
gentility, gentle or noble birth; polite manners
gentle, *n.*, of gentle birth; gentlemanly; *pl.*, gentlefolk; *v.*, to ennoble
gentry, gentle birth; polite accomplishments; courtesy
George, a jewel representing Saint George and the Dragon (in the insignia of the Order of the Garter)
germains, *see* germens
german, a kinsman, a near relation
germane, related by blood
germens (germains), seeds
gest, end of the time allotted for a visit (in a royal progress)
gests, exploits in war
gesture, bearing, demeanour
ghost, to appear to one as a ghost
gi', give
gib (gib-cat), a tomcat
gibbet, to hang
giddily, carelessly
giddiness, precipitancy (*A. Y. L.*, v, 2, 6)
gig, a top
giglot (giglet), trollop
gild, to smear, colour; make drunk
gill, *see* flirt-gill *and* Jill
gillyvor, gillyflower, clove pink
gilt, gold
gimmaled, jointed
gimmors, jointed machinery
gin, a snare, trap
gin, begin

gi'n, given
ging, a gang, a pack
Ginn, Jenny
gird, *n.*, gibe, reproof; *v.*, to gibe, taunt
girdle (turn his), to shift his girdle (so as to make it easy to draw his dagger), *with a pun* — to change his temper or mood (*M. Ado*, v, 1, 142)
girt, to gird
Gis, Jesu
give, to give as a name, apply as an epithet; to display in one's coat of arms
give out, to show, report, publish
glad, gladness, joy (*Per.*, ii, Gow., 38)
glance, *n.*, indirect hit, hint, allusion; (at), *v.*, to hint at, allude to
glass, mirror
gleek (glike), jest, jeer, gibe
glib, geld, castrate
glike, *see* gleek
glimpse, the lustre; the glamour (of novelty); a tinge or touch
globy, swollen, protuberant (*T. N. K.*, v, 1, 113)
glorious, eager for glory
gloze (glose), *n.*, a subtlety; *v.*, to comment, interpret; talk cleverly or speciously; use flattering words
glut, to swallow
gnarl, to snarl
go, to walk; (through), to make a bargain; (go to), go away — used as an exclamation of protest, impatience, etc.
goatish, lecherous
gobbet, piece of raw flesh
god, to deify, idolize
god-a-mercy, God have mercy; gramercy, thank you
god-den (good-den, good-en), good e'en (evening)
God-dild (God 'ild, God 'eild), may God reward
God gi' go-den (God ye good-den, God-i-god-en, God dig-you-den), God give you good evening!
Gogs-woons (by), by God's wounds
Golgotha, Calvary
gondilo (gundello), gondola
good, *adj.*, of sufficient means; *n.*, my good friend (*vocative*); (a), a good deal, heartily (*Two G.*, iv, 4, 170)
good cheap, *adv.*, cheap
good-deed, in deed, in very deed
good life (with), in a lifelike manner (*Temp.*, iii, 3, 86); (of), moral, edifying (*T. N.*, ii, 3, 37)
good-nights, good-night songs, farewells (2 *Hen. IV*, iii, 2, 343)
goodyear, goodyears, goodyere, pox
gorbellied, fat-paunched
gorge, throat, stomach; (cast or heave the), to be nauseated, vomit
gorget, armour for the throat
gospelled, converted to gospel teachings
gossamer, filmy thread of cobweb
gosse, gorse
gossip, *n.*, a sponsor, a godfather or godmother; *fem.*, familiar friend; busybody; *v.*, to stand sponsor for; make merry at a christening
gourd, a kind of false dice
gout, a drop
government, behaviour; conduct; self-control
governor, tutor; manager
grace, *n.*, any pleasing quality;

favour, honour; virtue; *v.*, to honour; gratify; beautify
graced, honourable
graceful, favouring; holy
gracious, well-pleasing; virtuous, holy; lovely
graciously, persuasively, eloquently; virtuously
graff, *n.*, *v.*, graft
graft, *p.p.*, grafted
grafter, the tree from which the scion was taken
grain, cochineal dye; (in), dyed in a fast colour, grained
grained, dyed in grain; discoloured by age; tough-grained (*Cor.*, iv, 5, 113); forked (*Compl.*, 64)
gramercy (gramercies), much thanks, many thanks, thank you
grand-guard, a piece of armour for the left side
grandsir, grandsire
grange, farmhouse, country house
grate, vex, annoy; disturb; (on), pester, harass
gratify, reward, repay
gratility, small gratuity (*T. N.*, ii, 3, 27)
gratulate, *v.*, greet, congratulate, wish joy; *adj.*, gratifying
grave, dignified, reverend
grave, bury; engrave
graved, furrowed, frowning
greaves, armour for the leg below the knee
'gree, agree
Greek, lively fellow, featherbrain
green, fresh, young; immature, unsophisticated; foolish; sallow
greenly, like a novice, foolishly
grievance, trouble, distress
grisled, grisly, fierce (*Per.*, iii, Gower, 47)
gripe, griffin
grize (grise), a step or stair
grizzle (a), a crop of grey hair
grizzled, grey-haired; dark with some white hairs
groat, a fourpenny piece
groom, a menial; a fellow; bridegroom
gross, *adj.*, large; coarse; stupid; manifest, obvious; *n.*, full amount; *adv.*, plainly
grossly, stupidly, foolishly; obviously; in a gross (unpurified, unabsolved) condition
grossness, absurdity
ground, plain-song, melody
groundling, a spectator in the pit
ground-piece, a model
grow, to accrue
grunt, to groan
guard, trimming
guardage, protection, guardianship
guardant, *n.*, protector; *adj.*, on guard
guess, *n.*, opinion; *v.*, to think, believe
guidon, a small flag
guiled, full of guile, treacherous
guinea hen, loose woman
gules, red colour (in heraldry)
gulf, abyss; whirlpool; belly
gull, *n.*, young bird, nestling; dupe, simpleton; imposture; *v.*, to dupe
gundello, *see* gondilo
gunstone, cannon ball
gurnet, a gurnard (fish)
gust, appetite; indulgence; *v.*, to taste, perceive
gyve, *n.*, *v.*, fetter

Glossary

habit, fashion; behaviour, demeanour

habitude, one's nature, natural qualities

hack, see hick

hackneyed, made too familiar

haggard, n., a wild hawk; adj., unchaste

haggle, to hack, gash

hag-seed, witch's offspring

hair, nature, character

hair-worth, the worth of a hair, a jot

halcyon, kingfisher

hale, v., pull, draw, drag, haul; maltreat

half-achieved, half-won

half-blooded, of good blood on one side only

half-caps, slight salutes with one's cap

half-cheek, profile

half-cheeked, having but one side-piece

half-face, thin face

half-faced, showing only half the face; thin-faced; miserable

half-kirtle, a short kirtle or gown

half-sights, purblind persons

half-sword (at), in close combat

halidome (holidam, holidame), holiness, all that one holds sacred

hall (a), make room (for dancing) (R. and J., i, 5, 28)

Hallowmas, All Saints' Day (November 1)

halt, to limp

hand (at), when checked; (at any), by all means, at any rate, in any case; (in), by the hand; (out of), immediately; (to make a fair), to do a good job

handfast, close custody; contract of marriage

handkercher, handkerchief

hands (of all), in any event, at any rate; (of his), in action, in fight

handy-dandy, the formula in a childish game of choosing which of two closed hands holds an object

hanger, a strap or loop by which a rapier hangs from the belt

hanging, arras

hangman, n., executioner; adj., rascally

happily, haply, perchance, perhaps

happiness, felicity (of phrase); comeliness

happy, adj., well-expressed, felicitous; cultivated, accomplished; v., to make happy

hard-haired, with a heavy crop of hair

hardiment, prowess

hardly, with difficulty

hardness, hardship

hardock, hardhack, a kind of wild flower (Lear, iv, 4, 4)

Harflew, Harfleur

Har'ford, Haverford

harlot, n., base man, rascal; adj., lewd

harlotry, n., harlot; wayward creature; adj., rascally

harp, to sound, give expression to

Harpier, the name of a demon (perhaps suggested by 'harpy') (Macb., iv, 1, 3)

Harry ten-shillings, pieces coined by King Harry (really by Henry VII) (2 Hen. IV, iii, 2, 236)

hatch, n., half-door, the lower half of a door that opens in two segments

hatch, v., to ornament with plates of metal (fig., T. and C., i, 3, 65)

hatched, closed with a half-door

hatchment, a tablet with coat of arms set up on the house of a deceased person

hateful, full of hate, malignant

haught, haughty

haunch, the latter end

have, catch one's meaning (Haml., ii, 1, 68)

have-at-him, an attack, assault

have at you, let me get at you (as a notice of attack etc.). Similarly, have to it (let's get at it), have after, amongst, through, with

having, possession, estate, allowance

haviour, behaviour, demeanour, bearing

havoc, the cry 'No quarter!' 'Spare none!'; v., to rend in pieces

hawking (eye), quick and bright, like a falcon's

hay, a country dance like a reel

hay, home thrust (R. and J., ii, 4, 27)

hazard, a game at dice; one's stake; a winning opening in a tennis court

head, an armed force

headland, a strip left unploughed at the end of a field and ploughed afterwards in cross furrows (2 Hen. IV, v, 1, 16)

heap, a crowd, throng, band

hearse, bier, coffin

hearsed, coffined

heart, an oath 'by God's heart'

hearted, deep-seated in the heart

heartlings, little heart (M. W., iii, 4, 59)

heat, to run across (W. T., i, 2, 96)

heave, a sigh

heavily, mournfully

heaviness, drowsiness; sadness

heaving, a sigh

heavy, sad; sleepy

hebona, ebony

hectic, a continual fever

hedge, to turn aside; use shifts; sneak along

hedge-pig, hedgehog

hefts, retchings (W. T., ii, 1, 45)

heighth, height

hell, a prison for debtors (C. of E., iv, 2, 40)

helm, to steer, manage

helpless, unavailing; irremediable

hempen caudle, the hangman's noose

hempseed, one worthy to be hanged (2 Hen. IV, ii, 1, 64)

hence, not here, absent; henceforth

hent, v., to seize, take; n., time for being grasped (Haml., iii, 3, 88)

heraldry, warrant (All's W., ii, 3, 280)

herb of grace, rue

Herculean, descended from Hercules

hereby, near at hand; (that's), that depends, that's as may be

hereto, hitherto

hermit, beadsman, one bound to pray for a benefactor

hest, command; exploit

hether, hither

heyday, liveliness, youthful ardour

hick and hack, to cut and slash (M. W., iv, 1, 68)

hide fox and all after, a game in which one hides and the rest try to find him

high and low, false dice

high-battled, commanding victorious armies

high-blown, puffed up, inflated

high-lone, on one's own feet (R. and J., i, 3, 36)

high-sighted, arrogant

high-stomached, of haughty and irascible temper

hight, is named

highth, height

high-witted, quick-witted and ingenious

hild, held (Lucr., 1257)

hilding, n., a worthless creature; adj., worthless, insignificant

hind, farm labourer; servant, menial; low fellow

hint, occasion, opportunity

hip (on or upon the), at one's mercy, in one's power

hipped, lamed in the hip

his, its

history, n., story; historical drama; v., to tell the story of

hit, to succeed; to interpret; (together), coöperate

hitherto, until now, up to the present

hizzing, whizzing (Lear, iii, 6, 18)

ho, interj., stop, whoa (T. N. K., v, 2, 18)

hoar, adj., ghastly white; v., to grow stale; to smite with leprosy

hobby-horse, simpleton; prostitute

hob nob, give or take (T. N., iii, 4, 263)

hodge-pudding, a big sausage; a mishmash

hoise, to hoist; p.p., blown up

hold, to interpret; wager; hold back, refrain; hold out; profit; hold good, prove true; (in), keep a secret

holding, burden (of a song); consistency

holidame, see halidome

Holland, linen

holp, helped

holy-ale, holiday celebration (Per., Prol., 6)

home, adv., to the destination intended (as by a home thrust), to a finish, thoroughly; to the point

honest, honourable, chaste

honesty, honour, decency, chastity

honeyseed, for homicide, homicidal (2 Hen. IV., ii, 1, 57, 58)

honeysuckle, for homicidal (2 Hen. IV, ii, 1, 56)

honoured, honourable

honour-owing, honourable

hoodman, the blindfolded player in blindman's buff

hoodman-blind, blindman's buff

hoodwink, to blindfold; make invisible

hook of, that which tempts to (Cymb., v, 5, 167)

hoop, to cry out, whoop

hope, n., expectation (good or ill); v., to expect

hopeful, hoped for, expected

horn, the mark of a cuckold

hornbook, a primer

horned man, a cuckold

horning (in), in making cuckolds

horn-mad, mad enough to gore one; mad because of being a cuckold

horn-maker, maker of cuckolds

horologe, clock

horse-drench, a dose for a horse

horse-leech, a large leech or bloodsucker

482

Glossary

hose, breeches
host, to lodge
hothouse, a house for hot baths; a brothel
hourly, marking the hours
house-clogs, fetters
housekeeper, a dog that guards the house
hovel-post, a post supporting an open shed or a stack
howlet, owlet, owl
howsoever (howsoe'er), although; in any case, anyhow
hox, to hamstring
hoy, a small vessel
hugger-mugger (in), in secrecy
hulk, a large ship of burden
hull, to drift about
humane, civilized, civilizing
humorous, damp; capricious; governed by a humour, eccentric
humour, *n.*, one of the four liquids in the body (blood, phlegm, bile, and black bile or melancholy); dominant humour, temperament, disposition; disordered humour; caprice, fancy, idea; *v.*, to indulge; influence; flatter
hundreth, hundred
hungerly, *adj.*, sparse, thin; *adv.*, hungrily, with appetite
hunt, game
hunt's-up, a song to awake one early
hurly, tumult, noise
hurricano, a waterspout
hurtle, to sound confusedly
hurtling, disturbance, tumult
husband, *n.*, the master of a house; careful manager; husbandman; *v.*, to manage
husbandry, management, care; economy
hush, silent, still
husht, *interj.*, hush (*Per.*, i, 3, 10)
huswife, hussy
hyen, hyena
Hyperion, the sun god
Hyrcan, of Hyrcania (in Asia on the Caspian Sea)
hysterica passio, hysteria

I, ay (*R. and J.*, iii, 2, 45)
ice brook's temper, of steel tempered by immersing it in an ice-cold stream
Iceland dog, a sharp-eared dog
idea, exact image, likeness; mental image
idle, empty, useless, vain; waste; absurd, silly, trifling; meaningless, mad, incoherent
idle-headed, empty-headed, silly
idleness, want of cultivation; folly, absurdity
idly, madly, absurdly, heedlessly
i' fecks, in faith
ignis fatuus, will-o'-the-wisp
ignomy, ignominy
ignorant, causing ignorance, stupefying; unknown to one's self
'ild, *see* God-dild
Ilion, Troy
Ilion (Ilium), Priam's palace
ill-composed, composed of evil qualities
ill-disposed, poorly arranged
ill-favoured, ugly
ill-favouredly, unbecomingly
illiad, *see* eliad
ill-inhabited, poorly lodged
illness, evil quality, fault
ill-ta'en, mistaken

ill-tempered, distempered
illustrate, *v.*, to indicate brilliantly; *adj.*, illustrious
illustrious, without lustre (*Cymb.*, i, 6, 109)
ill-wresting, twisting everything awry (*Sonn.*, 140)
image, idea, thought; likeness, form, exact copy
imaginary, imaginative
imagined, of the imagination
imbare, to uncover, expose (*Hen. V*, i, 2, 94)
imbecility, weakness
imbrue (embrew), stain with blood; stain one's sword with blood, shed blood (*2 Hen. IV*, ii, 4, 210)
immanity, ferocity
immediacy, condition of an immediate representative
immediate jewel, the very jewel (*Oth.*, iii, 3, 156)
immediately, expressly
imminent deadly, threatening death
immodest, immoderate, unrestrained
immoment, of no account, of slight value
immures, surrounding walls
imp, *n.*, scion, youngster; *v.*, to graft; to mend (a wing) by grafting
impair, *v.*, to weaken; *adj.*, unbalanced, unfit (*T. and C.*, iv, 5, 103)
impale (empale), to hem in, surround, encircle
impart, make the gift (of heirship), *or* express my feelings (*Haml.*, i, 2, 112)
impartment, communication
impawn, to pledge as security
impeach, *v.*, to discredit, impugn; *n.*, accusation; discredit
impeachment, discredit; hindrance, opposition
imperator, commander
imperceiverant, undiscerning (*Cymb.*, iv, 1, 16)
imperial, emperor (*Two G.*, ii, 3, 5)
imperious, imperial
impeticos, pocket up (*T. N.*, ii, 3, 27)
impleached, interwoven
implorator, solicitor
impone, to wager
import, bring with them (*A. and C.*, ii, 2, 135)
importance, business; import; importunity
importancy, importance
important, importunate
importing, important, of import
importless, without significance
importment, signification, meaning
impose, *n.*, injunction; *v.*, to enjoin (one)
imposition, something laid upon or ascribed to (one); charge, imputation of guilt; penalty
imposthume, abscess
impotence, weakness, feeble health
impotent, infirm
imprese, one's emblematic device and motto
impress, *n.*, impression; impressment, conscription; *v.*, to enlist by conscription
improve, utilize
impudency, impudence
impudent, shameless, immodest
impugn, withstand
imputation, reputation; inference
in, into; on; in custody or prison
in-a-door, indoors

incapable, unable to take in, hold, or realize
incardinate, incarnate (*T. N.*, v, 1, 185)
incarnadine, to stain blood-red (*Macb.*, ii, 2, 62)
incarnation, *for* incarnate (*M. of V.*, ii, 2, 28)
incense, to incite, instigate; inflame with the idea (*Hen. VIII*, v, 1, 43)
inchmeal (by), inch by inch
incidency, act of falling upon, incidence
incision, bloodletting; surgical cutting
incivil, boorish, rude
incivility, boisterously rude behaviour
inclining, *adj.*, disposed to grant requests, obliging; *n.*, one's party, side; partiality
inclip, to embrace
include, bring to harmonious conclusion (*Two G.*, v, 4, 160)
income, the coming in, safe arrival (*Lucr.*, 334)
incontinent(-ly), immediately, forthwith
incony, dainty, delicate (*L. L. L.*, iii, 1, 136)
incorporal, bodiless
incorpsed, made one body
incorrect, undisciplined, rebellious
increaseful, abundant (*Lucr.*, 958)
incredulous, incredible
Inde, India, the Indies
indent, make an indenture (contract)
index, table of contents, prefatory summary; introduction, prologue
indifferency, moderate bulk; impartiality
indifferent, *adj.*, impartial; ordinary; average; *adv.*, rather, tolerably
indifferently, impartially; tolerably
indigest, *adj.*, shapeless; *n.*, chaos
indigested, shapeless
indign, disgraceful
indirect, wrong, unjust, irregular
indirection, devious ways; crooked or dishonest means
indirectly, wrongfully
indisposition, disinclination
indistinguishable, of inextricably mixed breed, mongrel (*T. and C.*, v, 1, 33)
indistinguished, past the limit of vision, boundless (*Lear*, iv, 6, 278)
indite (endite), invite, engage
individable, observing the unities of time and place (*Haml.*, ii, 2, 418)
indubitate, undoubted, notorious
induction, beginning, outset; preparatory scheme; introductory play (as in *T. of S.*)
indue (endue), to provide, furnish, endow; (to, unto), to furnish with qualities that adapt one to; to bring into sympathetic agreement with (*Oth.*, iii, 4, 146)
indurance, submission, long suffering (*Hen. VIII*, v, 1, 121)
industrious, skilful, ingenious; zealous
industriously, on purpose, deliberately
inequality, incongruity (*M. for M.*, v, 1, 65)
infamonize, brand with infamy (*L. L. L.*, v, 2, 684)
infection, *for* affection (*M. W.*, ii, 2, 120); desire (*M. of V.*, ii, 2, 133)

infer, to bring about, procure; allege, adduce; imply

infest, to harass

infinitive, infinite (*2 Hen. IV*, ii, 1, 26)

inflame, set on fire, make excessive (*T. N. K.*, iii, 5, 130)

inflict, afflict

influence, the inflowing of power from (*or* as from) the stars

inform (thus), to give this (false) information (*Macb.*, ii, 1, 48); (with nobleness), imbue, inspire (*Cor.*, v, 3, 71)

informal, distracted

infusion, nature, character; medicinal quality

ingenious, clever, naturally able; intellectual; conscious

ingeniously, ingenuously, sincerely (*Tim.*, ii, 2, 230)

ingraffed (ingraft, engraffed), ingrafted

ingredience, ingredients (collectively), contents

inhabit, abide

inhabitable, uninhabitable

inhearse, to entomb

inherit, to possess; (of), to make one entertain (*Rich. II*, i, 1, 85)

inheritor, owner

inhibition, what hinders

inhooped, surrounded with the hoop within which quails or cocks were set to fight

initiate, *adj.*, of a novice (*Macb.*, iii, 4, 143)

injoint, unite, combine

injurious, unjust, unrighteous; insulting

injury, *n.*, insult; *pl.*, things whose loss is an injury

inkhorn mate, one of these writing fellows

inkle, a sort of tape

inland, internal; (bred), in refined society (not in the wild outskirts of the land); (man), cultivated

inly, *adj.*, inward; *adv.*, inwardly

inn, *v.*, to get in, harvest (*All's W.*, i, 3, 48)

innocent, *n.*, fool, idiot

inoculate, to graft

inprimis, imprimis, first in order

inordinate, beyond moderation (*Oth.*, ii, 3, 311)

inquire, *n.*, inquiry

insane, causing insanity

insanie, insanity (*L. L. L.*, v, 1, 28)

insconce (ensconce), to hide. *See* ensconce

inscroll, enter on a scroll

insculp, engrave

insculpture, inscription

inseparate, inseparable

inshelled, drawn into the shell

insinuate, ingratiate one's self; remind, make (one) think (*L. L. L.*, v, 1, 28)

insinuation, *n.*, worming one's way in

insisture, steady motion onward (*T. and C.*, i, 3, 87)

insociable, remote from society; eccentric

instalment, seat of installation (*M. W.*, v, 5, 67)

instance, example, illustration; proof; motive, cause; adage

instant, instantly

instantly, at the same time

instate, invest

---

instrumental, naturally serviceable

insult, to exult insolently

insultment, arrogant triumph

intellect, purport, signification (*L. L. L.*, iv, 2, 136)

intelligence, spying

intelligencer, secret agent; interpreter

intelligencing, *adj.*, acting as secret agent

intelligent, carrying information

intemperance, unruly conduct; incontinence

intend, tend; pretend; mean

intended, understood, implied

intendment, intention; design

intenible, unable to retain (*All's W.*, i, 3, 208)

intention, intentness; intensity

intentively, with continuous attention

intercept, interrupt

interest, a claim

inter'gatory, interrogatory

interlude, a short play; a farce

intermission, interruption

intermissive, discontinued for a time

intertissued, interwoven

intervallum, interval

intil, into

intituled, entitled

intrenchant, not to be cut, invulnerable

intrinse (intrinsicate), intricately tied

intrude, force one's way into

inurned, entombed (*Haml.*, i, 4, 49)

invectively, with abusive language

investments, attire

invincible, not to be taken by the eye, invisible (*2 Hen. IV*, iii, 2, 337)

invised, unseen (*Compl.*, 212)

inward, *adj.*, inmost; secret; (with), in one's confidence; *n.*, inside; an intimate

inwardness, intimacy

irregulous, unprincipled, lawless

Ise, I shall (*Lear*, iv, 6, 246)

issue, result, product; action, deed

issued, descended

it, its

iterance, iteration, repetition

iwis, certainly

Jack (jack), fellow, chap, rogue; a man's figure which strikes the bell on a clock; a drinking vessel (*with a pun*); a small bowl aimed at by the players; a key in a virginal

jack-a-Lent, a man's figure pelted in sport during Lent; a butt; a little fellow

jackanapes, an ape or monkey

Jacksauce, impudent fellow

Jack-slave, a low fellow (*Cymb.*, ii, 1, 22)

jade, *n.*, a poor or worn-out horse, a nag; a worthless woman (*or* man); *v.*, to trick, befool; drive away exhausted

jaded, contemptible (*2 Hen. VI*, iv, 1, 52)

jadery, a nag's tricks

jakes, a privy

jane, a kind of fustian; *adj.*, coarse, untaught

jar, *n.*, *v.*, tick

jaunce, *v.*, to prance; to trudge; *n.*, a hard jaunt

iaundies, jaundice

---

jay, a showy woman (*Cymb.*, iii, 4, 51)

jealous (-ious), suspicious; (hood), a jealous dame (*R. and J.*, iv, 4, 13)

jealousy, suspicion

jennet, *see* gennet

jerkin, a close-fitting jacket

jesses, straps attached to a falcon's legs and connecting with the leash

jest, to sport

jet, to strut, swagger; parade; encroach

jig, *n.*, a comic song (and dance) in dialogue; *v.*, to perform a jig; to sing merrily; to walk with a dancing gait

Jill, Gillian; girl

John-a-dreams, a dreamy fellow

John Drum's entertainment (i.e., treatment), dismissal with a beating (*All's W.*, iii, 6, 41)

joinder, clasping

joined-stool, *see* joint-stool

jointress, dowager

joint-ring, a ring of separable halves

joint-stool (joined-, join-), stool made by a joiner

jordan, a chamber pot

journal, diurnal, daily

journey-bated, exhausted by travel

jowl, to dash

judicious, judicial

jump, *n.*, chance, hazard; *v.*, to risk, hazard; agree; coincide; *adv.*, exactly

junkets, sweetmeats, delicacies

justicer, a judge

justle, to jostle, elbow, push, force, shock

justling, turbulent

justly, rightly, exactly, precisely

jutty, *n.*, projection; *v.*, to overhang

juvenal, a youth

kam, cam, crooked, askew

kecksy, dry stalk

keech, a round lump of fat

keel, to skim

keep, *n.*, keeping, charge; *v.*, to guard; reside, stay; stay in or with; keep up, maintain; (touch), stand the test, come to time, fail not

keeper, guarding angel or spirit; doorkeeper

keeping, maintenance

Keiser, the Emperor (Kaiser)

ken, *v.*, to know; recognize; descry; *n.*, sight, range of eyesight

kennel, gutter; pack

kern, a light-armed Irish or Highland foot-soldier

kersey, coarse woolen cloth

kettle, kettledrum

kibe, chilblain

kickshaws, dainty dishes

kickshawses, fanciful amusements

kicy-wicky, pet, darling wife

kid-fox, a young fox

kidney, constitution (*M. W.*, iii, 5, 117)

killen, kill (*Per.*, ii, Prol., 20)

Killingworth, Kenilworth

kiln-hole, the fire-hole of a kiln or oven

kind, *n.*, nature; *adj.*, natural

kindle, to bring forth, bear

kindless, unnatural

kindly, *adj.*, natural; *adv.*, according to one's nature

kingdomed, *adj.*, like a (tumultuous) kingdom (*T. and C.*, ii, 3, 185)

Glossary

kirtle, a gown
kissing comfits, perfumed sweet-meats
kitchen, to serve one as cook (*C. of E.*, v, 1, 415)
knack, gewgaw, knicknack; plaything (*W. T.*, iv, 4, 439)
knap, to snap off bit by bit; rap
knave, boy, youth; servant
knit, knitted texture
knoll, to ring, toll; sound, resound; call by a bell
knot, garden plot
knotty pated, with a head as dense as a knot in wood
koth-a, *see* quoth

label, an attached slip carrying the seal; a slip with writing on it
laboursome, elaborate
labras, lips (*M. W.*, i, 1, 166)
lace, to adorn
laced mutton, a strumpet
lade, to bail (*3 Hen. VI*, iii, 2, 139)
lag, *n.*, dregs, lowest sort; *adj.*, of old age; *adv.*, late; (of), behind, later than
lag-end, fag-end
Lakin (by'r) by our Lady (the Virgin)
lamentable, sorrowful
lamp, torch
lampass, a congestion of the mucous membrane in horses
lanch, to lance
land (laund), a forest glade
land-damn, *meaning unknown* (*W. T.*, ii, 1, 143)
land-rakers (foot), vagrant footpads
languish, *n.*, pining
lank, to grow thin
lanthorn, lantern; a turret with windows on every side
lap, to wrap
lapse, *n.*, slipping, loss of one's footing; *v.*, to fall into sin, to err
lapsed (if I be), if I do not heed my steps, walk circumspectly (*T. N.*, iii, 3, 36)
lapsed in, having proved dilatory and inconstant (*Haml.*, iii, 4, 107)
lard, to fatten; deck or strew (with); garnish
large, liberal; broad, loose; licentious
lark's-heel, larkspur
'larum: *see* alarum
'las, alas
latch, to catch; catch or bind as with a spell, enchant (*M. N. D.*, iii, 2, 36)
late, recent; lately, of late, once
lated, belated; overtaken by darkness
latten, made of latten (tin plate)
latter, last; (spring), coming late in the year, like Indian summer
laund (land), open space in the woods, glade
lavish, unrestrained, lawless, loose; wasteful
lavolt (lavolta), a high-capering dance
law of writ, drama that observes the classical rules (*Haml.*, ii, 2, 420)
lay, *n.*, stake, wager; *v.*, to stake, wager; beset; (by), lay down (one's pack); (for), set traps for, waylay; (up), fold up and lay in store
layer-up, preserver

lazar, leper
lead, to weight with lead
leading, command; military skill, generalship
leaguer, camp
leap, to leap into
learn, teach
learned, well educated
learning, an acquirement; information
leash, a set of three
leasing, lying; a falsehood
leather-coats, russet apples
leathren, leathern
leave, *n.*, permission to depart; liberty in excess, license; *v.*, leave off, cease, refrain from; give up; go out of business
leavened, matured, well-considered
leavy, leafy
lecture, instruction
leech, physician
leer, complexion, hue
leese, lose (*Sonn.*, 5)
leet, a manorial court; its day of session
leg, an elaborate bow, an obeisance
legatine, of a legate (an ecclesiastic representing the Pope)
'lege, allege
legerity, lightness, nimbleness
leiger, a resident ambassador or agent
leisure (by), hardly ever, never (*T. A.*, i, 1, 301); (by my good), having a favourable opportunity (*M. for M.*, iii, 2, 261)
leman, lover, sweetheart
lend, give
lendings, unessential furnishings (lent to one) (*Lear*, iii, 4, 114)
length, *n.*, delay (*A. and C.*, iv, 14, 46); stride (*T. N. K.*, v, 4, 57); range (*Per.*, i, 1, 168)
lengthen, to defer, delay
lenten, befitting Lent; scanty, meagre
l'envoy, epilogue, addendum
leperous, producing leprosy or the like
lesson, to teach
let, *n.*, impediment, hindrance; *v.*, to hinder; forbear, refrain
let-alone, prohibition
lethe, death (*J. C.*, iii, 1, 206)
letters, a letter, an epistle
level, *n.*, line of aim, range; *adj.*, on an equality; just, fair; *v.*, to guess
lewd, mean, low, given to low society
lewdly, basely; (bent), with base designs
lewdster, licentious fellow
Lewis, Louis
liable, subject (to); fit
libbard, leopard
liberal, free; outspoken; refined, cultivated; licentious
liberal-conceited (of liberal conceit), elegantly designed
liberty, license; drama that does not observe the classical rules (*Haml.*, ii, 2, 421); (of sin), wicked transgressor (*C. of E.*, i, 2, 102)
licourish, lickerish, delicious
lie, to lodge, dwell; be in prison; stand in a defensive posture; (on), depend on
lief, dear, beloved
lien, *p.p.*, lain
lieutenantry (deal on), to act by

means of one's lieutenants or sub-stitutes (*A. and C.*, iii, 11, 39)
lieve (live), lief, dear
lifelings, little life (*T. N.*, v, 1, 187)
lifter, a thief
liggens (God's), an oath
light, *p.p.*, alighted, arrived (*Per.*, iv, 2, 77)
lighten, enlighten
lightly, easily, readily, heedlessly; usually
like, to liken; to please, suit; (well), to be in good condition, to be fat
likelihood, probable indication; comparison
liking, bodily condition; (in some), not thin
limbeck, alembic; the cap of a still
limbmeal, limb from limb
limbo, a region on the border of hell; prison, captivity
Limbo Patrum (in), in prison (*lit.*, in the limbo reserved for the souls of the just who died before Christ's coming)
lime, *n.*, birdlime; *v.*, to smear with birdlime; to catch with (*or* as with) birdlime; to cement; to put lime into sack
lime-twig, a twig smeared with birdlime
limit, *n.*, appointed time; (strength of), strength gained during the period of lying-in (confinement); *v.*, to appoint
limiter, he who determines one's course
line, to delineate; to make strong, fortify
line, *n.*, lime tree, linden
linger, to protract, draw out
link, a torch
linsey-woolsey, a material of mixed linen and woollen; gibberish
linstock, the staff that holds the gunner's match
lip, to kiss
Lipsbury Pinfold (in), in the pound of Liptown, i.e. between my teeth, in my grip (*Lear*, ii, 2, 9)
liquor, to grease (boots)
list, boundary, limit; goal
list, *n.*, desire; *v.*, to desire, please
lither, pliant, yielding
live (lieve), lief
liveless, lifeless
livelihood, liveliness, life, vigour
lively, *adj.*, living, alive; lifelike; *adv.*, to the life
liver vein, the amatory style (the liver being regarded as the seat of the passion of love)
livery, *n.*, delivery of an estate to the heir; *v.*, to attire
live's, life's
loach, a small fish
lob, *n.*, bumpkin; *v.*, to lop, hang (the head), droop
lock, to restrain by embracing
lockram, a kind of linen
lodestar, guiding star, the polestar
loggets, a game like quoits but played with small logs
loggerhead, a blockhead
'long, to belong
longly, for a long while, intently
long of, on account of
'loo, halloo
loofed (being), having sailed off
look, to seek, search, search for.
look up

loon (lown), rogue, rascal, lout; man of low rank, peasant
loop, loophole
looped, full of holes or slits
loose, *n.*, the discharge (of an arrow); *v.*, to discharge, shoot
loosely studied, given to low ways
loose shot, marksmen not attached to a company
lop, trimmings of trees (*Hen. VIII*, i, 2, 96)
lord, husband
lording, a little lord, a fine youngster
Lord's sake (for the), in prison (from the cry of poor prisoners begging for alms)
Lord's tokens, spots indicating the final stage of the plague (*L. L. L.*, v, 2, 423)
lose, to let slip, forget; to cast away, ruin, destroy
loss, ruin, disaster; casting away (*W. T.*, ii, 3, 191)
lots, lottery tickets that draw a prize; lots (to blanks), everything to nothing, practically certain
lottery, prize, allotment
lout, to mock, flout
love-broker, a go-between
love-day, a day appointed for the friendly settlement of quarrels, a day of reconciliation
lover, sweetheart; friend
lovered, provided with a lover (*Compl.*, 320)
loves (of all), for love's sake, if you love him, by all means (*Oth.*, iii, 1, 13)
love-springs, young shoots of love (as of a plant)
lown, *see* loon
lozel, scoundrel, wretch
lubber, *for* leopard (*2 Hen. IV*, ii, 1, 31)
luce, pike (fish)
lucre, covetousness
Lud's town, London
lull, loll (*Rich. III*, iii, 7, 72)
Lumbert Street, Lombard Street
lumpish, out of spirits, dull
lunes, mad fits or notions, lunacy
lurch, to pilfer, filch; (of), rob of, win from
lure, a kind of decoy for a falcon
lush, luxuriant
lust, delight, pleasure (*Lucr.*, 1384)
lust-breathed, urged on by lust (*Lucr.*, 3)
lust-dieted man, one whose every desire is fed (*Lear*, iv, 1, 68)
lustihood, vigour of body
lusty, merry
luxurious, lustful
luxuriously, lasciviously
luxury, lust
lym, bloodhound

Machiavel (Machivel), Macchiavelli
machine, contrivance, device, invention
maculate, stained, impure, unclean
maculation, stain, impurity
made-up, perfect, complete
maggot-pie, magpie
magnanimity, heroism
magnanimous, heroic
magnifico, a Venetian nobleman
maidenhead, virginity
Maid Marian, a character in May games and rustic dances
mail, *n.*, wallet, budget (*L. L. L.*,

iii, 1, 74); *v.*, to cover, wrap (*2 Hen. VI*, ii, 4, 31)
main, *n.*, full strength; mainland; main part; stake (in diceplay)
main, *v.*, to maim (*2 Hen. VI*, iv, 2, 172)
main-course, mainsail
mainly, strongly; very (*Lear*, iv, 7, 65)
maintenance, bearing, behaviour
major, major premise in a syllogism (*1 Hen. IV.*, ii, 4, 544)
majority, superiority
make, to do; shut and bar (a door); collect, get together; make the fortune of; go; (dainty), to act coyly; (nice of), to reject fastidiously
makeless, mateless (*Sonn.*, 9)
malapert, saucy
malhecho, mischief, evil (*Haml.*, iii, 2, 147)
malkin (mawkin), a slattern, kitchen maid
mallard, drake
malmsey, a strong sweet wine
malthorse, a maltster's horse
maltworm, an ale-drinker
mammer on, to hesitate about
mammet, a doll; a babyish girl
mammock, to tear in pieces
man, to tame (a falcon); to provide with a manservant; to handle as a weapon (*Oth.*, v, 2, 270)
manage, *n.*, manège, art and practise of horsemanship; training; control; management; a course or short gallop; *v.*, to train; handle, wield; carry on
mandragora, mandrake
man-entered, initiated into manhood
mankind, *adj.*, masculine, mannish
manner (with the), in the act, in flagrante delicto
man-queller, man-killer
mantle, *n.*, scum; *v.*, to form scum
manure, to till, cultivate
mappery, map-making (*T. and C.*, i, 3, 205)
marches, border lands, frontier
marchpane, cake made of almonds, sugar, etc.
mare, the nightmare (a demon)
mare (the wild), a seesaw
margent, margin
marish, marsh
mark, two-thirds of a pound sterling
mark (God bless *or* save the), a phrase of unknown origin used to avert evil (like 'absit omen') or in apology
marmoset, a small monkey
marry, *an oath* 'by the Virgin Mary,' *but used as a light interjection*; indeed, to be sure, why
mart, *n.*, market, market place; market time; trading; bargain; *v.*, to bargain, traffic; to market
Martialist, follower of Mars, warrior
Martin, *see* Saint Martin
Martlemas, beef salted at Martinmas (St. Martin's day, November 11) — jocose nickname for Falstaff (*2 Hen. IV*, ii, 2, 110)
martlet, the martin
marvell's, marvellous
masked, *adj.*, with surface as unruffled as a mask is unchanging, calm (*Per.*, iii, 3, 36)
masoned, of masonry
Mary-buds, buds of the marigold

mastic, snarling (*T. and C.*, i, 3, 73)
match, appointment; bargain, agreement; plan, scheme
mate, *n.*, low fellow
mate, *v.*, to daze, stupefy
material, full of matter and sense (*A. Y. L.*, iii, 3, 32); that produces one's life and substance, elemental (*Lear*, iv, 2, 35)
matin, morning
matter, cause of complaint or quarrel, dispute
maugre, in spite of
maund, a hand basket
maw, stomach
mawkin, *see* malkin
maze, to daze, confound
mazzard, head, pate
meacock, cowardly, mean-spirited (*T. of S.*, ii, 1, 315)
mealed, spotted, stained (*M. for M.*, iv, 2, 86)
mean, *n.*, means; a part between treble and bass
mean, *v.*, to lament (*M. N. D.*, v, 1, 330)
measurable, fit, appropriate
measure, *n.*, a stately dance; tune; *v.*, to dance (a measure)
meat, food
meddler, trafficker, general agent (*W. T.*, iv, 4, 329)
medicinable (med'cinable), medicinal, curative
medicine, *n.*, drug, magic potion; the alchemist's tincture, the philosopher's stone; physician; *v.*, to restore
meditance, meditation
meditation, thought, a thought
medlar, a kind of pear
meed, *n.*, reward, pay; deserts, merit; excellence
meered, limited, sole and entire (*A. and C.*, iii, 13, 10)
meet, *adj.*, even, quits; *adv.*, fitly, successfully; *v.*, to meet with; acquire, gain
meeting, meeting place
meiny, household troop, retinue; multitude, common people
mell, to have to do, deal
memorize, make memorable or glorious
memory, a memorial, memento
mends, remedy (*T. and C.*, i, 1, 68)
mercatante, merchant (*T. of S.*, iv, 2, 63)
merchant, fellow; merchant ship
mercy (by), by a merciful interpretation (*Tim.*, iii, 5, 55); (cry one), to beg one's pardon
mere, absolute, entire, utter
merely, absolutely, utterly
merit, reward, recompense
mervailous, extraordinary (*Hen. V*, ii, 1, 50)
mesh, to brew (*T. A.*, iii, 2, 38)
mess, a portion of food; a group of four; (lower), less intelligent persons (*W. T.*, i, 2, 227)
metal, substance; character, nature; (good), a man of vigour and courage (*All's W.*, ii, 1, 42)
metamorphise, metamorphose
metaphysical, supernatural
mete, to measure; aim
mete-yard, a measuring rod
metheglin, a kind of spiced mead
mettle, spirit, high spirit
mew, to shut up (as a hawk in a mew or cage), to coop up

Glossary

mewl, to mew like a cat (*A. Y. L.*, ii, 7, 144)
micher, a truant
miching, sneaking
mickle, great, much
middest, midst
middle earth, this earth
milch, *adj.*, giving milk; tearful (*Haml.*, ii, 2, 540)
milk-livered, white-livered, cowardly
mill-sixpence, a milled sixpence
mince, to walk with short steps; talk with affected elegance; affect, counterfeit with a prudish air
mincing, affectation, prudishness
mind, *n.*, intention; disposition; opinion; memory; *v.*, to conceive; mean, intend; notice, attend to; remind; remember
minded, *adj.*, disposed
mindless, without a mind; forgetful
mine, to undermine, sap
mineral, a mine
mingle, *n.*, mixture; *v.*, to compound, unite
minikin, *adj.*, pretty little
minim rest, a rest equal to a half-note
minime, not at all, by no means
minimus, smallest of human beings
minion, *n.*, darling, favourite; paramour, mistress; hussy; saucy creature
minister, servant, attendant; agent, deputy
ministration, service
minstrelsy, entertainment in story-telling
minute-jack, fickle-minded creature
minutely, every minute
mirable, wonderful, admirable
mirth, joy, rejoicing; a sport or entertainment
miscarry, to come to harm; be lost, perish; fail
misconster, misconstrue
miscreate, illegitimate, spurious
misdread, fear of evil, anxiety
miser, miserable creature
misgoverned, unruly
misgoverning (misgovernment), misconduct
misgraffed, grafted amiss, ill-matched
misprise (misprize), to undervalue, disdain
misprised, *adj.*, mistaken
misprision, mistake, misconception; contempt
misprize, *see* misprise
misproud, arrogant
miss, *n.*, misbehaviour; loss, deprivation; *v.*, to do without
missingly, because I have missed him (*W. T.*, iv, 2, 35)
missive, messenger
mistake, to misjudge
mistempered, tempered for a bad use, misused (*R. and J.*, i, 1, 94)
mistreadings, transgressions
mistress, lady love; madam; the jack in bowling, a small bowl at which the players aim
mistress court, the chief court
mistrustful, that makes one suspicious (*V. and A.*, 826)
misuse, *n.*, misbehaviour; *v.*, to abuse (in speech); delude; misrepresent (*Sonn.*, 152)
mobled, with the head wrapped up
Mock-water, tricky diagnostician (*M. W.*, ii, 3, 60)
model, copy (on a small scale);

likeness; the very image; a small figure or shape
modern, commonplace, trite; ordinary, everyday
modest, moderate; decorous; mild
modestly, moderately, without exaggeration
modesty, moderation; sense of decency; restraint (in style)
module, mere image
moe, more
moiety, a part
moldwarp, the mole
mome, simpleton
momentany, momentary
Monarcho, a fantastical Italian well known at Elizabeth's court, famous for high-flown discourse (*L. L. L.*, iv, 1, 101)
monster, to make monstrous
monstruosity, monstrous inconsistency (*T. and C.*, iii, 2, 87)
montant, a swashing stroke from above (*M. W.*, ii, 3, 27)
month's mind, a strong inclination
monument, a memorial; a stately family tomb
monumental, memorial; handed down as an heirloom
mood, the mode (form of the scale) in music; *fig.*, the tune, style (*2 Hen. IV*, iv, 5, 200)
mood, anger, angry fit; bitter grief
moody, sullen, angry, irascible
moody-mad, mad with rage
moon, month
mooncalf, a monstrosity
moonish, fickle, capricious
mop, a grimace
mopping, *n.*, making affected faces
mope, to be in a daze; be stupefied; wander heedlessly
moped, out of sorts
moral, *n.*, a maxim, an adage; an emblem; the meaning; *v.*, to moralize; *adj.*, emblematical
moraler, moralizer
morality, moral instruction
moralize, to interpret, expound
Morisco, morris dance
Morning (the), Aurora
morris-pike, a pike invented by the Moors
morrow, morning
morsel, a trivial creature
mort, the notes on the horn to announce the deer's death
mortal, deadly, death-dealing
mortality, death; deadliness
mortified, deadened; withered and insensible to pain; paralyzed; moribund; dead to the world
mortifying, *adj.*, deadly; exhausting the vitality
mose in the chine, to suffer ulceration from glanders
mot, motto, emblematic device
mother, hysteria
motion, *n.*, proposal, suggestion; impulse, incitement; emotion, strong feeling, passion; mental action, perception; idea, notion; puppet show, puppet; *v.*, to propose
motive, moving cause; active force; incentive; occasion; limb or organ that moves
motley, the parti-coloured attire of a fool; a fool
motley-minded, foolish, fantastic
mought, *v.*, might
mould, earth

moulten, *adj.*, that has shed its feathers
mounch, to munch
mountainer, mountaineer
mountant, rising, raised
mountebank, *v.*, to win by artful speeches
mounted, *adj.*, high, on high
mouse, to bite and tear (like a cat)
mouse-hunt, a night-prowler (*R. and J.*, iv, 4, 11)
mouth, to declaim pompously
mouthed, *adj.*, gaping
move, *v.*, to propose, bring forward; anger; approach one with a suggestion or proposal
mow, a grimace
moy, Pistol's misunderstanding of the French pronoun *moi*, which he takes to be the name of a coin (*Hen. V*, iv, 4, 14, 23)
muddy, confused in mind
muddied, confused and suspicious
muddy-mettled, stupid, without sense or spirit
muleter, muleteer, mule-driver
mulled, stupefied, lethargic (*Cor.*, iv, 5, 239)
multiplying medicine, the philosopher's stone
multipotent, very powerful
multitude, the common herd
multitudinous, of the multitude (*Cor.*, iii, 1, 156); with its multitude of tossing waves (*Macb.*, ii, 2, 62)
mumble-news, a gossiping fellow
mummer, an actor in a dumb show or in a rustic play
mummy, human flesh dried and embalmed, used as a medicine or for magical purposes
muniments, furnishings
mural, wall
murdering piece, a cannon charged with many slugs
mure, wall
murk, darkness
murmur, rumour, gossip
murrion, *adj.*, killed by the murrain
Muse, poet
muse, to wonder, be surprised; wonder at
musit, a hole or gap in a hedge or thicket
Musko, a Muscovite, Russian (*All 's W.*, iv, 1, 76)
muss, a game in which the players scramble for some object
mute, an actor who has no speaking part
mutine, *n.*, mutineer, rebel; *v.*, to mutiny
mutiner, *n.*, mutineer; insurgent
mutiny, strife, uproar, tumult
mutton, a sheep; a harlot
mystery, trade, profession, art; skill

nail, the sixteenth of a yard
naked, unarmed
napkin, handkerchief
napless, threadbare
native, natural, genuine; related by birth, kindred; naturally adapted; by nature; at home
natural, *n.*, a born fool, an idiot; *adj.*, idiotic
nature, vitality; life
naught, good for nothing; wicked; naughty; come to naught, ruined; (a thing of), a wicked thing; (be naught awhile), efface yourself! get out!

487

naughty, good for nothing; bad; wicked

nave, navel; the hub of a wheel

nayward (to the), in the negative direction

nay-word, a watchword, a word for identification; a byword

ne, nor

neaf, fist

near, nearer

near-legged, knock-kneed

nearness, near kinship

neat, trimly dressed; foppish; elegant

neb, a bird's bill; the mouth

necessitied to, in pressing need of

needful, urgent; in need of troops

needless, not in want (*A. Y. L.*, ii, 1, 46)

needly, of necessity

needy, necessary, much needed

neele, needle (*Per.*, v, Prol., 5)

neeze, to sneeze

neglect, to let slip; do without; disregard; overlook

neglection, *n.*, neglect, disregard

neighbourhood, friendly relations

neither, not so either (denying an alternative)

nephew, cousin; grandchild

nerve, sinew, tendon

nervy, sinewy

nether, lower; on earth

nether-stocks, stockings

neuter, neutral

next way, the nearest (shortest) way

nice, precise; over precise, finical; squeamish; prudish; trivial, unsubstantial; foolish, silly

nicely, subtilely; punctiliously; foolishly

niceness (nicety), prudery; an overprecise scruple

nick, *n.*, a notch in a tally; (out of all), beyond reckoning, out of measure; (in the), in the nick of time; *v.*, to cut one's hair in a notched pattern as was done to fools; to mark with folly, to disgrace

niece, granddaughter

nighted, black as night; blinded

night-rule, actions by night (*M. N. D.*, iii, 2, 5)

nill, will not

nimble-set, agile (*T. N. K.*, iv, 2, 127)

nine men's morris, a game (not unlike hopscotch) played with nine 'men' (pebbles or discs)

nip, to force (as if by a rapture) (*Per.*, v, 1, 235)

nit, a louse's egg, a young louse

noble, a gold coin (one third of a pound)

noblesse, nobility

noddy, simpleton

noise, *n.*, rumour; music; band of musicians; *v.*, to rumour

nole, head

nonage, minority

non-come, the state of one *non compos mentis* (out of one's mind), utter confusion, a nonplus (*M. Ado*, iii, 5, 67)

nook-shotten, shot into a corner of the earth, remote

northen, from the north (*T. A.*, iv, 1, 104)

not, not only

note, *n.*, a mark, sign; brand of infamy, stigma; mark of inferiority   a letter, memorandum,

bill; distinguished position or quality; knowledge; remark; *v.*, to mark with infamy, disgrace; show, indicate

notedly, exactly

nothing, not at all

nothing-gift, worthless gift or distinction

notify, to take notice (*M. W.*, ii, 2, 85)

notion, mind

notorious, well-known; notable

notoriously, notably

not-pated, *adj.*, having the hair notted (cut short)

nouzle up, to pamper

no-verbs, mispronounced words (*M. W.*, iii, 1, 107)

novum, a game at dice of which the best throws were nine and five

noyance, harm, injury

number, versify

numbers, rhythm, metre; verses, poetry

nuncio, messenger

nuncle, mine uncle (a fool's term in addressing his master)

nursery, nursing, fostering care

nurture, culture, good breeding; moral training

nuthook, a catchpole, sheriff's officer, beadle

O, a cipher, zero

o', of, on

oak, wreath of oak leaves

oathable, fit to take an oath

ob., abbreviation for *obolus*, halfpenny

object, a sight; object of attention or love

obliged, bound by a legal obligation

obliquy, obliquity (*Tim.*, iv, 3, 18)

oblivion, forgetfulness, loss of memory

oblivious, causing forgetfulness

obscene, abominable

obscenely, Costard's word for 'becomingly' (*L. L. L.*, iv, 1, 145); Bottom's word for 'conveniently' (*M. N. D.*, i, 2, 111)

obsequious, befitting a funeral, funereal; passionately mournful

observance, observation; attention; care; devotion; obligatory rule

observancy, devotion, homage

observant, obsequious attendant, sycophant

observation, ceremonial rites

observe, to be attentive or show respect to; indulge

observing, deferential

obstacle, obstinate (*1 Hen. VI*, v, 4, 17)

obstruction, stagnation, stagnancy (*M. for M.*, iii, 1, 119)

occasion, favourable opportunity

occulted, closely hidden

occupation, handicraft, trade

occupy, to cohabit with

occurrents, occurrences, incidents

odd, at odds, at enmity (*T. and C.*, iv, 5, 265)

odd-even, a time about midnight when one cannot tell whether it is P.M. or A.M. (*Oth.*, i, 1, 124)

odds, a quarrel, enmity; advantage (in a wager or match)

odorous, *for* odious (*M. Ado*, iii, 5, 18)

Od's, God's (in oaths)

o'erbeat, to overflow with dashing waves (*Cor.*, iv, 5, 136)

o'erblow, to blow away

o'ercount, to outnumber; (me of), to win from me by getting an advantage in the accounting

o'ercrow, to triumph over, overpower

o'ereaten, *adj.*, that has served for two meals and of which only scraps are left (*T. and C.*, v, 2, 160)

o'erflourished, painted over with ornamental designs

o'erfraught, overladen (with grief)

o'ergalled, much inflamed

o'ergreen, to deck with verdure, to give a good appearance to (*Sonn.*, 112)

o'ergrown, hairy; enfeebled by age

o'erleaven, to pervade and modify

o'erlook, to bewitch with the evil eye

o'erparted, having too difficult a part to play

o'erperch, to fly over

o'erposting, getting quickly over

o'erraught, overtook and passed; (of), cheated out of

o'ersized, smeared over

o'erstrawed, overstrewed

o'erteemed, exhausted by bearing children

o'erwatched, exhausted by lack of sleep

o'erweigh, outweigh

o'erwhelm (overwhelm), to jut out over, overhang

o'erwrested, over-strained, exaggerated

of, from; by; in, during; on

off, off the mark, all wrong (*Cor.*, ii, 2, 64)

offal, what falls off, chips and shavings, rubbish

offer, to threaten; be on the offensive; undertake, attempt

office, *n.*, duty, service; *v.*, to act as servants in; officiously keep one away (*Cor.*, v, 2, 68); *pl.*, rooms where the servants perform their several duties (kitchen, buttery, etc.)

officed, *adj.*, having their required duties

officer, agent; attendant

officious, zealous in service

'old, wold, upland (*Lear*, iii, 4, 125)

old (*a general intensive*), plentiful, hard, much, etc.

omen, disaster (which omens portend)

omit, to pass or lay by; neglect

on, of; because of, on account of

once, once for all

oneyers (great), great ones (*1 Hen. IV*, ii, 1, 84)

open, to give tongue

opener, interpreter

operance, operation

operant, active; potent

opinion, public opinion; reputation; self-opinion, self-conceit

opinioned, *for* pinioned (*M. Ado*, iv, 2, 69)

oppress, put down, suppress

oppugnancy, opposition, antagonism

or (or ere), before

or . . . or, either . . . or

orb, circle, round; the sphere (of a star); this earth

orchard, garden

order (take), make arrangements

ordinance, rank in society; ordnance
ordinant, decisively operative
ordinary, a meal at fixed price
ore, precious metal
orgillous, proud, haughty
orient, pearly
orifex, orifice
orphan, without parents (*M. W.*, v, 5, 43)
ort, a scrap; *pl.*, bits of food left after a meal, leavings
ostent, show, appearance; display
ostentation, show, display; a spectacle
ostridge, ostrich
other, others
othergates, otherwise, in another fashion
otherwhere, elsewhere
Ottomite, Turk
ouch, a brooch or jewelled buckle
ought, owed
ounce, lynx
ouph, elf, goblin
ousel, *see* woosel
out, abroad; in the field (as a soldier); out of one's part, at a loss, embarrassed; off the track, wrong, mistaken; ended, finished; expired; at variance, vexed; fully, quite; with a hole in one's shoe; out of
outbreast, to surpass in singing
outbrave, defy; outshine
outcraft, outwit
outlook, to outstare
outpeer, excel, outvie
outprized by, less valued than
outrage, violence in speech or action; violent outbreak; frantic behaviour
outdure, hold out against
outspeaks, manifestly (as it were, outspokenly) exceeds (*Hen. VIII*, iii, 2, 127)
outvied, beaten by a higher bid
outward man, an outsider
overcome, to come or pass over
overgo, surpass; exceed; overwhelm
overhold, overrate
overscutched, worn-out, stale (*2 Hen. IV*, iii, 2, 340)
overseen, deluded, discomfited (*Lucr.*, 1206)
overshot, beaten in shooting, discomfited
overture, disclosure
overwhelm, *see* o'erwhelm
overture, revealing, disclosure
owe, to own, possess, have
oxlip, a variety of the cowslip
oyes, proclamation ('Oyes,' i.e., 'Hear,' being the crier's opening call)

paced, trained, broken in
pack, to be off; conspire, make arrangements
packed, *p.p.*, engaged in a conspiracy; implicated
packing, conspiracy, secret doings
paction, agreement
paddock, toad
page, to attend like a page
pageant, to mimic (as in a show)
pain, *n.*, pains, effort, toil; penalty; *v.*, to cause toil or trouble to
painted, falsified, unreal; (cloth), a cheap substitute for tapestry hangings
pajock, peacock
palabras, words

palate, to taste; to get (the taste); to have the flavour of
pale, pallor
palisado, a palisade, fence of stakes
pall, to wrap as in a cloak or pall
pall, to grow weak, fail
palliament, the white gown of a candidate (*T. A.*, i, 1, 182)
palmer, pilgrim
palter, to prevaricate, equivocate; shuffle
pantaloon, a feeble silly old man
pantler, a servant who manages the pantry
paper, to summon by letter (*Hen. VIII*, i, 1, 80)
paragon, *v.*, to set up as a model; compare; excel
parasits, parasites (*Ven.*, 848)
parcel, *n.*, part, an item; party, group; *v.*, to increase by an item (*A. and C.*, v, 2, 163)
parcel-bawd, partly a procurer
parcel-gilt, partly gilt, gilded on the inside
parcelled, *adj.*, distributed, particular, separate
pard, leopard
pardon, *n.*, leave, permission; *v.*, to excuse
parfect, to enact, perform (a part)
Parish Garden, Paris Garden
parish top, a large top spun in parish sports
paritor, apparitor, an officer of an ecclesiastical court
parle (parley), *n.*, talk, conversation; conference (*esp.* as to truce or surrender); *v.*, to speak; confer, negotiate
parlous, perilous, hazardous; pert and clever
parmacity, spermaceti
part, *n.*, party; deed; quality; *v.*, to depart; depart from
partake, to take sides, side; impart, communicate
partaker, confederate, accomplice; sharer
parted, *adj.*, gifted, accomplished (*T and C.*, iii, 3, 96)
partialize, to make partial, unfair
partial slander, a slanderous censure for partiality (*Rich. II*, i, 3, 241)
participate, *adj.*, coöperative
particular, *n.*, one's own special case; special or personal part; personal relation; personal interests or concerns
particularly, with my individual self (*Tim.*, i, 1, 46)
partisan, a long-handled weapon with a piercing and cutting blade
Partlet, a name for the hen (Chaucer's 'Pertelote')
party, part, side
party-verdict, one's own part in a collective verdict
pash, *n.*, the head; *v.*, to strike with a smashing blow; mangle
pass, to pass by, disregard; manage; play the part of; decide, pass sentence; thrust (in fencing); die; happen; care; go beyond bounds or belief; *n.*, license; transgression; thrust, bout (in fencing); predicament; (of pate), an intellectual thrust, a witty speech (*Temp.*, iv, 1, 244); (of practice), a plotted thrust (*Haml.*, iv, 7, 139)
passable, enough to serve as a pass-

word (*Cor.*, v, 2, 13); that admits free passage (*Cymb.*, i, 2, 10)
passado, a forward thrust
passage, *n.*, course; procedure; wandering; act, action; occurrence; fact; passing away, death; time when the streets are thronged with people; (no) nobody passing
passant (*in heraldry*), walking
passenger, wayfarer
passing, *adj.*, exceeding, transcendent; *adv.*, exceedingly
passing bell, a bell rung to call for prayers for one who is dying
passion, any stormy emotion or its expression in words or action; grief, suffering; the sufferings and death of Christ; frenzy; mental disorder, insanity; a passionate speech in a play; *v.*, to grieve passionately
passionate, *adj.*, sorrowing; expressive of strong feeling; *v.*, to express with adequate emotion
passive, submissive
passport, a paper certifying a soldier's discharge and licensing his journey
passy measures pavin, a stately Italian dance; a solemn humbug (*T. N.*, v, 1, 206)
past-proportion, an amount too vast for computation
pastry, the room where pastry is made
patch, a fool
patched, *adj.*, motley
patchery, roguery, chicanery
patens, metal plates
path, *v.*, to walk abroad (*J. C.*, ii, 1, 83)
pathetical, *adj.*, touching
patience, calmness, fortitude; kind permission
patient, *adj.*, calm; *v.*, to compose (one's self)
patronage, *v.*, to protect; maintain, avouch
pattern, *n.*, a precedent; supreme exemplar; specimen of one's handiwork or skill; *v.*, to prefigure; match
pauca (pauca verba, paucas pallabris), few words
paunch, to stab in the belly
paved, covered with a slab of stone (*M. for M.*, v, 1, 440)
pax, a sacred tablet passed to the congregation to be kissed at mass
peach, to denounce (one) as; to become an informer
peak, to waste away; to move about feebly and dazedly; to sneak
pearl, *pl.*, pearls
peascod, peapod
peascod time, the season of early peas
peat, a pet, little girl
pebble, *pl.*, pebbles (*Lear*, iv, 6, 21)
peck, to pitch (*Hen. VIII*, v, 4, 94)
peculiar, personal; private; one's own
pedant, schoolmaster
pedascule, schoolmate, tutor
peeled, *adj.*, shaven, tonsured
peep, a pip, a spot on a die or playing card; (a peep out), not quite up to the mark
peer, to appear, show one's self; show
peevish, childish, silly; trivial
peevish-fond, childishly foolish

Glossary

Peg-a-Ramsey, an old song and dance

peise (peize), to poise, balance; weigh down; (the time), to weight it so that it may not pass so quickly (*M. of V.*, iii, 2, 22)

pelf, goods, property, riches

pellet, to form into round drops (*Compl.*, 18)

pelt, to scold, rail (*Lucr.*, 1418)

pelting, paltry, insignificant

pencilled, painted, depicted

pendulous, overhanging (*Lear*, iii, 4, 69)

penitent, *adj.*, doing penance; *n.*, one who is doing penance

penner, pen case

pennorth, pennyworth, bargain

pensioner, one of the royal bodyguard

pensived, made pensive (*Compl.*, 219)

penthouse, a lean-to (with a single-pitched roof)

penurious, needy

pen'worth, pennyworth, bargain

perch, resting place, station (*Per.*, iii, Prol., 15)

perdie (perdy), pardieu (a trivial oath)

perdition, loss, destruction

perdu, a soldier set to watch at a dangerous post

perdurable, never-ending, lifelong

perdurably, eternally

perdy, see perdie

peregrinate, foreign in one's ways, affected

peremptory, imperious, domineering; resolved, determined

perfect, *adj.*, fully informed; fully equipped, ready; trustworthy; very proficient; *v.*, to finish, accomplish; instruct fully

perfection, achievement; accomplishment; acquisition

perforce, forcibly, by force; of necessity

perge, proceed, go on

periapt, a magic girdle

period, *n.*, end, close; goal; peroration; *v.*, to bring to a close, put an end to

perish, to destroy

perishen, perish (*Per.*, ii, Prol., 35)

perjure, *n.*, perjurer; *v.*, to make false to one's oath

peroration, elaborate oration

perpend, consider; pay attention

per se, all by himself, unique, peerless

persever, persevere

persistive, persistent, enduring

person, parson (*L. L. L.*, iv, 2, 84, 85)

personage, figure, personal appearance

perspective, a glass or optical instrument which distorts objects

perspectively, as seen in or through a perspective

persuade, to urge; win over

persuaded well of, having a favourable opinion of

pert, brisk, lively, animated

pertly, promptly; boldly, defiantly

pervert, turn aside

pester, to crowd, throng; infest

pestilent, plaguy

petar, petard, a small bomb

pettitoes, toes (*lit.*, pig's feet) (*W. T.*, iv, 4, 619)

pew-fellow, an associate, sharer

phantasime, a fantastic fellow

phantasma, an illusion

Pheazar, a comic name (*from* pheeze) (*M. W.*, i, 3, 10)

pheeze (pheese), to settle, fix (in a hostile sense); take down by a flogging

Philip, a proverbial name for a sparrow

Philip and Jacob (i.e., James), the day sacred to those saints, May 1

Philippan, wielded at the Battle of Philippi

Philomela (Philomel), the nightingale

philosopher, man of science

philosophical, scientific

Phœbus, the sun god, the sun

phrase, a word, a term

phraseless, of indescribable beauty (*Compl.*, 225)

physic, *n.*, medicine; curative treatment, remedy; medical art or knowledge; *v.*, to cure, heal; restore

physical, curative, remedial; good for one's health

pia mater, the delicate membrane that envelops the brain; the brain

pick, to pitch

picked, refined, fastidious; carefully chosen

pickers (i.e., pilferers) and stealers, the fingers

picking, trivial

pickthank, a sycophantic talebearer

Pickt-hatch, a low quarter of London

piece, a work of art; masterpiece; accomplishment; creature

piety, devotion, patriotism

pight, pitched; determined

pilcher, pilchard, a kind of fish; scabbard

piled, stripped of hair (*with a pun on* furnished with a pile or velvet nap) (*M. for M.*, i, 2, 35)

pill, to pillage; take by robbery

pin, a peg at the centre of a target

pin and web, a disease of the eye, cataract

pinch, to pinch away (*Two G.*, iv, 4, 160)

pinched thing, a dupe (*W. T.*, ii, 1, 51)

pinfold, a pound

pink, half-closed, drowsy (*A. and C.*, ii, 7, 119)

pinked, perforated (for ornament)

pioned, *adj.*, trenched (*Temp.*, iv, 1, 64)

pioner, pioneer, a soldier who digs trenches, makes roads, etc.

pip, see peep

pipe-wine, wine from the pipe (from the wood) *with a pun on* musical pipe (*M. W.*, iii, 2, 90)

pitch, *n.*, height; the highest point reached by a soaring falcon; *v.*, to throw one's self, fall

pittikins (*diminutive*), pity (*Cymb.*, iv, 2, 293)

place, mansion; pitch (of a falcon)

placket, the slit at the top of a skirt

plain, *adj.*, smooth and level; out-and-out; simple; *v.*, to make plain, interpret

plain, to complain, lament

plain-song, simple melody

plaintful, lamenting, doleful (*Compl.*, 2)

planched, made of boards

plant, sole of the foot

plantage, vegetation, herbage

plantation, colonizing

plash, a shallow pool or puddle

plat, *n.*, a plait, braid; *v.*, to plait, braid

plate, *n.*, a coin; *v.*, to cover (with armour)

plated, *adj.*, wearing plate armour

platform, a paved level in a fortification; a careful plan

plausibly, with enthusiastic applause

plausive, pleasing, agreeable; plausible

play, to gamble for

playfeere, playfellow

pleached, interlaced; folded

pleasance, merriment

please-man, a sycophant, flatterer

pleat, a plait

pliant, susceptible to request (*Oth.*, i, 3, 151)

plight (in), in condition, ready, prepared

plighted, folded (so as to conceal); pledged, betrothed

pluck, to pull

plume up, to adorn (as with plumes); accomplish brilliantly

plurisy, excess, plethora

pocket up, to accept without resentment

poem, a drama in verse

point, a tagged lace; a trumpet signal (*2 Hen. IV*, iv, 1, 52); *pl.*, orders (*Cor.*, iv, 6, 125); (at), on the point of, ready; (at) completely; (at a), fully prepared; (at ample), amply

point-devise (-device), precise, exact in every detail; finical

'pointed, *p.p.*, appointed

pointing stock, an object of scorn

poise, *n.*, weight, importance; *v.*, weigh

poke, pocket, wallet

poking stick, a rod for adjusting the plaits of a ruff

Polack, Pole

pole, standard (*A. and C.*, iv, 15, 65)

pole-clipt, *adj.*, whose poles are embraced by vines (*Temp.*, iv, 1, 68)

policy, statecraft; diplomacy; strategy; politics; cunning

politic, treating of statecraft

polled, bald; stripped bare, cleared (*Cor.*, iv, 5, 215)

polusion, *for* allusion (*L. L. L.*, iv, 2, 47)

pomander, a ball of aromatic substances

Pomgarnet, Pomegranate (name of a room) (*1 Hen. IV*, ii, 4, 42)

pomp, procession; festal ceremony

Pompion (i.e., pumpkin), Costard's slip of the tongue (or joke) for Pompey (*L. L. L.*, v, 2, 503)

pompous, magnificent, glorious

pomwater, a large sweet apple

Pont, Pontus in Asia Minor

Pontic, the Black Sea, the Euxine

poop, to play (one) a foul trick

poor-John, dry salt hake

poother (pudder), turmoil

popingay, popinjay, parrot

pop'rin, a Flemish pear

popular, vulgar; ordinary

popularity, low company

populous, containing many men

porpas, porpoise

porpentine, porcupine

porringer, a cap shaped like a porridge bowl

port, *n.*, a gate, portal; mien, bear-

ing; style of living; v., to bring to harbour
portable, easy to bear, tolerable
portage, portholes; cargo
portance, conduct
portly, stately, imposing; dignified and courteous
posied, inscribed with a posy (motto)
position, proposition
possess, to inform
possession, state of being possessed by an evil spirit; madness
posset, v., to curdle
possitable, for positively (M. W., i, 1, 244)
post (off), to put off, defer
poster of, one who courses over
posture, style, fashion (J. C., v, 1, 33)
posy, motto (especially in verse)
pot (to the), to certain death (Cor., i, 4, 47)
potable, drinkable (of gold in the form of aurum potabile) (2 Hen. IV, iv, 5, 163)
potch, to make a stab
potent, potentate
potential, powerful
pother, see poother
potting, n., drinking
pottle, a two-quart tankard
poulter, a poulterer, dealer in poultry
pouncet box, a small box (with perforated top) for carrying perfume
pound, to shut up as in a pound
powder, to salt, pickle
powdering tub, a tub for pickling; sweating tub for the treatment of disease
power, an armed force, army
Powl's, Saint Paul's Church
pow, waw, interj., pooh, pooh
practice, n., plot, artifice, treason; treachery
practisant, partner in stratagem
practise, to plot, scheme, work craftily; (on, upon), work craftily upon or against, plot against
præmunire, the act of asserting or maintaining the authority of the Pope in England
praise, n., merit, virtue; v., to appraise
pray in aid, to ask for assistance
precedence, that which precedes
precedent, former
precedent, the original; indicative sign
precept, a written order, mandate, summons (as from a court or magistrate)
preceptial, in the form of precepts
precipitance, the act of casting one's self down from a height
precurrer, forerunner
precurse, a foretokening (by omens)
predicament, category, class; situation
predict, prediction
predominance, controlling astrological influence
preface, prologue
prefer, to present; advance, promote; recommend (for service)
prefixed, previously appointed
pregnancy, quick wit
pregnant, ready; quick-witted, clever; evident, obvious
pregnantly, readily and clearly
premised, sent before the appointed time

prenominate, v., to name in advance; adj., foresaid
prenzie, an unknown word, probably a misreading (M. for M., iii, 1, 94, 97)
prepare, preparation
preposterous, extraordinary (W. T., v, 2, 159)
prescript, n., an order, mandate, instructions; adj., prescriptive, regular and proper
presence, assembly, noble company; person; presence chamber
present, adj., immediate, instant; n., present time (moment) or occasion or business; ready money
present, to show, figure, represent; personate; bring a charge against
presentation, semblance
presently, immediately, instantly
presentment, presentation; representation (in portraiture)
press, n., crowd, throng; conscription, impressment; v., to crowd; force to enlist
press money, money paid to one on enlistment
pressure, shape, figure; impression on the mind, idea
prest, ready
Prester (n., priest) John, a fabulous Eastern ruler (both priest and king)
presupposed (upon), ascribed to (one) beforehand
pretence, purpose, intention
pretend, to intend, purpose; indicate; allege, lay claim to
pretender, claimant
prevail, avail
prevailment, persuasive force
prevent, anticipate; forestall
price, prize
prick, n., a point on the dial; the bull's-eye; a dot in writing, a slight thing (T. and C., i, 3, 343); a skewer; a spine (of a hedgehog); pl., archery; v., to spur, incite; to indicate or check by a puncture or dot; to stick, insert
pricket, a buck in the second year
pricksong, song with written notes
pride, display (in dress, etc.), fine attire, pomp; glory; height, highest pitch, prime; heat (Oth., iii, 3, 404)
prig, thief
prime, adj., first; chief; lustful; n., the spring
primer, more pressing or immediate
primero, a kind of card game
primerose, primrose
primest, first; best
primy nature, the springtime of life
prince it, to act like a prince
principality, an angel of high rank
principals, the main timbers or posts (Per., iii, 2, 16)
princox, a saucy youngster
print (in), by rule, methodically
prisonment, imprisonment
private, privacy; private (unofficial) communication
prize, n., a match for a prize, an athletic contest; (war's), the rule in the game of war (3 Hen. VI, i, 4, 59); v., to appraise, rate
prizer, a professional athlete; an appraiser, valuer
probal, adj., such as to win assent, probable
probation, proof, demonstration; examination

process, the course of events; a story, an account; legal method; summons; mandate
process-server, a sheriff's officer, bailiff
procreant cradle, cradle for offspring
procurator, agent, proxy
procure, to bring (one); carry on the trade of procuress
prodigiously, by monstrous births
proditor, traitor
proface, may it do you good! your health!
professed, full of professions of love (Lear, i, 1, 275)
profession, occupation, trade
professor, a teacher or professor of religion
progeny, ancestry; lineage
progress, a formal journey by a sovereign
proin, to prune
project, to set forth, expound
projection, planning
prolixious, long drawn out
prolong, postpone
prompture, incitement, instigation
prone, eager, headlong
proof, n., tested armour; impenetrability; experience; adj., invulnerable, impregnable
propagate, to hand down; increase
propagation (for), in order to procure the handing down (due payment) (M. for M., i, 2, 154)
propend, incline
propension, inclination
proper, one's own, peculiar; appropriate; (to), characteristic (of), appropriate (to); handsome; fine
properly, peculiarly
propertied, endowed with qualities
property, n., identity; essential or characteristic quality; a thing to make use of, a tool; v., to make subsidiary; to make (one) a mere agent or tool or chattel
proportion, portion, fortune; preponderance (Macb., i, 4, 19); pl., levies
propose, v., to imagine; contemplate (as in the future); appoint; talk; n., conversation
proposer, talker, speaker
propriety, one's self, own identity
propugnation, defensive strength
prorogue, to put off, postpone; prolong; make torpid by procrastination
prosperous, favourable, propitious
protest, v., to proclaim, declare; n., protestation, asseveration
protractive, long drawn out
proud, gorgeous (esp. of attire); high-mettled
provand, provender
provincial (here), belonging to this province or division of my order (M. for M., v, 1, 318)
provoke, incite
prune, to trim and adjust the feathers, preen; trim and deck out
pudder, see poother
pudding, sausage
pudency, modesty
pugging, thievish
puisny (puny), raw, untrained
puissance, power; strength; armed forces
puissant, powerful, mighty
puke-stocking, wearing dark woollen stockings (1 Hen. IV, ii, 4, 78)

pullet-sperm, eggs

pulsidge, *for* pulse (*2 Hen. IV*, ii, 4, 26)

pumpion, pumpkin

pun, to pound

punk, a strumpet

punto, a thrust; (reverso *for* riverso), a back-handed thrust

puny, *see* puisne

purchase, *n.*, acquisition, gain; booty, loot; *v.*, to acquire, get; get by robbery

purgation, a cleansing of the system by cathartics; a cleansing of the conscience by confession

purge, to take physic

purl, rise in a spiral (*Lucr.*, 1407)

purple, the purple orchis

pursuivant, heraldic officer; a king's messenger

purveyor, an officer who arranges for the supplies on a royal progress

push, *interj.*, pshaw, pish; *n.*, a scoff (*M. Ado*, v, 1, 38)

pushes, straits, difficulties

push-pin, a children's game with pins

pussel, a harlot

put (*with inf.*), to cause, make; (forth), to emerge, appear; venture, hazard; show one's self; utter; (in), to interpose, intercede; present one's claim; (o'er), to refer; (on), to urge on, prompt, instigate, encourage; (to't), to put to the test, put to straits; (up), to pocket; tamely submit to, endure without resenting; (upon, on), to report, bring to one's attention; address (words) to one; force or inflict on, apply to; lay to one's charge

putter-on, inciter, instigator

putter-out, one who puts out or deposits money as a stake

puttock, a kite (the bird)

pyramis, pyramid

quail, *n.*, a wanton

quail, *v.*, to intimidate; destroy

quaint, ingenious, elaborate; fine, elegant; skilful; dainty, delicate

quaintly, ingeniously, skilfully; delicately

quaked, *p.p.*, made to shiver

qualification, pacification

qualify, to moderate; mitigate; calm, pacify; dilute

quality, the essential and characteristic quality, nature; an accomplishment; profession (*esp.*, that of an actor); ability, professional skill; rank

quantity, a small amount; small piece, bit; diminutive creature

quarrel, complaint; cause or ground of complaint or of dispute, cause; case

quarrelous, quarrelsome

quarry, all the deer killed in a hunt; heap of slain

quarter, a division of an army; range or limit; post; point of the compass; friendly relations, concord; (good) order

quartered, *adj.*, in the different quarters of the camp (*Cymb.*, iv, 4, 18)

quat, pimple

quatch, broad and fat

quean, wench, hussy

queasiness, nausea, loathing

queasy, inclined to nausea, qualmish; fastidious; nauseated, disgusted; ticklish (*Lear*, ii, 1, 19)

quell, *v.*, to kill, destroy; *n.*, slaughter

queller, killer

quench, become calm

quern, hand mill

quest, inquest

questant, seeker after honour, aspirant

question, *n.*, talk, conversation, dialogue; converse; subject of talk or dispute; *v.*, to discuss; talk, converse; speak to

questionable, demanding to be spoken to

questrist, seeker, one in quest of

quick, living, alive; lively, sprightly, quick-witted; with child

quicken, bring to life; revive; refresh; come to life

quiddity (quiddit), a subtle definition or distinction (*esp.* in law), quibble

quid for quo, tit for tat

quietus, receipt in full, final settlement

quill (in the), in concert, all together (*2 Hen. VI*, i, 3, 4)

quillet, a legal subtlety, quibble

quintain, a post or block set up to tilt at

qui passa, a certain tune (*T. N. K.*, iii, 5, 86)

quire, *n.*, company

quire (quier), *v.*, to sing in harmony; harmonize

quirk, a flourish (with the pen); evasion; eccentricity; odd variety; quip

quit, to release; remit; acquit; repay, reward, requite; avenge

quite, to repay in kind (*Rich. II*, v, 1, 43); requite

quittal, requital (*Lucr.*, 236)

quittance, *n.*, discharge (from debt); recompense; *v.*, to repay

quiver, nimble (*2 Hen. IV*, iii, 2, 301)

quoif, *see* coif

quote, to note, observe; scrutinize; set down, designate; mark (by contrast); show, exhibit; interpret, understand

quoth 'a? (koth-a?), did he say? (used to express or suggest dissent or irony)

quotidian, a fever that recurs daily

rabbit-sucket, a sucking rabbit

rable, rabble (*T. N. K.*, iii, 5, 106)

race (raze), a root

race, herd; native disposition, temper

rack, *n.*, floating cloud or mist; *v.*, to drive before the wind

rack, *v.*, to stretch, strain; raise unduly, exaggerate

racker, one who tortures and distorts

raddock, the ruddock, robin

rage, to enrage

ragged, rough; harsh

rag-of-muffin, ragamuffin

rake up, to cover lightly (*Lear*, iv, 6, 281)

ramp, a strumpet (*Cymb.*, i, 6, 134)

rampallian, rampant creature

rampired, barred and barricaded

randon, random

range, *n.*, a rank; *v.*, to rank, take rank; stand in order

ranged, *adj.*, arranged in order

rank, *n.*, a line, row; *adj.*, too luxuriant, overgrown; full, great; insolent; coarse, foul; fetid; in heat

rankle, to cause a festering wound

rankness, exuberance; arrogance

ransacked, *adj.*, carried away as booty

rap, to carry away (with emotion), transport; *p.p.*, enraptured; in a trance; beside one's self

rapture, delirious fit; paroxysm; violent robbery (*Per.*, ii, 1, 161)

rascal, a deer in poor condition

rase (raze), to erase; wipe out, destroy; pull (off)

rash, quick, sudden, hasty; operating quickly; urgent

rashly, hastily

rate, *n.*, estimate; estimation; number; price, value; rank; scale (of living); degree

ratified, duly observed, kept (*L. L. L.*, iv, 2, 125)

ratolorum, *for* rotulorum (of the rolls) (*M. W.*, i, 1, 8)

raught, reached

ravel, to become tangled; (out), unravel, disentangle

ravelled, *adj.*, tangled

ravin, *adj.*, ravening, raging with hunger

ravin (raven), to swallow or devour greedily

ravined, ravenous

ravished, *p.p.*, torn or snatched away from (*T. N. K.*, ii, 2, 22)

rawly, in an unprovided condition

rawness, inconsiderate haste

rayed, befouled; bedraggled

raze (race), *n.*, a root

raze, *v.*, *see* rase

razed, with ornamental slashes or openwork

razure, erasure

reach, far-reaching mental powers

read, to lecture, give instruction, teach

reading, *n.*, learning, erudition; interpretation

ready, dressed

re-answer, compensate, balance

rearward, the rear guard, rear

reason, *n.*, talk; a remark; (do), to give one satisfaction; *v.*, to talk, converse; discuss; explain

reave, bereave, deprive

rebate, to dull

rebato, a kind of high collar (*M. Ado*, iii, 4, 6)

rebellious, fighting against, meeting blow with blow (*Macb.*, i, 2, 56)

rebuke, *n.*, a shameful defeat, discomfiture; chastisement; *v.*, to check, repress; discomfit; cow, overawe

rebused, *for* abused (*T. of S.*, i, 2, 7)

receipt, what is received; size, capacity; reception; receptacle

receive, to accept as true, believe

received, *adj.*, accepted, approved

receiving, *n.*, receptivity, apprehension

recheat, a set of notes on the horn to call back the dogs

reck, to care

reclaim, to restrain, check

reclusive, retired (as a recluse)

recognizance, a token, keepsake; a bond given (to appear, pay a debt, etc.)

recoil, to go back, revert; give way; degenerate

recollect, to collect, gather

Glossary

recollected, *adj.*, studied and elaborate (*T. N.*, ii, 4, 5)
recomforted, restored to happiness
recomforture, consolation
recompt, to recount
record, *n.*, a witness; *v.*, to bear witness; vouch for; sing. *See* recorder
recordation, memorial; repetition from memory (*T. and C.*, v, 2, 116)
recorder (record) a kind of musical pipe
recountment, narrative, story
recourse, repeated flowing
recover, to revive, restore, cure; get, obtain, win; reach
rectorship, authority as ruler
recure, to cure, restore to health
rede, advice, counsel
redeliver, to report in reply
redemption, ransom; rescue
red lattice, a mark of an alehouse
reduce, bring back; bring
reechy, smoke-begrimed; reeking, filthy
reed, *adj.*, piping (*M. of V.*, iii, 4, 67)
reeky, malodorous
reeling ripe, ready to stagger
refel, refute
refer (one's self), to appeal; stipulate for; take up with
reference, assignment; appeal; (have ... to), to centre in
reflect, to shine
reflection, shining
reflex, *n.*, reflected light; *v.*, to shed, direct
reform, *for* inform (*M. Ado*, v, 1, 262)
refrain, hold back
refuge, plead in excuse of
refuse, renounce, disown
regard, *n.*, a look; view, sight; consideration, attention; respect; *pl.*, conditions, terms; *v.*, to look at; notice; honour; consider
regent, ruler, governor
regiment, authority as a ruler; regularity, rule
region, the sky, upper air, heavens; station, rank
regreet, *n.*, greeting; *v.*, to greet again; greet; return to; address; send greetings
reguerdon, *n.*, *v.*, reward
rehearse, relate, recite; pronounce
reinforce, to rally (*Hen. V*, iv, 6, 36); bring up reinforcements (*Cymb.*, v, 2, 18)
reinforcement, a fresh assault (*Cor.*, ii, 2, 117)
rejoindure, reunion
rejourn, adjourn
relapse, a rebounding, recoil
relation, story, report, account, discourse
relative, going back to the fact, decisive, conclusive (*Haml.*, ii, 2, 632)
religion, religious devotion or obligation
religious, devoted; conscientious (*Hen. VIII*, iv, 2, 74)
relish, *n.*, a taste, smack; quality; meaning; *v.*, to taste; recognize; enjoy; have the taste of
relume, rekindle
remain, *n.*, stay; residue
remediate, curative
remember, to remind; mention
remonstrance, manifestation

remorse, compassion, pity
remorseful, compassionate
remote, distant
remotion, keeping away, aloofness
remove, a stage (of a progress); the raising of a siege; removal (by death)
removed, sequestered, recluse; remote, solitary
removedness, frequent absence
render, *v.*, to report, repeat; surrender; *n.*, an account, statement; payment
renegado, apostate (*T. N.*, iii, 2, 74)
renege, deny; renounce
renew, rally, renew the fight
renouncement, withdrawal from a worldly life
renowmed, renowned
rent, to rend, tear
reny, to deny
repair, *n.*, amendment, restoration; coming, arrival; *v.*, to revive, restore; come, go
repast, to feed, nourish
repasture, sustenance
repeal, *n.*, *v.*, recall
replenished, *adj.*, complete, perfect; well-stored
replication, echo; reply, answer
report, *n.*, a reporter, informant; *v.*, (themselves), to speak and tell what they were (*Cymb.*, ii, 4, 83)
reportingly, by report, on hearsay evidence
reprehend, *for* represent (*L. L. L.*, i, 1, 184)
reprisal, prize
reprobance, reprobation
reproof, disproof, refutation
reprove, disprove
repugn, contend against
repugnancy, active resistance
repugnant, refractory
repured, *see* thrice-repured
reputing of, making much of, vaunting (*2 Hen. VI*, iii, 1, 48)
requicken, revivify
require, to request, ask for; call for, deserve
required, *adj.*, requisite, due
requiring, *n.*, asking, requesting, petition
requit, requite
reremice, bats
reserve, preserve, keep safe, keep
resist, to be distasteful to (*Per.*, ii, 3, 29)
resolute, a stout-hearted fellow (*Haml.*, i, 1, 98)
resolution, a state of freedom from doubt (*Lear*, i, 2, 108)
resolve, to explain to (one), clear up one's doubts, satisfy, inform; solve, clear up; dissolve; (one's self), make up one's mind; *n.*, resolution
resolvedly, with detailed explanation (*All's W.*, v, 3, 332)
resorters, regular visitors
respect, *n.*, attention; regard, esteem; reputation; propriety; *v.*, to regard; consider; care for; hold in honour or regard
respected, *for* suspected (*M. for M.*, ii, 1, 170)
respective, considerate, scrupulous; worthy of regard
respectively, respectfully
respite, end of the period of respite (*Rich. III*, v, 1, 19)

responsive, accordant, well-suited (*Haml.*, v, 2, 159)
rest, *n.*, abode, stay; final stake, firm resolution; *v.*, to remain
rest (to set up one's), to risk one's final stake, to be resolved (at all hazards, to make up one's mind; make one's abode.
'rest, to arrest
restem, to hold (their course) in the opposite direction (*Oth.*, i, 3, 37)
restrain, to pull back tightly; withhold
resty, torpid, sluggish, slothful
resume, take (*Tim.*, ii, 2, 4)
retail, hand down by retelling, recount, relate
retain, take into service; recover
retention, limitation; capacity; detention; (poor), thing of slight capacity (*Sonn.*, 122)
retentive, *adj.*, detaining, imprisoning; (to), strong enough to restrain
retire, *n.*, retreat, falling back; withdrawal; repair, resort
retort, to repay (*M. W.*, ii, 2, 1)
retrograde, moving backward, i.e. in a direction from east to west, contrary to the order of the signs of the zodiac
return, send or make answer
revenge, *n.*, vengeance, retribution; *v.*, to avenge
revengement, retribution, condign punishment
reverb, reverberate
reverberate, *adj.*, re-echoing
reverent, reverend
reverse, a backhanded stroke
revolt, *n.*, a rebel; *v.*, to draw back (from a wrong course) (*2 Hen. VI*, iv, 2, 133)
revolted, unfaithful
reword, to repeat by echoing
rheum, a watery discharge (tears, saliva, mucus); cold in the head, catarrh; rheumatic disorder
rheumatic, affected with catarrh; damp and misty; irritable; delirious (*Hen. V*, ii, 3, 40)
rheumy, damp
rib, to enclose
ribald-rid, ridden by ribalds
riband, ribbon
rid, to dispatch, destroy; get over, put behind one; (way), make quick progress (*3 Hen. VI*, v, 3, 21)
riggish, wanton
right, regular, thoroughgoing
rigoll, circle; ring
rim, midriff
ripe, ready
ripely, fully, decidedly
ripeness, *n.*, being prepared, a state of preparation
rivage, shore
rival, partner, associate
rivality, copartnership
rivelled, dry and furrowed
rivo, a reveller's interjection of no definite meaning, apparently an incentive to drink and be merry
road, a place where ships ride at anchor, harbour or roadstead; stage of a journey; inroad, raid; strumpet
Roan, Rouen
roast, *see* rule
robustious, violent; boisterous, noisy
rod, a staff carried as a symbol of office; sceptre

493

roguing, *adj.*, wandering
roguing thieves, roving pirates
roguish, vagrant
roisting, *adj.*, blustering, rousing
romage, turmoil of labour
Romish, Roman
rondure (roundure), circle
ronyon (runnion), a mangy creature, hag
roofed, under one roof (*Macb.*, iii, 4, 40)
rook, to perch in huddled fashion
rooky, frequented by rooks
ropery, knavish talk (*R. and J.*, ii, 4, 154)
rope-tricks, knavish tricks and talk (*T. of S.*, i, 2, 112)
roping, *adj.*, hanging in ropes
Rossillion, Rousillon
roted, learned by heart (*Cor.*, iii, 2, 55)
rother, ox
round, *n.*, a dance in a circle; *adj.*, plain, honest; outspoken, blunt; *adv.*, without mincing matters; *v.*, to surround, encircle
round, to whisper
roundel, a dance in a circle
roundly, outspokenly; without ceremony; in thoroughgoing fashion
roundure, *see* rondure
rouse, a bumper; (takes his), carouses
rout, company; gang; rabble; brawl
row, line, verse (*Haml.*, ii, 2, 438)
Rowland, Roland the most famous of Charlemagne's Twelve Peers
royal, a gold coin worth half a pound
roynish, scurvy, paltry
rub, *n.*, impediment (in bowling), obstacle; annoyance; a rough place (not well finished); *v.*, to hinder; (on), to go on in spite of difficulties
rubied (rubious), ruby-red
rudesby, insolent fellow
ruffle, *n.*, bustle, noisy life (*Compl.*, 58); *v.*, to swagger; bluster; maltreat; outrage; (up), rouse to anger
ruffling, *adj.*, rich and showy (*T. of S.*, iv, 3, 60)
rug-headed, shaggy-haired
ruinate, to ruin, bring to destruction
rule, behaviour, conduct; manner of proceeding
rule the roast, to be master of the feast, carry all before one
rumour, noise, din, uproar
rump-fed, fat-rumped (*Macb.*, i, 3, 6)
runagate, renegade, traitor; runaway, fugitive
running, *adj.*, hasty, hurried, slight (*Hen. VIII*, i, 4, 12)
runnion, *see* ronyon
rush aside, to force or push aside
rushle, to rustle (*M. W.*, ii, 2, 68)
rustle, to rush noisily
ruttish, lecherous

'S, God's
's, us; she is (*Per.*, iv, Gow., 4)
s', so (*Cor.*, iv, 6, 120)
Saba, the Queen of Sheba
sack, a general term for sherry and similar wines
sackbut, a kind of trumpet or trombone
Sackerson, a famous Paris Garden bear

sacrificial, expressing devotion (*Tim.*, i, 1, 81)
sacring bell, a bell rung at mass at the elevation of the host
sad, grave, serious; glum, morose
sadness, seriousness; (in, in good), in earnest, in very truth
safe, *adj.*, sound; *v.*, to conduct in safety; make safe, obviate anxiety about (anything)
safety, safe custody
Sagittary, a Centaur; a house in Venice with the sign of the Centaur
sain, *p.p.*, said (*L. L. L.*, iii, 1, 83)
Saint Martin's summer, Indian summer
Saint Nicholas' clerks, robbers
salamander, a fabulous animal that lives in the element of fire
sale-work, wares made for sale (not for one's own use), hence of inferior quality
sallet, salad; a kind of helmet; spicy passage (*Haml.*, ii, 2, 462)
salt, *adj.*, stinging, mordant; lustful
saltiers, jumpers, *for* satyrs (*W. T.*, iv, 4, 334)
salute, to affect, stir (*Hen. VIII*, ii, 3, 103)
salvage, a savage
Samingo, *for* San (Saint) Domingo (*2 Hen. IV*, v, 3, 79)
sampire, samphire
sanctimonious, sacred, holy
sanctimony, a sacred obligation; faithfulness to such obligations
sanctuarize, to afford the protection of a sanctuary
sand-blind, dim of sight, purblind
sanded, of a sandy colour
sanguine, blood-red; ruddy; of a sanguine temperament physically
sans, without
sarcenet, a fine soft silk fabric; flimsy
Sarum, Salisbury
satire, satirist (*Sonn.*, 100)
saucy, insolently insistent; lascivious
savage, growing wild (*Hen. V*, iii, 5, 7)
savagery, wild vegetation, weeds
savour, get the taste of (*Lear*, iv, 2, 39)
sawn, sown (*Compl.*, 91)
say, *n.*, touch, trace
say, a kind of cloth resembling serge
'say, to assay, to make trial (*Per.*, i, 1, 59)
'Sblood, God's blood (an oath)
scaffolage, scaffoldage, wooden platform, stage
scald, scabby; scurvy, miserable
scale, to weigh in the balance
scall, *for* scald (*M. W.*, iii, 1, 123)
scamble, to scramble; struggle confusedly; fight
scamel, some kind of sea bird (*Temp.*, ii, 2, 176)
scandal, *n.*, censure; *v.*, to defame; cause to be defamed
scandaled, scandalous
scandalized, defamed; held in ill repute
scant, *adv.*, hardly, scarcely
scantling, a small pattern or specimen
scantly, grudgingly; with slight appreciation
scape, escape; escapade, prank; *pl.*, doings (*with a pun on* escape) (*M. of V.*, ii, 2, 174); *v.*, to escape
scarf, to wrap; (up), muffle, blindfold

scarfed, *adj.*, adorned with pennants and flags
scarre, a rock, precipice (*All's W.*, iv, 2, 38: *probably a misprint*)
scath (scathe), harm, injury
scathful, harmful, damaging
school, schooling, learning
school-doing, the actions and behaviour in which one has been schooled (*T. N. K.*, v, 4, 68)
science, knowledge, learning
sconce, a small fort, an earthwork; head, pate
scornful, disdained, bemocked (*Lucr.*, 520)
scot and lot, a municipal tax; payment in full
scotch, *n.*, a gash; *v.*, to gash, slash
scour, to run fast; purge
scrimer, fencer
scrip, a written list; a wallet or satchel; (and scrippage), a wallet and its contents (*A. Y. L.*, iii, 2, 171)
scripture, a sacred writing
scrowl, to scrawl, write clumsily; signify one's meaning (*T. A.*, ii, 4, 5)
scroyle, a scurvy wretch
scrubbed, stunted
scuffle, to fight or fence hand to hand or at close quarters
scull, a school of fish (*T. and C.*, v, 5, 22)
'scuse, an excuse
scut, tail (of a deer)
'Sdeath, God's death
seal, *n.*, confirmation, fulfilment; *v.*, to confirm, ratify
sea-like, in naval array (*A. and C.*, iii, 13, 171)
seam, fat, grease
seamy side without, wrong side out
search, *n.*, band of searchers; *v.*, to probe
season, a preservative; soundness; *v.*, to ripen; make ready; pickle, preserve; to control, moderate
seconds, inferior flour, second-rate matter (*Sonn.*, 125)
sect, class; party, faction; cutting; sex
secure, *adj.*, free from care; overconfident, careless, heedless; unsuspecting; *v.*, to make confident or careless
securely, without foreboding; heedlessly, without caution
security, lack of care or caution
seeded, run to seed, full-grown
seedness, the state of being just sown
seel, to sew up the eyes of (a falcon); *fig.*, to blind
seely, *see* silly
seeming, *n.*, appearance; false appearance; likelihood; *adv.*, becomingly
seen (well), well-skilled
segregation, dispersion
seignory, older rank, seniority (*Rich. III*, iv, 4, 36)
seized of, legally possessed of
seld, seldom
seldom, infrequent
seld-shown, rarely appearing in public
self, one's own; same
self-abuse, self-deception
self-admission, personal preference (*T. and C.*, ii, 3, 176)
self-affected, partial to one's self

self-assumption, self-conceit
self-bounty, natural goodness of heart
self-breath, one's own speech
self-comparisons (with), in actions that matched his own (*Macb.*, i, 2, 55)
self-covered, whose (woman's) self is covered (by a monstrous appearance) (*Lear*, iv, 2, 62)
self-figured, planned by one's self
self-gracious, spontaneously kind
self-substantial, consisting of one's own substance
self-unable, inadequate in itself (*All's W.*, iii, 1, 13)
semblable, *adj.*, similar; in seeming; *n.*, one's like
semblably, in appearance
semblative, in appearance (*T. N.*, i, 4, 34)
sempster, tailor (*T. N. K.*, iii, 5, 44)
sennet, a trumpet signal
se'nnight (sev'nnight, sevennight), a week
Senoys, Sienese, inhabitants of Siena
sense, sensuous perception; mental perception; sensual passion; (to the), to the quick
senses, good sense (*Hen. V*, ii, 3, 51)
sensible, capable of feeling, sensitive; keenly or deeply felt; of the senses or one of them (*Haml.*, i, 1, 57)
sensibly, intensely, acutely; in conscious being (*T. A.*, iv, 2, 122)
sentence, axiom, sententious remark
separable, *adj.*, that separates (*Sonn.*, 36)
Septentrion, the North
sequent, following; follower
sequester, sequestration
sere, a part of a gun-lock between the hammer and the trigger
sergeant, a sheriff's officer
serpigo (suppeago), a skin disease
servant, lover, suitor
servanted to, in the service of
sessa, *interj.*, come! away!
set, to value, appraise; wager, stake, risk; (down), encamp or lay siege; (off), compensate, atone for
Setebos, the chief deity of Sycorax (in fact, of the Patagonians) (*Temp.*, i, 2, 373)
setter, one who arranges opportunities for highwaymen (*1 Hen. IV*, ii, 2, 53)
sevennight (sev'nnight), *see* se'nnight
several, different, distinct; distinctive; privately owned
severals, individual persons or things; details, particulars
sewer, an attendant in charge of the service (at a feast)
'Sfoot, God's foot
shades, Hades, the world below
shadow, *n.*, protecting shade, shelter; shady spot; *v.*, to shelter
shadowing, *adj.*, darkening, obscuring one's consciousness
shadowy, frequenting the shady woods
shag, shaggy
shag-eared, with shaggy hair hanging about the ears (*Macb.*, iv, 2, 83)
shale, shell (of a nut)
shall, inevitably will
shall 's, shall we
shard, a potsherd, fragment of pottery

shard-borne, borne up by wings (or wing cases) like shards or bits of pottery (*Macb.*, iii, 2, 42)
sharded, having shard-like wing cases
shark up, to gather up hastily and indiscriminately
sharp-looking, lean-faced
shealed, *adj.*, shelled
shearman, one whose trade is to shear woollen cloth
sheaved, made of plaited straw (*Compl.*, 31)
sheed, to shed (*Sonn.*, 34)
sheep-biter, a dog that bites sheep, a malicious fellow
sheep-biting, *adj.*, snarling, ill-tempered
sheer, clear, pure; mere
shent, *p.p.*, scolded, taken to task
sheriff's post, a post at a sheriff's door (for notices, etc.)
sherris (sherris sack), sherry
shield, to forfend, forbid
ship-tire, a headdress like a ship
shive, a slice
shock, to meet in clash of arms
shog, to jog, walk
shoon, shoes
shore, sewer, cesspool
short, to shorten; come short of (*Cymb.*, i, 6, 200)
shot, tavern reckoning; expenditure
shot-free, without paying one's reckoning
shotten, *adj.*, that has cast the roe
shough, a rough-haired lapdog
shoulder in, to push aside into
shouldering, *n.*, jostling, insolent crowding
shoulder-shotten, with lame or dislocated shoulder
shovegroat, a game like shuffleboard played with coins
shovelboard, a shilling used in a game like shuffleboard (*M. W.*, i, 1, 159)
show, a pictured representation (*Lucr.*, 1507)
shrew, to curse (a light word), beshrew
shrewd (shrowd), shrewish, petulant; biting, mordant; harsh, hard; mischievous; bad, ill
shrewdly, sharply, keenly; badly; confoundedly, deucedly
shrieve, sheriff
shrift, confession, whether followed by absolution or not; confessional
shrill-gorged, shrill-throated (in its song)
shrive, to hear confession and absolve
shriver, confessor
shrow, shrew
shrowd, *see* shrewd
shut up, to conclude (*Macb.*, ii, 1, 16)
sib, related, kin
Sicil, Sicily
sick, to fall ill
sicken, to fall ill; impair
sicle, shekel (*M. for M.*, ii, 2, 149)
side, to take sides with (*Cor.*, i, 1, 197)
side-sleeve, a wide, open, hanging sleeve (*M. Ado*, iii, 4, 21)
siege, seat; rank; excrement
sightless, invisible; unsightly, repulsive
sights, the eyeholes in a helmet
sign, *n.*, outward appearance; image; signal flag; *v.*, to mark, designate

significant, sign, significant action; a letter that explains a story (*L. L. L.*, iii, 1, 131)
signiory, the Venetian government
signory, domain of a nobleman, dukedom, etc.; authority as a noble, lordship
silly (seely), innocent, harmless, inoffensive; plain and simple; poor, wretched
silverly, like drops of silver
simple, *adj.*, uncompounded; *n.*, medicinal herb (used in compounding remedies); ingredient
simple-answered, truthful in reply (*Lear*, iii, 7, 43)
simular, *adj.*, counterfeit, specious; (of virtue), simulating goodness
simulation, enigmatical expression
since, when in the past (once upon a time)
single, weak, feeble; sincere
singleness, simplicity
single-soled, thin, miserable
singly, uniquely; by any one man (*Cor.*, ii, 2, 91)
singularity, personality; an artistic rarity
singuled, segregated, separated
sinister, left; illegitimate
sink, to cause to fall or bend
sinking-ripe, all ready to sink
sir, lord; gentleman; dignitary; title of a priest or a university graduate
sirrah, sir (used in anger, insult, or familiarity, or as a title for a servant or an inferior)
sir-reverence (*for* save reverence, *salva reverentia*), with all due respect; *adj.*, not to be mentioned without apology (*R. and J.*, i, 4, 42)
sister, to match, equal (*Per.*, v, Prol., 7)
sistering, *adj.*, close-neighbouring (*Compl.*, 2)
sith, since
sithence, since
sizes, allowances (*Lear*, ii, 4, 178)
skains-mates, swaggering fellows (*R. and J.*, ii, 4, 162)
skiff, to cross in a skiff (*T. N. K.*, i, 3, 37)
skill, reasonable cause, reason
skilless, ignorant
skillet, a kind of saucepan
skills not, makes no difference, matters not
skimble-skamble, incoherent, nonsensical
skipper, saucy youngster (*T. of S.*, ii, 1, 341)
skirr, to scurry, scour; ride rapidly about
slab, viscous
slack, to neglect; be remiss in serving one
slander, *n.*, disgrace; *v.*, to calumniate; disgrace; denounce, upbraid
slanderous, disgraceful, bringing shame (to)
slave, to make a slave of, make subservient to one's own will
sleave, a skein
sleave silk, floss silk
sledded, *adj.*, that ride in sledges (*Haml.*, i, 1, 63)
sleeve-hand, wrist-band, cuff
sleeveless, futile, bootless
sleided, divided into threads
'Slid, God's lid
'Slight, God's light
slight, inattentive, negligent; *v.*, to

throw contemptuously; (off), to put aside with contempt

slightly, carelessly, inconsiderately, without serious attention

slip, a counterfeit coin; a kind of leash

slipper, slippery, shifty

slipshod, wearing slippers

slobbery, dank and muddy

slops (slop), loose breeches or trousers; loose jacket

slow, to retard, check

slubber, to soil; to do hurriedly, huddle up

sluggardized, made sluggish

sluttery, sluttishness

sly-slow, passing with an imperceptible motion (*Rich. II*, i, 3, 150)

small, the slender part of the leg

smallness, shrill and high quality (of voice)

smatch, *n.*, smack, taste

smatter, to chatter, jabber

smile, to smile at

smilet, little smile

smoke, to torment (as with smoke), baste, thrash; to smell out, detect

smooth, to flatter; foster, encourage; talk insinuatingly

smoother, to smother

smother, stifling smoke

smug, neat and trim, spruce

sneak-cup, one who avoids drinking his share

sneap, *n.*, a snub, a sharp rebuke; *v.*, to nip with cold

sneck up, be hanged, go hang

snipe, insignificant creature

snort, to snore

snuff, open resentment; (to take in), to resent

so, very well, well and good

sod (sodden), *p.p.*, boiled

soft, hold! wait a moment!

soil, explanation (*Sonn.*, 69)

soiled, full-fed with green fodder (*Lear*, iv, 6, 124)

soilure, defilement

sola (sowla), *interj.*, halloo

solace, *n.*, happiness; *v.*, to entertain; take pleasure

soldieress, female warrior

sole, to pull by the ears, pull the ears of

solely, alone

solemn, ceremonial, formal, in due form; stately, state

solemnity, festival, festivity, celebration; solemnizing; dignity, stateliness

solicit, move; allure; prevail with soliciting, *n.*, prompting, instigation

solidare, a gold coin

something, *adv.*, somewhat

sometime, sometimes; formerly, once

sometimes, formerly

somewhither, to some place or other

sonance, sound, signal

sonties (by God's), an oath of doubtful meaning, perhaps 'sanctity'

soon at night, to-night, this coming night

sooth, *n.*, truth; bland compliance (*Rich. II*, iii, 3, 136); *adj.*, true

soothe, to humour, indulge; flatter

soother, flatterer

sop, anything thoroughly saturated with a liquid

Sophy, the Shah of Persia

sore, a buck in the fourth year

sorel, a sorrel, a buck in the third year

sorrow-wreathen knot, the arms folded in sorrow (*T. A.*, iii, 2, 4)

sort, *n.*, rank; company; manner, way, fashion; lot (to be drawn); *v.*, to sort out, select; ordain; fit, adapt; keep company; be fit, suit, accord; come to pass, come out, result

sortance (hold), to accord

sot, fool, idiot

sotted, besotted, become utterly foolish

sottish, befitting an idiot

soul-fearing, striking terror to the soul

sound, *n.*, *v.*, swoon

soundless, unfathomable

sour (one's cheek), to scowl

souse, swoop down upon

soused, *adj.*, pickled

south, south wind

sovereign, efficacious (as a remedy)

sovereignly, supremely

sovereignty, efficacy

sow (of lead), a large mass

sowla, *see* sola

space, time, interval

span, *n.*, a measure of length, the distance from the tip of the thumb to that of the little finger when both are extended, about nine inches; a short time; *v.*, to limit, measure, bring to an end

span-counter, a game in which the player tries to throw his counter (a small disc) within a span's distance of his opponent's

spaniel, to follow like a spaniel

spare, to be scrupulous about offending (*M. for M.*, ii, 3, 33)

specialty, the essential quality; a particular document; a special contract or bond

speciously, *for* specially (*M. W.*, iii, 4, 113)

speculation, looking on, gazing; the act or faculty of sight; intelligent sight; a scout

speculative, having the faculty of sight

sped (to be), to be finished, done for

speed, *n.*, success, welfare; helper, patron saint, help to success; *v.*, to prosper, succeed; help, cause to prosper

speken, speak (*Per.*, ii, Prol., 12)

spent, used up

sperr, to bar (*T. and C.*, Prol., 19)

spet, to spit

sphere, one of the concentric hollow spheres in which (according to the Ptolemaic astronomy) each planet is fixed; eye socket

sphered, set in a sphere

spherical, planetary

sphery, starry

spill, destroy

spilth, spilling, pouring out

spinner, spider

spinster, spinner; unheroic emotional creature (*T. N. K.*, i, 3, 23)

spirit, vital power, vitality; *pl.*, certain subtle fluids supposed to permeate the blood and organs (classified as 'natural,' 'animal,' and 'vital'); vital powers

spital, hospital

splay, castrate

spleen, impetuosity; impetuous force or fury; passion; malevolence;

irascible temper; grudge, ill will; capricious temper or impulse; restlessness; laughter, a fit of laughter, hysterics; a sudden action, flash

spleenful, impetuous, eager; angry

spleeny, ardent, headstrong

splenitive, irascible

splinter, to join and bind up in splints

spoil, to despoil; lay waste, ruin, destroy; seize as prey

spoon, to let (a ship) run before the wind

sportive, wanton

spot, figure in embroidery (*Cor.*, i, 3, 56)

sprag (*for* sprack), quick (*M. W.*, iv, 1, 84)

sprightful, spirited

spring, earliest part, beginning; a shoot

springe, a snare

springhalt, a kind of lameness in horses

sprite, spirit

sprited, haunted

spritely, ghostly, in the form of spirits

spurs, the main roots of a tree

spy, *n.*, note, observation (*Macb.*, iii, 1, 130)

squandered, *p.p.*, scattered

squandering, *adj.*, straggling, random

square, *adj.*, fair, just; *n.*, rule, regularity; a body of troops in square formation; troop; the bosom or breast-piece of a garment; *v.*, to rule, regulate; judge; quarrel, fall out

squarer, a quarrelsome fellow

squash, an unripe peapod; youngster

squier, *see* squire

squiny, peep, look with half-open eyes

squire (squier), a carpenter's square

stablish, establish

stablishment, confirmed possession

staff, stanza

stage, to exhibit publicly; bring on the stage

stagger, to assault, fell; hesitate, be in doubt

staggers, a disease of horses; dizziness; staggering condition, perplexed and ill-regulated life

stain, *n.*, tinge; a nonpareil that puts all others to shame; *v.*, to darken, eclipse; be darkened

stale, *n.*, decoy; laughingstock, butt; prostitute; urine; *v.*, to make stale, cheapen

stall, shut up, keep close; install

stammer, to report or describe imperfectly

stamp, *n.*, a coin; *v.*, to coin; vouch for, mark as true

stanch, satisfy

stanchless, insatiable

stand (on, upon), insist on; make much of; plume one's self on; depend on; concern

standing, *n.*, duration; high rank; *adj.*, stagnant

standing bed, a bed with a bedstead

standing tuck, a rapier standing upright

staniel, a kind of hawk, kestrel

stanze (stanzo), stanza

staple, fibre

star, lodestar; sphere, rank; *pl.*, fortunes

Glossary

star-blasting, malign influence of the stars

star-crossed, thwarted by evil stars, ill-fated

stare, stand on end

stargazer, astrologer

starting hole, hole in which to take refuge, evasion

start-up, upstart

starve, benumb or kill with cold; paralyze; perish with cold; (out), outwatch

starved, shrunken, mean

state, *n.*, attitude in standing; estate; rank; high rank, majesty; appearance in state; a person of high rank or authority; chair of state

station, attitude when standing

statist, statesman, politician

statute, a special kind of bond

statute cap, a plain woollen cap prescribed by statute for persons below a certain rank

stead, to be of use, assist, oblige; (up), supply

stealth, theft; imperceptible movement; stealing away

steely, made of steel; unbending, inflexible

steepy, steep; precipitous

steerage, steering

stell, to fix, place

stelled, starry (*Lear*, iii, 7, 61)

sternage, the sterns

stick, to place, set; scruple, hesitate

sticking place, the place where it will remain fixed

stickler-like, like one who separates combatants

stiff, formidable, harsh (*A. and C.*, i, 2, 104)

stigmatic, one marked with deformity as with a brand of infamy

stigmatical, marked with deformity, misshapen

still, ever, always, constantly

still an end, without ceasing (*Two G.*, iv, 4, 67)

stillatory, a still

still-piecing, always closing again (*All's W.*, iii, 2, 113)

still-vexed, constantly buffeted by storms

sting, instinctive impulse

stitchery, needlework

stithy, *n.*, smithy; *v.*, to fashion at the anvil

stoccado (stoccata), a thrust

stock, stoccado, thrust; stocking

stockfish, dried codfish

stockish, stupid, insensible

stomach, *n.*, appetite; anger, resentment; arrogance; high spirit, courage; *v.*, to resent

stomaching, *n.*, quarrelling

stone, *n.*, see thunder-stone; *v.*, to make as hard as stone

stone-bow, a bow used for shooting stones

stonish, to confuse, astonish, disconcert

stoolball, a game resembling cricket (stool = wicket)

stope, see stoup

store, abundance, plenty; stuff, material; progeny

story, *n.*, history; *v.*, to recount, relate

stoup (stope), a large glass or tankard

stout, brave, bold; haughty

stoutness, arrogance

stover, winter food for cattle

straight, straightway, immediately

straight-pight, erect in carriage (*Cymb.*, v, 5, 164)

strain, *n.*, lineage, race; inherited or native character; trait of character; sort, kind; tendency; difficulty in believing, doubt; *v.*, to force; exaggerate; do violence to one's nature (*W. T.*, iii, 2, 51); (at), make a difficulty about, object to

strained, *adj.*, forced, artificial, exaggerated

strait, stingy; strict; pressing, rigorous

straited, *adj.*, in straits, at a loss

straitness, strictness, rigour

strange, foreign, alien; distant (in manner); extraordinary, remarkable

strange-achieved, acquired by extraordinary efforts or in foreign lands (*2 Hen. IV*, iv, 5, 72)

strangely, extraordinarily, surprisingly; like a stranger, as a foreigner (*W. T.*, ii, 3, 181)

strangeness, coldness of manner, aloofness

strangered, cast off as an alien

strappado, a torture in which the victim was hoisted by a pulley attached to his hands (which were strapped together behind him) and was let part way down with a jerk

stratagem, a frightful deed

stray, *n.*, straggler; *v.*, to lead astray

streamer, banner

strength, forces, army

strewments, flowers strewed

stricture, strict self-restraint

stride, to step over

strike, *n.*, a measure, a bushel; to strike (lower, take in) sail; smite with malign influence; broach (a cask)

striker, footpad

strond, strand

strossers, trousers

strow, strew

stroy, destroy

stubborn, rough, harsh, rude

stubbornness, roughness

stuck (stuck-in), a thrust, stoccado

studied, inclined, disposed

study, commit to memory

subdue, to, to bring into conformity with

subduement, subdual

subject, subjects (collectively)

suborn, corruptly or by underhand means to procure or induce one to commit an unlawful or unworthy deed

subscribe, to sign away, renounce; to yield, submit, give way; declare, publish; assent to; (for), vouch for

subscription, deference, submission

substractor, calumniator, detractor

subtile (subtle), fine, delicate; crafty, artful, deceitful; deceptive

subtilly (subtly), artfully, craftily, deceitfully

subtility (subtlety), craft; artful plan; illusion

succeeding, sequel, consequence

success, succession; what ensues, the course of time; the outcome (good or ill), the issue

successantly, immediately (*T. A.*, iv, 4, 113)

successive, hereditary, next in succession

successively, by hereditary succession

sudden, speedy, prompt; impromptu; hasty

suddenly, immediately, without delay

suffer, to suffer death, be executed

suffered, *p.p.*, let alone, allowed, permitted

sufferance, suffering; damage; forbearance, indulgence, acquiescence

suffering, submissive, tame

sufficiency, ability

sufficient, able; of adequate means

suffigance, for sufficience (*M. Ado*, iii, 5, 56)

suggest, tempt; insinuate to; woo

suggestion, temptation; wily insinuation (*Hen. VIII*, iv, 2, 35)

suit, *n.*, obligatory attendance; *v.*, to dress, attire; agree, accord

suited, adapted, nicely adjusted

suits (out of), out of favour

sullen, dismal, dark

sullens, moroseness, the dumps (*Rich. II*, ii, 1, 139)

sumless, countless, inestimable

summer-seeming, befitting the summer of life (*Macb.*, iv, 3, 86)

summoner, a sheriff's officer

sumpter, packhorse

sup, provide supper for, feed

superfluous, having more than one needs

superflux, superfluity

superpraise, to praise in excess

superscript, superscription, address (on a letter)

superserviceable, officious (*Lear*, ii, 2, 19)

superstitiously, with punctilious exactness (*W. T.*, iii, 3, 40)

supervise (on the), immediately after reading it over (*Haml.*, v, 2, 23)

supervisor, looker-on

suppeago, see serpigo

supplant, uproot, get rid of; knock out (*Temp.*, iii, 2, 55)

suppliance, what fills up, pastime

supply, to satisfy one's desire

supplyant, supplementary (*Cymb.*, iii, 7, 14)

supplyment, continued supply

supposal, opinion

suppose, supposition; expectation

supposed, for deposed (*M. for M.*, ii, 1, 163)

sur-addition, surname

surance, assurance

surcease, *n.*, coming to an end; *v.* to cease

surety, *n.*, confidence in one's safety; *v.*, to be surety or bail for

surprise, seize, capture; overpower

sur-reined, exhausted by hard riding, overridden

survey, to note, perceive (*Macb.*, i, 2, 31)

surveyor, supervisor, overseer; official in charge of the lands of an estate

suspect, *n.*, suspicion; *v.*, for respect (*M. Ado*, iv, 2, 77)

Sutton Co'fil', Sutton Coldfield in Warwickshire

swabber, a petty officer in charge of keeping the decks clean

swaddling, see swathling

swag-bellied, with hanging paunch

swarth (swart), swarthy, black, dark

swarth (swath), what is cut by one sweeping of the scythe

497

Glossary

swasher, swaggerer, bully
swashing, adj., swaggering
swath, see swarth
swath, swaddling clothes
swathling (swathing) clothes (swaddling clouts), clothes in which one is swaddled or wrapped
sway, n., balanced motion; drawing or controlling force; v., to turn aside; move
swayed, having a depression because of strain (T. of S., iii, 2, 56)
swear, to invoke in swearing (Lear, i, 1, 163)
sweep, pompous motion, procession (Tim., i, 2, 137)
sweet, fond of sweets (Two G., iii, 1, 330)
sweet and twenty, one twenty times sweet, superlatively sweet (T. N., ii, 3, 52)
sweeting, a sweet apple; sweet one
sweet-suggesting, sweetly seductive (Two G., ii, 6, 7)
swelling, rising in clouds
swilled, washed (by dashing waves)
swinge, impetus, sway
swinge-buckler, one who strikes a buckler with dashing blows, swash-buckler, dashing fighter, roisterer
Switzers, Swiss bodyguard
swoond, to swoon
swoopstake, sweeping up all the stakes at one swoop, without discrimination
sword-and-buckler, adj., using the weapons of the common people, swaggering in low company (1 Hen. IV, i, 3, 230)
'Swounds (Zounds), God's wounds
sympathize, agree, accord; sympathize with
sympathized, harmoniously arranged, consistent; harmoniously associated; described or expressed in one's veritable likeness
sympathy, agreement, conformity, equality

ta, thou (2 Hen. IV, ii, 1, 63)
table, n., tablet; palm of the hand; v., to set down in a list or catalogue
table book, memorandum book
tables, tablets for memoranda; backgammon
tabour, a small drum
tabourer, drummer on the tabour
tabourin, a kind of drum
tackled stair, rope ladder
taffeta, n., a kind of silk; adj., fine as silk
taffety, finely dressed in silk
tag, the rabble
taincture, defilement
taint, n., loss of reputation, discredit; v., to find fault with, discredit, disparage; hold culpable
take, to charm, enchant, please; strike with malignant power (by witchcraft or demonic influence), blast, infect; (to), betake one's self to; leap over; give (a blow, etc.); (air), come out, become known; (head), move violently away; (in), take, capture, subdue; (me with you), let me understand you; (off), kill; (on), pretend; (order), make arrangements; (out), copy; (peace, truce), come to terms; (scorn), disdain; (thought), become melancholy, grieve; (up), make up, settle,

reconcile; purchase on credit; levy, enlist; rebuke; cope with
taking, infectious, blasting
tale (as thick as), in succession as rapidly as could be counted (Macb., i, 3, 97)
talent, talon
talents, treasures, precious locks (Compl., 204)
tall, lusty, valiant
tallow-catch, a tub for tallow (1 Hen. IV, ii, 4, 253)
tame, to repress, put down
tamed, adj., gone stale, vapid (T. and C., iv, 1, 62)
tang, n., a sharp note (Temp., ii, 2, 52); v., to sound, ring; ring out
tanling, sun-tanned child (Cymb., iv, 4, 29)
tardily, slowly
tardy, to hold in check
targe (target), a light shield, buckler
tarre, to set on, incite
tarriance, tarrying, waiting
Tartar, Tartarus, hell
task, to challenge, put to the test; call to account; tax
task (at), taken to task (Lear, i, 4, 366)
tasking, challenge
tassel-gentle, tercel-gentle, a male falcon
taste, n., test; specimen; (in some), in some measure; v., to try, test; taste (to), to be a taster for one (to guard against poison, hence taste to you all, die first) (T. N. K., v, 4, 23)
tasteful, full of sweet taste
tawdry-lace, a kind of necktie
tax, n., reproach, accusations; v., to blame, reprove, reproach; (with), accuse of
taxation, demand, claim; satirical talk
tediosity, tediousness (T. N. K., iii, 5, 2)
teem, to bring forth; bear children
teen, grief, sorrow
teeth (from his), grudgingly
tell, to count
temper, n., temperament, disposition; v., to mix, compound; mould, fashion; soften; dispose; bring to the proper state of mind for anything
temperality, for temper, i.e., physical condition (2 Hen. IV, ii, 4, 25)
temperance, climate; calmness, self-control; continence, chastity
temperate, chaste
tempered, adj., disposed, in the right temper; (ill-), distempered
temporary meddler, one who meddles with worldly matters
tenable, held (Haml., i, 2, 248)
tend, to attend, be ready; pay attention
tendance, service; attention; attentive visitors
tender, n., v., regard; adj., dear
tender-hefted, stirred by tender feelings only (Lear, ii, 4, 174)
tenner, tenour, purport of a speech (T. N. K., iii, 5, 123)
tent, n., a roll of lint used in cleaning a wound or keeping it open; a probe; v., to treat with a tent; to probe
tenure, purport, tenour
tercel, male falcon

Termagant, n., a supposed god of the Saracens (of violent nature); adj., furious, raging
terminations, the sharp points of her words (M. Ado, ii, 1, 257)
termless, fair beyond words (Compl., 94)
terrene, terrestrial, earthly
tertian, a fever recurring every other day
tester, a sixpence
testern, to present with a sixpence
testimonied, p.p., evidenced
testril, a sixpence
tetchy, irritable, touchy, fretful
tetter, to affect with a tetter or rash
than, then
thane, a Scottish title, earl
that, that which, what
that, so that; for if, since, etc.
thence, away, absent
theoric, theory
thereabout, at about that place (Haml., ii, 2, 468)
thereabouts, something like that (W. T., i, 2, 378)
thereafter, according (2 Hen. IV, iii, 2, 56)
thereto, in addition to that
thews, muscles and sinews
thick, hurriedly (2 Hen. IV, ii, 3, 24)
thicken, to grow dim
thick-eyed, dim-sighted
thick-pleached, see pleached
thick-skin, stupid fellow
thief, robber, highwayman
thievery, plunder, booty
think, to be melancholy, despond; seem
thirdborough, town constable
this, thus (V. and A., 205)
this' (this), this is
thorough, through
thought, melancholy, despondency, sorrow
thoughten (be), consider (Per., iv, 6, 115)
thought-executing, acting with the speed of thought (Lear, iii, 2, 4)
thoughtful, solicitous
thought-sick, sick at heart
thou's, thou shalt
thousand, thousandth
thrasonical, worthy of Thraso (the braggart soldier in Terence's Eunuchus)
three-farthings, an Elizabethan coin (thin, with an image of the Queen and the figure of a rose) (K. John, i, 1, 143)
three-man beetle, a heavy ramming implement worked by three men
three-pile, the heaviest velvet
three-piled, superlative
three-suited, having an allowance of three suits a year
threne, a funeral song, dirge
thrice-repured, thrice purified and refined
thrift, economy, frugality
thriftless, unprofitable, unavailing
thrifty, well-husbanded
throe, to agonize; (forth), give birth with throes
thronged, shrunk (Per., ii, 1, 77)
through, adj., thoroughgoing; adv., thoroughly
throughly, thoroughly
throw, n., the right distance (in bowling, the limit; (at this), at this cast of dice, this time; v., to win at a throw of the dice

Glossary

thrum, end of the warp

thrummed, ornamented with thrums or tufts

thunder-stone, thunderbolt

thwart, adj., perverse; v., to cross, traverse

'tice, to entice, lure

tickle, adj., insecure; delicate, precarious; (of the sere), discharged at a touch (see sere); v., (up), to finish up summarily

tickle-brain, dispenser of potent drink

ticklish, wanton

tick-tack, a kind of backgammon

tide, n., time; a festival of the Church; course; v., to betide

tidy, plump

tight, skilful

tightly, promptly; soundly

tile (to wash a), to labour in vain

tilly-vally (-fally), interj., fiddlesticks

tilt, see a-tilt

tilth, tillage, agriculture; husbandry

time, the time, the age; the people of the time, the world

timeless, unseasonable, ill-timed; untimely

timely, early; in good season

timely-parted ghost, the body of one who had died at his appointed hour (a natural death) (2 Hen. VI, iii, 2, 161)

tinct, colour; the elixir that turns base metals to gold, the philosopher's stone; its transmuting potency

tincture, colour; blood-stained relics (J. C., ii, 2, 89)

tire, n., headdress; equipment, furnishings; v., to attire

tire, to tear and feed ravenously; exercise one's self; glut

tire-valiant, a showy headdress

tiring house, dressing room (in a theatre)

tirrits, for terrors (2 Hen. IV, ii, 4, 219)

tisick, disease of the lungs

Titan, the sun god, the sun

tithe, n., tenth part; adj., tenth

tithe-pig, a pig due to the parson as a tithe

tithing, a district of a county

titler, claimant (T. N. K., v, 3, 83)

tittles, very small things; poverty and obscurity (L. L. L., iv, 1, 84)

to, in comparison with; according to; in addition to, besides

toaze (touse), to tear roughly, worry

tod, n., twenty-eight pounds of wool; v., to yield a tod

todpole, tadpole

tofore, before

toge, toga, gown

toged, wearing the toga, in the garb of peace

together, together

token, a plague spot

tokened, marked with plague spots

tolerable, for intolerable (M. Ado, iii, 3, 37)

toll, to take toll; gather; (for), to pay toll and enter in the toll book at a fair in order to have the right to sell

tomboy, a strumpet

tongue, n., voice, vote; v., to speak; denounce

to-night, last night

top, n., height; v., to surpass, rise above, outdo; to poll, cut off the top; haul up

topless, supreme (T. and C., i, 3, 152)

torcher, torchbearer (All's W., ii, 1, 165)

tortive, twisted aside

touch, n., test (by or as by the touchstone); the touchstone; a trait of countenance or of character; feeling; v., to test, try

touse, see toaze

toward, promising, tractable, docile; forward, bold; at hand, coming, in preparation

towardly, ready to be influenced, docile

tower, to mount up, soar aloft

toy, n., a trifle; an idle fancy, whim; (take), to take fright, be startled, shy (T. N. K., v, 4, 66), v., to dally amorously

trace, to follow, keep pace with; tread, walk along or through; move forward; carry out, perform

tract, visible track, trail, course

trade, resort; business, dealings; way, path

traded, adj., practised, experienced

trade-fallen, bankrupt, ruined

traducement, slander, calumny

traffic, business

train, n., allurement (lit., line of bait); v., to allure, entice

trammel up, to catch as in a trammel or net

Tranect, the Venetian ferry (M. of V., iii, 4, 53)

transfix, remove, take away (Sonn., 60)

translate, transform

transparent, bright

transport, to remove from this world to the next

transpose, to change, transform

trash, to hold back (a dog by a clog tied to the collar)

travail, n., toil and trouble; v., to toil

traverse, v., to march; move from side to side, dodge; cross, fold; adv., across

tray-trip, a game at dice

treacher, traitor

treasury, treasure

treatise, speech, discourse, story, tale

treaty, negotiation, conference; proposal; entreaty

treble-dated, living for three generations of men

trench, to turn aside by digging a trench

trenchant, cutting, keen-edged

trencher, a wooden plate

trencher friend (trencher knight), a parasite

trencherman, eater, feeder

Tribunal Plebs, for tribunus plebis (T. A., iv, 3, 92)

trick, n., knack; characteristic, one's way; touch; peculiarity; trifle; caprice; v., to dress

tricking, n., costumes

tricksy, sportive; fine, ornate

trifle, to make a trifle of, reduce to insignificance (Macb., ii, 4, 4); waste

trigon (fiery), a triplicity, the three fiery signs of the Zodiac (Aries, Leo, and Sagittarius) in the form of an equilateral triangle

trill, to trickle

trim, adj., fine; adv., accurately; v., to fit out (a ship); dress up

tripe-visaged, pale, sallow

triple, adj., third

triple-turned, three times faithless

triplex, triple measure

tristful, sorrowful

triumph, splendid show or festival; trump, winning card (with a pun) (A. and C., iv, 14, 20)

triumviry, triumvirate

troll-my-dames, a game like bagatelle

tropically, metaphorically

trot, old woman, hag

troth, truth; faith

trow, to believe, think; (I trow or trow after a question), pray, I wonder

Troyan, Trojan; fellow

truant, to play truant

truckle-bed, trundle-bed

true, honest; trustworthy, faithful

true-love, a betrothed lover; sweetheart; (knot), a double bowknot

truepenny, honest fellow

truest mannered, most trustworthy in character

trumpet, trumpeter

truncheon, to cudgel

truncheoner, a man carrying a club

trundle-tail, a dog with a long draggly tail

trunk sleeve, a full puffed sleeve

try, n., a test; (bring to try), bring (a ship) into the position of lying-to, as close to the wind as practicable

tub, sweating tub

tub-fast, the fast prescribed for a patient in the tub

tuck, rapier

tucket, a flourish or marching signal on the trumpet

tug, to contend in a hand-to-hand struggle

tuition, protection

tumble, perform a tumbler's feats

tun-dish, a kind of funnel

turband, turban

Turk (the), the Sultan; (turn), to become a Mohammedan, apostatize, prove utterly false, play the traitor

Turlygod, a name by which mad beggars called themselves (Lear, ii, 3, 20)

turn, to change; return; tune (A. Y. L., ii, 5, 3)

Turnbull Street, Turnmill Street, a disreputable neighbourhood in London

turtle, turtledove

tush, tusk

twelf, twelfth (T. N., ii, 3, 91)

twelve score, twelve-score yards

twiggen, covered with wickerwork

twilled, ridged (Temp., iv, 1, 64)

twink, twinkling of an eye

twire, to peer, peep out (Sonn., 28)

tyke, dog, cur

type, sign, mark, indication

tyrannically, boisterously

tyrannous, cruel, savage, fierce

tyranny, fury, rage

tyrant, usurper

umber, a brown pigment

umbered, coloured like umber

umbrage, shadow

unaccommodated, not furnished with artificial fittings, naked

unadvised, unintended; carelessly,

heedlessly; without due consideration, precipitate; inconsiderate

unadvisedly, inconsiderately

unaneled, not having received extreme unction

unapproved, unsupported by evidence

unapt, unfit; not prompt or quick; disinclined

unaptness, unreadiness, disinclination

unattainted, not infected by love; unprejudiced

unavoided, inevitable

unbaked, raw, unsophisticated

unbarbed, with bare (unarmed) head (*Cor.*, iii, 2, 99)

unbated, unblunted

unbent, smooth, unwrinkled (*Lucr.*, 1509)

unbid, uninvited, unwelcome, disconcerting (*3 Hen. VI*, v, 1, 18)

unbolted, unsifted, out-and-out (*Lear*, ii, 2, 71)

unbonneted, bareheaded (*Lear*, iii, 1, 14); cap in hand, with all due modesty, without boasting (*Oth.*, i, 2, 23)

unbookish, uninstructed

unbraced, unfastened, unbuttoned; with doublet open at the neck

unbraided wares, honest goods, not counterfeit or adulterated

unbreathed, unpractised

uncandy, to melt

uncape, off with your mantle, come out of your hiding-place (*M. W.*, iii, 3, 176)

uncase, to undress

uncharge, exonerate, acquit

uncharged, unassailed (*Tim.*, v, 4, 55)

unchary, unsparingly

unchecked, uncontradicted

unchild, to make childless

uncivil, uncivilized

unclew, to undo, ruin

unclog, to unburden

uncoined, not counterfeit, sound, genuine

uncomprehensive, beyond comprehension

unconfirmed, untrained, inexperienced

uncontrolled, unconquered; unsubdued; beyond control

uncouple, to let loose (hounds)

uncouth, unknown, strange; pathless, wild

uncrossed, uncancelled, with the account not crossed out as being settled (*Cymb.*, iii, 3, 26)

unction, salve, ointment

unctious, unctuous, oily, fat

uncurrent, improper, objectionable

undeeded, without having performed any action

under, under the sun, earthly; underground, of hell

underbear, to submit to, endure; trim on the lower edge

undercrest, to wear as an honour and justify (*Cor.*, i, 9, 71)

undergo, to be subjected to, endure; sustain; undertake

under-skinker, subordinate wine-server

undertake, to assume; take in charge; engage in combat with; accept a challenge; have to do with; vouch, warrant; (for), act or intercede in one's favour

undertaker, a contractor, one who takes charge; one who accepts a challenge or is ready to fight; champion

undervalued, inferior in value or reputation

underwrite, to confirm, as by signature (*T. and C.*, ii, 3, 137)

underwrought, undermined (*K. John*, ii, 1, 95)

undistinguished, extending beyond the limits of vision (*Lear*, iv, 6, 278)

undoubted, dauntless (*3 Hen. VI*, v, 7, 6)

undressed, rude, unrefined (*L. L. L.*, iv, 2, 17)

uneared, unploughed

uneath, hardly (*2 Hen. VI*, ii, 4, 8)

unequal, unjust

uneven, disturbing (*1 Hen. IV*, i, 1, 50)

unexperient, inexperienced (*Compl.*, 318)

unexpressive, inexpressible (*A. Y. L.*, iii, 2, 10)

unfair, to deprive of beauty (*Sonn.*, 5)

unfashionable, in misshapen wise (*Rich. III*, i, 1, 22)

unfolding, announcing the time to release the sheep from the sheep-fold (*M. for M.*, iv, 2, 219)

unfool, to relieve of the imputation of folly (*M. W.*, iv, 2, 120)

unforced, self-evident (*Oth.*, ii, 1, 240)

unfurnish, to deprive

unfurnished, unprovided with a mate (*M. of V.*, iii, 2, 126)

ungalled, unhurt, without a scratch

ungenitured, impotent (*M. for M.*, iii, 2, 184)

ungird, to put off, lay aside (*T. N.*, iv, 1, 16)

ungracious, displeasing; graceless, wicked

unhaired, beardless (*K. John*, v, 2, 133)

unhandled, untrained, unbroken

unhandsome, inappropriate, unfitting; unfair

unhap'ly, unhappily, unfortunately (*Lucr.*, 8)

unhappily, with unpleasant accuracy; to one's disadvantage or discredit

unhappiness, evil nature; mischief (in speech or action); something amusing (*M. Ado*, ii, 1, 361)

unhappy, ill-omened; mischievous; sharp-tongued, satirical; sharp, ill-tempered

unhatched, not yet come to action; unhacked

unheart, to dishearten, discourage

unhopeful, unpromising

unhoused, unconfined by domesticity

unhouseled, not having received the Eucharist

unimproved, unused, not put to use

unintelligent of, not perceiving

union, a fine large pearl

unity, consistency

universal, constant, unrelieved, unvaried (*L. L. L.*, iv, 3, 305)

unjust, dishonest; false, faithless

unjustice, injustice

unkept, uncared-for

unkind, unnatural; childless

unlace, divest one's self of, cast off (*Oth.*, ii, 3, 194)

unlike, unlikely, improbable

unlimited, not observing the unities of time and place (*Haml.*, ii, 2, 419)

unlived, deprived of life (*Lucr.*, 1754)

unmanned, not trained (of a hawk), unruly

unnerved, weak in sinews, enfeebled (*Haml.*, ii, 2, 496)

unowed, having no recognized owner

unpack, to relieve

unpanged, suffering no pangs of grief

unparagoned, unmatched, matchless

unpaved, castrated

unpay, to undo, make good (*2 Hen. IV*, ii, 1, 130)

unpeaceable, incurably quarrelsome

unpinked, not furnished with scallops

unpitied, pitiless, unmerciful

unplausive, not expressing approbation, neglectful

unpolicied, lacking sagacity, senseless

unpossessing, having no right of inheritance

unpregnant, unready; (of), without due sense of

unprevailing, unavailing

unprizable, priceless, inestimable; contemptible

unprized, unvalued (*Lear*, i, 1, 262)

unprofited, profitless

unproper, not exclusively one's own

unproportioned, unsymmetrical, out of accord with a consistent plan of conduct

unprovide, to render irresolute

unqualitied, deprived of one's natural qualities

unquestionable, disinclined to conversation

unraised, uninspired

unraked, not raked together and covered with ashes

unready, not dressed

unrecalling, past recall (*Lucr.*, 993)

unreclaimed, untamed, undisciplined

unreconcilable, irrevocably at odds (*A. and C.*, v, 1, 47)

unrecuring, incurable

unresisted, irresistible

unrespected, not noticed, unheeded, uncared-for

unrespective, unthinking; indiscriminate

unreverent *and* unreverend, used indiscriminately in both senses

unrolled, struck off the official register

unrough, beardless

unsatisfied, uninformed

unscanned, heedless

unseam, to rip up

unseasoned, unripe, immature

unseen, invisible

unseminared, emasculated

unshape, to derange, disorder

unshaped, incoherent

unshunned, inevitable

unsisting, shaken, made to vibrate (*M. for M.*, iv, 2, 92)

unskilful, undiscriminating, uncritical

unsorted, unfit

unsought, unsearched (*C. of E.*, i, 1, 135)

unsquared, shapeless, uncouth (*T. and C.*, i, 3, 159)

unstanched, unquenchable; leaky

unstate, to deprive of rank and fortune; resign one's superiority in

untempering, not ingratiating

untented, too deep for the probe

unthrift, unthrifty, prodigal

unthrifty, prodigal; heedless; misbehaving; unfortunate

Glossary

untoward, perverse, unmannerly
untowardly, to ill fortune, disastrously (*M. Ado.*, iii, 2, 134)
untraded, unhackneyed, novel
untried, untouched in presentation (*W. T.*, iv, 1, 6)
untrimmed, divested of bridal array (*K. John*, iii, 1, 209)
untrussing, *n.*, undoing one's breeches
untucked, dishevelled (*Compl.*, 31)
unvalued, of ordinary rank; priceless
unwappered, not worn out (*T. N. K.*, v, 4, 10)
unwares, without knowing what one does
unwarily, when off one's guard
unwit, to deprive of one's wits, drive mad
unworthy, undeserved, unmerited
unyoke, call it a day's work
up, in the field, in arms; in confinement; in power; (and down), exactly, out and out
upcast, a cast in bowling (*Cymb.*, ii, 1, 2)
upon (on), because of, as a result of
uprighteously, uprightly, righteously (*M. for M.*, iii, 1, 206)
upshoot, the final shot
upspring, a wild kind of dance
upswarm, to raise in large numbers
up-till, up against
upward, *n.*, the top (*Lear*, v, 3, 136)
urchin, hedgehog; imp in hedgehog's shape
urchin-shows, visions of imps
urchin-snouted, with a snout like an urchin imp
urge, to mention, speak of; allege; propose
urn, a grave
usance, interest on money
use, *n.*, interest; advantage; profit; usufruct, possession for one's use; habit, custom; (*pl.*), ways, practices; *v.*, to make a practice of, practise; (one's self), conduct one's self, behave
usurer, one who lends money at interest
usuring, usurious
usurp, to exercise power without right; use unrighteously or without right or by imitation; be a usurper
usury, the taking of interest
utis, noisy merry-making, high jinks
utter, to sell, bring to market
utterance (at), at all hazards; (to the), in a duel to the death (*Macb.*, iii, 1, 72)

vacancy, leisure time; intermission
vade, to fade
vagrom, *for* vagrant (*M. Ado.*, iii, 3, 26)
vail, *n.*, setting; *v.*, to lower, let fall, bow; do homage
vails, gratuities
vain, empty-headed; deceitful (*C. of E.*, iii, 2, 27)
vainly, mistakenly
valance, drapery, especially on a bed canopy
valanced, draped (with a beard)
validity, strength; value
valued, furnished with notes of the several qualities (*Macb.*, iii, 1, 95)
vanity, worthlessness; frivolity in character or conduct, triviality; foolishness; a matter of no importance; a frivolous person

vantage, *n.*, advantage, favourable situation or opportunity; profit; superiority, overplus; (at), (of), advantageous, convenient; from an advantageous position; (to the), to boot, in addition
vantbrace, defensive armour for the forearm
vara, very (*L. L. L.*, v, 2, 487)
varlet (varlot), a knight's attendant; fellow, rascal, knave
varletto, varlet, fellow (*M. W.*, iv, 5, 66)
varlotry, rabble (*A. and C.*, v, 2, 56)
vassal, *n.*, fellow, wretch; *adj.*, low, servile
vassalage, vassals, subjects (collectively)
vast, an immense space, an expanse; waste, abysmal region
vastidity, vastitude (*M. for M.*, iii, 1, 69)
vastly, in a desolate condition
vaultages, vaulted or cavernous places
vaulty, arched like a vault; cavernous
vaunt, outset, beginning (*T. and C.*, Prol., 27)
vaunt-courier, forerunner, precursor
vaward, vanguard; early part
vegetives, plants (*Per.*, iii, 2, 36)
veins (bloody), bloody-minded men (*Per.*, i, 4, 94)
velure, velvet
velvet guards, velvet trimmings
veney (venew), a hit (in fencing or in a witty contest); a bout
vengeance, harm; God's vengeance (as a curse); *adj.*, cursed, confounded; *adv.*, cursedly (*Cor.*, ii, 2, 5)
venom, venomous
vent, a discharge (of blood); utterance, talk; energy, energetic action (*Cor.*, iv, 5, 238)
ventages, air holes (*Haml.*, iii, 2, 373)
ventricle, a cavity in the brain
Ver, the Spring
verbal, oral; outspoken, blunt (*Cymb.*, ii, 3, 111)
verge, circle, circlet
verify, to speak the truth in commendation of; affirm, maintain
verity, fidelity
Veronesa, a Veronese ship (*Oth.*, ii, 1, 26)
versal, universal (*R. and J.*, ii, 4, 218)
via, *interj.*, forward! away! come!
vice, a fault; a comic character (personifying iniquity in general or some fault) in the moral plays (moralities)
vice, to force (as by vice, screw, or winch)
vicious, faulty, erroneous
victoress, victress
vie, to wager, stake (at card play); make play with; compete with one in regard to (something)
viewless, invisible
vigil, the eve of (i.e., preceding) a holy day or festival
vigitant, *for* vigilant (*M. Ado.*, iii, 3, 100)
vile, low in rank; poor, mean; worthless, contemptible
villager, countryman, rustic (*T. N. K.*, iii, 5, 104)
villain, bondman; fellow; rascal (as a term of endearment)

villiago, base peasant (*2 Hen. VI*, iv, 8, 48)
vindicative, vindictive, revengeful
viol-de-gamboys, a viol held between the legs
violent, to be violent, rage (*T. and C.*, iv, 4, 4)
virgin, to be a virgin
virginal, *n.*, an instrument like a spinet; *v.*, to tap the fingers (as upon the keys of a virginal)
virtue, excellence of any kind; an accomplishment; power; essence, essential quality
virtuous, medically powerful
visit, to attack, assail; punish (by divine judgment)
visitate, to visit
visitation, a visit
visited, attacked by the plague; afflicted with disease
visitings of nature, natural feelings or impulses (*Macb.*, i, 5, 46)
visitor, an ecclesiastical inspector or examiner; a spiritual adviser (*Temp.*, ii, 1, 11)
visor, a mask; a masked person; visage
vizaments, *for* advisements, i.e., thoughtful consideration (*M. W.*, i, 1, 39)
vizard, a mask
vizarded, masked
voice, *n.*, vote, suffrage, expressed choice or approval; *v.*, to elect by oral voting; acclaim
void, to leave, abandon
'void, to avoid, shun
voiding lobby, anteroom, waiting room
Volquessen, a district in France, formerly the country of the Velocasses (a Gallic tribe)
Volsce, Volscian
voluble, fickle, changeable
voluntary, a volunteer
voucher, the process of summoning one into court to vouch for the title to property
vouchsafe, to deign to receive (*J. C.*, ii, 1, 313)
vulgar, *adj.*, common, ordinary; public; *n.*, the common people; the vernacular
vulgarly, publicly

waft, to beckon; turn; transport by sea
waftage, passage by water, transportation
wafture, a waving motion
wag, *n.*, rogue; *v.*, to stir; be gone
wage, to wager; risk; carry on; pay wages to; (with), balance, be in proportion with
waggish, sportive, roguish
wagon, chariot, carriage, coach
wagoner, charioteer
wailful, doleful, lamenting
wain, wagon
waist, a waistband, girdle, belt
wait, to watch; be in attendance; (on, upon), attend; be on the watch for; be subservient to, tend
wake, *n.*, a festival on the vigil (eve) of a holiday; *v.*, to be awake; to sit up late; to revel at night
wall-eyed, with staring light-coloured eyes
Wallon, the borderland between France and the Netherlands
Walloon, a native of Wallon

501

Glossary

waned, diminished; past its prime (*A. and C.*, ii, 1, 21)
wanion (with a), with a vengeance (*Per.*, ii, 1, 17)
wanton, *n.*, a spoiled child; cockered creature; a sportive person, playful creature; *adj.*, unrestrained, untamed; self-willed; lawless; perverse; sportive, playful; fanciful; effeminate; luxurious, self-indulgent; *v.*, to play, sport; dally
wantonly, sportively, in lively fashion
wantonness, sportiveness; self-indulgence, luxury; whimsicality, affectation
wappened, faded and worn out (*Tim.*, iv, 3, 38)
ward, *n.*, guard; posture of defence; cell; *pl.*, the projections in a lock, locks; *v.*, to guard, protect
warden, a kind of pear
warder, a kind of truncheon
wardrop, wardrobe
warn, to notify; summon officially or formally; defy, meet in combat (*J. C.*, v, 1, 5)
warp, to distort; deviate; change
warped, distorted; perverse
warrant, to guard, protect; assure; make good, stand to
warranted need (upon a), if ever the occasion justifies such a requirement or demand (*M. for M.*, iii, 2, 151)
warrantise, guaranty; assurance; one who serves as a surety
warrener, the keeper of a rabbit warren
waste, *n.*, ruin, destruction
Wat, Walter (nickname for the hare)
watch, *n.*, state of being awake; wakeful condition, insomnia; fixed interval; timepiece; circle of figures on a dial; *v.*, to tame by depriving of sleep
watcher, one who is awake
water-gall, a kind of feeble rainbow, supposed to foretell rain
water-rug, a kind of shaggy waterdog
waters (for all), fit to play any part, ready for anything (*T. N.*, iv, 2, 68)
waterwork (in), painted in water colours
wawl, to howl, squall
wax (a man of), as finely moulded as a wax figure
waxen, *v.*, increase
waxen, *adj.*, engraved in wax, and thus not permanent (*Hen. V*, i, 2, 233)
way, persuasion, faith (*Hen. VIII*, v, 1, 28)
waylay, to dog the steps of
weal, the commonwealth, the body politic
wealsman, statesman (*Cor.*, ii, 1, 59)
wealth, welfare, prosperity
wear, *n.*, fashion, style; *v.*, to be worn, be in fashion; become adapted; wear out, wear or waste away
weather, the windward
web and pin, cataract (of the eye)
weed, garment, attire
weeding, the weeds (*L. L. L.*, i, 1, 96)
week (in by the), thoroughly caught (*L. L. L.*, v, 2, 61)
ween, to expect
weet, to wit, know
weigh out, to weigh fully and ac-

curately in order to repay in full (*Hen. VIII*, iii, 1, 88)
Weird Sisters, the Fatal Sisters, the Fates
welkin, the sky; blue as the sky
well, in a blessed state (euphemism for 'dead')
well-a-near, wellaway (*Per.*, iii, Prol., 51)
well-breathed, sound of wind (*Ven.*, 678)
well desired, made heartily welcome (*Oth.*, ii, 1, 206)
well-found, thoroughly versed; approved, sound
well-governed, well-behaved
well-graced, *adj.*, very popular, favourite
well-liking, plump, fat (*L. L. L.*, v, 2, 268)
well-respected, well-considered (*1 Hen. IV*, iv, 3, 10)
well said, well done
well seen, skilful, expert
Welsh hook, a weapon with a hooked cutting point and blade, like a billhook
wench-like, womanish
weraday, well-a-day, alas
wesand, windpipe, gullet
what, whatsoever
what . . . for, what kind of
wheel, *n.*, spinning wheel
wheeling, *adj.*, wandering, having no settled abode
Wheeson, Whitsun, Whitsunday
whelk, a knob, swelling, pustule
whelked, knobbed, knobby (*Lear*, iv, 6, 71)
when, an exclamation of impatience, much like 'make haste!' 'quick!'
when as, when
whe'r, whether
where, whereas; *n.*, a place elsewhere
whereagainst, against which
where as, when
wherein, in what attire
whereon, because of which
whereout, out of which
wherewithal, by means of which
whether, which of the two
whiffler, an officer who goes ahead to clear the way
while, until
whilere, a little while ago
whiles, while; until
whinid'st, very mouldy (*T. and C.*, ii, 1, 15)
whipping cheer (have), to be regaled with whipping (*2 Hen. IV*, v, 4, 5)
whipster, youngster (*Oth.*, v, 2, 244)
whissing, wheezing
whist, silent, quiet
white, the white circle at the centre of the target round the pin or bull's-eye; a fair pet or darling (*Oth.*, ii, 1, 134)
whitely, pale-faced (*L. L. L.*, iii, 1, 198)
whiting time, bleaching time (*M. W.*, iii, 3, 140)
whitster, bleacher (*M. W.*, iii, 3, 14)
whittle, a large knife
whole, sound, in good health, cured
whoobub, hubbub
whoreson, bastard; fellow, rascal
wide, far from the mark; much mistaken; astray; wildly; (of), far from
widow, *v.*, to endow with a widow's right to property; to survive as a widow

widowhood, widow's right to property (*T. of S.*, ii, 1, 125)
wight, person
wild, precipitate, headlong; without plan or forethought, at random
Wild, *n.*, the Weald (a tract of country, formerly a forest) in Kent
wilderness, wild growth (*M. for M.*, iii, 1, 142)
wild mare (ride the), to play at seesaw
wilful, willing; on purpose
wilful-blame, blameworthy for wilfulness (*1 Hen. IV*, iii, 1, 177)
will, sexual desire
wimpled, blindfolded (*L. L. L.*, iii, 1, 181)
Winchester goose, syphilitic person
wind, to blow (on a horn); to scent
wind, to insinuate, work one's way by subtlety
windgalls, soft tumours above the fetlock
windlasses, roundabout methods
window bars, openwork in a dress
windowed, full of great holes
windy, windward
wing-led, swept on, as with strong pinions (*Cymb.*, ii, 4, 24)
wink, *v.*, to shut the eye; *n.*, eyeshut, death
winter-ground, to protect from the cold by covering (*Cymb.*, iv, 2, 229)
wipe, a welt, wale, scar from the lash (*Lucr.*, 537)
wish, to recommend for service (*T. S.*, i, 1, 113)
wishtly, wistfully, eagerly (*Rich. II.*, v, 4, 7)
wist, knew
wistly, intently
wit, *n.*, mind, intellect; good sense; cleverness; *v.*, to know
witch, a sorcerer or sorceress, wizard or witch
with, by (of the agent); (to be), to attend to, settle one's case, see to one; (himself), in his right mind (*T. A.*, i, 1, 368)
withal, with this, with it; at the same time; with (at the end of a sentence); (do), help it (*M. of V.*, iii, 4, 72)
within him (get), to close with him so that he cannot use his sword (*C. of E.*, v, 1, 34)
Withold (Saint), Saint Vitalis (*Lear*, iii, 4, 125)
without, beyond the limit of; unless
without-door, external
witness (with a), with a vengeance, and no mistake (*T. of S.*, v, 1, 122)
wittol, a contented cuckold
witty, clever, keen-witted; artful
wive's, wife's
woe, *adj.*, sorry
wolt, wilt
wolvish, wolfish; like a wolf in sheep's clothing (*Cor.*, ii, 3, 122)
woman, to make one womanish
womaned, accompanied by a woman
woman-queller, woman-killer
woman-tired, torn by a woman as by a bird of prey, henpecked
womb, *n.*, belly; *v.*, to enclose
wornby, cavernous
wonder, to wonder at
wondered, having wonderful (magical) powers
wonder-wounded, amazed, astounded
wood, mad, insane
woodbine, honeysuckle; bindweed

502

woollen, with a woollen bag (*M. of V.*, iv, 1,56); (in the), between woollen blankets, without sheets (*M. Ado*, ii, 1, 33)

woolward, with woollen next the skin, as a penance (*L. L. L.*, v, 2, 717)

woosel, ousel, blackbird

woo't, (wo't), wolt, wilt thou

word, *n.*, watchword, motto, the right word; order, command; the word of God, the Scripture; *v.*, to utter; express or represent in words; address persuasively, cajole

word (to be at a), to speak no more than one means, briefly and to the point

work, a fortification

working, any operation of the mind or emotions

workyday, everyday, ordinary

world, a wonder, a marvel, a great sight; (to go to the), to abandon the celibate life, marry; (a woman of the), a married woman

worm, serpent; feeble creature

worship, *n.*, reverence, honour; *v.*, to honour

wort, a vegetable; unfermented beer

worth, wealth; (to have one's worth of), to have one's way against or in spite of (*Cor.*, iii, 3, 26)

worth, befall

worthy, *adj.*, honourable; *v.*, to make one highly esteemed

wot, know

wo't (woo't), wolt, wilt

woundless, invulnerable

wrack, *n.*, *v.*, wreck

wrackful, destructive, ruinous (*Sonn.*, 65)

wrangler, opponent

wrastle, wrestle

wrath, wroth, angry (*M. N. D.*, ii, 1, 20)

wreak, *n.*, vengeance, revenge; *v.*, to avenge, revenge

wreakful, avenging, revengeful

wrest, a tuning key, a person indispensable for the regulation of affairs (*T. and C.*, iii, 3, 23)

wretch, a term of endearment (*Oth.*, iii, 3, 90)

wretched, abominable

wrinch, rinse (*T. N. K.*, i, 1, 156)

wring, to writhe, suffer extremely

wringing, torturing pain

writ, Holy Writ, Scripture; a writing; (law of), the classical rules, the unities (*Haml.*, ii, 2, 421)

write, to subscribe, entitle, use the style of; certify (*All's W.*, iii, 5, 69)

writhled, wizened, shrivelled

wroth, discomfiture (*M. of V.*, ii, 9, 78)

wrying, *n.*, leaving the straight path, going astray

yare, ready, prompt, quick

yarely, actively, nimbly

yaw, to follow a zigzag course. be unsteady

yclad, *p.p.*, clad, clothed

ycliped, *p.p.*, named, called

Yead, Ed, Edward (*M. W.*, i, 1, 160)

yea-forsooth, *adj.*, obsequious and hypocritical

yearn (ern), to grieve

yeast, foam

Yedward, Edward

yellowing, yelping, baying (*T. A.*, ii, 3, 20)

yellowness, jealousy (*M. W.*, i, 3, 111)

yellows, jaundice in horses

yeoman, a bailiff's man

yerk, to jerk, kick; give a quick thrust

yesty, foaming; frothy

yield, to report; reward (*A. and C.*, iv, 2, 33)

yielded, born

yokes, branching horns (*M. W.*, v, 5, 111)

youngling, a youth, youngster

youngly, in youth

younker, youngster; greenhorn

yravish, to ravish, delight (*Per.*, iii, Prol., 35)

yslacked, *p.p.*, quieted, relaxed (*Per.*, iii, Prol., 1)

zany, a clown's subordinate jester; a buffoon, a foolish fellow

zeal, devotion

zealous, devout

zed, the letter *z*

zone, the sphere of the sun

Zounds, *see* 'Swounds